THE GROWTH OF THE
AMERICAN REPUBLIC

Franklin Delano Roosevelt
Portrait by Douglas Chandor, in the State Capitol,
Austin, Texas

THE *GROWTH* OF THE

AMERICAN REPUBLIC

SAMUEL ELIOT MORISON
JONATHAN TRUMBULL PROFESSOR OF AMERICAN HISTORY
IN HARVARD UNIVERSITY
AND
HENRY STEELE COMMAGER
PROFESSOR OF HISTORY, COLUMBIA UNIVERSITY

Volume Two

New York
OXFORD UNIVERSITY PRESS

Fourth Edition, Revised and Enlarged

Fifth Printing, 1955

Printed in the United States of America
by the Plimpton Press, Norwood, Mass.

PREFACE

The Growth of the American Republic appeared in 1930 as a single volume, beginning the story in 1763 and terminating it in 1917. In 1936–7 we rewrote the entire book, greatly enlarging the period since the Civil War, and carrying the story down to the second inauguration of President Franklin D. Roosevelt. In the third edition, of 1942, we extended the story backward to the origin of man in America and forward to cover America's entry into World War II. Now, when World War II has become history, we have prepared a fourth edition which covers that conflict as well, and ends with the presidential election of 1948. By eliminating some of the data on the pre-war period that no longer seems significant, this fourth edition is not substantially longer than the third. Throughout, the text has been revised to correct errors and the bibliographies have been completely reworked.

Our sincere thanks are extended to the many readers who have notified us of mistakes in earlier editions; to our colleagues who have read parts of the copy; to authors and publishers severally mentioned in the footnotes, who have allowed us to quote passages from prose and poetry; to the Carnegie Institution of Washington and Harper and Brothers for permitting us to use maps from the *Atlas of Historical Geography* and *Harper's Atlas of American History*.

We write for young men and women of all ages, for whom economy in truth-telling is neither necessary nor appropriate. We believe that history embraces the whole of a people's activity: economic and social, literary and spiritual, as well as political and military. We have endeavored therefore to give such stress to these different aspects that our story will be that of a growing and changing civilization in an expanding United States of America.

This new edition is dedicated to the veterans of World War II. May they continue to further the Growth of the American Republic!

SAMUEL ELIOT MORISON

HENRY STEELE COMMAGER

July 1950

CONTENTS

VOLUME II

I. THE AFTERMATH OF THE WAR 1

1. The Heritage of the War. 2. The Revolution. 3. The Triumphant North: wealth, natural resources, industry. 4. Prostrate South: physical devastation, administrative collapse, social disorganization. 5. The Freedmen: black codes, Freedmen's Bureau, Union League, economic progress. 6. Beginnings of the New South: physical restoration, agricultural revolution, industrial revolution.

II. RECONSTRUCTION, POLITICAL AND CONSTITUTIONAL, 1865–1877 31

1. Reconstruction during the Civil War: Presidential plan, Congressional plan. 2. Andrew Johnson takes Charge: Johnson, South accepts defeat. 3. Congress Intervenes: Radical leaders, Joint Committee of Fifteen, election of 1866. 4. Congressional Reconstruction: Reconstruction Acts, military rule, impeachment. 5. Black Reconstruction: carpet-bag and scalawag rule, taxes and debts, constructive achievements. 6. Reconstruction and the Constitution. 7. Restoration of White Rule in the South: Ku Klux Klan, Force Acts, election of 1876 and the end of carpet-bag rule.

III. POLITICS OF THE GRANT ADMINISTRATION, 1869–1877 56

1. The Election of 1868. 2. President Grant: character, cabinet. 3. Foreign Affairs: expansion under Seward, Cuban rebellion, the Fenians, Geneva arbitration. 4. Domestic politics: Southern question, greenbacks and resumption, tariff and civil service. 5. The Liberal Republican Movement: revolt against Grantism, the Cincinnati convention, campaign of 1872. 6. Scandal and Stagnation: Credit Mobilier, Whisky Ring, corruption in state and local politics, panic of 1873, the Centennial. 7. The Disputed Election of 1876.

IV. THE PASSING OF THE FRONTIER, 1865–1890 . 79

1. The Last West: the Plains barrier, bases for a new sectionalism. 2. The Indian Problem: corruption and mismanagement, peace policy and Dawes Act. 3. The Mining Frontier: gold and silver mines, Nevada and Comstock lode, social and legal institutions of mining kingdom. 4. The Cattle Kingdom: run of cattle industry, long drive, social and cultural institutions, collapse of cattle industry. 5. The Disappearance of the Frontier: settling the Plains area, fencing and dry farming, significance of passing of frontier. 6. Political Organization: admission of the Omnibus States, Oklahoma and Utah, constitutions of new states.

V. TRANSPORTATION AND ITS CONTROL, 1865–1900 105

1. The Railway Key. 2. Railroads and the West: railroad colonization, the Hill country. 3. Federal and Local Aid: land grants, financial aid. 4. Abuses and State Regulation: railroad malpractices, Granger laws, Granger cases. 5. The Advent of Federal Regulation: the Interstate Commerce Act of 1887. 6. The Decline of Steamboating.

VI. THE ECONOMIC REVOLUTION, 1865–1900 . 123

1. Hamilton Wins: the industrial state, Civil War and Industrial Revolution. 2. The Age of Invention: major inventions, social and economic consequences. 3. Iron and Steel: iron ore, Bessemer and open hearth, ironmasters, U.S. Steel Corporation. 4. Trusts and Monopolies: rise of trusts, consolidation in transportation. 5. Trust regulation: protest against trusts, Sherman Act of 1890, judicial interpretation.

VII. LABOR, 1865–1933 146

1. General Considerations: nature of labor problem, machinery and labor; corporations and labor, immigration, the double standard in labor and business. 2. The Rise of Organized Labor: Knights of Labor, Haymarket riot, Gompers and the A.F. of L., the I.W.W. 3. Industrial Conflicts: general causes, Great Strike of '77, Pullman strike, Altgeld and Cleveland, violence in coal, steel, and textile industries. 4. Labor Legislation and the Courts: right to strike, picketing, federal legislation, child labor, hour and wage legislation, and the courts.

VIII. IMMIGRATION, 1865–1936 174

1. The Melting Pot. 2. The Old Immigration and the New: change in source of immigration, geographical distribution, economic distribution, Mexican and Canadian immigration, immigrant constitutions. 3. Putting up the Bars: state regulation, Oriental immigration, Acts of 1917, 1921, 1924, and 1929.

IX. AGRICULTURE AND THE FARM PROBLEM, 1865–1920 189

1. The Agricultural Revolution. 2. Machinery. 3. Scientific Agriculture. 4. The Farm problem: physical problem, economic problem, social and political problems. 5. Agrarian Revolt: the Grange, the Alliance movement, the Non-Partisan League.

X. POLITICS, 1877–1890 214

1. Masks in a Pageant: bankruptcy of major parties, titular and real party leaders, evasion of issues. 2. Glimmerings of Reform: Hayes, Garfield, and Arthur, Civil Service reform. 3. The Administration of Grover Cleveland: election of 1884, Cleveland, land reforms, tariff. 4. The Climax of Reaction: election of 1888, pensions, McKinley tariff.

XI. THE BATTLE OF THE STANDARDS, 1890–1897 . 236

1. The Populist Revolt: agrarian distress, the Populist Party, election of 1892. 2. The Money Question: origin of the money question, greenbacks, crime of '73, specie resumption, silver, Bland-Allison and Sherman Acts, international bimetallism. 3. The President and the Panic: panic of 1893, repeal of Sherman Act, tariff of 1894, Coxey's programme, ebb-tide and elections of 1894. 4. Bryan, Bryan, Bryan, Bryan: organization of silver Democracy, Republican and Democratic conventions, Bryan and the Cross of Gold, campaign of 1896.

XII. ARTS, PHILOSOPHY, AND LETTERS, 1865–1920 . 266

1. The Gilded Age. 2. Transcendentalism to Pragmatism. 3. Legal and Religious Thought: pragmatism in law, the church and Darwinism, the socialization of Christianity. 4. Literary Currents: post-war decline, local color, Mark Twain, literature of protest, Howells, recorders of the social scene, historical fiction, popular

literature. 5. Journalism: changes in technique and organization, leading editors, Pulitzer and Hearst, magazines. 6. Art and Architecture: architecture, painting, sculpture, collections and museums. 7. Education: the South, elementary education, McGuffey's Readers, educational reforms, higher education, the Morrill Act and professional education, education for women, the public library.

XIII. IMPERIALISM AND WORLD POWER, 1865–1898 . 314

1. The United States in World Affairs: emergence from isolation, foreign trade, Pacific policy, Hawaii, Samoa, Pan-Americanism, Venezuela controversy. 2. Manifest Destiny in the Nineties: the rise of imperialism, expansionists of 1898. 3. Cuba Libre: the Cuban revolution, causes of American intervention, the martial spirit, war. 4. Exit Spain: American unpreparedness, military and naval campaign in Cuba, Manila Bay, peace.

XIV. THE AMERICAN COLONIAL EMPIRE, 1898–1913 . 336

1. The Fruits of Victory: the problem of the Philippines, the Peace of Paris, ratification, Philippine Insurrection, anti-imperialism, the campaign of 1900. 2. The Supreme Court follows the Election Returns: the insular cases. 3. The American Colonial System: Cuba and the Platt Amendment, Puerto Rico, the Danish West Indies, the Philippines, Philippine Independence. 4. The Open Door: the partition of China, American interest in China, Hays' open-door policy, Boxer uprising, closing the open door.

XV. THE PROGRESSIVE MOVEMENT, 1890–1917 . 354

1. The Promise of American Life. 2. Challenge to American Democracy: the double standard of private and business morals, the growth of big business, the distribution of wealth, the rise of the city, corruption and inefficiency in politics. 3. The Era of the Muckrakers. 4. Humanitarianism: social settlements, battle with the slums, charity organization, women and children, penal and prison reform, temperance crusade, Indians and Negroes. 5. Progressivism in Politics: philosophy of progressivism, national politics, reform in state politics, the shame of the cities, municipal reform.

XVI. THE REIGN OF ROOSEVELT, 1901–1909 . . 385

1. Theodore Roosevelt. 2. The Trusts: growth of trusts, malpractices, trust legislation, trust-busting. 3. The Extension of Government Regulation: railway regulation, pure food and drugs. 4. Conservation: the exhaustion of natural resources, Roosevelt's conservation policies. 5. The Big Stick: Panama, Venezuela, Cuba, and San Domingo. 6. World Politics: Russo-Japanese War, Algeciras Conference, the election of 1908.

XVII. THE TAFT ADMINISTRATION, 1909–1913 . . 410

1. Ineptitude and Insurgency: W.H.Taft, the Payne-Aldrich tariff, insurgent revolt, Taft's achievements. 2. Canadian Reciprocity and Dollar Diplomacy. 3. Roosevelt and the Progressive Party: the New Nationalism, LaFollette's campaign, Republican Convention of 1912. 4. Woodrow Wilson and the Election of 1912: Wilson, Democratic Convention of 1912, the election.

XVIII. THE NEW FREEDOM, 1913–1917 . . . 425

1. The Inaugural. 2. The Underwood Tariff. 3. Banking and Currency Reform: the Pujo Committee and the Money Trust, the Federal Reserve Act. 4. The Regulation of Business: the Federal Trade Commission Act, the Clayton Act, Democratic achievement. 5. Neighbors and Dependencies: Wilson's foreign policy, the Caribbean, Mexico.

XIX. THE ROAD TO WAR, 1914–1917 . . . 445

1. The United States and the World War — Factors and Conditions: the outbreak of the war, American neutrality, public opinion in the United States, propaganda, Economic factors — trade, munitions, loans. 2. The Struggle for Neutral Rights: inadequacy of international law, English violations of neutral rights, German submarine warfare, the *Lusitania* and Bryan's resignation. 3. Preparedness and the Election of 1916: efforts toward peace, preparedness, the election of 1912. 4. War: final appeal to belligerents, renewal of submarine warfare, break with Germany and its significance, moral cost of war, war.

XX. WAR AND PEACE, 1917–1920 . . . 469

1. Industrial and Financial Mobilization: Council for National Defense, shipping, railroads, industries, food,

money. 2. Mobilizing Public Opinion: committee on public information, attack on German morale, the Fourteen Points, espionage and sedition acts, persecution. 3. Naval and Military Operations: the navy, conscription, training, military organization, the crisis on the Western front, Belleau Wood and Château Thierry, St. Mihiel, Meuse-Argonne offensive, armistice. 4. The Peace Conference, the Treaty, and the League: position of Wilson, the American peace delegation, the Peace Conference, the Treaty of Versailles, the League of Nations, the struggle over ratification.

XXI. WORLD POLITICS, 1920–1937 497

1. The League, the World Court, and Peace: foreign policy of Republicans, relations with the League, disarmament and the Washington Conference, the outlawry of war, neutrality legislation, the World Court. 2. War Debts and Reparations: war debts, the Dawes and Young plans, moratorium and default. 3. Retreat from the Far East: Japanese hegemony in the Far East, Washington Conference, Japanese violation of treaties and of the open door. 4. The Metamorphosis of the Monroe Doctrine: Mexican relations, Caribbean, Clark Memorandum, good neighbor policy.

XXII. 'NORMALCY' AND REACTION, 1921–1933 . . 515

1. Politics and Personalities: the conservative reaction, election of 1920, the Harding administration, the election of 1924, Coolidge, the election of 1928, philosophy of the Hoover administration. 2. Liquidating the War: the railroads and the Transportation Act of 1920, Merchant Marine, aviation, veterans' benefits, prohibition. 3. Economic Policies: economic philosophy, taxes and debt, the Fordney-McCumber and Hawley-Smoot tariffs, foreign trade and markets, oil diplomacy, trusts and trade associations, concentration of control in industry and finance, public utilities, Muscle Shoals. 4. Agricultural Distress: collapse of farm prosperity, Republican farm policies, McNary-Haugen and export debentures plans, the Federal Farm Board. 5. The Depression: the boom; fundamental causes of the depression, the crash, government policies, the RFC.

XXIII. AMERICAN SOCIETY BETWEEN TWO WARS . 549

1. Prosperity and Disillusionment. 2. Intolerance. 3. Literary Interpretations. 4. Fine Arts and Music. 5. Science, Natural and Social.

XXIV. THE NEW DEAL, 1933– 580

1. The Election of 1932: issues and candidates, Franklin D. Roosevelt, the campaign, the election. 2. The Philosophy of the New Deal: Roosevelt's Inaugural Address, recovery and reform, the legislative lag in the United States, American precedents of new deal legislation. 3. Money, Banking, and Securities Legislation: emergency banking act, abandonment of gold standard, inflation and devaluation, credit policies, mortgage relief, Glass-Steagall Act, securities and securities exchange legislation. 4. Farm Relief: the AAA, effects on farm economy, the Hoosac Mills case, soil conservation and resettlement, farm mortgage and credit policies, reciprocity treaties. 5. Industry Under the New Deal: the NRA, the codes, operation and effect of the NRA, the Schechter case. 6. Labor Under the New Deal: administrative attitude, labor and the NRA, the NLRB and its activities, the Wagner case, the A.F. of L. and the C.I.O., strikes, violence, and terrorism. 7. Conservation and the Regulation of Utilities: conservation and the CCC, the Tennessee Valley Authority, regional planning, the Ashwander case, utilities control legislation. 8. Relief and Security: emergency relief, public works program and its achievements, mounting debt, Social Security legislation, judicial validation of legislation.

XXV. DOMESTIC ISSUES OF THE SECOND ADMINISTRATION 612

1. The Election of 1936. 2. Court Reform and Constitutional Revolution. 3. Farm and Labor Legislation. 4. Political and Administrative Reform. 5. The New Deal: An Evaluation.

XXVI. THE SECOND WORLD WAR 632

1. Isolationism and the Threat to Collective Security. 2. The Bell Tolls. 3. A Fortress on a Paper Pad. 4. War. 5. The Great Debate. 6. The Year of Decision.

XXVII. WORLD WAR II: THE FRAMEWORK . . 665
1. Basic Considerations. 2. Military Preparedness. 3. The Battle of Production. 4. Workers, Farmers, and Consumers. 5. Science Goes to War.

XXVIII. FIGHTING THE WAR 698
1. The Battle of the Atlantic, 1941–1944. 2. Active Defense in the Pacific, 1941–1942. 3. From Casablanca to Cape Bon. 4. Sicily and Italy.

XXIX. WINNING THE WAR 730
1. The Air War. 2. The Great Invasion. 3. Normandy to the Rhine. 4. Attack and Counterattack. 5. Across the Pacific. 6. Political Interlude. 7. Götterdämmerung. 8. Victory against Japan.

XXX. THE TRUMAN ADMINISTRATIONS . . 777
1. Reconversion. 2. Labor Unrest and Labor Gains. 3. Society, Education, and Civil Rights. 4. Politics and the Election of 1948.

XXXI. THE RESPONSIBILITIES OF WORLD POWER . 795
1. The New World. 2. Relief and Reconstruction. 3. Liquidating the War. 4. Organization for Peace. 5. The Control of Atomic Energy. 6. The Cold War.

BIBLIOGRAPHY 829

STATISTICAL TABLES 897

THE CONSTITUTION OF THE UNITED STATES OF AMERICA 925

INDEX 949

LIST OF ILLUSTRATIONS

VOLUME II

Franklin Delano Roosevelt . . . . . *frontispiece*
From a Portrait by Douglas Chandor, in the State Capitol, Austin, Texas

Average Value of Farm Land per Acre: 1910; Increase in Farm Property by States: 1860–1870 14
From Thirteenth Census of the United States, 1910, *Vol. V.*

Selected Plantation Area, Boundaries of Cotton Belt, etc., 1910 24
From Thirteenth Census of the United States, 1910, *Vol. V.*

Reconstruction in the South 44
From Charles O. Paullin, Atlas of the Historical Geography of the United States, *Plate* 164E

Great Plains, showing Indian Reservations 82
From Donaldson, Public Domain

Passing of the Frontier, 1870–1900. 2 maps 96

Railroad Systems. 4 maps 118
From Charles O. Paullin, Atlas of the Historical Geography of the United States, *Plates,* 140B, 141D,-E,-G

Value of Manufactured Products in 1919, by States . . 134

Membership of American Federation of Labor . . . 158

Sources of Immigration to the United States . . . 176
From Report of Industrial Commission of 1900, *Vol. XIX.*

Map of the United States showing Productive Areas . . 190
From U.S. Treasury Department, Bureau of Statistics

Irrigation Projects and Roster of Federal Dams, 1942 . . 198
Reproduced by permission of the New York Times

Tenant Farmers: 1880, 1930. 2 maps 202
From Charles O. Paullin, Atlas of the Historical Geography of the United States, *Plates,* 146N,-Q

Election of 1896 262

Population Map showing Urban Concentration . . 362
Reproduced by permission of the publishers and copyright owners, Erwin, Wasey and Co., Inc., N. Y.

The American Army in France 485
From U.S. War Department, The War with Germany: A Statistical Summary

American Interests and Possessions Abroad, 1930 . . 508
Figures are based upon Paul Dickens, A New Estimate of American Investment Abroad, *U.S. Dept. of Commerce Trade Infor., Bull. No.* 767

Presidential Elections: 1928, 1932. 2 maps . . . 520

The Depression. 2 charts 539
Reproduced by permission of the New York Herald Tribune *and the Bureau of Agricultural Economics*

Economic Interests: 1920 547
From Langley and Foley, Since the Civil War (*D. Appleton-Century, Co., Inc.*)

Congress since 1928 583

Concentration of Wealth. 2 maps 588
From Charles O. Paullin, Atlas of the Historical Geography of the United States, *Plates* 153C, 155D

Wholesale Prices and Purchasing Power of the Dollar . . 592
Based on U.S. Bureau of Labor Statistics

Employment and Unemployment, 1929–1949 . . . 602

The Tennessee Valley 604
From Unified Development of Tennessee River System (*Report of Tennessee Valley Authority*)

Elections of 1936 and 1940 614

The Caribbean: Bases Acquired by the United States from Great Britain, 1940 652
From Design for Power, *by Frederick L. Schuman, by permission of Alfred A. Knopf, Inc., authorized publishers*

Industrial Production Index, 1934–1946 684
From Board of Governors of the Federal Reserve System

Stages of the Solomons Campaign 716

The War in North Africa 720

Invasions of Sicily and Italy 724

Operations in Italy 728

The Air War in Europe 732
Adapted from U.S. Strategic Bombing Survey Reports

Invasion of Normandy 736

The Battle of France 744
From The War in Maps

Pacific Theater, 1941–1945 752

Liberation of the Philippines, 1944–1945 . . . 770

Consumers' Price Index in Two World Wars . . . 778

Labor Force, Employment and Unemployment, 1940–1947 . 780
From Department of Commerce, Bureau of the Census

Population Changes since 1940 786
From the New York Times, *13 November 1949*

Zones of Occupation, Germany and Austria . . . 806

THE GROWTH OF THE AMERICAN REPUBLIC

THE GROWTH OF THE AMERICAN REPUBLIC

Volume II

I

THE AFTERMATH OF THE WAR

1. *The Heritage of War*

Bow down, dear land, for thou hast found release!
  Thy God, in these distempered days,
  Hath taught thee the sure wisdom of His ways
And through thine enemies hath wrought thy peace!
  Bow down in prayer and praise!
No poorest in thy borders but may now
Lift to the juster skies a man's enfranchised brow;
O Beautiful! My Country! Ours once more!

THUS James Russell Lowell, at the Harvard commemoration service of 1865, saluted, as he believed, a reunited nation purged by war of all grossness that had accompanied its rise to power. But the fierce passions of warfare had burnt good with evil; and in the scorched soil the new growth showed more tares than wheat. Lowell was, in fact, delivering the swan song of the New England intellectuals and reformers. In the generation to come that region would no longer furnish the nation with reformers and men of letters, but with a mongrel breed of politicians, sired by abolition out of profiteering. Industry and commerce had the Middle States firmly in their grasp and were extending tentacles throughout the Middle West. The old simplicity and idealism retreated beyond the Mississippi, and materialism soon overtook them there.

The war had been fought for the preservation of the Union, yet this was not the sole object of the war. The nation whose endurance was to be tested was, as Lincoln said in his Gettysburg Address, 'a nation conceived in liberty and dedicated to the proposition that all men are created equal.' After 1862 the abolition of slavery came to be a second acknowledged objective of the war. And to many people, in Europe as in America, the maintenance of a 'government of the people, by the people, for the people' came to be a third. Union, freedom, and democracy, these things were legitimate objectives of the war, and it is proper to inquire to what extent they were achieved, and at what cost.

Union had been preserved, but only in the narrow sense of territorial integrity had the old Union been restored. The original Federal Union had disappeared, and in its place arose a strong national state, federal chiefly in administrative machinery. The long dispute over the nature of the Union had been settled, at last, and in favor of the nationalist contention, but the settlement had been brought about by violence; soon it was to be sanctioned by constitutional guarantees and accepted by common consent. Nor had sectionalism disappeared. The natural influences of geography and climate which had gone to create northern and southern sectionalism remained. And in the generation after the war a third powerful section came into existence — the trans-Mississippi West, whose regional consciousness, like that of the South, was accentuated by its politico-economic exploitation by the Northeast. Until the turn of the century American life was conditioned by this tripartite sectional division of North, South, and West.

Slavery, to be sure, was gone and no more would politicians proclaim the sophistry that black servitude was necessary for white freedom. But emancipation, too, had been brought about by violence rather than by reason or by natural law. Perhaps this was the only way by which it could have been brought about, but even the most ardent champions of freedom were forced to admit that the method was unfortunate alike for white and for black. Emancipation ended slavery, and that was a momentous thing, but it did not solve the Negro problem. But in the weird metamorphosis of race relations that followed Appomattox, the Negroes did have some voice in their own destiny, albeit for the most part they merely obeyed new masters.

And what shall we say of the third objective — government of, by, and for the people? Democracy, indeed, had not 'perished from the earth,' yet for a decade to come the essentials of self-government were denied to the South, and Americans witnessed what they had never before known: military government in time of peace. The Civil War destroyed slavery and the slave-holding class; but within a few years it strengthened corporate industry and sharpened class dissensions in the victorious North. Twenty years after the attack on Fort Sumter the railroads alone represented a greater investment and concentration of power than had ever the slave interest, and their influence in politics and in the economic activities of free men were scarcely less far-reaching. The Civil War advanced democracy in the South because there slavery was destroyed and almost everyone reduced to a uniform poverty; but in the North and the West it furnished an opportunity for the development of powerful industrial and financial interests with which democracy had to grapple, as it had with slavery. As early as 1873 Walt Whitman, apostle of democracy, looked out upon *Democratic Vistas* and was moved to solemn warning:

> Shift and turn the combinations of the statement as we may, the problem of the future of America is in certain respects as dark as it is vast. Pride, competition, segregation, vicious wilfulness, and license beyond example brood already upon us. Unwieldy and immense, who shall hold in behemoth? who bridle leviathan? Flaunt it as we choose, athwart and over the roads of our progress loom huge uncertainty, and dreadful threatening gloom. It is useless to deny it: Democracy grows rankly up the thickest, noxious, deadliest plants and fruits of all — brings worse and worse invaders — needs newer, larger, stronger, keener compensations and compellers.

And years later Justice Harlan of the Supreme Court, looking back upon this period, remembered that 'there was everywhere among the people generally a deep feeling of unrest. The nation had been rid of human slavery . . . but the conviction was universal that the country was in real danger from another kind of slavery, namely the slavery that would result from aggregations of capital in the hands of a few.'

The major objectives of the war, then, had been achieved, but only in a partial and inconclusive manner, and the post-Civil War generation was to learn what our own generation has learned, that war always creates as many problems as it solves. The cost, too, had been colossal, though Lincoln alone of the statesmen of that day seems to have realized how great it was and how hard its payment. 'Fondly do we hope,' he had said, 'fervently do we pray, that this mighty scourge of war may speedily pass away. Yet if God wills that it continue until all the wealth piled by the bondsman's two hundred and fifty years of unrequited toil shall be sunk, and until every drop of blood drawn with the lash shall be paid by another drawn by the sword, as was said three thousand years ago, so still it must be said, "The judgments of the Lord are true and righteous altogether."'

It is impossible, now, to compute with exactness the cost of the Civil War, but Lincoln's estimate was, if possible, too moderate. Deaths from all causes in the Union army totalled some 360,000, and in the Confederate army some 260,000. The number of wounded who recovered was far larger: but no reliable figures have ever been compiled. How many lives were lost because of malnutrition, disease, and the chaotic conditions of 1865 and 1866, it is impossible to say, nor can we count the cost in lives shattered by destruction and demoralized by defeat.

The money cost of the war was staggering; proportionally higher, indeed, than the money cost of the World War. Loans and taxes raised by the Federal Government came to a little less than three billion dollars, and the interest on the Civil War debt came to an additional two billion eight hundred million. The Confederacy floated loans of over two billion dollars, but the total financial loss of the South, in property confiscated, depreciated, and destroyed, in the losses of banks and insurance companies and businesses, and in the expense of reconstruction, was incalculable. Many states, North and South, went heavily into debt for the prosecution of the war. And although these debts have long been extinguished, the country is still paying for the war: pensions paid by the United States government to date have come to a little less than eight billion dollars, and large additional sums have been paid to Confederate veterans by Southern states. The total money cost of the war to North and South may be estimated at well over twenty billion dollars.

This does not mean the total cost. The war left a heritage not only of death, desolation and debt, but of practical problems of far-reaching importance and enormous complexity. The Union and Confederate armies had to be demobilized and upwards of one and one-half million men returned to the pursuits of peace. The administrative activities of the War Department and the Provost General's office had to be curbed and the supremacy of civil government restored. Currency and industry needed deflation to a peace basis and reinflation to provide for the needs of an expanding nation. There were staggering financial burdens of the war to be liquidated. Four million former slaves had to be readjusted to their new condition. Equally serious were the problems presented by the new industrial revolution in the North and the agricultural revolution in the South and the West. And foreign affairs of a most threatening nature, both in Europe and in America, called for immediate action.

The material problems of the war could be solved and the material devastation repaired; the moral devastation was never wholly repaired. The North was demoralized by victory, the South by defeat. During the war violence and destruction and hatred had been called virtues; it was a long time before they were recognized again as vices. The war had been brutalizing in its effects on combatants and noncombatants alike. Ruthlessness and wastefulness, extravagance and corruption, speculation and exploitation had accompanied the conflict, and they lingered on to trouble the post-war years. Above all the war left a heritage of misunderstanding and even of bitterness, that colored the thinking and conditioned the actions of men, North and South, for over a generation.

The United States stood on the threshold of a new era, and she was ill prepared to meet it. Modern America emerged from the period usually called 'Reconstruction.' In the fiery cauldron of the Civil War not only the Old South was melted down but the old America — the federal republic of Thomas Jefferson and Andrew Jackson — was volatilized. The Civil War, itself a political revolution, speeded up an inevitable revolution in material economy, society, and civilization.

2. *The Revolution*

To the South the fall of the Confederacy brought the overthrow of the planter and political aristocracy that had guided the destinies of that section since the days of Thomas Jefferson. A large part of this class was excluded, for some years, from participation in the government, and for some of the abler leaders such as Davis and Lee the disability was never removed. Slave property valued in 1860 at over two billion dollars was confiscated, and so were the savings and sacrifices represented by Confederate securities. A labor system which was the very basis of Southern society was overthrown, the agricultural régime which it served was disarranged, and a new system, no less wasteful and scarcely less oppressive, established in its stead.

As a result the old planter aristocracy almost disappeared from the South. This class had suffered in the war more severely than any other group; for if the war had been 'a poor man's fight,' the poor white had nothing to lose, and his condition was better in 1870 than it had been in 1850. But the planters lost not only their best blood but their means of recuperation. The blows of reconstruction, more staggering than those of defeat, wasted those impalpable moral values which had been accumulated during a century or more of stewardship. Well they learned what the Knights of Aristophanes declared twenty-four centuries ago:

> There are things, then, hotter than fire, there are speeches more shameless still
> Than the shameless speeches of those who rule the City at will.

Many gave up the struggle to maintain themselves on the land. A few fled to England, Mexico, or Brazil, others migrated to the Northern cities or started life anew in the West, many moved to the towns and tried to fit themselves for business or professional life. At the same time the small farmers and poor whites took advantage of the prevailing disorder to enlarge their farms, better their conditions, and elect men of their own kind, who shared instead of scorned their prejudices, to high office. A little while and the Tillmans, Watsons, and Rankins would sit in the seats of the Hamptons, the Cobbs, and the Clays.

Yet the most clean-cut stroke of the revolution in the South was the emancipation of four million Negro slaves. This process of emancipation had begun during the war; it was consummated by three Amendments to the Constitution. The Thirteenth, ratified in 1865, abolished slavery in places not reached by the Emancipation Proclamation. The Fourteenth Amendment extended federal protection to the freedmen for their personal and property rights, and the Fifteenth Amendment gave them the franchise. 'The bottom rail was on top' in the salty phrase of the time, but the whites did not let it stay there long.

While the old pattern of Southern society and economy was being rearranged into a new one, a corresponding revolution was effected in the North. With the representatives of the planter class out of Congress, the spokesmen of industry, finance, and of free western lands were unopposed, unless by one another. During the war they pushed through legislation to fulfil the frustrated desires of the fifties, and after victory they consolidated the fruits thereof.

The moderate tariff of 1857 gave way to the Morrill tariff of 1861, and that to a series of war tariffs with duties scaling rapidly upward, and carefully adapted to meet the need and greed of Northern business. By the National Banking Acts of 1863 and 1864 the Independent Treasury system of 1846 was swept away in favor of one more attractive to private finance; and an act of 1865 imposed a tax of ten per cent on all state bank notes, a fatal blow that none will regret. The money question which long agitated American politics was settled as the financial interests of the East wished, by the rejection of greenback inflation, the resumption of specie payments, and eventually by the establishment of the gold standard. That there might be no shortage of labor, Congress in 1864 permitted the importation of contract labor from abroad, and though this act was repealed within a few years, the practice itself was not discontinued until the decade of the eighties. At the same time the policy of internal improvements at national expense found expression in subsidies to telegraph and cable lines and in generous grants of millions of acres out of the public domain to railroad promoters and financiers.

While Northern industry and finance were reaping the fruits of loyalty and victory, the century-old ambition of Western farmers was satisfied by the passage of the Homestead Law in 1862. This act, limited temporarily in its application to those who 'have never borne arms against the United States Government,' granted a quarter-section (160 acres) of public domain to anyone who would undertake to cultivate it. The Morrill Act, passed the same year, subsidized agricultural education through public lands. At the same time easy access to the West was assured through the government-subsidized railroads. This legislation carried out the promise of the Republican party platform and brought to that party support from the agricultural West.

In order to secure these new acquisitions the Republican party sought to throw about them constitutional guarantees. The Fourteenth Amendment with its provision that no state could deprive any person of life, liberty, or property, without due process of law, was used to protect business interests from state regulation, and taught those interests to look to the Federal Government and the Republican party for protection. The Fifteenth Amendment, granting the franchise to the freedmen, was designed to secure the Negro vote to the Republican party.

Partly as a result of this legislation the Republican party, a sectional and, in all probability, a minority party,[1] was for two decades

[1] It is interesting to note that in four out of the five Presidential elections between the end of Reconstruction in 1876 and 1892, the Democratic candidate polled a larger popular vote than did the Republican. In the fifth election, that of 1880, the Republican

firmly intrenched in power. But the support which came from industry, finance, agriculture, pensioned veterans, and the Negro does not in itself explain the long tenure of power by that party. Perhaps even more important was the fact that the Republicans could claim to be the party that had saved the Union, and that they could brand the Democrats with the odium of secession. With a single exception, every candidate which the Republican party named for the Presidency between 1868 and 1900 had been an officer in the Union army. For a generation Republican orators rang the changes on Fort Sumter and Andersonville prison, and 'waved the bloody shirt of the rebellion,' and no appeal was more effective than that voiced by Colonel Robert Ingersoll in the campaign of 1876:

> Every State that seceded from the Union was a Democratic State. Every ordinance of secession that was drawn was drawn by a Democrat. Every man that endeavored to tear the old flag from the heaven it enriches was a Democrat. . . . Every man that shot down Union soldiers was a Democrat. . . . The man that assassinated Abraham Lincoln was a Democrat. . . . Every man that raised bloodhounds to pursue human beings was a Democrat. . . . Every man that tried to spread smallpox and yellow fever in the North was a Democrat. . . . Soldiers, every scar you have on your heroic bodies was given you by a Democrat. Every scar, every arm that is missing, every limb that is gone, is a souvenir of a Democrat.

The war, then, developed a revolution in industry, transportation, and finance that was already under way, and immensely strengthened the political party which came to be committed to these interests. Most of this development might have come about eventually by peaceful means, but the war accelerated the process and gave to it a drastic character. Industrial America, Alexander Hamilton's embodied vision, swaggered in under the cloak of patriotism, with the bayonet as a substitute for the slow process of education and economic revolution.

3. *The Triumphant North*

To the North the war brought not only victory, but unprecedented prosperity, a sense of power, a spirit of buoyant confidence, an exuberance of energy, that found expression in a thousand outlets.

candidate polled some 7,000 more votes than the Democratic. Or, to use another method of calculation, the total Democratic vote, from 1872 when for the first time all the Southern states voted, to 1892, was larger by some 4,000 than the total Republican vote.

Never before had the American people exhibited greater vitality, never since has their vitality been accompanied by more reckless irresponsibility. To the generation that had saved the Union everything seemed possible: there were no worlds, except the worlds of the spirit, that could not be conquered. Men hurled themselves upon the continent with ruthless abandon as if to ravish it of its wealth. Railroads were flung across mountain barriers, and settlers crowded into half a continent, while cattle swarmed over the grass lands of the High Plains. Forests were felled, the earth gutted of coal, copper, iron ore and precious metals; petroleum spouted from untended wells. Telegraph wires were strung across the country and cables stretched from continent to continent; factories sprang up overnight; new industries were established and old industries took on new form; speculators thronged the floors of stock and produce exchanges, inventors flooded the patent office with applications for new devices with which to conquer nature and create wealth. Cities grew so fast that no one could keep track of them, and the mansions of the rich were as vulgar as the tenements of the poor were squalid. And year after year, from every hamlet and farm, countrymen hurried in to the cities, and immigrants poured in to the mines and the mills, all anxious to participate in the great barbecue. Well might Walt Whitman ask, 'Who shall hold in Behemoth? who bridle Leviathan?'

Despite four years of war the resources of the North seemed little impaired. Population and wealth had increased; the output of factory and farm was larger than ever before. The national debt was close to three billion dollars, but no one doubted the solvency of the government. More money was in circulation than at any time in our history, and the census of 1870 revealed that the per capita wealth of the North had doubled in ten years. Sectional antipathies were for the time moderated, and East and West joined in the common enterprise of exploitation. There was a universal feeling that the resources of the continent were as yet untapped. 'The truth is,' wrote Senator Sherman to his brother, the General, 'the close of the war with our resources unimpaired gives an elevation, a scope to the ideas of leading capitalists far higher than anything ever undertaken in this country before. They talk of millions as confidently as formerly of thousands.'

The war had stimulated industry and banking and created new opportunities for the amassing of private wealth. The business of supplying the armies with food and clothing and munitions was immensely profitable, and behind the new tariff schedules the woolens industry and the iron and steel industry flourished as never before. More profitable still was the business of financing the war. Government bonds bore from five to seven per cent interest in gold. During the war they had sold at a discount; after the war they brought a premium, and many a fortune was founded upon speculation in these bonds. The National Banking Act, too, afforded a legitimate means to wealth, and in 1870 some sixteen hundred banks reported earnings of sixty million dollars on a capitalization of $425,000,000, while President Johnson estimated that banks which held government bonds received an aggregate of seventeen per cent interest annually upon their investment. The rewards of railroad organization, financing, and construction were even greater. At the end of the war there had been some thirty-five thousand miles of railroad in the country: ten years later the figure was seventy-four thousand, and the profits of construction and operation had gone, often by devious means, to establish the fortunes of Vanderbilt and Gould, Huntington and Stanford, and other multi-millionaires.

No less spectacular was the exploitation of natural resources, largely for the aggrandizement of private individuals. Oil was struck in western Pennsylvania in 1859, and soon thousands of fortune-hunters stampeded into the oil-soaked triangle between the Allegheny river and Oil Creek, and the stock of hundreds of new oil companies was hawked from town to town. During the war years the production of oil increased from twenty-one million to one hundred and four million gallons, and the capitalization of new oil companies was not far from half a billion dollars. Equally fabulous is the story of silver. In the year of Lincoln's election the production of silver was a paltry $150,000; by the end of Reconstruction the annual production had reached $38,000,000 and the silver barons of the West had come to exercise an influence in politics comparable to that held by bankers and industrialists in the East. During the same period the production of other basic minerals kept pace with that of oil and silver: coal production trebled, and iron ore production in the Lake Superior region alone increased more than ten-fold.

Business, responding to new and cheaper resources and to new markets, flourished as never before. Old factories expanded, and new factories were built, and in the decade of the sixties the number of manufacturing establishments in the entire country increased by eighty per cent. Wherever we dip into the economic statistics of the war and the post-war years we emerge with the same result. During these years the value of manufactured products in Maine more than doubled, in Illinois it trebled, and in Michigan it increased fourfold. Four times as much timber was cut in Michigan, four times as much pig iron was smelted in Ohio, four times as much freight was handled by the Pennsylvania railroad, four times as many miles of railroad track were laid, in 1870 as in 1860. The woolens, the cotton, the iron, the lumber, the meat, and the milling industries all showed a steady and even a spectacular development. All through the decade after Appomattox both imports and exports enjoyed a continuous increase. Three times as many patents were granted in 1870 as in 1860, and the transactions in the New York clearing house multiplied five-fold. And while property values in the South were suffering a cataclysmic decline, the census reported an increase in the total property value of the North and the West from ten billion dollars in 1860 to over twenty-five billion dollars a decade later.

Accompanying this extraordinary development of business enterprise was a steady growth in the population of cities and in immigration. Older cities such as New York and Philadelphia, Boston and Baltimore, continued the growth which had begun back in the forties, and newer cities such as Chicago and St. Louis, Cleveland and Pittsburgh, St. Paul and San Francisco, more than doubled their population in ten years. Immigration, too, responded to the new opportunities. Even during the war years some eight hundred thousand immigrants had found their way to the United States, and in the ten years after Appomattox no less than three and one quarter million immigrants flooded into the cities and the farms of the North and the West.

Industry, transportation, banking, speculation, the exploitation of natural resources and of labor, all contributed to the wealth of the country and, even more largely, to the wealth of individuals. Already observers began to remark that concentration of wealth in certain favored areas and in certain favored groups which has come to be so characteristic of the modern America. In 1870, for example, the wealth of New York State alone was more than twice as great as the combined wealth of all the ex-Confederate states; in that same year only 276,000 persons paid a tax on incomes of one thousand dollars or over. Every business grew its own crop of millionaires, and soon the names of Morgan and Cooke, Vanderbilt and Gould, Armour and Swift, McCormick and Pillsbury, came to be as familiar to the average American as the names of statesmen. A new plutocracy emerged from the war and reconstruction, masters of money who were no less self-conscious and no less powerful than the planter aristocracy of the old South. Rarely before had wealth been as irresponsible: the new rich were interested in government chiefly in so far as government had favors to bestow. Never before had wealth been more ostentatious: the mansions of the new rich sprouted vaingloriously along New York's Fifth Avenue and Chicago's Lake Shore and on the steep hills overlooking San Francisco's Golden Gate, while their owners tried to buy culture as they bought everything else. The war which had flattened out class distinctions in the South tended to accentuate class distinctions in the North.

4. *The Prostrate South*

Physical devastation without parallel until 1914–18 preceded the social and economic revolution in the South. Over large sections of the country Union and Confederate armies had tramped and fought, and parts of Virginia, Tennessee, South Carolina, Georgia, Alabama, and Arkansas had the appearance of enormous battlefields. Sherman had left a broad belt of blackened ruin from Atlanta to Savannah and from Savannah to Raleigh: 'where our footsteps pass,' wrote one of his aides, 'fire, ashes, and desolation follow in the path.' From Fairfax Courthouse to Petersburg the region was such a wilderness that nature came back and deer ran wild in the forests. Sheridan had swept down the fertile Shenandoah valley like an avenging fury, leaving a trail of wreckage and ruin. 'We had no cattle, hogs, sheep, or horses or anything else,' wrote a native of Virginia. 'The fences were all gone . . . the barns were all burned; chimneys standing without houses and houses standing without roofs, or doors, or windows . . . bridges all destroyed, roads badly cut up.' In the West conditions were just as bad. 'The Tennessee Valley,' wrote Robert Somers, an English observer, 'consists for the most part of plantations in a state of semi-decay and plantations of which the ruin is total and complete.' The Governor of Arkansas wrote of his state: 'The desolations of war are beyond description. . . . Besides the utter desolation that marked the tracks of war and battle, guerilla bands and scouting parties have pillaged almost every neighbourhood. . . . It would be safe to say that two thirds of the counties in the State are in destitute circumstances.'

Some of the cities presented a picture as appalling as the rural regions. Charleston, once the proudest city of the South, had been bombarded and partially burned; a northern visitor painted it as a city of 'vacant houses, of widowed women, of rotting wharves, of deserted warehouses, of weed-wild gardens, of miles of grass-grown streets, of acres of pitiful and voiceless barrenness.' Columbia, the garden city of South Carolina, had been left 'a wilderness of ruins. Its heart is but a mass of blackened chimneys and crumbling walls. Two thirds of the buildings in the place were burned . . . not a store, office, or shop escaped.' Of Richmond, the capital of the Confederacy, we read 'all up and down, as far as the eye could reach, the business portion of the city lay in ruins. Beds of cinders, cellars half filled with bricks and rubbish, broken and blackened walls, impassable streets deluged with *debris*.' In Atlanta, Sidney Andrews found masses of brick and mortar, charred timber, scraps of tin roofing, engine bolts and bars, cannonballs, and long shot filling the ruined streets. Mobile, Galveston, Vicksburg, and numerous other cities of the South were in a similar plight.

With the collapse of the Confederacy, civil government and administration all but disappeared throughout the South. There was no money for the support of government and no authority which could assess or collect taxes. The postal service was paralyzed and it was fully two years before normal service was restored. There were no courts, no judges, no sheriffs, no police officers with any authority, and vandalism went unrestrained except by public opinion or by lynch law. 'Our principal danger,' observed George Cary Eggleston, 'was from lawless bands of marauders who infested the country, and our greatest difficulty in dealing with them lay in the utter absence of constituted authority of any sort. Our country was full of highwaymen . . . the offscourings of the two armies and of the suddenly freed negro population — deserters from fighting regiments on both sides and negro desperadoes who found common ground upon which to fraternize in their common depravity. They moved about in bands, from two to ten strong, cutting horses out of plows, plundering helpless people, and wantonly destroying valuables which they could not carry away.' Fraud and peculation added to the universal distress. United States Treasury agents seized hundreds of thousands of bales of cotton, and other property as well. 'Agents frequently received or collected property and sent it forward which the law did not authorize them to take,' said Secretary McCulloch. 'Lawless men, singly and in organized bands, engaged in general plunder; every species of intrigue and peculation and theft was resorted to.' No less than forty thousand claimants were subsequently reimbursed by the Federal Government because of illegal confiscation of their property.

The entire economic life of the South was shattered and even agriculture was slow to revive. Alabama produced 989,955 bales of cotton in 1860 and only 429,472 in 1870; Mississippi produced 1,202,507 bales in 1860 and 564,938 in 1870. Not until 1879 did the seceding states produce a cotton crop as large as that of 1860. The rice industry of South Carolina and Georgia all but disappeared, and so too the sugar cane industry of Louisiana. In 1870 the tobacco crop of Virginia was one-third that of 1860 and the corn and wheat crop one-half. Between 1860 and 1870 the total value of farm property in the seceding states declined forty-eight per cent.

What manufacturing there was had been all but destroyed. Not a single Southern bank or insurance company was solvent and it was years before the banking system was even partially restored. Confederate securities into which the people had sunk their savings were now as worthless as continental currency. Shops were depleted of goods, and almost everything had to be imported from the North on credit. Labor was demoralized and property shockingly depreciated in value. Farm land that had once sold for a hundred dollars an acre went begging at five dollars, and in Mississippi alone almost six million acres of land were sold for non-payment of taxes. In the decade between 1860 and 1870 the estimated real value of all property in the eleven Confederate states decreased from $5,202,055,000 to $2,929,350,000: during the same period the estimated value of all property in the rest of the country more than doubled.[2]

The transportation system of the region was in a state of collapse. Roads were all but impassable, bridges destroyed or washed away, ditches filled in, river levees broken. What steamboats had not been captured or destroyed were in a state of disrepair. Railroad transportation was paralyzed, and most of the railroad companies bankrupt. Over a stretch of one hundred and fourteen miles of railroad in Alabama 'every bridge and trestle was destroyed, cross-ties rotten, buildings burned, water-tanks gone, ditches filled up, and tracks grown up in weeds and bushes.' On a splendid stretch of road be-

[2] Few things are more confusing or more unreliable than estimates of property values. It must be recalled that slaves were counted as property in the census of 1860. It is probable, too, that the values of 1860 were somewhat inflated, those of 1870 somewhat deflated. These estimates are not the same as the figures for assessed property value: the assessed values in the South reveal a more drastic depreciation.

tween Jackson and Canton, Mississippi, 'of the 49 locomotives, 37 passenger cars, and 550 freight, baggage and gravel cars, there remained fit for use, though in a damaged condition, 1 locomotive, 2 second class passenger cars, 1 first class passenger car, 1 baggage car, 1 provision car, 2 stock and 2 flat cars.' A similar story could be told for the railroads of Virginia, the Carolinas, and Georgia. Not for a generation was the railroad system of the South properly restored, and then it was restored by Northern capital.

Starvation was imminent in certain sections. In Richmond half the population was dependent upon government rations, doled out by federal relief; in Columbia ten thousand people were fed by the army and at Atlanta the army commissary distributed food to fifty thousand needy whites and blacks of the surrounding territory. The Negroes, indeed, suffered most, because less able to adjust themselves to the new situation. The Freedmen's Bureau and other Northern relief agencies did what they could to alleviate the suffering, but as late as December 1865 it was estimated that in Alabama, Mississippi, and Georgia there were over half a million white people without the necessities of life.

Social disorganization was scarcely less complete. The entire educational system of the South had been deranged. Schools were closed, pupils and teachers scattered. School funds had been used up in the war, endowments for colleges and universities squandered or confiscated. Churches had been destroyed and church money dissipated. Young men of family who had interrupted their education to fight for Southern independence had to labor in the fields to keep their families from starving; and a planter's family which still had young men was deemed fortunate. Seventy-year old Thomas Dabney, once a proud Mississippi planter, did the family wash for years after the war. General Pendleton plowed his few acres and General Anderson worked as a day laborer in the yards of the South Carolina Railroad. George Fitzhugh, the philosopher of the Cotton Kingdom who had lectured at Harvard and Yale, lived in a poor shanty among his former slaves. We hear of a Confederate colonel peddling his wife's pies to Northern soldiers, of a faithful black supporting his old master's family by wages earned in valeting a United States army officer, of white women yoked to the plow. 'Pretty much the whole of life has been merely not dying' wrote the Southern poet, Sidney Lanier.

5. *The Freedmen*

In Reconstruction the Negro was the central figure and the most difficult problem. Upwards of a million colored people had in one way or another become free before the end of the war; victory and the Thirteenth Amendment liberated about three million more, but in the worst possible manner for themselves and for their white neighbors. Never in the history of the world had civil and political rights been conferred at one stroke on so large a body of men, nor had any people ever been less prepared to assume a new status. Many Negroes thought that freedom meant no more work and proceeded to celebrate an endless 'day ob jubilo'; others believed that every Negro would be given 'forty acres and a mule' by the government, or that the property of their former masters would be divided among them.

> Every nigger's gwine to own a mule,
>   Jubili, Jubilo!
> Every nigger's gwine to own a mule,
> An' live like Adam in de Golden Rule,
> An' send his chillun to de white-folks' school!
>   In de year of Jubilo![3]

'Emancipation having been announced one day,' wrote Tom Watson about his Georgia home, 'not a Negro remained on the place the next. The fine old homestead was deserted. Every house in "the quarter" was empty. The first impulse of freedom had carried the last of the blacks to town.' Thousands took to the woods or to the road, or clustered around the United States army posts, living on doles or dying of camp diseases. As one of the colored leaders, Frederick Douglass, said, the Negro 'was free from the individual master but a slave of society. He had neither money, property, nor friends. He was free from the old plantation, but he had nothing but the dusty road under his feet. He was free from the old quarter that once gave him shelter, but a slave to the rains of summer and the frosts of winter. He was turned loose, naked, hungry, and destitute to the open sky.' Deaths among the black men from starvation, disease, and violence in the first two years of freedom ran into the tens of thousands. Fortunate indeed were those who remained faithful to their old masters and continued to work on the old plantation.

To the average Southerner emancipation changed the position of

[3] Stephen Benét, *John Brown's Body*, p. 344.

the Negro legally rather than socially or economically. The whites of the South were unable to realize the implications of freedom and unwilling to acquiesce in anything approaching race equality. The Negro was still thought of as an inferior being, incapable of real independence, impossible to teach. Some of the former slaveholders tried sincerely and with some success to assist the Negro in adjusting himself to his new status, and observers agreed that the planter was the Negro's best friend. But the small farmers, the laborers, and the poor whites were determined to 'keep the Negro in his place,' by laws if possible, by force if necessary. J. T. Trowbridge, for example, writing shortly after the war, remarked that 'there is at this day more prejudice against color among the middle and poorer classes . . . who owned few or no slaves, than among the planters, who owned them by the hundred,' and it was the universal opinion that emancipation sharply accentuated racial antipathies in the South.

Most planters sought to keep their former slaves as hired help or as tenant farmers, or on the share-crop system. But the freedman did not take kindly to labor during the first year of liberty. Reason and persuasion failing, the Southern states attempted to deal with the situation by a series of laws collectively known as the 'black codes,' which embodied the Southern solution to the Negro problem. Tennessee had none; the codes of the other states varied widely in scope and in character. The codes of Virginia and North Carolina, where the whites were in secure control of the situation, were mild; those of South Carolina, Mississippi, and Louisiana, where the blacks outnumbered the whites, were severe.

These black codes provided for relationships between the whites and the blacks in harmony with realities — as the whites understood them — rather than with abstract theory. They conferred upon the freedmen fairly extensive privileges, gave them the essential rights of citizens to contract, sue and be sued, own and inherit property, and testify in court, and made some provision for education. In no instance were the freedmen accorded the vote or made eligible for juries, and for the most part they were not permitted to testify against white men. Because of their alleged aversion to steady work they were required to have some steady occupation, and subjected to special penalties for violation of labor contracts. Vagrancy and apprenticeship laws were especially harsh, and lent themselves readily to the establishment of a system of peonage. The penal codes provided harsher and more arbitrary punishments for blacks than for whites, and some states permitted individual masters to administer corporal punishment to 'refractory servants.' Negroes were not allowed to bear arms or to appear in all public places, and there were special laws governing the domestic relations of the blacks. In some states laws closing to the freedmen every occupation save domestic and agricultural service, betrayed a poor-white jealousy of the Negro artisan. Most codes, however, included special provisions to protect the Negro from undue exploitation and swindling. On the whole the black codes corresponded fairly closely to the essential fact that nearly four million ex-slaves needed special attention until they were ready to mingle in free society on more equal terms. But in such states as South Carolina and Mississippi there was clearly evident a desire to keep the freedmen in a permanent position of tutelage, if not of peonage.

Southern whites who had never dreamed it possible to live side by side with free Negroes believed these new laws to be liberal and generous. They pointed out that the black codes were based upon vagrancy laws in Northern states. But Northerners regarded the black codes as palpable evasions of the Thirteenth Amendment, and were aroused to a frenzy of indignation. 'We tell the white men of Mississippi,' announced the powerful Chicago *Tribune,* 'that the men of the North will convert the State of Mississippi into a frog pond before they will allow any such laws to disgrace one foot of soil in which the bones of our soldiers sleep and over which the flag of freedom waves.' So the chief political significance of the black codes was an irresistible demand from the North that the Federal Government step in to protect the former slaves. This object, eventually embalmed in the Fourteenth and Fifteenth Amendments and the various Civil Rights Bills, was first pursued through the agencies of the Freedmen's Bureau, the Union League, and military government.

The Freedmen's Bureau of the War Department was created by Congress 3 March 1865, for a period of one year after the close of the war, and given general powers of relief and guardianship over Negroes and refugees, and administration of abandoned lands. General O. O. Howard, the 'Christian soldier,' was in charge of its activities, and hundreds of its agents were distributed throughout the South, charged with the responsibility of aiding the Negro to adjust himself to his new circumstances.[4] The chief activities of the Bureau

4 This work being still unfinished in 1866, the existence of the Bureau was extended to 1869 and its education activities to 1872.

were relief work for both races, administration of justice in cases involving freedmen, and development of education facilities for the colored people. In one month, September 1865, the Bureau distributed almost a million and a half rations, and altogether during its brief existence it established over a hundred hospitals, gave medical aid to half a million patients, distributed over twenty million rations to the destitute of both races, settled thousands of freedmen on abandoned or confiscated lands, and established over four thousand schools for Negro children. This was not Northern charity, for the total cost of the Bureau, seventeen million dollars, was more than covered by a heavy tax on cotton, which by 1869 had yielded over sixty-eight million dollars.

Opinion on the character and the achievements of the Bureau differed most sharply. Northern observers were lyrical in its praise; Southerners vituperative in criticism. In the opinion of Carl Schurz, 'no other agency . . . could have wielded that moral power whose interposition was so necessary to prevent southern society from falling at once into the chaos of a general collision between its different elements,' while Governor Humphreys of Mississippi thought that 'four years of cruel war were scarcely more blighting and destructive on the homes of the white man, and impoverishing, degrading to the negro than has resulted . . . from the administration of this black incubus.' However valuable was the work of the Bureau during the critical period of transition from slavery to freedom, there can be little doubt that it soon ceased to fulfil its original purposes and became a political machine of the Republican party. Many of its subaltern officials were men of low character who enriched themselves at the expense of both races. 'There *may* have been an honest man connected with the Bureau,' said General Wade Hampton caustically, and an official report described the agents as 'generally of a class of fanatics without character or responsibility.' They were charged with tyrannizing over the whites, keeping the Negro in a state of despondency, and fomenting ill feeling between the races. There can be no doubt that the Freedmen's Bureau did more than almost any other agency to exasperate the Southern whites and to complicate the problem of adjusting the Negro to his new status.

Despite the ignoble struggle for the control of the Negro, and with all the vicissitudes in his own fortunes, he made real progress during these years. Had it not been for the enlightened good will and intelligent co-operation of the best class of Southern whites, and for the surprising qualities of leadership developed by some of the Negroes, progress would have been well-nigh impossible. The Negroes themselves wanted principally land and education. Agitation for political rights came largely from northern politicians and idealists.

The most thorny question was that of political rights. The best opinion in the North was opposed to a blanket grant of suffrage to freedmen, while in the South there was no general inclination to permit the Negro any participation in politics whatsoever. Yet it was clear that if the freedman was to implement his new status, he must have some voice in politics. Perhaps if the South had been allowed to work out this problem, some compromise might have been effected. But because the Radical Republicans wished to secure the colored vote at the earliest opportunity, Negro suffrage was imposed upon the South by government fiat, and their votes were marshalled for the Republican party through the agency of the Union League. This political association, founded in the North in 1862, now extended its activities throughout the South and in 1867 began to enroll Negroes in large numbers. Its purpose was to exploit the freedmen for the benefit of the Republican party and to keep the carpet-baggers and scalawags in control of local politics; its methods were a combination of persuasion and intimidation. The success of this secret organization, controlling the votes of the Negroes for selfish purposes, permanently antagonized and disillusioned southern whites and forfeited the prospect of any subsequent compromise on the suffrage question.[5]

More substantial was the progress in education and in land ownership. As rapidly as educational facilities could be provided, freedmen took advantage of them. 'Few people,' wrote Booker T. Washington, 'who were not right in the midst of the scenes can form any exact idea of the intense desire which the people of my race showed for education. It was a whole race trying to go to school. Few were too young and none too old to make the attempt to learn. As fast as any kind of teachers could be secured, not only were day schools filled, but night schools as well. The great ambition of the older people was to try to learn to read the Bible before they died. . . . Day schools, night school, and Sunday school were always crowded, and often many had to be turned away for want of room.' The Freedmen's Bureau established hundreds of schools and enrolled several hundred thousand pupils; Northern philanthropic agencies helped, and the

5 The history of Negro political reconstruction will be found in chapter 2.

new constitutions of the reconstructed states made provision for free public education for blacks as well as for whites. By 1877 there were about six hundred thousand Negroes in Southern elementary and secondary schools, several normal and industrial schools, such as Hampton and Tuskegee, had been established, and Howard, Fisk, and Atlanta Universities were giving instruction in higher education.

In land ownership the freedmen made slow and halting progress. Northern statesmen like Stevens and Sumner had encouraged the Negro to look to the Federal Government for assistance in securing 'forty acres and a mule,' but in the end nothing was done to assist the Negro to become a landowner. This failure of the Federal Government to fulfil its responsibility is not easy to explain: the expectation of forty acres was perhaps excessive, but it would not have been either difficult or expensive to have established each colored family on a small plot of eight or ten acres; and a government that found it possible to give forty million acres of public land to a single railroad [6] might well have purchased ten million acres for the freedmen. It is probable indeed that in the depressed state of land values, the whole cost of such a plan might well have been financed by the cotton tax of sixty-eight million dollars. Without assistance from the government, the Negroes were unable to purchase even small farms, and the vast majority of them were forced to lease land on such terms as the whites were willing to grant. Not only this, but when the Negro did set up as an independent farmer he was severely handicapped by his unfamiliarity with farm management, and marketing. There were some 121,000 Negro landowners in 1890 and 187,000 ten years later. But by 1900 they owned only thirteen million acres of land, and as tenants cultivated about twice that amount. Fifty years after Emancipation there were only 218,000 Negro landowners, and their relative number was declining rather than increasing.

Emancipation altered the form rather than the substance of the Negro's economic status, for at least a generation after Appomattox. The transition from slave to independent farmer was a long and painful one, made generally through the medium of tenancy, and for many it was never completely made. Without the requisite capital to purchase a farm, a mule, and agricultural implements, and without credit except such as was cautiously extended by white bankers, storekeepers, or planters, the majority of the freedmen were unable to rise

[6] The Northern Pacific; see chapter 5.

above the share-cropper or tenant class. The transition is vividly described by an observer in 1880:

> The plantation underwent all of the changes of the transition period except that in mobility of labor, for none of the Negroes left. In 1860 the Barrow's plantation of a thousand acres at Oglethorpe, Georgia, contained about 25 Negro families living in the quarters centered around the big house. For several years following emancipation the force of laborers was divided into two squads, the arrangement and method of cultivating being very much the same as in the ante bellum days. Each squad was under the control of a foreman who was in the nature of a general of volunteers. . . . The laborers were paid a portion of the crop as their wages which made them feel interested in it. . . . After a while, however, even the liberal control of the foreman grew irksome. The two squads split up into smaller and smaller squads, still working for a part of the crop with the owners' teams, until this method of farming came to involve great trouble and loss. The mules were ill-treated, the crop was frequently badly worked, and in many cases not honestly divided. It became necessary to reorganize the plantation. The owner sold his mules to the Negroes on credit, thus placing the risk from careless handling upon the tenants. The gang system was abandoned, and the land was divided so as to give each family its individual tract. When some of them had to walk a mile it became impracticable to keep the cabins grouped. One by one the workers moved their house on to their farms, settling in convenient places near springs. The plantation now contained 999 acres as one acre had been given for a schoolhouse and a church. The system of sharing was abandoned for cash rent in kind, especially cotton. The Negroes planted what they pleased and worked when they liked, except that the landlord required that enough cotton be planted to pay the rent. . . .

Thus the blacks continued to work in the cotton fields, to live in the shacks provided for them by the former master or by his children, and on credit granted or withheld by the same hands. Their status was somewhat improved, and it was not difficult for the more industrious and brighter of them to make themselves independent. Some of the more ambitious drifted westward to the fertile lands of Texas or joined that curious exodus to Kansas in the late seventies. A few, indeed, achieved something more — a business or a profession which brought them social standing as well as a livelihood. Some became laborers in the coal mines or steel mills or tobacco factories that began to spring up throughout the South; others drifted northward to work in industrial centers. But the majority remained on land that belonged to others, plodding behind the plow in spring and picking cotton in the fall, reasonably sure of food and shelter and clothing, a Saturday afternoon in town, a Sunday at revival meetings, continuing in the ways of their fathers and their fathers' fathers.

6. *The Beginnings of the New South*

It is easier for an agricultural than for an industrial civilization to recover from the devastations of war, for though wealth may be destroyed, the land remains. Recovery began at once in certain sections of the South, and a crop was raised for market in 1865. With admirable courage the battle-scarred veterans turned to the task of reconstruction. Henry Grady celebrated this theme in one of the greatest of his orations: 'As ruin was never before so overwhelming, never was restoration swifter. The soldier stepped from the trenches into the furrow; horses that had charged Federal guns marched before the plow, and fields that ran red with human blood in April, were green with the harvest in June.' The old plantation régime was gone for ever, but gradually the Southern scene took on its familiar appearance. Fields bloomed white with cotton bolls; houses, roads, and fences were repaired; the wandering Negro returned to his farm, a tenant now. By 1879 the cotton crop surpassed that of 1860; by 1900 it was more than doubled. Almost overnight Southern cities arose from their ruins. A visitor to Atlanta found 'a new city springing up with marvellous rapidity. . . . Chicago in her busiest days could scarcely show such a sight as clamors for observation here. Every horse and mule is in active use. The four railroads centring here groan with the freight and passenger traffic, and yet are unable to meet the demands of the nervous and palpitating city.' Columbia, Charleston, Richmond, and New Orleans were rapidly rebuilt, and new cities like Birmingham and Durham sprang into existence. Physical restoration, however, was more rapid than cultural or social recovery; it was half a century before the South was able to repair the impalpable damage to her morale.

One of the most thorough changes was the redistribution of land and the rise of small farmers and poor whites to power. This occurred largely because the planters were forced to throw their lands on the market, at prices that the little fellows could pay, or on terms of hire that they could meet. The significance of this redistribution was, to be sure, in large part nullified by the subsequent development of the share-crop and the crop-lien systems. Yet admitting the importance of tenancy and of the crop-lien system in this distribution, it can nevertheless be maintained that because it broke up the old plantation system, the Civil War furthered economic democracy in the South.

It may be illuminating to analyze somewhat more closely this redistribution of land. In 1860 there were 33,171 farms in South Carolina, 55,128 in Alabama, and 17,328 in Louisiana; twenty years later the figures were 93,328 for South Carolina, 135,864 for Alabama, and 48,292 for Louisiana. As the number of farms doubled and trebled, the average acreage declined. In 1860 only 352 farms in South Carolina were under ten acres in size, while 1841 farms embraced more than five hundred acres. Ten years later there were 10,474 farms under ten acres in size and only 594 of five hundred acres or over. Mississippi, in 1860, reported 563 farms under ten acres; ten years later there were 11,003. In 1860 the average Georgia farm was 429 acres; by 1880 this had shrunk to 187; the average for Louisiana in 1860 was 536, in 1880, 171. The same tendencies were observable in every one of the Southern states, and continued unabated down to the twentieth century. In the half century after 1860 the average acreage of farms in eleven Southern states decreased from 335 to 114, while in the same period the average Northern farm increased from 126 to 143 acres. At the same time millions of acres were taken up in the land west of the Mississippi, indicating already before the close of the century the passing of the center of cotton production from the Atlantic seaboard to Louisiana and Texas. The significance of these figures, however, was qualified by the operation of the share-crop system. Actually most of the farms of under 10 acres and many under 20 were units in a large farm not unlike the ante-bellum plantation.

The share-crop and crop-lien systems arose out of the necessities of the post-war adjustment — out of the breakdown of the labor system and the collapse of credit. The share-crop system was an arrangement whereby planters could obtain labor without paying wages and landless farmers could get land without paying rent. Instead of an interchange of money for labor and rent, there was a sharing of crops. The planter furnished his tenant with land and a house, and generally with seed, fertilizer, a mule, and a cultivator; in return he received at the end of the year one-third to one-half of the crop which the tenant raised. The tenant furnished his labor and received, in return, the rest of the crop. At the close of the war most of the freedmen and

SELECTED PLANTATION AREA, BOUNDARIES OF COTTON BELT, AND COUNTIES HAVING 50 PER CENT OR MORE OF NEGRO POPULATION: 1910.

Thirteenth Census of the United States: 1910.

Department of Commerce, Bureau of the Census.

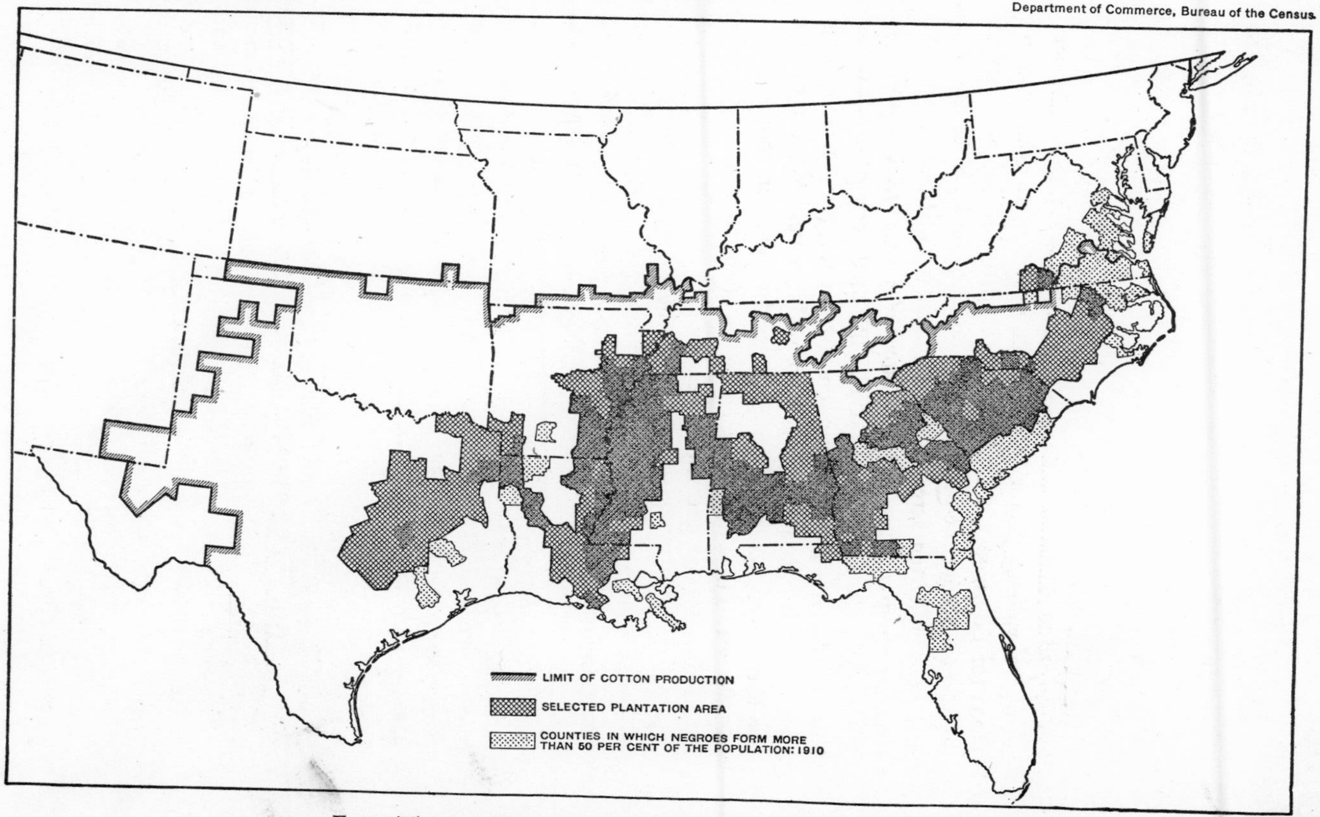

From Thirteenth Census of the United States, 1910, *Vol. V.*

many of the poorer white farmers entered into just such arrangement with the landowners. But this system which appeared at first to be mutually advantageous was really disastrous to all. The share-cropper was rarely able to escape from the tenant class into the farm-owning class; the planter was seldom able to farm profitably or scientifically with share-crop labor. With every year the number of tenant farmers increased, the profits of farming and the fertility of the soil decreased. In 1880, when the first records were made, one-third of the farmers of the cotton belt were tenants; forty years later the proportion had increased to two-thirds.

The crop-lien system was equally disastrous in its economic and social consequences. Under this system the farmer mortgaged his ungrown crop in order to obtain his supplies for the year. Rates of interest were usuriously high, and the merchant who supplied food, clothing, seed, and other necessaries customarily charged from twenty to fifty per cent above the normal price. Because cotton was the one sure money crop, the creditors generally insisted that most of the land be planted to cotton, thus discouraging diversification of crops. As early as 1880 two-thirds of the farmers of South Carolina had mortgaged their ungrown crops, and by 1900 this proportion was applicable to the entire cotton belt. Share-crop and crop-lien served to keep the poorer farmers of the South in a state of perpetual bondage to the large planters, merchants, and bankers, a state from which few were ever able to extricate themselves. The result was an increasing impoverishment of a large part of the farming population, a growing stratification of class lines, and a relative decline in the agricultural prosperity of the entire section. By the turn of the century sober observers warned that the Southern farmer, white as well as black, was in danger of becoming a serf.

Nevertheless, the agricultural revolution touched the South less than any other large section of the country. Despite the disappearance of the large plantation and the emancipation of the Negro, the Cotton Kingdom of 1900 was in many essential respects much as it had been before the Civil War. The old-fashioned planter was gone, but in his place was the merchant, banker, or loan-agent, controlling large aggregations of tenant farms. The labor force showed fewer changes than in other parts of the country: the Negro slave was no more, but in his place was the share-cropper. Though farms were smaller, tenancy was far more widespread. The South was still a one-crop section, less self-sufficient agriculturally in 1900 than in 1860, and what Rupert Vance calls the 'cotton culture complex' still dominated the psychology of that section. The application of science and invention to agriculture had wrought fewer changes in the Cotton Kingdom than elsewhere, for cotton was the one important crop that refused to yield to machinery; the boll weevil proved invincible, and proportionately less money was invested in machinery here than in any other section.

When Henry Grady, editor of the Atlanta *Constitution,* in a famous oration at New York in 1886, celebrated the 'New South' he used a phrase that stuck. What most strikingly differentiated the 'New' South from the 'Old' South was the rise of industry and manufactures. The effect of the plantation system was to stratify industrial activities and to tie up all available capital in slaves. The destruction of this system released capital for the new enterprises and directed energies into new channels. The result was the rise of an industrial system which profoundly affected the whole of Southern economy and society.

Manufacturing flourished in the South before the Civil War. By 1860 the South had some fifteen per cent of the manufacturing establishments of the country turning out approximately eight per cent of the total produce. The war destroyed most of these establishments, but even during the Reconstruction era industry showed signs of revival, and the eighties witnessed a recrudescence of manufacturing on a broader and firmer basis. By 1870 many industries, such as textile, flour, and lumber, had recovered lost ground, and new industries, such as the fertilizer and the iron, had developed. Throughout the decade of the seventies cities were growing rapidly, railroad mileage was extended by five thousand miles, and the value of manufactured products increased by leaps and bounds.

Indeed the natural resources of this section were as yet but little exploited; cheap labor was available in almost unlimited quantities; coal, iron ore, timber, and water power were as readily available as in New England or Pennsylvania, the transportation system was improved, and capital could be procured from the North. Grady boasted of these advantages, and prophesied a future of unparallelled prosperity: 'In 1880 the South made 212,000 tons of iron, in 1887 845,000 tons. She is now actually building, or has finished this year, furnaces that will produce more than her entire product last year. Birmingham alone will produce more iron in 1889 than the entire South produced in 1887. Our coal supply is exhaustless, Texas alone having 6000 square miles. In marble and granite we have no rivals, as to quantity or quality. In lumber our riches are even vaster. More than fifty per cent of our entire area is in forests, making the South the best timbered region in the world.'

Grady's predictions as to the development of mining, iron and steel manufacturing, and lumbering proved justified, but he neglected to emphasize the most notable of new Southern industries: textiles. For generations Southerners had been accustomed to send their cotton to the mills of Old England and New England where the manufacturing establishments, capital, and facilities for world marketing were well organized. The monopoly of New England mills was challenged in the seventies and eighties, and by the beginning of the twentieth century the competition from North and South Carolina and Georgia was so serious as to threaten the derangement of the entire fabric of New England economy. Proximity to raw material and to water power, cheap labor, freedom from legal restraints, and low taxes, all gave Southern mills an initial advantage. By the middle seventies the textile mills of the South had over half a million spindles; fifteen years later there were almost two million. Yet this was only a beginning. By 1920 the South was to have over half the active spindles in the country, and the leading textile states, North Carolina, South Carolina, and Georgia, ranked second, third, and fourth in the nation.

The development of the textile industry in the South necessitated grave social and economic readjustments. It introduced to Southern economy a labor problem of an explosive nature; to Southern society a social problem that has so far defied solution; to Southern politics new considerations that acted as a solvent on the old political solidarity. The transition from rural to urban culture, from an agrarian to an industrial economy, proved no less painful in the New South than it had been in early nineteenth-century New England. Small mills were established in scores of little North Carolina, South Carolina, and Georgia towns, financed by local capital, managed by local enterprise, supported by local pride and worked by labor recruited from the immediate neighborhood. Some were established for sheer economic motives, others to 'benefit the town' as a whole, still others for the ostensible purpose of providing employment for the poor. These, mostly from the poor-white class, welcomed the opportunity to exchange their drab and impoverished existence for the dubious attractions of the mill village. 'To such people,' wrote Holland Thompson, 'the cotton-mill offered a means of escape from bitter

.25
.50
8.50
12.50

poverty. A family whose crops often did not pay the store accounts, whose members handled almost no money, heard with amazement of twenty or twenty-five dollars earned by a family in a single week. The whole family had worked on the farm, as families have done since farming began, and for the family to work in the mill seemed a natural procedure. The usual result was that the children worked, though the father often failed to find employment and became a hypochondriac or a loafer. . . . Life, even in an isolated factory village, was more interesting than on a farm, and the houses in a mill village, however monotonous they might be in appearance, were much superior to the average tenant cabin.' [7] Woman and child labor was the normal result of this situation, and it was, until recently, unchecked either by public opinion or by law.

Though certain cities such as Albemarle, Durham, Gastonia, and Winston-Salem in North Carolina, Columbia, and Spartanburg, South Carolina, West Point, Georgia, and Elizabethtown, Tennessee, became textile centers, the industry was much less concentrated and much less specialized in the South than in New England. The establishment of local mills introduced a new element into many an old Southern town — the 'mill village,' inhabited by laborers recruited from near-by farms, its very existence often ignored by respectable people, much as respectable folks in Northern towns ignored their 'red light' districts. The mill village gathered around the factory as a medieval village clustered about a feudal castle, and the mill manager ruled his community as a feudal lord ruled his manor. 'It is not surprising,' said Mr. Thompson, 'that the manager came to think of himself as divinely appointed. In the village his word was law. He controlled the whole economic life. Any immoral or otherwise obnoxious person could be discharged from the mill and evicted from the factory tenement. No minister or teacher advanced doctrines contrary to the established mores.' By the opening of the twentieth century the New South had gone a long way toward substituting industrial autocracy for the old agrarian feudalism.

Scarcely less striking was the development of the tobacco, mining, iron and steel, lumbering and oil industries. Winston-Salem and Durham, North Carolina, became the greatest tobacco centers in the world and Reynolds and Duke were names to be conjured with in North Carolina, like Carnegie and Schwab in Pennsylvania. Birmingham rose to be a world steel center much like Pittsburgh. As the

[7] 'The Southern Textile Situation,' *South Atlantic Quarterly,* April, 1930.

timber stands of New England, New York, and Michigan were exhausted, lumbering moved south to the pine forests of Louisiana and Mississippi, exploiting and desolating here as in the North. And the plains of Texas and Oklahoma which were once the Cattle Kingdom became part of the domain of oil.

This industrialization of the South carried with it changes in the political and the cultural outlook of that section. The leaders of the New South were no less sensitive to the demands of industry than the leaders of the Old South had been to the demands of agriculture. The 'Bourbons' who ruled the South from Reconstruction to the turn of the century were, for the most part, thoroughly committed to a program of industrialization, and it was not long before the South, as well as the North, could boast its 'railroad Senators' and its 'coal and iron Senators.' William Mahone, for example, who dominated Virginia politics for twenty years after the war, was a railroad builder and industrialist. The three men who controlled Georgia politics in the post-war years, General Colquitt, General Gordon, and Joseph E. Brown, were all deeply involved in railroad promotion and manufacturing. Literature and the press, the pulpit and the school, all entered the service of the new economic order, and the common man of the South was easily persuaded that an industrial society could confer quicker and more obvious blessings than could an agricultural. The new philosophy of industrialism won Southerners to a more sympathetic attitude toward the North, and friendliness and understanding succeeded the bitterness of the post-war years.

It is to this industrialization that students refer when they speak of the New South. Yet we must not be deceived by the phrase, as many Southerners were. Industrialization is common to the whole of the post-Civil War United States, and there is no more a 'New' South than there is a 'New' West. Indeed, the Middle West and the Pacific coast both advanced more rapidly along the path of industry than did the seaboard South, and the South of 1900 accounted for a smaller proportion of the total manufacturing product of the country than did the South of 1860. Far more than other sections, the South escaped those two concomitants of industry — urbanization and immigration. The South was still in 1900, as in 1860, predominantly rural and a one-crop section; if King Cotton had been deposed he was still a lively pretender. The population of the Southern states remained almost entirely native-born. The problem of black and white still hung like a dark cloud on the Southern horizon, and the necessity of keeping his a 'white man's country' still dominated the Southerner's psychology. South of the Mason and Dixon line was still the 'Bible belt,' home of orthodoxy and revivalism, and whatever the economic or psychological attractions of Republicanism, that section continued to support the party of Jefferson, Calhoun, and Davis.

II

RECONSTRUCTION, POLITICAL AND CONSTITUTIONAL

1865–1877

1. *Reconstruction During the Civil War*

RECONSTRUCTION had been a subject of discussion in the North ever since the beginning of the war. As usual with American political issues involving sectional balance, the discussion took place on the plane of constitutional theory. It turned largely on the question whether the seceded states were in or out of the Union when their rebellion was crushed. From the Northern premise that secession was illegal, strict logic reached the conclusion that former states of the Confederacy were now states of the Union, with all the rights and privileges pertaining thereto. If, on the contrary, secession was valid, the South might consistently be treated as conquered territory, without any legal rights that the Union was required to respect. Yet both sides adopted the proper deductions from the other's premise. Radical Republicans, the most uncompromising nationalists, managed to prove to their satisfaction that the Southern states had lost or forfeited their rights, while former secessionists clamored for privileges in the Union they had declared irrevocably dissolved!

But the question of the status of the Southern states was to be decided not in accordance with theory but in accordance with political and economic realities. Lincoln, with his customary clarity, saw this, and saw, too, how dangerous was any theoretical approach to the problem. In his last speech, on 11 April 1865, he insisted that this question whether the Southern states were in or out of the Union was 'bad as the basis of a controversy, and good for nothing at all — a merely pernicious abstraction.' 'Finding themselves safely at home, it would be utterly immaterial whether they had ever been abroad.' Obviously, these states were 'out of their proper practical relation with the Union'; the object of all should be to 'get them into their proper practical relation' again.

Lincoln, indeed, had been pursuing this eminently sensible policy since the beginning of the war. As early as 1862 he had appointed provisional military governors in Tennessee, Louisiana, and North Carolina whose duty it was to re-establish loyal governments in those states. The North Carolina experiment came to naught, but in Tennessee Governor Andrew Johnson and in Louisiana General Banks made impressive progress toward the restoration of federal authority, and after the fall of Vicksburg Arkansas was similarly restored. Encouraged by this success, Lincoln, in a proclamation of 8 December 1863, formulated what was to be the Presidential plan of reconstruction.

The object of this plan was to get the seceded states back into their normal relations with the Federal Government as quickly and as painlessly as possible; the means was the Presidential power to pardon. The plan itself provided for a general amnesty and restoration of property to all who would take a prescribed oath of loyalty to the Union. Furthermore whenever ten per cent of the electorate of 1860 should take this oath they might set up a state government which Lincoln promised to recognize as the true government of the state. Whether Congress would recognize any such state government, or not, was of course a matter over which the Executive had no control.

This magnanimous plan, known as the ten-per-cent plan, was promptly adopted in Louisiana and Arkansas. Voters were registered, constitutional conventions held, new constitutions abolishing slavery drawn up and ratified, and these states prepared to reassume their place in the Federal Union. But all was not to be such easy sailing. Congress, which was the judge of its own membership, refused to recognize the validity of these reconstructed states or to admit their representatives, and in the Presidential election of 1864 their electoral votes were not counted.

The Congressional leaders, indeed, had a plan of their own for controlling the reconstruction of the seceded states. This plan was embodied in the Wade-Davis Bill of 8 July 1864, which provided that Congress, not the President, was to have jurisdiction over the process of reconstruction and that a majority of the electorate, instead of merely ten per cent, was required for the reconstitution of legal state governments. Lincoln averted this scheme by a pocket veto and brought down upon himself the bitter excoriation of the Wade-Davis Manifesto. 'The President . . . must understand,' said Senator Wade and Congressman Davis, 'that the authority of Congress is paramount and must be respected . . . and if he wishes our support he must confine himself to his executive duties — to obey and execute, not make the laws — to suppress by arms armed rebellion, and leave political reorganization to Congress.'

With the publication of the Wade-Davis Manifesto the issue between the President and Congress was fairly joined, and it was not to be settled until a President had been impeached and the Constitution altered to suit the Radicals. Congressional opposition to Lincoln's plan was due in part to legislative *esprit de corps,* in part to the hatred engendered by the war. To the Radicals it seemed monstrous that traitors and rebels should be readmitted to full fellowship in the Union they had repudiated. But the real motives behind this appeal to passion were political and economic. If the Southern states returned a solid Democratic contingent to Congress, as appeared inevitable, the reunited Democratic party would have a majority in both Houses and would be able to repeal a good part of the tariff, banking, and railroad legislation which the Republicans had placed upon the statute books. It would be the Union as in Buchanan's time, administered by 'rebels' and 'Copperheads' for the benefit of the agrarian South and the West. Even those Northerners who were willing to admit that Davis and Stephens might be honest men did not care to see them at their old desks in the Senate, shouting for 'Southern Rights.' As Thaddeus Stevens put it, the Southern states 'ought never to be recognized as capable of acting in the Union, or of being counted as valid states, until the Constitution shall have been so amended . . . as to secure perpetual ascendancy to the party of the Union' — the Republican party, of course. The amendment that Stevens had in mind was Negro suffrage. By this brilliant device, selfish and cynical politicians obtained the support of humanitarians and doctrinaires who believed political franchise necessary to protect and uplift the freedmen.

If Lincoln had lived, there is some likelihood that his policy of wisdom, justice, and magnanimity would have prevailed; for even after his death the Radicals had great difficulty in imposing their policy of vengeance upon the country. For about six weeks after the assassination there was a petty reign of terror, directed by Secretary Stanton, and supported by President Johnson who had always been in favor of hanging 'traitors' when apprehended. Only the stern intervention of Grant prevented the seizure of Lee and other Confederate generals. Colossal rewards for Davis and his cabinet, as alleged promoters of the murder of Lincoln, resulted in their capture.

But the charge of complicity in the murder was soon seen to be preposterous and, since it was obviously impossible to get a Virginia jury to convict Davis of treason, that charge was wisely directed to the circumlocution office. Thirst for vengeance appeared to be slaked by the shooting or suicide of the assassin Booth, and by hanging his three accomplices and the unfortunate woman who had harbored them, after an extra-legal trial by a military tribunal.

2. *Andrew Johnson Takes Charge*

The results of the election of 1864 indicated that the country was still willing to follow 'Father Abraham,' and up to the eve of his death Lincoln persisted in applying his own policy of reconstruction. But the entire situation was altered by the assassination of Lincoln and the accession to the Presidency of Andrew Johnson. Lincoln's political astuteness might have defeated the sharp-witted leaders of the Radicals; President Johnson simply played into their hands.

Like Tyler in 1841, Johnson was the nominal head of a party of which he was not really a member. A War Democrat from a seceded state, he had been placed on the same ticket with Lincoln to emphasize the Unionism of the Republican party in 1864. Of origin as humble as Lincoln's, in early life a tailor in a Tennessee mountain village and unable to write until taught by his wife, he possessed many of Lincoln's virtues but lacked his ability to handle men. Self-educated and self-trained, he possessed a powerful though not well disciplined mind, fine oratorical abilities, and a trenchant pen that was time and again to cast consternation into the ranks of his opponents. United with these intellectual qualities were the virtues of personal integrity, devotion to duty, and courage. Johnson had been the ablest spokesman of Southern democracy, and no truer democrat ever occupied the Presidential chair. Yet he is perhaps the most maligned and misunderstood of all our Presidents. In the historical literature of the half century after the war he is represented at the best as a pugnacious ignoramus, at the worst as a drunken ruffian. Actually he had most of the civil and moral virtues, and timidity rather than pugnacity was his failing. No President was ever in a more difficult situation. He had no personal following either in the South or in the North. He had none of the prestige that came to Lincoln from the successful conduct of the war. He had no party organization behind him; he had broken with the Democratic party and he had not been accepted by the Republican. The Radicals, including most of the professional Republican politicians, controlled the party machinery; and the civil service looked to them for leadership. Seward and Welles were loyal to Johnson, but Stanton, with his customary duplicity, used the machinery of the War Department against him, and kept the Radicals posted on Cabinet secrets. And his personality and his policies soon antagonized not only the professional politicians, but the financial and business interests, the press, and the pulpit as well.

Immediately upon his accession to the Presidency, Johnson appeared to be willing to co-operate with the Radicals. 'Treason is a crime and must be punished,' he said; 'treason must be made infamous, and traitors must be impoverished,' and bluff Ben Wade exclaimed exultantly, 'Johnson, we have faith in you. By the gods, there will be no trouble now in running this government.' But soon there was trouble enough, and Wade was one of those who made it. After a brief interval of vindictiveness, Johnson, influenced no doubt by Secretary Seward and sobered by responsibility, swung around and made Lincoln's policy of reconciliation his own. While Congress was not in session he proceeded to carry on Lincoln's reconstruction program. The theory underlying his policy was the indestructibility of the states. Johnson, like Lincoln, held that the Southern states never had been out of the Union, and that their constitutional relations to the Federal Government were unaffected; but that until loyal governments were re-established their vitality was suspended.

Beginning with North Carolina, therefore, Johnson proceeded to appoint provisional civil governors in all the Confederate states where Lincoln had not already done so. These governors were enjoined to summon state constitutional conventions, which were elected by the 'whitewashed rebels' — former citizens of the Confederacy who took the oath of allegiance required by the Presidential proclamation. Fourteen specified classes, assumed to be inveterate rebels, were excluded from this general amnesty and required to make personal application for pardon.[1] Although many of those thus proscribed did

[1] Including all civil and diplomatic officers of the Confederacy, and state governors, general officers of the Confederate Army, former U. S. army officers and naval officers who had resigned their commissions, Congressmen and judges who had resigned their seats, and other Confederates worth over $20,000. To these classes were eventually added all who had held federal office before 1861 — even coroners, constables, notaries public, and sextons of cemeteries — and who had afterwards entered the Confederate service or given aid and comfort to the rebellion. Confederate common soldiers were not disfranchised under this or any subsequent plan of reconstruction although they were ineligible for office under the Congressional plan.

receive special pardons from President Johnson, the general effect was to exclude natural leaders and experienced statesmen from participation in the task of establishing the new state governments. Broadly speaking, they were poor-white governments.

The constitutional conventions declared invalid the ordinances of secession, repudiated the state war debts, declared slavery abolished, and amended the former state constitutions. Elections were promptly held under these amended constitutions, and by the autumn of 1865 regular civil administrations were functioning in all the former Confederate states except Texas.

Yet the very ease with which reconstruction was being consummated excited distrust and criticism in the North. It was charged that political reconstruction had been accomplished before any genuine reconciliation had been achieved, and that the South was neither repentant for her sins nor reconciled to defeat. There were many in the North who professed to fear that the rebellious spirit of the South had been scotched, not crushed, and that the rewards of victory were being wasted. It was to meet this criticism that Johnson, in the fall of 1865, sent a number of observers to report on conditions in the South and to advise him on policies. These reports, as well as other information made public at this time, went far to prove that Southerners had fairly accepted defeat and its logical consequences and to justify the wisdom of the Presidential policy.

'I am satisfied that the mass of thinking people in the South accept the situation of affairs in good faith,' wrote General Grant to the President. 'Slavery and State rights they regard as having been settled forever by the highest tribunal — arms — that man can resort to. . . . I was pleased to learn from the leading men whom I met that they not only accepted the decision arrived at as final, but now that the smoke of battle has cleared away and time has been given for reflection, that this decision has been a fortunate one for the whole country.' Other observers, such as Harvey Watterson and Benjamin Truman concurred in this opinion; at the same time General Sherman was writing to his brother, the Senator, 'No matter what change we may desire in the feelings and thoughts of the people South, we cannot accomplish it by force. . . . You hardly yet realize how completely this country has been devastated, and how completely humbled every man of the South is.' Everyone now admits that Grant and Sherman were right. Without in the least confessing that her cause had been wrong the South acknowledged her defeat as final and irrevocable, and very definitely put aside all thought of revenge. The South accepted the advice of Lee, that her allegiance was now due to the United States, and that her duty was to create a new and better South within the Union. Lee himself set a noble example to his countrymen by his serene acquiescence in trial by battle, and by devoting the rest of his life to education as President of Washington College, at Lexington, Virginia.

This was the situation, then, when Congress prepared to meet in December 1865. The South had accepted the verdict of Appomattox, the North was not inclined to take advantage of its victory. Slavery was irrevocably gone, and the wounds of war were healing. The Presidential policy had apparently triumphed over Radical Congressional policy, and the process of political reconstruction seemed all but complete. In his first annual message President Johnson announced with pride the restoration of an indissoluble Union of indestructible states. Such was the fact; yet within a few months all Lincoln's and Johnson's work of reconstruction was undone, and the Southern states once more were cast into the political melting-pot.

3. *Congress Intervenes*

The Congress which met for the first time on 4 December 1865 showed its temper by forbidding the clerk of the House even to read the names of the members-elect from the reconstructed states at the first roll-call. The Radicals shrewdly postponed any definite decision on the status of these states on the ground that Congress was not yet properly informed. A joint committee of both Houses was appointed with authority to investigate and report on the title of Southern members-elect to be received. This Joint Committee of Fifteen, a resurrection of the old Committee on the Conduct of the War, was controlled by a Radical majority who soon proved themselves the most astute and skillful group of parliamentarians in our history. It was this Committee which formulated the theory and set the pace of Congressional reconstruction, dictated the tactics of the struggle against the President, and elaborated the Fourteenth Amendment to the Constitution. The Chairman of the Committee was the mild-mannered Fessenden of Maine, but the man who dominated its actions was Thaddeus Stevens of Pennsylvania, leader of the Republicans in the House, and for two years the virtual ruler of the United States.

Stevens is one of the most unpleasant characters in American history. A harsh, sombre, friendless old man of seventy-four, and with no redeeming spark of magnanimity, he was moved less by sympathy for the Negro than by cold hatred of the Southern gentry. The former he would exalt to a status of complete political and social equality, the latter he would humiliate, disfranchise, and despoil of all landed property in favor of the freedmen. 'I have never desired bloody punishments to any great extent,' he announced, 'but there are punishments quite as appalling and longer remembered than death. They are more advisable, because they would reach a greater number. Strip a proud nobility of their bloated estates; reduce them to a level with plain republicans; send them forth to labor and teach their children to enter the workshops or handle a plow, and you will thus humble the proud traitors.' Stevens regarded the Southern states as conquered provinces, and insisted that Congress should treat them as such — 'and settle them with new men and drive the present rebels as exiles from this country.' Upon the basis of this theory Congress could do just about as it pleased with the former Confederate states, and this theory underlay much of the reconstruction of the next two years.

Charles Sumner of Massachusetts, Republican leader in the Senate, was not on the Joint Committee, but next to Stevens he was the most powerful figure in Congressional reconstruction. An idealist by conviction, and a reformer by training, he was a complete doctrinaire, a Yankee Brissot. Against the ex-Confederates he cherished no vindictive feelings, but without personal knowledge of the Negroes he believed them no exception to the dogma of equality, and that they wanted only the vote to prove it. Sumner advanced the theory that the Southern states had committed political suicide, had extinguished their standing as states, and were in the position of territories subject to the exclusive jurisdiction of Congress. Vain, over-educated, humorless, and irritable, Sumner nevertheless had a distinguished record as a champion of good causes. The New England intellectuals looked to him for leadership, his polished orations impressed the commonalty, and he gave to the Radical movement a tinge of idealism and altruism that was badly needed.

The theory of reconstruction upon which Congress ultimately acted was not precisely that formulated either by Stevens or by Sumner, but a hybrid of the two. As drafted by the Joint Committee it announced that 'the States lately in rebellion were . . . disorganized communities, without civil government and without constitutions or other forms by virtue of which political relation could legally exist between them and the federal government,' that they had 'forfeited all civil and political rights and privileges under the federal Constitution,' and that they could be restored to their political rights only by Congress. In other words, the states were intact, but the state governments were, for most but not for all purposes, in a condition of suspended animation. Under this interpretation it was possible for Congress at once to deny representation to the Southern states and to accept the ratification of the Thirteenth Amendment by the legislatures of these same states!

The policy of Congress, then, was unequivocally opposed to that of the President. Johnson threw down the gauntlet to Congress in February 1866 by his veto of the Freedmen's Bureau Bill, and the war was on. Having accepted the issue Johnson should at once have remodelled his cabinet, and removed federal officials who were working against him. But he did not have the courage to split his adopted party. Consequently the Radicals were able to unfold their program with no opposition save the President's vetoes, and to continue their propaganda against him and against the South. Under the greatest provocation he remained silent, while Stevens on the floor of Congress referred to him as an 'alien enemy, a citizen of a foreign state,' and Sumner called him 'an insolent drunken brute in comparison with which Caligula's horse was respectable.'

The Radicals were unable to command enough votes to override the Presidential veto of the first Freedmen's Bureau Bill,[2] but this initial victory of the President was almost his last. Within a month Stevens and Sumner pushed through a Civil Rights Bill which forbade the states to discriminate between citizens on the ground of race or color, and when Johnson rejected this bill as both inexpedient and unconstitutional, it was promptly passed over his veto.

Yet even the Radicals were dubious of the constitutionality of this measure, and it was in part to allay these doubts that the Committee of Fifteen drafted the Fourteenth Amendment and presented it to the Southern states as a *sine qua non* of readmission to Congress. This Amendment, the most important that was ever added to the Constitution, was designed to guarantee the civil rights of the Negro against unfavorable legislation by the states, reduce Congressional representation in proportion to the denial of suffrage to Negroes,

[2] A second Freedmen's Bureau Bill was subsequently passed over the Presidential veto, 16 July 1866.

disqualify ex-Confederates who had formerly held state or federal office, invalidate the Confederate debt, and validate the federal debt. It was the first article of the Amendment, however, that was particularly significant. This article provided that 'No State shall make or enforce any law which shall abridge the privileges or immunities of citizens of the United States; nor shall any State deprive any person of life, liberty, or property, without due process of law; nor deny to any person within its jurisdiction the equal protection of the laws.' It thus threw the protection of the Federal Government around the rights of life, liberty, and property which might be invaded by the states, reversing the traditional relationships between these governments which had from the beginning distinguished our federal system. Ostensibly meant to protect the Negro, this provision actually came to be interpreted as extending the protection of the Federal Government to corporations whose property rights were threatened by state legislation. That the framers of the Amendment anticipated any such interpretation of this article is highly improbable.

The issue was now joined between the President and the majority in Congress. Everything turned on the election of a new Congress in the autumn of 1866, one of the most important Congressional elections in our history. A National Union Convention of moderate men from both sections pledged support of the President but it did not form a new party or create party machinery. Hence in most Congressional districts voters had to choose between a Radical Republican and a Copperhead Democrat. Faced with this prospect most of the moderate Republicans like Lyman Trumbull and John Sherman went over to the Radical camp. The business interests, concerned with the maintenance of tariff, railroad, and banking legislation, followed suit, and almost all the powerful papers in the country swung into line.

Johnson did not manage his campaign well. He failed to capitalize the underlying economic issues and permitted the Radicals to make the campaign one of personalities and of passions. He seemed incapable of advocating a policy of tolerance in a tolerant manner, and his 'swing around the circle,' a stumping tour of the Middle West, became in many instances an undignified contest of vituperation. He was, said Seward, the best stump speaker in the country, but as Secretary Welles shrewdly remarked, the President should not be a stump speaker. Instead of appealing to the memory of Lincoln, and to the finer popular instinct, he called names and rattled the dry bones of state rights. Probably no orator, the New York *Nation* caustically observed, ever accomplished so much by a fortnight's speaking. The Radicals, on the other hand, were remarkable political generals. Soft-pedalling the economic issues and concealing their intention to force Negro suffrage on the South, they made ' patriotism ' the single issue. Reiterated tales of Southern defiance and atrocity, lurid reports of race riots at Memphis and New Orleans for which Southern leaders were held responsible, bewildered Northern opinion. ' Jefferson Davis is in the casement at Fortress Monroe, but Andrew Johnson is doing his work ' declared Sumner.

> Witness Memphis, witness New Orleans. Who can doubt that the President is the author of these tragedies? Charles IX of France was not more completely the author of the massacre of St. Bartholomew than Andrew Johnson is the author of these recent massacres now crying out for judgment. . . . Next to Jefferson Davis stands Andrew Johnson as [the Republic's] worst enemy.

Under such circumstances it is not surprising that the Northern voters returned a majority sufficient to override the Presidential vetoes.

Johnson has been criticized for not bowing to the ' will of the people ' and advising the Southern state governments to ratify the Fourteenth Amendment in order to mollify Northern sentiment and get their representatives admitted. But he knew perfectly well that Congress had no intention of receiving Southern representatives until Negro suffrage had been established and Northern supremacy written into the Constitution. So Johnson nailed his colors to the mast, and defied Congress to do its worst.

4. *Congressional Reconstruction*

While the campaign was still under way, in August 1866, President Johnson formally declared the ' insurrection ' at an end, and that ' peace, order, tranquillity, and civil authority now exist in and throughout the whole of the United States.' But the Radicals took the results of the fall elections as a vindication of their ' thorough ' policy, and under the implacable leadership of Thaddeus Stevens a series of measures of far-reaching importance were whipped through a complaisant Congress. These measures undid the whole of Presidential reconstruction, placed the Southern states back where they were in April 1865, and temporarily revolutionized our political system by substituting a quasi-parliamentary for a presidential system of government.

The most important of these measures, indeed the most important piece of legislation of the entire period, was the First Reconstruction Act of 2 March 1867. This Act announced that 'no legal government' existed in any Southern state except Tennessee, and divided the territory of the South into five military districts subject to military commanders who were charged with the responsibility of protecting life and property throughout their districts. For this purpose they might use, at their discretion, the ordinary civil tribunals or military tribunals. Escape from this military régime and restitution of state rights was promised on condition that a constitutional convention, chosen by universal male suffrage, set up governments based on black and white suffrage; and that the new state legislatures ratify the Fourteenth Amendment.

Johnson returned the bill with a scorching message arguing the unconstitutionality of the whole thing, and the most impartial students have agreed with his reasoning, Professor Burgess writing, indeed, that 'there was hardly a line in the entire bill which would stand the test of the Constitution.' Yet the President thought that he had no choice but to enforce this and subsequent Reconstruction Acts. In March 1867 military rule replaced in the South the civil governments that had been operating for over a year. The military governors ruled with a firm hand, sometimes with a flagrant disregard for the civil rights of the inhabitants. Confederate veteran organizations, parades, historical societies, indeed the most innocent symbols and memorials of the lost cause, were suppressed. Thousands of local officials were removed to make way for carpet-baggers or Negroes; the governors of six states were displaced and others appointed in their place, civil courts were superseded by military tribunals, the legislatures of Georgia, Alabama, and Louisiana were purged of Conservatives, state legislation was set aside or modified, and an army of occupation, some twenty thousand strong and aided by a somewhat comic but irritating force of Negro militia, kept the South safe for democracy but highly unsafe for the Democracy.

The rule of the major generals was harsh but it had the merits of honesty and a certain rude efficiency. Particularly important were the efforts made by the military to cope with economic disorganization and to regulate the social life of their satrapies. Thus in South Carolina General Sickles abolished imprisonment for debt, stayed foreclosures on property, made the wages of farm laborers a first lien on crops, prohibited the manufacture of whisky, and abolished discrimination between the races. Similar regulations were enforced in other military districts.

The principal task incumbent upon the military commanders was the creation of new electorates and the establishment of new governments. In each of the ten states over which they had jurisdiction the commanders enrolled a new electorate; in South Carolina, Alabama, Florida, Mississippi, and Louisiana the black voters outnumbered the white. This electorate chose in every state a 'black and tan' constitutional convention which, under the guidance of Northern carpet-baggers, drafted new state constitutions enfranchising the blacks and disfranchising ex-Confederate leaders, and guaranteeing civil and political equality to the freedmen. These new state constitutions represented, in many instances, a definite advance upon the older constitutions. The Constitution of South Carolina, for example, set up a far more democratic, humane, and efficient system of government than that which had obtained during the ante-bellum régime. It abolished property qualifications for office holding, reapportioned representation in the legislature, reformed local government and judicial administration, outlawed duelling and imprisonment for debt, protected homesteads from foreclosure, enlarged the rights of women, and outlined a system of universal public education.

By the summer of 1868 reconstructed governments had been set up in seven of the Southern states; the other three — Mississippi, Texas, and Virginia — were admitted in 1870. After the legislatures of these states had duly ratified the Fourteenth Amendment, Congress formally readmitted them to the Union, seated their elected Representatives and Senators, and withdrew the army as soon as the supremacy of the new governments appeared to be reasonably secure. Yet Congressional reconstruction was by no means complete, and Congress reserved to itself, and continued to exercise, the right of interfering in the domestic affairs of the reconstructed states.

But Congressional reconstruction was by no means confined to the South, nor were the Radicals content with securing the ascendancy of their party in the South through Negro suffrage. They aimed, ultimately, at establishing a centralized parliamentary government for the Union. The majority of Congress, not the Supreme Court, was to be the final judge of the powers of Congress; the President a mere figurehead. This new dispensation was implicit in the Reconstruction Act of 2 March 1867 and in two other pieces of legislation pushed through Congress the same day. The first of these, the Command of the Army Act, virtually deprived the executive of control of the army by requiring that he issue all military orders through the General of the Army who was protected against removal or suspension from office. The second, the Tenure of Office Act, by denying the President the right to remove civil officials, including members of his Cabinet, without the consent of the Senate, made it impossible for him to control his own administration. The next move in the game was to dispose of Johnson by impeachment, when Benjamin Wade, president *pro tem.* of the Senate, would succeed to his office and title.

Impeachment had been proposed by Benjamin Butler as early as October 1866, and all through the following year a House committee had been trying to gather evidence which might support such action, but without success. Now Johnson furnished the House with the excuse for which it had so long waited. Convinced that the Tenure of Office Act was unconstitutional[3] he requested and then ordered Secretary Stanton to resign. When General Lorenzo Thomas, the new Secretary of War, sought to take possession of his office, Stanton barricaded himself in the War Department. On 24 February 1868, the House voted to impeach the President before the Senate 'for high crimes and misdemeanours' as the Constitution provides, and within a week eleven articles of impeachment were agreed upon by the Radicals. Ten of the eleven articles simply rang the changes on the removal of Stanton; the other consisted of garbled newspaper reports from the President's speeches. A monstrous charge to the effect that Johnson was an accomplice in the murder of Lincoln was finally excluded.

Altogether the impeachment of Johnson was one of the most disgraceful and vulgar episodes in the history of the Federal Government and barely failed to suspend the federal system. The impeachment was managed by a committee led by Benjamin F. Butler, Thaddeus Stevens, and John Bingham, unscrupulous parliamentarians who exhausted every device, appealed to every prejudice and passion, and rode roughshod over every legal obstacle in their ruthless attempt to punish the President for his opposition to their plans.

[3] President Johnson's contention that this law was unconstitutional was vindicated in the Supreme Court's decision in Myers *v.* U.S., 272 U.S. 52 (1926).

The President was defended by able counsel including William M. Evarts, leader of the American bar, and Benjamin R. Curtis, formerly a justice of the Supreme Court. These tore the case of the prosecution to shreds and it was soon apparent to all but the most prejudiced that there were no valid grounds, legal or otherwise, for impeachment. Yet the Radicals would have succeeded in their object but for Chief Justice Chase who insisted upon legal procedure, and for seven Republican Senators who sacrificed their political future by voting for acquittal: Grimes, Trumbull, Ross, Van Winkle, Fessenden, Fowler, and Henderson. One more affirmative vote and Ben Wade would have been installed in the White House. Then, in all probability, the Court would have been battered into submission, and the Radicals would have triumphed over the Constitution as completely as over the South.

When the trial took place, Johnson had less than one year to serve; and the Republican nominating convention met shortly after his acquittal. There was no longer any effective opposition to the Radicals within the party ranks, and the reconstructed states gave them faithful delegates. In the ensuing election General Grant was victorious over his Democratic rival, but his popular majority was dangerously narrow. Indeed, the election revealed unmistakably that the people were tired of Radical reconstruction and wanted a return to the traditions and practices of representative government. To the Radicals it indicated likewise that if the Republican party was to hold its gains it was imperatively necessary to insure Negro suffrage by Constitutional amendment. Within four months the Fifteenth Amendment to the Constitution, that 'the right of citizens of the United States to vote shall not be denied or abridged by the United States or by any State on account of race, color, or previous condition of servitude,' was passed by both Houses of Congress and sent to the states for ratification.

5. *Black Reconstruction*

The period from 1868 to 1877 was one in which the Radicals were in control, for varying periods, of most of the reconstructed states of the South. The extent of this control varied from state to state and from year to year. In North Carolina, for example, the Democrats recaptured control of the state as early as 1870; in South Carolina the Radicals were not ousted until 1877. Similarly the extent of Negro participation in politics varied in time and in place. In no state were the Negroes ever completely in control of the political situation, but in almost every one of the reconstructed states there was a Radical-Republican majority composed of Negroes and their white allies. These last consisted of two classes; 'carpet-baggers'—Northerners who went South after the war, largely for purposes of political profit; and 'scalawags'—or Southern white renegades. The term 'black reconstruction' therefore does not imply that the Negroes dominated the reconstruction process; it implies merely that this period of reconstruction was distinguished by the active and successful participation of Negroes in politics for the only time in the history of the South.

It was this participation of the Negroes in politics that arrested the attention of contemporaries and that has commanded the interest of students. Here was presented, in its most extreme form, the actualization of the theory of racial equality. What Charles Sumner and Wendell Phillips had elaborated in their studies, what Thaddeus Stevens and Ben Wade had proclaimed in the halls of Congress, was here put into effect. Yet the experiment was never given a fair trial, nor were the auspices under which it was conducted favorable. The vast majority of the freedmen were quite unprepared for the exercise of any political responsibility. They were catapulted into politics, without preparation or experience, and this at a time which would have tried the statesmanship of the wisest and most experienced political leaders; they were abandoned by the best men of the South and deceived by the worst; their innocence exposed them to temptation and their ignorance betrayed them into the hands of astute and mischievous spoilsmen who exploited them for selfish and sordid ends.

The resulting state administrations were characterized by extravagance, corruption, and vulgarity. The state treasuries were systematically looted and the credit of the states pledged to railroad companies and other corporations, while taxes and debts mounted to dizzy figures. In South Carolina, for example, the Radicals raised the state property tax until it was confiscatory, increased the state debt from seven to twenty-nine millions, multiplied legislative expenditures six-fold, floated millions of dollars of bonds at twenty-five cents on the dollar, and sold charters to corporations. The appropriations for public printing which during the sixty years before the war had come to less than one million dollars, mounted in a single session to almost half a million; over two hundred thousand dollars was paid out for furniture whose total value was less than eighteen thousand dollars, while a restaurant, maintained for the benefit of the legislators, cost one hundred and twenty-five thousand dollars for a single session. Under the head of legislative supplies members were furnished at the public expense with such articles as Westphalia hams, perfumes, wines and whiskies, Brussels carpets, gold watches, carriages, and ornamental cuspidors. Worse still was the all but universal corruption which accompanied almost every political transaction. Elections, judicial decisions, votes, and franchises were openly bought and sold, and even the carpetbag Governor Scott was moved to accuse the legislature of ' all sorts of villanies.'

The situation in Alabama, Louisiana, Mississippi, and other states was almost as bad. Taxes were everywhere increased — in Alabama four-fold, in Louisiana eight-fold, in Mississippi fourteen-fold, and local taxes soared even more spectacularly. So heavy was the taxation that in Mississippi alone not less than six million acres of land were offered for sale for unpaid taxes, and a similar condition obtained in other states. Everywhere lobbyists plied their trade, and railroad rings made states responsible for millions of dollars of worthless bonds.

As a result of carpetbag and scalawag misrule the public debt of most of the Southern states doubled and in some cases trebled and quadrupled. In the four and one-half years of Governor Warmouth's administration Louisiana suffered a saturnalia of corruption during which the government expended over twenty-six millions and ran up a state debt of over forty-eight million dollars, besides bartering away state property, franchises, and river rights and dissipating school funds. Warmouth himself succeeded in garnering a personal fortune of over half a million dollars as his share of the loot. North Carolina saddled itself with a reconstruction debt of almost twenty millions, Alabama ran up its debt to the staggering total of thirty-two millions, and even poverty-stricken Tennessee managed somehow to increase its debt by over twenty-one millions during these years.

Yet these figures of confiscatory taxation and mounting debt do not in themselves constitute an unqualified indictment of carpetbag and scalawag rule. It must be remembered that the normal costs of reconstruction were inevitably high, that the Radical legislatures undertook many long-needed but expensive reforms, that money was depreciated in value and prices inflated, and that most of the states were forced to float their bonds through Northern banking houses at outrageous discounts of from fifty to seventy-five per cent. At the same time, while expenses were thus increasing, the normal sources of revenue were drying up, and the Radical governments could scarcely avoid desperate expedients in taxation and finance.

Nor were corruption, extravagance, and maladministration confined to the South. It was during these unhappy years that the Tweed Ring robbed New York City of over seventy-five million dollars and the Gas Ring in Philadelphia increased the city's debt at the rate of three millions a year, and in national politics it was the era of the Crédit Mobilier, the Whisky Ring and the Navy Department frauds. The corruption of the Negro governments of the South was dictated largely by unscrupulous Northerners who harvested the profit, and in the end the Negroes had nothing better to show for their day of power than the plunder that their more fortunate fellows managed to carry off from the state capitols.

More important, indeed, was the constructive side of black reconstruction. Much of this had to do with mere physical rehabilitation necessitated by the ravages of the Civil War, but in almost every one of the Southern states a good deal of progressive legislation was written into the statute books. In South Carolina, for example, the Radical legislatures reformed the system of taxation, provided relief for the poor, distributed homesteads to Negroes, established numerous charitable institutions, encouraged immigration, and, above all, provided for the first time in the history of the state a system of free public schools. Everywhere, indeed, the Radical legislatures advanced political democracy, encouraged education, and inaugurated some social reforms, and these contributions go far to justify a judgment less harsh than that which is customarily pronounced upon them.

Yet the heritage of black reconstruction was an unfortunate one. Southerners drew from this experience certain conclusions which were more obvious than exact. They concluded that any Negro participation in politics was dangerous and that the maintenance of Democratic party solidarity was necessary to insure the rule of the white man. Because some progressive legislation was identified with carpet-bag and Negro rule, Southerners came to distrust such legislation and found reassurance in the return to power of an ultra-conservative Democracy. Because extravagance had accompanied Radical rule, Southerners came to believe that economy and good government were synonymous, and renewed their ante-bellum prejudice against governmental expenditure, even for legitimate purposes. And finally the readiness with which the colored people lent themselves to exploitation by unprincipled white men forfeited for the Negroes the respect of many Northerners and persuaded them that Negro participation in politics was a mistake.

6. *Reconstruction and the Constitution*

At no time in American history has the Constitution been subjected to so severe or prolonged a strain as during the era of Reconstruction. The theory *intra arma silent leges* had been tacitly acquiesced in during the actual conflict, but it remained to be seen whether reconstruction would be carried through on the same legal theory. There arose at once a number of knotty problems concerning the legal character of the war, the legal status of the seceded states after Appomattox, and the status of persons who had participated in the rebellion. There arose, too, with equal urgency, the problem of the division of powers in the Federal Government—whether Congress or the President was the proper authority to direct reconstruction. Finally there came the question of the real meaning of the three Constitutional Amendments which were pushed through during Reconstruction, particularly of the Fourteenth. Some of these legal questions were settled by the courts at the time, others were adjusted in later years, and still others remained unsettled except by rude extra-legal forces.

Throughout the war President Lincoln maintained the legal fiction that the states were indestructible; that they were never out of the Union. This theory, though vigorously controverted by the Radical leaders, received judicial support in the leading case of Texas *v.* White (1869). Chief Justice Chase, speaking for the majority, said:

> The Constitution, in all of its provisions, looks to an indestructible Union, composed of indestructible States. When, therefore, Texas became one of the United States, she entered into an indissoluble relation. . . . There was no place for reconsideration, or revocation. . . . Considered therefore as transactions under the Constitution, the ordinance of secession . . . and all the acts of her legislature intended to give effect to that ordinance, were absolutely null. They were utterly without operation in law. The obligations of the State, as a member of the Union, remained perfect and unimpaired. It certainly follows that the State did not cease to be a State, nor her citizens to be citizens of the Union. If this were otherwise, the State must have become foreign, and her citizens foreigners.

The war must have ceased to be a war for the suppression of rebellion and must have become a war for conquest and subjugation. . . . Our conclusion, therefore is, that Texas continued to be a State, and a State of the Union.

Upon what theory, then, could reconstruction proceed? If the states were still in the Union, it was only the citizens who were out of their normal relations with the Federal Government, and these could be restored through the pardoning power of the President. This at least was the Presidential theory, and when the President declared the insurrection at an end the Supreme Court accepted his proclamation as legally binding.

By virtue of what authority, then, did Congress proceed to impose purely military government upon the South, and set up military courts? The Supreme Court had already passed upon this question of military courts in *ex parte* Milligan. In this famous case which involved the validity of military courts in Indiana the Court laid down the doctrine that 'martial rule can never exist where the courts are open, and in the proper and unobstructed exercise of their jurisdiction,' and to the argument of military necessity the Court said, 'No doctrine involving more pernicious consequences was ever invented by the wit of man than that any of [the Constitution's] provisions can be suspended during any of the great exigencies of government. Such a doctrine leads directly to anarchy or despotism.' Yet within a year, in flagrant violation of this decision, Congress established military tribunals throughout the South; and when the validity of this legislation was challenged, in the McCardle case, Congress rushed through a law depriving the Court of jurisdiction over the case while the Supreme Court sat supinely by and submitted to the outrage.

While brushing aside embarrassing legal obstacles, Radical leaders nevertheless sought refuge in constitutional dialectics. The maintenance of military rule in the South and the insistence upon ratification of the Fourteenth and later the Fifteenth Amendments before re-admission, was based theoretically upon the clause in the Constitution that 'Congress shall guarantee to every state a republican form of government.' For three-quarters of a century this clause had been interpreted to mean that Congress would maintain the pre-existing governments, but now the Radicals wrenched it away from its traditional meaning and insisted that — for the Southern states at least — a 'republican' form of government included Negro suffrage, and the Court supported them to the extent of declaring that 'the power to carry into effect the clause of guarantee is primarily a legislative power, and resides in Congress.'

Many of the acts which Congress passed in order to carry into effect its reconstruction policy were palpably unconstitutional, but the attitude of the Radicals was well expressed by General Grant when he said of this legislation that 'much of it, no doubt, was unconstitutional; but it was hoped that the laws enacted would serve their purpose before the question of constitutionality could be submitted to the judiciary and a decision obtained.' This hope was indeed well founded for the validity of some of the reconstruction measures never came before the Court, and others were not passed upon until long after they had 'served their purpose.' In his messages vetoing the Freedmen's Bureau Bill, the Civil Rights Act, and the various Reconstruction Acts of 2 March, 23 March, and 19 July 1867, President Johnson scored their unconstitutionality with monotonous regularity. Nevertheless, once they were passed over his veto, he believed that he was required to carry out their provisions. It remained then for the aggrieved victims of these bills to test their validity in the courts. This object was sought in a number of cases, but in every instance the Federal courts succeeded in evading the issue or in escaping responsibility for a decision. The State of Mississippi asked for an injunction restraining Johnson from carrying out the Reconstruction Acts, but the Supreme Court, remembering the Dred Scott case, refused to accept jurisdiction. Georgia then brought suit against Secretary of War Stanton, but once again the Court refused to intervene in what it termed a political controversy.

Individuals fared somewhat better. Though some of the Radicals wanted to prosecute the leaders of the Confederacy for treason it was soon apparent that no jury would convict them, and the terms of military surrender guaranteed that there would be no military trial. Efforts to punish participants in the rebellion by discriminatory legislation were equally unsuccessful. In *ex parte* Garland the operation of the federal test oath to exclude lawyers from practicing in federal courts was declared invalid, because *ex post facto;* and in Cummings *v.* Missouri similar state legislation was held invalid on the same grounds.

More important was the judicial emasculation of the various acts to enforce the Fourteenth and Fifteenth Amendments. In a series of cases — United States *v.* Reese (1875), United States *v.* Cruikshank (1875), United States *v.* Harris (1883), and Civil Rights Cases (1883)

—the Supreme Court laid down the doctrine that the Civil War Amendments did not authorize the Federal Government to protect citizens from each other but only from discriminatory state legislation, that they gave protection only where such legislation discriminated because of race or color, and that they gave protection only to civil and not to social rights. These decisions indicated clearly that the courts could not be relied upon to secure for the Negro the rights presumably guaranteed him by the Fourteenth and Fifteenth Amendments.

The delicate question to which department of the government, executive or legislative, appertained the task of reconstruction, has never been legally settled, though at the time the legislative branch was victorious. The truth is that the theory of separation of powers played havoc with the realities of the situation. In the conflict between these two departments of the government, President Johnson conducted himself with circumspection and a nice regard for the law and the Constitution, while Congress rode roughshod over both, and the courts played a negative and ineffectual role.

7. *Restoration of White Rule in the South*

Inevitably the excesses of black reconstruction aroused organized and determined opposition throughout the South. This opposition took both legal and illegal forms. In some states in which the whites were in a preponderant majority, such as Tennessee and North Carolina, the Democrats were able to recapture control of their states by regular political methods. Elsewhere, however, it was thought necessary to resort to methods that were frankly terroristic. Adopting the technique of the Radicals who had organized the Negro vote, white Southerners played upon the blacks' timidity and superstition, and made life uncomfortable for carpet-baggers. The latter, for instance, were apt to find themselves bystanders in a shooting affair, 'accidental' targets for the bullets of participants. The Negroes were dealt with largely by secret societies.

Of these secret societies, the most famous, though not the largest, was the Ku Klux Klan. 'The origin of the Ku Klux Klan,' wrote a Southern editor, 'is in the galling despotism that broods like a nightmare over these Southern States.' Actually its origin was with a social *kuklos* (circle) of young men in Pulaski, Tennessee, who discovered that their initiation garb of sheets and pillow cases made them authentic spirits from another world to the blacks. Realizing the political possibilities of their society, they formed other *kukloi* which in 1867 organized as the 'Invisible Empire of the South.' The advent of military reconstruction, in 1867, gave an impetus to their growth, and during the next three years, this and other secret societies, notably the Knights of the White Camelia, policed unruly Negroes in the country districts and delivered spectral warnings against using the ballot, thus paralyzing Radical power at its source. But the work of the secret societies was not confined to politics. 'As bodies of vigilantes,' says their most careful historian, Professor Fleming, 'they regulated the conduct of bad Negroes, punished criminals who were not punished by the State, looked after the activities and teachings of Northern preachers and teachers, dispersed hostile gatherings of Negroes, and ran out of the community the worst of the reconstructionist officials.'[4] Yet there can be no doubt that the Klan and other societies pledged to the 'maintenance of white supremacy' were guilty of many crimes, and that all too often secrecy became a cloak for lawlessness and oppression directed against whites as well as against blacks. Partly for this reason, and partly because their work was so well accomplished, the Klan was formally disbanded in 1869 and the Knights of the White Camelia went out of existence in the following year.

The Radicals had no intention of acquiescing tamely to the violent undoing of reconstruction, and their answer to the Ku Klux Klan was renewed military occupation of evacuated districts, the unseating of Democratic state administrations on the ground of fraud, and a new crop of supervisory laws, the most important of which were the Force Acts of 1870 and the Ku Klux Act of 1871, authorizing the President to suspend the writ of habeas corpus and suppress disturbances by military force. Actually some 7,373 indictments were found under these acts, but there were relatively few convictions, and only once did President Grant find it necessary or expedient to establish military rule on a large scale.

Indeed, public opinion in the North was no longer ready to sustain a drastic policy toward the South. A large segment of the Republican party opposed the Radical policy, and in the election of 1872 this group threw its support to an independent candidate pledged to put an end to the Southern problem. Grant was elected, but two years later the Democrats captured the lower House, and the repudiation

[4] W. L. Fleming, *The Sequel of Appomattox*, p. 258.

of Radicalism was complete. Meantime, all the Southern states had been re-admitted to Congress, and by the Amnesty Act of 1872 almost all Southern whites who were still disfranchised were restored to full political privileges.

In the South, too, the Radicals were in full retreat. Factional struggles between the carpet-baggers and the scalawags split the Republican party in almost every Southern state; business demanded peace and security; and the Negroes began to desert their Republican allies. As the power of the Radicals waned, demands for military intervention became increasingly insistent, but in the end Grant revolted against these demands. 'The whole public,' he protested, 'are tired out with the annual autumnal outbreaks in the South and the great majority are ready now to condemn any interference on the part of the government.'

So in state after state the Southern whites recaptured control of the political machinery: in Tennessee, Virginia, North Carolina, and Georgia in 1869–71, in Alabama, Arkansas, Texas, and Mississippi in 1874–75. By the end of 1875 only South Carolina, Louisiana, and Florida were still under Radical control, and here that control was precarious and exercised with some degree of restraint. Once back in power, the Democrats proceeded to undo as much of Radical reconstruction as they could. By one means or another Negroes were eliminated from politics, carpet-baggers scared out, scalawags won over. Expenditures and taxes were drastically reduced, and some progressive legislation wiped off the statute books. More important was the wholesale repudiation of state debts. Acting on the assumption that a large part of these debts had been fraudulently contracted, state after state proceeded to repudiate them: altogether, by this convenient method, the Southern states rid themselves of between 125 and 150 million dollars of debts — a large part of the cost of Radical reconstruction.

When Rutherford B. Hayes was inaugurated President, 4 March 1877, the carpetbag régime had been overthrown in every Southern state save South Carolina and Louisiana, where it was still upheld by federal bayonets. By frankly terroristic methods the whites in South Carolina had, the previous autumn, elected General Wade Hampton governor, and returned a Democratic majority to the legislature. A Republican returning board cancelled the ballots, filled vacancies arbitrarily, and with the help of federal troops excluded the Democrats from the state capitol at Columbia. The newly elected

Democratic members then hired a hall, organized their own House, and with Speaker, clerks, and sergeant-at-arms forced their way into the representatives' chamber where the Radicals were sitting. During three days and nights the rival Houses sat side by side, every man armed to the teeth, and ready to shoot if the rival sergeants-at-arms laid hands on one of his colleagues. At the end of that time the Democrats withdrew, leaving the carpetbag Governor Chamberlain, and his legislature in possession of the State House; but the people of the state obeyed the government which Governor Hampton administered. A quarter-century later, Governor Chamberlain admitted:

> There was no permanent possibility of securing good government in South Carolina through Republican influences. . . . The vast preponderance of ignorance and incapacity in that party, aside from downright dishonesty, made it impossible. . . . The elements put in combination by the reconstruction schemes of Stevens and Sumner were irretrievably bad, and could never have resulted except temporarily, or in desperate moments, in governments fit to be endured.

President Hayes broke this deadlock on 10 April 1877 by withdrawing the federal troops from Columbia, when the Democrats peaceably took possession. Two weeks later, when the troops evacuated New Orleans, white rule was completely restored to the South. The principle of self-government was vindicated, and the world given another striking proof that government without consent is impossible to maintain in English-speaking countries. Ho Ho

Within less than twenty years the animosities between the North and South were all but forgotten, and in 1898 Congress removed the last political disabilities from ex-Confederates. But reconstruction left deep scars upon the South, physical and moral. Politics were forced into an unnatural racial groove, allegiance to the Democratic party became synonymous with white supremacy, and from 1876 to 1916 the South presented a united front politically. Race relations were poisoned, as the annual though diminishing crop of lynchings attests. The colored people were retarded at least a generation in their progress towards responsible citizenship; white men exhausted their energy in efforts to keep the Negroes down. Southern society remained relatively static, immune to modern movements in education and social regeneration, and in the twentieth century the South was hardly more prepared to meet the industrial invasion than New England had been a century before.

III

POLITICS OF THE GRANT ADMINISTRATION
1868–1877

1. *The Election of 1868*

EVEN as the Senate sat in solemn judgment over President Johnson, the triumphant Republicans met in party convention to nominate his successor, and to promise a continuation of Radicalism in politics and conservatism in economic policy. Any number of favorite sons were willing to accept the crown which sat so uneasily upon Johnson's head, but only one was considered worthy of that honor. General Grant was no party man and no politician. Before the Civil War he had seldom taken the trouble to vote, and the army was not a good school of politics. Such political principles as he professed had inclined him toward the Democratic party, but after McClellan's candidature it was inconceivable that he should have tied up with the Democrats. He had been to Lincoln a faithful subordinate, but to Johnson somewhat less than faithful, and after his break with Johnson he had been captured by the shrewd Radical politicians who saw in him an unbeatable candidate. On the first ballot Grant received a unanimous nomination; the selection of 'Smiling' Schuyler Colfax as his running mate did nothing to strengthen the ticket.

The Republican platform pledged the party to continue Radical reconstruction in the South, repudiated the 'Ohio idea' of payment of the government debt in greenbacks, committed the party to hard money, and preserved an eloquent silence on the tariff issue. The adoption of this platform indicated that the Republican party of Frémont and Lincoln was now controlled by a coalition of political Radicals (in the then special sense of that word) and economic conservatives.

No such unanimity characterized the Democratic convention which met in New York City some weeks later, for the deep gash cut in that party in 1860 had not yet fully healed. The Democrats still labored under the odium of secession, and were embarrassed by the leadership of the discredited President Johnson. Harassed by conflicting counsels and confused by rival claims for leadership, they adopted a platform that emphasized equally the reconstruction and the money issues, and named a candidate certain to repudiate the platform.

That platform arraigned the Radical Republican party 'for its disregard of right, and the unparallelled oppression and tyranny which have marked its career,' charged it with 'corruption and extravagance' exceeding anything known to history, declared its reconstruction acts 'unconstitutional, revolutionary, and void,' and prophesied that its victory would reduce Americans to 'a subjected and conquered people.' In addition the platform committed the Democratic party to the so-called 'Ohio idea' — that, wherever possible, the public debt of the United States should be paid in greenbacks rather than in gold. If the campaign was to be fought on the reconstruction issue, Andrew Johnson was the obvious candidate; if on the money issue, the logical candidate was 'Gentleman George' Pendleton, sponsor of the 'Ohio idea.' With an evasiveness that was coming to appear characteristic, the party chose instead a man who could not dramatize the reconstruction issue and who was committed to a hard money policy — the weak and the ineffectual Horatio Seymour, former Governor of New York!

The campaign that followed was one of the most bitterly fought in our history. The stakes of victory were large. To Republicans success promised an indefinite tenure of power, during which the party might be given a national basis through the extension of Negro suffrage to the South, and an untrammelled continuation of the program of economic exploitation through tariff, banking, and railroad policies already begun. To the Democrats victory promised the relegation of the Negro problem to local politics, the restoration of Southern states to the Union, and the modification of that far-reaching economic legislation which had been written into the statute books during the Civil War years. Republican strategy made reconstruction the major issue and the efforts of the Democrats to distract attention to economic issues proved unavailing. Again the Republicans waved the 'bloody shirt of the rebellion,' even more effectively than in 1866. When the electoral vote was counted, it was found that Grant had carried every state but eight, and rolled up a popular majority of some 300,000. Yet the victory was by no means as conclusive as might appear from these figures. It was the Negro vote of some 700,000 that gave Grant his popular majority, and it was the exclusion of three Southern states and the control of six others through reconstruction laws that gave him his large electoral college majority. Only by a wilful misreading could the election be interpreted as a vote of confidence to the Radicals or an enthusiastic endorsement of Grant.

2. *President Grant*

The problems which Grant faced were varied and complex, but he brought to their solution neither understanding nor competence. Of the new economic forces that were shaping the United States, he was completely unaware. With less equipment for the Presidency than any predecessor or successor, his temperament unfitted him for high political office, and he was unable or unwilling to overcome his temperamental deficiencies. Although a leader of men, he was not a good judge of men, and the very simplicity which had carried him safely through the intrigues of the Civil War exposed him to the wiles of politicians whose loyalty to himself he mistook for devotion to the public weal.

Brilliance, subtlety, urbanity — these qualities were not expected of Grant, but it came as a shock that he seemed to have lost the qualities he had shown in the war — a sense of order and of command, directness, resoluteness, consistency, and intellectual honesty. He was vacillating and undignified; his judgment was incalculable, his prejudices implacable. The magnanimous victor of Appomattox, revealed himself in office petty, vindictive, and shifty. To his friends, said Henry Adams, 'Grant appeared as intermittent energy, immensely powerful when awake, but passive and plastic in repose. . . . For stretches of time his mind seemed torpid. . . . They could never measure his character or be sure when he would act. They could never follow a mental process in his thought. They were not sure that he did think.' He was naïve rather than innocent, simple rather than unsophisticated, and his simplicity, as Adams shrewdly remarked, 'was more disconcerting than the complexity of a Talleyrand.'

Utterly untutored in politics, his political sense was as primitive as that of a Sioux Indian. He was curiously ignorant of the law and even of the Constitution, and he never came to understand properly the relations of the Executive to his Cabinet or to the other departments of the government. 'His Cabinet,' observed John Bigelow, 'are merely staff officers, selected apparently out of motives of gratitude for pecuniary favors received from them.' Nor did he ever come to understand the character of the Presidential office. To the end he regarded the Presidency as a personal prerogative, a reward for services rendered rather than a responsibility. Of the nature of political forces he had no comprehension, and he failed entirely to grasp the real character of the pressure groups who lobbied so successfully for favorable legislation on tariffs, finance, public lands, and even foreign affairs. He had, apparently, but one political principle — a profound faith in his friends; it was a faith often mistaken and often betrayed.

Without qualifications for his office, Grant's only hope lay in the wisdom and integrity of his advisers. But these were chosen with bizarre irresponsibility. Grant's cabinet contained some men of ability and a few of real talent, but these were accidents and in time Grant came to regard them as errors. Altogether, during his eight years of office, Grant appointed no less than twenty-five men to his cabinet. Some, such as the pathetic Borie or the addle-headed Ackerman were merely incompetent; others, such as Delano of the Interior Department or the Attorney-General, Williams, were corrupt. A few, such as Belknap, Secretary of War, or Boutwell, Secretary of the Treasury, were incompetent and corrupt. Six — Hoar, Cox, Creswell, Jewell, Bristow, and Fish — proved to be men of intelligence and integrity, and of these Grant managed to dismiss all but one, Secretary of State Fish.

It was fortunate, indeed, that Grant was able to command, throughout the eight years of his administration, the talents of Hamilton Fish. A New York aristocrat, Grant's third choice for the State Department, and relatively unknown when he took office, Fish proved himself one of the shrewdest men who have ever directed the foreign affairs of the nation. He had what most of his colleagues in Grant's cabinet so singularly lacked, integrity of character, disciplined intelligence, learning, experience, urbanity, and a tact and patience sufficient to win and retain the confidence of his chief. To Fish must be ascribed responsibility not only for the signal achievements of the administration in the field of foreign affairs but also for preventing many egregious mistakes in domestic policies.

Yet for all his obvious defects of character and of mind, Grant wielded an immense power. For the devotion which he commanded from millions of men was devotion to something stronger than integrity or political wisdom or character or intellectual preëminence. It was devotion to an ideal. 'The plain man,' as Allan Nevins so well observes, 'had not elected Grant; he had elected an indestructible legend, a folk-hero. . . . Mention that monosyllabic name, and the prosaic laborer, farmer, clerk, or business man for once in his life saw a vision. It was a vision of four years of terror and glory. Painted on the clouds above his farm or shop, he saw the torrent of muddied blue uniforms rallying on the bluffs of Shiloh; he saw the butternut rush dissolving against a smoke-wreathed wall at Gettysburg; he saw the night ripped by shells and rockets as gunboats spouting fire raced past Vicksburg; he saw the lines at Lookout Mountain waver, re-form, and go on up; he saw two armies wait as Lee walked into the parlor at Appomattox.' It was well for Grant that he brought to the Presidency this imperishable glamor, for he brought little else.

3. *Foreign Affairs*

It was in the field of foreign affairs, where Grant permitted himself to be guided by Hamilton Fish, that the administration won its most notable success. During almost the whole of Grant's two terms of office, American foreign relations were in a delicate and critical state. The outbreak of revolution in Cuba threatened to involve the United States in war with Spain; the activities of the Fenians along the Canadian border embarrassed our relations with Canada; and the unwillingness of Lord Russell to arbitrate American claims against Great Britain for alleged failure to observe neutrality during the Civil War strained Anglo-American friendship to the breaking-point.

Many vexatious foreign questions had grown out of the Civil War. Some had been liquidated; others remained to plague the Grant administration. Seward, by his firm attitude toward the French in Mexico and the Spaniards in Santo Domingo, had vindicated the Monroe Doctrine, and by his shrewd strokes of diplomacy had advanced his policy of imperialism in the Pacific. Spain's attempted conquest of Santo Domingo broke down of its own accord, but the Spanish withdrawal from that ill-fated island in 1865 appeared to be a diplomatic victory for Seward. It was not until two years later that Seward persuaded Napoleon III of the necessity of abandoning his Mexican venture: in June 1867 the puppet-Emperor Maximilian slumped before a firing squad and the cardboard Empire collapsed. Russia had long been eager to get rid of Alaska, and in 1867 Sumner in the Senate and a well-oiled lobby in the House permitted Seward to buy that rich domain for seven million two hundred thousand dollars. To round out his expansionist policy Seward annexed the Midway Islands, west of Hawaii, and, with a view to the construction of an isthmian canal at some future date, acquired the right of transit across Nicaragua. When he surrendered his office, a treaty for the purchase of the Danish West India islands was pending in the Senate.

Seward had misjudged the temper of the country, for the Senate promptly rejected the treaty. President Grant, although indifferent to the Danish West Indies (the present Virgin Islands), was enormously interested in another of Seward's Caribbean projects — the annexation of Santo Domingo. This hare-brained proposal had originated with two Yankee fortune-hunters who planned to secure for themselves half the wealth of the island. They managed to draw into their conspiracy powerful financial and commercial interests and bought the support of such men as Ben Butler, John A. Rawlins, and Grant's personal secretary Orville Babcock; these in turn persuaded the President to commit himself to the project. Grant sent Babcock on a tour of inspection to Santo Domingo, and Babcock returned with a treaty of annexation in his pocket. The treaty was eventually formalized and submitted to the Senate only to encounter the implacable hostility of Charles Sumner and Carl Schurz and fail of ratification. It was the most severe defeat that the administration was to suffer.

The Santo Domingo episode was not in itself of importance, but its consequences were important. It revealed how easily Grant could be won over to projects of a dubious character and how naïve was his understanding of foreign affairs. It led to the deposition of Sumner from his position as Chairman of the Senate Committee on Foreign Affairs and caused a rift in the Republican party that widened, by 1872, into a complete breach. It distracted the attention of Grant and the Radicals from the Cuban situation and enabled Secretary Fish to sidetrack the demand for a recognition of Cuban belligerency and preserve peace with Spain.

A Cuban rebellion had broken out in 1868 and dragged on for ten dreadful years before it was finally suppressed. From the beginning the sympathy of most Americans was with the rebels, and when the Cuban junta in New York spread stories of Spanish barbarism — stories for the most part true — sympathy flamed into indignation. Early in 1869 the House passed a resolution of sympathy for the Cubans, but the movement for recognition of Cuban belligerency encountered the firm opposition of Fish. Recognition, indeed, would have been a serious mistake. In the first place it would have compromised gravely American claims against Great Britain for premature recognition of the belligerency of the Confederate States; in the second place it would probably have meant war with Spain. So Fish permitted Grant to exhaust himself on his Santo Domingo project while he dragged out diplomatic negotiations with Spain. By 1871 the crisis was weathered, and even the capture in 1873 of the American ship *Virginius* on the high seas and the barbarous execution of fifty-three of her seamen was not enough to rupture Spanish-American relations.

To the northward as well as to the southward relations were strained. During the war Canada had furnished an asylum for Confederate plotters and a base for Confederate raids on Vermont and New York. In time of peace the Fenians, or Irish Revolutionary Brother-Republics, took similar liberties in the United States. Two rival Irish republics were organized in New York City, each with its president, cabinet, and general staff in glittering uniforms of green and gold. Each planned to seize Canada with Irish veterans of the Union army, and hold it as hostage for Irish freedom. From 1866 to 1870 the Fenians harassed the Canadian border. The first invasion, in April 1866, was promptly nipped by federal authorities at Eastport, Maine, but the ensuing howl from the Irish vote frightened President Johnson and his cabinet. Before the Attorney-General and the Secretaries of War and of the Navy could decide who should take the onus of stopping him, 'General' John O'Neil led fifteen hundred armed Irishmen across the Niagara river. The next day, 2 June 1866, the Canadian militia gave battle, and fled; but the Fenians fled farthest — to New York State, where they were promptly arrested and as promptly released. During the following three years the Fenians collected arms and money and girded themselves for a new attack, and in the spring of 1870 tatterdemalion armies moved on Canada from St. Albans, Vermont, and Malone, New York. This time both governments were ready for them. United States marshals arrested the Fenian leaders, and the armies disintegrated. Ridiculous as they were, these Fenian forays caused Canada much trouble and expense for which she was never reimbursed by the United States.

But the greatest achievement of the Grant administration was the liquidation of all outstanding diplomatic controversies with Great Britain. The sympathy of the English governing classes for the Confederacy and the lax enforcement of neutrality by the British government had aroused deep resentment in the United States. For some years after the war the psychological atmosphere was such that no calm adjudication of American claims was possible. The most important of these claims had to do with the alleged negligence of the British government in permitting the Confederate cruisers *Alabama, Shenandoah,* and *Florida* to be armed in, and escape from, British ports. Seward's persistent advocacy of these claims was finally rewarded in the last months of Johnson's administration by the so-called Clarendon Convention for their adjudication. But nothing that President Johnson did could then find favor with the Republican party. In April 1869 the Senate rejected this convention as insufficient, after Sumner had charged Great Britain with responsibility for half the total cost of the war: a mere $2,125,000,000. Sumner's speech shocked his English friends who so faithfully had sustained the Union cause; nor were they much comforted by his explanation that the cession of Canada would be an acceptable form of payment. Sumner loved England, but with characteristic lack of imagination failed to perceive that the tone as well as the substance of his speech stimulated Anglophobia.

After Sumner was eliminated as a result of the Caribbean question, negotiations went forward more successfully. The Canadian Sir John Rose staged with Hamilton Fish a diplomatic play of wooing and yielding that threw dust in the eyes of extremists on both sides. The covenant thus secretly arrived at was the famous Treaty of Washington (8 May 1871). It provided for submission to arbitration of boundary disputes, the fisheries question, and the *Alabama* claims: it determined rules of neutrality to govern the arbitral tribunal, and contained an expression of regret for the escape of the *Alabama* from British waters—a friendly gesture for which Americans had long been waiting.

In presenting their case to the arbitral tribunal at Geneva the United States claimed compensation not only for actual damage inflicted by the Confederate cruisers, but for the numerous transfers of registry occasioned by fear of capture. Hamilton Fish had no intention of pressing these 'indirect claims,' which he was anxious only to be rid of; but English opinion was deeply stirred by their presentation. An ill-tempered press discussion ensued. Gladstone would have withdrawn from the arbitration on that issue had not Charles Francis Adams, the American member, proposed that the Geneva tribunal should rule out the indirect claims in advance. This was done, and the arbitration proceeded smoothly to its conclusion: an award of $15,000,000 for depredations committed by the *Alabama, Florida,* and

Shenandoah. Even this sum was in excess of the actual damage, and part of it was never handed out to claimants.

Although the United States was thereby vindicated, the greater victory was for arbitration and peace. No threat of force affected the issue, for American ironclads had lost their primacy by 1871. Never before had questions involving such touchy matters of national honor been submitted to a mere majority vote of an international tribunal; and the good grace with which England as a whole accepted the verdict smoothed out the ill-tempered dissenting opinion of Sir Alexander Cockburn. Of other persons involved Charles Francis Adams never forgot that he was judge, not advocate. President Grant by his unwavering support of peaceful methods showed a quality not unusual in statesmen who know war at first hand; and in a later message to the Arbitration Union of Birmingham he confessed his guiding principle: 'Nothing would afford me greater happiness than to know that, as I believe will be the case, at some future day, the nations of the earth will agree upon some sort of congress which will take cognizance of international questions of difficulty, and whose decisions will be as binding as the decisions of our Supreme Court are upon us. It is a dream of mine that some such solution may be.'

4. *Domestic Politics*

No such idealism animated Grant in his handling of the more pressing problems of domestic politics. Three of these problems, reconstruction, the money question, and the tariff, were of urgent national importance; a fourth, civil service reform, was taken seriously only by a small group; but that group included many of the ablest men in American political life.

'Let us have peace,' the concluding phrase of Grant's letter accepting the Presidential nomination, had encouraged the country to believe that Grant would abandon Radical reconstruction and adopt toward the South a more conciliatory policy. In the beginning this hope seemed justified. The President suggested to his Cabinet a sweeping amnesty proclamation and urged Congress to complete the reconstruction process in Virginia, Mississippi, and Texas. By 1870 representatives from these three laggard states again took their places in Congress. But despite this good beginning it was soon painfully clear that, under pressure from such advisers as Boutwell, Butler, Morton, and Conkling, Grant had gone over to the Radical camp.

In his first annual message he recommended to Congress a drastic reconstitution of the legislature of Georgia and Congress responded with appropriate legislation. He gave his approval to the unfortunate Force Acts and the Ku Klux Act and applied them with uncompromising rigor. Faced with a revolt throughout the South against the carpetbag régime he fell back upon his military idea of restoring order, which he identified with carpetbag government. In South Carolina, Alabama, Mississippi, Louisiana, and Arkansas Grant supported the worst of the carpet-baggers and authorized the use of federal troops to overthrow duly elected Democratic governments and keep these states in the Radical Republican ranks.

The money question, like the Southern question, had been inherited from previous administrations. During the war the Government had issued $450,000,000 of legal tender notes, and at the close of the war some $400,000,000 of these so-called greenbacks were still in circulation. The presence of greenbacks in the currency gave rise to two issues that divided public opinion along class and sectional lines. The first involved the medium of payment of the interest and principal of government bonds. These bonds had been purchased with depreciated greenbacks, and it was urged that they should be redeemable in greenbacks unless otherwise specified. Farmers and workingmen who would ultimately pay the taxes for the redemption of these bonds supported this proposal as just. Bondholders and the business interests which they represented opposed it as a betrayal of national honor.

The Democratic party, as we have seen, endorsed this 'Ohio idea' of the payment of government securities in greenbacks. President Johnson, in his last annual message, went even farther and proposed that future interest payments be applied to the liquidation of the principal of the debt. 'It may be assumed,' he said, 'that the holders of our securities have already received upon their bonds a larger amount than their original investment, measured by the gold standard. Upon this statement of facts it would seem but just and equitable that the six per cent interest now paid by the Government should be applied to the reduction of the principal . . . which in sixteen years and eight months would liquidate the entire national debt. . . . The lessons of the past admonish the lender that it is not well to be overanxious in exacting from the borrower rigid compliance with the letter of the bond.' But the Democrats were defeated and Johnson discredited. In his first inaugural address Grant committed himself to payment of all government obligations in gold, and the first measure passed by the new Congress (18 March 1869) pledged the faith of the United States to such payment.

The second question raised by the presence of greenbacks concerned the policy of the Government toward the contraction of the greenback currency and the resumption of specie payments. The inflation of the currency through greenbacks had tended to raise commodity prices, make credit easier and money cheaper. The farmer and the debtor therefore regarded with dismay any proposal for the contraction of the currency by calling in these greenbacks. Business interests, on the contrary, looked upon contraction as financially sound and economically advantageous. Representatives of the farmer interest urged, correctly enough, that more rather than less money was needed to serve the needs of a rapidly growing nation. Representatives of business interests insisted, with equal correctness, that inflation, if it got out of hand, might prostrate the business of the nation and destroy the credit of the Government. They demanded that, in any event, the Government should stabilize the currency by pledging itself to redeem greenbacks with gold and thus bring greenbacks to par.

A powerful argument for stabilization of the currency was that constant fluctuation in the value of greenbacks opened a wide door to speculation. Because greenbacks were not legal tender for all purposes and because it was uncertain whether the Government would ever redeem them in gold, they circulated at a discount which varied from month to month. In 1865 the gold value of a greenback dollar was fifty cents; by the time Grant assumed office it had risen to seventy-three cents. In September 1869 two notorious stock gamblers, Jay Gould and Jim Fisk, took advantage of this fluctuation in the value of money to organize a corner in gold. With the passive connivance of persons high in the confidence of the President and the Secretary of the Treasury, the nefarious scheme was almost successful. On 'Black Friday,' 24 September 1869, the premium on gold rose to 162, and scores of Wall Street brokers faced ruin. Then the Government dumped four million dollars in gold on the market, and the corner collapsed. The whole country was aroused, and men everywhere blamed Grant for criminal incompetence in permitting himself to be enmeshed in the sordid affair. 'The worst scandals of the 18th century,' wrote Henry Adams, 'were relatively harmless by the side of this which smirched executive, judiciary, banks, corporate systems, professions, and people, all the great active forces of society.'

Yet the episode reflected not so much upon Grant's character as upon his judgment. The fact is that Grant knew little about finance and understood less, and the policy of the administration was from the beginning vacillating. Grant favored a resumption of specie payments but he was opposed to contraction of the currency and disposed to accept greenbacks as a permanent part of the currency. When in 1871 the Supreme Court announced that greenbacks were not legal tender for obligations entered into prior to the emission of the notes, and even made the alarming suggestion that they were completely invalid,[1] the government promptly moved for a rehearing of the case. Two vacancies on the Supreme Bench afforded Grant a propitious opportunity to strengthen the Government's position. In Joseph P. Bradley and William Strong, Grant found jurists upon whose faith in the constitutionality of the greenbacks he could with confidence rely. He was not disappointed. In the second Legal Tender decision, Knox *v.* Lee,[2] the Court reversed itself and sustained the constitutionality of the Civil War greenbacks; ten years later, in an even more sweeping decision, Julliard *v.* Greenman,[3] it was to proclaim the right of the Government to issue legal tender even in time of peace.

The Court having sustained the constitutionality of legal tenders, Secretaries Boutwell and Richardson found it proper to increase their number. When Grant assumed office there were in circulation $356,000,000 of greenbacks; by 1874 the total had been raised to $382,000,000. Congress, frightened by the panic of 1873, voted to increase the total to $400,000,000. The sum was not in itself too large, but the gesture toward inflation was alarming. Grant vetoed the bill, and the danger passed. Encouraged by the firm stand of the President and dismayed at the prospect of Democratic control of the lower House, Congress, in 1875, finally provided for the resumption of specie payments. This act settled, for the time being, the legal tender question, but it did not settle the money question. That remained to plague the next generation.

The tariff question was also settled to the satisfaction of the business interests. The Civil War tariffs, raising duties to unprecedented heights, were originally regarded as emergency revenue measures;

[1] Hepburn *v.* Griswold, 8 Wallace, 603 (1870).
[2] 12 Wallace, 457 (1871).
[3] 110 U.S. 421 (1884).

protected industries soon came to regard them as permanent. After Appomattox, Western farmers and Eastern progressives joined hands in demanding tariff reform, but the protected interests had no intention of yielding to a demand which they regarded as sentimental folly. In 1867 duties had actually been raised on a number of items, and throughout the following years Congress passed a series of 'pop' tariff bills which continued the upward course of protective duties. The administration was definitely hostile to tariff reform. Secretary Cox was forced out of the Cabinet in part because of his sympathy for it, and David A. Wells, the able economist who was a special commissioner of revenue, had to resign for the same reason. The approach of a Presidential election, however, scared the administration into temporary virtue on this issue, and in 1872 Grant signed a bill providing for a horizontal slash of ten per cent on many protected articles. At the same time, the last of the Civil War income taxes were repealed. After the election tariff duties were restored to their earlier status, but no effort was made to restore the income tax.

Nor did civil service reform fare better. In no department indeed was the record of Grant's administration more discreditable. Dissatisfaction with the spoils system was widespread, and when voiced by such leaders as Carl Schurz, Lyman Trumbull, and Charles Sumner it could not be disregarded. In the beginning it appeared that the reformers had Grant's support. In 1871 a Civil Service Commission, headed by George William Curtis, submitted a list of desirable reforms and Grant promised that 'at all events the experiment shall have a fair trial.' But Grant soon scuttled the Commission and jettisoned the reform. The recommendations of the Commission were ignored, the civil service packed with party henchmen, and the system of assessments on office-holders brought to a high state of efficiency. 'There is an utter surrender of the Civil Service to the coarsest use by the coarsest men,' observed Whitelaw Reid, and reformers everywhere echoed the sentiment. Curtis, wearied of shadow-boxing with the spoilsmen, resigned in disgust, and in 1875 the Commission itself was discontinued. With the appointment of the Republican boss, Zachary Chandler, to the Cabinet the administration abandoned even the pretense of interest in civil service reform and surrendered itself over to the spoilsmen.

5. *The Liberal Republican Movement*

The Civil War had obscured the deep differences within the Republican party, and Reconstruction served as a smoke-screen behind which Radicals captured control of the party organization. Grant had commanded the support of Eastern and Western business and farming interests alike, but his record soon forfeited the favor of those who looked to him to reform and to nationalize the party. Within less than a year after his assumption of office, revolt was in full swing.

Causes for dissatisfaction were numerous. The full measure of administrative corruption was indeed unknown, but enough was suspected to outrage men who cherished standards of political decency. Grant's Southern policy was a failure, his Caribbean policy an affront, and his repudiation of civil service and tariff reform alienated many of his followers. Above all there was a growing distrust of Grant himself, a distrust which found eloquent expression in Sumner's famous excoriation of May 1872 wherein the President was scored for taking and giving bribes, for nepotism, for neglect of duty, for lawless interference with the business of the other departments of the Government, and for half a dozen other misdemeanors, any one of which would have justified impeachment. Sumner's scorching disapproval was something which all Presidents had had to face, and was not taken too seriously; but soon many of the most distinguished of the elder statesmen were following his lead. Grant's abuse of the civil service alienated Cox and Schurz, his Southern policy antagonized Lyman Trumbull and Gideon Welles, his tariff policy cost him the support of David A. Wells and his money policy of Don Cameron, while outside the ranks of the politicians such men as Chief Justice Chase, Horace Greeley, and E. L. Godkin came to regard the President as unfit for high office.

This revolt against Grant was started by liberals and reformers, but old-line politicians and disappointed factional leaders soon flocked to it in embarrassing numbers. In the end it consisted of as heterogeneous a group as was ever gathered together in one political party. Free-traders like David A. Wells and high protectionists like Horace Greeley, Eastern conservatives like Charles Francis Adams and Western radicals like Ignatius Donnelly, civil service reformers like Carl Schurz and practical politicians like Reuben Fenton of New York, were all in the same boat. The one idea that animated them all was distrust or dislike of President Grant. It was a movement of opposition rather than of positive reform, and therein lay its chief weakness.

When the Liberal Republican convention met at Cincinnati 1 May 1872, this weakness became apparent. It was impossible for the discordant elements to agree upon a satisfactory platform or a logical candidate; 'coherence,' as one of its ardent supporters 'Marse' Henry Watterson observed, 'was a missing ingredient.' The platform as finally adopted called for the withdrawal of troops from the South, civil service reform, and a resumption of specie payments; as for the tariff, the convention 'recognizing that there are in our midst honest but irreconcilable differences of opinion' remanded 'the discussion of the subject to the people in their Congressional Districts.'

The task of choosing a candidate proved even more difficult. There were available half a dozen able men, any one of whom might have carried the new party to victory. The most obvious choice was Charles Francis Adams, son and grandson of Presidents, Minister to England during the critical days of the Civil War, and a man of distinguished intellect and irreproachable character. An equally satisfactory nominee would have been Lyman Trumbull, whom Lincoln had sent to the Senate back in 1855 and who had been for twenty years one of the ornaments of the Republican party. Two Supreme Court Justices, S. P. Chase and David Davis, were eager for the nomination, and Cox of Ohio and Brown of Missouri had their champions. Intrigues and jealousies defeated all of these, however, and in the end the convention was stampeded to Horace Greeley of New York.

No man in the country was better known than Horace Greeley, for over thirty years editor of the powerful New York *Tribune*. A Vermont Yankee who had kept his homespun democracy and youthful idealism in the atmosphere of New York, Greeley persistently championed the cause of the underprivileged, the worker, and the farmer. He had long been a power in the councils of the Whig and Republican parties, and his advocacy of high tariff, liberal land laws, and abolition had helped to shape the course of American history. Yet for all his intellectual abilities and idealism, Greeley lacked the first qualifications for responsible political position. He was impulsive and unpredictible, ambitious and intriguing, vain and vindictive. Worst of all, his eager promotion of every reform, his crotchets and caprices and carefully cultivated idiosyncrasies, laid him open to ridicule and caricature. He had championed Fourierism and vegetarianism, spiritualism and temperance, and a dozen other fads, and the average man did not see in these things the expression of a consistent social philosophy but rather the vagaries of a visionary and impractical nature.

The nomination of Greeley, therefore, came as a shock to the reformers who had organized the Liberal Republican movement, and many of them hastened to retreat from a position which they thought untenable. But the dismay of the reformers was as nothing to the dismay of Southern Democrats. For thirty years Greeley had castigated the South, and the Democratic party, and much of the responsibility for anti-slavery and, later, for Radical reconstruction could justly be laid at his door. Democrats might well feel that an endorsement of Greeley would be more stultifying than an endorsement of Grant. Yet they had no alternative, and bitterly they swallowed the bizarre pill presented to them by the Liberal Republicans.

Greeley proved himself, surprisingly enough, an excellent campaigner, but the odds against him were insuperable. Grant could command the support not only of the rank and file of the Republican party, the colored vote, North and South, and most of the German vote, but, above all, of the business and banking interests. These came to his aid in handsome fashion. Banking houses such as Jay Cooke and Co., and Henry Clews and Co., the iron interests of Pennsylvania, and the Whiskey Ring in St. Louis, all contributed generously to the Republican campaign funds. Yet although one of Grant's biographers admits that 'it was the efficient organization of the Republican campaign, the lavish use of money, and the constant contact with every locality' that brought Republican success, it is probable that Grant would have been re-elected even without these contributions. When the votes were counted it was found that Grant had carried every state but six and that he had a popular majority of over seven hundred thousand. Three weeks later Horace Greeley died, broken-hearted, and the promising experiment in political liberalism which had excited such high hopes collapsed.

6. *Scandal and Stagnation*

'It looks at this distance,' wrote Senator Grimes to Lyman Trumbull, 'as though the Republican party were going to the dogs. . . . Like all parties that have an undisturbed power for a long time, it has become corrupt, and I believe that it is to-day the [most] corrupt and debauched political party that has ever existed.' When this was written, in July 1870, it seemed an exaggeration, but within a few years a series of sensational exposures went far to prove its accuracy. While the campaign of 1872 was still under way the country was startled by charges of wholesale corruption in connection with the construction of the Union Pacific Railway, charges which reflected upon men high in the councils of the Republican party. The promoters of the Union Pacific, in order corruptly to divert the profits of construction to themselves, had organized a construction company, the Crédit Mobilier of America. To this company the directors of the Union Pacific awarded contracts of a fantastically profitable nature. As a result of this neat arrangement the Union Pacific was forced to the verge of bankruptcy while the Crédit Mobilier paid in a single year dividends of 348 per cent. Fearing lest Congress might interpose, the directors placed large blocks of Crédit Mobilier stock 'where they would do most good.' Exposure of the scheme brought disgrace to Representatives Oakes Ames of Massachusetts and James Brooks of New York, Senator Patterson of New Hampshire, and Vice President Schuyler Colfax, while others such as Wilson of Massachusetts and Garfield of Ohio were never able to explain away their connection with the unsavory affair.

Scarcely less excusable was the so-called Salary Grab. In the closing days of Congress, February–March 1873, Ben Butler pushed through a bill doubling the salary of the President and increasing by fifty per cent the salary of Congressmen. This could be justified; what particularly affronted public opinion was that the increases granted to Congressmen were made retroactive for two years: thus each Congressman voted to himself five thousand dollars of back salary out of public funds. The bill was an evasion if not an outright violation of the Constitution, but Grant signed it without demur. A storm of indignation against this 'steal' swept the country, and in the following session Congress hastened to restore the old salary scale.

The Crédit Mobilier and the Salary Grab were merely the most sensational of the exposures which indicated the demoralization of the administration. It soon appeared that the Executive Department as well as the Legislative was honeycombed with corruption.

The Navy Department sold business to contractors, and Secretary Robeson managed to accumulate a fortune of several hundred thousand dollars during his tenure of office. The Department of the Interior was working hand in glove with land speculators. The Treasury Department farmed out uncollected taxes to one J. D. Sanborn who promptly proceeded to highjack some $425,000 out of railroad companies and other corporations, one-half of which he took for himself. The American Minister to England, Robert Schenck, lent his name and position to the Emma Mine swindle, and the Minister to Brazil, J. W. Webb, defrauded the Brazilian Government of one hundred thousand dollars and fled to Europe, leaving the United States Government to refund the money, with apologies. The Custom House in New York was a sink of political corruption, and when Collector Thomas Murphy was finally forced out Grant accepted his resignation 'with regret,' while at the same time the skullduggery of Collector Casey of the Port of New Orleans was rewarded by Casey's reappointment to the office which he had disgraced. In the national capitol 'Boss' Shepherd, head of the local ring, ran up a debt of seventeen million dollars, a large part of which was graft, and found himself appointed by a grateful President Chairman of the Board of Public Works! It was Shepherd, too, who was largely responsible for the failure of the Freedmen's Bank, a failure which worked cruel hardship upon thousands of trusting Negroes who had deposited their savings in an institution supposedly philanthropic.

All of this was bad enough, but worse was still to come. The Democrats carried the Congressional elections of 1874, and the following year a Democratic House, the first since the Civil War, set afoot a series of investigations designed to cleanse the Government and to furnish campaign material for the impending Presidential contest. In the Treasury and the War Departments investigators uncovered sensational frauds. For years a 'Whisky Ring' in St. Louis had systematically defrauded the Government of millions of dollars in taxes on distilled whiskey. It was inescapably clear that the Ring had operated with the collusion of Treasury officials and of the President's private secretary, Babcock. When Grant was appraised of the situation he said 'Let no guilty man escape. Be especially vigilant against all who insinuate that they have high influence to protect or to protect them.' But most of them did escape — Babcock with the President's connivance. No sooner had the Whisky Ring been exposed than the country was confronted with a new scandal. Exploitation of the Indians for political and financial graft had long been notorious. In the spring of 1876 Secretary Bristow found irrefutable proof that Secretary of War Belknap had sold Indian post-traderships.

Faced with impeachment, Belknap hurried to resign, and his resignation was accepted 'with great regret' by the President whom he had betrayed. Impeachment proceedings were instituted, but the Secretary was finally acquitted on the technical ground that the Senate no longer had jurisdiction over his case.

Corruption, however, was by no means confined to the national Government. It could be found in state and municipal governments, in business and finance and transportation, and even in the professions. There was everywhere a breakdown of old moral standards, and to many it seemed that integrity had departed from public life. The idealism of the pre-war years had been burnt out in the flames of the War and Reconstruction. The industrial revolution, the building of transcontinental railroads and the exploitation of new natural resources had called into existence a class of new rich untrained to the responsibilities of their position. Speculation had entered business more largely than ever before and the mania for making something out of nothing permeated American society. The rise of the corporation as an instrument of business involved a diffusion of responsibility so great that the sense of responsibility all but disappeared. Never before and only once since — after World War I — have public morals fallen so low.

State legislatures, everywhere, were suspected of gross corruption. The systematic looting in which the Southern carpetbag governments indulged could be matched in Northern and Western states. In the fierce struggle between Daniel Drew and Cornelius Vanderbilt for control of the Erie Railroad the legislature of New York State was auctioned off to the highest bidder, and both the bar and the bench proved that they too were for sale. In Pennsylvania the powerful Cameron machine bought and sold legislation with bare-faced effrontery. In Illinois a corrupt legislature jammed through, in flagrant disregard of the Constitution, over seven hundred acts of incorporation. In Iowa, Minnesota, and California it was charged that the legislatures were controlled by railroads, and the charges were not hard to substantiate. The cities, too, presented a sorry spectacle. The brigandage of the Tweed Ring cost New York City not less than one hundred million dollars, and the ravages of the Gas Ring in Philadelphia were scarcely less thorough.

Yet this political corruption was only symptomatic of corruption in the business world. Defalcations, bankruptcies, stock-watering, wildcat investment schemes, railway wrecking were accepted parts of commercial life. Oil wells, gold and silver mines, and, above all, railroad construction offered rich fields for speculation, and the absence of statutory regulation of business practices made speculation and trickery fairly safe.

The panic of 1873 was partly a consequence of these malpractices. The causes of business depressions are always obscure but it is safe to say that reckless speculation in railroads and wholesale stock-watering in many industries played an important part in precipitating this panic. Other causes are not to be ignored. The depression was world-wide: Germany, France, and England felt the hard times and European investors proceeded to call in their American loans. Over-rapid expansion of the agricultural West produced surplus crops which, after the Franco-Prussian War, could not be marketed abroad at satisfactory prices. At the same time there was over-expansion not only in railroads and in farming, but in business and industry as well. With a confidence that bordered on folly the country had mortgaged itself to the future; it now found itself unable to pay either interest or principal.

The crash came 17 September 1873 with the failure of the banking house of Jay Cooke and Co. — a failure as spectacular then as would be the failure of the house of Morgan today. Soon one substantial business firm after another toppled, and on 20 September the New York Stock Exchange took the unprecedented step of closing its doors. Soon the panic became a depression. Industrial plants shut down, railway construction all but ceased, long bread lines began to appear in the larger cities, and tramps swarmed through the countryside. Commercial failures increased to almost six thousand in 1874, to almost eight thousand in 1875 and to over nine thousand in 1876.

In the midst of political scandal and economic stagnation the United States prepared to celebrate the Centennial of her independence. The Exhibition at Philadelphia was an impressive one, but it emphasized the material rather than the intellectual or artistic accomplishments of Americans and Machinery Hall was, quite properly, the focus of attention. The Ode written for the occasion by Bayard Taylor revealed only the thinness of the man popularly accounted the first poet of his generation; Sidney Lanier's Cantata expressed wishful thinking. The most appropriate Ode was furnished by the bitter sarcasm of James Russell Lowell:

Columbia, puzzled what she should display
Of true home-make on her Centennial Day,
Asked Brother Jonathan; he scratched his head
Whittled awhile reflectively, and said,
'Your own invention, and your making, too?
Why any child could tell ye what to do:
Show 'em your Civil Service, and explain
How all men's loss is everybody's gain;
Show your new patent to increase your rent
By paying quarters for collecting cents;
Show your short cut to cure financial ills
By making paper collars current bills;
Show your new bleaching process, cheap and brief,
To wit: a jury chosen by the thief;
Show your State Legislatures; show your Rings;
And challenge Europe to produce such things
As high officials sitting half in sight
To share the plunder and to fix things right;
If that don't fetch her, why you only need
To show your latest style in martyrs, — Tweed:
She'll find it hard to hide her spiteful tears
At such advance in one poor hundred years![4]

7. *The Disputed Election of 1876*

Republican defeat seemed certain in 1876 as the bankruptcy of the Grant administration became increasingly apparent. James G. Blaine of Maine, in a speech deliberately calculated to arouse sectional animosities, tried to deflect public attention from corruption to the reconstruction issue. The attempt might have succeeded better had not the well-timed exposure of Blaine's corrupt connection with the Little Rock and Fort Smith Railroad hopelessly damaged his claim to leadership. In the Cincinnati Convention the Republicans passed up the magnetic Blaine and chose instead as their standard bearer the respectable but mediocre Rutherford B. Hayes. Thrice Governor of Ohio, Hayes' record was good enough to command the support of the Liberal Republicans; the Old Guard had no alternative but to support the one man who might save the party from disaster. The Democrats, determined to make reform the issue of the campaign, picked a reformer, Samuel J. Tilden of New York.

When the first reports came in Tilden appeared to have won a

[4] The poem does not appear in Lowell's *Collected Works*. It can be found in *The Nation*, 5 August 1875.

sweeping victory. He had carried New York, New Jersey, Connecticut, Indiana, and, apparently, the solid South and piled up a popular plurality of over 250,000. But, scanning the returns, the Republican campaign managers became convinced that the election might yet be swung to their candidate. The votes of four states — South Carolina, Florida, Louisiana, and Oregon — were apparently in doubt. Without the votes of these states Tilden had only 184 electoral votes; 185 were necessary for election. On the morning after election day Zachary Chandler dispatched telegrams to each of the doubtful states, 'Can you hold your state?' and that afternoon he announced, 'Hayes has 185 electoral votes and is elected.'

The situation was highly involved. In all three of the Southern states there had been intimidation and fraud on both sides. Hayes appeared to have carried South Carolina, but in Florida and Louisiana Tilden seemed to have a safe majority. Republican returning boards threw out about one thousand Democratic votes in Florida and over thirteen thousand in Louisiana and gave certificates to the Hayes electors. In Oregon a Democratic governor had displaced a Republican elector on a technicality and appointed a Democrat to his position. From all four states came two sets of returns.

The Constitution provided that 'The President of the Senate shall, in the presence of the Senate and the House of Representatives, open all certificates and the votes shall then be counted.' But counted by whom? If the President of the Senate did the counting the election would go to Hayes; if the House counted the votes, Tilden would be President. Congress solved the problem by establishing an Electoral Commission of fifteen, five from the House, five from the Senate, and five from the Supreme Court. It was originally planned to appoint to this committee seven Democrats and seven Republicans and, as the fifteenth member, the non-partisan Judge David Davis of Illinois. At the last moment, however, the legislature of Illinois elected Judge Davis to the Senate and, with the approval of both parties, Judge Bradley was named in his place.

As it turned out, it was Judge Bradley who named the next President of the United States. On all questions submitted to it the Electoral Commission divided along strict party lines, and Judge Bradley voted invariably with the Republicans. There is reason to believe that Mr. Bradley's vote represented neither his original opinion nor his conviction. Abram S. Hewitt, Democratic leader of the House, wrote of Judge Bradley's vote:

The history of this opinion forms an important feature in the final outcome of the electoral count. . . . Mr. Stevens was the intimate friend of Judge Bradley. He passed the night previous to the rendition of the judgment in the Florida case at my house. About midnight he returned from a visit to Judge Bradley and reported . . . that he had just left Judge Bradley after reading his opinion in favor of counting the vote of the Democratic electors of the state of Florida. Such a judgment insured the election of Tilden to the Presidency with three votes to spare above the necessary majority. We parted, therefore, with the assurance that all further doubt as to the Presidency was at rest. I attended the delivery of the judgment the next day without the slightest intimation from any quarter that Judge Bradley had changed his mind. In fact, the reading of the opinion, until the few concluding paragraphs were reached, was strictly in accordance with the report of Mr. Stevens. The change was made between midnight and sunrise. Mr. Stevens afterwards informed me that it was due to a visit to Judge Bradley by Senator Frelinghuysen and Secretary Robeson, made after his departure. Their appeals to Judge Bradley were said to have been reinforced by the persuasion of Mrs. Bradley. Whatever the fact may have been, Judge Bradley himself in a subsequent letter addressed to the Newark *Daily Advertiser* admitted that he had written a favorable opinion which on subsequent reflection he saw fit to modify.[5]

By a straight eight to seven vote the Commission awarded all four contested states to Hayes. On 2 March 1877, the Senate declared Hayes elected by a majority of one vote.

Public indignation was intense for Tilden had a clear majority over his rival and the vote had constituted a stinging rebuke to the Republican administration. Though later investigation revealed frauds on both sides, there seems little reason to doubt that the 'will of the people' had been defeated by the Electoral Commission. Party passions ran high, but there was no resort to violence, and the general willingness to acquiesce in a peaceful solution of the problem reflected credit on the good sense of the American people. Yet Hayes assumed office under a cloud from whose shadow he was never able to escape into the sunlight of popular approval.

[5] 'Secret History of the Election, 1876–77,' *Selected Writings of Abram S. Hewitt*, edited by Allan Nevins, pp. 172–73. Columbia University Press (1937).

IV

THE PASSING OF THE FRONTIER

1865–1890

1. *The Last West*

THE roaring vitality, the cascading energy of the American people in the post-war years are nowhere better illustrated than in the history of the West. The generation after the Civil War witnessed the most extensive movement of population in our history; a hundred per cent increase in the settled area; the rapid social and economic development of this population from primitive conditions to contemporary standards of civilization; the final disappearance of the wild Indian; the rise and fall of the mineral empire and of the cattle kingdom; the emergence of new types of agriculture and of economic life articulated to the geography and climate of the High Plains and the Rocky Mountains; and the organization of a dozen new states with a taste for social and political experiments.

The most notable of these achievements was the conquest of the Great Plains — that region extending roughly from longitude 98 to the Rocky Mountains, and from Texas to the Canadian border. This vast area, comprising roughly one-fifth of the United States, had long interposed a formidable barrier to settlement. In the decade of the forties the westward moving frontier had reached the edge of the Plains. Then, instead of moving progressively westward as it had always heretofore done, the frontier leaped fifteen hundred miles to the Pacific coast. For thirty years the intervening territory was practically uninhabited except by Indians and Mormons; not until the decade of the seventies did permanent settlers begin to close in on the Plains and Mountain regions; then the process went on with unprecedented rapidity until by 1890 it was almost complete and the frontier had disappeared.

The Plains region had long been known as 'the Great American Desert'; it was not, of course, a desert, but the designation was not without justification. For over two hundred years the American pioneer had moved westward from one woodland frontier to another, and in all that time it had never been necessary for him to make any radical readjustment to forest and prairie and stream. But when the pioneer came to the edge of the Great Plains he found an environment fundamentally different from that to which he was accustomed. Here was an immense grassland, sparsely wooded, with few navigable streams, and with a rainfall seldom sufficient for farming as practiced in the East. When the pioneer farmer tried to apply here the experience he had gained and the tools he had developed in the wooded East, he failed. 'The attempt,' as Walter P. Webb has said, 'of a migrating people to cross this line of the 96 or 98 meridian resulted in social chaos and economic ruin which continued until, through invention and much experiment, new weapons were adopted, new implements invented, new methods devised for getting water, making fences, and farming, until new institutions were evolved or old ones modified to meet the needs of a country that was level, devoid of timber, and deficient in rainfall; until a plainscraft took the place of woodcraft.'

Not until the 1870's did the industrial revolution, science and invention, come to the aid of the farmer and enable him successfully to invade the High Plains. Before the farmer could establish himself permanently on the Plains three things were necessary: new methods of farming to cope with inadequate rainfall; a substitute for wooden fencing; and transportation facilities to carry the crops to market. The railroads furnished transportation; barbed-wire solved the fencing problem; and the windmill, dry farming, and irrigation went far to overcome the effect of insufficient rainfall and intermittent droughts.

In the course of this long and arduous struggle with the Plains environment, the miner, the cattleman, and the farmer evolved social and economic institutions that differed markedly from those which had obtained in the woodlands of the East. The Plains environment necessitated a modification not only of the tools and methods of farming, but of social attitudes, economic concepts, political and legal institutions as well. 'The physical conditions which exist in that land,' as Major Powell said, 'and which inexorably control the operations of men, are such that the industries of the West are necessarily unlike those of the East and their institutions must be adapted to their industrial wants. It is thus that a new phase of Aryan civilization is being developed in the western half of America.'

Thus there emerged in this last American West a regional consciousness as distinct and characteristic as that of the Old South; a common feeling that expressed itself not only in politics and economics, but in social attitudes, legal institutions, art and literature.

This sectionalism of the last West, rooted in geography, was cultivated by the impact of the industrial revolution on the process of settlement, and by the manner in which the various stages of economic development — mining, cattle-raising, and farming — all came to be controlled by outside interests. This interplay of basic local forces with absentee political and economic interests in the creation of this last West makes a fascinating study in the history of sectionalism.

2. *The Indian Problem*

The first step in the conquest of the last West was the solution of the Indian problem. The Indians of the Great Plains and the Rocky Mountain regions, some 225,000 in number, presented a formidable obstacle to white settlement. The strongest and most warlike of the tribes that the whites encountered were the Sioux, Blackfeet, Crow, Cheyenne, and Arapahoe in the North; the Comanche, Kiowa, Ute, Southern Cheyenne, Apache, and Southern Arapahoe in the South. Mounted on swift horses, admirably armed for Plains warfare, and living on the millions of buffalo that roamed the open range, these tribes for generations had maintained a stubborn and successful resistance to white penetration of their hunting grounds.

The first serious invasion of these hunting grounds came with the great migrations of the forties. The fate of the California Indians after the gold rush was prophetic of what was to happen elsewhere in the West. There were approximately one hundred thousand Indians in California in 1850; ten years later the number had been reduced to thirty-five thousand, and the Commissioner of Indian Affairs could write that 'despoiled by irresistible forces of the land of their fathers; with no country on earth to which they can migrate; in the midst of a people with whom they cannot assimilate; they have no recognized claims upon the government and are compelled to become vagabonds — to steal or to starve.' The advance of the miners into the mountains, the building of the transcontinental railroads, and the invasion of the grasslands by cattlemen, threatened the other Indian tribes of the West with the same fate. Most serious was the wanton destruction of the buffalo, indispensable not only for food but for hides, bowstrings, lariats, fuel, and a score of other purposes. Scarcely less ruinous were two other developments: the perfection of the Colt repeating revolver, fearfully efficient in Plains warfare, and the spread of small-pox and venereal diseases among the Indians.

It would be useless to trace in any detail the melancholy story of Indian relations in the period from 1860 to 1887, the year of the passage of the Dawes Act. It is a tale of intermittent and barbarous warfare, of broken pacts and broken promises, of greed and selfishness, corruption and maladministration, of alternating aggression and vacillation on the part of the whites, of courageous defense, despair, blind savagery, and inevitable defeat for the Indians. The sober historian, accepting neither the myths and legends that have clustered around the 'noble redman,' nor the bitterly prejudiced interpretation of Indian character by frontiersmen, must subscribe to President Hayes' indictment of our Indian relations in his annual message of 1877:

> The Indians were the original occupants of the land we now possess. They have been driven from place to place. The purchase money paid to them in some cases for what they called their own has still left them poor. In many instances, when they had settled down upon lands assigned to them by compact and begun to support themselves by their own labor, they were rudely jostled off and thrust into the wilderness again. Many, if not most, of our Indian wars have had their origin in broken promises and acts of injustice on our part.

Until 1861 the Indians of the Plains had been relatively peaceful, but in that year the invasion of their hunting grounds by thousands of frantic and ruthless miners, and the advance of white settlers along the Missouri frontier, together with dissatisfaction at their treatment by the Government and the breakdown of the reservation system, resulted in numerous minor conflicts. In 1862 the Sioux of the Dakota region went on the warpath, devastated the Minnesota frontier, and massacred and imprisoned almost a thousand white men, women, and children. Retribution was swift and terrible and fell indiscriminately upon the innocent and the guilty. For the next twenty-five years Indian warfare was a constant of Western history, each new influx of settlers driving the redskins to acts of desperation and bringing renewed outrage and punishment. In 1864 the Cheyenne, banished from their hunting grounds to the desolate wastes of southeastern Colorado, attacked Ben Halliday's stage and harried the mining settlements to the north; they were persuaded to abandon their depredations and concentrate at Indian posts, and at one of these posts Colonel Chivington ordered a savage slaughter of the Indian men, women, and children that sent a thrill of horror through the nation. Two years later a small force under Colonel Fetterman was in turn massacred by the discontented Sioux. All through the following decade the Sioux fought desperately for their hunting grounds; the famous massacre of Custer's regiment on the banks of the Little Big Horn (26 June 1876) served merely to accentuate the severity of their ultimate punishment.

In the mountains, as on the plains, the Indians were driven from their ancient homes. In Montana the Crow and the Blackfeet were ejected from their reservations; in Colorado the vast holdings of the Utes were confiscated and opened to settlement; in the Southwest ten years of warfare ended in the capture of the intractable Apache chief, Geronimo, and the practical destruction of the Apache tribe. The discovery of gold on the Salmon River in western Idaho precipitated an invasion of the lands of the peaceful Nez Percés. The Indians refused to surrender the lands once guaranteed to them, and fifteen years of intermittent warfare culminated in the decision to drive the recalcitrant tribe entirely out of their hunting grounds. Chief Joseph struck back, but in vain, and in 1877 there began that retreat eastward over fifteen hundred miles of mountain and plain that remains the most memorable feat in the annals of Indian warfare. In the end the feeble remnant of the Nez Percés tribe was captured and exiled to the South, and Chief Joseph spoke for all his race:

> I am tired of fighting. Our chiefs are killed. Looking-Glass is dead. Too-hul-hut-sote is dead. The old men are all dead. It is the young men now who say 'yes' or 'no.' He who lead the young men is dead. It is cold and we have no blankets. The little children are freezing to death. My people, some of them, have run away to the hills and have no blankets, no food. No one knows where they are, perhaps freezing to death. I want to have time to look for my children and see how many of them I can find. Maybe I can find them among the dead. Hear me, my chiefs. My heart is sick and sad. I am tired.

Altogether the Indian wars between 1865 and 1880 cost the Government millions of dollars and the lives of hundreds of men. Yet, in 1881, President Arthur could affirm:

> We have to deal with the appalling fact that though thousands of lives have been sacrificed and hundreds of millions of dollars expended in the attempt to solve the Indian problem, it has until within the past few years seemed scarcely nearer a solution than it was half a century ago.

A large part of this failure was no doubt inherent in the problem, but part of it rests squarely upon the Federal Government. The theory that each Indian tribe constituted a sovereign though dependent nation, to be dealt with as such through treaties, was completely divorced from reality. The Indians frequently failed to understand the terms of the treaties, nor did individual Indians consider themselves bound by tribal treaties. A further and fruitful source of difficulty was the fact that authority over Indian affairs was divided between the Departments of War and of the Interior, and that both departments pursued a vacillating and uncertain policy, the one failing to live up to treaty obligations, the other failing to protect the Indians on their reservations from the aggressions of white settlers.

These conflicting policies pursued by different departments of the Government were expressive of the conflicting policies entertained by the American people as a whole. Frontiersmen, in general, still subscribed to the traditional idea that the only good Indian was a dead Indian, and most soldiers were inclined to agree with them. But Easterners, removed by a century from the Indian menace, had developed a different attitude. Here churchmen and reformers united to urge a policy of humanitarianism toward Indian wards. Statesmen like Carl Schurz, religious leaders like Bishop Whipple, literary figures like Helen Hunt Jackson, were loud in their criticism of the Government's treatment of the Indian, and their attitude was effective in bringing about important changes in Indian policy.

In 1865, in the breathing space permitted by the conclusion of the Civil War, Congress had created a Committee on the Condition of the Indian Tribes which recommended, among other things, the practice of dealing with the Indians as individuals and concentrating them in reservations. This substitution of a 'peace' policy for the more belligerent one of the sixties was dictated partly by humanitarian considerations, and partly by the more cogent argument of economy — for it was obviously cheaper to herd the Indians into government reservations and feed them than it was to fight them. The new plan was carried forward under the administration of Hayes, Arthur, and Cleveland, and culminated, in 1887, in the passage of the Dawes Act which established the modern Indian policy.

The Dawes Act was the first serious attempt to civilize the Indian, teach him the practices of agriculture and social life, and merge him in the body politic of the nation. It provided for the dissolution of the tribes as legal entities and the division of the tribal lands among the individual members. To protect the Indian in his property the right of disposal was withheld for a period of twenty-five years; upon the expiration of this probationary period the Indian was to become unrestricted owner, and to be admitted to full citizenship in the United States. In October 1901 the Five Civilized Nations of Oklahoma, already thoroughly assimilated to American social and political institutions, were admitted to citizenship, and in 1924 Congress granted full citizenship to all Indians in the country. Thus the long process of struggle and assimilation reached an undramatic climax.

The Indian problem is rapidly disappearing with the approaching extinction of full-blooded Indians. The proud savages who once ruled undisputed the American continent are now settled on some two hundred government reservations, eking out an existence on government doles, cut off from the free life of an earlier day, losing the power to fend for themselves, disintegrating economically and physically, pitiful and tragic representatives of the race which helped the white man to adjust himself to the American scene, of the Hiawathas and Pocahontases who for so long fired the imagination of the American people.

3. *The Mining Frontier*

The territory between the Missouri and the Pacific had been crossed and recrossed by emigrants along the great trails, but it was the miners who first revealed to the nation the resources and possibilities of this country. The first frontier of the last West was the miners' frontier. In 1849 the lure of gold had drawn to California a turbulent, heterogeneous throng of miners who later formed the nucleus of a large permanent population and who developed the varied agricultural resources of the state. This process was to be repeated time and again in the decade of the sixties: in Colorado, Nevada, Arizona, Idaho, Montana, and Wyoming. In each case precious metals were the magnet that attracted the first settlers and advertised the resources of the territory; then, as the big pay dirt was exhausted, the mining population receded, and its place was taken by ranchers and farmers who established, with the aid of the railroads and the Government, the permanent foundation of the territory.

In 1859 the discovery of gold in the foothills of the Rockies, near Pike's Peak, drew thousands of eager prospectors from the border settlements and from California, bent on repeating here the fabulous story of California gold. Within a few months the roads from Council

Bluffs and Independence to western Kansas were crowded with wagons bearing the slogan 'Pike's Peak or Bust' scrawled on their canvas. Soon brash little mining camps dotted the hills all along Cherry Creek, a branch of the South Fork of the Platte. Denver City, Golden, Boulder, and Colorado City arose almost overnight, the Territory of Jefferson — changed later to Colorado — was organized, and the census of 1860 recorded a population of some thirty-five thousand. The mining boom soon spent itself, and the development of Colorado was somewhat retarded by the Civil War and Indian uprisings as well as by inadequate transportation and a failure to appreciate the agricultural and grazing resources of the country. During the ensuing decade population barely held its own, and it was not until the advent of the railroads in the seventies, the influx of farmers, and the readjustment of the region to a new economic basis, that the foundations for a sounder development were laid.

In the same year that gold was discovered in Colorado, came the announcement of a rich strike of silver on the eastern slopes of the Sierra Nevada, near Lake Tahoe. Here was located the Comstock Lode, one of the richest veins in the world. Within a year the roaring towns of Virginia City, Aurora, and Gold Hill sprang up in the desert waste, the Territory of Nevada was carved out of Utah, and ten thousand men were digging frantically in the bowels of the earth for the precious silver stuff.

Nevada furnishes the most extreme example of a mining community; nowhere else in history do we find a society so completely and continuously dependent upon mineral wealth. And the history of this mining commonwealth for the first decade of its existence is largely that of the Comstock Lode. Within twenty years the lode yielded no less than $306,000,000. Very little of this enormous wealth, however, remained in Nevada, most of it going to California mining companies or to gamblers and speculators in the East. The Comstock Lode is notable not only as the foundation of the mineral wealth of Nevada, but as the location of one of the greatest engineering enterprises of the nineteenth century — the Sutro Tunnel. It was this tunnel, penetrating into the heart of the mountain to the depth of three miles, and built by Adolph Sutro over a period of eight years, that made possible the continuous and profitable mining of the fabulous lode.

The application of engineering skill, machinery, and capital to mining the Comstock illustrates a process that was universal in the history of the mining kingdom. Panning and placer mining as practiced in the diggings of early California and Colorado was not only wasteful, but entirely unsuitable for getting the silver out of the quartz veins of such a mine as the Comstock. It was necessary to change from placer mining to quartz mining, and this change required the purchase of expensive machinery, the hiring of engineering skill and the organization of mining as a big business. So outside capital came in and took over the mining industry; the miners became day laborers working for wages, and the profits went to stockholders scattered throughout the United States and Europe. This was the history of Comstock, and it was to a greater or less extent, the history of most of the mines of the West in the following decade.

The story of Idaho and Montana runs parallel to that of Colorado and Nevada. Gold was discovered in 1860 on the Nez Percés reservation in the extreme eastern part of Washington Territory. Within a year a wave of prospectors from Washington and Nevada was rolling into the region. Lewiston, and farther to the south, Boise City, sprang into existence; and in 1865 the Territory of Idaho was carved out of Washington and Montana. 'The Idaho miners,' wrote the historian of the West, H. H. Bancroft, 'were like quicksilver, a mass of them dropped off in any locality, broke up into individual globules, and ran off after any atom of gold in the vicinity. They stayed nowhere longer than the gold attracted them.' But mining furnished a most insubstantial foundation for the development of Idaho, and the census of 1870 showed a population of less than 15,000 for the Territory.

Gold was discovered east of the Continental Divide along the headwaters of the Missouri, and in the Bitter Root valley in the eastern part of Washington Territory, and soon Alder Gulch (later Virginia City), Last Chance Gulch (Helena), and Bannack City enjoyed a flush rivalling that of the Colorado and Nevada camps. Although Montana produced over one hundred million dollars in precious metals in the first decade, the mining kingdom was short-lived, and the census of 1870 recorded a population of only slightly over twenty thousand. Like other mining camps those of Montana soon died out or were transformed into respectable towns, with schools, churches, and other institutions of civilization. For a brief time the activities of the notorious Henry Plummer and his gang threatened the prosperity of the Montana camps, and it required a Vigilante organization such as that which arose in California fifteen years earlier to restore law and order. Virginia City, which may well serve as typical of the mining towns of the West, was thus described by M. P. Langford in his *Vigilante Days and Ways:*

> This human hive, numbering at least ten thousand people, was the product of ninety days. Into it were crowded all the elements of a rough and active civilization. Thousands of cabins and tents and brush wakiups . . . scattered at random along the banks, and in the nooks of the hills, were seen on every hand. Every foot of the gulch, under the active manipulations of the miners, was undergoing displacement. . . . Gold was abundant, and every possible device was employed by the gamblers, the traders, the vile men and women that had come in with the miners to the locality, to obtain it. Nearly every third cabin in the towns was a saloon where vile whiskey was peddled out for fifty cents a drink in gold dust. Many of these places were filled with gambling tables and gamblers, and the miner who was bold enough to enter one of them with his day's earnings in his pocket, seldom left until thoroughly fleeced. Hurdy-gurdy dance-houses were numerous, and there were plenty of camp beauties to patronize them. . . . Not a day or night passed which did not yield its full fruition of fights, quarrels, wounds, or murders. The crack of the revolver was often heard above the merry notes of the violin. Street fights were frequent, and as no one knew when or where they would occur, everyone was on his guard against a random shot.
>
> Sunday was always a gala day. The miners then left their work and gathered about the public places in the towns. The stores were all open, the auctioneers specially eloquent on every corner in praise of their wares. Thousands of people crowded the thoroughfares, ready to rush in any direction of promised excitement. Horse-racing was among the most favored amusements. Prize rings were formed, and brawny men engaged at fisticuffs until their sight was lost, and their bodies pummelled to a jelly, while hundreds of onlookers cheered the victor. . . . Pistols flashed, bowie-knives flourished, and braggart oaths filled the air, as often as men's passions triumphed over their reason. This was indeed the reign of unbridled license, and men who at first regarded it with disgust and terror, by constant exposure soon learned to become part of it, and forgot that they had ever been aught else. All classes of society were represented at this general exhibition. Judges, lawyers, doctors, even clergymen, could not claim exemption. Culture and religion afforded feeble protection, where allurement and indulgence ruled the hour.[1]

'But,' Langford adds, 'underneath this exterior of recklessness, there was in the minds and hearts of the miners and business men of

[1] N. P. Langford, *Vigilante Days and Ways* (1912 ed.), pp. 222–224.

this society a strong and abiding sense of justice — and that saved the Territory.' It would indeed be a mistake to picture the mining camps as mere nests of lawlessness or to argue from the accounts of Easterners an abandonment of the institutions of civilized society. They had, to be sure, few of the institutions taken for granted in the East — churches, schools, newspapers, theatres, and so forth — but they hastened to establish such institutions as quickly as they could. Nor did the miners conform to the standards of society or of law which obtained elsewhere; instead they very sensibly formulated their own social standards and developed their own laws. The evolution of common law institutions in the miners' camps is one of the most illuminating chapters in the history of American law. Each miners' camp was an administrative and a judicial district. It had its own executive officers, judges, recorders, it voted laws and regulations suited to its own peculiar needs, and it enforced these laws through public opinion and police officers.

> The Argonauts [said Senator Stewart, himself once a miner] found no laws governing the possession and occupation of mines but the common laws of right. . . . They were forced to make laws for themselves. The reason and justice of the laws they formed challenge the admiration of all who investigate them. Each mining district . . . formed its own rules and adopted its own customs. The similarity of these rules and customs throughout the entire mining-region was so great as to attain the beneficial results of well-digested general laws. These regulations were thoroughly democratic in character. . . .

The legal codes and practices of these mining communities were eventually recognized in the American courts and many of them were incorporated into the constitutions and laws of the Western states.

The early development of Wyoming and Arizona followed the same general lines of the other mining communities. The mines along the Sweetwater River at South Pass City, Pacific City, and Miners' Delight were soon played out, and after 1865 the future of Wyoming Territory was almost wholly dependent upon ranching. In the Southwest, silver had been mined by the Spaniards in Santa Cruz valley and by Americans in the Gadsden purchase for many years, but the brisk development of mining in Arizona begun along the Bill Williams fork of the Colorado River was a by-product of the Civil War. Though a few mushroom mining towns sprang up in the Arizona and New Mexico deserts, the majority of the prospectors had poor luck and soon limped back to more promising territory to the north. Far more important than silver mining was the growth of copper mining in this region: the single mine of Copper Queen at Bisbee, opened in 1875, yielded its fortunate owners more than all the gold and silver mines of the Territory.

The last gold rush came in the Black Hills region of western Dakota Territory, on the reservations of the warlike Sioux. In 1874 the news of the discovery of gold here rioted along the frontier and through the mining kingdom and precipitated a lively gold rush. The railroad to Bismarck and the stage-coach from Cheyenne gave access to this region, and four thousand feverish prospectors rushed into the desolate hills between the forks of the Cheyenne. Deadwood had its brief day of glory; here 'Calamity Jane' enjoyed her merited notoriety; here 'Wild Bill' Hickok handed in his checks; here a stock company played Gilbert and Sullivan's *Mikado* for a record run of one hundred and thirty nights. Within a short time heavily capitalized companies, like the Homestead, took over the mining, and the days of glamor were gone.

Ephemeral as it was, the mining frontier played an important part in the development of the West and of the nation. The miners familiarized the American people with the country between the Missouri and the Pacific and advertised its magnificent resources. They forced a solution of the Indian problem, emphasized the need for railroads, and laid the foundations for the later permanent farming population. Out of the necessities of their situation they developed codes of law admirably suited to their needs and contributed much of value to the legal and political institutions of the West. They produced, in the thirty years from 1860 to 1890, $1,241,827,032 of gold and $901,160,660 of silver, enabled the Government to resume specie payments, and precipitated the 'money question' which was to be for well-nigh twenty years the major political issue before the American people. They added immeasurably to American folklore, enriched the American idiom, and inspired lasting contributions to American literature.

4. *The Cattle Kingdom*

One of the most dramatic shifts in the screen-picture of the West was the replacement of millions of buffalo that had roamed the Great Plains by cattle, and of the Indian by the cowboy and the cattle king.

The territory between the Missouri and the Rockies, from the Red River of the South to Saskatchewan — an area comprising approximately one-fourth of the United States — was the cattle kingdom, the last and most picturesque American frontier. Here millions of cattle — Texas longhorns, full-blooded Herefords, Wyoming and Montana steers — fatted on the long luscious grasses of the public lands. The cowboys and their liege lords, the cattle barons who ruled this vast domain, developed therein a unique culture, folklore, and society, and then passed away forever.

The development of the cattle industry on a large scale was due to a peculiar combination of factors: the opening up of the public domain after the Civil War, the elimination of the Indian danger and of the buffalo, the extension of the railroads into the High Plains, the decline in the number of cattle raised in the Middle West and the East, the increased consumption of meat here and abroad, the invention of the refrigerator car, and the growth of great packing centers and of world markets.

Since the days when the American Southwest belonged to Spain, the sturdy Texas longhorn, descendant of Spanish *toros* from the plains of Andalusia, had grazed on the limitless prairie grasses north of the Rio Grande. Wild as the buffalo they supplanted, and valued only for their hides, it was not until 1846 that the first herd was driven northward to Ohio, though long before that many had found their way to California. In 1856 a drove of Texas cattle reached Chicago, but not until the middle sixties did the 'long drive' to the region of rich grasses and good prices cease to be an experiment. In 1867 the Kansas Pacific began to reach out in the Plains, and in the same year J. G. McCoy established the first of the cow towns, Abilene, Kansas, from which live cattle were shipped to slaughter houses in Chicago. The refrigerator car, in common use by 1875, delivered the western dressed beef to the great eastern centers of population.

On the first of the organized long drives, 35,000 longhorns pounded up clouds of dust all along the famous Chisholm Trail, across the Red and Arkansas rivers and into the land of the Five Nations, to Abilene, Kansas. Two years later no less than 350,000 longhorned kine made their way along the Chisholm and Goodnight trails to fatten on the long northern grasses and find a market at one of the several roaring cattle towns on the Kansas and Pacific Railroad: Abilene, Dodge City, or Newton. Later the 'long drive' extended north to the Union Pacific and even to the Northern Pacific.

In after years [writes the historian of the cattle kingdom] the drive of the Texas men became little short of an American saga. To all who saw that long line of Texas cattle come up over a rise in the prairie, nostrils wide for the smell of water, dust-caked and gaunt, so ready to break from the nervous control of the riders strung out along the flanks of the herd, there came a feeling that in this spectacle there was something elemental, something resistless, something perfectly in keeping with the unconquerable land about them.[2]

Altogether some six million cattle were driven up from Texas to winter on the High Plains of Colorado, Wyoming, and even Montana, between 1866 and 1888. It was this new industry of fattening cattle on the Great Plains that produced the last phase of the Wild West, and the highest and most picturesque development of the ancient art of cattle droving. The experience of cattlemen along the Oregon and California trails and in western Montana in the decade of the forties had long proved the practicability of wintering cattle in the northern ranges. Now Easterners and Englishmen of a sporting or speculating turn put their money into cattle, establishing their headquarters anywhere from the Rio Grande to the Canadian border, and in the absence of law managed their affairs through some de facto commonwealth such as the Wyoming Stock Growers' Association. Texas borderers who learned their horsemanship and 'cowpunching' from the Mexican *vaqueros* were the first and the best *bucaroos* or cowboys. Every spring they rounded up the herds in designated areas, all the way from Texas to Wyoming and the Dakotas, identified their owners' cattle by the brands, and branded the calves, dividing up pro rata the strays or 'mavericks.' The breeding cattle were then set free for another year while the likely three- and four-year-olds were conducted on the 'long drive' to the nearest cowtown on a railway. Each 'outfit' of cowboys attended its owner's herd on the drive, protecting it from wolves and cattle rustlers, sending scouts ahead to locate water and the best grazing. The long drive seems romantic in retrospect, but to the cowboys it was hard and often hazardous work. Andy Adams, later one of the cattle barons of Texas, describes a dry drive along the Old Western Trail:

Good cloudy weather would have saved us, but in its stead was a sultry morning without a breath of air, which bespoke another day of sizzling heat. We had not been on the trail over two hours before the heat became

[2] E. S. Osgood, *The Day of the Cattleman,* p. 26, U. of Minnesota Press.

almost unbearable to man and beast. Had it not been for the condition of the herd, all might yet have gone well; but over three days had elapsed without water for the cattle, and they became feverish and ungovernable. The lead cattle turned back several times, wandering aimlessly in any direction, and it was with considerable difficulty that the herd could be held on the trail. Our horses were fresh, however, and after about two hours' work, we once more got the herd strung out in trailing fashion; but before a mile had been covered, the leaders again turned, and the cattle congregated into a mass of unmanageable animals, milling and lowing in their fever and thirst. . . . No sooner was the milling stopped than they would surge hither and yon, sometimes half a mile, as ungovernable as the waves of an ocean. After wasting several hours in this manner, they finally turned back over the trail, and the utmost efforts of every man in the outfit failed to check them. We threw our ropes in their faces, and when this failed, we resorted to shooting; but in defiance of the fusillade and the smoke they walked sullenly through the line of horsemen across their front. Six-shooters were discharged so close to the leaders' faces as to singe their hair, yet, under a noonday sun, they disregarded this and every other device to turn them, and passed wholly out of our control. In a number of instances wild steers deliberately walked against our horses, and then for the first time a fact dawned upon us that chilled the marrow in our bones — *the herd was going blind.*

The bones of men and animals that lie bleaching along the trails abundantly testify that this was not the first instance in which the plain had baffled the determination of man.[3]

The cowboy developed his own lingo, folklore, and customs. His high-horned Mexican saddle, lariat, broad-rimmed sombrero, high-heeled boots, and shaggy chaparajos were perfectly adapted to his work. His jangling spurs with their enormous rowels were not too severe for his bronco — vicious little mustang of Spanish origin, hardy as a donkey and fleet as an Arab. The clownish posturing of film heroes has obscured the authentic cowboy: spare of frame and pithy of speech, reserved and courteous as the true gentleman that he was, yet with the cavalier's eternal swagger; alert with the sort of courage needed to fight Indians and bad men, to break broncos and rope steers, or to deal with stampedes and prairie fires; enduring and uncomplaining, asking no better end than to die with his boots on. Finest of our frontier types, he flourished for a brief score of years, and faded into legend with the passing of the open range.

Wyoming was the most typical of the cattle states as Nevada was

[3] Andy Adams, *The Log of a Cowboy,* pp. 63–4. Boston, Houghton, Mifflin Co.

the most typical of the mining states. Here was a country admirably suited by nature for large-scale ranching but almost entirely unsuited for farming, and here for twenty years the great cattle companies ruled supreme. The cattlemen seized most of the public and most of the Indian lands, controlled the politics and wrote the laws of the Territory, and successfully resisted the invasion of their domain by sheep-raisers or by farmers. For almost twenty years the powerful Wyoming Stock Growers' Association was the de facto government of the Territory: it formulated laws and regulations governing land and water rights, the round-up, the disposition of estrays, breeding, and similar matters, and enforced them upon members and non-members alike; it agitated ceaselessly for the revision of the land laws of the West and for the recognition of the prior rights of cattlemen; it attempted, by fraud, intimidation, and violence, to keep Wyoming as the exclusive preserve of the ranchers.

It is clear that a system of land laws based upon conditions in the well-watered East and designed to encourage farming was not suitable for the needs of the semi-arid West nor for the purposes of ranching. As early as 1879 Major Powell of the United States Geological Survey had recommended to Congress a thorough revision of the land laws of the West based upon realities — upon a recognition of the importance of water rather than acreage. These recommendations had been ignored and the Government continued its misguided effort to confine the cattle industry within a framework of sections and quarter-sections. It was inevitable that the cattlemen should evade and flout these laws, so irrelevant to their needs, and should make their own laws. Land frauds in the cattle kingdom were so universal as to make impertinent the suggestion of mere individual wrong-doing. It was impossible to indict an entire section and, clearly, it was the laws that were at fault, not the cattlemen. By hook or by crook the cattle companies seized control of the grasslands. They leased millions of acres from Indians, they strung barbed wire fences around other millions of acres, they staked out claims along the water-courses, denying farmers access to water. In 1886 Secretary Lamar reported that 'substantially the entire grazing country west of the 100th meridian' was fenced in by cattlemen. Cleveland moved with characteristic energy to destroy these illegal enclosures, and in the end the inexorable advance of the farmer forced the cattlemen to accommodate themselves to the law.

The cattle boom reached its acme about 1885. By that time the range had become too heavily pastured to support the long drive, and was beginning to be criss-crossed by railroads and the barbed wire fences of homesteads. By that time, too, the range had ceased to be a frontier industry and had become a corporate enterprise, organized, capitalized, and directed in the East or in Europe. New factors had begun to increase enormously the hazards of ranching. The rapid fencing-in of the open range, the appearance of cattle diseases and the passage of state quarantine laws, the conflict between the cattlemen and shepherds, between Northern and Southern cattlemen, and between cattlemen and settlers, and the determination of the Federal Government to enforce its land laws in the West — all these factors presaged the decline of the cow kingdom. Then came the two terrible winters of 1885–86 and 1886–87 which almost annihilated the herds on the open ranges. Cattle owners began to stake out homestead claims in the names of their 'outfit' and to fence off their lands. Almost in a moment the cattle range replaced the open ranges. Cowboy custom and tradition died hard; in 'dude ranches' they still flourish; but the cowboy turned cattleman or ranch employee, penned in behind wire, and knowing not the joys and dangers of the long drive, was a clipped eagle.

5. *The Disappearance of the Frontier*

What marked the end of the picturesque mining and cattle kingdoms, and of the old, romantic 'wild west,' was the irresistible pressure of farmers, swarming by the hundreds of thousands out onto the High Plains and into the mountain valleys, subduing this wilderness of prairie and mountain land to cultivation and civilization. During the Civil War the discoveries of precious ores, the necessity of maintaining communication with the Pacific coast, and the insatiable demand for wheat, all served to advertise the West. War dangers and uncertainties, especially in the border states, induced many to try their luck in the new regions, while the liberal provisions of the Homestead Act, the low cost of railroad lands, and the high rewards of farming proved an irresistible magnet for thousands of others. During the war years the population of nine Western states and Territories increased by over 300,000, while the agricultural states of Illinois, Wisconsin, Minnesota, Iowa, Kansas, and Nebraska received 843,000 immigrants from Europe and the East. It is recorded that in the year 1864 no less than 75,000 persons passed westward bound through Omaha alone. From Council Bluffs, Iowa, in 1864, the Reverend Jonathan Blanchard wrote:

> When you approach this town, the ravines and gorges are white with covered wagons at rest. Below the town, toward the river side, long wings of white canvass stretch away on either side, into the soft green willows; at the ferry from a quarter to a half mile of teams all the time await their turn to cross. Myriads of horses and mules drag on the moving mass of humanity toward the setting sun; while the oxen and cows equal them in number.

All this seems incredibly remote from the Wilderness and marching through Georgia. It was one of the great pulses of American life that went on beating amid the din of arms.

The close of the war brought an enormous acceleration of this movement. It was in great part the absorbing power of the West which enabled one million soldiers to resume civilian life without serious economic derangements. Southerners by the tens of thousands, despairing of recouping their fortunes in the war-stricken South, migrated westward although excluded temporarily from the privileges of the Homestead Act. Immigrants, mostly from northern Europe, found their way to the prairies of Minnesota and eastern Dakota by the hundreds of thousands.

Yet it was the twenty years following 1870 that witnessed the greatest expansion of the West, the overwhelming of the mining and cattle kingdoms, the taking up of most of the good public and railroad lands, and the disappearance of the frontier. The railroads, crossing the continent along half a dozen lines, and immigration, which reached a total of over eight million in these twenty years, were the most influential factors in the process. Not only did the railroads provide transportation and insure markets, but they were the active colonizing agents of the time. Whole Territories, such as the Dakotas, came into existence largely by virtue of the railways, while scores of towns and cities, such as Cheyenne, Council Bluffs, Kansas City, Spokane, Portland, and Seattle were created by and completely dependent upon them.

But it was not enough to provide land and transportation for eager immigrants to the West. Some method had to be found for overcoming the natural handicaps to agriculture in the semi-arid Plains region. The first and most urgent problem was to provide fencing. Even in the East, where timber was available, the cost of fencing was

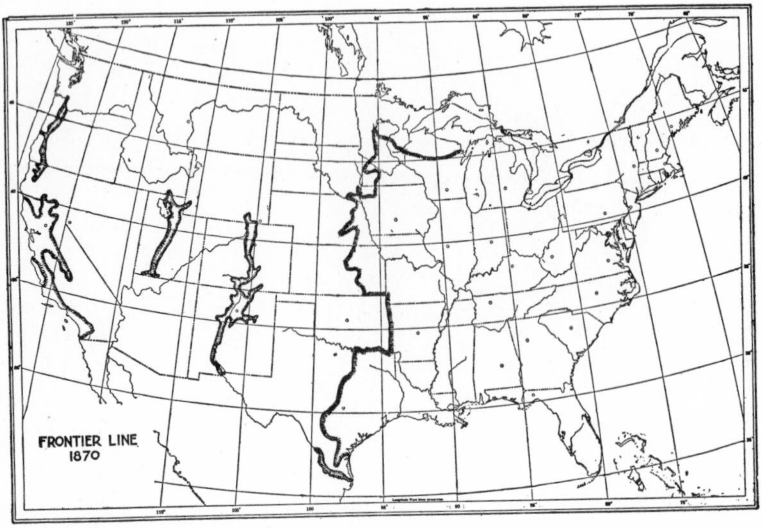

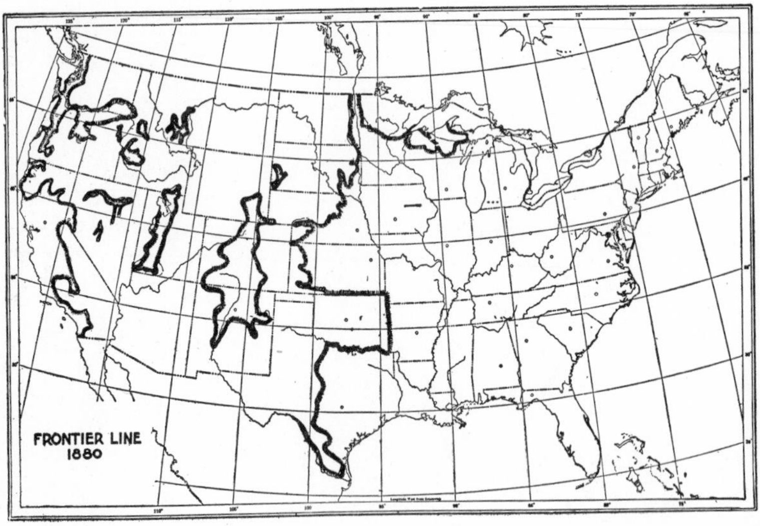

PASSING OF THE

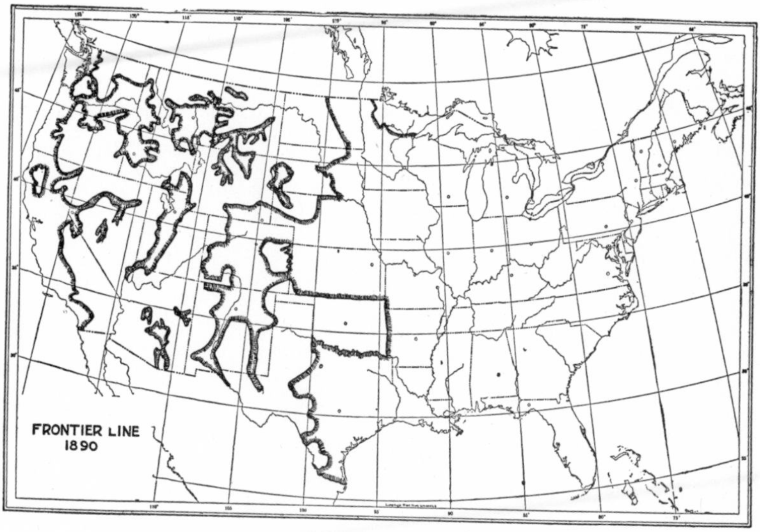

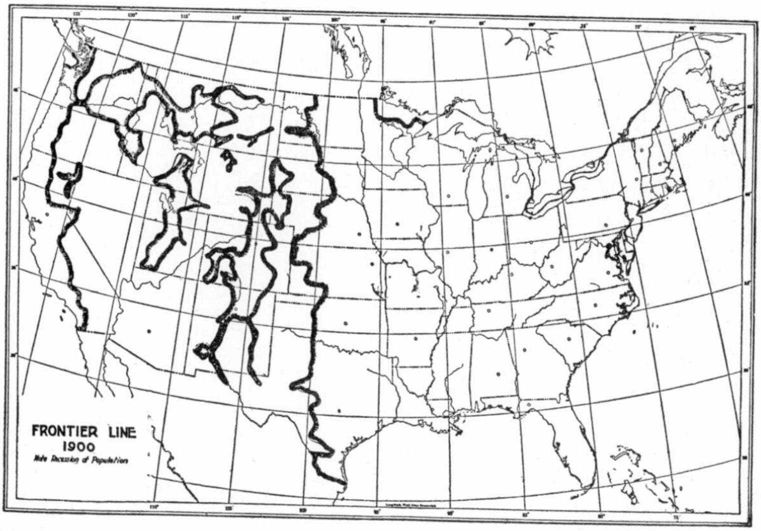

FRONTIER, 1870–1900

an important item: in 1870 the Department of Agriculture estimated that the total cost of fencing in the entire country was not far from two billion dollars and that the annual upkeep consumed almost two hundred million dollars. In the Plains, where lumber had to be imported, the cost of timber-fencing a quarter-section of land was prohibitive. Yet if cattle were to be controlled, manure saved, crops protected from the ravages of cattle, and water-holes preserved, fencing was absolutely necessary. Plains farmers experimented for years with various substitutes such as earth embankments, and osage orange hedges. In 1874 J. F. Glidden of DeKalb, Illinois, put barbed wire on the market and the fencing problem was solved! By 1883 Glidden's company was turning out 600 miles of barbed wire daily, and the expense of fencing had been reduced to a mere fraction of its former cost. The importance of barbed wire to the development of the Great Plains was comparable to that of the cotton gin in the development of the South.

Fencing made farming on the High Plains possible, but not necessarily profitable. There was still the question of water. 'The Great Plains,' wrote an observer of the Department of Agriculture, 'can be characterized as a region of periodical famine. . . . Year after year the water supply may be ample, the forage plants cover the ground with rank growth, the herds multiply, the settlers extend their fields, when, almost imperceptibly, the climate becomes less humid, the rain clouds forming day after day disappear upon the horizon, and weeks lengthen into months without a drop of moisture. The grasses wither, the herds wander wearily over the plains in search of water holes, the crops wilt and languish, yielding not even the seed for another year.' The great droughts and dust storms of 1934–1937 have brought home to us in dramatic fashion the dangers that have always threatened farmers in the Plains.

Scientific farming and invention modified, though they did not overcome, the menace of drought. For a time irrigation promised to solve the farming problem of the West. The Pueblo Indians were familiar with irrigation, and the Mormons had reclaimed thousands of acres of arid land by this ancient method. In 1894 Congress passed the Carey Act, turning over to the Western states millions of acres of public lands to be reclaimed through irrigation. The Act was ineffective, and by the Reclamation Act of 1902 the Federal Government took charge of irrigation. By the turn of the century some four million acres had been reclaimed: twenty years later this acreage under irrigation had been multiplied five-fold. Yet irrigation has not been an unqualified success, and its effects have been limited to a comparatively small area of the mountainous West and to California.

Far more effective than irrigation was the use of deep-drilled wells and of the windmill, and the practice of dry farming. By drilling from fifty to three hundred feet below the surface it was possible to tap ground water. Such water was brought to the surface not in the romantic 'old oaken bucket' lowered and raised by hand, but in slender metal cylinders lowered and raised by never failing windmills. Windmills were introduced to the Plains in the middle seventies; within a short time they became a familiar feature on the Plains landscape, and assured to the Plains farmer a steady though sometimes meagre supply of water. Dry farming — the scientific conservation of moisture in the soil through the creation of a dust blanket to prevent evaporation — made it possible to grow cereal crops successfully over large parts of the Plains area, though in the more arid sections it failed to bring satisfactory results.

As a result of all these factors: transportation, immigration, the growth of domestic and foreign markets, new methods of fencing and of soil cultivation, the settlement of the last West went on with unprecedented rapidity. In the twenty year period from 1870 to 1890 the population of California doubled, that of Texas trebled, that of Kansas increased four-fold, of Nebraska eight-fold, of Washington fourteen-fold, and of Dakota Territory forty-fold. Altogether the population of the trans-Mississippi West rose from 6,877,000 in 1870 to 16,775,000 in 1890. General Phil Sheridan described the process with prophetic pen:

> As the railroads overtook the successive lines of frontier posts, and settlements spread out over the country no longer requiring military protection, the army vacated its temporary shelters and marched into remote regions beyond, there to repeat and continue its pioneer work. In the rear of the advancing line of troops the primitive 'dug-outs' and cabins of the frontiersmen were steadily replaced by the tasteful houses, thrifty farms, neat villages and busy towns of a people who knew how best to employ the vast resources of the great West. The civilization from the Atlantic is now reaching out toward that rapidly approaching it from the direction of the Pacific, the long intervening strip of territory, extending from the British possessions to Old Mexico, yearly growing narrower; finally the dividing lines will entirely disappear and the mingling settlements absorb the remnants of the once powerful Indian nations, who,

fifteen years ago, vainly attempted to forbid the destined progress of the age.

These 'dividing lines,' which were a thousand miles apart when Sheridan wrote, had, by 1880, become so irregular as to be well-nigh untraceable, and ten years later, in his annual report for 1890, the Superintendent of the Census announced that

Up to and including 1880 the country had a frontier of settlement, but at present the unsettled area has been so broken into by isolated bodies of settlement that there can hardly be said to be a frontier line.

The 'disappearance of the frontier' was shortly hailed by a great American historian, Frederick Jackson Turner, as the close of a movement that began in 1607, and the beginning of a new era in American history.

After a lapse of almost sixty years, however, it is difficult to discern any fundamental break in the rhythm of American life that can properly be ascribed to the passing of the frontier. If the frontier represented an opportunity to stake out a farm in the West, that opportunity did not disappear in the nineties, for more land was patented for homestead and grazing purposes in the generation after 1890 than in the previous generation. The great wheat fields of western Canada, too, offered opportunities to American farmers. If the frontier represented, as one distinguished historian has said, 'not merely a staked claim to a farm' but 'a state of mind and a golden opportunity,' then it is clear that the 'golden opportunity' went glimmering when the overhead of farming in the West came to equal or to exceed that in the East, and that the psychological change was not an effect of the passing of the frontier but a cause.

The driving force which swept the pioneer westward from the Alleghenies to the Pacific, the dynamic energy which for two generations concentrated on the taking up of land, has disappeared or changed directions. The frontier as a possible safety valve for economic unrest, a social laboratory, a democratizing process, a spur at once to individual initiative and to collective social action, and a psychological attitude or state of mind, has disappeared; but its disappearance is rather the result of complex economic and psychological forces than a cause of great changes. The relatively lower returns from agriculture than from other forms of industry, the heavier cost of labor and the higher risks of farming, the greater social and cultural attractiveness of urban than of rural life, the transformed values and standards of living in the last generation, have made Americans shun rather than seek the great open spaces. The ideal of the sturdy, self-sufficient, independent farmer, so seldom realized in fact, has been supplanted by the ideal of the middle-class city-dweller, drawing a good salary and making money on the stock market.

This change in ideals is associated with a sense of frustration and of dissatisfaction that was part of the westward movement and of pioneer life. Both have been the subject of so much romantic sentimentality that we are apt to overlook some of the more realistic aspects. The continuous exodus of a large part of the population meant the unsettling, in a social sense, of the more settled regions of the East and South. Western colonization went on at the expense of older communities and contributed greatly to that process of social and cultural disintegration which has long been one of the characteristics of American life. What it meant for the men and women who participated in it is more difficult to determine, for the pioneers were not given to writing their memoirs; glimpses of it can be caught from the moving pages of Rölvaag's *Giants in the Earth* or the brutal pages of Sandoz's *Old Jules* or the nostalgic *Grandmother Brown's Hundred Years*. Often it meant release from hardship, a chance to be a man among men, and grow up with a new country. Often, too, it meant the exchange of an ordered, civilized, neighborly community with hard-won standards of propriety, for primitive conditions, an unequal contest with the wilderness, with loneliness and fear and disease. To break new pathways into the West and to wrest a living from the soil was not easy; and the process laid a heavy hand upon those who were not rough-hewn for pioneering. The pioneer women, laboring beneath intolerable burdens, denied the homely pleasures of social intercourse, cut off from aid in time of need, suffered the most, as the stories of Hamlin Garland and of Rölvaag have revealed. The terrible toll that pioneering exacted from the men and women who engaged in it can be neither discounted nor overlooked in any evaluation of the westward movement and the significance of the frontier.

6. *Political Organization*

In 1860 something over one-third of the area of the United States was divided into Territories and under the control of the Federal Government. From Minnesota to Oregon, from Texas to the Canadian border, there were no states. Within thirty years all this territory, comprising something over a million square miles, had been organized politically, and the major part of it included in states. Statehood was an important step in the assimilation of the West. Federal political control and the frontier disappeared simultaneously.

The admission of Nevada in 1864 had been dictated by the desire to obtain its three electoral votes for Lincoln. The inhabitants of Colorado had rejected the proffer of statehood in the same year, but in 1876 Colorado was admitted as the Centennial State. Nebraska was brought into the Union in 1867 over President Johnson's veto, in time to cast her vote for the impeachment of that unfortunate chief magistrate. With the creation of Wyoming Territory in 1868 the territorial subdivisions of the West had been rounded out, but few of these Territories, most of them based upon mineral wealth, showed any prospects of being prepared for statehood in the immediate future.

The building of the transcontinental railroads, however, put an entirely different face upon the situation, for they brought to the Western Territories a permanent farmer population and a solid economic foundation for statehood. This first became apparent in the northernmost tier of Territories. In 1870 the population of the Dakota, Idaho, and Washington Territories was only 60,000; by 1890, after the Northern Pacific had been completed and the Great Northern almost completed, their population had increased to 1,000,000. The influence of the railroads, both in bringing a permanent population and in providing markets, was a controlling factor in the creation of most of the other Western states.

Agitation for statehood, especially in the Dakotas and Washington Territory, was continuous. It is somewhat difficult, however, to distinguish between popular enthusiasm and that of professional politicians, eager to become congressmen and state officials. The situation in both Washington and Dakota was complicated: the inhabitants of Washington sought to incorporate the Idaho panhandle in their state, and in Dakota Territory there was an irresistible popular demand for a separation into two states. Though these and other Territories were amply entitled to statehood, on the score of population, action was held up for a full decade by political differences in Washington. The decisive influence of Colorado's vote in the disputed Presidential election of 1876 brought the statehood question into party politics. Except for the two years of the forty-seventh Congress, 1881–83, control of the Government was divided between the two parties during the entire period from Hayes to Harrington. Favorable action upon the demand of the Dakotas for admission in 1881 was held up by Eastern fear of Western radicalism, and Eastern resentment over the repudiation of certain railway bonds by Yankton county. Senator Ingalls of Kansas was led to exclaim, 'I believe that all the objections which have been hitherto urged against the passage of that bill are purely partisan, and malignant.' But by playing politics shamelessly with the fortunes and the futures of the Western Territories, both parties forfeited the confidence of these embryo states and made them the more willing to follow the banner of Populism in the early nineties.

The so-called blockade, however, came to an end abruptly in 1888, with the election of Harrison and the prospect of complete Republican control of the government. Both parties and both Houses then made frenzied efforts to get the credit for the admission of the Western states. The result of this eager rivalry was the Omnibus Bill of 1889 which, in its final form, provided for the admission of North and South Dakota, Montana, and Washington. No provision had been made in the Omnibus Bill for Wyoming and Idaho, but in both of these Territories constitutional conventions met without specific authority, and a few months later both were admitted by a debate-weary but vote-hungry Republican Congress.

With the admission of these six states there existed for the first time a solid band of states from the Atlantic to the Pacific. The same year that the Omnibus Bill was passed, the Government purchased a large part of the lands of the Five Civilized Tribes and threw Oklahoma open to settlement under the provisions of the homestead laws. The fertility and accessibility of its soil attracted thousands of prospective settlers and speculators, and when the gun was fired on 22 April 1889 there ensued a scene without parallel in the history of the West. Let Edna Ferber's Yancey Cravat describe it:

> Well eleven o'clock and they were crowding and cursing and fighting for places near the line. They shouted and sang and yelled and argued, and the sound they made wasn't human at all, but like thousands of wild animals penned up. The sun blazed down. It was cruel. The dust hung over everything in a thick cloud, blinding you and choking you. The black dust of the prairie was over everything. We were a horde of fiends with our red eyes and our cracked lips and our blackened faces. Eleven-thirty. It was a picture straight out of hell. The roar grew louder. People fought for an inch of gain on the Border. . . . Eleven-forty-five. Along the Border were the soldiers, their guns in one hand, their watches in the

other. Those last five minutes seemed years long; and funny, they'd quieted till there wasn't a sound. Listening. The last minute was an eternity. Twelve o'clock. There went up a roar that drowned the crack of the soldiers' musketry as they fired in the air as the signal of noon and the start of the Run. You could see the puffs of smoke from their guns, but you couldn't hear a sound. The thousands surged over the Line. It was like water going over a broken dam. The rush had started and it was devil take the hindmost. We swept across the prairie in a cloud of black and red dust that covered our faces and hands in a minute, so that we looked like black demons from hell.[4]

The towns of Guthrie and Oklahoma City sprang up overnight. By November Oklahoma had sixty thousand settlers and the following year it was organized into a Territory. Within a decade the population had reached almost 800,000 and the question of statehood became urgent. The problem of the disposition of the Indians of Indian Territory complicated matters considerably, and it was not until 1907 that Oklahoma and Indian Territory were admitted as one state.

It was in 1890 that the Mormon government in Utah accepted the inevitable and promised to abandon polygamy, thus removing the last objection to its admission to statehood. Under the able administration of the Mormon Church the Latter-day Saints had prospered amazingly, and when Utah was finally admitted to statehood, in 1896, it was with a flourishing population of some 250,000. The Territories of Arizona and New Mexico, both containing a large admixture of Mexicans and Indians, had rejected joint admission as a single state in 1907, and it was five years before they were admitted individually.

Thus was completed a process inaugurated by the Northwest Ordinance of 1787. Since that time the United States had grown from thirteen to forty-eight states. Texas came in as an independent Republic, Maine and West Virginia were separated from other states, Vermont and Kentucky were admitted without previous Territoritorial organization; but all the others, after passing through the Territorial stage, were admitted as States in a Union of equals, in accordance with the policies laid down by the enlightened Ordinance. The greatest experiment in colonial policy and administration of modern times had been brought to a conclusion successful beyond the wildest dreams of those who inaugurated it.

[4] Edna Ferber, *Cimmaron*, pp. 23–25, Doubleday, Doran.

The constitutions of the new states differed little from those of the older entities. Americans, on the whole, have hesitated to seize the opportunity for political experiment and differentiation offered by our federal system. What differences there were took a radical form. The constitutions of Wyoming and Utah provided for woman suffrage from the beginning, and Colorado and other Western states incorporated this provision in their constitutions shortly after. Some of the constitutions provided for the initiative, the referendum, and the Australian ballot, while all contained lengthy and stringent provisions for the control of railroads and other corporations. All of them reflected, too, a more liberal attitude toward labor and social reform. There were provisions for the eight-hour day, for the limitation of the hours of labor for women and children, for arbitration of labor disputes and employer liability, and prohibitions against the use of the blacklist or the employment of Pinkerton detectives. In form, too, these constitutions varied somewhat from those of the Eastern states: they were remarkably detailed and remarkably long, they strengthened the executive at the expense of the legislative power, and they provided for the creation of numerous boards and commissions to supervise new governmental functions. On the whole they resembled codes of law rather than basic principles of government, and constituted striking documents in the 'case of the American People *versus* Themselves.'

V

TRANSPORTATION AND ITS CONTROL

1865–1900

1. *The Railway Key*

ECONOMICALLY the era after the Civil War was marked by the application of machine power, in constantly increasing units and over a widely expanded area, to the processes of industry and of agriculture. Transportation was the key; mass production the result. We have already seen how railroads developed from the local feeders into the eastern trunk lines, which connected the Mississippi valley with the northern Atlantic coast and helped the North to win the war. Immediately after the war came mechanical improvements such as the gradual replacement of the old type of engine (which looked like a wash boiler hitched to a big funnel and a cow-catcher) by coal-burning expansion-cylinder locomotives, the Pullman sleeping car (1864), the safety coupler, and the Westinghouse air brake. This last, invented in 1869, did more than any other invention to transform the original string of boxes on trucks to the modern train, and to make possible safe operation at high speeds. But it was the old wood-burning, spark-belching 'bullgine,' gay with paint and sporting a name instead of a number, tugging unvestibuled coaches with swaying kerosene lamps and quid-bespattered wood stoves, which first wheezed across the Great Divide and linked the Atlantic to the Pacific.

There were 35,000 miles of steam railway in the United States in 1865, practically all east of the Mississippi. During the next eight years as many more were constructed. In the years 1874–87 some 87,000 additional miles of track were laid, and in 1900, with just under 200,000 miles in operation, the United States had a greater railway mileage than all Europe.

A transportation system such as this required state and federal legislation, colossal sums of money, and the labor of myriads. It affected the fortunes of almost everyone in the country, and of millions abroad as well. It gave a new wrench to the body politic, already distorted by the war. Railway expansion touched American life at countless points. It closely interacted with western migration and settlement, with the iron and steel industry, and with agriculture: it greased the way for big business and high finance, helped to pollute politics, and gave birth to the new type of successful corporation lawyer. Another revolution in transportation wrought by the internal combustion engine and the motor-car have so over-shadowed the railroads that it is difficult for the present generation to realize how completely they dominated the industrial and political world for almost fifty years after the Civil War.

We have already seen how the agitation for transcontinental railroads affected the fortunes of Stephen A. Douglas, and helped the Republican party to ride into power on a wholly different issue; how competing routes were advocated and surveyed, but deadlocked by sectional jealousy and politics. While the Civil War was wrecking the railway system of the South, it accelerated railway development in the North and across the continent. As a connection between the Mississippi valley and the Far West, Halliday's Overland Stage was more picturesque than efficient; but military necessity brought the dream of Asa Whitney and Stephen Douglas to fulfilment. With the active co-operation of the War Department, and under the supervision of Generals Dodge and Sherman, the first transcontinental line was projected and constructed.

On 1 July 1862 President Lincoln signed the first Pacific Railway Bill. This bill provided for the construction of a transcontinental railroad by two corporations — the Union Pacific, which should build westward from Council Bluffs, Iowa, and the Central Pacific, which should build eastward from Sacramento, California. Liberal aid was pledged in the form of alternate sections of public lands to the depth of ten miles on either side of the road and of loans ranging from $16,000 to $48,000 for every mile of track completed. Active construction on the Union Pacific, financed by the notorious Crédit Mobilier, was begun in 1865 and the road was pushed rapidly westward from Omaha through Nebraska and Wyoming Territories, near the line of the old Oregon and Mormon Trails, and across the Wasatch Range of the Rockies into the Great Salt Basin. In the meantime the Central Pacific, chartered in 1858, and directed by Collis P. Huntington and Leland Stanford, was pushed eastward over the difficult grades of the Sierras and across the arid valleys of Nevada to meet the U. P. The lurid details of their race have lost nothing in their telling by Zane Grey; but there is no need to exaggerate or to idealize this spectacular achievement. The obstacles to be overcome seemed almost insuperable: engineering problems, labor and financial difficulties, the constant struggle with mountain blizzard and desert heat. That they were overcome must be attributed not only to the indomitable energy and perseverance of men like Dodge and Huntington, but also to the courage and devotion of the thousands of laborers — the ex-soldiers, Irish immigrants, and Chinese coolies — upon whose brawny shoulders the heaviest part of the task rested.

When I think [wrote Robert Louis Stevenson] of how the railroad has been pushed through this unwatered wilderness and haunt of savage tribes . . . ; how at each stage of construction, roaring, impromptu cities full of gold and lust and death sprang up and then died away again, and are now but wayside stations in the desert; how in these uncouth places pigtailed Chinese pirates worked side by side with border ruffians and broken men from Europe, talking together in a mixed dialect mostly oaths, . . . how the plumed hereditary lord of all America heard in this last fastness the scream of the "bad medicine wagon" charioting his foes; and then when I go on to remember that all this epical turmoil was conducted by gentlemen in frocked coats, and to nothing more extraordinary than a fortune and a subsequent visit to Paris, it seems to me . . . as if this railway were the one typical achievement of the age in which we live. . . . If it be romance, if it be contrast, if it be heroism that we require, what was Troytown to this.[1]

Both the Union and the Central Pacific roads were pushed forward in record time, twenty thousand laborers laying as much as eight miles of track in a day in the last stages of the race. The prime motive for this feverish haste was the greed of each group of promoters to obtain the lion's share of federal bounties and land grants. When, amidst universal rejoicing, the two sets of rails were joined with a golden spike at Promontory Point, Utah, 10 May 1869, the Union Pacific was regarded as the winner, but the Central Pacific promoters had made enough to enable them to buy the state government of California.

Meantime there was a wild scramble among other groups of promoters for charters and favors, and within a few years Congress chartered and endowed with enormous land grants three other lines: (1) the Northern Pacific — from Lake Superior across Minnesota, through the Bad Lands of Dakota up the valley of the Yellowstone, across the continental divide at Bozeman, to the headwaters of the Missouri, and by an intricate route through the Rockies to the Columbia river and Portland; (2) the Southern Pacific — an out-

[1] *Across the Plains,* pp. 50–52, Scribner's.

growth and development of the Central Pacific and the short-lived Atlantic and Pacific — from New Orleans across Texas to the Rio Grande, across the Llanos Estacados to El Paso, and through the territory of the Gadsden Purchase to Los Angeles, up the San Joaquin valley to San Francisco; (3) the Santa Fé — following closely the old Santa Fé Trail, from Atchison, Kansas, up the Arkansas river to Trinidad, Colorado, across the Raton spur of the Rockies to Santa Fé and Albuquerque, through the country of the Apache and the Navajo, parallel to the Grand Canyon of the Colorado — which thrusts its impassable barrier for three hundred miles athwart the southern railway routes — and across the Mojave desert to San Bernardino and San Diego. By 1884, after numerous bankruptcies and reorganizations, all three reached the Pacific coast.

2. *The Railroads and the West*

These transcontinental lines were promoted largely with a view to profit from construction and from manipulation of securities, but the peopling of the vast region between the Missouri and the Pacific proved to be their most valuable function. In this respect they performed a work comparable with that of the Virginia Company of 1606 and the Ohio Company of 1785.

At the end of the Civil War the Plains west of eastern Kansas and Nebraska, the High Plains, and the Rocky Mountain regions were practically unpeopled, save for mining towns in Colorado and Nevada and the Mormon settlements in Utah. Mail coaches of the Overland Stage Line required at least five days to transport passengers and mails from the Missouri river to Denver, where flour was sold for twenty cents a pound and potatoes for fifteen dollars a bushel. Pre-war pioneers had been confined to subsistence farming until the railway connected them with markets; but the transcontinental railways pushed out into the plains far in advance of settlers, advertised for immigrants in the Eastern states and Europe, transported them at wholesale rates to the prairie railhead, and sold them land at from one to ten dollars an acre. Thus James J. Hill settled his great domain in the far Northwest, his agents scouring Europe for settlers and meeting new arrivals at the piers in New York City; Henry Villard of the Northern Pacific employed almost a thousand agents in England and continental Europe; the immigration department of the Santa Fé Railroad brought to Kansas in 1874 fifteen thousand German Mennonites whose ancestors had colonized the Crimea and Caucasus. Thousands of section-hands entered a free homestead right, saved their wages to buy farm equipment and a team of horses, built a sod-house or cabin, and became permanent settlers as soon as the steel road was built. The termini and eastern junction points of these lines — like Omaha, opposite the old Council Bluffs of the Indians; Kansas City, hard by the old jumping-off place for the Oregon Trail; Duluth, the 'Zenith City of the Unsalted Seas'; Oakland on San Francisco bay; Portland, Oregon; Seattle and Tacoma, Washington — places non-existent or mere villages before the Civil War, became in thirty years metropolitan cities.

Railroading was the biggest business of a big era, and the railway builders were of the metal that makes leaders and conquerors. The new Northwest was the domain of James J. Hill, the 'Empire Builder,' and the Great Northern Railway his individual path of empire. St. Paul was a small town on the edge of the frontier when he migrated thither from eastern Canada just before the Civil War, and Minneapolis a mere village at the St. Anthony falls of the Mississippi. Such importance as they had was due to their position at the end of a trail from the Red river of the North, which connected Winnipeg with the outside world. Long trains of two-wheeled ox-carts transported the peltry and supplies in forty or fifty days' time. In the winter of 1870 Donald Smith, resident governor of the Hudson's Bay Company, started south from Winnipeg, and James J. Hill north from St. Paul, both in dog-sleds. They met on the prairie and made camp in a snowstorm; and from that meeting sprang the Canadian Pacific and the Great Northern railways.

In the panic of 1873 a little Minnesota railway with an ambitious name, the St. Paul and Pacific, went bankrupt. Hill watched it as a prairie wolf watches a weakening buffalo, and in 1878, in association with two Canadian railway men, wrested it from the Dutch bondholders by a mere flotation of new securities.

The day of land grants and federal subsidies was past, and Hill saw that the Great Northern Railway, as he renamed his purchase, could reach the Pacific only by developing the country as it progressed. 'We consider ourselves and the people along our lines as co-partners in the prosperity of the country we both occupy,' said Hill, 'and the prosperity of the one should mean the prosperity of both, and their adversity will be quickly followed by ours.' So this empire builder undertook to enhance the prosperity of what came to be known as the

'Hill country'; he introduced scientific farming, distributed blooded bulls free to farmers, supported churches and schools, and assisted in countless ways in the development of the communities of the Northwest. 'It was,' observes one commentator, 'largely due to his unceasing interest in all that pertained to getting the most out of the soil that the "Hill country" developed more evenly and with fewer tragedies than any other large-scale land enterprise of these years.'

In the construction of his railroad Hill showed equal forethought and shrewdness. Construction costs were low, the financial management was skillful and conservative, and the Great Northern was the one transcontinental line that managed to weather every financial crisis. Hill first made connection with Winnipeg by the Red river valley; then, anticipating a diversion of Winnipeg traffic by the Canadian Pacific, he struck almost due west across the Dakota plains, sending out branches in order to people the region and carry its wheat to market. In the summer of 1887 he made a record stride, 643 miles of grading, bridging, and plate-laying from Minot, North Dakota, to the Great Falls of the Missouri, at the rate of over three miles per working day. Two years later, the Rockies yielded their last secret, the Marias pass, to a young engineer named John F. Stevens. In 1893 the trains of the Great Northern reached tidewater at Tacoma, Washington. Ten years more, and Hill had acquired partial control of the Northern Pacific Railroad, had purchased joint control of a railway connecting its eastern termini with Chicago, and was running his own fleets of steamships from Duluth to Buffalo, and from Seattle to Japan and China.

The Great Northern, the Northern Pacific, and the Union Pacific (which sent a tap-root northwesterly) were responsible for the opening of the great 'Inland Empire' between the Cascades and the Rockies, and for an astounding development of the entire Northwest. This once isolated Oregon country, with its rich and varied natural resources, magnificent scenery, and thriving seaports, has become as distinct and self-conscious a section of the Union as New England. The three states of this region — Washington, Oregon, and Idaho — increased their population from 282,000 in 1880 to 763,000 in 1890, and 2,140,000 in 1910, while California, which contained only half a million people when the golden spike was driven in 1869, kept pace with them. The population of Kansas, Nebraska, and the Dakotas, starting at the same level in 1870, increased six-fold in two decades; Utah and Colorado, where there was a great mining boom in the seventies, rose from 125,000 to 624,000 in the same period; Oklahoma and the Indian Territory, where not a white man was enrolled in 1880, had over a million and a half palefaces in 1910; and Texas, with the aid of a network of railways, doubled its population of 1,600,000 between 1880 and 1910.

King Cotton's crown passed to King Wheat, whose dominions increased. Railway penetration of the far Northwest, improved agricultural machinery, the handling of grain in carload lots, transhipment to lake or ocean steamers by grain elevators, and a new milling process which ground northern spring wheat into superfine flour—all these factors combined to move the center of wheat production north and west from Illinois and Iowa into Minnesota, the Dakotas, Montana, Oregon, and the Canadian Northwest. In this new wheat belt the bonanza farms, veritable factories for wheat production, were well established by 1890. The wheat crop increased from 152 to 612 million bushels between 1866 and 1891. With the low prices that prevailed after the panic of 1873 this meant ruin to the wheat farmers of the Eastern states. The silo, enabling dairy farmers to turn corn into dairy products, saved Eastern farming from disaster; but enormous areas within a few hours of the great industrial centers on the Atlantic coast have reverted to shrub since 1870.

3. *Federal and Local Aid*

When railroads began to supplant rivers and canals as highways of commerce, connect isolated rural regions with markets, and open up new land to settlement, they were looked upon as unmixed blessings, and their promotors were admired as public benefactors. Since every route decided upon by surveyors and railway promoters brought prosperity to some communities and threatened ruin to others, towns, counties, and states outdid one another in bidding for the iron tracks. The Federal Government, too, having definitely abandoned the embarrassing strict construction theories that bothered an earlier generation, regarded the roads as military and postal necessities and aided them with a liberality which at the time seemed commendable but which a later generation might well regard as fabulous.

This policy of government aid to internal improvements had its beginnings in grants of land to canal, turnpike, and railroad companies in the decades before the Civil War. In the fifties no less than twenty-eight million acres of public lands were granted to states for the purpose of subsidizing railroad construction; the Illinois Central alone got some 2,600,000 acres from the states through which it passed. With the enactment of the Pacific Railway Bill of 1862 the Government inaugurated the practice of making land grants directly to railway corporations. Certainly very few of the western railroads could have been built by private capital alone without generous aid from federal, state, and local governments.

Beside charters and rights of way across the territories, federal aid was extended to the roads in a number of ways such as land grants, loans, subsidies, and tariff remission on rails. The land grants were by far the most valuable. The Union Pacific was given some twenty million acres of public lands in alternate sections along its track; the Santa Fé system got seventeen million acres; the Central and Southern Pacific systems got twenty-four million acres; while the Northern Pacific obtained the enormous total of forty-four million acres, an area equal to the entire State of Missouri. Altogether the Federal Government gave to the railroads 158,293,377 acres — almost the area of Texas — of which some forty-two million acres were later declared forfeit because the roads failed to fulfill the conditions of the grants.

As most of this land was worth nothing to the roads until it produced crops to be hauled to market, and because they were in urgent need of money, the railway companies generally disposed of it as rapidly as possible, and at a price averaging about five dollars an acre. Some of the land, however, covered extensive deposits of coal and other minerals, and much of it was heavily timbered. So while disposing rapidly of their agricultural and grazing lands, the roads consistently followed the policy of reserving mineral lands, timber lands, and potential town sites for speculative purposes. Some of these holdings eventually proved fabulously rich. All in all these land grants, designed to assist railroads in financing construction where as yet there was no basis for revenue, paid a considerable part of the total construction costs. The lands granted to the Illinois Central, for example, brought in a sum equal to the entire construction cost of that railroad. It cost some seventy million dollars to build the Northern Pacific, but in 1917 the Northern Pacific reported gross receipts from land sales of over $136,000,000, with much of its most valuable lands still unsold. The lands granted to both the Union Pacific and the Central Pacific brought in enough money to have covered all legitimate costs of building these roads.

Direct financial aid was given by the Federal Government only to the Union and Central Pacific railways, and their subsidiaries, and in the form of a loan for every mile of track. These loans, aggregating over sixty million dollars, were eventually repaid with interest, but not before the question of repayment had troubled the political waters for a decade.

Aid from states, counties, and municipalities, often competing with one another, was even more lavish. The states often granted tax-exemption, protection from competition, and liberal charters. Some states lent the roads their credit, others subscribed outright to the stock of railway companies. Many states, especially Texas, Minnesota, Illinois, and Wisconsin, made extensive land grants; these totalled over fifty million acres. Counties and municipalities subscribed liberally to railway stock and often donated money outright. Counties and towns of Kentucky incurred a debt of over thirteen million dollars for railroad construction; eighty-six counties in Illinois subsidized railroads to the extent of over sixteen million dollars; the municipalities of Kansas contributed well over twelve million dollars to the railroads of that State. Careful estimates of total subsidies to railroads by various governmental agencies of western states indicate that Kansas contributed some seventy-five million dollars, Nebraska and Iowa each some sixty million dollars, and Wisconsin over thirty million dollars. It is impossible to avoid the conclusion that the aggregate subsidies received by the western railroads from federal, state and local governments covered the original cost of construction.

4. *Abuses and State Regulation*

This rapid extension of railroads was not followed by the expected wave of prosperity. On the contrary, within a few years the farmers of the West began to feel the effects of the post-war deflation, followed by the panic of 1873, and many laid the blame on the railroads. The advantages for which Westerners had paid so handsomely seemed to bring only hard times. How far the railroads were responsible for the hard times of the early seventies by stimulating production ahead of market needs is a matter of dispute; but there is no question of the reality of grave abuses connected with railway expansion in the post-war years.

Easily the most grievous of these abuses were the high freight rates charged by the western roads — rates so exorbitant that the farmers at times burnt their corn for fuel rather than ship it. The question of rates is, of course, inextricably connected with the question of the capitalization upon which the roads expected to pay dividends. The railway masters argued that they were barely able to maintain dividend payments, and it is true that in periods of depression, such as those following upon the panics of 1873 and 1893, many of the roads were in receivership. Yet it is clear that both the extortionate freight rates and the financial difficulties of the roads are traceable to over-high construction costs, fraudulent manipulation of stock, and incompetent management. These evils, equally glaring in the East and the South, were felt more immediately in the West than in any other section. The total construction cost of the Central Pacific, for example, from Sacramento to Ogden was something over ninety million dollars, and upon this investment the directors of the road expected to pay dividends; but a Congressional committee estimated that 'a road similar to that of the Central Pacific could probably be built for $22,000,000.' The same committee estimated that the cost of five transcontinental roads was $634,000,000 and that these same roads could be duplicated for $286,000,000. But the evil of over-capitalization was by no means confined to the West, and the editor of Poor's railroad manual for 1885 estimated that approximately one-third of the railroad capitalization of that year represented water.

Other abuses against which complaint was loud and persistent were discrimination in rates and in service, the granting of secret rebates to powerful shippers, free passes to state legislators, men of influence, and all actual or probable friends of the railroads, slashing freight rates at competitive points and making up the loss at non-competitive points, railroad control of warehouse facilities, retention of railroad land for speculative purposes, and the corrupt activities of railroads in politics.

The power of the western railways over their exclusive territory was nearly absolute, for until the age of automobiles, the people of the West had no alternate means of transportation. Such railways could make an industry or ruin a community by a few cents more or less in a rate on wheat or cattle. The funds at their disposal, often created by financial manipulation and stock-watering, were so colossal as to overshadow state governments. Railway builders and promoters had the point of view of feudal chieftains. They regarded the farmers, whom they had placed on the land, as ignorant and ungrateful boors who must be coerced and bribed into doing right by the railroad if milder methods would not serve. Railroading, in their opinion, was a business wholly private in its nature, no more a fit subject for government regulation than a retail store. 'There is no foundation in good reason,' said Leland Stanford to his stockholders in 1878, 'for the attempts made by the General Government and by the States to especially control your affairs. It is a question of might and it is to your interest to have it determined where the power resides.'

The determination of this question was not difficult. Leland Stanford, Collis P. Huntington, and their associates who built the Central Pacific and controlled the Southern Pacific, had the might, and in the exercise of that might they were indifferent to all save considerations of private gain. By distributing free passes to state representatives, by paying their campaign expenses, and by downright bribery, they prevented just taxation of their railroad properties and evaded all regulation. By discriminating in freight charges between localities, articles, and individuals, they terrorized merchants, farmers, and communities 'until matters reached such a pass, that no man dared engage in any business in which transportation largely entered without first . . . obtaining the permission of a railroad manager.'[2] Through the press, the professions, and even the pulpit they wielded a power over public opinion comparable to that of the slaveowners over the old South. The same methods were imitated by the eastern and middle western railways so far as they dared. In New Hampshire as in California, the 'railroad lobby,' ensconced in an office near the state capitol, acted as a chamber of initiative and revision; and, as Winston Churchill has told us in his *Coniston* and *Mr. Crewe's Career,* few could succeed in politics unless by grace of the Boston and Maine. 'The railroad corporations,' asserted Governor Larrabee of Iowa, 'were in fact rapidly assuming a position which could not be tolerated. Sheltering themselves behind the Dartmouth College decision, they practically undertook to set even public opinion at defiance. . . . They thoroughly got it into their heads that they, as common carriers, were in no way bound to afford equal facilities to all, and indeed, that it was in the last degree absurd and unreasonable to expect them to.'

These exactions and abuses of power were tolerated by the American people with what Europeans deemed a remarkable patience, so imbued were they with laissez-faire doctrine, so proud of progress,

[2] *Report* of the U.S. Pacific Railway Commission (1887), vol. I, 141.

improvement, and development, and so averse from increasing the power of government. But the deflation of the post-war years and the panic of 1873 brought an inevitable reaction against the roads in the early seventies. This reaction centered in the Mid-Western states of Illinois, Iowa, Wisconsin, Minnesota, Missouri, and Nebraska, but it also found expression in Eastern states such as Massachusetts and in Western such as California. It took several forms: prohibition of further state aid, as in the constitutions of California, Kansas, and Missouri; recovery of land grants; prohibition of specific abuses; and positive regulation of rates and services. The Eastern state governments inclined to supervision by special railway commissions, and that of Massachusetts, under the leadership of the gifted Charles Francis Adams, Jr., attracted widespread attention and was the model for numerous states.

The Mid-Western states were more direct in their methods. The Illinois Constitution of 1870 contained a clause directing the legislature to 'pass laws to correct abuses and to prevent unjust discrimination and extortion in the rates of freight and passenger tariffs on the different railroads of the state.' Pursuant to this clause the legislature of Illinois prohibited discrimination, established a maximum rate, and created a Railway and Warehouse Commission to regulate roads, grain elevators, and warehouses. These laws, though bitterly denounced as socialism throughout the East, served as models for similar legislation in other states. At the demand of the farmers, the example of Illinois was followed in 1874 by Iowa and Minnesota, and by Wisconsin with its drastic Potter law.

Thus within a few years the railroads of the Middle West found their independence severely circumscribed by a mass of highly restrictive regulatory legislation. The day of individualism and laissez-faire theories was passing away.

The validity of this legislation, shortly contested in the courts, was upheld in the 'Granger' cases. The first and most important of these was Munn *v.* Illinois (1876) involving the constitutionality of a statute regulating the charges of grain elevators. The warehouse owners contended that the act was a deprivation of property without due process of law and thus constituted a violation of the Fourteenth Amendment. In one of the most far-reaching decisions in American law, Chief Justice Waite upheld the validity of the Illinois statute. Basing his opinion upon the historical right of the state, in the exercise of its police power, to regulate ferries, common carriers, inns, etc., he announced that

When private property is affected with a public interest it ceases to be *juris privati* only. . . . Property does become clothed with a public interest when used in a manner to make it of public consequence, and affect the community at large. When, therefore, one devotes his property to a use in which the public has an interest, he, in effect, grants to the public an interest in that use, and must submit to be controlled by the public for the common good, to the extent of the interest he has created.[3]

The warehouse owners not only challenged the right of the state to regulate their business but contended further that rate-fixing by a legislative committee did not constitute 'due process of law.' This contention the Court disposed of in cavalier fashion:

It is insisted, however, that the owner of property is entitled to a reasonable compensation for its use . . . and that what is reasonable is a judicial and not a legislative question. . . . The controlling fact [however] is the power to regulate at all. If that exists, the right to establish the maximum charge, as one of the means of regulation, is implied. . . . We know that this is a power which may be abused; but that is no argument against its existence. For protection against abuses by legislatures, the people must resort to the polls, not to the courts.

On the same day that the Court sustained the validity of the Illinois statute, it handed down decisions in the important cases of Peik *v.* Chicago & Northwestern R. R., Chicago, Burlington & Quincy R. R. *v.* Iowa, and Winona & St. Peter R. R. *v.* Blake. These cases involved the validity of Granger laws establishing maximum freight and passenger rates. The laws had been attacked on the ground that they violated not only the Fourteenth Amendment, but also the interstate commerce clause of the Constitution. The Court, however, sustained the validity of these laws against both charges. The railroad, said the Court,

is employed in state as well as interstate commerce, and until Congress acts, the State must be permitted to adopt such rules and regulations as may be necessary for the promotion of the general welfare of the people within its own jurisdiction, even though in so doing those without may be indirectly affected.

[3] Munn *v.* Illinois 94 U.S., 113 (1876).

These decisions gave laissez-faire the air and inaugurated the period of public regulation of public utilities. They aroused, however, a storm of protest from conservative and financial circles in the East. They were branded as socialistic and revolutionary, as irreparable blows to private enterprise. Even the liberal New York *Nation* joined the hue and cry. But despite important modifications in later decisions, the fundamental principle here announced of the right of government to control business of a public character has never been repudiated, and the Granger cases remain as landmarks in American constitutional law and in the history of public regulation.

Within a decade the composition of the Supreme Court became more conservative, and the Granger decisions were duly modified with respect to the interpretation of the commerce power and of the meaning of 'due process.' In 1886, in the Wabash case, the Court held invalid an Illinois statute prohibiting the 'long-and-short haul' evil on the ground that it infringed upon the exclusive power of Congress over interstate commerce. In the same year, in the case of Stone *v.* Farmers' Loan & Trust Co. the court intimated that the reasonableness of the rate established by a commission might be a matter for judicial determination. Three years later, in the case of Chicago, Milwaukee & St. Paul R. R. *v.* Minnesota this *obiter dictum* became the basis for a decision declaring rate regulation by a legislative commission invalid. These decisions practically put an end to state regulation of roads and rates, and placed the burden squarely upon the Federal Government. Congress responded with the Interstate Commerce Act of 1887.

5. *The Advent of Federal Regulation*

Agitation for federal rather than state regulation of railroads began with the Senate report of the Windom Committee (1874) which advocated federal construction and operation of railways to compete with the private roads. In the same year the House passed and the Senate rejected the McCrary Bill providing for federal regulation of rates charged by interstate carriers. Three years later Congressman Reagan of Texas introduced a bill looking to the elimination of railway abuses, and got it through the House in 1878, but again the Senate, influenced by a powerful railroad lobby, failed to take action.

In the meantime interest had shifted somewhat from the problem of rates to that of pooling and of discrimination. The report of the

Cullom Committee of 1886 made clear the need for immediate reform in these matters. 'The paramount evil chargeable against transportation systems,' observed the Committee, 'is unjust discrimination between persons, places, commodities, on particular descriptions of traffic.' Almost equally dangerous, in the view of the Committee, was the effect of pooling agreements in creating regional monopolies and sustaining high charges.

The Wabash decision of 1886 made Congressional action imperative. The Interstate Commerce Act of 4 February 1887 represented in its substance a compromise between the Massachusetts or supervisory type of regulation and the Granger or coercive type of regulation. It specifically prohibited pooling, rebates, discrimination of any character, and higher charges for a short haul than for a long haul. It provided that all charges should be 'reasonable and just' but failed entirely to define either of these ambiguous terms. It required the roads to post their tariffs, and established the first permanent administrative board of the American Government, the Interstate Commerce Commission, to supervise the administration of the law. Enforcement was left to the courts, but a large part of the burden of proof and prosecution was placed upon the Commission. Although the bill was popularly regarded as a victory of the public, it had the support of the railroads, and railway stocks rose in the market upon its passage.

Administrative regulations, however, were still so foreign to the American conception of government that the federal courts insisted upon their right to review orders of the Interstate Commerce Commission, and took the teeth out of the Act by a series of decisions. In the Maximum Freight Rate case (1897), the Supreme Court held that the Commission did not have the power to fix rates, and in the Alabama Midlands case of the same year it practically nullified the long-and-short-haul prohibition. It was found almost impossible to require agents of the railroads to testify about railroad malpractices, and it was customary for witnesses to introduce into the court new testimony which had been withheld from the Commission, thus requiring an entirely new adjudication of the case. Reversals of the Commission's rulings were frequent; in the entire period from 1887 to 1905 fifteen of the sixteen cases appealed to the Supreme Court were decided adversely to the Commission. Even where the rulings of the Commission were sustained it was found almost impossible for shippers to collect refunds from recalcitrant roads: down to 1897 shippers had succeeded in getting refunds in only five out of two hundred and twenty-five cases. Indeed, the roads evaded the provisions of the Act so successfully that Justice Harlan declared the Commission to be a 'useless body for all practical purposes,' and the Commission itself, in its annual report for 1898, confessed its failure. Nevertheless the principle of federal regulation of railroads was established, and the machinery for such regulation created. It remained for a later administration to apply the principle and make the machinery effective.

6. *The Decline of Steamboating*

> I saw the boat go round the bend,
> Good-by, my lover, good-by!
> All loaded down with gentlemen,
> Good-by, my lover, good-by!

The generation that flung the iron tracks across the prairies and mountains of Western America witnessed the passing of one of the most characteristic and colorful phases of American life — steamboating. From the eventful day that Henry Shreve launched the *George Washington* on the Ohio (1817), until the Civil War, steamboats were the major means of inland transportation. For fifty years the waters of the Mississippi and her tributaries floated hundreds of steamboats great and small, their main decks laden with cotton and cattle, grain and furs, and 'fellows who have seen alligators and neither fear whiskey nor gunpowder'; their upper decks, which to the simple dwellers of the valley, appeared 'Fairy structures of Oriental gorgeousness and splendor,' bearing planters, merchants, dandies, and fine ladies. Swift passenger steamers raced each other recklessly on the lazy Father of Waters or the riotous Missouri, lashing the waters into foam with their churning paddles. While the North and East followed the fortunes and compared the records of the Yankee clippers, the people of the interior bet their shirts on the *Robert E. Lee* and the *Natchez* in their historic race from New Orleans to St. Louis, won by the *Lee* in the record time of three days, eighteen hours and fourteen minutes. Mark Twain has preserved for us the talk in the pilot's Texas, the jabber of the Negro roustabouts, the glamor of gilded cabins and the tense excitement of steamboat racing, in his immortal *Life on the Mississippi*.

It was in the decade of the fifties that river traffic reached its zenith.

The value of the river trade at New Orleans was over $289,000,000 in 1860. In those piping times before the war hundreds of new steamboats were launched on the inland waters, and on the outbreak of the conflict there were over two thousand of them on the Ohio-Mississippi system alone. Before the coming of the railroads the steamboat almost succeeded in tying the upper part of the great valley to the Cotton Kingdom. At one time eighty per cent of the pork and grain from Cincinnati was floated down the Ohio, and Southern Congressmen so far waived their strict-construction principles as to vote over three million dollars for river improvements.

The greater part of the produce that came down-river was reshipped by sea to Atlantic ports and to Europe. In the 1850's the Eastern trunk lines provided a short cut, right across this roundabout route, and struck at the fancy profits of river steamboating just as on the high seas the steamships got the cream from the clipper ships. As in that rivalry, so in this, the Civil War accelerated the movement tremendously. The steamboat fought gallantly for life, readjusting itself to new circumstances, compromising with new conditions. As Mark Twain tells it:

> Boat used to land — captain on hurricane roof — mighty stiff and straight — iron ramrod for a spine — kid gloves, plug hat, hair parted behind — man on shore takes off hat and says:
>
> 'Got twenty-eight tons of wheat, cap'n — be great favor if you can take them.'
>
> Captain says:
>
> 'I'll take two of them' — and don't even condescend to look at him.
>
> But Nowadays the captain takes off his old slouch and smiles all the way around to the back of his ears, and gets off a bow which he hasn't got any ramrod to interfere with, and says:
>
> 'Glad to see you Smith, glad to see you — you're looking well — haven't seen you looking so well for years — what you got for us.'
>
> 'Nuthin,' says Smith; and keeps his hat on, and just turns his back and goes on talking with somebody else.

But the river captains were not always as unsuccessful as this. Although passenger traffic almost disappeared from the inland waters, there was an absolute, though not a relative, gain in freight traffic. In 1879 no fewer than 3,372 boats and 1,320 barges passed Winona, Minnesota, loaded down with lumber and grain, and 1880 witnessed the high-water mark of freight transportation for the lower Mississippi with over a million bales of cotton unloaded on the levee at New Orleans. After that the decline of river shipping was precipitous.

Shipping in the Great Lakes was a different story. The enormous iron ore deposits of the Lake Superior region and the products of the forests and the wonderfully productive soil of the Northwest now brought under cultivation increased Great Lakes tonnage from 500,000 in 1869 to 2,600,000 in 1920. In 1885 traffic through the Sault Ste. Marie canals amounted to 3,256,628 tons; by 1920 it had increased to 79,282,000. Both river and Great Lakes transportation of the post-Civil War period exhibited the same tendencies we have observed in the railroads: combination, absorption of the weaker by the stronger lines, local and federal aid.

With the decline of the steamboat passed another phase of American frontier life as unique and as rich as the cattle kingdom. Only a few rusty, battered stern-wheelers survive to bring down cotton, hops, and pipestaves from the tributaries, and remoter reaches of the Black, the Arkansas, and the Ouachita rivers. There, as Roark Bradford's stories remind us, we may still see the Negro roustas toting heavy burdens with their peculiar shuffling gait, the 'coonjine,' and hear them sing:

De Coonjine, jine de Coonjine!
De Coonjine, jine de Coonjine!
Roll dat cotton bale down de hill,
De Coonjine, jine de Coonjine.

VI

THE ECONOMIC REVOLUTION

1865–1900

1. *Hamilton Wins*

IT was the dream of Jefferson that his country—'with room enough for our descendants to the hundredth and thousandth generation'—was to be a great agrarian democracy. 'While we have land to labor,' he wrote, 'let us never wish to see our citizens occupied at a work bench, or twirling a distaff,' for 'those who labor in the earth are the chosen people of God.' Yet it is one of the ironies of our history that the Sage of Monticello himself, through his own pet embargo, should have given the first impetus to factory development in America, and that his own party should have passed the first protective tariff. Within two generations of Jefferson's death the value of American manufactured products was almost treble that of the agricultural, and the spokesmen of big business were appealing to his laissez-faire principles against the regulatory ideals of his rival Hamilton. For a hundred years America has progressed economically in the direction that Alexander Hamilton wished: that of a diversified, self-sufficing nation, ruled by the people who control the nation's prosperity. When the census of 1920 recorded over nine million industrial wage-earners producing commodities to the value of some sixty-two billion dollars, and over fifty per cent of the population crowded into towns and cities, surely Hamilton was able to collect some bets from Jefferson in the Elysian Fields!

By 1910 the United States, hitherto a debtor nation of extractive and predominately agricultural industry, had become the leading industrial and manufacturing power of the world; the World War made it the predominant financial power as well. The power and responsibilities that this achievement has thrust upon the United States are as yet imperfectly apprehended by her people.

What were the bases of this economic revolution? It depended to a large extent upon half a dozen obvious factors: the discovery and large-scale exploitation of natural resources such as iron ore, coal, coke, natural gas, copper, gold and silver, and oil; the application of science, invention, and machine power to the processes of extraction and manufacture; the acquisition of a labor supply sufficiently large, steady, and cheap for the purposes of industry; the construction of a transportation system adequate to the needs of an industrialized nation; the growth of the domestic market and the development of foreign markets; the creation of capital at home and the ability to borrow abroad. In addition the economic revolution was fostered and aided by the Federal Government, positively through protective tariffs and other indirect subsidies, and negatively through a policy of laissez-faire.

The consequences of this revolution are not so easy to summarize, but some of them are by now sufficiently clear. It enhanced national wealth, raised the standards of living, produced cycles of prosperity and depression with attendant periodical unemployment and emphasized class divisions in the American people. It depressed agriculture and speeded up urbanization, encouraged immigration and made possible the more rapid growth of population. It led to mechanization and standardization of social life, modified social institutions such as that of the family, and changed the intellectual outlook of the people. It brought the United States into world affairs, economically and politically, and emphasized American nationalism. It led to a concentration of wealth and placed the control of the natural resources and the machinery of production and distribution of the country in the hands of a small group of men, so creating, in a nation brought up to Jeffersonian principles, a whole series of antagonisms and difficulties on which the teachings of the Fathers threw little light, to say the least.

It is another, and cruel, irony of our history that the South which cherished the agrarian Jeffersonian tradition and which had most to fear from the industrialization of America, should have greatly accelerated its coming by her secession and the consequent Civil War.

> The Civil War [says Lewis Mumford] cut a white gash through the history of the country; it dramatized in a stroke the changes that had begun to take place during the preceding twenty or thirty years. . . . When the curtain rose on the post-bellum scene the old America was for all practical purposes demolished; industrialism had entered overnight, had transformed the practices of agriculture, had encouraged a mad exploitation of mineral, oil, natural gas and coal, and had made the unscrupulous master of finance, fat with war-profits, the central figure of the situation.[1]

Indeed it is now so evident what the Civil War accomplished in the long run that Charles and Mary Beard have gone so far as to assert

1 *The Golden Day*, pp. 158–9. Boni and Liveright.

that industrialization was the conscious purpose of the Republican party or of those who supplied the brains and the funds of the Republican party during the period of the War and Reconstruction. We can find no evidence of this nigger in the woodpile — or Ford car in the heavy artillery. No one looked forward to this end, or foresaw what was coming. It was simply another case of what Euripides said through the chorus in the Medea, twenty-four centuries ago:

> And the end men looked for cometh not,
> And a path is there where no man thought;
> So hath it fallen here.

America, where society was fluid, and neither established Church nor feudal aristocracy stood up for the ancient ways, America, where success had always been its own justification, was the land first destined for complete conquest by the industrial Moloch. Yet England, France, Germany, where all the forces of resistance were intrenched in government and society, fell; Jefferson's America must have fallen sooner or later. But the Civil War, like every great war, depressed the forces which were declining in the nation's life, and gave tenfold vigor to those which were active, vigorous, and positive.

The issue of the war, while not absolutely unfavorable to farming and the farmer class, was so highly profitable to manufacturing and finance that small-scale, subsistence farming was doomed. War needs enormously stimulated manufacturing and banking in the North, and a complaisant government prolonged the high profits of the war period with tariff and banking legislation largely dictated by the interests which were benefited. At the same time the immigration policy of the government enabled industry to import cheap labor and thus keep wages down. The construction of the great transcontinental railroads opened up new markets for exploitation and furnished employment for additional capital. Within thirty years the ultimate control of a large part of the transportation system of the country was in the hands of a few men in the East.

After all, the Civil War was a mere speeding-up process which eliminated the weak and strengthened the strong. The fundamental factors were the march of science and invention and the exploitation of new resources of iron and of power.

2. *The Age of Invention*

The United States Patent Office was created in 1790 largely through the efforts of one of the greatest American inventors, John Stevens of Hoboken, New Jersey. So numerous were the patents granted to ingenious Americans in the following years that in 1833, it was said, the head of the Patent Bureau decided to resign because he felt that everything of importance had been invented! Yet the 36,000 patents granted before 1860 were but a feeble indication of the flood of inventions that was to inundate the Patent Office in the years following the Civil War. In the period from 1860 to 1890 no less than 440,000 patents were issued, and in the first quarter of the twentieth century the number reached the staggering total of 969,428. The average number of inventions patented in any one year since 1900 exceeds the total number patented in the entire history of the country before 1860.

While the beginnings of many important inventions can be traced to the late eighteenth and early nineteenth centuries, their application on a large scale to the processes of industry and agriculture came after the Civil War. Thus James Watt in Glasgow and Oliver Evans in Philadelphia developed the steam engine before the close of the eighteenth century, but it was not until the construction of the railroad system and the introduction of the De Laval steam turbine in 1882 that steam reached its peak in American development. And even at this time, the age of electricity was portended. A hundred years earlier Franklin, Galvini, and Oersted had experimented with electricity; Michael Faraday of England and Joseph Henry of the Smithsonian Institution had developed the principle of the dynamo as early as 1831, but it was not until after 1880 that the genius of Thomas A. Edison, William Stanley, Charles Brush, and a host of others revolutionized American life with the dynamo. Thus Charles Goodyear discovered the secret of the vulcanization of rubber in 1839 but it was not until the coming of the automobile that it assumed an important place in the economic order. Elias Howe invented the sewing machine in 1846, but it did not come into general use until popularized by Isaac Singer after 1860, and was first applied to the making of shoes by Gordon McKay in 1862. Eli Whitney of cotton-gin fame adapted for firearms the revolutionary principles of standardization and interchangeability of parts as early as 1798; but the general application of this principle to manufacturing, which has given precedence to American mass production, did not come until after the achievements of Kelly, Holley, and Bessemer ushered in the age of steel; and the full meaning of it did not appear until Henry Ford reorganized the automobile industry, and Herbert Hoover became Secretary of Commerce. Dr. N. A. Otto of Germany invented the internal combustion engine in 1876, but it did not mean much to the average American until Henry Ford in 1908 placed a motor-car on the market that was not a rich man's toy but a poor man's instrument.

A reference to some of the more important inventions developed since the Civil War will indicate something of their dominant place in modern American life. In the field of railway transportation the Westinghouse air brake of 1869, the Janney automatic coupler of 1871, the interlocking block signals introduced on American railroads in 1874, and the wide use of all-steel trains after 1900 insured a higher degree of safety to passengers, while the introduction of the Pullman car, in 1864, changed traveling from an ordeal to a pleasure, and the use of refrigerator cars after 1875 revolutionized the slaughtering and meat-packing industry of the country.

At the same time other forms of transportation — the electric railway, the automobile, and the airplane — were being developed. Between 1870 and 1880 Stephen Field and Thomas A. Edison in America and the Siemens firm in Berlin were perfecting the first electric railway, and inside of ten years there were 769 miles in operation in the United States. Thus within a short time the street car, elevated and subway train, all based upon the dynamo, accelerated that concentration of population in cities which is one of the characteristics of modern America. It is one of the dramatic things in our history that the steam railway dispersed population all over the land, and the electric railway and motor-car then pulled it, for working-day purposes at least, into a few hundred civic centers, and concentrated one-twelfth of the population of this vast country in a single urban conglomeration, New York.

George Selden of Rochester, New York, had experimented with gasoline cars as early as 1879, but it was not until the turn of the century that the industry of Henry Ford and the genius of Charles Duryea bore fruit in the modern automobile. By 1920 Ford was making over six thousand cars a day in his Detroit factories, and the automobile industry ranked first in the country in the value of its finished products. 'Darius Green and his flyin' machine' was a favorite comic recitation in the gay nineties; 'God never intended man to fly' was a serious conviction in 1900. Yet the vision of Samuel P. Langley, and the perseverance of the Wright brothers and Glenn Curtiss, lifted the airplane out of the experimental stage into the practical, around 1908. Langley died broken-hearted in 1906 at the failure of his flying machine; in 1919 two Englishmen, John Alcock and Arthur Brown, made the first non-stop trans-Atlantic flight from St. Johns, Newfoundland, to Clifden, Ireland; and in 1927 Charles Lindbergh made his non-stop flight from New York to Paris.

Other forms of communication: the telegraph, the cable, the telephone, and wireless telegraphy, helped to revolutionize modern life. It was in 1844 that Samuel Morse, a Yankee painter with a flair for mechanics, flashed over the wires from Washington to Baltimore, the first telegraphic message: 'What hath God wrought!' In 1856 the Western Union Company was organized and soon the whole country was criss-crossed with a network of wires. In 1858 the duplex telegraph was invented and on the modern multiplex telegraph eight messages can be sent simultaneously on one line, and over 100,000 words transmitted within an hour. Efforts to lay a trans-Atlantic cable had gone on since 1850, but it was not until 1866, and then after repeated failures, that the courage of Cyrus Field and the faith of Peter Cooper were rewarded, and communication between Europe and America became a matter of seconds instead of days. And in 1896 the Italian, Marconi, discovered the secret of wireless telegraphy.

In the Centennial year of 1876 Emperor Dom Pedro of Brazil, attending the Philadelphia Exposition, sauntered up to the booth of young Alexander Graham Bell; he picked up the cone-shaped instrument on display there, and as he placed it to his ear Bell spoke through the transmitter. 'My God, it talks!' exclaimed His Majesty; and from that moment the telephone became the central feature of the Exposition. Within half a century sixteen million telephones had profoundly affected the economic and social life of the nation. The tempo of business life was enormously quickened, too, by the invention in 1867 of the typewriter by an erratic printer, Christopher Sholes of Milwaukee; of the cash register in 1897 by James Ritty; of the adding machine by Burroughs in 1888; of the dictaphone — an outgrowth of the phonograph — by Edison; and hundreds of other office and business accessories. The linotype composing machine invented by Ottmar Mergenthaler and first used by Whitelaw Reid in 1886 in printing the New York *Tribune,* Hoe's rotary press, the web press, and folding machinery, have made it possible to print as many as 240,000 eight-page newspapers in an hour; and the electrotype has worked a comparable change in the printing of magazines and books. This book costs you the same as a volume of Hildreth's *History of the United States* cost your grandfathers; but the printers, papermakers, binders, and others who produce it get three to five times the wages that their forbears did in 1865; the cost of selling it to you has multiplied in the same degree or more; but the authors get a smaller amount on each copy than Hildreth did on his. Such are the benefits of modern inventions!

Just as science and invention have revolutionized transportation, communication, business, and the conditions of urban living, so they have wrought profound changes in agriculture and in the daily life of the American people. Postponing to another chapter the influence of the new machinery on the development of American agriculture, we will here merely call attention to a few of the inventions that have carried the industrial revolution to the rural regions. In 1868 a Scotch immigrant, James Oliver, perfected the chilled plow; in 1873 John Appleby took out a patent for a twine binder; in 1881 Benjamin Holt turned out the first combined harvester and thresher designed for the great bonanza farms of the Far West; in 1888 A. N. Hadley invented a combined corn cutter and shocker; and after the opening of the twentieth century gasoline power was widely applied to farm machinery. Thus the industrial revolution went beyond the walls of the factory and the streets of the city and transformed the very processes and conditions of farming.

Meantime a host of inventions affected the life of the American people, especially those who flocked to the towns. The 'Wizard of Menlo,' Thomas Edison, gave the world the incandescent lamp in 1880, and within a few years it supplied millions of homes with better, safer, and cheaper light than had ever been known before. It was Edison, too, who perfected the talking machine, and in conjunction with George Eastman, developed the motion picture; two inventions that provided employment to tens of thousands, and entertainment to millions of people everywhere.

The immediate material consequences of the application of machinery and of the inventive genius to the processes of extraction and manufacture are not difficult to ascertain. Machinery, science, and invention enabled man to increase his productivity a hundred-fold and — it may be added — to exploit with hundred-fold efficiency the natural resources of the continent. Thus in 1830 it was estimated that the production of a bushel of wheat required something over three hours of human labor; by the turn of the century the application of machine labor — machine seeders and harrows, steam reapers and threshers — had reduced the time to less than ten minutes. Thus under primitive conditions of weaving it required 5605 hours of labor to produce five hundred yards of cotton sheeting; by 1900 cotton manufacturers were able to produce the same amount with only 52 hours of human labor, and in the last thirty years machinery has materially reduced even this time requirement. One hundred and fifty years ago Adam Smith celebrated the efficiency of machine production with his famous illustration of the pin. Without machinery, he observed, a workingman would need a full day to make a single pin, but machinery then enabled a workingman to manufacture five thousand pins in a single day. A century later the great economist might have pointed his moral even more effectively, for then a single workingman could supervise the manufacture on automatic machines of fifteen million pins each day.

Such illustrations could be multiplied indefinitely, but it is unnecessary to belabor a point so obvious. The economic and cultural consequences of machinery and invention, however, are less easy to determine. That improvements in the processes of manufacture produce technological unemployment cannot be denied; it is equally true that until our own generation, at least, invention and machinery created more jobs than they destroyed. It is asserted, too, that recognition of the importance of machinery has tended to subordinate men to machines and to dehumanize industry. Such a charge is not susceptible to proof and it cannot be shown that industry today is less humane than it was in the eighteenth or early nineteenth century or that other values have not compensated workingmen for the alleged blunting of the creative instinct. But if we look away from the question of cultural values to that of social consequences, it is clear that invention and scientific discoveries have presented to us a series of complex social problems and have required, inescapably, a series of readjustments.

Social institutions [observes a group of distinguished sociologists] are not easily adjusted to inventions. The family has not yet adapted itself to the factory; the church is slow in adjusting itself to the city; the law was slow in adjusting to dangerous machinery; local governments are slow in adjusting to the transportation inventions; international relations are slow in adjusting to the communication inventions; school curricula are slow in adjusting to the new occupations which machines create. There is in our social organizations an institutional inertia, and in our social philosophies a tradition of rigidity. Unless there is a speeding up of social invention or a slowing down of mechanical invention, grave maladjustments are certain to result.[2]

3. *Iron and Steel*

'The consumption of iron,' wrote the great ironmaster, Abram S. Hewitt, 'is the social barometer by which to estimate the relative height of civilization among nations.' If this is true, the progress of civilization in the United States from the Civil War to the World War was indeed remarkable. The works of man in the United States of 1860 were constructed of wood and stone, with a little brick and iron; by 1920 this had become a nation of iron, steel, and concrete. The United States of 1860 produced less than one million tons of pig-iron; sixty years later production had mounted to almost thirty-six million tons and the United States was easily foremost in the manufacture of iron and steel products among the nations of the world. This transformation resulted from the exploitation of new resources of iron, the discovery of new processes for converting it into steel, the contribution by the government of indirect subsidies in the form of a prohibitive tariff, and the rise of a group of ironmasters with a genius for organization and production.

Iron ore had been mined in the Appalachians from early colonial days; in the early nineteenth century the industry was concentrated in eastern Pennsylvania and northern New Jersey. By the middle of the century the Trenton Iron Works, controlled by the philanthropist Peter Cooper, were producing thirty-five thousand tons of iron annually, but even then the industry was moving westward to the Pittsburgh region and geologists were hunting eagerly for new iron ore deposits. In the late 1840's enormous iron ore deposits were discovered in the northern Michigan peninsula, and the year of the rush to the California gold diggings witnessed a rush to the iron ore fields around Marquette scarcely less spectacular and no less significant for American economy. But even the deposits of the Marquette and the Menominee in northern Michigan were inadequate for the needs of the American iron and steel industry. It was in 1844 that the great

[2] *Findings of the President's Research Committee on Social Trends,* vol. I, p. xxvii.

Mesabi iron range at the head of Lake Superior was first discovered, but it was not until over forty years later that the energy and faith of the Merritt family made the ore commercially available and guaranteed the supremacy of the American steel industry. For within a short time this region proved to be the greatest ore producer in the world. The ore of the Mesabi region had, in addition, two inestimable advantages: it lay on the surface of the ground and was therefore easy and cheap to mine, and it was remarkably free of those chemical impurities that made difficult conversion into steel. In 1860 the tonnage of vessels passing through the 'Soo' canal between Lakes Superior and Huron was 403,000, and in 1870 only 691,000, but in 1901 it was almost 25,000,000 and in 1920, 58,000,000, and ore furnished the bulk of these increasing burdens.

The ore fields of the Lake Superior region are hundreds of miles distant from coal deposits, but cheap lake and railway transportation brought the two together. Ore and coal met in smelters of Chicago where the first American steel rails were rolled in 1865, and in Cleveland, Toledo, Ashtabula, or Milwaukee. Much of the ore was carried to Pittsburgh, center of the great Appalachian coal fields and strategically located with reference to water and rail transportation. In the eighties the iron and coal beds of the southern Appalachians were first exploited and soon Birmingham, Alabama, became a southern rival to Pittsburgh and Chicago. The twentieth century has witnessed a great development of the industry in Colorado with apparently inexhaustible resources of minerals.

The Bessemer and open-hearth processes and the application of chemistry and electricity to the making of steel were as fundamental as the new ore beds. The Bessemer process, which consists merely in blowing air through the molten iron to drive out the impurities, was anticipated in America by William Kelly of Kentucky, a prophet without honor in his own country; but it was not until Henry Bessemer had demonstrated the utility of his process in England that American iron manufacturers adopted it. The Bessemer process gave to American steel manufacturers one incalculable advantage: it was effective only where the phosphorus content of the iron ore was less than one-half of one per cent; comparatively little of the English iron ore was thus free from phosphorus, but practically all the ore of the Lake Superior region was. By 1875 Carnegie had recognized the advantages of the Bessemer process and adopted it in his great J. Edgar Thomson steel works. Shortly after the Civil War Abram

Hewitt had introduced to this country the Siemens-Martin open-hearth method of smelting, and despite the increased time and expense it involved, the superiority of the steel it produced was soon apparent. In 1880 ten times as much steel was manufactured by the Bessemer as by the open-hearth process, but by 1910 the latter method accounted for 20,780,000 tons of steel and the Bessemer for only 10,328,000 tons. The Bessemer and open-hearth processes not only made steel of superior quality and in enormous quantities but reduced the price from $300 to $35 a ton.

The application of chemistry to steel-making introduced further economies and solved many technical problems. 'Nine-tenths of all the uncertainties were dispelled under the burning sun of chemical knowledge,' affirmed Andrew Carnegie. Finally the introduction of electric furnaces has made it possible to produce hard manganese steel for automobiles and machines and 'high-speed' steel for tools. Carnegie could boast with truth:

> Two pounds of iron stone mined upon Lake Superior and transported nine hundred miles to Pittsburgh; one pound and one-half of coal mined and manufactured into coke, and transported to Pittsburgh; one-half pound of lime, mined and transported to Pittsburgh; a small amount of manganese ore mined in Virginia and brought to Pittsburgh — and these four pounds of materials manufactured into one pound of steel, for which the consumer pays one cent.

Well might the great ironmaster congratulate himself on this combination of engineering and technical skill, science and business enterprise. By 1890 the United States had passed Great Britain in the production of pig-iron; by 1900 American furnaces produced as much steel as those of Great Britain and Germany combined; and this supremacy in iron and steel manufacture, once attained, was never surrendered. Yet it would be naïve to suppose that this supremacy was due entirely to the combination of raw materials, science, and business enterprise. An important element in the growth of the iron and steel industry was the protective tariff. From the beginning the ironmasters of Pennsylvania had insisted upon protection for their infant industry, and long after that industry had outgrown its swaddling clothes it continued to enjoy the blessings of government paternalism. It was this tariff which enabled American manufacturers to compete successfully with their English and German competitors and to pile up fabulous profits. Abram Hewitt, himself one of the greatest of the ironmasters, put the matter succinctly: 'Steel rails . . . were subject to a duty of $28 a ton. The price of foreign rails had advanced to a point where it would have paid (the manufacturer) to make rails without any duty, but of the duty of $28 a ton he added $27 to his price and transferred from the great mass of the people $50,000,000 in a few years to the pockets of a few owners who thus indemnified themselves in a very short time, nearly twice over, for the total outlay which they had made in the establishment of their business.' Even Carnegie himself, when his Company showed a profit of $40,000,000 in a single year, felt that the time had come to abandon protection.

The story of the steel industry cannot be related without reference to those Titans of industry who presided at its birth and nurtured its giant growth. Alexander Holley of Troy, New York, was the first to apply the processes of Kelly and Bessemer in America, and for a decade after the Civil War he was active in introducing these processes to steel manufacture throughout the country. Equally active in laying the foundations of the industry, and a pioneer in the use of the open-hearth process was Abram S. Hewitt of New York whose distinguished career in industry was matched by a career no less distinguished in politics. But the greatest leader in the American iron and steel industry and perhaps the most typical figure of the industrial age, was undoubtedly Andrew Carnegie. A poor emigrant boy from Scotland, he followed and helped to perpetuate the American tradition of rising from poverty to riches, and his success he ascribed entirely to the political and economic democracy which obtained in this country. By dint of unflagging industry and unrivalled business acumen and resourcefulness and especially through his extraordinary ability to choose as his associates such men as Charles Schwab, Henry Frick, and Henry Phipps, and to command the devotion of his workmen, Carnegie built up the greatest steel business in the world, and retired in 1901 to chant the glories of 'Triumphant Democracy' and to give away his enormous fortune of four and a half hundred millions. This was made possible by the sale of his holdings to a rival organization, directed by the Chicago lawyer Elbert Gary and the New York banker J. Pierpont Morgan. The result was the United States Steel Corporation, a combination of most of the important steel manufacturers in the country, capitalized at the colossal sum of $1,400,000,000 — a sum greater than the total estimated national wealth of the United States in 1800. Seven

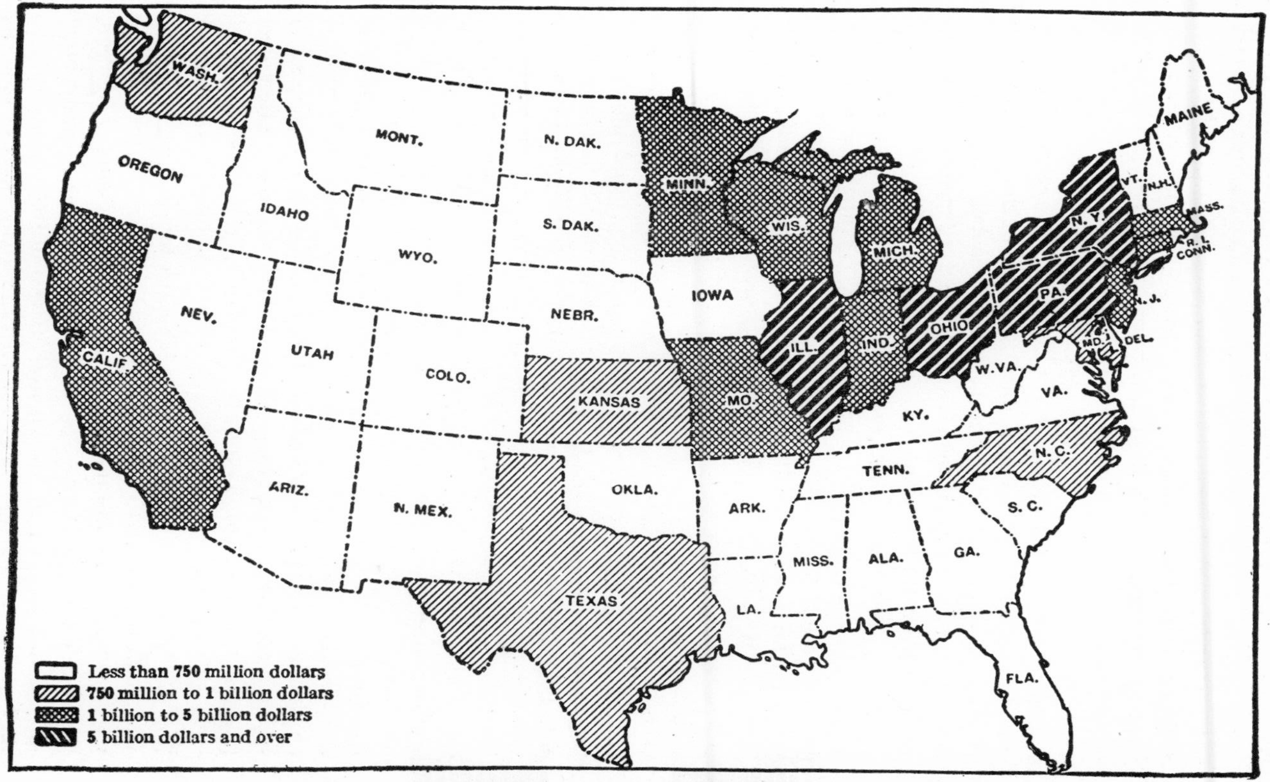

VALUE OF MANUFACTURED PRODUCTS IN 1919, BY STATES

hundred million of this capitalization was 'water,' but by 1924 the company had earned aggregate net profits of $2,108,848,640 and no one could deny that its sponsors were vindicated in their business acumen.

4. *Trusts and Monopolies*

The organization of the United States Steel Corporation in 1901 came as the climax to an economic movement which had been under way for a generation. This was the concentration of industry and transportation in large units — a concentration taking various forms such as pools, trusts, corporations, and holding companies.

The advantages of combination were numerous. It tended to eliminate competition, removing many of the hazards of unregulated competitive production, and facilitating great economies in manufacture, transportation, marketing, administration, and finance. Through combination capital reserves could be built up as a means to stabilize or expand industry. Where combination was along horizontal lines — the combination, for example, of all manufacturers of rubber or of typewriters — it was easy to control production and price. Where combination was along vertical lines — the control, by one corporation, of all the elements of raw materials, transportation, manufacture, marketing, and finance of a single product, like the Ford car — it gave a degree of independence and of power that no isolated industry could expect to enjoy. In the steel and the oil industries combination was both horizontal and vertical, and there it created industrial sovereignties as powerful as states.

The creation of an industrial monopoly did not require that all the plants under one control be concentrated at a particular place, but only that legal control be concentrated in the hands of a particular group. The legal instrument of this process was incorporation. Business corporations were not new in our history, but the widespread use of the corporate device came in the years after the Civil War. Incorporation gives permanence of life and continuity of control, elasticity and easy expansion of capital, limited liability for losses in case of disaster, the concentration of administrative authority and the diffusion of responsibility, and the 'privileges and immunities' of a 'person' in law and in interstate activities. With these immense privileges went responsibilities, but for the most part corporations chose to recollect their privileges and ignore their responsibilities until these were called to their attention by legislative or judicial bodies.[3]

Already as early as 1873 a Congressional Investigating Committee had announced that

The country is fast becoming filled with gigantic corporations wielding and controlling immense aggregations of money and thereby commanding great influence and power.

Yet at this time the trust movement was only in its infancy. In 1860, 140,433 manufacturing establishments turned out products to the value of $1,895,861,000. In 1900 the number of establishments had increased slightly to 207,514,[4] while the value of their products had increased eight-fold to $11,406,977,000. Even more illuminating are the statistics of concentration of manufacturing in particular industries. In 1860, 2116 manufacturers of agricultural machinery turned out products which averaged $9845 in value; forty years later the number of companies had been reduced by two-thirds to 715 but the average product had increased fifteen-fold. Five hundred and forty-two iron and steel companies, in 1860, produced goods with an average value of a little less than one hundred thousand dollars; by 1900 the number of companies had increased very slightly but the average product had increased more than twelve-fold. The number of establishments engaged in tanning and curing leather in 1880 was 5425; twenty years later this number had declined to 1306 but the value of the product had been multiplied five times.

If we direct our attention to the growth of large establishments at the expense of smaller ones, the statistics are equally significant. In 1904 ninety-eight per cent of all the manufacturing establishments in the country had an annual output of less than one million dollars, while but one per cent of the establishments boasted an annual output of over that sum. The former, however, turned out sixty-two per cent of the manufactured products of the country, while the latter turned out no less than thirty-eight per cent, and of these no less than thirty-three manufactured products to the value of over one hundred million dollars each. Yet even this concentration was but a faint indication of the concentration that was to come in the first quarter of the twentieth century.[5]

[3] See above p. 116 ff.

[4] The comparison here is only relatively accurate because the method of ascertaining what constituted a 'manufacturing establishment' was changed.

[5] See below, ch. 22.

The trust movement grew out of the period of fierce competition following hard upon the Civil War. Competing railways cut freight rates between important points, in the hope of obtaining the lion's share of business, until dividends ceased and railway securities became a drug on the market. The downward trend of prices from 1865 to 1895, specially marked after 1873, put a premium on labor-saving machinery, on new processes of manufacture, and on greater units of mass production, just as did the recent downward trend of 1929–35. Pooling — 'gentlemen's agreements' between rival producers or railroad directors to maintain prices and divide business, or even to pro-rate profits — was characteristic of the period after 1872. But on the whole it was found so difficult to maintain these rudimentary monopolies that a 'gentlemen's agreement' came to be defined as one that was certain to be violated. Pools were forbidden in the Interstate Commerce Act of 1887, and the prohibitions of the Sherman Law were extended to them in the Trans-Missouri Freight Association Case of 1897. By that time they were no longer necessary.

About 1880 pools began to be superseded by 'trusts,' a form of combination in which affiliated companies handed over their securities and their power to a board of trustees. A trust, according to Eliot Jones, 'may be said to exist when a person, corporation, or combination owns or controls enough of the plants producing a certain article to be able for all practical purposes to fix its price.' The first important trust was the Standard Oil Company, organized by John D. Rockefeller in 1870 and reorganized as a trust in 1882. A large measure of Rockefeller's success was due to improvements, economies, and original methods of marketing; his monopoly was secured by methods that were condemned even by the tolerant business ethics of the day, and pronounced criminal by the courts. Yet it is only fair to say that his competitors were no less unscrupulous than himself. By playing competing railways one against another, the Standard Oil trust obtained rebates from their published freight rates,[6] and even forced them to pay over to the Standard rebates from competitors' freight bills! If competing oil companies managed to stagger along under such handicaps, they were 'frozen out' by cutting prices in their selling territory until the Standard Oil had all the business. The situation was so notorious that the Hepburn Committee of New York reported in 1880 that the Standard Oil

[6] The practice of securing rebates was not original with the Standard Oil but dated back to the period of the Civil War.

owns and controls the pipe lines of the producing regions that connect with the railroads. It controls both ends of these roads. It ships 95 per cent of all the oil. . . . It dictates terms and rebates to the railroads. It has bought out and frozen out refiners all over the country. By means of the superior facilities for transportation which it thus possessed, it could overbid in the producing regions and undersell in the markets of the world. Thus it has gone on buying out and freezing out all opposition, until it has absorbed and monopolized this great traffic.

The Supreme Court of Ohio declared the trust dissolved in 1892, only to have it reorganize under the more lenient laws of New Jersey a few years later.

The Standard Oil trust was soon followed by a number of similar business combinations. The movement for consolidation gathered momentum in the eighties and early nineties, and reached its climax in the piping years of prosperity around the Spanish War. Altogether in this period something over 5000 industrial establishments were consolidated into about 300 trusts or corporations, and of these no less than 198 were formed in the period from 1898 to 1902. The combined capitalization of the consolidations formed in the single year of 1899 was no less than $2,243,995,000 — a sum greater than the total national debt at the time. The most important of the industrial combinations, besides the Standard Oil Co. and the United States Steel Corporation, were the Amalgamated Copper Co., the American Sugar Refining Co., the American Tobacco Co., the United States Rubber Co., the United States Leather Co., the International Harvester Co., and the Pullman Palace Car Co., no one of which had a capitalization under fifty million dollars.

Nor was the process of combination confined to the field of industrial manufacturing. In the exploitation of natural resources of coal, iron, oil, gas, copper, and timber, in transportation by land and by sea, in communication by telegraph and by telephone, in banking and finance, the same inevitable tendency toward combination and concentration was discernible. In no field was it more impressive, nor were its consequences more serious, than in transportation. By the turn of the century the major part of the railroad mileage and the railroad business of the country was in the hands of six groups: the Morgan and the Morgan-Belmont group controlling 24,035 miles, the Harriman group with 20,245 miles, the Vanderbilt group with 19,517 miles, the Pennsylvania group with 18,220 miles, the Gould group with 16,074 widely scattered miles, and the Hill group with

COMMUNITY OF INTEREST AMONG RAILROADS IN THE UNITED STATES

Lines	Miles
I.—Vanderbilt Group	
New York Central lines	10,016
Delaware, Lackawanna and Western	951
Chicago and Northwestern	8,550
	19,517
II.—Morgan Group	
Southern Railway	6,807
Mobile and Ohio	879
Queen and Crescent	1,115
Central of Georgia	1,835
Georgia Southern and Florida	285
Macon and Birmingham	97
Philadelphia and Reading	1,891
Lehigh Valley	1,404
Erie	2,271
Central of New Jersey	677
Atlantic Coast Line	1,812
	19,073
III.—Harriman Group	
Illinois Central	5,000
Union Pacific	3,029
Oregon Railroad and Navigation Co.	1,137
Oregon Short Line	1,498
Chicago and Alton	918
Southern Pacific	7,723
Kansas City Southern	833
Chicago Terminal Transfer	107
	20,245
IV.—Pennsylvania Group	
Pennsylvania system	10,031
Buffalo, Rochester and Pittsburg	650
Western New York and Pennsylvania	633
Chesapeake and Ohio	1,476
Norfolk and Western	1,671
Baltimore and Ohio system	3,156
Long Island	603
	18,220

Lines	Miles
V.—Gould Group	
Missouri Pacific	5,326
Texas and Pacific	1,599
St. Louis and Southwestern	1,265
International and Great Northern	825
Denver and Rio Grande	1,675
Missouri, Kansas and Texas	2,423
Rio Grande Western	603
Wabash	2,358
	16,074
VI.—Hill Group	
Great Northern	5,185
Northern Pacific	5,188
	10,373
VII.—Belmont Group	
Louisville and Nashville	3,235
Nashville, Chattanooga and St. Louis	1,195
	4,430
VIII.—Belmont-Morgan	
Georgia Railroad	307
Atlanta and West Point	87
Western of Alabama	128
	532
IX.—Independent Systems	
Seaboard Air Line	2,591
Plant System	2,170
Chicago, Milwaukee and St. Paul	6,592
Rock Island	3,819
Chicago, Burlington and Quincy	8,070
Atchison, Topeka and Santa Fe	7,808
St. Louis and San Francisco (K. C. M. & B.)	3,000
Chicago & Great Western	1,023
Colorado Southern	1,142
Pere Marquette	1,762
	37,977

SUMMARY

Groups	Mileage	Groups	Mileage
Vanderbilt	19,517	Belmont	4,430
Morgan	19,073	Belmont-Morgan	532
Harriman	20,245		
Pennsylvania	18,220		108,464
Gould	16,074	Independent	37,977
Hill	10,373		

From, *Final Report* of Industrial Commission of 1900, p. 308.

10,373 miles of track flung across the Great Northwest. Of the total railway mileage in the country only some forty thousand was still in the hands of independents. So, too, with other forms of transportation and communication: the expressing business of the country was apportioned out between three companies which by their united influence prevented the United States mails from taking parcels until 1912; the Western Union, until the rise of the Postal Telegraph, had a virtual monopoly on the telegraph business of the nation; and the American Telephone and Telegraph Co., capitalized in 1900 at one-quarter of a billion dollars, was already on its way to becoming the greatest of modern combinations.

These facts and figures spelled the doom of local industry, of the local self-sufficient community. They bespoke the concentration of manufacturing in large corporation-owned factories where economies could be attained through the elimination of unnecessary duplication and centralized control. They revealed an ever-increasing specialization in industry, both of the community and of the individual laborer and indicated an ever-increasing burden upon the transportation system of the country and greatly increased costs of distribution. The economic implications of these developments are writ large in the census reports; the social implications can best be read in such novels as Louis Bromfield's *Green Bay Tree,* or in Sherwood Anderson's *Poor White:*

In the days before the coming of industry, before the time of the mad awakening, the towns of the Middle West were sleepy places devoted to the practice of the old trades, to agriculture and merchandising. In the morning the men of the towns went forth to work in the fields or to the practice of the trade of carpentry, horse-shoeing, wagon-making, harness repairing, and the making of shoes and clothing. They read books and believed in a God born in the brains of men who came out of a civilization much like their own. On the farms and in the houses in the towns the men and women worked together toward the same ends in life. They lived in small frame houses set on the plains like boxes, but very substantially built. The carpenter who built a farmer's house differentiated it from the barn by putting what he called scroll work up under the eaves and by building at the front a porch with carved posts. After one of the poor little houses had been lived in for a long time, after the children had been born and men had died, after men and women had suffered and had moments of joy together in the tiny rooms under the low roofs, a subtle change took place. The houses became almost beautiful in their old humanness. Each of the houses began vaguely to shadow forth the personality of the people who lived within its walls. . . . A sense of quiet growth awoke in sleeping minds. It was the time for art and beauty to awake in the land.

Instead the giant, Industry, awoke. Boys, who in the schools had read of Lincoln, walking for miles through the forest to borrow his first book . . . began to read in the newspapers and magazines of men who by developing their faculty for getting and keeping money had become suddenly and overwhelmingly rich. Hired writers called these men great, and there was no maturity of mind in the people with which to combat the force of the statement, often repeated. . . .

Out through the coal and iron regions of Pennsylvania into Ohio and Indiana, and on westward into the States bordering on the Mississippi River, industry crept. . . .

A vast energy seemed to come out of the breast of the earth and infect the people. Thousands of the most energetic men of the Middle States wore themselves out in forming companies, and when the companies failed, immediately formed others. In the fast-growing towns, men who were engaged in organizing companies representing a capital of millions lived in houses thrown hurriedly together by carpenters who, before the time of the great awakening, were engaged in building barns. It was a time of hideous architecture, a time when thought and learning paused. Without music, without poetry, without beauty in their lives or impulses, a whole people, full of the native energy and strength of lives lived in a new land, rushed pell-mell into a new age.[7]

5. *Trust Regulation*

It was not until the eighties that the American public began to demand effective regulation of trusts; and the problem of regulation was seriously complicated by the federal form of government. Corporations are chartered by the states, not the nation. The constitutions of many states contained general prohibitions of monopolies or conspiracies in restraint of trade, but such prohibitions were singularly ineffective, especially after the federal courts began to interpret broadly the interstate commerce clause of the Constitution and the first article of the Fourteenth Amendment. A corporation chartered by one state has the right to do business in every other. Hence it was easy for corporations to escape the restrictions and limitations of strict state laws by incorporating in states such as New Jersey, West Virginia, or Delaware where the laws as to issuing stock, accountability of directors, and the like were very lax. Furthermore a cor-

[7] *Poor White*, pp. 131 ff., by permission of the author and the publishers.

poration is a 'person' before the law, and enjoys the inestimable privilege of protection by the Federal Government from state legislation which might be thought to deprive it of property 'without due process of law.' And in its ordinary operations the average corporation came into contact only with state and municipal governments. Railway companies, except certain transcontinental lines, obtained all their privileges from the states, and were taxed only by them, but where they engaged in interstate commerce they could not be regulated by the states nor, after the Fourteenth Amendment, could they be assessed a confiscatory or even a punitive tax. Lighting and water companies, and street railways, on the other hand, depended for their very existence on municipalities. Hence the corrupt alliance that was cemented after the Civil War between politics and business. Plain bribery was often practiced with municipal councils, which gave away for nothing franchises worth millions, while their cities remained unpaved, ill-lit, and inadequately policed. As Brand Whitlock, reform mayor of Toledo, observed:

> Out of these privileges to conduct public utilities, e.g., privileges to absorb social values, enormous fortunes were made, with all the evils that come with a vulgar newly rich plutocracy. To keep, extend, and renew these privileges, they must have their lawyers, and their newspapers to mislead and debauch the public mind; they must go into politics, organize and control the machines of both parties, bribe councilmen and legislators and jurors; and even have judges on the bench subservient to their will, so that the laws of the state and the grants of the municipality might be construed in their favor.

Opposition to trusts and monopolies, however, was not aroused so much by corruption and dishonest practices, which were looked upon with a leniency characteristic of the American people, as by the fear that the natural resources of the country were being ruthlessly exploited and rapidly exhausted by a group of men who used them for the aggrandizement of their own fortunes. Equally effective was the hostility of labor to powerful corporations, the opposition of the small businessman who in many instances was faced with the choice of surrender or ruin, and the widespread disapproval of the growth of great fortunes and the concentration of wealth.

> All who recall the conditions of the country in 1890 [said Mr. Justice Harlan in the Standard Oil case] will remember that there was every-

where among the people generally a deep feeling of unrest. The nation had been rid of human slavery . . . but the conviction was universal that the country was in real danger from another kind of slavery, namely the slavery that would result from the aggregation of capital in the hands of a few . . . controlling, for their own advantage exclusively, the entire business of the country, including the production and sale of the necessities of life.

In the eighties began the first concerted attack upon monopolies and upon the theory and practice of laissez-faire behind which monopolies flourished. This attack had been anticipated by such radicals as Wendell Phillips and Peter Cooper, but the animadversions of Henry George, Edward Bellamy, and Henry Demarest Lloyd reached a wider audience and inspired a more effective protest. Soon the spokesmen of labor, which found itself at an enormous disadvantage in bargaining with gigantic corporations, took up the cry and, supported by independent producers and by many plain people, forced the issue into politics. The Populist party was the first instrument of control, and Populist sentiment forced a dozen Southern and Western state legislatures to enact anti-trust laws. President Cleveland forced the issue to the front in his tariff message of 1887 and the next year stressed it with even greater urgency.

As we view the achievements of aggregated capital [he wrote] we discover the existence of trusts, combinations and monopolies, while the citizen is struggling far in the rear or is trampled to death beneath an iron heel. Corporations which should be carefully restrained creatures of the law and servants of the people, are fast becoming the people's masters.

And that same year the platforms of both the major parties pledged them to oppose trusts and monopolies.

The result of this widespread opposition was the Sherman Anti-Trust Act of 1890. This famous law, the joint product of Senators Sherman of Ohio, Edmunds of Vermont, Hoar of Massachusetts, and George of Mississippi, passed Congress by an almost unanimous vote and received the signature of President Harrison 2 July 1890. Its central provisions are to be found in the first two articles:

1. Every contract, combination in the form of trust or otherwise, or conspiracy, in restraint of trade or commerce among the several States, or with foreign nations is hereby declared to be illegal. . . .

2. Every person who shall monopolize, or attempt to monopolize . . .

any part of the trade or commerce among the several States, or with foreign nations, shall be deemed guilty of a misdemeanor. . . .

It is somewhat difficult to determine what was the precise purpose of this bill. It was alleged at the time that the purpose of the Act was to give to the federal courts common law jurisdiction over the crime of monopoly and conspiracy in restraint of trade; if so the law should have been interpreted in accordance with common law precedents to the effect that only *unreasonable* restraints of trade, or monopolies contrary to public interest, were illegal. But there are no such qualifications in the provisions of the Act itself. Nor are there any definitions of the terms 'trust,' 'conspiracy,' and 'monopoly,' while the term 'in the form of trust or otherwise' left much to the imagination. The student must conclude that the provisions of the Act were purposely couched in general and indefinite terms, leaving to the courts the tasks of interpreting and applying them. In thus placing responsibility upon the courts the legislators evaded the problem, and put off its solution indefinitely, for the courts were, for over a decade, singularly ineffective. Indeed, the Sherman law, as a weapon against trusts, proved a broken reed.

The first important case involving the interpretation and application of the anti-trust law was that instituted by the Government against the whisky trust. This suit, United States *v.* Greenhut, was summarily dismissed by the Court on the ground that no restraint of trade had been proven. Discouraged by this rebuff, the Government abandoned the prosecution of the whisky trust and allowed an indictment against the cash register trust to lapse. The attempt to dissolve the powerful sugar trust met with a similar fate. In this case, United States *v.* E. C. Knight and Co., 1895, the Supreme Court held that the mere control of ninety-eight per cent of the sugar refining of the country did not in itself constitute an act in restraint of trade, since trade was merely incidental to manufacture. The vigorous dissenting opinion of Mr. Justice Harlan was fraught with significance, for he warned that

Interstate traffic . . . may pass under the absolute control of overshadowing combinations having financial resources without limit and audacity in the accomplishment of their objects that recognizes none of the restraints of moral obligations controlling the action of individuals; combinations governed entirely by the law of greed and selfishness — so powerful that no single State is able to overthrow them and give the required protection to the whole country, and so all-pervading that they threaten the integrity of our institutions.

But the Government was not similarly concerned, and Attorney-General Olney wrote complacently, 'You will observe that the government has been defeated in the Supreme Court on the trust question. I always supposed it would be, and have taken the responsibility of not prosecuting under a law I believed to be no good.'

Obviously, when the Attorney-General came so near as this to sabotaging the Sherman law, it could not be effective. In case after case the courts emasculated or nullified the act, leading Theodore Roosevelt to declare, later, that the 'courts . . . had for a quarter of a century been . . . the agents of reaction and by conflicting decisions which, however, in their sum total were hostile to the interests of the people, had left both the Nation and the States well-nigh impotent to deal with the great business combinations.' Yet responsibility for the failure of the anti-trust act should not be charged exclusively to the judiciary. The legislature failed to amend the act; the Executive failed to enforce it. Altogether only seven suits under the Sherman Act were instituted by Harrison, eight by Cleveland, and three by McKinley; by contrast it may be noted that Roosevelt instituted forty-four and Taft eighty suits against trusts. Only when the law was applied to labor unions — happily embraced in the term 'or otherwise' — was it effective; here the Government won many a famous victory. But more business combinations were formed during the McKinley administration than in any years of our history, and it remained for the administrations of Roosevelt, Taft, and Wilson to discover whether the American people would be able to control them.

VII

LABOR

1865–1933

1. *General Considerations*

THE efforts of society and government to adjust themselves to the rise of big business and the nationalization of industry were energetic and fairly effective; the efforts of labor to effect a similar adjustment were convulsive but singularly ineffective. American labor was unable to achieve any satisfactory adjustment to industrial capitalism, largely because it was unable to act as a unit or to agree upon the nature of the problem, the instrument of action, or the proper objectives. Throughout the past century labor has contended among itself whether to accept or reject capitalism, whether to welcome or to sabotage inventions, whether to trust laissez-faire or seek government patronage, whether to organize on a broadly industrial or on a narrow craft basis.

Although labor is fundamental to industry, the labor problem has been set by industry rather than the other way around. From the beginning of the industrial revolution in America, labor has been exposed to a series of influences that conditioned if they did not absolutely fix the course of its development. Some of these influences dated back to the beginnings of the factory system; others appeared in more recent years; all have made themselves felt with augmented force in the period after 1890. Among these influences the most important were the increased mechanization of industry, the evolution of the giant corporation as an employer, the nationalization of industry and of the transportation system, the decline of agriculture as a potential safety valve, the change in the character of immigration, and a popular psychology which regarded unsympathetically the efforts of labor to achieve its objectives and which persistently refused to regard the labor problem realistically, or to admit that class lines could exist.

The benefits of the application of science and invention to industry have redounded to the advantage of society as a whole, but especially to capital, rather than to labor. Machinery has made enormous savings in manufacturing, and a vast increase in productivity, but only a small proportion of these savings has been passed on to labor in the form of wages, and the decrease in the hours of labor has not kept pace with the increase in productivity. Such decreases as have been wrested from employers have been in part nullified by the increasing fatigue and nervous strain of modern machine labor. As early as 1886 the United States Commissioner of Labor, Carroll Wright, observed that 'If the question should be asked, has the wage-earner received his equitable share of the benefits derived from the introduction of machinery, the answer must be, no,' and not until fifty years later was there any justification for an answer to the contrary.

That the increasing mechanization of industry had in general the effect of lowering the standards and the position of skilled labor, there seems to be no reason to doubt. The skill and experience of the craftsman no longer had their old-time value or gave the skilled worker any considerable advantage over the unskilled. It takes little training to tend machines. In 1922 Henry Ford estimated that forty-three per cent of the jobs in his automobile factories required only one day of training, and only fifteen per cent of the jobs required as much as one month of training. It was because artisans recognized that machinery threatened their only asset — skill — that they turned, in self-protection, to organization along craft lines. It is suggestive that it was from the ranks of such groups as the shoemakers, tailors, iron-moulders, typesetters, stone-cutters, cigar-makers, and machinists, that the impetus for organization first came. The Knights of St. Crispin, for example, was composed of shoemakers, the National Labor Union was organized by iron-moulders, and the Knights of Labor by garment-cutters, while the American Federation of Labor had its genesis among cigar-makers.

As machinery came to represent a large part of capital investment, it was thought necessary to accommodate the worker to machinery rather than machinery to the worker. Thus if economy required that machines be run twenty-four hours a day and seven days a week, the workers were expected to adjust themselves to that requirement regardless of the social desirability of such a schedule. Furthermore machinery constituted a fixed capital charge which could not well be reduced; when economies were necessary there was a temptation to effect them at the expense of labor. Finally the introduction of increasingly efficient machinery resulted in throwing large groups of laborers out of work. While most of these were eventually absorbed in other industries, the process worked severe hardship on the individual laborer and was accompanied by a staggering social waste. At the same time the increasing efficiency of machinery sometimes resulted in the production of more commodities than the public could or cared to buy, and thus in creating unemployment or in lowering the wages and standards of labor. Industrial unemployment is a product of the machine age, and has grown proportionately with the development of a machine economy.

The rise of the giant corporation as employer had for labor consequences almost as serious as those which flowed from the mechanization of industry. Such corporations subjected the laborer to a new set of circumstances, impersonal and complex as those introduced by the machine. The fiction that a corporation was a person had a certain legal usefulness, but every laborer knew that the distinguishing characteristic of a corporation was precisely its impersonality. A person was responsible for his acts to his own conscience; a corporation was responsible to its stockholders. As individuals, the directors of a corporation might be willing to make concessions to labor, even at personal sacrifice; but as directors they could not indulge themselves in this pleasure, for their first duty was to maintain dividend payments. Stockholders, too, might be willing to make concessions, but the gap between ownership and management was so great, and the machinery for bridging that gap so cumbersome, that it was almost impossible for stockholder opinion to become articulate or effective.

It was in relation to the bargaining power of labor that the change from individual employer to impersonal corporation was most keenly felt. It was one thing for an iron-puddler in the mid-nineteenth century to strike a bargain about wages and hours with the owner of a small iron works; it was a very different thing for a 'roller' in the twentieth century to strike a bargain with the United States Steel Corporation. Theodore Roosevelt put the matter with characteristic clarity:

The old familiar relations between employer and employee were passing. A few generations before, the boss had known every man in his shop; he called his men Bill, Tom, Dick, John; he inquired after their wives and babies; he swapped jokes and stories and perhaps a bit of tobacco with them. In the small establishment there had been a friendly human relationship between employer and employee.

There was no such relation between the great railway magnates, who controlled the anthracite industry, and the one hundred and fifty thousand men who worked in their mines, or the half million women and children who were dependent upon these miners for their daily bread. Very few of these mine workers had ever seen, for instance, the president of the Reading Railroad. . . . Another change . . . was a crass inequality in the bargaining relation between the employer and the individual employee standing alone. The great coal-mining and coal-carrying companies, which employed their tens of thousands, could easily dispense with the services of any particular miner. The miner, on the other hand, could not dispense with the companies. He needed a job; his wife and children would starve if he did not get one. What the miner had to sell — his labor — was a perishable commodity; the labor of today — if not sold — was lost forever. Moreover, his labor was not like most commodities — a mere thing; it was part of a living, breathing human being. The workman saw that the labor problem was not only an economic but also a moral, a human problem.[1]

It was in response to this situation that laborers organized 'to secure,' as Roosevelt says, 'not only their economic but their simple human rights.' Here, too, the giant corporations possessed immense advantages not vouchsafed to the small employers. Great corporations representing the combined wealth and strength of scores of companies and thousands of stockholders could afford to fight a strike for months, to import strike-breakers, to hire Pinkerton detectives, to carry their battles through the courts with high-paid lawyers, to buy the press and influence politicians, and, if necessary, to close down their plants and starve the workers into submission. Until the rise of the C. I. O. labor was least successful in building up and maintaining unions in those industries dominated by great corporations — the coal, the iron and steel, the oil, and the automobile industries.[2]

At the same time the rise of the giant corporation led to the development of an industrial dominion menacing not only to labor but to American society. The enormous wealth of corporations enabled them to acquire not only mining or manufacturing properties, but not infrequently whole towns and counties, so that they became, to all intents and purposes, sovereignties within states. Many textile companies in the South came to own the villages in which mills are located — the streets, houses, stores, schools, churches, and utilities, and to control, inevitably, the local administration and police; the inhabitants of such mill villages, most of them operatives in the mills, could remain and work only on sufferance of the mill

[1] *Theodore Roosevelt: An Autobiography,* pp. 470–71. N. Y., Charles Scribner's Sons.

[2] Railroads, where the Four Brotherhoods were strong, furnish an exception to this generalization.

owners. Similar conditions, in even more aggravated form, were to be found in Colorado, Kentucky, and Pennsylvania mining communities and in many of the lumber camps of the South and the West. In 1914 a United States Congressman testified that he had to have a pass to enter one of the towns of Colorado situated on the property of the Colorado Fuel and Iron Company; in the 1920's the Constitution was suspended in Harlan County, Kentucky, and as late as 1933 the Secretary of Labor, Frances Perkins, was forcibly prevented from speaking in the streets of a Pennsylvania coal town. Thus there developed in certain major industries a species of industrial feudalism in which the laborer occupied a position less secure than that enjoyed by the medieval serf.

In two ways the nationalization of industry and transportation operated to the disadvantage of labor. It made labor competition nationwide, and tended to establish labor standards at the lowest common denominator. With flexibility of capital and an efficient transportation system, it became possible for some industries to take advantage of cheap labor wherever it was available and thus largely to eliminate the influence of local conditions and to nullify the gains which labor might make under such conditions. The shift of the textile industry from New England to the South is a case in point, but such shifts were not generally necessary. Labor was as mobile as capital, and the importations of cheap labor from southern Europe to the industrial East, and of cheap Negro labor from the South to the North, were continuous and effective. In the second place the nationalization of industry and transportation and the growing interdependence of industries, tended to make labor disturbances national rather than local in character, thus bringing into play forces of public opinion and of government more likely to be hostile to labor than to capital. A reduction of wages in a single corporation might affect tens of thousands of workers in widely separated parts of the country and a strike against a corporation, such as the Pullman strike of 1894 or the coal strike of 1902 or the steel strike of 1919 or the automobile strike of 1936, affected not only the workers and stockholders in that industry but the workers and stockholders in scores of related industries, and became, inevitably, a matter of grave national concern. Thus the three great railroad strikes of 1877, 1894, and 1922 were all national in character and in effect, and on each occasion the Federal Government intervened in a manner harmful to the interests of the strikers.

The extent to which agriculture and the frontier functioned as safety valves for labor discontent is difficult to determine. Probably only a comparatively small percentage of discontented laborers actually threw up their jobs and trekked to the open lands of the West. There is little evidence that the existence of cheap agricultural land operated in any effective fashion to raise wages or standards of labor. For the workingman, indeed, the alternative between industrial labor and farming was rarely a very real one; after 1865, it became even more unreal. Throughout the period of industrialism, from the eighteen-thirties to the present, the movement of population from the country to the city has been greater than the movement from the city to the country, and it may be supposed that the movement from agriculture to industry has been at least as great as that from industry to agriculture.

Yet despite these necessary qualifications of the safety-valve theory, the significance of open land to labor must not be ignored. Agriculture and the frontier constituted, throughout the nineteenth century, a potential alternative to industrial labor, and it was an alternative that was accepted by many. The real significance of the frontier to labor is that it attracted to agriculture millions of immigrants and discontented or adventurous farmers and townsmen from the East and the South, who might otherwise have been forced into the ranks of industrial labor. The passing of good cheap farming land in the nineties, the increasing specialization and mechanization of agriculture, the rising investment and overhead charges and the declining economic and social returns, all combined to eliminate agriculture as an effective alternative to industrial labor for the immigrant and for the farmers of the East in the twentieth century. The 'new immigrants' from Russia and Italy and Austria settled down in the mining and industrial regions of the East; the sons and daughters of Eastern and Southern farmers moved to the city instead of going West. Both groups swelled the ranks of industrial labor and made the labor problem increasingly acute.

Immigration, indeed, presented the most serious problem with which labor had to contend. In the single generation from 1880 to 1910 almost eighteen million persons entered the United States; most of the men were farmers or unskilled laborers from the countries of southern and eastern Europe. Unable or unwilling to undertake farming, these 'new immigrants' took what work they could find in the factories, shops, or mines of the North. Even subtracting the number of immigrants who returned to their Old World homes and the women and children who did not enter industry, there remained several hundred thousand industrial workers who annually had to be absorbed into the body of American labor. Since the majority of these new recruits to American labor were unskilled they formed a body of cheap laborers whose presence tended to depress labor standards. This danger might have been in part mitigated by skillful organization, but such organization was not effected, partly because labor unions made but feeble effort to attract the unskilled or semi-skilled immigrant and partly because of the racial and religious antagonisms that embittered relations between native and foreign-born workers and between various emigrant groups. Labor has experienced its most serious difficulties in those industries where the proportion of foreign-born workers is highest — the meat-packing, iron and steel, and mining industries. Organized labor has always recognized in unrestricted immigration the most serious threat to its progress, and the persistent demand for immigration restriction has come largely from labor.

Finally the development of labor and the solution of the labor problem has been conditioned by public opinion. The tradition that America was a land of equal opportunity for all, that in America there were not and never would be any classes, and that here any laboring man could rise by his own efforts — the tradition, in short, of rugged individualism and laissez-faire — was a very tenacious one. The average American looked with suspicion upon any tendency to consider the problems of labor as distinct from those of capital or to develop class consciousness among workingmen, and he regarded with positive distrust the entry of labor into politics.

These attitudes were reasonable, and even wholesome, but from them flowed certain corollaries distinctly injurious to the interests of labor. Throughout the nineteenth century there was widespread hostility toward labor unions and the closed shop, and even so liberal a man as President Eliot of Harvard could assert that the closed shop was un-American. The strike, which as late as the 1840's was regarded as a conspiracy against public interest, continued to be in bad odor, and in 1886 the New York banker Henry Clews identified the strike with treason. 'Strikes may have been justifiable in other nations,' he said, 'but they are not justifiable in our country. The Almighty has made this country for the oppressed of other nations and therefore this is the land of refuge . . . and the hand of the laboring man should not be raised against it.' If the strike was looked upon as unpatriotic, picketing and the boycott were regarded as downright illegal, and labor has only recently won immunity from judicial interference with the use of these weapons.

The climate of opinion in which these ideas flourished was hostile to organized labor, but not until comparatively recent years was that climate moderated by new intellectual currents. Meantime there developed in the nineteenth century a double standard of social morality for labor and capital. Combination of capital was regarded as in accordance with natural laws; combination of labor as a conspiracy. Monopoly was good business, and business men denounced or evaded the Sherman Act, but the closed shop was un-American. It was the duty of government to aid business and to protect business interests, but government aid to labor was socialistic. That business should go into politics was common sense, but that labor should go into politics was contrary to the American tradition. Property had a natural right to a fair return on its value, but the return which labor might enjoy was to be regulated strictly by the law of supply and demand. Appeals to protect or enhance property interests were reasonable, but appeals to protect or enhance labor interests were demagogic. Brokers who organized business combines were respectable public servants, but labor organizers were agitators. The use of Pinkerton detectives to protect business property was preserving law and order, but the use of force to protect the job was violence. To curtail production in the face of an oversupply of consumers' goods was sound business practice, but to strike for shorter hours in the face of an oversupply of labor was unsound. The list might be extended, but the principle is more interesting than the practice. The double standard was illogical, but it was real, and labor had the choice of conforming to it, defying it, or changing it. Conformation was not to be expected, and defiance was generally suicidal, so labor naturally directed its efforts toward changing it. The story of the gradual modification of this double standard can be read in the history of labor organization and in the record of social legislation of state and federal governments over the past fifty years.

2. *The Rise of Organized Labor*

Organized labor passed through phases of bewildering complexity before it won the power to meet organized capital on nearly equal terms. There was little continuity of personnel with the ante-bellum period: wage-earners of the forties had largely become farmers, shopkeepers, and small capitalists by the seventies. Their places were taken by farmers' sons, discharged soldiers lured by the attractions of urban life, and a new wave of immigrants, continental rather than British. Ignorant of what had been tried before, the American labor leaders passed through the same cycle of experiment as in the thirties and forties. There were national trade unions and local trade unions, efforts to escape from the established order through co-operation, to ameliorate it by devices like the single tax, to break it down with socialism, political parties, and attempts to form one big union. Yet in spite of European dilution, the ideas of Marx, Lassalle, and Bakunin exerted less influence than did those of Owen, Cabet, and Fourier in the forties.

Labor began to turn away from Utopian escapes and humanitarian panaceas to the more practical agencies of trade unionism and collective bargaining as early as 1850 when the National Typographical Union was founded. Within a few years the hat-finishers, stone-cutters, iron-puddlers, and machinists had perfected national organizations. These and other national unions were in a flourishing condition in the early years of the fifties, but the panic of 1857 devitalized the entire labor movement, and by 1861 only a few struggling unions maintained a precarious existence.

The Civil War speed-up to industrial development created new opportunities for labor organization, while the sky-rocketing cost of living and currency inflation made organization imperative, if labor wished to protect the gains which war demands made possible. A score new craft unions were established and workingmen experimented with local trade assemblies representing different crafts. By 1863 these mixed assemblies of trades' councils had been established in all the larger cities of the East and the next year witnessed the brief appearance of an International (Canadian and United States) Industrial Assembly. More important were the new labor organizations that appeared shortly after the war: the National Labor Union, founded at Baltimore in 1866, the Knights of St. Crispin, established in Milwaukee the following year, and the Knights of Labor, founded in 1869.

The National Labor Union was a curious conglomeration of trades' assemblies, national and local unions, farmers' societies, women's suffrage leagues, and various other reform groups with a program as miscellaneous as its membership. It lasted only six years, but attained a maximum membership of over six hundred thousand and helped to push through two laudable pieces of federal legislation: the eight-hour law for employees on government works, and the repeal of the Contract Labor law of 1864. The Knights of St. Crispin, a shoemakers' union, had some fifty thousand members, scattered from Massachusetts to Wisconsin. Its policy was reactionary and unsuccessful, for it tried to maintain the old apprenticeship system under gild control, and opposed the introduction of shoe machinery.

By far the most important of the early labor organizations was the Noble Order of the Knights of Labor, founded in 1869 by a Philadelphia tailor, Uriah S. Stephens. Native-American in leadership and largely in personnel, it was an attempt to unite the workers of America into one big union, under centralized control. Membership was open to all workers — men and women, white and black, skilled and unskilled, laborers and capitalists, merchants and farmers. Only liquor dealers, professional gamblers, lawyers and bankers were excluded! The professed object of the order was 'To secure to the toilers a proper share of the wealth that they create; more of the leisure that rightfully belongs to them; more societary advantages; more of the benefits, privileges, and emoluments of the world; in a word, all those rights and privileges necessary to make them capable of enjoying, appreciating, defending, and perpetuating the blessings of good government.' The Order hoped to secure these laudable but somewhat vague ends by co-operation, arbitration of industrial disputes, an eight-hour day, the abolition of child labor, and many other social and economic reforms that were eventually incorporated into state and federal laws and accepted by even the most conservative.

The growth of the Knights of Labor was nothing short of phenomenal. When a Pennsylvania machinist named Terence V. Powderly became Grand Master in 1878, the membership was under fifty thousand. Powderly was an idealist who disliked the tactics of combative unionism, but it was the fate of the Order to become powerful not through co-operation, but by winning a great railroad strike in the Southwest in 1884. Capital then, for the first time, met labor on equal terms, when the New York financier, Jay Gould, conferred with the Knights' executive board and conceded their demands. The prestige of this victory was so great that the Order reached a membership of over 700,000 the following year. The Knights helped to push the Chinese Exclusion Act through Congress in 1882, and were largely responsible for the law of 1885 forbidding the importation of contract labor.

Parallel with the rise of the Knights of Labor, non-political trade unions of skilled workers grew and multiplied, as did a few unions affiliated with the 'Black' International, an anarchistic organization introduced into the United States in the early eighties by the German Johann Most. Knights of Labor, trade unions, and socialist unions struck for the eight-hour day in 1886, when the country was prosperous and business was booming. The spectacular event of this great upheaval was the Haymarket bomb explosion in Chicago. A long-drawn out strike in the McCormick Harvester Company culminated, 3 May, in a riot in which the police killed and wounded half a dozen labor demonstrators. On the following day when the police broke up a mass meeting held to protest against this massacre, someone threw a bomb into their midst; seven persons were killed and over sixty injured. Though the actual perpetrator of the outrage could not be found, Judge Joseph E. Gary of the Cook County Criminal Court held that those who incited the deed by word or action were equally guilty with those who committed the actual murder. Under this ruling the jury found eight anarchists guilty of murder, and sentenced one to imprisonment and seven to death. Of these seven one committed suicide, four were executed, and the other two had their sentences commuted to life imprisonment. Six years later Governor Altgeld came to office. Alleging that 'the record of this case shows that the judge conducted the trial with malicious ferocity' he pardoned the three anarchists who were still serving prison sentences. Although there was, and is, no possible doubt of the innocence of these men, Altgeld was denounced from coast to coast as an aider and abetter of anarchy. The Knights of Labor was in no way responsible for the Haymarket affair and Powderly had even attempted to disassociate the Order from the eight-hour movement, but the popular revulsion against radical organization of any kind embraced them uncritically, and their influence began to wane. Indiscriminate strikes, the mismanagement of Powderly, and the difficulty of holding skilled and unskilled labor in the same union made serious inroads in their ranks. By the end of the decade membership in the Order had dwindled to about one hundred thousand, and, after a brief and half-hearted flirtation with the Populists, the Knights practically disappeared.

Thus the first experiment of one big union ended disastrously, yet the Knights contributed much of lasting value to the American labor movement. It contributed the democratic idea of the solidarity and unity of all labor, in contrast to the more exclusive principle of trade unionism. Through its emphasis on education and social democracy advanced the status and dignity of labor and prepared the public mind for the K. of L. reforms which were achieved after its demise.

As the Knights of Labor declined in membership and prestige, its place in the van of the labor movement was usurped by a new and more vigorous organization, the American Federation of Labor. This body, which was to dominate the American labor scene for the next half century, definitely rejected the idea of one big union and returned to the principle of unions of skilled workers on craft lines. The two organizations differed in other respects as well: the A. F. of L. was opportunistic and practical where the K. of L. had been idealistic and vague in its aim; the new organization abjured politics and relied on the traditional weapons of the strike and the boycott, whilst the old Order had, on occasion, embraced politics and theoretically discouraged strikes. The Federation from the beginning accepted capitalism and chose to work within the framework of the established economic order, whilst the Knights was tinged with revolutionary radicalism and looked forward to a co-operative republic of workers.

The A. F. of L., distinctively American as it is, issued from the brain of a foreign-born worker in the polyglot section of New York. In the late sixties a bullet-headed young fellow named Samuel Gompers, a British subject of mixed Hebrew and Flemish ancestry, was working in a highly unsanitary cigar-making shop in the lower east side, and speaking at the meetings of a cigarmakers' union — the famous Local No. 144. Cigar making was then a sociable handicraft. The men talked or read aloud while they worked, and both shop and union included German and Hungarian immigrants who could discuss socialism or positivism with equal facility. Gompers, as he rose in the councils of his fellow workers, learned to concentrate on the economic struggle, and to fight shy of intellectuals who would ride union labor to some private Utopia. He determined to divorce unionism from politics, which dissipated its energy, and from radicalism, which served only to arouse the fear of the public and the fury of the police. In the hard times of the seventies he experienced cold and hunger, the futility of charity, and the cowardice of politicians. At all times he had reason to bewail the lack of discipline in the labor movement. By 1881 he and other local labor leaders had thought their way through to a national federation of craft unions, economic in purpose, evolutionary in method, and contending for the immediate objects of shorter hours and better wages. Five years later the A. F. of L. was born, and as the Knights of Labor declined it became the fighting spearhead of the American labor movement.

There is a rough analogy between the A. F. of L. and the Federal Government. Each national union in the Federation has complete power to contract with or strike against employers within its own jurisdiction. The Federation decides matters of jurisdiction, prevents — or tries to prevent — the establishment of rival unions in the same trade, and endeavors to keep the ranks of the workers solid by salaried organizers and a labor press. Opportunistic rather than idealistic, animated by the philosophy of the job, the Federation is a purely economic organization of wage-earners for the business of collective bargaining. 'At no time in my life,' said Gompers, 'have I worked out definitely articulated economic theory,' and Gompers' co-worker, Adolph Strasser, was even more emphatic. 'We have no ultimate ends,' he testified. 'We are going on from day to day. We are fighting only for immediate objects — objects that can be realized in a few years.' In 1918 the economic platform of the Federation included opposition to the injunction in labor disputes; an eight-hour day and a six-day week; municipal ownership of public utilities; factory inspection; workmen's compensation laws; abolition of child labor; the initiative, referendum, and recall; free schools, free textbooks, and compulsory education; objectives that had already been realized in many states. State federations, cutting traversely the national unions, were created within the A. F. of L. in order to obtain legislation of this nature by bargaining with local political leaders.

Despite the loss of the great Homestead strike against the Carnegie Steel Company in 1892 and failure to co-operate in the Pullman strike, the A. F. of L. weathered the hard times of 1893–97 and turned the century with a membership of over half a million. The piping years of the first Roosevelt administration brought prosperity to labor as well as to industry, and by 1904 this membership was trebled and on the eve of the World War it reached two million. The World War stimulated American industry just as had the Civil War, and the stimulus was promptly reflected in the growth of the Federation. When the United States entered the World War, the membership

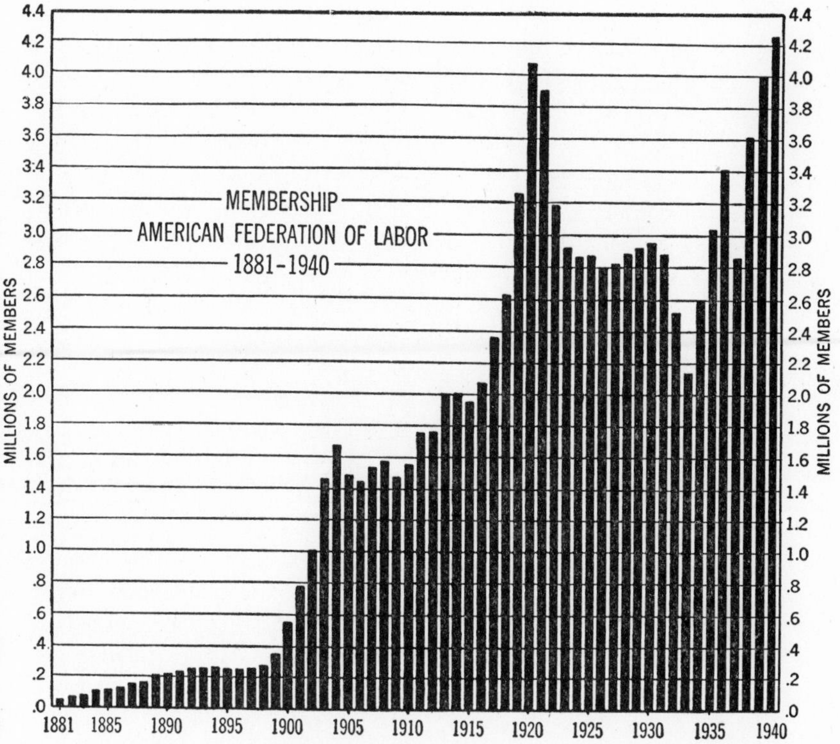
MEMBERSHIP
AMERICAN FEDERATION OF LABOR
1881-1940
MILLIONS OF MEMBERS
MILLIONS OF MEMBERS
4.4
4.2
4.0
3.8
3.6
3.4
3.2
3.0
2.8
2.6
2.4
2.2
2.0
1.8
1.6
1.4
1.2
1.0
.8
.6
.4
.2
.0
1881
1885
1890
1895
1900
1905
1910
1915
1920
1925
1930
1935
1940

was almost two and one half million, and the Federation embraced 111 national unions, 762 city central bodies, and 26,761 local unions.

This rapid growth of the Federation was in great part due to the leadership of Gompers who for forty years guided its destinies, impressed it with his personality, permeated it with his ideas, inspired it with his stubborn courage, held it steadily to the course of aggressive self-interest, and steered it clear of the shoals of politics upon which so many earlier labor movements had grounded. 'We must be partisan for a principle,' said Gompers, ' and not for a party.' From time to time the A. F. of L. threw its influence to some candidate who was favorable to the labor program or supported a party which adopted a good labor platform. Thus in 1908 Gompers supported Bryan and in 1912 Wilson; and the Federation has frequently made its power felt in local or state contests. But it has never listened to radical counsels or yielded to radical leadership, never formally, tied up with the Socialist or the Socialist Labor parties, never, except in 1924, entered politics in any formal manner.

By 1920 the Federation boasted a membership of well over four million, but throughout the following decade it suffered a continuous decline in membership, strength, and prestige, which was sharply accentuated by the depression of 1929. The decline may be attributed to a variety of causes: the inevitable post-war industrial readjustment, the disappearance of many of the war industries such as munitions, and of the brewery business, the rise of independent trade organizations such as the Amalgamated Garment Workers, the growth of company unions, the spectacular failure of the steel strike of 1919 and of the railroad strike of 1922, the death of Gompers, and the growing conservatism and timidity of the Federation under the leadership of President William Green.

Although the American Federation of Labor was for forty years the acknowledged spokesman of American labor, at no time did its membership embrace a majority of the working class, and certain unions of skilled laborers have steadily refused to join it. Not until 1935 did the powerful Amalgamated Clothing Workers affiliate with the A. F. of L., and the aristocratic Four Brotherhoods of railroad workers are still independent. Membership of the Federation was limited on the whole to the skilled crafts, while the great mass of unskilled labor long remained unorganized. In 1920, for example, when the Federation was strongest, only twenty-three per cent of the workers in manufacturing plants, twenty-five per cent in the building trades, and thirty-seven per cent in transportation, were organized. Not until 1936 when John Lewis of the United Mine Workers founded the Committee for Industrial Organization was there any serious effort to organize the great mass of unskilled and semi-skilled workers, and the astonishing success of the C. I. O. indicates how grave was the need for such an undertaking.

It was from the ranks of the unskilled and the casual laborers that the International Workers of the World, popularly known as the 'Wobblies,' recruited the greater part of its membership. Born out of the terrible Cripple Creek coal strike of 1904, the I. W. W. became the radical left wing of American labor. Despite a fluctuating and uncertain membership, its policy was consistently aggressive, and before its practical destruction in 1918 it led almost one hundred and fifty strikes, most notably the textile strikes of 1912. The I. W. W. was committed to the idea of industrial unionism, and socialism, and some elements were frankly anarchistic; its unalterable opposition to the capitalistic system was well expressed in one of its songs:

> We hate their rotten system more than any mortals do.
> Our aim is not to patch it but to build it all anew.
> And what we'll have for government, when we're finally through
> Is One Big Industrial Union!

3. *Industrial Conflicts*

As, after the Civil War, labor shifted its objectives from social reform to wages and the job, it resorted with increasing frequency to the weapons of industrial warfare — the strike and the boycott — and business retaliated with the lock-out, the blacklist, the injunction, and the employment of company police or the National Guard. The result was an uninterrupted industrial conflict that all too frequently broke out into violence and assumed the ominous character of warfare. In 1900 the Industrial Commission concluded that strikes and lock-outs were far more prevalent in the United States than in other industrial countries, and the experience of the next forty years furnished no ground for modifying that melancholy estimate.

The basic causes of the American industrial conflict are not hard to find. There was everywhere among laborers a persistent feeling that labor was being denied its proper share of the benefits that accrued from the exploitation of natural resources and the savings made possible by machinery. The great majority of strikes that have occurred since the 1870's have involved either hours or wages or both, and even a cursory examination of conditions that obtained before World War I will explain this fact. Agitation for the eight-hour day began in the 1860's, but as late as 1900 seventy per cent of the industrial workers in the country worked ten hours or more each day, and ten years later only eight per cent of the workers were on an eight-hour day. In many industries the hours were shockingly long: the steel industry had a twelve-hour day and a seven-day week, and this schedule was maintained until 1923; hours in the textile industry ranged from sixty to eighty-four a week; trainmen commonly worked over seventy hours a week; and in New York City bakers were expected to put in from eighty-four to one hundred or more hours each week. The wage situation was equally dismal, and until the second World War wages failed to keep pace with the costs of living. Investigation after investigation proved that in the decades from 1880 to 1910 the unskilled laborer commonly earned less than ten dollars a week and the skilled worker rarely more than twenty, while the earnings of women ranged from a low of $3.93 a week in Richmond to a high of $6.91 in San Francisco. During the whole of this period the annual average income of industrial workers was never more than six hundred dollars, or of farm laborers more than four hundred, figures considerably below that fixed as necessary for a decent standard of living. When we recall that unemployment was a constant and that even those employed rarely enjoyed continuous work throughout the year,[3] we can understand better the deep discontent of labor and the resort to conflict and violence.

The strike had been a familiar phenomenon in our history ever since the 1790's, but before the Civil War strikes had been localized and, on the whole, peaceful. The first great industrial conflict in our history came in 1877 when the four eastern trunk lines jauntily announced a wage-cut of ten per cent, the second since the panic of '73. Without adequate organization the railway employees struck, and with the support of a huge army of unemployed, hungry and desperate, the strike flared up into something like rebellion. During one week in July traffic was entirely suspended on the trunk lines and demoralized elsewhere in the country, and every large industrial center from the Atlantic to the Pacific was in turmoil. In Baltimore, Pittsburgh, Martinsburg, Chicago, Buffalo, San Francisco, and else-

[3] In 1898, for example, 14 per cent of the workers in manufacturing and transportation were unemployed. In this same year the average miner in the bituminous coal mines worked 211 days a year and in the anthracite coal mines 152 days a year.

where, there were pitched battles between militia and the mob, and order was restored only by federal troops. Pittsburgh was terrorized for three days; the fatalities ran into the scores, and property damage was estimated at ten million dollars. American complacency received a shock which was only partially alleviated by the notion, so precious to Americans then and since, that foreign agitators alone were responsible for the disorder. Only the most far-sighted realized that the country had reached a stage of industrial evolution which created a labor problem, or that the 'Great Strike' of '77 would be only the first of a long series of battles between labor and capital.

The decade of the eighties was a turbulent one, and almost four hundred thousand workers participated in the eight-hour movement that ended so disastrously in the Haymarket riot. Not until 1892 was the nation again to witness so menacing an outbreak in the labor field. In that year occurred the terrible strike in the Homestead works of the Carnegie Steel Company which culminated in a pitched battle between infuriated strikers and an army of Pinkerton detectives hired by the president of the Carnegie Company, Henry C. Frick. The strikers won the sanguinary battle, but the attempted assassination of Frick alienated public opinion and state militia broke the backbone of the strike. Two years later the country was distracted by a strike against the Pullman Palace Car Company in the model town of Pullman, Illinois. The strike resulted originally from the arbitrary refusal of Mr. Pullman to discuss grievances with representatives of his employees, but it came eventually to involve far larger issues. The cause of the Pullman workers was taken up by the American Railway Union, a powerful body of railway workers under the leadership of the magnetic Eugene V. Debs, and when this Union voted a boycott against all Pullman cars, the cause of the Pullman Company was as promptly championed by the newly organized General Managers' Association of Railroads. The result was a paralysis of transportation throughout the North. Disorder was widespread and the situation was packed with dynamite. The railroads succeeded in enlisting the sympathies of President Cleveland and the aid of Attorney-General Olney, a former railroad attorney who had not forgotten his earlier obligations to the railroads nor failed to consider the railroads' future obligations to him. On 1 July Olney appointed as special counsel for the United States a prominent railway attorney named Edwin Walker, at whose suggestion the federal circuit court at Chicago served on the officers of the American Railway Union a 'blanket injunction' against obstructing the railways and holding up the mails. Hooligans promptly ditched a mail train, and took possession of strategic points in the switching yards. Walker as promptly called for federal troops. Cleveland declared that he would use every dollar in the Treasury and every soldier in the army if necessary to deliver a single postcard in Chicago. On 4 July he ordered a regiment of regulars to the city. The effect was like that of sending British regulars to Boston in 1768.

Cleveland's antagonist in this conflict was not so much Debs and the railway union as Governor John P. Altgeld. This honest and fearless statesman had already been marked for destruction by big business because he had helped Jane Addams to obtain factory regulations in Illinois and because he had pardoned the men imprisoned for presumed participation in the Haymarket bomb outrage of 1886. During the Pullman strike Altgeld was ready and able to protect law and order with state militia. He sent troops to every point in the state where the authorities called for them, and had an ample force ready to use in Chicago, where, as yet, there was no disorder with which police and militia were unable to cope. The real reason why Walker called for a federal injunction and federal troops was to break the strike, not to preserve order; and the most serious disorder came after the federal injunction had been issued. Altgeld's eloquent protest against this gratuitous interference by the Federal Government and his demand for the withdrawal of federal troops was cavalierly disregarded. Debs defied the injunction, a prosecution for conspiracy failed, but he was given six months' imprisonment for contempt of court. By early August the strike was smashed.

The dramatic events of this Pullman strike raised weighty questions of law, and placed the Federal Government in direct antagonism to union labor. The President simply saw the issue of law and order, but through permitting Olney to appoint a railroad attorney special council of the government, he played into the hands of those who wanted federal troops to break a strike, and not state militia to preserve order. Governor Altgeld had no desire to foment disorder; but his stout protest against a dubious assumption of federal authority placed him in the position of a rebel. Debs was merely trying to help the Pullman employees by boycotting the company; but the movement got out of his hands and became something like a labor insurrection. The Supreme Court of the United States, to which Debs appealed his sentence, upheld the Government, declaring that even in the absence of statutory law it had a dormant power to brush away obstacles to interstate commerce — an implied power that would have made Hamilton and Marshall gasp.[4] Yet the whole affair was not without a certain educational value to all concerned. Debs, in his prison cell, studied socialism and in time became the organizer and leader of the Socialist party in America; the workers learned the real meaning of the Sherman Anti-trust Act; business awoke to the potentialities of the injunction in labor disputes; and the country at large was taught a new interpretation of the sovereign powers of the Federal Government. Only George Pullman emerged innocent of new ideas.

Scarcely less spectacular than the Pullman strike was the outbreak in the anthracite coal fields of Pennsylvania in 1902. Then, as later, the coal industry was in a chaotic condition, and the position of the miners was depressed and insecure. In the nineties organization had made some progress in the bituminous fields, but the racial antipathies among the miners, and the bitter hostility of the railway-controlled operators delayed unionization among the anthracite miners. In 1898, however, the youthful John Mitchell became president of the United Mine Workers union which then numbered some forty thousand members. Within two years he whipped it into shape, extended its membership to the anthracite fields, and wrested favorable terms from the powerful coal companies of eastern Pennsylvania. Two years later the operators abrogated this agreement, and the miners struck for recognition of their union, a nine-hour day, and an increase in wages. The operators were obdurate, and for four tense months the strike dragged on while the strikers maintained an unbroken front and won the support of public opinion. It was in the course of this struggle that President George F. Baer of the Philadelphia and Reading Railroad announced that 'the rights and interests of the laboring man will be protected and cared for, not by the labor agitators, but by the Christian men to whom God in His infinite wisdom, has given control of the property interests of the country.' Eventually President Roosevelt stepped in and threatened to take over the mines and run them with militia unless the stubborn operators came to terms with the miners. This threat, and the force of public opinion, persuaded the mine owners to arbitrate, and the strike ended in a signal victory for the miners, enhancement of the prestige of John

4 *In re* Debs, 158 U.S. 564 (1895).

Mitchell and of President Roosevelt, and a triumph for the cause of arbitration.

Labor unrest in the coal fields has been chronic. The murderous activities of the Molly Maguires in the eastern Pennsylvania coal fields in the early seventies and the ruthlessness with which they were suppressed, the terrible outbreak in the mines of Cripple Creek, Colorado in 1894 and again in 1903–04, the pitched battle at Ludlow, Colorado in 1914, the violent struggle in the mines of West Virginia in 1913 which burst out into civil war six years later, the Herrin massacre in southern Illinois in 1922, the prolonged and bitter war in the mines of Harlan County, Kentucky, as recently as 1931, all testify to a pervasive mismanagement and social waste in the coal industry of the country. In the twenty years from 1910 to 1929 no less than four million coal miners were out on strike at one time or another, and not until the forties was there any significant improvement in conditions.

The textile industry, North and South, has been subject to labor conflicts and disorders in a similar fashion. In 1912 the I. W. W. came East to organize the workers in the mills of Lawrence, Massachusetts and Paterson, New Jersey. The subsequent strikes in which the workers aroused the sympathy of those intellectuals whom Gompers so profoundly distrusted, were characterized by violence on both sides and by a ruthless disregard for legal rights and liberties. In the decade of the twenties the struggle was transferred to the mills of the South where the operators combatted by every possible means the unionization of their workers. In this they were largely successful, but the murderous outbreaks in Gastonia, N.C., in 1929 and in Marion, S.C., the following year, and the prolonged and bitter strikes of 1935 indicated that the industrial conflict was by no means confined to the North and the West.

The steel industry, too, experienced continuous maladjustment in the labor field. From the beginning the giant corporation that dominated the iron and steel industry set itself with adamantine stubbornness against unionization of its workers, and the smaller companies hastened to make this policy their own. Twice in the first decade of the new century efforts to unionize the steel mills collapsed; the third and most ambitious attempt came in 1919 when almost four hundred thousand steel workers struck for recognition of their union, higher wages, and the eight-hour day. An impartial commission of the Federal Council of Churches reported 'We find the grievances to have been real: the average week of 68.7 hours . . . and the underpayment of unskilled labor, are all inhuman. . . . The "Boss system" is bad, the plant organization is military, and the control autocratic.' The strike was attended with customary violence and lawlessness, and in large parts of Pennsylvania the Constitution was, in effect, repealed. But the strike was ill-timed and inadequately supported by organized labor. The country was in the grip of the conservative reaction and the anti-red hysteria which followed the World War, and public opinion was easily persuaded that the steel strike was the entering wedge of communism. The strike collapsed, and though within a few years the Steel Corporation made many of the concessions which the workers had demanded, it maintained until 1937 its inflexible opposition to unionization of its workers.

The statistics of strikes and lock-outs present a shocking picture of economic maladjustment and go far to justify the conclusion of a recent careful student that 'American labor history has been principally a fighting history.' Statistics are not available for every year, but in the twenty-five year period from 1881 to 1906 there occurred some thirty-eight thousand strikes and lock-outs, involving almost two hundred thousand establishments and over nine and one-half million workers. World War I and the post-war years witnessed some abatement of the industrial conflict, but the twenty-six thousand strikes that broke out between 1916 and 1935 indicated that the struggle was a continuous one.

4. *Labor Legislation and the Courts*

If the struggle has been continuous, so too have been efforts toward peace. Both capital and labor have attempted to abate the industrial conflict, and not without some degree of success. Capital has placed reliance upon company welfare work, pension, compensation, and insurance plans, profit-sharing schemes, labor representation in business, and company unions; labor upon collective bargaining and arbitration. These devices have done something to mitigate the distress incident to the industrial conflict, but they have done little to remove its fundamental causes or to advance the welfare of society as a whole. Business has looked askance at governmental intervention in the relations of capital and labor, and labor was, until very recently, equally sceptical of the advantages of legislative reform. But the interest of society in industrial peace is as great as the interest of either capital or labor, and real progress in labor and social reform has come about through the development of an enlightened public opinion expressing itself through progressive legislation.

It is a truism that until the 1930's, American social legislation lagged almost a generation behind that of the more progressive European states, but it must be remembered that the difficulties of dealing with the various social and economic aspects of the labor problem are greater in the United States than in England or continental Europe. This is due largely to three factors: the tradition of rugged individualism which made Americans reluctant to acquiesce in legislative regulation of business; the limitations of written constitutions embodying out-worn laissez-faire ideas and rigidly interpreted by the courts; and the existence of a federal rather than a centralized state. Important, too, has been the indubitable fact that the American workingman was more highly paid than any other worker in the world, which led unthinking people to snap at the comfortable theory that all agitation for social reform was inspired by socialistic teachings dangerous to American institutions and not by any real need or suffering.

The very existence of organized labor has often been threatened; its chief weapons, the strike and the boycott, have frequently been paralyzed by injunction or judicial decision. Early in the nineteenth century labor unions were sometimes held to be illegal in themselves; but by the time of the Civil War the right of workingmen to organize had been everywhere accepted.[5] Yet the strike remained at best an uncertain weapon. Business and government invoked the injunction against it time and again — in the great railroad strike of 1877, in the Pullman strike of 1894, and on scores of other occasions. The Clayton Anti-trust Act of 1914 contained a special article forbidding the use of the injunction in labor disputes, except to 'prevent irreparable injury'; but the intent of this article was defeated by a series of court decisions,[6] and eight years after its enactment the United States Attorney-General demanded and secured the most sweeping injunction in American history. Not until 1932 did the Norris-LaGuardia anti-injunction bill erect apparently invulnerable safeguards against the misuse of the injunction in labor disputes. The boycott of employers who would not accept union terms has been adjudged an unlawful combination in restraint of trade, and thus a violation of the

[5] Commonwealth *v.* Hunt (Mass. Reports, 4 Metcalf 45) is the leading case.

[6] Especially Duplex Printing Press Company *v.* Deering *et al.* 254 U.S. 443 (1921).

Sherman Act, in two leading cases,[7] and the secondary boycott, too, has come under the judicial ban.[8] The Supreme Court has held that labor organizations, even though unincorporated, may be prosecuted for violations of the Sherman Law.[9] Similarly the practice of picketing was so hedged about with judicial restrictions as to be until recently practically impotent.[10]

More has been accomplished by labor through social legislation than through strikes and other violent methods. This, in a general way, includes the establishment of an eight-hour day in most industries, limitation of the hours and regulation of the conditions of women's labor, abolition of child labor, factory inspection, safety and sanitation regulation, arbitration of industrial disputes, workmen's compensation laws or insurance provisions, minimum wage regulation, unemployment insurance and old-age pensions, restriction of immigration and protection of native labor against foreign competition.

Outside the limited field of interstate commerce, and except for federal employees the Federal Government was thought to have no jurisdiction over most of these matters, and it was not until the New Deal that ways were found to achieve indirectly what could not be achieved directly. As early as 1868 Congress established an eight-hour day on public works and in 1892 enacted an eight-hour day for all government employees. The Adamson Law of 1916 extended this boon to all railway employees. In other ways, too, the Federal Government has responded to the demands of organized labor. In 1884 a Bureau of Labor was created, and this was elevated to cabinet rank in 1913. An act of 1885 prohibited the importation of contract labor, and a whole series of laws since that time have regulated, restricted, or excluded immigration. In 1898 Congress passed the Erdman Act providing for the arbitration of labor disputes on interstate carriers, and in 1908 an Employers' Liability Act whose provisions were likewise confined to railway employees. The La Follette Seamen's Act of 1915 regulated the conditions of employment in the merchant marine and elevated the seamen for the first time to the full status of free men. Twice Congress attempted to prohibit

[7] Gompers *v.* Bucks' Stove and Range Company, 221 U.S. 418 (1907), and the Danbury Hatters' Case, Lawlor *v.* Loewe, 208 U.S. 274 (1908).

[8] Bedford Cut Stone Co. *v.* Journeymen Cutters Association, 274 U.S. 37 (1927).

[9] United Mine Workers of America *v.* Coronado Coal Co., 259 U.S. 344 (1922).

[10] Truax *v.* Corrigan, 257 U.S. 312 (1921) in which the Supreme Court held unconstitutional a law of Arizona forbidding the use of the injunction in labor disputes.

child labor through statutory enactment — in 1916 under the guise of a regulation of commerce, and again in 1919 through the medium of taxation. Both attempts were declared unconstitutional by the Supreme Court.[11] Within two years after the failure of the second attempt, the opponents of child labor succeeded in pushing through a Constitutional Amendment giving Congress the 'power to limit, regulate and prohibit the labor of persons under eighteen years of age.' By 1937 twenty-eight states had ratified this amendment. A Supreme Court reversal of the first child labor decision validated federal legislation and made a ratification seem less urgent.

Labor and social legislation lay, however, for the most part in the domain of the states, and here there was notable progress along certain lines, particularly in the more progressive states such as Massachusetts, New York, Kansas, Oregon, and Washington. The first labor law to be adequately enforced was the Massachusetts Ten-Hour Act of 1874 for women and children in factories. It was not so hard to get such laws passed as to provide proper administrative machinery for their enforcement; and until judges began to lose their laissez-faire prepossessions, there was constant danger that courts would declare such laws unconstitutional. A case in point was the New York Act of 1882 prohibiting the manufacture of cigars in tenement houses, which Gompers persuaded young Theodore Roosevelt to sponsor and Governor Cleveland to sign. It was intended as an entering wedge to break up the 'sweating' system, a rapidly growing menace. On a test case the constitutionality of the law was brought before the highest court of the state, which found against it on the ground that it interfered with the profitable use of real estate without any compensating public advantage. 'It cannot be perceived how the cigarmaker is to be improved in his health or his morals by forcing him from his home and its hallowed associations and beneficent influences to ply his trade elsewhere,' declared the court.[12] Roosevelt, who had personally inspected these one room 'homes' where whole families and their lodgers ate, slept, and rolled cigars, then began to revise his conception of justice.

It was this case [he recorded in his *Autobiography*] which first waked me to a dim and partial understanding of the fact that the courts were not necessarily the best judges of what should be done to better social and in-

[11] Hammer *v.* Dagenhart *et al.,* 247 U.S. 251 (1918) and Bailey *v.* Drexel Furniture Company, 259 U.S. 20 (1922).

[12] *In re* Jacobs, 98 New York 98 (1885).

dustrial conditions. The judges who rendered this decision were well-meaning men. They knew nothing whatever of tenement-house conditions; they knew nothing whatever of the needs, or of the life and labor, of three-fourths of their fellow-citizens in great cities. They knew legalism, but not life. . . . This decision completely blocked tenement-house reform legislation in New York for a score of years, and hampers it to this day. It was one of the most serious setbacks which the cause of industrial and social progress and reform ever received.[13]

And by what theory did the courts declare such labor laws unconstitutional? It is forbidden in most state constitutions and in the Fourteenth Amendment to the Federal Constitution to deprive persons of property without due process of law. As no reform can be effected without depriving some one of something that he may deem to be a property right, the American courts early elaborated the doctrine of a superior 'police power'—the reserved right of a state to protect the people's health, safety, morals, and welfare. This police power had been held to justify even confiscatory reforms, such as the prohibition of lotteries, or of the manufacture and sale of alcoholic liquors; but when labor and factory laws began to appear on the statute books, judges began to draw the line. Corporations, engaging the best lawyers, found it easy to convince courts that such laws were not a proper and reasonable exercise of the police power; and to point out conflicts with the Fourteenth Amendment, or other parts of the Federal Constitution. Where such a conflict could not be discovered, judges in the eighties began to postulate a theoretical liberty of contract, 'the right of a person to sell his labor upon such terms as he deems proper.'[14] Some feared that labor laws constituted an 'assault upon capitalism' or conjured up 'the spectre of Socialism,' and they wrote their fears into legal doctrine. In 1913 Justice Holmes observed that 'When twenty years ago a vague terror went over the earth and the word socialism began to be heard, I thought and still think that fear was translated into doctrines that had no proper place in the Constitution or the common law.' Others pored deeply over old English law reports, in the hope of construing conspiracy out of labor unions. A Pennsylvania statute forbidding payment of miners in truck orders was judicially nullified in a decision declaring such a law 'insulting and degrading' to the laborer, and

[13] *Theodore Roosevelt: An Autobiography,* p. 81, (Scribner's).

[14] Justice Harlan in Adair *v.* U.S., 208 U.S. 161 (1908). This theory first appears in American law in 1886, and is first discussed in Herbert Spencer's *Justice* (1891).

'subversive of his rights as a citizen.' An Illinois court declared unconstitutional a statute limiting the hours of labor for women in sweatshops on the ground that women had the same liberty of contract as men, a decision which inspired the Chicago *Evening Post* to protest that 'when Dora Windeguth, her employer at her elbow, says that she cannot earn enough in ten hours to live our whole chivalry rises to her defense; let her work twelve hours then. We have always contended that nobody need starve in America!'[15] And a few years later the New York Court of Appeals declared void a law prohibiting night work for women. 'When it is sought,' said Judge Gray on behalf of the Court, 'under the guise of a labor law, arbitrarily, as here, to prevent an adult female citizen from working any time of day that suits her, I think it is time to call a halt.' In 1905 the Supreme Court of the United States in the case of Lochner *v.* New York took a similar view of a New York statute prescribing the hours of labor in bakeries.[16] If, said the Court in effect, long hours of bakers could be shown to affect the quality of bread, something might be said for the regulation under the police power; but bakers were sufficiently intelligent to make their own labor contracts in their own interest, and 'we think the limit of the police power has been reached and passed in this case.' Justice Holmes, however, entered a vigorous dissenting opinion in which he observed that 'This case is decided upon an economic theory which a large part of the country does not entertain. . . . The Fourteenth Amendment does not enact Mr. Herbert Spencer's *Social Statics.*'

Many of these illiberal decisions have since been reversed, and the majority of states today have laws carefully regulating conditions and hours of labor for women and children, and in all dangerous occupations. As early as 1898 the Supreme Court, in the case of Holden *v.* Hardy[17] accepted a Utah law limiting to eight the hours of labor in mines, and this precedent has been commonly followed, though judges have differed on the question of what constituted a hazardous or fatiguing occupation. An Oregon law of 1903 limiting the hours of

[15] The *Post* continued: 'It is interesting to reflect that while Dora's feudal forebears fought for the right to work, it has been left for Dora's generation to fight for the right to work overtime. But there is still a chance — if we all stick together — to save this state from the fate of Massachusetts . . . and other commonwealths, which, given the choice between healthy womanhood and cheap paper boxes, are now going without paper boxes.'

[16] 198 U.S. 45 (1905).

[17] 169 U.S. 366 (1898).

employment for women to ten was upheld in the Supreme Court in the notable case of Muller *v.* Oregon [18] — notable not alone for the apparent change of attitude on the part of the Court, but because the mass of scientific, sociological, economic, and physiological data introduced by the counsel for Oregon, Louis D. Brandeis, was admitted as evidence. Thus the principle was established that the courts can take cognizance of the special circumstances that justified the exercise of the police power. This did not necessarily mean that the courts would accept expediency as a legal argument, but rather that they would acquiesce in legislative findings of reasonableness. By 1930 almost every state in the Union had limited the hours of labor for women, and most states either strictly regulated or wholly prohibited the labor of children under fourteen years of age. Under the impact of such legislation child labor declined from almost two million in 1910 to less than three-quarters of a million in 1930.

Legislative enactments of minimum wages were for a long time less successful. Organized labor itself long opposed such legislation as tending to level the general wage scale down rather than up, but in time labor withdrew its opposition to minimum wages for women and children. Following Australian and British precedents, Massachusetts in 1912 enacted the first minimum wage law for women and children, and within a few years fourteen states had followed suit. In 1916 the learning and logic with which Louis Brandeis and Felix Frankfurter had argued in the state court persuaded the Supreme Court to accept the Oregon minimum wage act,[19] and thereafter all seemed clear sailing. Seven years later, however, in one of the most remarkable reversals in our judicial history, the Court found a District of Columbia minimum wage law unconstitutional,[20] and on this rock of judicial intransigence the program of minimum wage legislation was wrecked. When in 1933 the legislature of New York attempted to fix minimum wages for women in laundries, the Court, by a five to four decision, invalidated the law, stating that legislatures are ' without power by any form of legislation to prohibit, change or nullify contracts between employers and adult women workers as to the amount of wages to be paid.' These decisions established, as President Roosevelt pointed out, a ' twilight zone ' in which neither federal nor state government had authority. In 1937, however, the

[18] 208 U.S. 412 (1908).

[19] Stettler *v.* O'Hara, 243 U.S. 629 (1916). On this case the court divided four to four, thus sustaining the act.

[20] Adkins *v.* Children's Hospital, 261 U.S. 525 (1923).

Court, by a divided vote, once more reversed itself, and sustained a new minimum wage law. Thus the long controversy ended in favor of the police power of the state.

Another series of laws safeguard the health and lives of workers through provisions for safety devices, fire prevention, sanitary inspection, and standards of sanitation and of cleanliness, light, and ventilation. Yet the hazards of industry remain appallingly great, and there are proportionately more industrial accidents in the United States [21] than in any other civilized country. The question of compensation for the disabled and pensions for the retired veterans of the armies of labor is one of the most urgent in American life today. Fortunately the old common law theory that the employer was responsible for injuries only when negligence could be definitely proved has been abandoned in favor of the responsibility of industry and of society as a whole. Montana led the way in compensation legislation in 1909 and Wisconsin, Washington, and Kansas followed in 1911. Since then every state but two has made some provision for accident insurance or compensation.[22] Not until the 1930's did agitation for unemployment insurance and old age pensions such as exist in all the more advanced European countries, make any real progress. The growing practice of laying off mass-production workers before middle age, and the widespread unemployment that accompanied the great depression of 1929, brought these problems squarely and inescapably before the American people. Before 1929 six states had adopted old age pension systems and between 1929 and 1933 nineteen more states placed such laws on their statute books. Wisconsin and Ohio led the way in unemployment insurance and during 1935 eight more states adopted such legislation. It was apparent, however, that the problems of unemployment and of insecurity were national rather than local in character and that the states alone could not be expected to solve them. The passage of the Social Security Act of 14 August 1935 inaugurated a nation-wide system of unemployment insurance and old age pensions through federal grants-in-aid to co-operating states, and the validation of this legislation by the Supreme Court in May 1937 justified those who believed that a problem national in character might be solved by national action.

[21] In New York State alone there were reported 4,366,168 industrial accidents in the ten years from 1925 to 1934. Different standards and statistical methods, however, make comparisons risky.

[22] It is interesting to note that compensation legislation was inaugurated in Germany as early as 1884 and by 1910 every leading European state had such legislation.

VIII

IMMIGRATION
1865–1936

1. *The Melting Pot*

IMMIGRATION is the oldest and most persistent theme in American history, and though the character of immigration has changed drastically within recent years, the nature of the process has remained essentially the same. For three hundred years immigrants to America have shared common experiences: the English and Dutch of the seventeenth, the German, Scotch, Irish, and Scandinavian of the eighteenth and nineteenth, the Italian, Slav, and Greek of the early twentieth century, all had to uproot themselves from Old-World homes, break away from familiar folk-ways, and adjust themselves to a new environment and new social institutions in the New World. With the early settlers, that process of adjustment was largely physical; with those who came after the pattern of American life had in some measure been fixed, it was largely social and economic; but the cultural and psychological implications of the process were substantially the same. And the United States continued to serve as a melting pot, to fuse the characteristics of all peoples into a new and unique metal, to pour it into the mold of the American environment, and temper it with American ideas. It was the most notable and the most extensive experiment of the sort since the barbarian invasions of Rome, and it may be assumed that if sociology is ever to become a science it must draw its materials largely from the facts of the American experience with the interaction of a complex racial and cultural inheritance and a common environment.

The decades of the forties and fifties had seen the influx of immense numbers of immigrants from Ireland, Germany, and Scandinavia. The Civil War dammed up the stream of immigration, but after Appomattox the pent-up waters flowed once again into familiar channels. In the next three-quarters of a century some thirty-three million emigrants sought the American melting pot,[1] swarming out

[1] Total immigration from 1820 to 1930 was 37,762,012. There has been, however, a continuous return emigration to the Old World, and in the decade 1930–40 this emigration more than equalled immigration. One authority has estimated that the total net increase from immigration from 1820 to 1930 may be placed at 26,180,000.

onto the rich prairie lands of the West, transforming the cities into enormous cosmopolitan beehives, performing the back-breaking labor that made possible the economic expansion of the nation, creating new problems of social assimilation and adaptation, and bringing to the United States the richest and most varied cultural heritage that was ever vouchsafed any nation — though one all too often dissipated or betrayed. This immigration from the Old World to the New represents the greatest folk movement in history, ancient or modern. After a century and a half of colonization and of unprecedented natural increase, the population of the English colonies in America was but slightly over two millions; every decade since 1860 has witnessed an immigration large enough to replace this entire population.

In attempting to analyze and interpret the significance of this immigration it may be well to dispose of certain misconceptions at the outset. Neither immigration nor racial heterogeneity are recent developments; immigration was as large, proportionately, in the later colonial period as in the latter part of the nineteenth century, and the population of the colonies on the eve of the Revolution, though predominantly English and African, represented six or seven races and three or four languages. Nor does there seem to be any valid ground for believing that the 'native stock' will succumb to the new alien invasion, or that the foreign infiltration has upset the equilibrium of the American population. Despite the fecundity of many of the immigrant groups, and the very general intermarriage of native and foreign born, the number of Americans of foreign or mixed parentage constituted only one-fifth of the population in 1930. And though the number of foreign born in the country more than doubled in the fifty years after 1880, so too did the population, and the foreign born made up a smaller percentage of the population in 1930 than in 1880. Nor do mortality statistics give any support to the theory that large-scale immigration has seriously impaired the quality or the vitality of the American people. More reasonable was the fear that the changing sources of immigration after 1880 would impede the process of assimilation and Americanization; yet the experience of World War II and of recent years has not justified these fears, nor is there any good evidence that recent immigrant stock has shown itself less intelligent politically than the earlier stock, or less faithful to democracy. At one time the notion that the foreign-born element in the population was largely responsible for crime and disease and the perpetual object of charity, was widely prevalent, but a more careful examination of this question over a longer period of time has not substantiated this belief. That the foreign born figured more largely than the native born in the statistics of crime and charity appears to have been an index of opportunity rather than of ability. Nor does there seem to be any scientific ground for holding that those of North European stock are in any fundamental way superior to those of the South, or any rational ground for accepting the theory of 'Nordic supremacy.' Whether immigration has lowered the American standard of living is not so easy to determine. Cheap immigrant labor unquestionably threatened the gains of organized labor from time to time, and tended to depress money wages; but the material standard of living in America generally kept ahead of that in Europe, and after half a century of immigration on an unprecedented scale remains still higher than in all but a few countries such as Denmark and Sweden. The infiltration of new blood into a given industry usually makes the people already there ambitious to move on and up; yesterday's pick-hand becomes today's riveter and tomorrow's construction boss. Standards of living are lower among the Anglo-Saxon mill hands in the South, where there has been no push from below, than among the Finnish and Lithuanian textile workers in New England; Polish truck-farmers in New Jersey have their cars, radios, and plumbing, while 'Nordic' farmers in Georgia cannot afford electric light. The oft-repeated charge that the immigrant unduly exploited this country loses sight of the extent to which he himself has been exploited, and of his indispensable contribution to developing the natural resources of the nation.

2. *The Old Immigration and the New*

The facts and figures of immigration can be told briefly; [2] their implications are not so easy to evaluate. In the decade from 1850 to 1860 about two and one-half million aliens came to this country; in the forty years from 1860 to 1900 about fourteen million; in the first thirty years of the twentieth century over eighteen million. Of these thirty-five million immigrants the largest number were from the United Kingdom — some sixteen million in all — of which well over ten and one-half million came from Ireland. Germany accounted for ap-

[2] For the statistics of immigration, see appendices.

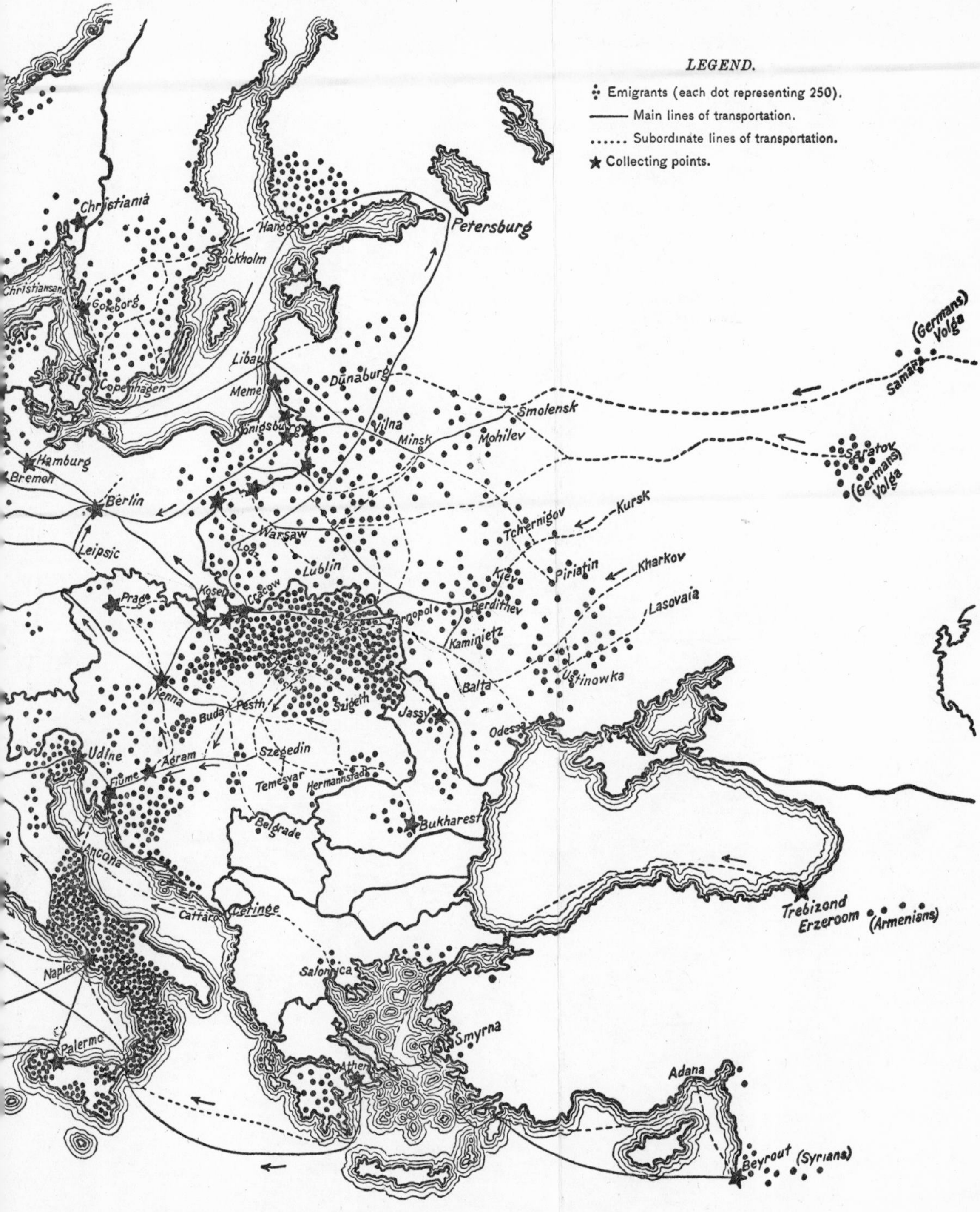

, Contributing Districts, Collecting Points, and Routes Followed, 1900.

M. V. Safford, M. D., U. S. Marine-Hospital Service.

f Industrial Commission of 1900, *Vol. XIX*

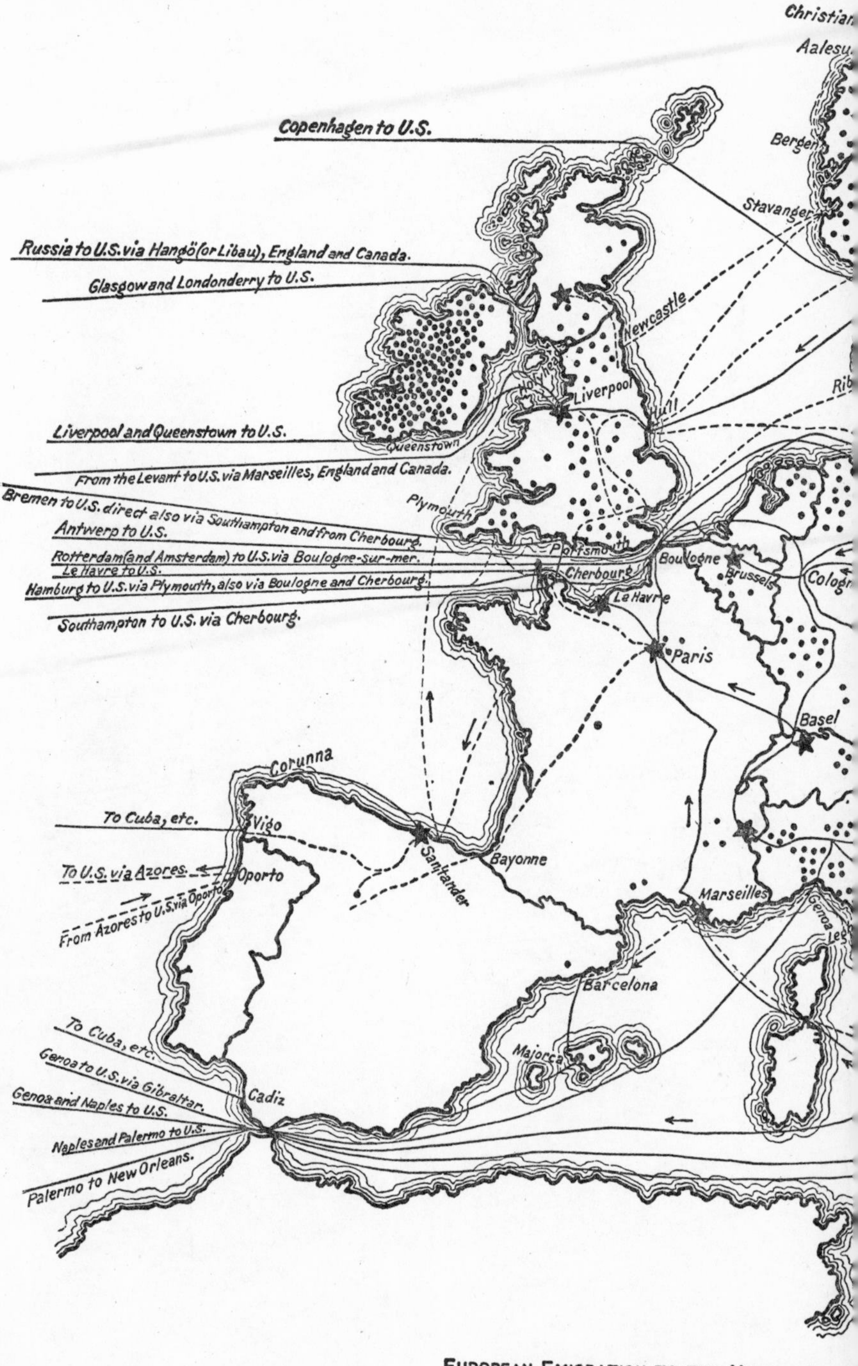

Christian
Aalesu
Bergen
Stavanger
Copenhagen to U.S.
Russia to U.S. via Hangö (or Libau), England and Canada.
Glasgow and Londonderry to U.S.
Newcastle
Liverpool
Holyhead
Hull
Liverpool and Queenstown to U.S.
Queenstown
From the Levant to U.S. via Marseilles, England and Canada.
Bremen to U.S. direct also via Southampton and from Cherbourg.
Plymouth
Antwerp to U.S.
Rotterdam (and Amsterdam) to U.S. via Boulogne-sur-mer.
Le Havre to U.S.
Hamburg to U.S. via Plymouth, also via Boulogne and Cherbourg.
Southampton to U.S. via Cherbourg.
Portsmouth
Boulogne
Cherbourg
Le Havre
Brussels
Cologn
Paris
Basel
Corunna
To Cuba, etc.
Vigo
Santander
Bayonne
To U.S. via Azores.
Oporto
From Azores to U.S. via Oporto
Marseilles
Genoa
Leg
Barcelona
Majorca
To Cuba, etc.
Genoa to U.S. via Gibraltar.
Genoa and Naples to U.S.
Naples and Palermo to U.S.
Palermo to New Orleans.
Cadiz

European Emigration to the United Stat

Compiled aft

From Report

proximately four and one-half million, and the three Scandinavian countries for two and one-quarter million. The larger part of the immigrants from northern and western Europe came in the generation immediately following the Civil War — there was a notable decline in immigration from Germany and the United Kingdom after 1890 and from Scandinavia after 1900.

As these figures indicate, the racial ingredients that made up the American population in 1870 or 1880 were not markedly different either in character or in relative strength from those which had made up the population a hundred years earlier. But already in the seventies there began to appear new types among the thousands who swarmed in at Castle Garden, New York. Austrians and Hungarians from the valley of the Danube, Bohemians from the river Moldau, Poles from the Vistula and Serbs from the river Save, blue-eyed Italians from the banks of the Arno and olive-skinned Italians from the plains of Campania or the mountains of Sicily, Russians from the Volga and the Dnieper and the steppes of Ukraine, all poured to the promised land. Almost seventy-five thousand of the many peoples of the old Dual Monarchy came over in the seventies, over fifty thousand Italians and as many Russians. By the eighties this trickle from southern and eastern Europe had become a stream, by the nineties a torrent, and in the early years of the new century a veritable flood. Altogether, in the fifty years between 1880 and 1930, Italy sent us over four and one-half million emigrants, Austria, Hungary, and the succession States over four million, Russia and Poland some three and three-quarters million — a total from these countries alone of over twelve millions.[3]

This change in the source of immigration is fundamental to recent American social history. It is to be accounted for partly by overpopulation in southern and eastern Europe, the desire to escape military service, and the persecution of Jews, Poles, Czechs, and other

[3] Change in source of immigration from Europe, 1860–1930.

Period	*Total Admitted*	*Northern & Western Europe*	%	*Southern & Eastern Europe*	%
1861–70	2,314,824	2,031,624	87.8	33,628	1.4
1871–80	2,812,191	2,070,373	73.6	201,889	7.2
1881–90	5,246,613	3,778,633	72.0	958,413	18.3
1891–1900	3,687,564	1,643,492	44.6	1,915,486	51.9
1901–10	8,795,386	1,910,035	21.7	6,225,981	70.8
1911–20	5,735,811	997,438	17.4	3,379,126	58.9
1921–30	4,107,209	1,284,023	31.3	1,193,830	29.0

minority groups, but more largely by the advertising of railroads and steamship companies and the demand of American industry for cheap labor.[4] It is the conclusion of one careful student, John R. Commons, that the demand for cheap labor, the competition for steerage passengers, and the need of transcontinental railroads to unload their large landholdings, have brought more immigrants here than were ever sent by hard conditions in the Old World.

The distribution of these new elements in our population is important. Immigrants from northern Europe, with the exception of the Irish, tended to go West and take up land. Large numbers of Germans, it is true, congregated in the cities of the Middle West, giving a distinctive flavor to such places as Cincinnati, St. Louis, and Milwaukee which has not yet entirely disappeared, but the majority probably became farmers. In the Scandinavians this tendency to go out to the land was even more marked: the great agricultural states of Minnesota, Illinois, North and South Dakota, Nebraska, and Iowa have a considerable Scandinavian population, and the influence of these industrious and intelligent farmers is felt south to Texas and west to California. Few Irish, on the other hand, moved away from the seaboard. Although most of the Irish who came here were farmers, the technique of American agriculture was strange to men used for generations to raising potatoes and cattle, there was a demand for their labor in the cities and on the railroads, and many of their religious leaders, like Bishop Hughes, feared lest dispersion would destroy the Catholic faith and impair the high moral standards of their flocks. In consequence of this urban concentration, the Irish were slow to achieve economic independence, but their group loyalty and talent for politics in a democratic medium made them the first and most enduring of racial blocs in politics. Their absolute control of the local government of New York was long proverbial, and their conquest of New England was so complete that in 1915 an Irish mayor of Boston could boast that his people had first 'made Massachusetts a fit place to live in,' and get away with it.

The later immigrants — Italians, Russians, Austrians, Poles, Jews, and others from southern and eastern Europe — showed this same predilection for the cities. Most of them were far too poor to buy a farm or invest in the machinery and stock necessary for modern agriculture, and people whose language, customs, and religion were very

[4] One witness stated to the Immigration Commission of 1911 that two of the leading steamship lines had 5000 to 6000 ticket agents in Galicia alone.

different from those of the older stock naturally tended to live together in colonies rather than isolate themselves on farms or in small towns. For many of them, too, migration to America was their urban movement — inspired by the same notions that took native Americans from the farms to the cities. In 1900 two-thirds and in 1930 three-fourths of the foreign born were living in towns and cities. The proportion of foreign born in such large cities as New York, Chicago, Cleveland, and Detroit was impressive, but the concentration in the smaller industrial cities, such as Passaic and Paterson, New Jersey, or Lawrence and Fall River, Massachusetts, was even more extraordinary. In 1930 it was not New York City but the industrial town of Hamtramck, Michigan, that had the largest percentage of foreign born in its population. But New York City, with almost half a million Italians and Russians, a quarter of a million Poles and Germans, and large numbers of every European and some Asiatic nationalities, presented the most variegated racial picture. Jacob Riis thus describes the city in 1890 when the new immigration was just beginning on a large scale:

A map of the city, colored to designate nationalities, would show more stripes than on the skin of a zebra, and more colors than any rainbow. The city on such a map would fall into two great halves, green for the Irish prevailing in the West Side tenement districts, and blue for the Germans on the East Side. But intermingled with these ground colors would be an odd variety of tints that would give the whole the appearance of an extraordinary crazy-quilt. From down in the Sixth Ward . . . the red of the Italian would be seen forcing its way northward along the line of Mulberry Street to the quarter of the French purple on Bleeker Street and South Fifth Avenue, to lose itself, after a lapse of miles, in the 'Little Italy' of Harlem. . . . Dashes of red would be seen strung through the District, northward to the city line. On the West Side the red would be seen overrunning the Old Africa of Thompson Street, pushing the black of the negro rapidly uptown. . . . Hardly less aggressive than the Italian, the Russian and the Polish Jew . . . is filling the tenements of the old Seventh Ward to the river front, and disputing with the Italian every foot of available space in the back alleys of Mulberry Street. . . . Between the dull gray of the Jew, and the Italian red, would be seen squeezed in on the map a sharp streak of yellow marking the narrow boundaries of Chinatown. Dovetailed in with the German population the poor but thrifty Bohemian might be picked out by the sombre hue of his life as of his philosophy. . . . Down near the Battery the West Side emerald would be soiled by a dirty stain, spreading rapidly like a splash of ink on a sheet of blotting paper, headquarters of the Arab tribe. Dots and dashes of color here and there would show where the Finnish sailors worship their God, the Greek pedlars the ancient name of their race, and the Swiss the goddess of thrift. . . .[5]

The same phenomenon could be observed in Boston, Chicago, San Francisco, and the other big cities of the country. Problems of housing, of sanitation and health, and of education inevitably resulted. American cities came to have their 'ghetto,' their 'little Italy,' or their 'Chinatown,' and 'slum' became a familiar word in the American vocabulary. By the decade of the eighties tenement conditions in American cities were as sordid as in the industrial centers of the Old World: breeding places for vice, crime, and epidemics. In 1890 two-thirds of the population of New York City was crowded into tenements. The situation was so serious that civic authorities, churches, and private philanthropies were aroused to remedy or eradicate it. In New York Jacob Riis, a Danish emigrant who had gained the confidence of Police Commissioner Theodore Roosevelt, told the story of *How the Other Half Lives,* and led a crusade against the worst of the tenements, and the Henry Street Settlement was established under the energetic leadership of Lillian D. Wald. In Chicago Jane Addams founded the famous Hull House, a social settlement which served as a clearing house for the social reform movement throughout the Middle West. Considerable progress was made, especially in the realm of sanitation, while 'Americanization' was accomplished largely by the American-born children of the immigrants themselves. The tenement problem, however, touched important property interests, and while hundreds of the worst tenements were condemned, housing conditions among the foreign-born remained disgraceful.

While the northern Europeans became farmers, or entered business or the skilled professions, immigrants from southern and eastern Europe became, for the most part, unskilled laborers in mine, in factory, or on the railroad. 'Historically,' according to a government report, 'the American origin of the more recent immigration, so far as such a movement can have a specific origin, seems to have been the desire of certain Pennsylvania anthracite mine owners to replace the employees that they found hard to deal with, and especially the Irish, with cheaper and more docile material. Strikes were

[5] Jacob Riis. *How the Other Half Lives,* pp. 25–27. Scribner's.

a frequent cause of friction . . . and it was natural that employers should be on the lookout for new sources of labor supply. In a number of places these raw recruits of industry seem to have been called in as the result of a strike, and there probably were plenty of instances of sending agents abroad to hire men or of otherwise inducing labor to immigrate either under contract or with an equivalent understanding.'

The Italians, Magyars, Slovaks, Hebrews, Czechs, Croats, Poles, and others who came over in the booming years of the eighties and the nineties were generally illiterate, ignorant, and poor, and unable to strike out for themselves in a new country. They naturally took what work was available, in the steel mills of Pennsylvania or the mines of West Virginia, in the lumber camps of Michigan or the textile mills of Massachusetts, in the stockyards of Chicago or the sweat-shops of New York. In 1907 a study of the Carnegie steel works revealed that of 23,337 laborers, 15,858 were foreign-born; two years later a survey of the workers in the bituminous mines of Pennsylvania discovered 76 per cent of foreign birth, and of these 92 per cent from southern and eastern Europe. The 'new' immigration was crowding out the native and Irish laborers in the field of unskilled labor, but though this worked hardship in individual cases, it was in general advantageous; until the thirties there was work enough for all in American industry. The ever-ready supply of unskilled and unorganized foreign labor at the beck and call of industry was a serious obstacle to American labor organizations, and it is not a mere coincidence that the corporation which only recently abandoned the open shop system — the United States Steel Corporation — recruited its labor force largely from immigrants of southern and eastern European extraction. The presence of large members of unskilled workers in manufacturing states such as Pennsylvania, Illinois, and Michigan and mining states such as West Virginia and Colorado tended to accentuate the grave industrial problems already pressing for solution, and the states achieved a distressing notoriety in the frequency and seriousness of their industrial disturbances. Though the 'great upheaval' of 1886 was to some extent the work of German anarchists, the tendency to ascribe social unrest to the 'foreign agitator' or to the unassimilated laborer is for the most part veriest sophistry.

Two other groups of immigrants have come into the United States in increasing numbers since the turn of the century: Canadians and Mexicans. It was easy for Canadians to drift into the United States, and after the Civil War many of them, attracted by the opportunities for work in the textile or the lumber mills, found their way to the Northern and Western states. But Canadian immigration did not take on any large proportions until after 1910. Since that time over one and one-half million Canadians, one-third of them French and about two-thirds English-speaking, crossed over the border, cementing the strong friendship already existing between the two neighboring democracies. Immigration from Canada was not accompanied by any problems of assimilation or Americanization, except among some of the French, but immigration from Mexico was a more serious matter. The census figures of 1930 revealed that not far from three-quarters of a million Mexicans were domiciled in the United States, the vast majority of them in the border states of Texas, New Mexico, Arizona, and California. For the most part poor and illiterate, casual laborers who worked in the cotton, rice, and beet-sugar fields or in the oil fields of the Southwest, they presented an ominous problem of labor and race relations. That Southerners, already perplexed with one racial problem, should permit the creation of a second, was not to be supposed, and the sharp decline of Mexican immigration after 1930 testified to the inauguration of a policy of rigid restriction. By 1940 the Mexican-born population had been cut almost in half.

Aside from the special problem presented by Orientals and Mexicans, the process of assimilation has not been as difficult as was prophesied by most observers. Such assimilation did not necessarily mean the supplanting of native culture with an artificial American one, but the cheerful acceptance of American social and political institutions. The opposition of certain patriotic groups to what Theodore Roosevelt called 'hyphenated Americanism' led frequently to an unfortunate and misguided effort to crush out those heritages of foreign culture and customs, language and literature, that give variety and flavor and richness to American life. The extreme and often touching eagerness of newcomers to abandon their Old World loyalties and profess those of the New World is one of the most striking characteristics of the whole immigration movement.

It is customary to interpret immigration from the point of view of the native American, but the persons chiefly affected by it were the immigrants themselves. The story of immigration cannot be read in the cold statistics of the census bureau, in the reports of labor surveys, of charity organizations, or of educational institutions. To the American already here, immigration has been merely one of a number of challenges to his social and political institutions. But for the immigrant who has torn up his roots from the Old World and transplanted them to new soil, who has abandoned the familiar ways and fields of his forefathers and is attempting to adapt himself to new and strange conditions of life, this is the great adventure of his life. No historian has yet cut through the statistics of immigration to the psychological realities that underlie them and give them meaning, but the stirring and often splendid story can be read in the moving pages of Rölvaag's *Giants in the Earth,* of Jacob Riis' *Making of an American,* of Mary Antin's *The Promised Land,* and of Michael Pupin's *From Immigrant to Inventor.*

These books, all by immigrants, emphasize the immigrant contribution to American society.

> We came not empty-handed here
> But brought a rich inheritance.[6]

wrote one of the immigrant poets, and no student of American culture can fail to appreciate the validity of the boast. The immigrant contribution of muscle and brawn is obvious; the contribution to politics and public affairs, industry and labor, science and education, arts and letters is scarcely less apparent, though to be sure, in these fields it has been an individual rather than a group contribution. It is necessary for us to remember only the achievements of Carl Schurz and John Peter Altgeld in politics, of Jacob Riis and Nathan Straus in social reform, of Joseph Pulitzer, James Gordon Bennett, and E. L. Godkin in journalism, of Andrew Carnegie, James J. Hill, and Henry Villard in business, of Samuel Gompers and Daniel de Leon in labor, of Alexander Graham Bell, Elilie Berliner, John Ericson, and Nikola Tesla in the field of invention, of Louis Agassiz, Charles Steinmetz, and Michael Pupin in science, of Francis Lieber and Michael Heilprin in scholarship, of Karl Bitter and Augustus Saint-Gaudens in fine arts, and of Theodore Thomas and Walter Damrosch in music[7] to persuade us that the foreign-born have enriched American life.

[6] The Danish poet, Adam Dan.

[7] The foreign-born have exercised, from the beginning, almost a monopoly over musical activities in the United States. A partial list of conductors of the leading symphony orchestras illuminates the situation in the 1930's:

Boston	Serge Koussevitsky
Buffalo	Lajos Shuk

3. *Putting Up the Bars*

The story of governmental regulation of immigration, important as it is, can be told briefly. It is a suggestive fact that though, in our constitutional system, the regulation of immigration is a function of the Federal Government, it was not exercised for well-nigh a hundred years. The traditional policy was that of unrestricted admission to all who sought our shores. Political opposition to foreigners, to be sure, had flared up in the Know-Nothing movement of the fifties, but this represented a passing phase, and it remained the boast of most Americans that their country was a refuge to the poor and oppressed of all nations. This attitude found expression in the popular ballad:

> Of all the mighty nations in the East or in the West
> This glorious Yankee nation is the greatest and the best;
> We have room for all creation and our banner is unfurled,
> Here's a general invitation to the people of the world.
>
> Come along, come along, make no delay,
> Come from every nation, come from every way;
> Our lands are broad enough, don't be alarmed,
> For Uncle Sam is rich enough to give us all a farm.

From the first regulation of immigration was left to the states and shortly after independence the states undertook to exclude undesirables. South Carolina passed an Act for Preventing the Transpor-

---

Chicago	Frederick Stock
Cincinnati	Eugene Goossens
Cleveland	Artur Rodzinski
Detroit	Ossip Gabrilowitch
Kansas City	Karl Kreuger
Los Angeles	Arnold Schönberg
Minneapolis	Eugene Ormandy
New York	Arturo Toscanini; John Barbirolli
Omaha	Rudolph Ganz
Philadelphia	Leopold Stokowski
Portland	William van Hoogstraten
Rochester	José Iturbi
St. Louis	Valdimir Golschmann
San Francisco	Pierre Monteux
Syracuse	André Polah
Washington	Hans Kindler

tation of Malefactors in 1788 and Pennsylvania a similar law in the following year. For the next half century the states of New York, Massachusetts, and Pennsylvania, to whose ports most of the arrivals came, attempted, through the exercise of the police power, to exclude criminals, paupers, and diseased immigrants. The constitutionality of such legislation was sustained, but when New York State, faced with the heavy burden of receiving and protecting the throngs of immigrants who poured in during the thirties and forties, assessed a small head tax on each immigrant, the Supreme Court declared the tax unconstitutional as an interference with the Congressional control of commerce. It was obviously unjust for one or two states to carry the entire burden of welfare work which unrestricted immigration entailed, but the Federal Government steadfastly refused to assume any part of that burden.

It was not indeed until 1882 that Congress finally undertook to regulate immigration, and then it acted only because its hand was forced by a situation which was rapidly getting beyond control. This was the threat of an inundation of the Pacific coast by Chinese coolies. It was the discovery of gold in '49 and the consequent demand for cheap labor that first brought the Chinese to California and the great Taiping rebellion of 1850 accelerated the movement. By 1852 there were some twenty-five thousand Orientals on the Pacific coast and thereafter they came at the rate of four thousand a year, their numbers augmented in the sixties by the demand for laborers on the Central Pacific Railroad. By the end of the seventies there were almost one hundred and fifty thousand Chinese in California alone, and their low standards of living, long hours of labor, and tractability were said to constitute a serious menace to native labor. At the same time they aroused racial prejudice by their obstinate adherence to the Chinese ways of life and religion, their exotic appearance, customs, and language, and their obvious intention to return to China with their savings. As a result of these factors an anti-Chinese movement developed in the mid-seventies under the leadership of an Irish agitator, Dennis Kearney. Taken up by the California Workingmen's party, it culminated in discriminatory legislation and a demand for the prohibition of further Oriental immigration.

It was in response to this demand that Congress, in 1882, passed an Act excluding Chinese laborers for a period of ten years—a prohibition that was extended in 1890 and again in 1902 until it became permanent. As a result of this policy of exclusion the Chinese population of the country declined from 107,000 in 1890 to 75,000 in 1930, and with that decline came a virtual disappearance of the anti-Chinese agitation that had for some time disturbed the relations of the United States and China.

Japanese immigration did not become a serious problem until some years later. There were less than twenty-five thousand Japanese in the country at the beginning of the twentieth century, but when the following decade witnessed an extraordinary upturn in immigration from the Nipponese Empire, the Pacific coast became alarmed and demanded that the policy of exclusion be extended to embrace the Japanese as well as the Chinese. Anti-Japanese agitation crystallized into discriminatory legislation, and in order to avoid an international crisis, President Roosevelt, in 1907, reached a 'gentlemen's agreement' with the Japanese government whereby it pledged itself to continue 'the existing policy of discouraging emigration of its subjects of the laboring classes to continental United States.' Despite this agreement a small stream of Japanese continued to trickle into the Pacific coast, and between 1911 and 1913 California and other Western states enacted a series of laws designed to prevent Japanese from owning or even leasing real estate. Once again a diplomatic rupture was threatened. The personal intervention of Secretary of State Bryan was effective in softening the language but not in modifying the meaning of the California laws, and the crisis was temporarily averted. Ten years later the Supreme Court sustained the California alien land law, and the Immigration Act of 1924 finally put an end to further Japanese immigration into the United States.

Once embarked upon a policy of regulation, Congress was faced with a number of alternatives among which to choose. Should it adopt a policy of restriction, of selection, or of exclusion? If restriction were to be adopted, how far should the government go in denying entry to prospective immigrants; if selection, upon what basis should it be made? The first general immigration law, that of 1882, was based upon the theory of selection; it placed a head tax of fifty cents upon every immigrant admitted, and excluded convicts, idiots, and persons likely to become public charges. From this time on a long series of federal acts elaborated the policy of selection, increased the head tax, prohibited contract labor, considerably extended the classes excluded, and provided for more efficient enforcement of the laws. In a general way the laws excluded the sick and diseased, paupers, polygamists, prostitutes, anarchists, alcoholics, and — by the Act of 1917 — persons with constitutional inferiority complexes!

While this policy of selection afforded protection against some unwelcome additions to the population, it scarcely affected the total number of immigrants. There arose therefore an insistent demand that some plan be formulated whereby the number of newcomers might be reduced and only the best ones admitted. The criterion of selection was to be literacy, and an historic battle was waged over this issue. Agitation for a literacy test came from two groups: labor which saw in such a test a means of reducing the 'new' immigration, a large percentage of which was illiterate, and reformist groups who felt that the American stock was being coarsened by intermixture with southern and eastern European stock, and who deplored the

> Accents of menace alien to our air,
> Voices that once the Tower of Babel knew.[8]

A bill incorporating a literacy test passed one of the two Houses of Congress no less than thirty-two times, and on four occasions it was passed by both Houses and went to the President, only to be vetoed each time. Cleveland, in 1897, characterized the measure as 'a radical departure from our national policy.' Taft, in 1913, declared that a literacy test violated a principle which he believed should be maintained. Wilson in 1915 and again in 1917 denounced it as a test of opportunity rather than of character or of fitness. On the last occasion, however, the bill was passed over the presidential veto and became a law. By its terms no alien over sixteen years of age who cannot read the English language or some other language or dialect is to be admitted to the United States.

The Immigration Act of 1917, in method selective, in purpose restrictive, marks the transition from the earlier to the modern policy of immigration regulation; since that time regulation has become increasingly restrictive in character until it finally reached the point of exclusion. During the World War immigration from Europe fell off sharply, but the fear of a renewal of the influx on an unprecedented scale after the cessation of arms led Congress definitely to abandon the policy of selection for one of absolute restriction. By the Immigration Act of 1921, the number of aliens admitted from any

[8] Thomas Bailey Aldrich, 'Unguarded Gates.' 'A poem,' wrote Aldrich, 'in which I mildly protest against America becoming the cesspool of Europe.'

European, Australasian, Near Eastern, or African country [9] was to be limited to three per cent of the total number of persons of that nationality residing in the United States in 1910. This so-called quota system, specifically designed to reduce the number of immigrants from southern and eastern Europe, drastically restricted the total number that could be admitted in any one year to 357,802. This act, however, was severely criticized on two counts: that it admitted too many immigrants and that it failed to discriminate sufficiently in favor of northern and western Europeans. Consequently a new and more drastic law was passed in 1924 which reduced the annual quota from three to two per cent, and which, by taking the census of 1890 as a basis, effectually favored English, Irish, German, and Scandinavian, and discriminated against Italian, Austrian, Russian, and other southern and eastern European immigration. Finally by the National Origins Act of 1929 the total number of immigrants who might be admitted in one year was reduced to 150,000 to be apportioned among the various European countries in proportion to the 'national origins' of the American people in 1920.[10] Immigration from other American countries was left undisturbed, except by a Department of Labor ruling that no immigrants should be admitted who might become public charges.

The enactment of the first quota law of 1921 ended an era. In a hundred years the tide of immigration had risen to a flood, engulfing the whole country and depositing millions of people from every land and the cultural accretions of centuries. Then suddenly it ebbed. The statue of Liberty still stood guard over New York harbor, its beacon light held proudly aloft, the inscription on its base not yet erased:

> Give me your tired, your poor,
> Your huddled masses yearning to breathe free,
> The wretched refuse of your teeming shore,
> Send these, the homeless, tempest-tost to me:
> I lift my lamp beside the golden door.[11]

But it was a symbol of things strange, and but faintly remembered.

[9] The Act of 1917 created a Barred Zone, including India, Siam, Indo-China, and other parts of Asia from which no immigrants were to be admitted. Immigration from China and Japan, already limited by law and by the 'Gentlemen's Agreement' was in 1924 absolutely barred.

[10] See table in appendix.

[11] 'The New Colossus,' *Poems* of Emma Lazarus, I, p. 202. Houghton Mifflin.

IX

AGRICULTURE AND THE FARM PROBLEM
1865–1920

1. *The Agricultural Revolution*

WHILE manufacturing, transportation, and business were advancing with giant strides in the half century following the Civil War, agriculture still remained the basic industry, and the one which engaged the labor of the largest number of people and upon which industrial development largely rested. But agriculture itself was undergoing a revolution brought about through the operation of three basic factors: the expansion of the agricultural domain, the application of machinery and biological science to the processes of farming, and the use of modern transportation to convey the products to world-wide markets. This revolution meant a shift from husbandry to machine farming, and from subsistence to commercial farming. It made agriculture an intimate though subordinate part of the industrial system. It brought a vast increase in productiveness and efficiency, with diminishing returns to owners and tillers of the soil, depression of the farmer class, and agitation for government relief.

In the fifty years from 1860 to 1910 the number of farms in the United States trebled, increasing from 2,033,000 to 6,361,000; the acreage more than doubled, from 407,212,000 to 878,798,000, and the acreage of improved farm land trebled; while the production of wheat rose from 173 to 635 million bushels, of corn from 838 to 2,886 million bushels, and of cotton from 3,841,000 to 11,609,000 bales. More land was brought under cultivation in the thirty years after 1860 than in all the previous history of the United States. While the value of farms and farm products increased, they did not keep pace with returns from manufacturing and business, and there were serious decreases in parts of New England and the South. Farm population increased absolutely, but the proportion of people living on farms steadily declined; while the agricultural domain expanded, the relative political and social position of the farmer contracted.

By 1910 agriculture had reached a condition of comparative stability, but throughout the preceding half century farming had been subjected to a series of shocks. The first, which we have already studied, was the impact of the Civil War and Reconstruction on the South, involving the partial destruction of the plantation system, the redistribution of land, and the rise of the crop lien and share crop systems. The second came from opening up the Far West and the over-rapid extension of farmers westward, with a consequent depression of agricultural activities in the Middle West and the East. American crops moved westward with the American people. In 1860 Illinois, Indiana, and Wisconsin were the leading wheat producing states; fifty years later the cereal empire had passed to North Dakota, Kansas, and Minnesota. In 1860 the heart of the corn belt was the Ohio Valley; in 1910 it was the Mississippi Valley from the Wabash to the Platte. In 1860 Mississippi was the leading cotton state of the South; by the turn of the century the Cotton Kingdom's capital was somewhere on the plains of Texas. All this meant readjustment in the older states, and the transition from staple crop farming to truck or dairy farming, or the snuffing out of agriculture except as a rich man's hobby. Equally disturbing to the agricultural equilibrium were the impact of new machinery, the introduction of new crops and of countless varieties of old crops, the substitution of staple crop for diversified agriculture, and the growing importance of the world rather than the domestic market.

Agriculture, historically the most static of all industries, has thus been forced to adjust itself rapidly to changing conditions. Except in isolated regions like the Southern highlands or the rich Pennsylvania and Maryland country, the average farm ceased to be a self-sufficient economic unit, where a man and his family raised most of what they ate, wore, and used, and provided their own amusement in neighborhood groups. It became, like West Indian sugar plantations, a cog in an industrial system, devoted to the raising of a staple crop, mechanized, and tied up with banking, railroading, and manufacturing.

One thing, however, did not greatly change. American agriculture continued to be, as it had always been, extensive rather than intensive, robbing the land of its fertility and leaving desolation behind. Because land was abundant, fertile, and cheap, the American farmer had found it easier and more profitable to take up new land than to conserve the resources of the old. Just as speculators recklessly exploited mineral resources, so the farmer used up the soil, and the lumberman cut down the forest, leaving nature to do the replacing unaided. Everything conspired to encourage the farmer in his gutting of the soil: not only machinery and world markets, but constant change in farm ownership, Negro labor in the South, an increase in absentee ownership and in tenancy which destroyed the sense of responsibility toward the land, the laissez-faire of the government policy as to conservation, and generosity in free homesteads which tempted farmers to abandon their old lands for new. Not until the spectacular rise in farm land values in the early years of the present century dramatized the passing of cheap good land did the government realize the necessity for conservation, or the farmer for scientific farming. Then it was almost too late. When economists came to count the cost of our exploitative agriculture they found that one hundred million acres of land — an area equal to Illinois, Ohio, North Carolina, and Maryland — had been irreparably destroyed by erosion; that another two hundred million acres were so badly eroded that they were almost useless for agricultural purposes; that over large areas the grass lands of the Great Plains had been turned into deserts; that the forest resources of the eastern half of the country were disappearing; and that recurrent droughts and floods were the inevitable consequences of these malpractices.

This then was the result of that half century of unprecedented expansion which had excited the wonder and envy of the entire world: the public domain in which, said Jefferson, there was 'room enough for our descendants to the hundredth and thousandth generation' was all but gone; the crop lands of the East and the grass lands of the West were rapidly approaching complete exhaustion; and the American farmer — 'the chosen people of God, if ever he had a chosen people' — was in a desperate plight. It remained to be seen whether the efforts of science and technology could repair the material devastation that had been wrought, whether the drastic remedies of the economists could heal the economic malaise, and whether the costly expedient of government relief could rehabilitate the farmer class.

2. *Machinery*

It is a curious and suggestive fact that the application of machinery to agriculture lagged fully a century behind the application of machinery to industry. The eighteenth century witnessed a thoroughgoing mechanization of many mining and manufacturing operations, but Henry Adams could truthfully observe that

> The Saxon farmer of the eighth century enjoyed most of the comforts known to Saxon farmers of the eighteenth. . . . The plough was rude and clumsy; the sickle as old as Tubal Cain, and even the cradle not in general use; the flail was unchanged since the Aryan exodus; in Virginia, grain was still commonly trodden out by horses.[1]

Mechanization of agriculture did not really begin until the thirties and forties, when Obed Hussey and Cyrus McCormick were experimenting with the reaper, A. D. Church and George Westinghouse with a thresher, and John Lane and John Deere with the chilled plow. Agricultural machinery, however, remained relatively unimportant, except in parts of the Middle West, before 1860. The Civil War, robbing the farms of their laborers and increasing the price of grain, induced farmers generally to adopt machines such as the reaper, which enabled a woman or even a boy to perform the work of several men. Over a hundred thousand reapers were in use by 1861 and during the four years of the war the number increased by a quarter of a million. After the war came countless new inventions — there were over twelve thousand patents on plows alone prior to 1900 — and the pressure of competition eventually made the use of agricultural machinery almost universal in the North. Soon almost every operation from preparing the ground to harvesting the product was transformed by machinery. The Oliver chilled plow meant an enormous saving in time and money; within a few years the simple plow had been developed into the wonderfully efficient rotary plow which plowed and harrowed the soil and drilled the grain in a single operation. In 1867 George Appleby invented a twine binder which increased greatly the amount of grain a farmer could harvest, and about the same time the steam threshing machine was perfected to a point where it was both efficient and safe. Within twenty years the bonanza farms of California were using 'combines' which reaped, threshed, cleaned, and bagged the grain in a single operation. During these same years the lister, the mowing machine, the corn planter, corn binder, husker, and sheller, the manure spreader, the four-plow cultivator, the potato planter, the mechanical hay drier, the poultry incubator, the cream separator, and innumerable other machines entirely transformed the ancient practices of agriculture, lightened the drudgery, decreased the amount of labor, and in-

[1] Henry Adams, *History of the United States during the Administration of Thomas Jefferson,* vol. 1, p. 16. Scribner's.

creased the efficiency. If the process continues much longer only retired capitalists will be able to afford farm equipment.

How great was the saving in labor made possible by the use of farm machinery can best be discovered from a few specific examples. In 1830 it required something over half an hour to prepare the ground and sow one bushel of wheat; in 1900 two minutes sufficed for this operation. With the hand cradle of 1830 a man could harvest twenty bushels of grain in sixty-one hours; by 1900 he could perform the same work in less than three hours. It took twenty-one hours to harvest a ton of timothy hay in 1850; four hours half a century later. It was this vast saving in labor which made it possible for a proportionately smaller number of farmers to feed an ever-increasing number of city-dwellers and have a surplus left over for export.

In the twentieth century came a further development of industrialization with the application of steam, gasoline, and electricity to the farm. The huge 'combines,' formerly drawn by twenty or thirty horses, are now propelled by gasoline tractors, and in 1930 almost one million tractors were in use on the farms of the United States. The kindly beasts which have accompanied mankind from the dawn of civilization, and whose care, training, and breeding have entered into human discipline, and culture, have been forsaken in favor of impersonal machinery. This substitution of power for horses has released not less than thirty million acres formerly devoted to pasture and forage. Electric power is used in all up-to-date dairies. The motor truck has altered to some extent marketing conditions, while the motor car, the telephone, and the radio have enlarged the social radius of the farm and led farmers to forget their rich heritage of folklore and song in favor of canned entertainment of various sorts.

Varied farming still exists in many parts of the country, and mechanization has never reached an extreme in New England, with its rolling topography and little specialties, or in the South with Negro labor, cotton, and tobacco. For although the cotton gin was the first important agricultural machine invented, no inventor has since been able to find a machine to supersede the hand cultivation of cotton — unless indeed the Rust cotton-picking machine, invented in the 1930's, proves a mechanical and commercial success. Nor does tobacco lend itself readily to the use of machinery. The value of farm implements and machines in the whole country increased from about $500,000,000 in 1890 to $749,000,000 in 1900 and to no less than $3,594,000,000 in 1920. This increase was distinctly sectional in character. It was the Middle West and the Far West that absorbed the reapers, mowers, tractors, harvesters, and threshers as fast as they could be turned out of the factories. In 1910 the value of machinery on Northern farms was $800,000,000 and by 1920 this had increased to over $2,300,000,000, while the corresponding figures for the South are $293,000,000 and $771,000,000. In 1920 the average value of farm implements and machinery on each South Dakota farm was $1,500; on each farm in the cotton belt it was $215.

Farming as a way of life is giving way to farming as a business. The farmer has become an industrial worker, as much bound up to the complex industrial and fiscal system of the country as if he had a boss over him. A stout heart and willing hands are no longer the only necessary equipment for farming, or a cabin roof and the sky the only 'overhead.' Increase in land value, heavy costs of machinery, and the substitution of chemical fertilizer for manure require considerable capital, and often involve the farmer in heavy indebtedness which in turn add to his overhead. The small diversified farm of the sixties, with fields of wheat, corn, oats, and barley, orchard and vegetable garden, pasture mowing and woodlot, gave way to the large farms specializing in staple crops which could be produced with one kind of machinery and sold for cash. Another result was the ominous increase in farm mortgages and in tenancy. By the turn of the century every third farmer was a tenant; thirty years later almost every second farmer was a tenant, and one-fifth of the total value of American farms was mortgaged.

3. *Scientific Agriculture*

There had been considerable interest in scientific agriculture in the second half of the eighteenth century, both in Europe and in America. Progressive Virginia planters like Washington and Jefferson adopted the new methods and implements which had been proved in England, and added some of their own; agricultural societies had been formed in all the thirteen original states by 1800. The rise of the Cotton Kingdom after the invention of the cotton gin in 1793, however, made it more profitable to take up virgin land in the newer South than to reclaim farms in Virginia and the Carolinas. Interest in scientific agriculture waned, except in New England where agricultural societies founded in the eighteenth century are still flourishing, where Elkanah Watson inaugurated the agricultural fair, where the first agricultural school in the United States opened in 1822, and where Benjamin Bussey's will anticipated the Morrill Act by twenty-five years. The *American Farmer,* the first agricultural journal in the United States, was established in Baltimore in 1819. By 1840, when the prevalence of 'old-field' land worn out by successive cropping with tobacco in tidewater Virginia and Maryland had become an eye-sore, Edmund Ruffin of Virginia began to devote himself to disseminating knowledge of scientific agriculture, and much of the abandoned land was regenerated by the use of marl. Lord Playfair's translation of Baron von Liebig's great treatise, *Chemistry in its Application to Agriculture and Physiology* (1840), was read with avidity by the more progressive farmers. By 1860 there were fifty farm papers in the country, many of them in the South; and if the Civil War had not broken out, the teachings of Ruffin and De Bow would undoubtedly have borne fruit in a more diversified and economical agriculture in the South. For these were directed away from specialization, just as those of the last generation have been diverted toward it.

Yet the average farmer had little patience with scientific agriculture, and some of them doubtless read with approval the dictum of one book on farming that was published in 1860: 'Scientific agriculture stands today with phrenology and biology and magnetism. No farmer ever yet received any benefit from any analysis of the soil and it is doubtful if any one ever will.' As long as there was an abundance of cheap land and a shortage of labor — a condition which obtained until some time after the Civil War — it was more economical for farmers to abandon worn-out soil and move on to virgin land than to cultivate intensively and invest in expensive fertilizers. The passing of these conditions led inevitably to scientific agriculture, conservation, and reclamation.

Scientific agriculture in the United States has depended largely upon government aid. A number of states subsidized agriculture in one way or another even before the Civil War. The Constitution gives Congress no explicit jurisdiction over agriculture but as early as 1839 Congress made its first appropriation, one thousand dollars, for agricultural research. One of the most useful results of the loose-constructionist thinking in the Republican party was the creation by Congress in 1862 of a Department of Agriculture, under the direction of a commissioner; in 1889 this department was raised to executive grade with a secretary of cabinet rank.

The activities and influence of the Department of Agriculture have grown rapidly, until by 1930 it included some forty subdivisions and bureaus and operated with an appropriation of not far from one hundred million dollars. State and federal departments of agriculture maintain experiment stations, issue valuable crop reports and other bulletins, encourage farmers to introduce new plants and improve old ones, fight plant and animal diseases, attempt to solve problems of management and marketing, and offer advice on innumerable subjects, from alfalfa and applesauce to zygophyllum and zymotic diseases.

In the year 1862, which saw the passage of the Homestead and Pacific Railway Acts, Congress passed the most important piece of agricultural legislation in American history — the Morrill Land-Grant College Act. This law, the joint product of Justin Morrill of Vermont and Jonathan B. Turner of Illinois, provided for the appropriation of public land to each state for the establishment of agricultural and industrial colleges. Under its wise provisions sixty-nine land-grant colleges have been established, some as agricultural colleges, others as state universities.

Scarcely second to the Morrill Act in importance is the Hatch Act of 1887. Influenced by the valuable work performed by the experimental station of Wesleyan University in Middletown, Connecticut, Congress provided in this act for the creation of agricultural experiment stations in every state in the Union; since that time Congress has steadily supported and expanded the work of education and experimentation in the field of agriculture. In 1930 some sixty experiment stations were carrying on scientific research of incalculable benefit to the nation. For the most part the experiment stations concentrate their efforts on local problems: the boll weevil in Alabama, red rust in Minnesota, dry farming in the West.

Scientific farming, the conquest of plant and animal diseases, the surmounting of natural obstacles, and the adaptation of plants to American conditions has its own roll of pioneers and heroes. Mark Alfred Carleton who experienced on the Kansas plains the devastations of wheat rust and rot and the vagaries of Kansas weather, scoured the wilds of Asia for a wheat strong enough to withstand the rust, the droughts, and the frosts of the Middle West. He returned with the famous Kubanka wheat and later introduced the Kharkov wheat to the American farmer. Within a few years these plants demonstrated their superiority to the domesticated variety, and by 1919 over one-third of the American wheat acreage was of the varieties introduced by Carleton. William Saunders and Angus Mackay of Canada succeeded in crossing Red Fife with Calcutta wheat, and produced the hardy Marquis, thus opening up millions of acres of land in the Canadian Northwest to winter wheat. Niels Ebbesen Hansen of the South Dakota Agricultural College explored the steppes of Turkestan and the plateaus of inner Mongolia and brought back a yellow-flowered alfalfa that would flourish in the American Northwest. From Algeria and Tunis and the oases of the Sahara came the famous white Kaffir corn, introduced by Dr. J. H. Watkins, and admirably adapted to the hot dry climate of the great Southwest. George Hoffer conquered the insidious rot that destroyed the corn of the Middle West; Marion Dorset found the remedy for hog cholera; and George Mohler helped to stamp out the dread hoof and mouth disease that threatened to wipe out a large part of American livestock. Dr. Stephen M. Babcock saved the dairy farmers of the nation millions of dollars through the use of the Babcock milk test which determined the amount of butter fat contained in milk. Seaman Knapp found in the Orient varieties of rice wonderfully adapted to the Gulf region, and today Louisiana exports rice to China and Japan. Luther Burbank, working in his experimental garden at Santa Rosa, California, succeeded in creating a host of new plants by skillful crossing. David A. Coker, on his South Carolina experimental farm, improved upland cotton and added immeasurably to the wealth of his section, and George Washington Carver of the Tuskegee Institute developed hundreds of new uses for the peanut, the sweet potato, and the soy bean. To be sure the cinch bug, the boll weevil and his cousin the alfalfa weevil, and many other insect pests have so far refused to yield to science, but the triumphs of science over plant and animal diseases have been as notable as the triumphs of medicine over the diseases which afflict mankind.

While American farmers have accepted government co-operation to increase the yield of their farms in order to meet rising costs, they have, of necessity, required government aid to reclaim desert wastes by irrigation. Artificial irrigation was practiced by the Pueblo Indians even before the coming of the white man, and later by the Spanish missions of the Southwest, but it first came into general use with the Mormon settlements in Utah. The Carey Act of 1894 and especially the Reclamation Act of 1902 opened up millions of acres of western lands to irrigation through government co-operation and financial subsidization, and by 1930 not far from twenty million acres of land were under irrigation, most of it in California, Colorado, Idaho, Montana, and Utah. Meantime the Federal Government inaugurated a stupendous program of irrigation and reclamation projects with a view not only to reclamation but to drought relief, flood control, soil conservation, and the manufacture of electric power.[2] Necessarily involved in such a program was the consideration of a whole series of questions about the control of marginal and sub-marginal lands, the regulation of crops, the disposition of surplus crops, and the relation of the government to agriculture — questions whose significance was not to be fully appreciated until the decade of the 1930's.

4. *The Farm Problem*

When we've wood and prairie land,
Won by our toil,
We'll reign like kings in fairy land,
Lords of the soil.

So sang Richard Garland and the 'trail-makers of the Middle Border' as they pushed hopefully westward from the forests of Maine to the coulees of Wisconsin, the prairies of Iowa, and the sun-baked plains of Kansas, Nebraska, and the Dakotas. They won their wood and prairie land, but often won it for others — for absentee landlords, railroads, banks, and mortgage companies — and they lingered on as slaves, not lords, of the soil. Within a generation the 'marching song of the Garlands' gave way to a different tune:

There's a dear old homestead on Nebraska's fertile plain,
  There I toiled my manhood's strength away:
All that labor now is lost to me, but it is Shylock's gain,
  For that dear old home he claims today.

And when young Hamlin Garland wrote his *Main Travelled Roads* he dedicated it to 'my father and mother, whose half century of pilgrimage on the main travelled road of life has brought them only pain and weariness.'

The history of a half century of American agriculture is implicit in the story of the Garlands, and well might the student ask why the pilgrimage of the farmer toward the sunset regions should have ended in weariness and pain, why the conquest of a continent and the creation of a great agricultural domain should have resulted not in the realization of Jefferson's dream of a great agrarian democracy,

[2] See accompanying map of irrigation projects.

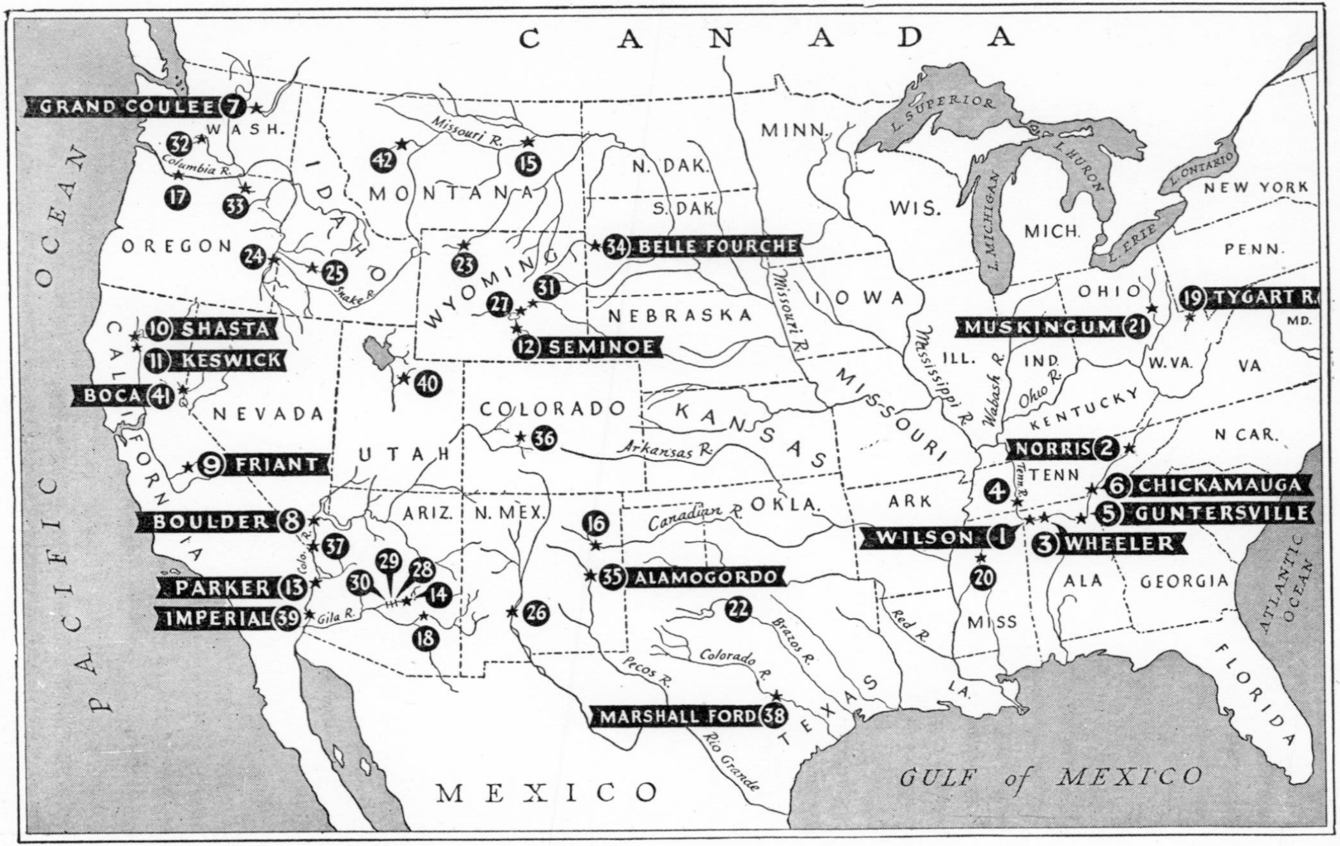

Irrigation Projects and Roster of Federal Dams, 1942

ROSTER OF FEDERAL DAMS, 1942

	Dam	Purpose	Completed Cost
1.	*Wilson, Alabama	Navigation, power	$41,694,819
2.	*Norris, Tennessee	Storage, power	30,855,815
3.	*Wheeler, Alabama	Navigation, flood, power	39,064,847
4.	**Pickwick Landing, Tenn.	Navigation, flood	38,130,845
5.	**Guntersville, Ala.	Navigation, flood	34,074,740
6.	**Chickamauga, Tenn.	Navigation, flood	37,650,035
7.	*Grand Coulee, Wash.	Flood, irrig., power	193,990,000
8.	*Boulder, Ariz.-Nev.	Flood, irrig., power	137,879,000
9.	*Friant, Calif.	Irrigation, flood	20,059,000
10.	**Shasta, Calif.	Flood, irrig., power	96,725,000
11.	***Keswick, Calif.	Power	12,430,000
12.	*Seminoe, Wyoming	Flood, irrig., power	9,500,000
13.	*Parker, Arizona	Water supply, power	19,228,000
14.	*Roosevelt, Arizona	Irrigation, power	3,890,000
15.	**Fort Peck, Montana	Flood, irrig., power	115,764,795
16.	*Conchas, New Mexico	Flood, water supply	15,452,000
17.	*Bonneville, Oreg.-Wash.	Navigation, power	80,860,000
18.	*Coolidge, Arizona	Flood, power	4,500,000
19.	**Tygart River, West Va.	Navigation, flood	18,500,000
20.	**Sardis, Miss.	Flood	14,514,000
21.	*Muskingum, Ohio (14 dams)	Flood	
22.	**Possum Kingdom, Texas	Flood, conversion	3,000,000
23.	*Shoshone, Wyoming	Irrigation, power	1,500,000
24.	*Owyhee, Oregon	Irrigation	5,400,000
25.	*Arrowrock, Idaho	Irrigation	4,300,000
26.	*Elephant Butte, New Mex.	Irrigation, power	4,100,000
27.	*Pathfinder, Wyo.	Irrigation	1,800,000
28.	*Horse Mesa, Ariz.	Power	2,873,000
29.	*Mormon Flat, Ariz.	Power	1,559,000
30.	*Stewart Mountain, Ariz.	Power	2,515,000
31.	*Alcova, Wyoming	Irrigation	3,339,000
32.	*Tieton, Wash.	Irrigation	3,756,000
33.	*McKay, Oregon	Irrigation	3,124,000
34.	*Belle Fourche, So. Dak.	Irrigation	1,230,000
35.	*Alamagorda, New Mexico	Irrigation	3,465,000
36.	*Taylor Park, Colorado	Irrigation	2,000,000
37.	***Davis Dam, Ariz.-Nev.	Power	32,656,000
38.	*Marshall Ford, Texas	Irrig., flood, power	23,595,000
39.	*Imperial, Calif.-Ariz.	Irrigation	8,926,760
40.	*Deer Creek, Utah	Irrigation	3,531,429
41.	*Boca, Calif.	Irrigation	997,404
42.	*Gibson, Montana	Irrigation	2,512,308

*Completed **Construction under way ***Preliminary work started

but in a 'farm problem.' For sixty years after 1870, the farm problem was a constant in American history, and with every decade it thrust itself more insistently upon the public consciousness. With every decade it became increasingly apparent that agriculture was headed toward ruin, and that the destruction of the independent farmer would rend the whole fabric of American economy, society, and government.

We can distinguish, for purposes of convenience, four aspects of the farm problem. There was the physical problem of soil exhaustion and erosion, of drought and frost and flood, of plant and animal diseases; the economic problem of over-expansion and over-production, of rising costs and declining returns, of exploitation in the domestic market and competition in the world market, of mortgages and tenancy; the social problem of isolation and drabness, of inadequate educational, religious, medical, and recreational facilities, of narrowing opportunity and declining prestige. Finally there was the political problem of wresting remedial legislation from intransigent state and federal governments, which were much more responsive to the demands of industry, transportation, and finance, than to the appeals of the farmer.

Of all these problems, the physical problem was perhaps the most serious. The reckless mining of the soil, the cultivation of staple crops, the destruction of the forests, resulted in soil erosion, drought, and flood. The use of Negro labor, the concentration upon cotton and tobacco which more rapidly than other crops exhaust the soil, and heavy rainfall, made the problem of soil erosion peculiarly grave in the South. Almost one hundred million acres of that section — approximately one-sixth of the total, had been hopelessly lost or seriously impaired through erosion, and in some sections of the Piedmont as much as half of the arable land had been swept of its topsoil by 1930. Early travelers in the South recorded that the streams were as clear as those of New England, but today the rivers of the South, which every year carry out to the ocean over fifty million tons of soil, are mud-black or clay-red. The abuse of the southern uplands, says one distinguished geographer, 'is well nigh incredible under the cotton economy, and the necessary breaking of that socio-economic pattern if the country is not ultimately to be left to the foxes and the briars is about as tough a task of regeneration as one can imagine.' Southern farmers have tried to replenish their worn-out soil with fertilizer, but that means an intolerable financial burden on the agricultural overhead of that section. South Carolina, for example, long spent fifteen per cent of its total farm income on fertilizer, and the proportion was almost as great in the other seaboard states.

In the grasslands of the West, too, erosion reached staggering proportions, necessitating irrigation and dry farming, and making the farmer helpless before dust storms and droughts.

> The primeval sod [writes Stuart Chase] has been burned, over-grazed, plowed up and destroyed. Where dry farming for wheat lands has been practised on the Great Plains, the Dust Bowl spreads. Where corn has been planted on the slopes of the tall grass regions, water erosion spreads. The sharp hooves of too many cattle and the close cropping of the grass by too many sheep have torn the cover from the open grazing lands, loosened the ancient sod, and started gullies and dunes of both water and wind erosion. One hundred and sixty-five million acres of grazing lands has been seriously depleted.[3]

Closely connected with erosion, and more serious to the individual farmer, are the recurrent droughts which have brought crop failures, bankruptcy, and ruin to the farmers of the High Plains ever since they first ventured out on that forbidding land. Mari Sandoz has graphically described for us the effect of drought in western Nebraska in the early nineties:

> The drought exceeded all probability. Corn did not sprout. On the hardland fringe the buffalo grass was started and browned before the first of May. Even lighter soil south of the river produced nothing. The sandhills greened only in stripes where the water-logged sand cropped out. The lake beds whitened and cracked in rhythmical patterns. Grouse were scarce and dark-fleshed. Rabbits grew thin and wild and coyotes emboldened. Covered wagons like gaunt-ribbed, gray animals moved eastward, the occupants often becoming public charges along the way.[4]

Since that time the drought has been an ever-present menace; that it is recurring with increasing frequency seems probable from the experience of the 1930's with devastating droughts in 1930, 1934, and 1936. So hazardous, indeed, is farming in parts of the High Plains that officials of the Department of Agriculture have concluded that nature did not design this section for intensive agriculture and have seriously proposed the abandonment of farming over large areas.

Outraged nature has taken her revenge on the farmer not only in erosion, dust storms, and droughts, but in floods. The long-continued

[3] *Rich Land, Poor Land,* p. 41. McGraw-Hill Book Co.

[4] *Old Jules,* p. 179. Little, Brown & Co.

practice of denuding the land both of topsoil and trees resulted, finally, in a series of calamitous floods, such as those which inundated the Middle States in the spring of 1936 and the great flood on the Ohio which inflicted incalculable damage throughout the entire Ohio valley in the winter of the following year.

The ravages of insect pests have been scarcely less serious than erosion, drought, and flood. 'Every year,' writes Dr. L. O. Howard of the Bureau of Entomology, 'the damage wrought by insects nullifies the labor of a million men.' Before the attack of the cinch bug and the corn borer, the boll weevil and the alfalfa weevil, the average farmer is all but helpless, and the plagues of grasshoppers have been like the locust plagues of ancient Egypt. Who that has read the glowing pages of Rölvaag's *Giants in the Earth* can forget how the grasshoppers destroyed not only the wheat but the morale of the farmers of the west:

> And now from out the sky gushed down with cruel force a living, pulsating stream, striking the backs of the helpless folk like pebbles thrown by an unseen hand. . . . This substance had no sooner fallen than it popped up again, crackling and snapping — rose up and disappeared in the twinkling of an eye; it flared and flittered around them like light gone mad; it chirped and buzzed through the air; it snapped and hopped along the ground; the whole place was a weltering turmoil of raging little demons; if one looked for a moment into the wind, one saw nothing but glittering, lightning-like flashes — flashes that came and went, in the heart of a cloud made up of innumerable dark-brown clicking bodies. All the while the roaring sound continued. . . . They whizzed by in the air; they literally covered the ground; they lit on the heads of grain, on the stubble, on everything in sight — pepping and glittering, millions on millions of them. The people watched it stricken with fear and awe.[5]

More complex, but more readily susceptible to remedial action, was the economic problem of the farmer. Put in its simplest terms, this was the problem of rising costs and falling prices. So long as farm land increased in value it was possible for individual farmers to sell out at a profit and thus have something to show for a lifetime of toil. But with the collapse of land values in the 1920's and '30's even the most ingenious economists and the most agile politicians could no longer blink the truth that American farming was being operated at a loss.

The factors that account for this economic malaise were numerous,

[5] *Giants in the Earth*, pp. 342–343. Harper's.

and we can do no more than list them in some logical sequence. In the generation after the Civil War the agricultural domain expanded too rapidly. This expansion into the West and Southwest brought ruin to the farmers of New England and the seaboard South, but it did not bring prosperity to the farmers of the West, for it was paralleled by a no less remarkable expansion of the agricultural domain of Canada, the Argentine, Australia, Russia, and Brazil. So long as farming was primarily for subsistence and while the market was largely domestic, this situation was not serious. But when the American farmer grew more than the American market could absorb — a condition with which the cotton planter was long familiar — he had to sell his product in the world market, and the price which he received, at home as abroad, was determined by the world market. Industry, which could regulate its production and which operated behind tariff walls, bought in a world market and sold in a protected market; agriculture, which could not effectively regulate its production and very little of which could benefit from tariffs, bought in a protected market and sold in a world market.

There were two possible means by which the farmers might have overcome these disadvantages. The first was organization, looking to a limitation upon production. Transportation, finance, manufacturing, power, even labor, organized for self-protection, but the farmers were never able to organize successfully or to work out any voluntary limitation upon crops which would be at once effective and profitable. The second alternative was governmental action which would afford the farmers the same kind of protection and subsidization as that which the tariff gave to industry. Such action was proposed in the 1920's, only to encounter insuperable political opposition. Not until the administration of Franklin D. Roosevelt did the government undertake to aid agriculture as it had long aided industry, through loans, subsidies, and price guarantees.

Furthermore, as agricultural technology expanded, the farmer found himself more and more the victim rather than the beneficiary of the industrial revolution. The expansion of agriculture into the West meant an absolute dependence upon railroads, and freight charges came to consume an increasingly large share of the farmer's income. The *Prairie Farmer* asserted in 1867 that Iowa corn cost eight or ten times as much at Liverpool as the farmer received for it at the local grain elevator; thus corn that sold for seventy cents a bushel in the east might bring the farmer only ten or fifteen cents,

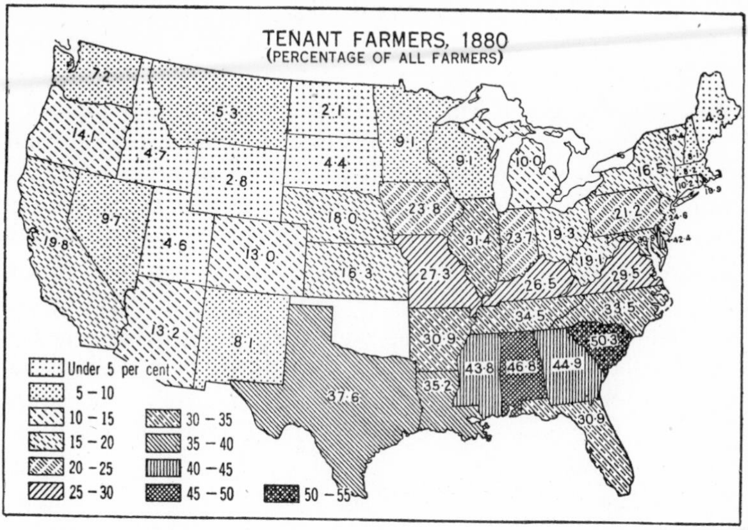

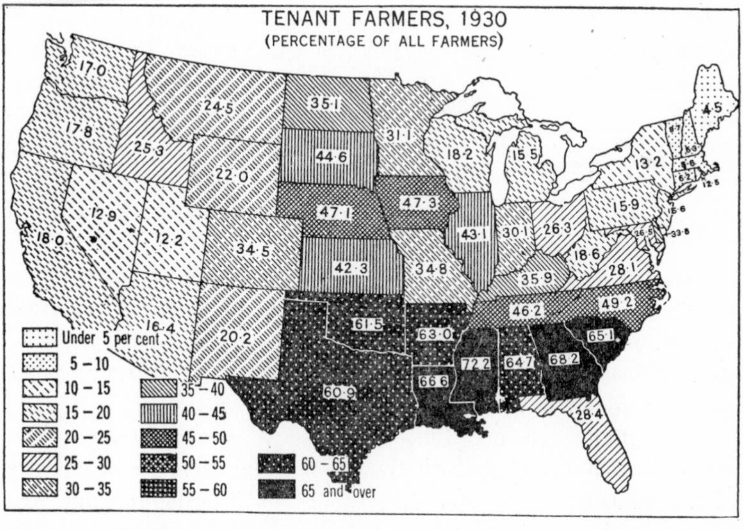

From Charles O. Paullin, Atlas of the Historical Geography of the United States, *Plates,* 146N,-Q

at the local exchange, and it was often cheaper for him to burn his corn as fuel than to ship it to market. In 1880 wheat fetched almost a dollar in the Chicago pit, but it cost forty-five cents to ship a bushel of wheat from central Nebraska to Chicago. Almost equally burdensome were certain railroad practices against which the farmer protested in vain. The railroads came to control the warehousing facilities of the West, fixed the price for storage, and controlled grading. In the late eighties Governor Thayer of Nebraska asserted that 'There is no question in my mind but that the farmers of Nebraska have been defrauded of hundreds of thousands of dollars within the last few years by the wrongful classification of corn at Chicago and other great corn centers.'

The farmer sold his product in a competitive market, but purchased supplies, equipment, and household goods in a market which was protected against competition. The cost of his transportation was fixed by the railroads, of his fertilizer by a fertilizer trust, of his farm implements by the McCormick Harvester Company, of his fencing by a barbed wire trust. The prices which he paid for daily necessities — for furniture and clothing, for lumber and leather goods — were artificially raised by the operation of protective tariffs. Above all, the price which he paid for money was prohibitively high. Some states attempted, through usury laws, to fix low interest rates, but such laws were flouted or evaded, and interest rates in the farm belts of the South and the West were often above twenty per cent and seldom below ten per cent. Inadequate banking facilities were in part responsible for this situation. In 1880, for example, the per capita banking power of the Eastern states was $176, of the Central states $27, and of the Southern states $10. Furthermore, with the rise in the value of money after the Civil War, the farmers' debt appreciated steadily. It took approximately twelve hundred bushels of wheat, corn, oats, barley, and rye to buy a one thousand dollar mortgage in the years 1867 to 1869; between 1886 and 1888 it took approximately twenty-three hundred bushels of the same crops to repay that mortgage.

This, indeed, was the heart of the matter. During most of the thirty years after the Civil War the farmer, south and west, was the victim not only of rising costs but of falling prices. Wheat which netted the farmer $1.45 a bushel in 1866 brought only $.76 in 1869, $.69 in 1889 and $.49 in 1894, so that while the wheat crop in 1878 and again in 1889 was double what it had been in 1867 the farmers received approximately the same amount on the three crops. Corn which brought $.75 at Chicago in 1869 fell to $.38 in 1879 and to $.28 in 1889. Twenty-three million bushels of rye brought $23,000,000 in 1867 and twenty-eight million bushels brought only $12,000,000 in 1889. Cotton sold at $.31 a pound in 1866, $.09 in 1886 and $.06 in 1893; less than six million bales of cotton sold, in 1884, for some $241,000,000; and approximately ten million bales sold, in 1894, for $220,000,000.

The result was to be read in the figures of farm values, farm income, mortgages, and tenancy. Agriculture, which represented approximately half of the national wealth in 1860, accounted for but one-fifth of the national wealth half a century later. The value of manufactured products was fifty per cent higher in 1870 than the value of all farm products; by 1910 it was over twice as large. The farmer received 30 per cent of the national income in 1860, 19 per cent in 1890, 18 per cent in 1910, 13 per cent in 1920 and, after the collapse of the early thirties, 7 per cent in 1933. Farm mortgages and tenancy increased correspondingly: 27 per cent of the farms operated by their owners were mortgaged in 1890; by 1910 the number had increased to 33 per cent and by 1930 to 42 per cent. The total mortgage indebtedness on these owner-operated farms increased from $1,726,000,000 in 1910 to $4,080,000,000 in 1930, while the mortgage indebtedness for all farms operated increased during the same period from three and one-half billion to nine and one-half billion dollars. As a large part of these farm mortgages were held by mortgage companies, banks, and insurance companies in the East, the interest payment drained the rural sections for the benefit of the urban sections of the country; to many farmers this annual interest charge came to seem more like a tribute than a just payment for services rendered. Even more alarming were the mounting figures of farm tenancy. In 1880 one-fourth of all American farmers were tenants; by the turn of the century one-third of all farmers were tenants; thirty years later almost half the farmers of the nation were cultivating land which they did not own. In the beginning tenancy was largely confined to the negroes of the South, but in the early years of the twentieth century it spread rapidly throughout the Middle West, and in the census of 1930 five of the leading Mid-Western farming states — Illinois, Iowa, Kansas, Nebraska, and South Dakota — showed over forty per cent tenant farmers.

The social problem of the American farmer lends itself less readily to statistical analysis, but its significance can be read in the pages of such stories as Garland's *Main Travelled Roads,* Rölvaag's *Giants in the Earth,* Willa Cather's *My Ántonia,* Ruth Suckow's *Folks,* and Ellen Glasgow's *Barren Ground.* It is abundantly clear that in the years before the New Deal farming yielded not only decreasing economic returns but also decreasing social returns. It was a glimpse of the drabness and isolation of farm life in the South that inspired Oliver H. Kelley to organize the Patrons of Husbandry, and it was the social and cultural attractions of that organization that brought farmers and farmers' wives flocking to it by the tens of thousands. Before the coming of the automobile, the telephone, and the radio, that isolation was a very real and a fearful thing. Thousands of families were cut off from companionship and conviviality, church and school. Thousands of mothers died in childbirth, thousands of children died through lack of simple medical care. Hamlin Garland tells us that when he wrote *Main Travelled Roads,* he determined 'to tell the truth.'

> But I didn't. Even my youthful zeal faltered in the midst of a revelation of the lives led by the women on the farms of the middle border. Before the tragic futility of their suffering, my pen refused to shed its ink. Over the hidden chamber of their maternal agonies I drew the veil.

And when he revisited the Dakota country, he

> revolted from the gracelessness of its human habitations. The lonely box-like farm-houses on the ridges suddenly appeared to me like the dens of wild animals. The lack of color, of charm in the lives of the people anguished me. . . . All the gilding of farm life melted away. The hard and bitter realities came back upon me in a flood. Nature was as beautiful as ever . . . but no splendor of cloud, no grace of sunset could conceal the poverty of these people, on the contrary they brought out, with a more intolerable poignancy, the gracelessness of these homes, and the sordid quality of the mechanical daily routine of these lives.[6]

It was the women who suffered most from the niggardliness and narrowness of farm life. The confession of Benét's John Vilas might have been that of a whole generation of pioneers:

> I took my wife out of a pretty house,
> I took my wife out of a pleasant place,
> I stripped my wife of comfortable things,
> I drove my wife to wander with the wind.[7]

[6] The quotations are from *A Son of the Middle Border,* pp. 356–65, 416. Macmillan.

[7] *John Brown's Body,* p. 143.

And it was the wives and the mothers who inspired the revolt against the farm, who encouraged their sons and daughters to try their fortunes in the cities.

It was inevitable that with the rise of the city, the social and cultural attractions of rural life should have been contrasted unfavorably with those of urban life. The cities offered not only business and professional opportunities, but facilities for education and recreation that were not to be found in the average rural community. City life conferred, too, a certain social prestige that no longer attached to farm life. The farmers, who had once been regarded as 'the chosen people of God,' came to be looked upon as 'hayseeds' and 'hicks,' fit subjects for the comic strip or the vaudeville joke. An ever increasing number of young people, unwilling to accept the drudgery and frustration that their parents had suffered, left the farms for the cities, and this movement from the farm to the city was almost as large and perhaps as significant as the immigration from Europe to the United States during these same years. Between 1870 and 1930 the rural population declined from over eighty to less than forty per cent of the total, and the decline in the actual farm population was even more precipitous.

It must not be supposed that the farmer made no effort to save himself from the social and economic difficulties that were rapidly crowding him to the wall. For almost every problem he had a solution, one that was usually reasonable and intelligent. But those solutions generally required legislative action from state or federal government, and in the generation after the Civil War the farmer was seldom in a position to obtain legislative action. From Jefferson to Jefferson Davis the politics of the nation had been guided chiefly by those who were responsible to the farmers, and where agrarian legislation had failed, such failure was to be charged rather to sectional conflict than to class conflict. But with the shift in population from the farm to the city, the rise of giant railroad and industrial corporations, and the concentration of financial power in the East, this situation changed. The farmers still constituted the largest single economic group in 1870, but they could not bridge the sectional barrier. Although the problems of the Southern planter and the Middle Western farmer were in many essentials the same, for a generation the Southerner insisted on voting Democratic, and the Western farmer just as stubbornly voted Republican. Railroad, banking, and industrial interests, however, were perturbed by no such sectional cleavage, but presented a united front, and political parties, always sensitive to economic forces, became increasingly subservient to these interests. Farmers everywhere wanted railroad regulation, but the railroad was the most powerful single interest in New Hampshire as in California, in Nebraska as in Georgia, and except for the brief Granger interlude the efforts of farmers to enact railroad rate bills met everywhere with insuperable political and legal obstacles. Most farmers wanted low tariffs, but even with the Democratic party in power the farmers were outwitted by industrial pressure-groups. The vast majority of farmers wanted cheap money and a more flexible banking system, but even Bryan was unable to overcome the well-financed propaganda of the banking interests of the East or to make any serious impression upon the tradition of loyalty to the Republican party which obtained among the farmers of the North. Nor were the farmers more successful in placing their representatives in state legislatures or in Congress. Lawyers and business men constituted the majority of the legislatures even in such states as Georgia and Nebraska, while in the halls of Congress a ' dirt ' farmer was something of a curiosity. It is suggestive that in the whole period from 1860 to 1928 no candidate of a major party was a genuine farmer and that only one candidate nominated to the Presidency by either major party came from west of the Mississippi, and he was not elected.

Failing to make any dent upon either major political party, the farmers inevitably turned to organizations of their own. These organizations were not always political in character, but they sought to do by common action what the government failed to undertake. From the Granger movement of the late sixties to the farm bloc of the Hoover administration, the story of the farmers' revolt can be told largely in terms of these organizations.

5. *Agrarian Revolt*

The bubble of Civil War prosperity burst in 1868 as did that of the World War in 1920, and the collapse of farm prices resulted in the first agrarian revolt. This revolt took various forms: the election of legislatures, governors, and often congressmen sympathetic to the farmers' demands; the passage of laws regulating freight and elevator charges; the organization of co-operative societies and eventually of local and even national political parties.

The first and most important of the societies that grew out of agrarian distress was the Patrons of Husbandry, commonly known as the Grange. It was in 1866 that President Johnson sent Oliver H. Kelley, a clerk in the Bureau of Agriculture, on a tour of investigation through the South. Kelley returned deeply impressed with the poverty, isolation, and backwardness of the farmers of that section of the country, and determined to organize a farmers' society which might in part ameliorate these evils. In 1867 he and a group of government clerks in Washington, D.C., founded the Patrons of Husbandry, and in the following year the first permanent Grange of this society was established in Fredonia, New York. By the end of 1870 there were Granges in nine states of the Union and when the panic of 1873 burst, the Grange had penetrated every state but four. Two years later it boasted a membership of over 800,000, organized in some 20,000 local Granges, most of them in the Middle West and the South.

The purpose of the Grange, as set forth in its Declaration of 1874, was 'to develop a better and higher manhood and womanhood among ourselves. To enhance the comforts and attractions of our homes, and strengthen our attachments to our pursuits. To foster mutual understanding and co-operation. . . . To buy less and produce more, in order to make our farms self-sustaining. To diversify our crops, and crop no more than we can cultivate. . . . To discountenance the credit system, the mortgage system, the fashion system, and every other system tending to prodigality and bankruptcy.' The major function of the Grange, as conceived by its founders and announced in its declarations, was social, and it was as a social institution that it made its most significant contribution. One secret of the success of the order was the policy of admitting women to membership, and for farmers' wives the Grange, with its monthly meetings and picnics, lectures and entertainments, offered an escape from the loneliness and drudgery of the farm. To the women of the Middle Border the Grange, and later the Alliance, suggested a more abundant, a more generous life, and when the heroine of Garland's *A Spoil of Office* spoke at the farmers' picnic, it was the cultural aspects of the movement that she stressed:

> I see a time [said Ida Wilbur] when the farmer will not need to live in a cabin on a lonely farm. I see the farmers coming together in groups. I see them with time to read, and time to visit with their fellows. I see them enjoying lectures in beautiful halls, erected in every village. I see them gather like the Saxons of old upon the green at evening to sing and

dance. I see cities rising near them with schools, and churches, and concert halls and theatres. I see a day when the farmer will no longer be a drudge and his wife a bond slave, but happy men and women who will go singing to their pleasant tasks upon their fruitful farms. When the boys and girls will not go west nor to the city; when life will be worth living. In that day the moon will be brighter and the stars more glad and pleasure and poetry and love of life come back to the man who tills the soil.[8]

This social program was too ideal and too remote to be dangerous. Not so with the political and economic program of the Grange. The Grange was formally non-political in character, but it was inevitable that the Grangers should use their influence in politics, and almost from the beginning the movement took on a distinctly political character. In Illinois, Iowa, Wisconsin, Minnesota, Kansas, California, and elsewhere the farmers entered politics, elected their candidates to legislatures and judgeships, and agitated for farm relief through railway and warehouse regulation. The result was the so-called Granger laws limiting railroad and warehouse charges and outlawing some of the grosser railway abuses.[9] Though these laws proved in the long run ineffective, they did teach the farmers the value of co-operation in politics and dramatize for the nation the necessity of political curbs on business and transportation.

Not only did the Grangers venture into politics; they embarked upon business enterprises as well. In an attempt to eliminate the middleman, they established hundreds of co-operative stores on the Rochdale plan — a plan whereby profits were divided among the shareholders, in proportion to their purchases. They set up co-operative creameries, elevators, and warehouses, organized farmers' insurance companies, and entered the manufacturing field, buying up patents and constructing their own factories which turned out excellent reapers, sewing machines, wagons, and similar things for half the price charged by private concerns. Kelley from the first opposed such business activities. 'This purchasing business,' he said, 'commenced with buying jackasses; the prospects are that many will be *sold*.' In the end his sour prophecy was justified. Owing to the relentless opposition by business and banking interests, the individualism of the farmers, over-expansion and mismanagement, most of the co-operative enterprises failed. Yet some good resulted from the

[8] *A Spoil of Office*, p. 14. D. Appleton & Co.

[9] See Chapter 5 for the legislative and judicial history of the Granger laws.

foray of the Grangers into business. Prices were reduced, thousands of farmers saved money, and with the establishment of Montgomery, Ward and Company in 1872 specifically 'to meet the wants of the Patrons of Husbandry' the mail-order business came into existence.

Prosperity returned to the farm in the late seventies, and membership in the Grange dwindled rapidly away until by 1880 it had fallen to one hundred thousand. A revival began in that year, but chastened by experience the Grange confined itself thereafter largely to social activities. Its place was taken by the more aggressive Farmers' Alliances, and the history of agrarian revolt during the eighties and early nineties is largely the history of the Alliance movement.

There were, from the beginning, a number of Alliances, but by the late eighties the process of consolidation and amalgamation had resulted in the creation of two powerful groups, the Northwestern Alliance, and the Farmers' Alliance and Industrial Union, commonly known as the Southern Alliance. The first effective organization of the Northwestern Alliance was undertaken by Milton George, editor of the *Western Rural* and the platform which he drew up in 1880 announced a purpose to 'unite the farmers of America for their protection against class legislation, and the encroachments of concentrated capital and the tyranny of monopoly.' The Northwestern Alliance was particularly strong in Kansas, Nebraska, Iowa, Minnesota, and the Dakotas, and during the hard times of the late eighties it increased its membership by leaps and bounds and became a major power in the politics of the Middle Border. The origin of the Southern Alliance dates back to a cattlemen's association in Lampasas County, Texas, in the middle seventies. Within a decade this Texas Alliance had spread throughout the state and in the late eighties, under the guidance of the astute C. W. Macune, it began to absorb farmers' organizations in other Southern states — the Arkansas Wheel, the Louisiana Farmers' Union, the Brothers of Freedom — and affiliated with the powerful Colored Farmers' National Alliance. By the early nineties the Southern Alliance boasted a membership of well over a million and was the most powerful farmers' organization in the country. Despite an obvious community of interest between the Northern and the Southern Alliances, all efforts to perfect an amalgamation of the two organizations foundered on the rocks of sectionalism.

The activities of the Alliances were as diverse as those of the Grange. Social activities embraced not only the customary meetings and picnics, but farmers' institutes, circulating libraries, and the publication of hundreds of farm newspapers and dozens of magazines, so that the Alliance became, in the words of one observer, a farmers' national university. The economic enterprises of the Alliance were more substantial and ambitious than those of the Grange. The Texas Alliance undertook co-operative buying and selling, the North Dakota Alliance underwrote co-operative insurance, the Illinois Alliance organized co-operative marketing. Thousands of farmer's 'exchanges' were established, and it was estimated that in 1890 the various Alliances did a business of over ten million dollars.

But historically the significance of the Alliance is to be found in its political rather than its social and economic activities. From the first the Alliances entered more vigorously into politics than had the Grange, and the Alliance programs called inevitably for political action. Those programs varied from year to year and from state to state, but in general they embraced demands for strict regulation or even government ownership of railroads and other means of communication, currency inflation, the abolition of national banks, the prohibition of alien land ownership, and of trading in futures on the Exchange, a more equitable system of taxation, and various progressive political reforms. An original contribution of the Alliance was the so-called Sub-Treasury scheme, a proposal which provided that the government should establish warehouses where the farmers might deposit non-perishable farm produce, receiving in exchange a loan of legal tender money up to eighty per cent of the market value of the produce, which might be redeemed when the farmer had sold his produce. This scheme had the triple advantage of enabling the farmer to borrow at a low rate of interest on his farm produce, sell his produce at the most favorable market price, and profit by an expanded and flexible currency. At the time when it was first advanced, it was regarded as merely a contribution to the gaiety of the nation; the Warehouse Act of 1916 adopted a similar proposal as a national policy.

Between 1890 and 1892, the Alliance became identical with the Populist Party.[10] The failure of the Populists to perfect and maintain a party organization brought about the disintegration not only of that party but of the Alliance, and induced an abiding distrust of direct political action on the part of the farmer. He snapped back into voting Republican if of the North or West, and Democratic if

[10] For the political history of the Populist movement, see Chapter 11.

of the South, or Southwest. The closing years of the nineteenth century brought temporary prosperity to the farmer, and though the value of agricultural products continued to be disproportionately low, a striking increase in the value of farm lands partly compensated the farmer for his low income.

After the debacle of the Alliance and the Populist movements, farmers turned once more from political to social and economic objectives. The Grange increased rapidly in membership and influence, but confined itself largely to educational and social activities. The American Farm Bureau Federation, with a membership of not far from one million, concerned itself primarily with problems of marketing and distribution and sponsored co-operative organizations of grain and cotton growers. The most promising recent agricultural development is the growth of farmers' co-operatives, particularly among the fruit growers of California, the wheat farmers of the West and the cotton planters of the South. In 1929 almost seven hundred thousand farms reported co-operative sales.

The World War, with its tremendous world demand for foodstuffs, brought a wave of prosperity to the American farmer similar to that of the Civil War, and history repeated itself in the post-war deflation. The decade of the twenties was one of almost unalleviated depression for the farmers. The number of farms declined from 6,448,000 in 1920 to 6,228,000 in 1930, the value of farm property from about seventy-eight billion to about fifty billion dollars, and the farm income from some twenty-one to some eleven billion dollars. Though the farm population constituted in 1930 some twenty-five per cent of the total, the farm income was only nine per cent of the total national income. In the face of this situation, farmers turned once again to politics. During the Wilson administration the Farmers' Non-Partisan League, organized in North Dakota, spread into fifteen states of the West. In 1916 the League captured control of the government of North Dakota and in the ensuing years enacted a farm relief program of a far-reaching nature. This legislation provided for state-owned warehouses and elevators, a state bank, exemption of farm improvements from taxation, creation of a hail insurance fund and a Home Building Association to encourage home ownership, and the establishment of an industrial commission to organize state-owned and financed industries. These laws, like the Granger and Populist laws of an earlier generation, were loudly denounced as class legislation throughout the East, for no axiom of politics was more widely cherished in that section than the axiom that legislation for farmer or labor interests was class legislation while legislation for manufacturing, banking, railroad, and shipping interests was broadly national.

Throughout the decade of the twenties a farm bloc agitated ceaselessly for relief and assistance. Congress was responsive, but Presidents Coolidge and Hoover were not, and though federal aid was extended to co-operative marketing and more generous credit facilities were provided, all effective efforts at crop reduction or control foundered on Executive vetoes.[11]

[11] For the farm malaise and farm relief in the post-war decades, see Chapters 22, 24, and 25.

X

POLITICS

1877–1890

1. *Masks in a Pageant*

THERE is no drearier chapter in American political history than that which records the period from the end of Reconstruction to the Populist revolt of the early nineties. The high political passions of the 1850's throw a fitful gleam upon the administrations of that triumvirate of nonentities, Fillmore, Pierce, and Buchanan, while the rascality and ineptitude of the 1920's give a morbid interest to the administrations of Harding, Coolidge, and Hoover. But the monotonous administrations of Hayes, Arthur, Cleveland, and Harrison are relieved neither by grand political passions nor by excess of virtue or of vice, but merely by labor troubles and a depression. Civil War issues were dead. National politics became little more than a contest for power between rival parties waged on no higher plane than a struggle for traffic between rival railroads. The vital interests of the era lay mostly outside politics, and for that reason must be studied separately.

During the whole of this period the electorate played a game of blind man's buff. Never before had American politics been so intellectually bankrupt. There were no clearly defined issues between the major parties, and the political leaders preferred to raise fake ones and attempt to be all things to all men, rather than tie up parties to the real forces that were transforming the country and which, in any case, they did not understand. Perhaps they were right, for the last time that a major party had adopted a vital issue, the country had been torn apart, and nobody wanted another Civil War. But the result was to make national politics unreal, and, except for electoral clowning and Congressional buncombe, very dull.

America was emerging from her isolation and becoming a part of the community of nations, but there was no intelligent appreciation of the responsibilities which this new position involved, and Blaine's gestures toward Pan-Americanism were all but futile. The country had recovered from the Civil War, but instead of encouraging sectional friendliness, politicians on both sides exploited patriotic and sectional animosities for the grossest purposes. The industrial revolution, as it unfolded, made traditional ideas of laissez faire less and less valid; but politics and law were still conducted on this outmoded principle and politicians still prated of individualism as if it were a reality in the economic and social spheres as in biology. Big business was growing bigger, trusts were becoming super-trusts, railroad monopolies placed unparalleled power in the hands of a few men, and the conflict of 'wealth against commonwealth' which Henry D. Lloyd was soon to dramatize, was recognized by thoughtful men, but political leaders showed no appreciation of the implications of these developments, and laws such as the Interstate Commerce Act or the Anti-Trust Act raised only the flimsiest of barriers against the onward march of privilege. Agriculture was fronting a series of grave crises and the independent American farmer was threatened on all sides by forces over which he could exercise no effective control; but politicians in Washington lacked the imagination to understand even the existence of a farm problem until it was called to their attention by political revolt. The money question, serious beyond any other in its possible consequences on the fortunes of that generation, demanded the most careful and impartial study; but it was either ignored or, when that attitude was no longer tenable, dealt with as a moral rather than economic problem. There were issues enough before the American people, issues involving in the most vital way the fortunes of the Republic and presenting valid alternatives, but candidates commonly evaded them and fought political campaigns on the basis of personality or inherited prejudice. So few fundamental political issues were agitated, so few new policies were inaugurated, that one distinguished historian has written, 'between 1865 and 1897 there were put upon the federal law books not more than two or three acts which need long detain the citizen concerned only with those manifestations of political power that produce essential readjustments in human relations.'[1]

And what of the lawmakers and political leaders, whose tattered banners Americans followed with such uncritical enthusiasm? It is a drab procession that passes before the historian, inspiring wonder and weariness, for the politicians of this era were mostly sad, solemn fellows. Clowns went out of fashion with Benjamin Butler and

[1] C. A. and Mary Beard, *Rise of American Civilization*, vol. II, p. 341.

Parson Brownlow, and did not return until the swashbuckling imperialists of '98 introduced a new note of humor into American politics. The titular leaders — Hayes, Garfield, Arthur, Cleveland, Harrison — were estimable men, who contributed nothing of lasting importance to American politics or American life. Orators extolled their virtues in oceans of words and biographers have embalmed their tenuous reputations in scores of books, but with the exception of Grover Cleveland it is not apparent that American history would have been in any essential different had none of them ever lived.

Behind these titular leaders were the real rulers — men who sat in committee rooms listening to the demands of lobbyists, bosses who sat in caucus selecting candidates, 'boys' who 'fried the fat' out of reluctant corporations, kept writers who flooded the country with 'educational' literature or with the poison of sectional hatred or with the stench of scandal that their candidates might gain office. At the head of the ranks of those who really ran the country were great bosses like Conkling and Platt and Hill of New York, Randall and Cameron and Quay of Pennsylvania, Hanna and Foraker and Brice of Ohio. Then there were the representatives of special interests — Standard Oil senators, sugar trust senators, iron and steel senators, and railroad senators, men known by their business rather than their political affiliations, like Aldrich of Rhode Island, Depew of New York, Elkins of West Virginia, Gorman of Maryland, Sawyer of Wisconsin, Mahone of Virginia, Dolph of Oregon, Cameron of Pennsylvania, and Clark of Montana. In close alliance were the spell-binders and propagandists — orators like Robert Ingersoll or editorial writers like Whitelaw Reid of the New York *Tribune*. Running through all ranks were the spoilsmen, interested only in office and patronage, like Platt and Fenton of New York, Alger of Michigan, Foraker of Ohio, Logan of Illinois, Ingalls of Kansas, and Allison of Iowa. Yet there was a small group of men in politics who preserved an old-fashioned integrity, patriotism, sense of duty and responsibility which transcended personal interest and occasionally even party interest — men like George F. Hoar of Massachusetts, John G. Carlisle of Kentucky, Lucius Q. C. Lamar of Mississippi, Abram Hewitt of New York, and Carl Schurz of Missouri.

James G. Blaine of Maine, Congressman, Senator, twice Secretary of State, and perpetual aspirant to the Presidency, was typical of this as Clay, Calhoun, and Webster of an earlier era. A man of indubitable intellectual power and of immense personal magnetism, Blaine was the most popular figure in American politics between Clay and Bryan. Year after year thousands of men marched, shouted, and sang for 'Blaine of Maine' whom devoted followers pictured as the 'Plumed Knight,' palladium of all virtues and defender of the true Republican faith. For thirty years he exercised a controlling power in the councils of his party, in legislation, foreign and domestic policies, party platforms and candidates. The perfect politician, he never forgot a name or a friend and always knew how to influence votes and manipulate committees. He was a magnificent orator and could inspire a frenzy of enthusiasm by twisting the British lion's tail or solemnly intoning the platitudes of party loyalty. Yet aside from his personality he made no impression upon American politics except to lower its moral tone. He was assiduous in cementing a corrupt alliance between politics and business. Deliberately and violently he fanned the flames of sectional animosity, waving the 'bloody shirt of the rebellion' for partisan and personal purposes. His name is connected with no important legislation; his sympathies were enlisted in no forward-looking causes. He was as innocent of economic as of political ideas and ignored when he did not oppose the interests of the laboring and the farming classes. His vision was narrow and selfish, his methods the methods of the spoilsman, his ambitions personal and partisan, yet for his little faith in democracy and his power to stimulate emotions and hatreds that a statesman would have laid at rest, he was rewarded with votes, office, power, and honor.

Politics was largely a Punch and Judy show, but though the puppets and even the voices changed, the hands that held the strings were the same. Business ran politics, and politics was a branch of business. The country, said John Sherman after the election of 1888, had 'reached the last stages in the history of the Roman Empire when offices were sold at public auction to the highest bidder,' and when some years later David Graham Phillips wrote *The Treason of the Senate* he merely recorded what was common knowledge as to the intimate relations of business and politics. The story can be read in the biographies of captains of industry like Carnegie and Rockefeller, of masters of capital like Morgan and Gould, of politicians like Blaine and Aldrich, and, told with more imagination but essential accuracy, in such novels as Winston Churchill's *Coniston,* W. A.

White's *A Certain Rich Man,* and Henry Adams' *Democracy*. The system was set forth most nakedly, perhaps, by Frederick T. Martin:

> It matters not one iota what political party is in power or what President holds the reins of office. We are not politicians, or public thinkers; we are the rich; we own America; we got it, God knows how, but we intend to keep it if we can by throwing all the tremendous weight of our support, our influence, our money, our political connections, our purchased Senators, our hungry Congressmen, and our public-speaking demagogues, into the scale against any legislation, any political platform, any Presidential campaign, that threatens the integrity of our estate.[2]

And since politics was a branch of business, the ethics of business became the ethics of politics. It was illogical of reformers to be shocked at corrupt practices in the one and not in the other. It is for this reason that much of the civil service reform movement, which looms so large in the history of these years, appears today unreal. Business had no party preferences except in so far as it preferred to invest in successful rather than unsuccessful candidates. Business contributed more generously to the Republican than to the Democratic coffers because the Republicans were more often victorious, but Democratic senators like Hill of New York, Gorman of Maryland, and Brice of Ohio could command the support of business quite as effectively as Morton of New York, Cameron of Pennsylvania, or Foraker of Ohio. Only rarely did parties divide along economic lines; for the most part both major parties straddled every important issue. Railroad and trust legislation were not party questions; both parties ostensibly favored regulation, neither gave such regulation sincere or intelligent support. Labor was not a political issue: Hayes in the 'Great Strike' of 1877 and Cleveland in the Pullman strike of 1894 permitted the use of the injunction and sent federal troops to protect business interests. Both parties were committed to a liberal and democratic land policy, but when it came to enforcing the provisions of the land laws and to stopping the gross frauds that made a mockery of those laws, Cleveland encountered as bitter opposition from his own party as from the Republican party. The Republicans espoused protection and the Democrats low tariff, but once in office the Democrats were unwilling to make any significant concessions to tariff reform. Both parties avoided the money question

[2] *Passing of the Idle Rich,* p. 149. Doubleday, Page & Co.

as long as they could; when evasion was no longer possible, they split along geographical lines.

Yet if the surface of the political waters was placid, underneath the currents flowed swift and treacherous, and when the ship of state, crazily rigged and manned by a piratical crew, drifted out of the quiet stretch of the eighties into the dangerous nineties, it was buffeted and battered and all but capsized.

2. *Glimmerings of Reform*

The administrations of Hayes and Arthur illustrate and emphasize some of these generalizations. A well-educated lawyer, officer in the Union army, elected twice to Congress and for three terms governor of Ohio, Rutherford B. Hayes was honest and able, but he was from the beginning seriously handicapped in his efforts to effect any constructive measures or to inaugurate necessary reforms. Not only the Democrats, but even many of his own party followers believed that he had achieved office through fraud, and he was never able to count on the moral support of the nation or to anticipate a second term in which he might consolidate his position. The factional disputes which had wrecked the harmony of the second Grant administration and of the Convention of 1876 were not allayed, and from the beginning Hayes incurred the animosity of Blaine and the implacable hostility of Conkling and his followers. The elections of 1876 had preserved Democratic control of the lower House, and two years later this opposition party captured control of the upper House as well. In the circumstances it is a tribute to Hayes that his administration was not a total failure.

That it was not a complete failure can be credited to the courage with which Hayes tackled the two immediate problems of reconstruction and civil service reform. The first and most important act of his administration was the recall of the federal troops from the South, an act which marked the technical end of political and military reconstruction. In order to dramatize the reconciliation of the sections, the President appointed an ex-Confederate, David M. Key, to his cabinet. Yet, with an inconsistency that was almost obtuse, Hayes refused to countenance the repeal of the hated Force Acts either directly or through 'riders' on appropriation bills, and the acts remained on the statute books to aggravate future relations between the North and the South.

Hayes' second task was to cleanse his party of the corruption which had so seriously damaged it during the Grant administrations and to fulfill his pledges of civil service reform. The appointment of the civil service reformer, Carl Schurz, to the Interior Department and of William M. Evarts, one of President Johnson's counsellors, to the State Department, was evidence of Hayes' sincerity. Yet excellent as were his intentions, he seriously compromised himself from the beginning by the scandalous manner in which he rewarded every member of the notorious Louisiana returning board as well as others who had been instrumental in awarding him the Presidency. Although he thereafter made genuine efforts towards reform, removing some of Grant's most offensive appointees and cleaning up the New York custom house, he was never able to win the complete confidence of the civil service reformers.

Indecisive as it was, Hayes' struggle with the spoilsmen had considerable effect on American political history. That struggle was precipitated by Hayes' attempt to oust Chester A. Arthur and Alonzo B. Cornell from the New York custom house which they had turned into a political machine of the most corrupt and disreputable character. Senator Conkling, already outraged by Hayes' Southern policy and embittered because he had not received the recognition which he thought was his due, took the removals as a personal affront and persuaded the Senate to reject the nominations of those whom the President appointed to succeed Arthur and Cornell. What was involved in this unseemly squabble was not merely a falling-out between two factions in the Republican party, or ' Senatorial courtesy,' but a larger issue of the American form of government. During the Johnson administration Congress had inaugurated a quasi-parliamentary form of government, and Grant had offered no effective resistance to the continuation of this parliamentary system. Congress, since the Civil War, had so largely eaten into the Presidential prerogative that the chief executive was by way of becoming a mere figurehead, like the President of the French Republic.[3] Under Hayes a Senatorial cabal, led by Conkling, Platt, Cameron, Ferry, Chandler, Boutwell, and Edmunds, proposed to continue their domination of the government. Against this plan the President set himself with adamantine stubbornness, and in the end, with the support of the Democrats, he was successful. His appointees were renominated and confirmed and

[3] This tendency was exposed in a book entitled *Congressional Government,* published in 1885 by young Dr. Woodrow Wilson who later did much to correct the evil.

Conkling retired from the struggle, only to renew it in the next administration without success. The normal and constitutional relationship between President and Congress was thereby restored.

For the larger task of articulating the government to the new economic forces, Hayes was not prepared. His only solution of the labor problem presented by the Great Strike of '77 was to send federal troops to put down the strikers. The resumption of specie payments, voted in 1875, caused an appreciation of greenbacks that worked hardship on many debtors, and when Congress tried a different solution of the money problem — the Bland-Allison Silver Act of 1878 — Hayes interposed his veto, an interposition which was quite unsuccessful. To the problems of railroad malpractices, trusts, and land frauds he gave no attention. He later confessed that 'the money-piling tendency of our country . . . is changing laws, government and morals, and giving all power to the rich, and bringing in pauperism and its attendant crimes and wickedness like a flood,' but when President he did not even hang out danger signals. His administration, indeed, for all of its political drama, was largely a negative one.

As the election of 1880 approached, the 'stalwart' Republicans who had been supporters of Grant's throne proposed the General for a third term. He was willing, but the Republican nominating convention was not; and another 'dark horse' from Ohio, General James A. Garfield, obtained the nomination. Garfield was an educated gentleman with a good military record and long experience in Congress; but his party made a greater virtue of his log-cabin birth and early exploits as a canal bargee. The nomination was a blow to Conkling, who had supported Grant; and in order to placate the New York Senator the convention named his henchman, Chester A. Arthur, to the vice-presidency. The Democrats, to confirm their loyalty, nominated General Winfield Scott Hancock of Pennsylvania, and the Greenback party, which had polled over a million votes in 1878, put up a third Civil War veteran, General James B. Weaver of Iowa. The campaign was fought largely on personalities and trumped-up issues, and money was used freely in critical states. Garfield won a thumping victory in the electoral college but his popular plurality was less than ten thousand in a total of over nine million votes.

Four months after his inauguration, while still struggling with questions of patronage, Garfield was shot by a disappointed office-seeker who boasted, 'I am a Stalwart; Arthur is now President of the United States.' After a gallant struggle for life, Garfield died on 19 September 1881. The new President, Chester A. Arthur, was a prominent lawyer and machine politician of New York, long a satellite of the lordly Conkling, and with nothing in his record to justify the hope that he would make more than a mediocre executive and much to arouse fear that he would make a very bad one. Handsome and affable, liked by business men and women of the world, he gave Washington its only 'society' administration between those of Buchanan and Theodore Roosevelt. Unexpectedly he developed a genuine independence and became something of a reformer. He severed his connections with the worst of the spoilsmen, vetoed an eighteen-million dollar river and harbor bill, and prosecuted, with some vigor, the so-called Star Route frauds in the Postoffice Department which had cost the government millions of dollars. Above all his administration is memorable for the enactment of the Pendleton Civil Service Reform Bill.

Every President since Polk had complained of the demands that patronage made on his time, energy, and judgment, and Lincoln had expressed fears that the spoils system was 'going to ruin republican government.' Scandal had followed scandal in the civil service; yet the spoils system had been extended even to scrubwomen in the public offices. Rotation in office was never complete, and a large residuum of trained servants was left undisturbed; but in general the federal service had become permeated with a class of men who were strongly tempted to anticipate future removal by present corruption. Federal office-holders were regularly assessed for campaign contributions and were expected to spend a good part of their time and energy in party activity.

The spoils system had been subjected to heavy criticism for two decades before Arthur's accession to office. As early as 1864 Sumner had introduced a bill looking to civil service reform, and three years later Representative Jenckes of Rhode Island, long the spokesman of this reform group, attempted to secure Congressional endorsement for a classified civil service modelled along English lines. Jenckes had the support of a number of eastern intellectuals — men of the type of E. L. Godkin of *The Nation,* G. W. Curtis of *Harper's Weekly,* and Thomas Wentworth Higginson, as well as active politicians like Carl Schurz, Senator Hoar, and Lyman Trumbull. In 1871 Grant came unexpectedly to the assistance of the reformers with a recommendation for a law governing 'the manner of making all appointments,' and in that same year a Civil Service Commission was established which was empowered to prescribe rules and regulations for admission into the civil service. Grant's enthusiasm was short-lived, and so was the Commission.

Hayes, as we have seen, had grievously disappointed party regulars by his friendliness toward the movement. He had announced in his acceptance speech his determination to institute reforms, and shortly after his accession to the Presidency he had informed Secretary Sherman that

> party leaders should have no more influence in appointments than other equally respectable citizens. No assessment for political purposes on officers or subordinates should be allowed. No useless officer or employee should be retained. No officer should be required or permitted to take part in the management of political organizations, caucuses, conventions, or election campaigns.

Sherman supported Hayes' efforts at reform, and Secretary Schurz introduced new standards of honesty and efficiency into the Department of the Interior and cleaned up the nauseating corruption which disgraced the administration of the Indian Bureau.

All this aroused the bitter hostility of politicians like Conkling, whose attitude toward civil service is indicated by his classic observation: 'When Dr. Johnson defined patriotism as the last refuge of a scoundrel, he ignored the enormous possibilities of the word *reform*.' The Stalwarts now looked to Arthur to undo the progress which his predecessors had made, but to their chagrin Arthur allied himself with the reform element, and in his first annual message to Congress came out squarely for the merit system.

It was the manner of Garfield's death that made possible the achievement that reformers and Civil Service Leagues had been advocating for years. Public opinion was finally aroused to the real dangers of the spoils system, and politicians were galvanized into action. Late in December 1882 the Senate passed, by a vote of 38 to 5, the Pendleton Civil Service Bill. The House majority was equally decisive, and on 16 January 1883, the bill became law. The Pendleton Act created a Civil Service Commission to administer a new set of rules which required appointments to be made as a result of open competitive examinations, and prohibited assessments on office-holders for political purposes. By law these new rules were applied only to some fourteen thousand positions, about twelve per cent of the total, but the President was empowered to extend them to other parts of the service at his discretion. Of Arthur's successors Presidents Cleveland, Roosevelt, Wilson, and F. D. Roosevelt have made large additions to the merit lists. At the turn of the century there were not far from one hundred thousand in the classified civil service; at the end of Theodore Roosevelt's administration the number had more than doubled and at the end of Wilson's administration it had increased to almost half a million.[4] At the same time most states were passing civil service laws of their own. Yet it would be idle to pretend that civil service reform has fulfilled the expectations of its advocates. The emoluments are not sufficiently high, or talent at such a premium as to attract university graduates and other able men from business and the professions. There has been, however, a great improvement in morale and efficiency; and it was fortunate indeed that the merit principle was adopted before the twentieth century when administrative expansion greatly increased the need of honest men and expert service.

In only one other field did the Arthur administration make any contribution to the development of the nation. The War of the Pacific between Peru, Bolivia, and Chile and the rising interest in an isthmian canal, awakened the American people to a realization of the decrepitude of their navy.[5] Twenty years after the building of the *Monitor* it was inferior to the navy of every principal European country, and to that of Chile. After long discussion Congress authorized on 5 August 1882 the construction of 'two steam cruising vessels of war . . . to be constructed of steel of domestic manufacture.' These were the *Chicago* and the *Boston,* which entered active service in 1887, and began a new era in American naval history. The program which Arthur had inaugurated was continued, with even greater effectiveness, by his successors: by the nineties the 'big navy' men could address their impassioned appeals to a public abundantly educated on the subject.

4 In 1940, 726,827 out of a total of 1,014,117 federal employees were in the classified civil service.

5 '"I don't think I should like America." — "I suppose because we have no ruins and no curiosities," said Virginia, satirically. — "No ruins! no curiosities!" answered the Ghost; "You have your navy and your manners."' — Oscar Wilde, *The Canterville Ghost.*

3. *The Administration of Grover Cleveland*

Arthur's placid administration ended in the most exciting Presidential campaign since the Civil War, although the only real issue between the parties was possession of the government. The Republicans, disappointed in Arthur, turned to the magnetic Blaine who had so narrowly missed the nomination in 1880. He had served for a few months as Secretary of State under Garfield and Arthur, and had retired to write *Twenty Years of Congress,* a thousand page celebration of the virtues and triumphs of the Republican party. Now it was his turn, and he was not to be denied; four ballots sufficed to give him the nomination. But Blaine was more than conscientious Republicans could swallow. To the rank and file of the party he may have been a 'plumed knight,' but to upright and intelligent Republicans, who were sick of the prevailing corruption, he was a simple grafter. The principal charge against him was the prostitution of the speakership to personal gain; in that connection he had never been able to explain the missive to a certain Fisher with the damning postscript, 'Burn this letter.' Even Conkling, when asked to campaign for Blaine, had replied, 'I don't engage in criminal practice.' Under the leadership of Carl Schurz and George William Curtis the reform wing of the party bolted from the convention, promised to support any decent nomination the Democrats might make, and proudly accepted the name 'Mugwump' which was given them in derision.[6] As bolting was the great offense in American political ethics, few of the Mugwumps managed to resume a political career; younger and shrewder politicians like Henry Cabot Lodge and Theodore Roosevelt, who supported Blaine while admitting the worst about him, had their reward.

With the Promised Land at last in sight, the Democrats made an admirable nomination. Grover Cleveland was a self-made man who as reform mayor of Buffalo and Governor of New York had distinguished himself for firmness and integrity, to the disgust of Tammany Hall. 'We love him for the enemies he has made,' said General E. S. Bragg of Wisconsin in the nominating speech, and it required only two ballots for the convention to endorse this tribute. Powerful journals such as the New York *Times,* the New York *Evening Post,* the Springfield *Republican, The Nation,* and *Harper's Weekly,*

[6] 'Mugwump' is the word for 'great captain' in Eliot's Indian Bible, applied on this occasion by the New York *Sun.*

with Nast's damning cartoons, shifted over to Cleveland, as did scores of independents and liberal Republicans of the stripe of Charles Francis Adams, James Russell Lowell, and Henry Ward Beecher. No campaign since the Civil War had played such havoc with party regularity.

As the campaign proceeded it became noisy and nasty. Cleveland was charged, among other things, with having an illegitimate child, which he admitted to the consternation of his supporters. But, as one of them concluded philosophically, 'We should elect Mr. Cleveland to the public office which he is so admirably qualified to fill, and remand Mr. Blaine to the private life which he is so eminently fitted to adorn.' Democratic torchlight processions paraded the streets, shouting,

Blaine, Blaine, James G. Blaine,
The continental liar from the State of Maine
Burn this letter!

To which Republican processions retorted:

Ma! Ma! Where's my pa?
Gone to the White House,
Ha! Ha! Ha!

The contest was bitterly fought throughout the North, Hendricks, the Democratic vice-presidential nominee, added to the strength of the ticket in the critical state of Indiana, and the Mugwumps played an important rôle in New Jersey and Connecticut. But New York was the decisive state. Here Blaine had a strong following among the Irish-Americans, which he lost at the eleventh hour through the tactless remark of a clerical supporter. As spokesman for a visiting delegation, a hapless parson named Burchard described the Democracy as the party of 'Rum, Romanism, and Rebellion.' Blaine neglected to rebuke this insult to the faith of his Celtic friends; Cleveland carried New York by a plurality of 1,149 in a vote of over one million; and New York's electoral vote gave him the Presidency.

For a person of such generous bulk, Grover Cleveland was remarkably austere, unbending, and ungenial. He was a man of integrity, courage, and steadfast devotion to duty; but singularly lacking in imagination and never quite at home in the rough and tumble of party politics. Though brought up in rural communities, he never understood the problems of the farmers of the South and the West nor the reasons for their discontent, but at least he made the effort. Conservative but not reactionary, he did not conceive of the government as an instrument for social reform but rather as a mediator between conflicting interests. Elected at a period when subservience to the popular will was supposed to be the first political virtue, he remained inflexible in the right as he saw it, and made slight departures from his pre-conceived notions upon any subject.

It was character that made Cleveland's administration the most distinguished between Lincoln's and Theodore Roosevelt's. He alone of the Presidents of this generation had some suspicion of the significance and direction of the economic changes that were transforming the country and made some effort to grapple with the problems created by changes. He alone of the titular leaders of either party had sufficient courage to defy the privilege groups and the pressure groups that were using the government for selfish purposes and to risk his political career in defense of what he thought was honest and right. He supported and advanced civil service reform; he challenged the predatory interests that were engrossing the public lands of the nation; he denounced the evils of protection and dramatized the tariff issue so effectively that it could not be evaded; he called a halt to the raids on the Treasury by war veterans and their lobbyists. If the total achievements of his administration were negative rather than positive, it may yet be maintained that the ability to say ' no ' and mean ' no ' was in itself no mean achievement.

Shortly after Cleveland's inauguration arose the question of patronage. Deserving Democrats, deprived of the sweets of office for twenty-five years, demanded as clean a sweep as the law would allow — eighty-eight per cent clean; virtuous Mugwumps insisted on no sweep at all. ' I have a hungry party behind me,' the President remarked sadly, and on another occasion he broke out, more expressively, ' the d—d everlasting clatter for office continues to some extent, and makes me feel like resigning, and Hell is to pay generally.' Congress repealed the Tenure of Office Act, which left the President free again to remove incumbents without permission of the Senate; and by the end of his term, Cleveland, despite his intense dislike for the spoils system, had replaced nearly all the postmasters, and about half the other officials. Yet the Democrats were not satisfied, and the Mugwumps were not pleased.

Cleveland stirred up the old soldiers by appointing General Lucius Quintus Cincinnatus Lamar, C.S.A., Secretary of the Interior; by proposing to return to their states the captured Confederate battle-flags; and above all by his attitude toward private pension claims and pension legislation in general. The pension situation had already become a scandal; it was shortly to become a disgrace. The first general Civil War pension bill had been passed in 1862 and was based upon the sound theory that it was the duty of the government to pension veterans who suffered from disabilities contracted while in military service, and to assist the widows and children of these veterans. Under this law not far from nine hundred thousand claims had been filed by veterans or their dependents prior to the accession of Cleveland to the Presidency. Of these some five hundred and twenty thousand had been allowed; the rest had been rejected as invalid. Many of those whose claims were thus rejected had recourse to private pension bills which were presented by greedy pension attorneys and pushed through by Congressmen anxious to make political capital. This particular form of raid on the public treasury disgusted right-thinking men everywhere. Charles Francis Adams wrote scathingly, 'We had seen every dead-beat, and malingerer, every bummer, bounty-jumper, and suspected deserter . . . rush to the front as the greedy claimant of public bounty. If there was any man whose army record had been otherwise than creditable . . . we soon heard of him as the claimant of a back pension . . . or as being in the regular receipt of his monthly stipend.' Cleveland actually signed no less than 1453 of these private pension bills — a larger number than any of his predecessors — but it was his vetoes that were remembered.

Soon a second pension theory emerged — a theory which insisted that all veterans who suffered from any physical disability, regardless of its origin or its cause, were entitled to pensions. This theory had the enthusiastic support of the Grand Army of the Republic, of thousands of pension agents, and of business interests anxious to dispose of surplus revenue in order that there might be no downward revision of the tariff. The G.A.R. which boasted by the middle eighties a membership of almost half a million, was one of the most powerful pressure groups in the country and had long maintained an intimate alliance with the Republican party. Like the American Legion of our own time it flooded the country with propaganda, bullied Congressmen, threatened Presidents, and intimidated political parties.

We flatter ourselves [said Senator Saulsbury in 1884] that we are great men. We are the Senators of the United States who make laws for the people; but behind us there is another power greater than ourselves, controlling our action if not our judgment. The pension agents who sit around this Capitol issue their circulars and decrees, and petitions come up for pensions, and the Senators of the United States, great and mighty as they may be, bow to the behests of the pension agents and vote the money that they require, and they are afraid not to do it for fear that they would lose political status at home. We all know it, and the country knows it.

In 1887 Congress, at the dictation of the G.A.R. and the pension agents, passed the Dependent Pension Bill granting pensions to all veterans suffering from any disabilities, regardless of how contracted. Cleveland vetoed the bill, and his veto was an important factor in defeating him for re-election the following year.

There was a roar of protest, too, from the predatory interests that were despoiling the lands and forests of the West when the President ordered an investigation into the fraudulent practices of cattle ranchers, railroads, timber companies, and squatters on Indian reservations. Lamar and his Land Office Commissioner, William A. Sparks, uncovered frauds that staggered the imagination. Most railroad lands had been granted on terms calling for forfeiture in the event of the non-fulfilment of the contract within a stated time, but during preceding administrations these forfeiture clauses had been blandly ignored. Not only this, but where railroad grants happened to embrace lands already settled, the railroads had been permitted either to take over the homesteader's land, with all improvements, or to indemnify themselves from valuable forest or mineral lands elsewhere. Lamar put an end to these practices and instituted suits to recover millions of acres of land from the railroads. He proceeded with equal energy against powerful lumber companies like the Sierra Lumber Company and the Montana Improvement Company, subsidiary of the Northern Pacific Railroad, who were ruthlessly despoiling the national forests. He nullified fraudulent leases of Indian lands like that whereby one cattle company leased from the Cherokees six million acres for which they paid an annual rental of only one hundred thousand dollars and which they subleased for five times that amount. He ordered cattle barons to take down their barbed wire fences enclosing millions of acres of public lands, and instituted reforms long overdue in the administration of the Land Office. Altogether, during his first administration, Cleveland forced the restoration of some eighty-one million acres of public lands. At the same time the Interstate Commerce Act of 1887 and the Dawes

Act of 1887 furnished useful points of departure for the more effective regulation of the railroads and of Indian affairs.

More dramatic was Cleveland's effort to force action on the tariff problem. In this effort he was moved by two considerations. The high tariff, adopted originally as an emergency Civil War measure, had come to be accepted as a permanent part of national policy. As such it had contributed, in Cleveland's opinion, not only to a general increase in the price level of protected goods, but to the encouragement and development of trusts. Government revenues had shown a consistent surplus over ordinary expenses of almost one hundred million dollars annually all through the decade of the eighties, and this surplus was a standing temptation to extravagance of the pork barrel and pension grab variety. Yet the tariff, which had divided parties so sharply prior to the Civil War, had almost ceased to be a party issue, or even a political issue. The Civil War tariffs had raised the average duties from eighteen to forty per cent, and successive tinkerings in 1867, 1870, 1872, and 1875 had not changed levels in any substantial way, though there had been a gradual upward trend on iron ore and woolens. Yet aside from the protests of the Liberal Republicans in 1872 there had been singularly little agitation of the subject. In 1880, however, the Democrats had demanded a 'tariff for revenue only' and soon the clamor for reform became so insistent that the Tariff Commission of 1882, composed though it was of protectionists, recommended a drastic downward revision of not less than twenty per cent.[7] Congress responded the following year with a 'mongrel tariff' that lowered some duties and raised others — a tariff which had the support not only of Republican protectionists like 'Pig Iron' Kelley of Pennsylvania but also of conservative Democrats like Randall of Pennsylvania and Mahone of Virginia.

This was the situation when Mr. Cleveland came to office. During the first two years of his administration the Democrats made no sincere effort to redeem their platform pledges of a downward revision of the tariff. In 1887, Cleveland, despite warnings to avoid

[7] 'The Commission' so read the Report, 'became convinced that a substantial reduction of tariff duties is demanded, not by a mere indiscriminate popular clamor, but by the best conservative opinion of the country. . . . Such a reduction of the existing tariff the Commission regards not only as a due recognition of public sentiment and a measure of justice to consumers, but one conducive to the general industrial prosperity, and which . . . will be ultimately beneficial to the special interests affected by such reduction.'

the explosive subject, startled the nation by devoting his annual message exclusively to the tariff. He denounced the fantastic extremes to which the principle of protection had been pushed, derided the 'infant industry' theory of high tariffs, emphasized the intimate relation of the tariff to trusts, and demanded a reduction which would be in harmony with the interests of society as a whole. 'Our progress toward a wise conclusion,' he wrote, 'will not be improved by dwelling upon theories of protection and free trade. It is a condition which confronts us, not a theory.' Reformers everywhere took heart. The New York *Nation* characterized the message 'the most courageous document that has been sent from the White House since the Civil War.' But Blaine denounced it as pure 'free trade,' and the Republicans prepared joyously to make this the issue of the forthcoming campaign. Roger Q. Mills promptly introduced a bill to the House looking to a downward revision of the tariff, but the measure was duly deadlocked by Senate Republicans led by the astute Nelson W. Aldrich, spokesman of Eastern manufacturing interests. Yet Cleveland had accomplished his purpose. He had brought the tariff issue sharply to the attention of the country and he had forced his own party to espouse tariff reform as the paramount issue.

4. *The Climax of Reaction*

Cleveland was renominated by the Democrats in 1888 without great enthusiasm, but with little opposition except from some of the disgruntled politicians, and the platform pledged the party to 'the views expressed by the President in his last message to Congress.' The Republicans pitched on the obscure Benjamin Harrison of Indiana as the most available and least offensive candidate, since he came from a critical state and had distinguished ancestry. The tariff was the issue of the campaign, but it did not decide the event. More important were such factors as Tammany's betrayal of Cleveland in the critical state of New York, the Republican campaign fund of over four million dollars, and the conversion of the G.A.R. to an instrument of the Republican party. The Democrats tried to round up the California vote by a bill which in effect denied treaty rights to Chinese immigrants; the Republicans, now that the issue of sexual immorality, so useful in the last campaign, was played out, resorted to the charge that the President beat his wife! Neither of these expedients had any effect, but another trick was more successful. The Irish vote had helped defeat Blaine in '84; now it was turned against Cleveland. A naturalized Anglo-American was inspired to inquire of the British Minister, Sir Lionel Sackville-West, how he should vote in order to serve the mother country. Sir Lionel, with incredible stupidity, advised him by letter to vote for the Democrats. Two weeks before the election, his letter was published, and the mischief was done. Though Cleveland's popular vote exceeded Harrison's by 100,000 the Republicans carried New York State, and again New York was decisive.

Benjamin Harrison, grandson of the hero of Tippecanoe, was an Indiana lawyer who made a dignified figurehead in the Presidency from 1889 to 1893. Aloof and aristocratic, honest and conscientious, he lacked the insight to comprehend the economic and imperialistic problems of a new day and the ability to control the spoilsmen of his party. Despite his character and attainments he made singularly little impression upon his own or later generations. James G. Blaine, who still considered himself the leader of the party, became his Secretary of State; the rest of the cabinet were nonentities. With the autocratic 'Czar' Reed as Speaker of the House, and with a majority in both Houses, the way was clear for constructive legislation. But the Republican party wanted little legislation that was not a raid on the treasury or a hold-up on the consumer, and in this administration statesmanship reached a new low-water mark.

For the Republicans returned to office with heavy political debts to pay. The machine politicians had performed yeomen service in rounding up votes, and they expected to be rewarded with the spoils of office. The old soldier vote had proved decisive in critical states, and the soldiers counted on more generous pensions. Business and manufacturing interests had contributed liberally to the campaign fund, and they expected to be rewarded with an upward revision of the tariff. To all these demands the administration showed itself remarkably complaisant. Rarely before in our history had an administration been more responsive to pressure groups; never since, unless in the 1920's, has the connection between government and business been more openly avowed or frankly accepted.

The appointment of John Wanamaker, the Philadelphia 'merchant prince,' to the office of Postmaster General indicated the repudiation of platform promises of civil service reform. Harrison had said, in his acceptance speech, that 'only the interest of the public service should suggest removals from office,' but it was quickly apparent that such interest required a clean sweep of Democratic office-holders. Within a year Wanamaker had removed over thirty thousand postmasters, more than double the number that Cleveland had dismissed in the same period. Cleveland had placed the railroad mail service under civil service rules, but Harrison suspended the operation of the rules until the service could be filled with Republicans, and at the same time refused to extend the rules to the new Census Bureau. Theodore Roosevelt was appointed, as window-dressing, to the Civil Service Commission, but the Civil Service Reform League denounced the President for violation of his campaign pledges and the New York *Nation* characterized him as a 'subservient disciple of the spoils doctrine.'

Harrison, during his campaign, had announced that 'it was no time to be weighing the claims of old soldiers with apothecary's scales,' and he lived up to the implications of that statement. 'God help the Surplus,' said Corporal Tanner who was appointed to the office of Pension Commissioner, and whose liberal interpretations of the existing pension legislation cost the Treasury millions of dollars. In 1890 Congress passed and the President signed a Disability Pension Act which provided pensions to all veterans who had served ninety days and who were unable to perform *manual* labor, regardless of the cause or origin of their disability. The bill cost the country something over sixty million dollars annually, and even the G.A.R. was satisfied for a time. 'While not just what we asked,' the pension committee of that organization reported, 'it is the most liberal pension measure ever passed by any legislative body in the world, and will place upon the rolls all of the survivors of the war whose conditions of health are not practically perfect.' Yet in course of time the veterans came to demand, and politicians found it expedient to grant, still more. After the turn of the century it was thought necessary to inaugurate a system of Universal Service Pensions, and by a Presidential ruling, in 1904, all veterans were granted pensions on the basis of service alone. By 1936 the Civil War pension bill had come to a little less than eight billion dollars.

The year 1890 is memorable, politically, for the passage of the Disability Pension Act, the Sherman Anti-trust Act, the Sherman Silver Purchase bill, the McKinley tariff, and for the admission of the last of the 'omnibus' states. Of these we have already discussed the Anti-trust Act and the omnibus states, and will reserve for later consideration the Silver Purchase bill. That the Harrison administration should fulfill its campaign promises by new tariff legislation was inevitable. Yet it was by no means clear, in the light of Cleveland's popular plurality, that the country wanted a higher tariff, nor was it certain that the administration could muster a majority on this issue. The McKinley tariff bill of October 1890 was pushed through as the result of a bargain between western Republicans who wanted silver legislation and eastern Republicans who wanted tariff legislation. Its provisions were formulated chiefly by William McKinley of Ohio and Nelson W. Aldrich of Rhode Island, but the important schedules were dictated by such pressure groups as the National Association of Wool Manufacturers, the Tin Plate and Iron and Steel Associations, and the Louisiana sugar growers. The bill was a frank recognition of the protective principle: it sought not only to protect established industries, but to foster 'infant industries' and, by prohibitory duties, to create new industries. It embodied three new and interesting provisions: it reached out for the farmers' vote with protective rates upon products of agriculture, duties which proved completely ineffective in the forthcoming agricultural depression; it placed raw sugar on the free list and compensated the Louisiana and Kansas beet sugar growers with a bounty of two cents a pound — a provision of dubious constitutionality; it included a reciprocity section which gave the President the authority to place duties on sugar, molasses, tea, coffee, and hides if he thought that nations exporting those articles to the United States were imposing unequal and unreasonable duties on American goods.

Pension legislation and tariff legislation helped to liquidate the troublesome surplus, and further support to this happy policy was found in additional legislation of a less important character. Postal subsidies to steamship lines were increased; the direct taxes collected during the Civil War were generously returned to the states where they had been paid; outbreaks among the Sioux culminating in the massacre of Indians at Wounded Knee Creek and the murder of Sitting Bull required enlarged expenditures for the army and the Indian Bureau; and finally Secretary Windom's policy of using surplus treasury funds to buy up and cancel government bonds took some $275,000,000 before the policy was reversed by Windom's successor. The total expenditures of the Fifty-first Congress, 2 December 1889 to 3 March 1891, reached the unprecedented sum of almost one billion dollars. 'This is a Billion Dollar country,' was the retort popularly attributed to 'czar' Reed.

The unpopularity of the McKinley tariff was largely responsible for the political revolution in the Congressional elections of 1890. Only 88 Republicans were returned to the new House, as against 235 Democrats and 9 Populists; and the Republican majority in the Senate was reduced to eight unstable votes from the Far West. Even rock-ribbed Republican states like Michigan and Massachusetts went Democratic, and McKinley himself failed of re-election. There was more to this verdict, however, than revulsion from the tariff and disgust at Republican chicanery and corruption. It registered a deep-lying unrest that was presently to break forth into a movement that carried Bryan to prominence, Roosevelt to achievement, and Wilson to apotheosis.

XI

THE BATTLE OF THE STANDARDS

1890–1897

1. *The Populist Revolt*

IN 1890 American politics lost their steady beat, and began to dip and flutter in an effort to maintain equilibrium among strange currents of thought that issued from the caverns of discontent.

Almost a generation had passed since the Civil War. The older Republicans had come to revere their 'Grand Old Party' only less than the Union and the flag, and indeed they often identified party loyalty with patriotism. They had come to regard their leaders as the beloved generals of a victorious army. It was difficult for the politicians to believe that anything was amiss. The Ohio and Middle Western men, average and representative of the party, had grown up with the country. Their experience of life had been utterly different from that of any European statesman. They had seen the frontier of log-cabins, stumpy clearings, and razor-back hogs replaced by frame houses and great barns, well tilled farms, and sleek cattle. Towns with banks, libraries, high schools, mansions, and 'opera houses' had sprung up where once as barefooted boys they had hunted squirrel and wild-cat; and the market towns of their youth had grown into great manufacturing cities. As young men they had enlisted in the crusade for the Union, and returned to take their part in progress, development, and expansion. The railroad, the telegraph, the sewing machine, oil and gas lighting, and a hundred new comforts and conveniences had come within reach of all but the poorest and remotest during their lifetime. If discontented workmen and poverty-stricken farmers sometimes intruded into the picture, it must be foreign agitators or the law of supply and demand that were to blame. How could there be anything wrong with a government which had wrought such miraculous changes for the better, or with a Grand Old Party which had saved the nation from disunion?

The Democratic party, too, was in danger of becoming conservative and content. The oldest, and during most of this period the largest political party,[1] it embraced the most diverse elements and was compelled to reconcile those elements by avoiding controversial issues. Its strongholds were in the most conservative sections of the country — the South and the East, and its strength in these sections rested not on any policies it might embrace but upon race, tradition, and the loyalty of local organizations interested primarily in spoils of office. There was little reason to believe that the Bourbon Democrats of the South would be friendly to new ideas of a liberal or radical character; there was no reason to suppose that Tammany Hall and kindred organizations in the North would be open to any ideas. The Solid South, irrevocably committed to the one principle of maintaining white supremacy, hung like a dead weight on party leadership; the local machines in the North, no less irrevocably committed to the single principle of getting and keeping office, were willing to sell out on any other issue to the highest bidder. There were independents, of course, in the Democratic as in the Republican party, men like Cleveland in New York, Thurman in Ohio, J. Q. Adams in Massachusetts, and Lamar in Mississippi, but only rarely could they carry their party with them on any controversial issue.

Yet the quarter-century of exploitation had its suffering victims, who felt that something was radically wrong and were groping for a remedy. Industrial unrest was acute; 1890 witnessed the largest number of strikes recorded in any one year of the nineteenth century, and the Homestead strike of 1892 recalled the scenes of violence and terrorism of the Great Strike of '77. Immigrants from southern and eastern Europe were pouring into the country in unprecedented numbers, threatening the wages and the standards of American workingmen. Railroad regulation had proved all but futile, and the anti-trust law was to prove effective only against labor organizations. Discontent with the McKinley tariff was widespread, and the prospect of any effective tariff reduction was dim. Money was tight, credit inflexible, banking facilities woefully inadequate, and the Sherman Silver Purchase Act did little to satisfy the advocates of free and unlimited coinage of silver and less to settle the money question. The political machinery was not articulated to democracy: the Senate, chosen not by popular vote but by state legislatures, was the stronghold of special interests; the Supreme Court reflected the ideas of the privileged.

[1] It is well to remember that the Democratic party polled a plurality of the popular vote in the Presidential elections of 1876, 1884, 1888, and 1892.

Dissatisfaction was most acute on the farms of the South and the West. The Middle Border began, in 1887, to suffer the devastating effects of deflation after a great land boom. Virgin prairie land, and peak prices of wheat and corn in 1881, had induced an excessive construction of railroads, largely financed locally, and an over-settlement of the comparatively arid western part of Kansas, Nebraska and the Dakotas. Small towns and counties indulged in lavish expenditure, and their citizens speculated wildly in building lots. These new farms were created largely on credit granted by mortgage companies in the East; in Kansas there was one mortgage, on the average, to every other adult in the state, and the situation in Nebraska and Iowa was almost as bad. After several years of excessive rainfall there came in 1887 a summer so dry that the crops withered all along the border of the Plains. In the four years from 1889 to 1893 over eleven thousand farm mortgages were foreclosed in Kansas alone and in fifteen counties of that state over three-quarters of the land was owned by mortgage companies. During these years the people who had entered that new El Dorado trekked eastward again; on their wagons one could read the scrawl, 'In God we trusted, in Kansas we busted.' William Allen White described some of these picturesquely.

There came through Emporia yesterday two old-fashioned mover wagons, headed east. . . . These movers were from western Kansas. . . . They had come from that wilderness only after a ten years' hard vicious fight, a fight which had left its scars on their faces, had beat their bodies, had taken the elasticity from their steps and left them crippled to enter the battle anew. For ten years they had been fighting the elements. They had seen it stop raining for months at a time. They had heard the fury of the winter wind as it came whining across the short burned grass and cut the flesh from their children huddling in the corner. These movers have strained their eyes watching through long summer days for the rain that never came. They had seen that big cloud roll up from the southwest about one in the afternoon, hover over the land, and stumble away with a few thumps of thunder as the sun went down. They have tossed through hot nights wild with worry, and have arisen only to find their worst nightmares grazing in reality on the brown stubble in front of their sun-warped doors. They had such high hopes when they went out there; they are so desolate now — no, not now, for now they are in the land of corn and honey. They have come out of the wilderness, back to the land of promise.

Others, made of sterner stuff, struggled on through the eighties and the nineties to better times. What was true along the Middle Border was almost equally true of other agricultural regions. In an Eastern state a survey of seven hundred representative farms discovered an average yield of $167. In the older Middle West farmers were glad to exchange places with immigrant factory hands who had at least a dollar a day. And in the South cotton growers struggled on from year to year against a falling market, overproduction, and the improvidence of Negro tenants, while mortgage indebtedness and tenancy grew at an ominous pace.

The stage was set for the entrance of a party of revolt, and with astonishing promptness the Populist party made its appearance. The rank and file of the new party was recruited from the Farmers' Alliances, Greenbackers, Knights of Labor, free-silverites, disciples of Edward Bellamy, and followers of Henry George; the leadership, drawn almost exclusively from the Alliances, furnished a refreshing contrast to the bankrupt and dismal leadership of the major parties during the eighties and nineties. There was 'Pitchfork Ben' Tillman, of South Carolina, who placed himself at the head of the underprivileged farmers of the Palmetto state, won the governorship from the 'Bourbon' Wade Hampton, pushed a series of reforms through the state legislature, and created a political machine which endures to this day. There was cadaverous Tom Watson of Georgia, apostle of the new Jeffersonianism, who championed the cause of the tenant farmers and the mill hands, ran for the presidency on the Populist ticket, wrote biographies of Jefferson and Napoleon, and earned the dubious title of the 'Sage of Hickory Hill.' There was David H. Waite, Governor of Colorado, friend of the farmers and the miners and of all the underprivileged of the earth, known by his admirers as the 'Abraham Lincoln of the Rockies' and by his critics as 'Bloody Bridles' Waite because he had said that it was better 'that blood should flow to the horses' bridles rather than our national liberties should be destroyed.' Minnesota boasted the Sage of Nininger, the inimitable Ignatius Donnelly, discoverer of the lost Atlantis, advocate of the Baconian theory, author of the prophetic *Caesar's Column,* undismayed champion of lost causes and desperate remedies. From Iowa came the upright and dignified James Baird Weaver who gave respectability to heterodoxy and who undertook the thankless job of representing the Greenbackers in the canvass of 1880 and the Populists in 1892, and who had every quality but magnetism. Abolitionist Kansas, where the farm revolt became 'a religious revival, a crusade, a pentecost of politics in which the tongue of flame sat upon every man and each spake as the spirit gave him utterance' was most prolific of leadership. Here the sad-faced Mary Lease went about advising farmers to 'raise less corn and more Hell.' Here Jerry Simpson, the sockless Socrates of the prairie, espoused the doctrines of Henry George and exposed the iniquities of the railroads. Here Senator William A. Peffer of the hickory-nut head and long flowing beard, whom Roosevelt, with his usual impetuosity denounced as 'a well-meaning, pin-headed, anarchistic crank,' presented with logic and learning *The Farmer's Side, His Troubles and Their Remedy*. And from Nebraska came the greatest of all the farmers' leaders, the Jefferson of the new dispensation, William Jennings Bryan.

Although the new party was not formally organized until 1891, it got under way in 1890, and that year succeeded in capturing control of the Democratic party in a number of Southern states and in effecting a working alliance with the Democrats in the West. As a result of this strategy it emerged from the fall elections of 1890 with four Senators and over fifty Congressmen and with partial or complete control of the legislatures of a dozen states. Flushed with this initial success the triumphant leaders prepared, through a series of conferences and conventions, to organize the new party in a formal fashion and to present a full ticket in the elections of 1892.

The Populist convention that met in Omaha on Independence Day of 1892 presented a sharp contrast to the conventions of the two major parties. Decorum and apathy had marked these conventions, and the nominations of Cleveland and Harrison had excited neither surprise nor enthusiasm. But a camp-meeting atmosphere characterized the convention of the People's party, and the speeches which the oddly assorted delegates greeted with such 'tumultuous applause' were old-fashioned camp-meeting harangues. The platform, drawn up by the eloquent Ignatius Donnelly, raked both the major parties and painted a melancholy picture of the American scene:

> We meet in the midst of a nation brought to the verge of moral, political, and material ruin. Corruption dominates the ballot-box, the legislatures, the Congress, and touches even the ermine of the bench. The people are demoralized; . . . The newspapers are largely subsidized or muzzled; public opinion silenced; business prostrated; our homes covered with mortgages; labor impoverished; and the land concentrating in the hands of the capitalists. The urban workmen are denied the right of organization for self-protection; imported pauperized labor beats down their

wages; a hireling standing army, unrecognized by our laws, is established to shoot them down, and they are rapidly degenerating into European conditions. The fruits of the toil of millions are boldly stolen to build up colossal fortunes for a few, unprecedented in the history of mankind; and the possessors of these in turn, despise the republic and endanger liberty. From the same prolific womb of governmental injustice we breed the two great classes — tramps and millionaires.

More specifically the platform demanded the free and unlimited coinage of silver; a flexible currency system, controlled by the government and not by the banks, with an increase in the circulating medium to fifty dollars per capita; a graduated income tax; the subtreasury scheme; postal savings banks; public ownership and operation of railroads, telegraph, and telephones; prohibition of alien land ownership and reclamation of railroad lands illegally held; immigration restriction; the eight-hour day for labor; prohibition of the use of labor spies; the direct election of Senators, the Australian ballot, the initiative and referendum. The platform was regarded throughout the East as little short of communism, yet within a generation almost every one of the planks had been incorporated into law in whole or in part.

For their standard-bearer the Populists chose James B. Weaver of Iowa, a veteran of the reform movement too well known to excite curiosity and too respectable to justify abuse. The ensuing three-cornered campaign was less exciting than might have been expected, but the election offered some suggestive comments on American politics. Cleveland swept the solid South and seven Northern states, including New York, and for the third successive time received a popular plurality. Harrison polled a smaller vote than he had in his first campaign, and the labor and tariff policies for which his party was held responsible forfeited the support of the industrial states of the East. Weaver received over a million popular votes and twenty-two electoral votes, but his efforts to rally the farmers of the nation to his standard had been successful only in the region of the High Plains. Southern farmers, regardless of grievances, preferred to vote for the party which to them represented white supremacy. It remained to be seen whether a Democrat could perform in '96 what a Populist had failed to achieve in '92 — the renewal of the traditional alliance of South and West which had been shattered by the Civil War, and the creation of an agrarian party which could command the support of labor.

2. *The Money Question*

American society appeared to be dissolving, but the same old Grover Cleveland, a little stouter and more set in his ideas, was inaugurated President on 4 March 1893. A large proportion of his vote had come from suffering farmers who looked for relief to the Democracy rather than to the Populists. Cold comfort they obtained from the inaugural address! The situation, as the President saw it, demanded 'prompt and conservative precaution' to protect a 'sound and stable currency.'

The trouble was, of course, that men disagreed violently as to the nature of 'a sound and stable currency,' and from that time to the present neither historians nor economists have been able to reach any agreement. No problem is of a more controversial character, and no controversy was ever more interpenetrated with emotion or more confused by the application of moral attitudes. But the money question, for all its complexity, had the merit of cutting athwart party lines and reflecting sectional and class alignments as did no other political issue of that time — not even the tariff. Yet it would be an error to suppose that party loyalties were completely shattered by the realignment over this question. Even at the height of the controversy, traditional party loyalties continued to animate thousands of voters; and that such predominately agricultural states as Iowa, Minnesota, and North Dakota cast their electoral votes for McKinley rather than for Bryan in 1896 must be credited, in the last analysis, not to economic determinism but to political habit and inheritance.

Put in its simplest terms — and nothing is more difficult to put in simple terms — the money question involved the relation of money to commodity prices, wages, and investments, and the function of the government in regulating that relation. The orthodox or classical theory of money, entertained by the business and investor classes generally, was the bullion theory. This theory held that money was actually only a token of coin, that its value was determined by the bullion which was held as security for its redemption, and that any interference by government with this value was economically unsound. It required therefore that all money in circulation have behind it some substantial metallic value, and that government confine itself to issuing money on security of bullion actually in the treasury vaults, either directly, or indirectly through banks. As long as the ratio between gold and silver remained relatively stable, the bullion theory of money accepted a bimetallic standard; when the decline in the value of silver disrupted that long-established ratio, orthodox economists turned to the single gold standard. This classical theory of money flowed from the philosophy of laissez faire which was so widely accepted in the whole field of economy and politics in the first half of the nineteenth century.

In the second half of the century, and especially after the Civil War, a new theory of money gained many adherents, a theory which regarded money as a token of credit rather than of bullion, and which maintained that it was the proper business of the government to regulate money in the interests of society at large. Advocates of this theory pointed out that bullion, and especially gold, did not provide a sufficiently large or flexible basis for the money needs of an expanding nation, and that any financial policy which tied money to gold placed the whole monetary system of the nation at the mercy of a fortuitous gold production. They insisted that bullion security for money was unnecessary or necessary only in part; that the vital consideration was the credit of the government, and that 'the promise to pay' of the United States was sufficient to sustain the value of any money issued by that government. These proponents of credit money demanded that currency be expanded whenever desirable to provide for the business needs of the country and to hold commodity prices stable. Enthusiastic support for this school of economic thought was found among the farmers of the South and the West, and among the debtor groups everywhere — groups who had favored easy money since the days of the Massachusetts land bank scheme and Shays' Rebellion.

The roots of the money question are to be found in the financing of the Civil War. At that time, it will be remembered, the Federal Government issued four hundred and fifty million dollars in greenbacks — money with no security but the promise of the government to pay. These greenbacks were legal tender for all purposes but customs duties and interest on certain government bonds. In part because of this discrimination against them, in part because of lack of confidence in the ability or the willingness of the government to redeem them in coin, they promptly depreciated in value. Yet though the fluctuation in the value of greenbacks was a constant temptation to speculation, they served nevertheless a useful purpose and came in time to command the confidence of a large part of the people. They not only helped to finance the war, but by expanding the currency they served to lower interest rates and to raise commodity prices.

On the conclusion of the war, however, conservative business interests presented three demands: the resumption of specie payments on all government obligations; the retirement from the currency of all legal tender notes; and the refunding of the national debt on a gold basis. These demands aroused the bitter opposition of such men as Thaddeus Stevens and Wendell Phillips, but they were in large part complied with. On 1 January 1879, the government resumed specie payments; the number of legal tender notes in circulation was contracted to $346,681,000; and Congress, in 1869, pledged the faith and credit of the United States to the payment of the principal and interest of government bonds in gold.

As a result of these policies, so their critics averred, commodity prices fell sharply and the public debt burden was vastly enhanced. The arguments which the Greenbackers advanced to support this charge are not hard to follow. As per capita circulation of money declined from $31 in 1865 to $19 in 1875, money became tight and therefore dear. Since there were fewer dollars to go around in 1875 than there had been a decade earlier, it took more corn, wheat, and cotton to buy a dollar than it had formerly taken. And as for the public debt, it was pointed out that the government had borrowed greenback dollars worth anywhere from fifty to eighty cents in gold; it was not morally obliged to pay back dollars worth a dollar in gold.

The Specie Resumption Act of 1875, however, ended the greenback question as a practical political issue. A Greenback party, to be sure, entered in the field; in 1878 it polled a million votes, and in 1880 and 1884 it offered presidential candidates to an indifferent electorate. But after the middle seventies the zeal of the inflationists was transferred from greenbacks to silver, and for the next twenty years 'free silver' was the most exciting and significant political issue before the American people. This shift from greenbacks to silver was brought about by three considerations. In the first place silver satisfied the requirement that there should be some substantial security behind money, for to the conservative economists silver bullion seemed a sounder security than the mere promise of the government to pay. In the second place, dependence upon gold and silver would insure a reasonable expansion of the currency, but guard against any such reckless inflation as might result from the use of mere legal tender notes. In the third place, silver had behind it the silver-mine owners and investors, a powerful group, vitally interested in silver legislation and prepared to finance 'educational' and political campaigns looking to such legislation.

In 1861 the mines of the country had produced approximately forty-three million dollars worth of gold but only two million dollars worth of silver. The coinage ratio between silver and gold of 15.988 to 1 actually undervalued silver, and in consequence silver was sold for commercial purposes and only gold was carried to the mints for purposes of coinage. During the sixties and early seventies, however, came the discoveries of immense deposits of silver in the mountains of the West; by 1873 the value of silver mined in the United States had increased to thirty-six million dollars while the value of gold had declined to the same figure. As a result of this relative and absolute increase in silver production, the price of silver gradually slumped until by 1873 it reached approximately the legal ratio. The next year, for the first time since 1837, it fell below the legal ratio, and it became profitable to sell silver to governments for coinage purposes instead of selling it for commercial purposes.

But when the silver-mine owners turned to governments, they found their market gone. Germany in 1871 adopted a gold standard; the Latin Union consisting of France, Italy, Switzerland, Belgium, and Greece promptly suspended the free coinage of silver; and all the other European states came tumbling after. Worst of all, from the point of view of the silver interests, the United States had, by the coinage act of 1873, demonetized silver. This demonetization had been effected by the simple device of omitting from the act any specific provision for the coinage of silver dollars. Silverites hotly charged a trick, and the act became known as 'the Crime of '73.' It is immaterial now to determine whether the demonetization of silver was without malice or guile; the significant fact is that for a quarter of a century a large part of the population sincerely and passionately believed that demonetization was part of a 'gold conspiracy' and that it constituted the greatest crime in history.

According to my views of the subject [said John G. Carlisle, who later became Cleveland's Secretary of the Treasury] the conspiracy which seems to have been formed here and in Europe to destroy by legislation and otherwise from three-sevenths to one-half of the metallic money of the world, is the most gigantic crime of this or any other age. The consummation of such a scheme would ultimately entail more misery upon the human race than all the wars, pestilences, and famines that ever occurred in the history of the world.

And the schoolmaster in *Coin's Financial School* described the act in even more hysterical terms:

> It is known as the crime of 1873. A crime, because it has confiscated millions of dollars worth of property. A crime, because it has made tens of thousands of tramps. A crime, because it has made thousands of suicides. A crime, because it has brought tears to strong men's eyes and hunger and pinching want to widows and orphans. A crime because it is destroying the honest yeomanry of the land, the bulwark of the nation. A crime because it has brought this once great republic to the verge of ruin, where it is now in imminent danger of tottering to its fall.

From the middle seventies to the middle nineties, then, the money question took the form of a demand for the free and unlimited coinage of silver. In 1878 the silverites pushed through, over a Presidential veto, the Bland-Allison Act which provided that the government must purchase each month not less than two nor more than four million dollars worth of silver, to be coined into silver dollars at the existing legal ratio with gold. Successive secretaries of the treasury followed the policy of purchasing the minimum amount, and the addition to the currency was not sufficient to increase in any appreciable way the per capita circulation of money or to halt the steady decline in the price of silver in the world market.

The hard times of the late eighties brought a renewal of the silver agitation, a demand from the farmers and the silver interests that the government abandon the faint-hearted gesture of the Bland-Allison Act and commit itself irrevocably to the policy of unlimited coinage of silver. Domestic production of the white metal increased from thirty-six million dollars in 1873 to fifty-seven million by 1890, and the increase in world production was proportionately great. This increase, of course, depressed the price of silver and raised the price of gold. At the same time per capita circulation of money in the United States barely held its own, and in some sections of the country declined sharply. The relation between the limited coinage of silver and the low price of silver was not lost upon silver-mine interests. The connection between low commodity prices and high gold prices, between low per capita circulation of money and high interest rates, was not lost upon the farmers.

Yet silver agitation might have come to naught had it not been for the admission of the 'Omnibus' states. The enabling acts of 1889 and 1890 brought into Congress representatives from six new Western states, and the Senate promptly became the stronghold of silver sentiment. The result was the enactment of a new and more generous silver bill — the Sherman Silver Purchase Act of 1890. This notorious measure, the product of a bargain whereby Western Republicans voted for a tariff bill which they disliked and Eastern Republicans voted for a silver bill which they feared, satisfied no one. It provided that the Treasury Department purchase each month four and one-half million ounces of silver, at the market price, paying for such silver with Treasury notes of the United States. It contained further the fateful provision that 'upon demand of the holder of any of the Treasury notes . . . the Secretary of the Treasury shall, under such regulations as he may prescribe, redeem such notes in gold or silver coin, at his discretion, it being the established policy of the United States to maintain the two metals on a parity with each other upon the present ratio.'

The Democrats opposed this measure not only on party grounds but because they regarded it as a futile and dangerous compromise. In this they were correct. The Sherman Act failed not only to increase the price of silver; it failed just as dismally to increase the amount of money in circulation or to affect the steady decline in the prices of farm commodities. The failure of the Sherman Act to effect these ends was variously explained by two opposing schools of thought. Gold monometallists insisted that the Act revealed the hopelessness of the effort to do anything for silver, and that it proved that the price of silver could not be raised artificially by government action. Silverites argued, on the contrary, that the Act proved the futility of compromise and the necessity for free and unlimited coinage. The act provided, to be sure, for the purchase of practically the entire domestic production of silver. But the world production was almost three times the domestic production, and as long as there were huge quantities of silver seeking a market, the price would be sure to slump. The solution, said conservatives, was to abandon silver to its fate and return to the gold standard. The solution, said the silverites, was to open our mints to unlimited coinage of silver, and peg the price at the traditional ratio of 16 to 1.

It is impossible now to determine which alternative was the better. In the end the gold standard was victorious, and prior to the 1930's historians were inclined to regard that victory as providential. Yet logic, at least, would seem to be with the bimetallists. Certainly if the United States stood ready to exchange, with all comers, one ounce of gold for sixteen ounces of silver, no one would sell silver for less than that sum. That is, if the United States could absorb all the silver that would be brought to her mints, she could peg the price, and bimetallism would be an established fact. But that *if* was crucial. The success of the operation depended upon the ability of the United States to pay out gold for silver until speculators were convinced of the futility of trying to break the price, or until the increased demand for silver raised its commercial value.

There was a third solution, one upon the desirability of which both monometallists and bimetallists were agreed. That was international bimetallism. If the United States could persuade the other great powers of the world to co-operate with it in re-establishing bimetallism, the normal market for silver would be restored, silver would rebound to its traditional price, and the money question would be solved. Hopefully, year after year, delegates journeyed to International Monetary Conferences. Practically every conference concluded that international bimetallism was economically expedient and financially sound — just as in our own time conferences have concluded that disarmament was economically expedient and morally sound. But on the political expediency of bimetallism there was no agreement. Each nation distrusted the sincerity of its neighbors, and no nation was ready to take the plunge. International bimetallism therefore served only the dubious purpose of furnishing bimetallists with arguments and permitting monometallists to hedge on the money question.

If bimetallism were to be tried, then, it would have to be tried as a national policy. The mere statement of this fact created an emotional tension unfavorable to the intelligent consideration of the question. On the one hand conservatives insisted that national finance and trade were so intimately connected with world finance and trade that it would be ruinous for the United States to embark upon a policy which might lead to economic isolation, and they painted in lurid colors the fearful consequences of such a development. On the other hand the silverites made the issue one of nationalism and patriotism, and the battle-cries of the Revolution echoed curiously across the plains of Kansas and Texas. 'It is the issue of 1776 over again,' said Bryan. 'Our ancestors when but three million in number, had the courage to declare their political independence of every other nation;

shall we, their descendants, when we have grown to seventy millions, declare that we are less independent than our forefathers?'

Consideration of the money question was confused not only by irrelevant issues of patriotism and nationalism, but of morals and ethics. 'Gold-bugs' talked of an 'honest dollar,' and, smugly appropriating all honesty to themselves, denounced their opponents as wicked and immoral men. 'The eagerness of the advocates of free silver,' wrote the conservative economist, J. Laurence Laughlin, 'is founded on an appeal to dishonesty and cheating on the part of those who would like to repudiate and scale one-half of their obligations.' Silverites retorted by branding the monometallists as 'Shylocks' and 'vampires,' and hurled back at them the charge of dishonesty. 'A dollar approaches honesty,' argued Mr. Bryan, 'as its purchasing power approaches stability. . . . Society has become accustomed to some very nice distinctions. A poor man is called a socialist if he believes that the wealth of the rich should be divided among the poor, but the rich man is called a financier if he devises a plan by which the pittance of the poor can be converted to his use. The poor man who takes property by force is called a thief, but the creditor who can by legislation make a debtor pay a dollar twice as large as he borrowed is lauded as the friend of sound currency. The man who wants the people to destroy the Government is an anarchist, but the man who wants the Government to destroy the people is a patriot.'

We can see now that the issue was both deeper and less dangerous than contemporaries realized. It was deeper because it involved a struggle for the ultimate control of government and of economy between the business interests of the East and the agrarian interests of the South and the West — a struggle in which gold and silver were mere symbols. It was less dangerous because, in all probability, none of the calamities so freely prophesied would have followed the adoption of either the gold or the silver standard at any time during these years. When the gold standard was finally adopted in 1900, the event made not a ripple on the placid seas of our economic life. When the gold standard was abandoned by Great Britain and by the United States, a full generation later, the event led to no untoward results. Historical parallels and analogies are always dangerous, but we are safe in saying that in the light of the experience of the 1930's much of the high-flown discussion of the 1890's was fantastic.

3. *The President and the Panic*

The Cleveland administration was just two months old when the failure of the National Cordage Company inaugurated the panic of 1893. The fundamental causes of this panic, as of all panics, are obscure, and the explanation that it was an inevitable curve of the business cycle merely begs the question. Yet it is possible to suggest some of the factors which contributed to the collapse of 1893. The long-drawn out agricultural depression which began in 1887 had seriously curtailed the purchasing power of one large group of consumers, and had similarly affected railway income. The collapse of our markets abroad, owing to business distress in Europe and Australia, had serious repercussions on American trade and manufacturing. Over-speculation attendant upon the organization of trusts and combines endangered the stability of the business world, while industrial disorders like the Homestead strike, the Coeur d'Alene strike, and the railway switchmen's strike, reduced profits and cut down purchasing power. Finally the silver policy of the government impaired confidence in the business world at home and abroad, and persuaded many European creditors to dump their American securities on the market and drain the nation of its gold.

By midsummer of 1893 the panic was in full swing. The Reading Railroad failed early in the spring. In July came the failure of the Erie, and shortly thereafter the Northern Pacific, the Union Pacific, and the Santa Fé all went into the hands of receivers. Within two years one-fourth of the railroad capitalization of the country was under control of bankruptcy courts, and sixty per cent of railroad stocks had suspended dividend payments. Banks everywhere felt the strain and called in their loans, often with consequences fatal to business firms and individuals unable to meet their obligations; in the single month of July 1893 commercial failures reached the sum of seventy-three million dollars and over fifteen thousand failures were recorded for the year. In the rural sections banks toppled like card-houses; of the 158 national bank failures in 1893, 153 were in the South and the West. 'Men died like flies under the strain,' wrote Henry Adams, 'and Boston grew suddenly old, haggard, and thin.' Adams was thinking of the Boston financiers; the characterization was equally applicable to the four million jobless who, by the summer of 1894, walked the streets of factory towns in a vain search for work.

President Cleveland believed that monetary uncertainty was the chief cause of the panic. He promptly summoned a special session of Congress to repeal the Sherman law, and to enact legislation which should 'put beyond all doubt or mistake the intention and the ability of the Government to fulfill its pecuniary obligations in money universally recognized by all civilized countries.' The result was the liveliest session of Congress in a generation. The administration forces were led by William L. Wilson of West Virginia and the eloquent Bourke Cockran of New York; silver was championed by the veteran 'Silver Dick' Bland and by young William Jennings Bryan of Nebraska.

> On the one hand [said Bryan] stand the corporate interests of the United States, the moneyed interests, aggregated wealth and capital, imperious, arrogant, compassionless. . . . On the other side stand an unnumbered throng, those who gave to the Democratic party a name and for whom it has assumed to speak. Work-worn and dust-begrimed, they make their mute appeal, and too often find their cry for help beat in vain against the outer walls, while others, less deserving, gain ready access to legislative halls.

In this instance the conclusion was right, however dubious the logic. Cleveland's discreet manipulation of the patronage provided enough Democratic votes to help the Republicans repeal their own silver-purchase act at the request of a Democratic President and a bimetallist Secretary of the Treasury! Business and finance breathed more freely, but the farmers cried out betrayal, and Bland warned the President that Eastern and Western Democrats had finally come to 'a parting of the ways.'

Nor did the repeal of the Sherman Act bring about that restoration of prosperity so hopefully anticipated and so confidently predicted. The Treasury Department was freed of its obligations to purchase silver but Secretary Carlisle's troubles had just begun. Distrust of the monetary policy of the government was by no means allayed, and there began a steady raid on the gold reserves of the Treasury. The Sherman Act had provided that silver certificates might be redeemed in gold or silver coin and had announced the 'established policy of the United States to maintain the two metals at a parity with each other.' Holders of silver certificates, fearful for the future, began to bring their certificates to the Treasury and ask for gold. Cleveland and Carlisle agreed that the government had no legal right to refuse their request. The resultant drain on the gold reserve not only carried that reserve below the established one hundred million dollar mark, but threatened to wipe it out altogether. To the frightened President it seemed that the hour was fast approaching when the government would be unable to meet its legal obligations in gold and would therefore be pushed onto the silver standard. There was, so he thought, but one recourse: to sell government bonds for gold. At his direction Secretary Carlisle, in January 1894, asked for bids on fifty million dollars of government bonds. Few bids were forthcoming, and as the deadline approached, with government credit dangerously threatened, Carlisle turned in desperation to the New York bankers. A banking syndicate, headed by the house of Morgan, took the issue, and a howl went up that the administration had sold out to Wall Street. Worst of all, this bond sale did not permanently help the Treasury. Purchasers of the bonds simply drew from it the gold with which to pay for their bonds. An 'endless chain' was thus set in operation, and the gold supply of the Treasury was depleted at one end as fast as it was replenished at the other. More bond sales thus became inevitable, and twice again, in November 1894 and February 1895, the same experience was repeated. Cleveland thought that he was doing the right thing, but the farmers of the country were convinced that a traitor was in the White House and a Judas in the Treasury Department. Morgan and his fellow-bankers thought that they were doing the patriotic thing, but even so cautious an economist as Alexander D. Noyes concluded that 'they measured with little mercy the emergency of the government.'[2] Finally in 1896, the Treasury floated a hundred million dollar bond issue through popular subscription. With the success of this fourth and last bond issue, the crisis was passed.

The financial difficulties of the government were ascribable not only to the gold drain, but to a sharp decline in government revenues. The McKinley tariff had actually reduced income from customs duties, and the depression cut into internal revenues, while the 'billion dollar Congress' had committed the government to a number of new and heavy expenditures. As a result the surplus of 1890 became a deficit of seventy millions by 1894. In the face of this situation Cleveland tried to force the Democratic party to redeem its pledge of tariff reduction. But vested interests had been built up under Republican protection, and Democratic Senators from the East were no less averse

2 Actually the Morgan Syndicate made only $248,773 on the whole issue!

to tariff reduction than their Republican colleagues. The Wilson tariff as prepared by the House represented an honest effort to reduce duties, but when it emerged from the joint committee of the House and the Senate it was no longer recognizable. Protectionist Democrats like Gorman of Maryland and Brice of Ohio had introduced no less than 634 changes, most of them upward. The new tariff abolished the sugar bounty, but restored the tariff on raw sugar, and fixed rates on refined sugar that were entirely satisfactory to the Sugar Trust. Cleveland, who had insisted that 'a tariff for any other purpose than public revenue is public robbery' denounced the bill as smacking of 'party perfidy and party dishonor,' and charged that 'the livery of Democratic tariff reform has been stolen and worn in the service of Republican protection.' Believing, however, that the Wilson-Gorman tariff was some improvement on the McKinley bill, he allowed it to become a law without his signature.

The sponsors of the Wilson bill had anticipated a reduction in customs duties, and they had wisely added a provision for a tax of two per cent on incomes above $4000. This income tax upon which the administration had confidently relied for necessary revenue was promptly declared unconstitutional by a five to four decision of the Supreme Court which fifteen years earlier had passed favorably and unanimously upon the war income tax. As some of the opinions, notably Mr. Justice Field's,[3] were characterized by gross prejudice and as it happened to be known that the odd judge, (Justice Brewer?), had changed his mind at the eleventh hour, this decision seemed a further proof to the farmers and workingmen that they had no voice in their government.

Even while the Senate was debating the Wilson bill and the House was making futile gestures toward free silver, one proposal was advanced which pointed the way to a sound and statesmanlike solution of some of the most pressing problems created by the money stringency and the depression. This proposal came from 'General' Jacob Coxey, a wealthy quarry owner of Massillon, Ohio, who with his wife and his infant son, Legal Tender Coxey, was shortly to lead an army of unemployed on a march to Washington. Coxey's attack on the depression and the money question was a double-

[3] Pollock *v.* Farmers' Loan and Trust Co. 158 U.S., 601 (1895). 'The present assault upon capital,' said Mr. Justice Field, 'is but the beginning. It will be but the stepping-stone to others, larger and more sweeping, till our political contests will become a war of the poor against the rich. . . .'

barrelled one: non-interest bearing bonds, and appropriations for good roads. One bill provided that any county or town desiring to undertake public improvements might issue non-interest bearing bonds which should be deposited with Secretary of the Treasury in exchange for legal tender notes, and which must be retired by taxation within twenty-five years. The public improvements thus financed were to be a form of work relief, employment being guaranteed to any idle man at not less than $1.50 for an eight-hour day. The Good Roads Bill called for an issue of five hundred million dollars of legal tender notes to be used for the construction of a county road system throughout the country at the same rate of pay. These measures were designed to inflate the currency, bring down interest rates, inaugurate much-needed public improvements especially in the rural regions, and provide work for the unemployed. The program was not unlike that later inaugurated by the administration of Franklin D. Roosevelt, but at the time it excited only contempt or amusement. Governor Greenhalge of Massachusetts, for instance, declared that it was immoral to tax people for public works that were not imperatively needed. Unemployment was an Act of God!

This year, 1894, year of the Wilson tariff and the income tax decision, was the darkest that Americans had known for thirty years. Everything seemed to conspire to convince the people that democracy was a failure. Prices and wages hit rock-bottom and there seemed to be no market for anything. Half a million laborers struck against conditions which they thought intolerable, and most of the strikes were dismal failures. Ragged and hungry bands of unemployed swarmed over the countryside, the fires from their hobo camps flickering a message of warning and despair to affrighted townsfolk. Coxey's army, consisting of broken veterans of the armies of industry, inspired by the pathetic delusion that a 'petition on boots' might bring relief, marched on Washington where they were arrested for trespassing on the Capitol grounds — a charge which somehow was never preferred against the silk-hatted lobbyists who presented their petitions for higher tariffs. The corn crop was a failure; wheat fell below fifty cents a bushel, cotton to six cents a pound, and bitterness swept over the West like a prairie fire. Never did the government seem more unfriendly, or democratic processes more futile. The Pullman workers struck for a living wage, and every agency of the government was enlisted to smash the strike. Representatives of the people in the lower House tried to reduce tariff duties, and representatives of privilege in the Senate made a farce of the effort. Congress passed an anti-trust law and it was enforced not against the trusts but against labor unions; when the great Sugar Trust was finally called into court, the Attorney-General of the United States sabotaged the prosecution. Congress enacted an income tax and it was voided in the highest court. And the President sold bonds to Wall Street, while silver, the poor man's friend, was disinherited and disgraced!

No wonder the Populists rolled up a vote of almost a million and a half in the Congressional elections of 1894. In countless country schoolhouses and Grange halls toil-worn men and women read from the graphic pages of *Coin's Financial School* the story of the Crime of '73, and auditors applauded with delight when the author refuted all the arguments of the 'gold-bugs.' Tenant farmers cheered lustily as 'Pitchfork Ben' Tillman demonstrated how he would stick his fork into the ribs of Grover Cleveland, and the rebel yell resounded again in the red hills of Georgia as flaming Tom Watson denounced the vampires of Wall Street. On the plains the 'Kansas Pythoness' Mary Lease warned the East that 'the people are at bay, let the bloodhounds of money beware,' and in Nebraska young William Jennings Bryan the 'Boy Orator of the Platte' rallied the farmers to a new crusade. There was ferment, too, in the intellectual world. Everywhere men were discussing the astounding revelations of Lloyd's *Wealth against Commonwealth,* the first great broadside against the trusts. Edward Bellamy's Utopian novel, *Looking Backward,* sold by the hundred thousand, and a chain of Nationalist Clubs, inspired by that book, planned hopefully for a new and saner world. Jacob Riis told the sordid story of *How the Other Half Lives* and respectable people, who had scarcely known the meaning of the word slum, were shocked into a realization of conditions in their own back-yards. And William Dean Howells, who had described American society in so many placid novels, wrote a poem called 'Society' which was published in the proper pages of *Harper's Magazine.*

I looked and saw a splendid pageantry
Of beautiful women and of lordly men,
Taking their pleasure in a flowery plain,
Where poppies and the red anemone,
And many another leaf of cramoisy,
Flickered about their feet. . . .

I looked again, and saw that flowery space
Stirring, as if alive, beneath the tread
That rested now upon an old man's head,
And now upon a baby's gasping face,
Or mother's bosom, or the rounded grace
Of a girl's throat; and what had seemed the red
Of flowers was blood, in gouts and gushes shed
From hearts that broke under that frolic pace,
And now and then from out the dreadful floor
An arm or brow was lifted from the rest,
As if to strike in madness, or implore
For mercy. . . .

4. *Bryan, Bryan, Bryan, Bryan*

The party in power is always blamed for hard times. The Congressional elections of 1894 resulted in a complete reversal of the political scene. Not only did the Republicans win an overwhelming majority in the House and a plurality in the Senate, but the Populists made heavy inroads upon the Democratic vote in the South and the West. The Democratic party, indeed, was on the verge of disintegration, and it was apparent that one of two courses was open to it. Either the silver wing of the party would capture control of the organization and unite all silver forces under the Democratic banner, or the silverites would secede to the lusty young Populist party and make that one of the great major parties. An analogous situation in the 1850's had resulted in the demise of the Whigs and the creation of the Republican party; in the 1890's fate and Bryan decreed a different solution.

It was Cleveland's insistence upon the repeal of the Sherman Act that drove the first wedge into the Democratic party. 'Silver Dick' Bland then warned the President that 'We have come to the parting of the ways. . . . I believe I speak for the great masses of the great Mississippi Valley when I say that we will not submit to the domination of any political party, however much we may love it, that lays the sacrificing hand upon silver.' In 1893–94 silver Democrats everywhere effected a fusion with the Populists, and in many Western states it was difficult to distinguish between the two parties. But the silver leaders were unwilling to abandon the party without a final effort to mold it to their way of thinking. In the closing days of the Fifty-third Congress, March 1895, Bryan and Bland drew up an eloquent 'Appeal of the Silver Democrats' calling upon the 'rank and file' of the Democratic party to seize control of the party organization. The tactics thus suggested were promptly put into effect, with results described by Bryan in his 'Cross of Gold' speech a year later:

> Then began the struggle. With a zeal approaching the zeal which inspired the Crusaders . . . our silver Democrats went forth from victory unto victory. . . . In this contest brother has been arrayed against brother, father against son. . . . Old leaders have been cast aside when they have refused to give expression to the sentiments of those whom they would lead, and new leaders have sprung up to give direction to this cause of truth.

Cleveland, of course, fought back, but his attempts to stay the tide of silver sentiment within his party were as futile as the efforts of King Canute to stay the tides of the ocean.

While the Democratic party was being torn apart, the Republicans looked on with complacency. Never indeed were Republican prospects brighter. The three years of Democratic administration had been depression years, and the Republicans did not fail to point the moral of that coincidence. The Democratic party had failed to solve the money question, or to reform the tariff; it had antagonized labor and the farmers without conciliating big business. So certain were the Republicans of victory in 1896 as to boast that any Republican could be elected—a boast that Mark Hanna made a prophecy.

Marcus Alonzo Hanna was the last great representative figure of the Ohio dynasty. A big business man satiated with wealth but avid of power, naturally intelligent though contemptuous of learning, personally upright but tolerant of corruption, shrewd and cynical in his management of men, but capable of deep loyalties and abiding friendships, Mark Hanna was the nearest thing to a national 'boss' that ever emerged in this country. Hanna was genuinely convinced that the business interests should govern the country, and he believed ardently in the mission of the Republican party to promote business activity, whence prosperity would percolate to the farmers and wage-earners below. Since 1890 he had been grooming for the Presidency his friend William McKinley, whom he rescued from bankruptcy in the hard times of 1893. Other Republicans like 'Czar' Reed of Maine and Shelby Cullom of Illinois were abler and more experienced, but the Ohio tradition and Ohio management prevailed. One by one McKinley's competitors were eliminated, as

'Uncle Mark' won over the delegations from the Southern and Mid-Western states. When the convention met, 'Bill McKinley, author of the McKinley Bill, advance agent of prosperity,' was nominated on the first ballot, 18 June 1896. The convention pointed with pride to Republican achievement, viewed with horror the 'calamitous consequences' of Democratic control, and came out somewhat equivocally for the gold standard. Only one untoward event marred the unanimity and jollity of the occasion: as the convention committed itself to the gold standard, the venerable Senator Teller of Colorado bade farewell to the party which forty years earlier he had helped to found. And up in the press gallery William Jennings Bryan looked on with palpitating interest as Teller led a grim band of twenty-two silver delegates from the convention hall.

Three weeks later, when the Democratic convention met at Chicago it became apparent that the tactics of Bryan and Bland had been successful. Instead of going over to the Populists, the silver Democrats had captured control of the party organization and were prepared to write a silver platform and name a silver candidate. Trainload after trainload of enthusiastic delegates swarmed into the streets of the Windy City, silver badges gleaming from their lapels, silver banners fluttering in the breeze. 'For the first time,' wrote one Eastern delegate, 'I can understand the scenes of the French Revolution!' It was indeed a revolution; the Democratic party had been taken over by the farmers of the South and the West. On the opening day of the convention the Eastern wing was snubbed by the election of Senator Daniel of Virginia as temporary chairman. The credentials committee was controlled by the silverites; the resolutions committee was controlled by the silverites. All that was necessary was to find a candidate.

'All the silverites need,' said the New York *World* on the eve of the Convention, 'is a Moses. They have the principle, they have the grit, they have the brass bands and the buttons and the flags, they have the howl and the hustle, they have the votes, and they have the leaders, so-called. But they are wandering in the wilderness like a lot of lost sheep, because no one with the courage, the audacity, the magnetism and the wisdom to be a real leader has yet appeared among them.' The lament was premature. In the person of William Jennings Bryan of Nebraska, the silver forces found a leader with courage, audacity, magnetism, and wisdom.

Only thirty-six years of age, Bryan had already distinguished himself as the most aggressive and eloquent spokesman of silver in the country. Elected to Congress in 1890 he had received the extraordinary tribute of appointment to the powerful Ways and Means Committee on his first appearance in that body; his speeches on the tariff, the income tax, and silver had attracted national attention and made him one of the leaders of his party. Defeated for election to the Senate in the landslide of 1894, he had turned his cascading energies and oratorical talents to the task of whipping up silver sentiment, organizing the silver forces within the party, and greasing the way for his own nomination. His pre-convention campaign was thorough and shrewd; his convention strategy astute; his nomination came as a surprise to the East only because the East did not know what was going on elsewhere in the country.

Bryan's opportunity came in the debate on the platform. Hill of New York and William E. Russell of Massachusetts had spoken eloquently for the gold plank; 'Pitchfork Ben' Tillman had failed to do justice to silver, and the great throng of twenty thousand sweltering men and women were anxious and impatient. Bryan's was the closing speech, and as he made his way nervously down the aisle, a great shout went up, and Bryan banners appeared miraculously in every part of the great hall. His opening words, clear and mellifluous, stilled the vast throng and set the tone of his speech — dignified but impassioned:

> It would be presumptuous, indeed, to present myself against the distinguished gentlemen to whom you have listened if this were a mere measuring of abilities; but this is not a contest between persons. The humblest citizen in all the land, when clad in the armor of a righteous cause, is stronger than all the hosts of error. I come to speak to you in defense of a cause as holy as the cause of liberty — the cause of humanity.

Bryan reviewed the contest between the silver and the gold forces within the party, and reminded the delegates that they were 'now assembled, not to discuss, not to debate, but to enter up the judgment already rendered by the plain people of this country.' That judgment might run counter to the interests of Big Business, but,

> when you come before us and tell us that we are about to disturb your business interests, we reply that you have disturbed our business interests by your course. We say to you that you have made the definition of a business man too limited in its application. The man who is employed for wages is as much a business man as his employer; the attorney in a coun-

try town is as much a business man as the corporation counsel in a great metropolis; the merchant at the crossroads store is as much a business man as the merchant of New York; the farmer who goes forth in the morning and toils all day, who begins in the spring and toils all summer, and who by the application of brain and muscle to the natural resources of the country creates wealth, is as much a business man as the man who goes upon the Board of Trade and bets on the price of grain; the miners who go down a thousand feet into the earth, or climb two thousand feet upon the cliffs, and bring forth from their hiding places the precious metals to be poured into the channels of trade, are as much business men as the few financial magnates who in a back room, corner the money of the world. We come to speak for this broader class of business men.

And they came, said Bryan, not as petitioners, but as a victorious army.

> We have petitioned, and our petitions have been scorned; we have entreated and our entreaties have been disregarded; we have begged, and they have mocked when our calamity came. We beg no longer; we entreat no more; we petition no more. We defy them.

The convention had found its spokesman at last, and every sentence was punctuated by a frenzied roar of applause. Like a skillful fencer Bryan found the weakness in the gold armor and drove home every thrust. Swiftly he reviewed the minor planks in the platform — the income tax which was 'not unconstitutional until one of the judges changed his mind, and we cannot be expected to know when a judge will change his mind'; the bank-note plank — 'the issue of money is a function of government, and banks ought to go out of the governing business'; the tariff, which was less important than the money question, for while 'protection has slain its thousands, the gold standard has slain its tens of thousands.' But the paramount issue was the gold standard, and

> If they come to meet us on that issue we can present the history of our nation. . . . We can tell them that they will search the pages of history in vain to find a single instance where the common people of any land have ever declared themselves in favor of the gold standard. They can find where the holders of fixed investments have declared for a gold standard, but not where the masses have. . . . Upon which side will the Democratic party fight; upon the side of the 'idle holders of idle capital' or upon the side of the 'struggling masses?'

Then followed the peroration which drew the class and sectional lines:

> You come to us and tell us that the great cities are in favor of the gold standard; we reply that the great cities rest upon our broad and fertile prairies. Burn down your cities and leave our farms, and your cities will spring up again as if by magic; but destroy our farms and the grass will grow in the streets of every city in the country. . . . Having behind us the producing masses of the nation and the world, supported by the commercial interests, the laboring interests and the toilers everywhere, we will answer their demand for a gold standard by saying to them: You shall not press down upon the brow of labor this crown of thorns, you shall not crucify mankind upon a cross of gold.

Bryan might have been nominated even without the 'Cross of Gold' speech, but that speech made his nomination a practical certainty. Yet five ballots were necessary before Bland's support disintegrated and the 'Boy Orator of the Platte' was selected as the Democratic standard-bearer in the Battle of the Standards.

Not only on the silver issue, but on banks, trusts, the injunction, and other issues, the Democrats had stolen the Populist thunder. When the People's party met in St. Louis the fusionists were in complete control. Under the skillful leadership of men like Weaver and Senator Allen of Nebraska, the Populists chose Bryan as their candidate, and then confused the situation by naming Tom Watson of Georgia for the Vice-Presidency. Within a short time silver Republicans bolted to Bryan; gold Democrats named a separate ticket but actually threw their support to McKinley. For the first time in thirty years the country divided roughly along class and sectional lines, and the electorate was confronted with a clean-cut issue. And that was not merely the money issue, but the more fundamental one of the control of the government by the business interests of the East or the agrarian interests of the South and the West.

And in Bryan the agrarians had an ideal leader:

> Prairie avenger, mountain lion,
> Bryan, Bryan, Bryan, Bryan,
> Gigantic troubadour, speaking like a siege gun,
> Smashing Plymouth Rock with his boulders from the West.[4]

Radical only on economic questions of money, banks, and trusts, strictly orthodox in matters of morality and religion, Bryan was an

[4] Vachel Lindsay, 'Bryan, Bryan, Bryan, Bryan,' *Collected Poems*, p. 99, The Macmillan Company, 1925.

honest, emotional crusader for humanity, with the forensic fervor and the political shrewdness that would have carried him to the Presidency in the age of Clay and Jackson. More fully than any candidate since the Civil War he represented the average middle class American, and it was because he was the common denominator of the American people of his generation that he was able to retain his extraordinary hold upon their affections for so many years. Everything about him illustrated that quality which justified his title, 'the Great Commoner.' Born in a small farming town in southern Illinois, he came from mixed Scotch, Irish, and English stock, from both North and South. One of his parents was Baptist, one Methodist; he himself joined the Presbyterian church. For generations his family had participated in the westward movement — from the Virginia Tidewater to the Valley, from the Valley to the banks of the Ohio, from the Ohio to the Mississippi valley; he himself continued the process by moving out to the last frontier in Nebraska. He attended a small denominational college, studied law, dabbled in politics, and finally found himself in the championship of a great popular cause. A man of no mean intellectual abilities, at least as well read as the average politician, enjoying a tremendous physical vitality, realist enough to appreciate the significance of the economic revolution, and astute enough to appeal to man's emotions as well as interests, he was thoroughly equipped for politics. But it was his qualities of character rather than of mind that won for him such loyalty as no other leader of his generation could command. Irreproachable in private and in professional life, his career was characterized by utter sincerity, passionate conviction, courage, audacity, genuine faith in the wisdom of the plain people and the processes of democracy, religious belief in the identity of morals and politics, and an unalterable assurance that the right must eventually triumph over the wrong.

The campaign was such a one as the country had not witnessed since Jackson and would not see again until 1928. For the farmers, wrote William Allen White,

> It was a fanaticism like the Crusades. Indeed the delusion that was working on the people took the form of religious frenzy. Sacred hymns were torn from their pious tunes to give place to words which deified the cause and made gold — and all its symbols, capital, wealth, plutocracy — diabolical. At night, from ten thousand little white schoolhouse windows, lights twinkled back vain hope to the stars. . . . They sang their barbaric songs in unrhythmic jargon, with something of the same mad faith that

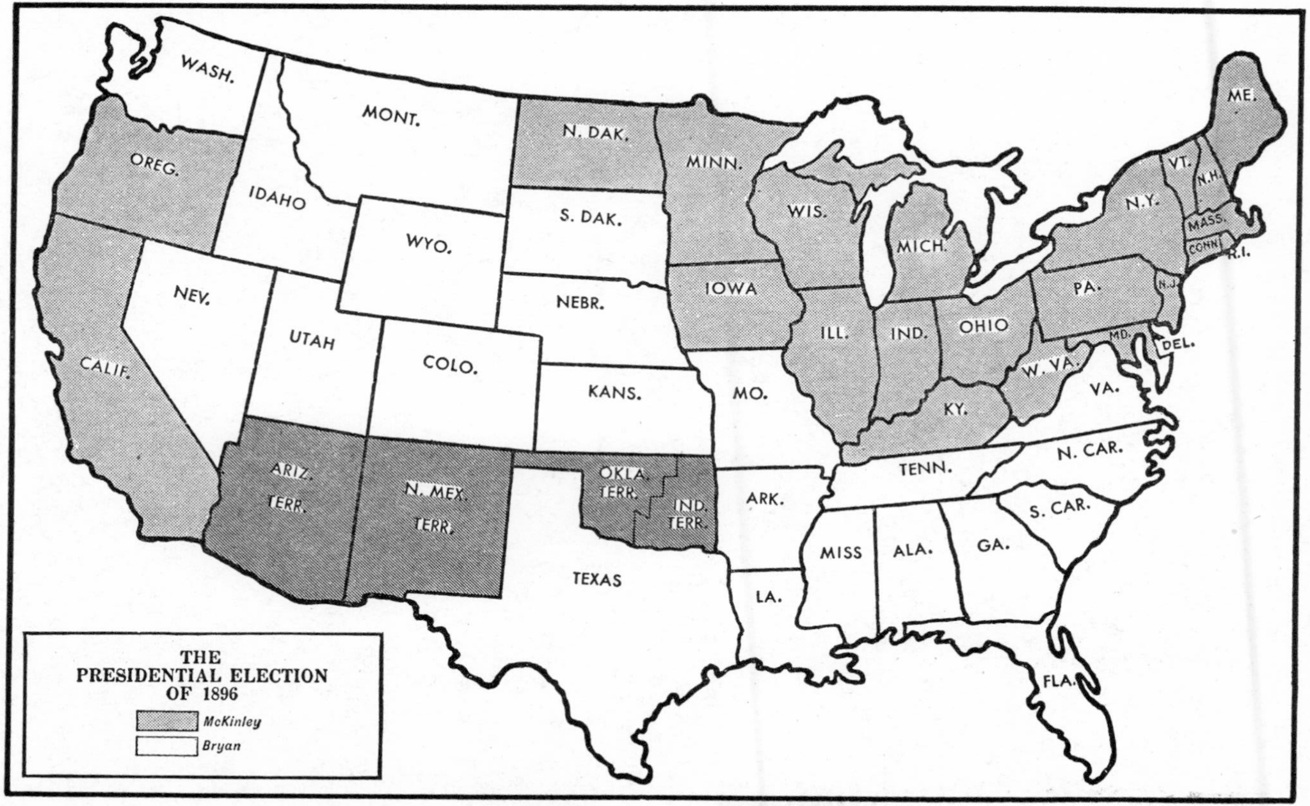
THE PRESIDENTIAL ELECTION OF 1896
McKinley
Bryan
WASH.
OREG.
CALIF.
NEV.
IDAHO
MONT.
WYO.
UTAH
COLO.
ARIZ. TERR.
N. MEX. TERR.
N. DAK.
S. DAK.
NEBR.
KANS.
OKLA. TERR.
IND. TERR.
TEXAS
MINN.
IOWA
MO.
ARK.
LA.
WIS.
ILL.
MICH.
IND.
OHIO
KY.
TENN.
MISS
ALA.
GA.
FLA.
S. CAR.
N. CAR.
VA.
W. VA.
MD.
DEL.
PA.
N.J.
N.Y.
VT.
N.H.
ME.
MASS.
CONN.
R.I.

inspired the martyr going to the stake. Far into the night the voices rose — women's voices, children's voices, the voices of old men, of youths and of maidens, rose on the ebbing prairie breezes, as the crusaders of the revolution rode home, praising the people's will as though it were God's will and cursing wealth for its iniquity.

Big business, fearing for its privileges, acted as if the Hun were thundering at the gates. Bryan's object was to reform government and curb privilege, not to reconstruct society; but McKinley stressed the 'danger to our institutions,' and the Republican candidate for the Vice-Presidency charged that the Democratic platform 'embodies a menace of national disintegration and destruction' and that it was animated by a spirit that would 'organize sedition, destroy the peace and security of the country, and is unworthy of the countenance . . . of any patriotic citizen of whatever political faith.' Others were not so mild in their remarks. The New York *Tribune* denounced 'the wretched rattle-pated boy, posing in vapid vanity and mouthing resounding rottenness,' and 'Marse' Watterson of Kentucky described Bryan as 'a dishonest dodger . . . a daring adventurer . . . a political fakir.' The churches were enlisted in the campaign of abuse; one clergyman called the Democratic candidate, 'a mouthing slobbering, demagogue whose patriotism was all in his jaw-bone'; and another announced, 'I must speak every Sunday from now until November. I shall denounce the Chicago platform. That platform was made in Hell.' 'Good and high-minded men,' observed Theodore Roosevelt justly, 'in their panic played into the hands of the ultra-reactionaries of business and politics.'

Mark Hanna, who was managing the Republican campaign, shook down metropolitan banks, insurance companies, and railroad corporations for colossal campaign contributions. His committee reported campaign expenditures of three and one half million dollars, but estimates of the amount actually spent by local and national organizations, ran up as high as sixteen million dollars. Over one hundred million tracts were distributed in the 'educational campaign,' and thousands of speakers toured the country charging the Democrats with 'anarchism' and 'sedition.' Employees were ordered to vote for McKinley on pain of dismissal, and their fears were aroused by the prospect of receiving wages in depreciated dollars or by the even more serious danger of wage-slashes and unemployment. On Wall Street there was even talk of an Eastern secession if Bryan should win. The silver-mining interests contributed to the Democratic funds, but their contributions were niggardly and the Democrats had not one-tenth of the 'sinews of war' that their opponents commandered. Bryan alone bore the brunt of the battle; travelling day and night, speaking ten, twenty times a day to vast throngs, he inaugurated a new kind of campaign and struck terror into the hearts of his opponents. Had the election been held in August, so it was said, he might have carried the country. But there were bumper crops that year throughout the West, and a crop failure in India, and farm prices bounded upward. The results of the election proved that the fears of conservatives had been somewhat exaggerated. Bryan carried the late Confederacy and most of the Far West; but the electoral votes of the populous East and the Middle West together with the trans-Mississippi states of Iowa, Minnesota, North Dakota, Oregon, and California gave McKinley an emphatic victory.[5]

> The great fight is won [wrote Mrs. Henry Cabot Lodge] a fight conducted by trained and experienced and organized forces, with both hands full of money, with the full power of the press — and of prestige — on one side; on the other, a disorganized mob, at first, out of which burst into sight, hearing, and force — one man, but such a man! Alone, penniless, without backing, without money, with scarce a paper, without speakers, that man fought such a fight that even those in the East can call him a Crusader, an inspired fanatic — a prophet! It has been marvellous. Hampered by such a following, such a platform . . . he almost won. We acknowledge to 7 millions campaign fund, against his 300,000. We had during the last week of the campaign 18,000 speakers on the stump. He alone spoke for his party, but speeches which spoke to the intelligence and hearts of the people, and with a capital P. It is over now, but the vote is 7 millions to 6 millions and a half.

The significance of the campaign, indeed, was not lost upon contemporaries. The election of McKinley constituted a triumph for big business, for a manufacturing and industrial rather than an agrarian order, for the Hamiltonian rather than the Jeffersonian state. 'For a hundred years,' Henry Adams observed, 'the American people had hesitated, vacillated, swayed forward and back, between two forces, one simply industrial, the other capitalistic, centralizing, and mechanical. . . . The issue came on the single gold standard, and the majority at last declared itself, once and for all, in favor of a capitalistic system with all its necessary machinery. All one's friends, all one's best citizens, reformers, churches, colleges, educated classes, had

[5] The electoral vote was McKinley 271: Bryan 176.

joined the banks to force submission to capitalism; a submission long forseen by the mere law of mass.'

Equilibrium was restored. Nothing had ever been the matter with the Grand Old Party. Now for high protection, plenty, and prosperity. Actually, the election of a Democratic administration could have served no useful purpose. The Democrats were not prepared, nor the country ripe, for measures to bring financial giants under control and the enormously increased production of gold, already under way, soon made the money question one of mere antiquarian interest. Yet Bryan's campaign had a significance quite independent of any question as to the soundness of its first principles. It was not only the last protest of the old agrarian order against industrialism, it was also the first attempt of the new order to clean house. Bryan was the bridge between Andrew Jackson and Franklin D. Roosevelt.

XII

ARTS, PHILOSOPHY, AND LETTERS

1. *The Gilded Age*

WITH the passing of ante-bellum America, and the transformation that we have already chronicled of industry, agriculture, and society, much of the old diversity and color disappeared from American life; and the levelling down of sectional diversity and local differences failed to bring any notable broadening of horizons or deepening of culture. The growth of wealth raised the standard of living in some quarters and introduced new luxuries, partly compensating for the greater variety and savor of life in an earlier generation; but while national wealth increased, the distribution of it was uneven, and the extremes of wealth and poverty were wider than ever before. New York's 'Four Hundred' were humorously but pointedly contrasted by O. Henry with her 'Four Million.' The new economic order, for all of its exploitation of natural resources and development of power, never achieved the social ideal of sufficient food, decent shelter and clothing, and a reasonable minimum of recreation.

That the scientific and mechanical revolution would complicate rather than simplify life was pointed out at the beginning of the process. 'We do not properly live these days,' wrote a disillusioned transcendentalist, John Sullivan Dwight, 'but everywhere with patent inventions and complex arrangements are getting ready to live. The end is lost in the means, life is smothered in appliances.' The pace of life increased, especially in the cities.

My heart rebels against my generation,
That talks of freedom and is slave to riches,
And, toiling 'neath each day's ignoble burden,
    Boasts of the morrow.

No space for noonday rest or midnight watches,
No purest joy of breathing under heaven!
Wretched themselves, they heap, to make them happy,
    Many possessions.

sang George Santayana.[1] As simplicity disappeared in the economic, so in the social organization. Even amusement became complicated and leisure a problem; sport too became organized and professional.

Social disintegration and economic upheavals were reflected in the cultural life of the nation. The years 1865 to 1890 were an era of parvenu standards, eclectic architecture and exotic art, literary sterility, and derivative, rather than indigenous culture. From North and South came the same complaint. A great scientist from Kentucky wrote:

> Not only did the Civil War maim the generation of Kentuckians to which I belonged, it also broke up the developing motives of intellectual culture of the commonwealth. Just before it I can see that while the ideals of culture were in a way still low and rather carnal, there was an eager reaching-out for better things; men and women were seeking, through history, literature, the fine arts, and in some measure through science, for a share in the higher life. Four years of civil war, which turned the minds of all towards what is at once the most absorbing and debasing interest of man, made an end of this and set the people on a moral and intellectual plane lower than that they occupied when they were warring with the wilderness and the savages . . . the tide which was setting towards the better life was stayed; the thoughts of men turned back towards the primitive.[2]

Emerson, who had pointed the way to the perfectibility of man, was equally disillusioned. He had hoped 'that in the peace after such a war, a great expansion would follow in the mind of the country; grand views in every direction — true freedom in politics, in religion, in social science, in thought. But the energy of the nation seems to have expended itself in the war.'

There was still energy enough in the America of the post-war years, but such 'grand views' as it entertained were material. The North, rich, lusty, arrogant, was pushing forward to ever greater wealth and power, feeding itself gluttonously at the 'great barbecue.' In the South the flame of life burned but feebly, the institutions and standards of the past had been destroyed, and men were busily engaged in repairing the material damages of the war. The West, raucous and raw, obstreperous and magnificently confident, was repeating the social experience of the frontier from the beginning of our history.

[1] Ode ii in *Poems,* p. 73. Scribner's, 1923.

[2] Nathaniel Southgate Shaler, *Autobiography,* pp. 76–77. Houghton Mifflin Company, 1909.

Blindly but undismayed, men were getting and spending and laying waste their powers; creating a new America on the ruins of the old — an America more like contemporary Germany or England than like the America of Jefferson's day; raising problems they could neither understand nor solve; assuming responsibilities for which they were unprepared; lightly abandoning the faiths of their fathers without substituting new gods, unless the gods of the mart, of the machine, and of science.

The acidulous E. L. Godkin, editor of *The Nation,* described the culture of this generation as a ' chromo civilization,' and even Walt Whitman, the poet of democracy, was assailed with misgivings as he surveyed the post-war scene. He wrote;

> Society in these States is cankered, crude, superstitious and rotten. . . . Never was there, perhaps, more hollowness of heart than at present, and here in the United States. Genuine belief seems to have left us. . . . The great cities reek with respectable as much as non-respectable robbery and scoundrelism. In fashionable life, flippancy, tepid amours, weak infidelism, small aims, or no aims at all, only to kill time. . . . I say that our New World democracy, however great a success in uplifting the masses out of their sloughs, in materialistic development, products, and in a certain highly deceptive superficial popular intellectuality, is so far an almost complete failure in its social aspects, and in really grand religious, moral, literary and esthetic results. In vain do we march with unprecedented strides to empire so colossal, outvying the antique, beyond Alexander's, beyond the proudest sway of Rome. In vain we annexed Texas, California, Alaska, and reach north for Canada or south for Cuba. It is as if we were somehow being endow'd with a vast and thoroughly appointed body, and then left with little or no soul.[3]

Yet the post-war period was, withal, a robust, fearless, and not ungenerous age, lawless and picturesque, full of the old-time gusto and joy of living, giving large scope even in corporate form to individual energy and material creation and challenging, by its very shoddiness, the genius of men. Beneath the tawdriness and materialism of society were stirring new forces of thought and expression, and occasionally these pushed their way to the surface. The impact of a new science forced a reformulation of philosophy and religion, and the impact of the industrial revolution did much to bring art and literature into contact with social realities. A generation that saw, even with indifference, the work of Richardson and Sullivan in archi-

[3] *Democratic Vistas* (1871).

tecture, of Homer and Eakins and Ryder in painting and of St. Gaudens in sculpture, of Clarence King and Raphael Pumpelly, Willard Gibbs and Jeffries Wyman in science, of William Graham Sumner and Lester Ward in sociology, Francis Parkman and Henry Adams in history, and Henry George in economics, of Oliver Wendell Holmes in law, of Charles Peirce and William James and John Dewey in philosophy, was not wholly sterile.

2. *Transcendentalism to Pragmatism*

From the year 1859, when Darwin published his *Origin of Species,* we can date a revolution not only in natural science but in thought. The new doctrine was accepted much more quickly on this side of the Atlantic than in Europe, just as inventions and technological advances were more promptly applied here. The leaders of practically every Christian sect except the Unitarians and Catholics fought hard for Genesis and special creation, and Louis Agassiz attacked evolution of species on scientific grounds. But the doctrine spread rapidly through magazine articles, lectures, and the writings of popularizers, just as had the doctrines of Newton in the previous century. And as with Newtonian physics, so Darwinian evolution created a new intellectual norm.

In 1860 almost everyone in America believed literally in the account of creation in the Book of Genesis, and supposed that species had been created by God for man's especial benefit. By 1870 people were joking about the 'missing link,' and being descended from a monkey or 'a protoplasmal primordial atomic globule.' By 1900 perhaps half of the white population held the belief that man was merely one of the countless organisms that had evolved from the primordial slime, and that this planet was millions instead of thousands of years old. Possibly this belief is no nearer the truth than the other; the important thing is that evolution and science created a new climate of opinion, and one in which we still live. It was not merely the change in man's views as to his origin on this planet that mattered. The implications of evolution were incorporated into every field of thought — law and history, economics and sociology, philosophy, religion, and art.

Evolution was chiefly responsible for the abandonment of transcendentalism and the formulation of a new philosophy known variously as empiricism, instrumentalism, or pragmatism. Transcendentalism had, indeed, served its purpose and served it well. Rooted in the eighteenth century, resting upon basic assumptions not susceptible to proof, cherishing truths that were intuitive rather than experimental, subjective rather than objective, employing the deductive rather than the inductive method, it admirably expressed the faith set forth in the Declaration of Independence, that reformers of the early nineteenth century endeavored to apply. Transcendentalists lived in a paradise of absolutes, where truths were 'self-evident,' laws immutable, right and wrong clear-cut. Their universe was fixed, not growing; their philosophy constant, not dynamic; their morals absolute, not relative.

Such a philosophy was obviously irrelevant to the kind of universe announced by Charles Darwin and described by Herbert Spencer. It was necessary to elaborate a new philosophy which would conform to and explain an organic world and a dynamic society. Truth could no longer be intuitive, plucked from the inner consciousness of man and beyond proof or disproof, nor yet what God revealed to man; but a hypothesis that could stand laboratory tests. Moral standards, when discovered to be the product of social evolution and environment, could no longer be absolute, and must change. Laws, by the same test, were neither eternal nor changeless, but the expression of a social conscience derived from the social needs of the moment. Fixed ideas were out of place in politics and economics as in science and religion.

Between transcendentalism, as expounded by Kant and Coleridge and Emerson, and the new doctrine of organic evolution as expounded by Darwin and Huxley and John Fiske, there could be no logical compromise. The St. Louis school of philosophy, founded in 1867 by William T. Harris, simply ignored the new science and devoted itself to the futile task of sowing the seeds of Hegelian idealism in the unfertile soil of the Middle West. The Scotch, or 'common-sense' school of philosophy, represented in the United States by President James McCosh of Princeton, attempted to effect a compromise and failed as lamentably as had the St. Louisians. It was clearly necessary to formulate a new philosophy, one which would harmonize with science and yet avoid the pitfalls of materialism. This task was undertaken and concluded by a brilliant group of philosophers who came to maturity in the last third of the nineteenth century: Charles Peirce, William James, and John Dewey. Pragmatism is the name of the philosophy that they formulated; and although European philosophers cried out with one voice that the demand that truth must 'work' and 'pay' was just a piece of American sordidness, it may yet be admitted that pragmatism was one of the really important novelties in the history of thought through the ages.[4]

It is not easy to define pragmatism; and one critic, the Italian Papini, has said that 'pragmatism is really less a philosophy than a method of doing without one.' James certainly, and Dewey probably, might willingly have admitted the validity of this criticism, for they had little patience with what passed for philosophy in the classroom or the textbook. The philosophy which they elaborated was meant for the world of affairs rather than the world of the cloister. 'Better it is,' wrote Dewey, 'for philosophy to err in active participation in the living struggles and issues of its own age and times than to maintain an immune monastic impeccability.' The pragmatists regarded truth not as an absolute, but as a social achievement. Truth was not something that was fixed, once and for all time, but something that each society and thinking individual made for himself. Truth was, to put it crudely, *what worked;* and the business of the philosopher was to find what worked to the best possible purposes. 'The ultimate test for us of what a truth means,' wrote William James, 'is the conduct it dictates or inspires. . . . The effective meaning of any philosophical position can always be brought down to some particular consequence.'

The pragmatists conceived of our world as a world in the making. They accepted the fullest implications of organic evolution and applied them to the field of morals and thought, and to social institutions. If asked to judge whether an act was right or wrong, an institution good or bad, they did not refer to some abstract measure of judgment but inquired into its consequences. The consequences might be unpredictable, or they might sustain the abstract judgment; but the effect of such an attitude on politics, law, economics, social institutions, education, religion, and morals was revolutionary, and the revolution is still going on. It is a natural result of their philosophy that many disciples of James and Dewey have been peculiarly active in political, legal, social, and educational reform.

It was natural that pragmatism should have received its earliest statement and most elaborate formulation in the United States, for to

[4] Parts of it, however, were as old as the fifth century B.C., when Protagoras was exiled from Athens for proclaiming the universal right of every man to find his own truth.

a striking degree pragmatism accommodates itself to the American environment and suits the American temper. 'It is beyond doubt,' observed John Dewey, 'that the progressive and unstable character of American life and civilization has facilitated the birth of a philosophy which regards the world as being in a constant formation, where there is still place for indeterminism, for the new, for a real future.' For Americans had always been inclined to put every idea to the test of utility, and even the Transcendentalists were actually less interested in absolutes than in their application. In a world that was constantly changing Americans welcomed with enthusiasm a philosophy which assured them that truth itself was constantly changing; in a society largely of their own making, they embraced with fervor the doctrine that even democracy, justice, and virtue could be created by society; that even immortality might depend upon the 'will to believe.'

So on all sides there was a courageous effort to accommodate institutions to the new teachings of evolution and instrumentalism. Progressive teachers abandoned the idea that education was the mere acquiring of a body of knowledge, and tried to make it 'functional,' though their inability to agree upon the social ends and needs to which education should be articulated, proved embarrassing. Progressive lawyers ceased to regard the law as a body of changeless truth and sacred precedent, and accepted the doctrine that law was a creation of society and that every generation must make its own precedents — a doctrine familiar, of course, to students of the common law. This aspect of pragmatism commonly accepted in the law schools, is just beginning to penetrate the courts. Economists reluctantly surrendered axioms which they had long regarded as invulnerable, and 'economic laws,' like supply and demand, are no longer regarded as less mutable than other laws. Moralists ceased to speak so pontifically of 'self-evident truths,' liberal clergymen cited the Ten Commandments less frequently than the Sermon on the Mount; even historians admitted that historical truth was relative to each generation. That is one reason why textbooks so quickly become out-of-date!

3. *Legal and Religious Thought*

The impact of evolution and of pragmatism upon the American mind is luminously illustrated in the history of legal and of religious thought in the last quarter of the nineteenth century. The most significant development in legal thought was the emergence of the idea that law, even 'fundamental' law, is an organic growth that must be molded to the changing needs of a changing society. The 'law of Nature and Nature's God' gave way, during these years, to law as a product of and a function of society. Historical jurisprudence was supplanted by sociological jurisprudence, a development which Roscoe Pound characterized as 'a movement for pragmatism as a philosophy of law; for the adjustment of principles and doctrines to the human conditions they are to govern rather than to assumed first principles; for putting the human factor in the central place and relegating logic to its true position as an instrument.' This meant a recognition of the fact, long forgotten and still sometimes ignored, that law was made for man, not man for law.

This concept of the law as a living, growing organism, owes much to the learning and genius of the most distinguished of all American jurists, Oliver Wendell Holmes. It is suggestive that Holmes was a friend of William James. 'The life of law,' wrote Justice Holmes in that great treatise on *The Common Law* which he published in 1881, 'has not been logic; it has been experience. The felt necessities of the time, the prevalent moral and political theories, institutions of public policy . . . have had a good deal more to do than syllogism in determining the rules by which men should be governed. The law embodies the story of a nation's development through many centuries, and it cannot be dealt with as if it contained only the axioms and corollaries of a book of mathematics.' The effort to accommodate law to the 'felt necessities of the time'—a perfect example of instrumentalism—opened the way to a more liberal interpretation of the Constitution and a more realistic interpretation of such legal concepts as 'due process,' 'police power,' 'property,' and 'liberty.' Intellectual disciples of Holmes such as Louis Brandeis, Roscoe Pound, Benjamin Cardozo, John Wigmore, and Ernst Freund have done much to rescue the law from the quicksands of abstract logic and root it again in the firm soil of realism. Yet even more remains to be done.

If law was an organic growth rather than an absolute abstraction, it could be studied as a science rather than as a system of morality, and by the scientific method. The creation of a science of law was a special function of the new law schools, the most notable of which was the Harvard Law School, revitalized by the appointment of C. C. Langdell as professor and dean in 1870. Here he introduced the case system, a laboratory method which has generally supplanted the textbook as a means of studying law. Here too began, in this country, the study of law as a science, rather than the mere mastering of sufficient knowledge to pass bar examinations.

The idea of organic evolution was perhaps most effective in the field of constitutional law and history. It made possible a reinterpretation of constitutional history that discarded Gladstone's dictum that the American Constitution was ' struck off ' by the genius of a few men, discovered that it was a product of century-long constitutional developments in England and in the Colonies, and worked out the idea that this organic development continued after 1787. Judges and patriotic societies are still hostile to this interpretation of the Constitution, and prefer to regard it as much as scholastic theologians did the sacred scriptures; but even St. Thomas Aquinas admitted more evolution in religious dogma than the judge who said, ' The Constitution is exactly the same now as in 1787, except for the Amendments. We know more about it, that's all.'

This idea of the organic evolution of law has contributed powerfully to the new nationalism that emerged from the chaos of the Civil War. If the relations of the states to the Federal Government were to be fixed for all time by the ideas of 1787, there was much to be said for the political philosophy of John C. Calhoun. But if the character of the Federal Government was to be determined by facts rather than theories, by organic growth rather than original conditions, then the doctrine of nationalism announced by Webster and defended by Lincoln was more nearly correct. A. C. McLaughlin's historical defense of nationalism as an organic creation of the American people is an example of the application of evolution and pragmatism to constitutional history.

The task of religion was similar to that of law. Just as the Bench had to recognize the new science, accommodate itself to the industrial revolution, and (however unwillingly and imperfectly) embrace a new philosophy, so the Church had to breast the waves of ' higher criticism ' and Darwinism that threatened to engulf it. The intellectual history of the Protestant churches in the nineteenth century is the story of an effort to harmonize dogma and revealed religion with these new forces of science and society. The Catholic Church made no such attempt to compromise concepts in different dimensions, but reaffirmed her infallibility at the Vatican Council of 1870, and, while accepting the ascertained facts of organic evolution in her schools and colleges, and rejecting laissez faire as a social philosophy, declined to alter a jot or tittle of her dogma.

It was the Protestant churches and the Jews who based their doctrine exclusively on the Bible that suffered most. For, beginning with the Tübingen school in Germany around 1830, Protestant and Jewish theologians applied to the Bible critical standards long accepted in other fields of scholarship. They tested the Scriptures by the known or unfolding facts of history, philology, archaeology, geology, and other sciences. In the hands of such devout religious leaders as Andrews Norton and Theodore Parker, this 'higher criticism' was employed to justify a figurative or allegorical rather than a literal interpretation of sacred Scripture. This application of the scientific method to religion paved the way for the rejection of much that seemed incongruous or inapplicable to modern life, and for a liberal Christianity based upon ethics, rather than upon revelation or authority; but in many instances the truths of religion were now authenticated by intuition, by the inner light, rather than by tradition or authority. Thus idealism went around the circle, ending in a vague sort of mysticism! In course of time much if not most of the higher criticism came to be accepted by the Protestant churches, and for them the Bible lost its supreme authority. Probably as much was lost in this process as was gained; for when the Bible ceased to be regarded as God's word, it was no longer read, and one of the priceless inheritances of English literature, that had imparted beauty, wisdom, and imagination to the race for three centuries, was neglected.

The Protestant churches were more afraid of Darwinism than of 'higher criticism'; several Southern states wrote laws forbidding the teaching of evolution in public schools onto their statute books. Darwinism, which announced the evolution of man from lower organisms, clashed squarely with the idea of special creation, long cherished as the cornerstone of orthodox faith. For a time leaders of all denominations joined in the hue and the cry against evolution, and a famous battle raged along the whole intellectual front. Orthodox defenders of the faith denounced Darwinism as a 'bestial hypothesis' and quoted with approval Disraeli's famous declaration, 'Is man an ape or an angel? I, my Lords, am on the side of the angels.' Stout champions of science countered with vigorous attacks upon what they denominated religious bigotry; John William Draper's *History of the Conflict Between Religion and Science* (1874) and Andrew D. White's *Warfare of Science* (1876) [5] ran through numerous editions. Moderates on both sides, meantime, attempted to effect a reconciliation between religion and evolution. The task was undertaken first by the English scientists, Huxley and Tyndall, who lectured widely in the United States. It was shortly taken up by a distinguished group of American scholars of whom the most notable was the philosopher and historian, John Fiske. Fiske, a very behemoth of a scholar, expounded a reconciliation of science and religion to the students of Harvard College in the late sixties and continued thereafter to spread his message by the written and the spoken word. Soon Henry Ward Beecher, the most popular of American preachers, signified his conversion and shortly thereafter such distinguished clergymen as Lyman Abbott, Beecher's successor at the Plymouth Church in Brooklyn, James Freeman Clarke of Boston, and William J. Tucker of the Andover Seminary came over to the side of the evolutionists.

The findings of the higher criticism and of science filtered down, in more popular and more radical form, through the lectures and writings of such men as Robert Ingersoll and Elizur Wright. Colonel Ingersoll, glorying in the title of 'the great agnostic,' was the Tom Paine of the new scientific dispensation; his lectures on 'Some Mistakes of Moses' and similar subjects were applauded by huge audiences throughout the regions where Paine had been denounced as an atheist. Elizur Wright, abolitionist, reformer, and insurance expert, began life as a devout Calvinist and ended it as an atheist. He was president of the Freethinkers' Liberty League, organized in 1876 to popularize Darwinism and the higher criticism, and, like Ingersoll, worked energetically to expose what he regarded as the bigotry of the orthodox churches. Agnosticism and 'free thought' made slight impression upon the mass of the American people, but there can be no doubt that the labors of men like Ingersoll and Wright facilitated the work of the modernists in combating fundamentalism in the Protestant churches.

While higher criticism and Darwinism caused some churchmen to gird on armor and do battle for their faith, others chose to meet a third challenge of the times, that of the industrial revolution which was making it all but impossible for people to lead the life that Christ commanded. And those who chose to meet this challenge

[5] This booklet was elaborated by President White into his *History of the Warfare of Science with Theology in Christendom* (2 vols. 1896).

rather than the others simply discarded all but the essentials of Christ's message, and endeavored to make the Church an instrument of social reform and regeneration.

> The religious effect of the social revolution [wrote the Reverend William J. Tucker] was in some respects deeper and more far-reaching than the political effect. It changed the prevailing type of religion. Individualism had been the foundation of the Protestant faith, especially of Puritanism. Now men began to think in terms of social Christianity. . . . Social settlements sprang up in the cities side by side with the religious mission and the charity organizations. The Church became as conspicuously the agent for 'social service' as it had been the 'means of grace' in the work of individual salvation.[6]

William Ellery Channing and Theodore Parker had already, in the forties and fifties, prepared the way for the 'socialization of Christianity' by their emphasis upon the duty of the Church toward such problems as labor, temperance, woman's rights, business practices, and war. Now in the post-war years the churches became effective instruments of social reform. From his parsonage in Columbus, Ohio, Washington Gladden championed the cause of industrial peace and succeeded in persuading labor and capital to arbitrate their differences. The venerable Edward Everett Hale of Boston applied Christian ethics to the problems of modern society and furnished a focal point for much of the reform activity of his day. Walter Rauschenbusch at the Rochester Theological Seminary and Shailer Mathews at the University of Chicago Divinity School taught and preached the relations of Christianity to the social order. The presses teemed with such volumes as George Herron's *The Christian Society,* Shailer Mathews' *Social Teachings of Jesus,* Richard Ely's *Social Aspects of Christianity,* Washington Gladden's *Applied Christianity,* and Francis C. Peabody's *Jesus Christ and the Social Question;* millions of copies were sold of C. M. Sheldon's *In His Steps,* describing a congregation which followed consistently the teachings of Jesus.

Thus the Protestant Churches, like the law, accommodated themselves to the new science and elaborated a new philosophy. They accepted new responsibilities and performed new duties; they reconciled evangelical Christianity to social Christianity and thus survived the impact of Darwinism and of the pragmatic philosophy and emerged better prepared to serve the spiritual and social needs of

[6] *My Generation,* pp. 16–17.

men. But, too often, they abdicated or watered down their prime function of worship, for which even the most sincere concern for the ills of human society was no substitute.

4. *Literary Currents*

As in philosophy, law, and religion, so in letters, the ferment and growth of this period was reflected, and the confusion recorded. The hold-over from an earlier age was impressive. Most of the great New England figures lived into the 1880's or 1890's — Holmes saluted the first trolley-car in his spirited *Broomstick Train* — but the Civil War seemed to have burnt out most that was original in their genius, or, as with Melville, filled them with frustration and disappointment. Whitman, dismissed from his government post in 1865 as the author of a 'scandalous book,' wrote some of his finest poems in these years — *Passage to India, Thou Mother With Thy Equal Brood, Song of the Exposition,* and most of the poem-sequence, *Whispers of Heavenly Death* — but he was chiefly occupied with revising the 'scandalous' *Leaves of Grass.* Whittier wrote his best poems on the vanishing New England of the Puritans, as *Snow-Bound, The Tent on the Beach,* and *Among the Hills* in the sixties, but lost his interest in good causes. Longfellow completed the *Christus* trilogy and his magnificent translation of Dante, but for the most part this was his well-deserved harvest season of praise and affection. Lowell's life was only half over at the end of the war; he now composed some of his best critical essays and enjoyed, as a Hayes supporter, a diplomatic career, but his poetry never again reached the splendid heights of the Harvard *Commemoration Ode.* Bryant was the 'first citizen of New York,' but his literary activity was confined to the translation of Homer. Emerson confessed in *Terminus,*

> It is time to be old,
> To take in sail: —
> * * *
> A little while
> Still plan and smile,
> And, — fault of novel germs, —
> Mature the unfallen fruit.

Minor poets such as Richard Watson Gilder, Henry Richard Stoddard, Louise Imogen Guiney, and Bayard Taylor, turning away from the realities of life and from the contemporary scene, celebrated esoteric themes of love and romance, composed

> Faint iambics that the full breeze wakens . . .
> Triolets, villanelles, rondels, rondeaus,
> Ballades by the score with the same old thought:
> The snows and the roses of yesterday are vanished
> And what is love but a rose that fades.[7]

'Do you call these genteel little creatures American Poets?' asked Whitman in his *Democratic Vistas*. 'Do you term that perpetual, pistareen, paste-pot work, American art, American drama, taste, verse? I think I hear, echoed as from some mountaintop afar in the west, the scornful laugh of the Genius of these States.'

Emily Dickinson, in whom burned the flame of true poetic genius, wrote only for herself and her friends, and it remained for a later generation to discover and evaluate her. Of the great Southern triumvirate, Paul Hamilton Hayne and Henry Timrod were silent; Sidney Lanier, while struggling for a bare living, was painfully penning that handful of poems which was to assure him immortality among American men of letters.

'For ten years,' said Edmund Stedman of the post-war period, 'the new generation read nothing but newspapers.' Yet good talent was developed in the local-color school of fiction which reached high tide around 1880. This school represented, in part, a nostalgia for the provincialism that was everywhere giving way to uniformity. Mark Twain, Bret Harte, and Joaquin Miller celebrated the early days of the Far West just as it was becoming respectable. Edward Eggleston, forerunner of Middle-Western local-colorists, described Hoosier Indiana, of which James Whitcomb Riley became the popular poet laureate. The gifted Constance Fenimore Woolson exploited the Great Lakes country as well as the South. Grace King, Kate Chopin, and Lafcadio Hearn recorded New Orleans life in loving pages, but George Washington Cable described Louisiana with such caustic realism that he had to find refuge in the North. Thomas Nelson Page, John Esten Cooke, and F. Hopkinson Smith sentimentalized 'Ole Virginia,' while James Lane Allen wrote his way out of the Blue Grass to New York, where he composed *A Kentucky Cardinal* and other idylls of his home state. Richard Malcolm Johnston described

[7] Edgar Lee Masters, 'Petit, the Poet,' in his *Spoon River Anthology*. Macmillan, 1915.

Georgia less romantically but more accurately in the *Dukesborough Tales;* Mary Noailles Murfree discovered and exploited the Kentucky and Tennessee mountaineers. Irwin Russell and Joel Chandler Harris (*Uncle Remus*) revealed the richness of Negro life and character in poetry and in fiction. In the seventies three talented women, Rose Terry Cooke, Sarah Orne Jewett, and Mary E. Wilkins Freeman, began tenderly and delicately to record rural New England. Mrs. Freeman excelled in dialect, Mrs. Cooke in humor, Miss Jewett in sentiment and observation; her Maine story, *The Country of the Pointed Firs,* was the finest product of the local-color school; for the local-colorists were primarily observers, only incidentally artists.

Mark Twain is in many respects the most typical American of all our prose writers, the most national, the most democratic. To call him a mere 'humorist' as his contemporaries did is the biggest joke connected with him; for he revealed — he was — America of the Gilded Age. He incarnated the pulsing energy and crude bravado, the generous big-heartedness, the naïve sentimentality of his generation; and no small measure of its frustration and vulgarity to boot. Born in frontier Missouri, where North meets South and East the West, Sam Clemens spent his boyhood on the banks of the great river whose epic he was to write, absorbing the rich human drama that passed before him as a living film. Part of his youth was spent as a Mississippi pilot, learning the great river, the varied country that it traversed, and the fabulous society that floated on its muddy waters. On the river were born his three immortal characters, Tom Sawyer, Huck Finn, and Nigger Jim, and from the steamboat leadsmen's cry at two fathoms, 'by the mark, twain!' he took his literary name. Mark Twain pictured not only this valley of democracy, but West and East as well. He fought briefly in the Civil War, staked out claims in the Nevada mines, turned his hand to journalism, and produced in *Roughing It* the liveliest if not the most accurate literary description of the mining frontier. *The Innocents Abroad* concealed under travel talk a typically American criticism of 'decrepit' European culture. And in *The Gilded Age,* which Mark Twain wrote in collaboration with Charles Dudley Warner, he painted the classic picture of American society of the post-war era.

For the generation 1865–1900 Mark Twain was a symbol not only for what he was and did, but in the measure that he failed to be or to do what he might have become or achieved. Though he made America rock with laughter at the conventions and archaisms of Europe, he accepted the conventions and standards of American post-war industrialism without serious misgivings. Magnificently 'natural' himself, he acquiesced in the proprieties of a respectable marriage, and settled down in the conventional society of Hartford, Connecticut, devoted himself to business and money-making, curbed his Rabelaisian humor, and aspired to be like the literary gentlemen of New England. Whether Mark Twain was a potential Swift, it is impossible to say. That ambition or environment stunted his natural artistic development is probable. His last years were marked by bitter disillusion and a sentimental and immature but none the less tragic pessimism. 'I have been reading the morning paper,' he wrote to his friend and mentor, Howells. 'I do it every morning, well knowing that I shall find in it the usual depravities and basenesses and hypocrisies and cruelties that make up civilization, and cause me to put in the rest of the day pleading for the damnation of the human race.' It was during these years that he wrote the moving *Personal Recollections of Joan of Arc,* the savage *Man that Corrupted Hadleyburg,* the allegorical *Mysterious Stranger,* and the naïvely atheistic *What is Man?,* the last two published posthumously. But if Mark Twain was not an original critic, he was our greatest creative prose artist since Hawthorne.

The very antithesis of Mark Twain, in the classic tradition of New England letters, was Sarah Orne Jewett. She represented an order of things that was passing, and recorded not a robust nationalism but an ingrown provincialism. Born of an old New England merchant family, from her childhood she felt the moist east wind upon her cheeks and smelled the faint perfume of bayberry and the pungent juniper. She was the quintessence of the more refined elements of coastal New England, and her pen chronicled a static society that was lovely and serene. She painted in delicate pastels, in subtle shadings, in grays and twilight colors, *The Country of the Pointed Firs.* She was one of the few local-colorists who rose above mere description and achieved a real literary distinction.

The local-colorists recorded an evanescent provincialism and Mark Twain and Whitman heralded a clamorous nationalism; beginning in the eighties a new school of writers in prose and poetry used literature as a vehicle of protest against the rising tide of materialism. The literature of social revolt was varied as the social scene itself, and embraced such diverse figures as Sidney Lanier and Edgar Lee Masters, William Dean Howells and Jack London. It was a natural and inevitable reaction from the crudities and shoddiness of industrialism, and the gross inequalities of modern economy. Some of it was broadly philosophical, some sheer propaganda: only a small part had any literary merit, but all is interesting to the historian.

The note was struck by a representative of the order that was passing away, and in a vernacular that ill accorded with the modern tempo. The sheer beauty, the haunting melody of Sidney Lanier's poetry has obscured for us much of its incisive social purpose. If the *Marshes of Glynn* (1879) is the height of his poetic genius, *The Symphony* (1875) is of greater historical import.

> Yea, what avail the endless tale
> Of gain by cunning and plus by sale?
> Look up the land, look down the land
> The poor, the poor, the poor, they stand
> Wedged by the pressing of Trade's hand . . .
> Does business mean, *Die you — live I?*
> Then 'Trade is trade' but sings a lie:
> 'Tis only war grown miserly.[8]

And William Vaughn Moody sang in a more philosophic vein, in his *Gloucester Moors* (1900):

> But thou, vast outbound ship of souls,
> What harbour town for thee?
> What shapes, when thy arriving tolls
> Shall crowd the banks to see?
> Shall all the happy shipmates then
> Stand singing brotherly?
> Or shall a haggard ruthless few
> Warp her over and bring her to,
> While the many broken souls of men
> Fester down in the slaver's pen,
> And nothing to say or do? [9]

Lanier and Moody spoke to limited audiences. A lesser poet, Edwin Markham, caught the popular fancy with his moving protest against the exploitation of labor, *The Man with the Hoe:*

[8] Sidney Lanier, *Poems,* pp. 60–61. Scribner's, 1886.
[9] William Vaughn Moody, *Poems,* p. 4. Houghton Mifflin, 1901.

Bowed by the weight of centuries he leans
Upon his hoe and gazes on the ground,
The emptiness of ages in his face,
And on his back the burden of the world. . .
Through this dread shape the suffering ages look;
Time's tragedy is in that aching stoop;
Through this dread shape humanity betrayed,
Plundered, profaned and disinherited,
Cries protest to the Judges of the World,
A protest that is also prophecy.

These were notes of solemn warning, notes that echoed the deep undertones of American life and flung them out in magnificent challenge.

In the meantime a corps of prose writers had assailed the intrenchments of industrial capitalism all along the line. Stephen Crane, a craftsman of rare promise, turned from realistic stories of the war to unconventional themes, and in *Maggie, A Girl of the Streets* revealed a brutal phase of life in a great metropolis that had been comfortably ignored by respectable society. A more significant literary figure was Frank Norris, a disciple of Zola, who, in one of the greatest novels of his generation, *The Octopus* (1901), told the story of the fight of California wheat-growers and sheep-ranchers against the choking tentacles of a dominant railroad. Far more popular than either was Jack London, who besides adventure stories wrote a few crudely realistic novels depicting the war of the classes. A more intelligent and philosophical indictment of modern society was drawn by Theodore Dreiser in a series of powerful novels stretching over a generation, from *Sister Carrie* (1900) to *An American Tragedy* (1925). Although he never attained high literary craftsmanship, Dreiser succeeded in arresting and holding attention by ability to tell a story and to create real characters such as Frank Cowperwood in *The Titan,* and by a sense of pity that resembled Dostoievsky's.

Nor did this criticism of American life emanate entirely from those upon whom the sun of economic success had not shone. Henry Adams, intellectual and social peer to any public man of his generation, drew so bitter an indictment of American politics in *Democracy* that he was moved to publish it anonymously. John Hay, who likewise moved in the best circles, described labor troubles, unsympathetically to be sure, in the pages of *The Breadwinners.* Robert Herrick, professor in the new University of Chicago, drew a sombre picture of

Chicago life upon the background of the Haymarket riot, in *The Memoirs of an American Citizen.* And even William Dean Howells, leader of New England literati and recorder of the *Rise of Silas Lapham,* was moved to scrutinize more critically the society into which he rose, and found it wanting. In *A Traveller from Altruria* (1894) Howells imagined a more rational and kindlier social organization, one not unlike that pictured by Edward Bellamy in his famous *Looking Backward.*

Long years of agrarian distress, the cruel contrast between the high ideal of the independent, self-sufficient farmer and the tragic reality of farm life on the middle border, brought a literary revolt similar to that against the industrial order. Something of this realistic attitude had already been expressed in the stories of Joseph Kirkland, Edward Eggleston, and Francis Grierson; but Edward Howe's grim *Story of a Country Town* (1884) fixed the type in our literature. Howe never again produced anything equal to this misanthropic masterpiece: it remains, with *The Spoon River Anthology* and *Winesburg, Ohio,* the most dismal picture of a small country town in our literature.

It was Hamlin Garland who was destined to be the literary spokesman of the middle border. In his first and best book of short stories, *Main Travelled Roads,* he presented farm life in Wisconsin and Iowa in all its unprepossessing actuality, 'with a proper proportion of the sweat, flies, heat, dust and drudgery of it all.' *Prairie Folks* and *Rose of Dutcher's Coolly* followed. Eventually Garland achieved eminence and prosperity, settled in the East, and in his old age waved the magic wand of romance over the scenes of his boyhood and enveloped them in a nimbus of romance and of beauty. The result was *A Son of the Middle Border,* a classic narrative of life in the West, portraying in colors of incomparable loveliness the heroic saga of the pioneer. If Garland himself had abandoned the hot realism of his youth, others had taken it up. Willa Cather in novels which lifted her to a high position in American literature — *My Ántonia,* and *O Pioneers* — painted the Nebraska prairie-land in sombre hues, 'its fierce strength, its peculiar savage kind of beauty, its uninterrupted mournfulness,' and in that exquisite and moving portrayal of *The Lost Lady* she presented a memorable example of the spiritual disintegration that was a part of the pioneering process. And, the Norwegian-American, O. E. Rölvaag, in *Giants in the Earth* (1927), wrote the epic story of the immigrant farmer in the Dakota country. *Giants in the Earth* chronicles, as no other volume has, that combination of physical and spiritual experience which is the warp and the woof of the westward movement; but instead of being the proud story of man's conquest of earth, it is the tragedy of earth's humbling of man.

Yet we would misconceive the American scene if we saw it only through the eyes of critics. They represented the same dissatisfied elements that found political expression in the Greenbacker and Populist programs, and later went Socialist or supported the Progressive movement. The majority of Americans were not dissatisfied with their life, viewed the American scene with neither indignation nor despair, and did not applaud those who saw it as through a glass darkly. Of all American writers, William Dean Howells perhaps best represents the normal American of this generation. Though his career was not as varied, his character as robust, his sympathies as broad, or his literary product as catholic as that of Mark Twain, Howells limned the average American — or in any event the average middle-class Easterner — with artistic accuracy. 'He was,' writes Carl Van Doren, 'the intimate historian of his age, who produced the most extended and accurate transcript of American life yet made by one man.' *A Foregone Conclusion* (1875), *A Fearful Responsibility* (1881), and *The Kentons* (1902), are concerned with the conflict between American and European manners, but a comparison of these with *Innocents Abroad* measures the advance in sophistication. In the *Rise of Silas Lapham* (1885) Howells drew the classic picture of the self-made man, so dear to the American heart, and hung another portrait alongside those of Colonel Sellers and Frank Cowperwood in the gallery of American characters. *A Hazard of New Fortunes* (1890), which Howells wrote after he had come under the influence of Tolstoy and Turgenev, takes New York and the industrial conflict for its background, but it never penetrates to the more brutal aspects of New York life as does Stephen Crane's *Maggie*.

For the most part Howells' America was a placid and happy country, his world one of gentility and middle-class correctness, his etchings like Whistler's rather than Pennell's. The emotions that he analyzed were not crude and passionate but delicate and sophisticated. Addressing an audience largely feminine, through the more dignified periodicals, he reflected the surface of American life; only after the mid-eighties did he penetrate to the deeper emotions and undercurrents; in *The Leatherwood God,* his last and one of his best novels, he returned to frontier Ohio for his setting and material.

Henry James, a few years younger than Howells, turned to literature as an escape from the menacing new world with which his brother William came to grips. Henry's lifelong concern was with subtle and sophisticated human relationships in an aristocratic society hedged about by social taboos; and as English society offered far greater scope for his talents, and richer rewards, he settled permanently in England in 1876. His characters toil not, neither do they spin; but the inadequacy of the society which produced them is evident, and against the international background he projected Americans who are at once alive, sophisticated, and complex, like the Englishmen of George Meredith. Indeed, in *An International Episode* (1878) and in the uncompleted *Ivory Tower* James saw through the flashy Newport of his day quite as clearly as did Edith Wharton, whose work falls wholly within the present century. Mrs. Wharton wrote of fashionable New York in the age of gaslight and horses. In a series that begins with *The House of Mirth* (1905) and ends in *The Age of Innocence* (1920), she presented now ironically, now tenderly, complex social problems against a background of upper-class New York where the Civil War profiteers and the plutocrats of the Gilded Age are breaking into society, shattering its old standards of elegance and good taste. Her greatest achievement, however, was *Ethan Frome,* a story of rural New England, Greek in its simplicity and tragedy, standing with Willa Cather's *A Lost Lady* and Ellen Glasgow's *Sheltered Life* in the very forefront of American letters.

Ellen Glasgow, of Mrs. Wharton's generation, traced the social history of Virginia — and, by implication, of the South — from the Civil War to the World War with a faithful and penetrating literary documentation. Deeply rooted in her provincialism, she brought to her monumental task narrative skill, wit and irony, art and philosophy. Her long series of novels, from *The Battle-ground* (1902) and *Virginia* (1913) to *The Romantic Comedians* (1926), *The Sheltered Life* (1932), and *Vein of Iron* (1935), records the disintegrating effect of the Civil War and Reconstruction on Southern society, the rise of the middle class, and the efforts of the 'first families' to adjust themselves to a society which they thought vulgar and a culture which they considered meretricious.

Nor did the Middle West lack for recorders of the social scene. Booth Tarkington traced the evolution of the small, provincial, and pleasant Mid-Western village into a large, but equally provincial and far less pleasant city, and described the social changes that accompanied the material ones. Tarkington belonged to the 'Hoosier' school of writers, sentimental and superficial, but the best of his novels—*The Midlanders, The Magnificent Ambersons,* and *Alice Adams*—clogged as they are with sentiment, do give a realistic picture of the time and the place. What Tarkington was doing for Indiana, young Brand Whitlock was doing for Ohio and William Allen White for Kansas, and White, at least, wrote one novel which will have a permanent place in the literature of this period. *A Certain Rich Man* (1909) describes the transformation of his state from the 'Bleeding Kansas' of the fifties to Populist Kansas of the nineties more realistically than has any historical work, and draws a portrait of a self-made man more convincing than Sinclair Lewis's famous *Babbitt* of 1922.

Despite undercurrents of unrest and protest, historical romance had its greatest triumph in the decade of the nineties. The local-colorists had already exploited historical material, and the Spanish-American War gave a final fillip. In rapid succession were published Harold Frederic's *In the Valley;* Richard Harding Davis's *Soldiers of Fortune;* S. Weir Mitchell's *Hugh Wynne* and *The Red City;* Mary Johnston's Civil War stories, *The Long Roll* and *Cease Firing;* Paul Leicester Ford's *Janice Meredith;* Owen Wister's *Lady Baltimore;* Edward Bellamy's *The Duke of Stockbridge;* and a series of notable novels depicting scenes in American history by Winston Churchill: *Richard Carvel, The Crossing, The Crisis.* All these dealt with the American scene; of authors who exploited the rich past of European history, Francis Marion Crawford was easily the most successful and popular.

No survey of the literature of this period would be complete without reference to the books that critics disdained but people read. There has never yet been a history of American letters that concerned itself with popular literature,[10] but the historian cannot be less interested in the reading habits of the common man than in his political or social interests. If we would penetrate to the character of the average American we must read such poets as James Whitcomb Riley and Eugene Field, humorists like 'Petroleum V. Nasby' (David R. Locke) and 'Josh Billings' (Henry W. Shaw) and the later O. Henry (William Sydney Porter), romancers like E. P. Roe and E. D. E. N. Southworth, and purveyors to juvenile taste such as Horatio Alger and Martha Finley. Neither Alger's monotonous stories of poor boys

[10] James Hart has one in preparation.

who made good, nor Mrs. Finley's lachrymose 'Elsie' books can qualify as literature, but it is probable that they exercised an influence broader than that of the writings of any other author we have named except Mark Twain. And the enormous popularity of the ponderous moral tales of the Rev. Mr. Roe and Mrs. Southworth indicates a characteristic sentimentality and a highly religious morality in the average middle-class American of the Gilded Age.

5. *Journalism*

If literature reflected the broad lines of national development and delineated the national character, journalism mirrored more faithfully the day-by-day activities and interests of the American people. The newspapers of the Civil War period were largely personal organs, their four or eight pages given over chiefly to politics, reprints of foreign dispatches, editorials, and personal advertisements. In the evolution of the newspaper of Greeley's or Bennett's day into the modern metropolitan daily such as the New York *Times* or the Baltimore *Sun* we can see not only the material growth of the nation and the expansion of their interests, but other factors which are at the same time characteristic of the development of the American people as a whole. Some of these are: 1. The subordination of politics to 'news,' with a consequent development of highly efficient machinery of reporting and news-gathering. This was made possible by mechanical and administrative improvement in the telephone, telegraph, cable, and printing machinery. 2. The passing of the personal element in journalism. With few exceptions newspapers ceased to be vehicles for the opinions of their editors, and became great and generally impersonal business organizations. This development, however, is probably less striking in journalism than in business generally. 3. Centralization and standardization through the creation of chains, the elimination of competition, and the use of syndicated editorials, features, and news. This is merely the horizontal trust extended to the field of journalism, through such agencies as Hearst and the Scripps-Howard corporation. More recently we have the beginning of the vertical trust in journalism through the centralized control of all processes of newspaper making from wood-pulp to distribution. 4. A notable enlargement and improvement in the physical appearance of the newspapers. This was accomplished by improved machinery such as the Hoe rotary press, the Mergenthaler linotype, and rotogravure processes, the organization of news-gathering agencies such as the United Press and the Associated Press, and the growth of advertising, which gave newspaper owners the necessary revenue with which to install expensive machinery and to maintain costly services. 5. Co-operation of the Federal Government in the form of low postal rates on newspapers, and rural free delivery. Thus we see that those processes of consolidation, standardization, capitalization, the scientific revolution, and governmental co-operation which characterize American life as a whole were changing the nature of American journalism.

In the sixties, as in the twentieth century, New York City was the newspaper center of the nation. Though such local papers as the Richmond *Enquirer,* the Toledo *Blade,* the Cincinnati *Commercial,* the Boston *Transcript,* the Louisville *Journal,* and the Springfield *Republican,* to mention only a few, were comparatively more influential than provincial papers of the present time, it was the great New York dailies — the *Tribune, Sun, Evening Post, Herald,* and *Times* that held a commanding position.

The dean of American newspapermen was the venerable William Cullen Bryant, for half a century editor of the influential *Evening Post.* The just fame of Bryant has been obscured by emphasizing his poetry at the expense of his splendid journalistic talents. It is the fate of the journalist to write in water, and most of Bryant's editorial work is forgotten; but few more vigorous, discriminating, and far-sighted critics have dealt with the American scene. He lifted American journalism to a higher literary and ethical plane than it had heretofore occupied, and gave not only to his editorial column but to his entire paper a refinement and dignity that assured it the leading place in American journalism. 'But,' writes Allan Nevins, historian of the *Evening Post,* 'he lacked the faculty for creating a broad newspaper which would appeal by enterprise in news-gathering and by special features to a great popular audience. He was responsible for few innovations in journalism, and they were not of high importance. His journalistic vein had something of the narrowness which marked his poetic genius, and though the *Post's* editorials, political news, literary articles, and foreign correspondence were of the highest merit, they were for the few and not for the many.'

At the farthest remove from Bryant in ability to gauge and to influence popular opinion and to create a broad national paper was Horace Greeley of the *Tribune,* by common consent the greatest of

American editors. Greeley was the spokesman of the plain people, liberal, practical, fearless, of cascading energy and boundless faith in democracy, a social reformer who fashioned a great paper as a flexible instrument to his purposes. He founded the *Tribune* in 1841, drove its circulation up over the hundred thousand mark, and until the close of the Civil War exerted a greater influence over public opinion in the North and the West than any other editor. He made his paper, especially the weekly edition, a family newspaper that was read all the way from Maine to Minnesota, his fierce denunciations of slavery doing more to consolidate Northern opinion than the agitation of all the other abolitionists combined. Greeley's erratic course during the Civil War cost him some popularity, and his vindictive attacks upon President Johnson contrast unpleasantly with the tolerant policies of Bryant or Raymond of the *Times*. Yet, he ended his career gallantly as a crusader for reform and a spokesman for tolerance; his thirty years as editor of the *Tribune* constitutes the greatest achievement of personal journalism in our history.

A very different sort of paper was the *Herald,* edited since 1835 by the James Gordon Bennetts, father and son. It was the elder Bennett's policy to create a paper that would be 'lively, saucy and spicy' and he succeeded in his ambition. The *Herald* was sensational and scandal-mongering from the beginning, but Bennett had an ear for news, and his social and financial columns were outstanding. He was never a molder of public opinion, but he anticipated the modern sensational newspaper in many respects.

The *Sun,* after 1868 under the control of Charles A. Dana, was closer to the *Herald* than to the *Tribune,* despite the fact that Dana was a graduate of Harvard and of Brook Farm, a scholar, and a man of taste, trained under Greeley himself. By emphasizing the news and feature articles Dana made the *Sun* the most popular paper of his time. He gathered around him a brilliant group of reporters — Arthur Brisbane, Richard Harding Davis, and Jacob Riis, to mention but a few — and made the *Sun* the liveliest and most vivacious and well-rounded paper between Greeley's *Tribune* and Pulitzer's *World*. Dana's incursions into politics were not always fortunate, as when he supported Ben Butler for the Presidency in 1884; but he rendered valiant service in exposing the corruption of the Grant administration.

Less influential than either Greeley or Dana was Henry J. Raymond of the *Times,* who, from the beginning, held faithfully to his ideal of an independent and decent newspaper. The *Times* under Raymond was, indeed, to its generation very much what the *Times* of today is to ours—cautiously liberal, eminently respectable, thorough and accurate. 'It probably came nearer the newspaper of the good time coming than any other in existence,' wrote Godkin of *The Nation*.

Undoubtedly the most powerful newspaper in the country outside New York City was the Springfield (Mass.) *Republican*, controlled and edited from 1844 to 1915 by three generations of Samuel Bowleses. Like the *Tribune*, the *Republican* was issued in a weekly as well as a daily edition, and the weekly had a much larger and wider circulation, spreading the liberal and independent doctrines of its editors throughout New England and the Ohio and Mississippi valleys. The second Bowles, who was probably the ablest, had charge of the paper during the critical years of the Civil War and Reconstruction: he supported Lincoln, advocated a magnanimous policy toward the South, fought corruption under Grant, denounced Tammany, and held fast to principles of independence, honesty, and courage that did much to raise the standards of American journalism. The *Republican* demonstrated the nation-wide power that a small provincial journal might wield, and set an example that was followed by William Allen White with the Emporia *Gazette*, Ed Howe with the Atchison *Globe*, William R. Nelson with the Kansas City *Star*, and Evan P. Howell with the Atlanta *Constitution*.

The decades of the seventies and the eighties marked a dividing line in American journalism. Raymond died in 1869, Greeley and Bennett in 1872, Bryant and the second Bowles in 1878. Joseph Pulitzer obtained control of the New York *World* in 1883, and William Randolph Hearst of the San Francisco *Examiner* in 1887. Samuel Bowles himself prophesied the significance of the passing of the older generation of editors:

> The growth of journalism as a business, and the extinction of the old party lines and divisions, have united to make a date, as it were, of its emancipation. With the deaths of James Gordon Bennett and Horace Greeley, personal journalism also comes practically to an end. They did much to create modern American journalism in its two different characters: both sought news as the first and chief element, — the one went farther and added criticism, opinion, reform; the one gathered and organized fact and recorded opinions; the other sought to control and make those opinions. Their personality was the necessity of their creative work;

it could not be suppressed by types and ink; but they have no successors, because there is no call for them, — the creators have given place to the conductors; and henceforth American Journalism, in its best illustrations will exhibit its outgrowth both of Partyism and Personalism. It will become a profession, not a stepping-stone; and a great journal will not longer be the victim of caprice and passion, or the instrument of the merely personal ambition, of its chance writer or conductor.

Joseph Pulitzer best represents the methods and the objectives of the new journalism. A Hungarian-German Jew, trained under Carl Schurz, he came to New York from the St. Louis *Post-Dispatch,* and purchased the almost defunct *World* from Jay Gould. By elaborating on the sensationalism of Bennett, he pushed the circulation of the *World* up to unprecedented figures, passing the million mark during the Spanish-American War. His paper, frankly popular in its appeal, played up crime, scandal, and sensational news in screaming headlines and illustrations, while its bold socialistic program established it definitely as the poor man's journal. Yet the *World* under Pulitzer was never merely a 'yellow sheet.' There was a wide gap between the news stories and the editorial page, which was conducted on a high intellectual, moral, and literary plane. Pulitzer's ambition was to reach the masses through sensationalism, and then indoctrinate them with his liberalism — an ideal in which he was not particularly successful. In course of time the *World,* like the *Herald* and the *Sun,* became more respectable and, after the retirement of Pulitzer and the accession of Frank I. Cobb, became the leading Democratic organ in the country, a position which it continued to maintain under the able direction of Walter Lippmann, until its lamented demise in 1931.

The success of Pulitzer in tapping substrata of newspaper readers was contagious. William Randolph Hearst, fresh from success on the California coast, came to New York in 1896 and purchased the *Journal.* In a short time he was out-sensationalizing Pulitzer, and there ensued one of the fiercest and most dramatic contests in the history of American journalism. Hearst, in the *Journal* and in the nation-wide chain of papers he subsequently acquired, brought 'yellow journalism' to its highest — or lowest — development, and without the editorial compensations of the *World.* Lavish use of enormous black leaders, of colored paper, of blaring full-page editorials, of illustrations, and of colored cartoon comic strips, gave the Hearst papers an extraordinary popularity. Sensationalism became a national menace when, in order to boost the circulation of his papers, Hearst exploited the Cuban revolution to whip up a popular demand for war with Spain. Godkin, in one of his last editorials, hotly denounced 'a regime in which a blackguard boy with several millions of dollars at his disposal has more influence on the use a great nation may make of its credit, of its army and navy, of its name and traditions, than all the statesmen and philosophers and professors in the country.'

Despite this vulgarization of the press the professional standards and ethics of journalism were on the whole improving. This was brought about partly through voluntary agreement, partly through the establishment of numerous schools of journalism, and partly through the example of such eminently respectable papers as the New York *Times,* which grew in circulation and in influence by concentrating on full and accurate reporting, and on the editorial page. The vigorous growth of other excellent papers such as the Baltimore *Sun,* the Chicago *Daily News,* and the St. Louis *Post-Dispatch* went far to off-set the strident inroads of the tabloid picture-papers which made their appearance in the years after the First World War.

More influential even than many of the great daily papers were weekly journals of opinion such as *The Nation,* the *Independent,* and *Harper's Weekly*. Of these three, *The Nation* under E. L. Godkin was for the thirty years after 1865 the leader of intelligent opinion in America. A great editor and critic, fearless, incisive, brilliant, penetrating, of high literary attainments and wide erudition, Godkin made his weekly, despite its limited circulation, the most powerful journal of opinion in the country. *The Nation* concerned itself chiefly with politics, the Negro, and literature; it was a strident critic of President Johnson, attacked corruption, national and local, and held aloft at all times the highest ideals of civic duty. Godkin, asserted Charles Eliot Norton, 'was the soundest and best trained writer on social and economical questions' in the country. His influence percolated down through editors, teachers, clergymen, and professional men until it indirectly affected the great mass of the people. 'To my generation,' wrote the philosopher William James, 'his was certainly the towering influence in all thought concerning public affairs, and indirectly his influence has assuredly been more pervasive than that of any other writer of the generation, for he influenced other writers who never quoted him and determined the whole current of discussion.' Yet Godkin lacked the common touch, lacked broad human sympathies. His liberalism had a doctrinaire tinge that reminds one unpleasantly of Charles Sumner. He had no understanding of either the Southern planter or the Western farmer, and generally identified good taste with righteousness. His opposition to Granger legislation and the Populist program was as uncomprehending as that of the most hide-bound reactionary. 'He couldn't imagine a different kind of creature from himself in politics,' wrote William James shrewdly. It is noteworthy that the most fervent appreciation of Godkin came from his New England and English friends who, like him, often confused form with substance, elegance with integrity.

More democratic, more in the American tradition, was *Harper's Weekly,* edited by the versatile and scholarly civil service reformer, George William Curtis. A family magazine, designed for entertainment rather than for agitation, it was nevertheless a force for political decency, and Curtis came in time to occupy something of the position formerly held by Horace Greeley. Yet the *Weekly* is chiefly remembered today as the vehicle of Thomas Nast's incomparable political cartoons. Less important than *Harper's Weekly* was the *Independent,* the leading religious paper of the post-war period, ably if somewhat contentiously edited by Henry Ward Beecher and Theodore Tilton.

The weekly journal of opinion went into something of an eclipse after the passing of Godkin and Curtis. The *Commoner,* edited by Bryan, and *La Follette's Magazine* were chiefly political propaganda for those left-wing leaders. But the second decade of the century witnessed a notable revival. In 1912 Oswald Garrison Villard obtained control of *The Nation,* and transformed it once more into a radical weekly similar to *The Nation* under Godkin. The *New Republic,* launched two years later under the auspices of Herbert Croly and with one of the most brilliant editorial staffs in the history of American journalism, assumed at once a commanding position in directing the political, social, and economic thought of the country along liberal channels, a position endangered but not entirely forfeited by its later drastic swing to the left.

6. *Art and Architecture*

American artistic development in this era was dominated by two factors: the growth of population and of cities, and the increase in national and individual wealth. Expansion created new fields for the architect and the artist in the construction of the numberless administrative, educational, and commercial structures, and presented new and enormously complex problems of construction, sanitation, transportation, lighting, decoration, and adjustment to real estate values. Increase of wealth made possible a patronage of the arts as lavish if not as discriminating as ever before in history, led to the establishment of museums and schools of art, to the wholesale importation of works of art from the Old World, and a wider and more intimate acquaintance with European art. Paradoxically, this led not to dependence upon European standards or schools, but to a general elevation of American taste and encouragement of native talent. Yet the fine arts, in so far as they attempt to create beauty out of the stuff of life, are universal rather than national in character, and it is a mistake to attempt to force artistic expression into artificial channels of nationalism. To speak of 'American architecture,' 'American painting,' or 'American sculpture' is largely an intellectual convenience: neither Richard Morris Hunt, nor John Singer Sargent, nor James McNeill Whistler, nor Frederick MacMonnies was 'American' except by accident of birth, and even those artists who most consciously tried to express American character, such as Thomas Eakins in painting and Louis Sullivan in architecture, received their advanced training and consequently much of their inspiration abroad.

Even before the Civil War the architectural renaissance, sponsored by Thomas Jefferson and Benjamin Latrobe and its offspring the Greek revival, had spent itself, and the most promising of American architects, James Renwick and Richard Upjohn, had turned to Gothic. St. Patrick's Cathedral, Grace Church, and Trinity Church, all in New York, gave promise of a Gothic revival. What came instead was a pseudo-Gothic that often goes by the name of Victorian. This style was used occasionally in larger public buildings such as the old Grand Central Station of New York, or the Smithsonian Institution at Washington, but it was ill-adapted to such structures, and found most extensive application in dwelling houses. Victorian Gothic was like much of the oratory of the period, florid, vain, and empty; characterized by over-decoration, over-ornamentation, and ostentation. Jig-saw scroll work, mansard roofs, useless gables, narrow windows, small dark rooms, long halls, ornate prettiness in interior decorations, and stuffy furniture, all reflected the decline in American taste since the simplicity of Jefferson, Latrobe and Bulfinch.

It was Henry Hobson Richardson who ushered in the new day of American architecture. Trained in Paris at the École des Beaux Arts, he brought back not the classic or renaissance styles then so popular in France, but the influence of Viollet le Duc. Richardson's fame is associated with the attempt to transplant Romanesque architecture to the United States — an attempt, it would seem, foredoomed to failure. Yet by contrast to the jerry-work of so much of the Gilded Age, Richardson's buildings have integrity and completeness that go far to explain the universal admiration they aroused. Such, indeed, was Richardson's power that he enjoyed a personal success greater than any other figure in American architecture. 'To live in a house built by Richardson,' writes T. E. Tallmadge, 'was a cachet of wealth and taste; to have your nest egg in one of his banks gave you a feeling of perfect security; to worship in one of his churches made one think one had a pass key to the Golden Gates.' Even the fastidious Henry Adams records with pride that he employed Richardson to build his house on Lafayette Square, Washington. His greatest monument was Trinity Church, Boston, a magnificent Romanesque structure for which John La Farge did the murals and the stained-glass windows. Although Richardson is best remembered for some of his churches, his influence on domestic architecture was profound, and massive fort-like dwellings of rough masonry built by him or his disciples are still to be found in many Mid-Western and some Eastern cities. Yet few styles of domestic architecture could be more ill adapted to the American temper than the Romanesque.

Contemporary with Richardson and, like him, trained in the École des Beaux Arts, was Richard Morris Hunt, brother of the eminent painter, and most exquisite of American architects. Hunt was the architect of the new American plutocracy. He introduced to America the beauty and lavishness of the French Renaissance, and built for American millionaires magnificent country houses patterned after French châteaux, or palatial town houses that resembled French hôtels-de-ville. While Richardson's influence was strongest in the Middle West, especially in Chicago and St. Louis, Hunt's genius found its field in New York City and in the more fashionable Eastern resorts such as Newport. The immense popularity of Hunt is eloquent of the advent of a wealthy leisure class of Americans who could afford to patronize artists after the fashion of Renaissance princes, and who were able to exercise some artistic discrimination. Yet French châteaux were no more suited to the genius of America than Romanesque fortresses, and though Hunt's work commended itself by its loveliness and grace, it was necessarily limited in its influence to a very exclusive group.

Scarcely less important in the development of architecture in America than Richardson and Hunt was the firm of McKim, Mead, and White, which designed more important public buildings than any other architectural firm in the country: the Pennsylvania station, the Morgan library, and the Columbia University buildings, in New York, the Boston Public Library, and the Union station in Washington, to mention but a few. Though devoted to no one style of architecture, the firm leaned toward the classical, and their influence is evident in scores of libraries, stations, educational institutions, and private houses scattered over the country. McKim, too, rendered signal service to American artists by establishing the American Academy in Rome — a gesture that was peculiarly appropriate coming from one who had done so much to cast American art in the models of imperial Rome.

The advance of architecture in America could be measured by comparing the buildings of the Centennial Exposition of 1876 with those of the World's Fair at Chicago in 1893. 'The Exposition,' wrote Henry Adams wonderingly, 'defied philosophy. As a scenic display Paris had never approached it, but the inconceivable scenic display consisted in its being there at all.' It was eloquent of the waning influence of Richardson and the rising influence of McKim and his associates, that the consulting architects chose the classical style for the Fair buildings. The Exposition enlisted a striking array of American artistic talent. Frederick Law Olmstead, who had laid out Central Park, New York, was the landscape architect. R. M. Hunt, C. F. McKim, Stanford White, Daniel Burnham, and Louis Sullivan were among the architects; Augustus Saint-Gaudens, Daniel Chester French, Lorado Taft, and Frederick MacMonnies contributed their skill as sculptors; and Kenyon Cox, Gari Melchers, and Edwin Blashfield as painters. Well might Saint-Gaudens exclaim, at a meeting of the architects, 'Look here, old fellows, do you realize that this is the greatest meeting of artists since the fifteenth century?' Daniel Burnham, indeed, remarked that the Fair was 'what the Romans would have wished to create in permanent form.' The remark revealed at once the achievement of American artists and their limitations, the triumph of taste and the decline of imagination. If the World's Fair was one of the great artistic exhibitions of modern times, it was imitative and derivative rather than American, and did not greatly further the development of native art. The most promising original artist discovered by the Fair, Louis Sullivan, whose Transportation building aroused the excited admiration of foreign critics, asserted that the influence of the Fair was little short of disastrous:

> The virus of the World's Fair . . . began to show unmistakable signs of the nature of the contagion. There came a violent outbreak of the Classic and the Renaissance in the East, which slowly spread westward, contaminating all that it touched. . . . Thus Architecture died in the land of the free and the home of the brave. . . . Thus did the virus of a culture, snobbish and alien to the land, perform its work of disintegration; and thus ever works the pallid academic mind, denying the real, exalting the fictitious and the false, incapable of adjusting itself to the flow of living things.[11]

Louis Sullivan, more clearly than any architect of his time, realized the connection between architecture and society, and tried, effectively, to articulate the one to the other. 'What the people are within,' said Sullivan, 'the buildings express without; and inversely, what the buildings are objectively is a sure index of what the people are subjectively.' This interpretation of the functional character of architecture in the Gilded Age was not a flattering one, and Sullivan observed somewhat acrimoniously that 'the unhappy, irrational, heedless, pessimistic, unlovely, distracted and decadent structures which make up the great bulk of our contemporaneous architecture point with infallible accuracy to qualities in the heart and mind and soul of the American people.' Sullivan allowed himself to be distracted by the problem of ornamentation, but his disciple, Frank Lloyd Wright, was more successful in an attempt to create an architectural style native to the American soil, and in harmony with the American environment.

What doomed Richardson's style, and made Hunt's and McKim's impracticable for commercial purposes, was the rising value of real estate, which placed a premium upon height and cheapness. Mason work was enormously expensive and could attain a height of at most

[11] *The Autobiography of an Idea,* p. 324. W. W. Norton.

seven or eight stories. The low-lying and luxurious buildings of a Hunt or a McKim are found chiefly on country estates, or, in cities, on public property. The elevator had been introduced before the Civil War, but it was not until the eighties that the perfection of cheap structural steel set American architecture free and, together with rising land values and the gregarious habits of the American business man, produced the skyscraper. Chicago was the center of the earliest efforts in this direction, and the Tacoma Building and Masonic Temple (1890) the earliest examples of all-steel skeleton buildings. Though Burnham and Sullivan worked capably in this medium, most of the artists who attempted to design curtain walls for these steel structures made a poor fist of it. By 1910, however, the skylines of New York and Chicago showed imposing dignity and genuine beauty, and European critics are agreed that the skyscraper is the one genuine American contribution to world architecture. The device of the set-back, required by law in New York City after 1916, revolutionized skyscraper design, and the buildings designed by such craftsmen as Raymond Hood and Cass Gilbert went far to invalidate the charge of Lewis Mumford that the skyscraper is 'an architecture for angels and aviators.' Yet the chief charge against the skyscraper can scarcely be denied: that it necessarily subordinated artistic considerations to real estate values, and that it added immeasurably to the complexity of modern urban life by concentrating thousands of workers in one spot during the working day, and concentrating business in one small section of a city.

More recently American architecture has been characterized by eclecticism. Harvard's new buildings followed closely on her own eighteenth-century models, but other great universities like Yale and Princeton abandoned the traditional Georgian for the alien Gothic. With the possible exceptions of Leland Stanford Jr. University in California, and Rice Institute, where Ralph Adams Cram married Ravenna Romanesque to the harsh, bright colors of the Texas plain, there is not today in the United States so satisfactory a group of university buildings as that designed by Thomas Jefferson for Virginia, over a century ago. Great office buildings like the Chicago Tribune Building were decorated to look like a birthday cake, and suburban developments spawned a miscellany of pseudo-Elizabethan, Queen Anne, and what Sullivan called 'Kickapoo Colonial' dwelling houses. The greatest triumphs of modern architecture have been in administrative and educational buildings, and its ablest representatives, Charles Platt, Bertram Goodhue, and Frank Lloyd Wright, have shown marked originality. At Deerfield and Phillips Andover Academies Platt re-adapted colonial Georgian to its environment; Goodhue designed the Nebraska State Capitol, one of the most notable achievements of modern architecture; while Wright's influence on domestic architecture has been world-wide. The work of societies that preserve ancient landmarks, and the restoration of an entire colonial capital, at Williamsburg, have made the American public more appreciative of their own architecture and eager to improve it than ever before. But at present architecture is in a state of suspension, 'functionalists' and traditionalists are at grips, the pre-fabricated house is being pushed, and the American Institute of Architects, allied with realtors and engineers, is at war with most of the university schools of architecture that represent training in design, taste, and experimentation.

The most striking characteristic of American painting after the Civil War, as in earlier years, was its dependence upon European and particularly French standards and training. The majority of American painters studied in France, at Barbizon or Paris; a smaller number derived their inspiration from Düsseldorf or Munich. A considerable number of the most distinguished American artists — Whistler, Abbey, Sargent, Cassatt, Harrison, to name but a few — took up their permanent residence abroad and belong to the history of English or French art as well as of American.

In no branch of the fine arts have Americans a more distinguished record than in painting, and the advance from the Hudson River School of landscape painters to Inness and Martin, or from portrait painters such as Peale and Trumbull to Eakins and Sargent, is notable. The most distinguished of American landscape painters was George Inness, who in his use of colors and of light anticipated the French luminists, and who combined with extraordinary technical skill a religious mysticism. Scarcely less talented than Inness in the field of landscape painting were Alexander Wyant and Homer Martin, the first drawing his inspiration from the English Constable, the latter in the Barbizon tradition. Martin was an ardent admirer of Corot, and in *Westchester Hills* and *View of the Seine* proved himself a worthy disciple to the great French master. The tradition of Inness, Wyant, and Martin was well maintained in the following generation by Dwight Tryon and John Twachtman.

The philosopher of luminism in painting was John La Farge, one of the most versatile and original geniuses of the nineteenth century. Like so many of our artists of recent foreign extraction, La Farge identified himself completely with America, and for a quarter of a century exerted a powerful influence in its development. In his youth a student in William Morris Hunt's atelier, he did his first important work on the murals and windows of Richardson's Trinity Church; yet he was a disciple of neither of these masters, but developed his own talents along independent lines. His most significant contribution was probably his experimentation in stained glass, and in the Church of the Ascension, New York, he revived something of the lost glory of medieval glass coloring. In his painting, particularly in his interpretation of light and the subtlety of his coloring, he anticipated many of the tenets of the Impressionists. That so exquisite, and by its very nature so exclusive, an art could thrive in America indicated that 'there must have been culture to recognize it, wealth to employ it, and some surrounding beautiful works of art to foster it, and all these to be found in his own country.'

Comparable to La Farge in influence, but utterly different in personality and career, was James McNeill Whistler, probably the most gifted of American painters. Like so many other artists, before and since, Whistler expatriated himself, and established himself in the more profitable, if scarcely more congenial, society of England. His vivid and belligerent personality, his aggressive egotism, his love of notoriety, served for a time to obscure his true gifts. By his portraits of *Carlyle, Sarasate,* and the *Artist's Mother,* he established himself at once as one of the great interpreters of the nineteenth century. But even more influential than these portraits were the *Nocturnes* and *Symphonies* with their original experiments in the use of color and of light.

During the era from 1880 to 1900 America had as competent a group of illustrators as could be found in any country: Howard Pyle, and his pupils such as Stanley Arthurs, Maxfield Parrish, and N. C. Wyeth; Arthur B. Frost, Walter Upton Clark, and Edwin Abbey. Abbey, who lived and worked in London, painted the official picture of the coronation of King Edward VII but was primarily a mural decorator, famous for his rich and elaborate recreations of historical scenes and for the colorful murals in the Boston Public Library and the Pennsylvania State Capitol. Another expatriated American, John Singer Sargent, was likewise an illustrator of superb talents. His versatility enabled him to paint landscapes, watercolors, and murals, but he is best known as a portrait painter in the tradition of Reynolds and Gainsborough, unmatched in the accuracy and intelligence, if not in the imagination, of his character reading.

It is a far cry from the academic perfection of Sargent and the elegance of his subjects to the dynamic native talent of Winslow Homer. Trained in a lithographer's shop and as an illustrator for *Harper's Weekly* during the Civil War, Homer is the most vital of American painters, important not only for what he accomplished but for his influence on younger painters and his contributions to the solution of technical problems. The subjects of his pen and brush were as native as his character: war pictures, scenes from Negro life in the South, rural and maritime New England, and the Adirondacks. His paintings are marked by originality of conception and boldness of execution, by primitive power and abounding energy.

A more original genius than either Sargent or Homer was Thomas Eakins, whose paintings brought him neither fame nor wealth but who came to exercise a more pervasive influence in American art than many painters with resounding reputations. 'Respectability in art,' said Eakins, 'is appalling,' and his own art was marked by a homespun realism that struck a new note in American painting. He is best remembered for his 'Clinic of Dr. Gross,' his realistic and unflattering 'The Thinker,' and his masterly portrait of Walt Whitman, but his greatest contribution came in his influence on a whole school of painters, of whom Robert Henri, John Sloan, and Joseph Pennell are the best known.

The richness and variety of the American scene was caught by a group of painters who had little else in common. Horatio Walker and George Fuller drew the homelier aspects of farm life in a manner and style reminiscent of Millet; Jonas Lie was inspired by the singular and primitive beauty of the building of the Panama Canal; Joseph Pennell, foremost of modern etchers, was fascinated by the spectacle of modern industry, railroads, and factories; Frederick Remington sketched life on the great plains; Elihu Vedder and George de Forest Brush painted, somewhat romantically, the vanishing Indians; and a group of 'New York Realists'—Robert Henri, George Bellows, John Sloan, George Luks, William Glackens, and Jerome Myers—caught the authentic flavor of life in the crowded streets and alleys and docks, the barroom and the dance hall, of New York City.

In sculpture, as in painting, American artists struck roots in the classic soil of Greece or Rome or in that of modern France. Here, too, the advance from the early nineteenth century to the modern period is a notable one. The statues and decorations of Hiram Powers, Thomas Crawford, Erastus Palmer, and Horatio Greenough had been excellent copies of Canova or Thorwaldsen, but they lacked originality or power. The first American sculptor to give evidence of either of these traits was John Quincy Adams Ward, whose statues of Henry Ward Beecher and President Garfield were completely divorced from the neo-classical insipidity of so many of his contemporaries.

Modern American sculpture dates from the Centennial Exposition of 1876, when the exhibition of modern French art made a profound impression upon Americans. Two young Americans, both trained at the École des Beaux Arts, exhibited at the Exposition: Augustus Saint-Gaudens and Olin L. Warner. 'To an intelligent foreigner,' writes Charles R. Morey, 'American sculpture would be summed up in a single name, that of Augustus Saint-Gaudens,' and so impressively does Saint-Gaudens tower above all of his contemporaries, indeed above all American artists, that few critics would quarrel with the generalization. Born in Ireland, of Irish and French parentage, he has nevertheless, more fully and sympathetically than any other sculptor, recorded the American genius. His 'Lincoln' in Lincoln Park, Chicago, with its intuitive comprehension of the combination of rugged shrewdness and spirituality, is so convincing that no one, 'having seen it, will conceive him otherwise thereafter.' The Farragut Monument, its base executed by Stanford White, and the Shaw Memorial in Boston established him as indubitably the foremost monumental sculptor of his day. Perhaps the most profound and the loveliest of all Saint-Gaudens' work is the figure which he did for the tomb of Mrs. Henry Adams. 'From Prometheus to Christ; from Michael Angelo to Shelley,' wrote Henry Adams, 'art had wrought on this eternal figure almost as though it had nothing else to say.'

Less powerful and less original than Saint-Gaudens, American trained, and in the American tradition, was Daniel Chester French, who executed the enormous bronze Lincoln for the Lincoln Memorial in Washington. Almost equally known is his youthful figure of the Minute Man, at Concord, Massachusetts, and his moving 'Death Stays the Hand of the Sculptor.'

Though Saint-Gaudens and French are the most distinguished of American sculptors, no account of American sculpture would be complete without mention of Frederick MacMonnies, whose rococo exuberance and grace remind one of Falguiere and Carpeaux, of George Gray Barnard, a disciple of Rodin who is perhaps best known for his collection of medieval art, of Karl Bitter, director of sculpture of three major Expositions, of Lorado Taft, whose work as a teacher and writer has tended to obscure his real talents, and whose 'Wave of Life' is one of the most impressive of modern monuments, and of younger and more original sculptors such as Paul Manship, Jo Davidson, and Malvina Hoffman.

Important in the creation of a background for the development of American art was the accumulation of great private collections, and the establishment of museums and schools of art. Civil War profiteers, bankers, and railway kings invaded Europe and captured 'old masters,' and though some of the early collections were meretricious, the great middlemen of art, such as Knoedler and Duveen, did the country a service by training the taste of the great collectors, such as J. P. Morgan, Martin A. Ryerson, Henry E. Huntington, and Andrew Mellon, whose collections have eventually become available to the public. More important in directing the taste of the public is the increase of museums of fine arts. In 1865 there was none in the country worthy of the name; by 1890, the greater cities had shown the way; and today there is hardly a city of over one hundred thousand population, or a university, that lacks a public art museum, often with a school of design attached. American art museums are not, like many of their European prototypes, mere mausoleums; with their lectures, guide information, and lending services they go more than half way to meet the public, and their influence on good taste has been incalculable.

7. *Education*

The effect of the Civil War and Reconstruction on education varied with the sections. On the South the effect was disastrous. A large part of the school funds of many Southern states had been invested in securities that were now worthless; what was salvaged from the devastations of war was dissipated by the ravages of reconstruction. School houses, never in too good repair, had fallen into ruin; teachers had been killed or scattered; and the South was less able to bear heavy educational taxes than ever before. Yet, impoverished and demoralized as the South was, she faced additional burdens in the form of providing education for the freedmen. Though the Freedmen's Bureau and Northern philanthropic agencies such as the Peabody, the Phelps-Stokes, and the Slater funds assisted, it was upon the Southern people that the burden ultimately fell. Higher education, too, was paralyzed; many private institutions lost part or all of their endowment; the very buildings of others had been destroyed; and few states were able to support their state universities. The University of North Carolina closed its doors for some years; the University of South Carolina was abandoned by white students when a carpetbag legislature threw it open to Negroes: the University of Louisiana was kept alive only by the heroic self-denial of a few loyal professors who refused to abandon the institution. Though students thronged to the colleges, and the faculties served them with unparalleled devotion and self-sacrifice, the story of such colleges as Washington and Lee (Virginia), Sewanee (Tennessee), and Davidson (North Carolina) is one of struggles against tremendous odds. Southern education did not fully recover from the effects of war and reconstruction until the twentieth century. Since 1900 the development in some Southern states, notably in North Carolina under the dynamic leadership of Governor Aycock, has been spectacular.

In the North, on the contrary, after a temporary setback, education profited by the peculiar temper and energy of the post-war period. The intimate relationship of a free public school system to democratic society had already been effectively demonstrated by great educational leaders such as Horace Mann of Massachusetts, Henry Barnard of Connecticut, and John D. Pierce of Michigan. 'The common schools are truly republican,' wrote Pierce, who waged an educational crusade in the West similar to that of Mann in New England. 'In the public schools all classes are blended together, the rich mingle with the poor, and both are educated in company. Let free schools be established and maintained in perpetuity, and there can be no such thing as a permanent aristocracy in our land: for the monopoly of wealth is powerless when mind is allowed freely to come in contact with mind.' The responsibility of the community to its children, then, had been pretty generally accepted by the middle of the century; but the conditions of education were far from satisfactory. Instruction was confined mainly to the elementary schools; not until as late as 1890 were there as many as two hundred thousand pupils in the public high schools of the nation.

The student of today, accustomed to a wide variety of courses, adequate equipment, well-trained teachers, and well-organized extra-curricular activities, might find the schools of this post-war generation shockingly primitive. Most American children of that generation went to a 'little red schoolhouse' where a student working his way through college, or a spinster who had not been fortunate enough to marry, taught all subjects and all grades. Teaching was largely by rote, discipline was severe, and corporal punishment everywhere taken for granted. The backbone of the curriculum — a term which few of the teachers would have recognized — was the 'three R's' — reading, writing, and arithmetic. History was a luxury in which some schoolmasters indulged; other subjects were taught chiefly in the schools of the larger cities or in the private academies. Children learned spelling out of the famous Webster's blue-backed *Speller,* a book which had already served two generations of American boys and girls, and which continued to do hardy service well into the new century; and 'spelling-bees' were as exciting a part of school life as were the ball games of later years. Even more important than the Webster Spellers were the McGuffey Readers, of which over one hundred million were sold in the years between 1836 and 1900. 'These books,' wrote the novelist Herbert Quick, 'constitute the most influential volumes ever published in America.' In an age when schools did not have libraries, and when few teachers were well-read, McGuffey's Readers, by introducing children to 'selections' from the best of English and American literature, performed a service of incalculable value and set the popular literary standard for two generations. 'For many a boy of the older West,' one distinguished clergyman later testified, 'McGuffey's varied and wise selections . . . were the very gates of literature ajar,' and Hamlin Garland remembered that 'from the pages of his readers I learned to know and love the poems of Scott, Byron, Southey, Wordsworth and a long line of English masters. I got my first taste of Shakespeare from the selected scenes which I read in these books.' The average schoolma'am of that day was no less concerned with molding character than with molding mind, and to this purpose, too, the McGuffey Readers, with their pious axioms of conduct and their moral tales, contributed powerfully.

Notwithstanding the inadequacies of many of the schools, no great nation was ever more fully committed to the ideal of a system of universal free public education than was the United States, and the statistics of school enrollment and expenditures are eloquent of her faithfulness to that ideal. A total of 6,871,000 pupils was enrolled in the public schools of the country in 1870; by 1900 this number had increased to 15,503,000; by 1920 to 21,578,000. In the same half-century the percentage of children between the ages of five and seventeen enrolled in schools rose from fifty-seven to seventy-eight — and illiteracy declined from twenty per cent to six per cent! The statistics of expenditures are even more illuminating. In 1870 Americans spent 63 million dollars on their public school system; in 1910, 214 million dollars, and in 1920 over one billion dollars — a sum greater than the entire expenses of the national government from its foundation to 1880 with the exception of the Civil War years. In another decade this figure had more than doubled. In the half-century from 1870 to 1920 the per capita expense for public education rose from $1.64 to $9.80; the expense per pupil, from $9.23 to $48.02, and in the next ten years, to $90.22. Even more striking was the progress in secondary education, indicative of the increased prosperity of the American people, and the assumption of responsibility for a complete educational system by the state. In 1890 there were only some 350,000 students in the secondary schools of the entire country, of which over one-third attended private schools. Twenty years later there were over a million pupils in the public high schools, and by 1930 the number had increased to about four and one-half million.

The war had drawn men from teaching into the ranks of the army and to business, and the feminization of teaching was in full swing. Already by 1870 over sixty per cent of public school teachers were women — a number which was to increase to eighty-five per cent by 1920. Though Horace Mann had established normal schools in Massachusetts in the thirties, there were only twelve in the country at the outbreak of the Civil War. The great majority of teachers were untrained and the idea generally obtained that any girl not otherwise occupied was competent to teach school. Gradually teaching became a profession and education came to be called a science. In due course of time every state in the Union established a board or commission of education which attempted to impose certain requirements and maintain high standards of teaching. States and cities vied with each other in establishing teachers' colleges, and by 1920 no less than 370 of these were training over 150,000 teachers — a number which doubled in the ensuing decade. In 1867 the office of United States Commissioner of Education was created 'to collect statistics and facts concerning the conditions and progress of education in the several States and Territories and to diffuse information respecting the organization and management of schools and school systems and methods of teaching.' Henry Barnard, who had rendered signal service in Connecticut and Rhode Island, was appointed first Commissioner of Education. Though this position was subsequently held by William T. Harris, distinguished philosopher and educator, and by Elmer Ellsworth Brown, later Chancellor of New York University, it never became an agency for centralization or standardization. The science of education received a powerful stimulus with the introduction of the doctrines of Pestalozzi, Froebel, and Herbart to America in the post-war decades, most notably by Edward A. Sheldon of the famous Oswego Normal School and William T. Harris, superintendent of schools in St. Louis and editor of the influential *Journal of Speculative Philosophy*. In 1882 was founded the National Herbart Society for the scientific study of education. Schools of education were established at the major universities such as Harvard, Columbia, Leland Stanford, and Chicago, in which latter school the nation's most distinguished philosopher, John Dewey, formulated a philosophy based squarely upon a democratic educational system.

It is in the field of higher education that we can best observe the extent to which education has become the national fetish, the depository for that idealism which in an earlier generation was directed toward religion. The objects of American philanthropy of the last half-century have been educational institutions or foundations rather than churches; the greatest architectural monuments are likely to be cathedrals of learning rather than of worship; the faith that men once had in religion to move heaven and earth has been largely transferred to organized education. Private philanthropy has combined with the state to create and maintain the most elaborate system of higher and professional education that has ever existed in any other nation, a system which has expanded in every direction in the last generation. Students by the hundreds of thousands throng the college halls; money without stint has been poured into educational coffers; old schools have been expanded beyond recognition and new ones have been created; professional schools of all kinds have come into existence; co-education has advanced with amazing rapidity; the scope and methods of education have been enlarged and standards generally raised.

The beginning of the educational renaissance came in the sixties, and can be traced to a number of causes: the appearance of a remarkable group of educational leaders, most of them trained abroad;

the Morrill Act of 1862 with its liberal provisions for mechanical and agricultural training; the demand of business and the professions for specialized knowledge; and the enormous increase in the financial resources of colleges, old and new, which enabled them to carry on their enlarged programs and to maintain their higher standards. Harvard, the oldest of American universities, led the way when a thirty-five year old chemist, Charles W. Eliot, assumed the presidency in 1869. Eliot summed up in himself many of the new forces abroad in higher education in America: he had spent some time in Germany, he was a scientist rather than a theologian, he was peculiarly sensitive to the changes which the Civil War and the industrial revolution had brought about in America, and prepared to adapt Harvard College to those conditions. He signalized his advent to the presidency by radical and far-sighted changes in organization, curriculum, and objectives. Though not the first to advocate an 'elective' college curriculum, in which the student was allowed to pick and choose his courses from a large offering, Eliot's tireless advocacy of liberty of choice, and the donations that made possible the adding of new subjects to the curriculum, set up new standards which most American colleges and universities were compelled to follow. Of greater ultimate significance was Eliot's rehabilitation of the Harvard schools of law and medicine, which he placed upon a sound professional basis. But more important than any single policy was Eliot's personality. He came, in time, to be a symbol for everything that was finest in American education, and, indeed, in American life — considered by many the first citizen of the land. His trenchant criticism and courage, liberal open-mindedness, ripe wisdom, and gallant faith added incalculably to the American tradition.

If Eliot was the most distinguished of American educators, he was by no means alone. Frederick Barnard was creating the modern Columbia University out of a small college, enriching the curriculum, establishing professional and graduate schools, and laying the foundations upon which Nicholas Murray Butler was to build. A. D. White, first president of the new Cornell University, was building a great co-educational school under peculiarly happy auspices, waging effective warfare on behalf of science and evolution, and drawing scholars of international repute to the shores of Lake Cayuga. Daniel Coit Gilman was inaugurating the most interesting and fruitful experiment in American higher education at Johns Hopkins University, established for the specific purpose of fostering graduate study, scholarship, and research. G. Stanley Hall, German trained psychologist and philosopher, came to the presidency of Clark University in 1889, and trained a school of psychologists who exerted a deep influence on public school education in the United States. And in 1892 a young Professor of Semitic at Yale, William Rainey Harper, took charge of the new University of Chicago and quickly made it the leading university west of the Alleghenies. At the same time Booker T. Washington, at Tuskegee Institute, was proving himself one of the great educators and statesmen of the country.

The second important factor in the development of higher education was the passage of the Morrill Land Grant Act of 1862. This Act gave to each state 30,000 acres of land per Congressman, to be used for the endowment and support of a college of agriculture and mechanical arts. Altogether over thirteen million acres of public domain were thus handed over to the states. The Morrill Act was, undoubtedly, the most important piece of educational legislation ever passed in this country. 'It recognizes the principle,' wrote L. H. Bailey, a prominent agriculturist, 'that every citizen is entitled to receive educational aid from the government, and that the common affairs of life are proper subjects with which to educate or train men. Its provisions are so broad that the educational development of all future may rest upon it.' Under the generous provisions of the Morrill Act sixty-nine land-grant colleges have been established. Many of the Western state universities sprang from the Act, and others received a decided impetus from its provisions: such typical and varied institutions as the University of Illinois, Iowa State College, Massachusetts Institute of Technology, and Cornell University have profited by the far-sighted wisdom of Justin Morrill.

The scientific revolution and the growing complexity of American economic life gave rise to a demand for education more closely articulated to the needs of the day. One result of this was the relative decline of classical and humanistic studies at the expense of the social and natural sciences, and the almost universal acceptance of the elective system. Another was the establishment of numerous professional schools, some in connection with older universities, others independently. Schools of law, medicine, architecture, engineering, education, and journalism began to turn out men who soon proved the superiority of professional training over mere experience, and schools such as the Harvard Law School, the Johns Hopkins Medical School, the Massachusetts Institute of Technology, the Columbia School of Architecture, the Colorado School of Mines, the Missouri School of Journalism, and the Chicago School of Education took their place among the leading institutions of their kind in the world.

All this expansion, academic and physical, was made possible by the steady flow of money which poured into the coffers of the older colleges or established new ones. The endowment of Harvard University, to take the most striking example, increased from not quite two and one-half million dollars in 1869 to approximately two hundred million by 1950. Yale, Columbia, Princeton, Rochester, Northwestern, and a score of other institutions were similarly enriched by private philanthropy. The total endowments of institutions of higher education exceeded one billion one hundred million dollars in 1928. Equally important with the expansion of older schools was the establishment of new. Of these Cornell (1868), Vanderbilt (1875), Johns Hopkins (1876), Tulane (1884), Leland Stanford (1891), the University of Chicago (1892), and Duke (1924) have assumed leading positions in American education.

A significant aspect of the educational renaissance was the development of facilities for graduate study in the United States. Before 1880 students anxious to carry their studies beyond the master's degree were forced to go abroad — generally to German universities. The leaders of American education in the post-Civil War period were for the most part German trained: the universities of Göttingen, Jena, and Berlin were particularly influential. Yale University conferred the first Ph.D. degree in America in 1861; ten years later she organized a graduate school, and Harvard followed in 1872. But the greatest impetus to graduate study came from the new Johns Hopkins University, the gift of a wealthy Baltimore railroad man. Here, under the inspiring leadership of Daniel Coit Gilman, the future leaders of American thought were receiving advanced training in history, philosophy, economics, and the sciences. Future President Woodrow Wilson, Josiah Royce and John Dewey, leaders of two schools of American philosophy, Richard T. Ely and D. R. Dewey, economists, J. Franklin Jameson, Frederick J. Turner, and Charles H. Haskins, historians, Walter Hines Page and Newton D. Baker, later distinguished in public affairs, to mention only a few, gave to the new institution in its early years a unique intellectual distinction. By the opening of the twentieth century most of the leading universities had established graduate schools and the number of graduate students registered was well over five thousand.

Higher education for women is comparatively recent in the United States. Emma Willard had established the Troy Female Seminary as early as 1821, and the gallant Mary Lyon had persevered against overwhelming obstacles in founding a school at Mount Holyoke, Massachusetts, which offered advanced work to girls, while Oberlin College, pioneer in co-education as in so many other respects, opened its doors to girls in the 1830's. But the first woman's college offering work on a level with the better men's schools was Vassar, the gift of Matthew Vassar, wealthy brewer of Poughkeepsie, New York, who hoped 'to inaugurate a new era in the history and life of woman.' Within twenty years four other colleges for women came into existence: Wellesley, Smith, Bryn Mawr, and Goucher, while Harvard and Columbia so far conceded to the demand for co-education as to establish affiliated colleges for women.

No account of American education would be complete without some reference to one of the most effective of all educational agencies, and the one most typically American — the public library. Libraries were not uncommon even in the colonial period, and several subscription libraries, such as the New York Society Library and the Library Company in Philadelphia, were in a flourishing condition before the Revolution. But the free public library, supported by taxation and open to all on equal terms, was a much more recent development. The first of the great modern public libraries was founded in Boston in the fifties, and it soon attracted not only generous public support but great private bequests. The Chicago Public Library was developed around the gift of seven thousand volumes presented after the great fire of 1871 by Thomas Hughes of England, author of *Tom Brown at Rugby*. The New York Public Library, the largest of its kind in the world, was formed by the merger of three great privately endowed libraries — the Astor, the Lenox, and the Tilden — with the library resources of the city. The Library of Congress, incomparably the most effective as it is the largest library in the world, was built about the nucleus of Thomas Jefferson's private library and has grown to some six and a half million volumes embracing many collections of priceless value.

The most effective impetus to the public library movement, however, came not from official sources or from public demand, but from the generosity of Andrew Carnegie. Inspired by a genuine passion for education, persuaded that the public library was the most democratic of all highways to learning, and mindful of his own debt to books and his love of them, the Pittsburgh iron-master devoted some forty-five million dollars of his vast fortune to the construction of library buildings throughout the country. His philanthropies were not only munificent but wise, for by requiring a guarantee of adequate support to the libraries which he built, he laid the foundations for healthy growth of library facilities after his own gifts had served their immediate purpose.

If, as Americans from Jefferson to John Dewey have confidently believed, education alone would provide a sound basis for 'a happy and a prosperous people,' Americans of the twentieth century had reason to be optimistic. Universal free education from the kindergarten to graduate school had become a fact. And if the results failed to come up to the most sanguine expectations, few but the more jaundiced critics concluded that the premises were erroneous, or questioned that Utopia could ultimately be reached along the broad road of democratic education.

XIII

IMPERIALISM AND WORLD POWER

1865–1898

1. *The United States in World Affairs*

WRITING in 1889 Henry Cabot Lodge, soon to win distinction as one of the most chauvinistic of American politicians, observed that 'our relations with foreign nations today fill but a slight place in American politics, and excite generally only a languid interest.' This generalization applied with equal force to the whole generation which had come to maturity since Reconstruction. From the settlement of the Alabama Claims and the successful weathering of the *Virginius* crisis to the eruption of Hawaii and Venezuela into American politics in the nineties, the relations of the United States with the outside world were singularly placid. The American people, proverbially parochial in their outlook, were busy with their internal affairs — repairing the devastations of the war, settling the continent, constructing their transportation and industrial system, absorbing new racial groups, and enjoying the game of politics.

The change came in the nineties, and it was more than mere coincidence that it synchronized with the passing of the frontier the shift from the 'old' to the 'new' immigration, and the coming of age of our industrial system. Fast as the population of the United States grew, the productivity of its agricultural and industrial organization grew still more rapidly. Almost every year prior to 1876 the United States suffered an unfavorable balance of trade; almost every year thereafter the balance was decidedly in its favor. In 1865 the foreign trade of the United States had been $404,000,000; by 1890 it had reached $1,635,000,000. More important than this quantitative increase was the fact that the increase in the export of manufactured goods was proportionately far greater than the increase in the export of agricultural products. The significance of this development was lost upon no realistic politician, and every President, from Grant to McKinley, was concerned with the expansion of our foreign markets.

Nor was the emergence of the United States as a world power a unique or isolated phenomenon. The closing years of the nineteenth century witnessed everywhere the rise of a new imperialism that was essentially an international struggle for new markets and sources of supply, such as had led to the colonization of America. Great Britain, after a long and sated indifference, was fired once more with enthusiasm for expansion and power; France found compensation for defeat by consolidating her African empire; Germany, having proved herself the strongest Continental power, demanded her share of colonial pickings; Japan startled the world with her smashing victory over China in 1895 and won recognition as a great power. Europe almost completed the partitioning of Africa, and, in rivalry with Japan, began to break pieces from the weak Chinese Empire. But in the Western Hemisphere the Monroe Doctrine stood as an insuperable barrier against fresh acquisition of American territory by European powers, although it did not prevent the exploitation of Latin America by European or North American capital. To European and African affairs the American people were completely indifferent; into the maelstrom of Far Eastern affairs they were drawn almost in spite of themselves. But the United States regarded affairs of this hemisphere as her particular concern, in time, as her exclusive province.

After the Civil War the two traditional policies in American foreign relations — the Monroe Doctrine and expansion in the Pacific area — persisted. American interest in the Pacific and the Far East dated back to the old China trade and became vital with the acquisition of Oregon and California. As early as 1844 Caleb Cushing negotiated a treaty with China granting trade and tariff concessions similar to those enjoyed by Great Britain. Nine years later Commodore Perry steamed past the forts at Yedo Bay and opened Japan to the commerce of the western world. 'It is self-evident,' wrote Perry, who anticipated much of our subsequent Pacific policy, 'that the course of coming events will ere long make it necessary for the United States to extend its jurisdiction beyond the limits of the western continent, and I assume the responsibility of urging the expediency of establishing a foothold in this quarter of the globe as a measure of positive necessity to the establishment of our maritime rights in the east.'

But the United States Government was not yet ready to assume such a responsibility; and Secretary Seward was the first to inaugurate a clean-cut Pacific policy. Declaring that our commerce in the East had 'already brought the ancient continents near to us and created necessities for new positions — perhaps connections or colonies there,' Seward embarked upon a design grandiose in conception. The purchase of Alaska was a major element in this design; other parts of it called for the cementing of friendly relations with China, an Isthmian canal and the annexation of Hawaii and whatever other coaling stations were available in the Pacific.

Hawaii, or the Sandwich Islands, had been discovered by Captain Cook in 1778, and early served as a convenient port of call in the China trade and recruiting station for Yankee whalers. By 1840 Honolulu, with whalemen and merchant sailors rolling through its streets, shops filled with Lowell shirtings, New England rum, and Yankee notions, orthodox missionaries living in frame houses brought around the Horn, and a neo-classic meeting house built of coral blocks, was a Yankee outpost. As early as 1842 Webster assured the Islanders that the United States could not permit Hawaii to become the possession of any other foreign power; but it just missed becoming a British protectorate in 1843. A few years later, Secretary Marcy negotiated with King Kamehameha III a treaty of annexation which failed of ratification only because Hawaii was to be made a state of the Union. Seward, too, moved toward annexation, but despite the approval of President Johnson and later of Grant, nothing was done. In 1875, however, the United States concluded with the Hawaiian monarch a reciprocity treaty which granted exclusive trading privileges to both nations and guaranteed the independence of the Islands against any third party; nine years later a new treaty renewed these privileges and ceded Pearl harbor on the island of Oahu to the United States.

These treaties greatly stimulated the sugar industry, which the sons of thrifty missionaries had established in Hawaii, on lands donated by the native princes for religious objects. American capital poured in, sugar production increased five-fold within a decade, and by 1890, ninety-nine per cent of the Hawaiian exports, then valued at twenty million dollars, went to the United States. The Islands had, in fact, become an American commercial appendage. In 1881 Secretary Blaine declared Hawaii to be part of the 'American system' and announced somewhat cryptically that if Hawaiian independence were endangered, the United States 'would then unhesitatingly meet the altered situation by seeking an avowedly American solution for the grave issues presented.' Even Cleveland, anti-imperialistic as he was, declared his 'unhesitating conviction that the intimacy of our relations with Hawaii should be emphasized.'

This was the situation when, in 1891, Queen Liliuokalani came to the throne, and inaugurated a policy looking to the elimination of American influence, and the restoration of autocracy. This policy, which threatened the position of the powerful American element, excited a prompt counter-offensive. After marines had been landed from the U.S.S. *Boston,* and probably with the connivance of the American minister John L. Stevens, a Committee of Safety consisting largely of missionaries' sons deposed the hapless Queen on 17 January 1893. A provisional government under Chief Justice Sanford B. Dole was set up, which promptly opened negotiations for annexation to the United States. 'I think we should accept the issue like a great Nation,' wrote Minister Stevens, 'and not act the part of pigmies nor cowards';[1] he did his part by hoisting the American flag over the government house at Honolulu. President Harrison, in full sympathy with this attitude, accepted a treaty of annexation on 14 February; but before the Senate got around to it, Grover Cleveland became President, and hearkened to the appeal of 'Queen Lil.' 'I mistake the Americans,' he said, 'if they favor the odious doctrine that there is no such thing as international morality; that there is one law for a strong nation and another for a weak one.' He withdrew the treaty from the Senate, sent out a special commissioner to investigate the situation, and, when the commissioner reported that the Hawaiian revolution was the work of American interests, aided by Minister Stevens, denounced the affair, and endeavored to persuade the provisional government to step down. The gesture was ineffective and, under the presidency of an American, the provisional government became a permanent one, and Cleveland was forced to recognize the Republic of Hawaii.

Our official relations with Samoa were equally unsatisfactory and confused. The Samoan, or Navigators', Islands were to the South Pacific what the Hawaiian were to the North, and from the 1830's on they had offered refuge to whalers and a virgin field of exploitation to missionaries. Not until the late sixties did American commercial interests with the Islands become sufficiently important to attract official attention; and in 1872 an American naval officer nego-

[1] Compare Tennyson's birthday tribute to Queen Victoria:

> We sailed wherever ship could sail;
> We founded many a mighty state;
> Pray God our greatness may not fail
> Through craven fear of being great.

tiated a treaty with some native chieftains granting to the United States exclusive control of the harbor of Pago Pago in the island of Tutuila. The treaty failed of confirmation, but the policy which it embraced was nevertheless adopted, and within six years a similar treaty was duly ratified. Shortly thereafter Great Britain and Germany secured comparable concessions in the Islands, and there followed ten years of ridiculous rivalry for supremacy between the three powers, each supporting a rival claimant to the native kingship. The danger of involving the United States in serious international complications was averted by the establishment of a tripartite protectorate guaranteeing the independence and neutrality of the Islands and confirming American rights to Pago Pago. Unimportant as this episode was, it constituted nevertheless, in the words of Secretary of State Gresham, 'the first departure from our traditional and well established policy of avoiding entangling alliances with foreign powers in relation to objects remote from this hemisphere.' President Cleveland asked Congress to withdraw from the agreement, but his request was ignored. After another embarrassing native civil war, the tripartite agreement was abrogated in 1900, and the Islands divided between Germany and the United States, Great Britain obtaining compensation elsewhere.

Thus, President Cleveland turned his back on the 'manifest destiny' to which his party had once summoned the United States, and the Republicans, reflecting the dominant and expansive forces of American life, somewhat timidly began to play the imperialist game.

In the years between Polk and Lincoln, the Monroe Doctrine had lapsed into something approaching desuetude; Seward's vigorous action against the French in Mexico proved that it was still a basic factor in American foreign policy. Other factors and objects were to maintain the leadership of the United States in all American questions, promote the commercial interests of the country, and keep peace, all of which involved diplomatic controversies with powers who still had colonies and capital in America.

A new contribution to our policy was Pan-Americanism; as formulated by James G. Blaine, it was primarily economic in character. Although the high priest of protection, Blaine realized that protective tariffs injured commercial relations between the United States and Latin America, because those countries, still regions of extractive industries, sold an excess of raw materials such as coffee, sugar, cocoa, sisal, hides, and wool to us, but purchased their manufactured articles in the cheaper markets of Europe. Since eighty-seven per cent of Latin American exports to the United States entered duty free, Blaine threatened to clamp a tariff on them unless the Latin American countries lowered their duties on United States products. What he had in mind was a Pan-American customs union, a series of uniform tariffs which would give reciprocal preference to American products or goods in all American countries; and it was with this in view that he called a Pan-American Conference in 1881. President Garfield's death was followed by a change in the State Department, and Blaine's successor revoked the invitations. A decade later President Harrison placed Blaine once more in a position to advance his cherished project. In October 1889 the first International American Conference, representing eighteen countries, convened at Washington. After a preliminary six weeks' junket which was designed to impress the delegates, the Conference met to consider Blaine's proposals for a Pan-American customs union and the arbitration of international disputes. Both seemed to the Latin Americans like the invitation of the spider to the fly, and were politely rejected. His ardor for Pan-Americanism somewhat dampened, Blaine endeavored to secure the same thing through reciprocity provisions in the McKinley tariff of 1890. Under the terms of this law reciprocity agreements were secured with ten nations. These agreements were abrogated by the Wilson tariff of 1894, but under the Dingley tariff of 1897 provision was made for a new series of reciprocity arrangements which were effected not only with the Latin American states but with European countries. On the eve of his assassination President McKinley announced his conversion to reciprocity as a universal policy:

> The period of exclusiveness is past. The expansion of our trade and commerce is the pressing problem. Commercial wars are unprofitable. A policy of good will and trade relations will prevent reprisals. Reciprocity treaties are in harmony with the spirit of the times; measures of retaliation are not. If perchance some of our tariffs are no longer needed for revenue or to encourage and protect our industries at home, why should they not be employed to extend and promote our markets abroad?

In spite of this persuasive argument from a high source, the Republican Senate, sensitive to the interests of American manufacturers, stubbornly refused to ratify any of the reciprocity treaties that were negotiated.

Although the Pan-American Conference did not accept arbitration as a formal policy, the principle itself was often invoked. President Hayes had arbitrated the Argentine-Paraguay boundary dispute, and Cleveland later arbitrated a similar dispute between the Argentine and Brazil. In another quarter, too, there was a notable victory for the principle of arbitration. This was in connection with the fur-sealing controversy in the Bering Sea. Anxious to prevent the ruthless extermination of the seal in Alaskan waters, and convinced that Canadian practices violated both property rights and morals, Blaine sought to extend American jurisdiction over the whole of the Bering Sea, and ordered the seizure of Canadian fishing vessels operating in these waters. He was right in ethics but wrong in law, and the controversy took an ugly turn. But at this juncture (1891) the United States and Great Britain had the good sense to resort to arbitration. The Tribunal decided all points of law adversely to the United States, but implicitly admitted the wisdom of Blaine's efforts to save the seal by drawing up regulations looking to that end.

Far more important than this sealing controversy was the dispute over the Venezuela boundary which afforded an opportunity both for an emphatic reaffirmation of the Monroe Doctrine and for a notable victory of the principle of arbitration. The dispute over the boundary-line between British Guiana and Venezuela was one of long-standing, but the whole question was suddenly given a new importance by the discovery of gold in the hinterlands of both countries. Overnight Great Britain extended her claims deep into the heart of Venezuela, and Lord Salisbury refused to submit the question to arbitration because of Venezuela's counter-claim to more than half the British colony. In a message of 17 December 1895 President Cleveland informed Congress of Lord Salisbury's refusal, proposed to determine the disputed line himself, and declared that in his opinion any attempt of Great Britain to assert jurisdiction beyond that line should be resisted by every means in the nation's power. Panic ensued in Wall Street, dismay in England, and an outburst of jingoism in the United States. Secretary of State Olney's note of 20 July, published with the message, announced a definition of the Monroe Doctrine that alarmed Latin America, insulted Canada, and challenged England:

> Today the United States is practically sovereign on this continent, and its fiat is law upon the subjects to which it confines its interposition. . . . Distance and three thousand miles of intervening ocean make any perma-

nent political union between a European and an American state unnatural and inexpedient.

No facts of the controversy could justify these extreme claims and provocative language. Why did Olney and Cleveland use it? Some have said that it was to win the Irish-American vote, or to create a new issue for the approaching Presidential campaign. But Cleveland's character was such as to stifle any suspicion of playing to the gallery. Probably Palmerston's seizure of Belize (British Honduras) was at the back of their minds, as the British seizure of the Nicaraguan customs in April 1895 was certainly in the fore. They feared that England was procrastinating, and that Venezuela, if abandoned to her own expedients, would declare a war in which the United States would be forced to participate. Seventeen years later Olney explained his language on the ground that 'in English eyes the United States was then so completely a negligible quantity that it was believed only words the equivalent of blows would be really effective.'

Actually it was only the absolute necessity for friendship with the United States that induced the Salisbury government to let this challenge lie. Of the British navy's preponderance over the American—at least five to one—there was no doubt. But 'Great Britain,' as Bayard wrote, 'has just now her hands very full in other quarters of the globe. The United States is the last nation on earth with whom the British people or their rulers desire to quarrel. . . . The other European nations are watching each other like pugilists in the ring.' And so they were. The first Boer War was already in the making, and England was beginning to find 'splendid isolation' a bit precarious. On 2 January 1896 came Jameson's raid in the Transvaal, and the next day the whole world was reading that incomparable masterpiece of diplomatic blundering, Kaiser Wilhelm's congratulatory telegram to the Boer leader Kreuger. There was a dramatic shift in English public opinion that the Government shortly reflected. On 25 January Joseph Chamberlain declared that war between the two English speaking nations would be an absurdity as well as a crime, and two weeks later Salisbury made a conciliatory statement in the House of Lords. After much secret diplomacy at London and Washington, a treaty was concluded between Great Britain and Venezuela submitting the boundary question to an arbitral tribunal, to be governed by the rule that 'adverse holding or prescription during a period of fifty years shall make a good title.' Thus Cleveland and Olney secured their principle that the whole territory in dispute should be subject to arbitration, and Salisbury his, that the British title to *de facto* possessions should not be questioned.

The tribunal, which included the Chief Justices of Great Britain and the United States, gave a unanimous decision in 1899, substantially along the line of the original British claim. So the Monroe Doctrine was vindicated, arbitration triumphed, and Anglo-American friendship restored. But outbursts of bad feeling like this always leave their mark; and the abusive language in the American press so affected Rudyard Kipling, then living in Vermont, that for the rest of his life references to the United States in his gifted writings were sarcastic and bitter.

2. *Manifest Destiny in the Nineties*

It is clear that in the nineties, the spirit of Manifest Destiny, long dormant, was once more abroad in the land. The precise manifestations of that destiny differed, but the idealogy was fundamentally the same as that which had animated an earlier generation. The phrase had once served as a rationalization for the conquest of Texas and California; it was now to serve as a rationalization for a 'large policy' in the Caribbean and the Far East. Now that the continent was conquered, it was obviously the ineluctable destiny of the United States to become a world power. 'Whether they will or no,' wrote Captain A. T. Mahan, the naval philosopher of the new imperialism, 'Americans must now begin to look outward.' The idea was echoed, in a great variety of forms, by a large number of politicians, business men, and scholars. The combination was irresistible. The scholars furnished the scientific and historical argument; the business men pointed to the potential profits; the politicians rang the changes on national honor and glory and party advantage. When, after a decade of tumult and shouting, the noise died down, the United States found herself in fact a world power, owning the extra-territorial possessions of Puerto Rico, Hawaii, Midway, Wake, Guam, Tutuila, and the Philippines, exercising protectorates over Cuba, Panama, and Nicaragua, and asserting interest and influence in the Far East.

The historical origins of this policy which within half a century carried the United States to world responsibility and world leadership are not without interest. That policy was merely one manifestation of a world-wide trend toward imperialism, and the rationalization which was furnished for it was equally common. Nowhere, however, was such rationalization more full-blown than in the United States. Captain Mahan, whose influence was world-wide, demonstrated in his brilliant series on the history of sea-power that not the meek, but those who possessed big and efficient navies, inherited the earth. Professor John W. Burgess popularized the German philosophy of nationalism and discovered that Teutonic and Anglo-Saxon nations were 'particularly endowed with the capacity for establishing national states, and are especially called to that work; and therefore, that they are intrusted, in the general economy of history, with the mission of conducting the political civilization of the modern world.' Sociologists like Frank H. Giddings thought nothing incompatible between Democracy and Empire. Even the clergy joined in the argument, and one missionary review announced confidently that 'to give the world the life more abundant both for here and hereafter is the duty of the American people by virtue of the call of God.'

It was the politicians and journalists, however, who gave imperialism the most enthusiastic support and energetic application. Nor were the political imperialists confined to any one party: Republicans, Democrats, and Populists alike joined in the hue and the cry for more land, more trade, and more power. Senator Henry Cabot Lodge analyzed for one of the popular magazines 'Our Blundering Foreign Policy,' and concluded that

> From the Rio Grande to the Arctic Ocean there should be but one flag and one country. . . . In the interests of our commerce . . . we should build the Nicaragua canal, and for the protection of that canal and for the sake of our commercial supremacy in the Pacific, we should control the Hawaiian islands and maintain our influence in Samoa. England has studded the West Indies with strong places which are a standing menace to our Atlantic seaboard. We should have among those islands at least one strong naval station, and when the Nicaragua canal is built, the island of Cuba . . . will become a necessity. . . .
>
> The tendency of modern times is toward consolidation. . . . Small states are of the past, and have no future. The great nations are rapidly absorbing for their future expansion and their present defence all the waste places of the earth. It is a movement which makes for civilization and the advancement of the race. As one of the great nations of the world the United States must not fall out of the line of march.

Other young Republicans like Theodore Roosevelt and Albert J. Beveridge were equally emphatic, but neither Democrats nor Populists were inclined to permit the Republicans to make political capital out of so popular an issue. Although Cleveland set his face sternly against imperialism, Democrats like Morgan of Alabama and Money of Mississippi and even Bryan supported an expansionist policy which was bound to eventuate in imperialism; Populists like Allen of Nebraska and Teller of Colorado were no less enthusiastic.

From the newspapers came the frankest expressions of imperialism and the most candid defense of a 'large policy.' It was not only the New York *Journal* and the New York *World* which fed the flames of chauvinism; throughout the country editors called upon Americans to take up new responsibilities. 'The subjugation of a continent,' wrote one Pacific coast journal, 'was sufficient to keep the American people busy at home for a century. . . . But now that the continent is subdued, we are looking for fresh worlds to conquer; and whether our conservative stay-at-homes like it or not, the colonizing instinct which has led our race in successive waves of emigration . . . is the instinct which is now pushing us out and on to Alaska, to the isles of the sea,—and beyond.' Some editors, like Pulitzer and Hearst, had circulation in mind, but most of those who clamored so loudly for expansion sincerely reflected what they thought to be the temper of the American people. And no better commentary on that temper was furnished than an editorial in the Washington *Post* published on the eve of the Spanish War:

> A new consciousness seems to have come upon us—the consciousness of strength—and with it a new appetite, the yearning to show our strength. . . . Ambition, interest, land hunger, pride, the mere joy of fighting, whatever it may be, we are animated by a new sensation. We are face to face with a strange destiny. The taste of Empire is in the mouth of the people even as the taste of blood in the jungle. It means an Imperial policy, the Republic, renascent, taking her place with the armed nations.

There is no doubt that the policy of expansion was popular in the late nineties, as in the forties and fifties. There was no need for Wall Street and big business to finance the movement or inspire propaganda; all they had to do was sit back and gather the fruit.

3. *Cuba Libre*

It was the Cuban revolution of 1895 that brought all of this chauvinism to a head, and furnished a focus for the imperialistic ambitions of the American people. From the days of Jefferson Cuba had been an object of peculiar interest to the United States, and regarded as properly within the American sphere of influence. As long as Spain owned the Island, most Americans were inclined to let matters rest, but the possibility of ultimate acquisition was never out of the minds of American statesmen. 'In looking forward to the probable course of events,' wrote John Quincy Adams, 'it is scarcely possible to resist the conviction that the annexation of Cuba to our Federal Republic will be indispensable to the continuance and integrity of the Union itself.' Polk had tried to purchase the Island, and the effort was renewed under the Pierce administration, but without results other than the aggravation of sectional hostilities in the United States. On the very eve of the Civil War a Senate Committee announced that 'the ultimate acquisition of Cuba may be considered a fixed purpose of the United States.' Yet curiously enough, when the opportunity came, during the Ten Years' War of 1868–78, the United States was coy.

That Ten Years' War was characterized by all the disorder, cruelty, and affronts to American interests and honor that later marked the course of the revolution of 1895. Yet in the first instance the United States carefully avoided any commitment to the cause of rebels, and in the second it entered the war on their side. How did it happen that the inhumanities of the sixties did not shock American sensibilities as did those of the nineties, that the spectacle of Spanish tyranny did not affront the spirit of American democracy in the sixties as in the nineties, and that the necessity for order and stability appeared so much less urgent in the earlier than in the later period? How did it happen that the murder of the crew of the *Virginius* in 1873 did not create a demand for war while the explosion of the *Maine* in 1898 was followed by a wave of war hysteria? How did it happen, finally, that the Destiny which necessitated American control of the Caribbean in the nineties, was not manifest in the sixties? The explanation of this change in the temper of the people and in the policy of the government is three-fold.

In the first place the technique of journalism had become enormously elaborated and the methods of journalism increasingly sensational. Newspaper editors found that circulation responded to atrocity stories, and it became immensely profitable to exploit them. The New York *World* and the New York *Journal,* then engaged in a titanic struggle for circulation, were the worst offenders in the business of pandering to the popular taste for sensation, but they were by no means alone. Most of the metropolitan papers throughout the country bought news service from the New York papers, and most of them subscribed to the Associated Press which served up daily concoctions of atrocities for the delectation of the public. For three years, from 1895 to 1898, this campaign of propaganda went on until at last the American people were brought to the point where they demanded intervention on behalf of 'humanity.'

In the second place the economic stake of the United States in Cuba had increased enormously during these thirty years. That economic stake did not consist merely of the fifty million dollars invested in Cuban sugar and mining industries, though these investments were important. More important was our trade with Cuba which by 1893 had passed the hundred million dollar mark, and all the varied business and shipping interests dependent upon that trade. Finally the American people and American business had adjusted themselves to the Cuban sugar economy; the destruction of the Cuban sugar industry which resulted from the insurrection seriously affected that adjustment. As the American Minister to Spain told one of his diplomatic colleagues: 'the sugar industry of Cuba is as vital to our people as are the wheat and cotton of India and Egypt to Great Britain.'

In the third place the United States had developed a new set of world interests which made it seem necessary that the entire Caribbean area be under American control. American interests in the Pacific and the Far East enhanced the importance of an Isthmian canal, and the prospect of having to defend an Isthmian canal made the islands that guarded the route strategically important. A big navy was necessary to protect our far-flung island possessions; new island possessions were necessary in order to provide harbors and coaling stations for our navy. Cuba was not the only object of American concern in the Cabibbean area. During this same decade President Cleveland asserted the Monroe Doctrine on behalf of Venezuela; Senator Morgan championed a Nicaraguan canal; Senator Lodge agitated the purchase of the Danish West Indies; and the State Department considered a revival of the proposal to lease Samana Bay in Santo Domingo.

It is in the light of these changing attitudes and interests that we must interpret the events leading up to the War of 1898. That war was fought ostensibly for the liberation of Cuba, but it did not begin until the Cubans had already fought three years for their own liberation. The fundamental cause of the Cuban revolution which broke out in 1895 was Spanish political oppression and economic exploitation; the immediate cause was the prostration of the sugar and tobacco industries which resulted from the operation of tariffs, both in the United States and in Spain. The McKinley tariff, by raising duties on tobacco and abolishing the duty on raw sugar, dealt a heavy blow to the Cuban tobacco planters and encouraged the extension of sugar plantations. Between 1889 and 1894 the production of sugar increased from 630,000 tons to 1,054,000 tons. The following year the Wilson tariff which taxed sugar up to 40 per cent went into operation, and the bottom fell out of the sugar market. The price of sugar which had been eight cents in 1884 fell to two cents in 1895. The consequent poverty and misery in Cuba furnished the impetus to the revolution.

From the very beginning the United States was inextricably involved in the Cuban revolution. With a Cuban 'junta' established in New York, spreading propaganda and selling bonds, and with scores of filibustering expeditions setting out from American ports, the United States found it difficult to enforce neutrality. Americans with property interests in Cuba clamored for intervention to protect those interests; Cubans with suspiciously fresh citizenship papers, claimed the protection of the United States government. When, within a fortnight of the outbreak of war, a Spanish gunboat fired upon an American vessel, the *Alliance,* an outburst of jingoism revealed the temper of the country. 'It is time,' said Senator Cullom of Illinois, 'that some one woke up and realized the necessity of annexing some property,' and this point of view was echoed by others no less prominent in public life. Thereafter one incident after another aggravated the relations between the United States and Spain and excited American sympathies for the insurrectionists, and when there was a dearth of such incidents, they were brazenly fabricated by the yellow press.

In the face of this demand for intervention, President Cleveland remained imperturbable and unmoved. He issued a proclamation of neutrality, recognizing the existence of a state of rebellion but not the belligerency of the rebels, and he did his best to enforce neutrality laws and protect American interests. Beyond that he would not go, and when Congress, in April 1896, passed a concurrent resolution recognizing the belligerency of the Cubans, Cleveland ignored it. To a friend who visited him in the summer of 1896 he confessed that 'he was willing to go a great way in insisting upon humanity — in fact, he feared there were some outrages upon both sides, if the truth were known. But in a general way he felt it incumbent upon him to be extremely careful; as the public mind seemed to be in an inflammable state, and a spark might kindle a conflagration. . . . There seemed to be an epidemic of insanity in the country just at this time.' Yet by the end of that year even Cleveland's patience had been strained well-nigh to the breaking point, and in his annual message to Congress he warned Spain that

> when it is demonstrated that her sovereignty is extinct in Cuba for all purposes of its rightful existence, and when a hopeless struggle for its re-establishment has degenerated into a strife which means nothing more than the useless sacrifice of human life and the utter destruction of the very subject matter of conflict, a situation will be presented in which our obligations to the sovereignty of Spain will be superseded by higher obligations, which we can hardly hesitate to recognize and discharge.

McKinley had been elected on a platform calling for Cuban independence, yet at first he too moved with the greatest circumspection. 'You may be sure,' he confided to Carl Schurz, 'that there will be no jingo nonsense under my administration,' and shortly after his inauguration he pledged his opposition 'to all acquisitions of territory not on the main land, Cuba, Hawaii, San Domingo, or any other.' In September 1897 McKinley tendered the good offices of the United States to restore peace to Cuba, but though a new and more liberal government had come to power in Spain, the American overture was rejected. But the Spanish government did inaugurate some long overdue reforms. General Weyler, who had earned the unenviable title of 'Butcher Weyler,' was recalled; the policy of herding Cubans into concentration camps, where many of them died of disease and mistreatment, was disavowed; all political rights enjoyed by peninsular Spaniards were extended to the Cubans, and a program looking to eventual home rule for Cuba was inaugurated.

Home rule no longer satisfied the Cubans. Reforms which might have headed off the revolution had they been offered in 1895, were now unacceptable and the war of extermination continued. Yet the sincere desire of the Spanish government for peace did much to mollify the attitude of the American government if not of the American people. In his annual message of December 1897 McKinley repudiated the idea of intervention and urged that Spain 'be given a reasonable chance to realize her expectations and to prove the asserted efficacy of the new order of things to which she stands irrevocably committed.' It was not to the interest, however, of the Cuban junta or of the American press to permit a policy of neutrality, and on 9 February 1898 the New York *Journal* printed a private letter from the Spanish Minister, Enrique de Lôme, which had been stolen from the Havana post-office. 'McKinley's message,' wrote the tactless Minister, 'I regard as bad. Besides the ingrained and inevitable bluntness with which is repeated all that the press and public opinion in Spain have said about Weyler, it once more shows what McKinley is, weak and a bidder for the admiration of the crowd, besides being a would-be-politician who tries to leave a door open behind himself while keeping on good terms with the jingoes of his party.' De Lôme resigned at once, but the relations of the United States and Spain were exacerbated.

At this juncture the nation was horrified by the news that in the night of 15 February 1898 the battleship *Maine* was blown up in Havana harbor with the loss of 260 lives. 'Public opinion,' Captain Sigsbee wired, 'should be suspended until further report,' but when a naval court of inquiry reported that the cause of the disaster was an external explosion by a submarine mine, 'Remember the Maine!' went from lip to lip. Without a dissenting vote Congress rushed through a bill appropriating fifty million dollars for national defense, and McKinley sent to Madrid what turned out to be his ultimatum, suggesting an immediate armistice, the final revocation of the concentration policy, and American mediation between Spain and Cuba. Spain's formal reply was unsatisfactory, but the Sagasta government, anxious to avoid war, moved toward peace with a celerity unusual at Madrid. Orders were given revoking the concentration policy and a desperate effort was made to persuade the Pope to request a suspension of hostilities — a request to which the Spanish government could agree without loss of face. The American Minister at Madrid cabled to know whether such a solution would be satisfactory to McKinley. 'I believe,' he said, 'that this means peace, which the sober judgment of our people will approve long before next November and which must be approved at the bar of final history. I believe that you will approve this last conscientious effort for peace.' But McKinley's reply was noncommittal. On 9 April the Spanish government caved in completely; hostilities were suspended, and the American Minister cabled from Madrid that if nothing were done to humiliate Spain further the Cuban question could be settled in accordance with American demands.

Any President with a backbone would have seized this opportunity for an honorable solution. McKinley, a veteran of 1861, was averse from war. Mark Hanna, Wall Street, big business, and the leaders of the Republican Old Guard backed him up. With such support McKinley needed less firmness than John Adams had shown in the XYZ affair or Grant in the *Alabama* case to preserve peace. But Congress, the press, and the country were clamoring for war. Theodore Roosevelt wrote in a private letter, 'the blood of the murdered men of the Maine calls not for indemnity but for the full measure of atonement, which can only come by driving the Spaniard from the New World.' McKinley became obsessed with the notion that if he did not give way, he would forfeit his leadership in the party. After much prayer and hesitation, he decided to yield to popular demand. One year later he recorded his conviction that 'if he had been left alone, he could have concluded an arrangement with the Spanish government under which the Spanish troops would have withdrawn from Cuba without a war.'

On 11 April the President sent Congress the war message which he had already prepared. At the very conclusion of that message he added a casual reference to the fact that Madrid had capitulated on every point at issue.

> This fact, with every other pertinent consideration, will, I am sure, have your just and careful attention in the solemn deliberations upon which you are about to enter. If this measure attains a successful result, then our aspirations as a Christian, peace-loving people will be realized. If it fails, it will be only another justification for our contemplated action.

That action, of course, was war.

4. *Exit Spain*

Light-heartedly the United States entered upon a war that brought quick returns in glory, but new and heavy responsibilities. It was emphatically a popular war. Although imperialistic in result, it was not so in motive, as far as the vast majority of its supporters were concerned. To the Joint Resolution of 20 April 1898, authorizing the use of the armed forces of the nation to liberate Cuba, had been added the Teller Amendment, declaring that 'The United States hereby disclaims any disposition or intention to exercise sovereignty, jurisdiction or control over the said Island, except for the pacification thereof, and asserts its determination, when that is accomplished, to leave the government and control of the Island to its people.'

No one who lived through them will forget those gay days of 1898. With what generous ardor the young men rushed to the colors to free Cuba, while the bands crashed out the chords of Sousa's *Stars and Stripes Forever!* And what a comfortable feeling of unity the country obtained at last, when Democrats vied in patriotism with Republicans, when the South proved equally ardent for the fight, and Joe Wheeler, the gallant cavalry leader of the Confederacy, became a high commander of the United States army in Cuba! It was more close and personal to Americans than World War I; it was their own little show for independence, fair play, and hip-hurrah democracy, against all that was tyrannical, treacherous, and fetid in the Old World. How they enjoyed the discomfiture of the continental powers, and how they appreciated the hearty good will of England! Every ship of the smart little navy, from the powerful *Oregon,* steaming at full speed round the Horn to be in time for the big fight, to the absurd 'dynamite cruiser' *Vesuvius,* was known by picture and reputation to every American boy. And what heroes the war correspondents created — Hobson who sunk the *Merrimac,* Lieutenant Rowan who delivered the message to Garcia, Commodore Dewey ('You may fire when ready, Gridley'), blaspheming Bob Evans of the *Iowa,* Captain Philip of the *Texas* ('Don't cheer, boys, the poor fellows are dying'), and Teddy Roosevelt with his horseless Rough Riders![2]

[2] Roosevelt's volume celebrating the deeds of the Rough Riders was the inspiration for one of Mr. Dooley's happiest comments:

'I haven't time f'r to tell ye the wurruk Tiddy did in ar-hmin' an' equippin' himself, how he fed himself, how he steadied himself in battles an' encouraged himself with a few well-chosen worruds whin th' sky was darkest. Ye'll have to take a squint into the book ye'erself to l'arn thim things.'

'I won't do it,' said Mr. Hennessy. 'I think Tiddy Rosenfelt is all r-right an' if he wants to blow his horn lave him do it.'

'True f'r ye,' said Mr. Dooley. . . . 'But if I was him I'd call th' book "Alone in Cubia".'

This was no war of waiting and endurance, of fruitless loss and hope deferred. On the first day of May, one week after the declaration, Dewey steams into Manila Bay with the Pacific squadron and without losing a man reduces the Spanish fleet to old junk. The Fifth Army Corps safely lands in Cuba, and wins three battles in quick succession. Admiral Cervera's fleet issues from Santiago Bay and in a few hours' running fight is completely smashed, with the loss of a single American sailor. Ten weeks' fighting, and the United States had wrested an empire from Spain.

Prince Bismarck is said to have remarked, just before his death, that there was a special providence for drunkards, fools, and the United States of America. On paper Spain was a formidable power. If the United States had more battleships, she had more armored cruisers and torpedo craft. Spain had almost 200,000 troops in Cuba before the war. The American regular army was as good as any in the world, but included less than 28,000 officers and men, scattered in small detachments from the Yukon to Key West. So weak were the harbor defenses of the Atlantic coast, and so apprehensive were the people of bombardment, that the North Atlantic fleet was divided: the one half blockading Havana, and the other, reassuringly called 'the Flying Squadron,' stationed at Hampton Roads. Against any other nation such strategy might have been disastrous. But the Spanish navy was inconceivably neglected, ill-armed, and untrained; while the United States navy — a new creation of the last fifteen years — was smart, disciplined, and efficient. John D. Long, Secretary of the Navy, was honest and intelligent; and when the energetic assistant secretary, Roosevelt, left to lead the Rough Riders, his place on the board of naval strategy was taken by Captain Mahan.

In a military sense the United States was entirely unprepared. An elderly jobbing politician was at the head of the War Department. There were enough Krag rifles for the Regulars, but the 200,000 volunteers, whom the President insisted on calling to the colors, received Springfields and black powder. There was no khaki cloth in the country, and thousands of troops fought a summer campaign in Cuba, clothed in the heavy blue uniform of winter garrison duty. The Commissary Department was disorganized, and soldiers complained that they were fed on 'embalmed beef.' Volunteers neglected even such principles of camp sanitation as were laid down in Deuteronomy, and for every one of the 289 men killed or mortally wounded in battle, thirteen died of disease. Transporting eighteen thousand men to Cuba caused more confusion than conveying two million men to France twenty years later. The Regulars were encamped at Tampa, Florida, but there was no adequate railroad connection between Tampa and Port Tampa, nine miles distant, and no adequate pier or transport facilities at the latter place. General Miles recorded his impression of conditions at Tampa:

> Several of the volunteer regiments came here without arms, and some without blankets, tents, or camp equipage. The 32nd Michigan, which is among the best, came without arms. General Guy V. Henry reports that five regiments under his command are not fit to go into the field. There are over 300 cars loaded with war material along the roads about Tampa. . . . To illustrate the confusion, fifteen cars loaded with uniforms were side-tracked twenty-five miles away from Tampa, and remained there for weeks while the troops were suffering for clothing. Five thousand rifles, which were discovered yesterday, were needed by several regiments. Also, the different parts of the siege train and ammunition for the same, which will be required immediately on landing, are scattered through hundreds of cars on the side-tracks of the railroads.

Yet the little expeditionary force which finally got under way was allowed to land on the beach at Daiquiri without opposition (20–25 June), and the Captain-General of Cuba, with six weeks' warning, almost 200,000 men in the Island, and 13,000 in the city of Santiago, was able to concentrate only 1,700 on the battlefields of Las Guasimas, El Caney, and San Juan, against 15,000 Americans. These 1,700 Spaniards, well armed and entrenched, gave an excellent account of themselves, and helped to promote Theodore Roosevelt from a colonelcy to the Presidency.

It was the Navy, however, that clinched the conquest of Cuba. Late in April the Spanish Admiral, Cervera, with four armored cruisers and three destroyers, had steamed out of the Cape Verde Islands to destinations unknown. There was panic all along the Atlantic coast, and the timid men hurried their valuables to points of safety well in the interior. But Cervera was not bound on offensive operations. On 19 May he sneaked into the narrow land-locked harbor of Santiago Bay, and was promptly bottled up by the American navy under Admiral Sampson and Commodore Schley. With the army closing in on Santiago, Cervera had no alternatives but surrender or escape, and he chose the latter. On 3 July the Spanish battle-fleet sailed forth from Santiago Bay to death and destruction:

Haste to do now what must be done anon
Or some mad hope of selling triumph dear
Drove the ships forth: soon was *Teresa* gone
Furór, Plutón, Vizcaya, Oquendo, and *Colón.*[8]

There never was such a Fourth of July in America as that Monday in 1898 when the news came through. Santiago surrendered on the 16th and except for a military promenade in Puerto Rico, which Mr. Dooley described as 'Gin'ral Miles' Gran' Picnic and Moonlight Excursion,' the war was over.

But the most important event of the war had occurred not in the Caribbean but in the Far East. Two months before the actual declaration of war Theodore Roosevelt, then assistant secretary of the Navy, had taken it upon himself to outline naval strategy and direct national policy. On 25 February he had cabled to Commodore Dewey in command of the Asiatic Squadron: 'Secret and confidential. Order squadron to Hong Kong. Keep full of coal. In the event of declaration of war Spain, your duty will be to see that the Spanish squadron does not leave the Asiatic coast, and then offensive operations in Philippine Islands. Keep Olympia until further orders.' As soon as war was declared, Dewey set out under full steam for the Philippines, and on the night of 30 April he slipped through the narrow channel of Boca Grande and into the spacious waters of Manila Bay, where a Spanish fleet was anchored. Gridley fired when ready; they all fired; and when the smoke and mist cleared away it was apparent that the Spanish fleet had been utterly destroyed. Dewey moved on the shore batteries, which promptly displayed a white flag, and the battle of Manila Bay was over. Not until 13 August — one day after the signing of the peace protocol did an American expeditionary force, with the support of Aguinaldo's Filipino army, take the city of Manila.

The collapse of her military and naval power everywhere forced Spain to sue for terms of peace. McKinley dictated them on 30 July — immediate evacuation and definite relinquishment of Cuba, cession of Puerto Rico, and an island in the Ladrones, and occupation of the city, harbor, and bay of Manila pending the final disposition of the Philippine Islands. Spain signed a preliminary peace to that effect on 12 August, sadly protesting, 'This demand strips us of the very last memory of a glorious past and expels us . . . from the Western

[8] 'Spain in America' in *Poems* by George Santayana, p. 118. Scribner's.

Hemisphere, which became peopled and civilized through the proud deeds of our ancestors.' But John Hay wrote to his friend Theodore Roosevelt in a very different vein: 'It has been a splendid little war; begun with the highest motives, carried on with magnificent intelligence and spirit, favored by that fortune which loves the brave.'

XIV

THE AMERICAN COLONIAL EMPIRE
1898–1913

1. *The Fruits of Victory*

IN the formal peace negotiations which began at Paris on 1 October 1898, the United States was represented by a Commission consisting of Whitelaw Reid, editor of the powerful New York *Tribune,* Secretary of State Day, and three Senators. Four of these commissioners had already committed themselves to a 'large policy' of imperialism and expansion; the fifth, Senator Gray, came around eventually to the majority point of view. To the American demand for the independence of Cuba and the cession of Puerto Rico and Guam, the Spanish representatives interposed no objections, and they even agreed to assume the Cuban debt of some four hundred million dollars. The question of the disposition of the Philippines, however, offered serious difficulties. If they had been contented under Spanish rule, there would have been no question of annexing them. An insurrection had just been partially suppressed when the Spanish War broke out, but Dewey had encouraged Emilio Aguinaldo, leader of the *insurrectos,* to return from exile after the battle of Manila Bay; and on the fall of the city of Manila, the Filipino leader had organized the 'Visayan Republic' in the province of Luzon and made a bid for foreign recognition. The obvious thing to do was to turn the Philippines over to the Filipinos, as Cuba to the Cubans. But Dewey cabled that the 'republic' represented only a faction, and was unable to keep order within its nominal sphere. Yet the fact remained that Aguinaldo represented government in the Islands, and that if the United States expected to retain the Philippines it would first have to conquer them.

McKinley was in a quandary. In his message of December 1897 he had laid down with respect to Cuba the rule that 'forcible annexation . . . can not be thought of. That, by our code of morality, would be criminal aggression.' Did the same rule hold good for the Philippines? The question was to be answered not by logic, but by a combination of interest and emotion. Already the newspapers had discovered that 'the commercial and industrial interests of America, learning that the islands lie in the gateway of the vast and undeveloped markets of the Orient, say, " Keep the Philippines." ' Already navalists were emphasizing the military importance of the Islands and suggesting the danger to American interests should Germany or Japan annex them. Already popular feeling was being aroused by the cry, 'Don't haul down the flag,' and when McKinley returned from a trip through the Middle West he found 'a very general feeling that the United States is in a situation where it cannot let go.' The President's instructions to the Peace Commission presented all of these considerations:

> The Philippines stand upon a different basis. The presence and success of our arms at Manila imposes upon us obligations which we cannot disregard. The march of events rules and overrules human action. . . . We cannot be unmindful that, without any desire or design on our part, the war has brought us new duties and responsibilities which we must meet and discharge as becomes a great nation. . . . Incidental to our tenure in the Philippines is the commercial opportunity to which American statesmanship cannot be indifferent.

Yet there were still several alternatives. The United States might simply guarantee and protect the independence of the Philippines as it was to guarantee and protect the independence of Cuba. It might take only the island of Luzon, leaving the rest of the archipelago to the Filipinos. Or it might annex all the Philippines. McKinley hesitated long and prayerfully, but finally concluded to fulfil manifest destiny by taking them all. 'One night it came to me this way,' he told his Methodist brethren, '(1) that we could not turn them over to France or Germany, our commercial rivals in the Orient — that would be bad business and discreditable; (2) that we could not give them back to Spain — that would be cowardly and dishonorable; (3) that we could not leave them to themselves — they were unfit for self-government, and they would soon have anarchy and misrule over there worse than Spain's was; and (4) that there was nothing left for us to do but take them all, and to educate the Filipinos and uplift and Christianize them.' So Spain was required to part with the Islands for twenty million dollars, and on 10 December 1898 the Treaty of Paris was signed, and the United States became, officially, a world power.

But the prospect of the annexation of an alien people without their consent aroused the fierce indignation of many Americans who thought it a monstrous perversion of the ideals which had inspired our crusade for Cuba. Old-fashioned Senators like Hoar of Massachusetts girded on their armor to fight for the principles of the Declaration of Independence, and for two months the fate of the Treaty hung in suspense. Lodge led the fight for ratification, and he was particularly concerned with the disgrace involved in repudiating what the President, through his envoys, had concluded in Paris. 'I confess,' he wrote, 'I cannot think calmly of the rejection of that Treaty by a little more than one-third of the Senate. It would be a repudiation of the President and humiliation of the whole country in the eyes of the world, and would show we are unfit as a nation to enter into great questions of foreign policy.' The administration invoked patronage and party regularity to save the Treaty, and in its efforts, it received unexpected aid from William Jennings Bryan. Bryan was unalterably opposed to imperialism, but he thought that a question of such magnitude as this should be decided on its own merits, and not as part of the general question of peace, and that it should be submitted to the verdict of the people at large.[1] On 6 February 1899 the necessary two-thirds majority for ratification was obtained, but Lodge called it 'the hardest fight I have ever known.'

McKinley, in 1897, had rejected a proposal to buy Cuba because he did not care to buy an insurrection; the United States now found that it had purchased, for twenty million dollars, a first-class Filipino insurrection. For the Filipinos, who had been good Catholics for over three centuries, did not wish to be 'uplifted and Christianized' by the Americans; but when on 4 February 1899 Aguinaldo's troops disregarded the command of an American sentry to halt, the United States army undertook to 'civilize them with a Krag.' Before the Philippine insurrection was stamped out it had cost the United States almost as many lives as the Spanish War, and more scandals; for a war between white soldiers and semi-civilized men of color is something worse than what Sherman said it was. Within a short time the United States found itself doing in the Philippines precisely what it had condemned Spain for doing in Cuba. Soon stories of reconcentration camps and 'water-cures' began to trickle back to the United States, and public opinion, already highly sceptical of a venture dubious alike in origin, method, and purpose, became inflamed. The result was a vigorous anti-imperialism crusade which commanded the support of men from all parties and all walks of life. It was not inappropriate that the nineteenth century should be

1 That Bryan was primarily interested in creating a campaign issue is unfounded.

ushered out with a passionate appeal to the Declaration of Independence, and the twentieth century ushered in with a victory for the forces of imperialism.

Never in our history had any reform movement attracted a more distinguished group of supporters than that which rallied to the banner of anti-imperialism. Party lines were disregarded: Republicans like Senators Hoar and Edmunds, Secretary Sherman, and Speaker Reed joined hands with Democrats like Cleveland and Bryan, Ben Tillman and John G. Carlisle. Samuel Gompers spoke for labor, and Andrew Carnegie paid the bills. The press was represented by E. L. Godkin of *The Nation* and Bowles of the Springfield *Republican*. President Eliot of Harvard spoke for the intellectuals of New England and President David Starr Jordan of Leland Stanford combatted jingoism on the Pacific coast. Philosophers like William James, historians like John Burgess, clergymen like Henry Van Dyke, social workers like Jane Addams, all worked together for a common cause. Effective aid came from the men of letters. Mark Twain was deeply embittered by our conquest of the Philippines, and in his letter 'To the Person Sitting in Darkness' he charged McKinley with 'playing the European game' of imperialism, and suggested that Old Glory should now have 'the white stripes painted black and the stars replaced by the skull and cross bones.' Through the inimitable Mr. Dooley, Finley P. Dunne passed in scathing review the whole imperialistic venture, and soon the whole country was laughing at his observation that ' 'tis not more thin two months since ye larned whether they were islands or canned goods,' and pondering his conclusion that 'they'se wan consolation; an' that is, if th' American people can govern thimsilves, they can govern anything that walks.' But the most powerful indictment of imperialism came from the young poet, William Vaughn Moody. In 'An Ode in Time of Hesitation,' he appealed from the chauvinistic spirit of the nineties to the idealism of the sixties:

> Lies! lies! It cannot be! The wars we wage
> Are noble, and our battles still are won
> By justice for us, ere we lift the gage.
> We have not sold our loftiest heritage.
> The proud republic hath not stooped to cheat
> And scramble in the market-place of war . . .
> Ah no!
> We have not fallen so.

We are our fathers' sons: let those who lead us know! . . .
We charge you, ye who lead us,
Breathe on their chivalry no hint of stain!
Turn not their new-world victories to gain!
One least leaf plucked for chaffer from the bays
Of their dear praise,
One jot of their pure conquest put to hire,
The implacable republic will require . . .
That insult deep we deeply will requite.
Tempt not our weakness, our cupidity!
For save we let the island men go free,
Those baffled and dislaureled ghosts
Will curse us from the lamentable coasts
Where walk the frustrate dead . . .
O ye who lead,
Take heed!
Blindness we may forgive, but baseness we will smite.

The argument against the annexation of the Philippines rested not only on an old-fashioned repugnance to government without the consent of the governed and a humanitarian revulsion against the manner in which the war of conquest was conducted, but on political, constitutional, and economic grounds as well. It was observed that the possession of colonies in the Pacific would require for their protection a larger military and naval establishment and would involve us in the whole complex of Far Eastern politics; and the observation was sound. It was pointed out that the conquest, defense, and administration of the Philippines would cost us far more than the Islands would ever bring; and the prediction proved to be correct. It was alleged that the flouting of the principles of democracy in the Philippines would impair the vitality and integrity of democracy at home; and the prophecy was not unjustified. Finally it was argued that the Constitution did not permit the acquisition of extraterritorial possessions and the government of alien peoples without their consent. This last argument was eventually rejected by the Supreme Court, but in a series of decisions so bewildering and so contradictory that no one has ever been able to understand their logic.

Bryan's leadership of the Democratic party was unchallenged and he determined to make imperialism the paramount issue of the campaign of 1900. The Democratic platform announced that all governments instituted among men derive their just powers from the consent of the governed; that any government not based upon the consent of the governed is a tyranny; to impose upon any people a government of force is to substitute the methods of imperialism for those of a republic.

The Republicans were glad to accept this issue, and they went before the electorate with the rallying-cry, 'Don't haul down the flag.' 'Who,' asked Bryan, in vain, 'will haul down the President?' But the real issue of the election was not imperialism, but prosperity. The Republicans held all the trump cards, and played them well. An upswing in foreign trade and the discovery of extensive new gold deposits had enabled them to settle the money question. Under the benevolent protection of the Dingley tariff of 1897 industry was flourishing and wages up. Higher prices for wheat, corn, and cotton allayed agricultural discontent, and McKinley's claim to be the 'advance agent of prosperity' appeared to be justified. The Republican party had carried the nation through a victorious war and raised its prestige in the eyes of the world. There was no inclination to repudiate the results of that war or the party that capitalized those results. The country was prosperous and contented and weary of idealism. The election proved that Bryan had misjudged the temper of the American people just as Wilson misjudged the popular temper in 1920. McKinley's victory was far more impressive in 1900 than it had been in 1896; in the electoral college he received 292 votes to 155 for Bryan, and his popular plurality was almost nine hundred thousand.

2. *The Supreme Court Follows the Election Returns*

The annexation of extra-continental territory, already thickly populated by alien peoples, created new problems in American politics and government. The petty islands and guano rocks that had already been annexed had never raised, as Puerto Rico and the Philippines did, the embarrassing question of whether the Constitution followed the flag, or the equally embarrassing question of the nature and extent of Congressional control. The Treaty of Paris had provided that 'The civil rights and political status of the native inhabitants hereby ceded to the United States shall be determined by Congress' but this provision threw little light on the subject. Opinions of the Supreme Court in the 'Insular Cases' left the status of the new possessions very muddled, but eventually, as in the British Empire, a theory was evolved from practice. Insular possessions are of two categories: incorporated and unincorporated; and the question of what constitutes incorporation is one to be determined on the basis of fact and intention as revealed in Congressional legislation. Thus Alaska is held to be incorporated,[2] but Puerto Rico is unincorporated, and this despite the fact that since 1917 its inhabitants have been citizens of the United States.[3] Unincorporated territories are not foreign, however, and their exports are not controlled by American customs duties unless by special act of Congress.[4] But Congress may, nevertheless, impose such duties as it sees fit.[5] This meant, according to Chief Justice Fuller, that

> if an organized and settled province of another sovereignty is acquired by the United States, Congress has the power to keep it like a disembodied shade, in an intermediate state of ambiguous existence for an indefinite period; and more than that, that after it has been called from that limbo, commerce with it is absolutely subject to the will of Congress, irrespective of constitutional provisions.

Thus the Republican party was able to eat its cake and have it; to indulge in territorial expansion, and yet maintain the tariff wall against such insular products as sugar and tobacco which might compete with the home-grown products.

The question of the civil and political rights of the inhabitants of these new territorial possessions was even more perplexing. Organic acts of Congress are the constitutions of the Philippines, Hawaii, and Puerto Rico, but to what extent was Congress bound, in passing these acts, and the Courts, in interpreting them, by the provisions of the Constitution? How far, in short, did the Constitution follow the flag? To this question the Court returned an ingenious answer. It neatly distinguished between 'fundamental' rights and 'formal' or 'procedural' rights. Fundamental rights are extended to all who come under the sovereignty of the United States, but mere procedural rights, such as trial by jury or indictment by grand jury, are not extended to the inhabitants of unincorporated territories unless Congress chooses so to extend them.[6] Thus, in fact,

2 Rasmussen *v.* United States, 197 U.S. 516 (1905).

3 Balzac *v.* Porto Rico, 258 U.S. 298 (1924).

4 De Lima *v.* Bidwell, 182 U.S. 1 (1901).

5 Hawaii *v.* Mankichi, 190 U.S. 197 (1903). Dorr *v.* U.S., 195 U.S. 138 (1904). Balzac *v.* Porto Rico, 258 U.S. 298 (1922).

6 See cases noted in 5.

the President and Congress, though limited in power within the United States, are absolute and sovereign over American dependencies. The parallel with the old British Empire is suggestive; and the government at Washington, like that of England, has been reluctant to admit the existence of an Empire. No colonial office has ever been established or colonial secretary appointed, and the administration of our colonies has been characterized by diversity and opportunism.

3. *The American Colonial System*

Cuba was not a colony, but until 1902 the Island was ruled by the United States army, with General Leonard Wood as military governor. The outstanding feature of this military régime was the remarkable clean-up of Havana under the direction of Major William C. Gorgas which cut the average annual death rate in half. In 1900 came one of the worst yellow-fever epidemics in years. A commission of four army surgeons under Dr. Walter Reed was appointed to investigate the cause. Working on the theory advanced by a Cuban physician, Dr. Carlos Finlay, they proved that the pest was transmitted by the stegomyia mosquito; and two of them, Dr. James Caroll and Dr. Jesse W. Lazear, proved it with their lives. Major Gorgas then declared war on the mosquito; and in 1901 there was not a single case of yellow fever in Havana. One of the greatest scourges of the tropics was at last under control.

By the Teller Amendment the United States had disclaimed any intention of exercising sovereignty over Cuba, and had promised to leave the government in the hands of the Cuban people. Few persons in Europe expected the United States to live up to this altruistic promise, and many Americans regarded it with scepticism. But on the conclusion of the war General Wood provided for the meeting of a constitutional convention to draw up a form of government. The convention met in November 1900 and drafted a constitution modelled upon that of the United States, but without any provision for future relations with that country. The American Government was unwilling to acquiesce in this situation, and discreet pressure was applied to induce the Cubans to add a series of provisions known collectively as the Platt Amendment, and formulated by Roosevelt's Secretary of War, Elihu Root. The chief provisions of the Platt Amendment were those giving to the United States an ultimate veto over the diplomatic and fiscal relations of Cuba with foreign powers, and recognizing the right to 'intervene for the preservation of Cuban independence, the maintenance of a government adequate for the protection of life, property, and individual liberty, and for discharging the obligations with respect to Cuba imposed by the Treaty of Paris on the United States.' The right of intervention was first exercised in 1906, upon demand of the President of Cuba. A provisional government was established under American authority, a new election was held, and the Island was eventually evacuated in 1909. But this was merely the first of a series of interventions. In 1912 President Taft thought it necessary to send marines to Cuba to protect American interests, and five years later President Wilson, despite his public repudiation of 'dollar diplomacy' followed the example of his two predecessors. During World War I Cuba experienced an unprecedented prosperity, but that prosperity was accompanied by extravagance and corruption. At the close of the war, the Cuban sugar market collapsed, and Cuban politics reflected the economic and financial disorder. At the request of Cuban liberals and of American investors, President Wilson sent a personal representative, General Enoch H. Crowder, to help the Cubans out of their difficulties. Crowder, for all his extraordinary abilities, was only partially successful; and when prosperity returned, he was discredited by the Cuban nationalists who resented his extra-legal status and who feared the economic implications of his advisory activities. His anomalous position was soon regularized by his appointment as Ambassador to Cuba, and thereafter, Cuban-American relations were on a more normal basis. Under the long reign of Machado unrest was chronic, but even when that unrest flamed into revolution, the United States avoided any official intervention. The fact is that by the nineteen-twenties the rising tide of Cuban nationalism made any intervention in Cuban affairs a highly dangerous business. There was a growing feeling, even during the Coolidge and Hoover administrations, that the Platt Amendment had outlived its usefulness. In 1934, President F. D. Roosevelt quietly negotiated a treaty with the liberal Mendieta administration abrogating the Platt Amendment.

Yet while the United States has withdrawn from Cuba politically, she has vastly extended her interests economically. Indeed Cuba is today an economic dependency of American utilities, railroads, mining, sugar, and tobacco interests. American investments in Cuba, which on the eve of the Spanish War totalled only some 50 million dollars, increased, in the next forty years, to over 1.2 billion. This enormous investment was controlled in large part by a few banking houses, the most powerful of which was the National City Bank of New York. This American economic penetration brought stability and some prosperity to Cuba, but it largely destroyed the economic freedom of the Island. What this meant to the average Cuban was stated with some exaggeration by a Cuban editor:

> Twenty-five years ago the rural Cuban squatted on the piece of land which produced most of what he needed for food and shelter with perhaps something extra which he could exchange for rice and cloth. The coming of the sugar industry on a large scale has completely changed his world. He now finds himself a part of a great industrial enterprise from which he receives his wages and which furnishes him a house. It has placed him in the stream of modern industrial progress. But he has no part in directing this industrial giant; he has no voice in its management. Yet to it he must look for education, recreation, and bread. . . . His future is not his own. It is determined for him in a directors' room in New York.[7]

Since the 1930's the growth of powerful trades unions, the enactment of enlightened social and labor legislation, and a rigorous control of sugar exports have combined to change this situation for the better.

Puerto Rico, like Cuba, was governed for a time by the United States military, but in 1900 the Foraker Act established civil government of the old crown colony type: an elective assembly, with an executive council appointed by the President, acting as upper house. Political parties quickly developed, the American governors were unable to keep neutral, and deadlocks came over the budget. This particular difficulty was solved by a law permitting the governor to reënact the previous appropriation, but such an arrangement was unsatisfactory to the Islanders. Another organic act, in 1917, granted American citizenship and a semi-responsible government, but the demand for complete home rule was still unanswered. From the beginning the Island was handicapped by a decrepit and unsatisfactory system of law and local government, an archaic economic order, and a densely overcrowded population of landless peasants enervated by hookworm and discouraged by the fluctuations of the sugar industry. There has been, under American rule, the usual advance in education, sanitation, and roads, and the usual increase in wealth and trade. But the authorities are still struggling with the

[7] Quoted in L. H. Jenks, *Our Cuban Colony*, p. 310. Vanguard Press.

problems of rural congestion that can be solved only by emigration, and the growing concentration upon sugar and dependence upon the American market has accentuated rather than retarded the development of peonage and the *latifundia* system. During the economic crisis of 1930, Governor Theodore Roosevelt reported that 'more than 60 per cent of our people are out of employment either all or a part of each year. The average yearly income of the working man or woman ranges between $150 and $200.' The United States has brought Puerto Rico the benefits of political democracy, but economic and social democracy remained as far distant as it was under Spanish rule.

As neither Cuba nor Puerto Rico afforded a first-class harbor for a naval base, negotiations were renewed with Denmark in 1900 for the purchase of the Danish West Indies, three small islands off the tip of Puerto Rico. In 1867 the United States Senate had rejected a similar treaty after Christian IX had bidden his West Indian subjects an affectionate farewell. This time (1902), it was the Danish Rigsdag that did the rejecting. During World War I rumors of possible German purchase impelled the State Department to increase its former offer to twenty-five million dollars. That was accepted, and in 1917 the Danish West Indies became the Virgin Islands of the United States. They have since remained a political appendage first of the Navy Department, and since 1931 of the Department of the Interior. Guam, acquired from Spain in 1898, and Tutuila, the American share of the partition of the Samoan group in 1899, had the same subordinate status until World War II.

In the years between 1893 and 1898 two developments in the Far East had sharpened the demand for the annexation of the Hawaiian Islands. The first was the rise of Japan to world power and the fear of a Japanese inundation of the Islands; the second was the prospective annexation of the Philippines, which gave Hawaii a new significance as a naval base. Toward annexation McKinley had no such scruples as had animated his predecessor, but there was still sufficient opposition in the Senate to necessitate action through a Joint Resolution instead of through the normal method of a treaty. Annexation was finally consummated by the Joint Resolution of 7 July 1898. An organic act of 1900 conferred American citizenship on all subjects of the former Republic, and the full status of a Territory of the United States, eligible for statehood, on the Islands. The government is of the usual territorial form, except that, as in the case of Puerto Rico, the Governor may make appropriations by his own authority for current expenses of government in case the territorial legislature refuses to do so. A similar provision in the charters of the Thirteen Colonies might have changed the course of history.

The problem of the Philippine Islands presented peculiar difficulties, especially because from the beginning it was felt that our tenure of these Islands was a temporary one. The Bacon Resolution, promising immediate independence upon the establishment of a stable government, had been defeated by the casting vote of Vice-President Hobart, but the McEnery Resolution had been adopted in its stead. This Resolution announced that 'it is not intended . . . permanently to annex said islands as an integral part of the territory of the United States; but it is the intention of the United States to establish on said islands a government suitable to the wants and conditions of the inhabitants . . . to prepare them for local self-government, and in due time to make such disposition of said islands as will best promote the interests of the citizens of the United States and the inhabitants of said islands.' There was, to be sure, a certain ambiguity about this declaration of intention, but the Filipinos were early given to understand that their aspirations for independence would have the sympathy and support of the United States. The first Philippine Commission, for example, was instructed to emphasize 'upon all occasions the just and beneficent intentions of the United States' and to represent 'the good-will, the protection, and the richest blessings of a liberating rather than a conquering nation.'

The Filipino Insurrection dragged on until 1902, but as early as 1900 military government was succeeded by a civil Philippine Commission. William Howard Taft was chairman of the Commission and first Governor-General of the Islands. The Commission was entrusted with executive, legislative, and judicial powers, and authorized to reconstruct the government of the Islands from the bottom up; that the interests of the natives might be represented in this work, the Commission was shortly enlarged by the addition of three Filipinos, and the Commission was instructed to 'bear in mind that the government which they are establishing is designed . . . for the happiness, peace and prosperity of the people of the Philippine Islands, and the measures adopted should be made to conform to their customs, their habits, and even their prejudices' so far as was consistent with the principles of good government. This executive arrangement was soon regularized by the passage of the Organic Act of 1 July 1902. This act recognized the Islands as unincorporated territory of the United States, and the inhabitants as 'citizens of the Philippine Islands,' and as such entitled to the protection of the United States; and provided for the ultimate creation of a bicameral legislature the lower house of which should be popularly elected.

American rule in the Philippines has been compared with that of Great Britain in India, with disparagement to the latter that is unfair; for the Americans had the simpler problems. The insular population in 1900 was about seven million, of which only four per cent were Mohammedans, and five per cent wild pagan tribes. Christian Filipinos, the 'little brown brothers' who comprised eighty-five per cent of the total, were a fairly homogeneous group, law-abiding and intelligent. Their ideas of justice and administration were Oriental, but caste distinctions were lacking; their thirst for education was keen, and Tammany Hall could teach them little in the way of politics. Under American rule they made a remarkable advance in education, well-being, and self-government. Through Taft's diplomacy at Rome, the United States acquired title to vast areas of agricultural land from the religious orders, and sold them on easy terms in small holdings, to the peasants. 'Uncle Sam' provided the Islands with honest, intelligent, and sympathetic, if somewhat expensive, administrators such as Taft, W. Cameron Forbes, and Hugh L. Scott; with schools, sanitation, good roads, a well-trained native constabulary, a representative assembly, and baseball. The number of pupils attending school rose from five thousand in 1898 to over one million in 1920, and all but three hundred of the teachers at that date were native. The infant death rate in Manila declined from 80 to 20 per thousand between 1904 and 1920; and small-pox and cholera were practically stamped out. Although the entire cost of civil administration has been defrayed by the Islanders, their per capita taxation in 1920 was only $2.50, and their per capita debt, $1.81. Civilization has penetrated to parts of the interior where the Spaniards never ventured. Remote forest glades where savage tribes once met in deadly combat are now the scene of baseball games between their respective sons, and the jungle resounds to cries of 'Strike him out!'

Despite these benefits which flowed from American assumption of the White Man's Burden, the Filipinos stubbornly continued to demand independence. Under the wise direction of Taft and his successors, administrative policies were pointed in this direction. The

Democrats, who had never abandoned their anti-imperialistic philosophy, pledged themselves, in 1912, to grant independence to the Philippines as soon as stable government could be established. President Wilson took this pledge seriously. The Jones Act, passed in 1916, formally announced the intention of the United States to withdraw from the Philippines 'as soon as a stable government can be established therein,' and inaugurated far-reaching political reforms. It abolished the Philippine Commission, provided for a legislature of two houses, both elected by popular vote, and gave the legislature authority to reorganize the government. At the same time Governor-General Harrison filled the civil service with native Filipinos, and encouraged the Philippine government to establish state-controlled railroads, banks, mines, and manufacturing industries. Under these auspices the Filipinos made such progress that President Wilson, in his last annual message, reminded Congress that the time had now come to fulfil the promise of the Jones Act by granting the Islands unconditional independence. But the incoming Republican administration had no sympathy with such a program. A new Commission, dominated by General Leonard Wood, reported that the Islands were not ready for independence, and Wood, who stayed on as Governor-General, reversed practically all of Harrison's enlightened policies. In 1927 Wood died, but not before he had destroyed in large part the reputation he had made in Cuba; his successor, Henry Stimson, returned to the policy of conciliation which had been so successful. Thereafter sentiment for independence grew, and in 1932 Congress passed the Hawes-Cutting Act granting independence after a ten-year probationary period. The economic features of the act, however, were so ominous, that the Filipinos refused to take advantage of it, and it lapsed by default. Two years later President F. D. Roosevelt revived the plan, and, revamped as the Tydings-McDuffie Bill, it was passed and tentatively accepted by the Filipinos.

This gesture was inspired, however, not by the altruistic motives which had animated the anti-imperialists of 1898, but by realistic economic and political considerations. Since 1913 all Philippine products, including sugar, had come into the United States duty free, and American beet and cane sugar interests looked upon this competition as highly injurious; it was no coincidence that among the most energetic proponents of Philippine independence were the Senators from Louisiana and Utah, the leading cane and beet sugar states. Furthermore American business men had been deeply disappointed in their expectation of commercial and industrial exploitation of the Philippines. That expectation had been an influential factor in bringing about annexation of the Islands, yet thirty years after annexation American investments in the Philippines, aside from government securities, were insignificant, and trade between the Islands and China had actually declined. Finally naval experts agreed that the Islands could not be defended, and that in case of a war with Japan they would prove a liability rather than an asset. In view of these considerations Americans were glad to escape from the responsibilities which ownership imposed upon them, and there were few so unkind as to contrast the vagaries of Destiny in the 1890's and in the 1930's. But America was not to get off so easily from her earlier commitments; the Philippine Independence Act of 1934 was wrongly interpreted as a 'retreat from the Far East,' which probably a majority of the American people wished it to be. That Act set up an almost completely autonomous government, but provided for complete independence only in 1945. During the next decade the United States was responsible for the defense of the Archipelago. What happened after Pearl Harbor is part of the history of World War II.

4. *The Open Door*

It was feared by many Americans and assumed by most Europeans that the annexations of the year 1898 were only a beginning; that the United States was destined to become a great colonial power. Imperialism in the Roman sense did not, however, make any permanent appeal to the American people, and even the word remains one of reproach. The political control of islands densely populated with inhabitants of foreign tongue and alien race was a very different matter from the traditional expansion into sparsely inhabited regions capable of full fellowship in the Union, and the 1934 decision to abandon the Philippines indicates how superficial was the imperialism of 1898. During Theodore Roosevelt's administration, and largely as a means of enforcing the Monroe Doctrine, the United States began to assume a financial responsibility for Caribbean republics that in several instances led to intervention; but it has not yet attempted to compete with Europe for colonies, or spheres of exclusive influence in weak and backward countries. On the contrary, it was John Hay, McKinley's Secretary of State, who proclaimed, if he did not originate, the policy of the 'Open Door' to China.

The Sino-Japanese War of 1894–95 had revealed to the world the weakness of China; to forestall the danger of Japan securing political and economic ascendancy in that Empire, the European powers hurried to obtain for themselves special concessions and spheres of influence. 'The various powers,' said the Dowager Empress of China, 'cast upon us looks of tiger-like voracity, hustling each other in their endeavors to be the first to seize upon our innermost territories.' Japan had already taken Formosa and established her ascendancy in the 'Hermit Kingdom' of Korea; in 1897 and 1898 Russia took Port Arthur and the Liaotung Peninsula, which gave her access to the interior of Manchuria; Germany seized Kiaochow in Shantung, France consoled herself with a lease to Kwangchow Bay, adjoining Indo-China; Italy got Sanmun Bay, south of the Yangtze river; and England added to her holdings the port of Wei-hai-wei. Along with these leases went valuable railway concessions, which promised to give to the European powers all but complete control over the internal trade of China.

Since the Cushing mission of 1844 the United States had demanded for itself the same commercial and extraterritorial privileges that were granted to other powers, and in this policy it has been entirely successful. Now with the acquisition of the Philippines, American interest in the Chinese trade was vastly enhanced. The carving up of China into foreign concessions, protectorates, and spheres of influence appeared to threaten American trade especially in Manchuria, and to nullify part of the value of the Philippines. But the United States was not alone in its concern over the consequences of the partition of China. Great Britain, which had long enjoyed a privileged position in the Far East, saw her markets threatened and her prestige damaged by the entry of the other powers into the game. Like the United States, she wanted an 'open door' in China, and as in 1823, she made overtures to the American government for a joint declaration of policy. These formal overtures were rejected, but the informal suggestions of that stalwart spokesman of British interests, Alfred E. Hippisley, were more effective. On 6 September 1899 John Hay, with the support of the British Foreign Office, announced what has come to be known as the 'Open Door' policy in China. In a circular note addressed to the major European powers, Hay recognized the existence of the 'spheres of influence,' and requested from each power a declaration that each, in its respective sphere, would maintain the Chinese customs tariff, and levy equal harbor dues and railway rates on the ships and merchandise of all nations. All the powers but Russia expressed approval, but only Great Britain formally agreed; Hay, however, promptly announced the agreement of all the powers as 'final and definitive.'

The Open Door policy, as originally announced, was concerned solely with safeguarding American commercial interests in China. Within less than a year, however, it was given a new and far-reaching modification. The brazen exploitation of China by the great powers had created a deep antipathy to foreigners, and in June 1900 a secret organization called the Boxers tried to drive the 'foreign devils' out of China. Within a short time the Boxers had massacred some three hundred foreigners, mostly missionaries and their families; others were driven into Peking where they took refuge in the British Legation. An expeditionary force to rescue the beleaguered whites was promptly organized, and the United States co-operated to the extent of some five thousand soldiers. There was grave danger that the relief expedition might degenerate into a general war, and Hay bent all of his energies to localizing the conflict. On 3 July, in a circular note to all the powers, he boldly announced the objectives of the joint intervention:

> The policy of the government of the United States is to seek a solution which may bring about permanent safety and peace to China, preserve Chinese territorial and administrative entity, protect all rights guaranteed to friendly powers by treaty and international law, and safeguard for the world the principle of equal and impartial trade with all parts of the Chinese Empire.

These were not the objectives that were entertained in the chancelleries of Berlin, St. Petersburg, and Tokyo, but the powers had no alternative but to concur. The danger of war was averted, and the Chinese government permitted the joint expedition to save the legations. Punishment, however, was exacted from the guilty Boxers, and China saddled with an outrageous indemnity of $333,000,000. Of this some $24,000,000 went to the United States; half of it was eventually returned to the Chinese government which established therewith a fund for sending Chinese students to American colleges.

The United States was now committed not only to an 'open door' to China, but to the maintenance of the political integrity of that decrepit Empire. This commitment was an executive one only, and was not sanctioned by the Senate or by public opinion. Only by alliance with some European power like England could the United

States have enforced this policy, and at no time did the exigencies of American politics permit such an entangling alliance. Tyler Dennett, an authority on American diplomacy in the Orient, states that 'the doctrine of the Open Door after 1899 was an academic phrase to which Europe consented for the sake of placating America. For ten years it existed as a phrase to conjure with, but not to be defined.' Or, as John Fairbank put it more recently, 'In its origin the Open Door was an Anglo-American defensive measure in power politics, without much thought for the interests of the Chinese State.' But both these authorities admit that the American sentimental stake in the welfare of China, as measured by the medical, cultural, and religious missions, was immense.

Even the Open Door policy was not without value. It delayed for some time the partition of China; enhanced American prestige in world affairs; and above all it was the consideration for which Great Britain gave the United States a free hand in the affairs of the Western Hemisphere. American support to England's Far Eastern policy bought English support to the American Caribbean policy and greatly facilitated the solution of such Anglo-American diplomatic controversies as the Isthmian question, the Alaska boundary dispute, and the Venezuela embroglio of 1903. And, it may be added, it inspired one poem which is worth all of the literature of imperialism together: William Vaughn Moody's 'The Quarry.'

XV

THE PROGRESSIVE MOVEMENT
1890–1917

1. *The Promise of American Life*

AT the turn of the century Americans could look back over three generations of progress unparalleled in history. The nation had advanced, in Jefferson's prophetic words, to 'destinies beyond the reach of mortal eye.' The continent was subdued, the frontier was gone, and already Americans were reaching out for new worlds to conquer. From a small struggling republic, menaced on all sides, the nation had advanced to the rank of a world power, its hegemony in the Western Hemisphere undisputed, its influence in the Eastern everywhere acknowledged. The political foundations upon which the nation had been established had endured the vicissitudes of foreign and civil war, of prosperity and depression. No standing army menaced personal liberty; no permanent bureaucracy endangered political liberty; and the institution of slavery which had threatened to destroy not only the Union but democracy, had been itself destroyed. Population had increased from five to seventy-six million, and tens of millions of Europeans of all races and peoples had been absorbed without any serious impairment of racial integrity or any dangerous warping of social institutions. The growth of national wealth had been no less astounding: in the half-century from 1850 to 1900 it had increased from seven to eighty-eight billion dollars, and the standard of living for the common man compared favorably with that to be found anywhere else on the globe. In agriculture and in industry the American people had advanced with giant strides, and progress in science and invention had been no less spectacular. Nor were the achievements of Americans material merely. The ideal of free public education had been realized; the ideal of a free press had been maintained; the ideal of religious freedom had been cherished. In literature, art, and science, Americans had made contributions of enduring value, and by every test of character or of achievement, America had proved herself worthy of her opportunities. Yet thoughtful Americans did not look with complacency upon their social, economic, and political institutions. For, as Woodrow Wilson said in that Inaugural Address which ushered in the 'New Freedom':

> The evil has come with the good, and much fine gold has been corroded. With riches has come inexcusable waste. . . . We have been proud of our industrial achievements, but we have not hitherto stopped thoughtfully enough to count the cost, the cost of lives snuffed out, of energies overtaxed and broken, the fearful physical and spiritual cost to the men and women and children upon whom the dead weight and burden of it all has fallen pitilessly the years through. . . . With the great Government went many deep secret things which we too long delayed to look into and scrutinize with candid, fearless eyes. The great Government we loved has too often been made use of for private and selfish purposes, and those who used it had forgotten the people.

The indictment was a general one, but it was all too easy to substantiate it with a bill of particulars. The continent had been conquered, but the conquest had been attended by an exploitation of soil and forest and water so reckless that the natural resources of the nation were nearing exhaustion. The agricultural domain had grown beyond the dreams of even a Jefferson, but the farmer was on the verge of ruin. The industrial revolution had made the United States the greatest of manufacturing nations, but the process had depressed a large element of society and had been accompanied by iniquitous practices in the employment of women and children and in the treatment of the aged, the incompetent, and the infirm. Unemployment and child labor went hand in hand; machinery was marvellously efficient, but no other industrial nation confessed to so many industrial accidents. The nation was fabulously rich but its wealth was gravitating rapidly into the hands of a small portion of the population, and the power of wealth threatened to undermine the political integrity of the Republic. In a land of plenty there was never enough of food, clothing, and shelter for the underprivileged, and cyclical depressions, apparently unavoidable, plunged millions into actual want. In the great cities the slums grew apace, and from the slums spread dirt and disease, crime and vice. Science told how to control many of the diseases that plagued mankind but poverty interposed between science and health, and tuberculosis, hookworm, malaria, and other diseases of poverty and ignorance took an annual toll that ran into the millions. The churches taught the Ten Commandments and philosophers the Golden Rule, but man's inhumanity to man was still illustrated in the penal code, in prison conditions, in the treatment of the aged, the poor, the incapacitated, the defective, and the insane, and in the attitude toward the criminal and the prostitute. The white race was sure of its superiority, but it had forgotten that code of chivalry which placed upon the strong responsibility for the weak, and the callous indifference toward the Indian and the exploitation of the Negro was a blot on American civilization. The educational system was an object of pride, but its benefits were unevenly distributed, and the census of 1900 discovered over six million illiterates. Everyone gave lip service to the principles of democracy, but political corruption cankered the body politic from top to bottom. On all sides thoughtful men feared that the nation which Lincoln had called 'the last best hope of earth' would prove instead the world's illusion.

Americans are not prone either to exaltation or to despair. Against the crowding evils of the time there arose a full-throated protest that was neither unrealistic nor ineffective. It is this protest which gives a peculiar character to American politics and thought from approximately 1890 to World War I. Its manifestations were as varied as the evils toward which it was directed. It took the form of an agrarian revolt, and in that form attempted to adapt the principles of Jeffersonian agrarianism to the facts of a modern industrial economy. It demanded the centralization of power in the hands of a strong government and the extension of regulation or control over industry, finance, transportation, agriculture, labor, and even morals. It found expression in a new and intelligent concern for the poor and the underprivileged, for women and children, for the victims and the derelicts of society, for the immigrant, the Indian, and the Negro. It called for new standards of honesty in politics and in business, for the reform of political machinery and the restoration of business ethics. It formulated a new social and political philosophy, which rejected political laissez-faire and justified public control of social and economic institutions on the principles of liberal democracy. This protest can be studied in political debates and campaign speeches, in laws and constitutions, in sermons and editorials, in the treatises of sociologists, historians, economists, and philosophers, in fiction, drama, and poetry, and in the voluminous writings of the journalists who came to be known as 'muckrakers.'

This progressive revolt of the nineties and the early years of the new century was clearly in the American tradition. It did not essentially differ either in its motivations or in its manifestations from the reform movement of the forties and fifties, and if it was on the whole more superficial than this earlier movement, the explanation can be found in the greater complexity of the problems which it attacked and the greater urgency of the reforms which it agitated. The new progressivism, like the old, had a distinctly moral flavor, and its leaders — Bryan, LaFollette, Roosevelt, Wilson — were moral crusaders. It was on the whole Jeffersonian rather than Hamiltonian in character; it was liberal rather than radical; it was optimistic rather than desperate. Its roots went down deep into American experience, but it profited immensely from the teachings and the practices of the more enlightened European nations. It was romantic in its philosophical implications, but realistic in the sense that it recognized the economic bases of politics. It was basic in its criticism, but opportunistic in its program, accepting in practice Justice Holmes' dictum that 'legislation may begin where an evil begins.' Its accomplishments, both social and legislative, were impressive, and though many of those accomplishments were forfeited in the war and the post-war years, it may be said to have laid both the philosophic and the legislative foundations for the New Deal of the 1930's.

2. *Challenges to American Democracy*

The problems which faced reformers, on the threshold of the new century, were many and complex. For the sake of convenience we may note five major problems which embraced, in one form or another, practically all of the particular evils and dangers to the amelioration of which the progressives addressed themselves. The first of these was the profound confusion of ethics which resulted from the attempt to apply the moral code of an individualistic, agrarian society to the practices of a highly industrialized and integrated social order. The second was the rise of big business and the control of the natural resources and the labor of the country by trusts and monopolies with the consequent exploitation of social wealth for private aggrandizement. The third was the grossly unequal distribution of wealth and the creation of social and class divisions along economic lines. The fourth was the rise of the city with its demand for a new type of social engineering. The fifth was the breakdown of political honesty and administrative system and the application of antiquated administrative institutions to the new problems of government.

The chief factors in the ethical confusion which overtook American society in the industrial age were the growing complexity and interdependence of the social organism and the diffusion of personal responsibility through the use of the corporate device. In a simple agrarian society, personal and social morals were much the same thing, and the harm that a bad man could do was pretty well limited to crimes against individuals. Such crimes — mainly violations of the Ten Commandments — were easy to recognize and comparatively easy to control. But in a highly complex industrial society personal crimes and social sins were very different things, and the old moral standards were no longer applicable. As society grew more interdependent, it grew more vulnerable. Society could be hurt in a thousand new ways, and few of them were recognized in the old moral codes, or in the law codes. 'The growth of credit institutions,' wrote the sociologist E. A. Ross, whose *Sin and Society* attracted the attention of such progressives as Theodore Roosevelt and Justice Holmes, 'the spread of fiduciary relations, the enmeshing of industry in law, the interlacing of government and business, the multiplication of boards and inspectors — all invited to sin. What gateways they open to greed! What fresh parasites they let in on us! How idle in our new situation to intone the old litanies!'

For the men who were guilty of the new sins against society were for the most part upright and well-intentioned gentlemen, often quite unaware of the consequences of their actions. 'Unlike the old-time villain,' Ross observed, 'the latter-day malefactor does not wear a slouch hat and a comforter, breathe forth curses and an odor of gin, go about his nefarious work with clenched teeth and an evil scowl. . . . The modern high-powered dealer of woe wears immaculate linen, carries a silk hat and a lighted cigar, sins with calm countenance and a serene soul, leagues or months from the evil he causes. Upon his gentlemanly presence the eventual blood and tears do not obtrude themselves.' These men, indeed, were caught in the meshes of a business system which had not yet developed a moral code of its own and to which the old codes were irrelevant. The manufacture and sale of impure foods, of dangerous drugs, of infected milk, of poisonous toys, might produce disease or death, but none of those involved in the process — retailers, wholesalers, manufacturers, advertisers, corporation directors, or stockholders — realized that they were guilty of murder. Misleading advertisements, the use of shoddy in manufacture, improper inspection and short-weight packages, might cheat purchasers, but none of those involved in the process realized that they were guilty of theft. Failure to observe fire regulations, to install safety appliances in factories and in mines and on railroads, to inspect unseaworthy boats, might take a fearful toll in lives, but none of those involved in the process realized that they were guilty of manslaughter. Improper inspection of banks, insurance companies and trust companies, false statements in a company prospectus, speculation in stocks, in gold, or in grain, might bring poverty and misery to thousands, but none of those involved in the process realized that they were guilty of larceny. Business competition might force the employment of children of eight or nine years of age in mines and in mills or dictate the use of woman labor in sweatshops, but none of those involved in the process realized that they were guilty of maintaining slavery. The purchase of votes, the corruption of election officials, the bribing of legislators, the lobbying of special bills, the flagrant disregard of laws, might threaten the very foundations of democratic government, but none of those involved in the process realized that they were guilty of treason to representative government.

For the new social sins were impersonal and without evil intent, and consequently produced no sense of guilt. The explanation of this may be found largely in the operation of the corporate device. For it is the essence of the corporation that it is a person for legal purposes but not for moral purposes. The corporation can manufacture shoddy products, exploit child labor, hire labor spies, bribe legislators and violate inspection laws, and neither the stockholders nor the directors nor the agents feel any direct personal responsibility in the matter. For 'the corporation is an entity that transmits the greed of investors, but not their conscience, that returns them profit, but not unpopularity.' Corporation employers were responsible to the management, the management was responsible to the directors, the directors were responsible to the stockholders, and the stockholders were too far removed from the business to exercise any intelligent control over its ethics even had they been inclined to do so. Occasionally there was a mild protest against 'tainted money' or against corporation malpractices, but for the most part it remained true that 'there is nothing like distance to disinfect dividends.'

The impersonality of 'social sin,' the diffusion of responsibility, presented perhaps the gravest problem which the reformers had to face. It was necessary for them to formulate a new social ethics and to educate the people to that new ethical code, and much of the work of the 'muckrakers' was directed toward this end. It was necessary to devise new administrative machinery for discovering the consequences of industrial malpractices and new legal machinery for fixing responsibility, and the effort to do this can be read in the struggle over trust, labor, factory, pure food, housing, and similar legislation. In the end many of the progressive reformers, persuaded that even 'good' men would not acquiesce in reforms that cut into their profits, despaired of any effective improvement within the framework of the capitalistic system. But that despair was premature.

We have already traced the rise of big business, the growth of trusts and monopolies, and the efforts to bring combinations of capital and industry under the control of the government. A large part of the reform movement was concerned with the problems that flowed from the new industrial order — problems of child labor, factory inspection, unemployment, the exploitation of immigrant workers, the aggrandizement of natural resources to private or corporate profit. Roosevelt's reputation as a progressive rests upon his gestures toward 'trust-busting,' railroad regulation, conservation, the 'square deal' for labor, and similar efforts to grapple with the social problems of the industrial revolution. Wilson's 'New Freedom' was largely directed toward these same ends: freedom of competition for the small business man, freedom from monopolistic control of prices for the public, freedom from industrial feudalism for the laborer. LaFollette inaugurated his reform career by attacking the railroads and the lumber interests that controlled Wisconsin, and throughout his long and honorable career he labored for social democracy through the regulation of industrial and financial monopolies. Bryan, after abandoning the money issue and imperialism, concentrated his energies upon the task of regulating business, industry, and finance. A host of lesser leaders in the progressive movement — Hughes of New York, Pingree of Michigan, Tom Johnson of Ohio, Altgeld of Illinois, Johnson of California, to name only a few, comprehended with equal realism the economic basis of the reform movement and fought the campaign for democracy by a series of flank attacks on the citadels of industrial and financial privilege. Political reformers learned that to cleanse politics it was necessary to regulate the business interests that controlled politics; social reformers learned that to eliminate child labor or the sweatshop or the slums it was essential to control the industrial and corporate interests that profited by these evils; humanitarian reformers discovered that the improvement of race relations, of penal conditions, and even of morals depended in the last analysis upon the improvement of general economic circumstances, and that this in turn required a more stringent regulation of business, a more intelligent conservation of natural resources. The 'Promise of American Life,' as interpreted by Herbert Croly, was not so much the promise of political democracy as of economic independence for the common man. And Henry Demarest Lloyd concluded his analysis of *Wealth Against Commonwealth* with the prophetic observation: 'The word of the day is that we are about to civilize industry.'

No less serious than the problems created by the industrial revolution, and intimately connected with them, was the problem of the distribution of wealth. Americans had once been able to congratulate themselves that they had achieved economic as well as political democracy, and Benjamin Franklin found in the American economic order 'a general happy mediocrity.'

There are few great proprietors of the soil [he wrote] and few tenants; most people cultivate their own lands, or follow some handicraft or merchandise; very few are rich enough to live idly upon their rents or incomes; or to pay the high prices given in Europe for Paintings, Statues, Architecture, and other works of Art, that are more curious than useful.

In the early years of the Republic there was little wealth and little poverty. Wealth was chiefly in land, and many of the greatest landowners, like Washington and Jefferson, were actually 'land poor.' The first half of the nineteenth century saw the rise of a few large fortunes, most of them either in land or in shipping, and the wealthy men of the time, like John Jacob Astor or James Lenox, were designated 'landlords' or 'merchant princes' rather than 'captains of industry' or 'titans of finance.' Moses Yale Beach of the New York *Sun* who published in the 1850's a pamphlet on 'Wealthy Men of New York' discovered only nineteen who could be called millionaires, and the richest, John Jacob Astor, boasted a fortune of only six million dollars.

But the Civil War, the industrial revolution, and the railway expansion into the West changed all this. Men discovered a hundred new ways of making money, and many of the new fortunes were gained through speculation, and carried with them no sense of responsibility, only a sense of power. As early as 1873 the Chief Justice of Wisconsin pointed out that 'The accumulation of individual wealth seems to be greater than it ever has been since the downfall of the Roman Empire. . . . For the first time in our politics, money is taking the field as an organized power.' Three years later the aged Peter Cooper, himself a millionaire, warned his countrymen that:

> The danger to our free institutions now is only less than in the inception of the rebellion. . . . It is only another oligarchy, another enslaving power, that is asserting itself against the interest of the whole people. There is fast forming in this country an aristocracy of wealth, the worst form of aristocracy that can curse the prosperity of any country. . . . Such an aristocracy is without a soul and without patriotism. Let us save our country from this, its most potent, and, as I hope, its last enemy.

And the perspicacious Lord Bryce told Americans that they had developed, in a century, greater extremes of wealth and poverty than were to be found even in old England. Soon the statisticians confirmed the fears of the critics. An estimate made in 1890 indicated that one-eighth of the people of the country owned seven-eighths of the property. Subsequent surveys revealed that this estimate was perhaps too moderate. Writing in 1896 Charles B. Spahr concluded that one per cent of the population owned over half the total national wealth, and that twelve per cent owned almost nine-tenths. This disparity between the rich and the poor did not decrease during the next twenty years, and when O. Henry contrasted New York's Four Million with her 'Four Hundred' the proportions were felt to be too embarrassingly close to truth for the purposes of humor.

The great fortunes of the day were obtained not from land but from the exploitation of natural resources, manufacturing, banking, and speculation. When in 1892 the New York *Tribune* compiled figures on the millionaires of the country, it discovered that almost a thousand had earned their fortunes in 'merchandising and investment,' over six hundred in manufactures, over three hundred in banking and brokerage, over two hundred in transportation. Some hint of the concentration of natural resources in the hands of the few could be found in the fact that there were 178 millionaires in the lumber industry, 113 in coal and lead mining, 73 in gold and silver mining, and 72 in oil. Sixty-five lawyers had become millionaires, but only twenty-six farmers had attained that happy status, and most of them were absentee landlords. It was clear that a handful of men had jockeyed themselves into a position where they could control the natural resources of iron, oil, copper, precious metals, timber, and water power, and all of the processes of extraction, manufacture, transportation, and finance whereby those resources were converted into the finished product.

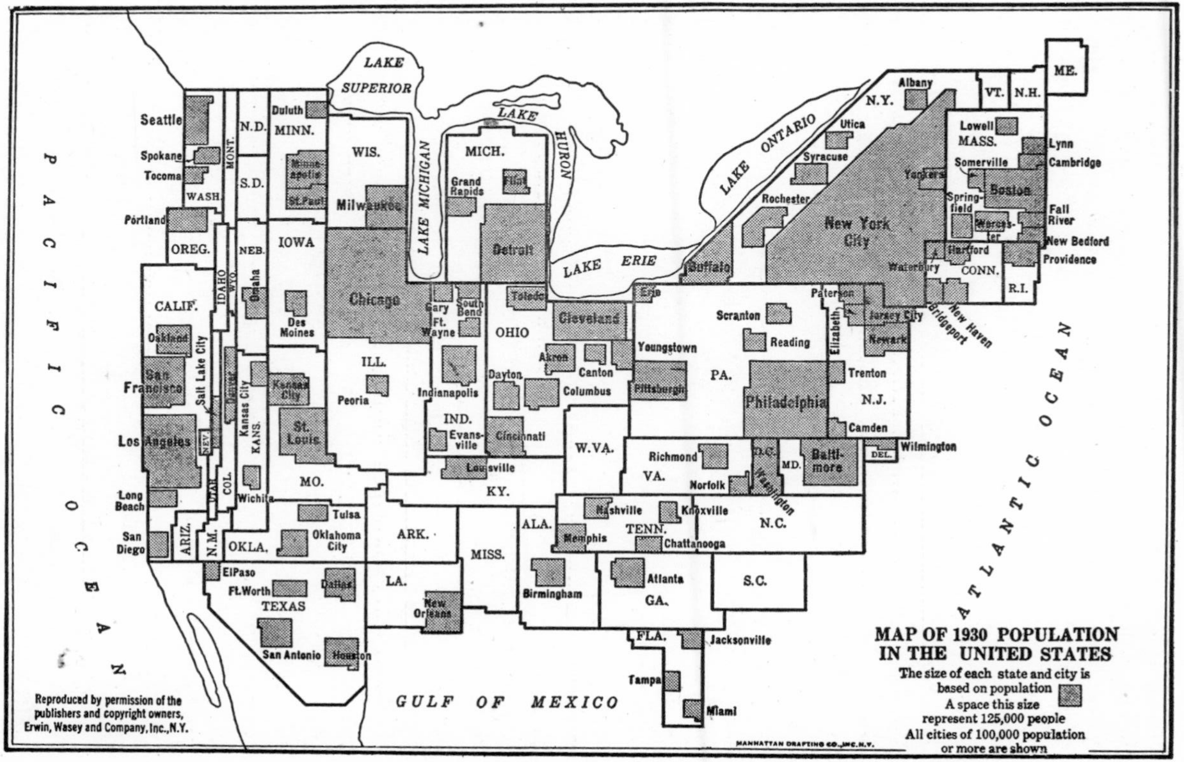
MAP OF 1930 POPULATION
IN THE UNITED STATES
The size of each state and city is based on population
A space this size represent 125,000 people
All cities of 100,000 population or more are shown
PACIFIC OCEAN
ATLANTIC OCEAN
GULF OF MEXICO
LAKE SUPERIOR
LAKE MICHIGAN
LAKE HURON
LAKE ERIE
LAKE ONTARIO
ME.
VT.
N.H.
MASS.
R.I.
CONN.
N.Y.
PA.
N.J.
DEL.
MD.
D.C.
VA.
W.VA.
N.C.
S.C.
GA.
FLA.
ALA.
MISS.
TENN.
KY.
OHIO
MICH.
IND.
ILL.
WIS.
MINN.
IOWA
MO.
ARK.
LA.
TEXAS
OKLA.
KANS.
NEB.
S.D.
N.D.
MONT.
WYO.
COL.
N.M.
ARIZ.
UTAH
NEV.
IDAHO
WASH.
OREG.
CALIF.
Seattle
Spokane
Tocoma
Portland
Oakland
San Francisco
Los Angeles
Long Beach
San Diego
Salt Lake City
Denver
Duluth
Minneapolis
St. Paul
Milwaukee
Omaha
Des Moines
Kansas City
St. Louis
Wichita
Tulsa
Oklahoma City
El Paso
Ft. Worth
Dallas
San Antonio
Houston
New Orleans
Chicago
Peoria
Gary
Ft. Wayne
South Bend
Indianapolis
Evansville
Louisville
Grand Rapids
Flint
Detroit
Toledo
Cleveland
Akron
Canton
Columbus
Dayton
Cincinnati
Youngstown
Pittsburgh
Erie
Buffalo
Rochester
Syracuse
Utica
Albany
Yonkers
New York City
Scranton
Reading
Philadelphia
Paterson
Elizabeth
Jersey City
Newark
Trenton
Camden
Wilmington
Baltimore
Washington
Richmond
Norfolk
Nashville
Knoxville
Memphis
Chattanooga
Atlanta
Birmingham
Jacksonville
Tampa
Miami
Lowell
Lynn
Cambridge
Somerville
Boston
Springfield
Worcester
Fall River
New Bedford
Providence
Hartford
Waterbury
New Haven
Bridgeport
Reproduced by permission of the publishers and copyright owners, Erwin, Wasey and Company, Inc., N.Y.
MANHATTAN DRAFTING CO., INC. N.Y.

Political power and social prestige naturally gravitated toward the rich. They were forced to protect their interests and investments by exerting a decisive influence in politics, and they did not hesitate to subsidize candidates and parties or to buy legislation. And as wealth came to dominate the economic and political scene, so it came in time to dominate the social scene. The new rich moved on to the great cities, built palatial mansions on Fifth Avenue, New York, or Michigan Boulevard, Chicago, or Euclid Avenue, Cleveland, or Commonwealth Avenue, Boston, and undertook to indulge themselves in luxuries that Franklin called ' more curious than useful ' and that Thorstein Veblen called ' conspicuous waste.' They filled their houses with art treasures from the Old World and the Orient, staffed them with innumerable servants, patronized the arts and charities, and, thus strengthened, crashed the gates of society. ' I remember very well,' wrote Frederick Townsend Martin, ' the first great march of the suddenly rich upon the social capitals of the nation. Very distinctly it comes back to me with what a shock the fact came home to the sons and daughters of what was pleased to call itself the aristocracy of America that here marched an army better provisioned, better armed with wealth, than any other army that had ever assaulted the citadels of Society.'

It was against the concentration of wealth and the power of wealth that the reformers directed some of their most vigorous assaults. In the opening gun of the battle, Lloyd announced that ' liberty produces wealth, and wealth destroys liberty. Our businesses — cities, factories, monopolies, fortunes — are the obesities of an age gluttonous beyond its powers of digestion.' Books like Thomas W. Lawson's *Frenzied Finance,* David Graham Phillips' *Treason of the Senate,* and W. J. Ghent's *Our Benevolent Feudalism* dramatized the rôle of wealth in business and in politics; books like Walter Weyl's *New Democracy* and Herbert Croly's *Promise of American Life* analyzed the menace of wealth to democracy; books like Jacob Riis's *How the Other Half Lives* and John Spargo's *Bitter Cry of the Children* told the other side of the story of wealth. Soon came protests from more respectable sources. Andrew Carnegie announced that it was a disgrace to die rich and John D. Rockefeller organized his charities as he had organized his industries. The conservative Senator Beveridge demanded an income tax to curb ' unhealthy fortunes so that they will not go on increasing in the idle hands of heirs who never earned a dollar,' and President Roosevelt confessed to

Jacob Riis his determination 'to favor . . . the diffusion of wealth in such a manner as will measurably avoid the extreme of swollen fortunes and grinding poverty. This represents the idea toward which I am striving.' In 1911 the venerable Wayne McVeagh appealed to President Taft to 'stop widening and begin narrowing . . . the gulf between the rich and the poor' by taxing surplus wealth out of existence. It was not given to Taft to respond to this appeal, but one of the purposes of the income tax which the Wilson administration enacted was the redistribution of wealth.

The fourth problem which challenged the ingenuity of the progressives was the rise of the city. In the generation from 1860 to 1900 the urban population had increased from sixteen to thirty-three per cent, but it was not so much the general increase in urban population as the increase in the size of the largest cities that created difficulties. Cities were growing more rapidly than small towns and villages. In the twenty years from 1880 to 1900 the population of New York City increased from a little less than two to almost three and a half million; Chicago grew from half a million to a million and a half, and became the second city in the nation; cities like Detroit, Cleveland, Buffalo, Milwaukee, Indianapolis, Columbus, Toledo, Omaha, and Atlanta more than doubled in size. In 1880 there were nineteen cities with a population of one hundred thousand or more; by 1900 the number had increased to thirty-six.

This rapid urbanization resulted from two streams of immigration, one from the country, one from abroad; both carried in their swollen currents a good deal of human debris. Those who came to the great cities, either from the farms or from foreign lands, had torn up their roots, and the process of transplantation was often a painful and sometimes a fatal one. The movement to the cities, like the movement to the West, created new and healthy communities, but both reflected a social disintegration of older and more stable communities, and both suffered from the consequences of that disintegration.

The rapid and unregulated growth of cities created problems of a new and complex character. How should the teeming thousands who thronged into the towns be housed? What provision could be made to guard against the diseases and epidemics that resulted from impure water, inadequate sewage disposal, filth, congestion and poverty? What measures should be adopted to control crime and vice; what measures to prevent the recurrence of fires such as that which devastated Chicago in 1871 and Boston in 1872? How were the streets to be lighted and paved, how were transportation facilities to be provided for the tens of thousands who lived far from their work? Could the children of the cities be afforded proper schooling, and could room be found between the crowded streets for playgrounds? All of these tasks of housing, sanitation, fire protection, policing, traffic regulation, education, and others of a similar nature devolved upon the city governments. Under their impact the administrative machinery of many cities broke down completely, and many governmental functions had to be assumed by purely private agencies. Yet private agencies, no matter how well intentioned or well financed, could not permanently carry on the administrative work of the great cities. What was needed was a new science of municipal government, a new philosophy of social engineering. In no department was the progressive movement more vigorous than in the realm of municipal reform, and cities like New York, Cleveland, Toledo, and Detroit were the training grounds for many reformers who later achieved national importance. In no department did the progressive movement borrow more liberally from European and especially English experience, and the cities were the experimental laboratories in which many of the new progressive ideas were tested.

But whether working within the framework of municipal, state, or federal government, the reformers were always under the necessity of operating through the established political channels, and allying with the major parties. Reform was never strong enough to get results independently of politics; it was never strong enough to organize its own political party. The consequence was that reform issues, no matter how nonpartisan in character, generally became party issues, and reform had to gamble on the vicissitudes of politics. And because reform was in politics, it had to grapple with political inertia and combat political corruption.

Observers like Lord Bryce, critics like E. L. Godkin, feared that inertia and corruption would, in the long run, destroy democracy, and the exposures of the 'muckrakers' proved that their fears were not unfounded. But what was the explanation of the phenomena of corruption in American politics? Corruption was not, of course, unique to the United States, but that it flourished more shamelessly in the United States than in other democratic nations, few could doubt. Its prevalence was to be explained in part by the American tradition of lawlessness, inherited from the Revolutionary era and from successive frontiers; in part by the unstable character of American social life which resulted from continuous social disintegrations involved in the westward movements, the movement from the country to the city, and the immigration from the Old World to the New. It was not disassociated with a philosophy which emphasized results rather than methods, and which made success the criterion of measurement — a pragmatic philosophy which grew naturally out of American experience. The explanation of popular inertia and administrative inefficiency is less difficult to discover. In the first place the administrative organization, inherited from an older and simpler day, broke down from sheer weight of the new and complex duties placed upon it. It took a long time for the science of government to catch up with the problems of government. In the second place the deep-rooted belief, inherited from the Jacksonian period, that any honest man could fill any office, and the fear of a permanent bureaucracy inherited from colonial days, kept the expert out of politics, and made municipal, state, and federal administration a paradise for the incompetent, and a happy hunting ground for privilege and wealth. Finally the legitimate financial rewards of politics were so meagre that able men preferred business or the professions, and incompetents brought the prestige of office so low that 'gentlemen' did not care or did not dare to go into politics.

A considerable part of the energy of the reform movement was dissipated in fighting corruption, and so spectacular did this struggle become that it seemed at times to be an end in itself. The result was that after the reformers had won a victory over the local 'ring' or the state 'boss,' the public often lost interest in the house-cleaning that followed, and permitted corrupt groups to regain lost ground. The exposure of the 'Shame of the Cities' or of dishonesty in state politics loomed large in the newspapers and magazines of the time, but was actually of little importance. Far more important was the effort of progressives to devise new political techniques and administrative agencies that might insure a more effective operation of democracy.

3. *The Era of the Muckrakers*

It was in 1906 that President Roosevelt applied to those engaged in uncovering corruption in American society the epithet 'muckrakers':

In Bunyan's Pilgrim's Progress, you may recall the description of the Man with the Muck-rake, the man who could look no way but downward with the muck-rake in his hands; who was offered the celestial crown for his muck-rake, but would neither look up nor regard the crown he was offered, but continued to rake the filth of the floor.

Like many other epithets — Puritan, Quaker, Yankee, Democrat — the term became in time almost a title of nobility. For the muckrakers did the work that no one else was prepared to do, and if Roosevelt had wished to find literary authority for his criticism he might better have reminded the country of George Herbert's

> Who sweeps a room as for Thy laws
> Makes that and th' action fine.

The muckrakers exposed the particular iniquities that afflicted American life, they aroused public opinion to the point where it was willing to support men like Roosevelt and Wilson in their reform programs, and they planted the seeds of progressivism which the politicians were to harvest. These muckrakers at whom Roosevelt hurled his anathema included many brilliant critics — not only journalists but novelists, historians, economists, sociologists, and philosophers. The task which they set themselves, consciously or unconsciously, was that of saving political and economic democracy, and realizing what one of them called the Promise of American Life. In so far as the progressive movement achieved this end, the credit belongs in part to the muckrakers.

Muckraking — by which we mean the entire literature of exposure and protest — did not begin in the Roosevelt administration. Its beginnings can be traced back to the eighties and the nineties, to the period of the agrarian revolt and the radical labor movement and the protest against the trusts. But not until after the turn of the century, when popular magazines like *McClure's, Everybody's, Cosmopolitan, Collier's,* and the *American Magazine* opened their pages to the literature of exposure, did the muckrakers really achieve popularity and influence. In its early phases muckraking was more philosophical and less spectacular; more concerned with general economic and social problems and less with specific grievances, and the difference may be explained in part by the fact that the later muckraking was to some extent a journalistic stunt.

Most of the literature of protest was ephemeral, but some of the books that were contributed to the progressive movement had qualities that insured them permanence, and others have an historical significance that derives from the interest which they excited. In the first category we can place the writings of two men who made lasting contributions to American economic thought: Henry George and Thorstein Veblen. Henry George's *Progress and Poverty,* published in 1879, is one of the great books of the nineteenth century, but like most great books its influence was provocative rather than didactic. George, who was one of the few original economic thinkers which this country has produced, set himself to resolve the paradox of progress and poverty through a 'formula so broad as to admit of no exceptions.' The formula which he found was the Single Tax — a tax which would wipe out unearned increment on land, insure equal access to the land and its resources, and thus destroy monopoly, eliminate speculation, and restore economic equality in all classes of society. George's diagnosis of the causes of poverty and inequality was more profound than his single-tax cure, and a whole generation of progressives confessed their indebtedness to this 'Bayard of the Poor' — men like Hamlin Garland, Tom Johnson, Clarence Darrow, and Brand Whitlock in the United States, Sidney Webb and Bernard Shaw in England, Tolstoi in Russia, and Sun Yat Sen in China. Nor was George's influence confined to the intellectuals. Over two million copies of his book were sold, and on the dusty plains of Kansas, in the slums of Liverpool and of Moscow, on the banks of the Ganges and of the Yangtsze, poor men painfully spelled out the message of *Progress and Poverty* to grasp a new vision of human society.

No such popularity greeted the writings of Thorstein Veblen, which were distinguished by an intricacy of style that discouraged all but the most persevering. Yet the *Theory of the Leisure Class* (1899) and the *Theory of Business Enterprise* (1904) constituted the most severe indictment of modern business that had yet been fashioned with the tools of scholarship. Veblen distinguished sharply between 'business' and 'industry'; the first, he contended, was concerned merely with profits and was therefore anti-social; the second was concerned with organizing the technological processes of production, and was therefore socially beneficial. It is impossible to follow here the ramifications of Veblen's thesis, but it is pertinent to point out that his books furnished many of the reformers with their most telling arguments against 'predatory wealth,' absentee ownership and the profit system.

Finally there were those in this era, as in the eighteen-thirties and forties, who wished to escape from complex modern society into some fond Utopia. The publication of almost fifty Utopian romances in the single decade of the nineties indicated something of the discontent that animated Americans, but it is significant that the Utopianism of the nineties, unlike that of the thirties and forties, spent itself in literary exercises. The most famous of the Utopian romances was Edward Bellamy's *Looking Backward, 2000–1887*. Bellamy's Utopia was a co-operative industrial society, where not only profit, but even money was eliminated: in some respects it resembled the industrial order set up in Soviet Russia in the nineteen-twenties. The book enjoyed an enormous popularity, and hundreds of Nationalist Clubs, dedicated to the nationalization of industries and natural resources, were established throughout the country. 'In those days,' wrote William Dean Howells, 'the solution of the riddle of the painful earth through the dreams of Henry George, through the dreams of Edward Bellamy, through the dreams of all the generous visionaries of the past, seemed not impossibly far off.' And Howells added his own fantasy to the dream, *A Traveler from Altruria,* a novel in which Mr. Homos contrasted the inequalities of American life with the ideal society of Altruria.

A third form which the literature of protest assumed was that of criticism against social as distinct from business conditions. This type of criticism, too, was inaugurated in the nineties with the publication of Jacob Riis's *How the Other Half Lives*. Riis was a Danish immigrant who had been disillusioned in his expectations of democracy in America and who, as police reporter for the New York *Sun,* had come into contact with aspects of life unfamiliar to the average middle-class American. *How the Other Half Lives* told in simple, anecdotal form the story of the slums of New York, of the disease and the crime and the vice that flourished in the dank tenements, of the grasping greed of landlords and the brutality of the police. Riis's revelations excited a shocked astonishment similar to that which greeted the revelations of conditions among the Southern tenant farmers in the 1930's. Subsequent books by Riis himself, by Jane Addams and Lillian Wald and Mary Antin, followed up this initial attack, and paved the way for the housing reforms of the next decade. Similar in character was John Spargo's *The Bitter Cry of the Children* which described with appalling detail the extent and conditions of child labor in America; Ray S. Baker's *Following the Color Line* which revealed the persistence of the exploitation of the Negro in agriculture and industry; and George Kibbe Turner's *Daughters of the Poor* with its damning exposures of the relations between politics and the white slave traffic.

Exposure of corporate malpractices and political corruption was the most characteristic form which muckraking took. This literature of exposure was voluminous, and we must content ourselves with a few representative samples. As early as 1894 Henry Demarest Lloyd fixed the type and the method of the later muckraking literature, with his *Wealth Against Commonwealth,* a devastating attack on the Standard Oil Company. Ten years later Ida Tarbell covered the same ground in her classic *History of the Standard Oil Company,* a book which analyzed with remorseless logic the methods by which the Standard Oil had crushed competitors, seized natural resources, and purchased legislative favors. Within a few years appeared a host of books of this type: Charles Edward Russell's *The Greatest Trust in the World,* an attack on the beef trust; Thomas Lawson's *Frenzied Finance,* the story of the Amalgamated Copper; Burton J. Hendrick's *Story of Life Insurance* which did much to create public demand for regulation of that business; and finally Gustavus Myers's *History of the Great American Fortunes,* which surveyed American fortunes from the colonial era to the twentieth century and concluded that many of them were piratical in origin.

Equally virulent were the exposures of political corruption, and of the alliance between business and politics. The most notable of all these was doubtless the series of articles on municipal misrule which Lincoln Steffens, greatest of the muckrakers, gathered into the classic *Shame of the Cities.* Studying one city after another — 'Philadelphia: Corrupt and Contented'; 'Pittsburgh, a City Ashamed'; 'The Shame of Minneapolis'; 'The Shamelessness of St. Louis'; 'Ohio; a Tale of Two Cities,' Steffens found everywhere conditions remarkably similar, and worked out something like a law of municipal politics. Privilege, Steffens concluded, controlled politics and neither morals nor laws had anything to do with the matter. Analyzing conditions in Colorado, Judge Ben Lindsey found the same rule applicable to state politics, and in *The Beast* told with compelling fervor the story of corporation control of the Centennial State. Nor were national politics immune from the muckraker's hoe; in *The Treason of the Senate* the novelist David Graham Phillips called the roll of Senators he found loyal to their business masters but traitors to their constituents: Depew of New York, Aldrich of Rhode Island, Gorman of Maryland, Spooner of Wisconsin, Lodge of Massachusetts, Elkins of West Virginia, and others of the same stamp.

The novelists, indeed, played an important rôle in the muckraking crusade. At no time in our history has American literature been more intelligently concerned with social problems, and at no time has it contributed more to the popular appreciation of those problems. Book for book the novelists matched the journalists, and for every volume of sociological analysis there was a companion volume of fiction. Stephen Crane's *Maggie, A Girl of the Streets* supplemented Riis's *How the Other Half Lives;* Jack London's *The Road* was a fictional version of Coxey's 'Petition on Boots.' Theodore Dreiser's *The Financier* and *The Titan* made it easier to understand *Frenzied Finance;* and Frank Norris' picture of wheat speculation in *The Pit* clarified much of the agrarian protest. Brand Whitlock's *Thirteenth District* anticipated Steffens' *Shame of the Cities,* and his *Turn of the Balance* was the most effective plea for penal reform in that decade. The moral of *Wealth against Commonwealth* could be read in William Allen White's *A Certain Rich Man* as well as in the pages of Lloyd; and the story of corruption in politics was never better told than in Winston Churchill's *Coniston* and *Mr. Crewe's Career*. One critic has characterized this literature of protest as the 'minority report of the novelists.' As we note its sweep and its depth and trace its influence, we must conclude that it represented rather a majority report.

4. *Humanitarianism*

'The world is too full of amateurs who can play the golden rule as an aria with variations,' wrote H. D. Lloyd in 1894. 'The only field for new effects is in epigrams of practice.' Into this field the reformers entered with buoyant enthusiasm. For every evil there was to be a remedy, and men and women banded together in innumerable charitable and rescue and humane societies to ameliorate social injustice. The methods of big business were introduced into the organization of philanthropy, and the study of social pathology became a science, with its own professional standards, technique, and vocabulary. Private philanthropy poured millions of dollars into the channels of reform; the churches adjusted themselves to the demands of 'socialized Christianity' and the state supplemented the work of private agencies through legislative regulations and appropriations.

Inspired by the example of Toynbee Hall in London, social workers established settlement houses in the slums of the great cities. The most famous of these social oases were Hull House in Chicago, Henry Street Settlement in New York, and the South End House in Boston, but altogether almost a hundred such settlement houses had been founded by the turn of the century. Designed originally to familiarize social workers at first hand with the lives of the poor, they became in time elaborate social service agencies and foci for social reforms. The experience of Hull House is typical:

> We early found ourselves [wrote Jane Addams] spending many hours in efforts to secure support for deserted women, insurance for bewildered widows, damages for injured operators, furniture from the clutches of the installment store. The Settlement is valuable as an information and interpretation bureau. It constantly acts between the various institutions of the city and the people for whose benefit these were erected. The hospitals, county agencies, and State asylums are often but vague rumors to the people who need them most. Another function of the Settlement to its neighborhood resembles that of the big brother whose mere presence on the playground protects the little one from bullies.

The influence of the social settlements was felt, in time, not only in the slums but in the legislative chambers, in labor reforms, in health and sanitation, in arts and handicrafts. Social workers like Jane Addams and Lillian Wald, once regarded as misguided zealots, came to be recognized as the most effective reformers of their generation.

The settlement houses were generally located in the most congested and the poorest parts of the great cities, and settlement workers early engaged in a 'battle with the slums.' Probably the most difficult of all the problems that had attended the growth of the city was that of housing. It was impossible to build dwellings fast enough to house the teeming thousands who poured in from the Old World and from the countryside to such cities as New York, Boston, and Chicago. Furthermore, land values and construction costs were so high that poor immigrants could not afford individual houses, even had they been available. Out of this situation came the tenement house of malodorous fame—a huge, compact structure of five or six stories, with scores and often hundreds of rooms and apartments. The rooms were small, dingy, airless and sunless; the halls long and dark; the sanitation shockingly primitive; and many of the tenements were fire traps. As early as 1866 a report of the New York City Council described the 'filth, overcrowding, lack of privacy and domesticity, lack of ventilation and lighting, absence of supervision, and sanitary regulation' prevalent in the tenements, and in the following decades conditions became worse rather than better. By 1890 over a million New Yorkers were packed into thirty-two thousand tenements; some of these were decent apartment houses, but many were 'crazy old buildings, rear yards, dark, damp basements, leaking garrets, shops, outhouses, and stables converted into dwellings though scarcely fit to shelter brutes.'

Doctors had long warned that these tenements were breeding places of disease and vice, and statistics revealed a death rate in New York and Boston fifty per cent higher than that of London. But it was not until 1890, the year of Jacob Riis' revelation, that public opinion was thoroughly aroused to the menace of the slums. Riis told of one of these tenements which housed over seven hundred and confessed a death rate of seventy-five per thousand. One typical block in New York's lower east side contained '2781 persons on two acres of land, nearly every bit of which was covered with buildings. There were 466 babies in the block, but not a bath-tub, except one that hung in an air-shaft. Of the 1588 rooms, 441 were dark, with no ventilation to the outer air; 635 rooms gave upon "twilight air-shafts." In five years 32 cases of tuberculosis had been reported from that block, and in that time 660 different families in the block had applied for charity.' The names of some of these tenement blocks — Blind Man's Alley, Murderers' Alley, Poverty Gap, Misery Row, and Penitentiary Row — were as eloquent of their character as pages of description.

The public response to these revelations led to 'a battle with the slums' and with the anti-social property owners who profited enormously from the rents derived from tenements. For as financial investments, tenements stood high. Of the tenement described above, for example, Riis remarked 'the rent-roll was all right. It amounted to $113,964 a year.' Despite opposition from vested interests, public opinion rallied to the reformers. A tenement house commission, appointed by Governor Theodore Roosevelt, made a series of recommendations for reform, and most of these were incorporated in the model tenement house law of 1901 which did away with the old lightless and airless 'dumbbell' tenements and insured more decent housing for the poor. State after state followed the example of New York, and by 1910 most of the great cities had inaugurated housing reform. Yet though the worst conditions were eliminated, the slums remained, and it was not until the 1930's that Americans were willing

— though apparently not able — to tackle the problem of slum clearance in any realistic fashion.

This same period witnessed the climax of the movement for the organization of charity. The unemployment and misery which accompanied the panic of 1873 had led to the establishment of a National Conference of Charities and Correction in the following year. Soon almost every large city in the country had a Charity Organization Society similar to that founded in New York in 1882, and designed to introduce science and efficiency into the haphazard administration of charity by scores of private agencies. These charity societies maintained shelters for homeless men, undertook the care of dependent children, engaged in rescue work among delinquent girls, offered legal aid to the poor, fought loan sharks, and attempted in scores of ways to alleviate the burden of poverty. Boards of Charity were created in almost every state, and cities made generous appropriations to supplement the contributions of private philanthropy. In 1909 the Russell Sage Foundation established a Charity Organization Department to serve as a clearing house for this work, and inaugurated a series of far-reaching investigations into the causes of poverty, crime, and disease.

Particularly notable was the solicitude for women and children. The latter, especially, were the innocent victims of urban growth and industrialism. High ground rents forced children out into the streets or into littered alleyways to play, tenements deprived them of air and light, and industry exploited them as a cheap source of labor. Two of Jacob Riis's most effective tracts described the *Children of the Poor* and the *Children of the Tenements,* while John Spargo, echoing *The Bitter Cry of the Children,* told of little girls working sixteen hours a day in factories and nine year old 'breaker boys' working ten hours a day picking slate out of moving coal. Society was aroused and there was a concerted effort to eliminate the grosser abuses of child labor, to protect the health and morals of children, and to supply adequate educational and recreational facilities. About the turn of the century the movement for community playgrounds gained headway, and shortly most of the large cities provided parks and playgrounds to take the children off the streets; by 1915 over four hundred cities had opened such playgrounds. Baby clinics and day nurseries were established for the benefit of mothers who had to work; free milk was distributed at milk depots, settlement houses and Visiting Nurses Associations gave medical care to children, and eventually medical and dental examination became a part of most public school routine.

The problem of juvenile delinquency was an especially vexatious one. At common law children above seven were held capable of crime, and those above fourteen had the same responsibility as an adult; as late as 1894 these common law principles were incorporated into the penal code of New York. Children were tried by the same laws as were applied to adults and, when convicted, were jailed with adult offenders, and thus all too often schooled in a career of crime. In 1899 Illinois established special courts for children, and soon the institution spread throughout the country. Most notable of those who labored for a more humane attitude toward the juvenile delinquent was Judge Ben Lindsey of the Denver Juvenile Court, whose judicial practices and writings eventually commanded a nation-wide attention.

The 'emancipation' of women had not proved an unmixed blessing; for many emancipation from the drudgery of the home merely meant a change to the drudgery of the sweatshop. The shift from the country home to the city apartment and the declining size of the family circumscribed the domestic activities of women, but when they turned their energies and talents into industry or business or the professions, they found discrimination everywhere. The principle of equal pay for equal work of the two sexes did not yet obtain in business or industry, and women who wished to enter the legal or medical or clerical professions found themselves at a heavy disadvantage. Scarcely less serious were the legal and political discriminations under which women labored. In few states did married women enjoy the same property rights as men; marriage and divorce laws worked to their economic and social disadvantage; and they were denied that participation in politics whereby they might improve their status. Socially, too, women suffered from inequalities. The strict social and moral codes of the time did not permit them the same degree of freedom that men enjoyed; the double standard of morality was almost everywhere accepted. Even in the field of education women by no means enjoyed the opportunities open as a matter of course to men.

The most spectacular aspect of the struggle for women's rights is that which led to the Nineteenth Amendment (1920) granting woman suffrage. Equally important, however, was the achievement of equality in the schools and in some of the professions, the improvement in the legal status of married women, the reform of marriage and divorce laws, the enactment of legislation regulating the hours and conditions of woman labor, the development of pre-natal care and maternity aid, and the growth of the woman's club movement which not only provided new outlets for the energies and talents of women but created an instrument for bringing their influence to bear on public affairs.

Society's misfits as well as society's wards excited the concern of humanitarians and particular attention was given to prison and penal reform. Everywhere efforts were made to improve prison conditions, mitigate the penalties of the law, and humanize the administration of justice. Since the 1840's the United States had been peculiarly 'the home of penitentiary science.' Under the leadership of Frederick Wines the Cincinnati Prison Conference of 1870 inaugurated a new era in penal and prison reform, and within a generation many of the recommendations of that conference had been incorporated into law. The fundamental idea that 'the supreme aim of prison discipline is the reformation of criminals,' was everywhere acknowledged in principle, if not in practice. Reformatories were established for juvenile delinquents; first offenders were separated from hardened criminals; the indeterminate sentence and the parole system was widely adopted; state prison farms were established; convict labor and the lease system were outlawed at least in some states; some of the most barbarous features of the penal codes were repealed, and a campaign against capital punishment led to its abolition in several states. The relation of feeble-mindedness to vice and crime was revealed by studies such as Dugdale's *The Jukes* and McCulloch's *The Tribe of Ishmael,* and eugenicists began to urge the sterilization of the feeble-minded as a policy fundamental to the protection of society.

Most notable of all the reforms of this generation was the crusade against liquor. The origins of the temperance movement in the United States date back to the early days of the Republic. Prior to the Civil War the fight on the Demon Rum was carried on through personal appeals for total abstinence. Temperance orators like Neal Dow and John Gough persuaded hundreds of thousands of men and children to 'sign the pledge,' and the Washingtonian Society for reformed drunkards had lodges throughout the country. As early as 1851 the temperance forces had established prohibition in Maine and had won minor victories in other states.

The traffic in liquor was growing by leaps and bounds, investment in the liquor business increased almost seven-fold between 1860 and 1880, and by the end of the century New York, Chicago, St. Louis, and other large cities with heavy Irish and German populations confessed to one saloon for every two hundred inhabitants. Not only was intemperance on the increase, but the liquor business entered everywhere into a corrupt alliance with vice and, through the National Protective Association, with politics. It was this development which aroused the temperance workers to renewed efforts. The churches denounced drinking as a sin; women attacked the saloon as a menace to the American home and the welfare of the women and children of the nation; reformers exposed the unholy alliance of the liquor business with crime and the connection between intemperance and poverty; business men discovered that drinking affected the efficiency of the workingman and increased the dangers of industrial accidents; while in the South it was urged that Negro sobriety was necessary for the protection of the whites. These various elements represented a public opinion so powerful that it could not long be denied.

The progress of prohibition, as distinct from temperance, was furthered by three well-organized agencies: the Woman's Christian Temperance Union, founded in 1874 and long dominated by Frances Willard; the Anti-Saloon League, founded in Oberlin, Ohio, in 1895 and financed by churches and business men; and the Methodist Church, most active of all religious denominations. By the turn of the century these organizations, working through the schools, the press, the church, and politics, had succeeded in drying up five states, all of them predominately rural. A sixth state, South Carolina, had embarked upon the experiment of a State Dispensary system not dissimilar from that subsequently adopted in Sweden, but the experiment did not prove a success. In the first fifteen years of the new century the cause of prohibition advanced with rapid strides, and by the time the United States entered World War I over two-thirds of the states were dry, and almost three-fourths of the population lived under 'local option' dry laws. The large cities, however, continued to be wet and from them supplies of liquor flowed unimpeded into thirsty dry areas.

The demand for national prohibition arose out of the ease with which liquor could be imported from wet into dry territory and the inadequacy of local enforcement machinery. State legislation restricting the importation of liquor had been held unconstitutional as early as 1888,[1] and subsequent efforts by Congress to delegate to the states control over the interstate liquor traffic proved ineffective.[2] 'The Interstate Commerce Clause,' said the United States Attorney-General, 'has been made a weapon of offense by which the liquor producing States have compelled prohibition States to receive intoxicating liquors willy-nilly, and thus have made the enforcement of local prohibition substantially impossible.' To remedy this intolerable situation Congress passed, in 1913, the Webb-Kenyon Act penalizing the shipment of liquor into any state where the sale of such liquor was illegal. During World War I, Congress, allegedly for reasons of national economy and efficiency, prohibited the wartime manufacture or sale of all intoxicants. While this law was still in force Congress wrote prohibition into the Constitution in the form of the Eighteenth Amendment. With a unanimity and promptness unique in our constitutional history up to that time, forty-six of the states ratified the amendment.[3]

In other fields, too, the quest for social justice was carried on with energy and intelligence. Helen Hunt Jackson's passionate protest against *A Century of Dishonor* (1881) aroused a new solicitude for the Indian, and within a year the Indian Rights Association was organized to agitate for a new orientation of the whole Indian problem — an agitation which was largely responsible for the enactment of the Dawes Act of 1887. Booker T. Washington's memorable *Up from Slavery* (1901) dramatized the progress that intelligent Negroes had made in one generation, while the shocking increase of lynchings in the South revealed the persistence of racial antipathies ominous for the future. In 1909 the Boston reformer, Moorfield Storey, organized the National Association for the Advancement of Colored People, and that organization undertook to protect the Negro in his legal and political rights, in the North as well as in the South, while Southerners like Walter Hines Page labored to improve the social and economic status of the colored race.

The achievements of the humanitarians were impressive, yet much that they did was palliative rather than curative. Increasingly as one of the reformers confessed, the conviction was growing

1 Bowman *v.* Chicago & Northwestern R.R., 125 U.S. 465; and Leisy *v.* Hardin, 135 U.S. 100.

2 Rhodes *v.* Iowa, 170 U.S. 412.

3 For the subsequent history of prohibition, see ch. 22.

that poverty would take care of itself if external conditions were made fairly tolerable, if children were not put at work prematurely, if exploitation of employees and purchasers were impossible, if sanitary homes were insured, if congestion . . . were controlled, if preventable diseases and accidents were prevented . . . if savings were safe, and schools provided an education, the police gave protection, the courts administered justice and charities relief.[4]

There was a growing impatience among the reformers themselves with concentration upon consequences rather than upon the causes of the social and economic malaise. The changing attitude is illustrated in the career of one of the most distinguished of the social workers, Josephine Shaw Lowell. Founder of the New York Charity Organization Society, active in work for dependent children, for delinquent girls, and for the insane, she decided finally to withdraw from much of this work. Explaining her decision to resign from the State Board of Charities, she wrote:

I think there is far more important work to be done for working people. Five hundred thousand wage earners in this city, 200,000 of them women, and 75,000 of those working under dreadful conditions or for starvation wages. That is more vital than the 25,000 dependents. . . . If the working people had all they ought to have, we should not have the paupers and the criminals. It is better to save them before they go under than to spend your life fishing them out when they're half drowned and taking care of them afterwards.

It was as a result of this more realistic attitude toward the problem of social reform that progressives turned from organized charity and humanitarianism to political and legislative action. The progressive movement in municipal, state, and national politics was associated at every point with the program of the social reformers.

5. *Progressivism in Politics*

In its political manifestations the progressive movement was directed toward a broader democracy and a greater efficiency in administration. It is clear that the reformers, however acute their disappointment in the actual functioning of political and economic institutions, were not inclined to despair of democracy. There was none of that tendency, so marked in European nations today, to

[4] Edward T. Devine, qt. in F. D. Watson, *Charity Organization Movement in the United States*, p. 331.

achieve order at the cost of liberty, to substitute efficient dictatorship for inefficient popular government. On the contrary most of the progressives had a boundless faith in the efficacy of democracy, and for all the ailments that assailed American institutions, their panacea was more democracy. The abandonment of traditional doctrines of laissez faire in favor of the principle of governmental regulation revealed not so much a disillusionment with liberty as a new confidence in government, and the growth of federal centralization pointed in the same direction. Yet the progressives were acutely aware that the administrative machinery inherited from a simpler age had broken down under the weight of new burdens, and they directed their energies toward the creation of more adequate administrative machinery and the formulation of a science of government. The effort to achieve democracy took the form of agitation for woman suffrage, the Australian ballot, direct primaries, direct election of Senators, the initiative, referendum and recall, municipal home rule, and governmental regulation of railroads, utilities, labor, banking, and finance. The attempt to improve administrative efficiency took the form of agitation for civil service reform, the short ballot, regulation of campaign expenditures, executive leadership, tax reform, the commission and city manager plans for municipal government.

In the arena of national politics, the progressive movement was organized by Bryan and LaFollette, Roosevelt and Wilson. Bryan inherited much of his progressivism from the Populists, with whom he was early affiliated, and throughout his long political career he ceaselessly advocated the extension of governmental regulation over business, and the adoption of 'anything that makes the government more democratic, more popular in form, anything that gives the people more control over the government.' La Follette, working through the State University, made Wisconsin an experimental laboratory for progressive ideas and, in the Senate, applied those ideas to the problems of national politics. Roosevelt made a reputation as a reformer by his support of trust and railway regulation, civil service reform, the 'square deal' for labor, and the conservation of natural resources, and in 1912 he named his new organization the 'Progressive Party' and adopted the whole of the reform program indicated above. Wilson announced that society stood ready to attempt a 'radical reconstruction' and that 'political society may itself undergo a radical modification in the process'; and as President he wrote a good part of the progressive program into the federal statute books.

But it was in state and municipal politics that the progressives achieved their most notable results. The constitutions of the Omnibus States had incorporated many of the items of the reform program, and the constitutions of Oklahoma, New Mexico, and Arizona went even further in this direction. Some of the older state constitutions were thoroughly revised; others were liberalized by amendments, over nine hundred of which were adopted in the first two decades of the new century. South Dakota in 1898, Utah in 1900, and Oregon in 1902 adopted the initiative and referendum, and by the time of the World War over twenty states had provided in some form or other for the use of these devices. In 1908 Oregon committed itself to the recall, and within six years its example was followed by ten states, all but one west of the Mississippi. At first confined to executive officers, the recall was extended by Arizona to judges, and by Colorado to judicial decisions, and this latter application of the recall received the approval of Roosevelt in his Presidential campaign of 1912. The campaign for direct primaries was even more successful. Governor LaFollette, who had been twice defeated for the governorship by a boss-ridden convention, persuaded Wisconsin to adopt this reform in 1903; Oregon followed in 1905, and within a decade two-thirds of the states had enacted direct primary and presidential preference laws. Yet the direct primary, which had aroused the enthusiasm of LaFollette and Roosevelt and Wilson, proved a distinct disappointment, for professional politicians quickly found ways to control the primaries, and by 1912 one advocate of the plan confessed that 'some bosses are wondering why they feared the law, and some reformers why they favored it.' No such dissatisfaction followed the adoption of the Australian or secret ballot which brought the control of parties and of elections more largely under the jurisdiction of the state. More popular than any of these was the demand for the direct election of Senators. Like so many of the progressive reforms, this one had its origins in the Populist movement of the nineties. As early as 1899 Nevada formulated a method for circumventing the constitutional requirement of election by state legislatures, and by 1912 some thirty states had provided for the expression of popular opinion in the choice of Senators. The Seventeenth Amendment, ratified in 1913, was therefore rather a recognition of an accomplished fact than an innovation.

From New York to California reform governors gave their support not only to these measures, but to enlarging the scope of governmental control over business. Charles Evans Hughes, elected Governor of New York after exposing spectacular corruption in the great insurance companies, obtained the establishment of a public utilities commission; Woodrow Wilson in New Jersey pushed through almost the whole progressive program and made that state, temporarily, a model of administrative efficiency and democracy; in Illinois John Peter Altgeld reformed the penal code, the prisons, and the eleemosynary institutions and fought the Yerkes interests that were trying to secure a perpetual franchise for the street railways in Chicago. In Wisconsin Robert LaFollette broke the power of the bosses, regulated railroads and public utilities, reorganized the system of taxation, established an industrial commission, made the State University an effective instrument of the social and economic regeneration of the state, and reconstructed the administration along more democratic lines. Hazen Pingree in Michigan, Albert Cummins in Iowa, and Hiram Johnson in California shattered the domination of the railways over state politics and brought the roads under strict governmental supervision. Even the South was not immune from the contagion of reform. Charles B. Aycock made North Carolina into the most progressive of Southern commonwealths, Charles A. Culberson brought Texas into the main current of the reform movement, and 'Alfalfa Bill' Murray, who had played a leading rôle in the Constitutional Convention of 1907, made Oklahoma for a brief time an experimental laboratory of Bryan democracy.

The same story can be repeated for municipal as for state politics. From Boston to San Francisco party bosses had captured control of city governments and used them for purposes of party advantage and personal gain. Venality, maladministration, and extravagance were the order of the day. Vice and crime were protected, public utility franchises sold for a song, and government was handed over to groups of cut-throats who had no interest but to serve themselves and their henchmen. Lord Bryce, in his *American Commonwealth,* observed that municipal government was the one conspicuous failure of American democracy and the revelations of Lincoln Steffens and his fellow-muckrakers furnished abundant evidence to substantiate this generalization. Corruption played a large part in the breakdown of municipal government, but it was not the whole of the story. The framework of American municipal governments had been designed for smaller and simpler communities and few cities were prepared to undertake the new tasks of traffic, lighting, sanitation, fire prevention, policing, education, and other costly and complex functions which the great cities demanded. Nor were the cities in a position to adapt their administration to these new duties.

> The ills from which our cities suffer [wrote Brand Whitlock, reform mayor of Toledo] are not the ills incident to democracy; they are ills incident to a lack of democracy. The American city is not fundamentally democratic, because it is governed from without. . . . Cities are ruled by legislatures from the State capital; they are governed, that is, by men from the country who know nothing of city problems or city life, and have indeed no real conception of just what cities need. In league with them . . . are the public utility corporations and political machines. The first requisite, therefore, for municipal reform, is home rule.[5]

It was for municipal home rule that men like Brand Whitlock of Toledo and Tom Johnson of Cleveland fought, but their efforts were only partially successful, and most of the larger American cities today suffer from absentee government and from under-representation in state legislatures.

Far more spectacular was the revolt against the boss rule and corruption which Steffens had described. Tom Johnson, a wealthy manufacturer who had come under the influence of Henry George, rescued Cleveland from the grip of the utilities and the domination of Mark Hanna and made it, for a time, the best governed city in the country. He left as his disciples two young men who later figured prominently in national politics: Frederic Howe and Newton D. Baker. In another Ohio city, Toledo, 'Golden Rule' Jones administered the city in accordance with his interpretation of the Golden Rule, and after his death Brand Whitlock carried on the work of reform in the same spirit and with even more acute understanding of the nature of the problem of municipal government. Emil Seidel, Socialist mayor of Milwaukee, gave that city a government as efficient and honest as was the government of the state. In Jersey City Mark Fagan fought the corrupt alliance of bosses and utility interests, and in San Francisco Fremont Older exposed the skullduggery of a political ring controlled by the president of the Union Pacific. Even New York, under mayors like Seth Low and J. P. Mitchell, lapsed into respectability, only to repent and reinstate the Tammany Tiger.

[5] *The Letters of Brand Whitlock*, edited by Allan Nevins, p. 114.

More fundamental than these crusades against corruption were the efforts to find a permanent solution to the vexatious problems of city government. The merit system was extended into municipal administration, and bureaus of municipal research inaugurated the study of the science of municipal government. Various schemes to divorce city government from politics were proposed, and two eventually found wide favor: the city manager and the city commission plans. Both plans were first adopted as a result of emergencies that necessitated honest and efficient administration. The commission plan grew out of the Galveston flood of 1900; adopted with modifications by Houston, Texas, and Des Moines, Iowa, it was soon widely copied throughout the country. The council-manager plan was Dayton's solution for a similar crisis—the Dayton flood of 1913. Both forms made rapid progress in the early years of the century, especially in cities of medium size. By 1940, 332 cities had adopted the commission, 315 cities the council-manager form of government.

XVI

THE REIGN OF ROOSEVELT

1901–1909

1. *Theodore Roosevelt*

WHEN McKinley had been renominated to the Presidency in 1900, the Republican Old Guard had named as his running mate the brilliant and bellicose young Governor of New York, Theodore Roosevelt. That action was dictated by three considerations: the desire to strengthen the ticket, the desire to head off Roosevelt's ambitions in national politics, and the desire to fill the New York governorship with a pliable figurehead. With a show of reluctance that was probably sincere, Roosevelt accepted the nomination to this high but inconspicuous office for the political oblivion that it usually meant, and prepared to study law for a professional career. But President McKinley was shot by an anarchist, on 6 September 1901, six months after his second inauguration. Eight days later his gentle spirit took flight, and Theodore Roosevelt became President of the United States.

Roosevelt at forty-three was the youngest by several years in the line of Presidents; yet few had been better equipped to administer the office. Building on a broad paternal inheritance of wealth, culture, and public service, he had already achieved prominence as a naturalist, a man of letters, a soldier, and a statesman. He had served his political apprenticeship as a member of the New York State Assembly and, later, as Civil Service Commissioner under Harrison and Cleveland, and in both capacities, he had identified himself with the reform element of his party. In 1895 he had returned to New York City and accepted the thankless post of Police Commissioner. His achievements were more sensational than permanent, but this work served to throw him into intimate contact with the social reformers and to give him a lasting sympathy with the underprivileged. Two years later McKinley was persuaded to offer him the position of Assistant Secretary of the Navy, but this office proved too confining for his cascading energies and with the outbreak of the Spanish War he organized the famous Rough Riders and fought his way to fame and glory at San Juan Hill. Elected Governor of New York in 1898 on his return from war, he had struck at corruption in that state with such vigor that in self-defense Boss Platt and the machine politicians had boomed him for the Vice-Presidency. His accession to the Presidency, regarded with dismay by the conservatives of his party,[1] inaugurated a new era in American politics in which his personality was a decisive factor.

No American of his time was more national in his interests or universal in his friendships than was Roosevelt. University men and the well-to-do in the Eastern states regarded him as one of themselves. He had identified himself with the West by ranching in the Bad Lands of Dakota, leading the Rough Riders, and writing western history. The South remembered that his Bulloch uncles had been warriors in the Lost Cause. People everywhere knew him as a red-blooded, democratic American whose every action showed good sportsmanship and dynamic vitality. Impetuous, temperamental, pugnacious, brilliant, Roosevelt promised to be the most colorful personality in American politics, and within a short time he had amply fulfilled that promise.

Like Bryan and Wilson, Roosevelt was a moralist in politics, a crusader for righteousness. Elihu Root accused him of imagining that he had discovered the Ten Commandments, and others remarked his tendency to see all questions as moral issues. His morality was positive, but not subtle; he was never in doubt as to the right or wrong of any question, and he regarded those who differed with him as either scoundrels or fools. His habit of injecting moral considerations into political and economic questions served to dramatize the need for reform, but tended to confuse rather than to clarify the problems with which he coped. He was a man of fixed convictions and implacable prejudices, but political realism and a positive talent for opportunism saved him from becoming doctrinaire and a robust sense of humor saved him from vindictiveness. He was an ardent nationalist, but his idea of nationalism was to some extent a matter of flags and martial airs. He was a faithful Republican, looked upon Democrats with deep suspicion and, until he himself bolted his party in 1912, upon bolters with positive loathing. He was a sincere progressive, but his progressivism was circumscribed by a limited understanding of economics. He was a thorough democrat, but his democ-

1 H. H. Kohlsaat tells of riding in the McKinley funeral train with Mark Hanna. 'He was in an intensely bitter state of mind. He damned Roosevelt and said, "I told William McKinley it was a mistake to nominate that wild man at Philadelphia. I asked him if he realized what would happen if he should die. Now look, that damned cowboy is President of the United States." ' *McKinley to Harding*, p. 101.

racy was a matter of intellectual conviction rather than of instinct, and he was always faintly embarrassed by his aristocratic background. He took a just pride in his versatility and in the catholicity of his taste: he could lasso a bucking steer, turn out an historical essay, hunt lions, run a political convention, play tennis, lead a regiment, and hypnotize an audience with equal facility; he could hold his own in the company of cowboys, ward politicians, Methodist clergymen, newspaper reporters, foreign diplomats, and Henry Adams. He read widely if not deeply, and his judgments on questions of literature and science were as dogmatic as his judgments on questions of politics and morals. He had a talent for friendship, and commanded a loyalty as worshipful as that which was given to Bryan, and more personal. Wonderfully energetic, bubbling over with good spirits, fascinating in private intercourse, and magnetic in public, he communicated to the American people something of his own wholesome enthusiasm for morality, his own zest for 'the strenuous life.' In time the legend grew that Roosevelt was the 'typical American.' Actually he was less typical, in background, in character, in mind, than Bryan or LaFollette or Wilson, but he was more exciting than any of them.

To the tenets of progressivism Roosevelt subscribed with more enthusiasm than understanding. His program was general rather than specific, moral rather than realistic. He advocated 'trust-busting' but his moral sense led him to distinguish between 'good' trusts and 'bad' trusts, and actually the trusts were more powerfully entrenched when he left than when he entered office. He espoused more effective railway regulation, but was unwilling to support measures which might have made such regulation possible. He denounced 'malefactors of great wealth' but was critical of the 'muckrakers' who exposed their malefactions, and took no positive steps to curb individual fortunes or to secure a more equitable distribution of wealth through taxation. He demanded a 'square deal' for labor, but no one in the country was more vitriolic in his denunciation of men like Altgeld, Debs, and Bryan, who tried to inaugurate the 'square deal.' He dramatized popular issues and avoided dangerous ones such as tariff and banking reform; and even on those issues to which he had committed himself, like trust and railway regulation, pure food, and child labor, he was always ready to compromise on 'half a loaf,' rather than risk a break with the Old Guard of his party. His chief service to the progressive cause was to dramatize the movement and make it respectable. Yet Roosevelt's dramatics often distracted attention from big tent to side shows, and his respectability required a conformity that seriously impaired the integrity of a reform movement. After the seven years of tumult and shouting had passed, many reformers came to feel that they had been fighting a sham battle and that the citadels of privilege were yet to be invested.

2. *The Trusts*

'It shall be my aim,' said the new President immediately upon his accession to office, 'to continue absolutely unbroken the policy of President McKinley for the peace, prosperity and honor of our beloved country.' But aside from reciprocity, in which Roosevelt had no interest, McKinley had formulated no policy except that of standpat, and it was inconceivable that Roosevelt should emulate him in this. Indeed, despite this gesture of respect, it was clear that Roosevelt's conception of the Presidency was utterly different from that which McKinley had entertained. McKinley had been willing to follow the leadership of Congress, but Roosevelt subscribed to the idea of executive leadership and gave an exhibition of it that recalled Andrew Jackson and anticipated his cousin. McKinley had been content to let well enough alone in business and politics, but Roosevelt was acutely discontented with existing practices in both, and demanded reform all along the line. According to his conception of the Presidency 'it was not only his right but his duty to do anything that the needs of the Nation demanded, unless such action was forbidden by the Constitution or by the laws,' and he soon indicated his conviction that the needs of the nation were multifarious. In his first message to Congress he gave the country a sample of his political program: that message called for the regulation of trusts, railroads, and banks, the creation of a Department of Commerce, new immigration legislation, conservation, irrigation and reclamation, improvement of the merchant marine, a larger army and navy, construction of an Isthmian canal, civil service reform, more generous support to the Smithsonian Institution and the Library of Congress, reform in the consular and the Indian service, and fifteen or twenty additional items.

What particularly arrested the attention of the country was the demand for a more effective enforcement of the anti-trust laws and for additional legislation empowering the Federal Government to regulate all corporations engaged in interstate business. It was clear that the Sherman Law had neither retarded the growth of trusts or monopolies nor stamped out the abuses which accompanied such growth. The revival of prosperity after the Spanish War, indeed, had been the occasion of a frenzy of consolidation that threatened to give control of business development to a few powerful interests. A governmental investigation of 1900 revealed the existence of one hundred and eighty-five manufacturing combinations, with a total capitalization of over three billion dollars. Seventy-three of these trusts had a capitalization in excess of ten million dollars. Four years later John Moody surveying the scene discovered the total of three hundred and eighteen manufacturing combinations with a total capitalization of over seven billion dollars — altogether some two-fifths of the manufacturing capital in the country.[2] Since one hundred and eighty-four of these trusts had been organized since 1898, it was clear that anti-trust laws were not taken seriously. This process of consolidation was even more marked in the realm of transportation, the control and exploitation of natural resources, and especially of finance. Gradually in the course of the first decade of the century, horizontal consolidations and vertical combinations came under the control of great banking houses located for the most part in New York City. The Houses of Morgan, Rockefeller, Vanderbilt, and Baker came to exercise an influence over the economic life of the nation comparable to that of the Houses of Bardi and of Fugger in the age of the Renaissance. Moody struck a popular note when he concluded that 'viewed as a whole, we find the dominating influences in the trusts to be made up of an intricate network of large and small capitalists, many allied to one another by ties of more or less importance but all being appendaged to or parts of the greater groups which are themselves dependent on and allied with the two mammoth, or Rockefeller and Morgan groups. These two mammoth groups jointly . . . constitute the heart of the business and commercial life of the nation.'[3]

In many cases the merger of competing or complementary industries marked a technical advance. But trust methods, however suitable for industries such as meat packing and oil refining, were also extended to others where they were less suitable, such as cotton spinning and piano making; and the economies of mass production were not often shared with laborer or consumer. The United States Steel Corporation combined the already swollen corporations of Gates, Rocke-

[2] *The Truth About the Trusts.*
[3] *The Truth About the Trusts*, p. 493.

feller, Carnegie, and others in a trust capitalized at $1,400,000,000, of which nearly one-half was water, and nearly one-tenth was issued to promoters for their services. Prices were maintained, although ten to twelve per cent was being earned on the real capitalization, and the wages of steel workers were kept down by importing cheap labor from southern Europe. The great insurance companies of New York, instead of reducing premiums to their policy holders, paid salaries of $100,000 or more to executives who were often mere figureheads, used their profits recklessly to form industrial consolidations, and corruptly to influence legislation. E. H. Harriman purchased the bankrupt Union Pacific Railway in 1893 with reserve funds of the Illinois Central system that he controlled, and made it one of the best railways in the country; but other lines that he absorbed were sucked dry and cast aside after the stockholders had been ruined. J. Pierpont Morgan, successful in reorganizing railroads and savings banks, came a cropper when at the end of his career he tried to unite all the transportation lines of New England under one management; his effort to consolidate the major transatlantic steamship companies into the International Mercantile Marine was equally disastrous to the stockholders.

As the Sherman Law had not been effectively invoked against these practices either by the Cleveland or the McKinley administrations, the public suspected corrupt collusion, and labor threatened to leave the guidance of Gompers for some more revolutionary dispensation, such as that offered by 'Gene Debs. Roosevelt himself pointed out that 'the power of the mighty industrial overlords of the country had increased with giant strides, while the methods of controlling them . . . through the government, remained archaic.' Much the same thing, to be sure, was going on in England and in Europe, but not to such an extent. The American theatre was so vast, and American resources so boundless, that financial or industrial consolidations found richer materials to work with. American financiers and industrialists were more sanguine and audacious than their transatlantic contemporaries; and the American government was decentralized, constantly changing in personnel, lacking organic strength and administrative traditions. It is hardly too much to say that the future of American industrial democracy was imperilled when Roosevelt came to office.

Yet Roosevelt proceeded with caution and circumspection. He had not come into power as an opposition leader, but was President 'by act of God,' and titular head of the party of big business. To most Republican leaders the election of 1900 appeared a mandate to let business alone, and Roosevelt knew that no one of the four Vice-Presidents who had succeeded to the Presidency had obtained the party nomination at the next election. He knew too, however, that the conscience of the people was aroused and their temper ripe for action. He tried to steer his way cautiously between laissez faire and socialism, to differentiate between trusts and monopolies, and to distinguish between the use and the abuse of corporations, and he had the common sense to see that the problem was complicated. 'In dealing with the big corporations we call trusts,' he said in 1902, 'we must resolutely purpose to proceed by evolution and not by revolution. . . . Our aim is not to do away with corporations; on the contrary these big aggregations are an inevitable development of modern industrialism. . . . We can do nothing of good in the way of regulating and supervising these corporations until we fix clearly in our minds that we are not attacking the corporations, but endeavoring to do away with any evil in them. We are not hostile to them; we are merely determined that they shall be so handled as to subserve the public good.'[4] To this end the President recommended the creation of a Department of Commerce, and a thorough investigation of the business of corporations. Both recommendations were accepted by Congress. In 1903 a Department of Commerce and Labor was established with Cabinet rank, and a Bureau of Corporations was authorized to investigate the operations and conduct of interstate corporations. At first the new Bureau was innocuous, but eventually it investigated the oil, packing, tobacco, steel, and other industries and furnished material for prosecution under the anti-trust laws. At the same time Congress enacted a law expediting trust suits in which the Government was a complainant, and appropriated generous funds for such prosecutions.

Far more dramatic was Roosevelt's decision to re-invigorate the Sherman Law. 'As far as the Anti-Trust Laws go,' he announced,

[4] Roosevelt's practice of arguing both sides of this question inspired one of Mr. Dooley's happiest comments: '"Th' thrusts" says he [Roosevelt], "are heejous monsthers built up by th' inlightened intherprise ov th' men that have done so much to advance progress in our beloved counthry," he says. "On wan hand I wud stamp them undher fut; on th' other hand, not so fast. What I want more thin th' bustin' iv th' thrusts is to see me fellow counthrymen happy an' continted. I wudden't have thim hate th' thrusts. Th' haggard face, th' droopin' eye, th' pallid complexion that marks th' inimy iv thrusts is not to me taste. Lave us be merry about it an' jovial an' affectionate. Lave us laugh an' sing th' octopus out iv ixistence."'

'they will be enforced . . . and when suit is undertaken it will not be compromised except upon the basis that the Government wins.' In 1902 he shocked Wall Street by instructing Attorney-General Philander C. Knox to enter suit against the Northern Securities Company, a consolidation of the Hill-Morgan and the Harriman railways, which embraced the Northern Pacific, the Great Northern, and the Chicago, Burlington and Quincy systems. Morgan and Hanna hurried to Washington to dissuade the President, but their intervention was futile.[5] Nor was their distinguished counsel more successful in the Supreme Court. By a five to four vote the Court sustained the government and overruled its previous decision in the E. C. Knight case,[6] thereby stopping a process of consolidation that Harriman proposed to continue until every important railway in the country came under his control. To Chief Justice White's lament that the parallel between the Knight and the Northern Securities cases was complete, Roosevelt replied that Mr. Justice White 'was entirely correct. . . . It was necessary to reverse the Knight case in the interests of the people against monopoly and privilege just as it had been necessary to reverse the Dred Scott case in the interest of the people against slavery.' This decision gave a serious setback to the use of the holding company device for the consolidation of businesses, aroused consternation in financial circles,[7] proved to the nation that industrial magnates were not immune from the law, and enormously enhanced the popularity of the President.

The trusts needed regulation more than dissolution, but Roosevelt was unable to get any legislation from Congress in the right direction. Bills initiated by his supporters in the House died in the Senate. A large part of the metropolitan press attacked his very moderate program as socialistic and subversive of the common weal, and himself as a reckless demagogue. The President, however, was steadily growing in popularity. Merely by being himself — greeting professors and pugilists with equal warmth, teaching his boys to ride and shoot, leading perspiring major-generals on a point-to-point

[5] On the conclusion of this interview, according to Roosevelt's biographer, J. B. Bishop, the President said to Mr. Knox, 'That is a most illuminating illustration of the Wall Street point of view. Mr. Morgan could not help regarding me as a big rival operator, who either intended to ruin all his interests, or else could be induced to come to an agreement to ruin none.' *Theodore Roosevelt and His Time,* vol. 1, p. 184.

[6] Northern Securities Co. *v.* U.S., 193 U.S. 197 (1904).

[7] 'It seems hard,' wrote J. J. Hill, 'that we should be compelled to fight for our lives against the political adventurers who have never done anything but pose and draw a salary. . . .'

ride, exercising with his 'tennis cabinet,' praising the good, the true, and the beautiful and denouncing the base, the false, and the ugly, preaching in hundreds of short addresses all over the country, with vigorous gesture and incisive utterance, the gospel of civic virtue and intelligent democracy — Roosevelt became an institution. Even the journals most opposed to his policies were forced to advertise him in their columns. When the election of 1904 came around, the Old Guard would have preferred to nominate Mark Hanna; but 'Uncle Mark' died, and Roosevelt was nominated for the Presidency by acclamation. The Democrats, hoping to attract the disgruntled reactionaries, discarded Bryan and put up a conservative New York Judge, Alton B. Parker. Roosevelt swept the country by a majority of over two and one-half million votes, and on 4 March 1905 became 'President in his own right.'

Encouraged by this mandate, Roosevelt turned with new enthusiasm to the enforcement of his trust policies. In the first two years of his second term, big business was further discredited by the muckrakers' attacks on the Standard Oil, the beef trust, and the railroads, by the shocking disclosures of the New York insurance investigations of 1905, by the discovery that the sugar trust had swindled the government out of four million dollars in customs duties and false weights, and by the panic of 1907. In that year Roosevelt sent Congress a pungent message in which he attributed the panic to 'the speculative folly and flagrant dishonesty of a few men of great wealth,' described the current malpractices of business and industry, and concluded that 'our laws have failed in enforcing the performance of duty by the man of property toward the man who works for him, by the corporation toward the investor, the wage-earner, and the general public.' Yet legislation giving the Federal Government plenary power to regulate all corporations engaged in interstate business was not forthcoming. Consequently Roosevelt could do little else than direct continued prosecutions under the Sherman Law. Such prosecutions were frequent, and in notable instances successful, but they simply punished the grosser mischief after it had been committed and did not always do that. The beef trust was dissolved, but managed somehow to reintegrate; the fertilizer trust was dissolved but miraculously reappeared some years later in different form; the American Tobacco Company was dissolved, but the constituent parts continued to maintain a community of interest.

Unscrambling the eggs, indeed, proved to be a delicate and often impossible operation. Roosevelt was forced to conclude that the mere size and power of a combination did not necessarily render it illegal; there were 'good trusts' such as the International Harvester Company, which traded fairly and passed on their economies to consumers; and there were 'bad trusts' controlled by 'malefactors of great wealth.' Curiously, this moral distinction was soon raised to the dignity of a legal one when the Supreme Court, in the Standard Oil case of 1911, accepted the common-law doctrine that only those acts or agreements of a monopolistic nature 'unreasonably' affecting interstate commerce were to be construed as in restraint of trade under the anti-trust law. Justice Harlan, in a vigorous dissenting opinion, denounced this 'rule of reason' as 'judicial legislation' and a 'perversion of the plain words of an Act in order to defeat the will of Congress.' But the 'rule of reason' became the guiding rule of decision, notably in the case against the United States Steel Corporation in 1920. Subsequent prosecutions have been based not on size or power, or community of interest which came in time to be encouraged rather than discouraged — but on unfair and illegal use of power.

3. *The Extension of Government Regulation*

'The great development of industrialism,' said Roosevelt early in 1905, 'means that there must be an increase in the supervision exercised by the Government over business enterprise.' In his efforts to regulate the trusts the President had already given a foretaste of this 'increase in supervision,' but the application of the new philosophy of government was not confined to this matter. Early in his first administration Roosevelt had extended the scope of supervision into the realm of labor relations. 'I found the eight hour law a mere farce,' he wrote. 'This I remedied by executive action.' Other aspects of the labor problem likewise felt the impact of 'executive action.' On demand of the President Congress enacted a workman's compensation law for all government employees, factory inspection and child labor laws for the District of Columbia, and safety appliance legislation for interstate carriers. But the most notable example of 'executive action' was Roosevelt's high-handed settlement of the anthracite coal strike of 1902, a settlement which revealed a resourcefulness that no former executive had possessed.[8] Yet despite

[8] See above, chapter 7.

his enthusiasm for the 'square deal' in labor, and for 'social and industrial justice,' Roosevelt failed to come to the support of Senator Beveridge in his struggle for national legislation against child labor.

The most striking example of the extension of government supervision, however, was in the field of railway regulation. The railways, indeed, furnished the fireworks for the second, as the trusts had for the first Roosevelt administration. Abandoned by Congress, ignored by Presidents Harrison, Cleveland, and McKinley, and emasculated by court decisions, the Interstate Commerce Act of 1887 had proved all but useless. Yet the necessity for regulation was as imperative in the first decade of the new century as it had been in the eighties. Concentration of control was greater, perhaps, in the field of transportation than in any other field: by 1904 six major railway systems, representing a combination of almost eight hundred independent roads and a capitalization of over nine billion dollars, controlled approximately three-fourths of the mileage of the entire country.[9] After the Spanish War freight charges had increased sharply without any corresponding increase in wages or improvement in service, while rebates, discrimination, and favoritism, forbidden by the Act of 1887, continued unabated and the activities of railroad lobbies in politics were notorious. The railroads, it will be remembered, had no real competition from motor transportation until after the first World War.

The railroads themselves were anxious to make the prohibition of rebates effective, and in 1903 they supported the Elkins Act, described as 'a truce of the principals to abolish piracy.' This act made the published freight rates the standard of lawfulness, substituted civil for criminal penalties, and provided that shippers were equally liable with the railroads for obtaining rebates. Under the provisions of this act Attorney-General Moody instituted prosecutions against the Chicago & Alton and the Burlington for granting rebates and against the Swift, Armour, Cudahy, and Morris packing houses for accepting them. Soon the government went gunning for bigger game. In 1907 Judge Kenesaw Mountain Landis assessed a fine of $29,240,000 against the Standard Oil Company for accepting rebates, but the sentence was set aside by a higher court.

In 1904 Roosevelt announced that railway regulation was the 'paramount issue.' The House promptly passed an act authorizing

9 The Vanderbilt, Morgan-Belmont, Harriman, Pennsylvania, Gould, and Hill systems. See p. 139.

the Interstate Commerce Commission to fix railway rates, but the Senate refused to concur and substituted instead a bill providing for an investigation of the entire subject. Testimony before the investigating committee revealed the continuation of malpractices and rallied the country behind the President. 'We must have railroad legislation,' wrote Roosevelt, and he charged Congress that 'the most important legislative act now needed . . . is this act to confer on the Interstate Commerce Commission the power to revise rates and regulations, the revised rate to at once go into effect, and stay in effect unless and until the court of review reverses it.'

Congress responded with the Hepburn Act of 1906, a compromise between the House demand for radical reform and the Senate desire for innocuous regulation. This Act made rate regulation for the first time possible and extended it from interstate railroads to storage, refrigeration, and terminal facilities, sleeping car, express, and pipe-line companies; regulation was further extended in 1910 to include telephone and telegraph companies. It authorized the Interstate Commerce Commission, upon complaint, to determine and prescribe maximum rates and order conformity therewith after thirty days. Owing to respect for the ancient principle of judicial review, appeals had to be admitted to federal courts, and the railroad's rate was to remain in effect pending appeal; but the burden of proof was now on the carrier, not the Commission. Free passes were prohibited for other than railroad employees, and by the 'commodity' clause the roads were required to disgorge most of the steamship lines and coal mines which they had bought up to stifle competition — a requirement which they managed to evade. The Commission was empowered to settle disputes between railroads and shippers, and a standardized accounting system was imposed upon all roads. The Hepburn Act represented a substantial advance in railway regulation, yet as Senator LaFollette contended, it did not go to the heart of the matter, for it failed to give the Commission power to evaluate railroad properties and the cost of service by which alone it could determine rates that were reasonable *per se*. Not until 1913 was provision made for any valuation of the railroads, and another decade was to elapse before that valuation came to be used for purposes of rate-making.

Equally important was the extension of governmental supervision over foods and drugs. Since 1890 there had been federal inspection of meat designed for export, but there was no inspection of meat or food consumed in the United States. Yet investigations of Dr. Harvey Wiley, chief chemist of the Department of Agriculture, and of Dr. E. E. Ladd, Food Commissioner of North Dakota, revealed an almost universal use of adulterants and preservatives in canned and prepared foods. In 1904 Dr. Ladd declared that 'more than 90 per cent of the local meat-markets in the State were using chemical preservatives. . . . In the dried beef, in the smoked meats, in the canned bacon, in the canned chipped beef, boracic acid or borates is a common ingredient.' Another chemist, Dr. Shepard, analyzing the adulterants used in common foods, found that an average menu for breakfast, dinner, and supper might contain forty different doses of chemicals and dyes. As early as 1905 Dr. Wiley had persuaded Roosevelt of the necessity of pure food legislation, and in his annual message for that year the President specifically recommended Congressional action. The packing interests fought tooth and nail against 'socialistic' interference with the sacred maxim of *caveat emptor,* but in March 1906 Upton Sinclair published *The Jungle* with its descriptions of loathsome conditions in the Chicago stockyards, and a shocked public demanded action. Representatives of the packing interests were forced to toe the mark, and in June 1906 a federal meat inspection law was placed upon the statute books.

Of the same nature was legislation designed to protect the American public against dangerous drugs and patent medicines. In 1904 the *Ladies Home Journal* inaugurated a campaign against poisonous patent medicines and misleading advertising, and in the same year Samuel Hopkins Adams contributed to *Collier's Weekly* a series of articles on 'The Great American Fraud.' The American Medical Association placed itself squarely behind the campaign and despite the frantic efforts of the Liquor Dealers' Association and the patent-medicine interests, Congress enacted in 1906 a Pure Food and Drugs Act which was strengthened in 1911 by an amendment forbidding misleading labelling on medicines. Though this legislation still left much to be desired, it did give consumers of American products better protection than the laws of any other country then afforded.

4. *Conservation*

Unquestionably the most important achievement of the Roosevelt administrations was in the conservation of the natural resources of the nation. Roosevelt's love of nature and knowledge of the West gave him a sentimental yet highly intelligent interest in the preservation of soil, water, and forest; and from the beginning 'conservation' became one of his leading policies. In his first message to Congress he announced that 'the forest and water problems are perhaps the most vital internal problems of the United States' and had called for a far-reaching and integrated program of conservation, reclamation, and irrigation. It was, indeed, high time to put some brake on the greedy and wasteful destruction of the natural resources that was encouraged by existing laws. Of the original 800,000,000 acres of virgin forest, less than 200,000,000 remained when Roosevelt came to the Presidency; four-fifths of the timber in this country was in private hands, and ten per cent of this was owned by the Southern Pacific, the Northern Pacific, and the Weyerhaeuser Timber Company. The mineral resources of the country, too, had long been exploited as if inexhaustible.

As early as 1873 the American Association for the Advancement of Science had called attention to the rapid and reckless exhaustion of our forest resources, but public opinion remained apathetic, and the majority of Americans continued to hug the comfortable delusion that our resources were infinite. It was not until 1891 that Congress was induced to pass a Forest Reserve Act authorizing the President to set aside timber lands. Under this authority Harrison withdrew some thirteen million, Cleveland some twenty-five million, and McKinley some seven million acres of forest from public entry. Despite this promising beginning, and the work of faithful public servants like Gifford Pinchot and F. H. Newell, the process of exploitation was going on more rapidly than that of conservation when Roosevelt assumed office. The official attitude, too, was distinctly hostile to conservation.

> A narrowly legalistic point of view toward the natural resources obtained in the Departments [Roosevelt later wrote] and controlled the Governmental administrative machinery. Through the General Land Office and other Governmental bureaus the public resources were being handled and disposed of in accordance with the small considerations of petty legal formalities instead of for the large purposes of constructive development, and the habit of deciding, whenever possible, in favor of private interests against the public welfare was firmly fixed.

Taking advantage of the law of 1891 Roosevelt set aside almost 150 million acres of unsold government timber land as national forest reserve, and on the suggestion of Senator LaFollette withdrew from public entry some 85 millions more in Alaska and the Northwest, pending a study of their mineral and water power resources by the United States geological survey. The discovery of a gigantic system of fraud by which railroads, lumber companies, and ranchers were looting and devastating the public reserve enabled the President to obtain authority for transferring the national forests to the Department of Agriculture, whose forest bureau, under the far-sighted Gifford Pinchot, administered them on scientific principles.

Realizing the necessity for arousing public opinion to the imperative need for conservation, Roosevelt secured wide publicity for the work of the Forest Service, and enlisted the co-operation of local and state groups throughout the country. In 1907 he appointed an Inland Waterways Commission to canvass the whole question of the relation of rivers and soil and forest, of water power development, and of water transportation. Out of the recommendations of this Commission grew the plan for a national conservation conference; in 1907 Roosevelt invited all the state governors, cabinet members, Justices of the Supreme Court, and notables from the fields of politics, science, and education to such a conference at the White House. This conference, one of the most distinguished gatherings in American history, focussed the attention of the nation upon the problem of conservation, and gave to the movement an impetus and a prestige that enabled it to survive later setbacks. The conference issued a declaration of principles stressing not only the conservation of forests, but of waters and minerals and the problems of soil erosion and irrigation as well. It recommended the retention by the government of all lands containing coal, oil, phosphate, natural gas, and power sites, the separation of title to surface and sub-surface, the regulation of timber-cutting on private lands, the improvement of navigable streams and the conservation of watersheds. As a result of its recommendations a number of states established conservation commissions, and in 1909 a National Conservation Association, with President Eliot of Harvard as chairman, was organized as a center for propaganda and education. Another outgrowth of the conference was a National Commission, headed by the indefatigable Gifford Pinchot, which undertook an inventory of the natural resources of the nation. Roosevelt realized that the problems of conservation were international in character, and through a North American Conservation Commission he succeeded in securing the co-operation of the other American States in the great work which he had at heart.

The hostility of the West to the program of conservation, aroused by the war on land frauds and the requirement that cattlemen pay for grazing on public lands, was allayed by a series of irrigation projects. The Carey Act of 1894, giving the states the right to appropriate public lands for irrigation, had proved inadequate, and in 1902 Roosevelt secured the enactment of a Reclamation Act providing that irrigation should be financed out of the proceeds of public land sales and under the supervision of the Federal Government. A new reclamation service, of which Frederick H. Newell was the guiding spirit, was established. Under the terms of this Act the government undertook the construction of the great Roosevelt dam in Arizona, the Arrowrock dam in Idaho, the Hoover dam on the Colorado River, the Grand Coulee on the Columbia River, and some ten others, bringing millions of acres of land into use through irrigation. In addition Roosevelt created five national parks together with four national game preserves and fifty-one wild bird refuges.

Much had been accomplished, but much remained to be done. The American people were still prodigal of their magnificent resources. Hundreds of millions of tons of coal were wasted yearly by inefficient methods of mining; hundreds of millions of barrels of oil wasted by unscientific and criminally reckless drilling and piping; billions of cubic feet of natural gas permitted to escape annually through improvidence and inefficiency. Forest fires continued to lay waste millions of acres yearly, and soil erosion destroyed additional millions. Lumber companies devastated the timber areas of the East and the South, and over fifty per cent of the annual cut was wasted by inefficient methods; while both lumber and coal companies soon resumed under more friendly auspices their depredations on the public domain. Alone of our Presidents up to his time Theodore Roosevelt had grasped the problem of conservation as a unit and comprehended its basic relationship to national welfare, and until the accession of Franklin D. Roosevelt to the Presidency, none of his successors had the boldness or the broadness of vision to carry on the work he so hopefully inaugurated.

5. *The Big Stick*

'There is an old adage that says, "speak softly, and carry a big stick, and you will go far."' This quotation from one of the President's earlier speeches provided cartoonists with another Rooseveltian attribute that proved most appropriate for his foreign policy. Not that the 'big stick' was used to incite war. It was Roosevelt who gave the Hague Tribunal its first case — the Pious Fund dispute with Mexico — who instructed his delegation at the second Hague Conference to work for the restriction of naval armaments, who was responsible for the return of the Boxer indemnity, who smoothed over a dangerous controversy with Japan, participated in the Algeciras Conference, and won the Nobel peace prize for successful mediation between Russia and Japan.

Roosevelt inherited from McKinley a Secretary of State, John Hay, whose experience as ambassador in London made him eager to meet the new British policy of friendship half-way. And that friendship persisted, despite the alarm over the invasion of England by American boots and shoes, steel rails and cottons, and despite some dissatisfaction with Roosevelt's belligerent attitude in the Alaskan boundary and the Venezuela controversies. There is no truth in the oft-repeated story of a secret Anglo-American alliance, but there was in effect, during the entire progressive era, an Anglo-American understanding. Downing Street freely conceded to Washington a free hand in the New World; and in return the State Department under Hay, Root, Knox, and even Bryan refrained from any act or expression that would unfavorably affect British interests, and supported British diplomacy in the Far East. The entente, if we may so call it, was consummated by the appointment of James Bryce to the Washington embassy in 1907.

A first fruit of this understanding was the Panama Canal. The voyage of the U.S.S. *Oregon* round the Horn in 1898 touched the popular imagination; and new island possessions in the Caribbean and the Pacific made the construction and operation of an interoceanic canal appear vital to American interests. The Clayton-Bulwer Treaty stood in the way, but not the government of Lord Salisbury. John Hay negotiated with Sir Julian Pauncefote in 1899 a treaty that the Senate, much to his chagrin, rejected, because it prohibited fortifying the canal and suggested instead an international guarantee. With the informal aid of Senator Lodge, chairman of the Committee on Foreign Relations, a new Hay-Pauncefote Treaty was signed on 18 November 1901, and promptly ratified.

The project for an Isthmian canal was no new thing; it had been talked of since the sixteenth century, and had entered into United States foreign policy since Polk's administration. In 1876 French interests purchased from Colombia the right to build a canal across Panama, and by 1889 de Lesseps, engineer of the Suez canal, had spent over $260,000,000 in a vain effort to cut a canal through the mountains and jungles of Panama. De Lesseps' company was forced into bankruptcy, but a new organization, the Panama Canal Company, was formed for the sole purpose of selling the dubious assets of the old to the United States.

With the quickening of interest in the canal project Congress became a battleground of rival groups: the new Panama Company, which wished to sell its concession on the Isthmus, and an American syndicate which had purchased a concession from the Republic of Nicaragua. McKinley appointed a commission to investigate the merits of the rival routes and that commission, finding that the Panama Company wanted $109,000,000 for its concession, reported in favor of the Nicaragua route. The Panama Company countered by reducing its price to a mere $40,000,000 and by engaging the services of a prominent New York lobbyist, William Nelson Cromwell, who tactfully contributed $60,000 to the Republican campaign fund and enlisted the powerful support of Senator Hanna. Heaven itself came to the aid of the Panama Company; in May 1902, while Congress was considering the rival routes, Mont Pelé in Martinique erupted with a loss of 30,000 lives. Mont Monotombo in Nicaragua followed suit, and when the Nicaraguan government denied that an active volcano existed in that republic, the Panama lobbyists triumphantly presented each Senator with a Nicaraguan postage stamp featuring a volcano in full action. Under these genial auspices Congress on 28 June 1902 passed the Spooner Act. This act authorized the President to acquire the French concession for $40,000,000 if the Colombian Republic would cede a strip of land across the Isthmus of Panama, 'within a reasonable time' and upon reasonable terms; if not the President was to open negotiations with Nicaragua. On 22 January 1903 Secretary Hay induced the Colombian chargé at Washington to sign a treaty granting the United States a hundred-year lease of a ten-mile wide canal zone, for the lump sum of $10,000,000 and an annual rental of $250,000.

The Colombian government procrastinated about ratifying the treaty — as other governments have been known to do — in spite of a truculent warning from Hay that something dreadful would happen in case of amendment or rejection. We need not take too seriously the constitutional scruples of the Colombian government, since after the dreadful thing did happen the President of the Republic offered to summon a congress with 'new and friendly members,' and rush the treaty through. Nor need we give much weight to Roosevelt's argument that 'foolish and homicidal corruptionists' placed him in a dilemma, the other horn of which was the inferior Nicaragua route. The real obstacle to ratification was the forty million dollars coming to the Panama Canal Company, whose financial affairs were now in the expert hands of Cromwell and the banking house of J. P. Morgan. That company had no right to sell its concession without the permission of Colombia, and there is some ground to believe that the charter of the company would have expired within a year, leaving it without anything to sell! There is no good evidence that Colombia attempted to 'hold up' the United States for a higher price than the treaty provided, although its chargé at Washington had not obtained the conditions required by his instructions.

Colombia's recalcitrance outraged Roosevelt. 'Those contemptible little creatures in Bogotá ought to understand how much they are jeopardizing things and imperiling their own future,' he wrote; and a little later he confessed to Hay, 'I do not think the Bogotá lot of obstructionists should be allowed permanently to bar one of the future highways of civilization.' Neither did Mr. Cromwell nor the Panama junta, dominated by the colorful Philippe Bunau-Varilla, and in July 1903 there was held at New York an informal meeting of Panama business men, agents of the Panama Company, and United States army officers, to plan a way out. That was, of course, the secession of Panama from the Republic of Colombia. Without making any promise or receiving any of the plotters, Roosevelt and Hay let their intentions become so notorious that Bunau-Varilla advised the revolutionary junta at Panama to proceed in perfect assurance of American assistance.[10] On 19 October three United States war vessels were ordered to the probable scene of hostilities, and on 2 November their commanders were instructed to occupy the Panama railway if a revolution broke out, and to prevent Colombia from landing

10 'Of course,' Roosevelt wrote some months later, 'I have no idea what Bunau-Varilla advised the revolutionists, or what was said in any telegrams to them as to

troops within fifty miles of the Isthmus. The acting Secretary of State cabled the United States consul at Panama, 3 November 1903, 'Uprising on Isthmus reported. Keep Department promptly and fully informed.' The consul replied that afternoon, 'No uprising yet. Reported will be in the night'; and a few hours later, 'Uprising occurred tonight 6; no bloodshed. Government will be organized tonight.'

The description was brief but accurate. The revolution had come off according to schedule. The Governor of Panama consented to being arrested, the Colombian Admiral on station was bribed to steam away, and United States warships prevented troops from being landed by the Colombian government to restore authority. Three hundred section hands from the Panama Railroad and the fire brigade of the city of Panama formed the nucleus of a revolutionary army commanded by General Huertas, former commander-in-chief of Colombian troops. On 4 November a Declaration of Independence was read in the Plaza, and General Huertas addressed his soldiers. 'The world,' he said, 'is astounded at our heroism. President Roosevelt has made good.' Two days later Secretary Hay recognized the Republic of Panama, which by cable appointed Mr. Bunau-Varilla its plenipotentiary at Washington. With him, twelve days later, Hay concluded a treaty by which the Canal Zone was leased in perpetuity to the United States. And while these negotiations were under way, Roosevelt wrote to his son: 'I have had a most interesting time about Panama and Colombia. My experiences in these matters give me an idea of the fearful times Lincoln must have had in dealing with the great crisis he had to face.'

As Roosevelt afterwards declared in a speech, 'I took Panama.' Considering the circumstances, one would wish that he had not defended himself by citing a treaty of 1846 with Colombia in which she guaranteed to the United States the right of transit and in return was guaranteed her 'right of sovereignty and property over the said territory.' It would also have been better taste on Mr. Roosevelt's part to have refrained from hurling opprobrious epithets at fellow-citizens who questioned the righteousness of his action. After all, the only

Hay or myself; but . . . he is a very able fellow, and it was his business to find out what he thought our Government would do. I have no doubt that he was able to make a very accurate guess and to advise his people accordingly. In fact he would have been a very dull man had he not been able to make such a guess.' J. B. Bishop, *Theodore Roosevelt and His Time*, vol. 1, p. 295.

issue at stake was the money to be paid to the speculators who controlled the Panama Canal Company and the construction of the canal might well have waited six months or a year. Colombia was hit by the big stick, but all Latin America trembled. Subsequently, in 1921, the United States paid twenty-five million dollars to quiet Colombia; it would have been better to have paid this sum eighteen years earlier.

Roosevelt was never scrupulous as to methods if a great end was in view, and he was most anxious to secure the Panama Canal as a permanent monument to his administration. 'The people of the United States,' he said, 'and the people of the Isthmus and the rest of mankind will all be better because we dig the Panama Canal and keep order in the neighbourhood. And the politicians and revolutionists at Bogotá are entitled to precisely the amount of sympathy we extend to other inefficient bandits.' Roosevelt certainly was not 'inefficient,' but over-eager to 'make the dirt fly' he made some ill-considered appointments to the first Canal Zone Commission. The dirt would have flown to little purpose if he had not appointed Colonel Goethals chief engineer and autocrat of the Canal Zone in 1907. Open to commercial traffic in August 1914, and formally completed six years later, the Panama Canal was a triumph for American engineering and organization. No less remarkable was the sanitary work of Colonel Gorgas, made possible by the discoveries of Ronald Ross and Walter Reed, which gave one of the world's greatest pest-holes a lower death-rate than any American city, and the policing of Colonel Goethals, which converted the spot described by Froude as 'a hideous dung-heap of moral and physical abomination' into a community of happy and healthy workers.

Elsewhere in the Caribbean area Roosevelt wielded the big stick with redoubtable energy. In 1902 a crisis arose over the question of international intervention for the collection of the Venezuelan debt. Great Britain, Germany, and Italy established a blockade to force the recalcitrant dictator, General Castro, to come to terms. Castro appealed to Roosevelt to arbitrate the claims, but inasmuch as American rights were involved, he very properly refused. Yet he deprecated the use of force for the collection of debts, and looked askance at the potential threat to the Monroe Doctrine. A crisis was avoided, however, when Germany, breaking away from the lead of Great Britain, agreed to submit her claims to arbitration. The Hague Tribunal settled the dispute satisfactorily, scaling down the demands from some forty million to eight million dollars[11] and accepting the so-called Drago doctrine which denied the propriety of coercion for the collection of claims. Roosevelt expressed the general satisfaction with this solution in a speech in which he said, 'Both powers [England and Germany] assured us in explicit terms that there was not the slightest intention on their part to violate the Monroe Doctrine, and this assurance was kept with an honorable good faith which merits full acknowledgement on our part.'[12]

Under the terms of the Platt Amendment the United States could intervene in Cuba when necessary to restore order. Such a situation arose in 1906, and on the request of the Cuban President, Estrada Palma, Roosevelt sent William H. Taft, then Secretary of War, to take charge of the Island. When peace and stability were restored, the United States once more withdrew, leaving the affairs of Cuba in excellent condition. At the same time, however, Roosevelt solemnly warned the Islanders that 'if elections become a farce and if the insurrectionary habit becomes confirmed . . . it is absolutely out of the question that the Island should remain independent; and the United States, which has assumed the sponsorship before the civilized world for Cuba's career as a nation, would again have to intervene, and see that the government was managed in such an orderly fashion as to secure the safety of life and property.'

Even more important as a precedent was Roosevelt's intervention in Santo Domingo and the enunciation of the so-called 'Roosevelt corollary' to the Monroe Doctrine. In his annual message of 1904 the President had announced that 'chronic wrong-doing or an impotence which results in a general loosening of the ties of civilized society, may . . . require intervention by some civilized nation, and . . . the adherence of the United States to the Monroe Doctrine may force the United States, . . . in flagrant cases of such wrong-doing or impotence, to the exercise of an international police power.' An occasion for such an exercise of police power arose when in 1905 the financial affairs of Santo Domingo fell into such a desperate condition that she was threatened with foreclosure by her European creditors. Roosevelt

11 The United States' claims were reduced from some four million to eighty-one thousand dollars.

12 Many years later Roosevelt gave an entirely different version of this incident. According to the story in his official biography and in his *Autobiography*, Germany was the ringleader in the intervention, and Roosevelt forced her to submit to arbitration only by threatening to send Dewey's fleet to Venezuelan waters inside of twenty-four hours if the Kaiser did not back down. The evidence to support this version of the story, however, is scant, conflicting, and unconvincing.

promptly announced a 'corollary' to the Monroe Doctrine: namely, that as we could not permit European nations forcibly to collect debts in the Western Hemisphere, we must ourselves assume the responsibility of seeing that 'backward' states faithfully fulfilled their financial obligations. In order to forestall European intervention in Santo Domingo Roosevelt placed an American receiver-general in charge of Dominican revenues, arranging to apply fifty-five per cent of customs receipts to the discharge of debts, and forty-five per cent to current expenses. The United States Senate refused to ratify this arrangement, but Roosevelt went ahead on his own authority. In a little more than two years Santo Domingo was transformed from a bankrupt island, without credit abroad or stability at home, into a prosperous and peaceful country, with revenues more than sufficient for ordinary expenses, and Roosevelt congratulated himself that he had 'put the affairs of the island on a better basis than they had been for a century.' But a dangerous precedent had been established, and within a decade the United States found herself inextricably involved in the domestic as well as the foreign affairs of other Caribbean and Central American nations. So burdensome did this responsibility become, that a quarter century later the Roosevelt corollary to the Monroe Doctrine was officially repudiated by the Department of State.

6. *World Politics*

For the first time the United States had a President whom the rulers of Europe looked upon as one of themselves, and who could play their game with their weapons. Roosevelt, like Edward VII, loved to inject his personality into world politics. The most conspicuous instance of this was his mediation in the Russo-Japanese War, undertaken on the suggestion of the Japanese and the German Emperors. Secretary Hay was then in his last illness, and the President negotiated directly with premiers and crowned heads. Perhaps none but he could have brought the two belligerents together at that time, or broken the deadlock from which the Treaty of Portsmouth emerged; but not everyone will admit the wisdom of that Treaty. Roosevelt preserved for the time being the integrity of China, but the Treaty of Portsmouth merely substituted Japan for Russia in Manchuria and embittered the Japanese people toward the United States. Yet Roosevelt's action had been dictated by friendship for Japan, and he himself later declared that he had served notice on France and Germany that the United

States would support Japan if either power went to the aid of Russia.[13] It is difficult to find any difference between this sort of thing and the system of secret treaties and balance-of-power diplomacy that Roosevelt, like other Americans, professed to abhor. He played the game of world politics with native audacity and amateur skill, sounding out every step in advance; but if something had gone wrong the American people would have found themselves morally committed by their President to a fighting membership in the Anglo-Japanese alliance. Yet it is inconceivable that the American people would have accepted any such commitments, and if the door held open by John Hay swung to shortly after his death it was, according to Tyler Dennett, because Roosevelt's policy 'could not be continued except at the expense of the Constitution of the United States.'

By the conclusion of the Treaty of Portsmouth, Roosevelt established for his country a right that she did not want, to be consulted in world politics. Again, in the Moroccan crisis of 1905–06, he quietly intervened to preserve peace with justice. French policy of hegemony in Morocco threatened a war with Germany that might easily have become a world conflagration. At the suggestion of the German Emperor Roosevelt urged France to consent to a conference on the North African question, and the American representative, Henry White, was in large part responsible for the Algeciras Convention which, whatever its inadequacies, did keep peace for some years. The Senate ratified the Convention, but with the qualifying amendment that ratification did not involve any departure 'from the traditional American foreign policy which forbids participation by the United States in the settlement of political questions which are entirely European in their scope.' It is interesting to note, by contrast, that President Taft carefully refrained from any participation in the second Moroccan crisis of 1911.

Roosevelt's growing radicalism had alienated conservatives and moderates even of his own party, and by his willingness to compromise he had forfeited the confidence of doctrinaire liberals and professional reformers, whom he denounced as 'muckrakers.' His vigorous assertion of executive leadership had antagonized Congress and powerful party leaders; and his sense of what constituted fair play brought down upon him at one time or another the wrath of

[13] It is difficult to know whether Roosevelt really made such a threat, or whether his memory played tricks on him, as with the Venezuela episode. Scholars have been unable to find any documentary evidence to support Roosevelt's story.

labor and of capital, of Negroes and of the Southern whites. Yet no President since Jackson was so popular with the 'plain people.' Only fifty years old in 1908, and at the height of his power and popularity, Roosevelt could have been renominated if he had only said the word. But he had declared in 1904 that 'under no circumstances' would he be a candidate to succeed himself; and in deference to the third-term tradition he contented himself with nominating his successor. Secretary of State Elihu Root, Charles E. Hughes, and William Howard Taft were the most available candidates, but Taft was closer to the President than any other man in high public office. Roosevelt held the Republican convention in the hollow of his hand, and Taft was duly nominated. It is probable that he would have been nominated even without Roosevelt's aid, although hardly without the pecuniary assistance of the Taft family. Bryan's control over the Democratic party was no less complete, and he was nominated by a convention subservient to his every wish. The differences between the two parties were insignificant, and except for charges and counter-charges of financial irregularities, the campaign was apathetic. Bryan carried only the Solid South, Kansas, Nebraska, Colorado, and Nevada, but his popular vote was a million more than that of Parker in 1904, and forty-three per cent of the total. The Republicans, however, captured not only the Presidency, but both houses of Congress.

To Taft, then, on 4 March 1909 Roosevelt handed over a government that had grown rapidly in prestige and power during the last seven years, a government that was by way of becoming once more a servant of the people. The entire civil service had been stimulated by Roosevelt's vitality, no less than by knowledge that efficiency and intelligence would be recognized and rewarded. The whole tone and temper of public life had changed for the better, and the popular interest in public affairs had never been more keen or intelligent. Yet in one respect Roosevelt had failed as a leader. He inspired loyalty to himself, rather than to his ideals and policies. With the conceit of a strong man he had forced and fascinated men of other beliefs to his and the public service, while neglecting to build up a progressive staff within the Republican party. It would never be quite the same old party again; but the Old Guard drew a sigh of relief when Roosevelt took ship to Africa.

XVII

THE TAFT ADMINISTRATION

1909–1913

1. *Ineptitude and Insurgency*

STRONG-WILLED Presidents of the United States have generally managed to nominate their successors; and if Roosevelt, unlike Jefferson and Jackson, did not bequeath the office to his Secretary of State, it was because his Secretary of War was more 'available.' William Howard Taft, fifty-one years old when he became President, had no less experience in public affairs than Elihu Root. He had been an excellent circuit court judge, Governor of the Philippines, Canal-Zone administrator, and Secretary of War. The President loved him as a brother, and believed him the ideal person to carry out his policies. Many progressives, indeed, welcomed the change; for Roosevelt's excessive use of opprobrious adjectives had become tiresome, as his voluminous messages were tedious; and the last year of his administration was consumed in frenzied futility, for as soon as the Republican leaders in Congress learned that Roosevelt would retire in 1909, they ignored alike his recommendations and his threats. 'Big Bill' Taft, it was hoped, would apply the emollient of his humor and good nature to the wheels of legislation.

If Roosevelt appeared to be less conservative than he really was, Taft appeared more. He genuinely wished to clinch the Roosevelt policies, but in his own fashion; and he was unprepared to go forward with a program of his own. Roosevelt was primarily a man of action, Taft essentially a man of deliberation. As a constitutional lawyer he could not share Roosevelt's view that the President could do anything not forbidden by law; rather he could do only those things for which he had specific authority under the Constitution. The difference between the two was much like the difference between Jackson and Buchanan. Roosevelt gave the Presidency an organic connection with Congress; under Taft the relationship became formal, almost diplomatic, and the initiative passed to House and Senate leaders who thought reform had gone far enough, if not too far.

In this they were wrong, but Taft was not prepared to disabuse them of their error. Cautious and vacillating, he was by instinct conservative, by training 'regular.' In theory he agreed with much of the insurgent program; actually he was unwilling to antagonize the Old Guard upon whom he relied increasingly for counsel and support. And it was during the first two years of the Taft administration that the Old Guard reached the zenith of its power. 'Uncle Joe' Cannon was its representative in the House, Nelson W. Aldrich in the Senate, and so certain were these men of their power that they openly professed a cynical contempt for democracy.

Roosevelt went to Africa in March 1909, as much to avoid embarrassing the new President by his presence as for the pleasure of big game hunting. The new President and the old parted with warm expressions of trust and affection. Yet Roosevelt returned fifteen months later to find the Republican party divided, the progressive program halted, and liberals everywhere alienated; and in fifteen months more the two old friends were exchanging bitter reproaches before the public.

That this happened was in large part President Taft's fault; the manner in which it happened was Roosevelt's. The Republican platform of 1908 contained a pledge to revise the tariff: an issue that Roosevelt had gingerly avoided, fearing lest it should disrupt his party. Revision was popularly understood as reduction and Taft had specifically committed himself to this interpretation of the term. 'It is my judgment,' he said during the campaign, 'that a revision of the tariff in accordance with the pledge of the Republican platform will be on the whole a substantial revision downward.' For a downward revision there was, by 1909, pressing need. The cost of living was rising, and the average worker was no better off than he had been a decade earlier. Trusts, which many thought were spawned by high tariffs, were growing stronger every year, and the investigations of the Pujo Committee were soon to reveal the existence of a 'money trust' unsuspected by most Americans. President Taft proposed in his inaugural address that 'a tariff bill be drawn in good faith in accordance with the promises made before the election,' and he suggested that the new tariff should afford merely a protection equal to the difference between the cost of production at home and abroad. Any consequent deficiency in the revenue, he added, might be made up by a graduated inheritance tax. In order to shorten the uncertainty of business men, he summoned a special session of Congress for immediate legislation along these lines.

When Congress assembled Sereno Payne of New York was ready with a tariff bill which placed iron ore, flax, and hides on the free list and reduced duties on steel, lumber, and numerous other items. The bill promptly passed the House and went to the Senate, where representatives of interested industries fell upon it. When it emerged from the Senate as the Payne-Aldrich tariff it was seen that of the 847 changes, some six hundred were upward and that the free list was a joke.[1] 'I have never come so close to tariff making before,' wrote Senator Lodge, 'and the amount of ruthless selfishness that is exhibited on both sides surpasses anything I have ever seen.' The progressive Republicans were outraged, and under the leadership of LaFollette they organized to fight the proposed measure item by item. There followed one of the most stirring debates in American political history. LaFollette attacked the woolens schedule, Beveridge the tobacco, Cummins the steel, Bristow the sugar, Dolliver the cotton, and if in the end their efforts failed to change the tariff, they did at least furnish the country with an edifying analysis of the connection between tariffs and trusts. The President was perturbed. The insurgents urged him to veto the bill as a violation of party pledges, but after painful vacillation he decided to sign it. And shortly after, in a most unfortunate speech at Winona, Minnesota, he aggravated his offence by pronouncing the Payne-Aldrich bill 'the best tariff bill that the Republican party ever passed.'

The progressive Republicans, led by LaFollette of Wisconsin, Beveridge of Indiana, and Norris of Nebraska, began to suspect Taft of playing traitor to the Roosevelt policies, and their suspicions were confirmed by Taft's conservation policy. James R. Garfield, Roosevelt's lieutenant in conservation, had been supplanted in the Interior Department by R. A. Ballinger, who was presently charged by chief forester Gifford Pinchot with letting the Guggenheim interests obtain reserved coal lands in Alaska. The President referred this quarrel in his official family to the House of Representatives, which whitewashed Ballinger, upon which Pinchot was dismissed. This action was naturally though mistakenly interpreted as a dramatic reversal of Roosevelt's conservation program. Actually Taft was not unfriendly to conservation. He was the first President to withdraw oil lands

1 'Th' Republican party,' explained Mr. Dooley to Mr. Hennessy, 'has been thru to its promises. Look at th' free list if ye don't believe it. Practically ivrything nicessary to existence comes in free. Here it is. Curling stones, teeth, sea moss, newspapers, nux vomica, Pulu, canary bird seed, divvy-divvy, spunk, hog bristles, marshmallows, silk worm eggs, stilts, skeletons, an' leeches. Th' new tariff bill puts these familyar commodyties within th' reach iv all.' Mr. Dooley on The Tariff in *Mr. Dooley Says.* Scribner's, p. 148.

from public sale. He asked for and obtained from Congress the authority to reserve the coal lands which Roosevelt had reserved without specific authority, and set up the Bureau of Mines as guardian of the nation's mineral resources. Pinchot was replaced by the head of the Yale School of Forestry, and his policy was continued by the purchase, in 1911, of great timbered tracts in the Appalachians.

The indignation of the progressives was directed not only against the President, but against the Old Guard upon whom he depended. In the Senate LaFollette, Beveridge, and Dolliver excoriated Aldrich to such effect that he decided not to stand for re-election. In the House insurgency took the form of a revolt against Speaker Cannon, 'a hard, narrow old Boeotian,' who controlled a well-oiled legislation mill which rejected progressive grist. On 18 March 1910 George Norris of Nebraska offered a resolution depriving the Speaker of membership on the powerful Committee on Rules, and making that committee elective. Democrats joined with progressive Republicans to pass the resolution, and Taft's prestige fell. The progressive cause gained, but legislative efficiency lost. Authority was needed to enforce party discipline in a body so unwieldy and fluctuating as the House of Representatives, and the Speaker's whip in due course was transferred to the floor leader.

Yet the ineptitude of Taft's administration and the growing revolt against him must not blind us to his achievements. During his term much valuable legislation was enacted. The Mann-Elkins Act of 1910 strengthened the Interstate Commerce Commission by empowering it to suspend any rate increases until and unless the reasonableness thereof were ascertained, and created a new Commerce Court to hear appeals from the Commission. The Department of Commerce and Labor, established at Roosevelt's instance in 1903, was wisely divided. A postal savings bank and a parcel post — reforms long overdue, much wanted by the people, but opposed by selfish interests — were provided. A Commission of Economy and Efficiency to examine into the national administration was created, and an act requiring publicity for campaign expenditures passed. The merit system was expanded by the addition of second and third class postmasters to the civil service list. A Federal Children's Bureau was established, and its activities entrusted to Julia Lathrop of Hull House. Alaska, peevish and discontented since the collapse of the Klondike gold bubble, at last obtained full territorial government in 1912. New Mexico and Arizona, last of the continental Territories save Alaska, became the forty-seventh and forty-eighth states of the Union; though here again Taft unnecessarily compromised himself with the progressives by refusing to certify the admission of Arizona until it expunged from its constitution a provision for the popular recall of judges. Once admitted as a state, Arizona promptly restored the device. Approximately twice as many prosecutions for violation of the Sherman Act were instituted during Taft's four years in office as during Roosevelt's seven. Significant of the rapidly expanding envelope of law were two amendments of the Federal Constitution. As James Bryce pointed out, the difficulties of this process were such that the Constitution had not been amended since 1802, excepting 'in the course of a revolutionary movement which had dislocated the Union itself.' The Sixteenth or income-tax Amendment, and the Seventeenth Amendment, transferring the election of United States Senators from state legislatures to the people, were adopted by Congress in 1909 and 1912 respectively and ratified by the requisite number of states in 1913.

Yet little of this legislation could be credited directly to the administration, and the public was more concerned with mid-term elections of 1910. Democrats and progressive Republicans won a smashing victory. The Democrats gained an impressive majority in the House and very much narrowed the Republican majority in the Senate. Democratic governors were elected in several Eastern states such as Maine, Massachusetts, Connecticut, and New York, and in New Jersey Dr. Woodrow Wilson, late president of Princeton University, made his first step towards a larger Presidency.

2. *Canadian Reciprocity and Dollar Diplomacy*

With a lawyer in the White House and in the Department of State, American diplomacy returned to its traditional channels. By an exchange of notes in 1908, Japan and the United States had agreed to support the independence and integrity of China, and the open door. Japan, nevertheless, with the full approval of the Triple Entente, began to consolidate her position in Manchuria. Secretary Knox attempted to meet this situation by proposing, in 1909, that the United States and European powers lend China sufficient money to buy back all the railroads controlled by foreign interests. This, said Knox, 'was perhaps the most effective way to preserve the undisturbed enjoyment by China of all political rights in Manchuria and to promote the development of those Provinces under a practical application of the policy of the open door.' But he had not felt out the Powers, as Roosevelt would have done, and his plan was rejected somewhat contemptuously by Russia and Japan. Failing in this effort to assist China out of her difficulties, Taft insisted that American bankers be allowed to participate in a four-power consortium to finance railway construction in the Yangtse Valley, 'in order that the United States might have equal rights and an equal voice in all questions pertaining to the disposition of the public revenues concerned.' But this plan, innocent enough in purpose, was repudiated by Wilson within two weeks of his accession to office.

It was fear of Japan, too, which provoked the so-called Lodge corollary to the Monroe Doctrine. In 1911 an American syndicate proposed to sell Magdalena Bay in Lower California to a Japanese fishing syndicate. On hearing of the proposal, Senator Lodge introduced and the Senate passed a resolution announcing that the purchase or control by any non-American government of any part of the American continents which had a potential naval or military value would constitute an unfriendly act. The resolution was effective, but it further aggravated Latin-American public opinion, already exasperated by Roosevelt's Panama and Caribbean policy.

A comparison of Roosevelt's and Taft's policies in Central America recalls the old adage that some persons can make off with a horse, while others cannot look over the stable wall. Secretary Knox signed treaties with Nicaragua and Honduras similar to Roosevelt's with Santo Domingo, underwriting American loans by guaranteeing the bankers against revolution and defalcation. But the Knox treaties were rejected by the Senate, and Taft's policy both in Central America and the Far East was denounced as 'dollar diplomacy.' In 1911 Taft, a warm friend to international peace, concluded treaties with both England and France for the arbitration of all disputes, including those involving 'national honor.' The German-American press and the professional Irish-Americans broke out into shrieks of dissent. A presidential election was approaching, and the Senate rejected the treaties.

Again it was Taft's misfortune, not his fault, that tariff reciprocity with Canada failed. In November 1910 three United States commissioners concluded with two members of the Dominion Parliament a reciprocity agreement to be adopted by identical legislative acts. The agreement provided free trade in primary food products, which would naturally flow from Canada southward, and a large reduction on manufactures, which would obviously go the other way. It was a sincere and statesmanlike effort by President Taft to cement friendly relations; but bad politics. The insurgent Republicans, representing for the most part Western agrarian states, were able to argue that reciprocity was a good bargain for the trusts, which would gain a new market and free raw materials at the farmer's expense. Democratic votes pushed the bill through Congress. In the debate, Champ Clark, the new Democratic Speaker, said, 'I am for it because I hope to see the day when the American flag will float over every square foot of the British North American possessions clear to the North Pole.' Mr. Clark awoke the next day to find himself notorious. His words may have been a joke, as he feebly explained; more likely they were spoken for effect, and certainly they expressed no current American sentiment. But they aroused the fighting spirit of Canadian loyalty, were repeated in Parliament, and awoke to loud entreaty Rudyard Kipling's lyre. Sir Wilfrid Laurier, the Canadian premier, was forced to appeal to his country. Canadian manufacturers, who feared to lose the protected home market they had so carefully built up, financed the conservative opposition, and in September 1911 Sir Wilfrid went down to defeat.

3. *Roosevelt and the Progressive Party*

Theodore Roosevelt, after enjoying good hunting in Africa and a triumphal progress through Europe, returned to New York in June 1910. Greeted with an hysterical enthusiasm that somewhat dismayed him, he insisted on settling down at Sagamore Hill to pursue his many non-political interests. The *Outlook* made him associate editor, and afforded him an organ. But the rôle of sage was not congenial to 'Teddy,' and the public would not be denied the delight of seeing and hearing their hero. Before the summer was over, he was making public addresses in the West, which showed unmistakably that shooting lions and dining with crowned heads had not dulled his fighting edge for reform. His ideas, clarified and systematized as the 'New Nationalism,' included not only the old Roosevelt policies of honesty in government, regulation of big business, and conservation of natural resources, but the relatively new conception of social justice — the reconstruction of society by political action. This principle involved some vigorous and wholly justified criticism of recent Supreme Court decisions, which had nullified social legislation in the states. In his Osawatomie speech of 31 August 1910 he announced, 'I stand for the square deal . . . I mean not merely that I stand for fair play under the present rules of the game, but that I stand for having those rules changed so as to work for a more substantial equality of opportunity and of reward for equally good service.' 'We must drive special interests out of politics,' he said, and hinted that unless the railroads behaved themselves the government might eventually be forced into a policy of public ownership. That autumn, at the request of Governor Hughes of New York, Roosevelt actively promoted the adoption of the direct primary, and soon found himself in the thick of the state gubernatorial campaign.

Conservative Republicans shuddered at the 'New Nationalism' and feared a complete breach with President Taft, who was worried. 'I have had a hard time,' he confessed to his old friend. 'I have been conscientiously trying to carry out your policies, but my method of doing so has not worked smoothly.' Roosevelt visited the President at the temporary summer capital, continued a friendly correspondence for several months, and refrained from public criticism of his administration. Yet the two men were being pulled apart. Insurgents and displaced progressives like Pinchot were continually telling Roosevelt that the President had surrendered to the Old Guard, and entreating him to be a candidate in 1912. Taft, on the other hand, was surrounded by friends and relatives whose advice resembled that of the Princess of Wales to George III: 'George, be a King!'

After the Democratic victories of 1910 and the Republicans' loss of the House, it was clear that Taft could not succeed himself. In December 1910, Senator LaFollette, spokesman for the insurgents, drafted a declaration of principles for a Progressive Republican League, and the next month the league was formally organized for the purpose of liberalizing the Republican party. On obtaining what he thought was Roosevelt's assurance that he would not enter the contest LaFollette became a candidate for the Republican nomination, and his prospects improved as the schism in the party deepened. His strength, however, was confined largely to the Mississippi Valley, and his radicalism frightened many who agreed in theory with the principles that he advocated. In the midst of a speech on the 'money trust,' on 2 February 1912, LaFollette collapsed. He recovered by the following day, but insurgents who had used him as a stalking horse for Roosevelt promptly deserted and went over to the old leader.

Roosevelt had declared in 1904 that 'under no circumstances' would he again be a candidate for the Presidency. Taft was his friend and his own choice; to oppose Taft would be to impeach his own judgment. But if he must confess that his judgment had been wrong, LaFollette was the obvious alternative. As late as 20 December 1911 Roosevelt wrote, 'I do not want to be President again, I am not a candidate, I have not the slightest idea of becoming a candidate.' This was true only in a purely technical sense, for Roosevelt had already assured his friend Lodge that if the nomination should be presented in the form of a patriotic duty, he would not decline. Even before LaFollette's candidacy fell flat, Roosevelt was planning how best to get into the race. At his own suggestion the Republican governors of seven states addressed to him, on 10 February 1912, an open letter urging that he announce his candidacy. A few days later President Taft publicly denounced persons who had supported the 'New Nationalism' as destructive radicals, 'political emotionalists,' and 'neurotics.' These words touched Roosevelt on the raw, since a rumor that he was losing his reason was being circulated. They were exactly the sort of challenge to dissolve his lingering doubts, and arouse a violent spirit of combat. 'My hat is in the ring,' he announced on 21 February.

That same day he delivered an address before the Ohio Constitutional Convention which must be regarded as the opening speech of his campaign. He urged that democracy be given economic as well as political connotations, that the rich man 'holds his wealth subject to the general right of the community to regulate its business use as the public welfare requires,' and that the police power of the state be broadened to embrace all necessary forms of regulation. Further, he advocated not only the initiative and the referendum, but the recall of judicial decisions. 'It is both absurd and degrading,' he said, 'to make a fetish of a judge or of any one else.' His radicalism alienated thousands of Republican voters, cost him the support of friends like Lodge, Knox, Root, and Stimson, and made his nomination by the Republicans extremely improbable.

LaFollette stayed in the fight, and the three-cornered contest for the Republican nomination became unseemly and bitter. Taft accused Roosevelt of appealing to class hatred, Roosevelt accused Taft of biting the hand that fed him, and many other things were said that would better have been left unsaid. Roosevelt knew that he could not win over the regular party organization, but wherever the law permitted he entered the presidential preference primaries in the hope that a display of popularity among the rank and file of the party might frighten the Old Guard. Thirteen states chose their delegates to party conventions through popular primaries, and in these states Roosevelt obtained 278, Taft 46, and LaFollette 36 delegates. There was no doubt that Roosevelt had the overwhelming support of the rank and file of the party, but the bosses were with Taft. Where delegates were chosen by conventions, the President was almost uniformly successful, and the Southern districts, the Republican rotten boroughs, returned a solid block of Taft delegates who represented little more than the federal office-holders in that region. The credentials of some two hundred delegates were in dispute. By electing Elihu Root temporary chairman, the conservatives retained control of the convention machinery, and awarded practically all the contested seats to Taft men.[2] On the ground that his legitimate majority had been stolen, Roosevelt instructed his delegates to take no further part in the proceedings; and Taft was renominated by a strong majority.

Roosevelt and his followers at once took steps to found a new party. Local organizations were rapidly formed, and on 5 August 1912 the first Progressive party convention met at Chicago amid scenes of febrile enthusiasm that recalled Populism and the early days of the Republican party. 'We stand at Armageddon, and we battle for the Lord,' announced Roosevelt to his enraptured followers, who paraded around the convention hall singing 'Onward Christian Soldiers' and

> We will follow Roosevelt,
> Follow! Follow!
> Anywhere! Everywhere,
> We will follow on.

[2] This question of the contested delegates is so enmeshed in precedent and party technique as to be almost insoluble for the layman. It is asserted on the one hand that the same 'steam roller' methods were used by Roosevelt in 1904 and 1908; on the other that there was no precedent for the action taken by Root. It seems on the whole probable that even if all the contests had been fairly decided, Roosevelt would not have had a majority. Yet if Roosevelt had allowed his avowed delegates to vote, it is possible though not probable that they might have won enough Taft votes to obtain the nomination. As one member said, the Negro delegates were 'straining on the leash' to vote for Roosevelt.

The convention adopted a platform embracing almost the whole of the progressive program and nominated Roosevelt by acclamation. A phrase of the beloved leader, 'I am feeling like a bull moose,' gave the new party an appropriate symbol, beside the Republican elephant and the Democratic donkey.

In the perspective of history the formation of the Progressive party appears to have been a mistake from every point of view save that of the Democrats. Roosevelt's secession with his following lost many good men their political careers, and ended all chance of liberalizing the Republican party in that generation; for although the Progressives eventually returned to the fold, it was with their tails between their legs. The true progressive strategy of the moment was that of LaFollette — to remain within the party, let the Old Guard lead it to defeat, and wait for 1916. Roosevelt's mistake was so colossal and irreparable, and so contrary to his long-settled principles of party regularity, that one naturally asks whether an appetite for power were not his moving force. Like the elder Pitt, Roosevelt believed that he, and he alone, could save the country; unlike Pitt, he did not win the opportunity to justify his faith.

The Progressives hoped that they would break into the solid South. But Roosevelt had invited the Negro leader, Booker T. Washington, to lunch at the White House, and appointed a Negro collector of the port at Charleston. And the South had a candidate of her own.

4. *Woodrow Wilson and the Election of 1912*

The young men of the South who lived through the dark days of reconstruction without allowing the bitterness of it to enter their souls came out clean as tempered steel. Such men were Chief Justice Edward D. White, Walter H. Page, and Thomas Woodrow Wilson. The year after Taft entered Yale, and the year before Roosevelt entered Harvard, Woodrow Wilson, son and grandson of Scots Presbyterian ministers, came up to Princeton. At the Hasty Pudding Club of Harvard, 'Teddy' would become so excited in debate as to lose the power of articulation. 'Tommy' was remembered at Whig Hall, Princeton, for having lost an interclub debating contest rather than defend protection against free trade. Before graduating from Harvard, Roosevelt wrote his first book, *The Naval History of the War of 1812,* which sounded the note of preparedness for war upon which his life closed. In his last year at Princeton, Wilson published an article exposing the irresponsibility of congressional government, which he did so much to remedy. Roosevelt entered public life in 1881; Wilson, after a brief and unprofitable practice of law, took his doctorate at Johns Hopkins, and began a quiet career of teaching and scholarship. In 1890, the year after Roosevelt was appointed to the Civil Service Commission, Wilson obtained a chair of political science at Princeton; and in 1902, the year after Roosevelt became President of the United States, Wilson was chosen president of Princeton University.

While Roosevelt fought political privilege in the nation, Wilson contended with social privilege at Princeton. Originally an austere Presbyterian college, Princeton had become a haven of the well-to-do, where young bloods monopolized the amenities of university life. Wilson attempted somewhat arbitrarily to transform the aristocratic undergraduate clubs into more democratic quadrangular groups. Dean Andrew F. West, a classical scholar, spoiled the symmetry of the scheme, and Wilson met his first defeat. Soon arose an even more important dispute over the organization and control of the graduate school which Wilson insisted must be integrated with the College. The whole country was interested when Wilson refused a bequest of half a million dollars which carried qualifying provisions that he deemed fatal to the proper functioning of the graduate school. The issue, to Wilson, was more than academic; it went to the very heart of the problem of democracy. 'The American college,' he said, 'must become saturated in the same sympathies as the common people. The colleges of this country must be reconstructed from the top to the bottom. The American people will tolerate nothing that savours of exclusiveness. Their political parties are going to pieces. They are busy with their moral regeneration, and they want leaders who can help them accomplish it. . . . The people are tired of pretense, and I ask you . . . to heed what is going on.' But Princeton refused to heed what was going on; and when a new bequest of several million dollars was placed at the disposal of Wilson's enemies, he stepped out of the academic picture.

As a scholar, publicist, and leader in education Wilson enjoyed a national reputation; but active politics were considered a closed sphere to professors. George Harvey, editor of *Harper's Weekly,* in search of a Democratic candidate for the Presidency, mentioned Woodrow Wilson in 1906. The suggestion was greeted with jeers, but the professor took it to heart. In 1910 the Democrats of New

Jersey — an amorphous state, half bedroom to New York and half to Philadelphia, controlled by corporations attracted by the laxity of its laws — wished to achieve respectability with a new sort of candidate. They had long been out of power and their none too savory reputation might be sweetened by a scholar. At George Harvey's suggestion the bosses nominated Wilson, and the people elected him governor. Chosen for the job of window-dressing, Wilson proceeded to clean up the shop. Within a year he had repudiated the bosses, broken the power of the sinister 'Jim' Smith, won the enthusiastic allegiance of reformers like George Record and Joseph Tumulty, and written more progressive legislation into the statute books than had been enacted in the previous half-century. He broke away from Harvey, but a silent politician from Texas, Colonel Edward M. House, took him up; and Wilson became a leading candidate for the Presidential nomination of 1912.

When the Democratic convention met in Baltimore, June 1912, the promised land was at last in sight. The split in the Republican party insured a Democratic victory on the single condition that the Democrats nominate a progressive candidate on a progressive platform. Bryan, thrice defeated, but still the most powerful figure in the party, made it his business to see that this condition was fulfilled. When the convention organized he dramatized his purpose by opposing his old rival Alton B. Parker for the temporary chairmanship. By a narrow margin Parker won, but the reaction from the country was critical, and Bryan emerged from this preliminary skirmish stronger than ever. The real battle came on the nomination. The largest number of delegates were pledged to Champ Clark of Missouri, the candidate of the party regulars and of William Randolph Hearst. Judge Harmon of Ohio had the support of Tammany Hall, Underwood of Alabama represented the Bourbon Democracy of the South, Governor Wilson commanded the progressive wing of the party. Before the balloting got under way Bryan forced the convention to adopt a resolution renouncing 'any candidate who is the representative of or under obligation to J. Pierpont Morgan, Thomas F. Ryan, August Belmont, or any other member of the privilege-hunting and favor-seeking class.' From the beginning Clark led the field, but when on the tenth ballot Tammany Hall threw its vote to the Missourian, Bryan by a dramatic repudiation of any candidate who had the support of the New York bosses, transferred his vote from Clark to Wilson. Once again the 'folks back home' were heard from, and as the balloting dragged on one delegate after another followed Bryan's lead. On the forty-sixth ballot Woodrow Wilson was nominated.

The Presidential election, then, became a three-cornered contest between Taft, Roosevelt, and Wilson; but really between the two last, as rival bidders for the popular feeling against privilege. It was a year of social unrest. The I.W.W. took charge of a great strike in the polyglot textile city of Lawrence, Massachusetts, and displayed to the shocked middle class red banners with lawless mottoes. The socialist nominee Eugene Debs was attracting more support than ever before in the history of the party. Samuel Gompers, analyzing the Progressive platform as mere eye-wash for Caesarism, advised labor to vote for Wilson but reformers generally were divided. Taft and the Republicans clearly represented the ultra-conservatives but there was little to choose between the Democratic and the Progressive platforms. Both denounced the Payne-Aldrich tariff, but the Democratic platform had the cleaner-cut tariff plank. The Progressive platform was more explicit on social and industrial reforms, but the influence of Roosevelt's financial backers, Frank Munsey and George W. Perkins, could be detected in the prudent avoidance of the trust issue which the Democrats emphasized. With the Roosevelt doctrine of regulation, the Democrats substantially agreed, and Wilson's 'New Freedom' was composed of the same ingredients as Roosevelt's 'New Nationalism.' Their methods of campaigning, however, had no more in common than their personalities. Roosevelt's tone was that of a fighting parson; Wilson already showed some glint of the spiritual quality of Lincoln. Roosevelt, with biblical imagery and voice like a shrilling fife, stirred men to wrath, to combat, and to antique virtue; Wilson, serene and confident, lifted men out of themselves by phrases that sang in their hearts, to a vision of a better world. It was the Old Testament against the New, and the New won.

Wilson polled only 42 per cent of the vote, but won an overwhelming victory in the electoral college. Roosevelt, with 27 per cent, carried six states. Taft, with 23 per cent, carried only Utah and Vermont. Nine hundred thousand voted for Debs! Technically, Wilson was a minority President, as Lincoln had been; actually the progressive principles which he, Roosevelt, and Debs alike espoused, commanded the support of over three-fourths of the voters. The Democrats swept Congress, carrying the House by 290 to 145 and the

Senate by 51 to 45, and they were victorious in twenty-one of the state gubernatorial contests. It was a complete repudiation of the old order.

Progressives thought of 1856 and were confident of triumph in 1916. The Grand Old Party, as they saw it, had gone the way of the Whig party — killed by a great moral issue that it would not face. Another bland Buchanan was in the White House. But the Old Guard neither died nor surrendered. The Progressives were little more than a candidate and his following, certainly not an organic party. And Woodrow Wilson, instead of playing the part of Buchanan, welded his party into a fit instrument of his great purpose 'to square every process of our national life again with the standards we so proudly set up at the beginning and have always carried at our hearts.'

XVIII

THE NEW FREEDOM
1913–1917

1. *The Inaugural*

FEW men have ever come to high office in the United States so unprepared politically as was Woodrow Wilson, but none ever showed a firmer grasp of the problems of statesmanship with which he had to cope, or a shrewder understanding of the game of politics which he was to play. Possibly the most remarkable characteristic of Wilson was his capacity for growth, his ability to orient himself in new problems and circumstances and reinterpret them in the light of the past and of his own convictions. Born an aristocrat, bred a conservative, trained a Hamiltonian, he became the greatest leader of the plain people since Lincoln, and a democrat who articulated the ideals of Jeffersonian democracy to the conditions of a new day.

Few even of the new President's friends expected more than a respectable Presidency. Wilson lacked the common touch, and loved humanity in the abstract rather than people in particular. Unlike Roosevelt, he could not descend into the market-place or emulate the prize-ring; throughout his eight years of office he was always aloof and often alone. His humor and warm affections appeared only to a few intimate friends. The obstinacy that had been his undoing in the academic world was not likely to be a useful virtue in the Presidency, if Cleveland's career were a fair test, and it was clear that Wilson would not sacrifice a principle or modify a policy either for friendship or for political expediency. And no President since Jefferson had been able to turn an intellectual equipment to public service. 'Wilson is clean, strong, high-minded and cold-blooded,' wrote the warm-hearted man who became his Secretary of the Interior; but he was also the kind of person to take refuge from facts in generalities. Loving the quiet places of life, his term was placed in an era of fierce contention; without Lincoln's power to express himself in simple, homely language, he was certain to be misunderstood.

The Democratic party for which he was now the spokesman had changed singularly little since Andrew Jackson's time. The elements in it that counted were the emotional and somewhat radical Western wing, represented by Bryan, Irish-Americans of the industrial states, who wanted power and office denied them during the Republican dynasties, and the solid South, including almost every white man in the late Confederacy, and many in the new Southwest — Oklahoma, New Mexico, and Arizona. Tradition and the hope of spoils held these sections together, but the issues of liquor and religion that almost split the party in 1924 and again in 1928 had not yet arisen; the small farmers of the South and West had much in common while the rural tories of the South could sympathize with rebels against the Northern industrial bosses. In only one election since Reconstruction had the party polled less than forty-two per cent of the popular vote cast for President, and in five of the ten presidential elections it received a plurality. But the Democratic party wanted leadership. Cleveland's victories had proved barren, Bryan had thrice failed, and the majority leaders in Congress were elderly and timid. For the task of leadership Wilson proved himself peculiarly equipped. He had been born with an intellectual arrogance which inclined him to rely largely upon his own judgment and he inherited a Calvinistic philosophy which placed the halo of moral necessity on expediency, while from a prolonged professional study of the science of government he had learned the necessity of executive leadership in the modern state. This conclusion emerged from all three of his earlier scholarly works, *Congressional Government, The State,* and *Constitutional Government in the United States,* and it was basic to his political thinking and practice. 'We have grown more and more inclined,' he said in 1908, 'to look to the President as the unifying force of our complex system, the leader both of his party and of the nation.' He had tested his theory of executive leadership in New Jersey and found it good; he was now prepared to justify it in a larger sphere.

Wilson's inaugural address, striking a note of high idealism and couched in words reminiscent of Jefferson's first inaugural, aroused the hopes and enthusiasm of liberals everywhere. 'No one can mistake,' he said boldly, 'the purpose for which the Nation now seeks to use the Democratic Party. It seeks to use it to interpret a change in its plans and point of view. Some old things with which we had grown familiar, and which had begun to creep into the very habit of our thought and of our lives, have altered their aspect as we have latterly looked critically upon them, with fresh, awakened eyes. . . . Some new things . . . have come to assume the aspect of things long believed in and familiar, stuff of our own convictions. We have been refreshed by a new insight into our own life.'

It was by the light of this new vision that Wilson examined the processes by which America had achieved her greatness and revealed the ruthlessness, waste and corruption, and reckoned anew the cost, not by the balance sheet of business but in the ledger of social well-being. 'We have been proud of our industrial achievements, but we have not hitherto stopped thoughtfully enough to count the human cost of lives snuffed out, of energies over-taxed and broken, the fearful physical and spiritual cost to the men and women and children upon whom the dead weight and burden of it all has fallen pitilessly the years through. The groans and agony of it all had not yet reached our ears, the solemn, moving undertone of our life, coming up out of the mines and factories and out of every home where the struggle had its intimate and familiar seat. . . . The great Government we loved has too often been made use of for private and selfish purposes, and those who used it had forgotten the people.'

The inaugural, however, was not a jeremiad, but a program of constructive reform. The Jeffersonian ideal of good government—that which governs least—was metamorphosed by Jefferson's spiritual successor into the ideal that 'our duty is to cleanse, to reconsider, to restore, to correct the evil without impairing the good, to purify and humanize every process of our common life.' Nor was this merely the vague and nebulous expression of a cloistered academic. 'We have itemized with some degree of particularity the things that ought to be altered,' Wilson said, and named the tariff, 'which makes the Government a facile instrument in the hands of private interests'; an antiquated and inadequate banking and currency system; a burdensome and wasteful industrial system which 'exploits without renewing or conserving the natural resources of the country'; an inefficient and neglected agricultural system; 'water-courses undeveloped, waste places unreclaimed, forests untended, unregarded waste heaps at every mine.' And not only was it the function of the government to serve and regulate the larger economic interests of the nation, but it must be 'put at the service of humanity, in safeguarding the health of the Nation, the health of its men and its women and its children, as well as their rights in the struggle for existence. . . . There can be no equality or opportunity . . . if men and women and children be not shielded in their lives, their very vitality, from the consequences of great industrial and social processes, which they can not alter, control, or singly cope with. . . . Sanitary laws, pure food laws, and laws determining conditions of labor which individuals are powerless to determine for themselves are intimate parts of the very business of justice and legal efficiency.'

This reinterpretation of democracy was to be no 'cool process of mere science.' The Calvinist in Wilson visualized the contest as one between the forces of good and of evil. 'The Nation has been deeply stirred by a solemn passion, stirred by the knowledge of wrong, of ideals lost, of government too often debauched and made an instrument of evil. The feelings with which we face this new age of right and opportunity sweep across our heartstrings like some air out of God's own presence, where justice and mercy are reconciled and the judge and the brother are one.' This was no mere political, no partisan task. It was the Armageddon of democracy. 'I summon all honest men, all patriotic, all forward-looking men, to my side. God helping me, I will not fail them, if they will but counsel and sustain me.'

No administration of modern times has been inaugurated with a greater passion for righteousness and justice. Yet it was not in the nature of American politics to move on a high level of idealism, nor to surrender without a struggle the stakes of battle. Nor did Wilson himself forego the advantages of partisanship; on the contrary he considered himself not only the head of the nation, but the head of his party as well, and no more consummate political strategist ever cracked the whip of party regularity. It was Wilson's fortune during his first administration to have behind him a reasonably united party, eager to follow his leadership. It was his misfortune, during his second administration, to conjure up the most bitter political and personal antagonisms in recent American history, and to have a large part of his reform program imperilled by the accident of foreign affairs.

2. *The Underwood Tariff*

Colonel E. M. House elected himself the political liaison officer of the Wilson administration. The cabinet was selected with his advice, though not by his dictation, in order to reunite a party considerably torn by the contest for the Presidential nomination. It was an able if not a brilliant cabinet, as good as any since the Hayes administration. Bryan was the inevitable choice for the State Department, not only by reason of his contribution to Wilson's nomination but because he would ensure the support of his immense following. William

G. McAdoo, Wilson's campaign manager and future son-in-law, became Secretary of the Treasury. L. M. Garrison as Secretary of War proved too warlike for his chief, and was dropped after three years for the more pacific Newton D. Baker. Franklin K. Lane, Canadian by birth and Californian by residence, proved an ideal Secretary of the Interior to reconcile the Far West to conservation. The appointment of Josephus Daniels, a North Carolina editor, to the Navy Department aroused criticism, but he showed himself a satisfactory administrator and a faithful ally in the fight for progressive legislation. David F. Houston, like Wilson a scholar and a university president, was an admirable choice for the Department of Agriculture. William B. Wilson of Pennsylvania, Secretary of the new Department of Labor, had begun life as a miner, and was eminently satisfactory to labor. For the important post of Attorney-General Wilson desired Louis Brandeis, but was dissuaded; the substitution of J. C. McReynolds, a Tennessee lawyer, was a mistake. Finally Wilson wanted ' one thorough-going politician ' in his cabinet, and in A. S. Burleson of Texas, as Postmaster-General, he found the ideal man. Four members of the cabinet were from the South and two from the West; New England was not represented, although Massachusetts, for the first time since 1820, had voted with Virginia.

When Congress met on 7 April 1913 President Wilson revived a practice abandoned by Jefferson, of addressing both Houses in person. A slight thing in itself, this act caught the popular imagination. It restored the President's initiative in lawmaking and established a relation between the ' two ends of Pennsylvania Avenue ' in the best sort of way. For Wilson's power over men left him when he stepped off the rostrum; unlike Roosevelt, he could not persuade or browbeat Congressmen in private conversation.

Congress had been summoned to special session, as in 1909, to revise the tariff. It was a dangerous issue; in the preceding twenty years only one tariff revision had failed to bring defeat at the polls, and the fate of the Wilson-Gorman tariff was as familiar to Democrats as the fate of the Payne-Aldrich to Republicans. But there was no hesitation, no compromise, in Wilson's position. ' The tariff duties must be altered,' he said. ' They must be changed to meet the radical alterations in the conditions of our economic life which the country has witnessed within the last generation. . . . Only new principles of action will save us from a final hard crystallization of monopoly. . . . We must abolish everything that bears even the semblance of privilege, or of any kind of artificial advantage, and put our business men and producers under the stimulation of a constant necessity to be efficient, economical and enterprising. . . . The object of the tariff duties henceforth laid must be effective competition, the whetting of American wits by contest with the wits of the rest of the world.' Hearings on the new tariff bill had begun as early as January 1913, and House leaders such as Underwood of Alabama, Kitchin of North Carolina, and Hull of Tennessee were ready with a bill. After a brief debate, the Underwood tariff, as it came to be known, passed the House by a strict party vote, 281 to 139. The real struggle, as everyone anticipated, came in the Senate.

On 8 May the Underwood tariff went to the Senate, and that body prepared to exercise its ancient prerogative of rewriting the House measure. To assist in this task representatives of vested interests descended upon Washington. Senator Thomas of Colorado described the scene:

> By telegram, by letter, by resolutions of commercial and industrial associations and unions, by interviews, by threat, by entreaty, by the importunities of men and the clamor of creditors, by newspaper criticism and contention, by pamphlet and circular, by the sinister pressure of a lobby of limitless resources, by all the arts and power of wealth and organization, the Senate has been and will be besieged, until it capitulates or the Underwood bill shall have been enacted.

Wilson did not intend that the circumstances of the Wilson-Gorman and the Payne-Aldrich tariffs should be duplicated. In a public statement of 26 May he lashed out at the sinister activities of the lobbyists. 'It is of serious interest to the country,' he said, 'that the people at large should have no lobby, and be voiceless in these matters, while great bodies of astute men seek to create an artificial opinion and to overcome the interests of the public for their private profit. . . . The Government ought to be relieved from this intolerable burden.' His appeal was effective, and consideration of the tariff bill went forward in a wholesomer atmosphere. Through the hot months of a Washington summer the President held Congress to its appointed task. He himself set an example of ceaseless vigilance, scrutinizing every section of the measure with meticulous care and appearing with embarrassing frequency at the Senate committee rooms to participate in conferences. In September the bill passed the Senate, and on 3 October 1913 it received the signature of the President, who announced that 'we have set the business of this country free from those conditions which have made monopoly not only possible, but in a sense easy and natural.'

The Underwood tariff was far from a free-trade measure, but it did reverse a tariff policy which had been almost unchallenged for fifty years. The average duties were reduced from some thirty-seven to some twenty-seven per cent, but more important than this were reductions in specific schedules and additions to the free list. Duties were reduced on 958 articles, raised on 86, and maintained on 307. Reductions embraced important raw materials such as cotton and woolen goods, iron and steel, while wool, sugar, iron ore, steel rails, agricultural implements, hides, boots, cement, coal, wood and wood pulp, as well as many agricultural products were to enter duty free. To meet the anticipated reduction in revenues, the bill provided for a graduated tax on incomes of three thousand dollars and over, ranging from one to six per cent. For all the jeremiads of the business interests, the new tariff worked admirably during the brief period of peace in which it could be tested, and the income tax brought not only abundant revenues but a mass of statistical information about the distribution of the national wealth that was of immense value to the lawmakers of the next decades.

3. *Banking and Currency Reform*

Reform of the banking and currency system was the second administration measure only in a strict chronological sense. Actually Wilson had from the first envisioned such legislation as an integral part of the reform program. In his inaugural address he had called attention to 'a banking and currency system based upon the necessity of the Government to sell its bonds fifty years ago and perfectly adapted to concentrating cash and restricting credits,' and in his tariff message of 8 April he had promised to call to the attention of Congress 'reforms which should press close upon the heels of the tariff changes . . . of which the chief is the reform of our banking and currency laws.' Actually the President presented his proposal for a reorganization of the banking system while Congress was still wrestling with the Underwood tariff.

The need for a thorough overhauling of our banking and currency system was almost universally recognized. The election of 1896 and the Gold Act of 1900 had settled only one aspect of the 'money question'; credit and banker control over money and credit remained to vex business men as well as farmers. The 'bankers panic' of 1907 reflected no basic unsoundness in the economic system, but a ruinous shortage of currency and inelasticity of credit; only by hasty importations of gold from abroad and by resort to extra-legal forms of currency was business able to weather the crisis. Out of this panic emerged the Aldrich-Vreeland bill which provided for a somewhat more flexible asset currency, based upon state and municipal securities and commercial paper. But this act, as Lyman Gage observed, was 'a patch' and Congress, in creating the National Monetary Commission, recognized that the whole question of banking and currency required further study. In its final report, the Commission listed seventeen serious defects in the American banking system, among them 'an unhealthy congestion of loanable funds in great centers,' and a 'concentration of surplus money and available funds in New York' which 'imposes upon the banks of that city the vast responsibilities which are inherent in the control of a large proportion of the banking resources of the country.'

But the extent of that concentration of money and credit was not fully realized until the investigations of the Pujo Committee of 1911 were made public. Those investigations revealed that the firm members or directors of two sets of New York banks, controlled by the Morgan and Rockefeller interests, held:

One hundred and eighteen directorships in thirty-four banks and trust companies having total resources of $2,679,000,000 and total deposits of $1,983,000,000.

Thirty directorships in ten insurance companies having total assets of $2,293,000,000.

One hundred and five directorships in thirty-two transportation systems having a total capitalization of $11,784,000,000 and a total mileage (excluding express companies and steamship lines) of 150,000.

Sixty-three directorships in twenty-four producing and trading corporations having a total capitalization of $3,339,000,000.

Twenty-five directorships in twelve public utility corporations having a total capitalization of $2,150,000,000.

In all, 341 directorships in 112 corporations having aggregate resources of capitalization of $22,245,000,000.

The members of the firm of J. P. Morgan & Co. hold seventy-two directorships in forty-seven of the greater corporations; George F. Baker, chairman of the board, F. L. Hine, president, and George F. Baker, Jr., and C. D. Norton, vice-presidents, of the First National Bank of New York hold forty-six directorships in thirty-seven of the greater corporations; and James Stillman, chairman of the board, Frank A. Vanderlip, president, and Samuel McRoberts, J. T. Talbert, W. A. Simonson, vice-presidents, of the National City Bank of New York hold thirty-two directorships in twenty-six of the greater corporations; making in all for these members of the group 150 directorships in 110 of the greater corporations.

Wilson himself was acutely aware of this condition, and of its significance to the agriculture and industry of the nation.

The plain fact is [he said in 1911] that control of wealth is dangerously concentrated. . . . The large money resources of the country are not at the command of those who do not submit to the direction and domination of small groups of capitalists who wish to keep the economic development of the country under their own eye and guidance. The great monopoly in this country is the money monopoly. . . . The growth of the nation, and all our activities, are in the hands of a few men who . . . are necessarily concentrated upon the great undertakings in which their own money is involved, and who necessarily . . . chill and check and destroy genius and economic freedom. This is the greatest question of all, and to this statesmen must address themselves with an earnest determination to serve the long future and the true liberties of men.

To this question, then, the new administration promptly addressed itself. Upon the necessity of reform all were agreed, but upon the precise nature of that reform there was widespread disagreement. Conservatives, even within the President's own party, wanted legislation along the lines of the Aldrich Act which would establish a central bank like the old B.U.S. without its branches, and place control of credit in the hands of the bankers. Bryan's followers, on the other hand, were determined that the power to issue notes should be a government, not a private, function, and that control of the new banking system should be exclusively governmental. Wilson was unfamiliar with the technical aspects of banking but, as Carter Glass later wrote, 'there was never a moment when he did not know what he wanted done or know what he would not permit to be done in this currency proceeding.' On 23 June he appeared before Congress to outline his own program for banking and currency reform.

We must have a currency, not rigid as now, but readily, elastically, responsive to sound credit. . . . Our banking laws must be mobilized reserves; must not permit the concentration anywhere in a few hands of the monetary resources of the country or their use for speculative purposes in such volume as to hinder . . . more legitimate uses. And the control of this system of banking and of issue which our new laws are to set up must be public, not private, must be vested in the Government itself, so that the banks may be the instruments, not the masters of business and of individual enterprise and initiative.

Carter Glass was ready with a bill which carried out in detail these general principles, and for six months Congress wrangled over this administration measure while metropolitan bankers and Western farmers criticized it with equal severity. Wilson had little to fear from the opposition of the bankers, but he could not afford to forfeit the support of Bryan and his followers, and in the end the provisions of the new law recognized both of Bryan's demands: that there should be no banker representation on the banking board, and that all notes of issue should be governmental obligations.

The Federal Reserve Act of 23 December 1913 provided for the creation of a new national banking system upon regional lines. The country was divided into twelve districts,[1] each with a Federal Reserve Bank owned by the member banks, which were required to subscribe six per cent of their capital. These regional banks did not engage directly in banking, but acted as agents for their members. All national banks were required and state banks permitted to join; within a decade one-third of the banks, representing seventy per cent of the banking resources of the country, were members of the Federal Reserve system. A Federal Reserve Board, consisting of the Secretary and the Comptroller of the Treasury and six others appointed by the President, supervises the business of the regional banks. A new type of currency was authorized: Federal Reserve notes secured by short-term commercial paper and backed by a forty per cent gold reserve. The new system was designed to introduce greater elasticity into the credit of the country, a sounder distribution of banking facilities, and more effective safeguards against speculation. All of these ends were realized, and in time the bankers themselves admitted that the Federal Reserve system had added immeasurably to the financial stability of the country.

One of the purposes of the Federal Reserve Act was to provide easier and more abundant credit for farmers, but despite the privileged position accorded to farm paper, the Act did little to bring

[1] District banks were established at Boston, New York, Philadelphia, Cleveland, Richmond, Atlanta, Chicago, St. Louis, Minneapolis, Kansas City, Dallas, and San Francisco.

down farm interest rates or ease farm credit. These objects were partially achieved, however, by the Federal Farm Loan Act of May 1916 which purposed to 'introduce business methods into farm finance . . . reduce the cost of handling farm loans, place upon the market mortgages which would be a safe investment for private funds, attract into agricultural operations a fair share of the capital of the nation, and lead to a reduction of interest.' More specifically the Act created a Federal Farm Loan Board and twelve regional Farm Loan Banks similar in general character to the Federal Reserve banks. These Farm Loan Banks were authorized to extend loans on farm lands, buildings, and improvements up to seventy per cent of their value to co-operative farm loan associations. Loans were to run from five to forty years, interest rates not to exceed six per cent, and profits were to be distributed to the members of the subscribing farm loan associations. By 1930 over four thousand such farm loan associations had been established and over one billion dollars of farm mortgages were held by the Farm Loan banks. A further step toward the creation of better credit facilities for farmers was taken in the enactment of the Warehouse Act of 1916 authorizing licensed warehouses to issue against farm products warehouse receipts which might be used as negotiable paper. Thus were the Populists vindicated a quarter-century after their sub-treasury scheme had been rejected with contempt.

4. *The Regulation of Business*

With the enactment of the Underwood tariff and the Federal Reserve Act the Democrats had gone far toward translating their platform promises into law, but the most emphatic of the party pledges was as yet unfulfilled. 'A private monopoly,' said the platform, 'is indefensible and intolerable. We therefore . . . demand the enactment of such additional legislation as may be necessary to make it impossible for a private monopoly to exist in the United States.' In the campaign, too, Wilson had stressed the trust problem as the paramount issue, and the heart of the 'New Freedom,' as he had elaborated it in his speeches, was the freedom of the consumer from monopolies.

Additional anti-trust legislation was long overdue. Roosevelt had recognized the need, but had failed lamentably to obtain such legislation from a recalcitrant Congress; Taft had not even tried. Yet the findings of the Pujo Committee and of the Commission on Industrial Relations revealed that trusts were more numerous and monopolies more powerful in 1913 than at the beginning of the century. Reliance upon the Sherman Law was clearly futile, and Wilson, in his acceptance speech, had called for ' new laws ' to meet ' conditions that menace our civilization.'

As soon as the tariff and banking reform bills were disposed of Wilson appeared before Congress to ask for legislation on trusts and monopolies. His address of 20 January 1914 included five specific legislative recommendations: the prohibition of interlocking directorates of corporations, banks, railroads, and public utilities; the grant of authority to the Interstate Commerce Commission to superintend and regulate the financial operations of railways: the explicit definition of the meaning of the anti-trust laws; the creation of a federal interstate trade commission to supervise, guide, and correct business; and the penalization of individuals, not business, for violations of the anti-trust laws. Congress promptly responded with three bills designed to meet executive specifications: The Federal Trade Commission Act, the Clayton Anti-trust Act and the Rayburn Securities Act. The first two became law in September and October 1914; the third was defeated in the Senate and was not successfully revived until 1933.

The Federal Trade Commission Act was preventative rather than punitive in character. It replaced Roosevelt's Bureau of Corporations with a new non-partisan commission of five, appointed by the President for seven year terms. Unfair methods of competition were declared unlawful, and the Commission was authorized to investigate corporations engaged in interstate commerce, and alleged violations of the anti-trust laws and to issue ' cease and desist ' orders against any corporation found guilty of unfair methods of competition. During Wilson's administration the Commission heard some two thousand complaints and issued three hundred and seventy-nine ' cease and desist ' orders against such malpractices as misleading advertising, bribery, adulteration, and unfair competition. In co-operation with the Department of Justice it brought about the dissolution of the International Harvester Company and the Corn Products Refining Company, and its subsequent investigations of electric light and power companies materially aided President Franklin D. Roosevelt in obtaining more adequate regulation of public utilities.

The Clayton Act was more radical in character and encountered bitter opposition. It prohibited discriminations in price which might tend to lessen competition or create monopoly, and 'tying' agreements limiting the right of purchasers to deal in the products of competing manufacturers. It forbade corporations to acquire stock in competing concerns, and outlawed interlocking directorates in corporations with a capital of more than one million and banks with a capital of more than five million dollars. In accordance with the President's recommendation, officers of corporations were made personally responsible for violations of the act. Labor unions were specifically exempted from the terms of the act, and the use of the injunction in labor disputes 'unless necessary to prevent irreparable injury to property . . . for which there is no adequate remedy at law' was explicitly forbidden. Gompers hailed these provisions as 'labor's charter of freedom,' yet the act did not outlaw the notorious 'yellow-dog' contracts nor, like the British Act of 1906, relieve unions from corporate responsibility for damage caused by their members.

'With this legislation,' said Wilson optimistically, 'there is clear and sufficient law to check and destroy the noxious growth [of monopoly] in its infancy.' But the courts reserved to themselves the right to determine what constituted 'unfair methods of competition' just as they reserved the right to interpret the phrase 'irreparable injury to property,' and in the war and post-war years judicial rulings became increasingly conservative. The effort to enforce the provision making directors responsible for corporation malpractices broke down when the government failed to prove its case against the directors of the New Haven Railroad. During the war the Clayton Act was tacitly suspended; and in the post-war period of Republican ascendancy it was seldom invoked, while the Federal Trade Commission, by encouraging the formulation of codes of trade practices, entered into something suspiciously like an alliance with the trusts. When, twenty years after the enactment of the Wilsonian anti-trust legislation, Franklin D. Roosevelt came into office, the trusts were as numerous and monopolies as powerful as ever, and the whole problem had to be studied afresh.

With the enactment of tariff, banking, and trust legislation the Democrats had carried out the most important of their pre-election promises, but this list by no means exhausts the reform and social legislation of the first Wilson administration. The LaFollette Seamen's Act of 1915 did much for the sailors' well-being and abolished the crime of desertion in the American merchant marine, while the Merchant Marine Act of 1916 created a government Shipping Board authorized to acquire and operate merchant ships. The Alaska Railway Act of 1914 provided for the construction, operation, and ownership of Alaskan railroads by the Federal Government. The Smith-Lever Act of 1914 provided millions of dollars for farm-demonstration work in every rural county in the country; the Smith-Hughes Act of 1917 made additional millions available for vocational and agricultural education; and the Federal Aid Road Act supplemented state and local with federal funds for the construction of highways. A Workmen's Compensation Act for the federal civil service, a law excluding from interstate commerce the products of child labor, and the Adamson Act establishing an eight-hour day on all interstate railways were passed in 1916. All in all the Democratic party made a splendid record of intelligent leadership and harmonious co-operation. They had proved that progress and statesmanship were not the monopoly of the Republicans, and that the progressive movement, which the Populists had begun and Roosevelt made popular, transcended party lines.

5. *Neighbors and Dependencies*

Wilson had not mentioned foreign affairs in his inaugural address nor had he discussed them in his campaign; yet his first administration was concerned largely, his second almost exclusively, with problems of international relations. When he assumed office the United States was at peace with the world, but faced with many vexatious controversies which demanded early attention. Japanese aggressions in Manchuria threatened the open door policy, and Japan was assuming a menacing attitude toward the anti-alien land laws of the Pacific coast states; Colombia was still sore over the Panama episode, and England was aggrieved at our discrimination in favor of American coast-wise shipping through the Panama Canal; American marines controlled Nicaragua, and conditions elsewhere in the Caribbean were unsettled, while Mexico was in the throes of a revolution which vitally affected American interests. To the solution of these difficulties the new President brought neither experience nor detailed information but a body of broad principles which not only required the maintenance of peace, but American leadership in that effort. And to those principles Secretary Bryan subscribed with more enthusiasm than understanding. For while Wilson was, for the most part, his own Secretary of State, Bryan's contributions to Latin-American policy were not negligible; his interpretation of the problem of neutrality, when that arose, was, however, less realistic than that of his chief.

In principle and, to some extent, in practice Wilson reversed the foreign policy of his predecessors. The first hint of that reversal was the statement of 19 March 1913, withdrawing administrative support from the proposed bankers' loan to China. That same week Wilson announced that 'one of the chief objects of my administration will be to cultivate the friendship and deserve the confidence of our sister Republics of Central and South America.' A few months later, in an address at Mobile, Alabama, the President announced that the foreign policy of his administration would be concerned more with 'human rights, national integrity, and opportunity' than with 'material interests,' and promised that 'the United States will never again seek one additional foot of territory by conquest.'

Yet it was soon apparent that the repudiation of dollar diplomacy was more of a theory than a fact. Actually Wilson and Bryan, despite their entirely sincere protestations of altruism, continued without modification the Caribbean policies of Roosevelt and Taft. The marines remained in Nicaragua, a new and exacting bankers' loan received the approval of the State Department, and in 1914 Bryan negotiated a treaty leasing the Gulf of Fonseca, the Great Corn and Little Corn Islands which so seriously infringed on Nicaraguan sovereignty that it was denounced by the Central American Court of Justice. In Santo Domingo Bryan authorized 'an enlargement of the sphere of American influence beyond what we have before exercised' and in 1916 Wilson ordered a military occupation of the Dominican Republic which lasted for eight years. Anarchy in Haiti led to American intervention in 1914; the following year the marine corps occupied the Island, and under the terms of a treaty which the Wilson administration dictated to the helpless Haitians, American control was continued until 1930 when public opinion in the United States forced its discontinuance.

Yet it would be a mistake to impeach the sincerity of Wilson and Bryan in their ambition for a more idealistic foreign policy. A fairer test of that policy was presented by Mexico, and one of the great achievements of the Wilson administration was the maintenance of peace with that distraught Republic. In 1911 Porfirio Diaz, dictator of Mexico for thirty-five years, resigned as the result of a revolutionary movement that he could no longer suppress. Diaz had given his country order at the expense of every sort of liberty. The national domain of 135 million acres was cut up into latifundia, or used to augment the already swollen estates of less than one thousand great landowners. At the same time Diaz pursued a policy resembling the enclosures of eighteenth-century England, expropriating and allotting in severalty the communal lands of the Indian villages. The new owners were able to exact forced labor from the landless peons by keeping them in perpetual debt for food and supplies. Education remained in the hands of the Church. The government was autocratic, the ruling class concentrated and powerful, the condition of the common people desperate. Foreign, especially English and American, mining and business interests, to which Diaz gave generous concessions and protection, enthusiastically supported his rule.

The revolution of 1910–11 was conducted by a small doctrinaire middle class under Francisco I. Madero, but supported by the peons in the hope of recovering their communal lands. Madero was installed as constitutional President in 1911, but neither kept order nor satisfied the aspirations of the landless. A counter-revolution of the landowners, supported by foreign investors, displaced him by assassination in February 1913, and installed Victoriana Huerta as President. Although unable to exert his authority over the greater part of the country, which was fast falling into anarchy, Huerta was promptly recognized by Great Britain and most of the Powers. Strong pressure was exerted on President Wilson by the American ambassador and by American business interests to do the same. How powerful those business interests were is indicated by reports of a congressional committee which calculated American investments in Mexico at one and one-half billion dollars and estimated that Americans owned 78 per cent of the mines, 72 per cent of the smelters, 58 per cent of the oil, 68 per cent of the rubber plantations, and some two-thirds of the railroads of Mexico.

But President Wilson refused to be moved by the importunities of business. In his statement of 11 March he anticipated his refusal to recognize Huerta:

> We hold that just government rests always upon the consent of the governed, and that there can be no freedom without order based upon law and upon public conscience and approval. . . . We can have no sympathy

with those who seek to seize the power of government to advance their own personal interests or ambition.

Such a policy, introducing moral considerations into the realm of international law, was a departure from the traditional practices of the United States as well as of other nations. The easy course, and perhaps the wise course, would have been to accord the Huerta government *de facto* recognition, and leave to the Mexicans the solution of their problems of constitutional law and democracy. The other policy was fraught with peril, for it placed upon the United States the responsibility of deciding which government was a moral one and of supporting that government. Furthermore, in the event that Huerta failed to back down, Wilson was faced with the awkward alternatives of active intervention — which would be an invitation to imperialism — or a serious loss of prestige.

The situation also threatened to becloud Anglo-American relations, for the United States government had reason to believe that the British ambassador at Mexico, a strong supporter of Huerta, represented British oil interests as well as the Foreign Office. And relations between the United States and Great Britain were momentarily strained by the action of Congress exempting American shipping from Panama canal tolls in contravention to the terms of the Hay-Pauncefote Treaty. Colonel House met Sir Edward Grey in July 1913 in order to talk these matters over. At a series of private and informal conferences in Washington the President agreed to press Congress to repeal the obnoxious legislation in return for the British Foreign Office withdrawing support from Huerta. The agreement, quietly concluded over the heads of the State Department and the British embassy, was carried out. On March 1914 the President appealed to Congress to withdraw 'from a position everywhere questioned and misunderstood.' 'I ask this of you,' he said, 'in support of the foreign policy of this administration. I shall not know how to deal with other matters of even greater delicacy and nearer consequence, if you do not grant it to me.' Congressional leaders fumed, but acquiesced. Equality of tolls was restored by Act of Congress, 15 June 1914, and from that date the British Foreign Office followed the American lead in Mexican affairs.

Huerta brought matters to a head early in April 1914 by arresting several sailors from an American warship. Admiral Mayo demanded not only an apology but a salute to the American flag, and the

President backed him up, though inasmuch as the United States had not recognized Huerta's government, the situation presented obvious and embarrassing legal difficulties. Huerta, hoping that American aggression might consolidate Mexican sentiment behind him, refused to budge. On 21 April a force of American marines were landed at Vera Cruz which they took with slight loss. Almost everyone expected that a second war with Mexico was about to begin. It did not begin, because Wilson desired no Mexican territory, and wished to help the Mexican people to find themselves. He distinguished between the Mexican people and the Mexican government — just as he later distinguished between the German people and the German government — and insisted that 'if armed conflict should unhappily come . . . we should be fighting only General Huerta and those who adhere to him, and our object would be only to restore to the people of the distracted republic the opportunity to set up again their own laws and their own government.'

The situation was growing acute when the President was rescued by a proposal from Argentina, Brazil, and Chile for a joint mediation. The President promptly accepted this solution, and a conference with these 'A. B. C.' powers met at Niagara Falls in May to compose the differences between the warring Mexican factions. The conference — the first of its kind in the history of the Americas — averted war and proposed a new constitutional government for Mexico. Huerta stood out stiffly against the terms of the mediation; unable, however, to obtain arms or credit from the United States or from an otherwise occupied Europe, he was practically starved out of office. Late in July he fled the country, and on 21 August Venustiano Carranza, leader of the Constitutional party, took over the Presidency. Two months later the United States government gave him *de facto* recognition.

During the six years that followed Mexico occasionally broke out into peace. Fundamentally the trouble was that the underlying force of the revolution — the land hunger of the peasants — was unable to find a leader with the honesty to adopt fundamental reforms. President Wilson maintained his policy of 'watchful waiting' while endeavoring without success to create a Pan-American machinery for dealing with the situation. The State Department advised all American citizens to withdraw from the country, and some forty thousand Americans did so. Many who remained to protect their property suffered at the hands of the revolutionists and bandits. Estimates of American losses vary, but it is probable that between 1910 and 1922 over four hundred American civilians lost their lives in Mexico or along the Mexican border and that property losses totalled not far from two hundred million dollars.

In 1916 the repeated raids of the bandit Villa across the Texas border forced the President's hand. The regular army and national guard were mobilized along the Rio Grande, and an expeditionary force under General John Pershing was sent in pursuit of Villa, who made good his escape. The practice it afforded the army may have been worth the cost, but failure to bring results discredited the policy of watchful waiting, and the violation of Mexican soil antagonized Carranza and aroused the suspicions of South American peoples. Armed intervention or even annexation would have been popular in the United States, and even with some members of the Mexican upper classes; but President Wilson again refused to take advantage of Mexican weakness and distraction. Probably no other nation unless Britain [2] and no other American statesman would so long and patiently have tolerated such conditions. Ultimately, favored by the 'hands off' policy of the United States, Mexico attained a certain degree of political stability. Carranza promulgated agrarian reforms, and, in 1917, a new constitution with stringent decrees in religious matters, and against foreign concessions, that he did not dare to carry out. In 1920 he was assassinated and Alvaro Obregon captured the government and was elected President. The diplomatic slate was wiped clean by treaties between the United States and Mexico in 1923. Another rebellion was suppressed that year; and in 1924 Plutarco E. Calles peacefully succeeded to the Presidency. The following year the Mexican Congress put into effect the retroactive and confiscatory land provisions of the Constitution of 1917, and thus raised a new dispute with the United States government, as well as anticlerical legislation that agitated Roman Catholics of this country. The astute and tactful diplomacy of Dwight W. Morrow forestalled an open rupture between the two countries, and brought about more amicable relations than at any time for a generation.

Wilson's achievements during his first term were indeed remarkable. The professor had become leader of a party refractory to leadership, and converted it from state-rights tradition to enlightened na-

[2] 'In my opinion,' said the Russian Minister of Foreign Affairs, 'the only satisfactory solution is annexation, and this action Russia would see with approval.' J. F. Rippy, *The United States and Mexico,* p. 334.

tionalism. In three years he had convinced the average citizen that the Federal Government was at last his servant, and had captured the loyalty of 'forwardlooking' men and women. The Democratic party, completely under his spell, renominated him by acclamation in 1916, but he had a stout fight to wage against the reunited Republican party. His internal reforms, excepting the Federal Reserve Act, were unpalatable to big business; and to many citizens his foreign policy appeared feeble, procrastinating, and pusillanimous.

XIX

THE ROAD TO WAR

1914–1917

1. *The United States and the World War: Factors and Conditions*

SINCE the early years of the twentieth century Europe had been preparing for war, and hoping to avoid it. Peace was maintained only by a precarious balance between two sets of alliances: the Triple Alliance or Central Powers (Germany, Austria-Hungary, Italy) and the Triple Entente (France, Russia, and Great Britain). A general war had been threatened on several occasions: by the Moroccan question in 1905, when Germany backed down; by the Agadir crisis of 1911; and two or three times during the Balkan Wars of 1912–13. The result of that local war was to lessen the prestige of the Central Powers which backed the wrong horse, and to increase both the power and the bumptiousness of Serbia and Rumania, the Balkan kingdoms that obtained the lion's share of the loot. And as soon as the war was over, Serbia went fishing in the troubled waters of the Dual Monarchy.

On 28 June 1914 the shot was fired that closed an era of progress, liberalism, and democracy and inaugurated the age of warfare, destruction, revolutionary upheavals, and dictatorships, of which we have not yet seen the end. Archduke Franz Ferdinand, heir to the throne of Austria-Hungary, was assassinated at Serajevo in the province of Bosnia. The murderer belonged to a Serbian revolutionary group active in breaking up the Dual Monarchy, but that was not generally known until after the war. Austria, determined once and for all to put an end to the Slavic threat and supported by Germany, presented stringent demands with which Serbia could not comply save at the cost of losing her independence. She made several concessions which Austria deemed insufficient, and on 28 July Austria declared war on her. Russia, as the leader of the Slavic world, could not stand by while Serbia, whom she had secretly encouraged, was crushed, and mobilized her army. Germany, fearing to be caught between two enemies, declared war first (1 August) on Russia and then (3 August) on France, which was bound to come to Russia's aid in any case. In order to crush France before unwieldy Russia fairly got going, Germany struck at her through Belgium, whose neutrality she and the other powers were bound by treaty to respect. Great Britain then (4 August) declared war on Germany. The World War was on.[1]

President Wilson at once tendered American good offices, which were politely but firmly rejected, and proclaimed the neutrality of the United States. 'The occasion is not of our making,' he said in his message to Congress of 4 September 1914. 'We had no part in making it. But it is here. It affects us directly and palpably almost as if we were participants in the circumstances which gave rise to it. . . . We shall pay the bill, though we did not deliberately incur it.' The statement was exact and the warning prophetic. From the very beginning the United States was vitally affected by the war. The most powerful of nations that remained neutral, we were likewise the most vulnerable. Our population included representatives of every racial group whose homelands were involved in the war, and their emotions were naturally aroused. Our commercial and financial relations extended to every European nation, and were particularly bound up with England and Germany. Our cultural relations were very close with England and France. And no European war in which England was involved could fail to raise problems of neutral rights, which, as the experience of Jefferson's time recalled, might easily become points of national honor.

Yet in 1914 the suspicion hardly dawned on the average American that his country might be drawn into the war, and there was an almost universal determination to stay out. A century had passed since the Treaty of Ghent and the fall of Napoleon; a hundred years for the sentiment of isolation from the 'broils of Europe' to deepen; a century of unparalleled growth in the power to maintain isolation. And although the United States, in view of her wars with the Indians and with Mexico and Spain, could hardly be called a pacific nation, she had early taken the lead in the peace movement and from the beginning of her history had subscribed to the principle of the arbitration of international controversies. The Jay Treaty, the Rush-Bagot agree-

1 Turkey joined the Central Powers about a month later. Italy disregarded her alliance with the Central Powers, and after a highly profitable neutrality and much astute bargaining, threw in her lot with the Entente Allies in 1915. Japan also joined the Allies before the United States came in, but confined her efforts to the Far East. Rumania and Portugal joined the Allies; Bulgaria, the Central Powers. Greece tried to remain neutral, but the Allies occupied Salonica as a base, and finally she joined their side.

ment, the Treaty of Guadalupe-Hidalgo, the Geneva arbitration, the arbitration of the fur-sealing, the Canadian, and the Venezuela boundary controversies, the provisions of various Pan-American conferences declaring arbitration to be a principle of 'American International law,' the Root and Bryan treaties, all testified to the persistence and the sincerity of American faith in this method of settling disputes.

There was a long American tradition of neutrality and neutral rights, and one of the most important of these rights was freedom of the seas. From the Franco-American treaty of 1778, the United States had made it a consistent policy to enlarge the right of neutrals and decrease the power of belligerents to disturb the peaceful part of the world. She had gone to war with England in 1812, ostensibly at least, to protect her rights as a neutral. She had adhered to the Declaration of Paris of 1856, which adopted the principle that free (neutral) ships make free goods. She had taken part in the Hague Conventions of 1899 and 1907, and had helped to draft the Declaration of London of 1909, which drew up a code of naval warfare based on the Declaration of Paris. American determination to preserve and enforce neutrality traversed class, sectional, and party lines. It was voiced in the press, in the churches, and on the street; it was reflected in Congress, and found eloquent expression from the President, who pled with the country to 'be neutral in fact as well as in name . . . impartial in thought as well as in action'; to 'keep herself fit and free to do what is honest and disinterested and truly serviceable for the peace of the world.'

There is no easy answer to the question of why we fought and those who look for simple explanations will be disappointed or misled. It is possible to discover the causes of wars such as that of 1812 or the one with Mexico, but after a century and a half, no two scholars are agreed upon the precise causes of the American Revolution, and the schoolboys of North Dakota and South Carolina grow up with very different notions of responsibility for the Civil War. The immediate provocations of these wars, to be sure, can be readily fixed; the underlying causes are still in dispute. So, too, with our entry into the World War: the provocation is easy to discover, but the fundamental causes are lost in a maze of controversy, and most of the available literature on the subject is tinged by emotion. We must be wary of it, and above all we must guard against reading back into the period 1914–17 our present-day judgments and preconceptions. What seems obvious now was often obscure to that generation, and a logic that seemed compelling in 1917 appears only plausible today. We must appreciate the importance of what men thought was true as well as the importance of what we now know to have been true. And if our generation is disillusioned about 'making the world safe for democracy' we must not assume that the phrase was insincere or the ideal naïve.

Let us then retrace, as best we can, the path to war. It is necessary that we keep in mind several considerations of a general character as well as a particular train of facts and circumstances. For while it is true that American entry into the war was precipitated by the German submarine warfare, and that without this we probably should not have fought, it is important to know why Germany resorted to submarine warfare, and why the United States reacted to it as she did.

From the outbreak of the World War American public opinion was predominantly favorable to the Allies. This is a fact of primary importance. It matters little how much of this opinion was due to Allied propaganda, since propaganda can only be effective on friendly hearts and receptive minds. American friendship with England and France, and suspicion of Germany, was no sudden and artificial growth. It went deeper than that. The majority of Americans were English-speaking, and regarded some part of the British Empire as their mother country, with whom war would have seemed immoral. For one thing, it would have involved us in war with our sister democracy, the Dominion of Canada. Ties of language and literature, law and custom, as well as of a more personal character, bound America to the British Empire in a thousand ways. With France our relations were more sentimental than intimate, but the tradition of Franco-American friendship went back to the Revolution: Lafayette's gallantry was one thing that school children did not forget when they grew up, and Colonel Stanton's 'Lafayette we are here' was something more than dramatics. With Germany and her allies, on the other hand, American relations were amicable but not cordial. To be sure, the presence of millions of Germans in America made for understanding and even sympathy with the German people; but many even of these were critical of their fatherland's policies, and few, as Ambassador Von Bernstorff lamented, were inclined to place the interest of Germany before that of the United States. And since the Spanish War there had grown up in America a feeling that the German government was militaristic, hostile to democracy, and unfriendly to the United States. Secretary Bryan had induced Great Britain to sign one of his favorite 'cooling-off' arbitration treaties, but it was significant that Germany had declined.[2] To many Americans there was something ridiculous in the posturings and sabre-rattlings of William II, even when they were not odious.

This basic friendliness for the Allies and suspicion of Germany made our entry into the war on the side of Germany unthinkable, our entry on the side of the Allies unpalatable though not inconceivable. Wilson himself furnishes an illustration of this attitude. Of mixed Scots and English ancestry, steeped in English literature, a student of English history and admirer of British political institutions, it was easier for him to grasp the British than the German point of view and his emotional and intellectual sympathies were from the first enlisted on the side of the Allies. He tried to be neutral, but he was willing to endure outrageous provocations rather than risk a war with England; and Bryan was right in protesting that he was quicker to hold Germany than England to 'strict accountability' for violations of neutral rights. And when Russia went republican, just as we were about to enter the war, Wilson found it easy to identify the cause of the Allies with that of democracy and of civilization itself.

American suspicion of Germany was intensified by her cynical violation of Belgian neutrality, and by the widespread conviction, assiduously cultivated by Allied publicists and supported by seemingly irrefutable documentary evidence, that she alone was responsible for the war. American opinion was further alienated by the sinking of the *Lusitania* and exacerbated by Germany's persistence in her U-boat policy, which most Americans regarded as a flagrant violation of international law and of morality.

With Belgium and the *Lusitania* in mind, it was easy for Americans to believe the anti-German propaganda which the Allies sponsored. Yet we must not exaggerate the importance of Allied progaganda: that propaganda probably did not hasten by a day the decision to fight. It did break down resistance in some quarters and silence it in others, and encourage Americans to rationalize their war on

[2] These Bryan arbitration treaties pledged both parties, in the event of a dispute, to wait twelve months after all means of composing their differences otherwise than by war had been exhausted.

broad humanitarian grounds. No one now believes the more preposterous atrocity stories, to the authenticity of which even Lord Bryce lent his name; but the hatred that they engendered served to give the war the moral character of a wolf hunt.

France was the most popular of the countries at war. Germany had declared war upon her, apparently without the slightest provocation, caught her unprepared, and taken an unfair advantage by striking through Belgium; yet the French armies aroused admiration by their desperate stand along the Marne. American writers such as Edith Wharton and correspondents such as Frank Simonds glorified France. A group of wealthy young Americans formed the *Lafayette Escadrille* in the French flying corps; thousands of other youngsters enlisted in the Foreign Legion and the British and Canadian armies, and their letters and articles all stimulated the feeling that the least America could do was not to let our historic ally be crushed by insisting on too strict a neutrality. While the American friends of France worked for her, the British issued first-class propaganda for themselves. They had an initial advantage in speaking the same language as the Americans and having much the same modes of thought. The Allies, moreover, controlled the most important avenues of communication; had indeed a monopoly of all but wireless telegraphy and special correspondence. They had ready access to American newspapers and journals, and could command the services of many intellectuals and leaders of American society.

The relative ineffectiveness of German propaganda is not to be measured by relative yardage in the New York *Times* and other metropolitan papers. The official German wireless station was able to send its news across regularly, and practically all the leading newspapers printed their *communiqués*. Several influential papers, such as the Chicago *Tribune,* made a specialty of German news, or employed military experts who interpreted events to show German victory inevitable, or sent popular correspondents to the German armies. But the German propaganda, designed largely for groups that were favorable anyway, such as German-Americans and the anti-British Irish-Americans, was singularly inept, pompous, and ineffective. Its arguments were legal, technical, and intellectual, rather than emotional. It failed to play up 'human interest' material such as the children doomed to malnutrition by the British blockade, or the good humor and the *Gemütlichkeit* of the average soldier. And whenever the German propaganda began to get going nicely, something happened — the sinking of the *Lusitania* or the deportation of Belgian civilians in 1916 — that undid everything. After the *Lusitania* the German Ambassador confessed 'our best plan is frankly to acknowledge that our propaganda in this country . . . has completely collapsed.' Subsequent resort to sabotage in munitions works and to acts of violence merely emphasized the growing German desperation.

Next in importance to the psychological was the economic factor. Even before the war a large percentage of American trade was with the Allied nations. On the outbreak of the war the Allies began to apply trade-restriction measures — commonly called the blockade — to the Central Powers; and they were very shrewd in developing these restrictions progressively. Cotton, for instance, was added to the list of contraband only after the *Lusitania* was sunk; and when a Southern Senator complained, Senator Lodge remarked that he was more moved by the spectacle of American women and children drowning in the ocean than by that of American cotton sitting on a wharf. Trade with Germany became negligible; trade with Great Britain and France mounted impressively. This increase in our foreign trade, in full swing by the middle of 1915, rescued the United States from a commercial depression that had lasted a year. 'The brutal facts,' wrote the English Ambassador, Cecil Spring-Rice, in November 1915, 'are that this country has been saved by the war and our demand from a great commercial crisis. . . . We have therefore the claims of their best customer and at the present moment our orders here are absolutely essential to their commercial prosperity.' Cotton, wheat, and beef, as well as manufactures, found a ready and highly profitable market; and when the Allies seized American cargoes destined directly or indirectly for Germany, it was possible to claim and eventually to collect damages. Within a year after the outbreak of the war the whole fabric of our economic life was so closely interwoven with the economy of the Allies that any rupture would have been ruinous. It was the realization of this, in addition to sympathy for the Allies, that persuaded Wilson and his cabinet to reject an embargo on munitions of war.

This trade in munitions was particularly important. Countenanced by international law it was open alike to all belligerents. But this impartiality was theoretical rather than real. Allied sea power prevented the Central Powers from procuring American munitions; the Allies got all they wanted; and our munitions exports increased in value from some $40,000,000 in 1914 to $1,290,000,000 in 1916. Germany never officially denied the legality of this trade, but she protested that it did violate the spirit of neutrality. To the suggestion that the United States place an embargo upon munitions exports, the American government replied that it could not change the rules of neutrality to the advantage of one and the disadvantage of another belligerent while the war was in progress. As a technical defense this was sound; but both belligerents were changing the rules of war, and it was within the rights of Congress to stiffen our neutrality requirements as, for instance, the Dutch did, by treating armed merchantmen as warships and interning them. The point is, neither Congress nor public opinion wished to do so.

Credit was essential for trade; without credit the belligerents could not buy American goods. At the beginning of the war the United States was a debtor nation; this situation was promptly reversed as foreign investors dumped their securities on the American market. Soon the Allies found it advisable to finance their purchases in the United States through loans floated in Wall Street. This scheme Bryan opposed. 'Money,' he said, 'is the worst of all contrabands because it commands everything else. . . . The powerful financial interests which would be connected with these loans would be tempted to use their influence through the newspapers to support the interest of the government to which they had loaned because the value of the security would be directly affected by the result of the war. . . . All of this influence would make it all the more difficult for us to maintain neutrality.' The State Department accepted this point of view and, on 15 August 1914, informed American bankers that 'in the judgment of this Government, loans by American bankers to any foreign nation which is at war are inconsistent with the true spirit of neutrality.' Yet within a month this position was modified to authorize 'credit loans,' and bank credits were promptly extended to belligerent governments. By the late summer of 1915 Bryan was out of the cabinet, and his successor Secretary Lansing, as well as Secretary McAdoo, warned the President that the country was 'face to face with what appears to be a critical economic situation.' 'Popular sympathy,' wrote Lansing, 'has become crystallized in favor of one or another of the belligerents to such an extent that the purchase of bonds would in no way increase the bitterness of partisanship or cause a possibly serious situation.' Before this united pressure Wilson gave way, and on 14 September 1915 the State Department withdrew altogether its opposition to loans. Before the United States entered the war about one and one-half billion dollars had been lent by the American public to the Allied governments, as opposed to only twenty-seven million to the Central Powers.

In 1934–35 the Nye committee of the Senate made public a vast body of data bearing on the relations between American bankers and munitions manufacturers and the Allies. These data were more sensational than important. That the American financial stake in an Allied victory may have influenced some people is possible. But the financial community as a whole, it was well known at the time, favored American neutrality rather than American participation; for neutrality afforded Wall Street all the profits of war without the compensating sacrifices and taxation. And there is not a shred of evidence to support the allegation that Wilson was at any time influenced by the financial 'stake' in his relations with Germany, or that the decision to fight in April 1917 would have been retarded or reversed had financial relations been otherwise. It was neither trade, nor munitions, nor loans, nor propaganda that persuaded the administration of the inescapable necessity of war; it was the German submarine policy.

2. *The Struggle for Neutral Rights*

From the beginning the United States was engaged in a losing struggle for the preservation of her rights as a neutral. The fundamental difficulty was lack of international law to deal with unforeseen conditions and circumstances. Laws purporting to protect the rights of neutrals had been formulated with reference to the last naval war, the Russo-Japanese conflict of 1905; but at that time the big naval powers were neutral, and the technique of offense developed so fast in the World War that there was no generally recognized law to deal with it. The Declaration of London of 1909 represented a hopeful effort to codify and modernize the laws of neutrality, but that Declaration had been rejected by Great Britain as too favorable to neutral rights, and had no legal standing. With reference, therefore, to many controversial matters international law was vague; with reference to new problems presented by the submarine, it was silent. And as Lloyd George subsequently remarked: 'Nations fighting for their lives cannot always pause to observe punctilios. Their every action is an act of war, and their attitude to neutrals is governed, not by the conventions of peace, but by the exigencies of a deadly strife.'

America's first and most prolonged dispute was with Great Britain. Promptly upon the outbreak of the war, Britain blockaded Germany. This was no mere policing of German ports, but a new type of blockade which, as elaborated in a series of Orders in Council, involved a considerable extension both of the contraband list and of the 'continuous voyage' doctrine which justified confiscating cargoes of enemy destination in neutral ships, even when billed for neutral ports; and a declaration that the North Sea and the English Channel were 'military areas.' The Allies' command of the sea enabled them to enforce these Orders in Council, even when their diplomacy was hard put to justify them on legal grounds. American direct trade with the Central Powers was entirely, her indirect trade largely, cut off. And in addition the Allies employed such devices as the rationing of trade to neutrals and the blacklisting of firms suspected of trading with the Central Powers.

Against these palpable violations of American neutral rights, the United States protested in vain. England's determination to enforce her own interpretation of neutral rights was inflexible. Three possible courses of action were open to the United States: war, an embargo partial or complete, or temporary acquiescence accompanied by formal protest. But from the start our means of defense and retaliation were circumscribed by pro-ally sentiment; and by 1916 they were still further restrained by the economic tie-up with the Allied cause which affected farmers and business men alike. And it was inconceivable that the United States should have gone to war over questions affecting property rights alone.

Wilson and the State Department certainly had no intention of taking a stand for neutral rights which, if persisted in, might land us in war on the side of autocracy, as had happened in 1812. They remembered that Jefferson's embargo had hurt us more than it had the belligerents in 1808. So they chose the course of protest and persuasion, a course designed to keep the record clear while avoiding the catastrophe of war.

The British and French continued to violate neutral rights, and the State Department to protest, down into the beginning of 1917. At any time after the middle of 1915 a real threat of an embargo on munitions of war would probably have brought the Allies to book. Their own factories were unable to supply the enormous demand of their armies for high explosives; the cutting off of supplies from America would have lost them the war. Jefferson's embargo had not accomplished anything, but Madison's non-intercourse, it will be remembered, forced the repeal of the Orders in Council; and the situation of 1915–17 was analogous to that of 1811–12, not to that of 1807–09.

Faced with economic strangulation, Germany struck back with the only weapons at her disposal: mines and submarines. As early as August 1914 she began to plant mines in the North Sea and the Irish Sea, and on 4 February 1915 she announced that all the waters around the British Isles constituted a war zone in which all commerce with the Allies would be destroyed. Thus was inaugurated the submarine warfare which eventually forced the United States into war. That the sinking of unarmed neutral ships was a clear violation of existing international law, Germany did not deny; but she justified her policy on the ground that it was necessitated by the equally lawless British blockade.

To Wilson, and to most Americans, the distinction between British and German violations of neutral rights was clear. As Mr. Asquith said, 'Let the neutrals complain about our blockade and other measures taken as much as they may, the fact remains that no neutral national has ever lost his life as the result of it.' But the U-boat warfare took a toll of two hundred and nine American lives on the high seas — twenty-eight of them on American ships.[3] Damages for property losses entailed by Allied violations of American rights could be settled after the war; damages for American lives that had been lost in the U-boat campaign could never be adequately paid.

Alarmed at the threat of submarine warfare, Wilson informed the

[3] Borchard and Lage give the number as 195. Other neutrals suffered far more. During the war over 3,000 Norwegian sailors lost their lives through submarine and mine, and over fifty per cent of the Norwegian merchant marine was destroyed.

German government on 10 February 1915 that 'the United States would be constrained to hold the Imperial German Government to a strict accountability' for 'property endangered or lives lost.' Thereby the Wilson administration took the stand that must inevitably lead to war, unless either the United States or Germany backed down.

The trouble with requiring submarines to follow the time-honored procedure of visit and search was that U-boats were extremely vulnerable; and a merchantman armed with a single 6-inch rifle could sink any that appeared above the surface. The Dutch government early in the war adopted the principle for which there was ample precedent in earlier naval wars, that armed merchantmen were warships, and refused to allow them to trade with the Netherlands. If the United States had adopted and enforced a similar law, the Allies would have had to stop arming their merchantmen, and the German submarines in that event could have afforded to observe the properties and humanities when making captures at sea. Our government might also have warned American citizens from travelling on belligerent merchant ships. But we must remember that they had the right, as neutrals, to do that, and to expect that if the ship they travelled in was sunk they would first be placed in safety. And the American public, with its strong tradition of defending neutral rights, would have treated any failure to hold the U-boats to 'strict accountability' as pusillanimous and the Democratic party would have lost the election of 1916. As it was, Wilson was accused of insincerity, cowardice, and pro-Germanism by the Republican press and also by the growing proportion of the American people who sincerely believed that the Allies must win, or the Prussian heel would be upon our necks.

Soon came a test of the meaning of 'strict accountability.' On 28 March 1915 an American citizen went down with the British ship *Falaba;* on 29 April an American merchant vessel, the *Cushing,* was attacked by a German airplane; and on 1 May the American tanker *Gulflight* was torpedoed. Germany offered to make reparations for an 'unfortunate accident' but refused to abandon submarine warfare.

Matters were brought to a head when on 7 May 1915 the crack Cunard liner *Lusitania* was torpedoed off the coast of Ireland with a loss of life of over eleven hundred, including 128 American citizens. The sinking of the *Lusitania* was criminally stupid; it was no mitigation of the crime to point out that the German embassy had warned passengers not to sail on the ill-fated ship, and that she carried munitions for the Allied armies. A thrill of horror ran through the American people; public leaders like Theodore Roosevelt clamored for war, and the press took up the cry.

That, as it turned out, might have been the best moment for the United States to have entered the war. Had we been able to bring our strength to bear in 1916, the war would probably have been over within a year, and the disastrous loss of life, destruction of spiritual values, and breakdown of civilized standards would have ceased two years earlier than it did. But the country was not yet mentally prepared for war, and Wilson in 1915, like Jefferson in 1807, refused to be stampeded into any irrevocable act. On 13 May he demanded that the German government disavow the sinking of the *Lusitania,* 'make reparation so far as reparation is possible for injuries that are without measure, and take immediate steps to prevent the recurrence of anything so obviously subversive of the principles of warfare.' But Germany, persuaded that Wilson was playing to the gallery, tried to drag out the issue by a series of technical objections. Impatient of procrastination, Wilson sent, on 9 June, a second peremptory note:

> The Government of the United States cannot admit that the proclamation of a war zone from which neutral ships have been warned to keep away may be made to operate as in any degree an abbreviation of the rights either of American shipmasters or American citizens bound on lawful errands as passengers on merchant ships of belligerent nationality. It does not understand the Imperial German Government to question those rights. It understands it, also, to accept as established beyond question the principle that the lives of noncombatants cannot lawfully or rightfully be put in jeopardy by the capture or destruction of an unresisting merchantman and to recognize the obligation to take sufficient precaution to ascertain whether a suspected merchantman is in fact of belligerent nationality or is in fact carrying contraband of war under a neutral flag.

Bryan, who felt that this protest was dangerously close to an ultimatum, resigned from the cabinet rather than sign the note. His own solution for the difficulty was to renounce responsibility for the lives of Americans who chose passage on belligerent ships. 'Germany,' he said, 'has a right to prevent contraband from going to the Allies, and a ship carrying contraband should not rely upon passengers to protect her from attack — it would be like putting women and children in front of an army.' This plausible argument, not without precedent in our own history, commanded the support of many of the most influential Congressional leaders — Senators Stone and Gore, Congressmen Clark, Lindbergh, Kitchin, and McLemore, among them. It was embodied, early in 1916, in the Gore-McLemore Resolutions refusing passports to American citizens who purposed to travel on the armed ships of belligerents. Wilson moved promptly to defeat the resolutions. 'Once accept a single abatement of right,' he wrote to Senator Stone, 'and many other humiliations would certainly follow, and the whole fine fabric of international law might crumble under our hands piece by piece.' As a result of executive pressure, the resolutions were defeated, and the 'whole fine fabric of international law' was saved — for the moment.

On 19 August 1915, before the *Lusitania* controversy had been settled, the English liner *Arabic* was torpedoed with the loss of two American lives. A diplomatic rupture seemed inescapable, but Von Bernstorff, fully alive to the seriousness of the situation, hastened to disavow the action, and to promise that in the future 'liners will not be sunk by our submarines without warning and without safety of the lives of non-combatants.' A month later his disavowal was confirmed by the German government, and the crisis passed. For six months American relations with Germany were undisturbed by any new U-boat sinkings, but this peaceful interlude was rudely shattered when in February 1916 the German government announced a renewal of submarine warfare on armed merchant vessels. On 24 March the unarmed channel steamer *Sussex* was torpedoed without warning; many Americans were aboard, and several were injured. Outraged at this violation of the pledge which had been given after the *Arabic* affair, Wilson warned Germany that unless she immediately abandoned her submarine warfare against freight and passenger vessels the United States would be forced to break off diplomatic relations. Faced with this threat, the German government capitulated, promising, on 4 May, that henceforth no more merchant vessels would be sunk without warning, provided the United States held England also to 'strict accountability.' The

State Department continued to protest England's violations, and German submarines spared merchant vessels until February 1917; during the intervening nine months American relations with Germany were less disturbed than at any time since the *Lusitania* tragedy.

3. *Preparedness and the Election of 1916*

Despite this apparent settlement of the U-boat controversy, President Wilson became more and more persuaded that the only way in which the United States could avoid war was to end the war. Proffers of good offices and of mediation had been repeatedly rejected, but all through 1916 Wilson labored to bring about a peace on the basis of mutual compromises and concessions. The task was hopeless from the first, for none of the belligerents wanted such a peace; none of the politicians dared face their peoples without some compensation for their terrible sacrifices. In all Europe there was no statesman with vision to foresee and courage to proclaim the disastrous consequences of a Punic victory.[4] Wilson alone appreciated the ultimate cost of a dictated peace to victors and vanquished alike; he alone had the courage to call for a 'peace without victory.'

So eager was Wilson to achieve peace that he went to the somewhat inconsistent extreme of offering to fight for it. In February 1916 Lord Grey, after a series of conferences with the ubiquitous Colonel House, was able to assure his government that 'President Wilson was ready . . . to propose that a Conference should be summoned to put an end to the war. Should the Allies accept this proposal, and should Germany refuse it, the United States would probably enter the war against Germany. . . . If such a Conference met, it would secure peace on terms not unfavorable to the Allies; and if it failed

[4] 3 January 1917. 'The Allies' reply to the peace overture of Germany is published today; about as weak a document as could be imagined. Neither the German proposal nor the Allies' response rises to any level of statesmanship. The chancelleries of Europe, so far as character is concerned are bankrupt, and the conceptions of the men in them are no higher than those of the fish-wives down at the Fish Market; they plot and wrangle all the time.' Allan Nevins, ed., *The Letters and Journal of Brand Whitlock* (*The Journal;* 1936), ii, 341. Cf. the situation in our own Civil War, above, vol. i, pp. 628–31.

to secure peace, the United States would probably leave the Conference as a belligerent on the side of the Allies, if Germany was unreasonable.' For reasons that were not entirely clear, the British cabinet rejected this overture, and it was never renewed. Efforts to enlist the interest both of France and of Germany were equally fruitless.

Profoundly discouraged, Wilson turned early in 1916 toward a program of military preparedness. This policy was in part the result of conviction, in part of political expediency. A Presidential campaign was in the offing, and the Democrats could not afford to permit their Republican opponents to capitalize the popular issue of national defense. As early as November 1915 Wilson had set forth a program of preparedness, justifying his conversion by a reference to *Ezekiel* xxxiii: 'But if the watchman see the sword come, and blow not the trumpet, and the people be not warned; if the sword come, and take any person from among them, he is taken away in his iniquity; but his blood will I require at the watchman's hand.' And in the following months Wilson blew the trumpet, and the people were warned. A series of monster preparedness parades in Eastern cities indicated support from the business and industrial sections of the country, but the South and the Middle West were lukewarm. Nevertheless, during the summer of 1916, the administration drove through Congress a series of acts strengthening the military and naval forces of the nation. The National Defense Act of 3 June enlarged the regular army to 175,000, strengthened the national guard, and provided for an officers' reserve corps; the Naval Appropriation Bill of 29 August authorized the construction of a large number of new battleships, cruisers, and smaller men-of-war. The handicap American trade was under, by having to depend on belligerent or Scandinavian merchantmen to carry its exports, converted the Democratic party to building up an expensive merchant marine, and the United States Shipping Board Act of 7 September 1916 appropriated fifty million dollars for the purchase or construction of merchant ships. Finally, to co-ordinate industries and resources for defense, Congress created a Council of National Defense consisting of six cabinet members and an advisory board drawn from the ranks of industry and labor.

Having thus made appropriate gestures toward the more militant elements, the President embarked upon a campaign for re-election under the slogan, 'He kept us out of war.' As a statement of fact it was accurate; those Americans who read into it a promise of future policy failed to consider the possibility of a change of the circumstances on which the promise was conditioned.

The Republican party was pro-ally in leadership, but dared not avow it for fear of losing the German-American vote; the Progressive party was moribund. Quondam Progressives hoped that the Republican convention would nominate Roosevelt, but the Republicans wished to punish him for his secession and feared the effect of his vigorous support of the Allies and of preparedness on German-American voters. Instead Charles Evans Hughes, Associate Justice of the Supreme Court, was placed in nomination; and Roosevelt dismissed the last Progressive convention with the advice to follow him back to the Grand Old Party. Some did; others, more concerned than he with the problems of domestic reform, went over to the Democrats.

By adding together the Republican and Progressive votes of 1912 Justice Hughes appeared certain of victory. All the well-known portents — the September election in Maine, the trend in New York, the betting odds of ten to seven — indicated a Republican victory. But Hughes proved a disappointing candidate; Wilson's progressive reforms were not forgotten; and hundreds of thousands of Socialists, more loyal to peace than to party, gave their votes to the candidate who had kept us out of war. When the early returns showed that Mr. Hughes had carried New York, New Jersey, and Indiana, his election was taken for granted. But the Far West was not yet heard from; and the electoral vote of the Far West had grown with its population. Mr. Hughes had made several errors during an electioneering tour of California. He lost that state by less than four thousand votes, and its electoral vote was just sufficient to give a majority in the electoral college to Wilson. The margin was dangerously narrow, but Wilson's popular plurality of six hundred thousand was a better indication of the relative strength of the two candidates.

4. *War*

As soon as his re-election was assured, Wilson determined to renew his appeal to the belligerents for a negotiated peace. Such an appeal seemed well-timed. The Battle of the Somme cost a million casualties; the Russian offensive in Galicia a million and a half more. Unfortunately, Wilson postponed his overture a week too long. Germany, having beaten Rumania to her knees in a quick summer campaign, issued an invitation to the Allies to open direct negotiations (12 December 1916). Six days later President Wilson addressed to every belligerent government a note asking for a statement of 'the precise objects which would, if attained, satisfy them and their people that the war had been fought out.' Coming at that time, this seemed an echo of the German invitation, which queered the Wilson overture in the sight of the Allies. Lloyd George announced that Britain's terms would be 'complete restitution, full reparation, and effectual guarantees' for the future; Germany's terms, announced confidentially to Washington, included a slice of France, economic control of Belgium, and plenty of indemnities. Clearly there could be no getting together on either basis; and although Wilson had at his hand one weapon — embargo — that could have forced the Allies to a conference, he had as yet no means to compel Germany.

Faced with this intransigence on the part of the belligerents, and convinced that the time had come when the United States must co-operate in securing and maintaining world peace, Wilson, in a memorable speech on 22 January 1917, formulated the conditions upon which such co-operation might be extended. Those conditions anticipated, in a general way, the subsequent 'Fourteen Points.' They included government by the consent of the governed, freedom of the seas, limitation of military and naval armaments, and a League to enforce peace. But fundamental to all of these principles was the requirement that the peace must be a 'peace without victory.' Victory, said the President prophetically,

> would mean peace forced upon the loser, a victor's terms imposed upon the vanquished. It would be accepted in humiliation, under duress, at an intolerable sacrifice, and would leave a sting, a resentment, a bitter memory upon which terms of peace would rest, not permanently, but only as upon quicksand. Only a peace between equals can last.

This appeal fell upon deaf ears, and even in the United States the phrase 'peace without victory' was criticized as pusillanimous. There was no hope that the Allies, bound hand and foot by secret treaties, or that Germany, now that Rumania was crushed and Russia reeling, would agree to a reasonable settlement; and though

Wilson proposed, the Allies disposed. Yet it was not pressure from the Allies, or even from American interests favorable to the Allies, which within two months swept the United States into war. Actually the die was cast, even before Wilson made his 'peace without victory' speech. Late in August 1916 the war-lords Hindenburg and Ludendorff had been elevated to the supreme military command in Germany. Determined to break the blockade and to destroy British morale, they insisted upon the reopening of unrestricted U-boat warfare, and on 7 October the German Reichstag approved their demand, though an announcement of this change of policy was delayed until Wilson had exhausted the possibilities of mediation.

The decision to embark upon unrestricted submarine warfare was made with a full comprehension of its effect upon relations with the United States. 'I know full well,' wrote Chancellor Bethmann-Hollweg to Bernstorff, 'that by taking this step we run the danger of bringing about a break and possible war with the United States. We have determined to take this risk.' And on an official Admiralty memorandum suggesting that war with the United States might be avoided if submarines 'overlooked' American boats, the Kaiser pencilled, 'Now, once and for all, an *end* to negotiations with America. If Wilson wants war, let him make it, and let him then have it.' The German high command believed that American participation in the war would not materially increase their contributions of money, munitions, and supplies, and they discounted American naval and military assistance. With over 120 submarines ready for service they calculated to a nicety the destruction of British and neutral merchant tonnage and promised a victory in six months. In that time, the United States, it was thought, could do nothing important.

On 31 January 1917 Von Bernstorff reluctantly informed the American government that after 1 February German submarines would sink on sight all merchant vessels, armed or unarmed, within a military zone around the British Isles and in the Mediterranean. Diplomatic relations between the two nations were promptly severed, and though Wilson still shrank from war, and hoped that Germany would not commit the supreme folly of aggressive acts against the United States, the nation prepared for war. Wilson himself took the first step in this direction by calling upon Congress for authority to arm American merchant vessels; he was apparently thinking in terms of the armed neutrality of 1798 that fell just short of war. A Senate filibuster, led by LaFollette and what Wilson described as 'a little group of willful men,' prevented Congressional action until the adjournment of 4 March, when the President discovered a statute of 1797 that authorized him to act. But events moved so rapidly that armed neutrality was soon forgotten. Late in February the British secret service handed over to the American State Department a copy of the incredibly stupid 'Zimmermann note' in which the German government proposed that, if the United States declared war, Mexico conclude an offensive alliance with Germany and Japan; Mexico to have Texas for her share of the loot. This note was released to the newspapers on 1 March and immensely strengthened the popular demand for war. On 17 March came the news that a revolution in Russia had overthrown the Tsar and established a provisional republican government; the last taint of autocracy in the Allied cause disappeared. When, also during March, German submarines torpedoed five American merchant vessels, Wilson decided that Germany was warring upon the United States and that the time had come to proclaim the existence of this war.

In the twenties and thirties that decision was denounced as a mistake. American participation, it was argued, made Allied victory possible, but that victory was not sealed by a just peace and in the end the war brought the United States nothing but debts and disappointments. Yet what was the alternative? We must not let ourselves be deceived by wishful thinking into the theory that a fair and lasting peace would have been negotiated in 1917 if the United States had stayed neutral. Those who indulge in that hypothesis are invited to examine the terms of the Treaty of Brest-Litovsk that Germany concluded with Russia early in 1918. The Russian revolution took that great country out of the war. The submarine campaign would shortly have starved England. France, unable to budge the German armies from the Hindenburg line, had shot her bolt; there were mutinies on the Western front even after the United States entered. Germany would have won the war had the United States not come in; and the resulting peace settlement would have left Imperial Germany — which was essentially the Germany of Hitler, with slightly better manners — bestride the narrow world like a colossus. Men at some times are masters of their fates; but April of 1917 was not one of those times. The hour for negotiated peace had passed. Mankind was destined to a year and a half more of warfare that did far more to destroy the accumulated values of civilization than what had already occurred. President Wilson, looking ahead, and faced by the most terrible alternative that any statesman since Lincoln had faced, doubtless felt that the lesser evil was for America to join the conflict and try to direct the peace that must eventually come into channels that would justify the sacrifice. Few doubt now that he was right.

Turning to the United States alone, and assuming that we could afford to be indifferent to a German victory, it is true that Wilson could have kept the United States out of the war had he been determined to preserve peace at the going price and had the American people been willing to pay the price. It was a price that not very many Americans were willing to pay, since it involved not only an embargo upon American shipping with disastrous consequences to American economy, but a complete submission to German demands and a consequent surrender of national honor. Perhaps the concept of national honor, like that of nationalism itself, is a figment of the imagination; but to most Americans of 1917, as of today, it was a very real and cherished thing. In January 1916 Wilson had warned his countrymen that considerations of national honor might require participation in the war:

> I know that you are depending upon me to keep this Nation out of the war. So far I have done so and I pledge you my word that, God helping me, I will — if it is possible. But you have laid another duty upon me. You have bidden me see to it that nothing stains or impairs the honor of the United States, and that is a matter not within my control; that depends upon what others do, not upon what the Government of the United States does. Therefore there may at any moment come a time when I cannot preserve both the honor and the peace of the United States. Do not exact of me an impossible and contradictory thing.

The preservation of both honor and peace, in March 1917, seemed to Wilson an 'impossible and contradictory thing.' Whatever others might think of the desirability of war in order to protect investments, enhance munitions profits, or preserve gains in trade, Wilson himself was insensible to these considerations, and it was Wilson who made the decision to fight. To him the logic of that decision was crystal-clear. 'The United States entered the war,' he said,

> not because our national interests were directly threatened or because any special treaty obligations to which we were parties had been violated, but only because we saw the supremacy and even the validity, of right everywhere put in jeopardy and free government likely to be everywhere imperilled by the intolerable aggression of a power which respected neither

right nor obligation. . . . We entered the war as the disinterested champions of right.

This was idealism — an idealism too lofty even for Americans. But there is no reason to impeach either the sincerity or the intelligence of the man who espoused it. That Wilson's faith in a peace without victory was betrayed, that his vision of a new and better world order was dissipated, was not his fault, but the fault of the European and American peoples who proved themselves incapable of living up to his ideal. Wilson's error was in failing to take a sufficiently cynical view of human nature, and it was an error that a later generation found difficult to condone.

And yet, even here, the evidence is conflicting. It is folly to suppose that Wilson, a student of history and a practical politician, was unfamiliar with the character of war and with its consequences. On the night before he delivered his war message to Congress he summoned Frank Cobb of the New York *World* to the White House. Cobb's recollection of that visit, as reported by Maxwell Anderson, is worth quoting in full:

> 'What else can I do?' he asked. 'Is there anything else I can do?'
>
> I told him his hand had been forced by Germany, that so far as I could see we couldn't keep out.
>
> 'Yes,' he said, 'but do you know what that means?' He said war would overturn the world we had known; that so long as we remained out there was a preponderance of neutrality, but that if we joined with the Allies the world would be off the peace basis and onto a war basis.
>
> 'It would mean that we should lose our heads along with the rest and stop weighing right and wrong. It would mean that a majority of the people in this hemisphere would go war-mad, quit thinking and devote their energies to destruction.' The President said a declaration of war would mean that Germany would be beaten, and so badly beaten that there would be a dictated peace, a victorious peace.
>
> 'It means,' he said, 'an attempt to reconstruct a peacetime civilization with war standards, and at the end of the war there will be no bystanders with sufficient peace standards left to work with. There will be only war standards.' . . .
>
> He said when a war got going it was just war and there weren't two kinds of it. It required illiberalism at home to reinforce the men at the front. We couldn't fight Germany and maintain the ideals of Government that all thinking men shared. He said we would try it but it would be too much for us.

'Once lead this people into war,' he said, 'and they'll forget there ever was such a thing as tolerance. To fight you must be brutal and ruthless, and the spirit of ruthless brutality will enter into every fibre of our national life, infecting Congress, the courts, the policeman on the beat, the man in the street.' Conformity would be the only virtue, said the President, and every man who refused to conform would have to pay the penalty.

He thought the Constitution would not survive it; that free speech and the right of assembly would go. He said a nation couldn't put its strength into a war and keep its head level; it had never been done.[5]

Despite his keen intelligence and sensitiveness, Wilson did not sufficiently appreciate the strength of Old World diplomatic traditions or of New World traditions of isolation. He did not contemplate the betrayal of his peace program by the Allies or realize that his own power and influence would be drained from him by repudiation at home.

So on 2 April 1917, President Wilson appeared before Congress and read his war message:

With a profound sense of the solemn and even tragical character of the step I am taking and of the grave responsibilities which it involves, but in unhesitating obedience to what I deem my constitutional duty, I advise that the Congress declare the recent course of the Imperial German Government to be, in fact, nothing less than war against the Government and people of the United States; that it formally accept the status of belligerent which has thus been thrust upon it; and that it take immediate steps not only to put the country in a more thorough state of defence, but also to exert all its power and employ all its resources to bring the Government of the German Empire to terms and end the war. . . .

It is a fearful thing to lead this great peaceful people into war, into the most terrible and disastrous of all wars, civilization itself seeming to be in the balance. But the right is more precious than peace, and we shall fight for the things which we have always carried nearest our hearts,—for democracy, for the right of those who submit to authority to have a voice in their own Government, for the rights and liberties of small nations, for a universal dominion of right by such a concert of free peoples as shall bring peace and safety to all nations and make the world itself at last free. To such a task we can dedicate our lives and our fortunes, everything that we are and everything that we have, with the pride of those who know

[5] John L. Heaton, *Cobb of 'The World,'* pp. 268–70. E. P. Dutton & Co., N. Y., 1924.

that the day has come when America is privileged to spend her blood and her might for the principles that gave her birth and happiness and the peace which she has treasured. God helping her, she can do no other.

In the small hours of Good Friday morning, 6 April 1917, Congress passed a joint resolution declaring war on the German Empire.

XX

WAR AND PEACE

1917–1920

1. *Industrial and Financial Mobilization*

'IT is not an army that we must shape and train for war,' said President Wilson, 'it is a nation.' And the real history of American participation in the World War is not so much the story of Belleau Wood and St. Mihiel and Château-Thierry as of mobilizing industrial resources at home. The task was not only gigantic, but urgent. In April 1917 German submarine warfare was succeeding beyond the expectations of the Germans themselves, and the Allies were almost at the end of their resources; Great Britain had, in April, grain enough for only six weeks and the government had fixed November first as the utmost limit of British endurance. Few Americans realized at the time the gravity of the situation, and Admiral Sims, who had been dispatched to consult with the British Admiralty, recorded his own consternation when Admiral Jellicoe assured him 'it is impossible for us to go on, if losses like this continue. . . . The Germans . . . will win unless we can stop these losses — and stop them soon.' Shortly, allied commissions came to the United States with the same story of desperate need for ships, food, munitions, and credit; direct military assistance was not as yet seriously contemplated.

It was not easy to transform the highly individualistic American economic system into a well integrated military machine, but the task was performed with commendable speed and efficiency, though at a staggering cost. Spurred by necessity Congress conferred upon the President powers more extensive than those possessed by any other ruler in the Western world — powers to commandeer essential industries and mines, requisition supplies, control distribution, fix prices, and take over and operate the entire system of transportation and communication. The President in turn delegated these powers to a series of boards, organized under the general supervision of the Council for National Defense. These boards in turn mobilized America's industrial, agricultural, and even intellectual resources for war purposes; the result was the nearest approach to a socialized state which it was possible to achieve where the profit system was undisturbed.

The first task was to provide ships to replace the tonnage which the submarines were destroying at the rate of over half a million tons monthly. Fortunately the United States Shipping Board Act of 1916 had already called into existence an organization prepared to deal with the complex problems of a government owned and operated merchant marine. On 16 April Congress further authorized the creation of an Emergency Fleet Corporation with broad powers to requisition, purchase, construct, and operate ships without limitation. Edward Hurley was made chairman of the War Shipping Board and in co-operation with the Interallied Shipping Council proceeded to build a 'bridge to France.' By seizing interned German ships, commandeering or buying neutral ships, taking over all private shipping, constructing enormous new shipyards at Hog Island in the Delaware River and elsewhere, building steel ships, wooden ships, fabricated ships, even concrete ships, the Emergency Fleet Corporation succeeded in increasing the available tonnage from one million to ten million tons.[1] By thus laying down two ships for every one sunk by the U-boats, the submarine danger was circumvented and the total shipping available to the Allied powers was steadily increased.

Scarcely less important was the reorganization of transport within the United States. Under the impact of war orders and troop movements the American railroad system broke down. On 26 December 1917 the government took it over, and proceeded to operate the railroads as a unified system, guaranteeing adequate compensation to the owners. William G. McAdoo, undismayed by his duties as Secretary of the Treasury, was made director-general of the railroad administration. By consolidating terminal facilities, standardizing equipment, shutting down little-used lines, discouraging passenger traffic, and co-ordinating all freight traffic, he succeeded in bringing the railroads to a peak of effectiveness heretofore unknown. Because the rental paid was too high, and the freight rates too low, this experiment in federal ownership and operation of the railroads cost

1 'Appalling prices,' wrote Sec. McAdoo, 'were paid for everything that had to do with a ship. Engines and other equipment were purchased at such a staggering cost that I fancied more than once that the machinery we were buying must be made of silver instead of iron and steel.' *Crowded Years.*

the government $714,000,000. During the war the government took over other agencies of transportation and communication as well—terminals, express companies, sleeping-car companies, elevators, warehouses, and telephone, telegraph, and cable lines.

Mobilization of the nation's industrial resources was effected by the War Industries Board under the direction of the astute Bernard Baruch, for two years economic dictator of the country. The task of this Board was to regulate all existing industries that produced war materials, develop new industries, facilities, and sources of supply, enforce efficiency and eliminate waste, fix prices, determine priorities of production and delivery, and manage all war purchases for the United States and the Allies. The production of some thirty thousand articles came under the supervision of the War Industries Board, and that supervision was almost incredibly minute. In order to save coal, the service of elevators was regulated even to the number of stops and the number of passengers they must carry; the number of colors on typewriter ribbons was reduced from one hundred and fifty to five, styles of pocket knives from six thousand to one hundred and forty-four. Baby carriages were standardized; travelling salesmen limited to two trunks; and the length of uppers on shoes was cut down. New regulations for the manufacture of corsets released eight thousand tons of steel annually; the elimination of tin from children's toy carts saved seventy-five thousand tons of tin; thirty-one thousand gallons of varnish were saved by leaving painted lines off rubbers. 'Women's waist factories made signal flags, radiator manufacturers turned to making big guns, automobile body builders made airplane parts, gear plants made gun-sights, piano factories made airplane wings.'[2] Ordinary peace-time production all but ceased, the government forbidding any work which might interfere with war manufacturing and conscripting labor to war purposes. It was such a regimentation of national economy as had never before been known; yet it was carried through with little friction and accepted in good spirit.[3]

The Food Administration more than any other government agency brought the war home to the American people. It was a stroke of genius to place Herbert Hoover in charge of this work, for

[2] Mark Sullivan, *Our Times,* vol. v, p. 382. Scribner's.

[3] The two men chiefly instrumental in working out the details of this mobilization of industrial and agricultural resources were Hugh S. Johnson and George Peek, who later applied to the N.R.A. and A.A.A. the technique they learned under Baruch.

as chairman of the Commission for Relief in Belgium he had gained invaluable administrative experience and prestige second only to the President's. Mr. Hoover's task was to increase the production and decrease the consumption of food in America so that the Allies might be adequately supplied. For the accomplishment of this task he displayed extraordinary ingenuity. By law Mr. Hoover was empowered to fix the prices of staples, license food distributors, co-ordinate purchases, supervise exports, prohibit hoarding or profiteering, and stimulate production. He fixed the price of wheat at $2.20 a bushel, established a grain corporation to buy and sell it, organized the supply and purchase of meat, corralled the supply of sugar. Meantime a systematic campaign persuaded the American people to cut down food wastes and reduce food consumption. 'Wheatless Mondays,' 'Meatless Tuesdays,' and 'Porkless Thursdays' became an accepted part of the national regimen, and Americans experimented with such unattractive comestibles as sugarless candy, vegetable lamb chops, whale meat, and shark steak. As a result of 'Hooverizing' the United States was able to export in 1918 approximately three times her normal amounts of breadstuffs, meats, and sugar.

These were the most important of the new war agencies that brought about an unprecedented regimentation of American economic life, but they by no means exhaust the list. A fuel administration, under the direction of Harry A. Garfield, introduced daylight saving and 'fuelless Mondays,' banned electric displays and closed down non-essential manufacturing plants in an effort to conserve coal. A war trade board licensed exports and imports and blacklisted firms suspected of trading with the enemy. A labor administration regulated relations between capital and labor, arbitrated industrial disputes, fixed hours and wages in certain industries, and banned strikes contrary to public interest. A war finance corporation was authorized to supervise the flotation of all security issues of one hundred thousand dollars or over and in addition was empowered to underwrite loans to industries engaged in the production of war materials.

The financial problem was indeed crucial. It was necessary to find money not only for our own but for Allied expenses. As early as July 1917 the British Chancellor of the Exchequer, Lord Northcliffe, informed Colonel House that 'our resources available for payments in America are exhausted. Unless the United States government can meet in full our expenses in America . . . the whole financial fabric of the alliance will collapse.' During and immediately after the war the United States government lent some ten billion dollars to the Allies and associated governments, practically all of which was spent in this country. American expenditures prior to October 1919 came to well over twice this sum — twenty-six billion. The total direct cost of the war was therefore about thirty-six billion dollars; indirect costs in the form of interest on the national debt, pensions, soldiers' bonus and so forth brought the total to well over forty-two billion by 1936.

To meet this staggering financial burden which in the last six months of the war came to forty-four million dollars a day, the government had recourse to heavy taxation and to loans. Approximately one-third of the war costs were financed by taxation — a record which compares favorably to our experience in earlier wars. Income, inheritance, corporation, and excess profits taxes were stepped up, and new taxes were laid on transportation, spirits, gasolene, amusements and entertainments of all kinds, and almost every other source which the ingenuity of treasury-department officials could discover. Wartime prosperity had made so many new millionaires and prosperous workingmen that these taxes were borne without protest. That the nation was enjoying unprecedented prosperity was evident from the extraordinary success of the five war loans which were floated between May 1917 and May 1919. The first of these loans was for two billion dollars, the second and third for three, the fourth for six, and the fifth for four and one-half; all were handsomely oversubscribed.

2. *Mobilizing Public Opinion*

Unless the American people had believed that the war was both righteous and necessary, they would not have supported these inconveniences and sacrifices, let alone the drain of man-power of which we shall speak presently. Yet when war was declared, a very large part of the public were indifferent, and an important minority disaffected. The leaders of opinion were, to be sure, more than ready for the fray; but the boy on the farm and the man in the street, who were to do the fighting, the girl in the factory who was to make supplies and the woman in the kitchen who was to do the saving, had very little idea what the war was about, and needed to be told. Congress knew this very well, and by act of 14 April 1917 established the Committee on Public Information, of which George Creel was appointed chairman by the President. Mr. Creel combined, as Mark Sullivan has observed, 'incredibly efflorescent imagination, fertile ingenuity, and prodigious energy.' He promptly undertook to mobilize the mind of America as Baruch was mobilizing industry and Baker the man-power. Artists, advertisers, poets, historians, photographers, educators, actors were enlisted in the campaign and the country was inundated with a flood of propaganda pamphlets, posters, magazines, and newspapers. Altogether over one hundred million pieces of 'literature' were distributed by the indefatigable Creel, while some seventy-five thousand 'four-minute men' let loose a barrage of oratory at movie houses and public gatherings which prostrated the intelligence of the country. Motion pictures displayed to horrified audiences the barbarities of the 'Hun'; pamphlets written by learned professors proved to the more sceptical that the Germans had always been a depraved people; and thousands of canned editorials taught the average man what to think about the war. In this campaign of education none was neglected: school children learned to lisp the vocabulary of hatred; women's clubs titillated to atrocity stories; and foreigners were taught to be ashamed that they had not been born in America. Nor were the delights of education confined to the United States; in the spirit of Garrison's 'our country is the world; our countrymen all mankind' Creel launched out to conquer the world with the spirit instead of the sword. No people was safe from his zeal, no country too remote for his concern. Three hundred Chinese newspapers supplied the palpitating celestials with The Truth About the War, and pictures of the American President and the American flag hung on walls of cottages of Russian peasants and Peruvian *mestizos*. It was such a triumph of the spirit as the world had never known, and brought about an intellectual uniformity and a social conformity from the effects of which that generation never fully recovered.

Equally important was propaganda directed toward breaking down the will to fight in the Central Powers. From the first Wilson had distinguished between the German people and their government and had held out to minority races of the Dual Monarchy the hope of independence from the Hapsburgs. In his war message of 2 April he had announced that 'we have no quarrel with the German people. We have no feeling toward them but one of sympathy and friendship,' and throughout the war he reiterated his policy of 'war on the German government, peace with the German people.' He emphasized the fact that the United States was fighting for no material gain, but for peace and justice and democracy and appealed to the people of the Central Powers to justify this crusade. The war was, indeed, 'a war for freedom and justice and self-government amongst all the nations of the world, a war to make the world safe for the peoples who live upon it and have made it their own, the German people themselves included.' In all this Wilson was entirely sincere, and his policy was designed to achieve two ends: to establish a moral basis for peace upon which all belligerents — including the Allies — must agree, and to impair the military strength of the Central Powers by sowing dissatisfaction among the peoples of Germany and Austria-Hungary.

These purposes were clearly in Wilson's mind when he announced, on 8 January 1918, the Fourteen Points upon which it would be possible to formulate terms of peace. Since the Fourteen Points subsequently served as the basis for the peace negotiations and the Versailles Treaty they are worth noting in detail:

1. Open covenants openly arrived at.
2. Freedom of the seas alike in peace and in war.
3. The removal of all economic barriers and the establishment of an equality of trade conditions among all nations.
4. Reduction of national armaments.
5. A readjustment of all colonial claims in which the interests of the population concerned must have equal weight with the claims of the government whose title is to be determined.
6. The evacuation of Russian territory and the independent determination by Russia of her own political development and national policy.
7. The evacuation and restoration of Belgium.
8. The evacuation and restoration of France and the return of Alsace-Lorraine.
9. A readjustment of the frontiers of Italy along national lines.
10. Self-determination for the peoples of Austria Hungary.
11. A redrawing of the boundaries of the Balkan states along historically established lines of nationality.
12. Self-determination for the peoples under Turkish rule and freedom of the Dardenelles under international guarantees.
13. The independence of Poland with free access to the sea guaranteed by international covenant.
14. The formation of a general association of nations under specific covenants for the purpose of affording mutual guarantees of political independence and territorial integrity to great and small states alike.

This moral offensive was a major factor in breaking down German resistance and hastening the conclusion of the war. Wilson's appeal to the German people, assiduously circulated throughout Germany, helped to drive a wedge between the people and government, and when Ludendorff's army met defeat on the Western front, Germany hastened to comply with Wilson's insistence upon a popular government, and opened negotiations for an armistice upon the basis of the Fourteen Points.

Propaganda justifying the war at home and abroad was not enough. It was thought necessary to search out disloyalty and punish it. 'If there should be disloyalty,' said Wilson, 'it will be dealt with with a firm hand of stern repression.' Despite large and active disloyal groups, North and South, both the Confederate and the Federal governments had managed to get through the Civil War without enacting sedition laws, but in 1917–18 the United States abandoned itself to an hysteria of fear. The Espionage Act of 15 June 1917 and the Sedition Act of 16 May 1918 were as extreme as any legislation of the kind anywhere in the world. The Espionage Act fixed a fine of ten thousand dollars and twenty years' imprisonment upon anyone who interfered with the draft or attempted to encourage disloyalty; the Sedition Act extended this penalty to anyone who should obstruct the sale of United States bonds, incite insubordination, discourage recruiting, 'wilfully utter, print, write or publish any disloyal, profane, scurrilous, or abusive language about the form of government of the United States, or the Constitution . . . or the flag . . . or the uniform of the Army or Navy . . . or bring the form of government . . . or the Constitution . . . into contempt . . . or advocate any curtailment of production in this country of any thing necessary or essential to the prosecution of the war.'

Under these harsh laws the government arrested over fifteen hundred persons for disloyalty; among those convicted and sentenced to prison were Eugene V. Debs, who had polled almost one million votes in the Presidential contest of 1912, and Victor Berger, Socialist Congressman from Milwaukee. A drive against 'conscientious objectors,' who were theoretically excluded from the draft, netted four thousand, of whom over four hundred were hurried to military prisons.

More disturbing even than this official crusade against sedition was the unofficial witch-hunting that engaged the energy of sundry old ladies of both sexes. It was a great opportunity to bring patriotism to the aid of personal grudges and neighborhood feuds; the intelligent and independent-minded sort of citizen who was known to his conforming neighbors as a 'tory' in the Revolution, a 'Jacobin' in 1798, and a 'copperhead' in the Civil War, became a 'pro-German traitor' in 1917, and was lucky if he did not have disjointed and garbled scraps of his conversation sent in to the Department of Justice or flashes from his shaving-mirror reported as signals to German submarines. The German-Americans, of course, had the worst experiences of this sort. Many of them were opposed to our entry into the war, but the vast majority were loyal to the United States and did their part as well as the native-born. They were subjected, however, to all sorts of indignities. Schools dropped German from their curricula, and even some universities abolished their German departments; German books were withdrawn from public library circulation, and German publications driven under cover. The Governor of Iowa even promulgated an edict that 'conversation in public places, on trains, or over the telephone should be in the English language.' Frederick Stock, distinguished conductor of the Chicago Symphony Orchestra, was deprived of his baton; the patriotic mayor of a Jersey town refused to permit Fritz Kreisler to appear on the concert stage; and some universities even revoked the honorary degrees which they had conferred upon distinguished Germans.

'We are glad to fight,' said Wilson in his war message, 'for the privilege of men everywhere to choose their way of life and of obedience.' But this exalted ideal did not apply to the United States, and one of the most appalling revelations of the entire war was the ease with which modern technique and mass-suggestion enables a government to make even a reasonably intelligent people, with an individualistic, democratic background, believe anything it likes. Wilson's melancholy prophecy that 'to fight you must be brutal and ruthless, and the spirit of ruthless brutality will enter into the very fibre of our national life, infecting Congress, the courts, the policemen on the beat, the man in the streets,' was fulfilled.

3. *Naval and Military Operations*

'Force to the utmost, force without stint or limit' had been Wilson's promise, yet the Germans had deliberately discounted America's military and naval contribution and the Allied powers clearly expected little aid from the United States. And in one sense the

German estimate was correct; it was fully a year after the declaration of war before American soldiers were available in sufficient numbers to affect the military situation on the Western front, and the Germans confidently expected to win the war in less than a year. When American military aid did come, it was decisive. But even before American soldiers turned the tide at Château-Thierry, the navy had co-operated to destroy the effectiveness of German submarine warfare and thus prevented U-boats from winning a decision.

General Joffre early assured American officials that half a million soldiers was the largest number the Allies expected the United States to send to France, but the government organized its military machine upon a far more ambitious basis. The task was not one of getting men alone; it involved complex problems of training, equipping, transportation, supply, medical and hospital service, intelligence service, and the maintenance of morale, first in the United States and then in France. Within eighteen months the United States created an effective army of four million men, transported over two million to France, and placed one and one-third million on the firing line. This was a tribute to the organizing genius of Newton D. Baker, who, despite pacifist inclinations, proved himself one of the ablest of all Secretaries of War.

Even before the actual declaration of war, General Hugh L. Scott, Chief of Staff, had convinced Mr. Baker of the desirability of raising an army by conscription rather than by the volunteer system. He in turn won over Wilson. Although our experience with the Civil War draft had not been happy,[4] European experience in the World War proved conscription to be a necessity. Weeks before the Selective Service Act passed Congress (18 May 1917) the details had been worked out, the machinery set up, and the co-operation of state and local authorities enlisted. It was wisely decided that the draft should be carried through by civilians, and that registration day should be a 'festival and patriotic occasion.'

The Selective Service Act provided that all men between the ages of twenty-one and thirty, inclusive, must register for service. Congressional leaders, recalling the New York draft riots of 1863, prophesied that conscription would be attended by 'rioting all over the United States,' and that 'we will never get a conscript on the firing line in France,' but all these predictions proved mistaken. When the registration offices closed at sundown of 5 June, 9,586,508

4 See above, vol. i, p. 600 ff.

men had registered and nowhere had there been the slightest disorder or opposition. Subsequent registrations on 5 June and 12 September 1918 embracing all men between the ages of eighteen and forty-five brought the total registration up to 24,234,021. Of these altogether 2,180,296 were inducted into the army. The regular army, the national guard, navy, and marine corps continued to be recruited by voluntary enlistment. Including these and 'minor branches of service,' the total number of men in the armed forces of the United States at the end of the First World War was about four million.

The rigorous physical examinations to which the drafted men were subjected revealed much of interest and value as to the health of Americans. In the solid tier of states from Texas to North Dakota between seventy and eighty per cent of the registered men passed the physical examination; in the industrial states of New England, New York, and Michigan and in the far west, the percentage of those found fit was only a little over fifty. 'Further analysis of the records . . . shows that the country boys made better records than those from the cities; the white registrants better than the colored; and native-born better records than those of alien birth. These differences are so considerable that 100,000 country boys would furnish for military service 4,790 more soldiers than would an equal number of city boys. Similarly 100,000 whites would furnish 1,240 more soldiers than would an equal number of colored. Finally, 100,000 native-born would yield 3,500 more soldiers than would a like number of foreign-born.'[5]

Raising an army was only a part of the military task which the United States was called upon to perform. It was necessary to make or purchase clothing, arms, ammunition and explosives, light and heavy artillery, gas and gas masks, airplanes and balloons, and many other things equally essential. It was necessary to supply transportation across the Atlantic for both troops and supplies, to build dockage facilities and develop new railroad, motor, and horse transportation in France, to set up a signal corps, string thousands of miles of telephone wires, create a vast medical and nursing corps, and construct hundreds of hospitals in the United States and overseas. No task of similar magnitude had ever been attempted before by any nation.

When the war broke out the United States had actual military equipment for an army of approximately half a million men. In the

[5] Leonard Ayres, *The War with Germany, A Statistical Summary*, p. 21. Washington, Government Printing Office.

course of the war she produced two and one-half million rifles, one hundred and eighty-one thousand machine guns, three thousand artillery units, twenty-million rounds of artillery ammunition, three and one-half billion rounds of small arms ammunition, over five million gas masks, and over eight thousand training planes. Yet at no time was the American army entirely independent of English and French arms and supplies; the Liberty aviation engine was just getting into production when the Armistice came, our field artillery was almost exclusively supplied with French 75 mm. field guns, and more American troops went to Europe in British than American transports.

The first American contingent, the 1st Infantry Division, arrived in France in June 1917, and on Independence Day paraded through the streets of Paris. Brand Whitlock, American Minister to Belgium, describes the enthusiasm with which they were greeted:

I heard the band, it was playing Marching Through Georgia. I could not withstand that! And so downstairs, and out into the rue de Rivoli bareheaded. There was the crowd sweeping along the street below the great iron fence of the Tuileries, from curb to curb, with no order, men, women, children, trotting along, hot, excited, trying to keep up with the slender column of our khaki-clad regulars, who marched briskly along. French soldiers in their light blue trotted beside them, as closely as they could get, looking at them with almost childish interest and wonder, as boys trot hurrying beside a circus parade. Our soldiers were covered with flowers — and always the steady roar of the crowd and now and then cries of *Vive l'Amérique. . . .*[6]

The purpose of this and subsequent contingents in 1917 was chiefly to bolster up Allied morale, and for this purpose the Americans were distributed among French and English troops along the quieter sectors of the front. By the end of 1917 some two hundred thousand American soldiers were in France, but only a few Engineer Regiments of the 1st Division had seen active service at the front in the Cambrai offensive.

The United States Navy had been, somewhat unwillingly it must be admitted, in the war from mid-April 1917. Although Secretary Daniels and his Assistant Secretary, Franklin D. Roosevelt, had done a great deal to build up the morale and efficiency of the fleet, the new construction provided for in the summer of 1916 was still mostly in the blueprint stage and the 'bridge' of merchant ships to France was

[6] *Journals of Brand Whitlock*, ed. by Allan Nevins, p. 423. Appleton-Century Co., N. Y., 1936.

as yet largely a bridgehead, at Hog Island on the Delaware. Admiral William S. Benson, the Chief of Naval Operations, had no war plan ready when war was declared, and the one he promulgated on 11 April looked to little more than a defensive patrol by battleships and cruisers on the American side of the Atlantic, and a considerable Pacific Fleet to watch Japan which was an Ally! Fortunately, the President had been prevailed upon by Ambassador Page to send the gifted and energetic Rear Admiral William S. Sims to London a few days ahead of the declaration of war; and the situation, as Sims pungently described it in his despatches, was so appalling that the navy almost completely altered its plans.

Admiral Jellicoe, First Lord of the Admiralty, told Sims that sinkings of Allied merchant vessels averaged almost 570,000 tons per month in February and March, and bade fair to reach 900,000 tons in April 1917.[7] There was only a three weeks' supply of grain on hand in England, the German U-boats were increasing in numbers and efficiency, and if something was not done promptly to stop these losses and repair the life line, the Allies would have to throw in the sponge before the end of the year. Sims found, to his surprise, that the Allies had not yet adopted the convoy system of operating merchant ships in groups so that they could be protected from submarine attack by an escort of cruisers and destroyers. Although many British officers had been advocating for months a return to these tactics of the days of sailing navies, the opposition of merchant skippers, who preferred to take their chances of dodging torpedoes to being herded by 'gold braid,' and who declared that steamships could never keep station in a convoy, prevented anything being done. Sims threw his influence on the side of convoys, they were promptly adopted, the predicted frictions and collisions proved to be few and unimportant, and the convoy system, more than any single factor (and this was as true of World War II as of World War I) enabled American troops and supplies to cross the Atlantic safely.[8]

Sims also persuaded the navy to send as many destroyers as it could

[7] Compare figures for World War II: in six months only of 1942 and in March 1943, sinkings by submarines in the Atlantic and Arctic passed 500,000 tons, the highest being 637,000 tons in November 1942. Morison, *Battle of the Atlantic,* 1947, p. 412.

[8] The comparatively small U-boats of 1917–18 had so short a cruising range that it was necessary to convoy vessels for only a few hundred miles west of Europe. It is true that the German navy, as a stunt, sent six submarines into U. S. coastal waters in 1918 but they sank only 24 ships of 2000 tons and over, and their operations were little more than a nuisance raid which failed even to disrupt coastal shipping.

spare to Queenstown (Cobh, Ireland) to be operated for escort-of-convoy and anti-submarine patrol under the British. The first six of them arrived on 4 May and went right to work; by 5 July there were thirty-four American destroyers at Queenstown together with six converted yachts and several ancient 400-ton torpedo boats of the Asiatic Fleet, which Lieutenant Commander Harold R. Stark had brought halfway around the world.

This was the first time in history that American warships had operated under British, or indeed any foreign command. The British commander, Vice Admiral Sir Lewis Bayly, was an austere, crusty old sea-dog, but the experiment was a success. The American destroyer officers (including in their junior ranks such men as Nimitz, Halsey, Carpenter, Hewitt, and Lee, who emerged as distinguished admirals in World War II) came to have a feeling amounting almost to veneration for 'Uncle Lewis'; while he, after they for a year had loyally obeyed his maxim 'Pull together!' issued an order which ended, 'To command you is an honor, to work with you is a pleasure, and to know you is to know the best traits of the Anglo-Saxon race.'

These destroyers experimented successfully with listening gear that detected submarines' propellers, and with depth charges ('ashcans') which could destroy a submerged U-boat if properly placed; both were primitive in comparison with the sonar and depth weapons of World War II, but effective against the small submarines of World War I. It was not until 17 November that American destroyers made their first kill of a U-boat, but in the meantime the new convoy tactics and aggressive patrolling had reduced Allied monthly shipping losses from 881,000 tons (April) to 289,000 tons (November), a figure that was more than surpassed by new construction; submarine operations now became very hazardous and the United States could send troops and supplies abroad with confidence that they would arrive. Not one loaded transport was lost. In several other ways, too, the United States Navy contributed to put the squeeze on Admiral Tirpitz's underwater fleet. A fleet of 120 SCs (subchasers) of the same 110-foot model that proved serviceable twenty-five years later was sent to European waters, commanded entirely by naval reservists fresh out of college; these boats proved their value against the Austrian navy in the Adriatic. Naval aviators, flying the old Curtiss float planes that few would dare to fly now, began operating in Europe promptly, and by the end of the war the United States had some 500 planes and 3 'blimps' on 27 different European bases. These planes did valuable work detecting convoys and reporting U-boats, and before the end of the war they joined the Army Air Force in bombing raids on Germany. Finally, it was the United States Navy that initiated, planned, and (under Rear Admiral Joseph Strauss) executed the colossal mine barrage across the North Sea which, beginning in June 1918, practically closed that exit to enemy submarines.

Previous to the laying of this barrage, an American battle fleet under Rear Admiral Hugh L. Rodman, including the *New York, Arkansas,* and *Texas* which were still slugging in 1945, with a complement of destroyers, was sent to augment the British Grand Fleet at Scapa Flow in the Orkney Islands. These combined fleets were more than sufficient to contain the German high-seas navy in port and to reduce its efficiency and morale to a point that contributed strongly to the German surrender in November 1918.

Without the excellent work by the United States Navy, the Allies would have been defeated before American help could have arrived. Nevertheless, it was the American Expeditionary Force which, in conjunction with the British, French, and (to a limited extent) the Italian armies, secured Allied victory.

Late in 1917 the military situation turned radically against the Allies. In October the Italian army cracked at Caporetto and the Austrians poured onto the plains of Friuli; the Italians dug in along the Piave, but it was necessary for the Allies to hurry troops from the Western front to stem the Austrian tide. A month later came the Bolshevik revolution in Russia; the new Soviet government sued for peace, and the inauguration of negotiations at Brest-Litovsk, 22 December 1917, released hundreds of thousands of German soldiers for the Western front. By the spring of 1918 the Germans had a clear numerical superiority in the West, and the German high command prepared with confidence for a drive on Paris which should end the war.

A Macedonian cry went up for American troops, and there began a 'race for France,' the outcome of which was to determine the outcome of the war itself. Could the United States speed up sufficiently her troop shipments to restore the numerical balance between the Allies and the Central Powers? 'Would she appear in time to snatch the victor's laurels from our brows?' asked Hindenburg. 'That, and that only was the decisive question! I believed I could answer it in the negative.' Troop shipments were given right of way over supplies, new transports were pressed into service, and soldiers were rushed from American training camps to France. In March 80,000 troops were shipped abroad, in April 118,000, in May 245,000. Altogether during the critical months from March to October 1918 1,750,000 American soldiers landed in France. 'America,' said the German Commander-in-Chief von Ludendorff, 'thus became the decisive power in the war.'

The great German offensive began on 21 March 1918 with a terrific assault on the British line from Arras to LaFère. Within a week the Germans had severely crippled the British Fifth Army, captured 90,000 prisoners, and rolled the British line back twenty-five miles. On 9 April came the second offensive; once again the British were hurled back on a broad front from Ypres to Armentières, and General Haig issued his famous appeal, 'Every position must be held to the last man: there must be no retirement. With our backs to the wall and believing in the justice of our cause, each one of us must fight on to the end.' In late May and early June the Germans launched their third offensive, this time against the French armies along the sector between Noyon and Rheims. Within a week the Germans smashed supposedly impregnable defenses, captured 40,000 prisoners and 650 guns and, standing on the right bank of the Marne, threatened Paris. At this crisis of the war the Allies placed General Foch in supreme command of all their forces, and the premiers of Great Britain, France, and Italy warned the United States that 'as there is no possibility of the British and French increasing the numbers of their divisions . . . there is great danger of the war being lost unless the numerical inferiority of the Allies can be remedied as rapidly as possible by the advent of American troops.'

American troops were already supporting the English and French at the front lines. Pershing, Baker, and Wilson were all determined that the American army in France should eventually form a separate and independent unit, but temporarily Pershing waived this demand, and placed all his forces at the disposal of Foch, who dispersed them among the Allied armies where they were most needed. On 28 May the famous 1st Division helped to repulse the German drive on Montdidier and in a counter-attack captured the heights of Cantigny. A few days later a marine brigade of the 2nd Division was rushed to the front to stop the German onslaught at Château-Thierry; for ninety-six hours the marines, assisted by the French colonials, fought off the Germans, hurling them back to the right bank of the Marne. On 5 June the 2nd Division took the offen-

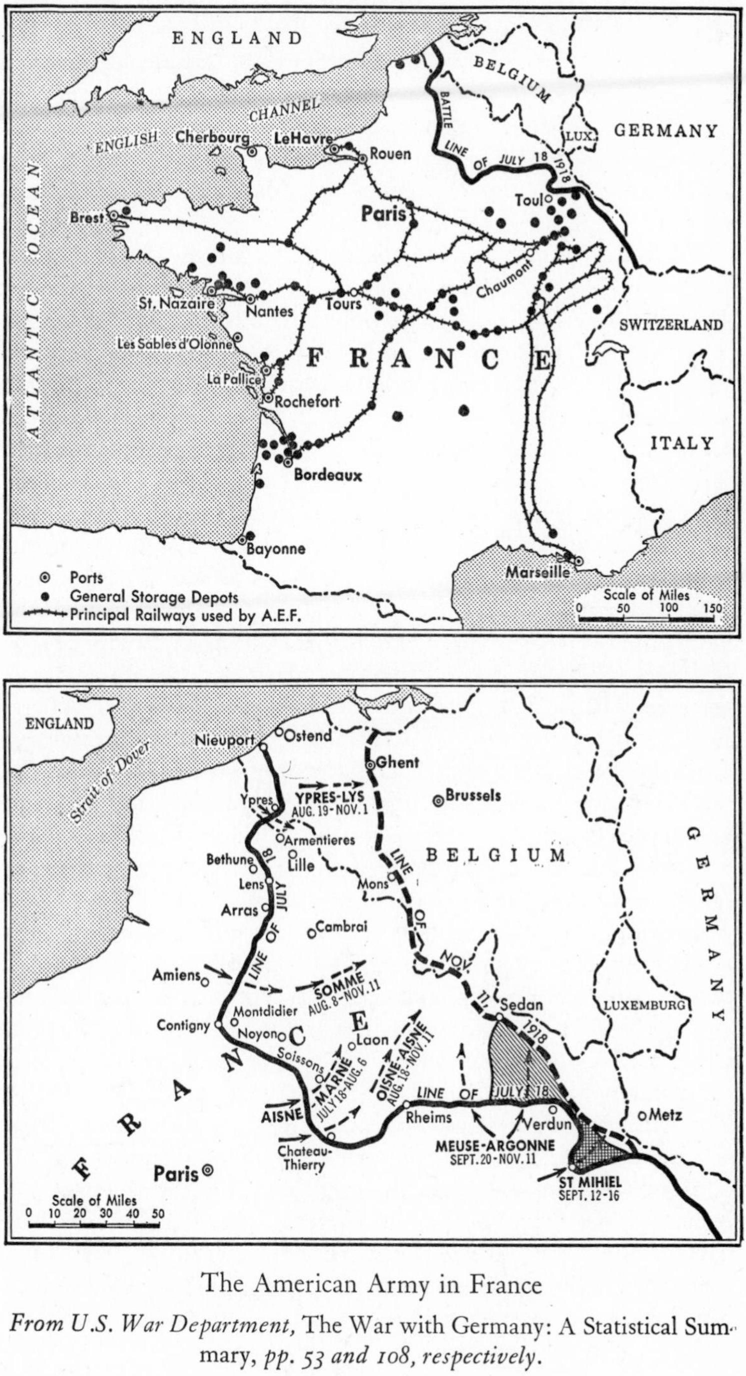

The American Army in France

From U.S. War Department, The War with Germany: A Statistical Summary, *pp. 53 and 108, respectively.*

sive at Belleau Wood and after three weeks of fighting succeeded in clearing the woods of Germans and penetrating their lines to a depth of over three miles. The actual military importance of these engagements was not great, but their moral importance was incalculable.

On 15 July came the fourth and last phase of the great German offensive, known as the Second Battle of the Marne. The Germans launched their heaviest attack at the Château-Thierry salient; had they broken through Paris could not have been saved. The American 1st, 2nd, 3rd, 4th, 26th, and 42nd Divisions, 275,000 strong, supported the French in stemming a tide which at first seemed irresistible. We have the testimony of the German Chief of Staff, General Walther Reinhardt, as to the effectiveness of the American resistance:

> Right here on the Marne . . . we well-nigh reached the objectives prescribed for our shock divisions for July 15th and 16th. Especially all divisions of the Seventh Army achieved brilliant initial successes, with the exception of the one division on our right wing. This encountered American units! Here only did the Seventh Army . . . confront serious difficulties. It met with the unexpectedly stubborn and active resistance of fresh American troops. While the rest of the divisions . . . succeeded in gaining ground and tremendous booty, it proved impossible for us to move the right apex of our line, to the south of the Marne, into a position advantageous for the development of the ensuing fight. The check we received was one result of the stupendous fighting between our 10th Division of infantry and American troops.

In three days the German attack was played out, and on 18 July, without giving the enemy an opportunity to consolidate his position, Foch called upon the 1st and 2nd American and the First French Morocco Divisions to form the spear-head of a counter-attack. It was brilliantly executed and completely successful. 'Due to the magnificent dash and power displayed on the field of Soissons by our 1st and 2nd Divisions,' wrote General Pershing, 'the tide of war was definitely turned in favor of the Allies.' And the German Chancellor Hertling later confessed that 'at the beginning of July 1918, I was convinced . . . that before the first of September our adversaries would send us peace proposals. . . . That was on the 15th. On the 18th even the most optimistic among us knew that all was lost. The history of the world was played out in three days.'

With the passing of the crisis on the Marne, Pershing revived his cherished plan for an independent American army. The Allied command of necessity acquiesced and on 10 August the American army began its official existence. It was assigned the task of straightening out the St. Mihiel salient, south of Verdun. St. Mihiel, which had been in the possession of the Germans since September 1914, was strategically important because it commanded the Mézières-Sedan-Metz railway and the great Briey iron basin. The Germans had long recognized that their position, exposed as it was on two flanks, was untenable in the face of a determined attack. They were preparing to withdraw when, early in the morning of 12 September, blanketed by a heavy fog, the American army of over half a million men went into battle. 'The rapidity with which our divisions advanced overwhelmed the enemy,' wrote Pershing, 'and all objectives were reached by the afternoon of September 13.' In two days the American army wiped out the St. Mihiel salient, captured sixteen thousand prisoners and over four hundred guns and established their line in a position to threaten Metz, all with only seven thousand casualties. Above all, as Pershing pointed out, 'no form of enemy propaganda could overcome the depressing effect on the morale of the enemy of this demonstration of our ability to organize a large American force and drive it successfully through his defenses.'

General Foch was unwilling to authorize a continuation of the St. Mihiel offensive because he had other plans for the American army. These involved American co-operation in a gigantic Allied offensive all along the line from Ypres to Verdun. The time was propitious for such drive. The last Austrian offensive against Italy had ended in failure and the revived Italian army was prepared to take the offensive; Bulgaria had cracked up in September, and Turkey was about to follow; while the uninterrupted Allied success all along the Western front since July proved the disintegration of German morale. American contingents were fighting alongside the Belgians in the North and played an important part in the British offensive on the Somme, but for the main attack the American First army was assigned the sector between the Meuse and the Argonne Woods, with Sedan and the Sedan-Metz railway as the ultimate objective.

The Meuse-Argonne battle, launched on 26 September, was the greatest in which American troops had ever been engaged. It was stretched out over a period of over forty days, engaged 1,200,000 soldiers, 840 airplanes, and 324 tanks, and caused 117,000 American casualties. That these casualties were proportionately higher than those suffered by the French and English troops was due in part to the formidable nature of the task to which the Americans had been assigned, in part to the American preference for open-field tactics, and in part to insufficient training and experience.

Despite an heroic resistance from the badly depleted German troops, the entire movement was a complete success. The famous Hindenburg line was broken, and day by day the American troops pushed toward their objective. In the course of the prolonged battle American forces and their French allies captured over 25,000 prisoners, 874 cannon, and 3000 machine guns, and inflicted over 100,000 casualties on the enemy. Similar success attended the Allied offensive along the whole front from Flanders to Rheims.

As early as August it was apparent to Ludendorff, if not to the Allied high command, that the end was near. Foch was planning for a new offensive in the spring of 1919 and Pershing was asking for an army twice the size of that already under his command, but on 2 October Ludendorff informed the German government that the army could not hold out forty-eight hours. In this he was, as events proved, mistaken, but the German government was panic-stricken. In the hope of conciliating Wilson a parliamentary system was hastily established and Prince Max of Baden was called upon to form a liberal government. On 3 October Prince Max addressed to President Wilson the first overture for peace.[9] 'The German Government,' he said, 'accepts, as a basis for peace negotiations, the program laid down by the President of the United States in his message to Congress of January 8, 1918, and in his subsequent pronouncements, particularly in his address of September 27, 1918.' The references were, of course, to the Fourteen Points, with their subsequent elaboration. After a month of diplomatic fencing, in which the Germans were necessarily worsted, Foch was instructed by the Allied governments to negotiate for an armistice. Mutiny in the German navy and revolution in Munich, the Rhine cities, and Berlin, rendered the Germans impotent to offer further resistance; but in the vain hope that a complete change in the form of government might win milder terms of peace, the Kaiser was forced to abdicate, and on 9 November he fled across the border to Holland. Two days later an armistice was officially proclaimed, and the greatest and most costly war that the world had yet known came to an end.[10]

[9] Austria-Hungary had inaugurated peace overtures as early as 14 September, but without success.

[10] For casualties, see statistical table in the appendix.

4. *The Peace Conference, the Treaty, and the League*

Wilson had been successful in carrying the war to a victorious conclusion; he was to discover that it was easier to win a war than to make a peace. Like Lincoln he failed to guard against the forces of vindictiveness, hatred, and greed that are inevitably loosed by war. Yet the problems which faced Wilson were infinitely more complex than those which faced Lincoln and Johnson at the close of the Civil War, and the opposition which he encountered at home and abroad, more powerful, more firmly entrenched, and more brazen. Nor was Wilson well equipped for the task of overcoming or outwitting this opposition. The only statesman representing a major power who combined intelligence, magnanimity, and vision, he was nevertheless constitutionally unable or unwilling to play the game of politics and of diplomacy as it was being played in the United States and in Europe. His only weapons were intellectual conviction and moral inspiration; he was 'too proud to fight' with the piratical weapons used by his opponents.

Yet though Wilson himself was guiltless of vindictiveness or greed, he was not without responsibility for inspiring these emotions in others or for creating a situation where they would have free play. He had acquiesced in the suppression of liberalism, of freedom of speech and of the press, in the United States, and he had supported George Creel's campaign to inoculate Americans with the germs of hatred for the Central Powers. And finally it was American intervention in the war which had made possible a dictated, not a negotiated, peace.

Even before the armistice Wilson determined to shatter precedent by taking personal charge of the peace negotiations. On 24 October 1918 he had appealed to the American electorate for a vote of confidence: 'If you have approved of my leadership and wish me to continue to be your unembarrassed spokesman in affairs at home and abroad, I earnestly beg that you will express yourselves unmistakably to that effect by returning a Democratic majority to both the Senate and House of Representatives.' Two weeks later Americans went to the polls and chose a majority of Republicans to both houses of Congress. The damage to Wilson's prestige was irreparable, and when on 13 December he sailed for France ex-President Roosevelt warned 'our allies, our enemies and Mr. Wilson himself' that 'Mr. Wilson has no authority whatever to speak for the American people at this time. His leadership has just been emphatically repudiated by them. Mr. Wilson and his Fourteen Points and his four supplementary points and all his utterances every which way have ceased to have any shadow of right to be accepted as expressive of the will of the American people.'

As members of the American peace delegation Wilson took with him Secretary of State Lansing, General Tasker H. Bliss, Colonel House, and Mr. Henry White, a career man in the diplomatic service. It was not a strong delegation. Prudence would have counselled the appointment of representatives of the Senate and of the Republican party; common sense would have dictated the appointment of men of international repute and experience such as William H. Taft, Elihu Root, or A. Lawrence Lowell. Along with the American delegation went hundreds of experts to assist in the historical, ethnographical, and economic work of the peace commission. The Paris Conference, whatever its defects, had the benefit of more expert advice than any political arrangement ever concluded.

In the preliminary armistice negotiations with the Allies, Wilson had been made painfully aware of the conflict in war aims between the United States and the Allied powers. While he had clung tenaciously to his Fourteen Points, he had been forced to admit qualifications with respect to the important items of 'freedom of the seas' and reparations. That he knew of the existence of the secret treaties which in part nullified the Fourteen Points is clear; that he ignored their significance is equally certain. These secret treaties, which had been revealed by the Soviet government in Russia to discredit imperialist diplomacy, had been concluded between the major Allies and powers like Japan, Italy, and Rumania, in order to induce them to join the Allied side. This did not indicate any peculiar obliquity on the part of the Allies — for Italy and Rumania would certainly have joined the Central Powers otherwise — but the treaties were completely contrary in spirit and letter to the principle of self-determination, and Wilson should have tried to obtain formal abrogation before sending American troops to Europe. Why he did not attempt to do so, why the Department of State remained indifferent to them, is still a mystery.

In the Peace Conference which held its first formal session 18 January 1919, all the Allied and Associated powers were represented, but the 'Big Four' — England, France, Italy, and the United States — made the important decisions. Like the conference at Brest-Litovsk, this gave the defeated powers no part in the negotiations; they were merely called in when the treaty was ready, and ordered to sign on the dotted line. Nor was Russia officially represented, since the Allies hoped that the Soviet government would shortly collapse. Moreover, the jingo atmosphere of Paris and the personalities of the leaders made a just peace exceedingly difficult to attain. David Lloyd George, the British prime minister who represented his country, was an able administrator, but a self-seeker and demagogue. He had won a general election since the armistice on the slogans 'Hang the Kaiser' and 'Make Germany Pay'; he was to learn before the conference was over that you could not do either. Georges Clemenceau, the 'tiger' of French politics, was a cynical, able, and disillusioned old man who regarded Wilson liberalism with complete scepticism and assailed it with mordant wit: 'Mr. Wilson bores me with his Fourteen Points; why, God Almighty has only ten!' Clemenceau cared only for France, and France wanted but one thing, security; the English and Americans were never able to convince the 'logical' French that the worst way to security was the way that had always made for insecurity in the past — a humiliating peace that placed intolerable burdens on the vanquished. Orlando, the prime minister who represented Italy, was the exponent of *sacro egoismo,* the prisoner of his own propaganda; he must bring home the Austrian bacon to Rome. All four leaders were responsible to the public opinion of democratic states, and had to work in a democratic medium; which meant that the most enlightened and generous statesmen had to reduce the standards of their own thoughts to the level of other people's feelings. People everywhere had been hurt, exasperated, wounded, by a war which they regarded as all Germany's fault; they were in no mood to support the sort of peace that Wilson wanted and that would have saved us from most of the post-war agony.

Wilson, who had insisted that 'punitive damages, the dismemberment of empires, the establishment of exclusive economic leagues, we deem . . . no proper basis for a peace of any kind,' stood out as best he could for his Fourteen Points. Once, exasperated by the greed of his three associates, he was on the point of giving up and going home. But it is easy to see why he stayed. His departure would have been a confession of failure, and would have opened him to the charge of caring more for Germany than for the Allies — a charge that leading Republicans were already making. And, above all, there was the menace of Bolshevism that hung over Paris like a dark cloud. Everyone was thinking of it; many were talking of it. At one point Hungary went Bolshevik, rumors that Germany and Italy were slipping kept coming in, the entire bourgeois-capitalist world was terrified! Any peace was better than prolonging the uncertainty, and if America deserted the Allies would not Bolshevism reap the profit? So Wilson stayed. In the end he was forced to acquiesce in many compromises, but he imposed upon his colleagues something of his own ideas of a 'just' peace, and wrung from them many concessions.

The Treaty of Versailles to which the Germans affixed their signature on 28 June, after a purely interallied peace conference of over six months' duration, was not as drastic as France wanted, or harsh enough to keep Germany down. It required Germany to admit her war guilt, stripped her of all colonies and commercial rights in Africa and the Far East, of Alsace-Lorraine, Posen, and parts of Schleswig and Silesia, rectified the Belgian boundary line, confiscated the coal mines of the Saar basin, imposed military and naval disarmament upon her, saddled her with an immediate indemnity of five billion dollars and a future reparation bill of indeterminate amount, and placed practically the whole of her economic system under temporary Allied control. Other treaties drawn up simultaneously or shortly after recognized Czecho-Slovakia, greatly enlarged the territories of Italy, Rumania, and Serbia at the expense of the old Dual Monarchy, and created a new Poland with a corridor to the sea, from the historic Polish territories that had been parts of three empires.

Wilson successfully resisted some of the more extreme demands of the Allies. He prevented France from annexing the Saar basin, substituting instead a temporary control under League mandate. He denied Fiume to Italy — an action which caused Orlando to withdraw from the Conference in a huff. He protested against the cession of Shantung to Japan and finally wrung from her the promise of an early evacuation of that province — a promise which was fulfilled. He refused to permit the Allies to charge Germany with the whole cost of the war — a sum which Lloyd George estimated at approximately 120 billion dollars — pointing out that this was 'clearly inconsistent with what we deliberately led the enemy to expect.' He resisted Clemenceau's desire to detach the entire Rhineland from Germany, the Polish demand for East Prussia, and the desire of many to intervene actively in Russia. And finally he wrote into the treaty the covenant of the League of Nations. This, he felt, was the heart of the treaty, the part that justified the whole. 'The settlements,' he said, may be temporary, but the processes must be permanent.'

It was Wilson who insisted that the League should be an integral part of the treaty, and on 25 January the Peace Conference sustained him and assigned to a special committee, of which he was chairman, the task of drawing up the league covenant. For this task he and his advisers were abundantly prepared. Since 1915 the idea of a League to Enforce Peace had been agitated in the United States and in Great Britain. The American society of that name, a British committee, and various individuals like Colonel House had plans, and all these contributed something to the final draft of the league covenant, drawn up by Sir Cecil Hurst and David Hunter Miller. This Hurst-Miller draft was adopted by the Peace Conference on 14 February 1919.

The function of the League of Nations, as set forth in its preamble, was 'to promote international co-operation and to achieve international peace and security.' Membership was open to all nations and self-governing dominions; every member nation should be represented and have an equal vote in the Assembly, which was a deliberative body, while the United States, Great Britain, France, Italy, and Japan should be permanent and four other nations temporary members of the Council, which was more largely an executive body. A secretariat, attached to the League at Geneva, and an independent Permanent Court of International Justice, established at the Hague, completed the machinery for world organization. The members of the League pledged themselves to 'respect and preserve as against external aggression the territorial integrity and existing political independence of all Members of the League' (Art. X); to bring to the attention of the League any circumstance threatening international peace; to give publicity to treaties and to armaments; to submit to inquiry and arbitration all disputes threatening international peace, breaches of treaties, and questions of international law, and refrain from war until three months after the award by the arbiters; to refrain from war with the nations complying with the award of the League; and to employ on the recommendation of the League Council, military, naval, financial, and economic sanctions against nations resorting to war in disregard of their covenants under the League. The Council was further authorized to formulate plans for the reduction of armaments and mitigate the evils of the private manufacture of armaments; to investigate disputes brought before it by member or non-member nations and recommend effective action; to give publicity to treaties; to exercise mandates over the former colonies of Germany and Turkey; to set up a Permanent Court of International Justice and International Labor Bureau which should have jurisdiction over conditions of labor, traffic in women and children, drugs, arms, and munitions, and the control of health. The Covenant specifically recognized 'the validity of . . . regional understandings like the Monroe Doctrine.'

The President had called Congress into special session to consider ratification of the Treaty and the League of Nations, but when he arrived in the United States, early in June, he found debate already under way and the Senate in an ugly mood. Opposition to the League had been growing from the time of the armistice, and prospects for ratification seemed unfavorable. The opposition was compounded of varied and diverse elements; personal hostility to Wilson, partisanship, and senatorial pique; indignation of German-Americans who felt that their country had been betrayed, Italian-Americans angry over Fiume, Irish-Americans stirred up against England, then engaged in trying to suppress the Sinn Fein revolution; conservative disapproval of what was alleged to be leniency toward Germany, liberal disapproval of severity toward Germany; and a general feeling that Wilson and America had been tricked, and that we should avoid future European entanglements. In the Senate three groups could be discerned. At one extreme were the 'irreconcilables'—Lodge,[11] Borah, Johnson, Knox, Moses, McCormick, LaFollette, and others who were adamant against any departure from the traditional policy of isolation and determined to undo the whole of Wilson's handiwork; at the other extreme were the faithful followers of the President who were ready to ratify the Treaty as it stood. In between was a large number of moderates, made up of members of both parties, who believed in the wisdom of a few reservations to protect American interests. At all times, during the prolonged debate over the Treaty, more than three-fourths of the members of the Senate were ready to accept membership in the League in some form or other.[12]

But Wilson, unwilling to accept any but the mildest 'interpretations,' showed himself no less stubborn than the irreconcilables. Failing to make headway against the senatorial clique, he resorted to a

[11] Lodge is included with this group because, though he sponsored reservations, his purpose was clearly to defeat, not to ratify.

[12] See the careful analysis of the votes in **W. S. Holt**, *Treaties Defeated by the Senate*, pp. 294–301.

policy which he had often before employed with spectacular success — a direct appeal to the people. On 4 September he set out on a speaking tour which carried him through the Middle and Far West. He spoke with superb eloquence and passionate conviction, but against the rising tide of isolationism and illiberalism he made little headway, and much of the effect of his speeches was spoiled by the counter-arguments of the irreconcilables who stalked him relentlessly from city to city. On 25 September he spoke at Pueblo, Colorado; that night as his train sped eastward to Wichita he suffered a physical collapse. And with his collapse went all brave hopes of a new world order.

On 19 November 1919 the Treaty of Versailles was defeated in the Senate. Brought up for reconsideration in the next session of Congress, it once more failed of two-thirds majority, and on 19 March 1920 the Senate returned it to the President with formal notice of inability to ratify. 'If the President desires to make a campaign issue on the treaty,' said Henry Cabot Lodge, 'the Republicans are willing to meet that issue.' The President did so desire. Calling for a 'solemn referendum' on the League of Nations, Wilson and his followers made that the issue of the Presidential campaign of 1920. The Republican candidate carried the country by a plurality of six million votes. On 25 August 1921, almost three years after the armistice, Congress by joint resolution officially declared the war with Germany at an end.

XXI

WORLD POLITICS

1920–1937

1. *The League, the World Court, and Peace*

THE foreign policy of the Republicans, who guided the affairs of the nation from 1921 to 1933, was dictated by facts rather than theories. Committed in theory to isolation, they were in fact forced to participate in the liquidation of old and the solution of new problems that affected vitally American interests: war debts and reparations, armaments, Japanese aggression in the Far East, and the peace movement. Subscribing to the policy of economic nationalism and the erection of trade barriers, they were in fact forced in the interests of their supporters to fight for raw material and markets with the weapons of reciprocal bargains and trade agreements. Actually, therefore, despite professions to the contrary, we can discern considerable continuity in American foreign policy throughout the whole period from the Wilson to the first Franklin D. Roosevelt administrations.

In their relations with the Old World the Republicans repudiated the spirit of Wilson, yet in time accepted the substance; in their relations with Latin America they repudiated the substance but acknowledged the spirit. The same basic interests that shattered American isolation after 1914 continued to operate after 1920; the same considerations that justified Wilson's retreat from the Far East in 1917 dictated the diplomatic retreat of the Washington Conference in 1922; the same factors that inspired Wilson's Mobile address and 'watchful waiting' toward Mexico in the end brought about the retreat from dollar diplomacy and the 'Roosevelt corollary' that marked the administrations of Coolidge, Hoover, and F. D. Roosevelt. For, as Secretary of State Hughes pointed out:

> Foreign policies are not built upon abstractions. They are the result of practical conceptions of national interest arising from some immediate exigency or standing out vividly in historical perspective. . . . They express the hopes and fears, the aims of security or aggrandizement, which have become dominant in the national consciousness and thus transcend

party divisions and make negligible such opposition as may come from particular groups.

And 'practical conceptions of national interest' indicated the espousal of policies not dreamed of in the Republican philosophy of 1920.

For upon one thing, the Republicans were agreed: that Wilson's League was 'intolerable.' Aside from that, however, the Republican policy was shrouded in an impenetrable obscurity unrelieved by the floundering explanations of candidate Harding. The Republican platform committed the party to 'an international association' to 'secure instant and general conference whenever peace shall be threatened by political action,' and promised to bring about 'such agreement with the other nations of the world as shall meet fully the duty of America to civilization and humanity in accordance with American ideals.' Harding, in the course of his campaigning, approved of the League with reservations, suggested the substitution of a new for the existing League, and denounced any League. His masterly obfuscation of the issue was perhaps his supreme intellectual achievement.[1] To add to the general confusion irreconcilables assured the electorate that the election of Harding would mean the end of the League of Nations while thirty-two distinguished Republicans, including Hughes, Taft, Root, Hoover, Butler, and Lowell, announced that the election of Harding was the surest way to 'bring America into an effective league to preserve peace.'

Although the new Vice-President, Calvin Coolidge, expressed doubt whether 'any particular mandate was given in the last election on the question of the League of Nations,' Harding apparently entertained no such doubts. The issue, he said, was a closed one; the League — then composed of forty-eight nations — was 'deceased.' Secretary Hughes adopted toward the League a policy of calculated disparagement; for months communications from that body were ignored until at last the situation became both embarrassing and ridiculous. Once having committed itself to the bold policy of recognizing the existence of the League, the Harding administration found it convenient to co-operate with it. In 1922 the United States began to send 'unofficial

[1] One Republican commentator observed with pardonable pride that: 'One half of the speeches were for the League of Nations if you read them hastily, but if you read them with care every word of them could have been read critically against the League of Nations. The other half were violent speeches against the League of Nations if you read them carelessly, but if you read them critically every one of them could be interpreted as in favor of the League of Nations.'

observers' to League conferences on the white slave and opium traffic, and by 1925 this policy had been extended to the point where the United States was officially represented at the League conference on traffic in arms and munitions.

From that time to 1939 co-operation with the League was constant. The United States was represented at numerous League conferences, participated in many of its social and cultural activities, contributed, publicly and privately, to its work, and established a permanent secretariat at Geneva to co-ordinate American to League activities. In 1934 the United States officially joined the International Labor Organization, and on several occasions it supported the efforts of the League to enforce peace. In 1932 an American representative sat on the commission which investigated Japan's invasion of Manchuria, and the next year Norman Davis, speaking for President Franklin D. Roosevelt, announced that if the United States concurred in the wisdom and justice of sanctions against an offending nation, 'we will refrain from any action tending to defeat such collective effort which these states may make to restore peace.' This promise of support was shortly implemented by Congressional legislation looking to the imposition of an embargo against Italy during the Ethiopian crisis of 1935. Since 1920 no party had dared advocate membership in the League of Nations, but the United States had gone far toward active and effective co-operation with that organization.

American traditions dictated effective co-operation for disarmament and the outlawry of war. In his first year of office President Harding, at the suggestion of Senator Borah, called a conference of the nine powers with interests in the Pacific area to consider a limitation on armaments. On 12 November 1921 delegates from the United States, Great Britain, France, Italy, Belgium, Holland, Portugal, China, and Japan heard Secretary Hughes propose an itemized plan for scrapping warships and limiting naval armaments to prevent a naval 'race.' The United States, Great Britain, Japan, France, and Italy finally agreed upon a program calling for the maintenance of a naval ratio of 5-5-3 for the first three and 1.7 for each of the others, the scrapping of designated ships, and a ten-year naval holiday in the construction of capital ships.

At the time, this Washington Treaty of 1922 and the London Naval Treaty of 1930, which extended its provisions to some non-capital classes of ships, were regarded as outstanding victories for peace. Yet no well-meaning reform of the twentieth century, except prohibition, was so disappointing as naval limitation. The United States sacrificed an opportunity to become the world's greatest naval power, which in the troublous years ahead could have made her an effective keeper of the world's peace. The United States Navy scrapped fifteen new capital ships on which over $300,000,000 had already been spent, and no other nation had a comparable building program with which to match this sacrifice. Britain retained the prestige of parity at the expense of weakening the naval power that in a few years' time would be essential to her existence. And, in order to induce Japan to consent to the 5–5–3 ratio, the United States and Great Britain had to agree not to strengthen any of their fortifications and naval bases in the Pacific between Singapore and Hawaii. This action virtually doubled the value of Japanese tonnage quotas for naval operations in the Orient and rendered the defense of Guam, Singapore, and the Philippines virtually impossible. Moreover, in spite of these concessions, Japan was insulted rather than appeased; their militarists used the slogan '5–5–3' much as in other days we had used '54–40 or fight,' to discredit the liberal government which had accepted limitation and to get into power. When that had been accomplished, at the end of 1934 Japan denounced the naval limitation treaties and started a frenzied building program that, by the time war broke out in the Pacific, rendered the Japanese Navy more powerful in every type of ship than the United States and British Pacific and Asiatic fleets, combined. But American and British budgets, now geared to meager naval appropriation, followed suit slowly and reluctantly.

Naval limitation saved the American taxpayer of 1922–37 millions of dollars, but the taxpayer from 1942 to the present has paid a hundredfold for this futile gesture. If the United States had gone ahead resolutely with the Daniels building program of 1916, the Japanese militarists might have been kept within bounds; Anglo-American naval power was the only force they feared.

Equally soothing at the time, but of no practical effect in preventing World War II, were the various treaties for the arbitration of international disputes and the outlawing of war that the United States sponsored in the nineteen-twenties and thirties. Arbitration, as we have seen, was in the American tradition. The United States submitted to the Hague Permanent Court its first case — the Pious Fund case. Both Taft and Wilson had attempted to extend the scope of arbitration to embrace disputes of all kinds, even those involving 'national honor.' The Taft treaties, to be sure, had been amended beyond recognition, but those which Bryan proposed had successfully hurdled all Senate opposition. By the time of the First World War Bryan had negotiated with thirty nations treaties providing for a commission to investigate all disputes not otherwise arbitrable and for a 'cooling-off' period of one year pending the settlement during which neither party to the dispute should resort to any act of force.

When in 1927 the French Premier, Aristide Briand, offered a bilateral treaty to the United States for the outlawry of war, Secretary of State Frank B. Kellogg countered with the suggestion of a multilateral treaty of the same character. The result of these negotiations was the Pact of Paris, sometimes known as the Kellogg Peace Pact, of 27 August 1928. It provided that the contracting powers 'condemn recourse to war for the solution of international controversies, and renounce it as an instrument of national policy,' and that 'the settlement or solution of all disputes or conflicts of whatever nature or of whatever origin they may be . . . shall never be sought except by pacific means.' Adhered to eventually by sixty-two nations, it was ratified by the United States 15 January 1929 by a vote of 81 to 1. The most thoroughgoing commitment to peace that great powers had ever made, the Pact of Paris may fairly be called an attempt to keep peace by incantation.

In view of its readiness to accept the Kellogg Pact, it is strange that the Senate until 1946 could never be induced to adhere to the World Court,[2] although repeatedly urged to do so by Presidents Harding, Coolidge, Hoover, and Roosevelt.

All these methods of preserving the peace — by limitation, by incantation, and (in the next administration) by negation (the Neutrality Acts) — would have been effective among nations that wanted peace. They were worse than useless in a world where three nations — Germany, Italy, and Japan — wanted war; for they merely served to lull the democracies into a false feeling of security, while giving the militarists elsewhere a chance to plot, plan, and prepare for a war that would enable them to divide up the world.

2. *War Debts and Reparations*

However disinterested America professed to be in European politics, it was of necessity deeply interested in European economy. Dur-

[2] The Permanent Court of International Justice, established 1922 under Article XIV of the League of Nations Covenant. Yet one of the judges of the Court, from the beginning, was an American.

ing the war the United States government had lent to the Allies something over seven billion dollars, practically all of which was spent in the United States. These were the original 'war debts,' but after the armistice loans and credits to the sum of three and a quarter billion more were extended to our late associates and to some of the succession states. These were used for purposes of reconstruction, and were 'peace' rather than 'war' debts. The original terms of these loans provided for payment of 5 per cent interest; in 1922 Congress provided that the loans should not run longer than to 1947 and fixed the minimum rate of interest at 4¼ per cent.

The payment of war debts was complicated by two other factors. The first, of minor importance, was the existence of a system of interallied debts. Thus Great Britain, who owed the United States over four billion dollars, had extended loans to her allies to the sum of ten and one-half billion dollars. France had borrowed some seven billion and loaned some three and one-half billion; Italy had borrowed almost five billion and loaned a little less than four hundred million dollars. Italy and France would clearly profit from an all-round cancellation of war debts; Great Britain, though her credits were six billion more than her debts, would profit directly because she had little prospect of collecting debts owing to her and indirectly because speedy restoration of purchasing power and world trade would bring her prosperity. As early as August 1922 Balfour approached the United States with a proposal for a general cancellation of war debts and at the same time announced that Great Britain would not attempt to collect from her debtors more than enough to cover her own debts to the United States. The United States, refusing to be embarrassed at this attempt to shift responsibility, ignored the proposal.

The second factor affecting the war-debt situation was reparations. From the beginning it was the avowed intention of the debtor nations to pay all their debts out of German reparations. Precisely how large those reparations were to be was not settled until 1921 when a Reparations Commission fixed the total at thirty-three billion dollars, a sum more than sufficient to cover all debts to the United States. It was one thing, however, to exact reparations; another to collect them. The burden was probably not too heavy for Germany to carry, but within a year payments were in default. So too, since the Allies insisted upon coupling reparations with war debts, were payments to the United States.

The United States never officially accepted this theory of the connection between reparations and debts, but it indicated its willingness to refund the war debts at a more reasonable rate of interest and it co-operated, unofficially, in attempts to solve the reparations problem. In June 1923 a settlement was negotiated with Great Britain reducing interest to 3.3 per cent and extending payment over sixty-two years; thereafter settlements of a similar though more generous nature, based upon alleged capacity to pay, were made with the other debtor nations. The Belgian debt was funded at 1.8 per cent interest, the French at 1.6, and the Italian at 0.4. Based upon the original 5 per cent interest rate, these funding arrangements represented a total cancellation of approximately fifty per cent, ranging from thirty per cent for Great Britain to eighty per cent for Italy. Americans considered these arrangements generous; most Europeans regarded them as proof that 'Uncle Shylock' was grasping and mercenary.

The necessity of getting money from Germany with which to pay these newly funded debts led to a reconsideration of the whole problem of reparations. France, less patient with German failure to meet her obligations than was the United States with her debtors, had attempted to compensate herself by occupation of the Ruhr, but such coercion was a dismal failure. At the suggestion of the American Secretary of State Hughes a committee of experts was appointed to find some way out of the impasse. Under the chairmanship of Charles G. Dawes this committee worked out a new and less onerous scale of reparations payments, arranged for a loan to stabilize German currency, and recommended the prompt evacuation of the Ruhr. Under this so-called Dawes plan Germany faithfully met her reparations payments until 1928, but only by extensive borrowing in the United States. When in 1929 the rival attractions of stock-market speculation dried up American loans, Germany once again faced default. To avert this disaster a new reparations committee, headed by the American financier Owen D. Young, formulated the Young plan. Under this plan the total reparations bill was reduced to approximately twenty-seven billion dollars and payment was spread over a period of fifty-nine years. Furthermore the Young plan specifically recognized the connection between reparations and the Allied war debts, by providing that reparations payments might be scaled down in the same proportion that the United States permitted the scaling down of the war debts.

Additional borrowings in the United States financed reparations until 1931, but by that time the depression made further borrowings impossible, and Germany once more defaulted, never to resume payments. Altogether Germany had paid in reparations $4,470,300,000, and had borrowed in the United States, $2,475,000,000. During this same period the Allies had paid to the United States only $2,606,340,000. The United States therefore had paid over half the reparations bill and almost the whole war-debt bill.

The year 1931 brought a major banking crisis in Austria which spread throughout central Europe, forcing Germany to abandon further reparations payments and Great Britain to abandon the gold standard. Faced with a collapse of the world financial structure President Hoover advised and Congress ratified a one-year moratorium on all war-debt payments. The following year a conference at Lausanne drastically reduced reparations payments to a mere $750,000,000. Great Britain and France at once made overtures to the United States for a revision of the war debts. Hoover replied that 'reparations are a solely European question in which the United States is not concerned' and repudiated the contention that the Lausanne settlement 'was made in reliance upon any commitments given by this government.' But when war-debt payments fell due in June 1933 there was a general default. Some states paid nothing, some made 'token' payments, Finland alone met her obligations in full. Faced with this effective if one-sided cancellation of the war debts, Congress in April 1934 passed the Johnson Act forbidding Americans to make loans to any foreign government which was in default on its debts to the United States.

The question of voluntary cancellation of the war debts is intricate and controversial. On the one hand it is alleged that most of the money advanced to the Allied and associated powers was spent in the United States, that a good part of it might reasonably be regarded as America's financial contribution to winning the war, that war-time prosperity brought to the United States more money than was loaned, that the American tariff policy was responsible for the inability of European nations to meet their obligations, that payment would prolong the world depression and adversely affect the United States, and that in any event the debtor nations were quite unable to make payments. On the other hand it is asserted that the money was loaned with the full understanding that it was to be repaid, that the United States was never formally allied with the Allied powers, that the American financial contribution to the war was proportionately greater than that of any of the Allies, that at least one-third of the debt was extended after the armistice for constructive purposes and a good part of it to nations with which we were not associated in the war, that while the Allies were pleading poverty they were spending huge sums on armaments and themselves lending large sums to satellite states, that they did not even turn over to the United States what they obtained from Germany in reparations, and that if the European nations failed to pay their debts, the burden would be transferred to the American tax-payer. Into this maze of conflicting assertions it is difficult for the historian to enter. One thing, however, is clear: the average American took the attitude expressed in President Coolidge's classic remark, 'They hired the money, didn't they?' and no American political party dared come out openly in favor of cancellation.

3. *Far Eastern Affairs*

The economic possibilities of the Far East proved disappointing, and, after World War I, the great majority of Americans came to think Far Eastern diplomacy as distasteful as European power politics and even more mysterious.

In fact, it was far more simple. There was the great and ancient empire of China, nominally a republic in the western model since 1912 but actually, since 1920, in a state of civil war between generals that left little power to the national government. And, on the other side, there was the ancient but streamlined empire of Japan, nominally a constitutional monarchy but actually at the mercy of the Emperor's army leaders whenever they chose to assert their authority. Japan by 1920 had acquired an economic position in the Orient similar to that of Britain in the Occident a century earlier; by technique learned in the West, combined with native energy, the so-called Mitsubishi group of interests had built up an industrial empire in textiles, steel, and consumer goods that was capturing the former European-dominated markets all around the Pacific. Underneath all this modern industrial skill, however, Japan was a country of primitive ideas, where the military were venerated, 'Bushido' (the code of the warrior) was the highest morality, and *Hakko Ichiu* — 'bringing the eight corners of the world under one roof,' the probably mythical slogan of a possibly mythical emperor in 600 B.C. — was in the back of the popular mind. This meant that, unless westernized liberal elements kept control of the Japanese government, Japan, like Germany in 1914, would not be content with industrial expansion but would go in for foreign conquest. And it was not yet certain whether revolutionary Russia or distracted China would be the first victim.

American policy toward the Orient remained the same after as before World War I: to keep the peace, maintain the Open Door policy both for business and missionary effort, and by diplomacy to check the efforts of Japan, Russia, or any other power to take advantage of Chinese weakness or impair her territorial integrity. There was no 'retreat,' as some writers have alleged, from our earlier policy; but there was less vigor in maintaining it, and no disposition whatever to enlarge our own sphere of influence in the Philippines. The Tydings-McDuffie Act of 1934, promising independence to the Philippines in 1946, looked like a retreat, but in reality it was but a wise advance step toward the withdrawal of western control from the Orient, one that all Western nations were forced to take after World War II.

The Anglo-Japanese alliance gave Japan a welcome excuse to participate in World War I, from which she profited greatly. First she seized the islands in the North Pacific and the German concession in Shantung. Then she took advantage of the involvement of the European powers and the isolation of the United States to consolidate her position in Manchuria and to browbeat China into submission to her will.

Early in 1915 the Japanese government presented to China, in the form of an ultimatum, Twenty-one Demands that would give her a practical protectorate over China more complete than any the United States had ever exercised over Cuba. They were a gross violation of the Root-Takahira agreement of 1908 to maintain the independence and integrity of China, and the Open Door for commerce. Bryan promptly protested; the United States, he said, 'could not regard with indifference the assumption of political, military or economic domination over China by a foreign power,' and would not recognize any impairment of American rights, the Open Door policy, or the territorial integrity and political sovereignty of China. His protest, however, was qualified by a recognition that Japan had 'special interests' in contiguous territories such as Shantung, Manchuria, and Mongolia. China accepted the Demands in somewhat modified form, the American protest was evaded, and Japan continued a stealthy but sure ad-

TABULAR VIEW OF THE WAR DEBTS

	Pre-armistice	Post-armistice		Total Indebtedness	Funded Debt	Average Interest Rate
	Cash Loans	Cash Loans	War and Relief Supplies			
Armenia *	....	....	$ 11,959,917.49	$ 11,959,917.49	....	....
Austria	....	....	24,055,708.92	24,055,708.92	$ 24,614,885	3.3%
Belgium	$ 171,780,000	$ 177,434,467.89	29,872,732.54	379,087,200.43	417,780,000	1.8%
Cuba †	10,000,000	....	....	10,000,000.00	....	....
Czechoslovakia	....	61,974,041.10	29,905,629.93	91,879,671.03	185,071,023	3.3%
Estonia	....	....	13,999,145.60	13,999,145.60	13,830,000	3.3%
Finland	....	....	8,281,926.17	8,281,926.17	9,000,000	3.3%
France	1,970,000,000	1,027,477,800.00	407,341,145.01	3,404,818,945.01	4,025,000,000	1.6%
Great Britain	3,696,000,000	581,000,000.00	....	4,277,000,000.00	4,600,000,000	3.3%
Greece	....	27,167,000.00	....	27,167,000.00	32,497,000	3.3%
Hungary	....	....	1,685,835.61	1,685,835.61	1,982,555	3.3%
Italy	1,031,000,000	617,034,050.90	....	1,648,034,050.90	2,042,000,000	0.4%
Latvia	....	....	5,132,287.14	5,132,287.14	5,775,000	3.3%
Liberia	....	26,000.00	....	26,000.00	....	....
Lithuania	....	....	4,981,628.03	4,981,628.03	6,432,465	3.3%
Nicaragua *	....	....	431,849.14	431,849.14	....	....
Poland	....	....	159,666,972.39	159,666,972.39	178,560,000	3.3%
Rumania	....	25,000,000.00	12,911,152.92	37,911,152.92	66,560,560	3.3%
Russia *	187,729,750	....	4,871,547.37	192,601,297.37	....	....
Yugoslavia	10,605,000	16,175,465.56	24,978,020.99	51,758,480.55	62,850,000	1.0%
	$7,077,114,750	$2,533,288,825.45	$740,075,499.25	$10,350,479,074.70	$11,671,953,489	2.1%

* Not funded † Paid

vance toward domination of the Far East. Secret agreements with the European powers secured support for the Japanese claim to Shantung, the German islands in the Pacific, and special concessions in China. In 1917 Viscount Ishii came to the United States on a special mission to quiet American apprehension of Japanese policies and obtain definite recognition of Japan's 'paramount' interest in China. From the point of view of the Japanese, the Lansing-Ishii Agreement of 2 November 1917 accomplished just that, but the American interpretation of the agreement was very different. It reaffirmed the Open Door, pledged both nations to respect the independence and territorial integrity of China, and disclaimed any desire for 'special rights or privileges.' At the same time, however, it specifically recognized that 'territorial propinquity creates special relations, and that Japan has special interests in China, particularly in that part to which her possessions are contiguous.'

In 1918 Japan took advantage of the Russian Revolution to intervene in Eastern Siberia. The United States joined this intervention in order to exercise a moderating influence. By 1920 the United States and other Allied powers had withdrawn their forces from Siberia; Japan alone stayed on. And at the Versailles conference Japan succeeded in legalizing her claims to Shantung and the former German islands in the Pacific.

This, then, was the situation which confronted President Harding in 1921. The 'open' door had been partly shut, the territorial integrity and political sovereignty of China had been impaired, and Japan had entrenched herself firmly in Shantung, Manchuria, Mongolia, and Eastern Siberia. Most of the agreements, declarations, and understandings by which the United States had sought to impose her own policy upon Japan had proved to be scraps of paper, and short of war — which nobody wanted — there was no way by which she could enforce them. From this embarrassing situation the United States tried to extricate herself by the Washington Conference.

The Washington Conference was designed to achieve two major objectives: disarmament and an avoidance of conflict in the Far East. The first we have already discussed;[3] the second was attempted by converting bilateral into multilateral understandings, thus freeing the United States from sole responsibility for a policy which she could

[3] Above, pp. 500–501.

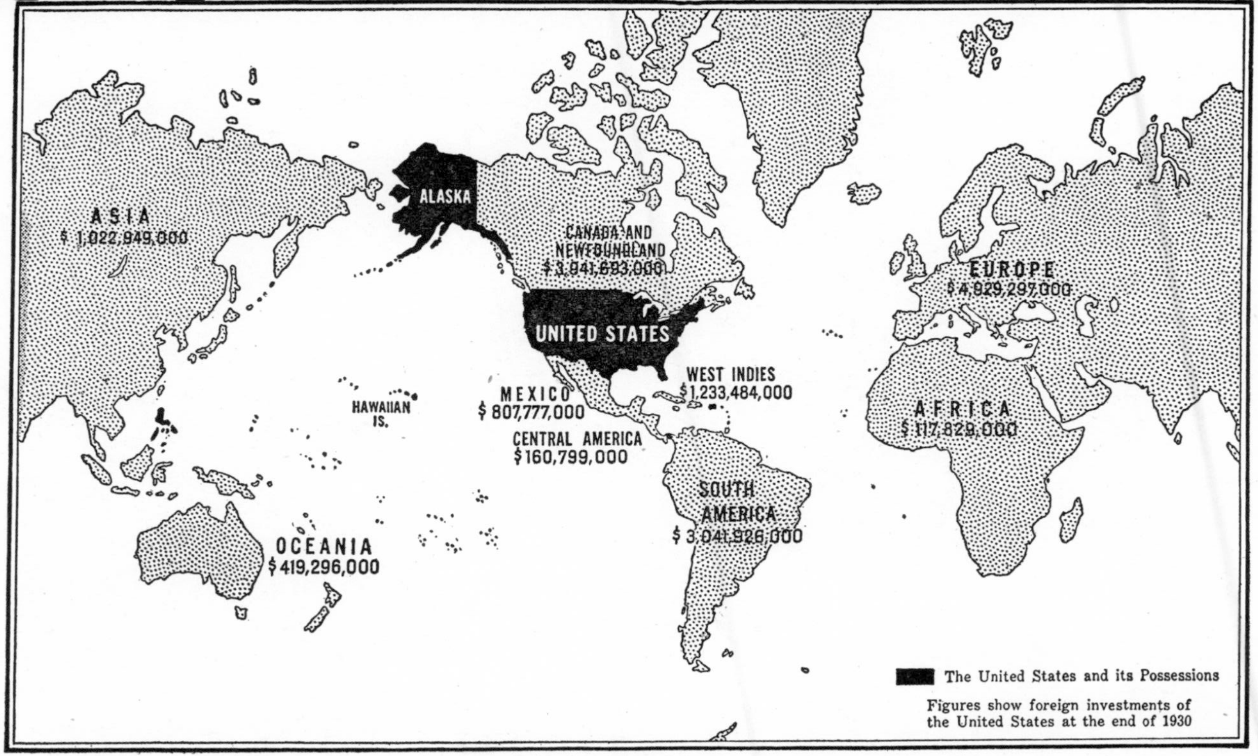

American Interests and Possessions Abroad, 1930

Figures are based upon Paul Dickens, A New Estimate of American Investments Abroad, *U.S. Dept. of Commerce Trade Infor., Bull. No. 767*

not in any event enforce and making that responsibility a common one. By the Four Power Treaty (13 December 1921) the United States, Great Britain, France, and Japan engaged mutually to 'respect their rights in relation to their insular possessions in the region of the Pacific Ocean' and pledged themselves to settle any controversy that might arise over these rights by a joint conference. By the Nine Power Treaty (6 February 1922) the same powers plus Italy, Belgium, the Netherlands, Portugal, and China, in order to 'stabilize conditions in the Far East' and 'to safeguard the rights and interests of China,' agreed mutually to respect its sovereignty, independence, and territorial and administrative integrity, maintain the principle of the open door, and refrain from creating 'spheres of influence,' seeking special privileges or concessions, or abridging therein the rights and privileges of citizens of friendly states.

The Japanese government, then in the hands of liberals, made great concessions. It forced the army to withdraw from Siberia and Shantung and agreed to construct no fortifications in the Mandated islands, in return for our not fortifying any of our Pacific possessions west of Hawaii. Three things weakened the Japanese liberals, who were our only hope of preserving peace in the Orient, and strengthened the militarists. These were, the 5–5–3 ratio in the naval limitation treaties, which the militarists found insulting and (from their own point of view) unconstitutional; the American Immigration Act of 1924, which excluded Japanese from entering the United States; and the British denunciation in 1922 of their Japanese treaty, which was a concession to Canadian and American pressure. These things, together with too frequent instances of American intolerance toward Japanese-Americans, offended Nipponese pride and offset gratitude for American help after the Tokyo Earthquake of 1923. That earthquake did, however, postpone a crisis because the havoc that it created and the superstitious dread it aroused caused the military secret societies to postpone to 1931 the coup d'état they had planned to execute in China.

China invited Japanese intervention by her weakness and division among a number of war lords, although there was always a nationalist government that attempted to act for the entire republic. In the meantime the Japanese militarists, who bore a strong resemblance both in methods and objectives to Hitler's Nazis, were organizing in order to seize the Japanese government in the name of Emperor Hirohito (a well meaning but weak young man) and to throw the detested white man out of Eastern Asia. World War II in the Far East really began on 18 September 1931 when General Hayashi, seizing the excuse of a bomb explosion on the South Manchuria Railway, moved his army from Korea into Manchuria and overran that great Chinese province. The Japanese government, ignorant of this 'Manchuria Incident' until it was all over, was forced to acquiesce under threat of assassination, and in 1932 Japan declared Manchuria the independent kingdom of Manchukuo, under a puppet monarch.

All this was, of course, a clear violation of treaties, the Kellogg Pact, and the Covenant of the League of Nations, by all of which Japan was in theory bound. All but the last of these engagements concerned the United States, and without waiting for League action, Secretary of State Stimson informed Japan that the United States would not recognize the legality of any development which impaired American treaty rights, or violated the open-door policy. The League of Nations, invoking the Kellogg-Briand Pact, appointed a commission to investigate, and its report (September 1932) condemned the Japanese aggression against China on every count. Japan replied by withdrawing from the League. In the meantime, the militarists consolidated their power by assassinating the Japanese premier and other important ministers of state, and entered on a vigorous program of economic and military preparation for invading China proper. That invasion began on 7 July 1937 with the 'China Incident,' a planned clash between Japanese troops on maneuver and Chinese troops on the Marco Polo bridge near Peiping. In the then state of American public opinion, the Department of State could do nothing but vigorously protest and piously hope that Chinese resistance or a domestic turnover would bring Japan to her senses.

4. *The Metamorphosis of the Monroe Doctrine*

Modification of the Monroe Doctrine had been inaugurated, in theory at least, by Wilson's administration. The Mobile Address had held out the promise of a new Latin-American policy, and the A.B.C. Conference at Niagara Falls and Colonel House's plan of a Pan-American League of Nations recognized the right of South American states to co-operate in the formulation of policies affecting the Western Hemisphere. Yet Wilson himself, as we have seen, was not constant to his ideal; the occupation of Vera Cruz, and intervention in Nicaragua and Hispaniola caused his sincerity to be seriously questioned south of the Rio Grande. To his successors he left a heritage not only of fine principles but of tough problems, such as the protection of oil and mineral investments in Mexico, the Caribbean occupations, and the struggle for markets and raw material in South America. His successors subscribed to his principles but liquidated his problems.

Mexico was the center of trouble for six years. Article 27 of the Constitution of 1917 had vested in the Mexican nation ownership of all mineral and oil resources, and limited future concessions to Mexican nationals. American investments in mining and oil amounted to about 300 million dollars; if Article 27 should be interpreted as retroactive, all that would be confiscated and future earnings endangered. President Obregon, who succeeded Carranza in 1919, would not at once commit himself in regard to the interpretation of this Article. Consequently President Wilson refused to recognize his government, and the Harding administration declined to do so unless Mexico gave formal guarantees that American interests would not suffer. Obregon, resenting this demand as an affront to Mexican sovereignty, refused. There followed a war of hard words for two years, during which American troops were deployed along the Rio Grande, and war seemed imminent. At this juncture a timely decision of the Mexican Supreme Court, holding that Article 27 was not retroactive, averted a crisis, and negotiations in the summer of 1923 resulted in the resumption of friendly relations between the two nations.

The new President, Plutarco Calles, favored nevertheless a retroactive interpretation of the troublesome Article 27, and at the same time promoted agrarian legislation that threatened American land investments and ecclesiastical legislation that affronted Roman Catholics. Secretary Kellogg, who had succeeded Hughes in the State Department, declared:

> The government of Mexico is now on trial before the world. . . . We have been patient and realize, of course, that it takes time to bring about a stable government, but we cannot countenance violation of her obligations and failure to protect American citizens.

Despite this threat, the Calles government remained firm. Secretary Kellogg, unable to enlist popular support for an aggressive defense of American oil interests, early in 1927 dragged the red herring of Communism across the controversy and, further to complicate the issue, accused the Mexican government of offensively opposing American policy in Nicaragua. Nevertheless, on 25 January 1927 the Senate voted unanimously to arbitrate the Mexican controversy. Sobered by this rebuke, President Coolidge appointed as ambassador to Mexico his Amherst classmate, Dwight W. Morrow, a member of the House of Morgan who had publicly avowed his opposition to 'dollar diplomacy.' Through a remarkable combination of character, intelligence, shrewdness, and charm, Mr. Morrow succeeded in repairing most of the damage that his predecessors in Mexico City and his superiors in Washington had done. In response to new Supreme Court rulings the Mexican Congress modified some of its oil and mineral legislation in line with American objections, while Morrow obtained an adjustment of land questions, claims, and the Church question. Throughout the decade of the 1930's this new understanding so auspiciously inaugurated by Morrow remained undisturbed, while in the United States a widespread admiration for Mexican culture (especially the paintings by Rivera and Orozco), and a growing appreciation for the social ideals of the Mexican revolution, made a good base for the future. And, in contrast to World War I, when Mexico was a center of German propaganda, the Southern Republic loyally supported the United States in World War II.

Elsewhere in the Caribbean the United States declined to pick up the 'big stick' that Theodore Roosevelt, Taft, and Wilson had successively brandished. Impatience of public opinion with 'dollar diplomacy' was back of it, but the Caribbean countries co-operated by an awakened sense of order, and American investments in them increased to a point where their direct influence on the local governments rendered the old cry 'Send the Marines!' unnecessary. Americans owned about one third of the wealth of Cuba, while investments in Haiti amounted to seventy-five million, in Santo Domingo ninety million, and in Central America almost three hundred million dollars. In 1922 the State Department promised to evacuate Santo Domingo, and two years later the Dominican flag displaced the American in that distracted republic. In 1925 United States marines were withdrawn from Nicaragua; they returned again the following year, but the acrimonious criticism which greeted this brief revival of intervention led to a more circumspect policy and eventually to a final withdrawal in 1933. Haiti was freed from American military control in 1934 and that same year Franklin D. Roosevelt's 'good neighbor' policy was dramatized by the abrogation of the Platt Amendment — those clauses in the 1903 treaty with Cuba that gave the United States the right to intervene at its own judgment for the preservation of order.

It was the Republicans, however, who sloughed off the embarrassing Theodore Roosevelt corollary to the Monroe Doctrine. A State Department memorandum, dated 17 December 1928, asserted that the Monroe Doctrine was directed toward Europe, not Latin America. Shortly thereafter the Assistant Secretary of State, William R. Castle, Jr., admitted that 'the Monroe Doctrine confers no superior position on the United States.' President Franklin D. Roosevelt built upon this foundation, and committed the United States even more firmly to the doctrine of non-intervention. In a speech shortly after his inauguration he observed:

> The maintenance of constitutional government in other nations is not a sacred obligation devolving upon the United States alone. The maintenance of law and orderly processes of government in this hemisphere is the concern of each individual nation within its own borders first of all. It is only if and when the failure of orderly processes affects the other nations of the continent that it becomes their concern; and the point to stress is that in such an event it becomes the joint concern of a whole continent in which we are all neighbors.

This conception of the Monroe Doctrine as the joint concern of American nations had first been broached by Woodrow Wilson, but it remained for the Roosevelt administration to implement it. A series of treaties and conventions, formulated by successive Pan-American Conferences, outlawed all wars of aggression, provided for the arbitration of all disputes, called for the removal of trade barriers, and announced that 'no state has the right to intervene in the internal or external affairs of another.' More important even than these formal assurances was the indubitable evidence of repentance and reform furnished by Secretary Hull's overtures to Latin America and the good-will visit of President Roosevelt in 1936. The Monroe Doctrine remains the most vital consideration of American foreign policy, but the interpretation of that doctrine is more circumspect and more disinterested than at any time since the Civil War.

XXII

'NORMALCY' AND REACTION

1921–1933

1. *Politics and Personalities*

THE decade after the World War like the decade after the Civil War, was a period of conservatism in politics and in social philosophy. In both eras the Republican party was in almost undisputed control of national affairs and regarded itself as an instrument for the advancement of business; the philosophy of laissez faire toward business was avowed, but the policy of government support to business was practiced. Both decades were necessarily taken up with the liquidation of the war: the restoration of industry, transportation, finance, and agriculture to a peace-time basis, payment of the public debt, reduction of taxation, and veterans' benefits. Both witnessed a rapid change in manufacturing and business technique and a florid but badly distributed industrial prosperity accompanied by agricultural distress and succeeded by acute and prolonged depression. And both were characterized by political and business corruption, decline in liberalism, apathy toward reform, and an ardent nationalism that took repressive and intolerant form.

The point of view of the dominant group in the 1920's was best expressed by the titular leaders of the party in power. President Harding called for a 'return to normalcy,' President Coolidge announced succinctly that 'the business of the United States is business,' and President Hoover insisted that 'rugged individualism' was basic to the 'American system.' There was a frank confession that the nation was in greater danger from 'mistaken government activity' than from 'lack of legislation,' and an acknowledgment that 'the government should assist and encourage business' — negatively by a policy of laissez faire, positively by high tariffs, the search for markets and raw materials, a suspension of embarrassing regulatory legislation, a reduction of taxation, and outright subsidies to merchant marine and aviation.

Yet the philosophy which animated the Harding-Coolidge-Hoover administrations was at no time integrated or consistent. It was on the contrary a curious amalgam of laissez faire and regimentation. The war had revealed the effectiveness of a planned, if not a socialized, economy; had organized and integrated the whole of American industry, transportation, and finance, and placed them at the service of the nation. This wartime control had brought not only efficiency but profits, creating thousands of new millionaires. Business men wished a return to private operation of business, but they were disposed to retain the advantages of nation-wide organization and integration, of the regimentation of industry and labor, of price-fixing and monopoly. Despite official repudiation of a planned economy — which smacked somehow of Communism — business was willing enough to accept such an economy provided that it could do the planning. It was willing enough to suffer regimentation provided that it could command the regiments. Actually the regimentation of American economy, about which so much was said during the Franklin D. Roosevelt administration, grew out of the war and post-war years; the N.R.A., for example, so frequently cited as the most thorough-going effort toward regimentation, was based squarely upon previous experience and many of the N.R.A. codes were mere copies of codes under which trade organizations had been operating for years. So during the period of Republican reaction we have the paradox of the triumph of the philosophy of laissez faire and of the policy of socialized control.

The Republicans naturally argued that this philosophy of conservatism had been endorsed by an overwhelming majority of the American people in 1920; obviously it was so endorsed in 1924 and 1928. For while the precise issues of the election of 1920 were obscure, the general issue was clear. Howsoever the electorate might be confused by the equivocal position of the Republican party on foreign affairs, there was no ambiguity about the economic philosophy which was celebrated in the party platforms and which animated the candidates. James Cox, the Democratic standard-bearer, was not himself a man of any strong liberal principles, but as a stalking horse for Wilson he represented what liberalism still flourished in the Democratic party. Warren G. Harding, nominated after Frank Lowden and Leonard Wood had exhausted each other, because 'there was nothing against him and the delegates wanted to go home,' was the choice of the Republican 'Old Guard' — Boies Penrose, Reed Smoot, Joseph R. Grundy, and the members of the 'Ohio gang.' A vice-presidential candidate was then offered to the convention by the same crowd, but the delegates gagged at this second course, and with some show of independence nominated Calvin Coolidge. Fame had recently thrust herself upon Governor Coolidge when, in the course of a Boston police strike, he declared that there was 'no right to strike against the public safety by anybody, anywhere, anytime.' This resounding declaration caught the imagination of a public jittery about the 'red menace.'

During the election the voters knew that Harding represented a return to conservatism, and Cox a continuation of Wilsonian progressivism; they gave Harding 16,152,200 votes and Cox 9,147,353. Eugene V. Debs, intellectually the most respectable of the three candidates, received a little less than one million votes. Since at that time he was serving a term in the Federal penitentiary at Atlanta for sedition, this vote constituted perhaps a tribute to rather than a reflection upon his character. Although less than half the potential electorate had troubled to go to the polls, the election indicated that the temper of the country was no less reactionary than that of the successful candidate.

Warren Gamaliel Harding of Marion, Ohio, was a small town politician and newspaper editor whose appearance and career recalled his old neighbor William McKinley. Like McKinley, Harding seemed to represent virtues dear to the American heart: simplicity, friendliness, generosity. He was a thoroughly commonplace person, without intellectual or social pretentions, easy-going and conservative, disposed to let well enough alone, and sure that in the United States everything was well enough. Like McKinley, too, he was politically regular, convinced that the Republican party was the only one fit to rule and that the 'Old Guard' had accumulated most of the wisdom in the United States. His political advancement, as McKinley's, had been promoted by local bosses and friends who expected gratitude, and Harding was not inclined to disappoint their expectations. But unlike McKinley, Harding was morally weak, unable to resist the influence of stronger and more unscrupulous wills, unable to deny the importunities of his friends.

When Harding moved into the White House he took with him his Ohio friends, and for three years the 'Ohio gang' had pretty much their own way in national politics. One of them, Harry Daugherty, was awarded the position of Attorney-General. The other cabinet appointments aroused mixed emotions. The country looked with satisfaction upon the choice of Charles E. Hughes for the State and of Herbert C. Hoover for the Commerce departments, and business men were gratified to see the aluminum millionaire, Andrew W. Mellon take the portfolio of the Treasury. The appointment of such men as J. W. Weeks to the War and H. C. Wallace to the Agriculture departments was unobjectionable, but that of Albert B. Fall to the Department of the Interior aroused dismay except among his Senatorial colleagues and the oil interests.

'There can be no doubt,' wrote William Allen White, 'that oil controlled the Republican convention of 1920.' This is something of an exaggeration; the manufacturing interests, represented by Joseph Grundy of Pennsylvania, were scarcely less influential. But it was the oil interests who made history, and the Harding administration will be longest remembered not for the Fordney-McCumber tariff or even for the Washington Conference, but for Teapot Dome. It is unnecessary to retrace here the tortuous and sordid details of the oil scandals of the Harding administration, but the evidence of the various civil and criminal prosecutions makes it clear that Secretary Fall, with the passive connivance of Secretary of the Navy Denby, entered into a corrupt alliance with the Doheny and Sinclair oil interests to give them control of immensely valuable naval oil reserves. The Elk Hill oil reserve in California was leased to Doheny; the Teapot Dome oil reserve in Wyoming to Sinclair. In return the government obtained some oil storage tanks in Pearl Harbor, Hawaii, and Fall got at least $100,000 from Doheny and $300,000 from Sinclair. Investigations conducted by Senator Walsh of Montana forced the resignations of Denby and Fall; civil prosecutions in the Federal Courts brought the cancellation of the oil leases; criminal prosecutions sent Fall and Sinclair to prison and threw a lurid light upon the activities of other oil men connected with the Sinclair and Doheny interests.

Other scandals, too, besmirched the Harding administration. Colonel Charles R. Forbes, director of the Veterans' Bureau, was charged with the corrupt sale of government property, liquor and narcotics, reckless waste, and misconduct in office, and sentenced to a term in the federal penitentiary. Colonel Thomas W. Miller, the alien property custodian, who sold invaluable German chemical patents for a song, was dismissed from office and convicted of a criminal conspiracy to defraud the government. Daugherty, who regarded his office as an opportunity to reward his friends and smite the 'Reds,' was dismissed for misconduct involving the illegal sale of liquor permits and pardons; a Senate committee found him guilty of these and other malpractices, but on a criminal trial he escaped conviction.

Harding seems to have been personally innocent of participation in or profit from this orgy of corruption, but he could not have been entirely unaware of it nor of the consequences when the inevitable exposures came. Demoralized by these betrayals, his health broke; a trip to Alaska failed to reinvigorate him, and on 2 August 1923 he died. Eight years later, at the belated dedication of the Harding Memorial at Marion, Ohio, President Hoover said, 'Warren Harding had a dim realization that he had been betrayed by a few men whom he trusted, by men whom he had believed were his devoted friends. It was later proved in the courts of the land that these men had betrayed not alone the friendship and trust of their staunch and loyal friend, but they had betrayed their country. That was the tragedy of the life of Warren Harding.' Considering the occasion, and the fact that Mr. Hoover had served in the Harding cabinet since it was formed, this admission is worth pondering.

Harding was succeeded by Vice-President Coolidge, and Republicans breathed a sigh of relief. For Calvin Coolidge, whatever his limitations, represented probity and economy; if he displayed little zeal in tracking down the malefactors who had wrecked the Harding administration, he did not permit a continuation of their malpractices, and it was possible for the Republican party to go before the electorate in a reformed if not repentant mood. Yet, as the event proved, even reform was probably unnecessary. Toward the spectacle of corruption and maladministration the country was profoundly apathetic, and the efforts of the Democrats to capitalize the scandals of Harding's administration were completely futile. In 1924 the nomination of Coolidge to succeed himself was not seriously contested, nor, for that matter, was the election. The Democrats, sensing the temper of the country, repeated the mistake of 1904 when they tried to compete with the Republicans by nominating an ultra-conservative. John W. Davis 'of West Virginia,' the Democratic nominee in 1924, had been Solicitor-General in Wilson's administration and Ambassador to Great Britain; but he was also the head of a highly successful firm of New York lawyers. The choice of Charles W. Bryan, brother to the Great Commoner, as Davis's running-mate did little to remove from the nomination the taint of Wall Street.

Despairing of both major parties, leaders from the ranks of labor and farming joined with the Socialists to organize a third party — the Conference for Progressive Political Action — and called on 'Fighting Bob' LaFollette to run on his own platform. That platform included public ownership of water power, downward revision of the tariff and railway rates, farm relief, abolition of the injunction in labor disputes, a federal child labor amendment, the election of all federal judges, legislation permitting Congress to override a judicial veto, the abolition of conscription, and a popular referendum on declarations of war. Almost five million votes for LaFollette testified to the strong undercurrent of liberal sentiment in the country, but 15,725,000 voters were satisfied with the Coolidge policies and 8,386,500 were content to follow their traditional allegiance to the Democratic party.

Calvin Coolidge was the first President from New England since Franklin Pierce. Like Pierce he came from a small farming community in the hills, worked his way through college, became a small-town lawyer, and made his way cautiously and painfully from the lower to the higher brackets of state politics. It was Coolidge luck that made the Vice-Presidency, which for most men is the gate to oblivion, for him a step to the Presidency. A respectable mediocrity, he had little to his credit in the way of constructive legislation or political ideas, and equally little to his discredit. So completely negative a man never before lived in the White House; it is characteristic that Coolidge is best remembered for his vetoes. Yet this dour, abstemious, and unimaginative figure became one of the most popular of all American Presidents. For 'Silent Cal' was the symbol of what Americans wanted to be. His frugality, unpretentiousness, and taciturnity gave vicarious satisfaction to a generation that was extravagant, pretentious, and voluble. To people who had pulled up their roots and were anxiously engaged in 'keeping up with the Joneses,' there was something vaguely comforting about the fact that Coolidge had been born in a village named Plymouth, that his first name was Calvin, that he had attended an old-fashioned New England college, that he had been content with a modest law practice and half of a two-family house in a small Massachusetts city, and that the oath of office which inducted him into the Presidency had been administered in a Vermont farmhouse by his aged father, and by the light of a kerosene lamp. Actually Coolidge was democratic by habit rather than by intellectual conviction; his frugality indicated no distrust of wealth; his taciturnity no philosophic serenity; his simplicity no

PRESIDENTIAL ELECTION of 1928

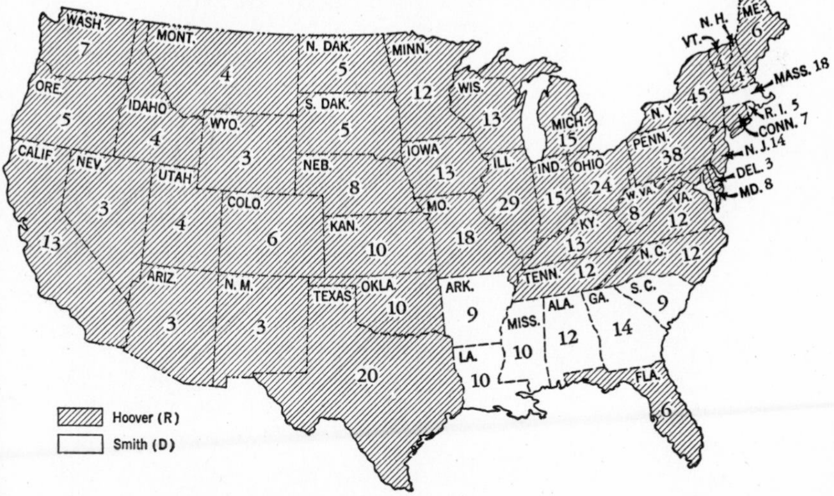
WASH. 7
MONT. 4
N. DAK. 5
MINN. 12
ORE. 5
IDAHO 4
WYO. 3
S. DAK. 5
WIS. 13
MICH. 15
N.Y. 45
VT. 4
N. H. 4
ME. 6
MASS. 18
R. I. 5
CONN. 7
N. J. 14
DEL. 3
MD. 8
CALIF. 13
NEV. 3
UTAH 4
COLO. 6
NEB. 8
IOWA 13
ILL. 29
IND. 15
OHIO 24
PENN. 38
W. VA. 8
VA. 12
KAN. 10
MO. 18
KY. 13
TENN. 12
N. C. 12
ARIZ. 3
N. M. 3
TEXAS 20
OKLA. 10
ARK. 9
MISS. 10
ALA. 12
GA. 14
S. C. 9
LA. 10
FLA. 6
Hoover (R)
Smith (D)

PRESIDENTIAL ELECTION of 1932

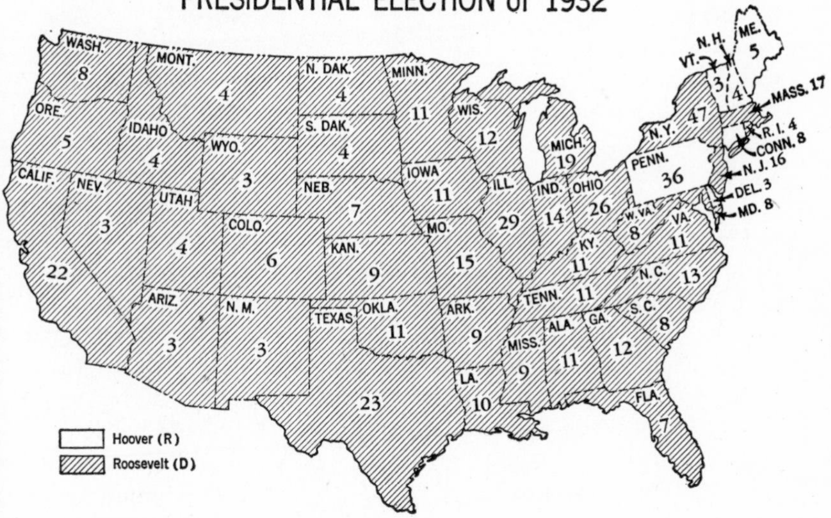
WASH. 8
MONT. 4
N. DAK. 4
MINN. 11
ORE. 5
IDAHO 4
WYO. 3
S. DAK. 4
WIS. 12
MICH. 19
N.Y. 47
VT. 3
N. H. 4
ME. 5
MASS. 17
R. I. 4
CONN. 8
N. J. 16
DEL. 3
MD. 8
CALIF. 22
NEV. 3
UTAH 4
COLO. 6
NEB. 7
IOWA 11
ILL. 29
IND. 14
OHIO 26
PENN. 36
W. VA. 8
VA. 11
KAN. 9
MO. 15
KY. 11
TENN. 11
N. C. 13
ARIZ. 3
N. M. 3
TEXAS 23
OKLA. 11
ARK. 9
MISS. 9
ALA. 11
GA. 12
S. C. 8
LA. 10
FLA. 7
Hoover (R)
Roosevelt (D)

depth. The Yankee traits left out in Coolidge were idealism, a desire to make the world better, and a fighting devotion to a cause. He believed in the *status quo,* and regarded the entire progressive movement since Theodore Roosevelt's day with cynical distrust. Consequently, although he had a moral integrity wanting in his predecessor, there was no break in administrative continuity between the Harding and the Coolidge administrations; no change in political or economic policy. Indeed, more fully even than Harding's, the administration of Coolidge represented a return to 'normalcy.' Under his auspices the policies of high tariff, tax reduction, and government support to industry were pushed to extremes, and the high plateau of prosperity was attained. In time, business men came to long for a restoration of the good old days of Coolidge as they once had longed for those of McKinley; and in the feverish days of the Hoover and Roosevelt administrations, the inane phrase 'keep cool with Coolidge' came to sound like a benediction.

Coolidge's success can best be gauged by the election of 1928. He had early announced, with an emphatic old Yankee phrase which the country insisted upon regarding as equivocal, that he did not 'choose to run'; and the Republicans turned perforce to the logical successor, Herbert C. Hoover. By his brilliantly successful administration of relief organizations in Belgium, Russia, and the Mississippi valley, Mr. Hoover had earned the reputation of a great humanitarian; by his active and progressive administration of the Commerce Department he had won the confidence of business. Innocent of any previous elective office, Hoover seemed to be a new type of political leader, a socially minded efficiency expert, able and ready to chart a new Utopia. The people who had come to regard wealth as the infallible hall-mark of success, did not resent the fact that he had become a millionaire; a society which had come to regard the mechanics of life as of primary importance took pride in the fact that he was a world-famous mining engineer. And though Hoover was a man of wealth and of the world, that he had been born on an Iowa farm and had worked his way to success gave him the right to speak of 'rugged individualism' and satisfied the American demand for democracy.

The Democratic nominee, Alfred E. Smith, represented a different and less traditional type of democracy. A product of the 'Sidewalks of New York' and of the Fulton fish market, he was the first lifetime city dweller and the first Irish Catholic ever to receive the presidential nomination of a major party. 'Al' Smith, rising superior to his Tammany associates, made a brilliant record as governor of New York, and won golden opinions from liberals and social workers, without losing his common touch or his transcendent ability as urban vote-getter. He had acquired a real comprehension of administrative problems and government finance; on questions of power regulation, labor, and social reform he was thoroughly progressive; on the prohibition issue, then agitating American politics, he was an out-and-out 'wet.' Smith had been a leading contender for the Democratic nomination in 1920 and again in 1924; in 1928 he was no longer to be denied, and received the nomination on the first ballot.

The campaign of 1928 was more exciting than any in American politics since 1896, but the radio had altered the character of campaigning and there were none of those whirlwind speaking tours with which an earlier generation had been familiar. Mr. Smith addressed immense and enthusiastic crowds in the cities of the North and the East, but when he invaded the rural regions of the South and West he found a chill reception. Both parties raised enormous campaign funds, the Republicans over ten, the Democrats over seven million dollars, but it was not money that defeated 'Al' Smith. He carried all the great urban centers, yet Hoover won by the decisive vote of twenty-one to fifteen million, and by an electoral college vote of 444 to 87, carrying every state but eight, and smashing the solid South. Explanations of this overwhelming defeat are not hard to find. The average workingman was contented, the average business man prosperous; neither had any desire for change. In addition, as a Catholic, a Tammany brave, a New Yorker, and a wet, Mr. Smith was alien to small-town, middle-class, and rural America. His speech, manners, and background did not seem to be those proper to a President. The kind of Protestant who belonged to the Ku Klux Klan feared that if 'Al' were elected, the Pope would move from Rome to Washington; Southern drys expected him to open a saloon at every crossroads; and there was a general feeling of apprehension that Tammany methods would be introduced into national politics.

The Hoover administration is significant in American history not so much for the great depression — which would have come no matter who had been President — but because it represented the last stand of rugged individualism and the beginnings of a socialized economy. It constituted, therefore, a watershed between the old and the new, and will doubtless serve to demarcate an historical era. For Hoover was at once a Manchester liberal who subscribed to laissez faire and an engineer who had faith in social planning; and he was sufficiently intelligent to attempt a synthesis of the two philosophies. He envisioned a nation where unrestrained individual enterprise was directed solely toward social good, where a balanced economy was achieved by co-operative action, and where order and liberty were reconciled, and to this vision he gave the name 'the American system.' Historically he was right; the reconciliation of order and liberty is one of the themes of American history. But the methods by which he sought to implement his philosophy, which might have been effective in Cleveland's day, were ineffective and unrealistic. Equally unrealistic, but equally understandable, was Hoover's theory that government was a science rather than an art, and that it was a mechanical rather than a political science. He placed his faith not so much in the traditional instrumentalities of democracy as in blue-prints, charts, graphs, and commissions. Faced with the greatest economic crisis in the history of the nation, Hoover, for all his engineering skill, failed to organize in any comprehensive or effective fashion the resources of the country in the fight against the depression, and left to his successor the tasks he was unable to perform. Whatever may be the historical verdict on Hoover himself, the experience of his administration seemed to indicate that government in a democracy is not primarily an administrative but a political task.

2. *Liquidating the War*

'When the war closed,' said Herbert Hoover, 'the most vital of all issues both in our own country and throughout the world was whether governments should continue their wartime ownership and operation of many instrumentalities of production and distribution.' The principle involved in that issue was easily settled; the details required careful and prolonged attention. Even Wilson had called for a rapid liquidation of governmental activities, and legislation returning the railroads to private operation and promoting privately owned merchant marine was passed during his administration. There was obviously no disposition on the part of the Republicans to reverse this policy. On the contrary the Republicans took an advanced position in favor of private ownership and operation even of such things as air mail and hydro electric power. 'We want,' said Harding, 'a period in America with less government in business and more business in government,' and the sentiment was echoed, in varying forms, by his successors.

The most urgent problem concerned the railroads which, under the act of 21 March 1918, had been taken over and operated by the Federal government. That act had been definitely of an emergency character, but it was felt that the roads should not be relinquished to private operation without some positive guarantees that the advantages of unified operation, achieved under government control, should be retained. 'It would be a disservice alike to the country and to the owners of the railroads,' said President Wilson, 'to return to the old conditions unmodified.' The Esch-Cummins Transportation Act of 28 February 1920 differed from previous railroad regulation in that it sought to encourage rather than discourage consolidation. Dealing with the railroad system of the nation as a unit, it provided that the Interstate Commerce Commission should evaluate all railroad property and fix a 'fair return' to the stockholders and fair rates on freight and passenger traffic. A so-called recapture clause provided that all net earnings over six per cent should be divided equally between the carrier and the government, the latter to use such earnings as a revolving fund for the benefit of weaker roads. Furthermore the Commission was given complete jurisdiction over the financial operations of the railways in order to protect the investing public and its stockholders. A Railway Labor Board was established to mediate all disputes about wages, hours, or working conditions.

This act, together with subsequent Supreme Court decisions, effectually deprived the states of control over a large part of even intrastate commerce, for with the railroad system considered as a unit it became almost impossible to distinguish between interstate and intrastate commerce. 'Effective control of the one must embrace some control over the other, in view of the blending of both in actual operation,' said Chief Justice Taft in 1922. 'The same rails and the same cars carry both. The same men conduct them. Commerce is a unit and does not regard state lines, and when . . . the supreme authority of the nation, cannot exercise complete effective control over interstate commerce without incidental regulation of intrastate commerce, such incidental regulation is not an invasion of state authority.'[1]

Under plenary government regulation the necessity for artificial competition was ended, and the railways were authorized and encouraged to combine with a view to economical operation. 'The new act,' as Taft said in another decision, 'seeks affirmatively to build up a system of railways prepared to handle promptly all the interstate

[1] Railroad Commission of Wisconsin *v.* C. B. & Q. R. R. Co., 257 U.S. 563 (1922).

traffic of the country.' In order to further this end the Interstate Commerce Commission, under the guidance of Professor W. Z. Ripley, worked out a plan for the consolidation of all railroads into nineteen major systems. The revolutionary character of the Esch-Cummins Act is perhaps best indicated by the fact that this Ripley plan called for the consolidation of the Northern Pacific, Great Northern, and Chicago, Burlington and Quincy railroads into one system — which had been prohibited by the Northern Securities decision of 1904 — and for the combination of Central and Southern Pacific railroads — which had been attempted in 1911 but forbidden by the Supreme Court in 1922. Opposition to the Ripley plan, however, was so strong that it was proposed to permit the railroads to submit their own plans, and in 1930 the railroads of the Northeast agreed to consolidate all roads into four major systems: the Pennsylvania, New York Central, Baltimore and Ohio, and Chesapeake and Ohio. Three years later a federal co-ordinator of railroads, Joseph B. Eastman, undertook to work out a scheme for the combination of all the railroads in the country in regional systems.

The other features of the Transportation Act did not work well. The Railway Labor Board was unable to prevent the railway shopmen's strike of 1922, and it was replaced, in 1926, by boards of adjustment, mediation, and arbitration with which the Federal government had only the most tenuous connection. The recapture clause proved in practice unworkable; it was eventually repealed and the money collected from the few railroads which had earned over six per cent was returned. And the attempt to fix a 'fair rate' of return ran afoul the old difficulty of evaluation. Should evaluation be based upon original cost, reproduction cost, earning power, capitalization, or a combination of all these factors? The effort of the Interstate Commerce Commission to estimate values upon reproduction costs of 1914 — which was thought to be near 'actual original costs' — encountered bitter opposition from the carriers who much preferred an estimate based upon costs in the 1920's. This difference of opinion — involving billions of dollars — was threshed out in the Supreme Court, and in the O'Fallon decision of 1929 the Court sustained the contention of the roads.[2]

Another step toward the liquidation of the wartime structure was taken with the passage of the Jones Merchant Marine Act of 5 June 1920. Nothing better indicates the effect of the war on nationalism

[2] St. Louis and O'Fallon Railway Co. *v.* U.S., 279 U.S. 461 (1929).

than the fact that this law, embodying eighteenth-century principles of mercantilism, received the signature of a President who had originally confessed free-trade sympathies. The Merchant Marine Act authorized preferential tariffs on goods imported in American vessels, restricted trade with American colonies to American ships, provided generous mail subsidies, and permitted the Shipping Board to sell the government-owned merchant fleet to private companies. Albert D. Lasker, the new chairman of the Shipping Board who had characterized government ownership as ' poison ivy in the garden of industry,' hastened to dispose of the government ships on liberal terms. Yet the Act of 1920 failed to revive the languishing merchant marine, and in 1928 Congress passed the Jones-White Bill, increasing mail subsidies, appropriating $250,000,000 for construction loans, and authorizing the sale of the remaining government-owned vessels. This Act permitted private companies to obtain first-class ships at about one-tenth original cost and underwrote the construction of sixty-eight new vessels. The drastic decline of international trade which set in with the depression made it impossible to know whether our merchant marine might have prospered under these liberal arrangements, and the United States was as far from having a self-sufficient merchant marine in 1934 as in 1920.

Aviation was similarly encouraged by a policy of government subsidy to private operation. The first air mail lines had been operated by the government, but from the beginning the ultimate objective of private operation was kept in view; in 1925 Congress authorized contracts for the transfer of air mail to private air lines, and during the following years the shift was effected. Encouraged by air mail subsidies of approximately eight million dollars annually and by municipal construction of air ports for the use of commercial companies, the airplane industry prospered and air transportation began to compete seriously with railroad transportation. In 1934 the Black Committee of the Senate revealed that during the Hoover administration the government had co-operated with private companies to discourage competitive bidding, encourage monopoly, and enlarge subsidies, a policy which brought dizzy financial rewards to favored speculators and support to the party in power, but did little to foster aviation. As a result of these disclosures President Roosevelt, in 1934, cancelled all air mail contracts and turned over to the Army Air Corps the task of carrying air mail. A series of disasters, resulting in eleven fatalities, excited a public demand for the restoration of the air mail to private companies. Responding to this demand the administration called for competitive bids, and the air mail was returned to private lines at a saving of some eleven million dollars annually.

A far more vexatious problem created by the war was that of veterans' benefits. The experience of the Civil and Spanish-American Wars suggested that the government's account with its soldiers was not closed when they received their discharge. As late as 1932, twenty-three thousand Civil War veterans and one hundred and twenty-five thousand Civil War widows were receiving nearly a hundred million dollars in pensions from the Federal Government. In the years after the World War agitation for veterans' benefits took two forms: disability compensation and adjusted compensation for war service. To the first there could be no reasonable objection, and from the beginning the government adopted a singularly liberal policy toward disabled soldiers and their dependents. It provided not only outright pensions and hospitalization, but undertook an extensive program of vocational rehabilitation. By 1936 almost five hundred thousand World War veterans and dependents were receiving aid, and appropriations to the Veterans Administration were over six hundred million dollars.

Of a different character was the demand for adjusted compensation, commonly called a bonus. Many soldiers who had served for thirty dollars a month while their civilian friends were earning ten or twelve dollars a day in industry or high salaries in business felt that the government owed them additional compensation. On the conclusion of the war seventeen states provided bonuses ranging from ten to thirty dollars for each month of service; but the veterans wanted something more liberal than this and found it logical to look to the Federal government for satisfaction. In 1922 representatives of the American Legion succeeded in pushing through Congress a bill calling for a bonus of fifty dollars for each month of service, but were unable to override the Presidential veto. Two years later Congress, bowing to pressure which it was no longer expedient to resist, passed over Coolidge's veto an Adjusted Compensation Act. This Act gave every world war veteran an endowment and insurance policy computed at the rate of $1.25 for each day of overseas and $1.00 for each day of home service. Some three and one-half million veterans thus received policies whose average value was about one thousand dollars, and though the nation was prosperous no provision was made for carrying this additional burden of three and one-half billion dollars on the public debt.

The depression brought a demand for the immediate payment of the face value of these endowment policies; this demand was coupled with the suggestion that the bonus payment be made in greenbacks, thus seriously inflating the currency. An act of February 1931 permitting the holders of bonus certificates to borrow up to one-half their face value failed to satisfy the veterans, and in June 1932 a 'bonus army' marched on Washington to present its 'petition on boots.' Camping on the flats within sight of the Capitol building, this bonus army seemed to President Hoover an offense against the dignity of the government and with singular ineptitude he called on the National Guard to break up the camp and drive out the bonus marchers. The army performed this task with an efficiency and thoroughness that shocked public opinion and gained for Hoover the enmity of many who had little sympathy with the bonus army but less with measures that smacked of militarism.

From 1932 to 1936 the bonus question continued to agitate American politics. The Patman Bill providing for the payment of bonus certificates through currency inflation passed Congress in 1935 but was vetoed by President Roosevelt. It was clear, however, that only its inflationary provisions prevented its passage over the Presidential veto. In January 1936 a simple bonus act, innocent either of inflationary or taxation features, was passed over Roosevelt's veto, and the Treasury, already burdened by a staggering deficit, was called upon to find the one and one-half billion dollars immediately necessary to meet this new obligation. The bonus question was thus finally eliminated from American politics; it had the unique distinction of having elicited vetoes from four successive Presidents.

One other inheritance from the war proved equally troublesome until removed from the political area: prohibition. The roots of prohibition, to be sure, go back deep into the nineteenth century,[3] but it was the war psychology that made it possible to write prohibition into the Federal Constitution. The Eighteenth Amendment, forbidding the 'manufacture, sale or transportation of intoxicating liquors' was submitted to the states in December 1917, ratified within thirteen months, and proclaimed in effect in January 1920. The Volstead Act, passed over President Wilson's veto, 28 October 1919, defined intoxicating liquor as any beverage containing over one-half of one per cent

[3] See above, ch. 15.

alcohol and provided stringent regulations for the enforcement of prohibition.

Despite the apparent enthusiasm which had attended the enactment of the Eighteenth Amendment, enforcement proved to be a difficult business. Once national prohibition was a fact the country seemed to regret its gesture of self-denial. The Federal government made heroic efforts to enforce the Volstead Act: annual appropriations ran to over ten millions, and in the ten years from 1920 to 1930 prohibition officers made over half a million arrests and the courts secured over three hundred thousand convictions. Yet drinking continued, and, what was worse, became fashionable. The corner saloon gave way to the speakeasy, home-brewing became a national pastime, and many families substituted cocktails for wine. Opposition to prohibition, once strongest among the foreign born workingmen, spread through every class of society and the thirst for liquor was rationalized and sublimated into a philosophy of 'personal liberty.' The recalcitrance of the public was not the only cause for the collapse of prohibition. States with large urban populations sabotaged prohibition laws just as Northern States had once nullified the fugitive slave laws. Agents of the Prohibition Bureau entered into corrupt alliance with 'bootlegging' interests, and the Bureau itself became enmeshed in party politics.

Both parties tried to avoid the troublesome issue, but without success. The Republican party, in office during most of the life of national prohibition, and strongest in the rural communities and among the middle and upper classes of the cities, was inclined to stand behind what Hoover called, 'an experiment noble in motive and far-reaching in purpose.' The Democrats were in a quandary. Their strength was drawn in almost equal proportions from Southern constituencies that were immovably dry and Northern industrial constituencies that were incurably wet. This division almost split the party in 1924 when for 104 ballots the drys supported McAdoo and the wets Smith; the nomination of Davis did little to heal the breach. By 1928 the wets had gained the upper hand in the Democratic party; Smith's nomination was not seriously contested and in his campaign he boldly proposed the practical abandonment of national prohibition enforcement and the return of the problem to the states. His stand on the prohibition question was largely responsible for his spectacular success in the urban centers of the North and his victory in Rhode Island and Massachusetts; it was partly responsible, too, for his loss of traditional

Democratic states such as Virginia, North Carolina, Florida, and Texas.

President Hoover made a genuine effort to enforce the prohibition laws, and at the same time appointed a commission to investigate the whole question of law observance and enforcement. This so-called Wickersham Commission submitted, in January 1931, a confused report to the effect that federal prohibition was unenforceable but should be enforced, that it was a failure but should be retained — a conclusion which inspired one columnist to observe that 'the distinguished jurists seem t' feel that if we'd let 'em have it the problem o' keepin' 'em from gettin' it would be greatly simplified.' By 1932 opposition to federal prohibition, even among drys, had gone so far that the Republican party favored a 'revision' of the Eighteenth Amendment with a view to returning the question to the states, and the Democrats demanded outright repeal. Following Roosevelt's overwhelming victory, Congress passed, in February 1933, the Twenty-First Amendment, repealing federal prohibition, and within less than a year it was ratified by the requisite number of states. The problem of liquor control was thus back where it had been before the World War; whether the country has learned anything from the 'experiment noble in motive' remains to be seen.

3. *Economic Policies*

It was in the realm of economic policy that the conservatism of the Harding, Coolidge, and Hoover administrations was most apparent. The progressive principles of the pre-war era were in part discredited, in part outmoded. The function of the government, as interpreted by the Republican party, was no longer limited to the policeman's task of keeping the peace and punishing offenders, but was directed to the positive task of encouraging business development. The new ideal, as elaborated during these twelve years, sought to foster economic self-government and economic nationalism. 'Without intrusion,' said President Hoover, 'the government can sometimes give leadership and serve to bring together divergent elements. . . . That is re-enforcement of our individualism. It does not cripple the initiative and enterprise of our people by substitution of government. . . . Self-government outside of political government is the truest self-government.' At the same time the traditional Republican policies of tax reduction, high tariffs, the promotion of foreign trade, and the encouragement of private ownership of utilities were reinterpreted in the light of changing economic conditions. The unprecedented prosperity which the nation enjoyed during this period appeared to justify the new dispensation.

One of the most urgent economic questions with which the Government had to cope was the payment of the national debt, which by 1920, had reached the unprecedented total of twenty-four billion dollars. The Civil War debt had been liquidated within a generation, and the prosperity of the 1920's justified the supposition that the World War debt might be disposed of with equal rapidity. But Secretary Mellon was not disposed to continue wartime taxes in order to achieve this laudable end. Convinced that high taxes would discourage business enterprise and thus defeat their own purpose, he embraced instead the more popular policy of tax reduction. The Revenue Act of 1921 repealed the wartime excess-profits tax and reduced the surtax, while increasing slightly the corporation tax; the Act of 1924 raised exemptions in the lower brackets, reduced the normal rate of taxation, and permitted rebates on so-called 'earned income.' The Act of 1926 introduced more drastic reductions in the normal tax, the surtax, and the estate tax, and this policy was continued still further by reductions in 1928 and 1929. Yet notwithstanding these successive reductions, the national debt was lowered by 1930 to approximately sixteen billion dollars. Whether a less generous tax policy would have brought better results it is impossible to say; it is probable that it would, in any event, have discouraged the excessive speculation of 1927–30.

This policy of tax reduction, however, was not maintained with respect to the most pervasive of all taxes — the tariff. The Underwood tariff had never really been tried under normal conditions, for the war itself afforded protection to American manufactures and fostered the establishment of new industries. On the conclusion of the war these new 'infant' industries — chemicals, dyes, toys, hardware, rayon, and so forth — clamored for protection. Yet in May 1919 President Wilson assured Congress that 'there is, fortunately, no occasion for undertaking in the immediate future any general revision of import duties.' The Republicans, however, thought differently. Fearful that the United States would be inundated with the produce of depressed European labor, a Republican Congress, in March 1921, pushed through an emergency tariff bill which was promptly vetoed by Wilson. 'If there ever was a time when America had anything to fear from foreign competition,' he observed in his veto message, 'that time has passed. If we wish to have Europe settle her debts, governmental or commercial, we must be prepared to buy from her.' But it took fifteen years for this elementary logic to sink in.

Within a month of his accession to the Presidency, Harding announced that 'the urgency for an instant tariff cannot be too much emphasized.' Congress responded with the emergency tariff of 27 May 1921, historically important because its prohibitive agricultural schedules, while affording no actual relief to farmers with surplus crops to sell, did commit them to the principle of protection. Far more important was the Fordney-McCumber tariff of 19 September 1922, which established rates higher than ever before in our history. Duties on sugar, textiles, pig iron, rails, and chinaware were restored to the old Payne-Aldrich level, while increases on toys, hardware, chemicals, dyes, and lace ranged from sixty to four hundred per cent. In order to provide some degree of elasticity, however, the law instructed the tariff commission to recommend such changes as were necessary to equalize production costs abroad and in the United States and authorized the President, on recommendation of the commission, to raise or lower duties as much as fifty per cent. This provision proved to be of little practical value. The tariff commission showed neither initiative nor impartiality, and both Harding and Coolidge often ignored its advice. Altogether Presidents Harding and Coolidge used their discretionary authority thirty-seven times. Thirty-two of these changes, including such things as butter, cheese, pig iron and chemicals, were upward; on five articles duties were reduced. These five were mill feed, bobwhite quail, paint-brush handles, cresylic acid, and phenol, but there was no Finley Peter Dunne to see the joke.[4]

The economic consequences of the Fordney-McCumber tariff were three-fold: it fostered the growth of monopolies in the United States, prevented Europe from paying her obligations to us in the form of goods, and brought reprisals from foreign countries. France was the first to strike back at the United States: in 1927 she boosted her duties on wheat, frozen meat, and other articles imported from this country; Great Britain followed suit. This tariff war had important repercussions in American economy. It cut seriously into our foreign trade, persuaded many manufacturers to establish branch plants abroad, and inspired among the large manufacturers and bankers their first serious misgivings as to the wisdom of protection.

[4] See above, p. 412.

Continued prosperity, however, confirmed the Republicans in their devotion to high tariffs and the shift in Democratic strength from the rural South to the industrial North tempered that party's traditional hostility to protection. In the campaign of 1928 the Republicans reaffirmed their faith in the economic blessings of high tariffs and the Democrats hedged shamelessly on the issue. There was apparently no urgent need for further tariff revision, but no sooner was Hoover inaugurated than he summoned Congress in special session to consider farm relief and 'limited changes in the tariff.' In April 1929 Representative Hawley of Oregon presented what was to be the Hawley-Smoot tariff bill. By the time it emerged from the Senate and from conference committees it represented increases all along the line, but particularly in minerals, chemicals, dyestuffs, and textiles. Objections from the American Bankers Association and from industries with foreign markets were brushed aside and a vigorous protest from 1028 economists had no effect on President Hoover, who signed the bill on 17 June 1930. The reaction was immediate: within two years twenty-five countries established retaliatory tariffs and American foreign trade took a further slump.

Yet the Republican administrations could not be impervious to considerations of foreign markets, raw materials and investments. During the World War the position of the United States had changed from a debtor to a creditor nation. American private investments abroad, estimated at less than three billion dollars before the war, increased to not less than fourteen billion by 1932. These investments were distributed to all parts of the globe and to every variety of business: government bonds, railroads, utilities, manufactures, mines, oil, fruit, sugar, rubber, and so forth. A considerable part of this investment was inspired by the determination of American industry to control its own sources of raw material, and in this policy the government co-operated, just as governments had co-operated in the analogous mercantilism of the seventeenth and eighteenth centuries. It authorized and encouraged foreign trade associations; discovered and publicized new trade opportunities abroad, warred on foreign monopolies, state or private, and helped American oil interests to obtain concessions in Latin America and in the Orient. Perhaps the most illuminating example of this neo-mercantilism of the nineteen twenties was the struggle for oil.

The United States, in the post-war years produced, and consumed, about three-fourths of the world's petroleum, but mounting consumption seriously depleted her oil reserves and geologists predicted their exhaustion within a generation. The result was a determined effort on the part of American producers to obtain concessions in oil fields abroad. This attempt encountered few difficulties as far as Mexican and South American fields were concerned, but many in Persia, Mesopotamia, and the Dutch East Indies. At the close of the World War the British and Dutch oil interests were prepared to dispute world supremacy with the Americans. Combining their resources in the Royal-Dutch Shell they attempted to exclude the Standard Oil from the oil fields of the Near and Far East, and both the British and the Dutch governments supported them in this policy. As early as 1919 one British oil promoter boasted that 'wherever Americans turn they find that British enterprise has been before them and that the control of all the most promising properties is in British hands. . . . The British position is impregnable.' The United States State Department, which had earlier taken a comparable attitude toward British concessions in Mexico and South America, now responded to this challenge with a threat of more direct retaliation. The threat was effective, and by private agreement the Standard Oil interests were given a cut in the gigantic Turkish Petroleum Company, and permitted to exploit oil reserves in the Dutch East Indies.

But the most characteristic example of the new economic philosophy was the official encouragement of large-scale combinations in business. The theory of competition, embodied in the Sherman and Clayton anti-trust laws, had long been discredited by business men; it was now scuttled by the government simply by not prosecuting suits for dissolution of trusts and combinations under the Sherman Act.

Herbert Hoover, as Secretary of Commerce, inaugurated a policy of 'alliance with the great trade associations and the powerful corporations.' His sense of engineering efficiency was outraged at the spectacle of competition, with its inevitable waste, and in his first report as Secretary of Commerce he proposed modifications of the Sherman Act to permit business organizations to combine for purposes of information, standardization, uniform credit policies, arbitration of industrial disputes, elimination of unfair practices, transportation, and research. He placed his Department at the disposal of business as a clearing house for exchange of information, and under his auspices, trade associations not only pooled information, advertising, insurance, traffic, and purchases, but drew up codes of fair practice. Over two hundred such codes were in existence at the end of the

Hoover administration, and the cotton, woolen, carpet, and sugar codes later accepted by the N.R.A. with Roosevelt were copies of those already in use. 'We are passing,' said Hoover aptly, 'from a period of extreme individualistic action into a period of associated activities.'

In part as a result of this official encouragement, the concentration of control in American industry and banking, once regarded as dangerous to the common weal, grew apace. The decade from 1919 to 1929 saw 1268 combinations in manufacturing and mining, involving the merging of some four thousand and the disappearance of some six thousand firms. The same process was discernible in the field of utilities, finance, transportation, and trade. In the eight years after the war, for example, 3744 public utility companies disappeared through merger. In 1920 there were 30,139 banks; fifteen years later the number had been reduced by failures and mergers to 16,053. One great corporation came to dominate the telephone, and one the telegraph systems. Even in the realm of retail trade, chain stores ate heavily into the business of the independent shopkeeper. The inevitable result of this process of combination and consolidation was the domination of American industry, transportation, and finance by giant corporations. In 1933 five hundred and ninety-four corporations, each capitalized at fifty million or more dollars, owned fifty-three per cent of all corporate wealth in the country: the other 387,970 owned the remaining forty-seven per cent.

Interlocking directorates and the holding-company device added to the concentration of power in the hands of a few persons. The Senate Committee on Banking and Currency estimated that through interlocking directorates and investments the J. P. Morgan banking house controlled, directly or indirectly, about seventy-four billion dollars of corporate wealth — approximately one-fourth the total corporate assets of the country.

More important than the decline in the number of banks was the concentration of their resources in the hands of the most powerful. In 1920, the twenty largest banking institutions in the country held about 14 per cent of all loans and investments; in 1931 the proportion had increased to 27 per cent.

This concentration of control extended, inevitably, to the field of natural resources. Fear of private aggrandizement of natural resources had inspired ineffective protests from the reformers and muckrakers of an earlier generation. By the 1920's four companies owned over one-half of the copper resources of the country, the United States

Steel Corporation controlled between one-half and two-thirds the total iron ore, the International Nickel Company of Canada nine-tenths the world supply of nickel, the Aluminum Company of America held a practical monopoly of bauxite deposits, eight corporations owned three-fourths the anthracite coal, and five companies produced one-third of the oil.

In few fields had concentration gone further than in the realm of hydroelectric power, and in none was better revealed the economic philosophy of the Republican party. In the years after World War I the electric light and power industry grew with extraordinary rapidity; between 1917 and 1932 production had increased more than three-fold and capitalization more than fourfold, to over twelve billion dollars. Investigations conducted by the Federal Trade Commission, Governor Pinchot, and others revealed that, largely through the holding-company device, control over power production was concentrated in the hands of six giant financial groups — General Electric, Insull, Morgan, Mellon, Doherty, and Byllesby.

Senators Walsh of Montana, Couzens of Michigan, LaFollette of Wisconsin, and the indomitable Norris of Nebraska led the most important contest in this sphere, that for government operation of the water-power dams at Muscle Shoals on the Tennessee river. These had been constructed to furnish power for nitrate plants during World War I, at the conclusion of which conservative interests insisted on turning them over to private companies. President Coolidge recommended that the property be sold to the highest bidder and vetoed a bill providing for government operation of the dams. But the high cost of privately produced electricity and the depression kept the power issue alive, and in 1931 the Norris bill calling for the construction of a second dam on the Tennessee river, and for government manufacture and sale of fertilizer and power, once more passed Congress. President Hoover, conscious of his reputation as an engineer, issued a preliminary statement that 'this happens to be an engineering project, and . . . is subject to the cold examination of engineering facts. I am having these facts exhaustively determined by the different departments of the government.' The exhaustive determination took three days; on 3 March 1931 came the anticipated veto, a reiteration of the doctrine of rugged individualism:

I am firmly opposed to the Government entering into any business the major purpose of which is competition with our citizens. . . . This bill raises one of the important issues of Federal Government ownership and operation of power and manufacturing business not as a minor by-product but as a major purpose. Involved in this question is the agitation against the conduct of the power industry. The power problem is not to be solved by the project in this bill. The remedy for abuses in the conduct of that industry lies in regulation and not by the Federal Government entering upon the business itself. . . . I hesitate to contemplate the future of our institutions, of our country, if the preoccupation of its officials is to be no longer the promotion of justice and equal opportunity but is to be devoted to barter in the markets. That is not liberalism, it is degeneration.

Even this *ex cathedra* statement as to the nature and purposes of government, however, did not settle the matter. Two years later, with the creation of the Tennessee Valley Authority the Roosevelt administration entered jauntily upon the course of ' degeneration.'

4. *Agricultural Distress*

The prosperous condition of American business during the twenties was not reflected in agriculture. Indeed during most of this decade the farmer was in distress, and the end of the period of Republican domination coincided with an agrarian depression deeper and more serious than any since the early 1890's. Between 1920 and 1932 total farm income declined from fifteen and one-half to five and one-half billion dollars. Wheat which sold for $1.82 a bushel in 1920 brought 38¢ in 1932; corn fell from 61¢ to 32¢; oats from 53¢ to 16¢; cotton from 16¢ a pound to 6¢ a pound. The size of the cereal and cotton crops of 1920 and 1932 was approximately the same; the 1932 value was slightly over one-third that of 1920.[5]

This catastrophic collapse of agricultural prosperity is to be accounted for by a number of factors. Nineteen hundred and twenty values were abnormally high, 1932 values abnormally low, not only in agriculture but in business of all kinds, and it is not remarkable that farming should, in some degree, have shared the war-time prosperity and the later depression. Yet in the first the farmers' share was dispro-

[5] Statistical Abstract of the U.S., 1936, pp. 632ff:

	1920		1932	
	Production	Value	Production	Value
	1,000 bu.	*1,000 dollars*	*1,000 bu.*	*1,000 dollars*
Wheat	843,277	1,539,584	756,927	289,096
Corn	3,070,604	1,899,136	2,926,871	934,682
Oats	1,444,291	777,179	1,250,955	195,826
Cotton (bales)	13,429,000	1,069,257	13,003,000	424,013

portionately low, in the second disproportionately high. Even in 1920 the farmer received only fifteen per cent of the national income; in 1933 he received only seven per cent. High war prices had resulted in expansion, with a consequent increase in borrowings and mortgage indebtedness, but farm prosperity did not last long enough to enable farmers to liquidate their debts. More important than this was the lowering of the world price for cereals and cotton and the collapse of foreign markets. Farm exports, which had averaged over two billion dollars annually from 1917 to 1925, fell to an average of three-quarters of a billion from 1931 to 1935. This precipitous decline can be largely explained by three developments: increased production of grain in Canada, Russia, Australia, and the Argentine; inability of Europe to continue borrowing from the United States after 1929; and the effect of the Hawley-Smoot tariff on European purchasing power and retaliatory legislation.

The Republican panacea for agricultural depression was the tariff. Tariff acts of 1921, 1922, 1924, and 1926 imposed increasingly higher duties on farm products, but since the American farmers raised, during most of this period, an exportable surplus these tariffs were ineffective. In addition the Republicans, responding to the demands of a Congressional 'farm bloc,' continued and expanded those policies of farm credit, co-operative marketing, education, and research inaugurated by the Wilson administration.

But the laws they passed were for the most part negative rather than positive in character, and accomplished little. Nor were the farm co-operatives, which grew rapidly during this decade, effective except in special fields such as dairying and fruit. The farmers themselves proposed legislation which would enlist government support to agriculture as fully as the tariff enlisted government support to industry. Out of a medley of ideas two plans emerged: the equalization fee and the export debenture. Both proposed, in effect, to extend the protective system to the farmers; both were regarded as socialistic by the more conservative members of the Republican party; both were vetoed by Presidents Coolidge and Hoover.

Hoover's solution for the farm problem was embodied in the Agricultural Marketing Act of 15 June 1929. This act authorized a new Federal Farm Board to extend loans to agricultural co-operatives, create stabilization corporations for the purpose of controlling surpluses, and insure both co-operatives and stabilization corporations against losses. The Board established a number of new co-operative

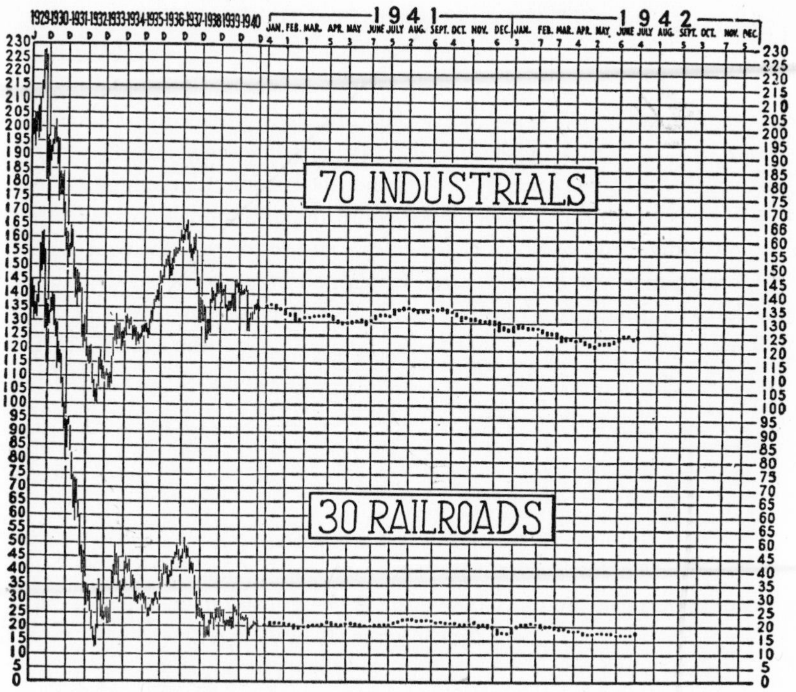

Price Trend of the New York Stock Exchange Market since 1929

Reproduced by courtesy of the *New York Herald Tribune*

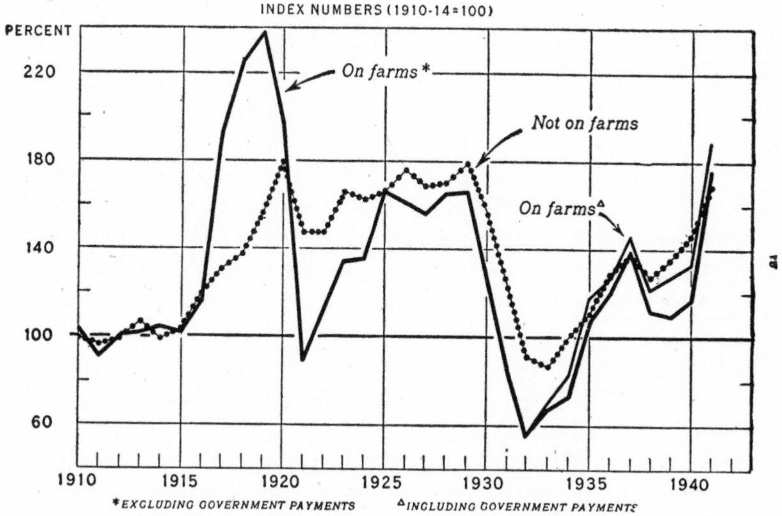

Income Per Capita on Farms and not on Farms, 1910–41

Bureau of Agricultural Economics

marketing organizations, subsidizing them with loans to the extent of $165,000,000. In 1930 it set up Grain and Cotton Stabilization Corporations. In an effort to peg the price of wheat and cotton these Corporations bought altogether over 300,000,000 bushels of wheat and 1,300,000 bales of cotton, losing in these operations not less than $184,000,000. This loss would not have been a matter of grave concern had it promoted its objective: higher prices. The prices of both commodities, however, were distinctly lower at the end than at the beginning of the experiment.

More effective was the work of the Reconstruction Finance Corporation, authorized in 1932 to extend aid to farmers through agricultural export agencies and, subsequently, through agricultural credit corporations. By the middle of 1937 the RFC had lent some $400,000,000 to Federal Land Banks, $192,000,000 to livestock and agricultural credit corporations, and $18,000,000 to Joint Stock Land Banks. Through the Commodity Credit Corporation it extended loans directly to 1,629,889 cotton producers, pegging the price of cotton at between ten and twelve cents a pound, while some 250,000 corn producers were granted loans of forty-five to fifty-five cents a bushel on their corn.

5. *The Depression*

President Hoover came to office committed to the ideal of abolishing poverty. 'We in America are nearer to the final triumph over poverty,' he said during the campaign, 'than ever before in the history of any land. . . . We have not reached the goal, but, given a chance to go forward with the policies of the last eight years, we shall soon with the help of God be in sight of the day when poverty will be banished from this nation.' Swept into the Presidency by an overwhelming majority, supported by a complaisant Congress and an enthusiastic public opinion, Hoover prepared to go forward with the policies of the previous eight years which he had, in large measure, inspired. His election was the signal for a boom on the Stock Exchange, and most business men and investors prepared to reap still higher profits and to enjoy a still higher standard of living.

For a time their confidence seemed justified. The average value of common stocks soared from 117 in December 1928 to 225 the following September, and certain stocks such as United States Steel and General Electric rose to dizzy heights. Inspired by these dazzling profits stockbrokers increased their bank borrowings from a mere three and one-half billion dollars in 1927 to eight and one-half billion two years later, hundreds of new investment trusts were organized, and during 1929 a total of 1,124,990,000 shares were sold on the New York Stock Exchange alone. The public appeared willing and able to absorb limitless quantities of stock: in the single month of January 1929 no less than one billion dollars' worth of new securities were floated. Factory employment, freight car loadings, construction contracts, bank loans, almost all the indices of business, showed a marked upward swing.

Yet even as Hoover announced in his inaugural address that 'in no nation are the fruits of accomplishment more secure,' shrewd investors were cashing in on their paper profits and pulling out of the market, and the Federal Reserve Board, alarmed at the speculative mania, was preparing to reverse the policy of easy credit which it had inaugurated in 1927. There were, indeed, many factors to excite concern. The world economic situation was discouraging. War debts were uncollectable, foreign trade had declined precipitously, and the interest on billions of dollars of private investments was in default. Prosperity, even during the height of the boom, was a spotty affair. Agriculture was depressed and the farmers' purchasing power severely reduced. Industries such as the coal and textile had not shared in the general well-being, while technical improvements worked hardships on many older industries and created temporary unemployment. Unemployment, indeed, was a constant throughout the decade; in 1921 it was estimated at over four million, and at no time did it fall below one and one-half million. Much of the new wealth had gone to the privileged few, and consumer purchasing power had not materially increased; between 1923 and 1928 the index of wages rose from 100 to 112 while the index of speculative profits jumped from 100 to 410! Meantime public and private debts had mounted to staggering sums; by 1930 the total debt burden was estimated at between one hundred and one hundred and fifty billion dollars — approximately one-third the national wealth. Above all, debts, installment buying, and speculation had strained credit to the breaking point, and, because few understood the dangers involved in the process, credit was gravely abused. 'Credit on the great scale,' as Edwin F. Gay observed, 'is a modern invention, an instrument of immense power, comparable with the prime-movers in the physical field for whose introduction through industrial revolution it had prepared the way. . . . But the engineers of credit know less about the limitations and control of their new organ than the engineers of steam and electricity do about theirs.' Too many Americans were living on the margin of existence, or, worse yet, on the future. When confidence in the future disappeared, they discovered their error.

The crash came in October 1929. On the twenty-first of that month the prices of stocks began to sag; on the twenty-fourth over twelve million shares changed hands; on the twenty-ninth came a catastrophic crash. In less than a month stocks suffered an average decline of forty per cent. Sage observers regarded this deflation of values as inevitable, but the collapse caught the country as a whole unprepared, and the first reaction was one of shocked incredulity. Bankers and public officials whistled shrilly to keep their courage up. 'I know of nothing fundamentally wrong with the stock market,' said Charles E. Mitchell of the National City Bank, 'or with the underlying business and credit structure,' while John J. Raskob, chairman of the Democratic National Committee and reputed financial wizard, announced that 'prudent investors are now buying stocks in huge quantities and will profit handsomely when this hysteria is over and our people have opportunity in calmer moments to appreciate the great stability of business.' Those who followed the advice of these experts lived to regret it. In the course of the next three years the prices of fifty leading industrial stocks declined from an average of 252 to 61, of twenty railroad stocks from 167 to 33, and of twenty public utility stocks from 353 to 99.

Once under way the spiral of the depression swept out in an ever-widening curve. Millions of investors lost their savings; thousands were forced into bankruptcy. Debts mounted, purchases declined, factories cut down production, workers were dismissed, wages and salaries slashed. Farmers, already hard hit, were unable to meet their obligations, and mortgages were foreclosed, often with losses to all concerned. Real estate sagged in value and tax collections dropped alarmingly, forcing governmental economies. Commercial failures increased from 24,000 in 1928 to 32,000, in 1932, and over five thousand banks closed their doors in the first three years of the depression. By 1930 there were a little over three million unemployed; in 1933 the number was variously estimated at from twelve to fifteen million. Factory pay-rolls fell to less than half the level of 1929 and the total wages paid out declined from fifty-five billion dollars in 1929 to thirty-three billion in 1931. Construction work, except for government operations, practically ceased. Foreign trade declined in three years from nine to three billion dollars. Only taxes and incomes from dividends and interest held up. Government expenditures in 1929 were thirteen billion dollars; by 1932 public works and relief had pushed them up to fifteen billion. But interest and dividend payments reached in 1931 an all-time high of eight billion dollars; at no time during the depression did they fall below the 1928 level. Since the whole national income declined from an estimated eighty-five billion dollars in 1929 to an estimated thirty-seven billion in 1932 it can be seen that the burden of the depression fell unequally upon the less privileged groups.

The Hoover administration promptly adopted a policy of deprecating the seriousness of the depression. To those who had guided the destinies of the nation throughout the unprecedented prosperity of the twenties, it seemed inconceivable that the economic structure could collapse. The panic, they were convinced, was a stock-market panic, induced by speculation and precipitated by fear. All that was necessary for a return of prosperity was a restoration of confidence. To this end the administration directed its energies. In conference after conference with the industrial leaders of the country President Hoover urged the maintenance of employment and wages; in speech after speech he exhorted the nation to keep a stiff upper lip. The President did recommend a modest program of public works, the Federal Farm Board extended aid to depressed farmers, and Congress voted relief to those who had been made destitute by the great drought of 1930. Yet these half-hearted measures were largely nullified by other administrative policies, notably the Hawley-Smoot tariff and feeding relief to banks and railroads rather than directly to the people.

'As a nation,' said President Hoover just a year after the crash, 'we *must* prevent hunger and cold to those of our people who are in honest difficulties.' But the administration was unwilling to grant direct relief; that burden was one for local governments and private charity to shoulder. In vain did Progressives like LaFollette, Costigan, and Cutting plead for a large-scale program of public works, financed directly by federal funds. In vain did they present statistics proving the breakdown of private charity and the inability of municipal and state authorities to carry the burden any longer. Every proposal for generous relief was met by the stubborn opposition of Republican Tories and Bourbon Democrats whose devotion to the fictions of states' rights and the shibboleth of a balanced budget blinded them to realities. When the House threatened to pass a bill appropriating some two billion dollars for public works, the President himself intervened with the warning that 'This is not unemployment relief. It is the most gigantic pork-barrel ever perpetrated by the American Congress.'

Not until 1932, when the Democrats controlled the House and a coalition of Democrats and Republican progressives ran the Senate, were important measures taken to cope with the depression. In January Congress passed and the President signed an act creating the Reconstruction Finance Corporation to lend money to railroads, banks, agricultural agencies, industry, and commerce. By subsequent amendments the RFC was authorized to purchase preferred stock of banks, and extend loans to local government agencies for self-liquidating projects; during the Roosevelt administration it became the banker for many of the new relief and recovery agencies. It inaugurated at once that policy of 'priming the pump' which should have been adopted two years earlier.

In the course of the next three years the RFC came to the aid of over seven thousand banks and trust companies, to the tune of three and one-half billion dollars. Loans to mortgage-loan companies aggregated some three hundred million and to insurance companies another hundred million dollars. Advances of some seven hundred million dollars to railroads enabled many of them to refinance their outstanding obligations and greatly to improve their facilities. Loans to industry totalled over one hundred million dollars, and to Agriculture, in one form or another, over two and one-half billion. Altogether authorizations and commitments of the RFC, including advances to other government agencies and disbursements for relief, came to over eleven billion dollars.

This timely assistance to banks, mortgage and insurance companies, railroads, and industries, undoubtedly saved many of them from serious losses and to that extent checked the downward spiral of the depression, while assistance to city and state governments enabled many of them to meet their more pressing pay-roll obligations. At the same time, by setting up certain standards to which borrowers must conform, the RFC was able to introduce minor reforms into banking, transportation, and industry. On the other hand many of the loans, especially those extended to banks during 1932, merely put off the day of reckoning and involved investors and depositors in losses which might have been avoided by a more circumspect policy. And the RFC gave little effective relief to those who needed it most urgently. For the theory behind it was that of the protective tariff — that prosperity would somehow trickle down from banks and industries to the workingmen at the base of the economic pyramid. Mounting figures of unemployment proved the theory fallacious and indicated the necessity for a more realistic view of the whole economic problem.

XXIII

AMERICAN SOCIETY BETWEEN TWO WARS

1. *Prosperity and Disillusionment*

THE World War, like the Civil War, was followed by an era of materialism, and if its manifestations were less gaudy they were more profound. Disillusion and cynicism spread, like a poison gas, to every part of the social body, inducing a paralysis of will and a flight from reason strange to American experience. Everywhere there was a profound distrust of reason, and as men lost faith in reason they ceased to use the discredited instrument. They lost faith, too, in the values that had long been taken for granted, and even, it would seem, the capacity to believe in the existence of values. There were no grand ideas, only a sophisticated rejection of ideas; there was no faith, only renewed superstitions masquerading as faiths. For all its cascading energy the age was negative rather than affirmative, incontrovertible in repudiation but feeble and unconvincing in its affirmations. Never before had so many men known so many excellent arguments for rejecting the heritage of the past; seldom did a generation bequeath so little that was permanent, so much that was troublesome, to the future.

Weary of reform and disillusioned by the crusade for democracy, Americans turned with unashamed enthusiasm to the business of developing their technical skills and exploiting their natural resources, getting rich, and enjoying themselves. During the piping years of the twenties they succeeded in realizing these ends. Population grew by 17 millions in a decade,[1] but the increase in national wealth outstripped the increase in population, and those who enjoyed this new prosperity congratulated themselves that it was universal and permanent, that the millennium had indeed arrived. The wealth of the nation was unevenly distributed,[2] yet during the twenties the average

[1] The increase in the nineteen-thirties was not so rapid: from 122,775,000 to 131,669,000.

[2] The National Resources Commission revealed that of 29,400,000 families, 25 million or over 87 per cent had incomes less than $2,500, while only about 1,000,000 or 2.8 per cent had incomes over $5,000. Those receiving $10,000 a year constituted less than 1 per cent of the total population of the country.

man in America enjoyed a higher income than he had known in the past. Part of that income went, in the form of taxes and philanthropy, to permanent improvements in the nation's physical plant — roads, schools, hospitals, libraries; part of it went to create a higher standard of living — cars, radios, improvements in home and office, education and medical care; part went to luxuries and entertainment — candy, tobacco, liquor, cosmetics, sports; too much went to speculation.

Americans had never been a patient people, and a generation that had witnessed a revolutionary speeding up of industry and transportation, and the destruction, in a few years, of the accumulation of centuries, was not disposed to take the long way. Conscious, as no previous generation had been, of change and impermanence, this one demanded immediate gratification and indulgence in appetites. People mortgaged their futures, straining credit to buy on the installment plan. Not content with the modest accumulation of saving and no longer inclined to regard thrift as a virtue or even as a sound economic policy, they speculated wildly on the stock market, thinking it proper to enjoy what they had not earned except by cleverness. This mass optimism and heedlessness was reflected in government policies and in mounting debts and taxes. Never before had Americans so cheerfully charged benefits to future earnings, or so needlessly and recklessly piled up debts for their children to pay. And with the depression the folly was continued — of necessity.

Nor were they less impatient in the social than in the economic realm. Married people were increasingly unwilling to take time for the rearing of children, and the birth rate showed a drop from 25 per 1000 in 1915 to about 17 per 1000 twenty years later, especially in those classes best able to afford large families. Marriage, too, came to seem a less permanent arrangement than had long been supposed; even the remarkable increase in the Catholic population did not retard the mounting divorce rate. In 1890, out of every 100 marriages 6 ended in divorce; 50 years later, 18 of every 100 marriages were thus terminated. In many respects, family life came to be less stable. Those who lived in the town where they were born became objects of interest if not of curiosity, and for the inhabitants of the large cities, moving came to be an almost annual junket. With the passing of the family home the old bonds and disciplines that had moulded generations slipped away, and the cities furnished no immediate substitutes. For millions of Americans, the depression was to reveal that

Home is the place where, when you have to go there,
They have to take you in,[3]

but for millions it was that and nothing more.

Socially perhaps the most notable phenomenon of this period was the rapid growth of the city and, even more important, the urbanization of the whole of society. The process of city growth can be read in statistics, its history and significance in the studies of such scholars as Schlesinger, Mumford, and Lynd. In 1900 the population was 60 per cent rural; in 1940 a little over 43 per cent. The depression somewhat retarded the growth of the large cities, but with the return of prosperity attendant upon the Second World War the process of draining the countryside to the industrial centers was sharply accelerated.

The whole nation became urbanized—in its psychology as well as its economy. Big towns copied the cities and little towns copied the big towns, while no cross-roads village was so isolated as to be without neon lights, juke boxes, and its row of boys and girls sipping cokes and solemnly discussing the respective merits of Duke Ellington's or Guy Lombardo's orchestras. Nearly half the population of the country lived within easy access of cities of 100,000 or more: these cities became the shopping, entertainment, educational, cultural, and political centers of the country. To this process the automobile, the radio, the moving picture, and the newspaper all contributed. Especially the automobile. At the close of the First World War there were some 9 million motor vehicles in use; a decade later the number had soared to 26 million and, even in the decade of the depression, the number continued to increase. The automobile, originally a luxury, had become the indispensable necessity; when hard times hit a family, the car was the last thing to go, and with the return of prosperity it was not a home but a car that the workingman bought. For the automobile came to be a symbol of freedom, a badge of equality, a vehicle of opportunity, it was useful for transportation, essential for social intercourse and self-respect. Tire and gasoline rationing, even more than Pearl Harbor, brought World War II home to the average American.

With the automobile the national characteristics of mobility and restlessness and the mania for speed were given new and easy outlets. On a typical summer day it would seem as if every house in the land had emptied itself onto the roads; no road-building program

[3] Robert Frost, 'Death of the Hired Man.'

was sufficient to take care of the traffic jams of a normal Sunday. But the automobile did more than carry restless city-folk into the country and the country-folk to the city; it broke down isolation and provincialism, promoted standardization, accelerated the growth of the city at the expense of the village, trained young Americans — girls as well as boys — to mechanical ingenuity, created a hundred new industries and millions of new jobs, required the construction of thousands of miles of roads, especially in the rural regions, created new problems of morals and of crime, and took an annual toll of life and limb as high as that exacted by the First World War. Henry Adams, who had seen in the dynamo the symbol of the twentieth century, was, ironically, vindicated.

The radio, like the automobile, began as a plaything and became both a necessity and a promoter of social and economic change. The first broadcasting station opened at Pittsburgh in 1920; within a decade there were almost 13 million radios in American homes, and by 1940 there were almost 900 broadcasting stations and 52 million receiving sets, and television was already planned. Radio commanded a far wider audience even than the newspaper, and it was in almost continuous use. The statistics of the radio business can be readily disposed of; it is far more difficult to evaluate the significance of this new form of communication, nor have numerous investigations served to throw light on the problem. It is to be observed that notwithstanding the multiplicity of broadcasting stations, most of the wave-lengths were controlled by a few great networks — the Columbia, the National, and the Mutual leading the field. Here, as in all other fields of American business, organization and concentration of control proceeded apace, and the success of municipal stations such as New York's famous WNYC did not convert the average listener to the British policy of government-owned radio stations.

Over the air waves went forth the most varied agglomeration of entertainment, education, advertisement, and propaganda that had ever assailed the ears of men. The entertainment feature, most prominent, was probably least important, for it may be doubted that Amos and Andy or Charlie McCarthy left any permanent impression on the American mind. More significant was the rapid development of news broadcasting — a service which, with the coming of the world crisis and the war, threatened to supplant that given by the daily newspaper. Radio news commentators' analyses were heard daily by millions who never read newspaper editorials, and skillful, conscientious commentators like Kaltenborn and Swing, as well as shameless demagogues like Father Coughlin and Gerald Smith, came to wield an influence comparable to that of Horace Greeley a century earlier. This instrument, which brought world affairs hourly into the home and made it possible for any and every American to hear the friendly 'fireside chats' of Roosevelt, the bitter harangues of Hitler, and the somber eloquence of Churchill, must have done a great deal to break down provincialism and isolation, while preserving a new freedom, to listen or not to listen to a distasteful voice or doctrine.

Second only to the radio as entertainment and diversion, but far behind it as education, were the moving pictures. Invented by the resourceful Thomas Edison at the turn of the century, the motion picture grew steadily in popularity. David Griffith's *Birth of a Nation,* shown to audiences in 1915, revealed unsuspected possibilities of drama and technique in this new art, and introduced the spectacle film which another producer, Cecil B. de Mille, shortly made his peculiar property. Stars of the silent screen supplanted luminaries of the 'legitimate' stage in the democratic heavens: Mary Pickford, 'America's sweetheart'; Charles Chaplin, comedian extraordinary; Douglas Fairbanks, handsome and acrobatic; Bill Hart, always in cowboy costume; Pearl White, whose endless series of escapades left her audience palpitating each week for the next installment; and a host of others now forgotten. The use of sound introduced in 1927 expanded film potentialities as television later did radio, and allied movies to the theatre. Many former stars had no voice appeal and disappeared; the talking cinema increasingly recruited artists and adapted dramas from the sophisticated boards. Film versions of *David Copperfield, Wuthering Heights, Captains Courageous, Anna Karenina, Little Women,* and other books introduced millions to classics they would never have read; Greta Garbo, Charles Laughton, Bette Davis, and many others gave performances worthy of the best stage tradition. Technicolor added to the beauty of the film, and the development of the cartoon movie by Walt Disney, creator of *Mickey Mouse* and *Donald Duck,* delighted adults as well as children and opened up a new dimension of the art. By 1937 the motion-picture industry was fourteenth in volume of business, eleventh in assets, among the industries of the nation, and it was estimated that not less than 75 million persons visited the movies every week. It was from the movies, indeed, that the new generation obtained its notions, for the most part highly romantic and dangerously misleading, about life. Circumscribed by the requirements of the box office, directed to vast and uncritical audiences, subjected to a censorship often unintelligent and sometimes vulgar, the movies hesitated to undertake a realistic portrayal of life as it actually was in the United States. They appealed rather to the wishful thinking of their patrons. The vast majority of films portrayed romantic love, with emphasis upon its more biological aspects. Crime, high life, and comedies were always popular, while films critical of society were usually box-office failures, though in the forties such films as *The Snake Pit, Gentlemen's Agreement,* and *Home of the Brave* furnished encouraging exceptions to this generalization. On the whole, however, movies represented an escape into a fairyland of love, adventure, or riches. Inevitably the *mores* and the vocabulary of the movies were imitated by those to whom they represented the fulfillment of every ambition. They set the fashion in dress, in home furnishings, in play, even in marriage and family life, and more and more human nature came to conform to commercial art. Hollywood advertised the gaudiest aspects of American life in every nation of the world, and in the realm of values challenged the sovereignty of home, school, and church.

Every other field of entertainment revealed the same tendency toward commercialization. Sport became a big business. Professional baseball teams played to capacity crowds; Babe Ruth and Joe Di Maggio were national heroes to millions of boys who had never heard of Charles W. Eliot or Justice Holmes. Intercollegiate football attracted millions of spectators who thus came to appreciate one of the advantages of higher education, and many university presidents could not resist the demand of their communities or alumni for a football team of hired oafs. High school basketball tournaments became events of state-wide importance. Prize-fighting, too, became respectable as well as profitable; fight fans in 1927 paid two and one half million dollars to see Gene Tunney beat Jack Dempsey, and in 1940 a presidential candidate was glad to have the support of the heavyweight champion, Joe Louis. Daylight-saving time and the five-day week gave a new popularity to tennis and golf, while such old-fashioned games as croquet, which required well-kept lawns and family groups, all but disappeared. Card games, once looked upon as a form of gambling, became fashionable, and adeptness at bridge something of a social necessity. No previous generation had made such progress in the art of being amused. None had been less capable of amusing itself.

2. *Intolerance*

Busily engaged in getting and enjoying wealth, and sure that they were at last on the road to Utopia, Americans were peculiarly intolerant of criticism or heterodoxy. The seeds of intolerance had been planted during the war, and in the post-war years they sprouted strange and noxious weeds. So admirable did this business civilization appear to those who enjoyed its benefits that they found it difficult to understand how honest men could find fault with it, and fault-finding was ascribed to depravity or disloyalty. Surely no good American would criticize the United States; criticism itself was a sign of un-Americanism. Nationalism, glorified during the war, took on an especially virulent form. It manifested itself in a bewildering variety of ways — in the revision of history and history textbooks, the requirement that school teachers subscribe to loyalty oaths, the denial of citizenship to pacifists, the deportation of aliens, the suppression of economic unrest through laws against syndicalism and anarchism, the purging of legislatures and other organizations, a repudiation of liberalism in arts and literature, a celebration of fundamentalism in religion, and a legislative and judicial emasculation of state and federal bills of rights.

Religious fundamentalism took on an aggressive form. Colleges and theological seminaries were purged of 'modernists' and, under the leadership of William J. Bryan, now turned crusader for the true faith. Several Southern states enacted laws forbidding the teaching of evolution in state-supported schools which even the notoriety of the Dayton 'monkey-trial' failed to erase from their statute-books. Censorship and Comstockery burgeoned under official sanction. Six states established boards of censors for moving pictures — enough to control a product dependent upon nation-wide favor — and the Treasury Department and the Post Office connived with self-appointed guardians of the public morals to protect the public from 'immoral' books and works of art.

The most notorious chapter in the history of intolerance was written by the Ku Klux Klan. This secret society, organized in Atlanta, Georgia, in 1915, had nothing in common with the Klan of Reconstruction days but a name and a purpose to keep the Negro down. It made little progress during the war years, but in the nineteen-twenties it flourished like the green bay tree. During this decade it dedicated itself to the old Know-Nothing program of nativism and anti-Catholicism, and added, for good measure, anti-Semitism. The Klan's cult of secrecy, elaborate rituals and ceremonials and gaudy paraphernalia appealed to many who were indifferent to its objectives, and soon it spread from Georgia throughout the South and into the Middle West; even on the rolling hills of Pennsylvania and eastern Massachusetts fiery crosses blazed against evening skies. At its height the Klan boasted some six million members; it went into politics, intimidated candidates for office throughout the South and in Indiana, elected governors and senators friendly to its program. For a decade the Klan went its violent way, and thoughtful men saw in it the potential basis for an American fascist movement. It declined, in the end, from internal rot rather than from external opposition.

The Klan represented a widespread hostility to minority and nonconformist groups — hostility shared, actively or passively, by the great majority of Americans. Rarely had the emphasis upon conformity been so insistent, and never before had bills of rights proved so impotent as barriers against popular persecution. The demand for conformity and orthodoxy was proclaimed in a bewildering body of laws, and where the laws were silent vigilante groups spoke for them. In the South, Negroes were increasingly denied rights supposedly guaranteed to them by the Fourteenth and Fifteenth Amendments. Jim Crow laws, segregation ordinances, denial of equal facilities in education or public services were taken for granted, and archaic legislation from slavery or reconstruction days was resurrected as a weapon to break Negro labor and tenant farmer organizations. Grandfather clauses, party control of primary elections, poll taxes, and sheer intimidation were used to circumvent the Fifteenth Amendment.

Twenty-four states enacted criminal-syndicalism or criminal-anarchy laws, directed chiefly at radical labor agitators, and one, West Virginia, safeguarded future generations by making unlawful any teachings of 'ideals hostile to those now or *henceforth* existing under the constitution and laws of this State.' California outlawed any doctrine advocating the use of force to accomplish a change in industrial ownership, and under the esoteric terms of this law over five hundred persons were arrested in a period of five years. One of them, a venerable and distinguished social worker named Anita Whitney, was arrested for the crime of attending a meeting of the Communist Labor party in order to oppose its program. Miss Whitney's sentence of one to fourteen years in the penitentiary evoked from Justice Brandeis an eloquent protest:

> Those who won our independence believed that the final end of the state was to make men free to develop their faculties; and that in its government the deliberative forces should prevail over the arbitrary. They valued liberty both as an end and as a means. They believed liberty to be the secret of happiness, and courage to be the secret of liberty. They believed that freedom to think as you will and to speak as you think are means indispensable to the discovery and spread of political truth; that without free speech and assembly, discussion would be futile; that with them, discussion affords ordinarily adequate protection against the dissemination of noxious doctrine; that the greatest menace to freedom is an inert people; that public discussion is a political duty; and that this should be a fundamental principle of the American government. But they knew that order cannot be secured merely through fear of punishment for its infraction; that it is hazardous to discourage thought, hope, and imagination; that fear breeds repression; that repression breeds hate; that hate menaces stable government; that the path of safety lies in the opportunity to discuss freely supposed grievances and proposed remedies; and that the fitting remedy for evil counsels is good ones. Believing in the power of reason as applied through public discussion, they eschewed silence coerced by law — the argument of force in its worst form. Recognizing the occasional tyrannies of governing majorities, they amended the Constitution so that free speech and assembly should be guaranteed.[4]

The most sensational attack upon persons entertaining radical ideas came with the deportation delirium of 1919–20. President Wilson had predicted, 'once lead this people into war and they'll forget there ever was such a thing as tolerance'; and his Attorney General, A. Mitchell Palmer, hastened to embrace the opportunity of justifying that prediction. After the war was over, Palmer, whose role in the cabinet had been insignificant but who entertained presidential ambitions, proceeded to win a famous victory over alien radicals in the United States. Using private spies and *agents provocateurs,* Palmer conducted a series of lawless raids on private houses and labor headquarters, rounded up several thousand aliens, held them incommunicado and subjected them to drumhead trials. In the end only a few hundred were deported; the vast majority of those arrested were found to be harmless.

The Courts, too, felt the repercussions of the war, and in two notable cases construed the wartime Espionage and Sedition Acts se-

[4] Whitney *v.* California, 274 U.S. 257, at 375.

verely to limit freedom of speech in time of national danger. Schenck *v*. United States [5] involved criticism of conscription, and although the defendant was found guilty the decision is memorable rather for the establishment of the criterion of 'clear and present danger' as the only justification for qualifying the constitutional guarantee of freedom of speech. This standard, however, was not adhered to in the more controversial case where a miserable garment worker, Jacob Abrams, was sentenced to twenty years' imprisonment for distributing a ragged little pamphlet suggesting that the workers of the world arise against the American military expedition to Siberia. The opinion of the Court in this case evoked from Justice Holmes perhaps the most moving of his many eloquent dissents: [6]

> When men have realized that time has upset many fighting faiths, they may come to believe even more than they believe the very foundations of their own conduct that the ultimate good desired is better reached by free trade in ideas — that the best test of truth is the power of the thought to get itself accepted in the competition of the market, and that truth is the only ground upon which their wishes can be safely carried out. That at any rate is the theory of our Constitution. It is an experiment, as all life is an experiment. Every year if not every day we have to wager our salvation upon some prophecy based upon imperfect knowledge. While that experiment is part of our system I think that we should be eternally vigilant against attempts to check the expression of opinions that we loathe and believe to be fraught with death, unless they so imminently threaten immediate interference with the lawful and pressing purposes of the law that an immediate check is required to save the country.

Socialism as well as Communism and pacifism came under the ban, and in 1920 the Empire State distinguished herself by expelling five Socialist members from the state legislature. It was not alleged that the party was an illegal one or that the Socialist members were guilty of any crime, but merely that Socialism was 'absolutely inimical to the best interests of the State of New York and of the United States.' This palpable violation of elementary constitutional rights inspired vigorous protests, even from conservatives. The distinguished Charles Evans Hughes, later to be elevated to the Chief Justiceship, hastened to expose the illogic of the Albany legislature: [7]

[5] 249 U.S. 47 (1919).

[6] Abrams *v*. U.S. 250 U.S. 616 (1919).

[7] *New York Times,* 10 January 1920.

> I understand that it is said that the Socialists constitute a combination to overthrow the Government. The answer is plain. If public officers or private citizens have any evidence that any individuals, or group of individuals, are plotting revolution and seeking by violent measures to overthrow our Government, let the evidence be laid before the proper authorities and swift action be taken for the safety of the community. . . But I count it a most serious mistake to proceed, not against individuals charged with violation of law, but against masses of our citizens combined for political action, by denying them the only resource of peaceful government; that is, action by the ballot box and through duly elected representatives in legislative bodies.

But his call for sanity fell on deaf ears. Even the Supreme Court shortly revealed a spirit scarcely more enlightened than that of legislative bodies. In two notable cases [8] it denied citizenship to a woman and an elderly professor in a theological school who proclaimed their pacifism. 'I would suggest,' wrote Justice Holmes in one of the last of his many dissenting opinions — subsequently accepted by the Court —, 'that the Quakers have done their share to make the country what it is, that many citizens agree with the applicant's belief, and that I had not supposed hitherto that we regretted our inability to expel them because they believed more than some of us do in the teachings of the Sermon on the Mount.'

Hostility to radicals, antipathy to foreigners, and jealousy for the maintenance of the status quo were revealed in the most sensational murder case since that of the Haymarket anarchists — the Sacco-Vanzetti case. The principals, again, were foreigners and philosophical anarchists — Nicola Sacco and Bartolomeo Vanzetti — accused of murdering a paymaster at South Braintree, Massachusetts. Although appearances were against them, the actual evidence against them was slight and their alibis were sound. When they were convicted and sentenced to death there was a widespread belief that the jury had been moved more by their radical views and their evasion of military service than by the evidence. For seven years men and women of all shades of opinion and in almost every country of the globe labored to obtain a retrial, and Governor Fuller of Massachusetts so far heeded this opinion as to appoint an investigating committee consisting of the Presidents of Harvard and Massachusetts Institute of Technology and a judge of probate. Although this committee found the trial judge guilty of 'grave breach of official decorum,' it

[8] U.S. *v.* Schwimmer, 279 U.S. 644, and U.S. *v.* Macintosh, 283 U.S. 605.

reported, on the basis of evidence even more slight than that of the original conviction, that justice had been done. When Sacco and Vanzetti were electrocuted, on 23 August 1927, a cry of horror at the injustice of it went around the world, and those citizens of Massachusetts who loved justice remembered John Adams and the Boston massacre case and Judge Sewall's retraction in the case of the Salem witches, and hung their heads in shame. For such people Edna St. Vincent Millay spoke in her sonnet:

> As men have loved their lovers in times past
> And sung their wit, their virtue and their grace,
> So have we loved sweet Justice to the last,
> That now lies here in an unseemly place.
> The child will quit the cradle and grow wise
> And stare on beauty till his senses drown;
> Yet shall be seen no more by mortal eyes
> Such beauty as here walked and here went down.
> Like birds that hear the winter crying plain
> Her courtiers leave to seek the clement south;
> Many have praised her, we alone remain
> To break a fist against the lying mouth
> Of any man who says this was not so;
> Though she be dead now, as indeed we know.[9]

In the main, the record of the Supreme Court gratified those who still cherished the guarantees of the Bill of Rights. Conservative on most economic issues, it was distinctly liberal on questions involving personal liberties. Particularly notable was a series of decisions extending Federal protection to the right of minority groups to freedom of speech, freedom of assembly, and a fair trial. Thus in De Jonge *v.* Oregon,[10] the Court voided a criminal-syndicalism law which would have made mere attendance at a Communist meeting a crime. 'The greater the importance of safeguarding the community from incitements to the overthrow of our institutions by force and violence,' said Chief Justice Hughes,' the more imperative is the need to preserve inviolate the constitutional right of free speech, free press, and free assembly in order to maintain the opportunity for free political discussion, to the end that government may be responsive to the will of the people and that changes, if desired, may be obtained by peaceful means.' Again, in Herndon *v.* Lowry [11] the Court ruled that the mere

9 Edna St. Vincent Millay, *Wine from These Grapes*, p. 43 (Harper & Brothers).
10 299 U.S. 353 (1937).
11 301 U.S. 242 (1937).

possession of Communist literature could not be held to be an 'incitement to riot.' Stromberg *v.* California [12] nullified a loosely drawn 'red-flag' law; and Thornhill *v.* Alabama [13] interpreted picketing as a form of expression and extended to it the constitutional guarantees of free speech. Hague *v.* C.I.O.[14] vindicated the right of liberal groups to hold public meetings in boss Frank Hague's bailiwick, Jersey City. Powell *v.* Alabama [15] — the notorious Scottsboro case — was remanded to the State courts on the ground that failure to include Negroes on the panel from which jurors were drawn constituted in effect a denial of due process, while in Chambers *v.* Florida [16] a unanimous court, speaking through the new Associate Justice of Alabama, Mr. Black, reversed the conviction of a Negro obtained through the use of the 'third degree.'

Equally significant was the judicial insistence upon a broad reading of the guarantee of a free press. American devotion to freedom of the press was a deep-rooted one, and not until the First World War was there any serious challenge to the principle that there should be no previous restraint upon any publication. When, in 1925, Minnesota provided punishment — without jury trial — for any 'malicious, scandalous and defamatory' newspaper article, making truth a defense only if the motives were good and the ends justifiable, the Supreme Court voided the law.[17] A more dangerous, because more subtle, attack upon the freedom of the press came when Huey Long's pliant legislature in Louisiana imposed a discriminatory tax upon newspapers of over twenty-thousand circulation — a tax neatly designed to embarrass the few papers still opposed to the Long regime. Refusing to be diverted by the vexatious question of the taxing power of the state, the Court nullified the act squarely on the ground of its conflict with the guarantees of the First Amendment.[18]

In thus striking down state legislation impairing personal liberties, the Court was immensely aided by a new constitutional weapon which it had only recently forged. That was the doctrine whereby the Federal Bill of Rights was interpreted as a limitation upon state as well as upon national action. Ever since Barron *v.* Baltimore, back in 1833,[19] it had been assumed that the Bill of Rights limited only

12 283 U.S. 359 (1931).
13 310 U.S. 88 (1940).
14 307 U.S. 496 (1939).
15 287 U.S. 45 (1932).
16 309 U.S. 227 (1940).
17 Near *v.* Minnesota, 283 U.S. 697 (1931).
18 Grosjean *v.* American Press Co., 297 U.S. 233.
19 7 Peters 243.

the national Congress, and this position was long unchallenged. Beginning, however, in the nineteen-twenties — and definitely with the case of Gitlow *v.* New York in 1925[20] — the Court intimated that the rights of 'life, liberty and property,' guaranteed against state impairment by the Fourteenth Amendment, might be presumed to embrace those rights set forth in the Federal Bill of Rights. This dictum, at first only cautiously suggested, was within a decade completely incorporated into constitutional law. Since, historically, most limitations upon personal liberties had come from the states, this new principle of law gave support to the hope that the Fourteenth Amendment might at last be interpreted to mean what its framers had originally intended.

3. *Literary Interpretations*

Nationalism, materialism, and orthodoxy aroused dissent and inspired protest. A new school of humanists, led by the intrepid Professor Irving Babbitt, raised aloft their classical standards and judged severely the tawdriness of contemporary society; their inability to formulate a positive program persuaded many that they understood the past better than the present. Twelve Southerners collaborated in a declaration of spiritual independence, *I'll Take My Stand,* which argued with more charm than logic the beauties of an idyllic Southland that never existed and the ugliness of an industrial civilization. In the realm of education humanism was most energetically represented by President Hutchins of the University of Chicago; his protest against the growing materialism of higher education in America was wholesome, but his worship of metaphysics and of scholastic philosophy seemed as divorced from the realities of twentieth-century America as did the Gothic architecture of his university.

More important was the contribution of critics like Randolph Bourne, Van Wyck Brooks, and Vernon L. Parrington, who recalled the long and splendid history of American liberalism and idealism, and who did concern themselves energetically with the contemporary scene. There was thunder on the left, too. Thorstein Veblen, most penetrating critic of the economy of the leisure class and of capitalist business enterprise, was rescued from the neglect which had too long obscured his work. Other students of American economy, such as

[20] 268 U.S. 652.

Richard T. Ely and E. A. Ross, were given a more friendly hearing than they had enjoyed when they first turned their literary batteries upon the ramparts of laissez-faire capitalism. Publicists like Herbert Croly, Walter Weyl, and Walter Lippmann found in *The New Republic* and *The Nation* vehicles for criticism that was penetrating enough to command attention even from conservatives, while from Joseph Wood Krutch came an examination of *The Modern Temper* that remains one of the most revealing analyses of the spiritual confusion of this age. Easily the most vociferous of the critics, however, was Henry L. Mencken, who made it his special business to expose bourgeois complacency, and whose 'Americana,' extracts from the current press, recorded with melancholy faithfulness the fatuousness of contemporary life. Through his personal organ, *The American Mercury,* through his interminable series of *Prejudices,* and through a host of rapt disciples, Mencken imposed his peculiar style on smart young writers and his iconoclastic views upon the nation. As a critic of pretentiousness and vulgarity he performed a useful function; but the fumbling inconsistency of his attitudes became increasingly apparent as the volume of his negative criticism reached encyclopedic dimensions, and it was a sign of reviving national health that he lost influence more rapidly than he had gained it.

Imaginative literature reflected even more luminously the reaction from conservatism and orthodoxy, the confusion and fragmentation of life, the passing of the age of confidence. It would be misleading to suggest that this literature was neither materialistic nor nationalistic, but its materialism was more philosophical, its nationalism less ostentatious, than in the social or political arena. Influences from abroad continued strong; James Joyce, D. H. Lawrence, T. S. Eliot, and Thomas Mann supplanted the foreign preceptors of an earlier generation, George Moore, Zola, Ibsen, and Nietzsche. The most striking characteristics of the literature of the twenties and thirties were naturalism, sensationalism, social protest, and escape into the world of the past or of dreams. There was a tendency to description, faithful but dull, which made novels more useful as historical or sociological tracts than interesting as literature; a brave attempt to incorporate Freudian psychology into literature which usually took the form of emphasis upon sex; a cheerful zest for experimentation in subject matter and technique; an assiduous cultivation of indigenous historical material and a convulsive effort to substitute idiomatic American for academic English; and a consequential sensitiveness to the widening market of the book clubs, the popular magazines, the movies, and the radio.

The easiest weapon against the complacency and the vulgarity of the Harding-Coolidge era was satire, and the most popular of those who used this weapon was Sinclair Lewis, discoverer of *Main Street* and creator of George Babbitt. Lewis was the Mencken of American novelists; his function to satirize the ideals of the self-satisfied middle-class society in which he moved so uneasily. His satire, to be sure, was of manner rather than of fundamentals; his revolt was against dullness rather than evil, against provincialism rather than moral anarchy, against the Gopher Prairie or Zenith City rather than the world he lived in, and it was easy to discover in him a grudging affection for the characters whom he ridiculed and the society he derided. He was pre-eminently the historian of bad manners, and his immense popularity must be ascribed in large part to the timeliness of his stories. His portrayal of the small town was less faithful than that of Brand Whitlock, in *J. Hardin & Son,* his picture of the American bourgeoisie less acute than that of William Allen White in *A Certain Rich Man,* but the devastating accuracy of his reporting caught the imagination of a generation educated by journalism and advertising.

More penetrating in their criticism, more thorough-going in their 'revolt from the village,' were two very different artists — Edgar Lee Masters and Sherwood Anderson. In *The Spoon River Anthology* Masters recorded, in the style of the *Greek Anthology,* the monotonous existence of two hundred individuals in a drab midwestern town, where dreamers were always defeated and idealists ended as cynics or hypocrites. Sherwood Anderson, one of the first American authors to respond to the teachings of Freud and one of the precursors of the stream-of-consciousness technique, presented in *Winesburg, Ohio* a picture not only of narrowness but of social disintegration and moral anarchy. The reverse side of this revolt from the village was the satire on urban respectability and suburban sophistication. F. Scott Fitzgerald was the earliest historian of the Jazz Age, his *This Side of Paradise,* for a time, the Bible of undergraduates.

Satire and the reaction against provincialism petered out after the twenties. Lewis himself turned to more profitable and more significant themes; Anderson went over completely to Freudianism,

Masters fell silent, H. L. Mencken gave up the *American Mercury*. J. P. Marquand persisted in the technique, but in more urbane and mordant form. Marquand will be remembered as one of that small group of American authors whose fictional creations have entered into the national idiom: George Apley and H. M. Pulham Esq., symbols of Bostonian propriety, belong with George Babbitt, Silas Lapham, Colonel Sellers, and a half dozen other national characters.

Satire and irony, appropriate enough for the Jazz Age, were obviously inadequate for the depression, and the rebels of the thirties abandoned them for more forthright criticism. Of these the most notable were James Farrell, John Dos Passos, Thomas Wolfe, and John Steinbeck — a group who performed for that decade much the same service that Crane, Norris, London, and Dreiser had performed for the hard times of an earlier generation. Of this earlier group Dreiser alone lingered on, finding the new America no more to his liking than the America he had depicted in *Sister Carrie*. His two most important books of this period are entitled *An American Tragedy* and *Tragic America*. Dreiser's most faithful disciple was James Farrell, who in his *Studs Lonigan* trilogy — massive, formless, without pity or dignity — took a dismal view of life in the Chicago of the post-war years. In the Dreiser tradition, too, was Dos Passos, a more skillful and original technician than Farrell, more tolerant, dignified, and philosophical. In his *U.S.A.* trilogy Dos Passos portrayed a society rootless and disintegrated, hurrying to wealth and to pleasure, without faith or security or purpose, even without genuine passion. Thomas Wolfe, the promise of whose *Look Homeward Angel* was not fulfilled in his later and more popular books, belongs to this group. Gargantuan, tempestuous, capable at once of the most dreadful bathos and the most poignant beauty, passionately devoted to his country but fleeing it like the plague, Wolfe was something of a genius and something of a charlatan: his portrait of Eugene Gant remains one of the memorable achievements of our literature. In the Frank Norris, rather than the Dreiser, tradition is John Steinbeck. His earlier books revealed little more than technical skill and sympathy for the underdog, but in *The Grapes of Wrath*, he presented a great novel. This story of the trek of the Joad clan from their Oklahoma farm to the promised land of California was the one story to come out of the depression that caught up the tragedy of the dust bowl, the gallantry and vulgarity of the rural proletariat. It was a modern version of *The Octopus,* more penetrating and profound, a tribute to the enduring nobility of the human spirit in time of tribulation.

These were the satirists and the critics, writers who attacked the failings of society and thus admitted their faith in reformation. But the most significant writers of this era were the spokesmen of the 'lost generation' who celebrated moral chaos and confessed to despair. They had no faith in progress or in reform, and their reading of the new science which Jeans and Eddington were proclaiming taught them that man had no permanent or significant place in the universe, that human values were fictions or illusions, and that life was not only without dignity but without meaning. They were the victims, too, of the materialism of the twenties and the moral chaos of the thirties — the American equivalents of Jules Romains and Aldous Huxley. They were not rebels against society or against the world in which they lived; they had passed beyond rebellion into acquiescence. Theirs was the generation of 'the hollow men, the stuffed men' and their spiritual home was the 'waste land.' Some, like Jeffers, rejected moral values and found savage delight in an amoral universe; others, like Faulkner and Hemingway, took refuge in brutality and sadism; still others, like Conrad Aiken, found satisfaction in the trivialities and 'minute facets of minute experience.' [21]

A few cherished, like the Victorians, Browning and Arnold, the dignity of fortitude. All of them might have said, with Eugene O'Neill, that the writer 'must dig at the roots of the sickness of today as he feels it — the death of the old God and the failure of science and materialism to give any satisfactory new one for the surviving religious instinct to find a new meaning for life.' And the younger ones could confess, with Katherine Anne Porter, that 'for myself, and I was not alone, all the conscious and recollected years of my life have been lived to this day under the heavy threat of world catastrophe and most of the energies of my mind and spirit have been spent in the effort to grasp the meaning of those threats, to trace them to their sources and to understand the logic of this

[21] So, in Ireland, William Butler Yeats was writing

Though the great song return no more
There's keen delight in what we have
The rattle of pebbles on the shore
Under the receding wave.

The Nineteenth Century and After.

majestic and terrible failure of the life of man in the Western World.'

Easily the most distinguished of this group was Edwin Arlington Robinson, born in the same year as William Vaughan Moody, but whose most memorable work belonged to the war and post-war years. 'The world,' he wrote, 'is a kind of spiritual kindergarten where bewildered infants are trying to spell God with the wrong blocks.' For bewildered human beings — the inhabitants of his own Tilbury Town, or of King Arthur's England, or of the dream world of Amaranth, Robinson had neither bitterness nor indignation but only pity. Writing with austere detachment and a technique flexible and flawless, he concerned himself not with the problems of the passing day, but with those issues that have troubled man from the beginning of philosophy. He celebrated failures, but failures who triumphed through spiritual integrity; that defeat was inevitable for man was to him neither bitter nor outrageous. He drew a matchless gallery of derelicts — lost souls of Tilbury town, poor wretches who had to live with their pasts, or with their sins, the hopeless and the desperate. He is the poet of the might-have-been, of illusions, of the tragedy of greatness, of the futility of material strivings. Subtle, probing, endlessly analytical, he laid bare, even in the medieval narratives, the soul of the modern man.

T. S. Eliot, Missouri-born Harvardian, expressed more sharply than any of his contemporaries the post-war mood of futility. He wrote of a generation of 'hollow men' who exhibited

> Shape without form, space without color,
> Paralyzed force, gesture without motion

and in *The Waste Land* — an effort to portray the splintered fragmentation of life — he gave a name to the whole contemporary world which he interpreted with ironical detachment. He exerted an immense influence on the poets and poetry of that day; less, unfortunately, after he had embraced the Church and written profound and moving spiritual poems like *Dry Salvages.*

Robinson Jeffers was bitter where Eliot was urbane, violent where Robinson was tender. He represented in extreme form the revolt against accepted moral values and the glorification of pain, perversity, and death. In *Roan Stallion, Dear Judas, Give Your Heart to the Hawks,* and *Thurso's Landing* he is obsessed with themes of madness and horror and destruction. He moved spiritually in the opposite direction from Eliot, and his final rejection of Christianity and celebration of force suggest an intellectual kinship with Spengler rather than with the Anglo-American decadents.

The novelists of despair were less skillful but more elaborate. William Faulkner, like Jeffers, frankly embraced chaos and death. Employing the stream-of-consciousness technique borrowed from Joyce, Faulkner laid bare, in novel after novel, the misery, brutality, obscenity, and depravity of the degenerate first families and the poor whites of the South. 'No battle is ever fought,' says one of his characters, 'the field only reveals to man his own folly and despair, and history is an illusion of philosophers and fools.' This philosophy was scarcely novel, but Faulkner presented it with such rigorous faithfulness that he serves as a symbol and a type. Most of his novels, however, suffered from the connotation suggested by the title of one of them — *The Sound and the Fury:* they were tales signifying nothing. Erskine Caldwell, too, found material ready to his hand in the lives of the Southern poor whites. Yet Caldwell was a more robust figure — chiefly because he had humor. Competent in the short story, his longer tales — *God's Little Acre* and *Tobacco Road* — were sensational rather than profound. *Tobacco Road,* dramatized, ran for over four years on Broadway, where its portrayal of Southern depravity titillated the same people who greeted rapturously the screen versions of *Gone With the Wind* and *So Red the Rose.* Neither Jeffers nor Faulkner nor Caldwell grew like Eliot and Robinson; naturally so, for if you start with the premise that life is meaningless, there is nothing more to say.

Flight from realism took a somewhat more provocative form with the Imagist poets, practitioners of *vers libre,* who hotly abandoned ideas and experience for the satisfactions of surface impressions of color and sound and form; this group was assured a hearing more because of the eccentricities of its high priest and priestess — Ezra Pound and Amy Lowell — than because it represented anything of importance. Escape, finally, found concrete illustration in the flight of sensitive artists and authors who sought certitude and peace and help from pain in the sidewalk cafés of Paris or on the Riviera — and found only disillusionment.

A more robust form of divorce from reality was the historical romance, long cultivated by American writers. Joseph Hergesheimer was the legitimate successor to S. Weir Mitchell and Mary Johnston, his *Java Head* and *Balisand* entertaining costume pieces, historically sound. Kenneth Roberts brought a realistic technique to the reinterpretation of the Revolutionary era; his *Oliver Wiswell,* a celebration of the American Tories at the expense of the Patriots, was a subtle argument for Fascism at a time when many Americans were beginning to have misgivings about democracy. The Civil War lent itself even more eagerly to romance, and Stark Young's *So Red the Rose* and Margaret Mitchell's *Gone With the Wind* — in book and screen versions — converted millions of Northerners to the Confederate cause, though a less romantic but more sensitive interpretation by McKinlay Kantor — *Long Remember* — went almost unnoticed. Easily the most memorable literary foray into history, however, was Stephen Benét's epic poem *John Brown's Body,* which we have frequently quoted; for it was not only the best long poem in our literature but the best short history of the Civil War.

The revival of regionalism, which carried over into the thirties, represented in part a revolt from realism, in part a reaction from standardization, and in part a reflection of the historical study of regions, exemplified in Webb's *Great Plains* and Vance's *Human Geography of the South.* The local-color novels of the period are legion. Some of the best of them had elements of permanence — Louis Bromfield's *The Green Bay Tree* and *The Farm* (Ohio), Stark Young's *Heaven Trees* (Louisiana), Elizabeth Roberts' *Time of Man* (Kentucky), James Boyd's *Roll River* (Pennsylvania), Rachel Field's *Time Out of Mind* (Maine), Dorothy Canfield's *Hillsboro People* (Vermont), Allen Tate's *The Fathers* (Virginia). And throughout this period Willa Cather and Ellen Glasgow continued to write books that were regional in setting and background but had the universality of all works of art.

To this general school of regionalists belong, too, the poets John Neihardt, Carl Sandburg, Vachel Lindsay, and Robert Frost. Neihardt's *Song of Hugh Glass* and *Song of the Three Friends* are the most ambitious efforts yet projected to tell, in poetic form, the saga of the pioneer and the Indian. Sandburg is the poet of the prairies and the prairie metropolis, Chicago. In his uncritical affection for plain people, and in his stylistic barbarisms, Sandburg was the disciple of Walt Whitman; he celebrated Chicago as Whitman had celebrated Brooklyn and the streets of New York. It was natural that the author of *Cornhuskers* and *Slabs of the Sunburst West,* and

The People, Yes, should write, in the end, a poetical biography of the prairie democrat, Abraham Lincoln. Vachel Lindsay was a modern troubadour, a mixture of poet, reformer, and minister, who wandered from town to town preaching the 'gospel of beauty' and 'trading his rhymes for bread.' 'The Congo,' 'General Booth Enters Heaven,' 'The Santa-Fe Trail,' and the tributes to Lincoln, Altgeld, and Bryan were essentially folk-songs, fashioned from the experience of the common people. In Robert Frost one finds the beauty and serenity of the New England countryside, *North of Boston.* Equally adept at lyric and narrative poetry, Frost, like Whittier, sang the changing seasons and the homely duties of farm and shop; unlike Whittier he ignored alike social problems and philosophy.

More fully than any other man of letters of his time Eugene O'Neill represented all of these varied intellectual interests and spiritual forces. The most distinguished of American dramatists, imaginative, original and technically competent, O'Neill indulged himself in naturalism (*Anna Christie, The Hairy Ape, The Emperor Jones*), enjoyed his revolt from the village and took his fling at the contemporary Babbitts (*Ah, Wilderness, 'Marco Millions,'* and *The Great God Brown*), bathed in Freudianism (*Desire Under the Elms* and *Strange Interlude*), and worked his way from these provocative imitations of current intellectual fashions to philosophical mysticism. In *Mourning Becomes Electra* he boldly invited comparison with the Agamemnon trilogy of Aeschylus. Finally, in *Lazarus Laughed,* an allegory of the victory of life over death, O'Neill, like Eliot, shifted from a negative to an affirmative view of life.

There had been something artificial and Byronically vulgar about the studied cultivation of despair with which so many writers reacted to the lush materialism of the twenties. Imagism and Freudianism, fantasy and satire were all very well when there was nothing at stake but the comfort of artistic souls, but they were cheap, too. The long depression of the thirties tested the American spirit, and the spirit responded. Archibald MacLeish, gifted member of the newer generation of poets, addressed to his fellows a stirring appeal, *The Irresponsibles,* calling upon artists and scholars and men of letters to leave their ivory towers and return to the great tradition of setting the course of national life. And when, after 1935, the dark shadows of totalitarianism spread over the skies and a long night threatened to blot out all those values which civilized people had ever cherished, most American men of letters rallied to the defense of the human spirit and insisted that there were things worth living for and worth dying for. Sinclair Lewis in *It Can't Happen Here* sounded the alarm bell to a lethargic democracy. Ernest Hemingway, who had long worshipped at the shrine of moral nihilism, and whose *The Sun Also Rises* was one of the gospels of the 'lost generation,' found in the death struggle of Spanish democracy a spiritual catharsis. Robert Nathan, whose limpid and sensitive prose had been dedicated to the simple annals of the poor and the adoration of New York City, dramatized the impact of war upon the innocents in *They Went on Together*. Dos Passos, who had long wandered aimlessly over *U.S.A.*, found at last *The Ground We Stand On* — the ground of democracy and freedom. The poets rang true to the tradition of Whittier and Lowell, Whitman and Lanier and Moody. Carl Sandburg voiced his faith in *The People, Yes* — that 'The deathless dream will be the stronger' — and young Paul Engle told his fellows:

> Now the huge pendulum of history
> Begins to turn upon you, it is time
> To leave this wandering always on the earth
> And take from the hawk his flying wisdom, soar
> On the keen edge of the world's wind, veer and hover
> Until you take the very stars for eyes.

Stephen Benét turned from those Civil War themes which he had exploited so magnificently to a more menacing conflict, and his *Litany for Dictatorship* sounded solemn warning:

> Now the night rolls back on the west and the night is solid.
> Our fathers and ourselves sowed dragon's teeth.
> Our children know and suffer the armed men.

Edna St. Vincent Millay abandoned her love sonnets, and in *Conversation at Midnight, Huntsman, What Quarry?,* and *Make Bright the Arrows* appealed to her generation to prove all things by spiritual tests and hold fast to that which is good.

4. *Fine Arts and Music*

The most notable developments in the arts were the accent on nativism and the sensitive response to social and economic problems. Never before had 'art for art's sake' been in such disrepute; rarely has the emphasis on its social significance been so impressive, or its aesthetic quality so slight. That art became at once more indigenous and more democratic was in part a response to the times, and in part a result of the active intervention of the government both as patron and as collaborator.

Samuel Isham, the historian of American painting, could assert in 1905 that 'two or three centuries from now those curious to learn what manner of people lived at the beginning of the twentieth century can cull from the art production of France or Germany or England an infinity of pictures, many of them of high artistic merit. From America they will get hardly anything of that sort, at least in oil painting.' There was exaggeration here — Isham had forgotten Homer and Eakins — but on the whole the criticism was justified. Within twenty years the situation had changed dramatically, and the change appears permanent. American 'primitives' were rediscovered; there was a new appreciation of those earlier illustrators, Audubon, Bingham, and Mount, while Currier and Ives prints began to decorate the most respectable walls. A host of younger painters repudiated the 'salon' painting of an earlier generation and turned hopefully to limning the American landscape and interpreting the most varied aspects of American life.

The movement had its beginning with the New York realists — Sloan, Bellows, Glackens, Henri, Luks — who in turn acknowledged the inspiration of Eakins. Affectionately and sensitively these men painted the color of the great metropolis: McSorley's Bar, boys swimming off the East River piers, children playing in the teeming streets of the lower East Side, Bowery bums, Yeats at Pettipas, or a prize fight at Sharkey's. These pioneers broke with the Beaux-Arts tradition and discovered dignity in the life about them; in their wake came a host of eager younger men who refused to abandon their native regions for either the Left Bank or Greenwich Village and who recorded in paint what the regional novelists of an earlier generation had recorded in fiction. Thomas Hart Benton the painter was as authentically American as his ancestor the senator; like Mark Twain he transcribed the social history of the great River, of the South and the West. Grant Wood bathed the rolling hills and the gimcrack houses of Iowa in rich color and sentiment; John Steuart Curry chose the plains of Kansas and the cotton fields of Dixie; Edward Bruce divided his allegiance between New York and California; Charles Sheeler traced the farm houses and barns of the Pennsylvania Germans; William Lathrop painted the beauty of the Delaware Valley which had inspired Inness; Waldo Peirce was at his best depicting scenes on the coast of Maine. No part of the country was neglected, nor was interpretation sacrificed for photographic realism.

It was, indeed, the social consciousness of the American painters that was most striking: genre painting, itself, was nothing new. In 1936 the artist George Biddle, reviewing an exhibition of contemporary American and of French painting, found that while among the French pictures there was not one that was 'preoccupied with life, let alone social problems,' of the American works 'seventy-four dealt with the American scene or with a social criticism of American life; six with strikes or with strikebreakers; six with dust, sand, erosion, drought, and floods. There were no nudes, no portraits, and two still lifes. Out of the hundred not one could be said to enjoy, reflect, participate in our inherited democratic-capitalist culture.'[22] Certainly in Biddle's own work this preoccupation with the social scene is ever present. It is implicit or explicit in those paintings of Burchfield that record the ugliness of small Ohio towns as faithfully as does *Winesburg, Ohio;* in the political caricatures of William Gropper and Benton; in Henry Varnum Poor's murals of labor; in Alexandre Hogue's graphic pictures of the Dust Bowl, which might serve as illustrations to Steinbeck's *Grapes of Wrath.*

That art should have roots in native soil and should reflect the homely concerns of people is obvious enough to those familiar with Dutch or French painting, but persistent colonialism and rich but artistically illiterate patronage long combined to delay the recognition of these truths in the United States. The emergence from colonialism, inaugurated by Homer and Eakins, was complete by the thirties, and the New Deal provided new and more democratic patronage. The Federal Arts project, inaugurated in 1933, employed hundreds of artists to decorate public buildings, circulate art exhibits, teach art appreciation, and compile the vast and splendid record of American folk art. It proceeded 'on the principle that it is not the solitary genius but a sound general movement which maintains art as a vital, functioning part of any cultural scheme,' and is significant not only for what it accomplished but as the first genuine recognition of the fact that artists could make a contribution to society and that society, in turn, had a responsibility to art.

The Federal Arts project subsidized music as well as painting, and if the results were less impressive, the explanation was to be found in the immaturity of American music rather than in any want of

22 *An American Artist's Story,* p. 292.

zeal. For, with the notable exceptions of folk music and Negro spirituals, America had always imported her music and her musicians, and the most determined efforts to cultivate here a 'native' music had failed. Writing a century ago, the editor of the *Musical Journal* urged that 'no fine art can flourish at second hand. We believe it must be rendered national, and in the case of music, be presented through the language the people understand. . . We believe further that Europe cannot supply this country habitually with singers. Whatever may be the first and absorbing use to which the opera house may be put, it should be obliged to produce original works.' As far as 'singers' were concerned, the situation was remedied soon enough: the United States produced its own crop of nightingales. But the demand for original works was fulfilled only quantitatively. Ambitious compositions were produced by John Knowles Paine, George Chadwick, Arthur Foote, and Horatio Parker; Edward MacDowell's sonatas and concertos were applauded on two continents. But most of the music of this generation now seems second-rate and derivative.

More vitality and more native quality appeared in the new generation of composers that came to maturity after World War I — John Powell, Virgil Thomson, John Alden Carpenter, Roy Harris, Aaron Copland, Jerome Kern, and George Gershwin. Powell, Harris, and Gershwin exploited the resources of folk music and Negro spirituals, while Carpenter and Copland, influenced by such modernists as Stravinsky and Schönberg, were interested in exploring the symphonic possibilities of jazz or in translating into music the nervous and explosive character of our mechanical civilization. Many of these experiments were interesting sociologically rather than musically, but Harris' *American Overture,* Schelling's *Victory Ball,* Kern's *Show Boat* and Gershwin's *Rhapsody in Blue* and *Porgy and Bess* are nominated for permanence.

The American genius was not best revealed in music in the classical forms — sonata, quartette, symphony, opera. It was rather in folk melodies and their modern equivalents, ragtime, jazz, blues, and swing, that the authentic native note was sounded. The wealth of Negro folk music was first exploited by the greatest of American composers, Stephen Foster, and his melodious compositions remain our most widely loved songs. Blues and jazz, too, are heavily indebted to the Negroes, and the Jubilee Singers of their own university, Fisk, were the first American choir to be well received in Europe. Potentially more important is the wealth of folk music only now being discovered and exploited. Lumberjacks, miners, cowboys, sailors, Appalachian mountaineers, canal boys, all had their own body of songs, while each of our wars has produced a reputable crop of patriotic songs and the crisis of the thirties gave us Earl Robinson's stirring 'Ballad for Americans.' Whether all this is 'good' music or not must be left to those who use the adjective so glibly; certainly it is native music and, so far, the best we have to offer.

What we have lacked in music of our own has been made up for in appreciation of the music of others. The tradition of appreciation was an old one, and throughout the nineteenth century American audiences had given enthusiastic welcome to European artists and had listened appreciatively to classical concerts. Early in the nineteenth century, Lowell Mason introduced singing into the public schools, but it was not until World War I that music became a normal part of the curriculum of every school, and it was in 1911 that the Harvard Glee Club set a new fashion for collegiate singing, choosing the most difficult compositions of Bach and Palestrina rather than the sentimental college songs of earlier generations.

The new generation of boys and girls revealed an affection for and a ready mastery of such instruments as the saxophone, the trombone, the clarinet, astonishing to those who recalled their own resistance to the violin and the piano. The radio enabled the whole nation to enjoy symphonies and operas, and even chamber music found appreciative audiences. Supplementing the fifty million radios were some four million phonographs, and during the thirties and forties the sales of phonograph records reached fabulous heights. Few cities were so benighted as to lack a symphony orchestra — no less than eighty-four new ones were established in the depression decade — and if the nation could support few opera companies, that was rather a comment on the decline of the leisure-class tradition than an indictment of musical taste. Particularly encouraging was the growing support to native talent, while the totalitarian terror recruited to our shores some of the most disinguished of contemporary European composers — Stravinsky, Hindemith, Bartók, Schönberg, to mention only a few. Musical conservatories like the Juilliard, Eastman, and Curtis flourished, and great foundations like the Guggenheim stood ready to give such patronage to budding genius as Mozart and Schubert never knew.

5. *Science, Natural and Social*

Possibly American civilization during these years will be judged neither by material achievements nor by arts and letters, but rather by contributions to knowledge. Certainly these contributions affected more men and women, and affected them more immediately, than did any in the field of the arts. And it is suggestive that while the Nobel Prize in literature has gone to Americans only four times (Sinclair Lewis, Eugene O'Neill, Pearl Buck, T. S. Eliot), eight Americans have received the prize in physics, six in medicine, and three in chemistry.[23]

Science, to be sure, was put to the service of business and industry, but nowhere has pure science and research been more generously encouraged or more liberally supported than in the United States, by the great universities and by industry itself. The United States greatly benefited from the migration of European scientists, as well as other intellectuals, which set in with the advent of Hitler to power in 1933; Einstein was merely the most famous of hundreds of physicists, chemists, and physicians who found in America refuge from oppression and opportunities to continue their researches.

It is well to remember, in this connection, that science and medicine are not national but international, and that the intellectual and spiritual interdependence of the modern world is nowhere more self-evident than in the realm of science. As Mr. Raymond Fosdick has recently reminded us:

> In peace as in war we are all of us the beneficiaries of contributions to knowledge made by every nation in the world. Our children are guarded from diptheria by what a Japanese and a German did; they are protected from smallpox by an Englishman's work; they are saved from rabies because of a Frenchman; they are cured of pellagra through the researches of an Austrian. From birth to death they are surrounded by an invisible host — the spirits of men who never thought in terms of flags or boundary lines and who never served a lesser loyalty than the welfare of mankind.[24]

The most striking advances were doubtless in the fields of astronomy and of physics. Working with the giant telescope of Mt. Wilson observatory which enabled them to plot thousands of new galaxies,

[23] The Nobel prizes in physics went to A. A. Michelson, R. A. Millikan, Arthur Compton, Carl D. Anderson, Clinton J. Davison, E. O. Lawrence, Isidor Rabi, and Percy Bridgman; in medicine to Alexis Carrel, Karl Landsteiner, Thomas H. Morgan, G. R. Minot, W. P. Murphy, and G. H. Whipple; in chemistry to T. W. Richards, Irving Langmuir, and H. C. Urey.

[24] *The Rockefeller Foundation, a Review for 1941,* p. 11.

astronomers postulated an expanding universe. Physicists, meantime, invented the cyclotron to break down the composition of the atom and rearrange its elements, and held out the hope that we might obtain from some of these elements — uranium, for example — fabulous new sources of energy that would end dependence on fuel. Yet, able as they were to chart a new universe of infinite vastness or to penetrate to the secret of the atom, the new generation of scientists held out no assurance of ultimate understanding of the laws that governed the universe or even that there were any laws. Under the impact of the new science ancient certainties faded, and with them the illusions that the cosmos was governed by laws that man could comprehend. According to Professor Percy W. Bridgman:

> The physicist finds himself in a world from which the bottom has dropped clean out; as he penetrates deeper and deeper it eludes him and fades away by the highly unsportsmanlike device of just becoming meaningless. No refinement of measurement will avail to carry him beyond the portals of this shadowy domain which he cannot even mention without logical inconsistency. A bound is thus forever set to the curiosity of the physicist. What is more, the mere existence of this bound means that he must give up his most cherished convictions and faith. The world is not a world of reason, understandable by the intellect of man, but as we penetrate ever deeper, the very law of cause and effect, which we had thought to be a formula to which we could force God Himself to subscribe, ceases to have any meaning. The world is not intrinsically reasonable or understandable; it acquires these properties in ever-increasing degree as we ascend from the realm of the very little to the realm of everyday things; here we may eventually hope for an understanding sufficiently good for all practical purposes.[25]

The average man lived 'in the realm of everyday things' and these melancholy testaments of science did not seriously disturb him, nor did they exercise any conspicuous effect in upsetting traditional faiths, religious or philosophical. To the average man, indeed, science meant applied science, and here it continued to substantiate the notion of progress. It meant a host of inventions and techniques that contributed enormously to his convenience and his physical well-being. It meant electrical refrigeration, air conditioning, fluorescent lighting, television, frequency modulation, microfilming, the use of glass and of plastics for a thousand new purposes, the development of synthetic rubber, of new methods of cracking oil, of soil-less agriculture, the construction of bigger bombers and

[25] "The New Version of Science," *Harper's Magazine*, March 1929, p. 450.

of more accurate bomb-sights. Above all, it meant progress in the realm of medicine and public health. Throughout this generation doctors and chemists, bacteriologists and physicists, working in the laboratories of universities, the Federal Government, or the great foundations, waged war against diseases that had baffled medical science for centuries. The results were little less than spectacular. In the first third of the century, infant mortality declined in the United States by two-thirds and life expectancy increased from forty-nine to fifty-nine years. The death rate for tuberculosis dropped from 180 to 49 per 100,000, for typhoid from 36 to 2, for diphtheria from 43 to 2, for measles from 12 to 1, while pneumonia fatalities decreased from 158 to 50 and were still going down rapidly; sulfa drugs and, later, penicillin almost ended them. Yellow fever and smallpox were practically wiped out, and the war on malaria, pellagra, hookworm, and similar diseases was brilliantly successful.

A new study of the role of the glandular system led to the discovery of specifics against endocrine disorders. Within a few years insulin had cut the death rate of diabetes from over 700 to 12 per 1000 cases. Pernicious anemia, long regarded as fatal, yielded readily to the use of liver and liver extracts. Adrenalin proved wonderfully helpful in cardiac disorders and gave relief to sufferers from asthma. Tannic acid was found to work miraculous cures on apparently fatal burns. In the study of anesthesia, too, where Americans had long occupied a distinguished position, the perfection of avertin and cyclopropane made possible new miracles of surgery. Chemistry opened the way to an appreciation of the role of vitamins in maintaining health and building up resistance to diseases; numerous ailments like pellagra, rickets, and tooth decay yielded to vitamin treatment, and the discovery led to very general dietary reforms, as well as to considerable proprietary quackery.

Indubitably the most sensational development in the field of medicine was the successful fight against coccus infections. In 1935 the German Dr. Domagk announced that prontosil was effective in arresting streptococcal infection. At the Pasteur Institute in Paris, prontosil was broken down and sulfanilamide isolated as the effective ingredient. English and American doctors promptly experimented with sulfanilamide and its numerous derivatives and found that it could be used with spectacular success against a host of coccal infections — streptococcus, meningitis, gonorrhoea, gangrene, bacillar dysentery, undulant fever, pyelitis, and, above all, pneumonia.

These immense advances in medical science put better health

within the reach of all, yet the general health condition of the American people was not a matter for complacency. Infant mortality was still higher than in such countries as Norway and Sweden, draft statistics revealed that a substantial proportion of American men suffered from poor eyesight and bad teeth and that the incidence of venereal disease was still distressingly high, while surveys discovered many counties, especially in the rural regions, without adequate hospitals. Investigations proved a clear correlation between health and income and suggested the desirability of government support to a public-health program comparable to that given public education.

The answer to this paradox is that the social sciences had not kept pace with the physical sciences. The deductive method, to be sure, was abandoned in favor of the inductive, but the greater the accumulation of data the greater appeared the reluctance to interpret it, and many inquiries not only began but ended with description. The study of government was called 'political science' but few students were bold enough to claim for it more than an effort to apply the scientific method; and while scholars knew more about the mechanics of administration than ever before, they knew less about the State and its role in history. Sociologists like A. G. Keller published monumental studies of the *Science of Society* but no one was deceived by the title, and the most significant contributions in this field were case studies like the Lynds' *Middletown*. No major American historian since Henry Adams had dared formulate a law of history; Adams' experiment was not one to inspire a repetition of the effort. The 'laws' which jurists invoked were not laws in the scientific meaning of the term. Philosophers were not agreed on the nature of being or of knowing, and though they were zealous in criticism and history, neither Dewey nor Santayana appeared to have any successors among them. In none of the social sciences was confusion more notorious than in economics. Economists, indeed, were divided into schools which warred over every issue of importance: the nature of money, the function of credit, the social value of spending and of saving, the relation of technological changes to employment, the causes of prosperity and of depression. So acute were these differences that a humorist observed, 'If you laid all the economists in the world end to end they wouldn't reach a conclusion.' The judgment was perhaps over-harsh; yet few economists were able to diagnose the ailments from which American economy was suffering throughout the post-war years, and the problems of the depression and of the New Deal found most of them as bewildered as the common folk.

XXIV

THE NEW DEAL

1. *The Election of 1932*

THE Republican program for liquidating the depression came too late for political purposes as for economic results; every indication pointed to a Democratic victory in 1932. This prospect dampened Republican zeal; Hoover's renomination was neither contested nor greeted with enthusiasm, and the platform was ambiguous and evasive. A very different situation obtained in the Democratic camp where competition for the nomination was sharp. Alfred E. Smith's large popular vote in the previous election justified him in believing that he might now overcome the handicaps that had then thwarted him, and lead his party to victory. Others regarded the anti-Catholic prejudice as insuperable and called for new leadership. By far the most prominent of the several aspirants was Franklin Delano Roosevelt.

A distant connection of the famous 'T.R.,' and married to the former President's niece, Franklin D. Roosevelt had more than the magic of his name to commend him. Born to wealth and position, educated at Groton School, Harvard University, and the Columbia Law School, his interest in public affairs dictated a political career and his money enabled him to forego private practice and enter the political arena. Like all the Roosevelts except the Oyster Bay branch, he was born a Democrat. At the age of twenty-nine he was elected state senator from the 'silk-stocking' Dutchess County district, where he had inherited a country estate, and promptly distinguished himself by a successful fight against the election of boss Murphy's candidate to the United States Senate. After supporting Wilson in 1912, he was appointed Assistant Secretary of the Navy, an office in which he proved to be versatile and efficient. Contact with Wilson served to deepen Roosevelt's liberal convictions, companionship with Bryan and Daniels broadened his democratic sympathies, while acquaintance with party leaders taught him the political ropes. In 1920 he was nominated as Cox's running mate; the following year his promising political career was apparently ended by a severe case of infantile paralysis. During the next seven years, while he stubbornly fought his way back to health, he used his enforced retirement for study, thought, and correspondence; his convictions were deepened and his character strengthened. He returned to politics in 1928, rugged in health, rejuvenated in spirit, better known in the party than before, and one of the best-informed men in the country on a wide range of subjects.

Governor Smith persuaded Roosevelt to re-enter politics. The friendship between the 'happy warrior' from the sidewalks of New York and the gentleman-democrat of Hyde Park had begun early; Roosevelt had nominated Smith for the Presidency twice. New York was a critical state and Smith was convinced that Roosevelt's candidacy for the governorship would materially strengthen the national ticket. It did; in 1928, the voters of New York elected Roosevelt governor when they rejected Smith for President. Two years later Governor Roosevelt was re-elected by a majority of seven hundred thousand and thus became the leading contender for the next Presidential nomination. Smith, embittered, broke with his former friend; but the drift toward Roosevelt was irresistible, and when the Convention met he was nominated on the fourth ballot.

The Democratic platform, in contrast to the Republican, was clear-cut and brief. It promised unemployment relief, labor legislation, and the 'restoration of agriculture'; the conservation and development of power resources in the public interest; federal regulation of holding companies, securities exchanges, and utility rates; reciprocal trade agreements and other efforts to secure world peace; a balanced budget and a sound currency; and a prompt repeal of the Eighteenth Amendment. The 'continuous responsibility of government for human welfare' was held up as a guiding principle.

Roosevelt, who before his nomination had seemed to many people merely an amiable gentleman with philanthropic impulses and political ambitions, electrified the country by the boldness of his campaign. The radio had made possible a new type of campaign, but Roosevelt, partly to prove his physical vigor, partly to capitalize his personal magnetism, chose to embark upon an old-fashioned stump-speaking tour which took him into almost every state of the Union. He set forth a comprehensive scheme of reform and recovery, embracing the repeal of prohibition, unemployment relief, government operation of Muscle Shoals, lower tariffs, and legislation to save agriculture, rehabilitate the railroads, protect consumers and investors, and slash government expenses. The keynote was a 'new deal' to the 'forgotten man.'

President Hoover, laboring under the dead-weight of hard times, could only recite his efforts to cope with the depression, prophesy that a Democratic victory would mean that 'the grass will grow in the streets of a hundred cities, a thousand towns,' and reaffirm his faith in rugged individualism and the American system. In his last speech of the campaign he set forth eloquently his conception of the choice before the people:

It is a contest between two philosophies of government. . . . Our opponents . . . are proposing changes and so-called new deals which would destroy the very foundations of our American system. . . . You cannot extend the mastery of government over the daily life of a people without somewhere making it master of people's souls and thoughts.

Too many voters feared that the foundations of the American system were already being destroyed by attrition to take seriously this impassioned warning. On election day Roosevelt received almost twenty-three million, Hoover a little less than sixteen million votes. Roosevelt's victory in the electoral college was even more decisive, for he carried every state but six, four of them in New England. Democratic control of both houses of Congress was complete. No President or party ever came into power with a clearer popular mandate to carry out a program.

2. *The Philosophy of the New Deal*

When Roosevelt took the oath of office the depression had reached its lowest level and most dramatic stage. The heroic efforts of the R.F.C. had been insufficient to avert a banking crisis; by March 1933 two-thirds of the banks of the country had been closed by official proclamation, and the shock of this financial disaster was being felt throughout American economy. The new President made no effort to minimize the danger. He said, in his Inaugural Address:

Values have shrunk to fantastic levels; taxes have risen; our ability to pay has fallen; government of all kinds is faced by serious curtailment of income; the means of exchange are frozen in the currents of trade; the withered leaves of industrial enterprise lie on every side; farmers find no markets for their produce; the savings of many years in thousands of families are gone. More important, a host of unemployed citizens face the grim problem of existence and an equally great number toil with little return. Only a foolish optimist can deny the dark realities of the moment.

CONGRESS SINCE 1928

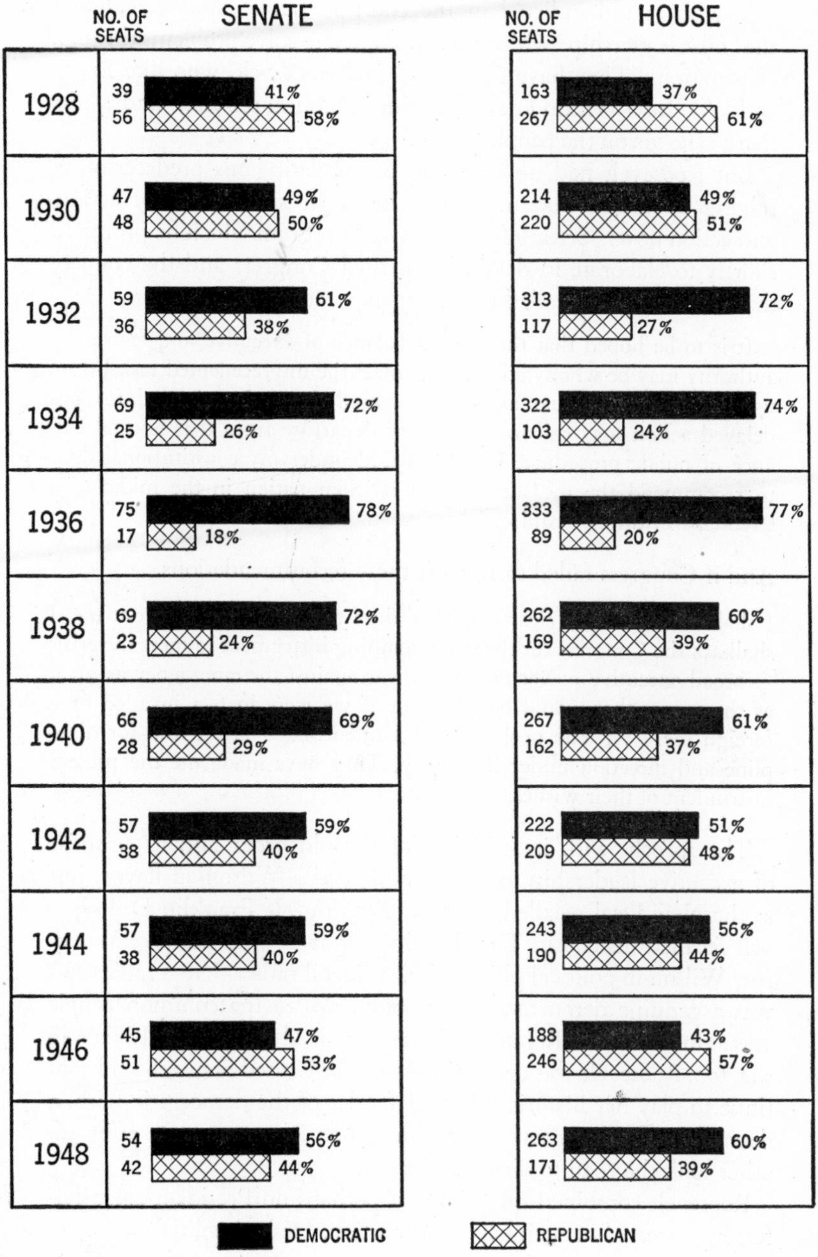

There followed an excoriation of the 'unscrupulous money changers' who 'stand indicted in the court of public opinion,' and of the 'false leadership' which had attempted to solve problems through exhortation. 'They have no vision,' said Roosevelt, who like Bryan and Woodrow Wilson knew the value of biblical phrases, 'and where there is no vision the people perish.'

But Roosevelt had no intention of emulating his predecessor in relying upon exhortation. 'This nation,' he said, 'asks for action, and action now!' Setting forth a general program which he promised shortly to elaborate in detail, he warned Congress and the country that the emergency called for emergency measures.

> It is to be hoped that the normal balance of executive and legislative authority may be wholly adequate to meet the unprecedented task before us. But it may be that an unprecedented demand and need for undelayed action may call for temporary departure from that normal balance of public procedure. I am prepared under my constitutional duty to recommend the measures that a stricken nation in the midst of a stricken world may require.

And if Congress failed to support these recommendations,

> I shall not evade the clear course of duty that will then confront me. I shall ask the Congress for the one remaining instrument to meet the crisis — broad executive power to wage a war against the emergency as great as the power that would be given me if we were in fact invaded by a foreign foe. . . . The people of the United States have asked for discipline and direction under leadership. They have made me the present instrument of their wishes.

The speech, with its criticism of the old order and its promise of executive leadership toward a new, had a Wilsonian flavor, just as the New Deal recalled the New Freedom. If Franklin D. Roosevelt recalled his cousin Theodore in personality, he was like Woodrow Wilson in political philosophy. A liberal rather than a radical, he was a genuine democrat, whose confidence in the common people was as instinctive as Bryan's and as rationalized as Wilson's. Like Wilson, too, Roosevelt was determined that the United States should continue to play her historic role as defender of the democratic faith, a determination that grew upon him as one European state after another took the road to dictatorship.

Roosevelt combined qualities that perhaps no President since Jefferson possessed in such happy proportion. He had political acumen, the ability to work through established political machinery and to champion reform without antagonizing party bosses. He had personal charm equally effective in social intercourse, in public appearances, and over the radio. Himself something of a scholar, he did not distrust scholarship in politics and was able to command the services of an enthusiastic and loyal group of experts to furnish ideas, formulate legislation, and implement policies. With shrewdness he combined audacity and courage; tenacious of ultimate ends, he was opportunist as to means and preferred compromise to strife. He knew how to dramatize himself and his policies and how to create a favorable climate of opinion in which to work, and he inspired loyalty to his ideas as well as to his person.

Those ideas, as they were unfolded to a bewildered nation, were a consummation of platform and campaign promises. Conservatives had not yet forgiven Wilson for taking his platform seriously, and the spectacle of another Democrat repeating the same process aroused widespread dismay. Yet the mass of the common people agreed that the desperate emergency justified radical measures. They felt that the Federal Government had been given back to them. Within a year Congress, under the relentless leadership of the President, had enacted a far-reaching program of social and economic legislation; at the end of four years that program had assumed the outlines of a revolution.

And yet the legislation of the first Roosevelt administration did not constitute a revolution. The popular name, New Deal, is more correct. Now that party passions have subsided it should be obvious that the Roosevelt philosophy was deeply rooted in the American tradition and the Roosevelt methods modeled on American precedents. The New Deal seemed revolutionary not because it introduced fundamental changes into American politics or economy, but because it was carried through with such breathless speed. Speed was imperative because of both the emergency situation and the legislative lag which dated from the period of World War I. The abandonment of laissez-faire and the development of social control, which had gone on steadily in both state and national politics from the middle eighties to the Wilson administration, had been interrupted by the World War and stalled by the post-war reaction. The twelve years of 'normalcy' had in truth been years of reaction, and this reaction distrusted panaceas, rejected government intervention in business, and refrained from tampering with the existing system or even questioning its ultimate validity.

The legislation of the Roosevelt administration, then, was an attempt to catch up with the political lag of well-nigh twenty years and to articulate government to the facts of a depressed economy. Three bodies of precedents illuminated the course of the new deal: the federal regulation of business and railroads dating back to the 1880's; the social legislation of more progressive states such as Massachusetts, New York, Wisconsin, Oregon, and Kansas; and the organization of American industry and business which had long accepted such practices as price-fixing agreements, codes and cartels, and the regimentation of labor in company-owned towns and company unions.

In so far, then, as the new deal was directed toward an extension of government control over national economy, it was in the progressive tradition; in so far as it was directed toward improving the welfare of the common man, it was in the democratic tradition. Yet, as with all hastily-prepared emergency legislation, much of it did not achieve the end for which it was designed. Taken as a whole, the new deal legislation contributed greatly to both recovery and reform, improved the status of the farmer and the laborer, prepared the way for a more equitable distribution of wealth, brought business, banking, securities, utilities, and transportation under more effective regulation, and, most important of all, helped to salvage the natural resources of the nation. At the same time it interfered seriously with the freedom of business enterprise, inaugurated far-reaching controls over labor and farming, encouraged the growth of bureaucracy, created administrative confusion, and pointed the way to administrative reforms, stimulated the fear of dictatorship and of class antagonisms, greatly increased the national debt, and at some points conflicted with the Constitution. However the historian may wish to strike the balance between credits and debits, three things are clear: the new deal, in one form or another, was inevitable; it was directed toward preserving capitalistic economy rather than substituting another system; and the methods employed were in the American tradition. Comparisons with European dictatorships are in order, yet misleading, for American democracy has always accomplished its purposes through powerful leaders such as Jefferson, Jackson, Lincoln, and the Roosevelts, and at no time in the past has power been exercised in a manner to menace the

American constitutional system. The logic of the new deal, indeed, and of Roosevelt's leadership, was suggested over a century earlier by William Ellery Channing:

There are seasons, in human affairs, of inward and outward revolution, when new depths seem to be broken up in the soul, when new wants are unfolded in multitudes, and a new and undefined good is thirsted for. There are periods when the principles of experience need to be modified, when hope and trust and instinct claim a share with prudence in the guidance of affairs, when, in truth, *to dare* is the highest wisdom.[2]

3. *Money, Banking, and Securities Legislation*

Roosevelt's first act upon assuming office was to decree a national bank holiday and place an embargo upon the export of gold and silver. Congress met in special session on 9 March 1933, and there followed with breath-taking rapidity a series of banking, financial, and revenue measures that went far to fulfill the Presidential promise of 'strict supervision of all banking and credits and investments . . . and an end to speculation with other people's money.' An Emergency Banking Law of 9 March provided for the early termination of the bank holiday, facilitated the reopening of liquid banks under proper regulation, created a bank conservator to supervise the operations of banks not prepared to resume business, permitted National Banks to issue preferred stock which might be purchased by the Reconstruction Finance Corporation, and liberalize the powers of the Federal Reserve Banks with respect to the issue of bank notes. The following day Congress listened to a Presidential message proposing drastic economies in administrative expenses and veterans' payments. Too disconcerted to offer serious objections, Congress granted authority to slash department budgets twenty-five per cent, cut federal salaries up to fifteen per cent, and reduce pension and benefit payments. These economies were effected, but within a short time Congress recovered sufficiently from its lapse to restore salary cuts, put practically all veterans back on the pension rolls and, eventually, vote a veterans' bonus; the economy measure, therefore, has a mere antiquarian interest.

It was clear, too, that with Great Britain and many other European nations off the gold standard, the United States could no longer afford to maintain it. On 5 April the President exercised his authority

[2] *The Complete Works of William Ellery Channing*, p. 459.

to forbid the hoarding of gold and gold certificates, and two weeks later the nation formally abandoned gold. A Joint Resolution of 5 June, designed to avoid the difficulties which had attended Civil War legal tender, cancelled the gold clauses in all government and private obligations and made all debts payable in legal tender. The validity of this repudiation of gold contracts was challenged in the courts. A long series of precedents gave the Court no choice but to sustain Congressional power over legal tender, and though it held that the cancellation of the gold clauses in government contracts was both illegal and immoral it added that the plaintiff had suffered no damages and had no ground for suit. The chief object of new deal financial legislation, however, was to raise commodity prices, and it was in this direction that the administration now moved. Late in April the President asked for authority to pursue a policy of inflation, and this was granted him in the Farm Relief and Inflation Act of 12 May. Under its terms the President might, at his discretion, inflate the currency by the addition of $3,000,000,000 of new treasury notes, or reduce the gold content of the dollar up to 50 per cent. Before exercising either alternative the President awaited the results of the London Economic Conference. Upon the failure of that Conference — a failure due largely to his refusal to consider international stabilization — he experimented with a 'managed currency.' His object was 'to establish and maintain a dollar which will not change its purchasing and debt-paying power.' This effort to establish a dollar which would have a fixed and constant relation to commodity prices and which would stay put had its champions among contemporary economists; but its real inspiration came from the spirits of James B. Weaver and William Jennings Bryan.

Currency manipulation did not effect any appreciable increase in commodity prices, and in January 1934 the President, 'to make possible the payment of public and private debts at more nearly the price level at which they had been incurred,' asked and obtained authority to devaluate the dollar, impound all gold in the Treasury and the Federal Reserve Banks, and create out of the accruing profit a stabilization fund of $2,000,000,000. He fixed the value of the dollar at 59.06, and the nation returned to this modified gold standard. Friends of the administration credited improvement of commodity prices to this dollar devaluation; critics averred that improvement would have come in any event, and that devaluation worked unwarranted hardship upon security holders. None could deny, however, that the administration's goal of con-

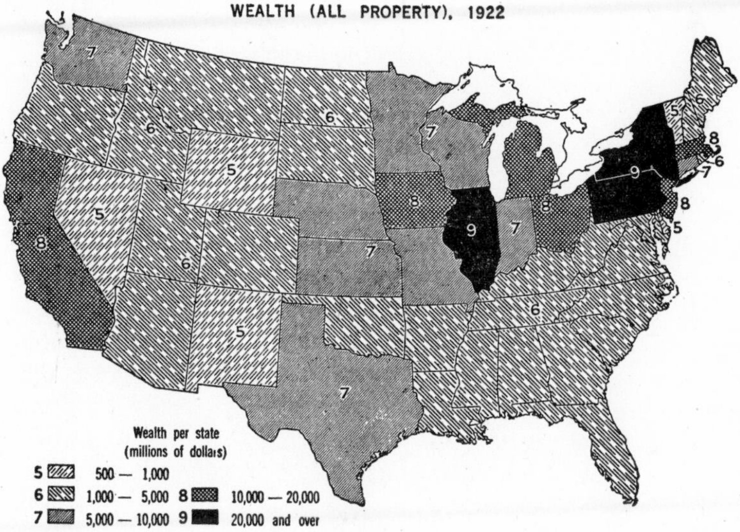

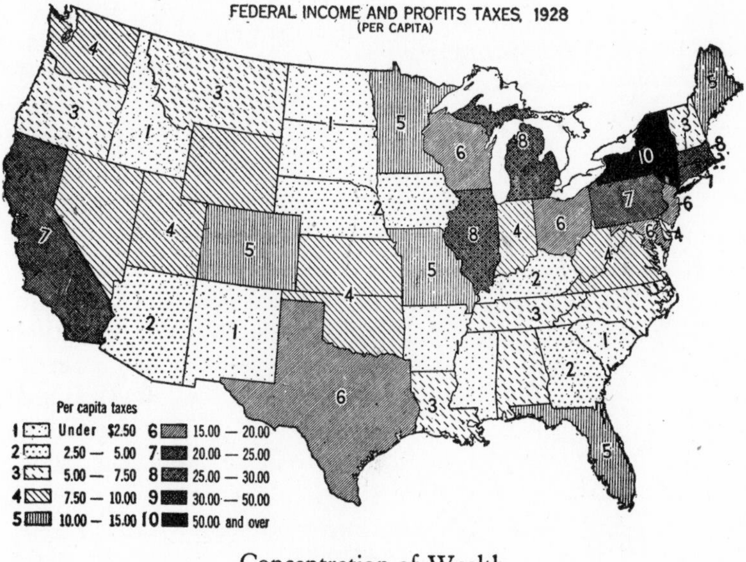

Concentration of Wealth

From Charles O. Paullin, Atlas of the Historical Geography of the United States. *Plates* 153C, 155D

trolled inflation had been carried through with utmost caution or that the dangers of printing-press money had been skilfully avoided.

In line with this inflationary policy was the effort to establish more generous credit facilities. High interest rates and frozen credit had forced an alarming number of foreclosures on both rural and urban properties, involving staggering losses to both owners and investors. In order to reverse this process, the Reconstruction Finance Corporation was allotted additional funds to place at the disposal of business, industry, and agriculture. A new Federal Farm Credit Administration made possible the refunding of farm loans at drastically lower rates of interest and provided money for new mortgages. In June 1933 Congress established a Home Owners' Loan Corporation to refinance small mortgages on privately owned homes; within a year this corporation had approved over 300,000 loans amounting to almost one billion dollars. Subsequent legislation to ameliorate municipal and farm bankruptcies was voided by the Supreme Court,[3] but a corporation bankruptcy act stood the test of constitutionality.

Reform rather than recovery was the object of the banking and securities exchange legislation of the Roosevelt administration. The demand for banking reform went back to the decade of the twenties, but it was the Congressional investigations of banking and securities practices under the skilful direction of Ferdinand Pecora which revealed conditions characterized as 'scandalous,' and the banking collapse of 1932-33 which dramatized the need and furnished the opportunity for reform. The result was the Glass-Steagall Banking Act of 16 June 1933. This measure, the most important since the Federal Reserve Act of 1913, provided for the separation of commercial and investment banking, severe restrictions upon the use of bank credit for speculative purposes, the expansion of the Federal Reserve system to embrace banks heretofore excluded, and permission to national banks to establish state-wide branch banking. To prevent a recurrence of the epidemic of bank failures in the 1920's, this Act set up a Federal Deposit Insurance Corporation to insure bank deposits up to a fixed sum; from the point of view of the average citizen this federal guarantee of deposits was by far the most striking feature of the new banking bill.

In accordance with platform and campaign promises the administration attempted a thorough-going reform of the whole security and investment business. In his message to Congress, the President

[3] Louisville *v.* Radford, 295 U.S. 555.

observed that 'there is an obligation upon us to insist that every issue of new securities . . . shall be accompanied by full publicity and information, and that no essentially important element attending the issue shall be concealed from the buying public. . . . This . . . should be followed by legislation relating to the better supervision of the purchase and sale of all property dealt in on exchanges, and by legislation to correct unethical and unsafe practices on the part of officers and directors of banks and other corporations.' Legislation designed to secure these ends, and modelled closely upon the British Companies Act and Directors' Liability Act, which had stood the test of long experience, was formulated by Professor Felix Frankfurter of the Harvard Law School and passed, as the Truth in Securities Act, 27 May 1933. It provided that all new securities offered or advertised for interstate sale should be registered before the Federal Trade Commission — subsequently the Securities and Exchange Commission; that every offering should contain full information to enable the prospective purchaser to judge the value of the issue and the condition of the corporation; and that the directors and officers of the corporation were to be criminally liable for any deliberate omission of significant information or any wilful misstatement of fact.

The following year came legislation to curb malpractices on the stock exchange which the stock exchange itself either could not or would not end. An act of 6 June 1934 created a Securities and Exchange Commission, licensed stock exchanges and required the registration of all securities in which they dealt, prohibited pools, options, and other devices for manipulating the market, and empowered the Federal Reserve Board to determine the extension of credit for marginal and speculative loans. Subsequent legislation extended and greatly enlarged the authority of the Securities Commission over public utilities companies.

4. *Farm Relief*

The efforts of the Hoover administration to alleviate farm distress had been unsuccessful, and 1932, as we have seen, marked the nadir of the agricultural depression. Prompt and drastic remedial action was necessary if the collapse were not to turn into catastrophe, and both Congress and the President were eager to take such action. With the assistance of advisers long familiar with the farm problem — Secretary Wallace, George Peek, and Mordecai Ezekiel — Roosevelt prepared a farm relief plan of unexpected boldness and, urging that 'an unprecedented condition calls for the trial of new means to rescue agriculture,' invited Congress to enter 'a new and untrod path.' Congress responded to the invitation and on 12 May the Agricultural Adjustment Act became law. This Act, the first of a series which involved the reconstruction of American economy, was intended to re-establish equality between agriculture and industry by raising the level of agricultural commodity prices and easing the credit and mortgage load. Its most interesting provisions authorized the Secretary of Agriculture to make agreements with farmers whereby, in return for government subsidies, they undertook to reduce production of certain staple commodities. The original act contemplated reduction of cotton, wheat, corn, hogs, rice, tobacco, and milk; subsequent amendments extended the provisions of the Act to rice, flax, barley, peanuts, grain sorghums, sugar, and beef cattle. Reductions were to be effected by renting to the government land taken out of cultivation or by benefit payments on restricted allotments grown. The costs of these payments were to be met from taxes on the processing of the products involved.

It was expected that this plan would not only bring cash payments but would raise the entire price level of agricultural commodities, and in this expectation farmers hastened to avail themselves of its benefits. Almost three-fourths of the cotton-growers agreed to reduce their acreage by approximately one-third in return for cash payments of from seven to twenty dollars an acre or an option on the purchase of some of the cotton held by the government. Altogether, in 1933, slightly over ten million acres of land were taken out of production, thus reducing the cotton crop by at least four million bales. For this reduction planters received from the government some two hundred million dollars in benefit payments. In addition the price of cotton rose from five and one-half to nine and one-half cents a pound. The total cash income of the cotton farmers for 1933 was thus more than double the income of the previous year.[4] Subsequent arrangements, in 1934 and 1935, buttressed by the Bankhead Cotton Control Act of April 1934, held the cotton crop down to about ten million bales, continued generous

[4] It must be remembered, in connection with these and subsequent figures, that the devaluation of the dollar by forty per cent as well as the general improvement in business conditions would normally have increased the price of cotton, even without the contributions of the A.A.A.

benefit payments to planters, and maintained the price at ten cents a pound or better.

The program for the reduction of wheat acreage was equally successful. Contracts with over 550,000 wheat farmers removed some eight million acres from production, brought the co-operating wheat growers over one hundred million dollars in benefit payments, and contributed to an increase in the price of wheat and in the total income of wheat growers of approximately one hundred per cent. The drought of 1934 and adverse crop conditions in 1935 necessitated a modification of the crop reduction program, and by the end of this period the government had disposed of surplus stocks held over from the Federal Farm Board operations and the nation was importing wheat. The effort to reduce corn acreage and remove hogs from the market was attended with even greater success. In 1933 over one million corn and hog producers signed contracts with the A.A.A. to reduce acreage by approximately twenty-five per cent; at the same time the government purchased and slaughtered for relief or other purposes some six million pigs and hogs. The result was the smallest corn crop since 1881, generous benefit payments totalling over three hundred million dollars, and substantially higher prices for corn and pork. The reduction of the tobacco crop was spectacularly successful — from the farmers' point of view. Over ninety-five per cent of Southern farmers entered into agreements to cut tobacco production by almost one-third. Southern tobacco-growers who had received $56,000,000 for their 1930 and $43,000,000 for their 1933 crop, got $120,000,000 for their 1934 crop. Comparable results were attained in other less important farm commodities. In part because of the A.A.A. program of crop reduction, in part because of drought and government payments, and in part because of the devaluation of the dollar, the national farm income increased from $5,562,000,000 in 1932 to $8,688,000,000 in 1935.

On 6 January 1936, the Supreme Court invalidated the A.A.A. as an improper exercise of the taxing power and an invasion of the reserved rights of states.[5] 'This is coercion by economic pressure,' said Justice Roberts, who conjured up the terrifying consequences that would flow from the taxation of one part of the community for the benefit of another.

The expressions of the framers of the Constitution, the decisions of this court interpreting that instrument, and the writings of great com-

[5] U.S. *v.* Butler, *et al.*, Receivers of Hoosac Mills Corp., 297 U.S.1.

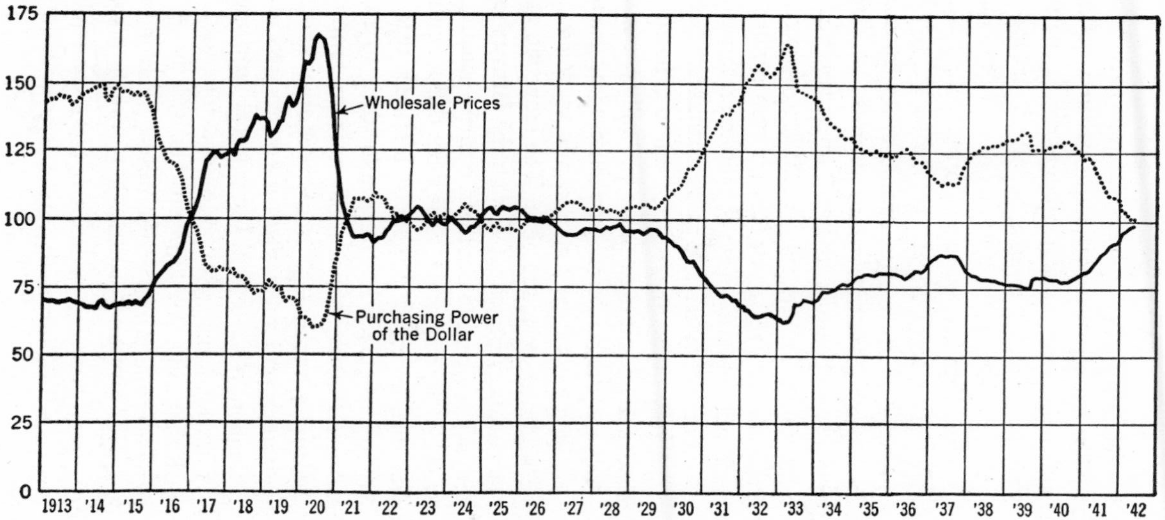

Wholesale Prices and Purchasing Power of the Dollar

Index Number, 1926 = 100

Based on U. S. Bureau of Labor Statistics

mentators will be searched in vain for any suggestion that there exists . . . in the Constitution the authority whereby every provision and every fair implication from that instrument may be subverted, the independence of the individual states obliterated, and the United States converted into a central government exercising uncontrolled police power in every state of the Union, superseding all local control or regulation of the affairs or concerns of the states.

But Justice Stone, in his powerful dissenting opinion, protested that this objection 'hardly rises to the dignity of argument,' pointed out that 'the present levy is held invalid, not for any want of power in Congress to lay such a tax . . . but because the use to which its proceeds are put is disapproved,' warned his colleagues against a 'tortured construction of the Constitution,' and observed, with some asperity, that 'courts are not the only agency of government that must be assumed to have capacity to govern.' Where judges confessed such irreconcilable differences on the meaning of the Constitution, laymen might well be confused.

The philosophy behind the A.A.A. was that of national self-sufficiency. It correctly assumed that the loss of foreign markets was one of the major causes of the agricultural depression, but it entertained little hope that those markets could be permanently recovered. It looked, therefore, rather to the development of a self-sufficient agrarian economy, independent — so far as that was possible — of the vicissitudes of foreign markets. Such a philosophy pre-supposed a 'planned economy.' It required not only a reduction of farm crops but of the number of farmers; it proposed the removal of millions of acres of 'marginal' land from cultivation and the resettlement of 'marginal' farmers on more fertile soil or in small semi-industrial communities; and it demanded that those farmers who were to continue farming be relieved of their burden of mortgage indebtedness and given a new impulse toward independence. Administrative opposition to this philosophy of autarchy and serious doubts as to the expediency of a planned agricultural economy prevented any full-hearted effort to carry this scheme into effect, but some parts of it were given a trial. In 1935 the President set up a Resettlement Administration which, under the guidance of Rexford Tugwell, embarked upon a program of rehabilitation. It removed from cultivation and attempted to improve some ten million acres of marginal land; extended financial aid to some 635,000 farm families, and adjusted farm mortgages to save debtors over twenty-five million dollars; built model farm-houses, suburban developments, and camps for migratory workers; and, through the development of health, education, and recreation services, attempted to make rural life more attractive.

An even more ambitious plan to rehabilitate agriculture was embodied in a Presidential proposal of 1937 to rid the country of the curse of tenant farming. In the five years between 1930 and 1935 the number of tenant farmers had increased by two hundred thousand, and in the latter year forty-two per cent of the farmers of the country were tenants. Efforts to organize the tenant farmers of the South had resulted in disorder and in violent reprisals, but had dramatized to the country a situation which called for prompt remedial measures. Representatives from some Southern states looked askance at federal interference in this new 'peculiar' institution, but it was everywhere admitted that only the national government could institute the necessary reforms.[6] In July 1937 Congress passed a bill providing that the Federal Government subsidize the purchase of farms for tenants on easy terms; it remained to be seen whether the provisions of the bill were sufficiently liberal to make any serious impression upon farm tenancy.

Far more important was legislation affording farm mortgage relief. In the five years from 1927 to 1932 not less than ten per cent of the farm property of the country had been foreclosed at auction; in certain sections of the West these foreclosures had become so numerous that farmers banded together to intimidate prospective purchasers, close courts, and terrorize judges, recalling the scenes of Shays's rebellion a century and a half earlier. The Federal Farm Loan Act of May 1933 authorized the Federal Land Banks to issue bonds up to two billion dollars for the refinancing of farm loans at four per cent interest which was guaranteed by the Federal government; the following year the extension of the government guarantee to both principal and interest permitted a reduction of interest rate to three per cent. Meantime the Reconstruction Finance Corporation organized a Commodity Credit Corporation to lend money directly to farmers. The liberal policies pursued by these agencies brought an end to the epidemic of foreclosures and, together with higher commodity prices, enabled hundreds of thousands of farmers to liquidate their debts.

[6] Ireland furnished an illuminating example of government co-operation to end tenant farming. In 1870, 97% of Irish farmers were tenants; by 1931 the number had been reduced to 2½ per cent.

At the same time Secretary of State Cordell Hull, unsympathetic to the philosophy of national autarchy, was exploring the possibilities of the recapture of foreign markets through reciprocity agreements. 'The United States,' he said, 'is at the cross-roads. Of all the countries in the world, it is in the freest position to assume a world leadership, in the adoption of saner commercial policies.' Under the terms of the Trade Agreements Act of June 1934 Secretary Hull negotiated unconditional most-favored-nation reciprocity treaties with Cuba, Canada, France, Russia, and some twenty other countries. The treaty with Canada was typical: in return for concessions on the importation of Canadian cattle and cheese, Canada granted concessions on American pork products, potatoes, corn, eggs, poultry, fruits, and sundry manufactured articles. The results of this new trade policy were gratifying: within a year trade with Cuba had doubled, and trade with Canada, Sweden, France, and South and Central American countries improved materially. It was the hope of Mr. Hull that the new commercial policy would operate not only for economic improvement at home and abroad but that it would break down nationalist barriers and advance international understanding and peace.

5. *Industry Under the New Deal*

The most spectacular, but by no means the most significant, of New Deal experiments was the effort to rehabilitate and regiment industry for purposes of recovery and reform through the N.R.A. There was nothing essentially new in the regimentation of industry: as Secretary of Commerce, Mr. Hoover had given official encouragement to the formation of codes of fair practices and price-fixing agreements. What was new in the Roosevelt program was the attempt to extend this type of organization to all types of industry, small as well as large, to protect labor and the consumer, and to insist upon effective government supervision of the process.

The National Recovery Act of 16 June 1933 had, like so many of the New Deal measures, the dual purpose of recovery and reform. It was designed to speed up industrial production, spread employment, reduce hours and raise wages, and provide funds for a system of public works and emergency relief; it proposed, at the same time, to eliminate child labor, throw new safeguards about the rights of labor to organize and strike, and reduce the waste of competition without encouraging monopolies.[7] Section 1 of the Act, formulated with an eye on the Supreme Court, declared the existence of 'a national emergency productive of widespread unemployment and disorganization of industry,' and announced the policy of Congress

> to remove obstructions to the free flow of . . . commerce; to provide for the general welfare by promoting the organization of industry for the purpose of cooperative action among trade groups, to induce and maintain united action of labor and management under adequate governmental sanctions and supervision, to eliminate unfair competitive practices, to promote the fullest possible utilization of the present productive capacity of industries, to avoid undue restriction of production, . . . to increase the consumption of industrial and agricultural products by increasing purchasing power, to reduce and relieve unemployment, to improve standards of labor, and otherwise to rehabilitate industry and to conserve natural resources.

To attain these laudable ends the law provided for the organization of industries through the mechanism of codes drawn up by representatives of the industries concerned in conjunction with government administrators, and subject to approval by the President. Monopolies or monopolistic practices were specifically prohibited, but at the same time the operation of the anti-trust laws was suspended during the duration of the Act. Pending the formulation of codes for major industries, the President was authorized to impose upon industry a blanket code. This blanket code, promulgated 27 July, was expected to serve as a model for industrial code-makers; it prohibited child labor, fixed the hours of labor at thirty-six for industrial and forty for clerical workers, established a minimum wage of forty cents an hour, and included the mandatory protection to labor provided for in the famous Section 7(a) of the N.R.A.

In the hot summer months of 1933 thousands of representatives of American industry descended on Washington to discuss, argue, and frame codes. The task was a titanic one and exhausted even the cascading energies of the national administrator, General Hugh Johnson. The problems which government authorities faced were bewildering and complex; codes had to be drawn up for hundreds of industries and businesses, each presenting special technical prob-

[7] 'It is not stretching the point to state categorically that there was not a major industry in the United States in the spring of 1933 that was not suffering either from over-production, or destructive competition, or unfair practices, or complete lack of planning.' President Roosevelt, in *On Our Way*, p.85.

lems. The N.R.A. administrators were familiar only with the general principles of the new program, business men and their legal advisers were familiar with all the details; the inevitable result was that business wrote its own codes of law and that big business imposed its ideas upon small business. Yet out of the welter of conference and debate there emerged a pattern of industrial organization that met most of the requirements laid down by the N.R.A. law and the President's blanket code. The Cotton Textile Code, for example, fixed minimum wages of twelve dollars in the South, thirteen in the North for a forty-hour week, outlawed the labor of children under sixteen years of age, created a Cotton Textile Industry Committee to co-operate with the government in fixing and enforcing rules of trade, and re-enacted the labor provisions of Section 7(a) of the N.R.A. Within a year some five hundred codes had been adopted and some two hundred more were in process of formulation, and it was estimated that over twenty-three million workers were under codes, and that over four million unemployed had been reabsorbed in industry.

The ideal of the new program was industrial self-government, with the N.R.A. as a basic constitution and the codes as laws. It was hoped that self-interest and public opinion would persuade industry to conform to both constitution and laws; in the event of non-conformity the codes could be enforced through a complex system of national, regional, state, and local compliance boards with ultimate recourse to the federal courts. Three features of the N.R.A. presented peculiar difficulties: the labor provisions (Section 7a) created confusion and excited opposition; the suspension of the anti-trust laws strengthened large at the expense of small business and raised prices; and doubts as to the constitutionality of the law encouraged noncompliance. The problem of labor under the N.R.A. will be considered below; the other two may be noted briefly here.

Shortly after the enactment of the N.R.A., President Roosevelt appealed to business to defer price increases until recovery was under way. 'If we now inflate prices as fast and as far as we increase wages, the whole project will be set at naught. We cannot hope for the full effect of this plan unless, in these first critical months, and even at the expense of full initial profits, we defer price increases as long as possible.' But industry was unwilling to defer profits, and for the most part Roosevelt's appeal was disregarded. Even more ominous was the growth of monopoly and the continuance of unfair practices under the N.R.A. codes, proved conclusively by investigations of the Brookings Institute, the Consumers' Advisory Board, the Federal Trade Commission, and, finally, by the so-called Darrow Committee which in July 1934 reported that the codes were controlled by the larger firms and were employed to foster and protect monopoly. Reforms were promptly inaugurated, but were ineffective, and during 1934 and 1935 the N.R.A. was assailed with increasing bitterness from all sides: by large business men who resented government control of their labor relations; by small business men dismayed at the growth of monopoly; by liberals who lamented the suspension of the anti-trust laws; by consumers outraged at price increases; by labor disappointed in the practical results of the codes; and by lawyers who insisted that the whole experiment was unconstitutional.

The N.R.A., then, was breaking down of its own weight when in May 1935 the Supreme Court destroyed it by undermining its legal foundations.[8] The opinion of the court was unanimous, and its decision so sweeping that it left no salvage. The N.R.A., said the Court, involved an illegal delegation of power, for 'Congress cannot delegate legislative power to the President to exercise an unfettered discretion to make whatever laws he thinks may be needed or advisable for the rehabilitation and expansion of trade or industry.' It constituted an improper exercise of the commerce power and an invasion by the Federal Government of the realm reserved to the states, for 'if the commerce clause were construed to reach all enterprises and transactions which could be said to have an indirect effect upon interstate commerce, the federal authority would embrace practically all the activities of the people and the authority of the state over its domestic concerns would exist only by sufferance.' And neither of these palpable violations of the Constitution could be justified on any plea of a 'national emergency,' for the Constitution was designed for emergencies as well as for periods of peace and prosperity.

Thus came to an end a law which President Roosevelt had described as 'the most important and far-reaching ever enacted by the American Congress.' Though many liberals felt that the Schechter decision had saved the administration from embarrassment if not from disaster, Roosevelt himself was reluctant to admit defeat or to abandon an experiment so hopefully inaugurated. The reappearance of destructive industrial competition, the hasty abandonment of

[8] Schechter Poultry Corp. *v.* U.S., 295 U.S.495.

wage and hour standards, the widespread re-employment of child labor, and the judicial nullification of the Guffey Coal Act[9] and the Railroad Retirement Act,[10] created a demand for the substitution of some new form of industrial regulation for the N.R.A. Before the end of his first administration Roosevelt was appealing for new wage and hour legislation, and early in his second administration an emasculated Black-Connery bill made feeble gestures in this direction.

6. *Labor Under the New Deal*

Labor had suffered reverses even during the prosperous twenties; the depression brought not only unemployment and wage slashes, but the extension of the stretch-out system, the sweatshop, and child labor, the widespread flouting of factory laws, and a concerted attack upon labor unions. Roosevelt came to office with the enthusiastic support of labor, and pledged to the reversal of the illiberal policies of his predecessor; the appointment of Frances Perkins, distinguished social reformer, to the post of Secretary of Labor augured well for the fulfilment of that pledge. The first and most important effort toward the rehabilitation of labor was the N.R.A. which attempted to spread employment, raise wages, reduce hours, eliminate child and sweatshop labor, and safeguard the right of organization and collective bargaining. This latter policy was embodied in the famous Section 7(a) of the National Recovery Act which provided that

> Employees shall have the right to organize and bargain collectively, through representatives of their own choosing, and shall be free from the interference, restraint, or coercion of employers of labor, or their agents, in the designation of such representatives or in self-organization or in other concerted activities . . . ; and that no employee and no one seeking employment shall be required as a condition of employment to join any company union or to refrain from joining, organizing, or assisting a labor organization of his own choosing.

To effectuate this policy there was created, in August 1933, a National Labor Board 'to settle by mediation, conciliation, or arbitration all controversies between employers and employees.' Without specific statutory foundation, this Board was merely an administrative agency which investigated and reported on violations of Section 7(a)

[9] Carter *v.* Carter Coal Co. *et al.,* 298 U.S.238.
[10] R.R.Retirement Board v. Alton R.R.Co. 295 U.S.330.

and extended its offices to the mediation of disputes. In this it was partially successful: in the first year of its existence the N.L.B. entertained 3755 grievances of which 3061 were mediated and investigated 1323 strikes of which 1023 were arbitrated. In June 1934 it was replaced by a National Labor Relations Board which, with its affiliated industrial boards, had jurisdiction over all controversies arising under the N.R.A. and was authorized to determine which of competing unions represented the majority of workers in any industry and to require that the majority union constitute the exclusive bargaining agency.

Under the impetus of the N.R.A. organized labor more than recovered all the losses which it had suffered in the preceding decade, and by 1936 the A.F. of L. boasted a membership of over four million. When employers who questioned the constitutionality of Section 7(a) refused to be bound by its provisions or to accept the rulings of the N.L.R.B., labor struck, and an epidemic of strikes and lock-outs swept the country. Labor, sure that the government stood behind it, presumed upon its new position and antagonized public opinion; industry, determined to recoup depression losses and unintimidated by the New Deal, employed the traditional weapons of the company union, the injunction, and violence. During 1934 the country witnessed, with conflicting emotions, a great strike in the automobile industry, a nation-wide textile strike, and a general strike in San Francisco; all three were unsuccessful, and the latter two were smashed by the militia and by lawless, self-constituted vigilantes. The government itself suffered a severe setback when the Weirton Steel Company invoked the Norris-LaGuardia Anti-Injunction Act to prevent the N.L.R.B. from supervising a vote of employees on union representation. Emboldened by this successful defiance of the government, corporations initiated a counter-offensive against labor that threatened many of the gains which labor had secured under the new deal.

The invalidation of the N.R.A. appeared to justify this counter-offensive, on legal grounds at least, but some of the labor provisions of that law were promptly re-enacted in the Wagner-Connery Act of 5 July 1935. This Act set up a permanent, independent National Labor Relations Board which was authorized to investigate complaints and issue 'cease and desist' orders against unfair practices in labor relations affecting interstate commerce. These 'unfair practices' included interference with or coercion of employees in collective bargaining, domination of labor union through financial contributions, discrimination against union members in employment or tenure, or refusal to bargain collectively with employees. Within two years this revamped N.L.R.B. handled over five thousand cases involving 'unfair practices.' Yet in many instances business, relying upon the precedent of the Schechter case, refused to comply with the terms of the law, and this recalcitrance was sustained on occasion by opinions of inferior courts. In April 1937, however, the Supreme Court, by a 5–4 decision, sustained the validity of the Wagner Act.[11] Speaking for the Court, Chief Justice Hughes insisted that the connection between manufacturing and commerce was obvious and that the protection of the 'right of employees to self-organization and freedom in the choice of representatives for collective bargaining' had an intimate relation with interstate commerce and was properly within the constitutional powers of Congress.

> The fact remains [said the Chief Justice] that the stoppage of those operations by industrial strife would have a most serious effect upon interstate commerce. It is idle to say that the effect would be indirect or remote. It is obvious that it would be immediate and might be catastrophic. We are asked to shut our eyes to the plainest facts of our national life and to deal with the question of direct and indirect effects in an intellectual vacuum. . . . When industries organize themselves on a national scale, making their relation to interstate commerce the dominant factor in their activities, how can it be maintained that their industrial labor relations constitute a forbidden field into which Congress may not enter when it is necessary to protect interstate commerce from the paralyzing consequences of industrial war?

This opinion was so sweeping as to raise the very natural question as to where the Court would draw the line between interstate and intrastate business and to suggest the suspicion that it constituted, in part, a modification of the Schechter decision.

The most important development in labor, however, was the emergence in 1935–6 of the Committee for Industrial Organization. The C.I.O., as it came to be known, was a secession from the A.F. of L. by workers impatient with the cautious policy of that organization; it represented, too, a revival of the philosophy of industrial unionism espoused in the decade of the 80's by the Knights of

[11] National Labor Relations Board *v.* Jones & Laughlin Steel Corp., 301 U.S. 1 (1937).

Labor.[12] Under the dynamic leadership of John Lewis, President of the United Mine Workers, the C.I.O. set out to unionize skilled, unskilled, and white-collar workers in industries which had heretofore successfully resisted unionization such as the steel, automobile, textile, and public utilities. Its success was, for a time, phenomenal. Union after union seceded from the A.F. of L. to the new organization; hundreds of thousands of unskilled and semi-skilled laborers signed up with the only union which appeared to have any interest in them; and newspapermen, teachers, and administrative officials indicated their sympathy with the philosophy of the C.I.O. by organizing professional affiliates. By mid-summer 1937 it was estimated that the C.I.O. had a membership of four million, and students predicted that it would, in the near future, supplant its older rival as the spokesman for American labor, a prediction that proved entirely erroneous.

Heady with the wine of success, Mr. Lewis instituted a series of strikes directed not so much to improvement in hours and wages as to the closed shop and the right of exclusive representation in collective bargaining. Disdaining traditional methods, strikers employed the new technique of the 'sit-down,' seizing possession of the machinery and property of employers and refusing to yield until their demands had been granted. To this new weapon many employers capitulated at once, and the acquiescence of the United States Steel Corporation in the demands of the C.I.O., in March 1937, was justly regarded as of historic significance. Others, notably the General Motors and Republic Steel corporations, challenged the legality of the sit-down, and called upon the courts to rescue their property. The courts responded with injunctions, and when workers resisted the court orders, violence ensued. The intervention of Governor Murphy of Michigan prevented widespread violence in the automobile industries of that state, but in June 1937 the nation was shocked by the outbreak of open warfare in South Chicago, where police, defending the property of the Republic Steel Company, killed ten strikers and strike sympathizers. Though a Senate Committee under Robert LaFollette scored the Chicago police for brutality, public opinion turned against the C.I.O. and the sit-down, and by mid-summer 1937 it appeared that the new organization might forfeit many of the gains it had achieved in its first year.

12 See above, Chapter 7.

EMPLOYMENT AND UNEMPLOYMENT

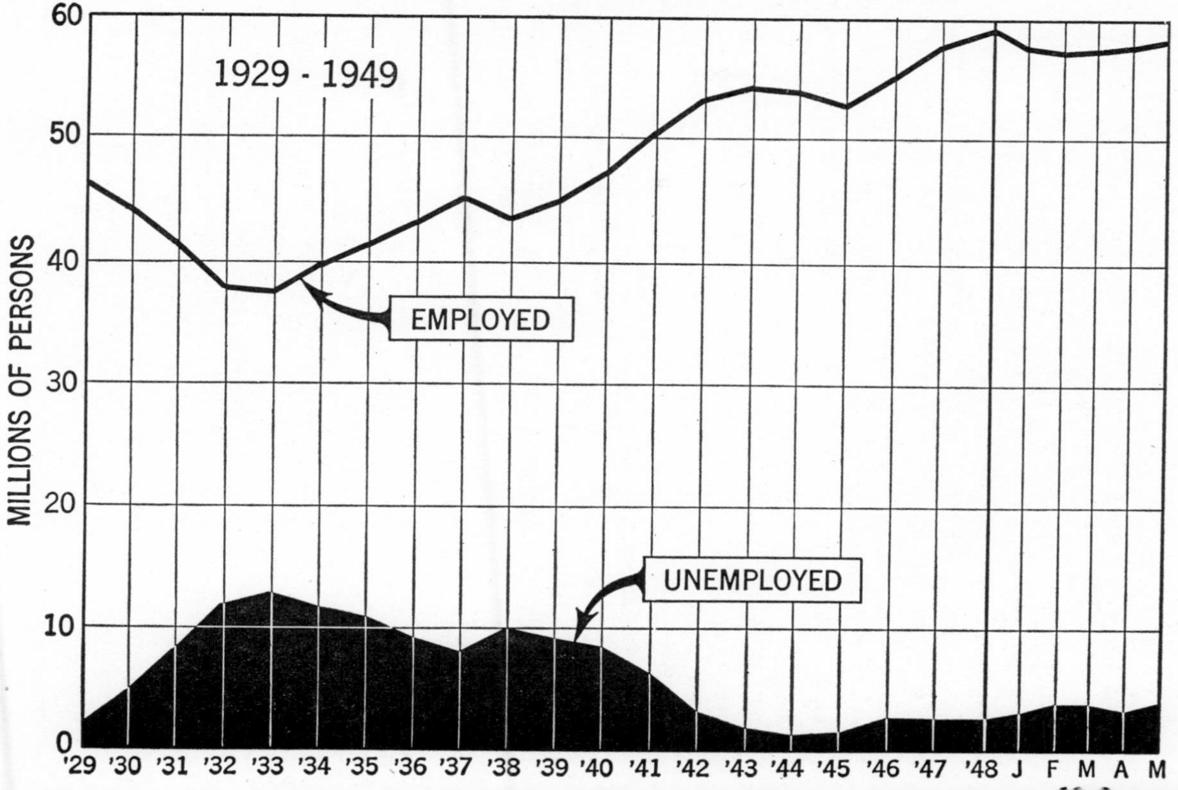

7. *Conservation and the Regulation of Utilities*

Nowhere did the New Deal institute more far-reaching changes than in the realm of power regulation and the conservation and utilization of natural resources. The conservation program of Theodore Roosevelt, the Water Power Act of 1920, and the Boulder Dam project initiated under President Hoover, served as precedents; yet the contrast between Mr. Hoover's veto of the Muscle Shoals Bill in 1931 and the enactment of the Tennessee Valley Authority in 1933 shows an almost complete reversal in policy and political philosophy. The change involved not only the first large-scale effort to save from destruction the natural resources of the nation, but a candid acceptance of socialism in the realm of public utilities and a commitment to an experiment in economic planning of a regional character.

The conservation work of the Roosevelt administration was directed both to emergency relief and to permanent reform; it constituted the most scientific effort yet made to analyze, preserve, and restore American soil, forest, water-power, and wild life. The initial step in this policy was the creation (31 March 1933) of the Civilian Conservation Corps designed to afford emergency work-relief to young men between the ages of seventeen and twenty-eight, and to carry through a program of conservation. In the first eight years of its existence the C.C.C. enlisted almost 3,000,000 youths who, under the direction of army officers and foresters, added over 17,000,000 acres of new forest land, checked forest fires, fought plant and animal diseases, stocked over a billion fish in hatcheries, and undertook to prevent soil erosion through the construction of 6,000,000 check dams, built thousands of bridges, strung hundreds of thousands of miles of telephone wire, and inaugurated ambitious projects of insect pest and mosquito control. And, as President Roosevelt observed, 'no one will ever be able to estimate in dollars and cents the value to the men themselves and to the nation as a whole in morale, in occupational training, in health, and in adaptability to later competitive life.'

The recurrent droughts of the 1930's led to the enactment of an Omnibus Flood Control Bill, the construction of a series of large reservoir and power dams and of many thousand smaller dams on streams. An alarming spread of the 'dust bowl' on the high plains inspired a gigantic campaign against soil erosion and the planting of a hundred-mile wide shelter belt of trees stretching from Texas to Canada. An erosion-prevention program inaugurated by the Department of Agriculture in 1935 embraced, five years later, over 270,000,000 acres, and enlisted the co-operation of one-fourth of the farmers of the country. Other important conservation work carried on by the Tennessee Valley Authority, the Resettlement Administration, and the Public Works Administration involved the elimination of pollution in streams, the creation of fish, game, and bird sanctuaries, the conservation of coal, petroleum, shale, gas, sodium, and helium deposits, the closure of grazing lands to homestead entries, and the addition of twelve million acres of land to the national forests.

Of all the measures of the new deal, possibly the most important for the future and certainly the most interesting to foreign observers was that establishing the Tennessee Valley Authority. The problem of Muscle Shoals had been inherited from the Hoover administration. Mr. Roosevelt was not content merely with government operation of these dams for nitrate production, as had been done in World War I, but insisted upon expanding the project into a vast experiment in regional reconstruction. A law of 18 May 1933 created the Tennessee Valley Authority with power to acquire, construct, and operate dams in the Tennessee Valley, manufacture and distribute nitrate and fertilizer, generate and sell electric power particularly with a view to rural electrification, inaugurate flood control through reforestation, withdraw marginal lands from cultivation, develop the Tennessee river for navigation, and advance 'the economic and social well-being of the people living in the said river basin.'

The Tennessee Valley embraces an area of some forty thousand miles in seven states — Tennessee, Kentucky, Alabama, Mississippi, Virginia, North Carolina, and Georgia — and constitutes a natural region which presented a tempting challenge to long-range economic and social planning. It was a region of varied agricultural and industrial possibilities, rich in natural resources which were rapidly being exhausted, and in water power which was going to waste. The experiment of government operation of power plants, government regulation of agriculture, and government control of social rehabilitation, if fairly and intelligently conducted, might be expected to throw some light on the whole problem of a planned economy. Success would point to an extension of the experiment in other regions; failure would suggest a return to rugged individualism.

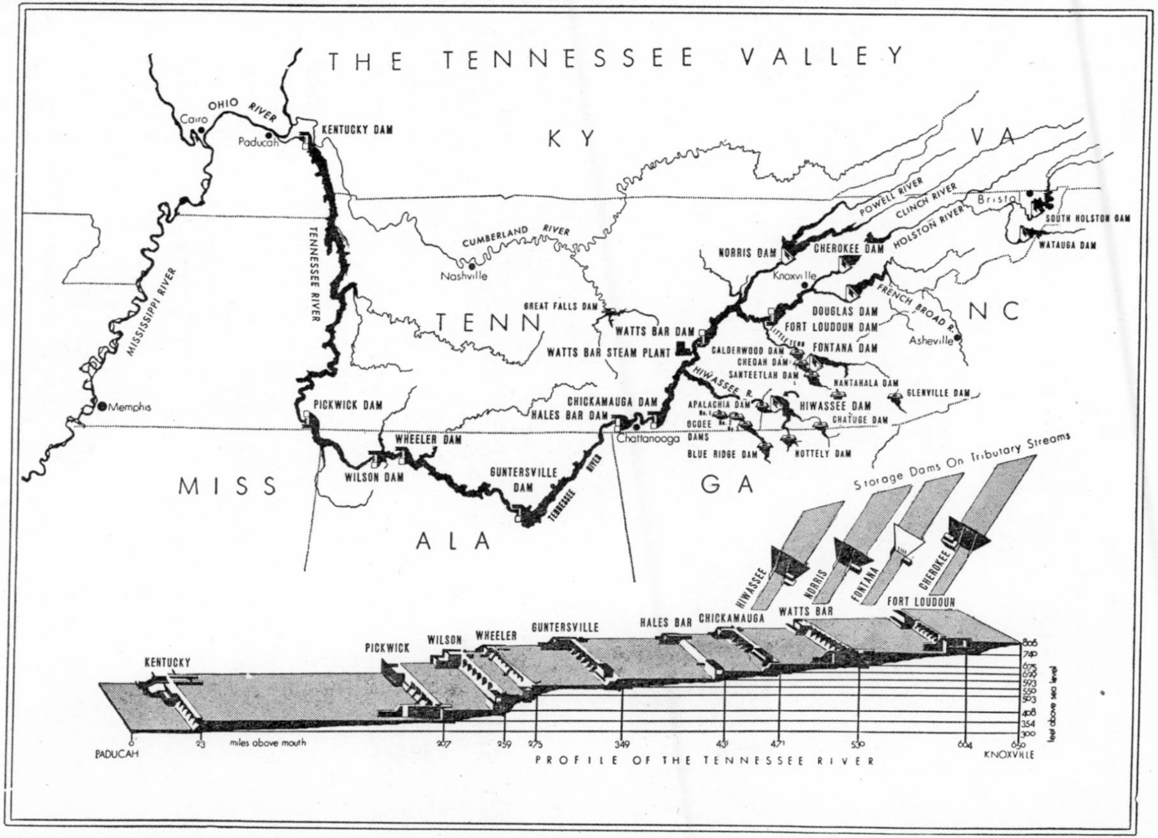

Courtesy of Tennessee Valley Authority

The directors of the T.V.A., interpreting the Act as conferring upon them broad authority to give a 'new deal' to the people of the Tennessee Valley, undertook at once to make the project a comprehensive laboratory for social and economic experiment. A series of tributary dams were constructed, and used for flood control, nitrate production, and the generation of electric power. The government constructed some five thousand miles of transmission lines and sold surplus power to near-by communities at rates sufficiently low to insure widespread consumption; a subsidiary to the T.V.A. promoted this scheme by financing rural electrification. By 1941 the Authority was serving over 400,000 customers. In 1934 only 1 farm out of 30 in Mississippi, Alabama, Tennessee, and Georgia received electricity; five years later the proportion was 1 out of 7. Government competition with private utility companies forced the latter to reduce their rates; the consequent increase in consumption appeared to demonstrate the profitableness of the experiment. As an agency to foster 'an orderly and proper physical, economic, and social development' of the Valley, the T.V.A. also undertook to withdraw marginal lands from cultivation, resettle marginal farmers, conduct agricultural experiments particularly in connection with the wider use of phosphate fertilizer, promote public health and recreational facilities, and, in a general way, 'use the facilities of the controlled river to release the energies of the people.'

The Tennessee Valley Authority was the most notable of several such experiments in the generation of hydroelectric power and regional rehabilitation. Almost as important for the future was the ambitious program for the Columbia River basin. In 1933 the government began construction work on the Grand Coulee Dam, some 70 miles west of Spokane, and in 1937 on the Bonneville Dam on the lower Columbia. These were expected to develop over two million kilowatts of electric power and to make possible the irrigation and reclamation of over a million acres of farm land.

Government competition with private power companies and the use of the 'yardstick' to determine fair rates inevitably evoked criticism and inspired challenge. The T.V.A. was attacked on economic grounds as a threat to the twelve billion dollar investment in private utilities; on social grounds as tending toward what President Hoover had called 'degeneration'; and on legal grounds as an exercise of power not authorized by the Constitution. The first two issues were fought out in the arena of public opinion and politics;

and in both arenas the government policy was endorsed. The third came before the courts. In a notable decision of 17 February 1936 the Supreme Court, with only one dissenting vote, sustained the constitutionality of everything that the T.V.A. was doing.[13]

The T.V.A. presented one form of approach to the utilities problem. A more direct and positive control was provided in the Wheeler-Rayburn Act of 26 August 1935. This law authorized the Federal Water Power Commission to regulate the production, transmission, and sale of electric power in interstate commerce and the Federal Trade Commission to exercise the same authority over gas. In its original form the Act contained a 'death sentence' provision designed to separate holding companies from their subsidiaries; this provision was defeated by a powerful lobby, but the Act as finally passed authorized the Commission to dissolve all holding companies contrary to the public interest.

8. *Relief and Security*

The most urgent problem facing the administration was that of relief for the twelve to fifteen million unemployed victims of the depression. Roosevelt had promised during his campaign that no one should starve, but millions of Americans were perilously near starvation, and the resources of state and local governments and of private charities were well-nigh exhausted. The emergency was clearly one that called for the energetic intervention of the Federal Government. What form that intervention should take was a matter of dispute. Outright relief had the advantages of economy and efficiency; work relief, on the other hand, promised to maintain morale, repair and improve the economic plant, and facilitate the transfer of workers to private industry. Relief, however, no matter how generously contributed or how intelligently directed, offered no solution to the problem of unemployment or guarantee of security, and from the beginning President Roosevelt took the position that it must be succeeded by a permanent program of security.

The first step in emergency relief was the creation of the Civilian Conservation Corps, to which we have already referred. The Federal Emergency Relief Administration of May 1933 appropriated half a billion dollars for direct emergency relief to states and local communities and eventually disbursed over three billion dollars for these

13 Ashwander *v.* Tennessee Valley Authority, 297 U.S. 288.

purposes. The National Recovery Act of June 1933, however, provided for a comprehensive system of public works embracing highways, parkways, river and harbor improvements, slum clearance, the conservation of natural resources and of water power, and the construction of public buildings, low-cost houses, hospitals, reservoirs, sewage plants, and similar projects. Under the terms of this Act a Public Works Administration was established to organize and co-ordinate the whole system of public works; operating through a Civil Works Administration it promptly set four million men at work on a variety of clearance, construction, and clerical projects supposedly of a socially desirable character, and at wages adjusted to prevailing rates in local communities. In addition, the government contributed direct relief to victims of droughts and floods and to marginal farmers and set up a United States Employment Service to co-ordinate state employment activities.

In January 1935 President Roosevelt proposed that a distinction be made between employables and unemployables, that new and more satisfactory provision be made for the former, and that the burden of supporting the latter be transferred to state and local governments. In accordance with this suggestion Congress, in April 1935, authorized the Works Progress Administration and appropriated $4,880,000,000 to be expended for relief, loans and grants on non-federal projects, highways, the CCC, rural rehabilitation, housing and slum clearance, reforestation, flood control, and soil erosion work, educational, professional, and clerical work, and rural electrification. Additional funds were subsequently appropriated for health and sanitation projects and for the assistance of students in colleges and graduate schools. The purpose of this legislation was to give work to the unemployed, to stimulate private business by 'pump-priming' with billions of dollars, and to inaugurate reforms that states were unable to subsidize.

The task of carrying through this gigantic program of public works was attended with inevitable confusion and waste. Some of the projects were ridiculous, some were useless, many were so ill directed as to be worthless. Administrative costs were high, construction was often shoddy, and politics influenced the choice of work, the hiring of workers, and the appropriation of money. Yet a partial list of WPA projects completed by the end of 1936 includes 1497 water works, 883 sewage plants, 741 street and highway improvements, 263 hospitals, 166 bridges, and 70 municipal power plants, while almost five hundred million dollars had been spent on school buildings and one hundred and fifty million on slum clearance. Particularly novel were federal arts, writers', and theater programs. Unemployed writers prepared state, regional, and city guides, organized state and local archives, indexed newspaper files, and undertook useful sociological and historical investigations. Artists decorated hundreds of post offices, schools, and other public buildings with mural paintings. Unemployed musicians organized symphony orchestras and community singing, and brought music to communities where it had been known only through the radio, while scores of stock companies toured the country with repertories of old and new plays.

The depression hit the middle class, too, and millions of families who had borrowed money to build or buy homes found themselves unable to keep up mortgage payments or finance necessary repairs. Congress set up the Home Owners' Loan Corporation to refinance small mortgages at low rates of interest, and this Corporation came to the rescue of over a million home owners. The Federal Housing Administration assumed the risk of insuring existing mortgages; by 1940 it had covered over four billion dollars in mortgages. And in 1937 Congress created the United States Housing Authority to assist local communities in slum clearance and the construction of low-cost housing. This program was fought bitterly by the real estate interests and by 1941 only 120,000 family dwelling units, designed for the lower-income groups, had been completed. Then war put an end to further construction and the housing shortage remained to plague the next generation.

The chief objection to the indefinite continuation of these relief projects was on the score of expense. Altogether in the three fiscal years of 1934, 1935, and 1936 the Federal Government appropriated $8,681,000,000, for relief and public works. This sum represented, to be sure, merely one-third the cost of World War I, and Roosevelt had promised, in his Inaugural Address, to 'treat the task as we would treat the emergency of a war'; yet it was generally supposed that the American people could not afford an indefinite continuation of such expenditures. Every year of the New Deal saw mounting deficits, and the national debt increased, between 1930 and 1936, from sixteen to thirty-six billion dollars, with no prospect of an immediate reversal of the trend.[14]

[14] Yet it must be noted that carrying charges for the national debt did not materially increase during these years. Interest on the public debt was $832,000,000 in 1926, $689,000.000 in 1933, and $749,000,000 in 1936.

As early as 1934 the President had called for a broad program of old-age and unemployment insurance. Investigations conducted by his Committee on Economic Security and hearings before House and Senate committees indicated the grave and urgent nature of the problem. Between 1920 and 1936 population had increased by approximately twenty per cent; in the same period the number of industrial jobs had declined by twenty-five per cent. At the same time the increase in life expectancy and the decline in the birth rate resulted in a disproportionate rise in the number of persons over sixty-five years of age. But industry was unwilling to employ men of advanced years; investigations of several hundred industrial establishments revealed that few hired workers over fifty years of age, and the situation in professional and white-collar establishments was much the same. The conclusion was inescapable that the aged would, in the future, constitute an ever-growing burden on the community. That burden was, indeed, already a present one. In 1937 the Social Security Board reported that 'one-fifth of the aged in the United States were receiving old-age assistance, emergency relief, institutional care, employment under a works program, or some other form of aid from public or private funds; two-fifths to one-half were dependent on friends and relatives. . . . Approximately three out of four persons 65 or over were probably wholly or partially dependent on others for support.'

Pressure for the enactment of federal unemployment and old-age insurance legislation mounted in the early years of the decade. Beginning in 1929 a number of states passed old-age pension laws, and by 1934 twenty-eight states provided old-age pensions to some 180,000 beneficiaries over sixty-five. Despite the efforts of Mr. Roosevelt, when Governor of New York, to bring other states into a joint system of unemployment insurance, only Ohio and Wisconsin had such legislation. It was clear that old-age and unemployment insurance placed an unequal burden upon those states which adopted and gave an unfair advantage to those states which rejected such a program. Pressure was also exerted by advocates of the so-called Townsend plan of old-age pensions and the Lundeen plan of unemployment compensation. The first, providing for monthly payments of two hundred dollars to all persons over sixty years of age, on the sole provision that they retire from work and spend the money, was championed by Townsend Clubs claiming close to a million members. The second, calling for weekly payments of not less than ten dollars to every unemployed person eighteen years of age and over, commanded the support of communists, labor organizations, and social reformers. Each would have cost the national treasury not far from ten billion dollars annually — approximately one-fourth the total national income during depression years! There was never the remotest chance that either would pass Congress, but pressure for such legislation made moderate social security legislation appear conservative.

The result was the enactment, 14 August 1935, of an elaborate Social Security Act providing for pensions to needy aged, old-age insurance, unemployment insurance, benefit payments to the blind, dependent mothers and children, and crippled children, and extensive appropriations for public health work. Pensions of not more than fifteen dollars a month were to be extended to indigent persons over sixty-five on the understanding that co-operating states would contribute a like amount. The system of old-age insurance provided benefits to participants in accordance with a complicated system of graduated premiums paid by both employer and employee. The unemployment insurance plan was designed to persuade the states to establish systems of unemployment insurance; to this end it required payments by employers of a percentage of their pay roll for insurance purposes, but provided that ninety per cent of the federal levy should be returned to states whose insurance plans conformed to standards approved by a Social Security Board. In addition the Act appropriated to the states twenty-five million dollars for aid to dependent children and called for annual appropriations of twenty-five million for maternal and child health service, crippled children, the blind, state and local public health service, and vocational rehabilitation.

In the course of the next two years practically all the states set up old-age pensions and unemployment insurance systems that met the requirements fixed by the Social Security Board. Inevitably, however, the Social Security Act was challenged on constitutional grounds, and conflicting opinions in inferior federal courts created uncertainty as to the effectiveness of the law. In a series of notable decisions handed down on 24 May 1937,[15] the Supreme Court sustained all the crucial provisions of the Act, and announced a concept of national welfare so broad that it constituted, in theory, if not in effect, a reversal of many of the conservative decisions of the early New Deal period and a return to the Marshall interpretation of the Constitution.

15 Carmichael *et al.* *v.* Southern Coal & Coke Co., 301 U.S. 495. Charles C. Steward Machine Co. *v.* Davis, 301 U.S. 548. Helvering *et al.* *v.* Davis, 301 U.S. 619.

Thus Justice Cardozo, sustaining the unemployment insurance provisions of the Security Act, observed of unemployment that,

> The states were unable to give the requisite relief. The problem had become national in area and dimensions. There was need of help if the people were not to starve. It is too late today for the argument to be heard with tolerance that in a crisis so extreme the use of the moneys of the nation to relieve the unemployed and their dependents is a use for any purpose narrower than the promotion of the general welfare.

Such an interpretation of the Constitution, had it been adopted earlier, might well have sustained the A.A.A. and Railway Pension legislation. Not the least significant aspect of the Social Security legislation was that it discovered a method for implementing nationalism.

XXV

DOMESTIC ISSUES OF THE SECOND ADMINISTRATION

1. *The Election of 1936*

THE Congressional elections of 1934 strengthened the Democratic control of Congress and revealed the popularity of the New Deal. Yet as the presidential election approached, signs of discontent multiplied; and as prosperity in some measure returned, business men became increasingly critical. The charges against President Roosevelt and the New Deal were numerous, varied, and urgent. Conservatives asserted that the President was destroying the 'American system' of individualism, undermining enterprise, and insinuating socialism if not communism into American economy. His policies, it was urged, had discouraged rather than encouraged recovery. There were still millions of unemployed and, despite extravagant government expenditures, the number was not being appreciably reduced. High taxes shackled industry, the Securities Act prevented new stock flotations, the T.V.A. was running the private utility business, the Home Owners' Loan Corporation undermining mortgage investments, the Wagner Act fomenting labor disorders, the monetary policy impeding the recovery of foreign trade, and the reciprocity treaties injuring the farmer. The President, it was alleged, had ignored the platform and flouted campaign promises. The platform had committed the party to 'sound money' and the party had promptly taken the nation off the gold standard and repudiated financial obligations; it had promised reduction in government expenses, and expenses had increased with every fiscal year. Money had been thrown away on relief, millions of men had been encouraged in idleness, a monstrous bureaucracy developed, taxes had mounted, and the national debt had reached the staggering sum of thirty-five billion dollars. The Constitution, it was said, had been betrayed, and there was the authority of the Supreme Court to prove that much of the new legislation was unconstitutional. The Bill of Rights had been violated, the jurisdiction of the states ruthlessly invaded, and the federal system shattered! The President was reaching toward dictatorship, Congress was a rubber stamp, the independence of the judiciary was threatened, and the tripartite division of the government ignored! The billions poured out for relief purposes constituted a party slush fund, the civil service had been prostituted to party ends, and Postmaster-General Farley had introduced Tammany methods into the national government.

Much of this criticism emanated from members of the Democratic party. The President's former friend, Alfred E. Smith, led a small but distinguished procession of Democrats including John W. Davis, presidential candidate in 1924, and Bainbridge Colby, Secretary of State under Wilson, in 'taking a walk' away from the Democratic camp. These men appealed to the party to preserve the traditional faith, and when their appeal was ignored, organized the 'Jeffersonian Democrats.'

Scarcely less acrimonious was criticism from liberal organs like *The New Republic* and *The Nation,* which thought Roosevelt overconservative. The NRA, it was asserted, had encouraged monopoly, and four years of the New Deal had strengthened big business at the expense of small. The administration had passed up the best opportunity ever vouchsafed for a thorough overhauling of the banking system and had given way again and again before the pressure of powerful business and utility lobbies. Labor was still oppressed, the farmer depressed, the middle class caught between the vise of soaring prices and stationary income. The relief problem had not been handled in an intelligent fashion, appropriations for relief were pitifully inadequate, and no effort had been made to discover the facts and causes of unemployment. The President had failed to inaugurate fundamental reforms in the economic system, and had failed to reveal any consistent philosophy of government. And although but a few of the many millions spent by the government had been devoted to a military and naval preparedness that later events revealed to be pitifully inadequate, the President was charged with encouraging navalism and militarism.

Throughout 1936 criticism mounted, becoming shriller every day. The din and clamor pouring from hundreds of radio stations and thousands of platforms seemed impressive, and some Republicans went so far as to prophesy defeat for the New Deal. It was incumbent upon the Republicans to find a candidate satisfactory alike to liberals and conservatives, and in Alfred M. Landon, Governor of Kansas, they thought they found one. He was in the oil business, yet appeared to understand the farm problem; he had followed Theodore Roosevelt in 1912, but had returned with him to the 'G.O.P.'; he was thrifty, 'folksy'; in a word, a Midwestern 'Cal' Coolidge. He could be trusted to abandon most of the New Deal experiments and return to that policy of laissez-faire which so many conservatives wistfully regarded as 'normalcy.' When the Republican convention met, Landon was nominated on the first ballot, and on a platform which asserted that

America is in peril. The welfare of American men and women and the future of our youth are at stake. We dedicate ourselves to the preservation of their political liberty, their individual opportunity and their character as free citizens, which today for the first time are threatened by the government itself.

The platform, however, promised to do all the things the Democrats had done, but in a different spirit and without violation of the Constitution or destruction of the 'American system of free enterprise, private competition, and equality of opportunity.' The party pledged itself to speed up employment, maintain relief, obtain old-age security, foster agriculture, destroy monopolies, regulate business, protect the civil service, and preserve a 'sound currency'; it would, at the same time, reduce expenditures, balance the budget, and free business from New Deal trammels. It was not to be expected that the platform should be more specific than this, but the nominee, in his speeches, was equally positive about the program and equally vague about the methods by which these apparently contradictory ends were to be achieved.

Despite opposition without and dissension within, the Democrats met in a jubilant mood. The convention dispensed with the hundred-year-old two-thirds rule, renominated Franklin D. Roosevelt by acclamation, endorsed the entire New Deal program, and promised its continuation and expansion, through legislative action if possible, through constitutional amendment if necessary. It declared:

The Republican platform proposes to meet many pressing national problems solely by action of the separate States. We know that drought, dust storms, floods, minimum wages, maximum hours, child labor and working conditions in industry, monopolistic and unfair business practices cannot be adequately handled exclusively by forty-eight separate State legislatures, forty-eight separate State administrations and forty-eight separate State courts. Transactions and activities which inevitably overflow State boundaries call for both State and Federal treatment.

PRESIDENTIAL ELECTION of 1936

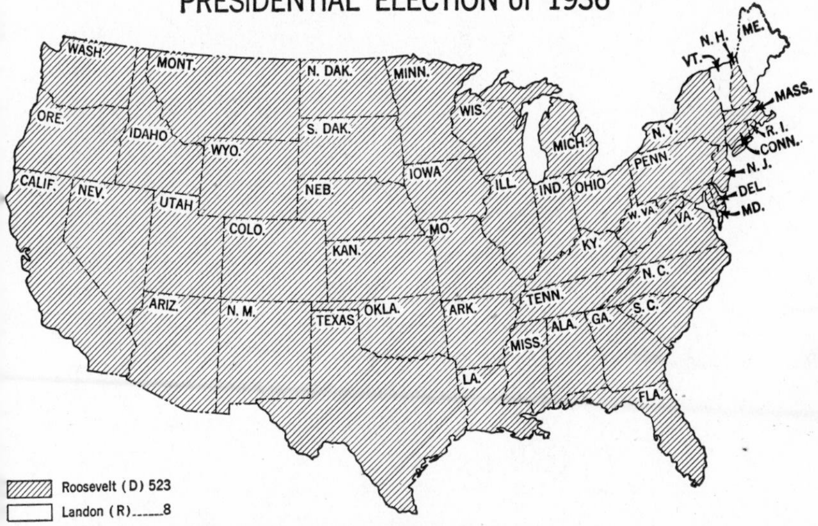

PRESIDENTIAL ELECTION of 1940

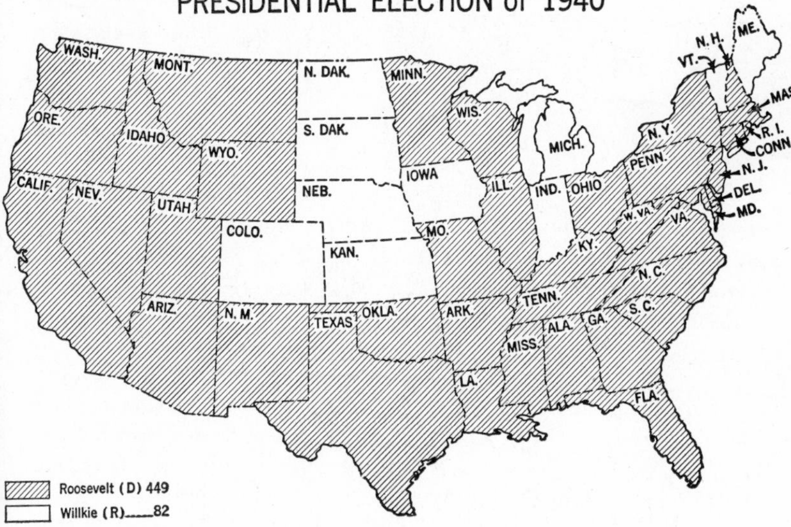

The campaign was more heated than any for a generation. Both parties collected enormous campaign funds, both launched elaborate radio campaigns. Governor Landon showed himself lacking in political finesse and personal magnetism; Roosevelt again revealed consummate skill in his appeal to public opinion. Most of the newspapers of the country supported Landon, as did a large proportion of professional and academic, and almost all business groups. So energetic was the Republican attack upon the New Deal that when 'straw votes' conducted by the *Literary Digest* and the Hearst press predicted Landon's election, many were inclined to doubt the evidence of their senses and accept the prophecy. Mr. Farley, unimpressed by these straw votes, predicted that Roosevelt would carry every state but two. His prediction was fulfilled. In the greatest landslide in American political history, Roosevelt polled a popular majority of ten million votes and carried every state but Maine and Vermont. Democratic victory in state and Congressional elections was equally overwhelming.

2. *Court Reform and Constitutional Revolution*

No more impressive vote of confidence had ever been given a candidate; his mandate to continue policies already inaugurated was unmistakable. In the last speech of the campaign the President declared 'we have just begun to fight,' and when Congress met in January 1937, he presented it with a series of far-reaching proposals designed to complete the structure of the New Deal: bills on farm tenancy, wages and hours of labor, housing, taxation, and hydroelectric development, together with a plan for sweeping administrative reorganization. Weakened but not chastened, the Republican minority was unable to offer effective opposition to these proposals. The elephant then lifted his eyes to the Supreme Court.

For the Republicans had 'retired into the judiciary as a stronghold, and from that battery all the works of republicanism were to be beaten down and erased.' So Jefferson had said of the Federalists over a century earlier, and his successor in the White House had reason to echo the bitter charge. Never before, indeed, had the Supreme Court worked such havoc with a legislative program as it did in 1935 and 1936 with that of the New Deal; never before, in so short a time, had it invalidated so many acts of Congress. It overthrew the NRA on the novel ground of improper delegation of power. It struck down the AAA through what a dissenting justice called a 'tortured construction of the Constitution,' which straitjacketed the taxing power and created a no-man's land where neither federal nor state power might be applied. It rejected the railroad retirement plan on the curious theory that there was no legitimate connection between interstate commerce and the welfare of those who conducted it, while the Bituminous Coal Act had gone into the judicial wastebasket because the court insisted that coal mining was a purely local business. It invalidated congressional legislation to protect farm mortgages on the ground of conflict with the esoteric 'due process' clause of the Fifth Amendment, and it nullified the Municipal Bankruptcy Act on the assumption that such legislation invaded the domain of the states — even though the Act required state consent, which many states had already given. The Federal Government had long been denied the power to enact minimum-wage legislation; now a twilight zone of political impotence was conjured up by denying this power to the states. In the realm of administration rather than legislation the Court rejected the clear implications of the Myers decision and denied to the President the power to remove a recalcitrant member of the Federal Trade Commission. Even in the two cases where the Court sustained the New Deal — the gold clause and the T.V.A. cases — it did so on narrow grounds and with ill grace.

Thus the modern 'miners and sappers' of the Constitution had undermined the legislative structure of the New Deal. And 'what was worse,' as Roosevelt insisted, 'the language and temper of the decisions indicated little hope for the future. Apparently Marshall's conception of our Constitution as a flexible instrument — adequate for all times and therefore able to adjust itself as the new needs of new generations arose — had been repudiated.' It had, indeed, and the prospect was a bleak one. For the 1935–36 decisions were so sweeping in character that they appeared to foreclose amendment of the objectionable legislation and to foredoom further legislation along liberal lines. The Court, in fact, had taken upon itself the responsibility of nullifying the electoral verdicts of 1932 and 1934 and of negativing in advance any possible consequence of a comparable verdict in 1936.

What to do? The question was not a new one; it had confronted Jefferson, Jackson, Lincoln, and Theodore Roosevelt, and had commanded the attention of a long line of political thinkers from Taylor of Caroline to Borah of Idaho. Yet the most anxious study of the problem had not yielded a solution. Impeachment had failed, with the acquittal of Justice Chase in 1805; withdrawal of jurisdiction had been tried during Reconstruction and proved unsatisfactory; proposals to require more than a mere majority of votes for the nullification of legislative acts or to permit Congress, by a two-thirds vote, to override such nullifications, were of dubious constitutionality; the process of constitutional amendment was slow and uncertain. In the past, indeed, the judiciary had customarily been brought to tardy acquiescence in majority will by the slow process of new appointments rather than by any drastic change in its constitutional position.

Roosevelt had early announced his determination to find constitutional sanctions for what the nation required, and he had been confirmed in this determination by the spectacle of democracies abroad yielding to dictatorship because 'too weak or too slow to fulfill the wants of their citizens.' Opportunistic in tactics, he confined himself to the immediate issues. 'I know,' he said, 'that the Constitution was not to blame, and that the Supreme Court as an institution was not to blame. The only trouble was with some of the human beings on the Court.' Seven of the nine members of the Court had been appointed by Republican predecessors, and although six of the judges were over seventy years of age Mr. Roosevelt had not yet been able to make a single appointment, and in Justices McReynolds, Van Devanter, Sutherland, and Butler there was a solid nucleus of the Court which appeared to think that the Fifth and Fourteenth Amendments had 'enacted Herbert Spencer's *Social Statics,*' as Justice Holmes once said.

If the trouble was merely in the weakness of the Court, that could be remedied by appointing new members. So at least Roosevelt thought, and this was the crucial part of the proposal for the reform of the federal judiciary which he submitted to a startled Congress on 5 February 1937.

In the proposed bill the 'addition of younger blood' was to be obtained by the appointment of one new judge, up to a maximum of six, for every justice of the Supreme Court who, having passed the age of seventy and served for ten years, failed to retire.

The proposal was simplicity itself, and on this score, at least, had much to commend it. It fixed upon seventy as the logical retirement age, and if the examples of Holmes and Brandeis made this age seem premature, the rules in effect in the civil service, the army and navy, universities, hospitals, and similar institutions, suggested that it was not unreasonable. The presidential proposal did not compel retirement at seventy, but merely provided an additional judge for every incumbent over seventy; if the incumbent wished to avoid an enlarged court he had the alternative of resigning, at full pay. The bill raised no constitutional question, for the power of Congress to control membership was clear. And while the bill made possible a change in the number of Supreme Court justices, the President was entirely correct in reminding the nation that there was nothing unprecedented about this; the number had been changed six times in the past.

Nevertheless, the proposal was greeted with cries of alarm and dismay. It was denounced as a plan to 'pack' the Supreme Court; as an example of the President's lust for power; as an attack on the independence of the judiciary; as the end of constitutional government in the United States. Conservatives rejoiced that they could now identify opposition to presidential policies with the defense of the Constitution; Southern Bourbons, long restless under the New Deal lash, found here an opportunity for opposition that had a powerful emotional appeal. Quondam liberals like Senators Wheeler, Borah, and Johnson, who had long held something of a monopoly on criticism of the highest court, ranged themselves on the side of judicial supremacy, and it was clear that hostility to the President was making strange bedfellows.

Throughout the spring and summer of 1937 as the debate went on, it became clear that the tide of public opinion was rising against the presidential proposal. Yet it was not logic or eloquence that insured the defeat of the bill, but rather the masterly retreat of the Court itself. For even as the bill was under consideration, and before there had been any change in its membership, the Court found ways of making the constitutional sun shine on legislation which had heretofore been under a judicial cloud. Nine months after the Court had struck down the New York minimum-wage law, it sustained a similar act of the state of Washington. On the same day it approved of a revised farm-mortgage act and a new Railway Labor Act. A few weeks later came five decisions, all upholding various provisions of the National Labor Relations Act which a committee of sixty distinguished lawyers had advised their clients to disregard as incontestably unconstitutional. A month later, and the highly controversial Social Security legislation was vouchsafed judicial blessing. In vain did a consistent, if stubborn, minority argue that these decisions were reversals of those recently announced. The new majority, made possible by a timely switch by Justice Roberts, was determined to be liberal!

Convinced, now, that reform had already been achieved and confident that public opinion would not support the presidential plan, the Senate Judiciary Committee voted 10–8 to reject it, and the bill went no further. The President, at the height of his power and his popularity, had suffered the most stinging rebuke of his political career.

Although Roosevelt lost this battle, he won the campaign. Even while the court debate was under way, Justice Van Devanter announced his retirement, and his example was shortly followed by a number of his brother judges on the bench. Within a few years, indeed, the Court was entirely remade. To fill vacancies created by retirement and death President Roosevelt appointed Hugo Black of Alabama, distinguished for his fight against the power trust; Stanley Reed of Kentucky, former solicitor-general; Felix Frankfurter of the Harvard Law School, teacher of a generation of social-minded lawyers and jurists; William Douglas of the Yale Law School and the Securities and Exchange Commission; Attorney-General Robert Jackson of New York; Frank Murphy, former governor of Michigan and Governor-General of the Philippine Islands; and James Byrnes of South Carolina, a consistent liberal; while the talents and tolerance of Mr. Justice Stone were recognized by his elevation to the Chief Justiceship.

This new court hastened to retreat from the untenable constitutional positions seized by its predecessor, back to the great tradition of Marshall, Story, Miller, Taft, and Holmes. There was a quick return to that broad interpretation of the commerce and the tax clauses which had made possible the adaptation of the Constitution to the varied needs of national growth, and to that judicial continence, best exemplified in Holmes, which preserved the equality and independence of the three departments and the dependence of all upon the Constitution.

The unrealistic limitation on the commerce power written into the Constitution by Hammer *v.* Dagenhart was repudiated and a series of decisions interpreting the Wagner Labor Act and the Fair Labor Standards Act finally nullified that divorce of commerce from manufacturing first announced in the E. C. Knight case and reaffirmed in the Schechter and Guffey coal cases. Another series of decisions, in 1939, swept away any lingering doubts about the power of the Federal Government to regulate agricultural production through marketing agreements. The limitation imposed upon congressional spending power by the Butler decision was withdrawn; uncertainties about federal control over navigable rivers and water power, conjured up in the T.V.A. decision, were swept away and the right of the Federal Government to regulate even potentially navigable streams and to exercise general jurisdiction over the development of hydro-electric power was re-established.

The judicial fiction of 'liberty of contract' endorsed in the Adkins case went by the board. The judicial amendment of the 'rule of reason' to the Sherman antitrust law was, in effect, repealed, and the complicated doctrine of 'fair value' formulated in Smythe *v.* Ames abandoned as useless or misleading. Limitations on federal regulation of primary elections, deduced, apparently, from the Newberry case, were dissipated, and congressional authority over the whole process of federal elections was established. In the Phelps-Dodge case the court held that those earlier monuments to judicial conservatism respecting labor legislation, Adair *v.* United States and Coppage *v.* Kansas, were 'completely sapped of their authority,' while the Hutcheson decision announced that the prohibitions on the use of the injunction in labor disputes provided for by the Clayton and the Norris-La Guardia Acts should be interpreted to mean what they said. Congressional authority to enact bankruptcy legislation, presumably fixed by the clear terms of the Constitution but denied in two recent decisions, was restored; Congressional jurisdiction over the business of employment agencies, heretofore seriously circumscribed, was enlarged. Collector *v.* Day and its successors, which had long served to create fields of reciprocal tax immunity, gave way to the insistent demands for realism in the realm of taxation, and both state and Federal Governments were permitted to tax each other's employees where such taxation did not impose an improper burden upon any governmental function.

Nor were all the new decisions in the direction of the enlargement of federal powers. Toward the exercise of state police power the Court took a sympathetic attitude, while in the complex and controversial domain of taxation, there was a ready acquiescence in the search for new sources of revenue and a distinct tolerance toward the discriminatory taxation of the business of out-of-state corporations. And, finally, Swift *v.* Tyson, which for a century had permitted the federal courts to disregard decisions of the state courts on matters of state law, was formally pronounced mistaken.

Within a few years the Supreme Court had carried through a constitutional revolution, but it was a conservative revolution, inspired by respect not only for the great traditions of constitutional interpretation but for the other two co-equal departments of the government. None who observed the functions of the government and the character of the commonwealth after ridding the Constitution of the judicial gloss of recent years could doubt that democratic government under law had met and surmounted one of its most crucial tests.

3. *Farm and Labor Legislation*

The long and acrimonious debate on judicial reform side-tracked consideration of the urgent measures which the President had submitted to Congress at the beginning of his second administration. Yet the session was not wholly barren. A new Bituminous Coal Act replaced the outlawed Guffey bill and stood the test of judicial scrutiny. The Wagner-Steagall Act created a Federal Housing Authority to finance and supervise slum clearance and the construction of low-cost housing, and if the quantitative results were disappointing, the principle of federal concern was a significant one. The Bankhead-Jones Farm Tenant Act extended government loans to tenant farmers and share-croppers eager to own their farms, and a new Farm Security Administration made available small loans for agricultural rehabilitation, maintained camps for the migratory farm workers whose lot was so movingly depicted in *The Grapes of Wrath,* and supervised a variety of projects designed to aid the underprivileged agricultural groups.

It was this farm problem which engaged the most anxious attention of the second Roosevelt administration until war broke out in Europe. The act of 1933 had been voided, and the Soil Conservation Act of 1936 was admittedly only a stop-gap until farm representatives and Congressional leaders could formulate a more comprehensive program. Executive pressure was not sufficient to obtain action on this program in 1937, but the approach of congressional elections was more efficacious, and early in 1938 Roosevelt had the satisfaction of signing a bill which he regarded as a marked improvement upon all previous agricultural legislation. The Agricultural Adjustment Act of February 1938 had five principal features. It authorized the Secretary of Agriculture, with the approval of two-thirds of the farmers involved, to fix the acreage to be planted in crops and establish artificial marketing control of surplus crops; it set up a system of 'parity payments' to producers who agreed to limit their crops; continued conservation payments to farmers who planted within certain acreage allotments and carried out soil-conservation practices; made available commodity loans on surplus crops and set up storage facilities to insure an 'ever normal granary'; and provided a system of federal insurance on wheat. Although the results of this comprehensive attack upon the problem of farm surpluses were at first disappointing, the program shortly commanded the approval of the vast majority of the farmers involved, which is not surprising when one views the results. The Secretary of Agriculture reported that between 1932 and 1939, cash income from wheat had doubled, and income from corn and cotton had increased four-fold. Besides relieving farmers, the maintenance of a normal granary and the accumulation of surplus crops stabilized the American economic system and held out hope for ultimate relief to the war-stricken peoples of the world.

The administration won a second major victory on the labor front. The situation here was far from satisfactory. The invalidation of the NRA had removed all semblance of federal control over hours and wages, and the 'recession' of 1937, brought about in considerable part by the curtailment of government spending and the sharp reduction of relief rolls, further threatened the gains which labor had achieved since 1933. A census of November 1937 revealed a total of 11,000,000 persons wholly unemployed and another 5,500,000 only partially employed. This was a year, too, of widespread industrial disorder and of declining wages. The efforts of the newly organized CIO to organize the heretofore invulnerable steel, automobile, and textile industries met with bitter opposition. Industrial unionism — and especially the new weapon of the sit-down strike — evoked charges of radicalism and Communism from the management. In Pennsylvania and Ohio the militia were employed to break strikes, at the River Rouge plant of the Ford Company near Detroit vigilante organizations beat up labor organizers, and at the Republic Steel Works in South Chicago striking steel workers were killed by police in the Memorial Day massacre. Altogether 1937 witnessed a total of almost five thousand strikes, involving some two million workers.

The situation obviously required legislative action, and in July 1937 the Senate passed a bill drawn by Senator Black of Alabama designed to put 'a ceiling over hours and a floor under wages.' The bitter opposition of Southern Democrats delayed enactment, until June 1938. This Fair Labor Standards Act had as its objective the 'elimination of labor conditions detrimental to the maintenance of the minimum standards of living necessary for health, efficiency, and well being of workers.' It provided for an eventual maximum working week of forty hours and an eventual minimum wage of forty cents an hour for all employees engaged in or producing goods for interstate commerce. Scarcely less important was the prohibition of child labor in all industries engaged in producing goods for interstate commerce and the severe limitation on the labor of boys and girls between sixteen and eighteen in hazardous occupations. The preliminary increase to thirty cents per hour increased the wages of some seven hundred thousand workers, and the hour provisions affected, ultimately, some thirteen million working men and women. With pardonable exaggeration President Roosevelt characterized this Act as 'the most far-reaching, far-sighted program for the benefit of workers ever adopted in this or any other country.'

Inevitably its constitutionality was challenged by those who relied upon the precedent of Hammer *v.* Dagenhart, but in a unanimous opinion the Supreme Court reversed the Dagenhart case and sustained the new law.[1]

Labor, meantime, was winning other victories in the courts scarcely less significant. The authority of the National Labor Relations Board sustained perhaps the most persistent and severe attack that had ever been directed against any of the New Deal agencies. Yet the record of the Board spoke for itself. In the five years ending January 1941, it had handled some 33,000 cases involving over seven million workers and including some 22,000 charges of unfair labor practices and over 11,000 petitions to determine collective bargaining agencies. More than 90 per cent of all these cases were disposed of amicably, and of the 3166 strikes certified to the Board, 2383 were settled peaceably. In the judicial arena, too, the success of the NLRB was little less than spectacular. In case after case its findings were sustained by the highest Court; the percentage of reversals was, indeed, the smallest in the history of any of the independent commissions. Sustained by these triumphs in the labor and the judicial arenas, the Board successfully

[1] U.S. *v.* Darby Lumber Co., 312 U.S. 100.

beat back all attempts to repeal its authority or curtail its powers and, by the beginning of the third Roosevelt administration, the opposition was silenced if not converted.

4. *Political and Administrative Reform*

The history of the NLRB was symbolic of a development long under way but not yet appreciated by the average citizen: the expansion of governmental functions and the burgeoning of administrative agencies. The number of civil servants in the employ of the Federal Government had increased from some 370,000 before World War I to over half a million during the Hoover administration. Under the New Deal, with the establishment of new boards and bureaus and the enlargement of old ones, the number rose from 583,000 in 1932 to 920,000 in 1939. Both the increase in governmental activity and in the number of civil servants had every appearance of permanence.

This situation was regarded with misgivings by many whose thinking about government had been moulded by the laissez-faire philosophy. But with most people the older notion that that government was best which governed least had given way to a more realistic appreciation of government as the servant of the people and the instrument of national welfare. The 'necessary evil' of Thomas Paine had become so necessary that it had ceased to be an evil. More and more Americans came to look to government to perform whatever individuals and groups were powerless to do for the control of national economy and the protection of society. Farmers looked to it to save them from the consequences of the vagaries of the weather or their own carelessness; the unemployed to provide them jobs or relief; the old and infirm for security; distressed borrowers to save their homes; the middle class to guarantee bank deposits; investors to safeguard investment; working men to protect labor organizations and regulate wages and hours; teachers to keep the schools open; scholars to keep them in school; while the whole people took for granted that government would regulate business and transportation, develop water power, preserve the soil and the forest resources, and generally supervise most aspects of national life.

Yet the government which had thus come to play so crucial a part in the life of the nation had developed in an opportunistic and haphazard fashion. Every student of government knew that the administrative machinery was characterized by confusion, inefficiency, and extravagance, while to the layman bureaucracy was synonymous with red tape. Scientific management, which had been applied to the business of large corporations, had never been tried out in this largest and most important of all businesses. Every President since Theodore Roosevelt had been aware of the problem and anxious for reform, but none had been able to achieve more than piecemeal improvement.

Franklin D. Roosevelt was convinced that a thorough overhauling of the executive branch of the government was imperative, and in 1936 he appointed a Committee on Administrative Management to formulate plans for reform. Early the next year he laid their recommendations before Congress: a reorganization of the civil service and an extension of the merit system; the addition of two new departments of cabinet rank; the establishment of budget and efficiency agencies, and of a planning agency through which the President might co-ordinate executive functions; an increase in the White House staff; and the creation of an independent auditing system for the executive departments. These reforms, the President asserted, would 'increase efficiency, minimize error, duplication and waste, and raise the morale of the public service.'

The proposals were innocuous enough, but Congress, alarmed by the presidential 'attack' on the Supreme Court, jealous of any enlargement of executive authority, and sensitive to the bogey of dictatorship, rejected them. The President, however, persisted, and in 1939 — after the Supreme Court issue had been settled and the Congressional elections were safely out of the way — had the satisfaction of obtaining Congressional approval for most of his program.

One important aspect of the problem remained — that concerned with the extension of the merit system and the divorce of administration from politics. Although the total number of federal employees covered by the merit system had increased steadily during the New Deal, the percentage had declined, and the suspicion that many of the relief agencies engaged in politics was widespread. To prevent any such exploitation of government employees or relief workers, Senator Hatch of New Mexico introduced and Congress passed two bills forbidding federal employees or state employees paid from federal funds from engaging in 'pernicious political activities.' More specifically these bills made it unlawful for any office-holder to coerce or intimidate any voter, or 'to use his official authority or influence for the purpose of interfering with an election or affecting the result thereof.' Just what these esoteric words meant was not entirely clear, nor was their meaning clarified in the following decade.

If politics were to be divorced from spoils, it seemed logical that they should be more closely wedded to principles and issues. This, at any rate, was the view which the President announced with reference to the Congressional elections of 1938. Exasperated by the persistent hostility of some reactionary Democrats to the New Deal program, and anxious that party labels should have meaning and that the Democratic party should be a liberal one, Roosevelt undertook what he thought was a vindication of political principles and what his critics called a 'purge.' Speaking — so he insisted — as party leader rather than as President, he appealed for the defeat of three conservatives in the Democratic primaries — George of Georgia, Tydings of Maryland, and O'Connor of New York. If parties really represented principles and if the Wilsonian theory of presidential responsibility as party leader was sound, the appeal was both logical and laudable. But American politics are not governed by considerations of logic or principles of political philosophy, and critics were quick to stigmatize the presidential intervention as dictatorial and to appeal to state pride to defeat it. The appeal was successful, notably in Georgia and Maryland, where the 'purge' was repudiated and George and Tydings triumphantly returned to the Senate. There was rejoicing among the Republicans, yet with the Democrats holding a majority of 262 to 169 in the House and 69 to 23 in the Senate, even the most critical could not believe that the President's popularity was seriously impaired.

5. *The New Deal: An Evaluation*

With the farm and labor legislation of 1938 the domestic reform program of the Roosevelt administration was rounded out. Much, to be sure, remained to be done, but what remained was in the nature of an extension and elaboration of policies already inaugurated rather than of new projects. Certainly by the close of the second Roosevelt administration the philosophical principles of the New Deal had been firmly established, the process of public education carried through, the political and administrative machinery set in effective motion, many essential economic and social reforms achieved, and prosperity largely restored. Roosevelt was to win another term in which to consummate his program, but that third term was primarily concerned with war. The end of the second administration, then, furnishes an appropriate opportunity for an evaluation of the New Deal.

What, then, would seem to be the significance of the New Deal in our history, what its permanent influences? First, there is the immensely important physical rehabilitation of the country. A century from now this may well seem the most important contribution on the domestic front. For three-quarters of a century, and more, Americans had been wasting their natural resources at an appalling rate, and efforts to halt this waste and to reverse the trend had been unsuccessful. The New Deal attack upon this basic problem was more ambitious and thorough-going than any other that had been launched. The fight on soil erosion, the building of dams and the planting of trees to prevent disastrous floods, the effort to halt the spread of the Dust Bowl and reclaim the Great Plains, the closing of the public domain, the reclamation of sub-marginal lands, the development of water-power resources, the inauguration of regional reconstruction projects like the T.V.A. and the Bonneville — all these changed the face of the country and at least halted if they did not reverse a long trend toward the exhaustion of our natural resources.

Second — and less assuredly — we can note accomplishments in the direction of human rehabilitation and the general acceptance of the principle that the State has an inescapable responsibility for the health, welfare, employment, and security as well as for the protection and education of all its citizens. This principle was implicit in the New Freedom, but only with the New Deal did it receive general application in federal and state governmental activities. The details of that application are familiar enough. It began with large-scale relief to the unemployed; it expanded into a systematized program of social security; it embraced medical services and socialized medicine; it entered the domains of agriculture and labor, established maximum hours, minimum wages, elaborate programs of rural rehabilitation; it revealed itself in an enlarged concern for the welfare of women and children. The principle was, in fact, accepted by the Republican as well as the Democratic platform of 1940, 1944, and 1948. Only in case of a political revolution beyond our ken can there ever arise any serious challenge to this realistic interpretation of the term 'commonwealth' to the principle of community responsibility for the welfare of all.

In the third place, developments in the realm of politics and government were of capital importance. One of these was the strengthening of the power of the executive and the reassertion of presidential leadership characteristic of every period of progressive advance in our history. Another was the revitalization of the political party as a vehicle for popular will and as an instrument for effective action; a vindication of the party system as the chief agency for harmonizing sectional and class conflicts and acting as a broker for clashing pressure groups and interests. In much the same category was the vast expansion of governmental activities and of administrative agencies and the effective adaptation of government to the problems of twentieth-century economy and society. If more was to be desired here on the score of efficiency and economy, few will doubt that government will continue to exercise most of the new activities and responsibilities which it has assumed.

More fundamental than these, but inextricably connected with them, was the rapid growth of federal centralization. This, too, had been under way a long time, but it was accelerated by the necessities of the depression, the practices of the New Deal, and, after 1939, by the requirements of national defense. The growth of centralization was apparent in the administrative field — with the increase of bureaus and departments, of the number of civil servants, and of government expenditures. It was apparent in the legislative field with the extension of federal authority over agriculture, industry, transportation, banking, labor, conservation, public works, health, education, and the arts. And it was ratified judicially by the application of a 'broad construction' of the Constitution where federal authority was involved. This development of federal centralization was attended by a corresponding growth of regional administrative activities — of which the T.V.A. was merely the most publicized — and the accommodation of administration to geographical and economic realities. State boundary lines lost much of their earlier importance; state loyalties perceptibly waned; state powers, while by no means diminished in their totality, were not permitted to interfere with the activities of the Federal Government with respect to problems that transcended state lines.

One of the most interesting New Deal developments was that of economic and social planning. Most Americans were naturally suspicious of governmental planning, and their distaste for it was accentuated by the reaction against the Russian 'five year plan.' Yet the immense tasks of physical and human rehabilitation, the incoherence and confusion attendant upon merely opportunistic reforms, and the practical necessities of co-operation between state and federal governments and between different departments within governments, all brought home to students the desirability of some form of planning. Tried out locally, as by city planning commissions, or regionally, as in the Great Plains or the Rio Grande Valley, planning seemed more reasonable. The National Resources Board shortly became a National Resources Planning Board, and concerned itself largely with research and over-all planning problems. 'Planning' came to lose its socialistic connotations and to be adopted by most of those who appreciated the staggering complexity of modern administration.

Of basic importance in this political arena was the growth of an appreciation of the nature and function of the state. The misleading notion that there was an inevitable conflict between man and the state had long embarrassed American politics. Distrust of the state, inherited from the revolutionary era, approved by Jefferson and his disciples, endowed with a perverse rationalization by Herbert Spencer and the laissez-faire school, gave way, at last, to a realization of the fact that the state was man, organized politically, and that man expressed himself naturally in the state. The old distrust of state action gave way to the realization that only the state could act effectively in the many crises of national affairs. Happily, this new attitude was unattended by that odious personification or deification of the state which developed contemporaneously in Europe.

This new and more reasonable political philosophy made possible the strengthening of the state not at the expense of society but for the benefit of society. It became clear, after a century and a half of discussion, that there was no necessary conflict between the ideal of order and the ideal of liberty. The age-old question whether democracy could function under self-imposed constitutional limitations was answered — temporarily at least — in the affirmative. The old but ever new question whether a democracy was strong enough to resist special pressure groups, to reconcile conflicting economic interests, to subordinate private to public welfare, seemed likewise to have received an affirmative answer.

The expansion of governmental regulation and functions meant a steady socialization of the economic life of the nation. The immediate impulse to socialization came from practical considerations of the inability of private enterprise to undertake necessary large-scale social and economic programs. Its manifestations were chiefly in the economic realm: government development of hydro-electrical power, government partnership in banking, government operation of merchant marine. More significant, if less dramatic, was the government participation in business activities that came first with the depression and then with the defense program. During the early years of the depression the Federal Government — of necessity rather than in response to policy — came to the rescue of banks, railroads, utilities, and industries, and financial aid involved supervision and effective partnership. War brought a vast expansion of governmental activity — the financing and operation of a number of defense industries, construction of low-cost housing, the financing of large-scale medical programs, and many others. States, too, expanded not only their regulatory activities but their participation in social and economic life, setting up systems of state insurance and employment agencies, while cities took on such diverse activities as transportation, the distribution of milk, and radio broadcasting.

It would be a mistake to assume that this socialization was developed entirely at the expense of private enterprise. Indeed it is certain that the New Deal did more to strengthen and to save the capitalist economy than it did to weaken or destroy it. That economy had broken down in many nations abroad, and its collapse contributed to the rise of totalitarian governments which completely subordinated business to the state. The system was on the verge of collapse in the United States during the Hoover administration, and it is at least conceivable that had that collapse been permitted to occur, it might have been followed by the establishment of an economy very different from that to which Americans were accustomed. Historically Franklin Roosevelt's administration did for twentieth-century American capitalism what Theodore Roosevelt's and Wilson's had done for nineteenth-century business enterprise: it saved the system by ridding it of its grosser abuses and forcing it to accommodate itself to larger public interests. History may eventually record Franklin D. Roosevelt as the greatest American conservative since Hamilton.

Closely associated with these political and economic developments was the expansion and extension of democracy under the New Deal. This was obviously in the American tradition. Political democracy had been, in large part, achieved before 1933; it was the peculiar function of the New Deal to give the term realistic economic implications, to bring home to the American people the fact that the common man must be assured of security as well as suffrage. In speech after speech Roosevelt pointed what he thought the moral of recent European history: that given a choice between liberty and bread men will choose bread, and that it was the task of democracy to provide bread as well as to secure liberty. In a 'fireside chat' of 1938 he said:

Democracy has disappeared in several other great nations, not because the people of those nations disliked democracy, but because they had grown

> tired of unemployment and insecurity, of seeing their children hungry while they sat helpless in the face of government confusion and government weakness through lack of leadership in government. Finally, in desperation, they chose to sacrifice liberty in the hope of getting something to eat. We in America know that our democratic institutions can be preserved and made to work. But in order to preserve them we need . . . to prove that the practical operation of democratic government is equal to the task of protecting the security of the people. . . The people of America are in agreement in defending their liberties at any cost, and the first line of that defense lies in the protection of economic security.

And to this task of providing economic — and psychological — security Roosevelt devoted the major energies of his administration.

Yet it is well to note that the New Deal concept of democracy was not egalitarian, that it did not propose a levelling of economic inequalities or a readjustment of class relationships. Great fortunes were to be taxed to rescue the one-third of the nation alleged to be underfed and ill-housed, but though organized wealth was antagonized, it was not attacked. Nor did the New Deal seek to operate within group organizations — industry, labor, corporations, the professions. These were left free — within the framework of the anti-trust and other laws — to work out their own policies, and it was clear that these groups had little interest in experimenting with democracy.

Even more significant than the extension of democracy in the domestic realm was the maintenance of a democratic system of government and society in a world swept by confused alarms of struggle and flight. 'The only sure bulwark of continuing liberty,' Roosevelt had observed, 'is a government strong enough to protect the interests of the people, and a people strong enough and well enough informed to maintain its sovereign control over its government.' The proof that in the United States it was possible for such a government to exist and such a people to flourish was of fateful significance, and it restored the United States to its traditional position as 'the hope of the human race.' For in the thirties it became doubtful that liberty or democracy could survive in the modern world, and at the end of that decade totalitarian states felt strong enough to challenge the democracies in a war for survival. It was of utmost importance to the peoples of the world that the American democracy had withstood the buffetings of depression and the vicissitudes of world affairs and emerged strong and courageous; that the American people were refreshed in their faith in the democratic order, prepared to defend it at home and to fight for it wherever it was threatened.

XXVI

THE COMING OF THE SECOND WORLD WAR

1. *Isolationism and the Threat to Collective Security*

ROOSEVELT'S second Inaugural Address, like Wilson's first, failed to mention foreign affairs, yet once again, as in the years after 1913, domestic issues were destined to be overshadowed by those of foreign relations. The most important development of these years was not the success of the New Deal in the realm of judicial, farm, labor, and administrative reform, but the catastrophic breakdown of international security in world affairs and the impact of international anarchy upon the United States. And it was fortunate indeed that the American people had weathered the worst of the depression and set their domestic affairs in some semblance of order before they were called upon to meet the greatest of all crises in their history — a crisis in which the survival of the nation was at stake.

The breakdown of collective security was neither sudden nor unexpected. It was a disintegration rather than a collapse, the causes of which were inherent in the First World War and the political and economic rearrangements that followed. There had indeed been little real security in the immediate post-war years, but there was peace, of a sort, and a general acknowledgement of the sanctity of treaties and the paramount necessity of preserving peace and international law. With the thirties peace was shattered, and both treaties and international law were formally repudiated.

For this distintegration the United States was partly responsible. She had participated in winning the war and making the peace, but rejected all responsibility for maintaining the peace. Disillusioned about the war, cynical about the treaties, critical of the political jockeying of the continental powers, indifferent to the fate of the new nations that she had helped create and that looked to her for inspiration, she had taken the road to isolationism. And, notwithstanding several sincere gestures in the direction of disarmament — the Washington Conference, the Pact of Paris, the Hoover moratorium — she had persisted on that road for almost two decades. Convinced that big navies made for war she had joined in scrapping hundreds of thousands of tons of capital ships, and, even after 1930, had discouraged rearmament, while regarding with approval or indifference the economic and military rehabilitation of Germany. The United States had withdrawn from the affairs of Europe, was playing a less vigorous role in the Far East, and seemed ready to abandon her interests in Latin America. She said, in effect, that the affairs of the rest of the world were of no concern to her.

This isolationism which the country had formally embraced in 1920 was not only diplomatic and political, but economic and even moral. Tariff barriers made it increasingly difficult for foreigners to sell or to buy from the United States or to pay their war debts. Many leaders dallied with the notion of economic self-sufficiency, refusing to recognize the international spread of American trade and investments or the dependence of American manufactures upon materials imported from abroad. And behind the economic and political isolationism was the vague but pervasive attitude that the United States was morally superior to the nations of the Old World, and that she could better safeguard her moral superiority if she avoided contamination with Old World secret diplomacy, wars, racial hatreds, and decadent cultures.

Isolation was the official American position throughout the twenties and well into the thirties, and it was fraught with peril. For in this policy of isolation the United States was not alone. Other democratic nations were following the American example and contributing, in one way or another, to the disintegration of collective security. The League of Nations, though repudiated by its original sponsor, had at first gone far to justify the ardent hopes of its friends; during the thirties, however, it steadily lost power and prestige. American failure to join the World Court made that body largely ineffective. Good will was plenty and cheap; but neither England nor France nor the United States cared to enforce by arms the provisions of the Versailles Treaty or the findings of the League Council or even international law. The democracies, rather, lulled themselves into the belief that trouble could be avoided by abandoning instruments of force. Thus, even this early, moral apathy, political timidity and mental laziness, inaugurated the policy which was later to be characterized as appeasement.

If the democracies were thus willing to let treaties and international law go by default, the non-democracies were prepared to repudiate and flout them. Across the seas, unappreciated by the average American there had arisen a new threat to peace, to law, and, ultimately, to American security. This was totalitarianism as expressed in the political organization of Italy, Germany, and Japan. The essence of totalitarianism was the subordination of all individual or social interests to the interests of a 'master race' represented by the State; its object, the division of the world into spheres of influence, each sphere to be controlled by a master nation; its method, the ruthless use of force. Italy, under Benito Mussolini, had inaugurated the first totalitarian state in 1922; Adolf Hitler, who became Chancellor of Germany in 1933, improved vastly on the Italian model; Japan, long inured to despotism, borrowed methods and techniques rather than philosophy from these European powers who were shortly to become allies.

Totalitarianism developed in countries which had suffered defeat in the First World War or in the subsequent treaty arrangements, or that had experienced economic collapse and social demoralization in the post-war years. These countries needed, or thought they needed, room into which their surplus populations might expand. To the discontented leaders of these states democratic processes seemed too slow and ineffectual for the accomplishment of domestic reforms, while the observance of international law and the maintenance of peace implied an acquiescence in the alleged injustices and inequalities of the *status quo*. Totalitarianism promised the articulation of every phase of economy and the regimentation of all activities of society to the service of the State, the suppression of protest and dissent, and the concentration of the whole energy of the nation on expansion and aggrandizement. It promised a solution of domestic difficulties, an escape from embarrassing international obligations, and, ultimately, power and prosperity in a new world order. That regimentation was to be achieved at the cost of liberty and democracy was no deterrent to those who thought liberty dangerous and democracy decadent; that the policy of expansion would usher in a new era of lawlessness and war did not discourage those who regarded law as an instrument for their oppression and who held war to be a positive good. And because the totalitarian achievements in the domestic field commended themselves on the score of efficiency, and the totalitarian protest against the distribution of territory and natural resources seemed plausible, the democratic peoples for years did not appreciate the fact that the totalitarian philosophy was a threat to world peace and a challenge to all the values of Christian civilization, and to the inherent dignity of man.

2. *The Bell Tolls*

Early in the thirties the first of these totalitarian nations felt strong enough to strike. Japan, long restless under the limitations of the Open Door policy and the Nine Power Treaty, and determined to establish her hegemony in the Far East, invaded Manchuria in September 1931, crushed Chinese resistance, and, a year later, set up the puppet state of Manchukuo. The United States protested and the League of Nations condemned the aggression, but Japan ignored the American protest, withdrew from the League, and prepared to extend her conquests.

The moral was not lost on other discontented nations. Throughout the twenties Germany had wrestled with the economic disorganization and social demoralization that followed her defeat, and although Britain and the United States had co-operated to ameliorate her condition, the crisis was, by 1931, acute. German democracy seemed unable to cope with this crisis, but Adolf Hitler and his National Socialist party promised relief from economic ills, escape from the 'bondage' of the Versailles Treaty, and the union of the entire German race under one strong government. In 1933 the aged President von Hindenburg was persuaded to appoint Hitler to the chancellorship, and within a few months all opposition leaders were in jail and the National Socialist party had a firm grip on the entire political and military machinery of the country. Hitler moved swiftly to consolidate his position and implement his promises. Determined to make Germany the greatest military power in the world, he contemptuously withdrew from both the Geneva Disarmament Conference and the League of Nations and embarked upon a full-scale program of rearmament. And, as if to dramatize his dissociation from the moral standards of the Western world, he invoked the discredited doctrine of Aryan superiority to justify a reign of terror against the Jews.

By 1935 Hitler felt sufficiently strong and sufficiently confident of democratic weakness openly to take the aggressive. In January of that year a plebiscite, provided for in the Versailles Treaty, returned the Saar to Germany; having used the treaty Hitler denounced it two months later, admitted that Germany had illegally created an air force, and openly reintroduced compulsory military service. Faced with these *faits accomplis,* distrustful of one another, and fearful of communist Russia, the European signatories of the Versailles Treaty meekly acquiesced, while Britain ratified the new arrangements by a formal agreement permitting Germany to build her navy up to thirty-five per cent of the total British tonnage, with an even more generous allotment for submarines.

As early as 1927 Benito Mussolini had declared that 1935 would be the turning point in European history and had promised the Italians that when that time came ' we shall be in a position to make our voice felt and to see our rights recognized.' Mussolini thought the time was now ripe to re-establish the Roman Empire of ancient days. Ethiopia, which blocked the way from Italian Libya to Italian Somaliland and which was reputed to be rich in raw materials and weak in military power, seemed an easy victim to start on. Early in 1935 Mussolini persuaded the slippery French Premier, Pierre Laval, to consent to an Italian conquest of Ethiopia, and during the winter of 1935–36 that conquest was consummated. Haile Selassie, the Negus of Ethiopia, appealed to the League of Nations, which, after tedious wrangling, denounced Italy as an aggressor nation and invoked against her the sanctions of arms, credits, and trade embargoes. Italy had arms enough, however, and the exemption of iron, steel, copper, and oil from the trade embargo made a joke of sanctions. It was inescapably clear that the League was impotent and that both France and Great Britain preferred the dubious course of appeasement to the more honorable one of resistance. On 7 March when the conquest of Ethiopia was all but complete, Mussolini agreed to arbitration ' in principle '; that same day Hitler denounced the Locarno Treaty, which he had expressly promised to observe, and ordered his army into the demilitarized Rhineland.

It was clear that similar philosophies produced similar consequences in the realm of power politics. Both Germany and Italy were on record as indifferent to the obligations of treaties and of international law, and contemptuous alike of the League of Nations and of the democracies who so feebly supported it. The identity of interest of these two totalitarian states was shortly dramatized in one of the great crises in the history of modern Europe and of modern democracy — the Spanish Civil War. Restless under an incompetent and oppressive dictatorship the Spanish people, in 1931, had overthrown their decrepit monarchy and proclaimed a republic. The following years were troubled by the conflict of extreme conservative and extreme radical groups. The indecisive election of 1936 placed a popular front coalition government in uneasy control of the nation, but reactionary groups still commanded the support of the Church, the great landowners, and — above all — the army. Emboldened by promises of support from Italy and Germany, the Nationalists, as these reactionary groups came to be known, raised the standard of rebellion, and in midsummer 1936 Spain was plunged into a devastating civil war that had much the same relation to the Second World War that the Kansas struggle had to the American Civil War.

Although the Republican regime was not a democratic one in the American sense, and although it had failed conspicuously to maintain order and safeguard liberty and property, it was clear that its defeat would constitute a severe setback for democracy and a signal triumph for the forces of reaction and of lawlessness. Nazi Germany and Fascist Italy saw this readily enough, and promptly made the cause of the Nationalists their own. The governments of Great Britain and France failed to appreciate the implications of this war, or feared that intervention might lead to a widening of the conflict which would involve all Europe. Russia alone actively supported the Loyalists, but was in no position to extend much assistance; and her support, raising as it did the bogy of Communism, further discouraged the timid governments of the democracies. So while Germany and Italy hurried hundreds of planes and tens of thousands of 'volunteers' and enormous quantities of war material into the Nationalist camp, Britain and France adopted the short-sighted and unheroic policy of non-intervention, and the United States Congress clamped an embargo on the shipment of munitions to either side. These divergent policies ultimately decided the outcome of the war, and a Nationalist dictatorship was set up under General Franco. The democracies condemned Republican Spain to defeat and dissolution; the totalitarian powers saw to it that their side won, and so gained an ally and enormous prestige.

Once more it was Japan's turn. On 7 July 1937 the militant government deliberately precipitated the 'China incident' which was to plunge the Far East into prolonged war. A hastily summoned international conference at Brussels formally adjudged Japan an 'aggressor' nation, proposed a truce, and offered mediation, but Japan replied that the 'China Incident' was her exclusive affair.

President Roosevelt might have declared that a state of war existed and so invoked the Neutrality Acts (which we shall describe presently) and prevented the export to Japan of oil, scrap iron, and other war materials. But any such embargo would have to be applied impartially and would have damaged China far more than it could hurt Japan. Ambassador Joseph Grew in Tokyo, moreover, warned the administration that if Japan was denied access to oil and iron products of the United States, or of other strategic materials in British and Dutch Malaya, her armed forces would go down there and take them — and war was the last thing the United States wanted or cared to risk. Not one 'interest' in America, even those most hurt by Japanese competition, not one admiral or general, not one pressure group, wanted war with Japan.

As they advanced into China, the Japanese bombed and looted American churches, hospitals, and schools, excluded American commerce from occupied provinces, and perpetrated outrages on American nationals; but America remained quiescent. Even a deliberately planned sinking of the gunboat *Panay* by Japanese Army aviators on 12 December 1937 aroused but slight indignation. When the Tokyo government apologized and paid reparation a sigh of relief went over America. What wonder the Japanese, German, and Italian militarists concluded that nothing could make Americans fight?

The pattern and the menace of totalitarian conquest were becoming clear enough, yet the democracies, unprepared to risk war, continued to follow a policy of appeasement. Germany, taking advantage of their military weakness and their spiritual timidity, moved swiftly and boldly to the creation of the 'new order' in which she should be the dominant world power. From the beginning of his political career Hitler had been committed to three major objectives: the reincorporation into a greater Germany of all German peoples, the control by Germany of Middle Europe and the road to the Middle East, and the erection of a totalitarian barrier against communism. By 1936 he had called into existence the 'Rome-Berlin' Axis, and an anti-Communist alliance which shortly embraced Japan, Italy, Spain, and Hungary. Secure in his new alliances, confident of the strength of the mighty military machine he was creating, and emboldened by the ineptitude and demoralization of France and Britain and the isolation of Russia, Hitler inaugurated a policy of territorial aggrandizement.

Austria was the logical place to begin: she was small and defenseless, her population was largely German, she occupied a strategic position on the road to Italy and on the flank of Czechoslovakia, and her seizure would serve as a laboratory for further aggrandizements. Late in 1937 Hitler decided that union now with Austria was imperative, and in February of '38 he promised the return to the Reich of ten million Germans beyond her frontiers. The next month the blow fell. While Britain and France held futile conferences, and Mussolini hid away, a Nazi fifth column in Austria took control of the army and the police. The plucky Austrian Chancellor, Schuschnigg, who had resisted Nazi aggression to the last, abdicated, and on the night of 11 March the German mechanized army pounded across the border and took over the helpless country. Two days later the union of Austria and Germany was formally announced. Without firing a gun Germany had added seven million people to her strength, had established her boundary at the Brenner pass, had flanked Czechoslovakia and interposed an effective barrier between Russia and France, and had vindicated her 'strategy of terror.'

Before the democracies had recovered from this shock, Hitler was ready for the next stroke. This time the prize was an even greater one. Czechoslovakia lay athwart German access to the Danubian Valley; she was rich in natural resources and in industry; her army and air force were powerful enough to be a valuable prize but not sufficiently powerful to resist German might; she was thoroughly democratic and therefore a standing rebuke to totalitarian pretensions. In the Sudetenland, along the German border, lived some three million Germans. By no stretch of the imagination could they be characterized as oppressed, but many of them did undoubtedly long for incorporation into the mother country. Hitler was ready to demand the cession of the Sudeten, yet the demand was not unaccompanied by risks. For little Czechoslovakia, it was thought, had powerful friends and allies. France was bound to her by the most solemn obligations; Russia was prepared to support her; Great Britain and the United States — which had been largely instrumental in her establishment — regarded her with affection. Throughout the spring and summer of 1938 Hitler stormed at the hapless Czechs while he alternately threatened and cajoled Britain and France. His tactics were successful. When, early in September, he demanded the immediate cession of the Sudeten, the British Government admonished the Czechs to yield. Abandoned by her friends Czechoslovakia capitulated, and the crisis seemed past. But apparently Hitler did not want so undramatic a victory, for he refused to await the outcome of a plebiscite or the slow processes of arbitration, and insisted on immediate and complete surrender. Determined to avoid war at all costs the British Prime Minister, Neville Chamberlain, flew to Hitler's mountain retreat at Berchtesgaden to plead for delay. The appeal seemed successful, but when the Czech Premier Beneš promised to resist invasion a new crisis arose. This time both Chamberlain and Daladier, Premier of France, made the pilgrimage to Hitler's Canossa. At the Munich Conference of 29–30 September, Britain and France abandoned the little democracy to her fate. 'I bring you peace with honor,' said Chamberlain on his return to London. 'I believe it is peace in our time.' But Winston Churchill said, 'Britain and France had to choose between war and dishonor. They chose dishonor. They will have war.' The diagnosis was correct, the prophecy true.

Thus by 1938 the system of collective security had completely disintegrated. The Versailles territorial settlements of 1919, which had followed racial lines and popular will as closely as possible, had been repudiated, international law flouted, promises broken, the League of Nations reduced to impotence, and the doctrine that might makes for success triumphantly vindicated. Ruthlessness, treachery, and violence had proved stronger than the armor of a righteous cause. Ethiopia, Spain, China, Austria, Czechoslovakia, each in turn had been sacrificed by the democracies to the principle of appeasement, until it was clear that that principle was bankrupt. 'If we have to fight,' Chamberlain had said fatuously of the Czech crisis, 'it must be on larger issues than this,' and in America as in England and France millions echoed the sentiment. But three centuries ago an English preacher-poet, John Donne, had pointed out that mankind is a unit and that injury to any part of it hurts the whole. Alluding to the custom of churches tolling a 'passing bell' when a parishioner died, he wrote:

> Who bends not his ears to any bell, which upon any occasion rings? but who can remove it from that bell, which is passing a peece of himselfe out of this world? No man is an Iland, intire of it selfe; every man is a peece of the Continent, a part of the maine; if a Clod bee washed away by the Sea, Europe is the lesse, as well as if a Promontorie were, as well as if a Mannor of thy friends or of thine owne were; any mans death diminishes me, because I am involved in Mankinde; And therefore never send to know for whom the bell tolls; *it tolls for thee.*

3. *A Fortress on a Paper Pad*

The bell tolled for the United States when Republican Spain, Austria, and Czechoslovakia passed, but its sombre notes were muffled and dim to American ears. To the vicissitudes of foreign affairs the average American was indifferent. About all that he thought of Europe was that it was decadent, given to wars, secret diplomacy, class conflict, and a tendency to evade payment of just debts; his attitude towards foreign policy could be summed up in the cliché, 'avoid foreign entanglements.' Isolationism was not so much a reasoned principle as an instinct. 'We are so snug here,' said President Coolidge to a visitor who described the state of Europe. 'Nothing they do can touch us.' We had always won our wars, we were fully protected by ocean barriers, we were powerful and invulnerable. Public opinion, to be sure, was shocked by the persecution of Jews and other minorities, but with respect to most other developments abroad it was indifferent or divided. Most conservative and Catholic opinion supported the Spanish Nationalists against the Loyalists: the argument of self-determination, invoked to justify the German annexation of Austria and the seizure of the Sudeten, seemed plausible; Ethiopians were said to be uncivilized; it was too bad about China, but there was nothing we could do about it, and China was big enough to take care of herself. Mussolini had spruced up Italy and made the trains run on time; Hitler was a champion defender of civilization against the Communists. As for the Versailles Treaties, they were scarcely worth sustaining; we had never thought enough of the League of Nations to join it, and international law was merely a fiction about which jurists argued. And finally, so it was said, we had trouble enough at home without going abroad for more. The rise of totalitarianism coincided with the depression and the New Deal; American attention was fixed on the rising curve of unemployment, the conflicts of labor and capital, the fate of banks and bank deposits, the distress of the farmer, and a hundred other matters of immediate and personal concern. It was too much to expect that the average American would realize that there was any connection between these domestic difficulties and foreign affairs, or that what happened in remote quarters of the globe could ever affect him.

This was the popular rather than the official attitude, to be sure, but in a democracy the two are not divorced. Officially the United States protested against the Japanese invasion of Manchuria in 1931 and denounced her invasion of China in 1937, but public opinion would not have permitted the Hoover or the Roosevelt administrations to support these protests by any show of force. Officially, too, we had from time to time reminded careless signatories of the obligations of the Pact of Paris and, in general terms, condemned the resort to force in international affairs. We had sought to build up friendly relations abroad — through reciprocity treaties, the recognition of

Russia, and the good neighbor policy in Latin America. Yet it was inescapably clear that without popular support the administration was in no position to interfere in the affairs of Europe or of Asia, or even to speak authoritatively in condemnation of aggression. And such popular support was conspicuously wanting; it was the isolationists who grew in strength. By 1935 isolationist sentiment was sufficiently strong to impose itself upon the government in a formal fashion.

All through the twenties American disillusion in regard to the World War crusade for democracy had deepened, and the revelations of European secret treaties and chicanery, the spectacle of confusion, compromise, and appeasement, accentuated that disillusionment. In 1934 a Senate Committee under the chairmanship of Gerald Nye of North Dakota undertook an elaborate investigation into the record of the munitions industry and the bankers during the First World War, and while the findings failed to prove that these interests were in any way responsible for our entry into the war, they did reveal scandalously high profits, outspoken sympathy for the Allies, and studied hostility to disarmament. The public did not distinguish between responsibility for war and profits from war, but concluded that Wall Street bankers and 'merchants of death' had cunningly sold the war to unsuspecting Americans. Publicists, historians, and journalists joined in the hue and cry against the Wilsonian venture, and converted a substantial part of public opinion to the naïve view that the American people had been stampeded into the war against their better judgment. They convinced millions of Americans that our participation in the war had been a mistake, that our intervention in any future European war would be a crime, and that the only way to escape involvement was to take the profits out of war and the risks out of neutrality. In 1934 the Johnson Act denied to nations that had defaulted on their debts the right to float securities in the United States; early the next year the Senate again rejected membership in the World Court. The outbreak of the Italo-Ethiopian conflict crystallized the demand for a more thoroughgoing attack on the entire problem of neutrality.

The philosophy behind the neutrality legislation of 1935–37 was set forth in an article by the lawyer, Charles Warren:

> In the future, in order to keep out of war, it will be necessary . . . for the United States to do far more than merely comply with its legal obligations of neutrality. In order to avoid friction and complications with the bellig-

erents it must be prepared to impose upon the actions of its citizens greater restrictions than international law requires. It must also be prepared to relinquish many rights which it has heretofore claimed and asserted, and to yield to contentions by belligerents, hitherto denied by it, with respect to interference with the trade and travel of its citizens on the high seas, if the interests of the belligerents seem to them so to require.[1]

The legislation itself, enacted piecemeal over a period of two years, may well be considered as a whole. It was designed to prevent, at almost any cost, the involvement of the United States in any non-American war. It prohibited loans or credits to belligerents, placed a mandatory embargo upon direct or indirect shipments of arms or implements of war to belligerents, gave the President discretion to require payment and transfer of title before export to belligerents of any articles whatsoever, forbade American citizens to travel upon the ships of belligerents, and prohibited the arming of American merchant vessels. By the act of 1937 these limitations were to be effective in the event of civil as well as international wars.

Technically this legislation did not surrender any of our rights under international law. It was purely domestic, controlled only our own policy, and was none of the concern of any foreign nation. Actually, however, it constituted an abandonment of the traditional American doctrine of freedom of the seas and waived rights under international law which we had thought sufficiently valuable to fight for in 1917. Even more significant was the principle, implicit in this legislation, that the United States would not distinguish between aggressor and victim nations — which was another way of saying that, as far as we were concerned, there was no moral distinction between them. As President Roosevelt, who disapproved this legislation, later observed: [2]

Our arms embargo played right into the hands of the aggressor nations. The aggressor nations knew that under our arms embargo the peace-loving nations of the world, which had not piled up as much armament as the aggressors had, were prevented from buying any war materials from us. The aggressors knew that as soon as they would declare war upon their victims, the victims would be shut off from obtaining implements of war from neutral nations. Of course the aggressors had spent many years and a large portion of their wealth in piling up armaments, and did not have to buy materials outside. The victims of aggression, how-

1 'Troubles of a Neutral,' *Foreign Affairs,* XII, 387–8.

2 *Public Papers and Addresses of F. D. Roosevelt,* 1939 vol., intro. p. xxxiv.

ever, who had not built up armament to the same extent, would have to look to neutral nations to sell the implements of war to them. It was clear, therefore, that so long as our arms embargo statute prevented the United States from helping all belligerents, the aggressor nations were given a tremendous advantage by it, and to that extent were actually encouraged by our laws to make war upon their neighbors.

Such arguments, though urged at the time and amply vindicated by subsequent events, fell upon deaf ears. Congress, like the people in general, was determined that, come what might, the United States would not again be involved in European or Asiatic wars. It believed that peace could be assured by withdrawing American ships and commerce from the areas of war, treating all belligerents with equal indifference, and giving neither aid nor offense to any warring nation. And this conviction had one almost fatal consequence. For the neutrality legislation assumed that the question of American involvement in war was one to be determined exclusively by the United States. It assumed that this country never could or would be attacked. It suggested the futility of rearmament and lulled Americans into a false sense of security. It constituted America's Maginot Line — and it was as easily breached.

Notwithstanding congressional action, American policy was not entirely negative. Neither President Roosevelt nor Secretary Hull was committed to the principle of retreat and surrender implicit in the neutrality legislation, and so far as was constitutionally possible they continued to throw the influence of the United States on the side of international law rather than international anarchy. Roosevelt, who was the most naval-minded of American presidents, had, from the beginning of his term, done his best to strengthen the American Navy. He continued the Stimson policy of refusing to recognize the puppet state of Manchukuo or any modification of the Open Door doctrine in China or of the Four and Nine Power Treaties.

Of positive importance were the efforts of the President and of Secretary Hull to build up hemispherical solidarity. The good-neighbor policy, the abrogation of the Platt Amendment, the withdrawal of American forces of occupation from Caribbean republics, the Hull reciprocity treaties, and the settlement of the long and vexatious controversy over the expropriation by Mexico of American oil properties on terms satisfying to the Mexican government had already testified to the sincerity of American intentions. In 1935 the United States concluded with six Latin American nations a treaty of non-aggression and conciliation which reaffirmed the provisions of the Pact of Paris, provided machinery for its enforcement, and pledged the signatories not to recognize territorial changes effected by force. The next year President Roosevelt himself attended the Pan-American conference at Buenos Aires which provided for mutual consultation on all matters affecting hemispheric peace. Soon the shadow of war fell athwart the Western Hemisphere and the question of collective security emerged from the abstract to the concrete. The eighth Pan-American Conference, meeting at Lima in 1938, adopted resolutions proclaiming 'their unshakable will for peace, their profound sentiment of humanity and tolerance, and their absolute adherence to the principles of international law, of the equal sovereignty of States and of individual liberty without religious or racial prejudices.' These sentiments were reinforced by an endorsement of reciprocal trade agreements and by the interchange of cultural and educational facilities.

Hemispherical solidarity was also developed northward. The administration made renewed efforts to strengthen ties between the United States and Canada. A proposal for a Great Lakes-St. Lawrence waterway, notwithstanding administrative endorsement, failed to command Senate approval, but the enactment of a sweeping reciprocal trade agreement did something to cement economic co-operation. Speaking at Kingston, Ontario, in August 1938, President Roosevelt said,

> The Dominion of Canada is part of the sisterhood of the British Empire. I give you my assurance that the people of the United States will not stand idly by if domination of Canadian soil is threatened by any other Empire.

To what extent the administration was prepared to implement this assurance remained to be seen. But it was clear that the Monroe Doctrine had been extended, in effect, to Canada. It was clear, too, that the famous doctrine was no longer a unilateral but a multilateral declaration of policy.

Meantime President Roosevelt watched, with growing concern, the collapse of collective security abroad. Speaking at Chicago, the heart of the isolationist camp, shortly after the beginning of the 'China incident,' he called for a quarantine against aggressor nations. If lawlessness and violence rage unrestrained, he warned, 'let no one imagine that America will escape, that America may expect mercy, that this Western Hemisphere will not be attacked.' But his prophetic words were denounced as 'war-mongering' at home, and his appeal for concerted action by the peace-loving nations was ignored abroad.

Again during the crisis of 1938 the President attempted to bring about a solution that would be both peaceful and honorable. In a message of 26 September he reminded the disputants of their obligations under the Pact of Paris and other 'binding treaties' and appealed for negotiation and arbitration of the Sudeten question. In an address a few weeks after the Munich surrender Roosevelt warned appeasers abroad as well as at home that 'peace by fear has no higher or more enduring quality than peace by the sword.'

The warning went unheeded, as had the appeal for negotiation. Americans preferred wishful thinking about peace to realistic thinking about war. European statesmen were more impressed with the neutrality legislation than with presidential eloquence. American gestures for the maintenance of law and of peace were admirable but largely futile.

> Longing to wed with Peace, what did we do? —
> Sketched her a fortress on a paper pad;
> Under her casement twanged a love-sick string;
> Left wide the gate that let her foemen through.[3]

4. *War*

For Hitler, Munich was not only a diplomatic triumph; it was a moral one. The democracies had been brought to the verge of war and on an issue which would have justified war in the eyes of the world; they had looked into the abyss and reeled back in dismay. Munich had revealed not only the unwillingness of Britain and France to stand by their commitments and fight for their principles; it had uncovered, too, the hollowness of the Franco-Russian agreement and the inability — or unwillingness — of the democracies to co-operate with the one European power that might have saved them. Emboldened by this spectacle of timidity and dissension, confident that his tactics were both sure and safe, Hitler drove implacably ahead. In March 1939 he sent his army into Czechoslovakia, and, while Britain and France looked helplessly on, dismembered that hapless country. Back in the United States, Senator Borah explained

[3] Edna St. Vincent Millay, *Make Bright the Arrows,* Harper & Brothers, 1942, copyright 1939, 1940, by author.

to a bemused Congress that this was not a violation of the Pact of Paris, and as if to confound him Mussolini three days later seized little Albania. In May the two totalitarian leaders concluded a formal military alliance, directed against France and Britain. When Roosevelt, in a message of 14 April, asked for specific guarantees that Germany would not attack some twenty little countries, Hitler replied with a masterpiece of evasion, defiance, and chicanery which revealed not so much his ingenuity as his contempt for American concepts of international morality. Then, drunk with success, the German Fuehrer turned on Poland, demanding the return of the Free City of Danzig and a wide zone across the Polish Corridor. Edified by the fate of Czechoslovakia when she had yielded to Hitler's demand for the Sudeten, Poland refused, but agreed to arbitrate. Hitler promptly inaugurated his 'war of nerves,' hitherto a prelude to surrender. This time it led to war of weapons.

Thoroughly frightened now, England and France attempted to repair the damage of prolonged appeasement. But the diplomatic humpty-dumpty had had so great a fall that it was quite impossible to put it together again. France distrusted Britain and Britain suspected France, each with some reason; Russia had lost confidence in both of them; the smaller nations could not fail to read the moral of Munich and of Prague. Yet Britain and France pushed doggedly ahead. They offered to guarantee Poland against aggression—though they failed conspicuously to indicate how they proposed to do this. They gratuitously presented guarantees against attack to Greece and Roumania, and Britain concluded a hasty alliance with Turkey. These tardy gestures heartened the democracies as little as they frightened the totalitarian states. As if to test the realism of the British, Russia proposed an alliance on the understanding that she be permitted to march troops into Poland and to take the Baltic states of Latvia, Lithuania, and Estonia into 'protective custody.' Acquiescence in this proposal might have exposed the British government to the charge of insincerity in its zeal for the welfare of the non-aggressor nations, and the proposal was rejected. Of necessity, perhaps, Russia turned to Germany, and on 23 August the world was startled to learn that the two great antagonists had concluded a non-aggression pact.

This was nothing less than a disaster, but though there was a strong faction in both Britain and France that advocated further appeasement, this time the two governments did not back down. Hitler promptly renewed his demands on Poland, but when he offered to 'guarantee' the British Empire in return for a free hand in Poland, the British reply was firm: 'His Majesty's government have obligations to Poland by which they are bound and which they intend to honour.' Perhaps Hitler did not take seriously this display of firmness; perhaps he was sufficiently confident of his military power to discount any aid which Britain and France might give Poland or any damage they might inflict on Germany. And when Roosevelt made a final plea for a peaceful solution of the Polish problem the Fuehrer replied almost contemptuously that he had 'left nothing untried for the purpose of settling the dispute in a friendly manner.'

In the early morning of 1 September the German army marched into Poland while German planes rained death and destruction on airports, railroads, and the civilian inhabitants of cities. Two days later Neville Chamberlain announced to a hushed Parliament that Britain was at war. Reluctantly, France followed.

For two dreadful weeks the German mechanized army smashed through Poland in a 'blitzkrieg' without parallel in modern warfare, while a vast armada of planes reduced Polish cities and villages to rubble. The Russians, meanwhile, moved in from the East, taking over what they held to be Russian Poland and setting up a boundary designed chiefly for future defense. Attacked from all sides by overwhelming force, without military aid from either Britain or France, Poland capitulated. Before the end of September the first stage of the war was over. At comparatively slight cost in men and arms, Germany had added twenty-one million to her population and had enriched herself with vast agricultural and industrial resources.

In the west Germany stood securely behind the newly completed Siegfried Line, while Britain and France, unable or unwilling to take the offensive, relied upon an imperfect blockade to bring her to reason. There ensued a period of inaction which was fatuously denominated a 'phoney' war. Russia, however, more realistic and more ruthless than the western democracies, was not inactive. Zealous to build up defenses against Germany, she demanded concessions from Lithuania, Latvia, and Estonia which were promptly forthcoming, and from Finland which were rejected. Determined to have her way, and anxious perhaps for an experimental test of her military machine, Russia then launched her might against little Finland, and for four months the world stood amazed at the unequal combat. The Finns fought heroically, and, for a time, successfully, and public opinion in Scandinavia, Britain, and the United States, already deeply antagonized by Russian perfidy and traditionally friendly to Finnish democracy, called for effective aid. Aid was forthcoming, but it was feeble and inadequate, and early in March Finland yielded to the inevitable and concluded a peace by which she preserved her independence, but lost territory along her eastern border and the strategic island of Hangoe. A few months later Russia took over the three Baltic states to the south and seized Bessarabia from Roumania, thus completing, as she thought, her system of barrier defense against Nazi might.

Early in April the 'phoney' war came dramatically to an end. Without warning Germany moved into Denmark — with whom she had just recently concluded a non-aggression pact — and then on to Norway. The attack on Norway was a marvel of planning, co-ordination, and efficiency. The Norse put up a stout resistance, but against the combination of surprise, superior force, tanks and airplanes, they were all but helpless. The British, to be sure, tried to help, landing forces at Namsos and Aandalsnes and fighting their way into far-northern Narvik, key to the nickel mines of the interior; within less than two months, however, they had been driven out and German supremacy was unchallenged.

Just a month after the invasion of Scandinavia came the blow in the west. On 10 May the German army invaded neutral Holland while the air force rained death over Holland, Belgium, Luxembourg, and France. In five days the Netherlands were conquered, Rotterdam laid in ruins by the most cruel of all air assaults. Three days later Antwerp fell. Already the Germans, flanking the vaunted Maginot Line, had crashed through the supposedly impenetrable Ardennes Forest, breached the French line at Sedan, enveloped the French Ninth Army, and smashed ahead toward the channel ports in an effort to trap the British Expeditionary Force that had been rushed to the aid of Belgium and France. With the French army thoroughly demoralized, hundreds of thousands of refugees jamming the roads, and the Germans supreme in the air, there seemed to be nothing but disaster ahead. On 21 May — just eleven days after the attack on Holland — the Germans reached the channel west of the British Expeditionary Force; a week later King Leopold of Belgium surrendered, and the British were left to their fate. Then came the miracle of Dunkirk. Every warship, sloop, cutter, launch, fishing boat, ferry, barge, and tugboat was pressed into service and, with a suicide division holding the front and the R.A.F. forming a screen overhead, the British Expeditionary Force, 334,000 strong, was rescued.

Then the Germans turned south, and in two weeks had broken through French defenses everywhere and cut the French army to pieces. On 10 June Italy, eager to be in at the kill, entered the war. Five days later Paris fell, and Reynaud, in desperation, appealed to Roosevelt for 'clouds of planes.' But Roosevelt could give only sympathy, and a hastily formed French government under the aged and undemocratic Marshal Petain sued for peace. Half of France was occupied, and unoccupied France was ruled by the 'men of Vichy' who readily adopted a policy of collaboration with the conquerors. In one month Hitler's mechanized armies had done what the forces of William II had been unable to do in four years.

Now England stood alone. 'We have just one more battle to win,' said Goebbels to cheering thousands, and had Hitler invaded at that moment he might have ruled the world. But he turned aside, instead, to complete the conquest of France and to consolidate his gains, and gave the British time to prepare to justify those proud lines from *King John:*

> This England never did nor never shall
> Lie at the proud foot of a conqueror,
> Come the three corners of the world in arms
> And we shall shock them. Nought shall make us rue,
> If England to itself do rest but true.

All that summer and fall Hitler hurled his mighty armada of Messerschmitts, Dorniers, and Heinkels at Britain in a determined effort to destroy her from the air. Through August and September the air assault rose to a crescendo of fury, and great cities like London, Manchester, and Birmingham and ports like Plymouth, Dover, and Portsmouth suffered wholesale destruction, while civilian casualties ran into the tens of thousands. But the R.A.F. fought heroically back, exacting a terrible toll of the invaders, and the English people showed an unflinching courage in the face of disaster. By October the German air force had to acknowledge that it had failed.

In its hour of mortal peril England had found its soul. It had found, too, a great leader. For the reins of government had passed now from the faltering hands of Chamberlain to the iron grip of Winston Churchill, and he aroused and inspired his countrymen as had no Englishman since Alfred. Undismayed by disaster, he confronted life with antique courage, and he infused that courage not only into his own countrymen, but into freedom-loving peoples everywhere. At the crisis of Dunkirk he had hurled defiance at the German legions:

We shall prove ourselves once again able to defend our island home, to ride out the storm of war, and to outlive the menace of tyranny, if necessary for years, if necessary alone. . . Even though many old and famous States have fallen or may fall into the grip of the Gestapo and all the odious apparatus of Nazi rule, we shall not flag or fail, we shall go on to the end, we shall fight in France, we shall fight on the seas and oceans, we shall fight with growing confidence and growing strength in the air, we shall defend our island, whatever the cost may be, we shall fight on the beaches, we shall fight on the landing grounds, we shall fight in the fields and in the streets, we shall fight in the hills; we shall never surrender, and even if, which I do not for a moment believe, this island or a large part of it were subjugated and starving, then our Empire beyond the seas, armed and guarded by the British Fleet, would carry on the struggle, until, in God's good time, the new world, with all its power and might, steps forth to the rescue and liberation of the old.

Would America answer the appeal?

5. *The Great Debate*

The attack on Poland shocked American public opinion and the revelation of German might in the swift conquest of that country jolted most Americans out of their complacency. 'When peace has been broken anywhere,' President Roosevelt said in his message to the nation at the beginning of the war, 'the peace of all countries everywhere is in danger.' And — in sharp contrast to Wilson, a quarter century earlier — he added, 'I cannot ask that every American remain neutral in thought. Even a neutral cannot be asked to close his mind or his conscience.'

Americans assuredly were not neutral in thought. The overwhelming majority of them ardently desired the defeat of Hitler and his satellites. But they desired, just as ardently, the maintenance of peace. They were eager that Britain and France should win, but unwilling to assist them to victory if such assistance involved any risk or cost any money. One concession, however, was wrung from a reluctant Congress — a modification of neutrality legislation which permitted belligerents to obtain war materials from this country on a 'cash and carry' basis. The neutrality law of 4 November 1939 did not repeal the earlier legislation. American ships were still banned from belligerent waters; Americans were still forbidden to travel on belligerent ships, lend money or grant credit to belligerents, or arm their own merchant vessels. But if Britain and France had the cash and the shipping, they could at least 'come and get it.' These two nations promptly took advantage of the new law by placing large orders with American manufacturers, but it would be many months before tanks began to roll off assembly lines and planes out of hangars in sufficient quantity to match German production.

In the fall of 1939 few Americans worried about that consideration. As the war settled down to an apparent stalemate, there seemed to be time enough. Then the swift rush of events in the spring and summer of 1940 put an entirely new face on the matter. As Hitler's armies overran Scandinavia and the Low Countries and knocked out France, as German planes bombed England, it became clear that Americans had underestimated the German might. After Dunkirk it seemed possible that Britain herself might fall, leaving Hitler bestriding the world like a colossus. We had always taken the British fleet for granted, and contented ourselves with a one-ocean navy. But what would happen if the British navy were at the bottom of the ocean — or in the hands of the Germans — and the United States were attacked simultaneously in the Atlantic and the Pacific? Senator Nye, to be sure, asserted that the notion that we depended in any way upon the British fleet was 'conceived in the brain of the Mad Hatter,' but few Americans agreed with this observation on naval strategy from the prairie statesman.

One thing we could do — rearm, and under the spur of presidential prodding Congress voted immense sums to build a two-ocean navy and tens of thousands of planes, and to raise and equip a vast army. Altogether, within a year after the invasion of the Low Countries Congress appropriated thirty-seven billions for rearmament and aid to the Allies — a sum larger than the total cost of the First World War. But this, too, was a long-range program: not until 1943, it was thought, would planes roll out in sufficient numbers to enable the United States to meet attack from all directions; not until 1945 or 1946 would the two-ocean navy be in a position to guard both the Atlantic and the Pacific. And until then the safety of the United States would depend upon the ability of Britain to hold out.

The President was prepared for even bolder steps. In a speech at

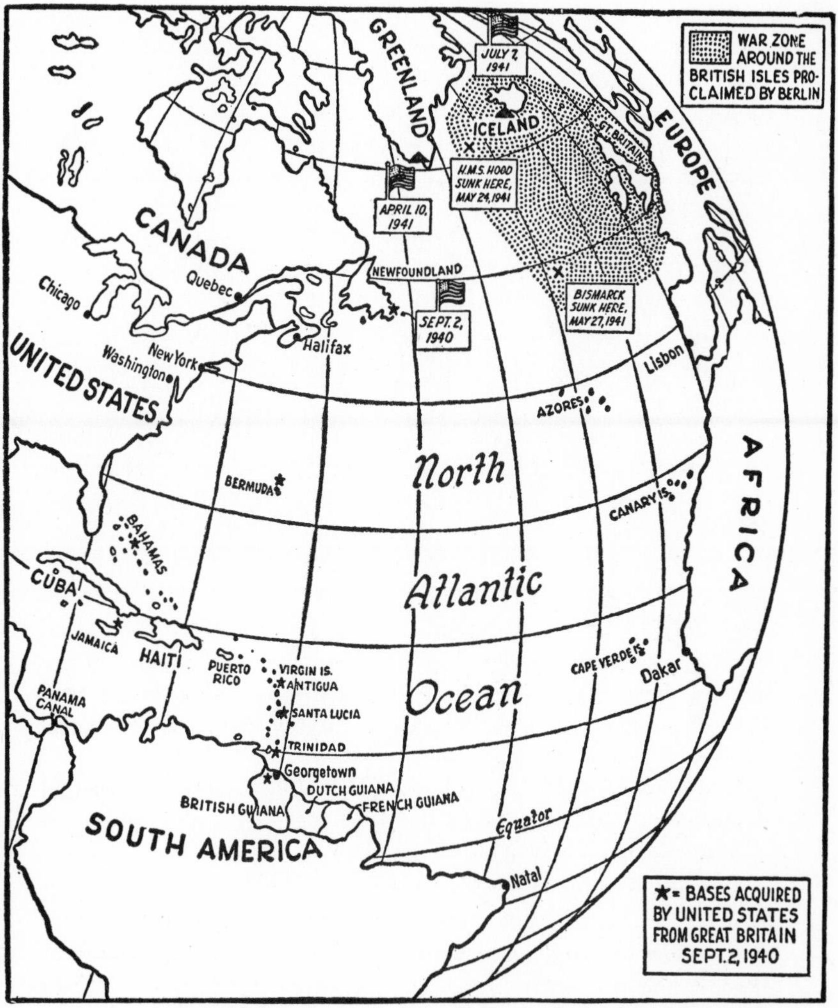

Reprinted from *Design for Power* by Frederick L. Schuman, by permission of Alfred A. Knopf, Inc., authorized publishers.

Charlottesville, Virginia, he had solemnly warned the nation against the 'delusion' that it could become 'a lone island in a world dominated by the philosophy of force,' and he had promised to 'extend to the opponents of force the material resources of this nation, and at the same time . . . harness and speed up the use of those resources in order that we ourselves in the Americas may have equipment and training equal to the task of every emergency.' In pursuance of this policy came a series of diplomatic, executive, and legislative acts. The Act of Havana of 29 July extended the protection of all the American Republics to the territory of any European power, thus effectively preventing the transfer of French or Dutch colonies to Nazi overlords. In August the United States and Canada set up a Joint Board of Defense designed to pool the defense facilities of the two nations. In mid-September came the first peace-time conscription in our history — the Burke-Wadsworth Bill, providing for the registration of all men between the ages of 21 and 35 and the induction into the armed services of eight hundred thousand draftees. And that same month Roosevelt announced to the nation the consummation of an arrangement whereby the United States transferred to Britain fifty over-age destroyers and received in return ninety-nine-year leases on a series of bases from Newfoundland to Georgetown in British Guiana. It was, said the President, 'an epochal and far-reaching act of preparation for continental defense in the face of grave danger,' and, he added, 'the most important action in the reinforcement of our national defense that has been taken since the Louisiana Purchase.' Churchill's comment was even more arresting:

> These two great organizations of the English-speaking democracies, the British Empire and the United States, will have to be somewhat mixed up together in some of their affairs for mutual and general advantage. For my part, looking out upon the future, I do not view the process with any misgivings. No one can stop it. Like the Mississippi, it just keeps rolling along. Let it roll. Let it roll on full flood, inexorable, irresistible, to broader lands and better days.

The destroyer deal met with all but universal approval, though there were many who lamented that it was consummated by executive rather than congressional authority. But with the exception of this and one or two other incidents, Roosevelt's conduct of foreign policy during these crises years sharply divided American opinion and precipitated one of the great debates in American history. Critics charged that it was dragging the United States inexorably into an 'imperialistic' war with which we had no legitimate concern; supporters insisted that only by helping Britain and France to defeat Hitler could we save democracy from destruction and ourselves from ultimate attack. Both 'isolationists' and 'interventionists' were anxious to avoid war, but they differed diametrically on the means by which that end should be attained and on the price that should be paid. The issue was fought out not only in the Halls of Congress, but in every city and village of the land, in the press, over the radio, on public platforms, and in private homes. Under its impact party lines were shattered, labor organizations split, scholars engaged in unacademic combat, business relations were strained, and old friendships broken. William Allen White's Committee to Defend America by Aiding the Allies organized branches in a thousand towns, sent out hundreds of speakers and millions of letters and pamphlets to arouse the nation to its danger. The opposition organization, the America First committee, paraded, picketed, protested, and preached an amalgam of isolationism and pacifism, old-fashioned Anglophobia and new-fangled anti-Semitism. Every week the Gallup poll took the public pulse, recording for the edification of the psychologist the curious dichotomy of the American mind. Great newspapers like the *New York Times* and the *Herald-Tribune* ranged themselves boldly behind the presidential policy, while the *Chicago Tribune* found itself in a congenial alliance with the Hearst papers ringing the alarm-bells of isolationism.

In the midst of this debate came the presidential election, in many respects the most important since 1860. Back in 1919 the Republican party, departing from its tradition, had espoused isolationism, and it had ever since clung to that unheroic position. Now again, as in 1919, political considerations appeared to dictate an isolationist policy, and spokesmen for the party, conscious that the domestic policies of the New Deal had been endorsed at every election since 1932, decided that the Democratic leadership was most vulnerable on its conduct of foreign relations. The three leading contenders for the presidential nomination — Senator Robert Taft of Ohio, Senator Arthur Vandenberg of Michigan, and District Attorney Thomas Dewey of New York, were all sincere isolationists, though of varying degrees. Of the three, Vandenberg was probably the ablest, Dewey the most spectacular, Taft the most conservative; none of them had given the faintest indication that he had learned anything from the domestic crisis of the last ten years or that he understood anything of the great revolutionary forces that were sweeping across the world.

Fortunately the Republican choice was not limited to these three respectables. A shrewd group of amateur politicians had been quietly building up a political maverick, Wendell Willkie, quondam Democrat, Wall Street lawyer, and President of the Commonwealth and Southern, which had fought a losing fight against the T.V.A. This record should have damned any candidate, but it was offset by qualities of mind and character that lifted Willkie far above the other candidates and won him a wide and enthusiastic following. For notwithstanding his wealth and his Wall Street and power affiliations, Willkie was a liberal conservative, critical not of the principles animating the New Deal but of the extravagance and inefficiency with which these had been implemented. He was no isolationist, but a frank proponent of aid to the Allies. His transparent sincerity, his freedom from obligations to political bosses, his homespun Americanism, his pronounced liberalism on questions of domestic and foreign policy, his personal charm and magnetism, appealed to an electorate wearied with political clap-trap, and inspired a devotion such as no Republican had enjoyed since Theodore Roosevelt. In a little over a month Willkie had forged to the front as the one dangerous rival to the three original contenders. It was clear that whatever the politicians wanted, the rank and file of the party were for him and it was arresting that the leading Republican organ, the New York *Herald-Tribune,* was demanding his nomination. When the Republican Convention met at Philadelphia in June, seasoned politicians found that they could not hold the delegates to their pledges against the rising tide of Willkie sentiment, the deluge of telegrams from Willkie supporters, the shouts from the galleries, and — above all — the growing conviction that only Willkie had a chance to win. On the first ballot Dewey was well in the lead; by the fourth Willkie had pushed ahead, and on the sixth he was nominated. On the one really important issue, the platform declared somewhat evasively ' we favor the extension to all peoples fighting for liberty, or whose liberty is threatened, of such aid as shall not be in violation of international law or inconsistent with the requirements of our own national defense.'

The Democrats meanwhile were in a quandary. The President had never been more popular, nor had his leadership ever appeared more essential, and Democratic state conventions had called for his renomination. But would he accept the nomination a third time, and would the American people acquiesce in this challenge to the sacrosanct third-term tradition? Roosevelt himself maintained an inscrutable silence; early in 1940 he still sincerely desired to escape a third term, and it is not yet known when the foreign crisis determined him to accept it if proffered. The Democratic Convention, left without guidance, renominated the President on the first ballot and by an all but unanimous vote, and Roosevelt replied by radio that 'in the face of the danger which confronts our time, no individual retains or can hope to retain the right of personal choice which free men enjoy in times of peace. He has a first obligation . . . to serve his country in whatever capacity his country finds him useful.' Largely at Roosevelt's insistence Henry Wallace was nominated to the vice-presidency.

The campaign that followed was, on the whole, encouraging to those who believed in democracy. Issues of foreign and domestic policy were debated candidly and forcefully, and the public response was intelligent. Willkie did most of the campaigning — the President declared himself too busy for politics! — and everywhere he went he was greeted with immense enthusiasm. Fortunately for the unity of the nation he refused to make political capital out of the President's conduct of foreign affairs, supported the conscription bill, applauded the destroyer deal, and urged, as eloquently as the President himself, 'all aid to Britain.' Inasmuch as he approved, too, of most of the New Deal domestic reforms, his campaign was lacking in real issues. The third-term issue, which had promised so much, actually proved to have little popular appeal.

From the beginning Roosevelt held the advantage, and he never lost it. He had proved so right in his diagnosis of the European situation, and so firm in his leadership, that most Americans were inclined to trust him to meet the crisis ahead. Willkie commended himself, even to his opponents, but it was not clear that he could do better what the President was doing so well, and he labored under the appalling handicap of Old Guard sponsorship and the support of malcontents. Politics makes strange bedfellows, but few candidates ever found themselves with a more heterogeneous group than did Willkie: Union League Club reactionaries who had convinced themselves that Roosevelt was more dangerous than Hitler; followers of the rabble-rousing Father Coughlin of Detroit who taught that the World Court was synonymous with communism; Irish-Americans who hated Britain and German-Americans who sympathized with totalitarianism; old-line politicians hungry for the spoils of office; midwestern farmers weary of crop control; Southern Bourbons who feared that democracy would mean race and class equality; doctrinaires who thought the republic could not stand the shock of a third term; avowed isolationists like Hamilton Fish and Charles Lindbergh. It was enough to wreck any candidacy.

It did. In the November elections Roosevelt for the third time rolled up impressive electoral college and popular majorities. The President carried 38 states, with 449 electoral votes, Willkie 10 states with 82 votes; the popular vote was somewhat closer — 27,000,000 to 22,000,000. Three minor parties polled a vote of less than one-quarter million.[4] The third-term tradition had been shattered, the Republican party revived, the validity of the two-party system reaffirmed.

6. *The Year of Decision*

The President naturally, if somewhat optimistically, interpreted his triumphant re-election as an endorsement of his foreign as well as his domestic policies. When Congress met early in January 1941 he appealed to it for the actualization of the 'four freedoms' — freedom of speech, freedom of religion, freedom from want, freedom from fear — and for the support of those peoples everywhere who were fighting in defense of these freedoms. Four days later he submitted a program designed to circumvent the limitations of the neutrality legislation and make American war material immediately available to the fighting democracies. This was the 'Lend-Lease' bill which authorized the President to 'sell, transfer, exchange, lease, lend' any defense articles 'to the government of any country whose defense the President deems vital to the defense of the United States,' and made available to such nations the facilities of American shipyards for repair and reconditioning. The President argued the necessity of his proposal with a simple analogy that reached the understanding of millions. 'Let me give you an illustration. Suppose my neighbor's house catches fire, and I have a length of garden hose. . .' The proposal precipitated prolonged and bitter debate which reached its climax, or nadir, in Senator Wheeler's statement that Lend-Lease would mean 'ploughing under every fourth American boy.' After the

[4] Willkie carried Colorado, Indiana, Iowa, Kansas, Maine, Michigan, Nebraska, North Dakota, South Dakota, Vermont. The popular vote was: Roosevelt, 27,243,466; Willkie, 22,304,755.

isolationists had exhausted themselves, administration supporters passed the bill by substantial majorities in both Houses of Congress and it became law 11 March. This act really made the United States the 'arsenal of democracy.' Under its far-sighted provisions the United States not only made available to the fighting democracies some eighteen billion dollars worth of arms,[5] foodstuffs, and services, but geared its own production to war needs a year earlier than might otherwise have been possible, and officially abandoned any pretense at neutrality and identified herself with the 'United Nations.'

After that events moved with breathtaking speed. A few weeks after the passage of Lend-Lease the United States seized all Axis shipping in American ports. In April it took Greenland under protection and announced that the American Navy would patrol the sea lanes in defense zones. In May came the transfer of fifty oil tankers to Britain, the seizure of French ships, and, after the sinking of the American freighter *Robin Moor,* the solemn proclamation of an 'unlimited national emergency.' In June the United States froze all Axis assets in this country and closed all Axis consulates. And on 24 June the President announced that American aid would be extended to a new ally — Russia.

For in the early dawn of Sunday, 22 June, Hitler had sent his legions hurtling across the border in Russia. 'I have today decided to give the fate of the German people and the Reich and of Europe again into the hands of our soldiers,' he said, and the world stood astounded at the audacity of the gamble — and the consequences of its success. Hitler himself had no misgivings. All through the year his mighty army had marched from triumph to triumph, his air force had rained terror and death on a hundred cities, his submarines had taken a terrible toll of British shipping. During the winter months he had waged a war of nerves against the Balkan nations; on 1 March his troops entered Sofia and Bulgaria hastened to join the Axis, and late that same month the government of Yugoslavia succumbed to the same intolerable pressure. And when the courageous Yugoslavs overthrew the government that had betrayed them, the German army smashed its way through the little country while its air force laid Belgrade in ruins. For six months Mussolini's soldiers had been waging a losing fight against the sturdy Greeks in the mountains of Albania; now in a single week the German

[5] The original appropriation was seven billion; altogether Lend-Lease aid totalled $50,226,845,387.

army fought its way to Salonika, flanked the Greek army to the west, pushed the weak British Expeditionary Force into the sea, and by the end of the month unfurled the swastika on the Acropolis. The remnants of the British and Greek armies retreated to Crete. In mid-May Hitler launched an air-borne offensive against that island, and within ten days had scored yet another triumph.

The British, to be sure, had re-established Haile Selassie on his Ethiopian throne, pushed the Italians back in Libya, and gained control of Syria and Irak. But these were minor successes, and the Germans all but ignored them. They were preparing, now, for the final blow — an all-out offensive against the British Isles, or an attack through the Middle East that would open the gates to India. But these were great projects, and Hitler did not dare risk them while the Russian armies stood massed on his eastern frontiers. So he turned first to Russia, where he expected a sure if not an easy victory and with it the wheat of the Ukraine, the oil of the Caucasus, the vast industrial resources of the Donets and the Volga basins, and access to the fabulous East. And, by posing as the leader in a crusade against communism, he expected to confuse the democratic world.

Never were greater expectations more grievously disappointed. The leaders of the democracies were not confused. Churchill told his people that whoever marched with Hitler was a foe, whoever fought him an ally. Roosevelt, undaunted by anti-communist sentiment in the United States, took the same position. The military strategy appeared at first to be more successful than the diplomatic, but here, too, Hitler was disappointed, for though the Russians were forced steadily back they were not defeated, and soon the world learned that the *Wehrmacht* was not invincible. By winter the Germans were pounding at the gates of Moscow and Leningrad, but the gates were not forced open, and that winter, as the Red armies seized the offensive and rolled the invaders back, enthusiasm for Russia swept the democracies.

In Russia, England found an ally of inexhaustible resources in men — and courage. And now, too, the New World was at last ' stepping forth to the rescue ' of the Old. The United States moved steadily toward a war basis and toward actual involvement in the conflict. Opposition, to be sure, was if anything more recalcitrant than ever. When the United States Navy occupied Iceland, Senator Wheeler revealed the fact while the operation was still in progress. The administration bill to extend conscription for the duration of the emergency passed by only a single vote — 203–202; House Republicans, who had already voted 143 to 21 against repeal of the Hines Embargo and 135 to 24 against Lend-Lease, advertised their persistent partisanship by voting 133 to 21 against this Selective Service bill. And that same month a group of isolationist leaders, including ex-President Hoover, John L. Lewis, and others scarcely less distinguished or perspicacious, announced that this was not our war and that we had no stake in its outcome. But public opinion was hardening against these naysayers. And when, after the German attack on the United States destroyer *Greer,* the President ordered the Navy to 'shoot on sight' any enemy submarines, the nation applauded.

Meantime, too, President Roosevelt, like Wilson a generation earlier, had moved to clarify American public opinion by obtaining a statement of war aims from the Allies. On 14 August he and Winston Churchill met at Argentia Bay, Newfoundland, and there drew up the Atlantic Charter, containing certain 'common principles' on which they based 'their hopes for a better future for the world.' These were: no territorial aggrandizement; no territorial changes that do not accord with the wishes of the people concerned; the right of all people to choose their own form of government, and the restoration of self-government to those deprived of it; the enjoyment by all states — victors or vanquished — of access to trade and raw materials; economic collaboration between all nations; freedom from war, from fear, from want, for all peoples; freedom of the seas; and abandonment of the use of force as an instrument of international relations. It was essentially a restatement of Wilson's Fourteen Points, and its reformulation in these circumstances was a monument alike to the wisdom of that original pronouncement and to the tragic failure of men to appreciate it and actualize it.

In the meantime, tension mounted in the Far East. The Japanese armies in penetrating China met unexpected resistance from Chiang Kai-shek's forces, so the Japanese navy's cherished plan came to the fore. This was to gobble up Malaya before proceeding further in China. The 'Greater East Asia Co-prosperity Sphere' was declared, and Prince Konoye, the Japanese premier, announced on 22 December 1938 that there would be no peace with the Chiang Kai-shek government. America continued to protest, and made futile gestures of appeasement, such as refusing to make a small appropriation for a submarine base at Guam (23 February 1939). The Japanese government was of two minds about risking open war with the western nations. It still had a considerable respect for the United States Navy, and it feared lest Hitler demand the old German colonies in the Pacific. But after the Germans overran the Low Countries and France in June 1940, it became more and more difficult to restrain the Japanese militarists. The French colonies of Indo-China and the Netherlands East Indies seemed to be ripe for the picking; British Malaya and Burma might be so any day, if Hitler invaded Britain.[6] In the summer of 1940 she wrested the first concessions from the helpless Vichy government — permission to build air fields in French Indo-China. When the United States struck back with a loan to China and a partial embargo, Japan defiantly joined the Axis as a warning that the United States could not hope to fight her alone.

The ABC–1 Staff agreement (of which more anon), concluded between the American and British Chiefs of Staff on 27 March 1941, gave the United States the invidious task of trying to keep Japan quiet while helping Britain with ' short of war ' measures to defeat Hitler. There was not much chance of doing this, since the Japanese navy, as a result of frenzied building since the naval limitation treaties were denounced, already outnumbered the combined fleets of the three potential Allies (United States, Great Britain, Netherlands) in the Pacific.[7] The American people, too, were becoming ashamed of a situation in which Japan was allowed to acquire from them the sinews of war to conquer China; while the Roosevelt administration was becoming fearful that mere protest and ' non-recognition ' of unpleasant facts would only enable Japan to get half the world's population under her thumb and divide the world with Hitler. Congress, in an Act of July 1940 for Strengthening the National Defense, gave the President power to restrict the export of any war materials required for American defense or to license their export to friendly nations. In the same month, Congress passed the Two-ocean Navy Act. Very cautiously, Roosevelt began imposing embargoes on various strategic materials,

[6] It must be emphasized here that Japanese aggression was not compelled by overpopulation (except perhaps in the white-collar class) or by need for ' living space.' Japan already had that, in Manchuria, and failed to use it. Her industry, suffering less and recovering earlier than that of the United States from the great depression, was rapidly conquering all Far Eastern and even Near Eastern markets. The great aim and objective of Japan, previous to taking over the whole of China, was Java, an island more heavily populated than Japan itself but possessing abundant raw materials that Japan lacked and a docile, hard-working native population to exploit. The Japanese ' Greater East Empire ' was defined even by themselves as a feudal empire in which the Sons of Heaven would play the rôle of master race, like the Germans in Europe.

[7] Table in S. E. Morison, *Rising Sun in the Pacific,* p. 58.

including scrap iron; and a Gallup poll actually showed 96 per cent popular approval. (These embargoes were on exports to all nations, but were really aimed at Japan because licenses for export were allowed to all friendly nations.) So things went on for almost a year.

In July 1941 began the crisis. On the 25th, Japan announced that she had assumed a protectorate of the whole of French Indo-China. This was her first overt seizure of another country, in imitation of Hitler's numerous grabs, assuming her partial occupation of China to be a mere 'incident' and not a warlike act. On the very next day, 26 July, President Roosevelt took two momentous steps. He received the armed forces of the Philippine Commonwealth into the United States Army, appointing General Douglas MacArthur Commanding General of United States Army Forces of the Far East; and he issued an executive order freezing Japanese assets in the United States. And, as Great Britain and the Netherlands followed suit, Japan's source of credits and imports of rubber, scrap iron, and fuel oil were completely cut off. The Japanese war lords decided they must make war on the United States, Great Britain, and the Netherlands within three or four months, unless these countries gave way and restored the flow of oil and other strategic supplies. For Japan was 'eating her own tail' in the matter of fuel oil; the armies must have oil or evacuate the mainland, and of course the military could not contemplate any such loss of face. It was the embargo on oil and credits that brought Japan to the point of war — Thomas Jefferson was vindicated after 130 years!

The final negotiations need not delay us here, as they were a mere sparring for time by two governments that considered war all but inevitable. The Japanese wanted time to organize their great military and naval push to the south; the United States wanted time to prepare the defense of the Philippines and strengthen its navy. Through the summer and fall of 1941 Mr. Hull made it clear that Japan could have all the materials and goods she wanted from America, if she would liquidate the 'China Incident' and begin a military evacuation of that country and of Indo-China. Prince Konoye, the Japanese premier, in vain sought some face-saving formula that would give America the shell and the Japanese army the oyster. Seeing that was impossible, Konoye on 14 October asked General Tojo, the war minister, to withdraw at least some troops from China. Tojo refused; the Japanese army, which he was confident could beat America, would do nothing of the sort; and a few days later the Emperor made Tojo his prime minister. On 20 November Japan presented her ultimatum to Washington. She would not occupy any more Asiatic territory if the United States would stop reinforcing the Philippines; she would evacuate southern Indo-China only if the United States would cease all aid to Chiang Kai-Shek (who had been advanced a credit of a few million dollars) and 'unfreeze' Japanese assets in the United States, leaving Japan free to complete her subjugation of China. Tojo did not expect that the United States would accept such terms, which were suitable only for a defeated nation. And, on 26 November 1941 without further delay, the Japanese carrier force, which for months had been practicing for an attack on Pearl Harbor, sortied from its rendezvous in the Kurile Islands for that fatal destination.

No inkling even of the existence of that force leaked out, but a few days earlier Japanese troop-laden transports with escorting warships were reported steaming south off Formosa, and on 27 November Washington sent a 'war warning' message to Pearl Harbor and Manila, indicating an amphibious attack against either the Philippines, Thai, or the Malay Peninsula. No one in a position of authority at Washington or Hawaii anticipated an attack on Pearl Harbor because they believed the Japanese navy to be incapable of more than one operation at a time and nobody imagined the Emperor would be so foolish as to bring America, angry and united, into the war.

So it was that when the Japanese carrier planes at 7:55 on Sunday morning 7 December began launching torpedoes and raining bombs on the Pacific Fleet in Pearl Harbor, the local commanders, the government at Washington, and the nation at large were taken completely by surprise. At noon on the same day (8 December in the Far East) Japanese planes from Formosa attacked the American Army airfields near Manila with an equally devastating blow; at 8:30 Guam had been bombed from nearby Saipan, and before dawn Japanese troops landed on the Malay Peninsula. To millions of Americans, sitting down to their Sunday dinner, their radios tuned in to some musical program, the news came as something fantastic and incredible. As the details of the disaster poured in, hour by hour, incredulity turned to anger and an implacable determination to avenge what President Roosevelt correctly called an 'unprovoked and dastardly' attack. The next day Congress declared a state of war with Japan; three days later Germany and Italy declared war on the United States.

On 9 December President Roosevelt delivered his war message to the nation. Reviewing the American efforts for peace and the events that led up to the attack on Pearl Harbor, he reminded the American people that this was a war not only for the survival of the nation but for the survival of all those spiritual values which Americans had from the beginning of their history cherished and defended.

The true goal we seek is far above and beyond the ugly field of battle. When we resort to force, as now we must, we are determined that this force shall be directed toward ultimate good as well as against immediate evil. We Americans are not destroyers — we are builders.

We are now in the midst of a war, not for conquest, not for vengeance, but for a world in which this nation, and all that this nation represents, will be safe for our children. We expect to eliminate the danger from Japan, but it would serve us ill if we accomplished that and found that the rest of the world was dominated by Hitler and Mussolini.

We are going to win the war and we are going to win the peace that follows.

And in the dark hours of this day — and through dark days that may be yet to come — we will know that the vast majority of the members of the human race are on our side. Many of them are fighting with us. All of them are praying for us. For, in representing our cause, we represent theirs as well — our hope and their hope for liberty under God.

XXVII

WORLD WAR II: THE FRAMEWORK

1. *Basic Considerations*

WHEN the United States entered the war, in December 1941, the military situation of the Allies was desperate. Triumphant Hitler controlled western Europe from the White Sea to the Aegean; German armies had overrun the Balkans and pushed deep into the heart of Russia. To most observers it seemed that Russia would have to give way, as had France, to irresistible force. France, half under German occupation, and Spain, also controlled by a military dictator, seemed ready to throw in their lot with the Axis. Packs of German submarines harried Allied shipping in the Atlantic, and the eastern Mediterranean had become so dangerous to British ships that the old, long Cape passage to India had to be used. North Africa from Tunis to the border of Egypt was under Axis control, and it needed but one determined push to carry Rommel's army to Alexandria, close the Suez Canal, and force Turkey into the Axis. In southern Russia the Germans were poised to drive through the Caucasus to Irak and Iran and join hands with the Japanese in India.

In the Pacific the situation looked just as dark. The blow at Pearl Harbor had crippled the United States Pacific Fleet, and with the sinking of the *Repulse* and the *Prince of Wales,* the British naval arm in the Far East was paralyzed. Now that the Japanese had won naval supremacy in the Western Pacific, the Philippines and Malaya were doomed. Hong Kong fell on Christmas Day, Rabaul in January 1942, Singapore in February, the Netherlands East Indies in March, and the Philippines in April. The Japanese had outdone even the Germans in rapid conquest.

On the surface, the two groups of combatants locked in global conflict seemed not unevenly matched. On the one side were Britain and her loyal Dominions, Russia, the United States, most of Latin America, and an incalculable China; on the other side were Germany, Italy, and Japan, with a number of small satellites. The Allies had clear superiority in manpower, but this superiority was partly offset by the fact that Germany was able to draw upon millions of non-German Europeans for forced labor, while Japan enjoyed a similar advantage in the Indies. It was a question, too, whether Russia's millions could be armed and equipped in time to fight, or America's armies be ferried across the submarine-infested Atlantic to engage in battle, or new naval and airplane construction replace the Pearl Harbor losses in time to prevent Japan from making herself impregnable. The Allies controlled plenty of oil and iron resources in the Western Hemisphere, but the Japanese now had all the Far Eastern oil deposits and controlled the main world sources of rubber, tin, tungsten, and quinine. The industrial potential of the Allies was far greater than that of their enemies, but only the future would reveal whether that capacity could be developed and brought to bear in time to be effective.

These were long-range considerations. In the early months of 1942 the Axis held all the trump cards. Germany and Japan had prepared for war for a decade, and their armed forces had had the advantage of combat experience before the United States entered the war. Both nations had speedily achieved positions that appeared invulnerable. Germany, now master of the European continent, appeared to enjoy that immunity from attack which Napoleon once imagined to be his, and which isolationists had long imagined to be the peculiar advantage of the United States. She seemed to be capable of making Europe an impregnable fortress, building up reserves and production, waging a submarine war of attrition against Britain, and concentrating all her army on the conquest of Russia, all at the same time. Japan enjoyed even greater advantages in the Far East. Naval and air supremacy gave her command of the Western Pacific; like Germany she held interior lines of communication and could fight, as it were, on her own ground and on her own terms. She had at her disposal the rich resources of the Netherlands Indies and of a good part of China. Her enemies had to guard against a northward thrust at Alaska, a southward advance on Australia, or a blow to the west toward India. The United States was the only nation that had the power to fight her, and to get at her, would have to develop a mighty long arm, for Tokyo is 3350 sea miles from Pearl Harbor and 5437 miles from San Francisco, and the air line from the Panama Canal to Australia measures 7390 miles.

It was a bleak prospect for the defenders of freedom — how bleak the average American never realized. Yet against this formidable array of power and strategic position, the Allies were far from powerless. What did they have to offer? Russia was still far from conquered, winter and Lend-Lease were coming to her aid, while behind the Volga massive new armies were being mustered and, deep in the Urals, hundreds of new factories were springing up. The Royal Air Force had warded off Hitler's planned invasion of their island, the British army was being rebuilt after its disaster in the Low Countries, and the Royal Navy was still a force to be reckoned with. If the British and Americans together could beat the U-boats, they could also build up ground and air forces in Britain for an eventual invasion of the Continent. Europe was crushed, but from Norway to Yugoslavia and from France to Greece, resistance forces were active, keeping alive the hope of freedom while teasing the German overlords. As the armed strength of the British Dominions grew, divisions from Australia, New Zealand, Canada, and South Africa were sent to the North African front or the mother country. The destroyer–naval-bases deal and the timely occupation of Greenland and Iceland had enabled the United States to prepare outposts in the Atlantic and the Caribbean from which to wage war on the U-boats, in spite of whose efforts Lend-Lease material flowed in an ever widening stream to Britain, to the Antipodes, and over various long and dangerous routes to Russia.

These considerations afforded some ground for confidence. Never for a moment did the political and military leaders of America and Britain doubt ultimate victory. In two other respects the Allies enjoyed a superiority that was important if not decisive. First the Allies (or, as one should say after 1 January 1942, the United Nations) were allied and united in fact as well as in name. There was not only co-operation but an actual merging of the sinews of war, far beyond anything of the sort in World War I. Internally, too, the Allied countries were united. There were no fifth columns, no military uprisings such as that which attempted to overthrow Hitler in 1944, no resistance forces, no heavy burden of hatred and sabotage from conquered peoples to drain off military strength. The Axis powers, on the contrary, never achieved real union, not even a sharing of weapons or scientific secrets. There was no Axis Combined Chiefs of Staff, no combined planning of grand strategy or of operations. Italy was, in large measure, a drain upon her senior partner; Japan fought her own war her own way, with no concern for German interests. For instance—the Japanese attack on Pearl Harbor was contrary to the wishes of Hitler and the German high command, who wanted Japan to pitch into Russia but leave America alone; and within Japan the army and navy were fighting different wars. Great Britain and the United States had their differences, but they never acted at cross purposes, and the various 'governments in exile' (Free French, Norwegian, Dutch, Polish) in London merged their resources with the Allies. And although Russia kept her 'capitalist' Allies suspiciously at arm's length, there was far closer co-operation between the western Allies and Russia than between Germany and Japan.

A second major Allied asset was in leadership. In her hour of mortal peril Britain found in Winston Churchill her greatest war leader since Chatham, and the United States was equally fortunate in Franklin D. Roosevelt, her greatest war President. There was strong opposition to 'F.D.R.' in America and to 'Winnie' in Britain, but each was popular in the other's country, and both commanded the confidence of the entire free world. Both Allied war leaders had a knowledge of history and geography that the Axis leaders did not possess, both were versed in naval strategy, a subject of which Hitler, Mussolini, and Tojo were completely ignorant. More important, however, was the fundamental difference between Allied and Axis leadership, rooted in different historical traditions and national characters. Roosevelt and Churchill directed the war with the active co-operation of their civilian cabinets, committees of Congress and of the House of Commons, and their high command. Hitler and Tojo did not even bother with legislatures, and they frequently overrode army and navy chiefs to exercise a direct and despotic control over detailed operations. American and British conduct of the war had nothing to parallel, for example, Hitler's direct and disastrous intervention in the conduct of campaigns.

Roosevelt and Churchill confirmed, when the Prime Minister visited the President at the sad Christmastide of 1941, the basic strategic concept of the war — to beat the Hitler-Mussolini team first. That idea — originally conceived by a United States committee of naval officers headed by Rear Admiral Richmond K. Turner in November 1940 — became part of an 'if and when the United States enters the war' plan that was adopted on 27 March 1941 by the American and British Chiefs of Staff, after a conference between them in Washington lasting two months. For the President and his chief military advisers, General Marshall and Admiral Stark, did not wish to be caught up in a war without plans, as Wilson, General Scott, and Admiral Benson had been in 1917. The decision to concentrate upon

Germany, even if we were at the same time at war with Japan, was dictated by common sense. If effective aid were not rendered Britain and Russia, the United States would be forced to fight two wars alone. And Germany, with her military and scientific potential, was by far the more formidable of the Axis partners. Without strong American aid to the Western Allies, Germany could (and undoubtedly would) have conquered Britain and Europe, and then challenged the United States; but Japan could be kept at bay until Germany was defeated, and then the Allies could concentrate on her. When we reflect that Germany almost had an unbeatable submarine weapon just before her defeat, we can appreciate how important this decision was. Right after Pearl Harbor, it did not seem at all obvious.

The second major decision was to make the war, in fact as well as in principle, a combined operation — to set up combined chiefs of staff; to work out all military, political, economic, and scientific plans in common; to share all resources of material, money, men, and brains. The pattern had been set by Lend-Lease and the Anglo-American staff conference of 1941; but nothing on this scale had ever before been attempted in the military or the political realms by the United States or any other country. Of this fateful decision, which Roosevelt and Churchill also confirmed at the White House in December 1941, General Marshall later wrote: 'It was the most complete unification of military effort ever achieved by two Allied nations.' And General Eisenhower, reviewing the lessons of the war, observed that

> Allied effectiveness in World War II established for all time the feasibility of developing and employing joint control machinery that can meet the sternest tests of war. The key to the matter is a readiness, on the highest levels, to adjust all nationalistic differences that affect the strategic employment of combined resources and, in the war theater, to designate a single commander who is supported to the limit. . . In World War II America and Great Britain, whose forces fought side by side in so many battles on the ground, sea and air, understood and applied these truths.[1]

2. *Miltary Preparedness*

Notwithstanding the most ample warning, the United States was not adequately prepared for war when it came. Most Americans persisted in regarding war as an aberration that might come upon other

[1] *Crusade in Europe*, p. 451. Doubleday.

countries, but not their own. Many so confused the potential with the actual armed strength of the United States that they could not conceive any nation having the effrontery to attack her; they felt that even if America decided to get into the war, she could choose her own time and method. There was also a powerful emotional bar to military preparedness. A whole generation of Americans had persuaded themselves that participation in World War I had been an avoidable mistake, one they would never, never repeat. The average American — especially if he had served in the last war — disliked generals, distrusted admirals, and declined to be 'cannon fodder' for the munitions manufacturers who had been blasted by Senator Nye. He had so hardened himself against propaganda that he was inclined to dismiss any unpleasant facts as propaganda. Never before had seeming sophistication been in fact such simple naïveté.

Fortunately this ostrich-like attitude toward world affairs was by no means universal. For several years Germany and Japan had been giving the American people an expensive education, complete with exhibits, in what a world dominated by fanatics, sadists, and militarists would be like. If Americans did not profit as much as they might have from the lessons of recent history and of current experience, they did not ignore them. Few, to be sure, anticipated a war that would send Americans fighting to the far corners of the world, but some of the more far-sighted had done so and tried to prepare for it. Fortunately President Roosevelt was one of these. 'Let's think back to June of 1940,' wrote Donald Nelson after the war was over.

> Who among us, except the President, really saw the magnitude of the job ahead, the awful mission of the United States in a world running berserk? I can testify that all the people I met and talked to, including members of the General Staff, the Army and Navy's highest ranking officers, distinguished statesmen and legislators, thought of the defense program as only a means for equipping ourselves to keep the enemy away from the shores of the United States. None of us . . . except the President saw that we might be fighting Germany and Japan all over the world. He took his stand against the advice of some of this country's best minds, but his foresight was superior to theirs, and this foresight saved us all.[2]

But by 1941 General Marshall, Admiral Stark, and the whole Joint Chiefs of Staff were fully alive to the grave peril in which their coun-

[2] *Arsenal of Democracy,* p. 85. Harcourt, Brace.

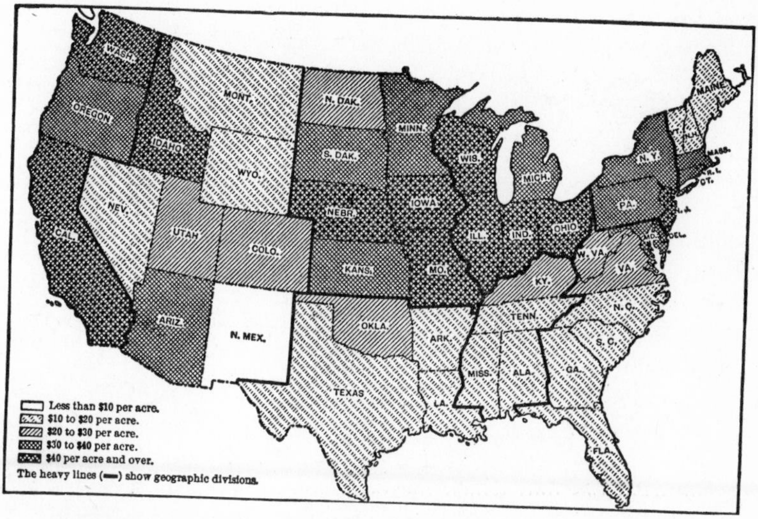

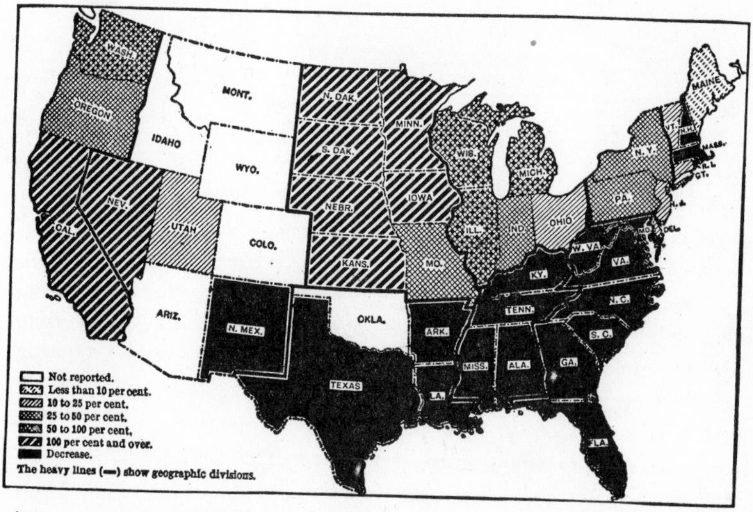

Average Value of Farm Land per Acre: 1910; Increase in Farm Property by States: 1860–1870

From Thirteenth Census of the United States, 1910, *Vol. V.*

try stood, and alert to prepare for the worst. The 'Joint Board Estimate,' which they submitted to the President in September 1941, envisioned a global war and formulated the grand strategy that was subsequently adopted. Assuming that we would be fighting Germany, Japan, Italy, and possibly other countries too, the estimate declared that national security could be attained 'only through military victories outside this hemisphere.' It recommended that both mobilization and production 'be designed to meet United States' needs while engaged simultaneously in war against Germany and Japan.' [3]

Despite shortcomings in the preparedness program, the United States was in a far better military position in December 1941 than it had been in April 1917. Selective service had provided an army of 1,600,000. The officer-procurement program was well under way with over one hundred thousand officers already commissioned, and twenty schools were training candidates for ordnance, chemical warfare, armored anti-aircraft, and other specialized branches. Over 900,000 troops had participated in battle maneuvers in the Carolinas and Louisiana.

The air corps was expanding rapidly. Schools were provided to train 30,000 pilots a year; production of planes was speeded up and plans were drawn for a variety of new types; bases were hurriedly built in Alaska, Panama, and the Caribbean, and those newly acquired from Britain and Denmark were enlarged. 'The entire year,' wrote General Arnold, 'was one of acceleration in building bases and training facilities, teaching aircrews and groundcrews, establishing supply depots and supply lines, strengthening our continental defenses, expanding our aircraft and engine factories, furnishing friendly nations with more planes and equipment than we could spare, and getting ready for war. When the Japanese attacked we may not have had a powerful air force, but we knew that we soon would have one. We had the plans and our organization was growing every hour.' [4]

The navy, too, had its plans. The disarmament movement of 1919–31 had seriously reduced its strength, but a new construction program, started in 1933, was accelerated and enlarged in 1938, and

[3] Robert Sherwood, *Roosevelt and Hopkins,* p. 415. 'Joint Board' because the term 'Joint Chiefs of Staff' had not yet been officially adopted.

[4] *First Report of the Commanding General of the Army Air Forces,* 4 January 1944, by General of the Army H. H. Arnold.

in July 1940 Congress passed the 'Two-Ocean Navy' bill, which would have made the United States Navy irresistible by 1944 — if Japan had kindly waited that long. The Navy Department promptly expanded its shipbuilding and repair facilities, officer procurement, naval air arm, and research programs. The Atlantic and Pacific Fleets had an annual get-together for a colossal war game; the marine corps practiced amphibious landings in the Caribbean. Best of all, the navy, in escorting ships to Iceland and Greenland and in patrolling wide out in the Atlantic, operated under war conditions from April 1941; and from 4 September 1941, when U.S.S. *Greer* was attacked by a U-boat, there was a 'shooting war' between the two navies in the Atlantic.

There were other items, too, on the credit side of the preparedness ledger. The destroyer-bases deal had given the United States new air, naval, and military bases from British Guiana to Newfoundland; these were supplemented by others in Greenland in April 1941, and in Iceland in July. Lend-Lease greatly stimulated war industries and production, at first for the British but to our own subsequent benefit; and in return the British imparted all their military secrets to United States army, navy, and air-force observers in London. Reorganization of the army, in full swing in December, was complete by the spring of 1942 with the creation of three major commands — ground forces, air forces, and service forces. The liaison between American and British staff officers had meshed the gears so that the Combined Chiefs of Staff started them revolving right at the outbreak of war. General Marshall, a warrior-statesman who saw eye to eye with Roosevelt and Churchill, had been head of the army since 1 September 1939; General Douglas MacArthur commanded the United States army forces in the Far East, and those younger generals who were to lead American armies to victory — Eisenhower, Bradley, and Patton — were already in responsible positions. The marine corps already had two divisions trained in amphibious warfare, of which it had made a special study. And thanks in part to the energy of scientist-statesmen such as Vannevar Bush and James B. Conant, a program of scientific research that proved indispensable to victory was well under way.

All this meant that when war actually came, the adjustments required were in quantity rather than quality, more of everything rather than rubbing out and starting afresh. And the people as a whole, little as they liked the prospect, knew they were in for a tough struggle. Pearl Harbor did not so much break the rhythm of American life as step it up.

The most urgent need was to build up the armed forces and give them the latest equipment. Congress promptly repealed its prohibition against sending draftees outside the Western Hemisphere, and extended their period of service to six months after the end of the war. All men between 18 and 45 were made liable to military service. The draft was administered by over six thousand local and five hundred appeal boards, whose members served voluntarily. The standards of physical fitness and of intelligence were more exacting than in any previous war, and the number who failed to come up to those standards shocked a public that had long been complacent about the American standard of living. About five million men were rejected on grounds of physical disability. Industrial areas and the South made the poorest showing. Rejections ran from less than 25 per cent in Iowa, Kansas, Wyoming, and Utah to over 40 per cent in Georgia, North Carolina, and South Carolina. Of the 31 million registered, over 17 million were examined and 9,867,707 inducted into service. Counting the voluntary enlistments, 15,145,115 men and women served in the armed forces during the war; 10,420,000 of these were in the army, 3,883,520 in the navy, 599,693 in the marines, and 241,902 in the coast guard.

Until December 1942, enlistments in the navy and marine corps were voluntary, but thereafter they were required to take draftees so that the army would not suffer. For the first time in American history women were permitted to serve in the armed forces. There were 'Wacs' in the army, 'Waves' in the navy, women marines, 'Spars' in the coast guard, and 'Wasps' in the air force, to the number of 216,000. Women were not permitted to engage in combat, as in Russia and even in Great Britain, but many saw service overseas and in dangerous positions at home.

The problem of training this vast force was tremendous. Fortunately the American soldier of 1941 was better prepared, in many respects, than the soldier of 1917; approximately half the draftees had high-school education, as contrasted with only one tenth for the earlier World War, and there was far more extensive and intelligent use made of the facilities of universities, research institutions, and laboratories. The early adoption of Selective Service and the inability to launch an offensive before the fall of 1942 gave the army time to provide all soldiers with some training (in theory a year's training) before they had to fight.

In the old days a soldier could be rushed into battle after learning little more than close-order drill and the manual of arms; modern warfare required him to be something of an athlete, a mechanic, a scout, and a scientist as well as a fighting man. 'An infantryman, for example,' wrote General Marshall, describing the army's training program,

> became proficient in his primary weapons and familiarized with the MI rifle, the carbine, the hand grenade, the rifle grenade, the automatic rifle, the .30 caliber medium machine gun, the 60-mm mortar, and the two-man rocket launcher. These were the weapons that every infantry rifleman might be called upon to use. Not only were men taught to handle their weapons with proficiency in the replacement training centers, but they were taught to take care of themselves personally. There was intensive instruction in personal sanitation, malaria control, processing of contaminated water, cooking, and keeping dry in the open, and all the other lore that a good soldier must understand. But most important, our replacements were taught the tricks of survival in battle. . . Training of replacements was made as realistic as possible to manage in training. Problems of street fighting, jungle fighting, and close combat were staged in realistic fashion with live ammunition, and men learned to crawl under supporting machine-gun fire, to use grenades, and advance under live artillery barrages just as they must in battle.[5]

Training for the air forces, whose expanding activities required over three million men, was naturally more complex than for ground forces. Air power meant fighter planes, high-level bombers, dive bombers, transport and troop-carrier planes, for which pilots and crewmen had to be trained; but it also meant research and planning, ground crews, and aircraft carriers in the navy with crews of 2500 men. To fly a combat plane required a high degree of intelligence, alertness, co-ordination, and mechanical skill; as one cadet observed, 'The cockpit of a basic trainer looks like the Grand Canyon full of alarm clocks.' A B-29 bomber carried a crew of only 14; but each B-29 required 18 additional men for operation, 20 for maintenance, 8 for transportation, 13 for administration, and 12 for 'housekeeping.' The army air force alone had to train 75,000 pilots and 80,000 gun-

[5] *Biennial Report of the Chief of Staff of the United States Army*, 1 July 1943 to 30 June 1945.

ners annually, as well as provide some 300,000 men for ground crews and other hundreds of thousands as technicians and administrators. The air-transport command grew to be bigger than all the commercial airlines of the world combined: the troop-carrier command, on the first day of the Allied invasion of Holland, used five times more planes than had ever been employed in all the commercial airlines of the United States. To fight a global war it was necessary to build hundreds of airfields and thousands of miles of landing strips all over the globe. To keep ahead of the enemy, research had to provide radar and radar interception, flak suits, precision bomb sights, jet propulsion, rocket guns, and global weather forecasting.

The work of the service forces was less dramatic than that of the air or ground forces but no less important.

> For instance, within a typical infantry division the transportation of men, equipment and supplies requires more than 1500 men. The preparation of food requires more than 650 men. The administrative duties in connection with food and supplies require more than 700 men; medical, 600; communications, 1500; repair and maintenance of equipment, 450; while a variety of other specialized services accounts for 1600 additional men. All of these soldiers receive not only intensive training in their specialties but also combat training to support effectively the 8000 men in the division whose principal job is at the fighting front.[6]

The service forces supplied food, clothing, munitions, and transportation for the army; handled pay and allowances; processed billions of dollars in contracts; managed posts in continental United States; operated base-port organizations; administered the medical services; ran the post exchanges, the entertainment and educational activities; administered redeployment and, eventually, demobilization. In these complex tasks of engineering and housekeeping the American talent for scientific management and business efficiency appeared at its best.

Remarkable progress was made by the medical corps. Deaths from wounds and disease had always been the bane of armies. In the Civil War, for example, deaths from wounds were far greater than the number killed outright; and in the Spanish War, deaths from disease far outnumbered battle casualties. Thanks to high standards of physical fitness for induction, abundant food, better clothing, more and better hospitals competently staffed, the health of the armed

[6] *Biennial Report of the Chief of Staff*, 1 July 1941 to 30 June 1943.

forces in World War II compared favorably with that of the civilian population in the same age groups. The development of sulfa drugs and penicillin injections against various diseases, the use of plasma for blood transfusions, control of mosquitoes and other soldiers' companions, new techniques for the treatment of burns and neuroses, and prompt evacuation of the wounded from battle areas reduced the death rate from wounds to less than half that of World War I, enabled about two thirds of all wounded to return to duty, and brought deaths from non-combat causes down to less than 1 per cent of officers and men annually.

This was, peculiarly, an engineers' war, and here American technical skill gave the Allies great advantages over the enemy. To the army's engineers and the navy's 'seabees' fell responsibility for the construction and administration of vast cantonments, roads, railroads, bridges, canals, airfields, ports, and a thousand other essential military facilities. In the United States alone, the Engineers' construction program required the acquisition of 38 million acres of land and the expenditure of ten billion dollars. The Engineers built thousands of miles of highways, constructed port facilities throughout the globe, repaired harbors like Marseilles and Cherbourg that had been systematically wrecked by the enemy, and constructed artificial harbors like Mulberry-A off Normandy. They built and operated thousands of miles of military railroads — in Persia, in North Africa, in France: the Avranches-Le Mans railroad, essential to General Patton's offensive, was reconstructed in 48 hours. Particularly notable were their achievements in building roads, laying pipelines, and throwing bridges across scores of rivers, streams, and ravines. The Alaska Highway was the largest, the Burma Road the most notorious, the hundreds of miles of roads in North Africa and Italy the most useful of their road-building achievements. The American motorized army was dependent on gas and oil, and the supplies in North Africa and on the European Continent were wholly inadequate; the Engineers performed seeming miracles of pipeline construction. The first pipeline was laid four days after the Normandy landings, from submarines offshore; within six months the Engineers had laid almost 3000 miles of pipelines from Cherbourg to the Rhine, from Marseilles to the Rhone, and, after the capture of Antwerp, from that city to Wesel across the Rhine — pipelines that furnished Allied armies with a flow of four million gallons of gasoline every twenty-four hours. Equally impressive was the achievement in bridge-building. Strategic air attacks had destroyed most of the bridges over French and German streams, and the retreating Germans accounted for the rest. In the course of the Allied advance toward Germany, American Engineers built 223 major highway and dozens of railroad bridges. The first railroad bridge, across the Rhine at Wesel, was finished in ten days; pontoon, treadway, and the famous Bailey bridges were finished in as many hours. In the Pacific and the CBI theaters, too, the Engineers laid the foundations for the military and naval advance, constructing huge harbors in New Caledonia, Australia, and India, laying a pipeline from Calcutta through Burma to Kunming, China, and preparing hundreds of air strips. And finally, it was the Engineer Corps that, in 1943, took over Manhattan District and provided the massive and complex technological facilities for making the atomic bomb.

The United States Navy entered the war adequately prepared for everything except anti-submarine warfare, which happened to be one of its first and most pressing duties. The navy had been air-minded since 1919, when it went in for supplying the fleet with an adequate air arm; not only the Catalina seaplane based on mobile tenders, but fighters, dive-bombing and torpedo-bombing planes based on carriers, of which five big ones were completed before the war. At the same time measures against hostile aircraft were developed by more and better anti-aircraft guns on all ships, special anti-aircraft cruisers and air-search radar. Next in importance in naval preparedness was the practice (in conjunction with the fleet marine force, established in 1933) and development of amphibious warfare. The navy realized in 1940 that, owing to Axis or Vichy French control of the entire European and North African littoral,[7] transporting troops overseas would not be a simple matter of avoiding U-boats, as in World War I; troops, military stores, and heavy armored equipment must be combat-landed on enemy-held shores, through mined waters and under hostile skies. And in the Pacific it was well known that the Japanese would fight hard for every island or atoll they might hold. Consequently the navy accumulated a flock of Higgins boats, a fleet of passenger ships, freighters, and tankers that were converted to transports, navy cargo ships, and fleet oilers, and a fleet of minesweepers; while contracts had been let for the first of the completely new assortment of vessels specially designed for amphibious warfare, from the 460-foot LSD (Landing

[7] Except the neutral Iberian peninsula.

Ship, Dock), which spawned landing craft from a miniature lake in its bowels, and the 330-foot LST (Landing Ship, Tank), down to the 12½-foot LCR (Landing Craft, Rubber), with a capacity of seven men. With F.D.R., always a sea-power enthusiast, in the White House, the long, lean years ended for the navy; and after 1940, with plenty of money available for high wages and overtime in the shipyards, it became possible to build a destroyer in five months instead of a year, and a big carrier in 15 months instead of three years. Naturally, as with the army, numerous training schools and research centers had to be set up for a 1000 per cent increase in personnel and for a type of naval warfare that depended as much on brains as on brawn.

Under Rear Admiral Emory S. Land, though not a part of the navy, was the Maritime Commission, created by Congress in 1936. After a slow start (only 102 vessels built in all the United States in 1939–40) the Commission was given new powers in July 1941, and drew up blueprints for an emergency freighter that could be built quickly and inexpensively; the first Liberty ship—appropriately named *Patrick Henry*—was launched in September, and that year 139 ships were launched. The United States Merchant Marine Cadet Corps, established in 1938, was expanded; the national maritime unions, with the slogan 'Keep 'em Sailing,' co-operated in keeping seamen on their jobs despite the U-boat menace, and in November 1941, when Congress finally repealed those clauses of the Neutrality Acts forbidding merchantmen to arm in self-defense, the navy began installing naval gun crews on merchant vessels.

At the end of the war over four million men and women were enrolled in the navy, coast guard, and marine corps, and the United States navy was more powerful than all the world's navies combined; the American merchant marine, too, headed the procession.

Americans had to learn to fight with new and complicated weapons and in every kind of terrain from snow-covered mountains to arid deserts and miasmic, sodden, tropical jungles. And, for the first time since the old Indian wars, they had to fight an enemy who tortured prisoners, who observed no rule of war except his own advantage, and who never surrendered until so ordered by his emperor. There was a flexibility in the American character that enabled soldiers to adapt themselves to new techniques and tough terrain and dirty fighting, in spite of the fact that to their high peacetime standards of comfort and sportsmanship such things were repugnant.

Early recognizing the necessity of training for new kinds of fighting, the armed forces set up a desert-training center in the Southwest, a mountain-combat school in California, and amphibious warfare-training centers along both coasts and in Hawaii. Both army and navy developed their respective intelligence services to find out what the country's enemies were about; and in addition there was the new Office of Strategic Services under Major General William J. Donovan, which spread a network of 'cloak and dagger' heroes ahead of the armed forces in Europe.

3. *The Battle of Production*

In the late afternoon of 15 January 1942, President Roosevelt called the Vice President and Donald Nelson into his White House study and outlined a plan for the War Production Board. 'The President told us,' Nelson later recalled,

> that all our problems of global and local strategy, with all of the stringencies experienced by Great Britain, Russia and China, were determined by our ability to produce war materials. The plain truth was this: our fate and that of our Allies — our liberties, our honor and our substance — depended upon American industry. That was the hardest and most uncompromising fact before us.[8]

It was, indeed. Even before we entered the war, Roosevelt had promised that America would be 'the arsenal of democracy.' Now she was called upon to make good. In productive capacity the United States was clearly supreme, and the outcome of the war would depend as much upon the speed and efficiency with which industry could be mobilized and its products made available, as on the ability of Americans to fight in the air, on the sea, and on land. In the realm of production the United States enjoyed advantages over all other belligerents: an immense labor force, a modern plant, ample ingenuity, and, not least, immunity from air attack and freedom from the blackouts, food and housing shortages, and all the other dangers and aggravations that handicapped allies and enemies alike.

Fortunately American industry was already on a partial war basis. Lend-Lease and the big defense appropriations of 1940–41 had enormously stimulated war production. Already over six million workers had been added to the payrolls; unemployment was a thing of the past. Already welders' arcs were glowing and spitting in more than

[8] Donald Nelson, *Arsenal of Democracy,* p. 17. Harcourt, Brace.

PRODUCTION OF SELECTED MUNITIONS ITEMS
1 JULY 1940—31 JULY 1945

Item	1 July 1940, through Dec. 1941	1942	1943	1944	1 Jan. 1945, through 31 July 1945	Cumulative 1 July 1940, through 31 July 1945
Military airplanes and special purpose aircraft	23,228	47,859	85,930	96,359	43,225	296,601
Naval ships (new construction; excluding small, rubber, and plastic boats)	1,341	8,039	18,431	29,150	14,099	71,060
Displacement tonnage of above new naval construction	270,000	846,000	2,569,000	3,224,000	1,341,000	8,250,000
Total Maritime Commission ships	136	760	1,949	1,786	794	5,425
Dead-weight tonnage of above maritime construction	1,551,000	8,090,000	19,296,000	16,447,000	7,855,000	55,239,000
Machine guns	126,113	666,820	830,384	798,782	302,798	2,724,897
Tanks	4,258	23,884	29,497	17,565	11,184	86,388

From *Public Papers of F. D. Roosevelt,* ed. by S. I. Rosenman, 1942 vol. Harper Bros.

a hundred shipyards. Plants by the thousand, and not only the major industries, converted from peacetime to war production. Radio manufacturers turned out radar equipment, piano manufacturers made plane wings, corset manufacturers fashioned parachutes, silverware companies produced surgical instruments, and so forth. Between 1939 and 1941 the index of industrial production rose from 109 to 169, while steel production, always a key item, soared by 16 million tons.

Yet there were ominous shortages and lags. In 1941, wrote Donald Nelson, 'we almost lost the war before we ever got into it. At best it was a hair-line verdict. Just a few more mistakes would have turned the trick—a little more unwillingness to look into the face of reality, a little more shrinking from hard facts and figures . . . a little more tremulous indecision.' Unwilling to believe that the United States would really be forced into the war, many leading industrialists were slow to convert to war production, and the armed forces were sometimes slow to place orders for essential tools and weapons, fearing that these would be obsolete before they could be used. The steel industry did not expand its capacity enough, and the automobile industry was reluctant to shift from pleasure cars to war vehicles just when prosperity gave them a flood of new-car orders. The administration had not built up adequate stockpiles of rubber, aluminum, copper, or chrome, and there were serious deficiencies in other essential items such as quinine.

Pearl Harbor gave an urgency to American production that it had heretofore lacked, and galvanized industry into high speed. In his message to Congress of January 1942 President Roosevelt set production goals for that year at 60,000 airplanes, 45,000 tanks, and eight million tons of merchant shipping; Axis propagandists derided these figures as an example of American bluff, and even the head of the War Production Board admitted, 'We thought these goals were out of the question.' With reasonable promptness the administration set up machinery for placing war orders, financing the construction of war plants, allocating raw material and manpower, settling labor disputes, and raising money to finance the war. A bewildering hierarchy of boards co-ordinated as best they could the competing demands of the United States and her Allies, the armed services and civilian economy, the army, navy, and air force, manufacturers, mining, transportation, and agriculture. Eventually all these boards were brought (in theory) under supervision of the Office of

War Mobilization headed by former Supreme Court Justice James F. Byrnes; but quarrels between them and the Executive Departments, each convinced that its special requirements deserved the highest priority, were many and violent. Thousands of industrialists hurried to offer their services to the government; thousands of technicians, scientists, and even scholars were placed where they thought they could contribute most effectively to the war. Half a million new employees were added to the civil service.

It was an all-out effort but not total war as the term was understood in Great Britain, Russia, and Germany. There was no firm control over all manpower, no implacable direction of talent to the activity where it could be most useful, no conscription of women for military service or for industry as in other countries. Meat, sugar, fats, coffee, and canned goods were rationed, but Americans ate more heartily than ever before. Gasoline and tires were rationed, but hundreds of thousands of cars managed to stay on the road for purposes only remotely connected with the war. Personal and corporation taxes were increased but there was no limit on profit. Nor was there any limit to what workers could earn, if they chose to work overtime; and as prices in general were kept down, the average worker's standard and style of living rose higher than ever before — which was very much to the general good. This war struck deeper into the life of the people than had any previous conflict, but it was not all 'blood, sweat, and tears' by any means.

Yet American industry produced not only enough materials and weapons for the United States but supplied the deficiencies of the Allies as well. American factories equipped French and Chinese armies; built harbor works in the Persian Gulf, India, and New Caledonia; provided millions of feet of steel landing mats for hundreds of airfields scattered around the earth; supplied locomotives to Iran, trucks to Russia, jeeps to Britain, aircraft to China; built the Burma Road; completed the Alaska Highway; constructed aluminum plants in Canada; laid oil pipelines in France, and performed a thousand similar tasks. To hard-pressed Russia went almost 400,000 trucks, 52,000 jeeps, 7,000 tanks, 130,000 field telephones, 420,000 tons of aluminum, and enough planes to equip two air forces the size of the United States Army Ninth Tactical Air Force, which was the world's largest. Britain received enough planes for four such air forces, over 100,000 trucks and jeeps, six million tons of steel, one billion dollars' worth of ordnance, thousands of radar sets, and millions of feet of radar-interception foil. One year after Pearl Harbor the United States was producing more war material than all the Axis nations combined.

Most important was the production of basic strategic materials such as steel, petroleum, aluminum, copper, and rubber, which went into essential instruments of war such as ships, planes, tanks, trucks, radar, and ammunition. Steel mills, which had produced less than 50 million tons annually during the 'thirties, turned out 86 million tons of steel in 1942 and 90 million in 1944. Although this was barely enough to meet the most urgent military needs, it was almost twice the output of the Axis powers even with the resources of the conquered countries at their disposal. Thanks in part to the great hydroelectric dams like the TVA built in the 'thirties, aluminum production soared from 435,000 tons in 1939 to 2,469,000 tons in 1943; while that of magnesium, one-third lighter than aluminum, was multiplied fortyfold. The production of bauxite, essential to the manufacture of aluminum, increased from less than half a million to some seven million tons in these same years. Notwithstanding a series of crippling strikes, coal production more than held its own. Copper, essential in the making of munitions, presented a serious problem and at one period shortage of this metal threatened to slow down essential parts of the war program. 'By the beginning of 1942,' writes Donald Nelson,

> we had had to disregard ordinary economic laws completely and offer premium prices to get copper from marginal deposits which would not and could not have been worked in any ordinary circumstances. We had to arrange for the production of new copper in South America and Africa, and we had to find the shipping — in the midst of what seemed at the time to be a highly successful Axis submarine offensive — to bring the metal to the United States. In mid-summer of 1942 the Army had to furlough some 4,000 soldiers who had previously worked in copper mines, in order to increase production.[9]

Air and naval forces made tremendous demands upon petroleum, and with Britain largely cut off from her Eastern supplies, the Royal Navy and Air Force depended on American fuel oil and aviation gasoline. Through the Office of Petroleum Administration the government took steps to assure an adequate supply, steps such as strict rationing of civilian use, the construction of Big Inch and Little Inch pipelines, and of new tankers. Thus oil production was in-

[9] *Arsenal of Democracy*, p. 173.

creased from 1264 million barrels in 1939 to 1678 million barrels in 1944.

The country followed with eager interest the growth of a new synthetic-rubber industry. Japanese conquest of the Malaya and East Indies rubber plantations had completely cut off basic supplies, and the American stockpile was only 600,000 tons, about the normal annual consumption. Without rubber the air force and mechanized armies would be immobilized. There was a period of confusion and controversy over the best methods for the manufacture of synthetic rubber; farmers wanted it to be made from an alcohol base, they to provide the potatoes and grains; oil men championed the use of petroleum. A compromise was finally effected, a rubber administration was set up under the direction of William M. Jeffers, new synthetic rubber plants were built, and by 1944 production reached 762,000 tons, while reclaimed rubber and a small dribble of wild-rubber imports from the Amazon lifted the total to over a million tons — enough to keep the war machinery functioning.

The shortage in rope and twine, 'must' products for the navy, merchant marine, mining, oil wells, trucking, fishing, and harvesting grain, was equally urgent if not so spectacular. The Japanese conquests cut off the only source of manila fiber and the principal source of sisal. Under the War Production Board, government and the rope industry co-operated to control and build stockpiles, revived the growth of American hemp in the Middle West, planted 28,000 acres with manila in Central America, increased sisal production in the same area, and tapped new sources of fiber in East Africa.

No single item in the war economy was more important than shipbuilding, and nowhere was the need for speed more urgent. All through 1942 and until April 1943, the U-boats took a heavy toll of Allied and neutral shipping; total losses to submarines, air attack, and marine casualty in those 15 months were close to ten million tons; ship production in United Nations shipyards did not even replace monthly losses until the end of 1942, after which the production curve went up and up, while destruction by the enemy went down and down. It was in April 1943 that the German Admiral Doenitz warned Hitler, 'Our war on shipping will fail if we don't sink more ships than the enemy can build,' and it was in that very month that the War Maritime Commission reached its goal of a monthly production of 140 ships, amounting to one million tons. By building ships in great segments for rapid assembly on the ways,

Industrial Production Index: 1934 to 1946

(Based on physical volume, adjusted for seasonal variation, 1935–39 average for total = 100)

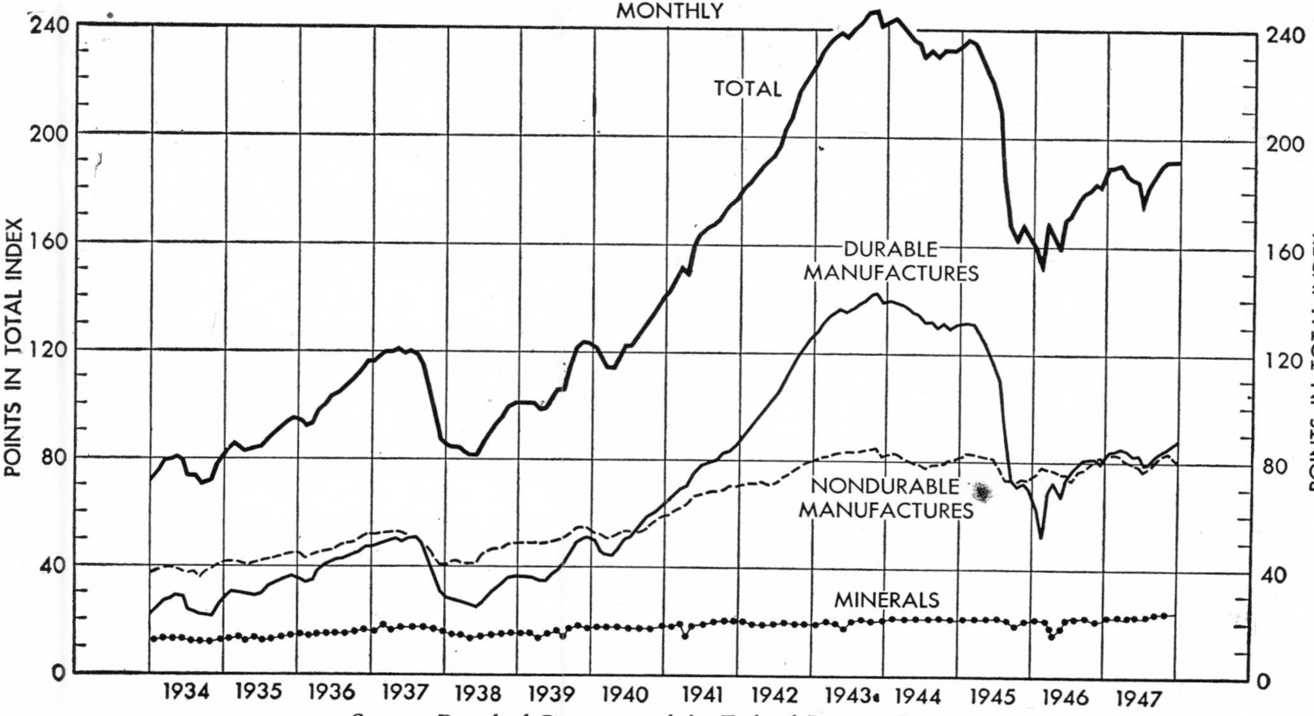

Source: Board of Governors of the Federal Reserve System.

by the use of electric welding and other improvements, the time for constructing a 10,500-ton Liberty ship was reduced from months to weeks; the first one required 244 days to build, but by 1944 the average construction time was 42 days. In all, 271 'Liberty ships,' 531 of the larger and faster Victory ships, and hundreds of tankers and other types were constructed during the war; British shipyards, equipped partly with American machinery, added their quota.

Equally important was the production of aircraft. 'The Americans can't build planes, only electric ice boxes and razor blades,' said Hermann Goering in one of his least happy prophecies. Fortunately, owing to the requirements of Lend-Lease and the foresight of the navy and air-force commands, airplane production was in full swing at the time of Pearl Harbor, and more combat planes were produced in January 1942 than in the whole of 1939. New plants like Willow Run outside Detroit, Grumman on Long Island, Glen Martin near Baltimore, and Douglas in southern California arose almost overnight. Automobile manufacturers, too, converted to aircraft production, and thousands of sub-contractors made the 400,000 component parts that go into a modern bomber. Special attention was given to three types, the Flying Fortress (B-17) — soon to be supplemented by the B-24 Liberator and the B-29 Superfortress — the SBD dive bomber, and the indispensable C-47 transport plane. Production in 1942 fell short of what Roosevelt demanded, but by 1944 it had reached 95,000 planes a year. Altogether, from Pearl Harbor to the end of the war, American factories turned out some 275,000 planes. These planes, together with those manufactured by the British, gave the Allies eventual mastery of the skies over both Europe and the Pacific; the Germans produced about one third as many planes as the United States alone, and the Japanese somewhat less.

Most war contracts went to the largest corporations, for obvious reasons of speed and efficiency, and out of habit. Thus ten giant corporations received one third of all war orders and one, General Motors, took on 14 billion dollars' worth of prime contracts. Much of the work for which they contracted percolated down through subcontracting to smaller plants, but in the course of the war some half a million small firms went under. The administration made energetic efforts to use the resources of small industries, but lack of time and of adequate machinery largely frustrated its efforts. So an inevitable consequence of the war was to speed up the concentration of economic control.

4. *Workers, Farmers, and Consumers*

So vast an industrial output made heavy demands upon labor, and this at a time when the armed services were using some 15 million men of the most productive age. The gap was made good in a variety of ways, some of them unfortunate: the addition of over six million women to the labor force, an increase in child labor, the return of older and unemployed men to work, the exemption of key labor in war factories from the draft. By these means the total labor force rose from 47 million in 1940 to over 55 million in 1943, and the typical work week was stepped up from 40 to 48 hours. Even more important in meeting the demands of war was an increased productivity of labor, brought about in part by the greater mechanization and the incentive of high wages, in part by the loyalty and enthusiasm of working men and women.

The most difficult of labor problems was the allocation of workers to industries and the adjustment of competing demands by military and civilian services. This task was entrusted to a manpower commission headed by the not very skillful Paul V. McNutt. Congress never authorized, as the British and Australian parliaments did, conscription for industry as well as for armed services, and the federal government had no counterpart to the British War Cabinet which controlled the civilian economy as well as military affairs. Yet, even if the nation did not use its reservoir of talents to the best advantage, it certainly drew on that reservoir more wisely than in any previous war.

The shift from peacetime to wartime production introduced violent dislocations in American economy and society. Labor gravitated naturally to the larger industrial centers, creating acute problems of housing, schooling, transportation, and policing. Between 1940 and 1946 American urban population increased by almost nine million, while the number of farm laborers actually declined. People followed industry to the West and Southwest, and during the war years the three Pacific Coast states gained one third in population. There were dislocations, too, within the labor force. Automobile mechanics could fit well enough into airplane plants, but it was not so easy for salesmen and gasoline-station attendants to adjust themselves to factory work. The rush of women into office and factory presented complex problems of social readjustment and doubtless contributed to an alarming increase in juvenile delinquency and in divorces. Several hundred thousand teachers left their underpaid profession for war work, and few cared to return; yet there was already an acute teacher shortage. With unemployment at an end and pay envelopes at an all-time high, there was a perceptible shift in the distribution of income and, with it, in demands that various social groups made for housing, food, liquor, and luxuries. Increased purchasing power in the hands of the middle-income groups made inflation a serious threat, and wise price-control, rationing, and tax policies became of crucial importance.

At the beginning of the war, the American Federation of Labor and the Congress of Industrial Organizations joined in a no-strike pledge in return for an understanding that the cost of living would be held down. A survey of newspaper editorials would suggest that this pledge was flagrantly violated, but an examination of labor statistics reveals that it was faithfully honored by the union officials. There were indeed strikes, euphemistically called work stoppages, but these were unauthorized. The government set up a War Labor Board which arbitrated critical industrial disputes and, through the so-called Little Steel formula — a wage increase of 15 per cent — tried to adjust wages to the cost of living. The major labor difficulties came in the coal mines, where John L. Lewis four times led his United Mine Workers out on strike. In 1943 coal strikes cost over nine million man-days; nevertheless coal production was higher in that year than in any previous year for a decade. These intemperate coal strikes were chiefly responsible for the enactment of the equally ill-considered Smith-Connally Act authorizing the government to take over any industries or plants whose contribution to the war was threatened by strikes, and forbidding strikes during government operation. Under the terms of this law, the government twice took over the coal mines and, for a short time, the railroads.

Most helpful in speeding up production were the labor-management committees, modeled on similar committees in Great Britain and Canada, established in each major industry and plant. These were designed to give labor a larger share in management and production; reduce turnover, absenteeism, and accidents; and encourage suggestions and inventions. Suggestions for improvements in production techniques sponsored by such committees saved the labor of over 100,000 workers in critical industries — a saving that more than made up for all the time lost in strikes.

During World War I, the government had found it necessary to seize and operate the railroads — a successful but costly experiment. At the outbreak of World War II, the railroads of the country were in a bad way. The depression and motor-car competition had eaten heavily into their revenues; 108 companies were in the hands of receivers. Road beds and rolling stock were badly run down and much of the equipment was obsolete. Railway mileage was less than it had been a quarter-century earlier, and the number of employees had dropped from over two million in 1920 to just over one million in 1940.

Yet, except for a brief period when a strike threatened to paralyze invasion preparations, the government made no move to take over the railroads. Management responded magnificently to the confidence reposed in it, and with a veteran railroad man, Ralph Budd, at the head of the government's war-transportation office, co-operation was excellent. The carriers were called upon not only to shift large segments of the population from one part of the country to another, and to transport millions of soldiers to camps and ports of embarkation, but to move the industrial produce of the country from mines, oilfields, and factories to assembly centers and ports. In 1944 the railroads carried twice as many passengers as in 1940, and carried them twice as far. Freight tonnage at the same time increased 50 per cent. The carriers managed to fulfill the responsibilities laid on them and emerged from the war in a stronger financial position.

Agricultural production also increased despite the migration of workers from farm to factory. The agricultural program of the New Deal — soil rehabilitation, rural electrification, and price subsidies — now paid handsome dividends. With the highest prices in history as an incentive, with an extensive use of fertilizer and modern machinery, and with ideal growing weather, American farmers brought 30 million more acres under cultivation in 1944 than in 1940, and produced bumper crops that broke all records. Between 1939 and 1944 the productivity of farm labor increased by one fourth; 477 million more bushels of corn, 324 million more bushels of wheat, 171 million more bushels of oats, and 500 million more pounds of rice were raised in 1944 than in 1939. Ten million more cattle and 32 million more hogs were slaughtered than in 1939; but first prize should have gone to the American hen, which laid one billion dozen more eggs than she had five years earlier! The United States was able not only to feed her own military and civilian population better than ever before, but to send six billion dollars' worth of foodstuffs to the Allies.

As food prices remained high, this meant unprecedented prosperity for the farmer, who, as a class, profited even more from the exigencies of war than did labor or the corporate stockholders. During the war years, farm income more than doubled, the value of farm property increased by 20 billion dollars, mortgages and debts were paid off. Gloomy prophets of a peasant status for the American farmer were confounded, and the 'husbandmen' began once more to play the active role in society and politics that they had before the Civil War.

High prices to farmers, high wages for workers, and big profits for corporations created a sellers' market at a time when the supply of consumer goods was inadequate to the demand. Under the stimulus of war the national income — that is, income left after taxes — rose from 73 billion dollars in 1940 to 140 billion in 1945. Real wages increased by 44 per cent and farm income by over 100 per cent; by the end of the war almost half the population had an income between \$2000 and \$5000 a year. Every other belligerent had faced the same problem with rigorous rationing and heavy taxation; but in the United States, because farmers wanted higher prices, and labor resented any limitation on wages, and because public opinion was fearful of bureaucratic interference in private lives, action was not so prompt.

The first requirement was to hold the line on prices and rents and to cut down consumer spending. Machinery for price regulation was set up in April 1941, but general price controls were not authorized until January 1942, by which time prices had already increased 25 per cent. Not until April of that year did the Office of Price Administration, then under the direction of the colorful Leon Henderson, fix prices on several hundred items of consumer goods and set up machinery for freezing rents. Another law passed in October extended government controls to wages and salaries in certain categories. But the President's plea that no one be allowed a net income of more than \$25,000 went unheeded. Consumer spending was restricted largely by the shortage of goods, by rationing, and by the prohibition of installment buying. These limited controls were successful in preventing serious inflation, as became clear enough when they were abandoned immediately after the war.

A second method of keeping prices down was to siphon off surplus income, which might otherwise go into the black market or pile up for postwar inflationary buying. Clearly the most effective method was high taxes, the easiest the sale of war bonds. Congress, which always hated to increase taxes, chose the easier way. President Roosevelt thought the tax bill of 1944 bad enough to veto, but it was passed over his veto. Taxes were, to be sure, increased. New income, corporate, excise, and inheritance taxes hit especially the middle- and top-income brackets, whose voting strength could be safely disregarded; and a 5 per cent 'victory tax,' collected at the source, took something from even the relatively poor. But the American tax burden never approached that to which the British subjected themselves. Only about 40 per cent of the cost of the war was met by taxation; the rest by borrowing, passing on the burden to posterity. The United States Treasury went into the red by 55 billion dollars in 1943, 49 billion in 1944, and 54 billion in 1945. It could borrow money from the banks at from 1 to 1½ per cent; but in order to siphon off surplus money it embarked upon a vigorous campaign of selling war bonds in denominations from $25 to $10,000. The purchase of these war bonds, like that of Liberty bonds during World War I, came to be regarded as a patriotic duty, and the public absorbed about 97 billion dollars' worth of government bonds. The total cost of the war came to about 350 billion dollars — ten times that of World War I — and before it ended, the national debt had soared to 250 billion dollars.

Nor were taxation and the national debt the only economic costs directly chargeable to the war. If previous wars were any guide, pensions would stretch into the limitless future; the wounded and the neurotics remained a national burden; the Servicemen's Readjustment Act, generally known as the 'GI Bill of Rights,' gave every veteran several years of free education or industrial training on Uncle Sam; and finally came the inescapable cost of helping the reconstruction of war-torn Europe, the cost of the military occupation of Japan and Germany, the paying of claims for war damages, and so forth.

In a sense the war vindicated the economic theories of both Thorstein Veblen and John Maynard Keynes. When production was entrusted to the engineers and the technicians and the question of profits ignored, production soared to an all-time high; when the government spent money lavishly, unemployment and the depression evaporated, and national income rose to the point where it could carry a heavy tax load. Because the war ended the depression and brought prosperity to almost every segment of American society—with notable exceptions of the fixed-income groups—and left the country with an expanded and modernized industrial plant, some cynics concluded that war was an economic panacea; and there were even those who saw in the perpetuation of war economy a cure for peacetime problems.

Another generation must pass before it will be possible to compute the economic incidence of the war. If we disregard the money, which was to a large extent a matter of internal bookkeeping, the real cost was its effect on mankind, the deaths of irreplaceable young men, and the deterioration of ethics.

5. *Science Goes to War*

When Robert P. Patterson, Under Secretary of War, was explaining the decision to 'beat Hitler first,' he listed as the most compelling reason 'the danger of the German scientists, the risk that they would come up with new weapons of devastating destructiveness.'

World War II, far more than any previous war, was fought with the weapons of science. Here, as it turned out, Britain and the United States were supreme. Allied victory in the war of science was basic to victory on the ocean, in the skies, and on the battlefield. This supremacy of Allied over Axis science, dramatized in the successful creation of the atomic bomb, was inherent in the conflicting systems. Axis scientists were as able as the British and American; indeed a significant number of those who contributed largely to American scientific progress came from Germany and the occupied countries. But German science labored under insuperable handicaps. The Nazi 'master race' idea, in itself a repudiation of the scientific attitude, had driven many of the ablest German, Austrian, and Italian scientists to other countries. And, in a country where Nazi officials were appointed university presidents and laboratory directors, and where everyone had to hew to a Nazi scientific 'line,' there was not the freedom of inquiry necessary for a healthy growth of science, or of any branch of learning. Hitler intervened personally in research as he did in military strategy: it was he, for example, who insisted that work on certain guided missiles be given priority over the atomic research.

The Germans and the Japanese, as Baxter points out, 'made almost every conceivable blunder.' Confident that the war would be short, the Nazi government failed to mobilize the scientific facilities of the nation. Distrusting the academic mind, it lodged control over research in the armed forces. Although in the realm of nuclear physics the Germans had made immense strides, they permitted the Allies to get ahead of them. There was no genuine co-operation between the Axis powers, no interchange of scientific discoveries or information, no joint planning. As for the Japanese, 'if we had planned the Japanese system for research on new weapons, we could scarcely have devised one better calculated to promote our interests.' [10]

The situation in the United States and Britain was in sharp contrast to the one that obtained in the Axis countries. Here science was free, and scientists were not intimidated by the specter of official disapproval or the peril of losing their jobs if they were not of a 'master race' or of a certain party. Here universities and laboratories were largely still free and independent, although many attempts had been made to place them under political direction. Here the political and military branches of the government co-operated with science not by imposing anything but by presenting their problems and accepting the scientists' guidance in the realms in which they were expert. Finally, Allied scientists worked as one team, in conjunction with distinguished refugees from Axis countries. If history ever proved anything, it proved this: that scientific supremacy goes to nations who put a premium on originality, where the spirit of free inquiry is untrammeled, and where government co-operates rather than controls.

Dr. Vannevar Bush of the Carnegie Institution of Washington brought the importance of scientific research forcibly to the attention of Harry Hopkins, who had no difficulty in winning Presidential approval for a proposal to mobilize the scientific talents of the nation for military purposes. The day after the fall of Paris, Roosevelt set up a National Defense Research Committee with Bush as chairman. That same summer of 1940 the Tizard Mission arrived in Washington to give the United States the benefit of British scientific research, especially in the crucially important fields of radar, mine, and submarine detection, chemical warfare, rockets, and explosives. 'There is no question,' says the historian of American wartime science, 'that in the early days of the scientific interchange, the British gave more than they received.'

10 James Phinney Baxter, 3rd, *Scientists Against Time*, pp. 7, 11. Little, Brown.

An Office of Scientific Research and Development, broader in authority and scope than its predecessor, was set up in May 1941 under the direction of Bush and President Conant of Harvard. Except for the armed services, no single government agency contributed more to Allied victory than this O.S.R.D. Staffed by the leading scientists of the nation, working in close co-operation with the army, navy, and air force on the one side and with the universities and research laboratories on the other, it sparked many of the important new weapons and fighting techniques. Radar and radar interception, rocket weapons, magnetic mines, explosives, smoke, proximity fuses, jet propulsion, guided missiles, military medicine, and, most vital of all, the atomic bomb were developed by and under this group of scientists.

The most urgent problem was that of anti-submarine warfare, for unless German submarines could be conquered, the Atlantic would become an iron curtain between the Allies. In this field an operational research group of scientists went out in ships and planes to see for themselves how anti-submarine measures worked, and to get the 'bugs' out of the devices they invented. Most important of these many devices was the microwave-search radar which enabled planes so equipped to detect and locate surfaced submarines far beyond the range of sight, so that bomber planes and surface craft could be coached in for the kill. At the same time new methods of attack were perfected—the most important, perhaps, the British 'Hedgehog' which fired clusters of depth charges with contact fuses. It was to these techniques and weapons that Admiral Doenitz referred in December 1943 when he told Hitler, 'For some months past, the enemy has rendered the U-boat ineffective. He has achieved this object through his superiority in the field of science; this finds its expression in the modern battle weapon, detection. By this means he has torn our sole offensive weapon in the war from our hands.'

As early as 1940 Hitler had stopped intensive research on radar; fortunately the British maintained it, and it was radar that had enabled British planes to intercept the Luftwaffe in the Battle for Britain. It proved less helpful, however, against the V-1 and V-2 bombs that threatened to destroy London in 1944 and 1945. In this crisis Allied science provided three countermeasures that prevented most of the V-1 buzz bombs from getting through: ground radar, the M-9 electrical director for anti-aircraft fire, and the proximity fuse. Even these were ineffective, however, against the giant V-2s, hurtling through the air at a speed of 3400 miles per hour. The proximity shell fuse, perhaps the most important innovation in artillery ammunition since the introduction of high-explosive shells, was used with devastating effect on enemy planes in the Pacific and in European waters and, eventually, in land warfare as well.

Radar had proved an invaluable defense against German and Japanese planes and submarines; when the Allies, in turn, mounted an offensive, it threatened them with defeat. Scientists applied themselves energetically to working out countermeasures, and in this they were successful beyond their anticipations. Ferret planes hunted out enemy radar stations, and other planes jammed them either by mechanical or by electronic methods. Mechanical jamming — actually merely deception — was achieved by dropping metallic or aluminum strips known as Chaff or long ribbons of aluminum known as Rope; the Eighth Air Force dropped over ten million pounds of aluminum foil for this purpose. Because the Germans had early standardized their radar, electronic jamming proved relatively easy and crippled the dangerous flak that had levied so heavy a toll on Allied bombers. At the same time radar permitted reasonably accurate (but not pin-point) bombing through overcast or cloud, enabling Allied bombers to carry out their missions in bad weather as in good.

Research contributed in various other ways to aerial warfare; for example, the rocket gun and the happily named Holy Moses or high-velocity aircraft rocket, used with gratifying results in General Patton's breakthrough at Coutances. And the perfected incendiary bomb, used chiefly in the attack on Japan, inflicted more damage and heavier casualties than even the atom bomb: the 9 March 1945 raid on Tokyo by 300 aircraft burned out sixteen square miles of that city — an area four times as large as that destroyed at Hiroshima.

By all odds the most spectacular and momentous of the triumphs of Allied science was the atomic bomb. Even before the outbreak of war, German scientists had succeeded in releasing energy by splitting the uranium atom; and in January 1939 the Danish physicist Niels Bohr revealed to American scientists the nature of the German experiments. There had indeed been preparatory research by many scientists of many lands, the chief American contributors being E. O. Lawrence, H. C. Urey, and A. J. Dempster. Physicists were working on various aspects of this problem all over the Western World, and by the time of Pearl Harbor the scientists of many countries had the theoretical knowledge to make an atomic bomb. But to adapt this theoretical knowledge to military use was a task of such complexity and magnitude as to stagger the imagination. First it was necessary to find sufficient quantities of uranium or uranium-bearing ores; then to devise some method of isolating the isotope, uranium 235; and finally — the most prodigious task of all — to build the plants and scientific machinery that would extract the isotopes in sufficient quantity and with sufficient speed to make them available for atomic warfare. It was indeed 'scientists against time,' for the Germans had a head start in the field of atomic fission.

As early as 1939 Albert Einstein, Leo Szilard, and Eugene Wigner — all foreign-born — warned President Roosevelt of the danger implicit in enemy supremacy in this field of research, and the President appointed an advisory committee on uranium, which at once swung into action. Invaluable help came from Britain, where the scientists were well ahead of Americans on atomic research, and it was not until they placed their knowledge at American disposal that the Roosevelt administration, in deepest secrecy, reached the momentous decision to go 'all out' on the project. The making of the atomic bomb was as much a combined operation as the invasion of Normandy.

Over-all direction of the atomic project was entrusted to the O.S.R.D. which enlisted many of America's leading physicists, chemists, and metallurgists. Research was farmed out to various universities. The crucial problem was to find some method of extracting U-235 that would be both speedy and practical. Five different methods were theoretically possible, and Dr. Bush succeeded in persuading the military and political authorities to gamble on all five simultaneously. By midsummer 1941, research had advanced to the point where the Atomic Research Committee was able to predict success. 'We entered the project with more skepticism than belief,' it reported. 'We have now reached the conclusion that it will be possible to make an effective uranium bomb which would be equivalent as regards destructive effect to 1800 tons of TNT.' A few months later the Committee reported that a fission bomb would result from 'bringing quickly together a sufficient mass of element U-235.'

But how to get a sufficient quantity of U-235; that was the rub. Of the five experimental methods, only three promised early results, and on these three, groups of scientists concentrated at the universities of California, Columbia, and Chicago. On 2 December 1942 the last group achieved the first self-sustaining nuclear chain reaction. It was 'the halfway mark on the road to the atom bomb.'

In ordinary circumstances scientists would have set up next a series of experimental or pilot plants to determine which of these three methods promised the most satisfactory results. Time did not permit this; the experimental pile at Chicago, for example, would have had to run 70,000 years in order to produce enough plutonium for a single bomb. Driven by the most compelling sense of urgency, Vannevar Bush and his associates persuaded the government to supply the money necessary to push ahead vigorously with the three most promising methods. The next step was to construct the vast plants necessary to apply these varying techniques to uranium or uranium-bearing metals. At this juncture the army corps of engineers took over, for only they were in a position to get the necessary priorities, command the engineering skills, impose effective security measures, and provide the money for so ambitious a series of undertakings. Under the authority of 'Manhattan District,' commanded by General L. R. Groves, a vast group of plants was erected in eastern Tennessee where power from the T.V.A. was available, and here the city of Oak Ridge, dedicated wholly to the atomic bomb, rose almost overnight. A plutonium plant was built at Hanford, Washington, on the banks of the Columbia. Eventually, 125,000 workers were employed in these plants and in the Los Alamos laboratory in New Mexico. The engineering problems involved were more intricate and extensive than any in history, and their solution represented a triumph of American technological genius.

By 1944 all three methods — the electromagnetic, the gaseous-diffusion, and the plutonium — were producing results. The next step was to make the bomb itself. The best-equipped physics laboratory in the world was erected at Los Alamos in the New Mexico desert, and Professor J. R. Oppenheimer of the University of California, with the assistance of Professors Compton, Rabi, Bohr, and Sir James Chadwick, was given responsibility for producing the bomb. By midsummer 1945 the Los Alamos scientists were ready to set off the first experimental bomb. On 16 July, in a remote corner of the Alamogordo Air Base, the atomic age was ushered in. 'We were reaching into the unknown,' said General T. F. Farrell, 'and we did not know what might come of it.' Nor do we yet.

The atomic bomb, wrote Secretary Stimson, 'was the greatest

achievement of the combined efforts of science, industry, labor and the military in history.' To this should be added the federal government, for without the support of the President from the very beginning in 1939, the project could never have been carried to completion. How was it, then, that Allied scientists won the race against time? First, by pooling of scientific resources of the United States, Great Britain, and Canada. Second, through co-operation between scientists and the armed forces. Third, American engineering capacities and natural resources enabled scientists to translate theoretical findings into reality more rapidly than was possible in any other country.

XXVIII

FIGHTING THE WAR

1. *The Battle of the Atlantic, 1941–1944*

SO much for the background and the basic considerations of American participation in World War II; now for the most important aspect of it, the actual fighting. In this, the most formidable and desperate armed conflict in which the United States ever engaged, there were so many theaters of war, so many kinds of warfare, so many countries involved, so many events going on simultaneously, that the story cannot help but be complicated, unless simplified beyond semblance of truth. Neither we nor our readers can be expected to keep our eyes on all aspects and theaters of the war at once, as the White House and the Joint Chiefs of Staff had to do at the time. Consequently, we are handling the war story by taking up one campaign or series of campaigns at a time, as nearly in chronological order as we can manage.

First to receive our attention must be the Battle of the Atlantic, because in that theater the Germans and British started to fight in September 1939 and the United States joined three months before Pearl Harbor. On 4 September 1941 a U-boat tried to sink U.S.S. *Greer* when she was steaming alone between Greenland and Iceland. President Roosevelt then issued orders to the navy to 'shoot on sight' any Axis vessels entering the waters of the Western Hemisphere.

Within two weeks the navy began to assist the Canadians and British in escorting transatlantic merchant convoys from a point off Newfoundland (where the leased port of Argentia made an excellent base) to a mid-ocean meeting point where the British took over; and the convoys to Iceland were entirely an American responsibility. Two United States destroyers were torpedoed and one, *Reuben James,* sunk in October when escorting convoys.

As we have seen, the basic strategic decision of the war was to beat the European Axis first. This meant intensified efforts by the United States and Canadian navies to protect transatlantic convoys, and so keep Britain going; also the building up of ground and air forces in the United Kingdom for an eventual invasion of Germany.

The fast (12- to 14-knot) troop convoys, which started across as early as January 1942, had the protection of battleships and cruisers all the way; and there were usually more warships than transports in such a convoy. The slower (6- to 9-knot) merchant convoys, numbering from 40 to over 100 freighters each, were lucky at this period to have one destroyer or Canadian corvette for every eight ships. Until mid-February 1942 the Germans left transatlantic convoys pretty much alone because Admiral Doenitz was assembling U-boats for a blitz on shipping lanes along the eastern seaboard of the United States.

The American top military commanders made a bad initial miscalculation. Expecting that Germany would make a bomber-plane attack on eastern cities, the army tied up thousands of aircraft guns and tens of thousands of men in useless anti-aircraft installations, and continued to tie them up for two years. But the Luftwaffe had no bombers with sufficient range to hit the east coast and get back again. Neither navy nor army air force had made any preparations to repel the U-boat attack that opened on 12 January 1942, off Cape Cod. Destroyers were tied up in escort duty; only five subchasers were in commission; there were less than a hundred planes to patrol coastal waters between Newfoundland and Trinidad; very few merchantmen had yet been armed. Under these conditions, frightful destruction was wrought by U-boats in the crowded shipping lanes off the Atlantic and Gulf coasts between the Canadian border and Jacksonville, Florida. Eighty-two ships of almost half a million tons were sunk during the first four months of 1942. When the navy adopted remedial measures, such as routing ships in daylight only between net- or mine-protected harbors and anchorages, Admiral Doenitz shifted his submarine wolf packs to the Straits of Florida, the Gulf of Mexico, and the Caribbean; and in those waters 142 ships totaling over 715,000 tons were sunk in May and June 1942. During the first six months of 1942, about 44 more ships were cut out from the North Atlantic convoys, 84 were sunk in waters around Bermuda, and many more in other areas. Vessels were sunk 30 miles off Ambrose Channel to New York harbor, two were torpedoed within sight of Virginia Beach, some were caught off the Passes to the Mississippi, others right off the Panama Canal entrance. Over half of the victims in southern waters were tankers, the sinking of which not only roasted water-borne survivors in burning oil, but caused coastwise shipments of fuel oil to be discontinued and threatened the success of military operations in Europe and the Pacific.[1] Puerto Rico suffered from inability to move crops or import necessary food; sugar and coffee had to be rationed in the United States, and 'good neighbors' in Latin America began to doubt big neighbor's ability to win. Most serious of all, during these six months the Western Allies sank only twenty U-boats, less than the monthly production of new ones; and of these, United States air and naval forces were responsible for only six.[2] Obviously, if this ratio of losses continued, there would soon be a 'torpedo curtain' dropped between the United States and Europe.

Fortunately Admiral Ernest J. King became commander in chief of the United States fleet before December was out, and at once took energetic measures to combat the submarine menace. A sailor's sailor, King had a vast naval experience and knowledge after 41 years' active service, and an immense capacity for work. A hard, grim, determined seaman who hated both publicity and politicians, he quickly acquired the confidence of President Roosevelt, whose qualities were complementary to his. These two in concert with General Marshall, who shared the qualities of both, formed a winning team. There had been nothing like that in American history since the Lincoln-Grant-Farragut team of 1864–5; and King had far more responsibility than Farragut, Marshall more than Grant.

The problem was immense. The west-east lifeline to Britain had to be maintained, and so did the north-south lifeline. That 250-mile-wide belt of ocean from Newfoundland, around the Atlantic and Gulf shores of the United States, through the Caribbean past the Panama Canal, Colombia, and the Guianas, and around the bulge of Brazil to Rio de Janeiro and the River Plate was one of the world's most crowded sea lanes. Through it ships must ply to carry oil, iron, steel, cotton, sugar, coffee, and bauxite from their sources to the most important Allied markets. The U-boats were playing ducks and drakes with these ships.

The most obvious means of protection was to route the ships in coastal convoys all the way from Canada to Brazil; but convoys were no use without escorts, and the first need was for small escort vessels.

[1] The navy obtained almost all its fuel oil for the Pacific fleet from the Gulf, Venezuela, and Aruba, via the Panama Canal.

[2] The first sinking of a U-boat by United States forces was not by 'Sighted Sub Sank Same' Mason — he got the second — but by Ens. Tepuni piloting a plane based on Argentia, on 1 March. The first sunk by a U.S. ship was by destroyer *Roper,* 14 April 1942.

The slogan 'sixty vessels in sixty days' was nailed to the mast in April 1942; and 67 vessels actually came through by 4 May, when a second sixty-sixty program was already under way. The British navy lent 22 little coal-burning armed trawlers, minesweepers were pressed into anti-submarine work, 30 new destroyers and large coast-guard cutters were commissioned, 54 Canadian corvettes were purchased, and large yachts were converted. As escorts became available, an interlocking convoy system was worked out in which two trunk lines, Key West to New York and return, were fed freight by numerous branch lines from Halifax to Trinidad and Brazil. In the second half of 1942 these coastal convoys lost only one half of one per cent of their ships; the transatlantic convoys lost only 1.4 per cent in a whole year. By April 1943 there were every day at sea in the American half of the North Atlantic and down to Brazil an average of 31 convoys with 145 escorts and 673 merchant ships, as well as 120 ships traveling alone and unescorted.[8]

Because most of the coastal convoy lanes, except the New York-Guantánamo, passed fairly close to shore, ships could be furnished air as well as surface escort during daytime. A great effort, therefore, was made by both army and navy to establish new airfields and train aviators for anti-submarine patrol. Such air coverage as the United States could supply in 1942 was not, however, very effective, partly because of constant wrangling between the army and navy high commands; partly because army aviators were not trained to fly over water and were apt to miss the convoy they were sent forth to protect; partly because the planes were too small, short-ranged, and not equipped with the right radar. War experience soon proved that the big, fast, four-engined planes like the Liberator, equipped with guns, radar, and depth bombs, were the most effective weapons against submarines. Their speed enabled them to catch and bomb the boats surfaced. The problem of connecting a lethal weapon with a submerged U-boat through the dense, opaque medium of salt water was never really solved. By September 1943, when the navy had enough long- and medium-range bombers to cover the coastal convoys as well as to protect a good part of the transatlantic route from Icelandic bases, it relieved the army air force, whose anti-submarine command shifted overseas to help the R.A.F. Yet even in the second half of 1942, only 64 U-boats — less than three months'

[8] These figures do not include the troop convoys, or convoys in the British strategic area, the eastern half of the Atlantic.

production at that time — were sunk by all Allied forces. Of these, only ten were credited, even in part, to United States forces; only one to a naval vessel.

In the meantime, the Battle of the North Atlantic had extended into the Arctic Ocean and the South Atlantic. The first, the most dangerous and disagreeable of all convoy routes, had to be undertaken to get Lend-Lease goods to Russia through Murmansk or Archangel. Although the British navy did most of the escorting over this route — losing in that service eleven warships — about half the merchantmen concerned were American. The convoys were formed up near Reykjavík, Iceland, passed through the Denmark Strait, and as far north as the ice pack would permit; but this was never far enough to escape the attacks of German bombers based on fields in occupied Norway and Finland. North Russia convoys were also attacked by German submarines camouflaged with white paint, and by cruisers and destroyers that issued forth from the Norwegian fjords. Winter was better for the Allied ships than summer, when there is perpetual daylight in those high latitudes. The North Russia convoy that sailed 27 June 1942 sustained one of the grimmest convoy battles of the entire war. It was attacked by six U-boats on 1 July, by 32 planes during the next two days; while the Glorious Fourth was celebrated in reverse by five air attacks, one of them frustrated by U.S.S. *Wainwright.* Hitler sent out his battleship *Tirpitz,* sister ship of the sunken *Bismarck,* to get this convoy; the escort scattered and then it was every merchantman for himself. Out of 33 merchantmen in this convoy, 22 — 14 of them American — were lost, a score so devastating that the British Admiralty refused to run any more North Russia convoys until fall brought shorter days. But Russia's need was so great that U.S.S. *Tuscaloosa, Emmons,* and *Rodman* carried 300 tons of supplies to Murmansk in August 1942. This dangerous route was no longer a necessity after July 1943, when the Mediterranean was reopened to merchant traffic and the Suez-Persian Gulf route could be used.

Another and happier extension of the Atlantic battle was to the southward. Although many Latin-American countries broke relations with or declared war on the Axis and Japan earlier,[4] Brazil

[4] All Central-American republics declared war on the Axis and Japan, and Colombia and Venezuela broke diplomatic relations with them, in December 1941. Ecuador and Peru broke relations in January 1942, Mexico in May. Chile broke relations in January 1943. Argentina broke relations only a year later. The countries

was the only nation south of the Rio Grande that gave the Allies substantial aid. And the strategic position of this great republic made her help highly important. With Cape São Roque only 1845 miles from the bulge of Africa, the Atlantic here became a bottleneck, control of which was vital for either side. From the start Brazil co-operated with the American navy, although she did not declare war on the Axis until 22 August 1942, when Doenitz pulled a minor Pearl Harbor on her by sinking five Brazilian ships within sight of shore.[5]

In conjunction with the British naval command in West Africa, an air-sea patrol of the Atlantic Narrows was established. By July 1942 United States army engineers had performed the supposedly impossible task of building an airfield on lonely, rugged Ascension Island about halfway between Brazil and Africa, guarding the southern entrance to the bottleneck. This setup proved so successful in catching German raiders and blockade runners trying to keep up Hitler's connection with Japan, that these vessels were all captured or driven home by 1944.

Patrolling for submarines, however, was like the proverbial hunting a needle in a haystack. Until 1943, when the United States and Brazilian navies were able to escort convoys to and from Rio, sinkings in the South Atlantic were numerous and serious. Thereafter warships and land-based planes killed so many U-boats that Admiral Doenitz pulled the rest out.

The crucial period in the Battle of the Atlantic was the twelvemonth between July 1942 and July 1943. At the turn of the year Hitler appointed his submarine expert, Admiral Doenitz, commander in chief of the German navy and concentrated on producing more and better U-boats. The number of them operating in the Atlantic more than doubled, and their effectiveness was increased by operating big supply subs — 'milch cows' they were called — around the neutral Azores, where U-boats could replenish without returning to France. But the number of Allied ships and planes capable of dealing with them, or at least of protecting convoys, more than quadrupled. The occupation of North Africa by American forces re-

who had not yet done so declared war in 1945 in order to be among the United Nations.

[5] To show how events interlocked, one primary mission of these U-boats, to break up an American convoy carrying General Sherman tanks around Africa to General Alexander in Egypt, failed; and it was those tanks that turned the tide at the Battle of El Alamein in October.

quired so many troop and supply convoys to Casablanca and the Straits that the North Atlantic route was denuded of American destroyers, and the British navy gradually took over. Admiral Doenitz sheered off from the Atlantic coast of the United States, now that coastal convoys and other measures made hunting unprofitable, and started a new blitz on the northern transatlantic route, which, in March and April 1943, accounted for 85 merchant ships aggregating over half a million tons. Echelons of wolf packs, preceded by U-boats whose sole duty was to shadow convoys, attacked by day as well as night. These sinkings, occurring at the worst season in the North Atlantic when the temperature of the water hovers around 30° F, were accompanied by heavy loss of lives. Hundreds of merchant and naval seamen were blown up, drowned, or frozen to death. And although the navy got all transatlantic troop transports across safely, as at every period of the war, it lost to submarine attack at this time three army transports en route to Greenland and Iceland.

As an example of the tribulations of a northern transatlantic convoy at this tough period, take a westbound convoy in February, escorted by United States coast-guard cutters *Spencer* and *Campbell,* five Canadian and British corvettes, and a Polish destroyer. Captain P. R. Heineman, USN, was the commander. Head winds slowed speed of advance to 4 knots; yet the escorts managed to fuel under way in tempestuous seas from tankers in the convoy. On 21 February the two cutters and a Liberator flying from the United Kingdom sank a U-boat. During the next three days, when the convoy was outside the range of air protection, it suffered six attacks by a large wolf pack of submarines and lost five ships. Polish destroyer *Burza* depth-charged one U-boat which dove to 130 fathoms; its commander then blew all tanks, surfaced at a steep angle, and was promptly rammed and sunk by the *Campbell.* The rest of the wolf pack continued to snap at the convoy for two days more, but the energy and skill of the escort got the ships through with the loss of but one more. Heineman's escort unit, relieved by the Canadian navy south of Newfoundland, had barely tasted the uneasy shelter afforded by Argentia harbor when it had to go out and take charge of an eastbound convoy of 56 ships. Westerly gales with hail and snow battered this convoy for nine days running. Though the escorts were now experts and the merchant crews showed both courage and discipline, six ships were lost in so rough a sea that few survivors could be rescued.

By April 1943 the Allies were definitely ahead in this contest with the submarine. At a conference with Hitler on the 11th, Doenitz admitted the loss of 40 U-boats and 6 Italian submarines since the New Year. The submarines were no longer paying their cost in shipping, and new construction had now replaced the heavy Allied losses. Hitler decided, however, to continue, partly because the U-boat campaign tied up Allied forces that might otherwise be used for the invasion of Europe, but mostly in order to gain time for the production of new types and gadgets. If only he could get out a few dozen of the new 250-foot, electric-drive submarine, which could stay under water indefinitely and make 17 knots submerged (as compared with 7.6 knots for existing boats), Allied anti-submarine warfare would be baffled. In the meantime existing U-boats were provided with more guns so they could shoot it out with attacking planes, and were fitted with the ' snorkel ' or breathing tube, which enabled them to operate their diesel engines under water.

So the real question in mid-1943 was whether the Allies could master existing submarines in order to enable America to get enough men and weapons across in time to beat Germany to her knees before the new U-boat was in production. It was a race against time, not only of scientists and shipyards but of navies and bomber planes. After May 1943, when Admiral King set up a unified anti-submarine command under his immediate supervision, the increased number of convoys and escorts, improved devices and training, and the work of the scientists and technicians put the Allies definitely in the lead. The British, organizing killer groups of R.A.F. and A.A.F. bomber planes assisted by combat ships, put on a great drive in the Bay of Biscay against U-boats that were approaching or departing from their French bases. This, in conjunction with successes elsewhere, brought the total bag up to 41 in May. At the same time the United States began using her new escort carriers in convoys between Norfolk and the Mediterranean. These, accompanied by two or three of the new destroyer-escorts, went out after every submarine detected within 300 miles of the convoy route and sank a considerable number, even some of the big ' milch cows.' The latter were soon driven from their pastures when Portugal permitted the Allies to use their air bases in the Azores; that closed the last stretch in the North Atlantic which long-range bomber planes had been unable to reach. Italy, which had operated an effective fleet of submarines in the Mediterranean and out to Brazil, was out of the war by September. Soon the Allies would be sinking more submarines per month than they lost merchant vessels to submarine attack.

Yet the Battle of the Atlantic was by no means over. Doenitz once boasted, 'Aircraft can no more eliminate the U-boat than a crow can fight a mole.' As long as the 'mole' had to come up to breathe, and the 'crow' had radar-eyes to detect him over the horizon, the bird and his surface-swimming friends had the edge. But if the 'mole' developed underwater lungs so that he never had to broach, what then? One thing is certain — it was air power, properly co-ordinated with the United States navy and the British Admiralty, that gave the Allies their advantage; without it, they would have lost the war. And, conversely, the German navy's want of an air arm to scout for its U-boats was a major factor in their ultimate defeat.

2. *Active Defense in the Pacific, 1941–1942*

'A dismal situation, waste and wild,'[6] faced every responsible officer of government or armed forces who heard the news of Sunday, 7 December 1941. The entire battle fleet and half the planes on

[6] *Paradise Lost* i. 60. In brief, the facts of the Pearl Harbor attack were as follows, but remember that this attack was only a part of a comprehensive scheme of conquest. General Tojo became premier of Japan on 18 October. On 1 November Admiral Yamamoto issued his order for the attack, rehearsals for which had been going on for several months, and on the 7th the Admiral designated 7 December as D day. On 26 November the Pearl Harbor Striking Force under Vice Admiral Nagumo, composed of six carriers protected by 2 battleships, 3 cruisers, and 9 destroyers, sortied from Etorufu in the Kuriles. On the same day the United States made its final proposals, to the effect that if Japan would evacuate China and Indo-China, the United States would restore full commercial relations and sign a non-aggression pact. On 27 November Washington sent a 'war warning' to Admirals Stark and Hart at Pearl Harbor and Manila, but predicted aggression in the Philippines or Malaya rather than at Pearl Harbor. Nobody in authority at Washington or Pearl Harbor believed that the Japanese either could or would strike Hawaii, because they underestimated Japanese capabilities, and overestimated Japanese intelligence. In the meantime Nagumo's striking force approached Hawaii, undetected, by a northern route. On 5 December a Japanese submarine force, some with midget subs on board, took up a scouting line around the mouth of Pearl Harbor. At 3:42 a.m. 7 December minesweeper *Condor* sighted one of the midgets. A destroyer sank it at 6:45, but owing to incredibly poor communications, neither sighting nor sinking was known in naval headquarters ashore until shortly before the bombs began to drop, too late to give warning. An army search radar picked up scouting planes from the Japanese carriers at 6:45 and the first attack wave at 7:02, but the watch officer laughed it off and failed to report to army headquarters. At 7:55 the first air attack came in. At 9:10 (Oahu time) the Japanese ambassadors in Washington waited on Secretary Hull to deliver Japan's ultimatum. Attacks continued on the ships in Pearl Harbor and the airfields and seaplane bases on Oahu until about 10 a.m., when the 360 planes used in the attack (less 27 shot down or crashed) returned to their carriers.

Oahu were wiped out at one stroke. Every hour brought news of another Japanese air attack — on Thailand, Singapore, Mindanao, Guam, and Luzon. People were dazed, incredulous. There had been no such disaster as this in American history: six battleships on the bottom and one grounded; over 2400 Americans killed. The navy alone, in this one treacherous attack before war had been declared, lost about thrice as many men as it had lost in the two last wars — the Spanish War and World War I. Everyone wondered, what next? Invasion of Hawaii or California? Attack on the Panama Canal?

Actually the results of Pearl Harbor were not nearly so bad as at first was feared, while the consequences of the other Japanese attacks in the Far East were much worse. Admiral Nagumo's carrier-plane blitz of the American battle fleet was no prelude to invasion. The Japanese had no intention of seizing Oahu; they were merely bent on preventing the Pacific fleet from interfering with their plans for conquest in Malaya and the Philippines. What colossal folly! For the Pacific fleet, even if intact, was so short of auxiliary ships as to be in no position to intervene across the Pacific for months; and Japanese treachery united a hesitant America, bringing her angry and determined into war. Moreover, the expensive and valuable installations at Pearl Harbor and the destroyers of the Pacific fleet were spared; its three carriers, *Lexington, Enterprise* and *Saratoga,* were providentially at sea. They and their air groups actually constituted a striking force ten times as valuable as the lost battleships, all but two of which were eventually salvaged.

In the Far East, on the other hand, the news was calamitous. Thailand surrendered to the Japanese, who promptly landed troops at various points on the Malay Peninsula and began a relentless march on the great British base of Singapore. Other amphibious forces captured Hong Kong and jumped the Borneo oilfields; Japanese bombers based in Indo-China sank H.M.S. *Repulse* and *Prince of Wales,* eliminating British naval strength in the Pacific.

In the Philippines our situation after the first twenty-four hours was hopeless, though no one in authority would admit it. General MacArthur's command at Manila was alerted by the news of Pearl

Nagumo retired without being detected. Of the 94 naval vessels in Pearl Harbor, 6 battleships were sunk and 1 grounded, 2 auxiliaries were a total loss, and a few others badly damaged; about 120 planes were destroyed; 2335 men of the armed forces and 68 civilians were killed, 1178 wounded. After an exhaustive investigation the Joint Congressional Committee found that the top commanders at Pearl Harbor had been guilty of negligence.

Harbor, of a dawn attack on an American tender in Davao Gulf, and of an air strike on Baguio at breakfast time. Yet a hundred Japanese bombers caught the American air squadrons grounded on their fields near Manila at noon 8 December (East Longitude date) and wiped out over half of them. Two days later, unopposed, the Japanese bombers destroyed Cavite navy yard, together with the Asiatic fleet's stock of spare torpedoes.

That in itself was a serious loss, because Admiral Thomas C. Hart had counted on the 30 submarines of his Asiatic fleet to repel any Japanese invasion of Luzon. He had fortunately sent away to Dutch waters his biggest ships — three cruisers and nine destroyers; for they would have been 'duck soup' for the 2 Japanese battleships, 3 carriers, 13 cruisers, 39 destroyers, and numerous smaller craft that covered the several invasions of the Philippines. All that the short-armed submarines could do was to snipe a few auxiliary vessels, whose loss hampered the Japanese less than did the weather. During the seventeen days before Christmas the enemy successfully effected nine amphibious operations in the Philippines, five of them on Luzon. Overwhelming forces under General Homma brushed aside such troops as MacArthur could deploy to meet them, and converged on Manila from the northwest and the southeast. In the vain hope of preserving the Philippine capital from destruction, MacArthur evacuated it on 27 December, withdrew his army to the Bataan Peninsula, and set up headquarters in the island fortress of Corregidor. From the beginning of 1942 the Philippines were a Japanese-occupied dependency under a puppet President.

The defense of Bataan and Corregidor, valiant and inspiring, had no other effect than to deny the use of Manila Bay to the enemy for three months. The campaign was a melancholy confirmation of Mahan's theory of sea power. The Japanese, controlling all sea approaches and the air as well, enveloped both the peninsula and 'the Rock' in a tight blockade, and landed fresh troops behind the American lines almost at will. Over half the American and Filipino troops were disabled by wounds or by disease; all were at the point of starvation when on 8 April Major General Edward P. King decided to surrender his 'battling bastards of Bataan,' about 12,500 Americans and over 60,000 Filipinos. Their ranks were promptly thinned by the infamous 'death march' from Bataan to the prison camps. American forces at Corregidor and in the southern islands held out almost a month longer.

In the meantime the Japanese had won all their main objectives in Southwest Asia. Rabaul, potentially a more valuable base than Singapore since it protected Truk and menaced Australia, fell in January. The Malay Barrier — Sumatra, Java, Bali, Timor, and smaller islands of the chain — which barred the enemy from the Indian Ocean and Australia, was stoutly defended by soldiers, sailors, and aviators of the United States, Great Britain, the Netherlands, and Australia under a combined ' Abda ' command. But this weak and loose-jointed Abda command had a hopeless task. The Japanese would seize a strategic point in Borneo or Celebes, operate or build an airfield there, soften up the next objective by air attack, occupy it with an amphibious force, and so on until they had won the prizes of the Far East — Sumatra and Java with their teeming population and valuable oil deposits and rubber plantations. There were a few American planes in this area; and the old Asiatic fleet was about one third of the Abda naval command. With British and Dutch allies it fought a series of valiant engagements — off Balikpapan, 24 January 1942; off Bali, 4 February; in Badung Strait, 19–20 February; the great Battle of the Java Sea on the 27th, and the Battle of Sundra Strait, in which *Houston* went down fighting, next day. On 9 March — ninety days after the war began in the Far East — Java surrendered, the Malay Barrier was completely broken, and the sea lanes to Australia lay open. It was partly to restore Australian confidence that President Roosevelt ordered General MacArthur to leave the Philippines and set up headquarters in the sub-continent. He left on 11 March, promising to return.

One disaster followed another. Rangoon, capital and chief seaport of Burma, was occupied by the Japanese on 8 March, and Mandalay, anchor of the Burma Road, on 1 May. China was now isolated from her allies; only the American aviators flying over ' the Hump ' from India could bring her a trickle of aid. On 6 May, after the Japanese had captured the main defenses of Corregidor, General Jonathan M. Wainwright was forced to surrender the Rock together with its 11,000 defenders and a Philippine army of over 50,000 on the Visayas and Mindanao. There had been no such capitulation in American history since that of Vicksburg in 1863. Several thousand troops in the southern islands refused to surrender and continued sporadic resistance to the Japanese as guerrillas.

Now the colonial empires of the United States, the Netherlands, and Great Britain as far west as India and as far south as Australia, with all their rich resources, were in Japanese possession. Never in modern history has the prestige of the so-called white race fallen lower, or that of an Oriental people mounted higher, than in June 1942.

On Christmas Eve 1941 Admiral King warned, 'The way to victory is long; the going will be hard.' And so it was. Admiral Chester W. Nimitz, who at the same time received the command of the Pacific Fleet, was forced to bide his time until new naval construction and more trained troops gave him adequate reinforcements.

Since no British fleet remained in the Pacific, the Combined Chiefs of Staff entrusted the conduct of the Pacific war to the American Joint Chiefs of Staff, and they perforce adopted a strategy of active defense. A glance at the map of the Pacific will show why: distances were immense, and the only hope of eventually defeating Japan was to hold fast to what we still had as bases for a future offensive. Islands still in American possession such as Hawaii and Samoa had to be defended; and the troops and planes to do that were still few. The sea-air lanes to New Zealand and to Australia, where General MacArthur would shortly begin to build up an offensive, had to be protected; and that meant tying up a large part of the fleet to escort transport and supply ships from the Panama Canal and California to the antipodes by a long, circuitous route. Fortunately Japanese submarines were less numerous and enterprising than their Axis counterparts so that Australia-bound convoys were seldom attacked. American carriers made nuisance raids on Wake and Marcus Islands, on the Marshall group, and on Japanese-held points in New Guinea; but the best of them was the one delivered on Tokyo 18 April 1942. That carrier raid was unique because, in view of the short range of navy bomber planes, it was delivered by Colonel James H. Doolittle's B-25's from a base that President Roosevelt humorously called 'Shangri-La.' That base turned out to be a carrier group commanded by a new naval luminary, Vice Admiral William F. Halsey. The planes did little damage, and most of their crews had to bail out over China; but the news that Tokyo had actually been bombed lifted American morale, then sorely in need of a victory, and stimulated the Japanese higher command to retrieve face by an imprudent offensive.

As April of 1942 turned into May, the Japanese began this forward movement, and it did them no good. Instead of sitting pretty in their new conquests until attacked, and organizing the annexed peoples and resources to make Japan impregnable, they succumbed to what one of their admirals after the war called 'victory disease.' They decided to establish a defensive perimeter starting at Attu in the Aleutians, running through Midway and Wake Islands to the Marshalls and Gilberts, then through the Fijis and New Caledonia to Port Moresby in New Guinea. These islands were near enough to one another so that patrolling planes could detect any attempt to repeat raids like the one on Tokyo, and also disrupt the lifeline between the United States and the British antipodes. Ships of the Japanese navy, waiting like so many spiders at Kure, Truk, Kwajalein, and Rabaul, could be quickly rushed to any point on the perimeter to fight any United States fleet that ventured through. Admiral Yamamoto very much hoped Admiral Nimitz would make the attempt: having been in the United States, he knew something of American productive capacity and believed that the only hope of Japanese victory lay in mopping up his enemy's navy before it could be reinforced. The Japanese higher command expected that after the United States navy had met a few more defeats like Pearl Harbor, the 'soft' American people would force their government to quit and leave Japan in possession of her most valuable conquests. Then she could proceed at her leisure to conquer the rest of China and so become the most powerful empire in the world — capable of defying even Germany, if Hitler conquered all Europe.

The Japanese navy in 1942 was, by any standards, a very fine navy. Owing to a lavish building program it was much greater than any force the Allies could possibly deploy in the Pacific before late 1943. Owing to excellent naval science, it was at least equal to the United States navy in quality. Japan had the two largest and most powerful battleships in the world, displacing 63,700 tons, with 18-inch guns; while the American *Iowa* class, none of which were completed before 1943, were of 45,000 tons with 16-inch guns. She had a fleet of fast and powerful 8-inch cruisers built in defiance of former treaty restrictions, comparable to the American *Baltimore* class, and mounting torpedo tubes that no United States cruisers had. She had the fastest and most modern destroyers, twice as many big carriers as the Americans, and her carrier planes were superior in the fighter and torpedo-bomber types. Japanese amphibious technique appeared to be irresistible. Japanese torpedoes were faster, more powerful, and more sure-firing than those made in the United States, and the employment of them was at once more lavish and more intelligent.

Japanese naval gunnery was excellent; their ships were intensely trained for night fighting, and American ships were not. They lacked radar, which American ships began to install in 1942, but their pyrotechnics were superior. Flushed with triumph after triumph in the Southwest Pacific, the Japanese navy was confident of victory; so was the army that would back it up, and the air force. After 8 March the United States was fighting alone in the Pacific, and with her left arm only; her right was jabbing U-boats.

Why, then, did Japan fail? Because, owing to a combination of stupid strategy on her part and good strategy and good luck (a tremendous factor in naval warfare) on America's, the numerically inferior Pacific fleet defeated her in the battles of the Coral Sea, Midway, and Guadalcanal. After 1942 it was too late. The United States navy had learned many salutary lessons, acquired unprecedented strength, and become an irresistible force in the air, on the surface, and under water.

The Battle of the Coral Sea frustrated the first lunge forward in the new Japanese offensive. Yamamoto's intention was to capture Port Moresby, a strategic base in southern New Guinea, which MacArthur needed for the start of his 'return,' and whose airfields the Japanese wanted in order to break the American-Australia lifeline. Observe how actual or potential air bases were always the big prizes in the Pacific war. No fleet could operate far from its base without air protection, either floating or fixed; and island bases had the merit of unsinkability. By the same token, the Coral Sea fight was the first naval battle in which no ship of either side sighted a ship of the other; all the fighting was done by carrier plane against carrier plane, or carrier plane against ship.[7] Yamamoto did not go all-out this time, as he was husbanding forces for an attack on Midway within a month; but the force commanded by Vice Admiral Inouye from Rabaul was formidable. One small amphibious group was to take Tulagi in the Solomons, while a large one steamed around the tail of New Guinea to Port Moresby, covered and supported by a heavy cruiser group with one light carrier, and by a force built around two of the big carriers whose planes had hit Pearl Harbor. Admiral Nimitz got wind of this in time, and sent carriers *Lexington* and *Yorktown* and a support group of two Australian cruisers and *Chicago* into the Coral Sea, the whole under the command of

[7] Some 40 or 50 land-based planes from both sides did get into it, but they hit nothing, not even friendly ships which they attacked by mistake.

Rear Admiral Frank Jack Fletcher. The resulting engagement was almost a comedy of errors; each side in this new sort of naval warfare made mistakes, but the Japanese made the most. After American carrier planes had sunk the small enemy flattop, Admiral Inouye — a timid soul for a Japanese — recalled the Port Moresby invasion force to Rabaul. The Japanese carrier planes then managed to sink 'Lady Lex,' but the two big enemy flattops retired because of damage inflicted by the American carriers' planes. Tulagi was occupied by the Japanese, but the big prize, Port Moresby, eluded their grasp; and never again did the keels of their warships vex the opalescent waters of the Coral Sea.

In the next and most vital Japanese offensive, Yamamoto did go all-out. Himself assuming the sea command in the super-battleship *Yamato,* he had with him almost every capital ship of the Japanese navy except the two carriers damaged in the Coral Sea. His first objective was to capture Midway, a tiny atoll at the tip end of the Hawaiian chain, 1134 miles northwest of Pearl Harbor and 2200 miles from Tokyo, where the United States had an advanced naval and air base. Midway was wanted as key to the new perimeter, and as a staging point for air raids to render Pearl Harbor unusable by the Pacific fleet.[8] The minor objectives were Attu and Kiska, two barren islands in the western Aleutians which were wanted as the northern anchor of the new defensive perimeter, and as stops to a possible invasion of Japan by the short high-latitude route.[9] Yamamoto's dearest object, however, was to force Nimitz to give battle with his numerically inferior Pacific fleet, and to wipe it out.

The naval force that Japan deployed was so overwhelming in strength that it should at least have won Midway; but it failed to do so, partly because of faulty strategy, partly because American naval intelligence was able to inform Admiral Nimitz of enemy movements. Yamamoto's plan was a complicated one, the success of which depended on complete surprise, and on Nimitz's reacting as expected. A light-cruiser force was sent ahead to pound Dutch Harbor in the Aleutians; that was expected to entice Nimitz's fleet up north, while a fast carrier force under Admiral Nagumo seized

[8] Several people in the Japanese high command thought that Midway was Doolittle's 'Shangri-La'; an additional reason to take it.

[9] It is a curious fact that both Japan and the United States feared lest the other use the Aleutians as steppingstones of invasion, yet neither planned to do so because the weather was generally too foul for flying and the anchorages were bad.

Midway Atoll. Nimitz was expected to make a bid to recapture Midway, even if he did not fall for the Dutch Harbor ruse; and when and if he did, Yamamoto would have ten battleships, ten heavy and three light cruisers, scores of destroyers, and the planes from five or six carriers and four seaplane tenders ready to pounce upon him.

Although Nimitz knew in part what Yamamoto was up to, and guessed the rest, he had but a small fleet to stop him. First, Midway was reinforced with planes to the saturation point, and as a result of Pearl Harbor experiences, air searches were sent 700 miles out. Next, Rear Admiral Raymond A. Spruance with the staff of Halsey (then ill) was sent out in command of carriers *Enterprise* and *Hornet* with their attendant cruisers and destroyers; and Rear Admiral Fletcher in carrier *Yorktown* hastened to join him. Admiral Kakuta started the campaign in the Aleutians, slipping his carrier-based planes through the fog to hit Dutch Harbor on 3 and 4 June. But Nimitz, knowing that the main blow would be struck at Midway, did not alter his dispositions. A few days later, Japanese occupation forces landed unopposed on Kiska and Attu.

On 4 June Nagumo's four-carrier force, advancing undetected under a foul-weather front, was near enough Midway Atoll to let the air base have it. One installation of search radar saved Midway: it detected the Japanese flight of 72 bombers escorted by 36 fighters almost a hundred miles away — which gave Captain Simard, the atoll commander, time to get every one of his planes aloft; the fighters to intercept, the bombers to counterattack Japanese carriers. A brave group of 26 obsolete marine-corps Buffaloes, together with anti-aircraft guns on the island, disposed of about one third of the enemy attackers. The rest bombed Midway severely but left both air strips intact. In the meantime the land-based bombers repeatedly attacked the Japanese carriers, but made not a single hit.

According to Japanese plans, Nimitz was not supposed to have any ships in the vicinity of Midway for at least a week. Consequently Nagumo, the carrier-force commander, did not search very assiduously that day; and it was a painful surprise to him when, early in the morning of 4 June, he learned from one of his cruiser float planes that at least one American flattop was up to the northeastward. Nagumo then made the fatal decision of the battle. He ordered his reserve attack group, then arming for a second strike on Midway, to be rearmed with the different sort of bombs used against ships, and turned his prows northeastward to close with the American carriers.

Fletcher and Spruance already had several flights of torpedo and dive bombers flying toward the Japanese; and, owing to Nagumo's mistake, they had the good fortune to catch three of his four carriers in the vulnerable situation of rearming and refueling planes. Nevertheless, the carrier-plane battle opened ill for the Americans, as Nagumo's combat air patrol of fast 'Zeke' fighter planes shot down 35 of the 41 slow torpedo bombers that came in first. Only minutes later, however, the American carriers' dive bombers planted bombs on flagships *Akagi, Kaga,* and *Soryu* and left them exploding and burning; United States submarine *Nautilus* came along in time to finish *Soryu.* The fourth Japanese carrier, *Hiryu,* unseen by the American fliers, got off two plane strikes, which found and disabled *Yorktown.* Fletcher's flagship, however, was promptly avenged, for an attack group from her deck and from *Enterprise* jumped *Hiryu* that afternoon and put her away. A Parthian shot by a Japanese submarine sank *Yorktown* on the 7th.

Yamamoto, having lost his four best carriers, ordered first a concentration of his battleship and cruiser forces to catch Spruance at night if he pursued; but Spruance, one of the cagiest naval officers who ever wore the broad stripe, disappointed him. Early in the morning of 5 June, Yamamoto ordered a general retirement of his vast fleet. He had sustained the first defeat to the Japanese navy in modern times. Four carriers and their air groups were wiped out, and the Stars and Stripes still flew over Midway; Kiska and Attu were but poor consolation prizes. The ambitious plans for taking New Caledonia, the Fijis, Samoa, and possibly Australia now had to be scrapped; and the Japanese high command was forced into an unaccustomed defensive position. Midway was a decisive battle.

For two months there was an ominous pause in the Pacific war; each contestant was licking his wounds. Then broke out a bloody and desperate six-month campaign at and over two focal points—Buna-Gona in New Guinea, and Guadalcanal.

Although the 'beat Hitler first' decision imposed a strategic defensive in the Pacific, that decision never implied a mere passive defense. It implied raids such as the one on Tokyo; attrition tactics by submarines that were already operating as far as the coast of Japan; and, where opportunity occurred, limited offensives. One such occurred shortly. The Japanese decided to make a new stab at

Port Moresby, New Guinea, this time sending troops over the mountains to take it from the rear. To protect their left flank from American naval interference, they already had a seaplane base at Tulagi in the Solomons; but they also wanted a bomber strip on the near-by island of Guadalcanal. News reaching Washington that Japanese labor troops had landed there and had begun felling trees sparked off the Guadalcanal campaign. That operation had been conceived some months earlier by Admiral King to provide the first leg-up for a gradual advance to Rabaul; for Rabaul would have to be recaptured or neutralized before General MacArthur could proceed very far on his return. But this operation 'Watchtower' had to be undertaken on a shoestring, and it required 18 months' fighting to get around Rabaul.

By 2 July 1942, when the Joint Chiefs of Staff issued the directive for the Guadalcanal operation, massive naval, ground, and air forces were being assembled for the invasion of North Africa. The South Pacific command entrusted with the capture and securing of Guadalcanal got only what was left, but that was not inconsiderable. Some 20,000 marines in 16 transports, escorted by cruisers and destroyers, with an air-support force of three carriers, converged on the mountainous, jungle-clad Solomon Islands, whose very names were all but unknown. The landings on 7 August 1942 were successful. Areas around Guadalcanal airfield (promptly renamed Henderson Field) and Tulagi across the sound were secured in 36 hours.

Then came a sharp reversal of fortune. In the small hours of 9 August a Japanese cruiser force surprised, completely outfought, and sank four of the five United States and Australian heavy cruisers that were protecting the unloading transports, and withdrew after suffering slight damage.[10]

This Battle of Savo Island was the worst defeat ever suffered by the United States navy, and it had severe consequences. The new defenseless transports hastily withdrew, half-unloaded, leaving the marines on half rations. The Japanese, commanding the sea routes to Guadalcanal from Rabaul and Truk, were able to reinforce their garrison almost at will. Fortunately, the high command was mainly interested for six weeks in the land campaign against Port Moresby and sent so few troops to Guadalcanal that General Vandegrift's marines were able not only to hold Henderson Field but to inflict a

[10] One of the Japanese cruisers was sunk by U.S. submarine *S-44* before reaching port.

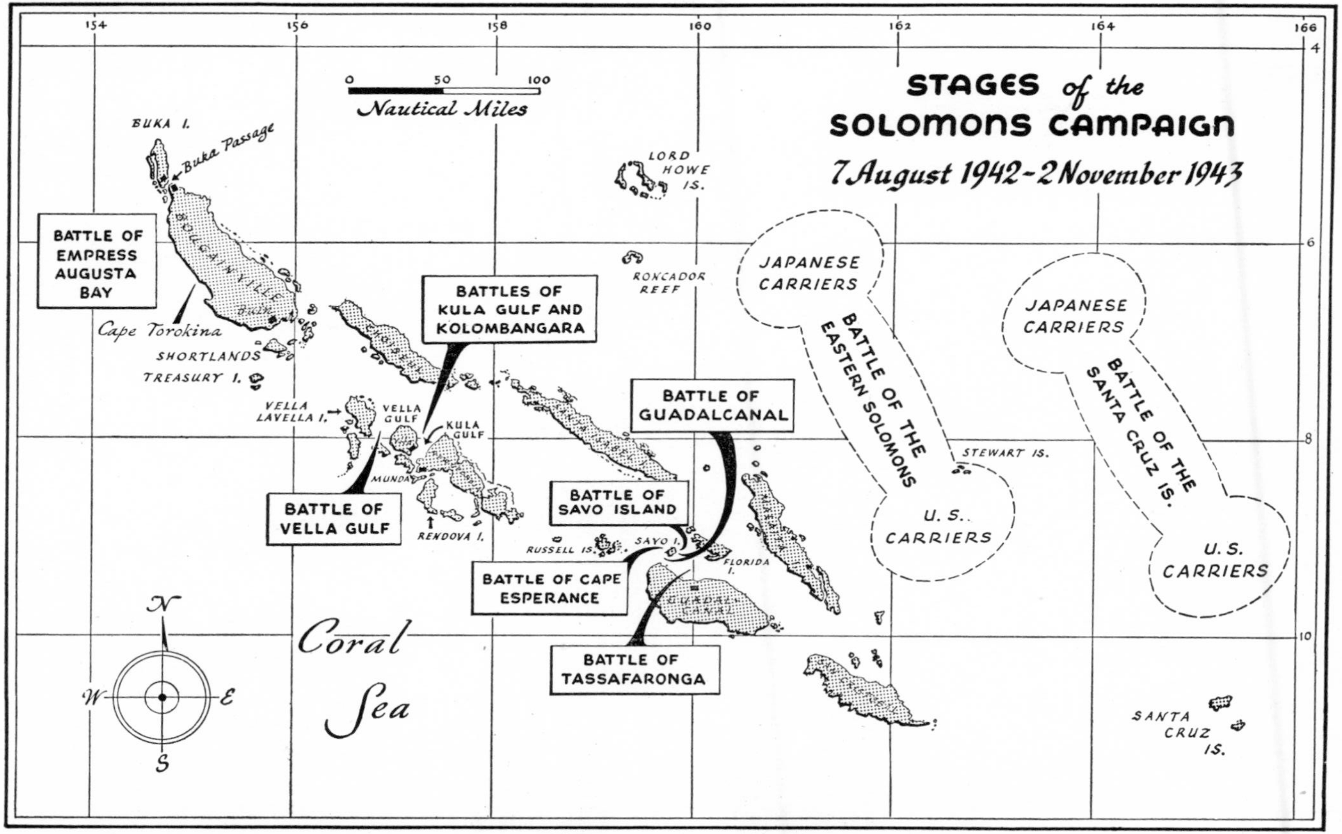
STAGES of the SOLOMONS CAMPAIGN
7 August 1942 - 2 November 1943
0 50 100
Nautical Miles
BUKA I.
Buka Passage
BATTLE OF EMPRESS AUGUSTA BAY
Cape Torokina
SHORTLANDS
TREASURY I.
BATTLES OF KULA GULF AND KOLOMBANGARA
VELLA LAVELLA I.
VELLA GULF
KULA GULF
MUNDA
RENDOVA I.
BATTLE OF VELLA GULF
LORD HOWE IS.
RONCADOR REEF
BATTLE OF GUADALCANAL
BATTLE OF SAVO ISLAND
RUSSELL IS.
SAVO I.
FLORIDA I.
BATTLE OF CAPE ESPERANCE
BATTLE OF TASSAFARONGA
JAPANESE CARRIERS
BATTLE OF THE EASTERN SOLOMONS
U. S. CARRIERS
STEWART IS.
JAPANESE CARRIERS
BATTLE OF THE SANTA CRUZ IS.
U. S. CARRIERS
SANTA CRUZ IS.
Coral Sea
N
W
E
S

signal defeat on an elite Japanese force at the Battle of the Tenaru River — a small action, but important because it proved that United States marines were better at jungle fighting than the formerly invincible Japanese.

We cannot begin to describe in detail the six-month campaign for Guadalcanal, crowded with events and fraught with valor and suffering. Controlling as he did the air and sea approaches down the 'Slot' — the wide channel between two rows of Solomon Islands — the enemy was able to bomb Henderson Field by day, bombard it with naval guns at night, and run fast 'Tokyo Expresses' with reinforcements and supplies to his garrison on the western end of the island. Regularly in mid-September, October, and November, the Japanese made all-out efforts to run in thousands of troops, break through the marines and their army reinforcements, defeat the supporting United States naval forces, and capture Henderson Field. The first two all but succeeded; the third was thrown back with heavy loss. There were two great carrier battles (Eastern Solomons, 24 August, and Santa Cruz Islands, 26–27 October), similar to that of the Coral Sea, and four night gunfire actions. Only two of these — Rear Admiral Willis A. Lee's battleship action off Guadalcanal and Rear Admiral Norman Scott's night cruiser action off Cape Esperance — were won hands-down by the American navy; but all added up to a strategic victory. There was a score of ground actions, such as the Bloody Ridge, 12–14 September, which would have been considered major battles in any previous war; there were air fights almost daily for six months. In mid-October it seemed that Guadalcanal could no longer hold out; Henderson Field was down to a handful of bombers and a few hours' rations of gas. Then, the appointment of Admiral Halsey as commander of the South Pacific force inspired new efforts from those on the spot and brought reinforcements. One month later, after the terrific naval battle of Guadalcanal (12–15 November) — in which the United States lost two cruisers, seven destroyers, and two admirals killed, the Japanese two battleships, a cruiser, two destroyers, and ten transports — the issue was no longer in doubt. On 4 January 1943 word went forth from Tokyo that Guadalcanal must be evacuated, and evacuated it was by night-running destroyers and barges, by 9 February 1943.

In the meantime the western prong of this Japanese offensive had been stopped on the north coast of Papua, New Guinea, in the villages of Buna, Gona, and Sanananda. This was done by General Mac-

Arthur's command, executed by American and Australian troops under General Eichelberger; and the fighting in malaria-infested mangrove swamps against a trapped and never-surrendering enemy was the most horrible of the entire war. With the aid of air power the combined army won through, and by the end of January 1943 all Papua up to Huon Gulf was back in Allied hands.

The Japanese were still building up air, naval, and ground forces on their island fortress at Rabaul and in the bastions at Lae, Salamaua, Kavieng, Bougainville, and the Central Solomons, and MacArthur and Halsey still had a long way to go, even to reach Rabaul. But the defensive period in the war with Japan was definitely at an end.

3. *From Casablanca to Cape Bon*

While Winston Churchill was conferring with President Roosevelt in the White House in June 1942, news came of the German capture of Tobruk in North Africa. Publicly, Churchill described the situation as 'a bit disconcerting'; privately, he confessed that he was the most miserable Englishman in America since the surrender of Burgoyne. For the fall of Tobruk with the loss of most of the British tanks opened a German road into Egypt and beyond. If Alexandria and the Suez Canal fell into Axis hands, nothing short of a miracle could keep them out of India, on whose eastern frontier the Japanese were already poised. But General Alexander and his staunch lieutenant, Montgomery, dug in at El Alamein, whither the American Joint Chiefs dispatched 400 General Sherman tanks to equip him afresh with those indispensable instruments of desert warfare. By October the situation had been reversed. Montgomery, superior in armor and in air power, prepared to launch the famous offensive that was to carry him, within six months, to Tunisia.

At their White House meeting neither Roosevelt nor Churchill nor their military advisers could agree on the time or place of the first Allied military operation against the Axis. The Americans wanted a cross-channel operation in France to come first, a beachhead to be secured in 1942, and the big invasion in 1943. The British feared lest any such attempt, before the Allies had overwhelming air and ground forces and plenty of amphibious equipment, would be thrown back with heavy loss. Roosevelt, who had received Molotov at the White House just before Churchill came, was deeply impressed with the sacrifices Russia was making, and the need for a 'second front in 1942' to divert enough German troops to prevent Russia from being overrun. The occupation of French North Africa, where the State Department was in touch with patriotic, anti-Vichy elements, was an obvious compromise, on which the Combined Chiefs of Staff decided 25 July 1942 — Operation Torch. Success here, in conjunction with General Alexander's army, would protect oil-fields of the Middle East and shorten the route to India, help to keep submarines out of the South Atlantic, checkmate any disturbance from Spain, acquire bases for an invasion of Italy, and provide invaluable combat and command experience for the great invasion of Europe still to come.

Yet the cost, too, was high and the risks were great. Spain might take alarm and throw open her gates to the Germans; the French in North Africa might resist, and so, too, the Moroccans; Germany might counterattack successfully through Sicily. And even if the Allied campaign went according to plan, the drain on men, shipping, planes, and war material would be so great as to postpone the cross-channel invasion until 1944.

However nicely these considerations balanced, once the decision to launch Operation Torch was made, there was no turning back. Logistics and weather prospects balanced each other to dictate an invasion early in November. Oran and Algiers on the Mediterranean and Casablanca on the Atlantic coast of Morocco were selected as the three strategic points, with good harbors, to be seized by amphibious forces. General Dwight D. ('Ike') Eisenhower, commanding in the European theater, was appointed commander in chief of the expedition, with Admiral Sir Andrew Cunningham as over-all commander of naval forces.

With less than four months in which to plan, equip, and launch a gigantic operation, it was decidedly risky. The United States and Great Britain had to train thousands of troops for amphibious warfare, divert hundreds of ships to new duties, provide for follow-up convoys, conduct secret and diplomatic negotiations with the French, and, as General Eisenhower wrote, occupy 'the rim of a continent where no major military campaign had been conducted for centuries.'[11]

It would be little use merely to occupy Casablanca, Oran, and Algiers; there must be a vigorous and rapid exploitation of these beachheads, in conjunction with General Alexander's army, to get

[11] *Crusade in Europe,* p. 72. Doubleday.

control of Tunisia as well as Algeria, and throw Axis forces out of North Africa.

The invasion forces were divided into three great groups. Of these the largest, and the one that had the longest journey to make, was all American — the Western Naval Task Force under Rear Admiral H. Kent Hewitt and General George S. Patton. The other two, the Center and Eastern Task Forces with destinations respectively Oran and Algiers, were mounted in Great Britain, and were composed of both British and American troops in British transports with British naval escort. General Alexander launched the great battle of El Alamein on 23 October, and on the same day Admiral Hewitt sailed from Hampton Roads.

The American Western Task Force was in itself a great feat of arms. America had gone into Africa before, back in Jefferson's day, and Africa had come willy-nilly to America, in the persons of her sable sons and daughters; but never in all history had a vast amphibious operation been projected across an ocean. Almost 35,000 soldiers, in or guarded by 101 ships manned by an equal number of sailors, including 5 aircraft carriers bringing 250 planes to cover the landings, and as many tanks (carried, for want of LST's, in an improvised train-ferryboat) steamed over 3000 miles, fueling from tankers at sea, dodging submarines, to establish American beachheads in Africa. Operation Torch came exactly 450 years after the discovery of America, and it marked almost as great a departure in the history of war as did Columbus's voyage in the history of navigation.

The whole complex operation went like clockwork. By midnight 7–8 November all three task forces, successfully eluding submarines, had reached their destinations unscathed, and unreported. The French — all except a few patriotic leaders who were in on the secret — the Spaniards, the Germans, and the Italians were caught completely off guard.

Every effort had been made to prepare the way for a favorable reception of the Americans in North Africa; but with the Department of State, the Office of Strategic Services, and British and American military intelligence acting independently and often at cross-purposes, it is not surprising that the French — ignorant whether the invaders were German, British, or American — received them with shells and bullets instead of brass bands and welcoming committees. Opposition at Algiers was negligible, but the landings at

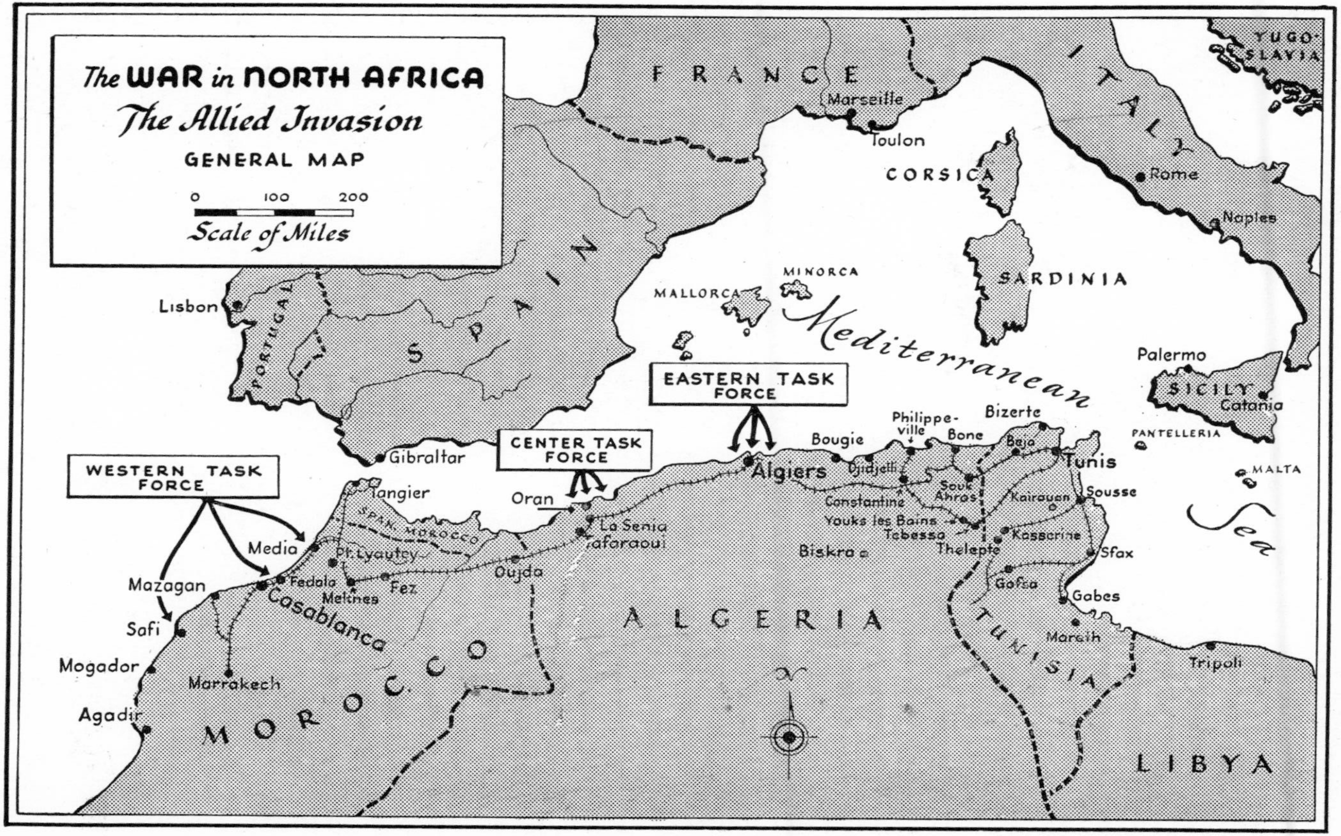
The WAR in NORTH AFRICA
The Allied Invasion
GENERAL MAP
0 100 200
Scale of Miles
FRANCE
Marseille
Toulon
CORSICA
ITALY
Rome
Naples
YUGOSLAVIA
SARDINIA
MINORCA
MALLORCA
Mediterranean
Sea
Palermo
SICILY
Catania
PANTELLERIA
MALTA
SPAIN
PORTUGAL
Lisbon
Gibraltar
EASTERN TASK FORCE
CENTER TASK FORCE
WESTERN TASK FORCE
Tangier
SPAN. MOROCCO
Oran
La Senia
Tafaraoui
Media
Pt. Lyautey
Fedala
Casablanca
Meknes
Fez
Oujda
Mazagan
Safi
Mogador
Marrakech
Agadir
MOROCCO
Algiers
Bougie
Djidjelli
Philippe-ville
Bone
Bizerte
Beja
Tunis
Souk Ahras
Constantine
Youks les Bains
Tebessa
Thelepte
Kairouan
Sousse
Kasserine
Sfax
Gafsa
Gabes
Mareth
Biskra
ALGERIA
TUNISIA
Tripoli
LIBYA

Oran and Casablanca ran into heavy fire, and Admiral Hewitt had to fight a naval battle with the French fleet off Casablanca, and sink most of it, in order to get General Patton's troops ashore safely.

General Henri Giraud, a French hero of both World Wars, was brought over by Eisenhower to take command of the French forces in North Africa; but they would have none of him. By a coincidence Admiral Darlan, second to Marshal Pétain in the Vichy government, happened to be in Algiers. He was so impressed by the strength of the Anglo-American landings that Eisenhower was able to persuade him to issue a cease-fire order to all French forces in North Africa, on 11 November. Unfortunately that was too late to save the French fleet in Toulon for the Allies; the French admiral scuttled it just before the Germans marched in. Darlan's assumption of command in North Africa did not mend the factions among the French there, but his assassination before the end of the year paved the way for the masterful General de Gaulle, and for full-hearted collaboration between French North Africa and the Allies.

Meantime the race for Bizerte and Tunis was under way. Although caught flat-footed by the invasion, the Germans reacted with great speed, flying 20,000 men across the Sicilian straits into Tunisia within a few days, and establishing fighter and bomber bases on easily captured Tunisian airfields. General Eisenhower moved with comparable speed, but the difficulties he faced proved insuperable. From Algiers to Tunis there were more than 500 miles of mountain and desert, with narrow twisting roads; the rainy season opened in November, and weather soon made flying all but impossible; a single rickety railroad from Casablanca could not begin to carry the heavy burden of supplies. Yet by the end of November the British army, operating out of Algiers, had reached Mateur, only 35 miles south of Bizerte. There the Germans held fast and soon compelled the Allies to give ground. The year 1942 ended with most of Tunisia strongly held by Axis troops, Anglo-American forces pressing them from the west, Alexander's army racing in from the east, and the French holding Lake Chad on the south.

Early in January 1943 Roosevelt and Churchill and their Chiefs of Staff met at Casablanca to plan future operations, if possible for the entire war. For the first time Allied prospects seemed favorable; this was, as Churchill said, 'the end of the beginning.' The Russians had turned the tide at the decisive battle of Stalingrad; Alexander had saved Egypt and all but destroyed Rommel's army; air and naval forces were fast being built up in Morocco and Algeria; and despite the efforts of enemy submarines, Mussolini could no longer call the Mediterranean *mare nostrum*. In the Pacific, Guadalcanal was in the bag; and although the invasion of North Africa was not the 'second front' that Stalin wanted, the R.A.F. was pounding German industrial centers with thousand-plane raids, and General Eaker's Eighth Air Force had joined in the air war.

The Allied chiefs at Casablanca gave anti-submarine warfare top priority, decided to invade Sicily and Italy as soon as Tunis was secured, allocated sufficient forces to the Pacific so that Nimitz and MacArthur could start an offensive there, and promised 'to draw as much weight as possible off the Russian armies by engaging the enemy as heavily as possible at the best selected points.' And they made the momentous announcement that the war would end only with 'unconditional surrender' of all enemies, European and Asiatic. Later that formula — borrowed from General Grant — would be sharply criticized. The most serious charges were that it unnecessarily prolonged the war by closing the door to a negotiated peace, and that by condemning Germany and Japan to destruction it paved the way for Communism.

It will be difficult in the future, and is impossible now, to determine the justice of these charges, or even their relevance; but at the time, when the Allies were fighting the most cruel, relentless, and barbarous enemies in modern history, they were in no mood to offer a negotiated peace. Memories of the Armistice of 1918 and the Treaty of Versailles, which Germany prepared to repudiate before it was even signed; of Hitler's repeated breaches of his plighted word to neighboring countries, and of his mass killings of civilians; fresh memories of Pearl Harbor, the Bataan death march, and other treacheries and cruelties of the Japanese, made it impossible to think of peace with Hitler, Mussolini, or Tojo.[12] Unconditional surrender did not delay the surrender of Italy. There is no persuasive evidence that it delayed the surrender of Germany. It is highly improbable that Hitler would ever have come to terms; had he desired to do so, he would not have been stopped by a phrase or a

12 Emperor Hirohito was a different matter; the Allied governments, realizing that he was a well-meaning figurehead who would be likely to co-operate with them after defeat — as he has — concentrated on Tojo in their anti-Japanese propaganda. So, too, with Victor Emmanuel II; he might have continued on the throne if he had not alienated his own people by subservience to Mussolini.

formula. Nor is there any evidence that a less drastic formula would have strengthened the weak and scattered anti-Nazi forces inside Germany herself sufficiently to enable them to overthrow Hitler and make peace.

While the Allies were bogged down in the mountains of western Tunisia, the Germans seized the initiative. Even as Roosevelt and Churchill were discussing grand strategy, the Germans, using the powerful new Tiger tank, launched an offensive. Swift counter-attacks and the arrival of Rommel's Afrika Korps early in February 1943 gave them a temporary ground superiority, which Rommel exploited in brilliant fashion. On 14 February he hurled his armor through Kasserine Pass, turned northward toward Tebessa, and threatened to cut the Allied armies in two. The untried American forces fell back in momentary confusion but soon steadied, and the timely arrival of two armored divisions from Oran, the skillful employment of powerful new tanks, and clearing skies that permitted the North African Air Force to deliver punishing blows, turned the tide. After five days of hard fighting, Rommel pulled back to the south.

It was his last offensive. Within a few days Montgomery had caught up with him, and the two ancient antagonists squared off for the last round at the strongly fortified Mareth Line stretching southward from the Gulf of Gabes to the desert. On 21 March Montgomery attacked. In a brilliant operation reminiscent of Lee's at Manassas, he hurled his main force at Rommel's front and sent two divisions on a wide sweep around his southern flank. Hammered front and rear, pounded by the most devastating aerial attack of the whole North African campaign, Rommel acknowledged defeat and retreated northward into Tunisia.

The Allied armies, now half a million strong, closed in for the kill. The British Eighth Army swept north along the coast, mopping up Sfax and Sousse. In the north the American II Corps and the British First Army fought their way from one mountain range to another, toward the coastal plain along the Gulf of Tunisia. There was the hardest kind of fighting for Hill 609 and Mateur, which the Americans captured on 3 May. Then, as Montgomery broke the German lines in the south and raced for Tunis, Omar Bradley smashed into Bizerte; both cities fell on 7 May 1943. The enemy, 300,000 strong, might still have put up a stiff fight in the rugged terrain of Cape Bon, but, as Alan Morehead wrote,

The Allied armies roared past German airfields, workshops, petrol and ammunition dumps and gun positions. They did not stop to take prisoners — things had gone far beyond that. If a comet had rushed down that road it could hardly have made a greater impression. . . In a contagion of doubt and fear, the German army turned tail and made for the Cape Bon roads looking for boats. When on the beaches it became apparent to them at last that there were no boats — nor any aircraft either — the army became a rabble.[13]

On 13 May, abandoned by their commander, Rommel, the remnants of the Axis armies surrendered. It was the most disastrous German defeat since Stalingrad, and the greatest victory that British and American arms had yet won. Total Axis losses in the campaign came to 350,000 men. Now that Africa was cleared of the enemy, the Mediterranean was open to Allied merchant ships throughout its entire length, although still subject to air attack from southern France and Italy. The severed lifeline of the British Empire, through Suez, was spliced again. Italy was in mortal danger, and the way was open at last for a blow at what Churchill mistakenly called 'the soft underbelly' of Europe. For this blow General Eisenhower and his associates now prepared.

4. *Sicily and Italy*

Two courses were open to the Allies. They could skip Italy, move into Sardinia and Corsica, and from these islands threaten northern Italy and southern France. This action would certainly have been bold and possibly decisive, but so big a jump, beyond fighter-plane range from North African fields, would have exposed transports and men of war alike to heavy German bombing attacks. The more cautious alternative was to overrun Sicily, cross the Straits of Messina to Calabria, and work up the Italian peninsula. This offered the chance of complete control of the Mediterranean, as well as an objective dear to Churchill's heart, knocking Italy out of the war. That is why Operation Husky — the attack on Sicily — was chosen at Casablanca, and D-day set for July. General Eisenhower, as Supreme Allied Commander Mediterranean, was designated to run the show; under him Admiral of the Fleet Sir Andrew B. Cunningham, General Sir H. R. Alexander, and Air Chief Marshal A. W. Tedder were the top naval, ground-force, and air commanders.

[13] *The End in Africa,* p. 201.

The INVASIONS of SICILY and ITALY
Milan
Verona
Trieste
Venice
Turin
Genoa
Bologna
Ravenna
Rimini
Spezia
Pisa
Florence
Ancona
Leghorn
Cecina
YUGOSLAVIA
Sarajevo
ITALY
Adriatic Sea
Grosetto
ELBA
Viterbo
Pescara
CORSICA
Civitavecchia
Rome
Termoli
Anzio
Foggia
Atella
Naples
Bari
Salerno
Brindisi
Taranto
NAVAL DIVERSION
Sapri
Tyrrhenian Sea
SARDINIA
Cagliari
MAIN ATTACK
Cosenza
Mediterranean
Messina
Palermo
Reggio Calabria
C. DELL' ARMI
FROM ORAN
Marsala
SICILY
SEVENTH ARMY
Catania
Licata
Syracuse
Bizerte
Tunis
PANTELLERIA
NAVAL DIVERSION
TUNISIA
Sea
LINOSA
LAMPEDUSA
MALTA
Kairouan
FROM TRIPOLI
EIGHTH ARMY
0 50 100 150
Miles

The invasion of Sicily on 10 July 1943 was the biggest and boldest amphibious operation of the war. About 250,000 British and American troops (increased to 450,000 before the campaign was over) landed simultaneously, eight divisions abreast, along 150 miles of coastline and in black darkness. The 300,000 Italian and 50,000 German defenders of Sicily were almost completely surprised and thrown off balance. The American Seventh Army (Lieutenant General George S. Patton, Jr.) was put ashore by the American Eighth Fleet (Vice Admiral H. Kent Hewitt) on the southwestern shore of Sicily at beaches near Licata, Gela, and Scoglitti; the British Eighth Army (Lieutenant General B. L. Montgomery), which included a Canadian division, landed on the American right flank and around Cape Passero up to Cassibile, a short distance from Syracuse. The new LST and other beaching craft, here employed in large numbers for the first time, assisted in getting troops, tanks, and field artillery ashore so promptly that within a few hours the invaders controlled 150 miles of coastline, and substantial beachheads. There was no attempt by the Italian Navy to interfere, because a strong battle fleet of the British Navy, roving around Sicily and feinting at Taranto, 'persuaded' it to stay quietly in Italian ports. The smoothness with which these landings were carried off, the celerity with which enemy opposition was overwhelmed, deeply impressed the German and Italian high commands. The one first concluded that only a delaying operation was possible; the Italians decided that it was time for them to get out of the war.

After a sharp battle at the Gela beachhead with a German armored division, in which several tank attacks were broken up by naval gunfire, the Seventh Army swept across Sicily, marching at a rate that matched Stonewall Jackson's 'foot cavalry' in the Civil War. On 22 July General Patton made his triumphal entry into Palermo, set up headquarters in the ancient palace of the Norman kings, and thence, like old Roger II in the twelfth century, directed the campaign along the north coast of Sicily.

In the meantime Montgomery's Eighth Army had slashed into the ancient city of Syracuse, which for some 2000 years had been considered the key to Sicily, seized Augusta, but met a sharp check from German paratroops and infantry on the Catania plain. That was unfortunate, because a quick capture of Messina and the Straits would have bottled up the Axis troops in Sicily and forced them eventually to surrender; as it was, the Germans had a week to rush in reinforcements and take up good defensive positions around Mount Etna.

On 1 August the forward movement was resumed. The British and Canadians swept around the southern and western slopes of Mount Etna, paralleled by the Americans advancing east from Palermo, mostly by land but partly by beaching craft along the north coast. Within a week the Axis forces were confined to the northeastern corner of Sicily, which they defended with great vigor and skill in order to cover an orderly evacuation to the mainland. By 17 August the great island was in Allied hands (greatly to the joy of the Sicilians, some of whom seriously proposed that Sicily be taken into the American Union). But some 40,000 German and 62,000 Italian groups escaped across the Strait of Messina with most of their weapons and equipment.

Italy, though not mortally wounded, was mortally sick of the war into which Mussolini had forced her. On 25 July, six days after the Allied air forces had delivered a 560-plane bombing raid on Rome, the little king of Italy summoned up enough courage to tell Mussolini to resign. The aged Marshal Badoglio, who frankly told the king that the war was *perduto, perdutissimo* (absolutely and completely lost), now headed the government and began to probe for peace with the Allies; but, owing to the Italian love of bargaining, and the Allies' 'Unconditional Surrender' slogan which made bargaining difficult, the negotiations dragged along until 3 September. This gave the Germans, who suspected what was cooking, plenty of time to rush reinforcements into Italy and to seize key points such as Genoa, Leghorn, and Rome.

Even before the Sicilian operation started, it had been decided at the 'Trident' Conference in Washington in May 1943 to invade Italy. The American Joint Chiefs of Staff were reluctant to accept this, wishing to get on with 'Overlord,' the invasion of Normandy; but it was already too late to start 'Overlord' in 1943, and there was no other place but Italy where German forces could be engaged during the following twelvemonth.

General Eisenhower was authorized to plan an invasion of Italy at the earliest possible date, 'using the resources already available.' That, in the main, he did; but limitations on the number of forces to be used in a given operation are seldom valid. Once you are in the thing, the enemy is apt to force you to throw in more and more, lest you lose all. And that happened in Italy too.

Salerno, south of the Sorrento Peninsula, was chosen for the main landing in Italy, as the farthest point where Allied fighter planes could protect the amphibious forces from German air attacks. Part of the plan was an air drop of the 82nd Airborne Division on Rome, to secure the Eternal City from German capture. Unfortunately it had to be called off because the Italian authorities were more afraid of the Germans than eager to help the Allies; Rome was promptly occupied by Marshal Kesselring's army, and it was not liberated for another ten months.

On 7 and 8 September 1943 the Allied Fifth Army, commanded by General Mark W. Clark U.S.A., with two British and two American infantry divisions in the assault and several more in reserve, took off from a dozen ports between Oran and Alexandria, including the newly won harbors in Sicily. Admiral Hewitt commanded the entire operation until the landings were effected. En route to the objective the familiar voice of General 'Ike' was heard broadcasting the news of the Italian surrender; so all hands expected a walk-over. They had a bitter surprise. Some very tough and unco-operative Germans were on the beachhead, and reinforcements were already being rushed in from beyond the mountains. D-day for Salerno, 9 September, was very costly. Most of the troops had to land under heavy gunfire, and many were pinned down on the beaches all day. Beachheads were established with great difficulty, and held precariously. The Luftwaffe was active and enterprising, and tried a new weapon, the radio-guided bomb, which put cruiser *Savannah* out of business. By 12 September when the Germans had built up their armored strength to some 600 tanks and mobile guns, they put on a series of vicious tank attacks designed to cut off the American from the British divisions. These were thwarted by the GIs, ably assisted by their own field artillery and by naval gunfire. And on 14 September the Germans started an orderly retirement northward.

The Fifth Army on 1 October entered Naples, which the Germans had done their best to destroy. Commodore William A. Sullivan U.S.N., with a mixed Anglo-American salvage team, did a remarkable job in clearing the bay and the waterfront, so that by the end of the year more tonnage was being discharged in Naples than in time of peace.

After the fall of Naples, the Italian campaign developed, in the words of General Maitland Wilson, into a 'slow, painful advance through difficult terrain against a determined and resourceful enemy, skilled in the exploitation of natural obstacles by mines and demolition.' The Apennines, rising three to six thousand feet from the coastal plain, criss-crossed by rapid streams and deep gorges, presented formidable obstacles to any offensive. Marshal Kesselring, fighting a series of delaying operations along prepared mountain intrenchments — the Volturno Line, the Winter Line, the Gustav Line, the Hitler Line, and finally the Gothic Line — exploited these natural advantages to the full. From Naples to Rome is but a hundred miles; yet even with numerical superiority on land and in the air, and control of the adjacent waters, it took the Allies eight months to cover the ground.

What fighting in the Apennines was like was graphically told by the war correspondent, Ernie Pyle:

> Our troops were living in almost inconceivable misery. The fertile black valleys were knee-deep in mud. Thousands of men had not been dry for weeks. Other thousands lay at night in the high mountains with the temperature below freezing and the thin snow sifting over them. They dug into the stones and slept in little chasms and behind rocks and in half-caves. They lived like men of prehistoric times, and a club would have become them more than a machine gun. How they survived the dreadful winter at all was beyond us who had the opportunity of drier beds in the warmer valleys. . . No one who had not seen that mud, those dark skies, those forbidding ridges and ghostlike clouds that unveiled and then quickly hid the enemy, had the right to be impatient with the progress along the road to Rome.[15]

By mid-October of 1943 the Allies had cracked the Volturno Line, and early in November their armies crossed the Sangros River. Then followed two months of tough fighting along the so-called Winter Line north of the Garigliano River. By mid-January of 1944 the Allies had shattered this defense system, only to find themselves up against the almost impregnable Gustav Line.

Rome was the objective of that winter's campaign — a political rather than a military objective — but some of the most mountainous terrain in all Europe barred the way to a frontal advance. As one attack after another bogged down in mud and rubble, the Fifth Army on 22 January 1944 made a bold landing in the rear of the Germans at Anzio, 37 miles south of Rome. It was hoped to cut the enemy's communications and force his withdrawal to the north. Although the landings were a complete surprise, these hopes were

15 *Brave Men,* p. 97. Henry Holt Co.

OPERATIONS in ITALY
From 9 Sept. 1943 to the end of the War
N
Milan
Verona
Padua
Venice
Trieste
Parma
Genoa
Bologna
Spezia
Ravenna
YUGOSLAVIA
15 JAN. 1945
Florence
Rimini
4 AUG.
Pisa
Cecina
Ancona
Arezzo
Sarajevo
17 JUNE
CAPTURED BY ALLIES 5 OCT. 1943
Grosseto
Adriatic Sea
9 JUNE
Viterbo
Pescara
15 JAN. '44
CORSICA
8 OCT. '43
5 JUNE
Rome
MONTE CASSINO
Anzio
Termoli
25 SEPT.
Foggia
22 JAN.
14 SEPT.
Naples
Atella
EVACUATED BY ENEMY 19 SEPT. 1943
28 SEPT.
Potenza
Salerno
Brindisi
SARDINIA
9 SEPT.
Sapri
Cagliari
9 SEPT.
14 SEPT.
Tyrrhenian Sea
Cosenza
Crotone
Catanzaro
9 SEPT.
Mediterranean Sea
Palermo
Messina
Reggio Calabria
Marsala
C. DELL'ARMI
SICILY
Bizerte
Catania
Tunis
Licata
PANTELLERIA
Syracuse
Kairouan
0 50 100 150
MALTA
Miles

not realized. Kesselring reacted swiftly; the Luftwaffe with new radio-guided missiles sank a number of British and American transports and warships, and the troops had to dig in on an open plain, where they were subjected to constant air attacks, heavy artillery bombardments, and counterattacks by German troops. Anzio beachhead, which should have been a spearhead, became instead a beleaguered fort.

To the south the Eighth Army launched a series of savage attacks against the ancient monastery-city of Monte Cassino, key stronghold on the Gustav Line. Tremendous artillery and aerial bombardment, though it reduced the city and the monastery to ruins, merely clogged the advance of armor and infantry, and for three months the Allies wore themselves out in futile attempts to take the place by storm. They had not heeded one lesson of the Stalingrad battle, that rubble is an almost impregnable defense.

Not until early May 1944 did weather permit a resumption of the Anzio and Cassino offensives. Then the Eighth Army, which by this time included American, British, Polish, and French divisions, enveloped and captured Monte Cassino (19 May); a Canadian force advanced up the Adriatic coast; the Fifth Army burst through the iron ring around Anzio on 25 May and advanced north against stubborn rear-guard resistance.

Kesselring spared Rome from the destruction and ignominy to which he had subjected Naples. By the morning of 4 June, as his forces were retiring northward toward a new defense line, flying columns of eager Allied troops were rushing along all roads that led to Rome. No sooner had the German rear guards departed from Rome, than window-shutters opened, Allied and Italian colors were displayed, and the streets filled with joyful crowds so dense that only with difficulty could the troops drive their flower-decked tanks and vehicles through. By midnight 4 June, the Fifth Army was deployed along the Tiber from its mouth to well north of the city.

For one brief day the liberation of Rome held the attention of the Allied nations. Then, on 6 June, came the news that the Allies had landed on the coast of Normandy.

XXIX

WINNING THE WAR

1. *The Air War*

SINCE the beginning of the war the American high command had taken for granted the necessity of an Allied invasion of the Continent from the British Isles, and to this plan Prime Minister Churchill and his staff reluctantly consented. The American planners hoped for a small-scale operation in the Cotentin peninsula of Normandy in 1942, and a full-scale invasion the following year. The necessity of mounting the North African invasion, however, and the lack of landing craft, planes, armor, and other essentials dictated a postponement of the great invasion until the spring of 1944.

Meantime the Allied war leaders launched an invasion by air, designed to reduce German war potential, shatter civilian morale, and pave the way for invasion by land, as well as to satisfy the insistent demands of the Russians for some relief from the intolerable pressure on the eastern front. In 1939 and 1940 the German air force had ruled the skies; with the defeat of the Luftwaffe in the battle of Britain, supremacy passed to the R.A.F. In 1941 British plane production surpassed German, and the R.A.F. took the offensive, dropping 46,000 tons of bombs on enemy targets. The next year the R.A.F. stepped up the air attack; all that year giant Halifaxes, Stirlings, Blenheims, and Lancasters sailed out over France, the Low Countries, and Germany, raining destruction on cities and industrial targets. On 30 May 1942 came the first thousand-bomber raid, with over three thousand tons of bombs hurled against the Rhineland city of Cologne. Two days later came a comparable raid on Essen, home of the giant Krupp works, and quickly thereafter a series of punishing raids on Ruhr and Rhineland cities and on submarine bases all the way from the Bay of Biscay to the Baltic. By 1943 the R.A.F. had Pathfinder planes, which located targets by radar and marked them — usually with incendiary bombs. This technique was used in what was perhaps the most devastating air attack of the European war — the week-long series of attacks on Hamburg in July 1943, which wiped out one third to one half of that great port and killed over sixty thousand civilians. 'Those who sowed the wind are reaping the whirlwind,' said Winston Churchill.

The United States Eighth Air Force had been activated in Britain as early as January 1942, and assigned airfields chiefly in East Anglia. Not until August of that year did the Americans launch their first raid over the Continent — a small-scale attack on marshaling yards outside Rouen — and so compelling was the demand for aircraft in the North African theater that not until 1943 did the A.A.F. join actively in the air war over Germany. Thus while the R.A.F. dropped some 75,000 tons of bombs on Germany and occupied territories in 1942, the A.A.F. dropped only 2000 tons that year. In 1943 the figures were 213,000 tons for the R.A.F. and 123,000 tons for the A.A.F.

Massive as was this attack, it was overshadowed by the prodigious efforts of 1944 when the Allies rained 1,600,000 tons of bombs on enemy targets, most of them on the German homeland. This was almost two hundred times the bomb tonnage that the Luftwaffe had cast on Britain. Of this the American Air Forces, the Eighth and the Ninth, accounted for about 900,000 tons and the R.A.F. for about 700,000.

The R.A.F. and the A.A.F. followed different but complementary bombing strategies. In part because Air Marshal Sir Arthur Harris thought German civilian economy and morale more vulnerable than German military objectives, in part because R.A.F. bombers were lightly armored and without adequate fighter protection, the British went in for saturation bombing, designed to destroy cities, disorganize labor, and shatter civilian morale. Because the Flying Fortress was better protected against flak and carried more guns than the British bombers, and because the A.A.F. developed in the Thunderbolt and the Mustang long-range fighter planes, the Americans adopted a program of so-called precision bombing. The British worked the night shift, the Americans the day shift; between them they achieved something like round-the-clock bombing. Both air commands followed a system of carefully selected targets and priorities: thus at one time, top priority was given to attacks on U-boat bases; at another to the German air industry; later to oil and aviation gasoline, and finally to transportation. At the same time the air forces were required to co-ordinate their offensive with the larger strategic scheme of the Chiefs of Staff. Thus the cross-channel invasion dictated a concentration of air power against transportation in northern France; the drive on Paris depended on the ability of the air force to close the Falaise gap and to protect General Patton's right flank; the Battle of the Bulge enlisted the air force in the closest kind of co-operation with ground forces; and the crossing of the Rhine was preceded by a vast air offensive against airfields, roads, bridges, and power plants in western Germany. Even closer co-operation was afforded by the air drops such as the paratroop landings that preceded the Normandy invasion, the spectacular paratroop and glider attack on Arnhem and Nijmegen designed to turn the Siegfried Line, and the airborne landings behind the German lines in March 1945.

By the spring of 1944 the air assault on Germany was so heavy that air leaders believed they could destroy the enemy without a land invasion. Whether the air forces could have beaten Germany to her knees without ground operations is a speculative question that will long engage the energies of armchair pilots and bombardiers. The findings of the Strategic Bombing Survey, however, throw a good deal of light on this vexed question as well as upon the entire history of the war in the West.

Most impressive was the sheer magnitude of the air war in western Europe. Altogether during the war the R.A.F. and the A.A.F. flew 1,442,280 bomber and 2,686,799 fighter sorties, and dropped 2,697,473 tons of bombs on enemy targets; over half on Germany proper, about one fifth on France, and about one seventh on Italy. This giant offensive was carried on by a maximum of 28,000 fighter and bomber planes, with a personnel of 1,335,000, and cost the Allies over 40,000 planes and 158,000 fliers. The air attack knocked out 57,000 German planes, killed about 300,000 and seriously wounded some 750,000 civilians, totally destroyed 3,600,000 dwelling units, and laid waste every large city in Germany. Many of the air raids were on a scale that made them comparable to major battles of earlier wars. Thus more soldiers were involved on the R.A.F. attack on Hamburg, in July 1943, than in the battle of Waterloo, and operation Clarion, the full-scale assault on German aircraft production of February 1944, was comparable to the battle of Gettysburg.

On the other hand, the Germans showed an amazing ability to sustain these attacks without loss of morale, and to recuperate. The Strategic Bombing Survey pointed out that

> Prior to the summer of 1943 air raids had no appreciable effect either on German munitions production or on the national output in general. The area attacks of the RAF did considerable damage to buildings and caused local delays in production by diverting labor to repair work and

The AIR WAR *in* EUROPE

(U.S. Strategic Bombing Survey Reports)

AIRCRAFT EMPLOYED IN EUROPE

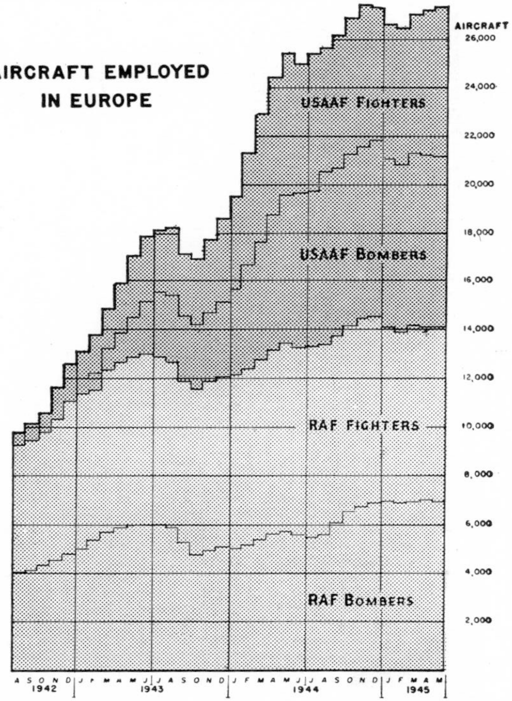

Note: The Strategic Bombing Survey covers American and British air forces employed against Europe from the European and Mediterranean theaters of operation.

TOTAL BOMB TONNAGE DROPPED IN EUROPE

SUMMARY

Year	USAAF	RAF	Totals
1940		15,610	15,610
1941		46,026	46,026
1942	2,003	74,489	76,492
1943	133,089	213,077	346,166
1944	890,661	703,075	1,593,736
1945	437,670	254,840	692,510
TOTALS	1,463,423	1,307,117	2,770,600

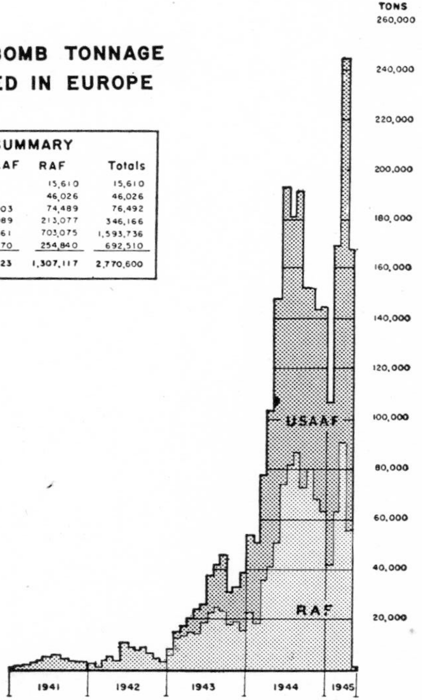

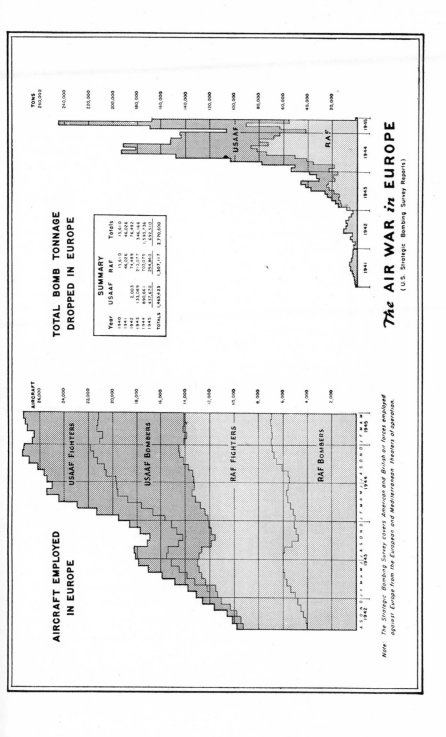

debris clearance. . . But considering the nature of the German economy during this period, it is impossible to conclude that either submarine production or munitions output as a whole was any smaller as a result of air raids than it would have been otherwise.[1]

From mid-summer 1943 on, the cumulative effect of the air war on Germany was serious, yet it is no exaggeration to say that not until after the summer of 1944 did the air attack vitally affect the German war economy. Notwithstanding the immense bomb tonnage dropped on German cities and factories, production in the most vital war industries increased steadily through 1943 and 1944. Thus the production index of all munitions output — aircraft, ammunition, weapons, tanks, half-tracks, naval vessels, and explosives — was substantially higher in 1944 than in any previous year. Germany built 15,000 planes in 1942, 25,000 in 1943, and 40,000 in 1944. Submarine production, too, reached its peak in 1944, with the construction of 387 U-boats; and even in the final four months of the war the Germans completed 155 submarines. Although some 20,000 tons of bombs were dropped on synthetic-rubber plants, rubber production increased until the summer of 1944, and lack of rubber did not at any time affect German military operations. The production of armor reached an all-time high in the last quarter of 1944, and began to decline only in February 1945. Steel was never a primary target, and although air raids and the capture of steel plants in occupied countries reduced production from thirty to twenty-five million tons in 1944, lack of steel did not slow up the German war machine. Despite the devastating and costly attacks on the ball-bearing factories at Schweinfurt, ball-bearing production reached its peak in September 1944.

In two areas of German war economy, however, the air attack achieved decisive results: transportation, and oil and aviation gasoline. Transportation was a major target, and during the war the Allied air forces — chiefly the A.A.F. — showered almost 900,000 tons of bombs on roads, bridges, ports, canals, railroads, and marshaling yards in France and Germany. During the weeks before invasion the Allied airmen concentrated on the transportation system north and west of Paris, and so successful was this attack that the invasion area was effectively sealed off from reinforcement. In September and October 1944 air attacks closed the Rhine, the Dort-

[1] *U.S. Strategic Bombing Survey: The Effects of Strategic Bombing on the German War Economy,* p. 11.

mund-Ems and the Mittelland canals, stopping all traffic between the Ruhr and points to the north. The last eight months of the war saw the attack on transportation rise to unprecedented heights. More than 40,000 tons of bombs were dropped on transportation targets in February 1945, and in March transport was designated the top target. The mass attack of February destroyed German capacity to resist the crossing of the Rhine and, by isolating the battle area, nullified German military protection. There seems no reason to challenge the conclusion of the Strategic Bombing Survey that 'the attack on transportation beginning in September 1944 was the most important single cause of Germany's ultimate economic collapse.'

The attack on oil and aviation gasoline was, however, equally decisive. From the beginning of the war Germany's petroleum situation was tight; when defeat at Stalingrad barred access to the rich Baku oilfields of the Caucasus, it became serious. Substantially half of German oil came from fields in Rumania, Hungary, and Poland; the rest was produced synthetically. The first major attack on oil came with the spectacular bombing of the Ploesti oilfields by the Fifteenth Air Force in August 1943. In the summer of 1944 the attack on oil refineries and synthetic plants was given top priority, and in the next ten months almost 200,000 tons of bombs were hurled at these targets. By July every major refinery and synthetic plant had been hit, and in August the Russians captured the Ploesti fields. As the savage assault continued, oil production dropped from 316,000 tons in April to 17,000 tons in September 1944, and monthly production of aviation gasoline was cut from 175,000 to 5000 tons. Typical of the war on oil was the long-sustained attack on the hydrogenation plant at Leuna near Magdeburg, the most heavily protected spot in Europe. Leuna was hit first on 12 May, and temporarily knocked out. Reconnaissance showed it back in operation in ten days, and it was attacked again on 28 May. By July, when production had climbed back to 75 per cent, it was given a series of 'treatments' that closed it for some weeks. Five heavy attacks in August and September kept it closed, but by mid-October it was once more back in operation. During November and December the A.A.F. visited Leuna six times more. Altogether from May to December 1944 the Allied air forces dropped 18,000 tons of bombs on Leuna, cutting production to less than 10 per cent of normal capacity.

The consequences of the attack on oil and gasoline were catastrophic. Although German aircraft production was on the upgrade throughout the year, a large part of the Luftwaffe was grounded for want of fuel. While British and American fliers averaged some 300 hours of training, German pilots were limited to about 100 hours. Lack of oil seriously impaired the German drive through the Ardennes in December 1944, and condemned to uselessness the 1500 tanks the Germans had massed along the Vistula to resist Russian crossing of that river in January 1945.

Why was Germany unable to repel or, in the end, to resist the Allied air offensive? It is not sufficient to say that the Allies outbuilt her in aircraft, or that Allied bombing wrecked her airplane factories and fuel facilities, for if Germany was able to build 40,000 planes in 1944, she could have built at least that many in 1942, and an adequate air force would have protected her against devastating attacks on factories and refineries. Germany's failure was not so much economic or technological as political and military, a failure of intelligence and control rather than of capacity. Hitler planned on a short war, and German industrial production was not geared to the demands of the war that actually developed. Confident of speedy victory, Germany early froze her airplane designs, and soon fell behind in the technological race; when it became clear that the war would be long, Hitler bet on the V-1 and V-2 weapons rather than on improved fighters, radar, or the atomic bomb. The Luftwaffe was built as an offensive weapon; large-scale production of fighter planes and adequate defense measures were put off until too late: anti-aircraft weapons, for example, had a low priority until 1943. The failure to push radar research and to develop to the full the potentialities of the ME-262 jet-propelled fighter plane — the most dangerous plane produced during the war — was attributable directly to Hitler's personal intervention in the conduct of research and production. These were the basic causes of Germany's failure in the air; the progressive destruction of cities, aircraft factories, oil and gasoline facilities, and, eventually, the Luftwaffe itself was a consequence inherent in the system of personal and party control.

2. *The Great Invasion*

Attacking Germany presented a very different problem in World War II than in World War I. The only factor in 1944 that recalled 1917 was the U-boats, which had to be eluded in order to get men and supplies across the Atlantic; but by 1944 the existing types of

U-boats were pretty well mastered by Allied air and surface attack, and the new, faster, and deadlier types had not yet come out. In 1917–18 France held firm, and the United States could land troops at docks in the French outports and take them to the front by train. But now all the French rolling stock — the old '40 hommes 8 chevaux' — , all French, Dutch, and most Italian ports were in the hands of the enemy, and the French coast was bristling with defenses. There was not one place north of Naples where Allied troops could get ashore without shooting their way in.

Plans for the eventual invasion had been under discussion for over a year when, in January 1943, the Casablanca conference set up a combined planning staff in London. The 'Trident' conference of May 1943 set the invasion date one year ahead. The Quebec conference of August elaborated details; and at Teheran, when the invasion plans were explained to and approved by Stalin, a diversionary landing in southern France was added to the plans. The American high command, eager to get on with the invasion and get the war with Germany over, took the initiative; the British, once the decisions were made, supported what seemed to them very dubious strategy with enthusiasm and energy.

Because operation Overlord was American in conception and would be to a great extent American in execution, it was appropriate that it should be under a United States army officer as supreme commander; and at Cairo in December 1943 Roosevelt and Churchill decided on the appointment of General Dwight D. Eisenhower,[2] who in the conduct of North African and Mediterranean operations had revealed military and diplomatic talents of a high order. At the same time it was agreed to continue the close integration of staff that had worked well in the Mediterranean theater. Both Eisenhower and his chief of staff, General Bedell Smith, had British officers (Sir Arthur Tedder and Sir Frederick Morgan) as deputies, and the Allied assault troops, air forces, and naval forces were under British command.[3]

Eisenhower flew to London in January 1944 to prepare for the

[2] Eisenhower's command extended to all arms of the service — ground, air, and sea, and to all the Allied forces in the West — French, Polish, Norwegian, Belgian, Czech, as well as British, Dominion, and American. At the same time he continued to hold the position of Commander in Chief of American Forces in the European Theater of Operations.

[3] General Montgomery, 21st Army Group; Sir Trafford Leigh-Mallory, air forces; Sir Bertram Ramsay, naval forces.

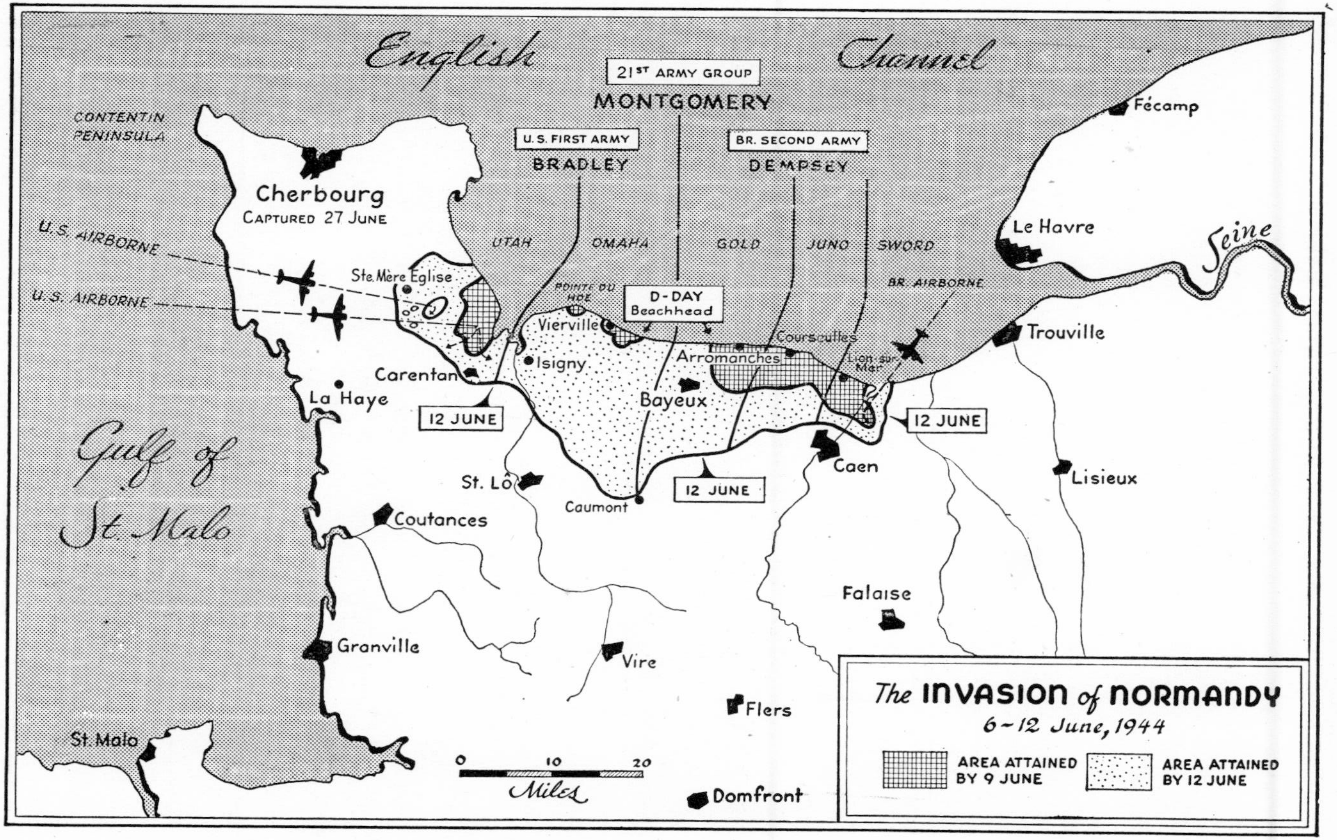
The INVASION of NORMANDY
6–12 June, 1944
AREA ATTAINED BY 9 JUNE
AREA ATTAINED BY 12 JUNE
English Channel
21ST ARMY GROUP
MONTGOMERY
U.S. FIRST ARMY
BRADLEY
BR. SECOND ARMY
DEMPSEY
UTAH
OMAHA
GOLD
JUNO
SWORD
D-DAY
Beachhead
POINTE DU HOE
BR. AIRBORNE
U.S. AIRBORNE
U.S. AIRBORNE
CONTENTIN PENINSULA
Cherbourg
CAPTURED 27 JUNE
Ste. Mère Eglise
Carentan
La Haye
Vierville
Isigny
Arromanches
Courseulles
Lion-sur-Mer
Bayeux
Caen
Caumont
St. Lô
Coutances
Granville
Vire
Flers
Falaise
Domfront
Lisieux
Trouville
Le Havre
Fécamp
Seine
12 JUNE
12 JUNE
12 JUNE
12 JUNE
Gulf of St. Malo
St. Malo
0
10
20
Miles

great invasion, and a month later received his directive from the Combined Chiefs of Staff:

> You will enter the continent of Europe and, in conjunction with the other United Nations, undertake operations aimed at the heart of Germany and the destruction of her armed forces. The date for entering the continent is the month of May 1944. After adequate Channel ports have been secured, exploitation will be directed toward securing an area that will facilitate both ground and air operations against the enemy.

Never before in modern times had an invading army crossed the English Channel against opposition and Hitler had had four years in which to fortify the coast of northern France. 'No power in the world,' he boasted, 'can drive us out of this region against our will.' His defenses were indeed formidable: underwater obstacles and mines, artillery emplacements, pill boxes, wire entanglements, tank traps, land mines, and other hazards were all designed to stop the invaders on the beaches. And behind these defenses stood 58 divisions — 17 of them in the Pas de Calais area, and 14 in Normandy and Brittany, the others scattered.

Yet the Allies had reason for confidence. They held the initiative; they could select their point of attack, engage in diversionary operations, and launch large-scale deceptive activities. They could count, too, on help from the French resistance. For six weeks Allied air forces had smashed roads and bridges in northern France, reducing the transportation system to chaos. The Allied force of soldiers, sailors, aviators, and service amounted to 2,876,000 men, all in England; that little country almost sagged under a stockpile of 2,500,000 tons of supplies. Thirty-nine divisions and 11,000 planes were available for the initial landings, and the Allied fleet was overwhelmingly superior. And Hitler's 'Atlantic wall,' despite prodigious efforts, was far from impregnable, its weak spots located by Allied Intelligence. The Germans, fighting on four fronts (Russia, Italy, France, and the Balkans), lacked strategic reserves. Their divisions were under strength, the Luftwaffe was whittled down to 2500 available planes, and the U-boat fleet had been decimated. Moreover, the German high command was riddled with dissension. Hitler guessed right that the invasion would hit the coast of Normandy, but the Wehrmacht guessed wrong, that it would come in the narrowest part of the Channel, the Pas de Calais, where the strongest forces accordingly were concentrated. Rommel, commander of the German armies in France, wanted to stop the Allies on the beaches; but Rundstedt, commander in chief in the West, preferred a defense in depth. Both were harassed by ex-corporal Hitler's interference in their strategy and tactics.

Why did the Allies reject the Pas de Calais with its four major ports, short sea crossing, and shortest roads to Paris and Antwerp? Because the Germans, expecting them there, had fortified it to the point of impregnability. Consequently the Allied command selected a forty-mile strip of beach along the Normandy coast between the Orne River and the Cotentin peninsula; the eastern sector was assigned to the British, the western one to the Americans. This area was within easy reach of such ports as Portsmouth, Southampton, Poole, Portland, and Plymouth; it offered long, broad beaches that were not too heavily defended, and the port of Cherbourg is on the Cotentin peninsula. D-day was set for 5 June.

> All southern England [wrote General Eisenhower] was one vast military camp, crowded with soldiers awaiting final word to go, and piled high with supplies and equipment awaiting transport to the far shore of the Channel. The whole area was cut off from the rest of England. . . Every separate encampment, barrack, vehicle park, and every unit was carefully charted on our master maps. The scheduled movement of each unit had been so worked out that it would reach the embarkation point at the exact time the vessels would be ready to receive it. The southernmost camps where assault troops were assembled were all surrounded by barbed-wire to prevent any soldier leaving the camp after he had once been briefed as to his part in the attack. The mighty host was as tense as a coiled spring, and indeed that is exactly what it was — a great human spring, coiled for the moment when its energy should be released and it would vault the English Channel in the greatest amphibious assault ever attempted.[4]

At the last moment bad weather threatened the whole operation. General Eisenhower postponed the invasion twenty-four hours, but on 5 June, despite winds up to 20 knots and choppy seas, he courageously decided to go ahead with it. All that night, Allied planes softened up the Normandy defenses and struck at the communications system of northern France. Shortly after midnight three paratroop divisions were flown across the Channel and dropped behind the beaches: a British division near Caen, and the two American ones on the Cotentin peninsula. At the same time a ghostly inva-

[4] *Crusade in Europe,* p. 249. Doubleday.

sion force of non-existent battleships, destroyers, transports, and aircraft simulated by radio transmission headed for the Pas de Calais shores in what has been called 'the most sophisticated faking in the history of man.' The Germans fell for the ruse and were confirmed in their belief that the main attack was coming at Calais; their Fifteenth Army was pinned down there.

During the night of 5–6 June the invasion armada of 600 warships and 4000 supporting craft, freighted with 176,000 men from a dozen different ports, was moving down the Norman coast. The transports and large landing craft anchored off the invasion beaches at 3 A.M.; battleships, cruisers, and destroyers closed the beaches and began hurling their shells on the bewildered defenders at 5:30. When the naval bombardment ended, small landing craft made their way through the surf and touched down at 6:30. The invasion was on!

Since the invaders achieved tactical surprise, the initial landings were everywhere successful. On the American right — designated as Utah beach — the VII Corps got ashore against light opposition, surmounted the barriers of marsh and swamp, captured the causeways into the interior, and linked up with elements of the 82nd Airborne Division at Ste. Mère-Eglise. The V Corps, assigned a four-mile strip between the Carentan estuary and the town of Port-en-Bessin (designated Omaha beach), found the going tough. Heavy overcast had prevented the Eighth Air Force from bombing Omaha; naval bombardment alone had not been enough to knock out German artillery emplacements; underwater obstacles were numerous and formidable; those who managed to make the beaches were exposed to murderous fire. 'For a time,' writes the historian of this famous operation:

> there was, definitely, a problem of morale. The survivors of the beach crossing, many of whom were experiencing their first enemy fire, had seen heavy losses among their comrades or in neighboring units. No action could be fought in circumstances more calculated to heighten the moral effects of such losses. Behind them, the tide was drowning wounded men who had been cut down on the sands and was carrying bodies ashore just below the shingle. Disasters to the later landing waves were still occurring, to remind of the potency of enemy fire. Stunned and shaken by what they had experienced, men could easily find the sea wall and shingle bank all too welcome a cover. . . Ahead of them, with wire and minefields to get through, was the beach flat, fully exposed to enemy fire; beyond that the bare and steep bluffs, with enemy

strongpoints still in action. . . Except for supporting fire of tanks on some sectors, they could count on little but their own weapons. Naval gunfire had practically ceased when the infantry reached the beach; the ships were under orders not to fire . . . until liaison was established with fire control parties. Lacking this liaison the destroyers did not dare bring fire on the strongpoints through which infantry might be advancing on the smoke-obscured bluffs. At 0800 German observers on the bluff, sizing up the grim picture below them, might well have felt that the invasion was stopped at the edge of the water.[5]

The British, too, had run into trouble. Caen was the hinge in the German line; if Montgomery succeeded in knifing through at this point, he would cut communications between the German Seventh and Fifteenth Armies. Resistance to the British landings on Gold, Juno, and Sword beaches, therefore, was fierce.

Yet the landings were everywhere successful. By the end of D-day the Allies had breached the Atlantic wall in three places, landed 120,000 men and parts of three airborne divisions, and had begun to bring in vehicles, supplies, and armor. Meantime naval and air bombardment prevented the enemy from bringing up reinforcements from the interior.

Once the initial landings had been effected, the Allies rushed over men, armor, and supplies in astonishing quantities and with amazing speed, building up the invading army faster than the Germans could reinforce theirs. By 12 June the Allies controlled a continuous beachhead some seventy miles in length and from five to fifteen miles in depth. On the left the British were battling for Caen; in the center the 101st Airborne had entered Carentan; and on the right the VII Corps was pushing swiftly across the Cotentin peninsula and sweeping north toward the great port of Cherbourg. In a single week the Allies had landed 326,000 men, 50,000 vehicles, and over 100,000 tons of supplies.

'The history of war,' said Marshal Stalin, 'does not know any such undertaking so broad in conception and so grandiose in its scale and so masterly in execution.'

The first task confronting the Allies was to capture the port of Cherbourg; the second, to get sufficient elbowroom in which to build up for a breakthrough to the south, west, or east as opportunity offered. The 'mulberrys,' two great artificial harbors made out of

[5] Charles H. Taylor, *Omaha Beachhead* (U.S. War Dept. Historical Division), p. 57.

sunken ships with connecting pontoon units, facilitated a rapid buildup of supplies, but a northwest gale beginning on 19 June and lasting three days beat up the 'mulberrys' badly, and wrecked over 300 landing craft on the beaches. This made the capture of Cherbourg highly urgent. The Americans had already sealed off the Cotentin peninsula and pushed north to the outskirts of Cherbourg. Bombarded from land, air, and sea, the city capitulated on 26 June, yet not before the Germans had wrecked all harbor installations. Foul weather and enemy resistance had combined to put the invading forces seriously behind schedule.

Another delaying factor was the *bocage* country of Normandy, where roads and tiny fields were lined by dense, high hedges growing out of earthen banks three or four feet in height — barriers as favorable for defense as the rubble of Cassino. The Germans put snipers in trees, hid tanks and machine guns behind the hedgerows, mined the narrow, twisting roads along which the motorized American army moved. As Ernie Pyle saw it,

> This hedgerow business was a series of little skirmishes . . . clear across the front, thousands and thousands of little skirmishes. No single one of them was very big. Added up over the days and weeks, however, they made a man-sized war — with thousands on both sides getting killed. But that is only a general pattern of the hedgerow fighting. Actually each one was a little separate war, fought under different circumstances. For instance, the fight might be in a woods instead of an open field. The Germans would be dug in all over the woods, in little groups, and it was really tough to get them out. Often in cases like that we just went around the woods and kept going, and let later units take care of those surrounded and doomed fellows. Or we might go through a woods and clean it out, and another company, coming through a couple of hours later, would find it full of Germans again.[6]

Fortunately, Sergeant Culin thought up the ingenious idea of securing two steel blades, capable of cutting through earth and root embankments, to the front of each tank. Steel was obtained from obstacles the Germans had strewn over the Normandy beaches, and soon the tanks were functioning once more as the spearhead of the offensive.

The battle of Normandy lasted from 6 June to 24 July. By that time the Allies had landed well over a million men and controlled over 1500 square miles of Normandy and Brittany from the Orne to

[6] *Brave Men*, p. 303. Henry Holt Co.

the Gulf of St. Malo. The British, after the toughest kind of fighting, had captured Caen; the Americans had taken not only Cherbourg but Saint-Lô, gateway to the south. The enemy, unable to bring up reinforcements, with communications wrecked and planes grounded, were confused and bewildered. Rommel, as we now know, thought the situation hopeless and was preparing to try to negotiate with Eisenhower for a separate peace when he was removed, and killed, on Hitler's orders. Yet the Germans continued to fight with pertinacity, and their new V-1 guided bombs, launched from positions in Belgium and northern France, were spreading death and destruction through London and the near-by English counties.

3. *Normandy to the Rhine*

On 25 July 1944 the battle of Normandy was over and the battle for France began. On that day General Patton's Third Army struck like a thunderbolt against the German lines west of Saint-Lô. First came a 'carpet-bombing' attack in which 2500 planes saturated a few square miles with almost 5000 tons of bombs. This was followed by a heavy artillery barrage; then the tanks began to move. A German commander described the scene at noon as 'like a landscape on the surface of the moon, all craters and death.' Within two days the VII Corps had reached Coutances ten miles to the south, hemming in remnants of the German army along the coast. By the end of July Avranches had fallen, and the Americans stood at the threshold of Brittany.

In the face of this fast and ferocious attack the German withdrawal turned into something like a rout. And after the breakthrough came the breakout. One wing of Patton's army turned west and within a week overran Brittany, stopping only at the fortified ports of Brest, Lorient, and St. Nazaire, which were left for leisurely reduction. Another wing turned east and within two weeks reached the Loire to the south and Le Mans to the west.

In a last desperate gamble Hitler ordered the German Seventh Army to break through the funnel of the American army at Avranches. 'To the best of my knowledge and conscience the execution of this order means the collapse of the whole Normandy front,' wrote General von Kluge, who had replaced Rundstedt; but his protest was unheeded. While the Germans were tangled up in this operation — rendered hopeless by Allied control of the air — the British and Americans cut through at Falaise, just south of Caen, and closed their own exit corridor on them. Most of what remained of the Seventh Army was destroyed in this battle of the Falaise gap; only remnants of armor fought their way through and sped to the Westwall to prepare for the defense of Germany.

Even as the Germans were being ground to bits in the Falaise gap, the Allies launched their long-awaited invasion of southern France. During the first two weeks of August, Allied bombers from Corsica and Italy hammered at the French Riviera while a great task force of United States, British, and French warships under Admiral Hewitt gathered off Corsica. Long-continued air and naval bombardment along the whole line of the Riviera neutralized the strong coast defenses and confused the enemy in regard to the actual points of landing; General Patch's Seventh Army went ashore at four places between Toulon and Cannes on the morning of 15 August, and once ashore, gobbled up the few German divisions in that region. By 17 August the invaders, 85,000 strong, held 50 miles of shoreline. Leaving the reduction of Toulon and Marseilles to the Free French forces, which here performed very effective service, the Seventh Army plunged northward in two great columns, one headed toward Grenoble 150 miles inland, the other up the Rhone Valley. By 25 August the German situation was desperate and Hitler ordered the First and Nineteenth Armies to extricate themselves as best they could, holding only a few ports on the Bay of Biscay. Pushing up the Rhone Valley, the Seventh Army took the industrial city of Lyon and raced to close the German escape corridor at Belfort Gap, between the Vosges and the Jura Mountains. By mid-September the Seventh Army had linked up with the Third. With total casualties of some 13,000, the Allies had cleared all of France south of the Loire, bagged 80,000 prisoners, and destroyed two German armies.

'Liberate Paris by Christmas and none of us can ask for more,' Churchill had said to Eisenhower. With the annihilation of the Germans in the Falaise gap, nothing stood between the Allies and Paris. Hodge's First Army raced for the Seine; Patton's Third Army boiled out onto the open country north of the Loire, reached Chartres in time to save the cathedral from irreparable damage, and swept eastward through Orléans to Troyes fifty miles southeast of Paris.

By 20 August American soldiers could see the Eiffel Tower. With liberation near, the Parisians rose against their hated masters, and with the aid of General Leclerc's 2nd Armored Division, Paris was freed on 25 August. Two days later General Charles de Gaulle entered the city in triumph and assumed the Presidency of the French provisional government.

In their desperate haste to reach the Westwall, the Germans put up no organized resistance. Third Army spearheads reached the historic Marne on 28 August; pushed through Château-Thierry, where an American army had fought in 1918; overran Rheims and the fortress city of Verdun. To the north of them, British and Canadian troops raced along the coast into Belgium, by-passing Calais and Dunkirk; captured Brussels and entered the great port of Antwerp on 4 September. By the 11th the American First Army, liquidating remnants of twenty disorganized German divisions, had liberated Luxembourg and crossed the border into Germany near Aachen. Within six weeks all France had been cleared of the enemy. The Germans had lost almost half a million men, and their losses in material included 20,000 vehicles, 1300 tanks, and 3500 aircraft. From Switzerland to Aachen, Allied armies stood poised for the advance into Germany.

Meantime the German position on other fronts was becoming increasingly desperate. Stalingrad had dammed up the main German offensive into Russia, and since then it had been one long ebb tide. The long-sustained Russian offensive that began in July 1943 had recovered most of the invaded territory, and in the spring of 1944 the Red Army stood poised on the Dnieper River in the north and on the Carpathians in the south. Stalin had promised to launch a new offensive when the Allies opened their second front, and even as Americans and British soldiers were landing on the Normandy beaches, his armies struck into Finland and within three months knocked that unwilling German ally out of the war. The major Russian offensive was launched on 23 June along an 800-mile front from Leningrad to the Carpathians, and in the space of five weeks swept 460 miles across the Ukraine and Poland and up to the gates of Warsaw. No sooner did this massive offensive grind to a halt than the Russians started another in the Balkans. Rumania threw in the sponge when the Red Army thundered across her borders, and the Germans were deprived of their last important source of crude oil. In September Bulgaria threw off the Nazi yoke and shifted

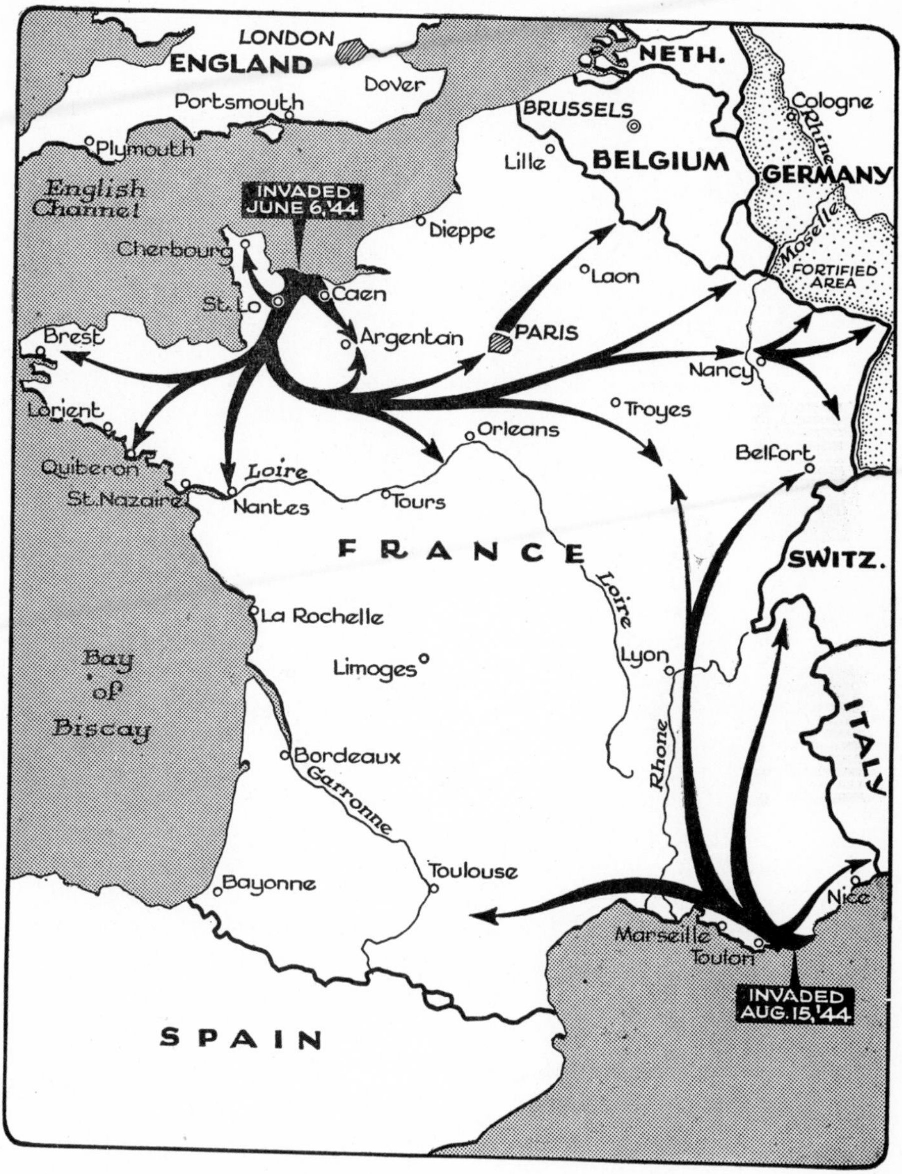

The Battle of France

over to the Allied side. By October the Russians had linked up with partisan forces in Yugoslavia. With most of the Balkans overrun, the road to Austria and Czechoslovakia was open.

In Italy, too, the Germans were being driven back on their last line of defense. The capture of Rome had not halted the Allied advance. Siena was occupied on 3 July and the great port of Leghorn, 250 miles north of Rome, fell to the American Fifth Army on the 19th. On that same day Polish troops advancing up the Adriatic captured Ancona. British troops coming up central Italy took Perugia in June, Arezzo in July, and Florence in August. By September the Allies had reached the powerful Gothic Line guarding the rich industrial Po Valley — a formidable barrier, which held up further advance that year.

While the Allies in France still held the initiative, they were unable to exploit it. They had run into a serious problem of logistics: the speed of their advance across France had outrun supplies. By September, cargo discharges were lagging behind schedule some 9000 tons daily, and in October by 20,000 tons. Stubborn German defense still denied the Allies important harbors on the Channel and in Brittany, as well as the water approach to Antwerp. Not until the Allies obtained adequate port facilities and base installations, repaired roads, railroads, and bridges, and laid down air strips and pipelines, could they renew a full-scale offensive.

> All along the front [wrote General Eisenhower] we felt increasingly the strangulation on movement imposed by our inadequate lines of communication. . . Regardless of the extraordinary efforts of the supply system, this remained our most acute difficulty. All along the front the cry was for more gasoline and more ammunition. Every one of our spearheads could have gone farther and faster than they actually did. . . Nevertheless we had to supply each force for its basic missions and for basic missions only.

This situation presented Eisenhower with one of his most difficult strategic decisions. Montgomery wanted to push ahead through Holland and around the flank of the Westwall into the heart of Germany; he was confident that with proper support he could plunge through to Berlin. Patton was no less confident of his ability to smash into Germany from the south. Logistics permitted a modest advance on a broad front, or a deep stab on a single front, but not both. Because it was essential to clear the way to the port of Antwerp, capture Calais and Dunkirk, and overrun the V-1 and V-2 bomb emplacements, priority was given Montgomery's British and Canadian troops.

To secure a bridgehead across the Rhine, the Allied High Command made one of the great gambles of the war—an end run around the right of the German line. The plan was for paratroops to seize crossings on the network of rivers that constitute the Rhine estuary, and for the British First Army to drive through and, in conjunction with the airborne troops, sweep around the Westwall into Germany. Two American divisions were assigned the task of capturing the key town of Eindhoven and seizing the Meuse and the Waal; a British airborne division was to come down at Arnhem. On 17 September 2800 planes and 1400 gliders flying from England dropped 34,000 paratroops on these little Dutch towns. The Americans succeeded in taking Eindhoven and, after some of the sharpest fighting in the war, Nijmegen; but the British were cut off and surrounded in Arnhem. Bad weather made it impossible to reinforce them by air; and for two weeks the British First Army hammered at the German ring in a vain effort to rescue them by land. As Eisenhower wrote, 'When in spite of heroic effort, the airborne forces and their supporting ground forces were stopped in their tracks, we had ample evidence that much bitter campaigning was still to come.'

4. *Attack and Counterattack*

It was indeed. With the failure of the Arnhem air drop, the war temporarily lost its blitz character and settled down to what General Eisenhower has called 'the dirtiest kind of infantry slugging.' The Germans now held a defensive position stronger than any they had enjoyed since the beginning of the invasion. They had lost much of their strength, but what they had left they were now able to concentrate. Their defensive line ran irregularly from the Maas (Meuse) River in the north, along the Roer River, the Hürtgen Forest, and the rugged Eifel in the center, and along the Moselle River and the Vosges Mountains in the south. A large part of this line was fortified in depth: the Westwall, or, as it came to be called, the Siegfried Line, stretched from Nijmegen to Switzerland. After the failure of the July plot against Hitler, General von Kluge had committed suicide, and von Rundstedt, ablest of German generals, was now commander in the West.

To defend the homeland he had parts of 48 infantry and 15 armored divisions, and by combing out idle members of the air force and the navy, drawing on the Home Defense, and raising Volksgrenadier Divisions, these were substantially reinforced. Fighting on shorter lines, on the defensive, and on home ground had certain advantages: one of the few compensations for the shrinkage of Nazi-held territory was that it enabled the German high command to shift troops back and forth from the Eastern to the Western fronts with relative ease, and sharply diminished the fuel requirements of the German air force. Both weather and terrain imposed heavy burdens on the Allied offensive. The winter of 1944–5 was one of the worst in memory: floods, cold, and snow combined to partially nullify Allied air supremacy and immobilize Allied armor.

In the confused fighting that stretched from October to mid-December 1944 we can distinguish a series of battles each as bitter as any of those that had been fought from Tunisia on, and as costly. The first of these — to take them pretty much in geographical order — was the Battle for the Scheldt Estuary. The Allies had occupied Antwerp on 4 September with its dock facilities almost intact, but as long as the Germans controlled its approaches from the islands at the mouth of the Scheldt, the great port was useless. The formidable task of clearing the enemy out of these islands was assigned to the Canadian First Army. South Beveland was overrun by 30 October, after a week of hard fighting. Walcheren was a tougher nut to crack. Its reduction, completed by 9 November, involved blowing up the dykes that held back the sea, and cost the Allies more casualties than the conquest of all Sicily. It was another two weeks before the mines could be swept out of the Scheldt, and the end of November before the first cargo ships were unloading at Antwerp.

The second major battle was for Aachen (Aix la Chapelle), at the juncture of Belgium, Holland, and Germany. The American First Army launched its attack on 2 October. First it had to fight through five miles of Siegfried Line fortifications. By the middle of the month the city was surrounded; then came a week of fighting street by street and house by house before the ancient city capitulated. Aachen was the first German city to fall to the Allies; the fanaticism with which it was defended was a foretaste of what was to come.

With the fall of Aachen General Bradley brought the Ninth Army north to co-operate with the First in a campaign to capture the Roer

River dams — the third of the major battles. As long as the Germans controlled these dams, seven in all, they could flood the whole area over which the Allies had to advance. Numerous attempts to bomb the dams were unsuccessful. Then came a large-scale assault by seventeen divisions through the Hürtgen Forest toward Duren. The country was not unlike that Wilderness in which Grant and Lee had tangled eighty years earlier, and — as General Eisenhower later wrote — 'Whenever veterans of the American 4th, 9th and 28th Divisions referred to hard fighting they did so in terms of comparison with the Battle of Hürtgen Forest which they placed at the top of the list.' Well they might, for these three divisions alone suffered casualities of almost 13,000. The Americans reached the Roer River on 3 December, and there they were stalled. Further progress was held up by the exigencies of the Ardennes campaign (see below), and the dams were not finally captured until early February — and then not before the Germans had released the pent-up waters of the Roer and flooded the whole of the lower valley.

To the south General Patton's Third Army was engaged in a fourth major battle — the capture of Metz, and the invasion of Lorraine and the great industrial Saar basin. Only once before in modern times — 1871 — had the fortress city of Metz fallen to an invader. Patton's attack jumped off early in November. First he enveloped Metz, reducing one by one the forts that encircled it. Then came a week of street fighting. The city fell on 22 November and the Third Army, fighting its way through the heaviest fortifications of the Siegfried Line, plunged into the Saar. This campaign cost the Americans 29,000 battle casualties, and netted them 37,000 prisoners.

In conjunction with Patton's advance to the Saar, General Devers' 6th Army Group launched an attack into Alsace, the French driving toward the Belfort gap, the Americans striking for Strasbourg, which fell on 23 November. The French then turned north along the Rhine, the Americans south; as they met, they pinched off a sizable body of Germans in the Colmar pocket. These operations, obscured by the more dramatic fighting to the north, cost the Allies no less than 33,000 casualties.

Thus by mid-December the Allied armies stood poised all along the border from Holland to Switzerland, ready to hurdle the Siegfried Line and plunge into Germany and beyond. Then came a dramatic, if temporary, change of fortunes: a German counteroffensive.

It was Hitler who decided to make the gamble of the Ardennes counteroffensive. The stakes were high; the risks did not seem greater than those of standing on the offensive and losing the war by attrition. At the very minimum a counteroffensive would stall the Allied advance, upset its timetable, and give Germany a breathing spell. At the most it might split the Allied 12th and 21st Army groups in two, and drive through to the coast, capturing badly needed fuel and munitions supplies and the port of Antwerp. Some Germans even dreamed of being in Paris by Christmas.

The Allies could not hold all of their 350-mile line in strength, and Eisenhower had taken the calculated risk of spreading his forces thin in the rugged region of the Ardennes mountains. To the Germans—and especially to von Rundstedt—this was familiar ground, and the pattern of attack, too, was familiar. In 1940 the French high command had regarded the Ardennes forest as wholly unsuitable for large-scale operations, and had failed to defend it. Feinting with his right, von Rundstedt had crashed through here with his main force in May 1940, brushed aside the Belgian and French defenses, reached the Meuse in two days, and swept up to the Channel coast. Now the Germans prepared to repeat this famous campaign. They knew that the Ardennes was thinly defended, and they banked on the weather playing into their hands—as it did. By scraping the bottom of the manpower barrel, they had managed to assemble 23 divisions and a formidable body of armor, and their air force was prepared to make its most ambitious effort since the invasion.

'The great hour has arrived and everything is at stake,' said Propaganda Minister Goebbels as, early in the morning of 16 December, three German armies began to grind forward into the Ardennes on a 50-mile front from Monschau to Enternach. They achieved surprise and initial success. The green 106th Division was swallowed up; the battle-weary 4th and 28th Divisions were forced to give way, fighting grimly. But after the first shock, Allied resistance stiffened and held. Balked in their plan to swing north toward Liege by heroic Allied defense of St. Vith, and held by stonewall resistance on the south, the Germans concentrated on the center of the Allied Line. It was here they achieved their most spectacular success, and here that, in the end, they were decisively defeated.

In four days the Germans advanced 20 miles; then their armies raced for the Meuse, which they all but reached on 26 December: a penetration of 50 miles! What frustrated them, however, was Bastogne, a name that will be remembered as long as Americans cherish valor. This little Belgian town, headquarters of the American VIII Corps, was a focal point of a network of roads, and the Germans thought its capture essential to the development of their campaign. General Troy Middleton decided to hold it at all costs. The decision was taken in the face of the fact that there were no forces adequate to the task. Middleton had at his disposal a handful of service troops, parts of two Engineer Combat Battalions, and remnants of the decimated 28th Infantry Division. Within two days elements of three other divisions had made their way to the beleaguered town. Of decisive importance was reinforcement by the 101st Airborne Division. This division was, at the time, in a rest center 100 miles behind the lines—its division commander in Washington, its deputy commander in England, many of its men on leave. Late in the night of 17 December it was ordered to Bastogne; piling pell-mell into trucks and jeeps, it set off on the 100-mile trip, and with lights blazing all the way, pulled into Bastogne on the 18th, just before the German tide flooded around the town. With the arrival of the 101st Division the strength of the defenders rose to some 18,000 men.

Then followed one of the epic battles of the war. The Americans seized the outlying villages, and set up a perimeter defense. For six days the enemy hurled armor and planes at the beleaguered town, and there was a whole series of little battles around the perimeter as they probed for a weak spot in the defense. Foul weather prevented aerial reinforcement of the defenders. On 22 December the situation of the Americans appeared hopeless and the Germans presented a formal demand for surrender, to which General McAuliffe gave the now classic answer, 'Aw, nuts.' On the 23rd the weather cleared, and for five hours C–47's dropped supplies; the next day, with bomber and fighter support, the situation looked more hopeful. Meantime the Third Army had made a great wheel to the left and started northward to the rescue of the besieged garrison. It was tough fighting all the way, but on 26 December the 4th Armored Division broke through the German encirclement and Bastogne was saved.

The German flood began to recede, but the Battle of the Bulge was far from over. Now the 21st Army Group hammered the bulge from the north, and the 12th Army Group from the south. Fighting savagely, the Germans pulled back, and the bulge shrank. By mid-January the original lines of mid-December had been restored. Von Rundstedt had held up the Allied advance by a full month, but at a cost of 120,000 men, 1600 planes, and a good part of his armor. Never thereafter were the Germans able to mount an offensive or even to put up an effective defensive against the Allied invaders.

5. *Across the Pacific*

The Casablanca decisions of January 1943, disappointing as they were to Americans who hoped to finish off Hitler that year, evened things up in the Pacific. For it was agreed that while the Mediterranean campaign continued and while preparations were made for a grand offensive in 1944, the United States should exploit her recent victories in the Pacific to keep the Japanese moving backward. Very few army divisions would be needed to augment the marines until the United States was ready to assault large land masses, and plenty of new naval vessels would shortly be available — notably the *Essex*-class carriers, which were not wanted in narrow European waters. Thus, there was every reason to believe that substantial gains could be made against the Japanese in 1943 by United States forces alone, aided by the little that Australia and New Zealand could supply.

Naval and air offensives against Japan could be mounted from three different regions — the Aleutians, Hawaii, and the South Pacific, including Australia. The first, the shortest route, was ruled out by bad flying weather. Nothing more was planned in those parts than to recover the western islands of Attu and Kiska, Japan's consolation for Midway.

Eliminating the Aleutians, the American Joint Chiefs of Staff studied possibilities in the Central and Southern Pacific. Japan itself was the final objective, but before invasion of her tightly defended home islands, positions must be taken within air-bombing distance. At the Quebec conference of May 1943, the Combined Chiefs of Staff decided that this base should be on the China coast somewhere between Shanghai and Hong Kong. But how to get there? Hundreds of atolls and thousands of islands — the Bonins, Marianas, Carolines, Marshalls, and Gilberts — plastered with airfields and bristling with defenses, sprawled across the Pacific like a series of gigantic spiders' webs, blocking all routes north of the equator; while south of the Line, Japan held the Bismarcks, the Solomons excepting Guadalcanal and Tulagi, and New Guinea excepting its very slippery tail. General MacArthur wished to advance by what he called the New Guinea-Mindanao axis; but Rabaul, planted like a baleful spider at the center of a web across that axis, would have to be eliminated first. As long as Japan held such a maze of islands on MacArthur's right flank, she could throw air and naval forces against his communications at will. So it was decided that Admiral Nimitz must take a broom to the Gilberts-Marshalls and Carolines while MacArthur and Halsey handled Rabaul.

Accordingly the plans for mid-1943 to mid-1944 included two preliminary operations (Western Aleutians and Central Solomons) to eliminate enemy nuisances and acquire more advanced springboards; and two major operations (Rabaul and Gilberts-Marshalls) to sweep up enemy spiders' webs. Following a notable naval victory off the Komandorski Islands on 24 March 1943, the 7th Infantry Division went into Attu and cleared the enemy out; he then evacuated Kiska. The Western Aleutians were then developed as air bases, to preclude any Japanese attempt to invade the United States by that route, and to prepare for eventual co-operation with Russia against Japan, which Russia did not want.

The second preliminary, the Central Solomons operation, was to improve the American position in the South Pacific by wresting Munda airfields in New Georgia from the enemy and rounding out American holdings in the New Guinea tail. Before it started, General Kenney's V Army Air Force sank an entire Japanese troop convoy by skip-bombing (Battle of the Bismarck Sea, 2–3 March 1943), and the Solomon Islands air force shot down and killed Admiral Yamamoto when he was making a routine inspection. Never again did Japan have a naval leader of his ability and resource. The Central Solomons offensive got under way at the end of June. After three sharp naval actions up the Slot (Battles of Kula Gulf, Kolombangara, and Vella Gulf), the United States navy won control of the surrounding waters, and Munda field with adjacent positions was captured by the army after a tough jungle campaign. In New Guinea and on Cape Gloucester off New Britain, a series of shore-to-shore amphibious operations secured the main passage from the Coral Sea into the Western Pacific.

Around September 1943 amateur strategists were very gloomy

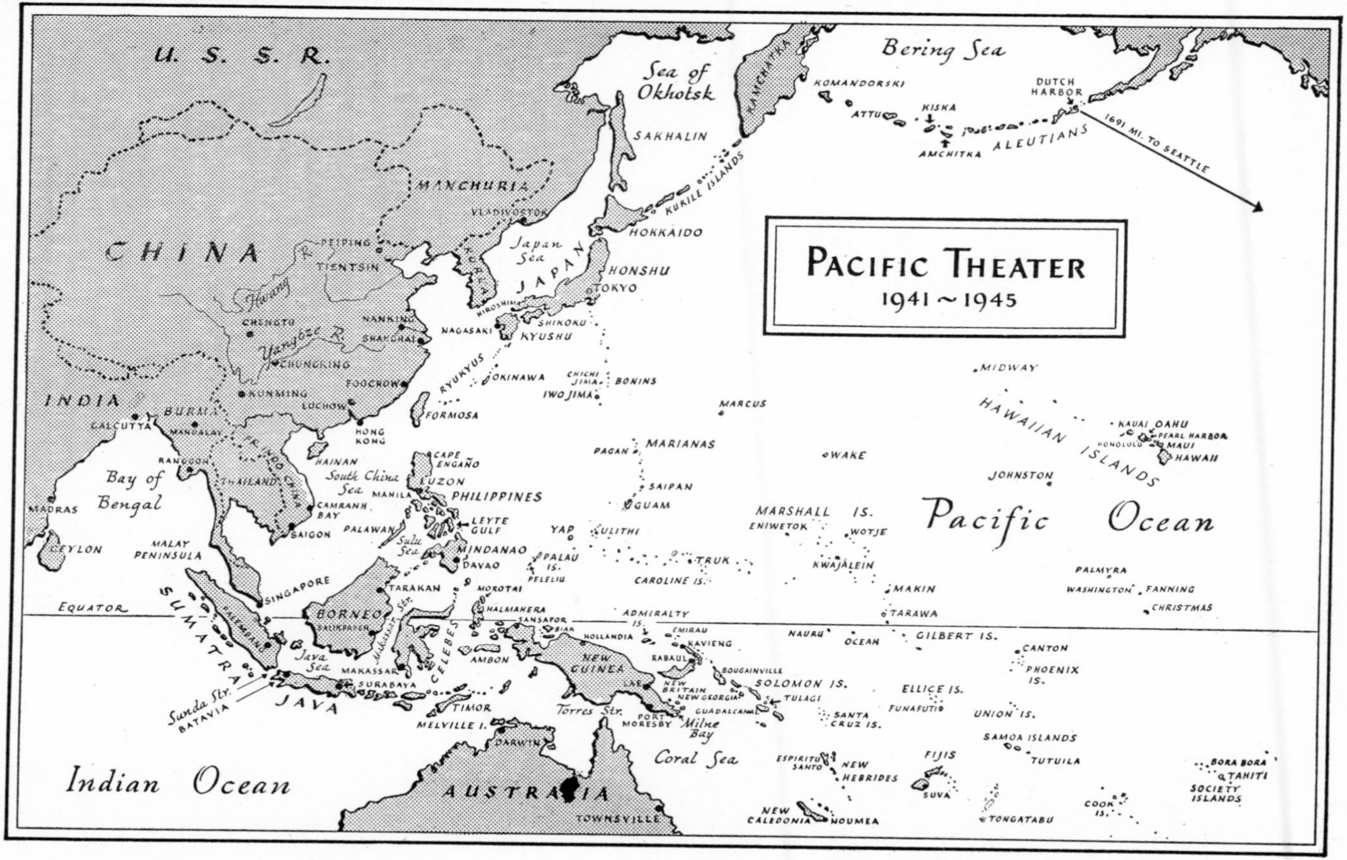
PACIFIC THEATER
1941 ~ 1945
U. S. S. R.
CHINA
MANCHURIA
VLADIVOSTOK
PEIPING
TIENTSIN
Hwang R.
Yangtze R.
CHENGTU
NANKING
SHANGHAI
CHUNGKING
FOOCHOW
KUNMING
LUCHOW
HONG KONG
INDIA
CALCUTTA
BURMA
MANDALAY
RANGOON
THAILAND
FR. INDO CHINA
HAINAN
CAMRANH BAY
SAIGON
Bay of Bengal
MADRAS
CEYLON
MALAY PENINSULA
SINGAPORE
SUMATRA
PALEMBANG
Sunda Str.
BATAVIA
JAVA
Java Sea
SURABAYA
MAKASSAR
BORNEO
BALIKPAPAN
TARAKAN
Makassar Str.
CELEBES
South China Sea
MANILA
LUZON
CAPE ENGAÑO
PHILIPPINES
LEYTE GULF
PALAWAN
Sulu Sea
MINDANAO
DAVAO
FORMOSA
RYUKYUS
OKINAWA
NAGASAKI
HIROSHIMA
KYUSHU
SHIKOKU
KOREA
Japan Sea
JAPAN
HONSHU
TOKYO
HOKKAIDO
SAKHALIN
Sea of Okhotsk
KURILE ISLANDS
KAMCHATKA
Bering Sea
KOMANDORSKI
ATTU
KISKA
AMCHITKA
ALEUTIANS
DUTCH HARBOR
1691 MI. TO SEATTLE
CHICHI JIMA
BONINS
IWO JIMA
MARCUS
PAGAN
MARIANAS
SAIPAN
GUAM
YAP
ULITHI
PALAU IS.
PELELIU
TRUK
CAROLINE IS.
MOROTAI
HALMAHERA
SANSAPOR
BIAK
HOLLANDIA
ADMIRALTY IS.
EMIRAU
KAVIENG
RABAUL
NEW GUINEA
LAE
NEW BRITAIN
NEW GEORGIA
BOUGAINVILLE
SOLOMON IS.
TULAGI
GUADALCANAL
PORT MORESBY
Milne Bay
Torres Str.
AMBON
TIMOR
MELVILLE I.
DARWIN
AUSTRALIA
TOWNSVILLE
Coral Sea
ESPIRITU SANTO
NEW HEBRIDES
NEW CALEDONIA
NOUMEA
SANTA CRUZ IS.
FIJIS
SUVA
TONGATABU
WAKE
MARSHALL IS.
ENIWETOK
WOTJE
KWAJALEIN
MAKIN
TARAWA
GILBERT IS.
NAURU
OCEAN
ELLICE IS.
FUNAFUTI
CANTON
PHOENIX IS.
UNION IS.
SAMOA ISLANDS
TUTUILA
COOK IS.
BORA BORA
TAHITI
SOCIETY ISLANDS
MIDWAY
HAWAIIAN ISLANDS
KAUAI
OAHU
HONOLULU
PEARL HARBOR
MAUI
HAWAII
JOHNSTON
Pacific Ocean
PALMYRA
WASHINGTON
FANNING
CHRISTMAS
EQUATOR
Indian Ocean

over slow Allied progress in the Pacific. If this island-hopping continued at the same pace, and with comparable losses, American and Australian forces would not be within striking distance of Japan for eight or ten years, and would then be woefully short of manpower. But there was no cause for worry. The whole object of these preliminaries was to secure positions for major offensives. If the navy could win control of the sea as far as ground forces could be ferried, and if carrier- and land-based air power could project the offensive in giant raids hundreds of miles farther, and if United States submarines could continue their successful attrition of the enemy merchant marine, Japan could be approached in a series of bold leaps instead of a multitude of short hops. And that was how it happened.

In November 1943 began the first great Pacific offensive, the campaign to break the Bismarcks barrier by neutralizing Rabaul, a place much too strong for direct assault. This was effected by a close co-operation between Admiral Halsey's South Pacific and General MacArthur's Southwest Pacific commands. Bougainville, the northernmost and largest of the Solomons, was within fighter-plane distance of Rabaul.[7] Admiral Theodore S. Wilkinson, commanding the III Amphibious Force, selected a slice of sodden coast on Bougainville far from all major concentrations of Japanese troops, and made a perfect landing on 1 November. His first wave of marines hit the beach forty minutes after the ships anchored; 14,000 men and 6200 tons of supplies were placed ashore in eight hours; and within a few days the troops had established a defensive perimeter inside which the Seabees (naval construction battalions) began building fighter and bomber strips. The Japanese fleet based on Truk and Rabaul promptly came south in the hope of pulling another Savo Island, only to be decisively beaten (Battle of Empress Augusta Bay, 2 November 1943) by Admiral Merrill's cruisers. And when more Japanese cruisers were sent from Truk to Rabaul, Admiral Sherman ordered down three fast carriers whose planes put several of them out of business. Joined by the new carriers *Essex, Bunker Hill,* and *Independence,* he paid a return visit on 11 November. Thus the American air base in Bougainville could be developed with none of that constant attrition by the Japanese navy that had prolonged the

[7] It had been conclusively proved, in Europe as well as the Pacific, that bomber missions accompanied by fighter planes to protect them from enemy fighters were several times as effective as unescorted bomber missions, at a time when Flying Forts (B-17) and Liberators (B-24) were the biggest available bombers.

struggle for Guadalcanal; and the Seabees completed air strips in time to keep Rabaul constantly on the defensive. Enemy air forces, even after stripping carriers of their planes to defend the place, were gradually worn away; and by 25 March 1944, when Barbey's amphibious force had occupied the Admiralty Islands with their great Seeadler Harbor, and Wilkinson's had taken Green Island north and east of it, Rabaul was ringed around and neutralized. The Bismarcks' barrier to MacArthur's advance was completely beaten down.

At the end of the war no fewer than 125,000 Japanese troops surrendered in New Britain, New Ireland, and Bougainville. How fortunate that no attempt was made to conquer the whole of those islands or to take Rabaul by assault!

If any one factor won the Pacific war, it was mobility. After the fast carriers had struck Rabaul in early November, they rushed north to participate in the great Central Pacific offensive, the object of which was to clean up the two spiders' webs (Gilberts-Marshalls, Carolines) that constituted Micronesia and obtain air bases to pound down the Marshalls. In this central area Admiral Spruance, the victor of Midway, commanded the Fifth Fleet, which, like Halsey's Third Fleet, was under Nimitz at Pearl Harbor.

The Gilberts and Marshalls campaigns were the first full-scale amphibious operations in the Pacific. It is necessary to have been through one to appreciate the difficulties of planning and executing a great amphibious operation. It is no wonder that top air-force strategists now declare there will be no more of that kind — but everyone said the same after World War I. Preparations for a large amphibious operation never even approach perfection, because the units employed cannot be trained as a team; no one base is big enough to hold them all. A division, a corps, or even an army can be trained together for a land objective, as on the European fronts; a naval task force can be trained together for almost any operation that is likely to occur, and the commander can know his every ship and captain. An air squadron can be trained to bomb, scout, or cover, and the commander can acquaint himself with the capabilities of every type of plane and of almost every pilot. Contrast the situation of Admiral Turner, commanding V 'Phib. An operation requiring the most detailed planning and the nicest timing included men of the navy, army, and marine corps attached to ships, planes, and ground forces in points as far apart as San Diego, New Zealand,

Hawaii, and Alaska. It is as if a football coach were required to form an all-star team from colleges all over the country, brief them with a manual of plays, and, without a single line-up, play a championship game. To make the parallel complete, this All-American team would not even know on what field they were going to play. Security was so essential that those engaged in training the V 'Phib did not themselves know what islands they were going to assault until after the units were embarked.

Never before had there been such intensive activity at Pearl Harbor and at Efate, Espiritu Santo, and the Fijis as during the last days of October and the first of November 1943. Then, of a sudden, those harbors and roadsteads were deserted; for 200 sail of ships, the great Fifth Fleet carrying 108,000 soldiers, sailors, marines, and aviators under the command of taut Raymond Spruance, bristling Kelly Turner, and General 'Howling Mad' Smith, were on the high seas. By devious routes they were converging on two coral atolls whose names will be long remembered: Makin and Tarawa.

Makin, where the enemy was in no great strength, was taken methodically by a regiment of the 27th Infantry Division, but Tarawa was a very tough nut, a small, strongly defended position behind a long coral-reef apron. The lives of almost a thousand marines and sailors were required to dispose of 4000 no-surrender Japanese on an island not three miles long. But Tarawa provided another airfield and it taught invaluable lessons for future landings.

The Gilbert Islands promptly became bases from which planes helped to neutralize the seven Japanese air bases in the Marshalls. Finally these were sealed off by the fast carrier forces under Rear Admiral Mitscher and protected by a screen of fast new battleships, cruisers, and destroyers. These roved about the Marshalls, the battleships pounding and the aircraft bombing. Consequently, not one Japanese plane was available in the Marshalls on D-day, 31 January 1944. Massive amphibious forces under Admirals Hill and Turner, with close air support furnished by escort carriers and the pre-Pearl Harbor battleships and cruisers, covered the landings of army and marine-corps infantry at two ends of the great atoll of Kwajalein, and on 17 February 1944 another force moved into Eniwetok, westernmost of the Marshalls group and only a thousand miles from Guam. The Japanese troops, as usual, resisted to the last; but the preliminary air and naval bombardment had reduced them to a state of desperation, and the Marshalls not only cost much less in dead and wounded than tiny Tarawa, but were conquered without the loss of a single United States ship. The Japanese navy dared not challenge these operations because its own air arm had been sliced off to defend Rabaul; and on 20 February 1944 its capital ships and aircraft were chased out of the important naval base of Truk in the Carolines, with heavy loss, by a round-the-clock carrier raid. American naval aviators had now learned to bomb by night as well as by day, with radar ranges.

Mobile surface forces and mobile naval air power needed mobile logistics, and got them. Outstanding in the pattern for Pacific victory was the mobile supply base — Service Squadron 10, a logistic counterpart to the fast carrier forces. While the flattops carried the naval air arm to within striking distance of the enemy, 'Servron 10,' composed of tankers, ammunition ships, refrigerator ships, repair ships, fleet tugs, escort carriers with replacement planes, and several other types of auxiliaries, acted as a traveling annex to Pearl Harbor and San Francisco in order to provide the fleet at sea with food, fuel, bullets, spare parts, and spare planes. In other words, the United States Pacific Fleet at last had recovered that independence of bases which had been lost when sail gave way to steam.

While Spruance and Turner were crashing through the Gilberts and Marshalls, Kinkaid and Barbey were leaping along the New Guinea coast. On that big island, as soon as naval and air forces controlled its coasts, one could 'hit 'em where they ain't' — leapfrog the strongest Japanese positions, land where an airfield was lightly held or where one could be quickly built, keep the isolated Japanese garrison pounded down, and push on. The Admiralties were secured before the end of March, Hollandia and Aitape airfields by the end of April. Biak Island, poised like a fly over the neck of the New Guinea bird, came next (17 May 1944). Admiral Toyoda, now commander in chief of the Japanese fleet, planned to stop the Americans right there with his two super-battleships; but before he got around to it, a more dangerous American offensive engaged his attention, and the VII 'Phib was able to take Noemfoor, Cape Sansapor, and Morotai by 15 September. MacArthur's forces were now within bombing distance of the Philippines.

The offensive that engaged Toyoda's attention was directed against the Marianas, of which the principal islands were Saipan and Tinian, which Japan had acquired in World War I, and Guam, which she had wrested from a weak American garrison in December 1941. A glance at the map will show the importance of this group. Together with the Bonins, the Palaus, and the Philippines, the Marianas were Japan's inner line of defense, an important link in the 'pipeline' by which Japanese planes flowed south to the Carolines and New Guinea; once it was broken, enemy garrisons in the Carolines could be left to 'wither on the vine.' Saipan was within flying distance of southern Japan by the new B-29 bombers, and Guam would be a natural staging point for the Pacific fleet in its next advance, against the Philippines or the China coast. So, when the victorious team of Spruance, Turner, Mitscher, and Smith moved into Saipan on 15 June, Japan had to do something better than the last-ditch local resistance she had offered in the Marshalls. And her Combined Fleet, hampered during the past year by lack of air power, had by now replaced its air groups.

Admiral Kurita, with five battleships, eleven heavy cruisers, and three carriers, moved directly north from Halmahera to a point about 300 miles east of Samar, where he rendezvoused with Admiral Ozawa's six big carriers, which had steamed through San Bernardino Strait. The Spruance-Mitscher fleet (seven *Essex*-class and eight light carriers, seven battleships, three heavy and six light cruisers) moved out to meet the Japanese, preceded by a screen of Pacific-fleet submarines. Spruance played his usual cool game, taking risks boldly when they seemed commensurate with the damage he might inflict, yet never forgetting that his main duty was to protect the amphibious forces at Saipan. Hence he dared not move too far west, lest the Japanese make an 'end run' and burst in on Kelly Turner. Thus the enemy was enabled to take the initiative.

The Battle of the Philippine Sea broke at 10 a.m. 19 June 1944, when hundreds of Japanese planes were detected flying toward the American carriers, then about 100 miles northwest of Guam. The resulting clash proved that American carrier planes and pilots were now vastly superior to the Japanese in performance and in tactics. Hellcat fighters intercepted Japanese planes 50 to 60 miles out, only 40 of several hundred planes broke through, and the anti-aircraft fire of Spruance's ships was so accurate and deadly that these scored only two hits, on tough battleships that were little damaged. The Japanese also tried to fly planes into Guam in order to use the airfield there as a base next day; but few of them reached Guam whole. As a result of this day's fighting in the air, the Japanese lost over 345 planes at the cost of only 17 American aircraft.

At nightfall of 19 June Spruance took the offensive, turning west in search of the Japanese fleet, now weaker by two big carriers sunk by United States submarines, and by its plane losses. Not until the next afternoon did American search planes find the elusive enemy, 250 miles away. Spruance closed at top speed and launched at 4:00 p.m., too late for his planes to return by daylight. They had just an hour to attack the Japanese fleet — sinking a third carrier and destroying about 80 more planes —when the sun set, and they started back to their own carriers. Unused as the pilots were to night landings on carrier decks, the scene that night was pandemonium, with crashes, splashes, and attempted landings on all types of warships. Some 80 of the 216 returning planes were lost, but of their crews all but 38 men were recovered.

The Japanese fleet had had enough, and high-tailed it toward Okinawa. Spruance again pursued but, traditionally, 'a stern chase is a long chase.' No more contacts were made, and with fuel shortage threatening, he was compelled to call off the pursuit on the evening of 21 June. Thus the major part of the Japanese fleet escaped; but its carrier air groups were wiped out, this time for good and all. And Admiral 'Jock' Clark, who commanded one carrier group, paid two visits to Iwo and Chichi Jima, where planes were being ferried down to Guam, and destroyed about a hundred more.

Now the conquest of the Marianas could proceed without outside interference. American amphibious technique by this time was so good that the Japanese retired from their beaches at Saipan and took to the limestone hills, from which they directed a bitter last-ditch resistance, which took one army and two marine divisions three weeks of hard fighting to overcome. Finally, on 6 July, the Japanese general and his staff committed suicide, and the rest of his army jumped over the cliffs or holed up in caves. Turner's amphibious forces then proceeded to assault and capture Tinian and Guam, which were much less strongly held. By 1 August 1944 the three islands of the Marianas were in American possession. Airfield and harbor development went on briskly, Admiral Nimitz moved his headquarters to the hills above Agaña, and by fall Marianas-based B-29's were bombing southern Japan.

It had taken a good two years for American forces to get from Midway, Australia, and Guadalcanal to the Marianas and western New Guinea; but the end was now in sight. The loss of Saipan was the most discouraging blow the Japanese war lords had yet suffered, and the success of the Normandy operation and of the Russian summer offensive on the other side of the world indicated that their European partner could not hold out for many months. The more sagacious of the Japanese now knew they were beaten; but they dared not admit it, and nerved their people to another year of futile resistance in the vain hope that America might tire of the war when victory was within her grasp.

6. *Political Interlude*

While the Allied armies were fighting their way into position for the final drive on Germany and Japan, the American people were called upon to give their verdict on the conduct of the war and to choose their leaders for the trying period of peace and reconstruction that lay ahead. There were some who deplored the intrusion of politics into the stern realities of war, but the vast majority rejoiced in the opportunity to show that the democratic processes worked as well in war as in peace. It was a tribute to the effectiveness of democracy and to the good sense of the American people that the task of electing a President and a Congress did not distract Americans from the main business of fighting the war, and that, on the other hand, the impact of war did not seriously interfere with the efficient working of the political machinery.

Party lines had been blurred during the war, but not wholly obliterated. In 1864 northern Democrats not only had attacked the conduct of the war but had called for an early peace; in 1944 Republicans supported the war enthusiastically and endorsed a bipartisan foreign policy and a postwar international organization. In the domestic arena, however, they were as critical of President Roosevelt as ever. They had scored substantial gains in the 1942 Congressional elections, increasing their strength in the House from 162 to 208 and in the Senate from 28 to 37, and they faced the Presidential election with quiet confidence.

Yet their position was politically difficult, if not embarrassing. They could not safely criticize Roosevelt's conduct of the war — as the Democrats had been able to criticize Lincoln's — for that conduct had been masterly and had brought victory in sight. They could not fairly charge — as could be charged against Wilson in 1918 and 1920 — that Roosevelt had exploited the war for partisan purposes, for the Vice President, the Secretaries of War, Navy, and

Interior, and many of the leading figures in the administration were Republicans or ex-Republicans, and political considerations had at no time affected military appointments or decisions. They could not consistently criticize Democratic insistence upon retaining the essentials of the New Deal, for they had adopted the New Deal policies as their own in 1940 and were preparing to reaffirm them in the 1944 platform. They concentrated, therefore, on the argument that three terms were enough, that no party could safely be entrusted with office for more than twelve years without getting hardening of the political arteries, and that however competent Roosevelt might be as a war leader, younger and more vigorous leadership was needed for the tasks of peace and reconstruction; in short that Roosevelt and his lieutenants were tired old men who should be put out to pasture.

The criticism was pertinent. Roosevelt was, indeed, tired, as were most of those of both parties who had labored day and night for years to prepare the country for war, conduct the war, and lay the groundwork for peace; but the Republicans failed to realize that tiredness, in 1944, was a distinction rather than a reproach. And the argument that responsibility for building the new world order should be entrusted to the party that had defeated the League of Nations and for twenty years opposed effective international co-operation failed to carry conviction.

When the Republicans met at Chicago, it was to ratify a nomination that, in effect, had already been made. Since his defeat in 1940 Wendell Willkie had become not only a national but a world figure; his experience as unofficial ambassador abroad confirmed him in his internationalism. His effort to return the Republican party to the progressive and internationalist tradition of Theodore Roosevelt had won him the support of the rank and file, but not of the party leaders, many of whom he had flouted. His defeat in 1940 was, moreover, a heavy handicap; not since the Civil War had a defeated candidate subsequently won a Presidential election.[8] When he attempted to capture the Republican primaries in Wisconsin in April 1944, he met with a stunning setback, and withdrew from the race. Easily the most prominent of his rivals was Thomas E. Dewey, who in 1942 had performed the seeming miracle of winning the governorship of New York State — the first Republican to ac-

[8] Cleveland is not an exception to this generalization. He had been elected in 1884 and had won a plurality of the popular vote again in 1888.

complish this since 1918. In two years Dewey had proved himself a popular leader and a competent administrator. Mildly liberal on domestic issues, open-minded on foreign, he was acceptable at once to the business community and to the farmers, and his qualities as a vote-getter assured him the support of the party bosses. All through the spring of 1944 he was busy capturing state delegations, and when the Republican convention met in Chicago, it nominated him on the first ballot. Second place on the ticket went to Governor John Bricker, whose chief claims to consideration were that he came from the politically doubtful state of Ohio,[9] and that his clear-cut conservatism furnished a neat balance to Dewey's ambiguous liberalism. The Republican platform criticized the techniques rather than the substance of the New Deal, promised to take the government out of business and to 're-establish' liberty at home, and reaffirmed the Mackinac Resolution of 1943, which had pledged the party to support a postwar international organization.

There is no evidence that Roosevelt wanted a fourth term and some that he did not. It was a fair criticism that, unlike Jefferson, Jackson, and Theodore Roosevelt, he had failed to train a successor, yet a consideration of the Presidential careers of Madison, Van Buren, and Taft gave no assurance that hand-picked successors succeeded to anything but trouble. Rightly or wrongly Roosevelt had come to think himself the best leader for war and for reconstruction. As his wife recalled, 'I knew without asking that as long as the war was on it was a foregone conclusion that Franklin, if he was well enough, would run again.'

The Democratic party shared this conviction. The convention renominated Roosevelt on the first ballot: the opposition was fairly represented by the vote of 1066 for the President, 89 for Senator Byrd of Virginia, and 1 for James Farley. The real battle came over the Vice Presidency. Henry Wallace had incurred the hostility of the southern Bourbons and the city machines, and the distrust of a good many of the rank and file of the party who felt that he lacked the stability and judgment necessary to the Presidency. Other candidates were Byrnes of South Carolina, of whom the CIO disapproved, William Douglas of the Supreme Court, and Senator Harry Truman of Missouri. Of these Truman was politically the most available. Missouri could be claimed by either North, South,

[9] Roosevelt carried Ohio in 1940, as Truman did in 1948, but the Dewey-Bricker ticket won in 1944.

or Middle West, and Truman was equally acceptable to all sections. Politicians noted that he had worked with the notorious Prendergast machine, liberals rejoiced that he had not been tarred by its corruption. His wartime record as head of the Senate Committee investigating national defense commended him to all who wanted a vigorous administrator; his World War I record made him acceptable to veterans; farmers trusted him and labor did not object to him. When Roosevelt let it be known that he would welcome either Truman or Douglas as his running mate, Truman was nominated on the second ballot.

The campaign that followed was characterized by heat rather than light. Dewey rang the changes on the 'tired old men' and the 'time for a change' themes; Roosevelt reminded the nation of the Republican record of hostility to progressivism, internationalism, and preparation for war, and asked for a vote of confidence. Two facets of the campaign were of more than passing interest. The first was the arrangements made for enabling members of the armed forces to vote; some 25 per cent of those otherwise qualified managed to comply with the complex requirements fixed by state and federal governments and send in their ballots.[10] The second was the formal entry of organized labor into the arena of politics through the Political Action Committee of the CIO, which enthusiastically and effectively supported the President. Dewey had to be content with the dubious boon of support by John L. Lewis.

The election showed that the country was, on the whole, content with Roosevelt's leadership and did not wish to 'change horses in mid-stream.' The President carried 36 states with 432 electoral votes; Dewey 12 states with 99 electoral votes; Roosevelt's popular plurality was about three and a half million. In view of the number of servicemen deprived of their vote by the failure of states to act in time, or by circumstances, and of the number of workingmen who lost their vote through change of residence, the result was roughly comparable to that of 1940 and showed that neither the President nor his party had lost strength. This conclusion was borne out by the fact that the Democrats increased their membership in the House to 242 while Republican strength dropped to 190. To those concerned for the ability of America to assume her responsibilities in the postwar world, the most heartening feature of the election was

10 The grand total of military votes cast, through both federal and state absentee ballots, was 2,691,160.

the defeat of such unregenerate isolationists as Hamilton Fish of New York, Gerald Nye of North Dakota, and Bennett Clark of Missouri.

The moral of the election was stated by President Roosevelt in his Inaugural Address of January 1945:

> We have learned that we cannot live alone, at peace; that our own well-being is dependent upon the well-being of other nations far away. We have learned that we must live as men and not as ostriches, nor as dogs in the manger. We have learned to be citizens of the world, members of the human community. . . We can gain no lasting peace if we approach it with suspicion and mistrust, — or with fear. We can gain it only if we proceed with the understanding and the confidence and the courage which flow from conviction.

7. *Götterdämmerung*

The Ardennes counteroffensive had delayed the Allied advance by fully a month; not until the end of January was Eisenhower able to regroup his armies and resume his advance toward the Rhine. Meantime the Russians had sprung their great winter offensive, which in numbers involved and territory recaptured dwarfed the fighting in the West. The Russian offensive jumped off on a thousand-mile front early in January 1945, crossed the Vistula, and swept toward Germany. While one group of armies in the center took Warsaw and raced across Poland to the Oder river, only fifty miles from Berlin, other prongs stabbed into Germany from the north and the south. One spearhead drove along the Baltic, overran East Prussia, and reached the Oder at Stettin; another struck from the south, captured Cracow, swarmed across the Oder and into the great industrial area of Silesia. Farther south, still other Russian armies moved into Hungary and Czechoslovakia and threatened Vienna. This gigantic pincer movement took a toll of over a million German casualties and inflicted incalculable damage on the German air force, armor, and war industry.

We can distinguish three stages — each one a confused series of battles — in the final Allied campaign in the West: the advance to the Rhine, from late January to 21 March; the crossing of the Rhine and the battle of the Ruhr, 21 March to 14 April; and the annihilation of all enemy opposition, 14 April to the surrender, 7 May.

First came a series of systematic mopping-up operations designed to clear the Germans out of all the territory west of the Rhine. The Canadian First Army launched an attack in the north and reached the Rhine at Cleve, near hard-fought Arnhem. The American First and Ninth Armies reduced the Roermont triangle, fought through the rest of the Hürtgen Forest, and, under cover of the heaviest aerial offensive since D-day, crossed the Roer river and plunged on toward Cologne. Patton's Third Army, wheeling to the right again after the Ardennes battle, fought its way through the Siegfried Line into Trier, and farther to the south the French First Army cleared out the Colmar pocket. 'The attacks we are seeing now should mark the beginning of the destruction of the German forces west of the Rhine,' said Eisenhower; this was an understatement. By the first week of March the Allied armies stood on the left bank of the Rhine almost everywhere from Holland to Switzerland except in the great triangle formed by the Eifel and the Palatinate.

This triangle did not remain long in German hands. Early in March Patton broke loose again and drove forward in a great sweeping advance like the one that followed the breakthrough at Saint-Lô. Within five days he reached the Rhine, then wheeled south and raced through the Palatinate, mopping up over 60,000 prisoners at a cost of less than 800 men killed. 'No defeat suffered in the war, except possibly Tunisia,' wrote Eisenhower, 'was more devastating in the completeness of the destruction inflicted upon his forces.'

The 7th of March was one of the dramatic days of the war. On that day the ruins of two once great cities, Cologne and Düsseldorf, fell to the Allies. And on that day, too, came what Eisenhower called 'one of those rare and fleeting opportunities which occasionally occur in war and which, if grasped, have incalculable effects in determining future success.' Retreating across the Rhine, the Germans had destroyed or arranged for the destruction of all the bridges that spanned that wide and dangerous stream. But at one crucial point the watch on the Rhine had failed. Driving south from Bonn, the ancient University city on which Beethoven had conferred immortality, a detachment of the 9th Armored Division of the First Army sighted the Ludendorff railroad bridge at Remagen, still intact. Colonel Engemann turned his tanks off the road and raced for the bridge, reaching it just as the first demolition charge went off. It did little damage, and before the bewildered Germans could repair defective fuses on the other charges, the Americans controlled both approaches to the bridge. Eisenhower had not planned a crossing here, but he hastened to capitalize on his good luck, ordering Bradley to throw five divisions across the river and try for a major breakthrough. Once across the Rhine, the First Army fanned out, securing the highway running south to Munich and threatening to drive north toward the Ruhr. As the Germans hurried up reinforcements to plug the gap in their line, they weakened their defenses elsewhere.

By now plans had been perfected for a large-scale crossing of the Rhine, an operation comparable in magnitude to the landings on Algiers and Sicily. It came on 23 March, and in such force that the Germans, their resistance weakened by the withdrawal of 15 divisions to the eastern front and by incessant bombing, were everywhere overwhelmed. Accompanied by a gigantic airborne operation, the British, Canadians, and Americans swarmed across the Rhine near Wessel, with Churchill looking on, puffing his inevitable cigar. Within twenty-four hours the Allies had established a firm bridgehead on the right bank and were rolling toward the Ruhr. Farther south, Hodges broke out of the Remagen bridgehead and headed toward the Ruhr, Patton crossed above Mainz and struck for Frankfurt, which fell on 26 March, and the armies of General Devers hurdled the Rhine near Mannheim and drove through Württemberg toward Bavaria. Within a week, General Eisenhower reported,

> the Rhine barrier, the greatest natural obstacle with which the Allied armies had been faced since the landings in France, had been breached all along the line; and the cost to our forces had been fantastically small. The enemy had committed the same error as in Normandy, and with the same fatal results. . . Instead of carrying out a planned withdrawal to the strong defensive positions afforded by the great river . . . he had chosen to stand and fight a hopeless battle in front of the Rhine. The result was that he was then too weak, when the withdrawal was eventually forced upon him, to hold the line which nature had offered him.

The next move, after vaulting the Rhine barrier, was the encirclement of the Ruhr, one of the greatest strategical operations of the war. Moving at breakneck speed — the 3d Armored Division covered 90 miles in a single day — Hodges' First Army swung north, Simpson's Ninth Army turned south, and a giant pincers closed on the Ruhr, trapping some 400,000 Germans. Encircled, pounded on all sides, hammered day and night by swarms of bombers, General von Model's armies disintegrated. In a period of two weeks the Ruhr pocket was compressed, then split in two, and each half systematically ground to pieces. By 18 April the bag of prisoners reached the staggering total of 325,000, and organized resistance ceased. It was, said General Marshall, the largest envelopment in the history of warfare; certainly it was the most one-sided victory in the history of American warfare. And while Simpson and Hodges were taking over the Ruhr, Montgomery drove relentlessly on Bremen and Hamburg, Patton raced for Kassel, and Patch sped through Bavaria toward Czechoslovakia.

As the Allied armies drove deep into Germany, they came upon one torture camp after another — Buchenwald, Dachau, Belsen, Auschwitz — and what they reported sickened the whole Western World. The atrocity stories of World War I had been, for the most part, concoctions of propaganda; the atrocity stories of World War II confounded the imagination of even the propagandists. These atrocity camps had been established in 1937 for Jews and anti-Nazi Germans and Austrians; with the coming of the war the Nazis used them for prisoners of all nationalities, civilians and soldiers, men, women, and children. In these camps, and in those of eastern Germany and Poland like Lublin, hundreds of thousands of prisoners had been scientifically murdered; other hundreds of thousands had died of disease, starvation, and mistreatment. Over 35,000 prisoners had been murdered in Buchenwald; the Oxfordshire Yeomanry found over 35,000 corpses when they captured Belsen. Much of this wholesale murder was done in the name of 'science' — thus prisoners were injected with typhus to provide typhus serum for Germans; all of it reflected the Nazi philosophy of contempt for human life and human dignity. Nothing in their experience had prepared Americans for these revelations of human depravity, and many were incredulous. But the evidence submitted to the Nuremberg War Trials Tribunal was conclusive and provided the basis for designating genocide as a crime in international law.

As German resistance crumbled everywhere, and the victory of Allied arms appeared certain, the civilized world was plunged into mourning by the news that its greatest leader was dead. President Roosevelt had returned from the Crimea Conference of February 1945 a sick man; after addressing Congress on the results of the Conference, he had gone to his winter home in Warm Springs,

Georgia, to prepare for the inauguration of the United Nations at San Francisco, which he fondly hoped would usher in a new era of peace. On 1 April, as he was drafting a Jefferson Day address, he suffered a 'massive cerebral hemorrhage,' which brought death. The last words he wrote were an epitome of his whole life: 'The only limit to our realization of tomorrow will be our doubts of today. Let us move forward with strong and active faith.'

By now the end was in sight. The western Allies were racing, unopposed, to the Elbe; the Russians were pounding on the gates of Berlin. On 25 April advance detachments of the two armies met at Torgau, on the Elbe, and Germany was completely severed. By the end of April Berlin was surrounded and in flames; on 2 May it surrendered. German resistance in northern Italy was collapsing as well. During April the Allies fought through the Gothic Line and out onto the Po valley; Bologna, Verona, Genoa, and Milan fell almost without an effort. On 3 May the Fifth Army made contact with the American Seventh, coming down through Austria, and on the next day German resistance in Italy ceased. On 28 April Italian partisans had captured the tyrant Mussolini and killed him; three days later came the news that Hitler had committed suicide in his bombproof shelter under Berlin. Thus ended, in ruin, horror, and despair, that Reich which was to have lived for a thousand years.

Now the Germans were trying desperately to surrender to the western Allies. A last-minute effort by Admiral Friedeburg to make a separate surrender to Montgomery of Germans who had been fighting the Russians was rejected. On 7 May General Jodl signed an unconditional surrender at Allied headquarters in Rheims, and the war in the West came to an end.

8. *Victory against Japan*

By 1 August 1944, when the three largest Marianas and the entire northern coast of New Guinea were in American hands, the question 'Where do we go from here?' became acute. All previous plans for defeating Japan had counted on establishing a great Allied base somewhere on the coast of China as the springboard for invading Japan, as Great Britain had been a springboard for invading Germany. But the situation in East Asia was very different from that in northern Europe, because Japan was not only a great military power but also a great sea power. The Japanese army and navy had sealed off China from her allies, except for the air route from India over the Himalaya 'Hump,' and that was good for a mere trickle of only 10,000 tons of supplies monthly.[11] Most of it, in fact, was needed to support the American air force in China under General Chennault; and Chennault's planes had neither the range to bomb Japan nor the technical skill to hit enemy convoys on China seas. Accordingly, at the Cairo conference of November 1943, Roosevelt, Churchill, and Chiang Kai-Shek agreed that all three Allies should attempt to drive the Japanese from northern Burma in order to reopen surface communications with China.

Burma was considered by most strategists the key to victory in Asia, but it was a key the Allies were unable to use. Striking through Thailand, the Japanese had overrun Burma early in the war, thus cutting off access to China from the south and threatening India on the east. In 1943 the famous Wingate's Raiders had harried the Japanese in the jungles of northern Burma, and their success encouraged the Combined Chiefs of Staff to plan a large-scale invasion from the north the following spring. The purpose of this campaign was to clear the Ledo Road leading from Assam province in India, and link up with the Burma Road leading to Kunming in China.

Geography, weather, and logistics prevented the consummation of this plan. Burma was at the end of a long supply line. From Calcutta, where American troops unloaded Liberty ships in conditions of heat, humidity, and disease that were paralleled only at the Persian Gulf railheads, a railroad ran to Ledo. Here the Himalayan foothills are steep, knife-edged, covered with disease-infected jungle, and impassable in the rainy season. General 'Vinegar Joe' Stilwell, commanding all Allied forces in the Burma-India theater under Chiang Kai-Shek, won his reluctant consent to train and rearm a few Chinese divisions, but the 'Gimo' was mainly interested in consolidating his own inefficient and corrupt regime. In the spring of 1944, as Wingate's Raiders and Merrill's Marauders were flown into the jungles of northern Burma to co-operate with these Chinese troops in protecting the slowly advancing Ledo Road, the Japanese struck across the Indian border for Imphal, threatening to cut the railroad linking Calcutta with Assam. Neither offensive was particularly successful. The Allies captured Myitkyina airfield in May but could not advance from there; the Japanese advance was contained and then repulsed. That fall Anglo-Chinese-American forces

11 By 1945 this had been increased to 46,000 tons monthly.

were preparing to advance on Bhamba, at the juncture of the Ledo and the Burma roads.

This Burma campaign was probably prophetic of the war of the future, because air power vanquished every terrestrial obstacle. At one time there were 100,000 Allied troops in Burma dependent entirely for food, bullets, and supplies on what could be flown in; and most of the troops, too, came by air. But the potentially strongest element on the Allied side, China, was actually the weakest. The Japanese, in April 1944, launched an offensive in Honan to pinch off the salient still in the hands of Chinese Nationalists between the Yellow and Yangtze rivers. Within a month they had secured a rail line between North and South China, and then continued on south from Tung-ting Lake, co-ordinating this drive with a northward one from Canton. These salients converged in September 1944 on Kweilin, the main American air base in South China, and during that fall overran seven of the principal airdromes from which Chennault's XIV Army Air Force had been operating. Since Chiang Kai-Shek either could or would do nothing to stop this offensive, and since Stilwell could not persuade him otherwise, that gallant if tactless general was relieved, and the Chinese front disintegrated.

It was fairly clear, then, by August 1944, that the Allies could not afford to wait for the capture of the Burmese key, and must get on with the war without using China as an ally, or even as a base. How then could they get at Japan? There were two schools of thought about this. The Pearl Harbor plan was to make a two-pronged advance from the new bases in the Marianas: the first, an aerial bombing ascent 'up the ladder' of the Bonin Islands, over Iwo and Chichi Jima; the second, an amphibious operation against Formosa, as a good substitute springboard for China, while MacArthur captured Mindanao. Luzon and the Visayas (the central Philippine Islands) would according to this plan be by-passed. General MacArthur, on the contrary, believed that the best road to Tokyo led through Manila, and that the Philippines, with 16 million people loyal to the Allies, could be wrested from Japan more easily than Formosa, and would be a better springboard for the final assault.

In July 1944 MacArthur flew to Pearl Harbor to meet President Roosevelt; and on the deck of U.S.S. *Baltimore* the following dialogue took place:

'Douglas, where do we go from here?'

'Leyte, Mr. President; and then Luzon!'

Admiral Nimitz agreed, and planning began for the great Philippine campaign.

Planning was complicated, but the timetable was stepped up two months as the result of a series of raids by the fast carrier forces under Admiral Mitscher. In a series of strikes on Japanese airfields in Mindanao and the Visayas, Task Force 38 [12] destroyed so many hundred enemy planes, and reduced the Japanese air force to so weak a state, that Halsey proposed to by-pass some of the small islands that were to have been seized as advance bases, and to skip even great Mindanao, and strike for Leyte.[13] It so happened that the Combined Chiefs of Staff were then meeting at Quebec with Roosevelt, Churchill, and Mackenzie King. It took them exactly one hour and a half after the signals from Nimitz and MacArthur had been received to give them both orders to invade Leyte on 20 October instead of 20 December. This was the quickest strategic decision of the war, and one of the most fortunate, for by December the Japanese would have had four big new carriers in commission.

Thus the success of fast carriers in raiding the Philippines had opened a new vista to victory. Naval strategists early in the war held that carriers could not venture safely within range of land-based planes. But here the big flattops steamed with impunity within sight of the Philippine mountains, protected from air and submarine attack by their own defensive screens and weapons, while their planes slashed at enemy airfields, planes, and installations.

So radical a change of plan, with only a month to prepare, meant extraordinary efforts and amazing improvisations; but they were made, and MacArthur was enabled to land some 145,000 troops on Leyte in the first five days, 30 per cent more than he had commanded in the entire Philippines at the start of the war.

While the amphibious forces were marshaling at the Admiralties and Hollandia, and slowly approaching their target, the fast carrier forces — four groups under Mitscher comprising 8 of the *Essex*

12 Called TF 58 when Spruance, who alternated with Halsey, was in command; the ships and subordinate commanders were the same in both, except that new ships were constantly being added.

13 The Joint Chiefs, however, felt they could not give up the seizure of Pelleliu and Angaur in the Palau group, 600 miles east of the Philippines, which was ready to start in a couple of days. The 1st Marine Division, now reinforced to 28,000 men, and 20,000 men of the 81st Infantry went in here, with suitable air and naval bombardment, on 15–17 September 1944. It took them two months to exterminate the holed-up Japanese garrison of half their numbers, but within a month a heavy bomber strip was operative, and the Kossol roadstead proved a valuable anchorage for the fleet.

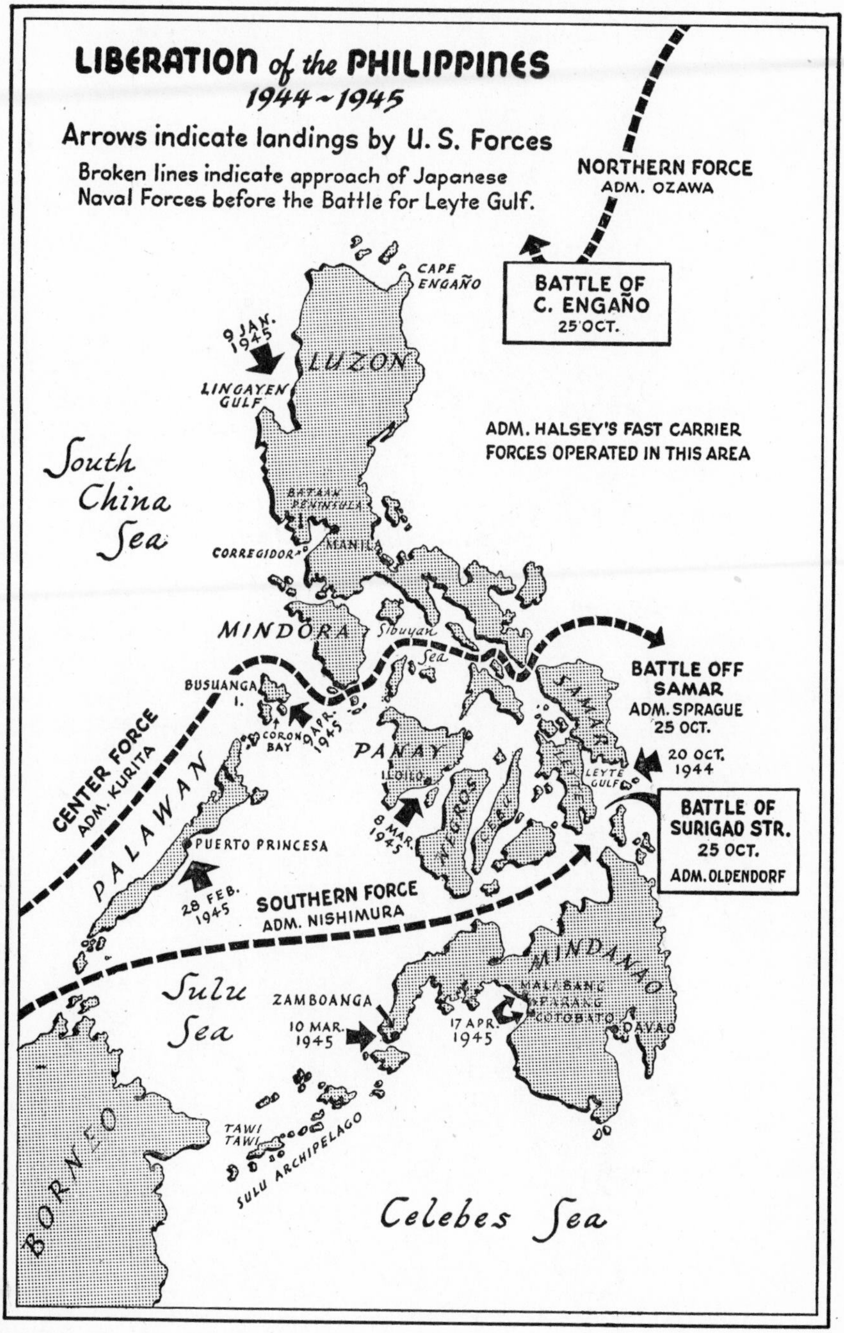

LIBERATION of the PHILIPPINES
1944–1945
Arrows indicate landings by U. S. Forces
Broken lines indicate approach of Japanese Naval Forces before the Battle for Leyte Gulf.
NORTHERN FORCE
ADM. OZAWA
CAPE ENGAÑO
BATTLE OF C. ENGAÑO
25 OCT.
9 JAN. 1945
LUZON
LINGAYEN GULF
ADM. HALSEY'S FAST CARRIER FORCES OPERATED IN THIS AREA
South China Sea
BATAAN PENINSULA
MANILA
CORREGIDOR
MINDORA
Sibuyan Sea
BATTLE OFF SAMAR
ADM. SPRAGUE
25 OCT.
BUSUANGA I.
CORON BAY
9 APR. 1945
SAMAR
PANAY
ILOILO
LEYTE
LEYTE GULF
20 OCT. 1944
CENTER FORCE
ADM. KURITA
PALAWAN
NEGROS
CEBU
8 MAR. 1945
BATTLE OF SURIGAO STR.
25 OCT.
ADM. OLDENDORF
PUERTO PRINCESA
28 FEB. 1945
SOUTHERN FORCE
ADM. NISHIMURA
MINDANAO
Sulu Sea
ZAMBOANGA
10 MAR. 1945
17 APR. 1945
COTOBATO
DAVAO
TAWI TAWI
SULU ARCHIPELAGO
BORNEO
Celebes Sea

class and the veteran *Enterprise,* 8 light carriers, 6 battleships, 14 cruisers, and 58 destroyers — rendezvoused in the Philippine Sea on 7 October, a clearing day of high, breaking seas, and then embarked on their preliminary raids. In the Ryukyus, 1200 miles from the outer base of Saipan, they cleaned up the airfields and war shipping. It was then the turn of Formosa, the biggest enemy air base outside Japan. Mitscher's Hellcats battled shore-based planes in the air while his bombers pounded installations ashore, for four days, during which Task Force 38 inflicted damage on the Imperial Japanese Air Force from which it never fully recovered, destroying over 800 planes. Meantime General Kenney's Far Eastern Air Force punished Mindanao, and Mitscher found time to pound Luzon before the invasion of Leyte started, with a minimum of interference from the air. American losses all told were less than 50 planes and two cruisers damaged. None of the supposedly vulnerable carriers was touched, although the Japanese claimed over the radio to have sunk them all — to which Halsey retorted in a dispatch to Nimitz, 'Ships reported sunk by Tokyo have been salvaged and are now retiring toward the enemy.'

Early in the morning of 20 October 1944, MacArthur's massive expeditionary force in 86 transports and 161 LSTs, covered by a dozen battleships and cruisers and a flock of escort carriers, destroyers, and smaller craft, entered Leyte Gulf — in the wake of Magellan 423 years before. The landings on Leyte were well managed by Admirals Barbey and Wilkinson, and a 20-mile-long beachhead was promptly secured. That afternoon General MacArthur and President Osmeña splashed ashore from a landing barge. Approaching a microphone, MacArthur delivered his impressive liberation speech beginning, 'People of the Philippines, I have returned.'

He certainly had, and in force; but could he stay? The Japanese were not taking this lying down. Here, decided the war lords, was the time to throw in the entire Japanese fleet, hoping that it might defeat the American forces afloat and isolate MacArthur so that his army would be back in a position similar to that of Bataan. From this decision there resulted, on 23, 24, and 25 October, the Battle for Leyte Gulf, the greatest sea fight of this or of any other war.

Admiral Toyoda, Commander in Chief of the Japanese navy, had all ready a plan to blast the United States navy out of Philippine waters; now he put it in execution. Most of his fleet at that time was based on Singapore, to be near its fuel-oil supply. As he knew his fleet was inferior to the United States Third and Seventh Fleets in every type except battleships, and as Mitscher had robbed him of most of his land-based air support, Toyoda's plan was based on ruse and surprise, factors dear to the Japanese strategists. Admiral Nishimura's southern force of battleships and cruisers was to come through Surigao Strait, break into Leyte Gulf at daylight 25 October, and there rendezvous with Kurita's powerful center force, which was to thread San Bernardino Strait and come around Samar from the north. Either separately was strong enough, once in the gulf, to make mincemeat of MacArthur's amphibious forces and cut off his troops from their lifeline. Way was to be cleared for Kurita by Admiral Ozawa's northern force of four carriers, whose mission was to entice the Halsey-Mitscher Task Force 38 up north. That was the only part of the plan that worked.

The rest of it worked very ill. Search planes tracked down the southern force in time for Admiral Oldendorf to deploy every battleship, cruiser, and destroyer that had supported the Leyte landings, and catch Nishimura as he came through Surigao Strait in the early hours of 25 October. First a flock of motor torpedo boats fired their 'fish'—and missed—but sent word ahead. Then, two destroyer torpedo attacks nicked Nishimura of one battleship and three destroyers. What was then left of his 'T' was crossed by Oldendorf's battleships and cruisers. This superb night victory was the battlewagons' revenge for Pearl Harbor—five of the six now engaged had been sunk on 7 December 1941. Their high-caliber fire sank the other enemy battleship and killed Admiral Nishimura, and what was left of his force limped away, to be harried and sunk after dawn by carrier planes.

Scarcely was this fight won when the Battle of Samar, the most critical action of all, began. Kurita was late for the rendezvous because his massive center force, built around five battleships and ten heavy cruisers, had been mauled and delayed en route, first by two American submarines, then by planes from Task Force 38 in the Sibuyan Sea. They sent the 18-inch-gunned *Mushashi* to the bottom with 26 aerial-torpedo and 30 bomb hits, and damaged other ships as well. The few land-based Japanese planes that counterattacked managed to sink the carrier *Princeton*. Halsey, however, did not wait to see whether Kurita would press through San Bernardino Strait with the rest of the force, because in the meantime his search planes found Admiral Ozawa's northern force coming down outside, with the express mission of luring him away. Without leaving even a destroyer to watch the strait, Halsey tore up north to dispose of the enemy flattops. And he failed to let MacArthur's command know what he was about.

Thus, Kurita, to his great astonishment, was able to thread the strait unopposed, and approach the northern entrance to Leyte Gulf undetected. It was one of the critical moments of the war. There, off the island of Samar, he encountered a force of six escort carriers under Admiral Sprague, one of three groups of the 'jeep' flattops that were providing air patrol for the amphibious craft in Leyte Gulf and close support for MacArthur's troops ashore. The ensuing Battle of Samar was the most gallant naval action of the war. Kurita, who still had the *Yamato* and 3 other battleships, 8 cruisers, and 10 destroyers, the slowest of which was capable of 24½ knots, should have been able to catch and destroy Sprague's escort carriers, none of which had a gun bigger than a 5-inch or was capable of higher speed than 17½ knots. But as soon as Kurita opened fire with his big guns from a distance of 14 miles, Sprague turned into the wind to launch planes, called for help from his sister 'jeeps,' and sent his three destroyers and destroyer escorts on repeated gunfire and torpedo attacks. One of his flattops, two destroyers, and a destroyer escort were sunk, but after a running fight of an hour and a half, he picked off two of Kurita's heavy cruisers and so badly mauled and slowed up his other ships by repeated air attack that the Japanese admiral broke off action and withdrew the rest of his force through Surigao Strait.

In the meantime, Halsey's and Mitscher's carrier planes, in the Battle of Cape Engaño up north, sank all three Japanese carriers (including the last of the six that had struck Pearl Harbor) and a few other ships as well.

The Battle for Leyte Gulf was decisive. It left the United States navy in complete command of Philippine waters; never again could the Japanese navy offer a threat. But there was much to do before the stubborn, hard-fighting Japanese infantrymen or the Japanese air force, which had now adopted a tactic of desperation, the *kamikaze* or suicide crash, could be overcome. During all these operations the Filipino guerrillas and civilians gave American troops valuable support; the much touted puppet republic under Laurel found no defenders except Japanese.

Landings were made on the backside of Leyte, and that island

and Samar were in MacArthur's hands by Christmas. The next big landing, at Lingayen Bay in northern Luzon, opened the way to Manila. Additional troops stormed ashore at Subic Bay and elsewhere; paratroops helped the infantry take Corregidor; and Manila fell on 23 February 1945. Already Admiral Barbey had organized a mobile amphibious force, which wrested the Visayas and Mindanao from the enemy by April so that, four months before the end of the war, the Philippines, fully liberated, were once more under their own commonwealth government. Immediately after the victory, the United States relinquished all control; but the Philippine Republic was not formally inaugurated until 4 July 1946.

Over a month before the landings at Leyte, the Joint Chiefs of Staff had decided that as soon as the Third Fleet could be relieved from supporting MacArthur in the Philippines, it should be used without delay to secure island bases for a final assault on Japan. On the map it will be observed that Tokyo, Saipan, and Formosa make an isosceles triangle with legs 1500 miles long. The eastern leg, Saipan–Tokyo, was already being used by the B-29 Superforts, but a halfway house was wanted through which they could stage for fuel or come down if damaged. Iwo Jima just fitted the bill. After a two weeks' preliminary bombardment, a three-day intensive naval and carrier-plane bombardment drove the Japanese from the landing beaches, and the old Fifth Fleet team went in on 19 February 1945. Mount Surabachi, scene of the famous flag-raising, was captured on 23 February; and after that it was a steady, bloody advance of the marines against the holed-up enemy, with constant fire support by the navy. Even before organized resistance ceased, on 14 March, the B-29's began using the Iwo airfields; and it is estimated that by this means more American lives were saved than the nearly 5000 men which the capture of the island cost.

In the meantime the other angle of the triangle, whose apex was Tokyo, had been shifted to Okinawa in the Ryukyus, as several hundred miles nearer Kyushu than Formosa is, equally valuable to mount a great air and amphibious assault, and less stoutly defended. Okinawa — known as the 'Great Loo-choo' when Commodore Perry called in 1853 — 60 miles long and 3 to 15 miles wide, was an integral part of Japan. It was expected that when we went in there, the Japanese would 'throw the book at us,' and they did. They had few surface ships left, but they had plenty of planes and there was no defense against the deadly *kamikaze* tactics. Again the same

Spruance-Turner team was in charge of the amphibious assault, with General Simon B. Buckner, U.S.A. (who lost his life there), in command of the ground troops. And, as the war in Europe was drawing to a close, the British contributed a task force built around four carriers with steel decks — useful insurance against *kamikaze*-kindled fires — which neutralized the islands between Okinawa and Formosa.

American amphibious technique was now so perfected that when, with the aid of a six-day preliminary naval bombardment, the four divisions went ashore on Okinawa on 1 April, the Japanese abandoned beaches and airfields and retired to prepared positions on the southern end of the island. Here they put up a desperate resistance, exacting a heavy toll of American lives, before the island was finally conquered late in June. In the meantime the navy, which had to cover the operation and furnish fire support, took a terrible beating from the *kamikaze* planes. Thirty-six ships, 17 of them destroyers, were sunk, and 158 were badly damaged; the United States lost 938 planes in the operation; the Japanese over 3800. Task Force 58, besides supporting this operation, made carrier-plane raids on Tokyo and on Kyushu airfields, and when the battleship *Yamato* sortied in early April, she was promptly sunk by air attack. Six carriers were badly damaged by *kamikazes* — but none was sunk.

Germany was now defeated and the Allies could give their undivided attention to knocking out Japan. A new Burma offensive, launched from the sea, captured Mandalay and Rangoon in the spring of 1945 and soon pushed the Japanese entirely out of Burma. While in great secrecy scientists were preparing the atomic bombs at Los Alamos, the navy and the army air force redoubled the fury of their attacks on the Japanese home island; the one by carrier-plane bombings, in-shore bombardments, and submarines cutting Japanese traffic with the mainland, the other by B-29 bombings from Saipan and Iwo. Large parts of Tokyo and other industrial cities were destroyed by incendiary raids; the rest of the Japanese navy was sunk in the inland sea.

On 26 July the Allied war leaders, meeting at Potsdam, presented Japan with an ultimatum. 'The alternative to surrender,' they said, 'is prompt and utter destruction.' Although the Japanese had already made peace overtures through Russia, they publicly announced that they would ignore the Potsdam ultimatum. Therefore on 6 August a lone B-29 dropped the first atomic bomb on Hiroshima, and on the 9th — the day after Russia finally declared war on Japan — a second atom bomb devastated Nagasaki.

Was this use of the deadliest weapon ever invented necessary, or even politic? Did the immediate advantages outweigh the long-range disadvantages? Were the military considerations of primary importance and the moral secondary? Could the Japanese government have been induced to surrender without its use? We may never know; the Japanese themselves can give no clear answer even to this last question. Joseph Grew, the former ambassador to Japan, believes that if an unequivocal declaration had been made in June 1945 that the unconditional surrender of Japan would not involve sacrificing their 'divine' Emperor, the Shimada government would have surrendered. Yet, even after two atomic bombs were dropped, strong elements in the Japanese army still resisted surrender, arguing that the United States could have only a few of the bombs, that she would not dare use them when about to invade, and that there was still plenty of food, bullets, and planes to sell Japan dear. It took all the Emperor's prestige to enforce the surrender, which was practically decided on at the cease-fire agreement on 15 August.

Be that as it may, the Pacific fleet entered Tokyo Bay on 27 August and took over the Yokosuka naval base; and on 2 September 1945 the Japanese foreign minister signed the surrender documents on the deck of the battleship *Missouri,* a few miles from the spot where Perry's treaty had been signed 82 years before. Thus, after 1351 days of war, the most powerful military empire of modern times, not excepting the German, was completely liquidated by armed forces of the nation that had been surprised at Pearl Harbor.

And thus came to an end after six years the greatest and most terrible war in history. Precipitated by the wickedness of ambitious men, it had convulsed the whole globe, consumed the wealth piled up by generations of men, exacted the lives of twenty million soldiers and civilians, and left in its train starvation, misery, and chaos. And the vision of the Apocalypse seemed to be realized by that generation which had thought itself the most civilized, as power was given unto the white horse and the red horse and the black horse and the pale horse over the fourth part of the earth to kill with sword and with hunger and with death.

XXX

THE TRUMAN ADMINISTRATIONS

1. *Reconversion*

NOW for the third time in a century the American people faced the problem of reconversion, reconstruction, and reformation. Some features of this problem were familiar enough from Civil War and World War I experience: the absorption of servicemen into civilian life, reconversion to a peacetime economy, and the restoration of normal constitutional and political practices, for example. Other features were new and unprecedented, and these mostly in the realm of foreign relations. The overshadowing fact, controlling both domestic as well as foreign policy in the postwar years, was that the United States emerged from the war the richest and most powerful of nations, and that upon it devolved responsibility for global relief and reconstruction, and for political and military leadership of all nations that did not look to Russia.

Economic and social readjustment after 1945 followed no familiar pattern. If the foreign situation was more troublesome than after any previous war, the domestic situation was less so. Reconversion presented fewer and less onerous problems than had been anticipated. Twelve million service men and women were absorbed into civilian life with no greater difficulty than half that number in 1919. Industry changed over easily from a war to a peace basis. Neither a depression nor a runaway inflation materialized. There was no political reaction comparable to that which had been dramatized by the change from Lincoln to Grant and from Wilson to Harding, no social upheaval, no jazz age; but there was something equally unpleasant — the cold war and the loyalty hysteria.

The most impressive fact about the domestic scene was the continuation and extension of wartime prosperity. Those who remembered the sharp recession of 1921 and the agricultural malaise that persisted throughout the decade of the 'twenties had feared a repetition of this economic crisis. This fear was not justified. Veterans had little difficulty finding work, and unemployment remained low; reconversion to civilian economy was swift; the dammed-up demand for consumer goods seemed insatiable. In the four years after the war, national production increased from 215 to 259 billion dollars, national income from 182 to 226 billion, and consumer income from 151 to 194 billion. More important than these general indications of continued prosperity was the maintenance of full employment, high wages, and high farm prices. What this meant was an acceleration of that redistribution of national income under way with the war itself. In 1935 over one half the workers of the country earned less than one thousand dollars; by 1948 only one tenth of the workers were in this unhappy category. In 1935 only one out of six American families enjoyed an income of over two thousand dollars a year, and only 6 per cent over three thousand; by 1948 three fourths of all families earned over two thousand and half over three thousand dollars a year. A 70 per cent increase in the cost of living, to be sure, qualified these statistics, but even so it was clear that the war and postwar prosperity, together with new tax policies, had achieved a greater approach to economic equality than Americans had known since the Civil War.

Even the farmers, the group most sensitive to the economic cycle, continued to enjoy unprecedented prosperity. Sustained by an insatiable demand for foodstuffs abroad, by higher standards of living at home, and by government subsidies, farm income actually increased by 5 billion dollars between 1945 and 1948: total farm income in 1948 was over 30 billion as compared with 11 billion in 1941 and 5½ billion in 1933! This meant a decline both in tenancy and in farm mortgages. Total farm mortgages fell by 2 billion between 1940 and 1948, and farm tenancy to the lowest point in the twentieth century.

What was the explanation of this phenomenon, which appeared to justify the claims of private enterprise and to confound the Communists, who had confidently expected an economic collapse in the United States? It was, in part, that five years of war had created a vast demand for consumer and durable goods; in part, the market for American surpluses created by the program of relief and reconstruction abroad; in part, the continuation of heavy government spending after the war. At the depth of the depression the federal government had spent about 9 billion dollars; five years after the war the federal budget was over 40 billion, and most of this was pumped into the domestic economy.

Neither demobilization nor reconversion created the problems that had been expected. Demobilization got under way with the surrender of Germany and proceeded swiftly after victory in the

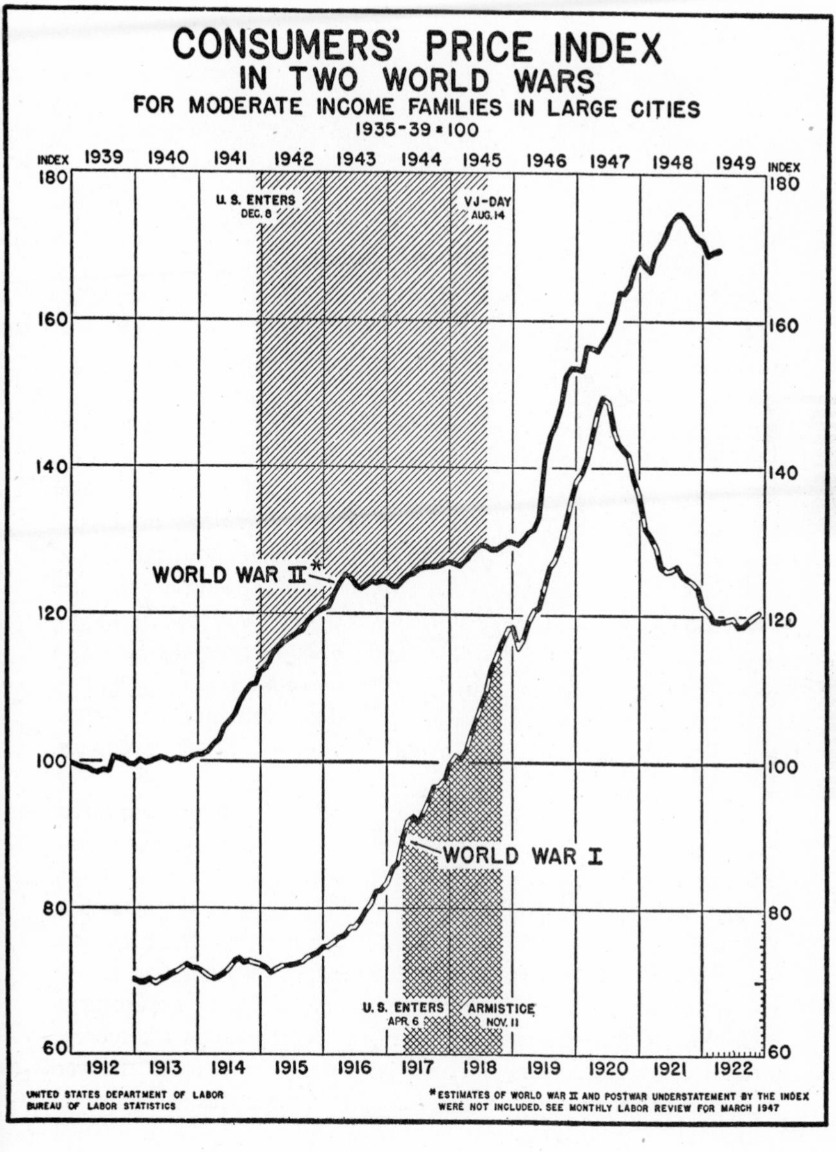

CONSUMERS' PRICE INDEX
IN TWO WORLD WARS
FOR MODERATE INCOME FAMILIES IN LARGE CITIES
1935-39 = 100
INDEX
1939 1940 1941 1942 1943 1944 1945 1946 1947 1948 1949
180 160 140 120 100 80 60
U. S. ENTERS DEC. 8
VJ-DAY AUG. 14
WORLD WAR II*
WORLD WAR I
U. S. ENTERS APR. 6
ARMISTICE NOV. 11
1912 1913 1914 1915 1916 1917 1918 1919 1920 1921 1922
UNITED STATES DEPARTMENT OF LABOR
BUREAU OF LABOR STATISTICS
*ESTIMATES OF WORLD WAR II AND POSTWAR UNDERSTATEMENT BY THE INDEX WERE NOT INCLUDED. SEE MONTHLY LABOR REVIEW FOR MARCH 1947

Pacific. Within a year the armed services had been reduced from 12 million to 3 million, and within another year to about a million and a half, at which figure the number was stabilized. The shock of the transition from the armed services to civilian life was cushioned by elaborate laws providing mustering-out pay, unemployment pay for one year, job reinstatement and seniority rights, civil-service preferment, insurance, loans for home building and the purchase of farms or businesses, generous subsidies for education or apprentice training. Eventually several million veterans took advantage of the education subsidies of the G.I. Bill of Rights, and the college population of the country increased by over one million.

Potentially the most serious threat to the orderly resumption of civilian economy was inflation. Wartime price controls had prevented any spectacular increase in the prices of basic commodities and rents, and these controls were retained until 1946. Then, yielding to pressure from manufacturers and farmers who preferred the 'law of supply and demand,' and from consumers who wanted goods at almost any price, Congress enacted a price-regulation measure so feeble that President Truman vetoed it. In three weeks prices increased more than in the previous three years. A stopgap law, which Truman reluctantly signed, was ineffective, except for rents, which increased from an index of 108 in 1945 to 117 in 1948, while the food index soared from 139 to 210 in this period. By 1949, however, production had caught up with demand in most fields, and, even with higher wages and corporation profits, prices were stabilized.

Closely related to the problem of inflation was that of the national debt and of tax policy. Under the impact of war the federal debt had soared to the astronomical figure of 260 billion; the carrying charges on this debt alone came to over 5 billion. After World War I government expenditures had declined from 18 to 6 billion, permitting a reduction in both debt and taxes. No such reductions appeared possible after 1945. Government expenditures dropped to about 34 billion in 1948, when there was a surplus of 8 billion dollars. The next year, however, expenses rose to 40 billion, and the budget for 1950 called for a further increase. Without either additional taxes or a sharp increase in taxable income, this spelled a deficit, and neither measure was forthcoming. On the contrary, political pressure led to slight reductions in income and excise taxes, and as the demands for national defense and international reconstruction remained high, the richest nation on earth resorted once again to deficit financing.

2. *Labor Unrest and Labor Gains*

Both the Civil War and World War I had been followed by depressions from which labor suffered acutely. The depression of the early 'seventies had broken the National Labor Union and retarded the growth of the Knights of Labor, reduced wages, and spread unemployment throughout the ranks of the workers. The 1920's had seen a steady decline in the membership of the A.F. of L. and other labor unions, and a marked weakening of labor's bargaining power. The two powerful labor organizations — the A.F. of L. and the C.I.O., each numbering over 6 million members — were determined to avoid a repetition of this history after World War II. Full employment, high wages, and overtime pay had brought labor earnings to an all-time high and labor leaders were not prepared to accept any diminution of these earnings, even with shorter hours. Fear of rising living costs, the prospect of a return to the forty-hour week — with consequent loss of overtime pay — and the belief that labor had not shared as fully in the general prosperity as had capital brought a demand for substantial wage increases. Clearly, too, this was the ideal time to strike: business was eager to get back to normal production and ready enough to pass higher costs on to the consumer; the public was eager to buy at almost any price.

During the war the unions had faithfully observed the no-strike pledge; with the end of the war the lid was off, and within a month after victory over Japan, half a million workers were out on strike. The year 1946 saw the greatest unrest in American labor history: 4,600,000 workers were involved in almost 5000 labor disputes, with a total loss of 116 million man-days of work. Almost every industry was affected, but the most serious strikes were in the steel, coal, automobile, and electrical industries, and on the railroads. The strike of bituminous coal miners, threatening not only American industry and transportation but European recovery, caused such grave concern that the government took over the mines. When John L. Lewis refused to order his men back to work, the Federal Court slapped a fine of three and a half million dollars on the United Mine Workers Union — a fine that was later reduced. Even the conservative Railroad Brotherhoods struck but the strike collapsed when the President sought for authority to use the army to run the railroads.

Labor Force, Employment, and Unemployment: 1940 to 1947

(Persons 14 years old and over)

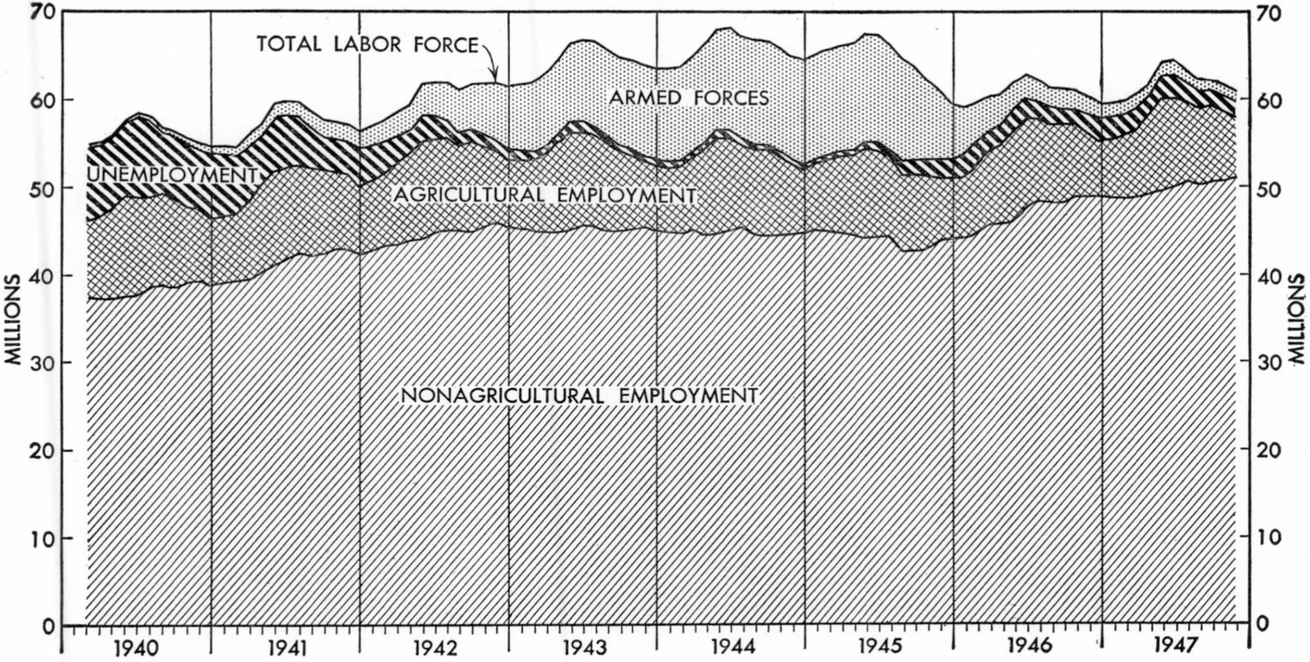

Source: Department of Commerce, Bureau of the Census.

The first series of strikes won wage increases of 18 to 19 cents an hour. Rising prices partly nullified this gain, and labor unrest continued. The years 1947 and 1948 both saw over 3000 strikes, and in 1949 the number rose to about 4000 with some 50 million work-days lost. These strikes extracted a second and third round of wage increases until, in the end, labor won substantially all that it asked in wages. An interesting feature of the postwar labor scene was the demand for those welfare payments and old-age pensions common in business and the professions, the military and the civil service. The pattern, originally set by the social-security program, was taken over by Lewis, who in 1946 succeeded in persuading the coal industry to set aside a 'royalty' of 20 cents on every ton of coal, to be used for health and welfare and for pensions of one hundred dollars a month. This demand was promptly taken up by the steel, automobile, and other workers. As only those who had been with their companies for long periods would be eligible for these benefits, the pension system put a premium on stability in labor, and indicated that the day of the casual laborer was becoming a thing of the past.

The stoppages in the coal industry, with their far-reaching repercussions in industry generally, and the threat of a nationwide tie-up of transportation, together with a widespread feeling that labor was irresponsible, that it encouraged inflation, meddled in politics, was susceptible to racketeering, and was permeated with Communism, all combined to produce a sharp anti-labor reaction in Congress. This reaction found expression first in President Truman's threat to use the army to run the railroads, and next in the Case bill of May 1946, which required a sixty-day cooling-off period in labor disputes and compulsory bargaining by unions. Truman, who had himself cooled off a bit after his denunciation of the railroad unions, vetoed this bill. The Republican 80th Congress of 1947, however, brought enactment of the controversial Taft-Hartley law. This elaborate Act outlawed the closed shop and the secondary boycott; made unions liable for breach of contract or damages resulting from jurisdictional disputes; required a sixty-day cooling-off period for strikes; authorized an eighty-day injunction against strikes that might affect national health or safety; forbade political contributions from unions, 'featherbedding,' and excessive dues; required union leaders to take a non-Communist oath; and set up a conciliation service outside the Labor Department, which was suspected of being too friendly to labor. Truman's veto argued that this bill

> would reverse the basic direction of our national labor policy, inject the government into private economic affairs on an unprecedented scale, and conflict with important principles of our democratic society. Its provisions would cause more strikes, not fewer. It would contribute neither to industrial peace nor to economic stability and progress. It would be a dangerous stride in the direction of a totally managed economy. It contains seeds of discord which would plague this nation for years to come.

Congress, however, re-enacted the bill by thumping majorities in both houses. Whether the Taft-Hartley Act 'plagued the nation' or not, it certainly plagued the parties: in the election of 1948 labor retired many Republican supporters of the Act to private life. Yet the most energetic efforts to repeal or modify it in 1949 were unavailing, and it lingered on as an issue for the 1950 Congressional elections.

The unrest of the late 'forties should not obscure the massive advances that labor had made in that decade. By mid-century the A.F. of L. numbered over 7 million members, the C.I.O. claimed over 6 million, and another 2½ million belonged to independent unions such as the Railroad Brotherhoods and the United Mine Workers. Total union membership had almost doubled since 1940. Organized labor generally had secured the forty-hour week, vacations with pay, welfare benefits, and, in some major industries, old-age pensions. A federal act of October 1949, raising minimum wages to 75 cents an hour, gave added protection to the mass of unorganized labor. Unemployment lingered at about 3 million, but many of these were 'unemployables.' Labor had vindicated its right to participate actively in politics and had avoided the dangers inherent in the creation of an independent labor party. Although Congress persisted in its refusal to enact a permanent Fair Employment Practices Act, at least ten states passed laws forbidding discrimination in employment because of race, color, creed, or national origins.

3. *Society, Education, and Civil Rights*

Social changes and readjustments in the postwar years were less striking than economic ones, but no less important. In most respects the war accelerated changes already under way rather than modifying or deflecting them. Mobility and adaptability had always characterized the American; the dislocations of war did not appear to work serious hardships, nor did the average American find any great difficulty in shifting from civilian to military and back to civilian status. The American was, traditionally, a Jack-of-all-trades; as he fitted well into the complex machinery of the army and the navy, so after the war he was prepared to try his luck with new jobs in new industries, enter new professions, or expose himself to more education. The American army was probably the most democratic in the Western World; with fifteen million Americans in uniform the war did not so much impose military standards on the civil population as civilian standards on the military. Yet in the postwar years the military came to play a larger role in politics and public affairs than ever before in American history.

The decade of the 'forties saw the largest population increase in the history of the Republic — from 131 to 150 million. This remarkable increase was brought about not by immigration — less than nine hundred thousand immigrants came in during the decade — but by a sharp reversal of the birth rate, which increased from 17 to 25 per thousand in a decade, and by a corresponding decline in the death rate. This change slowed up that trend toward an older population that had inspired the Townsend movement, and accentuated the crisis already existing in education. Particularly interesting was the sharp increase in Negro population — from 12 to 15 million — which resulted in a more even distribution of Negroes over the whole of the country and a nationalization of the race problem.

The city continued to grow at the expense of the country, and by mid-century urban population was 60 per cent of the whole. The most striking growth came in cities in the middle-population bracket, from 100,000 to 500,000. There were some spectacular regional shifts. The prophecy of Bishop Berkeley was vindicated two centuries later with the largest westward movement in American history. While New York and Pennsylvania showed modest increases of 7 and 8 per cent, the three Pacific coastal states boasted population increases of 50 per cent, and California emerged as the second state in the union. Equally interesting was the rapid growth of some states of the South and Southwest — especially Florida, Arizona, Texas, and Virginia. This shift in population had important political as well as social and economic implications: California, for example, was entitled to eight additional Congressmen in the next reapportionment, while Texas promised to be politically as powerful as Texans thought she should be.

The war had drawn perhaps four million women into the labor force; with the return of servicemen to their jobs some two million of these quit, and the percentage of women in the total labor force declined from 35 to 28 per cent. Following a familiar pattern, the war had spurred the marriage rate; but many war marriages ended in divorce, and in 1946 the divorce rate rose to an all-time high of one to every four marriages. Moralists feared that the institution of the family was about to break up, but the upswing in the divorce rate was probably to be explained by the ease with which divorces could be obtained, higher standards of marital happiness, and a tendency toward self-indulgence, rather than by any deterioration of the institution of marriage.

Of all the social problems of the postwar years those of education and of race relations were the most vexatious and commanded the most attention. The depression had sharply reduced school budgets, postponing new construction, the modernization of old buildings, and the improvement of teaching facilities. Prosperity might have enabled Americans to resume the interrupted program of school-building construction, but the war stopped all nonessential building, and schools were considered nonessential. The result was that the United States emerged from the war with the prospect of a largely increased school population and a badly run-down educational plant: in New York City alone, over two hundred school buildings were more than fifty years old, and the children of this richest city in the world went to school in buildings that had been condemned, twenty years earlier, as fire hazards. The situation with respect to teachers was equally serious. By 1938 the average salary of the public-school teacher was around $1400, and substantially lower than that in the South. With the coming of the war, teachers left their school rooms by the hundred thousand for better-paid jobs. The result was a progressive deterioration in the quality of teaching and in educational standards generally: in 1947, for example, 60,000 teachers had only a high-school education, and less than half of all public-school teachers had graduated from college.

The war and postwar boom in babies promised an enormous influx into the kindergarten and elementary grades in the late 'forties and early 'fifties. Under the spur of necessity, therefore, and of an aggressive campaign by teachers' organizations and by the *New*

York Times, most states increased their educational budgets sharply; total public-school expenditures in 1949 were around 4 billion. To be sure, this was not an impressive sum compared with national expenditures of over 7 billion dollars for liquor and over 3 billion for tobacco, and the observation of Roger Ascham in 1570 remained relevant four centuries later:

> Commonlie more care is had, yea and that amonges verie wise men, to finde out rather a cunnynge man for their horse, than a cunnynge man for their children. They say nay in words, but they do so in dede. For to the one, they will gladlie give a stipend of 200 crounes by years, and loth to offer the other 200 shillings. God that sittith in heaven laugheth their choice to skorne, and rewardeth their liberalitie as it should: for he suffereth them to have tame and well-ordered horses, but wild and unfortunate children.

A comparable crisis appeared in higher education, especially that which was privately supported. The G.I. Bill of Rights enabled several million veterans to go to college, and this together with continued prosperity raised the college and university enrollment to an unprecedented two and a half million. Most state legislatures made generous appropriations to meet this situation; the state schools, therefore, had little difficulty in expanding sufficiently to meet the influx of students. Privately endowed institutions, however, caught between rising costs and lower income from gifts and endowments, were very hard hit.

The inability of many poorer states and counties adequately to support their public schools led to a widespread demand for federal aid to education. This demand was based on the argument that the whole nation had a stake in the intelligence and competence of its youth, and that rejections from selective service on grounds of educational deficiency had run into the hundreds of thousands; it drew strength from statistics that revealed gross disparities between the educational facilities of northern and southern states and between those available to whites and Negroes. Senator Taft of Ohio, otherwise not notorious for his support of federal centralization, introduced a bill appropriating up to 250 million dollars a year to aid public schools in the poorer states and guaranteeing appropriations up to 40 dollars a year for every school child in the country regardless of race or color. The question of federal aid to parochial schools, however, cut athwart this proposal, and in the din of controversy over this issue and over larger questions of federal policy, the bill was lost.

In his famous Peoria speech Abraham Lincoln had charged that slavery

> deprives our republican example of its just influence in the world; enables the enemies of free institutions with plausibility to taunt us as hypocrites; causes the real friends of freedom to doubt our sincerity; and forces so many good men among ourselves into an open war with the very fundamental principles of civil liberty.

The denial of civil and political rights to Negroes and other minority groups during World War II and after had much the same effect. As Dean Acheson observed:

> The existence of discrimination against minority groups in this country has an adverse effect upon our relations with other countries. . . Frequently we find it next to impossible to formulate a satisfactory answer to our critics in other countries; the gap between the things we stand for in principle and the facts of a particular situation may be too wide to be bridged.

The war at once exacerbated race relations and advanced racial equality. Its total effect was to bring the whole issue of minority rights out into the open, expose the gap between the pretense of equality and the reality of inequality, and force the government to take action toward bridging that gap.

Notwithstanding official disapproval, segregation and discrimination persisted in the armed forces. Not until July 1948 did President Truman direct the armed forces to end segregation and inequality of opportunity for appointment and promotion. Far more serious was discrimination in employment, exercised by both management and labor. Even before Pearl Harbor President Roosevelt had proclaimed as official policy 'that there shall be no discrimination in the employment of workers in defense industries or government because of race, creed, color or national origin,' required that all defense contracts include a nondiscrimination clause, and set up a Fair Employment Practices Committee to enforce the order. In response to this policy Negro employment in war industries increased from 3 to 8 per cent of the whole, while employment in the federal government jumped from 40,000 to over 300,000. Labor proved, in fact, more recalcitrant on this issue than management, and it required court action to force the Railroad Brotherhoods to abandon their practice of writing racial discrimination into their contracts. Although the establish-

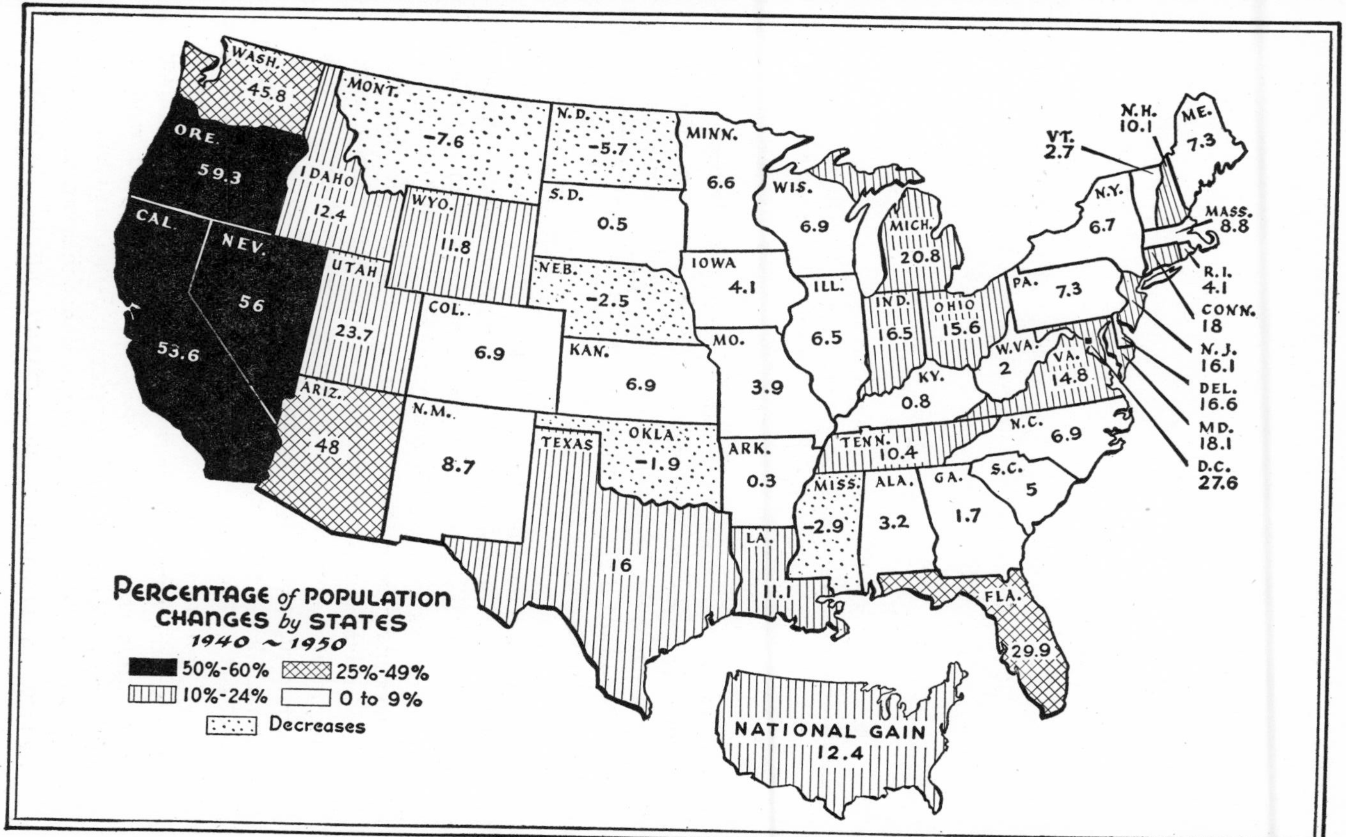
WASH.
45.8
ORE.
59.3
CAL.
53.6
NEV.
56
IDAHO
12.4
MONT.
-7.6
WYO.
11.8
UTAH
23.7
ARIZ.
48
COL.
6.9
N.M.
8.7
N.D.
-5.7
S.D.
0.5
NEB.
-2.5
KAN.
6.9
OKLA.
-1.9
TEXAS
16
MINN.
6.6
IOWA
4.1
MO.
3.9
ARK.
0.3
LA.
11.1
WIS.
6.9
ILL.
6.5
MICH.
20.8
IND.
16.5
OHIO
15.6
KY.
0.8
TENN.
10.4
MISS.
-2.9
ALA.
3.2
GA.
1.7
FLA.
29.9
S.C.
5
N.C.
6.9
W.VA.
2
VA.
14.8
PA.
7.3
N.Y.
6.7
VT.
2.7
N.H.
10.1
ME.
7.3
MASS.
8.8
R.I.
4.1
CONN.
18
N.J.
16.1
DEL.
16.6
MD.
18.1
D.C.
27.6
NATIONAL GAIN
12.4
PERCENTAGE of POPULATION
CHANGES by STATES
1940 ~ 1950
50%-60%
25%-49%
10%-24%
0 to 9%
Decreases

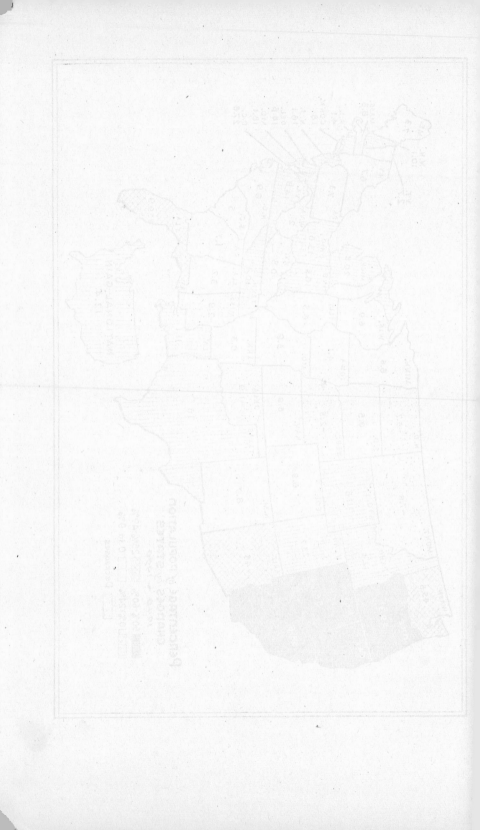

ment of a permanent Fair Employment Practices Committee was endorsed by both parties and supported, at all times, by a majority in both houses of Congress, every attempt to pass an FEPC law was frustrated by filibusters from southern Democrats.

Politically, too, the Negro made moderate advances during the war and postwar years. Southern states had long circumvented the Fifteenth Amendment and, except in some of the larger urban centers and in the border states, few Negroes voted. Eight southern states limited voting in Democratic primaries to white men; eleven required the payment of poll taxes — in some instances cumulative; others excluded Negroes from the polls by discriminatory application of literacy tests, requiring them to explain things in the Constitution that not even the Supreme Court has been able to explain. These laws and practices kept not only Negroes but whites from voting. The population of the state of Washington is slightly under that of South Carolina, but in 1944 there were 856,328 who voted in Washington and 103,375 in South Carolina. This discrepancy between poll-tax and non-poll-tax states was general: 18 per cent of those entitled to vote in poll-tax states actually voted, but 69 per cent in the non-poll-tax states.

A series of Supreme Court decisions — notably Nixon *v.* Herndon [1] and Smith *v.* Allwright [2] — nullified white primary laws, and when South Carolina attempted to evade these decisions by repealing all primary laws and maintaining the Democratic party as a purely private organization, the District Court rejected the subterfuge. 'Racial distinctions,' the court said,

> cannot exist in the machinery that selects the officers and lawmakers of the United States; and all citizens of this State and Country are entitled to cast a free and untrammeled ballot in our elections, and if the only material and realistic elections are clothed with the name 'primary' they are equally entitled to vote there.

Poll taxes, however, resisted both political and constitutional attack, though between 1921 and 1948 four southern states — North Carolina, Louisiana, Florida, and Georgia — abandoned them. There are no adequate statistics of Negro voting, but it seems clear that more southern Negroes voted in the election of 1948 than in any since Reconstruction.

The minority group that suffered most deeply during the war was

[1] 273 U.S. 536.

[2] 321 U.S. 649.

the Japanese. There were some 126,000 Japanese in the United States at the outbreak of the war; most of these lived in the Pacific coastal states, and two thirds of them were American-born (Nisei) and thus citizens. Alarmed by the supposed danger of a Japanese attack on the Pacific coast and fearful that persons of Japanese ancestry might prove disloyal to the United States, the War Department persuaded President Roosevelt to authorize the evacuation of some 112,000 west-coast Japanese to so-called relocation centers, which were actually prison camps. It was, said E. S. Corwin, a leading authority on American constitutional law, 'the most drastic invasion of the rights of citizens of the United States by their own government that has thus far occurred in the history of our nation.' It was also the most inexcusable. There was no evidence of disloyalty among the Japanese; no Japanese was convicted of sabotage or espionage during the war; and Nisei regiments were among the bravest of the brave in the Italian campaign. Efforts to get the Supreme Court to nullify the executive order were, however, unavailing until the very end of the war. 'Distinctions between citizens solely because of their ancestry are by their very nature odious to a free people whose institutions are founded upon the doctrine of equality' said the court, but

> it by no means follows that in dealing with the perils of war, Congress and the Executive are wholly precluded from taking into account those facts and circumstances which are relevant to measures for our national defense . . . which may in fact place citizens of one ancestry in a different category from others.[3]

After the war the Japanese were permitted to return to their homes. Many of them, however, found that they had no homes to return to, and many others found that they had lost not only their freedom during the war, but their businesses and jobs as well.

Apart from this injustice, however, the civil-rights record of World War II was better than that of World War I, and the record of the postwar years was no worse than that of the early 'twenties. This was partly because the country had learned something from that earlier experience; partly because the country was more united and racial groups more fully assimilated than a quarter-century earlier; partly because Attorney General Francis Biddle was genuinely concerned to maintain civil liberties.

Yet it was inevitable that the war with the Axis powers and then

[3] Hirabayashi *v.* United States, 320 U.S. 81.

the cold war with Russia should inspire fear of subversive activities in the United States. The totalitarian nations, Fascist and Communist alike, had perfected the technique of the Fifth Column, and Communism, at least, inspired in some of its inherents a fanatical loyalty that superseded national allegiance. There was a widespread suspicion that Communists had infiltrated into government service, labor unions, and schools, and that they were hiding behind the guarantees of the Bill of Rights to destroy freedom.

Even before the outbreak of the fighting war Congress took two steps to frustrate disloyal or subversive activities in the United States. As early as 1938 the House established a committee on un-American activities.[4] This committee, which at no point in its long and shabby career defined the term 'un-American,' embarked upon a relentless search for subversive activities—chiefly communistic and radical. Although it distracted Congressional attention from more important matters, spent millions of dollars, produced voluminous reports, and made the headlines of newspapers with great regularity, it found nothing that was not already known to the Department of Justice. The second measure was the enactment, in 1940, of a so-called Alien Registration Act, which was, in reality, a sedition Act. While the purpose of the Act was to prohibit the advocacy of revolution by violence, the Act itself unfortunately departed from Anglo-American traditions by embracing the doctrines of guilt by intent and guilt by association.

In part to counteract the excessive zeal and loose standards of the Un-American Activities Committee, President Truman in 1947 provided for an orderly investigation of the loyalty of civil servants in the executive department of the government. While this order set up intelligent standards and procedural safeguards and provided for non-judicial review, it, too, embraced the doctrines of guilt by intention and by association. Under its terms activities that might be evidence of disloyalty included 'membership in, affiliation with, or sympathetic association with . . . any organization, movement, group or combination of persons, designated by the Attorney General as having adopted a policy of approving the commission of acts of force or violence to deny other persons their rights under the Constitution.' Fortunately the enforcement of the order was characterized by moderation. Of the two and one half million persons

[4] Successively known as the Dies, the Rankin, the Wood, and the Thomas Committee.

passed on, only a few thousand were actually investigated and of these only a few hundred dismissed or persuaded to resign. Potentially the most ominous feature of the executive order was the one authorizing the Attorney General to prepare lists of subversive organizations and giving these lists a quasi-legal character. 'If there is any fixed star in our constitutional constellation,' Justice Jackson had said in the second flag-salute case, 'it is that no official, high or petty, can prescribe what shall be orthodox in politics, nationalism, religion or other matters of opinion or force citizens to confess by word or act their faith therein.' The most serious practical consequence of the executive order was to discourage independence, originality, and criticism in government employees, put a premium on conformity, and dissuade many otherwise valuable citizens from entering government service.

Loyalty investigations and purges, and the requirement of loyalty oaths were extended into many other fields, notably those of labor and education. The Taft-Hartley Act required union officials to take a non-Communist oath and inspired a wholesome housecleaning in some unions. A number of states and cities, convinced by the yellow press that the schools were rife with Communism, required loyalty oaths and character credentials from teachers, and two states made the flag salute compulsory for school children, until the Supreme Court struck down the regulation.[5] No evidence of Communism in the classroom was found, or any evidence that scholars and scientists in universities were infected with the Communist taint; the real harm was in making teachers afraid to discuss controversial issues with their pupils, and in putting them in a position where they were regarded with suspicion and where their reading, associations, and political beliefs were subjected to public scrutiny.

4. *Politics and the Election of 1948*

Every past war had been followed by political reaction, and most observers assumed that history would now repeat itself. After all the Democrats had controlled the Presidency for sixteen years and the Congress for fourteen, and that was as long a tenure as any party had enjoyed since Reconstruction. Expectation of change was strengthened by the consideration that the country had weathered both depression and war and was entering a new era, that the New

[5] West Virginia State Board *v.* Barnette, 319 U.S. 624.

Deal program had been largely achieved, and that the great leader who had so long proved politically irresistible was gone.

When the magnetic Roosevelt was replaced by the prosaic Truman, Republican hopes mounted. Truman's position, weak when he assumed office, appeared to grow progressively weaker. His experience in domestic politics was limited, his understanding of world affairs meagre. A loyal Democrat, there was no persuasive evidence that he was a loyal New Dealer, and the speed with which he replaced Roosevelt's cabinet with one of his own choosing, and his appointment of conservatives to key positions in the administration and the judiciary suggested that he would find his natural allies in the conservative wing of the Democratic party and thus forfeit much of the labor, liberal, and Negro vote that had contributed so generously to Roosevelt's successive victories.

The Congressional election of 1946 appeared to confirm the expectation that the Democrats were on the way out. Exasperated by the slowness of demobilization, blundering over reconversion, high prices, high taxes, and political incompetence, the voters turned to the Republican party for the first time since 1930. The 80th Congress numbered 51 Republicans and 45 Democrats in the Senate, 246 Republicans and 188 Democrats in the House.

The Republicans, however, misread the moral of this election. Having campaigned with the query 'Had Enough?' they not unnaturally interpreted their victory as a hearty 'yes.' Actually the election was an expression of impatience with the paucity of Truman's achievements rather than a demand for a return to 'normalcy.' The temper of the country remained liberal and affirmative.

Yet even with Republican control of the 80th Congress, Truman's accomplishments were far from negligible. In the domestic field he had succeeded in obtaining the creation of an Atomic Energy Commission with David E. Lilienthal as chairman; the enactment of an effective Rent Control law; a Presidential Succession Act making the Speaker of the House and the President of the Senate next in line of succession after the Vice President; a bill admitting some 200,000 displaced persons within a period of two years; housing and slum-clearance bills providing federal aid to low-cost housing; an increase in minimum wages to 75 cents an hour; a Legislative Reorganization Act streamlining Congress in so far as that cumbersome body could ever be streamlined; a Maximum Employment Bill setting up a council of economic advisers and pledging the government to such appropriations as were necessary to maintain full employment; and a National Security Act unifying the armed forces — on paper at least — in a single Department of Defense. And the record in the realm of foreign affairs — where the bipartisan policy was somewhat erratically pursued — was substantially better than that in the domestic.

Yet so sure were the Republicans of capturing the Presidency in 1948 that, for the first time in their history, they renominated a defeated candidate, Thomas E. Dewey. And so confident was Governor Dewey of victory that in his campaign he deliberately avoided any discussion of issues that might commit him to a particular policy or obligate him to particular groups. Despairing of success, the Democratic Convention met in an atmosphere of gloom. A revolt led by James Roosevelt of California fizzled out; a last-minute attempt to persuade General Eisenhower to take the nomination failed; and Truman was renominated by default. When Justice William O. Douglas refused to be a candidate for the Vice Presidency, the nomination went to seventy-year-old Senator Alben Barkley of Kentucky, who was thought to be acceptable to the restless southern wing of the party.

Democratic prospects were further dimmed by a revolt both of the right and of the left, which threatened to disintegrate the party. Henry Wallace, last remaining member of the original Roosevelt cabinet, broke with Truman in the fall of 1946 over the Administration's Russian policy, organized a progressive party, and ran for the Presidency. While there was little likelihood that his candidacy would develop any substantial strength throughout the country, it seemed probable that his aggressive championship of the interests of labor and of the Negro might wean enough votes from the Democratic ticket to swing such states as New York, Michigan, Illinois, and California into the Republican column. The revolt from the right was of longer standing. Woodrow Wilson had had trouble with the Bourbon Democracy of the South, and Franklin Roosevelt had been able to hold it in line only by his proved capacity to win elections. Truman inherited Bourbon enmity to Roosevelt, but not the ability to silence or to surmount it. When — for valid political as well as moral reasons — he took over Roosevelt's advocacy of a civil-rights program, forcing a strong civil-rights plank into the party platform, many southern Democrats revolted. Convinced that Truman was doomed to defeat in any event, they left the party and organized at Montgomery, Alabama, a states-rights or Dixiecrat party. Their candidate was Strom Thurmond of South Carolina, their platform states rights, and their method to exclude the regular Democrats from the ticket wherever possible.

Threatened thus from both right and left, Truman's chances of re-election seemed negligible. Largely abandoned by his own party, with inadequate campaign funds, and in the face of general apathy, Truman boldly waged an aggressive campaign. He attacked relentlessly the record of the Republican party as revealed in the 80th Congress and reaffirmed the principles of the New Deal — now named, somewhat unnecessarily, the Fair Deal. He defied the Dixiecrats and so held the Negro vote of northern cities. He countered the Wallace attack with an aggressive defense of his foreign policy and a strong intimation of a determination to seek military alliances with the nations of western Europe.

To the astonishment of almost every prognosticator, Truman won a resounding popular and electoral-college victory.[6] The Dixiecrats — though they garnered 39 electoral votes — proved less formidable than had been anticipated; Mr. Wallace was less popular with labor and the Negroes than had been supposed. Dewey's popular vote fell below that of 1944, and though he carried such powerful states as New York and Pennsylvania, he lost Ohio, Iowa, and Wisconsin, which he had carried four years earlier.

The Democrats, too, recaptured control of both houses of Congress, winning a majority of 12 in the upper chamber and of 93 in the House. Particularly interesting was the victory of such liberals as Kefauver of Tennessee, Humphrey of Minnesota, Douglas of Illinois, and Murray of Montana. The gubernatorial contests followed the national trend: the Democrats won 21 out of 33 contests, and among the Democratic victors were prominent liberals like Chester Bowles in Connecticut, Adlai Stevenson in Illinois, and Frank Lausche in Ohio.

The 1948 elections confirmed what had long been suspected: that

[6] The vote was:

	Popular	Electoral College
Truman	24,105,695	303
Dewey	21,969,170	189
Thurmond	1,169,021	39
Wallace	1,156,103	0

Americans do not take kindly to splinter parties; that labor was still loyal to the Democratic party; that the midwestern farm vote was by no means irretrievably committed to the Republican party; that the political temper of the country was still liberal; and that loyalty to Franklin Roosevelt was a factor to be reckoned with in the future.

XXXI

THE RESPONSIBILITIES OF WORLD POWER

1. *The New World*

THE problems of the postwar years were so many and so complex that neither the American people nor their government seemed able to understand or to master them: witness, for example, the turns and twists of American policy toward Palestine, Spain, Yugoslavia, China, and the Argentine in the five years after the close of the war. It was not merely that large areas of the globe had been laid waste and were ravaged by famine, disease, and anarchy, though this in itself placed a heavy responsibility upon the United States. Nor was it merely that Russia and the Western powers seemed unable to agree upon the solution of any of the important problems created by the war and by victory, though this disagreement threatened to prolong world unrest indefinitely. It was rather that profound and revolutionary changes were under way throughout the globe. Russia, like the United States, emerged from the war as a world power, and Communism as a world force. The British Empire was losing power, and Britain could no longer play her historic role or exercise her traditional influence in politics and economy. The so-called backward peoples of Asia and Africa were bursting out of the inferior position to which they had so long been condemned, and claiming the right to govern themselves and to have a voice in world affairs. Science and technology were binding nations ever closer together in time and space, making them at once more interdependent and more vulnerable than ever before.

Yet amid the vast confusion that obtained, the swift changes of light and shadow, it was possible to perceive a pattern that was almost elementary. In a century and a half — a short time in history — the United States had vaulted from insignificance to dominance, and from isolation to leadership. Not ambitious for power, America had achieved power. Rejecting responsibility, she had been unable to escape it. Inclined to parochialism, she had been thrust into the center of internationalism. Fundamentally peaceable, she had been led by circumstances to become the arsenal of the Western World. The only great nation to emerge from the war materially unscathed, she elected to assume responsibility for relief and reconstruction, and to put her technological skills and wealth at the disposal of less fortunate peoples. The only democratic power able to resist the advance of Communism, she was required to commit herself to that perilous task throughout the world.

As the global map underwent kaleidoscopic changes, the familiar features of global politics seemed to dissolve. National gave way to ideological antipathies, and the conflict was no longer between nations but between systems and philosophies. World War II, with its terrible destruction of the material, political, and spiritual resources of mankind, created immense vacuums, into which American and Russian power poured almost as if in response to natural forces. That Atlantic Community familiar to the Founding Fathers was recreated. A shift in the center of gravity from the Atlantic to the Pacific which Homer Lea had prophesied came to pass. The titanic conflict between Russian and American systems which Henry Adams had foreseen materialized.

Because America felt compelled to feed, clothe, and sustain the peoples of the Old World, to occupy parts of Germany, Austria, and Korea, defend Greece, rearm Turkey, establish air and naval bases across the world, become an Atlantic power, a Pacific power, and a Hemispheric power all at once, she stretched not only her physical but her intellectual resources thin. Because American wealth was essential to recovery almost everywhere, many Americans assumed that all that was needed for recovery was American wealth. Because so many ancient nations appeared unable to exist without American support, Americans were tempted to forget the force of tradition and history and assume that they could rearrange European politics as simply as they rearranged their own. Because American military might was the most formidable the world had ever seen, many Americans thought that it was absolute, and argued the necessity of using it wherever democracy or liberty was challenged by hostile forces.

But as the United States advanced in strength, so too did Russia. As the United States poured financial aid into western Europe, Russia revolutionized the economies of eastern Europe and of China through the application of Communism. As the United States built up a system of alliances, Russia gained allies through military or ideological conquest. And as the United States made atom bombs, so too did the Russians. With the emergence of the atom and the hydrogen bombs as absolute weapons, it became clear that notwithstanding her might, the United States was as vulnerable as any of her rivals. At the moment in history when Americans attained their greatest power, they were confronted with implacable limits on power.

Thus Americans were called on to make multiple adjustment. They had to adjust themselves first to the notion and the practice of world responsibility, and then to a host of particular problems connected with the exercise of that responsibility. This required a swift education in global affairs, and that education was inevitably superficial and confused. Americans who had barely acquainted themselves with the geography of their own country had to learn overnight about Burma and Indo-China, Pakistan and India, Eritrea and Ethiopia, Iran and Iraq, Palestine and Trans-Jordan, Manchuria and Korea, as well as about the geopolitics of a new Europe. They had to learn about foreign trade and currency controls, the intricacies of British, French, and Italian politics, the economy of a divided Germany, the strategic importance of the Scandinavian states, of Greece, Palestine, North Africa, Korea, and Formosa. They had to learn to work with new international organizations and administrations, and to acquire a new vocabulary and grammar of international politics. World responsibility meant, too, a new political orientation at home: a bipartisan foreign policy, a vastly enlarged State Department, a closer correlation between foreign and domestic policy and between civilian and military economy than ever before, the elaboration of far-reaching security controls, and the creation of an alert, intelligent, and prudent public opinion. The cost of national defense and the financing of relief, reconstruction, and defense abroad meant a terrific tax burden. Americans were called upon to display a degree of political maturity such as they had displayed only once before — in the Revolutionary generation, 1765–1800.

It was asking a good deal to expect Americans to learn all this at once. If the student were to judge by what appeared in the press or by what was said in Congress or in political campaigns, he might well conclude that it was asking too much. If he judged, however, by what was actually accomplished in the five years after the war, he would necessarily reach a more favorable conclusion. For, to an impressive degree, the American nation did fulfill the obligations that had been thrust upon it, and did seek, with patience and good will, the road to peace.

We are sometimes so impressed by the problems war creates that we forget those it solves. Just as World War I was followed by an era of disenchantment in which Americans argued that their participation had been a mistake, so within a few years of victory over Germany and Japan there were some who asserted that American participation in World War II had been an avoidable mistake. In some quarters it was thought clever to say that the United States had won the war but had lost the peace. For the most part this attitude was inspired by the exigencies of partisan politics, but some of it was inspired by a deep disillusionment with the post-war world, by frustration and fear. It is perhaps sufficient answer to these assertions to suggest the consequences to America had Germany and Japan been victorious, as they would inevitably have been had the United States stood aloof from the war. Shortly after Pearl Harbor President Roosevelt, asked to give a name to the conflict, suggested 'The War for Survival.' It was a good name, and however vexatious the problems of the postwar years, it is well to keep in mind that the United States and Britain survived, and with them a chance for democracy and freedom and for civilization itself in the modern world.

2. *Relief and Reconstruction*

The most pressing problem in foreign affairs was to bring relief to the stricken millions of the Old World. Over large areas of Europe economic life had come to a standstill. For five years the Nazis had systematically looted and destroyed wherever they went. Millions of workers had been drawn into nonproductive war industries; other millions had been killed, captured, or herded into concentration camps. Without adequate farm labor, fertilizers, machinery, or cultivation, food production had fallen to half the prewar level. Towns and cities were destroyed, factories smashed up, power plants wrecked, mines flooded, ports clogged, shipping sunk, railroads torn up, and rolling stock in ruins; money was almost worthless. Ten to twelve million bewildered refugees wandered aimlessly on the roads, or clung to the camps that had been hastily established for them. Herbert Hoover, sent abroad to survey the food situation, reported that 'It is now 11:59 o'clock on the clock of starvation.' Most continental Europeans were living on less than 1500 calories a day: the American average was 3500. Starvation, disease, and anarchy threatened to take more lives and to leave worse scars than war itself. Over large parts of Asia, too, the situation was desperate, and with crop failures in 1946, it grew worse: it was estimated that almost 400 million people of Asia were close to starvation.

The burden of relief fell most heavily upon the United States, which alone of major nations had a transportation system and shipping intact, and surplus food. As early as December 1942 President Roosevelt set up, in the Department of State, an Office of Foreign Relief, primarily concerned with the situation in North Africa. In June 1943 the United States proposed to her Allies the creation of an international relief organization, and out of this proposal came the United Nations Relief and Rehabilitation Administration (UNRRA), of November 1943, to which 48 nations eventually adhered. Under the vigorous leadership first of ex-Governor Herbert Lehman and then of Fiorella LaGuardia, UNRRA distributed not only food and clothing, but seed, fertilizer, livestock, machinery, and medicine. Altogether UNRRA spent some 4 billion dollars for relief purposes; of this sum the United States gave 2¾ billion. In addition the United States Army fed large areas of occupied Europe, Lend-Lease continued to pour foodstuffs and other supplies into Allied countries, and private gifts and CARE supplemented governmental contributions on a generous scale. Yet if the United States did much for relief, she did less than her resources permitted; there was no postwar rationing, cereals continued to be fed to livestock rather than exported direct to the starving abroad, and Lend-Lease was abruptly terminated in August 1945, one week after the capitulation of Japan.

Most of UNRRA's relief went to the peoples of eastern Europe — Poland, Yugoslavia, Russia, and Greece — and as the actual distribution of food and supplies was left to the various national authorities, UNRRA almost inevitably got mixed up in politics. With some truth it was charged that American supplies were being used to bolster Communist regimes abroad. Partly for this reason, partly because inadequate appropriations made for inefficiency of administration, and partly because of the widespread feeling that the crisis was ended, Congress got fed up with UNRRA and allowed it to die in 1947.

A major part of UNRRA's task was responsibility for the millions of refugees who came to be known as Displaced Persons. At the close of the war there were perhaps 10 million of these hapless victims of modern war; many of them had been pressed into Nazi military service and were mingled with other prisoners of war; others were labor slaves, or inmates of prison camps. By the end of 1946 the military had repatriated most of these refugees, but there remained a hard core of perhaps a million non-repatriables: Jews who wanted to go to Palestine, or Balts, Poles, Yugoslavs, and Russians who had fought Communism and were unable or unwilling to return to their own countries. Many of these were eventually resettled in Palestine, New Zealand, Brazil, Colombia, Britain, and other countries who were ready to welcome the labor and skills that they possessed. The United States lagged badly behind in this program of resettlement of Displaced Persons, admitting only some 6000 by the end of 1947. In 1948 Congress passed legislation to admit an additional 200,000, on terms far from generous. In 1950 this legislation was liberalized and additional refugees admitted.

The reconstruction of the war-shattered economy of western Europe called for boldness, imagination, courage, and intelligence. The depression of the 'thirties had demonstrated that American economy was irretrievably linked with European and that the United States could not remain prosperous in a bankrupt world. And complex as was the problem of economic reconstruction, its broad outlines were essentially simple. Europe needed everything but was able to buy nothing; the United States had — or was capable of producing — almost everything, but could sell nothing to a bankrupt Europe. If the European economy collapsed, the American economy would take a tailspin. Some method must be found, therefore, not only of getting the European economy functioning on an emergency basis, but of putting it on a permanently self-supporting basis, so that European countries could resume their traditional role in international trade. Clearly, too, more was involved than economic prosperity. If the United States stood idly by while western Europe plunged into economic chaos, she might be faced, within a few years, with a Soviet-dominated Continent.

Tinkering with tariffs, credits, and investment policies could ameliorate the immediate effects of the economic malaise, but could not cure it. Yet until such time as the true nature and extent of the problem became clear, palliatives were useful, and the United States moved on many fronts to ease restrictions on trade, stabilize currencies, and encourage investments. The Reciprocal Trade Agreements, inaugurated in 1934, had been renewed in 1945, and in 1947 some forty nations, meeting at Geneva, agreed on sweeping reductions in tariffs. Under the terms of this agreement the United States cut duties on thousands of items, including wool, copper, beef, sugar, and lumber; the general effect was to reduce duties to the 1913 level. At the same time the United States took the lead in establishing an International Trade Organization to promote the expansion of world trade. In response to these moves American imports increased from a prewar average of less than 3 billion to a total of over 7 billion dollars in 1948. Yet this still left a gap of almost 8 billion between what the rest of the world bought and what it sold to the United States: if trade were to continue this gap would have to be bridged.

Closely connected with the problem of trade was that of credit and currency. As early as 1943 the Treasury Department began laying plans for stabilizing national currencies, and making available credit for international trade and investment, and in the summer of 1944 a United Nations Monetary and Financial Conference met at Bretton Woods, New Hampshire, to crystallize these plans. This conference set up and Congress ratified two new agencies: an International Monetary Fund and an International Bank for Reconstruction. The first, designed to maintain stable exchange rates and discourage restrictions on the transfer of funds from nation to nation, was provided with a capital of 8.8 billion dollars, to which the United States contributed some 2⅔ billion. The World Bank, as it came to be called, was authorized to borrow and lend money and to underwrite private loans for production purposes. Most of the United Nations except Russia participated in setting up these two financial institutions. The Monetary Fund attempted to stimulate trade by effecting a general devaluation of the currencies of western European countries late in 1949. The achievements of the World Bank were, up to 1950, disappointing: by that time the Bank had made loans of only 700 million dollars and had been unable to attract private capital to any large-scale investment in European recovery.

One step that contributed to orderly economic reconstruction was the prompt settlement of Lend-Lease accounts. Lend-Lease had been terminated, with what Europeans thought unnecessary abruptness, in August 1945, but existing obligations called for the delivery of some 2 billion dollars worth of material and services during the following year. The final reckoning showed total Lend-Lease grants of some 50 billion dollars, and reverse Lend-Lease to the value of a little less than 8 billion dollars.[1] Roosevelt and Truman were both determined to avoid the war-debt business that had plagued American relations with her Allies after World War I, so Lend-Lease was settled on the simple principle of wiping all wartime debts and credits off the books, and requiring repayment only of postwar grants, and that on easy terms. Settlements were speedily concluded with Britain, France, China, and other wartime associates; only Russia refused to discuss the matter at all.

The end of Lend-Lease precipitated a serious economic crisis in Britain. Britain's balance of trade had long been unfavorable; before the war she had made up the deficit chiefly from foreign investments, shipping, and banking services. Six years of war had taken a heavy toll on these assets. The British had not only lost most of their foreign investments, but incurred heavy debts abroad; they had lost one third of their shipping as well as a substantial part of their foreign markets; and their industry was partially destroyed and almost wholly run down. They could neither recapture their export market nor pay for imports with accumulated capital. At the same time they were unable to escape heavy external financial commitments: occupation costs in Germany and Austria, military expenses in Palestine, Greece, and the Far East, assistance to their colonies, contributions to UNRRA, the Monetary Fund, and the World Bank, and so forth. To ward off a catastrophe Sir Stafford Cripps asked for a loan of 5 billion dollars from the United States. After protracted negotiations a sum of 3¾ billion was agreed upon, plus an additional credit for the 650 million outstanding on Lend-Lease; the loan was to run for fifty years and carry interest at 2 per cent.[2] In return Britain agreed to give up her system of blocked credits and exchange controls and to scale down her obligations to other countries. The British thought these terms pretty stiff; most Americans thought them generous, and Congress took seven months to ratify them. It had been hoped that the loan would carry Britain through the next five years but, notwithstanding the maintenance of wartime austerity and heroic efforts to regain foreign markets, the money ran out in two years, and by 1947 Britain was again faced with economic disaster.

The British crisis, together with the persistence of economic conditions that encouraged Communism in Italy and France, finally led to the formulation of a really adequate program of American

1 See table in Appendix.

2 Canada also lent Britain 1¼ billion.

aid. Early in May 1947 Under-Secretary Acheson announced that national self-interest required that the European nations become self-supporting, and that to this end the United States must be prepared with emergency financial measures. The next month Secretary of State Marshall, speaking at Harvard University, gave concrete form to this suggestion by advising Europe to work out a joint plan for reconstruction. 'Our policy,' he said, 'is directed against hunger, poverty, desperation and chaos. Its purpose should be the revival of a working economy in the world so as to permit the emergence of political and social conditions in which free institutions can exist.' Any government willing to assist in the task of recovery, he added, would find full cooperation on the part of the United States.

This was what Europe had been waiting for. The Prime Ministers of Britain and France promptly issued an invitation to twenty-two nations, including Russia, to meet at Paris the following month to draw a blueprint for European recovery. Though Molotov came to Paris with a staff of 89 economic experts to discuss preliminaries, it quickly appeared that while he was willing to accept American aid on a gigantic scale as nothing less than Europe's due, he thought America's role should be strictly limited to paying the bill. When it became clear that this pipe-dream was shared by neither Britain nor France — to say nothing of the United States — Molotov withdrew, and all the Soviet satellites followed; poor Czechoslovakia, which had already accepted an invitation to the Paris conference, sent regrets.

In the end representatives of sixteen nations met at Paris and, under the leadership of the Oxford philosopher Sir Oliver Franks, drafted an elaborate plan for European recovery. This plan fixed new production targets, promised financial and monetary stability, advised the abandonment of trade barriers, called for the restoration of the industrial economy of western Germany, and fixed the bill at approximately 22 billion dollars over a period of four years. It was assumed that most of this would come from the United States, but it was expected, too, that Canada and Latin America would help and that some money might be obtained from the World Bank and the International Monetary Fund.

In December 1947 President Truman submitted this plan to Congress together with his own recommendations for an appropriation of 17 billion dollars over a four-year period. The debate, in and out of Congress, was comparable to that over the not dissimilar Lend-

Lease bill of 1941. The opposition came chiefly from those who felt that the American economy could not stand so heavy a burden and those who regarded any further aid to the Old World as 'Operation Rat-hole.' It was led by Senator Taft, who was rapidly reverting to his prewar isolationism and who had his eye on the Republican nomination that summer. Liberals of both parties as well as powerful business, farm, and labor organizations rallied to the bill, whose leading senatorial champion was Senator Vandenberg, architect of the bipartisan foreign policy and most internationally minded of Republican leaders since Willkie. What finally turned the tide was not so much economic arguments as the Communist coup in Czechoslovakia in March 1948, together with new Russian demands on Finland. A program to halt the advance of Communism appealed to many who were immune to an appeal on mere economic or humanitarian grounds, and the Marshall Plan Act — providing an immediate grant of 5.3 billion for European recovery plus 463 million for China and 275 million for Greece and Turkey — passed both houses of Congress by thumping majorities and became law on 3 April 1949. Thus once more, in the great words of Churchill, 'the new world with all its power and might, stepped forth to the rescue and liberation of the old.'

3. *Liquidating the War*

It was the irrepressible Winston Churchill, too, who said, 'We shall not make the same mistakes after this war that we made after the last; we shall make a lot of new ones.' As it turned out, we made plenty of them and many of the old ones as well. The peacemaking of 1919, long the object of criticism and contempt, came to seem almost statesmanlike by comparison with the lack of it after 1945. The leaders of the Western democracies, Roosevelt and Churchill, had given — as we now know — immense thought and effort to laying the foundations for peace and an international organization, and a whole series of conferences — Quebec, Moscow, Teheran, Cairo, Crimea — had presumably prepared the way for the creation of a secure future. Yet five years after victory no permanent settlements had been arrived at, either for Germany or for Japan. Disagreements among the victors, restrained during the war itself, broke out virulently after the war, and grew increasingly acrimonious with the passing years. Of all the innumerable problems connected with the liquidation of the war — reparations, territorial settlements, the punishment of war criminals, the establishment of permanent governments, the restoration of self-supporting economies — not one was satisfactorily solved.

The unconditional-surrender formula, announced at Casablanca and reiterated at Moscow and Yalta, and imposed on the Germans and the Japanese, was no more than just that — a formula for surrender. Certainly it was not a formula for peace. Even as a formula for surrender it required very considerable elaboration, for the surrender of an army and a navy, and the dissolution of a government, is a complex and delicate process. And clearly the victors had to go on from there. They had to provide the mechanism for demobilization, dispose of the millions of prisoners of war, set up military government during the interregnum between surrender and peace, and get some temporary civil government under way. They had to start the economy functioning once more, supply food and clothing, heat and shelter, medicine and protection for the defeated populations, and recreate such social institutions as church, schools, and publishing.

What in fact was to be the Allied policy toward Germany? World War I afforded no precedent; when Germany quit, in November 1918, a German government was functioning and German economy was intact. Italy furnished no satisfactory precedent; her territory had not been devastated nor her economy shattered as had the German, and she had achieved the status of co-belligerent. The Allies — already by mid-1945 as much rivals as allies — had to tailor their policies to fit new and unpredictable circumstances. Unconditional surrender was not a conclusion but merely a point of departure. Two plans were discussed in the United States: the Welles plan of breaking Germany up into a group of small states, and the Morgenthau plan of reducing her to a pastoral economy. The first was never seriously considered; the second was tentatively endorsed at the Quebec Conference — over the protest of the British — and was then abandoned.

Some sort of plan was, however, essential. The Moscow Conference of 1943 set up a European Advisory Commission, which worked out the basic principles for the treatment of Germany after the war: the destruction of German militarism and military potential; the dissolution of the Nazi party and the punishment of war criminals; creation of zones of control; and the payment of reparations 'to the greatest extent possible.' The Yalta Conference reaffirmed these principles, added the provision that France might share in the occupation, named, as a basis for discussion only, the sum of 20 billion dollars for reparations, and tentatively conceded the territory east of the Curzon Line to Russia and the right of Poland to compensation from German territory. At the Potsdam Conference, held in July 1945, Truman, Stalin, and Attlee — who had replaced Churchill as spokesman for the British government — spelled out the details of these agreements and added certain others. That conference created a Council of Foreign Ministers, which was to draw up peace treaties with Italy and the Axis satellites; regularized an Allied Control Council for the military administration of Germany; gave Poland administrative control over all German territory east of the Oder and Neisse rivers; decided that notwithstanding the division into occupation zones Germany should be treated as an economic unit; and provided that each occupying power should take reparations from its own zone but that, in addition, the U.S.S.R. might receive reparations in the form of industrial equipment from the west in exchange for food and other products from the east.

Joint occupation was already under way, and was already revealing its inadequacies, yet it is difficult to know what alternative there was. Eastern Germany, including Brandenburg, Mecklenburg, Saxony, and Thuringia, was assigned to Russia; northwestern Germany, including Westphalia, Hannover, and Holstein, to Britain; southwestern Germany, including Bavaria, Württemberg, and Hesse, to the United States; while France received two smaller areas — Baden and the Saar. Austria, too, was carved up into four occupation zones, while both Berlin and Vienna were parcelled out to the victors. None of these zones was self-sufficient economically, and the principle of treating Germany as an economic unit broke down almost immediately. The Russians stripped their zone of whatever they thought they were entitled to, and made heavy demands for factories, power plants, rolling stock, and tools on the British and American zones. But the Potsdam declaration had included a precautionary clause to the effect that the conquerors 'should leave enough resources to enable the German people to subsist without external assistance.' If Britain and the United States permitted their zones to be gutted, German economy would collapse and Germany would become a permanent burden on their

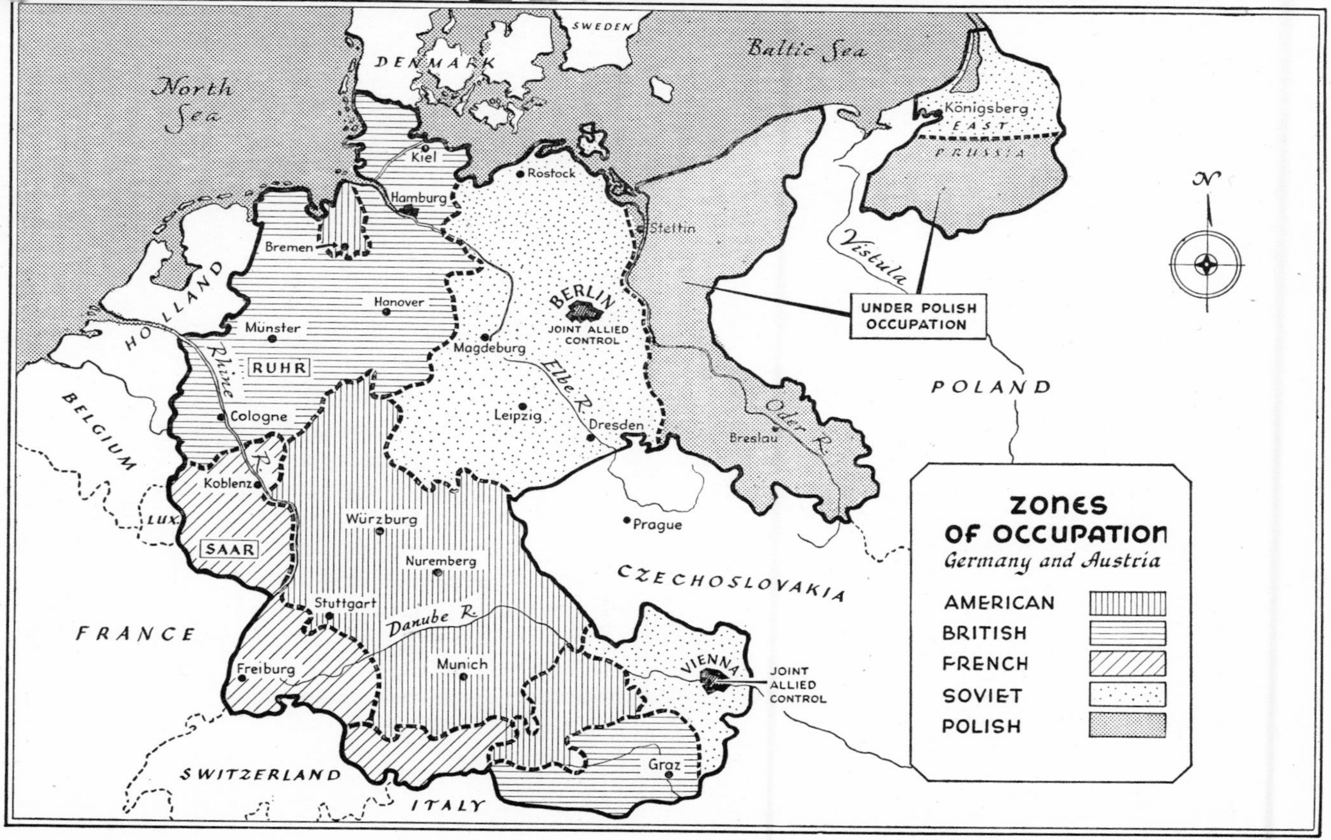
ZONES
OF OCCUPATION
Germany and Austria
AMERICAN
BRITISH
FRENCH
SOVIET
POLISH
North Sea
Baltic Sea
DENMARK
SWEDEN
HOLLAND
BELGIUM
LUX.
FRANCE
SWITZERLAND
ITALY
CZECHOSLOVAKIA
POLAND
EAST PRUSSIA
Königsberg
Vistula
UNDER POLISH OCCUPATION
Kiel
Rostock
Hamburg
Stettin
Bremen
Hanover
Münster
RUHR
Rhine
Cologne
Koblenz
R.
SAAR
BERLIN
JOINT ALLIED CONTROL
Magdeburg
Elbe R.
Leipzig
Dresden
Breslau
Oder R.
Prague
Würzburg
Nuremberg
Stuttgart
Danube R.
Freiburg
Munich
VIENNA
JOINT ALLIED CONTROL
Graz
N

taxpayers. Furthermore, if the industrial potential of the Ruhr and the Saar were destroyed, the consequences for European recovery generally would be disastrous. As a result of these considerations, and of growing antagonism between Russia and the Western Allies, reparations slowed down, and then stopped altogether in 1947.

Behind these sharp differences of opinion on reparations lay even deeper differences of general policy. The Russians made clear from the first that they aimed at nothing less than the communization of the whole of central Europe — Germany and Austria included. They proceeded as if the purely provisional agreements at Yalta and Potsdam were permanent. Thus Russia took over not only the Baltic states seized during the war — Estonia, Latvia, and Lithuania — but part of East Prussia as well and the whole of Poland east of the Curzon Line, and undertook a vigorous campaign to win eastern Germany for Communism. Poland regarded her occupation of Germany west of the Oder-Neisse line as equally permanent, and proceeded to oust some ten million Germans living in that rich area. In the circumstances, genuine co-operation between the East and the West appeared impossible. So within two years of the defeat of Hitler's Reich, Russia and the Western Allies were bidding against each other for control of the German people.

American policy, at first confused, was somewhat clarified by Secretary of State Byrnes in a speech at Stuttgart in September 1946. 'The American government,' he said, 'is unwilling to accept responsibility for the needless aggravation of economic distress that is caused by the failure of the Allied Control Council to agree to give the German people a chance to solve some of their most urgent economic problems.' The United States was unwilling to turn Germany into a poorhouse, and if Russia would not observe the terms of the Potsdam agreement, the whole reparations program would have to be revised. As a further gesture, Byrnes added that the United States would support revision of the eastern frontier, and regarded the Ruhr and the Rhineland as irretrievably German. 'It is not in the interest of the German people,' he asserted, 'that Germany should become a pawn or a partner in a military struggle for power between the East and the West.' Yet that is precisely what Germany had become!

All through 1947 relations between the East and the West became increasingly exacerbated. Early in 1948 a complete deadlock developed; when the Western powers decided to go ahead and establish a West German government, the Soviet representative on the Control Council charged that the four-power machinery had broken down and that the Council no longer existed. A crisis came in the summer of 1948 when Russia countered Western currency reform with a blockade of Berlin. Through some inexplicable oversight the Allied Control Council had not guaranteed the Western Allies access to their zones of Berlin, and as a result the Russians were able to cut all land communication by the simple device of erecting road blocks and stopping railroad trains. Confronted with the alternatives of mass starvation for the two million Germans of the western zones of Berlin or an ignominious evacuation of that city, the American Commander, General Lucius Clay, rejected both. 'We have lost Czechoslovakia,' he said,

> Norway is threatened. We retreat from Berlin. When Berlin falls, western Germany will be next. If we mean to hold Europe against Communism we must not budge. . . If we withdraw, our position in Europe is threatened. If America does not understand this now . . . then it never will, and communism will run rampant. I believe the future of democracy requires us to stay.

The American and British governments accepted this advice, and embarked upon an 'airlift' operation to supply the beleaguered capital not only with food but with coal and other necessities. To the consternation of the Russians the airlift was a spectacular success: by the spring of 1949 American and British planes were flying in up to 10 thousand tons of supplies daily. Confronted by the implacable determination of the West to supply Berlin indefinitely by this method — a method that incidentally provided admirable training for pilots and a dramatic display of power for continental Europe — Russia ended the blockade and negotiated the minor differences that had inspired it. It was a moral victory for the West, but an expensive one, and there was no assurance that Russia might not reimpose the blockade at any time.

Every effort to write peace treaties for Germany and Austria failed, but some progress was made on the lesser treaties. It would be tedious to follow these in detail. In accordance with instructions from the Potsdam Conference, the Council of Foreign Ministers — representatives of the Big Three with occasional spokesmen from France and China — met at London, Moscow, and Paris to air their differences and dramatize their disagreement. Pressure from other members of the United Nations, however, finally forced action, and in the closing weeks of 1946 the Council hammered out treaties with Italy, Finland, Hungary, Rumania, and Bulgaria. Russia acquired the Karelian Isthmus and part of Petsamo from Finland, and Bessarabia from Rumania; the Dodecanese Islands were ceded to Greece; Italy was required to pay 360 million dollars in reparations and Bulgaria 70 million — this in addition to reparations of 300 million each already exacted from Finland, Rumania, and Hungary. The settlement of Trieste and its hinterland — a question that had plagued the Peace Conference of 1919 — was the knottiest problem the Council faced; it was finally decided to make Trieste a free port under international control and cede the hinterland to Yugoslavia, but within a year this decision was revised, and Italy was encouraged by the Western powers to win back Trieste.

Meantime the Big Three went ahead with the trial of major war criminals, and the Western powers with their denazification program and with the re-establishment of a German government. From the beginning of the war Churchill and Roosevelt had made clear their determination to bring Nazi war criminals to trial. The Moscow Declaration on Atrocities of 1 November 1943 provided that persons responsible for atrocities would be tried in the countries where their crimes occurred and that 'major criminals whose offenses have no particular geographical location . . . will be punished by a joint decision of the Governments of the Allies.' The appointment of Associate Justice Robert Jackson to represent the United States in establishing an International Military Tribunal and to serve as chief counsel for the prosecution was an indication of the importance that Roosevelt and Truman attached to these trials. His report designated three major types of crime: violations of international law, crimes against humanity and against established criminal law, and aggressive warfare in violation of the Kellogg Pact and other international commitments. Jackson proposed the trial not only of major war criminals, but of criminal organizations such as the Gestapo, the SS, and the Nazi party, but left to military tribunals and to the German courts the punishment of lesser criminals.

The London Agreement of August 1945 accepted these proposals and established an international judicial tribunal with representatives from the four occupying powers. The International Military Tribunal then presented indictments against 24 major criminals and six criminal organizations. The trials, lasting ten months, published the whole ghastly record of Nazi aggression, atrocities, mass murders, looting, and destruction; this made no deep impression upon the German mind nor did it persuade the German people of their collective guilt. Nineteen war criminals were found guilty, and twelve, including such notorious figures from the Nazi high command as Goering, Keitel, Jodl, Ribbentrop, and Seyss-Inquart, were sentenced to death. In addition there were numerous trials of lesser war criminals by the military authorities and by denazified German courts. The Americans conducted a series of twelve trials, each centered on an occupational group — doctors and lawyers, military leaders, SS and police, industrialists, and government ministers. All the members of these groups were tried individually for specific crimes: 35 were acquitted, 24 given death sentences, and 128 condemned to varying terms of imprisonment.

The war trials came in for heavy criticism in Britain and the United States. It was alleged that by making aggressive warfare a crime the Tribunal was guilty of *ex post facto* legislation, that trials by judges from the victor nations did not deserve the term 'judicial,' and that trials by military tribunals were equally flawed with impropriety. Whatever the validity of these charges, much was to be said for the attempt to make aggressive warfare a crime; and by adopting the Universal Declaration of Human Rights, the United Nations in effect endorsed the principles and the findings of the Nuremberg tribunals.

While these trials were proceeding to their inevitable conclusion, the work of sterilizing German society of its Nazi infection went ahead. The Potsdam declaration had looked not only to the outlawing of the Nazi party and all of its affiliates, but to the elimination of Nazis from the civil service, schools, industries, and all important private organizations, and their replacement by persons 'who by their political and moral qualities are deemed capable of developing genuine democratic institutions in Germany.' This was easier said than done. The Nazi regime had so extended itself into almost every field of social and economic activity that almost the only Germans free of Nazi taint were those in exile, concentration camps, or cemeteries. Confronted with this situation, the military administration was forced to compromise, and the denazification that had begun with a bang petered out with a whimper. As General Clay wrote:

On the one hand it was certain that the 12,000,000 or more Germans who were identified in varying degree with Nazi activities could not be kept forever from political and economic life. On the other hand, it was clearly essential to any hope of a democratic Germany that the real Nazis be identified so that they could be excluded from positions of leadership until new leaders emerged. . . I had become convinced that this real task could not be accomplished by occupation officials without at some time making martyrs out of those we sought to condemn in the eyes of their countrymen, and that the long-range job was one for the Germans to undertake.[3]

Notorious Nazis were ousted from places of authority and, in some instances, punished, but most of the small fry went free or were subjected to mild penalties. Under the Germans, denazification became something of a joke. Thus of the 836,000 Nazis tried, less than 0.1 per cent were classified as major offenders, and as of May 1948 only 1677 were serving jail sentences.[4]

Notwithstanding the difficulties of denazification, the Military Government made substantial progress in the restoration of German economy and government in the years after the war. The task was not only enormously complex; it was one for which Americans were almost wholly without experience, and the wonder is not that so much was done badly, but that so much was done well. Even in the most favorable circumstances it would have been difficult to restore German economy; with the amputation of the agricultural east and Silesia by the Russians and of the Saar by the French, the influx of some 10 million German refugees from the Russian and Polish areas, the division of the west into three administrative zones, the reduction of German industry to the 1932 level, and the drain of reparations, complete restoration was impos-

[3] *Decision in Germany,* Doubleday.

[4] The figures may be of interest: in the American Zone

12,753,000	registered
9,073,000	were not charged
3,209,000	were processed
2,373,000	received amnesty without trial
836,000	were tried
503,360	were convicted
430,890	were fined less than 1000 RM
27,413	were sentenced to perform some community work
7,768	were given short sentences in labor camps
18,503	were pronounced ineligible to hold office
20,865	suffered partial property confiscation

See J. H. Herz, *Political Science Quarterly* (December 1948).

sible. After 1946 some of these obstacles to recovery were removed. The level of industrial production was raised; Britain and America combined their zones into an economic 'bizonia'; the United States poured half a billion dollars annually into western Germany and, in 1948, made it eligible for Marshall Plan aid. Gradually economic life revived and western Germany moved toward a self-supporting economy.

The establishment of German governments proved almost equally difficult. The collapse of the Nazi regime had left a complete political vacuum in Germany, and for the time being the military had to improvise administration as best it could, a task aggravated by the absence of any over-all policy and of clear-cut directives, and by the fact that the occupation zones cut athwart traditional state boundaries. Yet by July 1945 Military Government teams had restored city and county administrations, and in October a Council of States was set up to provide over-all administration in the American zone. The creation of a government for the whole of western Germany took another three years. A Parliamentary Council of elected delegates met at the university city of Bonn in September 1948 to draft a Basic Law; after six months of debate and negotiation a constitution creating a democratic federal state was finally hammered out, accepted by the occupation authorities, and adopted in May 1949.

The occupation of Japan was simple compared with that of Germany. The Imperial government was still functioning, the Japanese people were subservient and co-operative; their economy had not been destroyed as the German; and there was no problem of divided authority: General MacArthur handled the whole thing himself.[5] Japan, too, had surrendered unconditionally; the Potsdam Conference made clear that this did not involve the destruction of the Japanese nation, and subsequently it was decided that it did not involve the deposition of the Emperor. Within a few months after the surrender General MacArthur in co-operation with liberal elements in Japan revolutionized Japanese society and government. He demobilized four million Japanese soldiers, destroyed Japanese military potential, arrested and tried war criminals, purged the civil service, abolished the secret police and 'patriotic' societies, broke up cartels

[5] There were, however, two advisory bodies: a Far Eastern Commission in Washington and an Interallied Council for Japan in Tokyo. Each of the four major powers in the Far Eastern Commission had a veto, and if the Commission failed to agree, the American military administration could act unilaterally, as it almost always did; the Allied Council was limited to making recommendations.

and the family trusts, democratized the landowning system, ended press censorship, prohibited racial and religious discrimination, abolished Shintoism as a state religion, and required the Emperor to repudiate his own divinity. At the same time he inaugurated far-reaching political reforms. A new Diet, elected under a law permitting woman suffrage, drafted a democratic constitution that provided for popular sovereignty and parliamentary government, reduced the Emperor to a figurehead, and included a bill of rights and a permanent renunciation of war. But all efforts to write a peace treaty were frustrated by the recalcitrance of Russia.

Military occupation was as unsuccessful in Korea as it was successful in Japan. Long part of China, the 'Hermit Kingdom' had been annexed to Japan in 1910; the Cairo Conference had promised Koreans freedom 'in due course.' Russia's last-minute declaration of war against Japan enabled her to move troops into the Korean peninsula and, like Germany, Korea was divided into zones of occupation: the United States in the agricultural south and Russia in the industrialized north. All efforts to unify either administration or economy proved vain; as the Russians proceeded to communize their area, the American military authorities threw their support to the conservative elements of south Korea — the great landowners. Late in 1946 administration was turned over to the Koreans, and in 1948 a popular election adopted a Republican Constitution, and the American military government came to an end. The triumph of the Communists in the north and in China, however, made Korea's strategic position highly vulnerable, while economically the truncated nation continued to be a heavy drain on the American taxpayer.

4. *Organization for Peace*

We seek peace — enduring peace. More than an end to war, we want an end to the beginnings of all wars — yes an end to this brutal, inhuman and thoroughly impractical method of settling the differences between governments. . . We are faced with the pre-eminent fact that, if civilization is to survive, we must cultivate the science of human relationships — the ability of all peoples, of all kinds, to live together and work together in the same world, at peace. . . Today, as we move against the terrible scourge of war — as we go forward toward the greatest contribution that any generation of human beings can make in this world, — the contribution of lasting peace — I ask you to keep up your faith.

These were the last words that Franklin Roosevelt wrote, and they were eloquent of that profound concern for peace, and for the creation of machinery to keep it, that possessed him throughout the war years. Roosevelt's interest in peace went back to his service in the Wilson administration during World War I and to his candidacy, on a League of Nations platform, in 1920. That he had been deeply impressed by Wilson's idealism is clear; that he was determined not to repeat Wilson's mistakes is equally clear; 'the tragedy of Wilson,' wrote Robert Sherwood, 'was always somewhere within the rim of his consciousness.'

The Atlantic Charter had called for 'the establishment of a wider and permanent system of general security,' and thereafter, it is no exaggeration to say, the construction of a peaceful postwar order was second in Roosevelt's thoughts only to the war, and never wholly separated from it. The great coalition that was to guarantee peace took embryonic form in the United Nations of 1 January 1942, and thereafter every major conference of the Allied leaders gave increasing attention to this problem, and to its solution. Thus the Moscow Conference of October 1943 pledged the Big Three to

> recognize the necessity of establishing at the earliest practicable date a general international organization, based on the principle of the sovereign equality of all peace-loving states, and open to membership by all such states, large and small, for the maintenance of international peace and security.

And at the Teheran Conference Roosevelt outlined a specific plan for an international organization — a general assembly and an executive committee of 'Four Policemen' to enforce peace. All through 1944 the United States State Department and foreign-office officials of the major Allied powers were busily engaged in drafting proposals for a postwar international organization, and in August of that year their representatives met at Dumbarton Oaks, in Washington, and drew up the blueprint which was adopted, with some changes and additions, as the Charter of the United Nations.

The discussions at Yalta — the last and most important of the Roosevelt-Churchill-Stalin conferences — had addressed themselves to three major topics: the final defeat of the Axis powers, the problems of occupation (including what should be occupied and who should do the occupying), and the creation of an international organization. It was the last which Roosevelt emphasized in his report to Congress, and in the light of the subsequent breakdown of world peace, that report takes on an almost tragic character. 'I come from the Crimea Conference,' he said,

> with a firm belief that we have made a good start on the road to a world of peace. . . This time we are not making the mistake of waiting until the end of the war to set up the machinery of peace. . . The Conference in the Crimea was a turning point — I hope in our history and therefore in the history of the world. There will soon be presented to the Senate of the United States and to the American people a great decision that will determine the fate of the United States — and of the world — for generations to come. There can be no middle ground here. We shall have to take the responsibility for world collaboration, or we shall have to bear the responsibility for another world conflict.

Invitations had already gone out for a United Nations Conference to meet at San Francisco to draft a Charter for the new international organization, and late in April delegates from 50 nations gathered at that city whose very choice suggested the new importance of the Pacific area. Secretary of State Stettinius headed the American delegation, Anthony Eden the British, and — in the end — Molotov the Russian. Determined not to make the mistake Wilson had made in ignoring both the Republicans and the Congress, Roosevelt appointed two Republicans — Senator Vandenberg and Representative Eaton — and two Democrats — Senator Connally and Representative Bloom — to fill out the American delegation.

The conference lasted for two months, and was marked by many sharp disagreements over such matters as the Polish delegation, the admission of Argentina, separate votes for the Ukraine and White Russia, and the veto power; it ended on a note of surface harmony with all 50 nations signing the Charter, whose preamble announced the purpose of the organization:

> To save succeeding generations from the scourge of war . . . and to reaffirm faith in fundamental human rights, in the dignity and worth of the human person, in the equal rights of men and women and of Nations large and small, and to establish conditions under which justice and respect for the obligations arising from treaties and other sources of international law can be maintained, and to promote social progress and better standards of life in larger freedom, and . . . to ensure, by the acceptance of principles and the institution of methods, that armed force shall not be used, save in the common interest, and to employ interna-

tional machinery for the promotion of the economic and social advancement of all peoples.

Ratification followed swiftly. The United States was already committed to the Charter in principle, by the Fulbright-Connally Resolutions of 1943, and the Senate ratified the document on 28 July 1945 with only two votes in opposition. By October, 29 nations had ratified and the Charter went into effect.

The United Nations Charter was, in many respects, like the Covenant of the League of Nations. Like the League, it created an Assembly, whose functions were largely deliberative, and a Council whose functions were executive; like the League, it provided for a system of mandates, an International Court of Justice, a Secretariat, and other affiliated organizations; and like the League, too, it recognized the validity of regional agreements. It was unlike the League, however, in several important respects. It was not tied to the peace treaties, but existed independently of any that might be made; it permitted any one of the five great powers (the United States, Britain, Russia, France, and China) to exercise a veto on any but procedural questions; and it authorized the use of force against aggressor nations.

Specifically the Charter provided for a General Assembly in which each nation had one vote, and whose functions were limited almost entirely to discussion, investigation, and advice, and a Security Council to consist of five permanent [6] and six elected members, which alone had power to act in international disputes. The Assembly could call to the attention of the Council any situation likely to endanger peace, recommend measures for the settlement of disputes, and promote international co-operation in economic, social, and cultural fields. The Council, to which was assigned 'primary responsibility for the maintenance of peace and security,' was authorized to hear complaints from member nations, investigate disputes that might lead to war, and take such measures 'by air, sea or land forces' as might be necessary to preserve peace. All members agreed to make available to the Council such armed forces and facilities as were agreed on and called for. Article 52 of the Charter permitted the creation of regional agreements and agencies, and it was in ac-

[6] Great Britain, France, Russia, the United States, and China. The kind of problem presented, in 1950, by the existence of Nationalist and Communist governments each claiming to represent China was neither anticipated nor provided for in the Charter.

cordance with this permissive article that the Rio de Janeiro and the North Atlantic treaties were subsequently negotiated.

The Charter created a number of agencies designed to ease international tensions and promote co-operation of a constructive nature. There was to be an International Court of Justice with powers comparable to those formerly exercised by the World Court; an Economic and Social Council to promote social and cultural welfare and human rights; a trusteeship system to replace the unsatisfactory mandate system of the old League; a permanent Secretariat; a Military Staff Committee composed of the chiefs of staffs of the great powers and with authority over such military contingents as might be placed under it; and later an Atomic Energy Commission. Under the Economic and Social Council there was a proliferation of special agencies — UNESCO, a Food and Agricultural Organization, an International Labor Organization, a World Health Organization, and eventually many others of a technical character. Permanent headquarters of the United Nations were established in New York City.

Launched with high hopes, the United Nations soon ran aground on the shoals of the East-West conflict. Yet in the first four years of its existence it had some substantial accomplishments to its credit. It succeeded in settling — after a fashion — three major disputes: that between Russia and Iran, the series of problems connected with the emergence of Israel as a nation, and the complex and inflammable Indonesia issue. In addition, it took cognizance of the problem of Communist-inspired guerrilla warfare in Greece, the presence of British and French troops in Syria and Lebanon, a claim of Britain against Albania, and the position of Franco's government in Spain. Its principal achievements were not, however, in the settlement of explosive disputes, but in serving — in Senator Vandenberg's phrase — as a 'town meeting of the world,' and as a vehicle for important social and economic reforms. In a quiet way such agencies as the International Health and the International Labor organizations performed important services for the whole Western World.

Yet it could not be denied that the United Nations (as of 1950) disappointed those who had hoped that it would succeed where the League had failed. The ostensible difficulty was the veto; designed for use only in emergencies, and then to avoid a rupture between the great powers, it was invoked by Russia some fifty times in the first four years, often for purposes that were trivial. The real difficulty of the United Nations was, of course, not mechanical but substantial: the division of the world into hostile camps led by the United States and the Soviet Union. This division was dramatized by the Russian boycott of the Trusteeship Council; the veto on applications for membership from Ireland, Portugal, and Finland; the failure to bring important disputes before the International Court of Justice; and — most ominously — the failure of the Security Council to agree on the momentous question of the control of atomic energy.

5. *The Control of Atomic Energy*

The atom bomb, so soon to be detonated at Los Alamos, was the subject of Secretary Stimson's last talk with President Roosevelt. 'I went over with him,' Stimson records,

> the two schools of thought that exist in respect to the future control after the war of this project . . . one of them being the secret close-in attempted control of the project by those who control it now, and the other being the international control based upon freedom both of science and of access. I told him that those things must be settled before the first projectile was used. . . He agreed to that.[7]

This basic question of control was not, however, settled, and it remained to plague the world and perhaps to condemn it to destruction.

On the day the United Nations Conference convened at San Francisco, Stimson presented to President Truman a memorandum on the bomb, which pointed out that

> The world, in its present state of moral advancement, compared with its technical development, would be eventually at the mercy of such a weapon. . . Modern civilization might be completely destroyed. To approach any world peace organization of any pattern now likely to be considered without an appreciation by the leaders of our country of the power of this new weapon would seem to be unrealistic. No system of control heretofore considered would be adequate to control this menace. . . Our leadership in the war and in the development of this weapon has placed a certain moral responsibility upon us which we cannot shirk without very serious responsibility for any disaster to civilization which it would further.[8]

[7] Henry Stimson, *On Active Service*, p. 616.

[8] *Ibid.* p. 636.

The explosions at Hiroshima and Nagasaki and the 1946 experiments in the Bikini Lagoon [9] justified the truth of this prophecy and the validity of this warning. Thoughtful men everywhere in the world realized that atomic energy might be the Frankenstein monster that would destroy mankind. At the same time it was clear that, properly safeguarded and used for beneficent ends, atomic energy might usher in a new era of prosperity and well-being for the peoples of the earth. As David Lilienthal, chairman of the Atomic Energy Commission, pointed out:

> In the widening knowledge of the atom we have the means for making our time one of the two or three most vital and stimulating periods of all history. In the atomic adventure we sight one of those great mountain peaks of history, a towering symbol of one of the faiths that makes man civilized, the faith in knowledge.

How to prevent the use of atomic energy for destructive purposes and encourage its use for constructive purposes was the most urgent problem that confronted the statesmen of the world at mid-twentieth century.

It was a problem of peculiar difficulty as well as of peculiar urgency. In the first place, there were no 'secrets' about the atom bomb; physicists everywhere in the world knew how to make the bomb, and it was certain that within a few years any country that cared to spend the money and effort could have bigger and more devastating bombs than those that had already been exploded. In the second place, given existing international machinery, there was no effective means of controlling the manufacture of atom bombs; any method that would be effective required some surrender of national sovereignty. In the third place, there was no defense against an atomic attack except the desperate defense of counterattack.

American policy on atomic energy, first outlined by Secretary Stimson, was clearly formulated by two committees headed by Dean Acheson and David Lilienthal. This Acheson-Lilienthal Plan, published in March 1946, called for the creation of an International Atomic Development Authority, which should have exclusive control over such raw materials as uranium and thorium and over

[9] There were two tests. One bomb, dropped from the air, sank five ships and heavily damaged the superstructure of many more. The second, exploded under water, sank two battleships and an aircraft carrier and did major damage to many other vessels; it also created radioactivity in the water that lasted for several months.

every stage of the production of atomic energy throughout the world, and should act as custodian of atomic weapons and stockpiles of fissionable materials.

Meantime, at its first session the General Assembly of the United Nations created an Atomic Energy Commission to consist of representatives of all eleven of the members of the Security Council plus Canada. President Truman appointed the sage Bernard Baruch as American representative on this commission, and in a notable address in June 1946 Baruch presented a proposal that incorporated the main features of the Acheson-Lilienthal Plan plus provision for rigid international inspection and for the elimination of the veto in cases involving illegal manufacture of atomic bombs. Under the Baruch Plan, the proposed International Atomic Authority would control the whole field of atomic energy through ownership, licenses, operation, inspection, research, and management, and would concern itself not only with the prevention of the manufacture of atomic weapons but with the production of atomic energy for peaceful benefits. If this program were adopted, the United States stood ready to destroy its stock of atom bombs, stop further manufacture of bombs, and share its scientific knowledge with the rest of the world.

The United Nations Atomic Energy Commission endorsed the American plan by a vote of 10–0; Russia and Poland abstained from voting. Speaking for Russia, Gromyko found the Baruch plan unacceptable for two reasons: inspection would be an intolerable invasion of national sovereignty, and the suspension of the veto would destroy the unanimity principle that was the very basis of the Security Council. Gromyko proposed an alternative plan: the immediate destruction of all atom bombs and the prohibition of the manufacture of atomic weapons. Obviously such a plan was unacceptable to the United States or to her Western associates. It required the surrender of almost the only effective weapon the West had to restrain Russian aggression and, in the absence of inspection, gave no corresponding assurance that Russia would not proceed with the manufacture of atomic weapons behind her Iron Curtain.

Russian intransigence on the veto and on inspection condemned the work of the United Nations Atomic Energy Commission to futility, and in July 1949 the Commission suspended its deliberations. Meantime the United States pushed steadily ahead with her own atomic program. The atom bomb had originally been made by civilian scientists, but under the jurisdiction of the military. With the end of the war there was strong pressure for civilian control of the whole field of atomic energy. The plan worked out by Congress, after lengthy debate, placed the atomic-energy program under the jurisdiction of a five-man civilian Atomic Energy Commission but provided for close military liaison and elaborate security measures; the A.E.C. was to have a monopoly on all fissionable materials, processes, facilities, patents, and technical information. Lilienthal, whose administrative abilities had been tested by his work as head of the T.V.A., was appointed first chairman of the new Commission.

The whole atomic situation was changed radically by the announcement, in September 1949, that the Russians had detonated an atomic bomb. Clearly the Baruch Plan, which was based on an American monopoly of the atom bomb, was outmoded, and some new plan, which recognized Russia's altered position, was called for. The necessity of reopening the whole question of international control was dramatized by the announcement, a few months later, that the atom bomb would eventually be supplanted by the hydrogen bomb, a thousandfold as powerful. With the hydrogen bomb the annihilation of the human race became a grim possibility. Speaking with deep solemnity, the venerable philosopher-scientist Albert Einstein warned the world:

> The armament race between the U.S.A. and the U.S.S.R., originally supposed to be a preventive measure, assumes hysterical character. On both sides, the means to mass destruction are perfected with feverish haste, behind respective walls of secrecy. The H-bomb appears on the public horizon as a probably attainable goal. . . If successful, radioactive poisoning of the atmosphere and hence annihilation of any life on earth has been brought within the range of technical possibilities. The ghost-like character of this development lies in its apparently compulsory trend. Every step appears as the unavoidable consequence of the preceding one. In the end, there beckons more and more clearly general annihilation.

6. *The Cold War*

The wartime alliance between Russia and the Western powers was clearly a marriage of convenience, not of love. Yet it was no less effective for that. When Hitler invaded Russia, Churchill at once announced that 'any man or state who fights against Nazidom will have our aid,' and in this view Roosevelt concurred. The Western powers promised aid and fulfilled their promises: witness the 11 billion dollars of Lend-Lease that went to Russia, most of it freighted by British and American ships through the perilous North Atlantic and Arctic seas or on the long voyage around Africa and to the Persian Gulf. During the whole of the wartime alliance the leaders of the West hoped that after the war Russia, freed from the fear of Germany and Japan, protected by friendly border states, and strengthened by American help, might abandon her policy of isolation and hostility and associate herself with the work of creating a new international order. These expectations, it must be admitted, animated Roosevelt rather than Churchill, who was more cynical, or more realistic. Roosevelt saw clearly the importance of Russian co-operation to assure peace after the defeat of the Axis; he did not see so clearly the forces in Russia and in Communism militating against such co-operation. In short, he consulted his hopes rather than his fears; being Roosevelt, he could not have done otherwise.

Relations between Russia and the West were strained even during the war. Sharp differences over such matters as the sharing of military secrets, co-operation in the air war, the policy toward the Polish Army in Exile and the Polish underground and toward the contending forces in Yugoslavia, the timing of the second front, the treatment of Italy, and many other matters all foreshadowed the even deeper divisions that emerged after the war. Roosevelt hoped that these frictions would yield to the emollient of wartime comradeship, and that particular misunderstandings could be cleared up by personal consultations, and to this end he went to Teheran and to the Crimea.

The Yalta Conference of February 1945 in the Crimea appeared to have achieved the end to which Roosevelt so ardently looked. Later Yalta came to be regarded as a defeat for the West, but it was not so regarded at the time, nor is there any convincing evidence that it was so in fact. The Yalta agreements involved mutual concessions from Russia and the Western powers; on paper the concessions from the West seemed more far-reaching than those from Russia, but in reality the West conceded nothing substantial that Russia could not have taken anyway, while Russia yielded on important points to the Western point of view. Of primary importance was Russia's agreement to enter the war against Japan 'within two or three months' of the defeat of Germany. In return she was promised the Kurile Islands, the southern half of Sakhalin, an occupation zone in Korea, and privileges in Manchuria and at Port Arthur and Dairen: in all probability she could have taken all these as easily without as with Anglo-American permission. Nor should it be forgotten that when this agreement was made, the Allied armies had not yet crossed the Rhine, nor had the atom bomb been exploded at Los Alamos, and Roosevelt's military advisers anticipated that the war with Japan would go on for at least another year. As for the other postwar arrangements, Stalin acquiesced in the American formula for the admission of Latin American states to the United Nations and for their voting in the Security Council, withdrew his preposterous demand for sixteen votes in the General Assembly, agreed to permit France a zone of occupation in Germany, accepted the reparation figure as tentative only, waived insistence on the Polish boundary at the Oder-Neisse rivers, and left open to further negotiation the reorganization of the Polish government. Roosevelt and Churchill conceded the Curzon Line as Russia's western boundary, accepted a tentative reparations figure far beyond what they thought proper, promised Russia three votes in the General Assembly, and left open for future negotiation such thorny questions as Russian rights in the Dardenelles and in Iran, the future of the Baltic countries, and the disposition of Italian colonies.

Roosevelt, and his adviser Harry Hopkins, thought that the Yalta agreements ushered in a new era of peace and hope. 'We really believed in our hearts,' said Hopkins,

> that this was the dawn of the new day we had all been praying for and talking about for so many years. We were absolutely certain that we had won the first great victory for peace — and by we I mean *all* of us, the whole civilized human race. The Russians had proved that they could be reasonable and farseeing and there wasn't any doubt in the minds of the President or any of us that we could live with them peacefully for as far into the future as any of us could imagine.[10]

Actually the Conference was neither a victory nor a defeat for peace. Its principal achievements were in committing Russia to enter the war against Japan and to support the United Nations. As it turned out, the atom bomb made Russian entry an embarrassment rather than a help, and Russian membership proved an obstacle to the United Nations. It is doubtful whether the course of history was changed in any important particulars by the Yalta Conference.

The breakdown in East-West relations came after Yalta, and for

10 Sherwood, *Roosevelt and Hopkins*, p. 870.

reasons not wholly clear. Whether impelled by a sense of power, or by fear, or by the iron logic of Communism, Russia embarked upon a policy of defiance and aggression. She engineered Communist revolutions in Hungary, Bulgaria, and Rumania, and finally Czechoslovakia, reducing those countries to the position of satellites; Finland resisted, and kept her independence in domestic but not in foreign affairs — witness her inability to join in the Marshall Plan. In the Far East, too, Russia's policy was one of unblushing aggression. She engineered a Communist revolution in northern Korea, stripped Manchuria of her industrial wealth, brought Outer Mongolia into her orbit, supported the Chinese Communists in their successful war against Chiang Kai-Shek, inspired revolutionary movements in Indo-China, Malaysia, Burma, and Indonesia, and threatened Iran and even India.

It was in this area, indeed, that Communism scored its most spectacular success. The Chiang Kai-Shek regime, torn by dissension, corroded by corruption, and without strong popular support, proved wholly unable to stem the tide of Chinese Communism. Even during the war the Chinese had been as zealous to fight among themselves as to fight the Japanese; after the war, as the Japanese moved out, Russian and Chinese Communist armies moved in. Convulsive efforts by the United States to reform and strengthen the Nationalist regime and to force some settlement of the Chinese civil war proved abortive. Early in 1946 General Marshall arranged a truce between the Nationalists and the Communists, but it was speedily violated by both and, pronouncing a plague on both houses, Marshall withdrew American troops from China and washed his hands of the whole muddle. Yet notwithstanding this official shift in policy, the United States continued to pour military and financial aid into Nationalist China as long as there was any of it left. Altogether this aid came to some 2 billion dollars by 1950; its chief effect was to excite Nationalist hopes for further assistance, to embitter the Communists, and to persuade part of Asia that the United States had aligned herself with the forces of reaction in the Far East. When, in 1949, the Communists swept the whole of the mainland and Chiang took refuge on the island of Formosa, the problem of Chinese representation on the Security Council served further to embitter Soviet-American relations.

The deterioration of Russian relations with the Western powers, and especially with the United States, need not be traced in detail.

From the Russian point of view American military might, air and naval bases in far-flung quarters of the globe, and control of the atomic weapon, as well as American support to capitalism and socialism abroad, all constituted a threat to Communism; for Stalin clearly accepted Lenin's dictum that 'the existence of the Soviet Republic side by side with the imperialistic states for a long time is unthinkable. In the end either one or the other will conquer.' Soviet conduct, in any event, revealed a settled purpose to create a *cordon sanitaire* around Russia and aggrandize her territorial holdings, and to subvert democratic governments and extend Communism throughout the globe. Particular manifestations of Soviet policy fitted this pattern: Communist-inspired attacks on Greece, pressure on Turkey, invasion of Iran, demand for Italian colonies, revolution in Czechoslovakia, intransigence on the Polish boundary and the Polish-government issues, refusal to make peace with Austria, breakdown of four-power control in Germany, blockade of Berlin, the creation of the Cominform in 1947, boycotting of many agencies of the United Nations and of the Marshall Plan, frequent resort to the veto, scuttling of the Atomic Energy Commission, and Communist infiltration into western European states, Latin America, and even the United States.

It was, interestingly enough, in the Mediterranean and Near East that the first showdown came. The importance of the Mediterranean lifeline had been proved by the war, and the prospect of Russian dominance in this area raised questions of basic political and military strategy. If Russia could take over Iran with its rich oil resources, bring Turkey and Greece into her orbit, retain her strong ties with Yugoslavia, and get a foothold in North Africa, she would turn the flank of the West. Italy would be unable to resist Communism; the Near and Middle East would fall to Russia; the whole Moslem world would be threatened; and India would be open to attack from north, east, and west.

The British, who held a tenuous foothold in Greece and Palestine, announced early in 1947 that they could no longer carry this burden, and proposed to pull out. In desperation Greece and Turkey turned to the United States for financial and military assistance. On 12 March, President Truman sent a message to Congress embodying not only a request for appropriations for Greece and Turkey, but what came to be known as the Truman Doctrine. 'One of the primary objectives of the foreign policy of the United States,' he said,

> is the creation of conditions in which we and other nations will be able to work out a way of life free from coercion. We shall not realize our objectives unless we are willing to help free peoples to maintain their free institutions, and their national integrity against aggressive movements that seek to impose on them totalitarian regimes. . . I believe that it must be the policy of the United States to support free peoples who are resisting attempted subjugation by armed minorities or by outside pressures.

It was to be noted — and Russia did note — that while this doctrine affected immediately only Greece and Turkey, it was potentially world-wide in its application.

Congress voted the money — eventually close to 700 million — and American power moved into the Near East. After prolonged fighting the Greek guerrillas were beaten, Greek government and economy were reformed, Turkish defenses were strengthened. Russia withdrew from Iran, Palestine achieved her independence, Italy swung to the moderate de Gasperi government, and the situation in the Mediterranean was stabilized.

With the Truman Doctrine the United States took the offensive. What came to be regarded as official American policy was shortly stated by George Kennan of the State Department in an 'inspired' article in *Foreign Affairs,* which announced that

> the main element of any United States policy toward the Soviet Union must be that of a long-term patient but firm and vigilant containment of Russian expansive tendencies. . . The United States has it in its power to increase enormously the strains under which the Soviet policy must operate, to force upon the Kremlin a far greater degree of moderation and circumspection than it has had to observe in recent years, and in this way to promote tendencies which must eventually find their outlet in either the breakup or the gradual mellowing of Soviet policy.[11]

The next few years were to reveal that this represented, to some extent, wishful thinking: there was no 'mellowing' of Soviet policy!

Closely on the heels of the Truman Doctrine came the Marshall Plan, which, as we have seen, was designed to rehabilitate western Europe economically, and largely achieved that end. It soon appeared, however, that economic rehabilitation would not be enough: military support, too, was necessary. As Russia had in effect welded the whole of eastern Europe into a single system, so the United

11 *Foreign Affairs,* July 1947.

States and Britain would have to weld western Europe into a single defensive unit. This at least was the meaning of the Atlantic Pact. The idea of a postwar Anglo-American military alliance had first been broached by Winston Churchill in a notable speech at Fulton, Missouri, in the spring of 1946, and Churchill, too, had been the moving spirit in the creation of a Western European Union. 'The determination of the free countries of Europe to protect themselves will be matched by an equal determination on our part to help them to do so,' said Truman, and Congress responded by passing the Vandenberg Resolution, which pledged support to regional agreements for collective self-defense. Out of all this came the North Atlantic Treaty of 4 April 1949, which provided — in the words of the Rio de Janeiro Treaty of 1947 — that 'an armed attack against one or more of them shall be considered an attack against them all,' and pledged its signatories to mutual consultation and military assistance. While the North Atlantic nations found authorization for this agreement in Article 51 of the United Nations Charter, Russia regarded it as an open declaration of hostility.

The Atlantic Pact was an attempt to recreate the Atlantic Community. A very real thing in the seventeenth and eighteenth centuries, it had been ignored in the nineteenth as the United States turned westward and southward. History, tradition, interest, technological advances, sentimental and moral values had inevitably brought the United States back into the Atlantic Community, however, and twice in the twentieth century she had found it necessary to pledge all her resources to its salvation. Now at mid-twentieth century she prepared to recognize formally what she could no longer escape.

BIBLIOGRAPHY

I. *AFTERMATH OF THE WAR*

GENERAL HISTORY. There is no entirely satisfactory history of Reconstruction which fuses the political and economic material and presents the findings of recent research. Perhaps the most satisfactory account is still that by W.A.Dunning, *Reconstruction, Political and Economic,* in the *American Nation* series. J.G.Randall, *The Civil War and Reconstruction* is an admirable summary of recent scholarly findings. W.L.Fleming, *The Sequel of Appomattox* is one of the best of the Chronicles series, judicious and learned. E.M.Coulter, *The South During Reconstruction* is up to date and thorough but distinctly Southern in its point of view. E.P.Oberholtzer's *History of the United States since the Civil War* is a social history modeled on McMaster's *History,* with both the virtues and the defects of that work; vols.i and ii deal with the reconstruction period. J.F.Rhodes, *History of the United States,* vols.v-vii, neglects the economic aspects of reconstruction but is notably impartial. W.L.Fleming, *Documentary History of Reconstruction* (2 vols.), containing a wide range of source material, is indispensable for the student. Claude Bowers, *The Tragic Era* is a spirited but partisan narrative by an ardent Democrat. Allan Nevins, *The Emergence of Modern America,* in the *History of American Life* series, is the most satisfactory one-volume survey of the social and economic aspects of the period by one of the ablest practitioners of the new school of social historians. Paul H.Buck, *The Road to Reunion* traces the much-neglected history of the reconciliation of the North and the South in the post-war generation. No student should neglect the provocative chapter on 'The Second American Revolution,' in Charles and Mary Beard, *Rise of American Civilization,* vol.ii.

THE TRIUMPHANT NORTH. For the economic and political history of the North during the Civil War and post-war years see § VI. E.D. Fite, *Social and Industrial Conditions in the North during the Civil War* gives the background of the industrial revolution. V.S.Clark, *History of Manufactures in the United States, 1860–1914,* traces the development of the major industries. For economic and political developments in particular states, see Frederick Merk, *Economic History of Wisconsin during the Civil War Decade,* A.C.Cole, *The Era of the Civil War* (*Centennial History of Illinois,* vol.iii.), G.N.Fuller, *Economic and Social Beginnings of Michigan,* A.C.Flick (ed.), *History of the State of New York,* vol.viii, A.M.Dilla, *Politics of Michigan, 1865–1878,* George H.Porter, *Ohio Politics during the Civil War,* and C.M.Knapp, *New Jersey Politics during the Civil War.* Much valuable material can be found in the biographies of industrialists, see below, *passim*. S.M.Peto, *The Resources and Prospects of America, Ascertained during a visit . . . in 1865* is a useful commentary.

THE SOUTH AFTER THE WAR. Of the almost countless works of travel and description the following can be recommended: Sidney Andrews (a northern newspaper correspondent), *The South since the War,* J.T.Trowbridge (a popular novelist of the period), *The South,* prejudiced but vivid; Whitelaw Reid (the future editor of the New York *Tribune*), *After the War,* Robert Somers (an English observer), *The Southern States since the War,* and Charles Nordhoff, *The Cotton States in 1875*. The reminiscences of Southerners are not always reliable as to fact but afford an invaluable insight into the psychology of the defeated South. Joseph LeConte, *Autobiography,* Mary B.Chestnut, *A Diary from Dixie,* Francis Butler Leigh, *Ten Years on a Georgia Plantation,* Mrs. M.L.Avery, *Dixie after the War,* George C.Eggleston, *A Rebel's Recollections,* and Elizabeth W.Pringle, *Chronicles of Chicora Wood* are the best. E.P. Oberholtzer, *The United States since the Civil War,* vol.i, contains the best second-hand description. There is good material in some of the general histories of the South, notably Francis B.Simkins, *The South Old and New, 1820–1947,* W.B.Hesseltine, *The South in American History,* and J.G. Randall, *Civil War and Reconstruction*. H.L.Swint, *The Northern Teacher in the South, 1862–1870* illuminates an interesting minor subject.

THE FREEDMAN. There is no entirely satisfactory history of the Negro in America or of the freedman during reconstruction. W.E.B.Du Bois, *Black Reconstruction* is a brilliant and provocative interpretation of the period from the Negro and the economic point of view and goes far to challenge the orthodox interpretation of the role of the Negro in reconstruction. G.T.Stephenson, *Race Distinctions in American Law* is adequate on the black codes and other legislation dealings with the freedmen, and Paul Lewinson, *Race, Class and Party* traces the political evolution of the Southern Negro to the present. For the Freedmen's Bureau, see S.Pierce, *The Freedmen's Bureau,* Laura Webster, *Freedmen's Bureau in South Carolina,* V.L.Wharton, *The Negro in Mississippi, 1865–1890,* and A.A.Taylor, *The Negro in South Carolina during Reconstruction* and *The Negro in the Reconstruction of Virginia*. A vivid but not entirely reliable picture of Negro government is painted in James Pike, *The Prostrate State: South Carolina under Negro Government* with intro. by H.S.Commager. Material on the Negro as freedman may be found in the many general works on the Negro in America: B.G.Brawley, *Social History of the American Negro,* Charles R.Johnson, *The Negro in American Civilization,* G.W.Williams, *History of the Negro Race in America* (2 vols.), John Hope Franklin, *From Slavery to Freedom,* and — especially for the later period — the remarkable study of American race relations by the Swedish sociologist Gunnar Myrdal, *The American Dilemma:*

Negro Problem and Modern Democracy. For more recent economic development, see Charles S.Johnson, *Shadow of the Plantation,* Scott Nearing, *Black America,* S.D.Spero and A.L.Harris, *The Black Worker,* P.A.Bruce, *The Plantation Negro as Freedman,* and Arthur Raper, *Preface to Peasantry*. There is valuable material in Rupert Vance, *Human Factors in Cotton Culture* and *Human Geography of the South,* and in Howard Odum's massive *Southern Regions of the United States*. Two classic personal narratives that illuminate the problem of the Negro in America are Booker T.Washington, *Up From Slavery* and W.E.B.Du Bois, *The Souls of Black Folk*. On Booker Washington see Basil Matthews, *Booker T.Washington*. No student should fail to study race relations as presented in the literature of the South, notably the stories of Joel Chandler Harris, Thomas Nelson Page, Albion Tourgee, Ambrose Gonzales, Julia Peterkin, T.S.Stribling, DuBose Heywood, Stark Young, and, for the more recent period, Erskine Caldwell and William Faulkner.

THE NEW SOUTH. The literature on the New South is voluminous. Holland Thompson, *The New South* is a brief survey. Mr. Thompson has also written a valuable study, *From Cotton Field to Cotton Mill* and articles in *The South Atlantic Quarterly* and elsewhere. P.A.Bruce, *The Rise of the New South,* in the *History of North America* is a more popular study. Volume iv of Oberholtzer's *History* has an excellent chapter on the rise of industry in the South. A volume by C. Vann Woodward, *Origins of the New South, 1877–1913,* is announced for publication. Illuminating studies of particular states are R.P.Brooks, *The Agrarian Revolution in Georgia, 1865–1912,* S.H.Hobbs, *North Carolina, Economic and Social,* Robert Shugg, *Origins of the Class Struggle in Louisiana,* and Simkins and Woody, *Reconstruction in South Carolina*. W.K.Boyd has written the history of one typical city of the New South, *The Story of Durham* and T.J.Wertenbaker of another, *Norfolk, Historic Southern Port*. On the development of industry in the South see Broadus Mitchell, *Industrial Revolution in the South* and *The Rise of the Cotton Mills in the South,* M.B.Hammond, *The Cotton Industry,* M.Jacobstine, *Tobacco Industry in the United States,* Joseph C.Robert, *The Story of Tobacco in America,* H.L.Herring, *Welfare Work in the Mill Villages,* John Dollard, *Caste and Class in a Southern Town,* M.A.Potwin, *Cotton Mill People of the Piedmont,* E.Armes, *Story of Coal and Iron in Alabama,* and I.F.Marcossin, *The Black Golconda,* a study of the oil industry. Two biographies that recount the work of Southern industrial leaders are: B.Mitchell, *William Gregg, Manufacturer of the Old South,* and J.W.Jenkins, *James B.Duke*. Rupert Vance's *Human Factors in Cotton Culture* and *Human Geography of the South* are in a class by themselves as analyses of general socio-economic development, while Howard Odum's *Southern Regions of the United States* presents a wealth of statistical material for a comparative history of the New South. Two special studies that throw light on social conditions in the South are Thomas D.Clark, *Pills, Petticoats and Plows: the Southern Country Store* and *The Southern Country Editor,* both vastly entertaining. Of the many books interpreting the society and culture of the South, the most interesting is *I'll Take My Stand* by Twelve Southerners which presents a platform of southern regionalism and provincialism. Others of value are Howard Odum, *The Way of the South* and *Below the Potomac: A Book about the New South,* Virginius Dabney, *Liberalism in the South,* W.T.Couch (ed.), *Culture in the South,* B.B.Kendrick and A.M.Arnett, *The South Looks at its Past,* Clarence Cason, *Ninety in the Shade,* Josephus Daniels, *A Southerner Discovers the South,* and, dealing with a 'marginal' group, Horace Kephart, *Our Southern Highlanders.* R.B.Nixon, *Henry W.Grady* is a satisfactory biography of the Georgia editor who was so instrumental in creating the New South.

SOURCE SELECTIONS. W.L.Fleming, *Documentary History of Reconstruction* (2 vols.), H.S.Commager, *Documents of American History,* 5th ed., Nos.214–16, 231, 233, 245–47, 250, 257.

II. *RECONSTRUCTION, POLITICAL AND CONSTITUTIONAL*

PRESIDENTIAL AND CONGRESSIONAL RECONSTRUCTION. See bibliography in § I. John W.Burgess, *Reconstruction and the Constitution* is learned but vitiated by the author's preconceptions of the nature of nationalism and of Congressional powers. W.A.Dunning, *Essays on the Civil War and Reconstruction* presents the ripe conclusions of the foremost scholar in the field. R.S.Henry, *The Story of Reconstruction* is a useful general history, overburdened with detail. Lincoln's reconstruction policy may be studied in Charles H.McCarthy, *Lincoln's Plan of Reconstruction,* and J.G.Randall, *Constitutional Problems under Lincoln.* E.M.McPherson's *Political History of Reconstruction* contains a wealth of documentary material on the political side. There are monographs on reconstruction in every one of the seceded states: W.L.Fleming, *Reconstruction in Alabama,* J.W.Garner, *Reconstruction in Mississippi,* J.G. DeR.Hamilton, *Reconstruction in North Carolina,* Ella Lonn, *Reconstruction in Louisiana after 1868,* W.M.Caskey, *Secession and Restoration in Louisiana,* Garnie McGinty, *Louisiana Redeemed: The Overthrow of Carpet-Bag Rule, 1876–1880,* J.R.Flicken, *History of Reconstruction in Louisiana,* J.P.Hollis, *Early Reconstruction Period in South Carolina,* J.S.Reynolds, *Reconstruction in South Carolina,* F.P.Simkins and R.H.Woody, *Reconstruction in South Carolina,* W.Ramsdall, *Reconstruction in Texas,* C.M.Coulter, *Reconstruction in Kentucky,* H.J.Eckenrode, *Political History of Virginia during Reconstruction,* W.W.Davis, *Civil*

War and Reconstruction in Florida, J.W.Fertig, *Secession and Reconstruction in Tennessee,* J.W.Patton, *Unionism and Reconstruction in Tennessee,* T.S.Staples, *Reconstruction in Arkansas, 1862–74,* David Y.Thomas, *Arkansas in War and Reconstruction, 1861–1874,* John Wallace, *Carpetbag Rule in Florida,* J.C.McGregor, *The Disruption of Virginia,* Edwin C.Woolley, *Reconstruction in Georgia,* and Clara M.Thompson, *Reconstruction in Georgia, 1865–72.* Many of the essays in the *Studies in Southern History and Politics inscribed to W.A.Dunning* are indispensable. Valuable material can be found, too, in biographies: C.M.Coulter, *Parson Brownlow,* C.H.Ambler, *Francis H.Pierpont,* H.J.Pearce, *Benjamin H.Hill,* W.A.Cate, *L.Q.C.Lamar,* and Nelson M.Blake, *William Mahone.* The Reports of Grant and of Schurz on conditions in the South can be found in U.S. 39th Cong. 1st Sess. Sen. Ex. Doc.2, Truman's Report in ibid., Doc.43.

RECONSTRUCTION AND THE CONSTITUTION. The constitutional phases of Reconstruction may be studied in the general works of Dunning and Burgess already cited, and in C.Warren, *The Supreme Court,* vol.ii. On the Fourteenth Amendment see B.B.Kendrick, *Journal of the Joint Committee of Fifteen on Reconstruction,* H.E.Flack, *The Adoption of the Fourteenth Amendment,* W.D.Guthrie, *Lectures on the Fourteenth Amendment,* L.Boudin, *Government by Judiciary,* vol.ii. The judicial interpretation of the Fourteenth Amendment can be traced in F.J.Swayze, *Harvard Law Review,* vol.xxvi, and W.W.Davis, 'Federal Enforcement Acts,' in *Studies in Southern History and Politics.* Additional information on the formulation and purpose of the amendment can be obtained from the biographies of *Lyman Trumbull* by Henry White and of *William M.Evarts* by B.Dyer and C.L.Barrows, and in the articles by H.J.Graham in *Yale Law Journal,* vols.xlvii and xlviii. On the Fifteenth Amendment see J.M.Matthews, *Legislative and Judicial History of the Fifteenth Amendment.* For the background of the Milligan case see I.W.Ayer, *The Great Northwest Conspiracy.* The record of the trial has been republished with a brilliant introduction by S.Klaus.

GENERAL POLITICAL HISTORY. Howard Beale's *The Critical Year* is a study of the election of 1866, but contains material which illuminates the whole of reconstruction and has an exhaustive bibliography. C.H.Coleman has written a monograph on the *Election of 1868.* C.M.Chadsey has told the story of the *Struggle between President Johnson and Congress over Reconstruction.* The standard work on the impeachment of Johnson is D.M.DeWitt, *Impeachment and Trial of Andrew Johnson;* the essay in Dunning's *Essays on Civil War and Reconstruction* as well as the biographies of Johnson by Milton, Winston, and Stryker should also be consulted. There is a wealth of material in the diaries and biographies of public men of the time. *The Diary of Gideon Welles,* vol.iii, is the most illuminating source on Johnson and the struggle with Congress. Additional material can be found in James G.Blaine, *Twenty Years of Congress* (2 vols.), George Hoar, *Autobiography of Seventy Years,* C.R.Williams (ed.), *Diary and Letters of R.B.Hayes* (5 vols.), and Carl Schurz, *Reminiscences* (3 vols.). General Sherman reveals one of the most penetrating minds of the time in *The Sherman Letters,* ed. by R.S.Thorndike, and *Home Letters of General Sherman,* ed. by M.A.DeW.Howe. *The Education of Henry Adams* views the Reconstruction epoch through the eyes of the most brilliant and severe critic of his generation.

There are biographies of most of the figures prominent in the period, but they are of an uneven quality. George Fort Milton, *The Age of Hate* is the best biography of Johnson; Robert Winston, *Andrew Johnson, Plebeian and Patriot* is a fair interpretation; L.P.Stryker, *Andrew Johnson, a Study in Courage* is prejudiced. James A.Woodburn's and T.B.Miller's are satisfactory biographies of *Thaddeus Stevens;* the most recent is R.N.Current, *Old Thad Stevens.* A.B.Hart has written the life of *Samuel P.Chase;* Moorfield Storey that of *Charles Sumner;* W.D.Foulke has compiled two volumes on *Oliver P.Morton.* Henry White's *Life of Lyman Trumbull* is a first-rate piece of work; G.C.Gorham's *Life and Public Services of E.M.Stanton* (2 vols.) is less satisfactory. Some material can be found in C.L.Barrows, *William M.Evarts,* Margaret Clapp, *Forgotten First Citizen: John Bigelow,* and Glyden Van Deusen, *Thurlow Weed.* For biographies of other political leaders active in the Reconstruction period such as Roscoe Conklin, James G.Blaine, Benjamin Butler, Benjamin Wade, Zachary Chandler, W.P.Fessenden, etc., the student is referred to the *Dictionary of American Biography* and to § III below.

RESTORATION OF WHITE RULE IN THE SOUTH. There is no satisfactory account of the Ku Klux Klan. Stanley Horn, *The Invisible Empire* is the most satisfactory and most recent. The reports of the Ku Klux Klan Committee in thirteen volumes (U.S. 42d Cong. 2d Sess. Sen. Report No.41) contain a wealth of material on social conditions in the South, but most of the testimony is violently partisan. There is a valuable essay in W.G.Brown's *Lower South in American History.* Some aspects of the restoration of white rule can be found in the histories of reconstruction in individual states, above, and in C.Bowers, *Tragic Era.* On the situation in South Carolina, see W.Allen, *Governor Chamberlain's Administration in South Carolina* and C.G.Welles, *Hampton and Reconstruction.*

SOURCE SELECTIONS. Fleming, *Documentary History of Reconstruction* (2 vols.); Edward McPherson, *Political History of the United States during Reconstruction, passim;* H.S.Commager, *Documents,* 5th ed., Nos.229, 234–39, 244, 248, 249, 251–56, 258–67, 269–74, 291–93, 297.

III. *THE POLITICS OF THE GRANT ADMINISTRATION*

GENERAL. The political history of the Grant administration is adequately covered in the volumes of Rhodes, Oberholtzer, Schouler, and Dunning, cited above. The most thorough single volume on the administration is A.Nevins, *Hamilton Fish and the Grant Administration*, equally valuable for domestic and foreign affairs and throwing new light on every phase of the history of these years. Most biographies of Grant neglect his political for his military career: W.B.Hesseltine, *U.S.Grant* and Louis A.Coolidge, *The Life of Ulysses S.Grant* are exceptions. Of older works, Adam Badeau, *Grant in Peace* and Hamlin Garland, *Ulysses S. Grant* are still valuable. Other biographies which illuminate the Grant administration are Claude Fuess, *Carl Schurz*, Stewart Mitchell, *Horatio Seymour*, A.Nevins, *Abram Hewitt*, Alexander Flick, *Samuel Jones Tilden*, D.B.Chidsey, *The Gentleman from New York: A Life of Roscoe Conkling*, and W.A.Cate, *L.Q.C.Lamar*. There is a voluminous literature of memoirs and reminiscences. Some of the best of these are: *The Education of Henry Adams*, G.H.Hoar, *Autobiography of Seventy Years* (2 vols.), James G.Blaine, *Twenty Years in Congress* (2 vols.), Carl Schurz, *Reminiscences* (3 vols.), Hugh McCulloch, *Men and Measures of Half a Century*, John Sherman, *Recollections of Forty Years* (2 vols.), Andrew D. White, *Autobiography*, T.C.Platt, *Autobiography*, S.M.Cullom, *Fifty Years of Public Service*, and S.S.Cox, *Three Decades of Federal Legislation*. The election of 1868 is adequately covered by Coleman's monograph of that name, and in the various biographies of Grant, Johnson, and Chase cited above.

FOREIGN AFFAIRS. A.Nevins, *Hamilton Fish and the Grant Administration* covers the ground thoroughly. F.Bancroft's biography of *William H.Seward* and C.F.Adams' *Life of Charles Francis Adams* contain useful material. For the Alaska Purchase see J.M.Callahan, *The Alaska Purchase* and Jeanette Nichols, *Alaska*. Caribbean affairs are adequately covered in J.M.Callahan, *Cuba and International Relations* and C.L.Jones, *Caribbean Interests of the United States*. The most exhaustive treatment of Grant's Santo Domingo project is in Nevins' *Fish*, but see also Sumner Welles, *Naboth's Vineyard* (2 vols.) and E.L.Pierce, *Memoirs and Letters of Charles Sumner*, vol.iv. There is no good history of the Fenian raids, but for that and other aspects of Canadian relations see J.M. Callahan, *American Foreign Affairs in Canadian Relations* and H.Keenleyside, *Canada and the United States*. L.S.Shippee, *Canadian-American Relations, 1849–1874* is learned and exhaustive. For the Alabama claims and the Geneva arbitration see J.Moore, *International Arbitrations*, vol.i, ch.14; J.C.Bancroft Davis, *Mr. Fish and the Treaty of Washington*, and the chapter in the *Cambridge History of British Foreign Policy*, vol.iii. The treaty and award can be found in Malloy's *Treaties*, i.700–722, the *plaidoyers* and other records are collected in *Papers relating to the Treaty of Washington* in *Foreign Relations of the United States,* 1872, Part II (5 vols.).

DOMESTIC POLITICS. For the money question and the resumption of specie payments, see W.C.Mitchell, *A History of Greenbacks,* D.C.Barrett, *Greenbacks and the Resumption of Specie Payments, 1862–1879,* A.B.Hepburn, *A History of Currency in the United States,* A.S.Bolles, *Financial History of the United States,* vol.iii, D.R.Dewey, *Financial History of the United States,* and the *Recollections of John Sherman,* vol.i. The Legal Tender cases are adequately but controversially covered in the histories of the Supreme Court by Warren and Boudin. Other aspects of the cases are treated in E.J.James, *The Legal Tender Decisions,* G.F.Hoar, *The Charge of Packing the Court against President Grant,* and Sidney Ratner, 'Was the Supreme Court packed by President Grant?' *Pol.Sci.Qt.* vol.L (1935). For civil service see C.R.Fish, *The Civil Service and the Patronage.* The later stages of reconstruction are covered in the books listed under § II above. There are interesting chapters on 'Grantism' in Herbert Agar's provocative *The Price of Union.*

LIBERAL REPUBLICAN MOVEMENT. E.D.Ross, *The Liberal Republican Movement* is thoroughly satisfactory. There is a general account in Oberholtzer, vol.iii, ch.I. T.S.Barclay's *Liberal Republican Movement in Missouri* traces the local origins of the movement. There is valuable material in biographies of Schurz, Trumbull, Greeley, C.F.Adams, and Godkin, cited elsewhere.

SCANDAL AND STAGNATION. On corruption during the Grant administration Claude Bowers, *The Tragic Era* is readable but unreliable; Nevins' *Fish* is thorough and accurate. The pages of Henry Adams, *The Education of Henry Adams* are brilliant, and his novel, *Democracy,* is a clever indictment of Washington society. There is excellent illustrative material in A.B.Paine, *Thomas Nast and his Pictures. Chapters of Erie* by Henry and C.F.Adams brings the trail of corruption close to the White House. 'Black Friday' can be studied in the first of these Chapters, and also in R.I.Warshow, *Jay Gould* and R.H.Fuller, *Jubilee Jim: the Life of Colonel James Fisk.* Matthew Josephson, *The Robber Barons* emphasizes corruption in railroad building. Local corruption is described in S.P.Orth, *The Boss and the Machine,* Dennis T.Lynch, *Boss Tweed,* and A.C.Cole, *The Era of the Civil War.* On Jay Cooke, see E.P.Oberholtzer, *Jay Cooke* (2 vols.) and Henrietta Larson, *Jay Cooke, Private Banker.*

THE ELECTION OF 1876. P.L.Haworth, *The Disputed Election of 1876* is the standard monograph. New material can be found in A.Nevins, *Abram Hewitt.* The election is variously treated in Rhodes, *History,* vol. vii, H.J.Eckenrode, *R.B.Hayes, Statesman of Reunion,* C.R.Williams, *The Life of R.B.Hayes* (2 vols.), and Alexander Flick, *Samuel Tilden.* The monographs on reconstruction in South Carolina, Florida, and Louisiana, cited in § II, should be consulted for conditions in the states.

SOURCE SELECTIONS. Fleming, *Documentary History of Reconstruction,* 2 vols.; Commager, *Documents,* 5th ed., Nos.250, 274, 276–286, 288–293, 296.

IV. *THE PASSING OF THE FRONTIER*

GENERAL. Walter P.Webb, *The Great Plains* is indispensable to any understanding of the last west; the chapters on the institutional history of the Plains are particularly illuminating. LeRoy Hafen and Carl C.Rister, *Western America* covers the whole history of the trans-Mississippi region. Ray Billington, *The Westward Movement* is a capital general text with comprehensive bibliographies. Everett Dick, *The Sod-House Frontier* is a wonderfully interesting detailed social history; Harold E. Briggs, *Frontiers of the Northwest: a History of the Upper Mississippi Valley* is only less interesting. The concluding chapters of F.L.Paxson, *History of the American Frontier, 1763–1893* and his *Last American Frontier* are useful summaries. F.A.Shannon, *The Farmer's Last Frontier* is indispensable. Robert Riegel, *America Moves West* and Dan E.Clark, *The West in American History* are general accounts. Emerson Hough, *The Passing of the Frontier* is a vivid popular account of the last west. Glenn C.Quiett, *They Built the West* emphasizes the role of the railroads, and A.M.Sakolski, *The Great American Land Bubble* of land speculation. This story is more elaborately told in A.N.Chandler, *Land Title Origins: A Tale of Force and Fraud.* There is excellent material in E.P.Oberholtzer, *History of the United States,* vols.i-v, and in Allan Nevins, *The Emergence of Modern America.* The multi-volumed state histories by H.H.Bancroft contain invaluable material on the early history of all the western states (*Works,* 39, vols.); cf. his *Literary Industries and Retrospection, Political and Personal.* Useful regional histories of sections of the west are: George W.Fuller, *The Inland Empire* (3 vols.), Oscar Winther, *The Great Northwest,* B.N.Richardson and C.C.Rister, *The Greater Southwest,* and John C.Caughey, *The Pacific Coast.* Granville Stuart, *Forty Years on the Frontier* (2 vols.), and J.H.Cook, *Fifty Years on the Old Frontier* are perhaps the best of the personal narratives which cover the period from the Civil War to the passing of the frontier. For 'colonial' administration, see E.S.Pomeroy, *The Territories and the United States, 1861–1890.*

THE INDIAN PROBLEM. Most of the literature on the Indians is highly romantic and historically worthless. Some of the better studies of the Indian, giving adequate attention to the Plains Indians, are: G.B.Grinnell, *The Story of the Indian,* F.E.Luepp, *The Indian and his Problem,*

W.C.Macleod, *The American Indian Frontier,* John Collier, *Indians of the Americas,* and Paul Radin, *Story of the American Indian.* Valuable studies of particular tribes emphasizing the historical rather than the anthropological interest are: G.B.Grinnell, *The Fighting Cheyennes* and *The Cheyenne Indians* (2 vols.), Frank C.Lockwood, *The Apache Indians,* B.N.Richardson, *The Comanche Barrier to South Plains Settlement,* Grant Foreman, *The Five Civilized Tribes,* Angie Debo, *The Rise and Fall of the Choctaw Republic,* and Woodworth Clum, *Apache Agent.* Phases of Indian warfare are set forth in Robert Gessner, *Massacre,* Paul L.Wellman, *Death on the Prairie,* Stanley Vestal, *Sitting Bull* and *Warfare, The Story of the Fighting Sioux,* and W.P.Webb, *The Texas Rangers.* A valuable study of a special phase is L.B.Priest, *Uncle Sam's Step-children, 1865–1887,* and another is J.P.Kinney's *A Continent Lost, —A Civilization Won: Indian Land Tenure in America.* Additional material can be found in the *Memoirs* of General Sheridan (2 vols.), G.A.Custer, *My Life on the Plains,* Marguerite Merington (ed.), *The Custer Story,* Frederic Van de Water, *Glory Hunter, the Life of General Custer,* Frances C.Carrington, *Army Life on the Plains,* and N.A.Niles, *Serving the Republic.* The humanitarian crusade for a new Indian policy can be followed in Helen Hunt Jackson's passionate *Century of Dishonor,* G.W.Manypenny, *Our Indian Wards,* Ethelbert Talbot, *My People of the Plains,* James McLaughlin, *My Friend, the Indian,* and M.A.DeW.Howe, *Moorfield Storey.* Lewis Meriam, *et al., The Problem of Indian Administration,* and Lawrence Schmeckbier, *The Office of Indian Affairs* are thorough studies of that subject. For the disappearance of the buffalo, see E.D. Branch, *The Hunting of the Buffalo.*

THE MINING FRONTIER. Invaluable for a general introduction to the history of the mining kingdom are T.A.Rickard, *The History of American Mining* and *Man and Metals* (2 vols.). The various volumes of H.H.Bancroft's histories of western states all have valuable material on mining not elsewhere available. Glenn C.Quiett, *Pay Dirt, a Panorama of American Gold Rushes* is a popular account, as are C.B.Glassock, *Gold in Them Hills* and *The War of the Copper Kings.* C.H.Shinn, *The Story of the Mine* is chiefly concerned with the Comstock Lode, which is likewise described in C.B.Glassock, *The Big Bonanza* and George D.Lyman, *The Saga of the Comstock Lode.* For the institutional history of the mining kingdom see Rickard and Shinn, cited above, H.H.Bancroft, *Popular Tribunals* (2 vols.), and W.J.Trimble, *The Mining Advance into the Inland Empire* (U. of Wisconsin *Studies,* Hist. Ser.iii).

THE CATTLE KINGDOM. Walter Webb's *Great Plains* is the most valuable study of all aspects of the cattle kingdom, but three other works are substantial, scholarly, and original: E.S.Osgood, *The Day of the Cattleman,* Louis Pelzer, *The Cattlemen's Frontier, 1850–1890,* and E.E.Dale,

The Cattle Range Industry; cf. the more popular *Cow Country.* A special study that illuminates the whole field is O.B.Peake, *The Colorado Cattle Range Industry,* and another is Lewis Nordyke, *Cattle Empire,* the story of the 3-million-acre XIT ranch; see, too, Merrill G.Burlingame, *The Montana Frontier.* For the cowboy, his character and activities, see Emerson Hough, *The Story of the Cowboy,* P.A.Rollins, *The Cowboy,* E.D. Branch, *The Cowboy and his Interpreters,* and W.M.Raines and W.C. Barnes, *Cattle.* Andy Adams, *The Log of a Cowboy* and *Reed Anthony, Cowman* are authentic and realistic, as are, to a lesser extent, the volumes by Will James. For the trails, the long drive, and the cowtowns, see A.R.Hebard and E.A.Brininstool, *The Bozeman Trail* (2 vols.), Joseph A.McCoy, *Historic Sketches of the Cattle Trade of the West and Southwest,* and Stuart Henry, *Conquering our Great American Plains,* a picture of Abilene, Kansas. Struthers Burt, *Powder River* is a highly popular and vivid account of one important cattle country, and Charles Lindsay's *Big Horn Basin* of another. For the sheep frontier, see Edward N.Wentworth, *America's Sheep Trails* and Robert Cleland, *Cattle on a Thousand Hills.* For the balladry of the open range we have the admirable collections of John A.Lomax, *Cowboy Songs* and *Songs of the Cattle Trail and Cow Camp,* Badger Clark's poems, *Sun and Saddle Leather,* and E.F.Piper, *Barbed Wire and other Poems.*

THE DISAPPEARANCE OF THE FRONTIER AND POLITICAL ORGANIZATION. F.J.Turner's classic essay, 'The Significance of the Frontier in American History,' is the necessary starting point. Comments and criticism on the Turner thesis can be found in *Sources of Culture in the Middle West, Backgrounds versus Frontier,* edited by Dixon Ryan Fox, and in Benjamin Wright, 'American Democracy and the Frontier,' *Yale Review,* Winter 1931. See, too, E.E.Edwards, *References on the Significance of the Frontier,* published by the U.S. Dept. of Agriculture. An interesting commentary on the frontier thesis can be found in J.C.Parish, *The Persistence of the Westward Movement and Other Essays.* The efforts of men to adapt their institutions to the peculiar conditions of the high plains are best explained in Webb's *Great Plains.* F.L.Paxson has an illuminating article on the 'Pacific Railroads and the Disappearance of the Frontier' in Amer. Hist. Assoc. *Reports,* 1901, i, and some thoughtful comments on the significance of the frontier in *When the West is Gone.* R.P.Porter, *The West from the Census of 1880,* consisting largely of statistical tables, is useful to the student. P.W.Gates, 'The Homestead Law in an Incongruous Land System,' *Am. Hist. Rev.,* vol.xli, is indispensable. Of the state histories the most valuable are: Roy Gittinger, *Oklahoma,* Grant Foreman, *A History of Oklahoma,* R.N.Richardson, *Texas, the Lone Star State,* Richard Lillard, *Desert Challenge: An Interpretation of Nevada,* Robert Cleland's two volumes on California, W.W.Folwell, *History of Minnesota* (4 vols.), and E.M.Mack, *Nevada.* On the state constitutions see J.D.Hicks, 'Constitutions of the Northwest States,' U. of Neb. University *Studies,* xxiii, and on the Omnibus States, F.L.Paxson's 'Admission of the Omnibus States,' *Wis. Hist. Soc. Proceedings,* 1911, 77.

For subjects like the history of the West, a novel written from authentic materials is about ninety per cent history. Such are Ole Rölvaag, *Giants in the Earth,* Owen Wister, *The Virginian,* Willa Cather, *O Pioneers, My Ántonia,* and *A Lost Lady,* Herbert Quick, *Vandemark's Folly* and *The Hawkeye,* Hamlin Garland, *Boy Life on the Prairie,* Edna Ferber, *Cimmaron,* and Walter Clark, *The Ox-Bow Incident.*

There is a wealth of material on the West in the voluminous publications of the State Historical Societies, notably those of Minnesota, Wisconsin, Texas, Nebraska, Kansas, Iowa, and Oklahoma.

SOURCE SELECTIONS. Stanley Vestal, *New Sources of Indian History,* 1850–1891. Commager, *Documents,* 5th ed., Nos.302, 304, 315.

V. *TRANSPORTATION AND ITS CONTROL*

GENERAL. There is no good general history of American railroads, but John Moody, *The Railroad Builders* is a useful, brief sketch of some of the main roads. The most interesting works for the student are biographies such as J.G.Pyle, *James J.Hill* (2 vols.), and George Kennan, *Life of E.H.Harriman* (2 vols.), which resemble in tone and reliability the official biographies of crowned heads. H.G.Pearson, *An American Railroad Builder, J.G.Forbes* is detached and compendious. A.D.Smith and Wheaton Lane have written spirited popular biographies of *Commodore Vanderbilt.* There is a wealth of material in E.P.Oberholtzer, *Jay Cooke, Financier of the Civil War* (2 vols.). There are histories of most of the important roads, though of uneven merit. E.A.Mott, *Between the Ocean and the Lakes, the Story of Erie* is comprehensive, as is E.Hungerford, *Story of the Baltimore and Ohio* (2 vols.). A considerable literature has grown up about the Union Pacific. G.M.Dodge, *How We Built the Union Pacific* is by the chief engineer, and should be supplemented by J.R.Perkins, *Trails, Rails and War: the Life of Grenville Dodge.* Other volumes on the U.P. are Nelson Trottman, *History of the Union Pacific,* John P.Davis, *The Union Pacific Railroad,* H.K.White, *History of the Union Pacific Railway,* and E.L.Sabin, *Building the Pacific Railway.* Stuart Daggett, *Chapters on the History of the Southern Pacific,* G.D.Bradley, *Story of the Santa Fé,* and Eugene Smalley, *History of the Northern Pacific Railroad* are competent and impartial. Oscar Lewis, *The Big Four* is a biographical study of the building of the Central Pacific.

RAILROADS AND THE WEST. Robert E.Riegel, *The Story of the Western Railroads* is a model account, disappointingly brief. Paul Gates,

The Illinois Central Railroad and its Colonization Work is invaluable and illuminates the whole question of the relation of the railroads to colonization, as does R.C.Overton, *Burlington West: A Colonization History of the Burlington Railroad.* J.B.Hedges, *Henry Villard and the Railways of the Northwest* is equally authoritative for the story of immigration. L.H.Haney, *Congressional History of Railways, 1850–1887* is a standard work, old but not supplanted. There is a wealth of material in Thomas Donaldson, *The Public Domain.* G.W.Julian, 'Railway Influence in the Land Office,' *North Am. Rev.*, cxxxvi, 237 is a classic account by a politician who knew whereof he wrote.

RAILROAD ABUSES AND REGULATION. C.E.Russell, *Stories of the Great Railroads,* Gustavus Myers, *History of Great American Fortunes,* and Matthew Josephson, *The Robber Barons* are works of the muckrake type, giving the seamy side of railroad history for which the *Report* of the U.S.Pacific Railway Commission of 1887 (5 vols., 50th Cong. 1st Sess. Sen. Ex. Doc.51) furnishes abundant illustration. There are accounts of the Crédit Mobilier in Rhodes and Oberholtzer; for fuller treatment see J.B.Crawford, *The Crédit Mobilier of America.* S.J.Buck, *The Granger Movement* deals adequately with the Granger cases. The contemporary reaction to railroad malpractices in the West can be read in W.Larrabee, *The Railroad Question.* W.Z.Ripley, *Railroads: Rates and Regulations* (2 vols.) and *Railroads: Finance and Organization* are in a class by themselves. For the history of regulation see: A.T.Hadley, *Railroad Transportation, its History and its Law,* B.H.Meyer, *Railroad Legislation in the United States,* Robert E.Cushman, *The Independent Regulatory Commission,* and W.Thompson, *Federal Centralization.* F.A.Cleveland and F.W.Powell, *Railway Promotion and Capitalization in the United States* is the best work on that difficult subject. The constitutional aspects can be studied in E.S.Corwin, *The Commerce Power and State Rights,* and Felix Frankfurter, *The Commerce Clause under Marshall, Taney and Waite.* The history of the I.C.C. is comprehensively told in I.L.Sharfman, *The Interstate Commerce Commission* (5 vols.).

DECLINE OF STEAMBOATING. See Mark Twain's classic *Life on the Mississippi* and the colorful books by Herbert Quick, *Mississippi Steamboating,* and G.E.Eskew, *Pageant of the Packets.* F.H.Dixon, *A Traffic History of the Mississippi River System* is technical. For the Great Lakes, Norman Beasley, *Freighters of Fortune,* G.A.Cuthbertson, *Freshwater: a Narrative of the Great Lakes,* and Walter Havighurst, *The Long Ships Passing* are adequate.

SOURCE MATERIAL. W.Z.Ripley, *Railway Problems* is a collection of source extracts that includes such classics as Henry and C.F.Adams' *Chapters of Erie.* A.R.Ellingwood and W.Coombs (eds.), *The Government and Railroad Transportation* is useful for court decisions. Commager, *Documents,* 5th ed., Nos.215, 294, 314, 318, 319.

VI. *THE ECONOMIC REVOLUTION*

GENERAL. The 'facts' of American economic history are to be found in the voluminous *Reports* of the Census Bureau and the numerous state and federal investigating committees, but they have not yet been worked into anything like finished form. The most useful of the many economic histories of the United States are those by Chester Wright, F.A.Shannon, E.C.Kirkland, J.Barnes, and H.U.Faulkner. Sidney Ratner, *American Taxation: Its History as a Social Force* explores heretofore unfamiliar territory. The volumes in the History of American Life series, especially A.Nevins, *Emergence of Modern America,* Ida Tarbell, *Nationalization of Industry,* and H.U.Faulkner, *Quest for Social Justice,* are invaluable and all contain extensive bibliographies. Burton J.Hendrick, *The Age of Big Business* and John Moody, *Masters of Capital* are popular accounts that do not penetrate beneath the surface. V.S.Clark, *History of Manufactures in the United States, 1860–1914* is valuable for facts rather than for interpretation. Louis Hacker, *The Triumph of American Capitalism* is interpretative, but weak on the period since the Civil War. Thomas C.Cochran and William Miller, *The Age of Enterprise* is a general history and interpretation, well balanced and provocative. Incisive and provocative books on the economic revolution are those by Stuart Chase, *Men and Machines, The Tragedy of Waste,* and *Prosperity, Fact or Myth,* but neither the statistics nor the conclusions should be accepted without further investigation. Lewis Mumford, *Technics and Civilization* is an ambitious interpretation. Jerome Davis, *Capitalism and its Culture* presents a challenging interpretation. There is an immense amount of uncorrelated material in Herbert Hoover, *et al., Recent Economic Changes in the United States* (2 vols.). Constance McL.Green, *Holyoke, Massachusetts: A case study of the Industrial Revolution in America* is a model monograph.

Some of the more valuable histories of particular industries are: P.T.Cherrington, *The Wool Industry,* A.H.Cole, *The American Wool Manufacture* (2 vols.), M.T.Copeland, *Cotton Manufacturing Industry in the United States,* M.B.Hammond, *The Cotton Industry,* Paul Giddins, *The Birth of the Oil Industry,* I.F.Marcossin, *The Black Golconda,* R.C.Epstein, *The Automobile Industry,* C.B.Huhlmann, *Development of the Flour-milling Industry in the United States,* R.A.Clemen, *The American Live Stock and Meat Industry,* Thomas Cochran, *The Pabst Brewing Company,* and Ida Tarbell, *The Standard Oil Company.* Carl C.Rister, *Oil: Titan of the Southwest* is an admirable study of that new industry. Perhaps the best histories of business, as distinct from industry, are those by Marquis James: *The North American Insurance Company, Metropolitan Life,* and the forthcoming *Bank of America.* Biographies of businessmen are inadequate and uncritical, but there has been marked improvement here in recent years. W.T.Hutchinson, *Cyrus McCormick* (2 vols.) is a model of its kind. B.J.Hendrick, *Life of Andrew Carnegie* (2 vols.) is comprehensive but uncritical. A.Nevins, *John D. Rockefeller: The Heroic Age of American Enterprise* (2 vols.) is a masterly study of the greatest American businessman, thorough and scholarly. His *Abram Hewitt* is almost as good on the history of the iron industry; Ida Tarbell's *Life of Elbert Gary* is disappointing. Gustavus Myers, *Great American Fortunes,* and Matthew Josephson, *Robber Barons* are highly readable but propagandistic. Marquis James, *Alfred I. duPont, the Family Rebel* tells something of the history of the great Du Pont corporation.

SCIENCE AND INVENTION. Waldemar Kaempffert (ed.), *Popular History of American Inventions* (2 vols.) is indispensable. Roger Burlingame, *Engines of Democracy: Inventions and Society in Mature America* emphasizes the social implications of inventions. Herbert Casson has written three volumes that combine information with interest: *The Romance of Steel, The Romance of the Telephone,* and *The Romance of the Reaper*. Holland Thompson, *The Age of Invention* is a useful general introduction. Lewis Mumford, *Technics and Civilization* is original and important. For Edison see F.L.Dyer and T.C.Martin, *Edison, His Life and Inventions* and T.C.Martin and S.L.Coles, *The Story of Electricity*. Michael Pupin, *From Immigrant to Inventor* combines charm and interest. The best study of mechanization is Harry Jerome, *Mechanization in Industry*.

IRON AND STEEL. The two most valuable works are Nevins' *Hewitt* and Hendrick's *Carnegie,* cited above. Carnegie's *Autobiography* is illuminating of the character of the ironmaster, but the illumination is not always flattering. Paul de Kruif, *Seven Iron Men* is an exciting story of the Mesabi Iron Range, but is not reliable for facts or conclusions. S.H.Holbrook's *Iron Brew, a Century of American Ore and Steel* is a spirited popular story. James H.Bridge, *Inside History of the Carnegie Steel Company* is highly critical; there is no satisfactory history of the United States Steel Corporation.

TRUSTS AND TRUST REGULATION. John Moody, *The Truth about the Trusts* is old, and of the muckraking type, but has considerable data not elsewhere available. H.W.Laidler, *Concentration of Control in American Industry* presents the situation for 1930, and Horace Coon, *American Tel & Tel* is an excellent case study of the most successful consolidation. The most useful general histories of trusts are: Eliot Jones, *The Trust Problem in the United States,* J.W.Jenks and W.E.Clark, *The Trust Problem,* and H.R.Seager and C.A.Gulick, *Trusts and Corporation Problems*. W.Z.Ripley, *Trusts, Pools and Corporations* is an older study by an authority in the field. J.R.Commons, *Legal Foundations of American Capitalism* is suggestive, as is O.F.Boucke, *Laissez Faire and After*. The opening gun in the battle for trust regulation was H.D.Lloyd,

Wealth against Commonwealth, recently reprinted in a cheap edition. Equally effective was Ida Tarbell's notable *Standard Oil Company* (2 vols.). The campaign against the trusts can be followed in C.C.Regier, *Era of the Muckrakers.* Albert Walker, *History of the Sherman Law* is adequate for that subject prior to 1912. The history of regulation can be followed in M.W.Watkins, *Industrial Combinations and Public Policy,* J.D.Clark, *Federal Trust Policy,* and J.W.Jenks, *Economic Aspects of Recent Decisions of the Supreme Courts on Trusts, Journal of Political Economy,* xx, 346. See also general histories of the trust problem.

SOURCE SELECTIONS. Faulkner and Flügel, *Readings in the Economic History of the United States.* Commager, *Documents,* 5th ed., Nos.215, 231, 320, 339.

VII. *LABOR*

GENERAL. J.R.Commons, *et al., History of Labor in the United States* (4 vols.) is the standard authority. His *Documentary History of American Industrial Society* (10 vols.) has an enormous amount of source material but stops at 1880. Professor Commons has also edited a volume on *Trade Unionism and Labor Problems.* H.Harris, *American Labor* is the most recent general account. There is useful material in H.G.Taylor, *Labor Economics and Labor Problems.* The literature on trade unionism is extensive: S.Perlman, *History of Trade Unionism in the United States,* George Groat, *Organized Labor in America,* R.F.Hoxie, *Trade Unionism in the United States,* F.T.Carlton, *History and Problem of Organized Labor,* and Leo Wolman, *Growth of American Trade Unions, 1880–1923* are the best references. N.J.Ware, *The Labor Movement in the United States, 1860–1895* is chiefly a study of the Knights of Labor. An admirable special study is Herbert Lahne, *The Cotton Mill Worker,* in the Labor in the Twentieth Century series. For left-wing labor organizations, consult Morris Hillquit, *History of Socialism in the United States.*

There is much of value in the biographies and autobiographies of labor leaders. Samuel Gompers, *Seventy Years of Life and Labor* (2 vols.) is indispensable; see also, R.H.Harvey, *Samuel Gompers.* Terence Powderly's history of the K.of L., *Thirty Years of Labor,* is less satisfactory, but consult H.J.Carman (ed.), *The Path I Trod: The Autobiography of Terence V. Powderly.* E.Gluck, *John Mitchell* tells the story of the United Mine Workers. There is illuminating material in the *Autobiography* of Theodore Roosevelt, the *Autobiography of Lincoln Steffens,* Clarence Darrow, *My Life, Bill Haywood's Book, An Autobiography,* Mary H.Vorse, *A Footnote to Folly,* Tom Johnson, *My Story,* Ray Ginger, *The Bending Cross* (Debs), and Brand Whitlock, *Forty Years of It.*

THE RISE OF ORGANIZED LABOR. For general accounts see books listed above. Henry David, *History of the Haymarket Affair* gives the background of the Knights of Labor and of the Black International; it is the most satisfactory single volume on any phase of American labor history. For the A.F.of L. see L.L.Lorwin, *The American Federation of Labor.* P.T.Brissenden, *The I.W.W.* is entirely adequate on that organization, but see also J.G.Brooks, *American Syndicalism,* James Oneal, *American Communism,* and David J.Saposs, *Left-Wing Unionism.*

INDUSTRIAL CONFLICTS. Samuel Yellen, *American Labor Struggles* is valuable. There is a thorough if somewhat academic treatment of major industrial conflicts in vol.iv of Commons, *History.* For the Haymarket affair see David, above. The history of the Homestead Strike can be followed in B.J.Hendrick, *Life of Andrew Carnegie,* and in J.H.Bridge, *Inside History of the Carnegie Company.* For the Pullman strike, see chapter xi; and Almont Lindsey, *The Pullman Strike,* Harry Barnard, *Eagle Forgotten,* Ray Ginger, *The Bending Cross,* a biography of Eugene Debs, and A.Nevins, *Cleveland.* For the Molly Maguires, J.W.Coleman, *The Molly Maguires* is satisfactory; on labor warfare in Colorado see Benjamin Rastall, *Labor History of the Cripple Creek District.* The history of the coal strike of 1902 remains to be written, but much of value can be found in the *Autobiography* of Theodore Roosevelt, and in E.Gluck's *Mitchell* and C.Lloyd's *Henry Demarest Lloyd.* Tom Tippett, *When Southern Labor Stirs* is a fair introduction to textile strikes in the South, but see also G.S.Mitchell, *Textile Unionism in the South.* The problem of Negro labor is adequately treated in C.H.Wesley, *Negro Labor in the United States* and S.D.Spero and A.L.Harris, *The Black Worker.* H.Feldman, *Racial Factors in American Industry* is based upon the voluminous report of the Immigrant Commission; for a different interpretation see J.W.Jenks and W.J.Lauck, *The Immigration Problem* and E.A.Hourwich, *Immigration and Labor.*

LABOR LEGISLATION AND JUDICIAL INTERPRETATION. Volume iii of Commons, *History of Labor in the United States* contains an admirable and thorough study of Labor Legislation by Elizabeth Brandeis. For wages see Paul L.Douglas, *Real Wages in the United States, 1890–1926.* M.C.Cahill, *Shorter Hours: A study of the movement since the Civil War* is adequate for that subject. On the injunction, Felix Frankfurter and N.V.Greene, *The Labor Injunction* is definitive. For labor in politics, see John Lombardi, *Labor's Voice in the Cabinet: a History of the Department of Labor to 1921.* There is a convenient digest of labor legislation at the turn of the century in vol.v of the *Report* of the Industrial Commission of 1900 by Frederic J.Stimson. On labor and the Sherman Act see Edward Berman's monograph of that name, Edward E.Witte, *The Government in Labor Disputes,* M.R.Carroll, *Labor and Politics,* Charles O. Gregory, *Labor and the Law,* and A.T.Mason, *Organized Labor and the Law.* On workmen's compensation and social security, Abraham Epstein, *Insecurity* and Paul Douglas, *Social Security in the United States* are satisfactory. The problem of women in industry is treated in Edith Abbott, *Women in Industry* and Helen L.Sumner, *History of Women in Industry in the United States.* (Senate Doc. No.645, 61st Cong.2nd Session, 1910.) For industrial paternalism, see the material in Ida Tarbell, *Nationalization of Industry*. G.G.Groat, *Attitude of American Courts on Labor Cases* is thorough but somewhat antiquated. For an understanding of judicial interpretation of labor law, there is no substitute for the Court decisions themselves. On labor in politics see Nathan Fine, *Labor and Farmer Parties in the United States, 1828–1928,* E.E.Haynes, *Third Party Movements in the United States* and *Social Politics in the United States.*

Some of the better novels of the period have considerable historical value. Upton Sinclair, *The Jungle* exposes conditions in the Chicago stockyards; Robert Herrick, *Memoirs of an American Citizen* has the Haymarket riot for its background; Louis Bromfield, *The Green Bay Tree* and *The Good Woman* tell the story of the rise of labor in an Ohio town; W.D.Howells, *Hazard of New Fortunes* and Ernest Poole, *The Harbour* have New York labor disputes for their background.

SOURCE SELECTIONS. A.R.Ellingwood and W.Coombs, *The Government and Labor* and Carl Rauschenbush and Emmanuel Stein, *Labor Cases and Materials* are collections of source material on that subject and particularly valuable for court decisions. Commager, *Documents,* 5th ed., Nos.233, 295, 298, 301, 310, 326, 334–46, 364–66, 368, 403, 413–15, 421, 430, 434, 444, 451, 473, 474.

VIII. *IMMIGRATION*

GENERAL. J.R.Commons, *Races and Immigrants in America* is a classic discussion, though now somewhat antiquated. Maurice Davie, *World Immigration* is perhaps the most satisfactory recent discussion of the subject and is particularly valuable for its bibliographies. A new series, *The Peoples of America,* ed. by Louis Adamic, is designed to cover eventually all immigrant groups. G.M.Stephenson, *History of American Immigration, 1820–1924* and Lawrence G.Brown, *Immigration* are good but sketchy. Carl Wittke, *We who Built America: the Saga of the Immigrant* is particularly good on the old immigration. J.W.Jenks and W.J.Lauck, *The Immigration Problem* is a synopsis of the forty-volume *Report* of the Immigration Commission of 1911. Marcus L.Hansen, *The Atlantic Migration* is a brilliant study of the European background of immigration; it should be supplemented by his essays, *The Immigrant in American History.* A useful collection is Mary K.Reely (ed.), *Selected Articles on Immigration.*

There are a large number of studies of special racial groups. The best of these are: Marcus Hansen, *The Mingling of the Canadian and American Peoples,* A.B.Faust, *German Element in the United States* (2 vols.), A.J.Ford, *The Scotch-Irish in America,* William F.Adams, *Ireland and Irish Immigration to the New World from 1815 to the Famine,* Theodore Blegen, *Norwegian Migration to America* (2 vols.), Florence E.Janson, *Background of Swedish Immigration, 1840–1930,* John S.Lindberg, *Background of Swedish Immigration to the United States,* K.C.Babcock, *The Scandinavian Element in the United States,* E.G.Balch, *Our Slavic Fellow Citizens,* C.S.Bernheimer, *The Russian Jew in the United States,* H.P.Fairchild, *Greek Immigration to the United States,* Thomas Capek, *The Czechs in America,* R.F.Foerster, *Italian Emigration of Our Times,* Samuel Joseph, *Jewish Immigration to the United States from 1881 to 1910,* Jerome Davis, *The Russian Immigrant,* William Thomas and Florian Znaniecki, *The Polish Peasant in America,* and M.Gamio, *Mexican Immigration to the United States.*

For Oriental immigration see M.R.Coolidge, *Chinese Immigration,* G.F.Seward, *Chinese Immigration in its Social and Economical Aspects,* S.L.Gulick, *The American Japanese Problem,* and E.G.Mears, *Resident Orientals on the American Pacific Coast.*

Special studies of value are E.A.Hourwich, *Immigration and Labor,* E.S.Brunner, *Immigrant Farmers and their Children,* Grace Abbott, *The Immigrant and the Community,* and Herman Feldman, *Racial Factors in American Industry.* Elin L. Anderson, *We Americans* analyzes racial groups and adjustments in a typical 'American' city, Burlington, Vermont. Edward Steiner, *On the Trail of the Immigrant* follows the 'new' immigrant from the Old World to the New. R.L.Garis is satisfactory on *Immigration Restriction* and Jane P.Clark on *Deportation of Aliens from the United States to Europe.* Edward Corsi, *The Shadow of Liberty* is a study of Ellis Island, immigration, and deportation, by a former Commissioner of Immigration.

The social implications of immigration may be read in Jane Addams, *Forty Years at Hull House,* Jacob Riis, *How the Other Half Lives* and his classic *Making of an American,* Mary Antin, *The Promised Land,* Michael Pupin, *From Immigrant to Inventor,* Carl C.Jensen, *An American Saga,* and Lillian Wald, *Windows on Henry Street.* Louis Adamic, *The Native's Return* is a charming account of one aspect of immigration little appreciated.

Davie's *World Immigration* contains a bibliography of fiction dealing with the immigrant in America. O.E.Rölvaag, *Giants in the Earth* and *Peder Victorious* give the story of the first and second generations and the differing problems of adaptation. Edna Ferber, *American Beauty* and Gladys H.Carroll, *As the Earth Turns* tell of immigrants on New England farms. Abraham Cahan, *The Rise of David Levinsky* is a powerful picture of the New York Jew.

SOURCE SELECTIONS. Edith Abbott has edited two volumes of source material on immigration: *Historical Aspects of the Immigration Problem* and *Immigration, Select Documents and Case Records.* Commager, *Documents,* 5th ed., Nos.233, 257, 306, 307, 367, 372, 387, 404, 422, 435.

IX. *AGRICULTURE AND THE FARM PROBLEM*

GENERAL. There is need for a good history of American agriculture, particularly for the period after 1860; L.C.Gray, *History of Agriculture in the Southern States* (2 vols.) and P.W.Bidwell, *et al., History of Agriculture in the Northern United States* carry the story only to that date. There is an excellent survey of post-war agriculture in the U.S.Dept.of Agriculture, *Yearbook,* 1899, 'Progress of Agriculture in the United States,' and a mass of invaluable but undigested material in vol.v of the Thirteenth Census, *General Report and Analysis of Agriculture.* O.E. Baker (ed.), *Atlas of American Agriculture* is likewise a Census Bureau publication. Fred A. Shannon, *The Farmer's Last Frontier: Agriculture 1860–1897* is an altogether admirable survey of the farm problem after the Civil War. Brief accounts of a more general nature are A.H.Sanford, *The Story of Agriculture in the United States* and E.L.Bogart, *Economic History of American Agriculture.* There is a wealth of material in L.H. Bailey (ed.), *Cyclopedia of American Agriculture* (4 vols.). Joseph Schafer, *Social History of American Agriculture* is a series of lectures of a general character and should be compared to Robert T.Hill, *Public Domain and Democracy.* Rupert Vance, *Human Geography of the South* and Howard Odum, *Southern Regions of the United States* deal largely with farming in that section and contain data not elsewhere available. E.D.Fite, 'Agricultural Development of the West during the Civil War,' *Qt.Jour.of Econ.* xx, and J.L.Coulter, 'Agricultural Development in the United States 1900–1910,' ibid., xxvii, are useful studies of periods of transition.

There are several good histories for individual states: Joseph Schafer, *History of Agriculture in Wisconsin;* Ulysses P.Hedrick, *History of Agriculture in the State of New York;* Harold F.Wilson, *The Hill Country of Northern New England, 1790–1930;* and E.J.Wickson, *Rural California.* Some of the histories of individual crops are useful: E.C.Brooks, *The Story of Corn;* G.Bigwood, *Cotton;* M.B.Hammond, *The Cotton Industry* (2 vols.); M.A.Carlton, *The Small Grains;* and M.Jacobstine, *Tobacco Industry in the United States.*

MACHINERY AND SCIENCE. On agricultural machinery see the chapters in W.Kaempffert (ed.), *Popular History of American Inventions* (2 vols.) and H.W.Quaintance, 'The Influence of Farm Machinery on Production and Labor' which can be found most conveniently in L.B.Schmidt and E.E.Ross, *Readings in the Economic History of American Agriculture*. H.N.Casson, *The Romance of the Reaper* and W.Macdonald, *Makers of Modern Agriculture* are popular. W.T.Hutchinson, *Cyrus McCormick* (2 vols.), one of the notable biographies in our historical literature, tells in detail the story of the rise of the agricultural machinery business.

Paul de Kruif, *Hunger Fighters* is an account of the heroes of scientific agriculture. On Luther Burbank see D.S.Jordan and V.Kellogg, *The Scientific Aspects of Luther Burbank's Work* and H.S.Williams, *Luther Burbank, His Life and Work*. Joseph C.Bailey, *Seaman A.Knapp: Schoolmaster of American Agriculture* is a useful study of the most effective champion of scientific farming. Orville M.Kile, *The New Agriculture* is a popular work.

For the bonanza farms of the West see William G.Moody, *Land and Labor in the United States,* antiquated but valuable. The problem and technique of dry farming is adequately discussed in John A.Widstoe, *Dry Farming*. For irrigation see Ray P.Teile, *Economics of Land Reclamation in the United States;* William E.Smythe, *The Conquest of Arid America;* George Thomas, *The Development of Institutions under Irrigation,* and C.H.Brough, *Irrigation in Utah*.

THE FARM PROBLEM. There is an extensive literature on the 'farm problem,' much of it of an ephemeral nature. Charles H.Otken, *The Ills of the South* is old but valuable; on Southern agriculture see also the volumes by Vance and Odum, listed above. The National Industrial Conference Board, *Agricultural Problem in the United States* contains a useful tabulation of agricultural returns and throws light on conditions in the twentieth century, as does E.R.A.Seligman, *The Economics of Farm Relief: a Survey of the Agricultural Problem*. A.E.Sheldon, *Land Systems and Land Policies in Nebraska* (Nebraska State Hist.Soc. *Publications,* vol.xxii) is a historical treatment of immense value. R.P.Brooks, *Agrarian Revolution in Georgia* and E.M.Banks, *Economics of Land Tenure in Georgia* illuminate conditions throughout the South. Paul W.Gates, 'The Homestead Law in an Incongruous Land System,' *Am.Hist.Rev.* July 1936 is an admirable examination of a subject more elaborately interpreted in W.P.Webb's *Great Plains*.

Perhaps the most illuminating approach to the farm problem is through autobiographical and imaginative literature. Such volumes as Charles E.Russell, *Bare Hands and Stone Walls;* James W.Witham, *Fifty Years on the Firing Line;* Herbert Quick, *One Man's Life;* Mari Sandoz, *Old Jules;* Hamlin Garland, *A Son of the Middle Border;* and such stories and novels as Garland's *Main Travelled Roads, Other Main Travelled Roads,* and *A Spoil of Office;* Willa Cather's *O Pioneers* and *My Ántonia;* Ole Rölvaag's *Giants in the Earth;* Frank Norris' *The Octopus;* Herbert

Quick's *Vandemark's Folly* and *The Hawkeye;* William A.White's *A Certain Rich Man;* G.H.Carroll's *As the Earth Turns;* Ellen Glasgow's *Barren Ground;* Ed Howe's *Story of a Country Town;* Louis Bromfield's *The Farm;* Ruth Suckow's *Iowa Interiors* and *Folks;* and Josephine Johnson's *Now in November* give a more immediate and authentic impression of the nature of the farm problem than any number of statistical graphs. For an interpretation of this literature, see Parrington, *Main Currents,* vol.iii, Lucy Hazard, *The Frontier in American Literature,* and Dorothy A.Dondore, *The Prairie and the Making of Middle America.*

AGRARIAN REVOLT. The history of the Granger movement may be traced to Solon J.Buck's thorough monograph *The Granger Movement.* A.B.Paine, *Granger Movement in Illinois* suggests the need for other monographs of a similar character. For the Alliance, J.D.Hicks, *The Populist Revolt* is thorough, scholarly, and exciting. It may be supplemented by material in A.Nevins, *Grover Cleveland;* J.A.Barnes, *John G.Carlisle;* F.P.Simkins, *The Tillman Movement in South Carolina* and his *Pitchfork Ben Tillman, South Carolinian;* and F.E.Haynes, *James Baird Weaver.* For the political aspects of the Populist revolt see bibliography § X.

O.M.Kile gives the history of the *Farm Bureau Movement* and P.R. Fossum of the *Agrarian Movement in North Dakota.* There are no less than four histories of the Non-Partisan League: Bruce, Gaston, Russell, and Langer. Wayne C.Neely, *The Agricultural Fair* is a charming monograph on that institution.

SOURCE SELECTIONS. L.B.Schmidt and E.E.Ross, *Readings in the Economic History of American Agriculture.* Commager, *Documents,* 5th ed., Nos.214, 216, 287, 294, 316, 323–25.

X. *POLITICS* 1877–1890

GENERAL. There is no good general political history of the years after Reconstruction. Rhodes, *History,* vol.viii, is not up to the standard of his earlier volumes; Oberholtzer's *History* is superficial and prejudiced. Harry Thurston Peck, *Twenty Years of the Republic, 1885–1905* is a vivid and popular account. The chapters in C.A. and M.Beard, *Rise of American Civilization,* vol.ii, are brilliant and penetrating, but the material is necessarily highly condensed. E.E.Sparks, *National Development* and D.R. Dewey, *National Problems* in the *American Nation* series are fairly satisfactory though antiquated. Matthew Josephson's *The Politicos* is good narrative, highly critical of the political stuffed-shirts of the period but marred by an insistence on the economic interpretation. The best introductions to institutional history are Bryce's *American Commonwealth* and Herbert Agar's *The Price of Union.*

For memoir and autobiographical literature, consult bibliography in § III. W.A.White, *Masks in a Pageant* is a colorful and provocative analysis of political leadership during this and a later period. Arthur W.Dunn, *From Harrison to Harding* (2 vols.) is the work of a journalist. Though the volumes of the *American Political Leaders* series are uneven in merit, the standard is higher than that of the older *American Statesmen* series; particular volumes will be noted below. Some of the best biographical sketches of politicians of this era are to be found in the *Dictionary of American Biography,* which should be consulted for bibliographical suggestions as well.

The following biographical studies, listed alphabetically, are useful for an introduction to the politics of the period: Nathaniel W.Stephenson, *Nelson W.Aldrich,* based on voluminous source material but highly partisan; Harry Barnard, *Eagle Forgotten, the Life of John P.Altgeld;* G.F.Howe, *Chester A.Arthur,* a good book on a dull subject; S.H.Acheson, *Joe Bailey, Last of the Democrats,* a lively appreciation of the Senator from Texas; Margaret Clapp, *Forgotten First Citizen: John Bigelow;* David S.Muzzey, *James G.Blaine,* the best biography of that politician, which should be supplemented by reference to Blaine's *Twenty Years of Congress* (2 vols.); W.V.Byars, *Richard P.Bland, an American Commoner,* the only study of 'Silver Dick'; L.White Busby, *Uncle Joe Cannon,* an affectionate portrait of a second-rate politician; James A. Barnes, *John G.Carlisle,* one of the best biographies for the period and the best introduction to the background of the money question; L.B.Richardson, *William Chandler, Republican;* A.Nevins, *Grover Cleveland: a Study in Courage,* a biography, which should be supplemented by A.Nevins (ed.), *Letters of Grover Cleveland.* S.M.Cullom, *Fifty Years of Public Service* raises questions as to the validity of the title, as does Donald B. Chidsey's biography of Roscoe Conkling, *The Gentleman from New York.* For Debs, see Ray Ginger, *The Bending Cross, Eugene V.Debs.* T. C.Smith, *James A.Garfield* (2 vols.) is thorough and well written; little of importance is added in R.G.Caldwell, *James A.Garfield.* Herbert Croly, *Mark Hanna* is one of the best political biographies, but a different interpretation is presented in Thomas Beer's impressionistic *Hanna.* Tyler Dennett's biography of *John Hay* is more critical and more scholarly than the official biography by William R.Thayer (2 vols.). For President Hayes see Charles R.Williams, *The Life of R.B.Hayes* (2 vols.) and H.J.Eckenrode, *R.B.Hayes, Statesman of Reunion;* Mr.Williams has edited the *Diary and Letters of R.B.Hayes* (5 vols.). A.Nevins, *Abram Hewitt* uses material heretofore unavailable and illuminates Democratic politics during the seventies and eighties. George F.Hoar, *Autobiography of Seventy Years* (2 vols.) is good reading. Grace J.Clark has painted a Hoosier politician in her *George W.Julian.* W.A.Cate, *Lucius Q.C.Lamar* is one of the best biographies of a Southern statesman in our literature. Henry

Cabot Lodge, *Early Memories* is a charming picture of the only attractive period of the author's life. Karl Schriftgiesser, *The Gentleman from Massachusetts* is implacably hostile to Lodge. Robert McElroy, *Levi P. Morton* traces uncritically the rise to the Vice-Presidency of a New York banker. *Boise Penrose* is pictured in a biography by Robert D.Bowden; Boss Platt in a far better book, H.F.Gosnell, *Boss Platt and the New York Machine*. S.W.McCall, *Life of Thomas B.Reed* is eulogistic; William A. Robinson, *Thomas B.Reed* is more satisfactory. Royal Cortissoz, *Life of Whitelaw Reid* (2 vols.) is an official biography, uncritical but valuable for material not elsewhere available. Carl Schurz, *Reminiscences* (3 vols.) is somewhat overwhelming; a more satisfactory introduction to Schurz is through the biographies by Claude Fuess and Joseph Schafer. John Sherman's dullness is written into every page of his *Recollections* (2 vols.) and communicates itself to the biography by T.E.Burton. Elmer Ellis, *Henry Teller* is a thoroughly sympathetic biography of a neglected Western leader. For Tilden the biography by A.C.Flick supplants the older official work by John Bigelow (2 vols.). Fred Haynes, *James B.Weaver* is one of the best studies of political liberalism during this period. M.A.Hirsch, *William C.Whitney* is a solid study of that businessman-politician.

Some material of value can be found in the compendious state histories of which these are the most satisfactory: *The Centennial History of Illinois,* vol.iv and *The Commonwealth History of Massachusetts,* vol.iv. Consult also E.S.Bates, *The Story of Congress;* D.S.Alexander, *History and Procedure of the House of Representatives;* M.P.Follett, *The Speaker of the House of Representatives;* and Charles Warren, *History of the Supreme Court,* vol.ii.

GLIMMERINGS OF REFORM. On civil service reform, C.R.Fish, *The Civil Service and the Patronage* is a standard work. There is notable material in Bryce's *American Commonwealth,* vol.ii, and in Denis W. Brogan, *Government by the People*. E.L.Godkin, *Problems of Modern Democracy* contains some thoughtful essays on spoils in politics. There is abundant material in the *Reminiscences* of Carl Schurz and in the biographies of Schurz and Roosevelt. The best analyses of the American party system as it developed in the post-war period are C.E.Merriam, *The American Party System* and M.Ostrogorski, *Democracy and the Organization of Political Parties* (2 vols.).

CLEVELAND AND HARRISON ADMINISTRATIONS. The one indispensable work is A.Nevins, *Grover Cleveland;* Nevins has also edited a selection from *The Letters of Grover Cleveland*. H.C.Thomas, *The Return of the Democratic Party to Power in 1884* is thorough and scholarly. Stanwood, Taussig, and Tarbell cover the history of tariff during these years. For pensions, W.H.Glasson, *Federal Military Pensions in the United States* is satisfactory. For foreign affairs under Cleveland and Harrison, see § XIII, below.

SOURCE SELECTIONS. Commager, *Documents,* 5th ed., Nos.297, 299, 300, 303, 308, 312, 317.

XI. *THE BATTLE OF THE STANDARDS*

THE POPULIST REVOLT. Most of the books listed under 'Farm Problem' and 'Agrarian Revolt' in § IX and the political biographies listed in § X are useful for Populism and the battle of the standards. J.D.Hicks, *Populist Revolt* contains an exhaustive bibliography. Special aspects of the Populist revolt can be read in Paul R.Fossum, *Agrarian Movement in North Dakota;* A.M.Arnett, *Populist Movement in Georgia;* F.B.Simkins, *Tillman Movement in South Carolina;* John B.Clark, *Populism in Alabama;* and William D.Sheldon, *Populism in the Old Dominion.*

THE MONEY QUESTION. All of the literature on the money question is controversial and most of it is prejudiced. A possible exception is the account in D.R.Dewey, *Financial History of the United States.* A.B.Hepburn, *History of Currency in the United States;* A.S.Bolles, *Financial History of the United States,* vol.iii; and A.D.Noyes, *Forty Years of American Finance* are all anti-silver. For Greenbacks see W.C. Mitchell, *A History of Greenbacks.* J.Lawrence Laughlin, *History of Bimetallism,* M.S.Wildman, *Money Inflation in the United States,* and H.White, *Money and Banking* all present the monometallist point of view. The Bland-Allison Act can be studied in *Recollections* of John Sherman, Williams' *Life of R.B.Hayes,* and Byars' biography of Bland. For the Sherman Act and its repeal see material in Nevins' *Cleveland,* Barnes' *Carlisle,* and the biographies of Bryan listed below. F.Wellborn, 'Influence of the Silver Republicans, 1889–1891,' *Miss.Val.Hist.Rev.* xiv traces the legislative history of the Sherman Act.

CLEVELAND AND THE PANIC. The most satisfactory treatment of the second Cleveland administration is in Nevins, *Cleveland* and Barnes, *Carlisle;* G.H.Knowles has provided a satisfactory study of *The Presidential Campaign of 1892.* W.J.Lauck, *Causes of the Panic of 1893* confines itself to the money question and is highly unsatisfactory. D.L.McMurray, *Coxey's Army* traces the background of industrial unrest and does justice to Coxey. There is a good account of the income tax decision in Warren's *Supreme Court,* vol.iii, and a highly critical interpretation in Boudin's *Government by Judiciary,* vol.ii, and in S.Ratner, *American Taxation.* The story of the bond issues can be read in the biographies noted above and in Lewis Corey, *The House of Morgan;* the bond sale investigation is in 54th Cong.2d Sess.Sen.Exec.Doc.No.187. For a more friendly view of Morgan's role, see Frederick L.Allen's *Morgan.* Nevins' analysis of the Pullman strike is masterly, but see also the full text of the Altgeld-Cleveland controversy in Browne's *Altgeld,* and the discussion in Henry James, *Life of Richard Olney,* in Harry Barnard, *Eagle Forgotten,* in Almont Lindsey, *The Pullman Strike,* and in Ray Ginger, *The Bending Cross.* The Congressional investigation of the strike can be found in United States Strike Commission, *Report,* Sen.Exec.Doc.7, 53d Cong.3d Sess.

BRYAN AND THE ELECTION OF 1896. Bryan's own account of the battle of the standards has yet to be improved upon: *The First Battle.* There is no satisfactory biography of Bryan. M.Werner, *Bryan* is the most interesting; Wayne Williams, *William Jennings Bryan,* the most sympathetic; and Paxton Hibben, *The Peerless Leader,* the most critical. H.T.Peck, *Twenty Years of the Republic* contains a description of the campaign of 1896 as do Mark Sullivan, *Our Times: The Turn of the Century,* Herbert Croly's *Mark Hanna,* and Elmer Ellis' *Henry Teller.* The account in J.F.Rhodes, *The McKinley and Roosevelt Administrations* is dull; that in Oberholtzer, *History,* vol.v, incredibly biased. There is useful material on the revolt in the Democratic party and on the gold Democrats in Mark Hirsch, *William C.Whitney* and in James C.Olsen, *J.Sterling Morton.*

SOURCE SELECTIONS. W.J.Bryan, *The First Battle;* Commager, *Documents,* 5th ed., Nos.280, 288, 289, 299, 300, 311, 321–325, 327, 328, 332, 333, 337, 338, 341–43, 353.

XII. *ARTS, PHILOSOPHY, AND LETTERS*

THE GILDED AGE. To the scandal of American scholarship, there is no history of American thought, philosophy, religion, education, law, or social institutions that is wholly satisfactory. For literature we have the thoroughly conventional *Cambridge History of American Literature* (4 vols.) and the appropriate chapters in Spiller, Thorp, Johnson, and Canby, *Literary History of the United States,* vol.2, and the bibliographical vol.3. V.L.Parrington did not live to complete his magnificent *Main Currents,* but the fragment he left (*Beginnings of Critical Realism in America*) constitutes the best interpretation of the post-war years that we have. H.S.Commager, *The American Mind* picks up where Parrington left off. Ralph Gabriel, *The Course of American Democratic Thought: An Intellectual History since 1815* is particularly valuable for the post-war years. Lewis Mumford, *The Brown Decades* is provocative but unsubstantial, and the same can be said of his *Golden Day* and *Sticks and Stones.* Henry Adams, *The Education of Henry Adams* omits the years 1870–1890, but is the most interesting volume of its kind in our literature; it should be supplemented, however, by the two volumes of *The Letters of Henry Adams.* The most satisfactory introduction to the character of this period is through the letters, memoirs, and autobiographies of its spokesmen. Of these the following can be recommended: *The Letters of William James* (2 vols.); *The Letters of Henry James* (2 vols.); M.A.DeW.Howe, *John Jay Chapman and his Letters; The Autobiography* of Nathaniel S.Shaler; the *Reminiscences* of Raphael Pumpelly; W.D. Howells, *Literary Friends and Acquaintances;* E.Bisland, *Life and Letters of Lafcadio Hearn* (2 vols.); Rollo Ogden (ed.), *Life and Letters of E.L.Godkin;* John S.Clark, *John Fiske, Life and Letters* (2 vols.); Henry Holt, *Garrulities of an Octogenarian Editor;* Hamlin Garland, *A Son of the Middle Border; The Autobiography of William Allen White;* and Mildred Howells, *Life in Letters of William Dean Howells* (2 vols.). Three immensely valuable books are Elmer Ellis, *Mr.Dooley's America,* Walter Johnson, *William Allen White's America,* and Joseph Dorfman, *Thorstein Veblen and his America,* all covering broad ground. Interesting material may be found in E.W.Emerson, *Early Years of the Saturday Club* and M.A.DeW.Howe, *Later Years of the Saturday Club.* Novels such as Mark Twain's *The Gilded Age* and *Innocents Abroad,* Edith Wharton's *The Age of Innocence, The House of Mirth,* and *The Fruit of the Tree,* Henry James' *The Bostonians,* and the early novels of William Dean Howells, Ellen Glasgow, and Booth Tarkington faithfully recreate the character of the period.

TRANSCENDENTALISM TO PRAGMATISM. The best one-volume survey of American philosophy is Herbert Schneider, *History of American Philosophy,* particularly valuable for its elaborate bibliographies. Woodbridge Riley, *American Thought* is more technical in character and overly brief. There is useful material in Harvey Townshend, *Philosophical Ideas in the United States* and Ralph B.Perry, *Philosophy of the Recent Past,* which covers chiefly the twentieth century. No student should neglect the essays by George Santayana in his *Winds of Doctrine.* The beginnings of pragmatism can be read in Philip Wiener, *Evolution and the Founders of Pragmatism.* Something of value may be gleaned from G.P.Adams and W.P.Montague (eds.), *Contemporary American Philosophers* (2 vols.) and T.V.Smith, *American Philosophy of Equality* and *The Democratic Way of Life.* John Dewey has an essay on *The Influence of Darwin on Philosophy* in a volume by that title. The impact of Spencerian thought on America can be read in *Social Darwinism in America,* by Richard Hofstadter; there is much of interest, too, in S.Chugerman, *Lester F.Ward, the American Aristotle.* There are chapters on William James and on Ward in Commager, *The American Mind;* the bibliographies list further readings on pragmatism. The most illuminating approach to pragmatism is through the exciting pages of Ralph B.Perry, *Thought and Character of William James* (2 vols.), which should be supplemented, of course, by the earlier *Letters of William James.* James, too, has written the best explanation of pragmatism: see *Pragmatism* and

The Will to Believe and Other Essays. The *Collected Papers of Charles S. Peirce* (6 vols.) are for the most part highly technical in nature, but the lay student may understand some of the papers in vol.i and vol.v. Such a sampling of John Dewey as appears in *Characters and Events* (2 vols.) is instructive. The story of the popularization of Darwinism can best be read in Clark's *John Fiske* (2 vols.).

The impact of pragmatism on law may be read in O.W.Holmes, *The Common Law;* Benjamin Cardozo, *The Growth of Law, The Nature of the Judicial Process,* and *Paradoxes of Legal Science;* Roscoe Pound, *Introduction to the Philosophy of Law, Law and Morals, Interpretations of Legal History, The Spirit of the Common Law,* and, particularly, 'Scope and Purpose of Sociological Jurisprudence,' *Harvard Law Review,* xxiv and xxv. The *Collected Papers of Mr.Justice Holmes;* Felix Frankfurter (ed.), *Mr.Justice Holmes;* and Catherine D.Bowen, *Yankee from Olympus* suggest something of Holmes' contribution to the reinterpretation of American Law. M.A.DeW.Howe (ed.), *The Holmes-Pollock Letters* (2 vols.) is one of the great collections of letters in our literature. There is no substitute, however, for the reading of leading decisions over a period of a half-century. There are chapters on sociological jurisprudence in Commager, *The American Mind* and in C.E.Merriam, *American Political Ideas, 1865–1917.* E.R.Lewis, *A History of American Political Thought from the Civil War to the World War,* while far from satisfactory, is almost the only thing on this much-neglected subject; a second volume covering the period to 1950 is promised. There is useful material in H.E.Barnes and C.E.Merriam (eds.), *History of Political Theories, Modern Times.* For historical writing, see Michael Kraus, *History of American History,* and some of the essays in W.T.Hutchinson (ed.), *The Jernegan Essays in Historiography* and in Howard Odum (ed.), *American Masters of Social Science,* which contains Carl Becker's masterly essay on Turner.

The adjustment of religion and of the church to the new philosophy has been the subject of numerous studies. The great work on religion in America is Anson P.Stokes, *Church and State in the United States* (3 vols.). Of the monographs the most useful are C.H.Hopkins, *The Rise of the Social Gospel, 1865–1915* and H.F.May, *The Protestant Churches and Industrial America.* There is a large literature on Christian Socialism: a good sample is Francis Peabody, *Jesus Christ and the Social Question;* another is Walter Rauschenbusch, *Christianity and the Social Crisis.* Of personal material the best are William J.Tucker, *My Generation, Diary and Correspondence* of James F.Clarke, *Reminiscences* of Lyman Abbott, the *Recollections* of Washington Gladden, William Lawrence, *Memoirs of a Happy Life,* and Mary Ellen Chase, *A Goodly Heritage.* Two good general histories of religion are William Sperry, *The Story of Religions in America* and W.E.Garrison, *The March of Faith.* For revivalism see

H.D.Parish, *The Circuit Rider Dismounts: A Social History of Southern Methodism, 1865–1900* and William W.Sweet, *Revivalism in America: Its Origin, Growth and Decline.* Stewart G.Cole has written a *History of Fundamentalism.* Probably the best history of the Catholic Church in America is that by Theodore Maynard, *The Story of American Catholicism.*

LITERATURE. The two large co-operative surveys of American literature are indispensable, if only for their comprehensive bibliographies: *The Cambridge History of American Literature* (4 vols.), and Spiller, *et al.* (eds.), *Literary History of the United States* (3 vols.). The bibliographies in Walter F.Taylor, *History of American Letters* are likewise exceptionally full. The most satisfactory treatments of literature from the Civil War to World War I are Alfred Kazin, *On Native Grounds* and Walter F.Taylor, *The Economic Novel in America.* Van Wyck Brooks, *New England: Indian Summer* and *The Times of Melville and Whitman* have all the literary charm and brilliance of the earlier volumes on New England letters and cover less familiar ground. Ludwig Lewisohn, *Expression in America* is a Freudian interpretation; for a criticism of this interpretation see H.S.Commager, *The American Mind,* chapters 6 and 7. The comprehensive bibliographies in the *Literary History of the United States* make it superfluous to list individual biographies here, yet a few of the more notable or useful should be mentioned. For Mark Twain the classic biography is A.B.Paine, *Life of Mark Twain* (3 vols.). Howells, *My Mark Twain* is a tender, personal appreciation. Van Wyck Brooks, *The Ordeal of Mark Twain* develops the thesis that Clemens was frustrated by his social environment; this thesis is heatedly refuted by Bernard De Voto, *Mark Twain's America.* Dixon Wecter had in preparation a biography of Mark Twain and an edition of his correspondence. For Sidney Lanier see A.H.Starke, *Sidney Lanier;* for William V.Moody, David Henry's biography of that name. Biographies of Whitman are legion; the student can take his pick among those by Emory Holloway, Henry S. Canby, and Newton Arvin. For Howells see the *Life in Letters,* above, O.W.Firkins, *William Dean Howells,* and Delmar G.Cooke, *William Dean Howells.* There are admirable chapters in Parrington, *Beginnings of Critical Realism* and in Kazin, *On Native Grounds.* Howells' autobiographical writings are essential: *A Boy's Town, Years of My Youth, Literary Friends and Acquaintances.* There is a Howells omnibus edited by H.S.Commager. The literature on Henry James, too, is voluminous. Perhaps the best of all studies are Francis O.Matthiessen, *The James Family* and *Henry James: The Major Phase.* See also Rebecca West, *Henry James* and Van Wyck Brooks, *The Pilgrimage of Henry James.* F.O.Matthiessen has written an exquisite appreciation of *Sarah Orne Jewett* and Genevieve Taggard a satisfactory explanation of the *Life and Mind of Emily Dickinson.* John Manly's edition of the *Poems and Plays of William Vaughn*

Moody (2 vols.) contains a lengthy introduction, as does R.M.Lovett's more recent edition of the *Poems*. Thomas Beer, *Stephen Crane* is brilliant impressionism. Useful biographies of secondary figures are Ferris Greenslet, *Thomas Bailey Aldrich;* Irving Stone, *Sailor on Horseback,* the biography of Jack London; G.M.Gould, *Life and Letters of Edmund C.Stedman* (2 vols.); A.R.Burr, *S.Weir Mitchell;* Franklin Walker, *Frank Norris.* For the literature of social revolt see O.Cargill's anthology under that title. The literature of the Middle Border can best be studied through the books by Lucy Hazard and Dorothy Dondore, listed in § IX. H.R.Mayes has a biography of *Horatio Alger* and Mary A.Roe of *E.P.Roe,* and Edmund Pearson has a book on *Dime Novels.* James Hart has written *The Popular Book.* There are biographies of practically every major and minor figure in our literature; for these see the *Dictionary of American Biography.*

JOURNALISM. Frank L.Mott, *American Journalism, 1690–1940* is an entirely satisfactory study, but most other books concentrate on a few of the larger metropolitan papers to the exclusion of the Southern and Western ones. The best brief accounts are those of F.Hudson, *Journalism in the United States from 1690 to 1872,* and W.G.Bleyer, *Main Currents in the History of American Journalism.* F.L.Mott has given us, too, an exhaustively thorough *History of American Magazines* (3 vols.). The introductions by Allan Nevins in his collection of *American Press Opinion* are valuable, as are the numerous sketches of leading journalists which he contributed to the *Dictionary of American Biography.*

There is considerable biographical literature for leading editors and there are histories of many of the more important newspapers. G.S.Merriam, *Life and Times of Samuel Bowles* (2 vols.) is especially valuable; it should be supplemented by R.Hooker, *The Story of an Independent Newspaper.* For Greeley see his own *Recollections of a Busy Life.* The old *Life of Horace Greeley* by James Parton is written with vivacity and understanding. Don Seitz has written a journalistic biography of *Greeley* and also of *Joseph Pulitzer* and *The James Gordon Bennetts.* Royal Cortissoz, *Whitelaw Reid* is uncritical. Other biographies are Gerald Johnson, *An Honorable Titan, a Life of Adolph Ochs;* E.S.Bates and O.Carlson, *Hearst; Lord of San Simeon;* and George Britt, *Forty Years, Forty Millions, a Biography of Frank Munsey.* C.H.Dennis, *Victor Lawson* is a history of the 'Chicago Daily News.' Oliver Gramling, *AP The Story of News* reminds us of the declining importance of editors and the increasing importance of business organization in journalism. Of histories of individual papers the best are: Allan Nevins, *The Evening Post: a Century of Idealism;* F.M.O'Brien, *The Story of the Sun;* Elmer Davis, *History of the New York Times;* Harry Baehr, *The New York Tribune Since the War;* J.E.Chamberlin, *The Boston Transcript;* and Gerald Johnson, *et al., The Sun Papers of Baltimore.* O.G.Villard, *Some Newspapers and News-*

papermen contains brilliant pen portraits by one of the ablest of contemporary editors. The best of all personal accounts of journalism is *The Autobiography of William Allen White.* C.H.Levermore has an excellent article on 'The Rise of Metropolitan Journals,' in *Amer.Hist.Rev.*vi.

ART AND ARCHITECTURE. Lewis Mumford, *Sticks and Stones* is a brilliant interpretation of American architecture, looked upon with suspicion by professional students. Oliver W.Larkin, *Art and Life in America* is a remarkable survey of architecture as well as art, perhaps the best in our literature. T.E.Tallmadge, *The Story of American Architecture,* Fiske Kimball, *American Architecture,* and James H.Fitch, *American Building* are briefer histories. T.F.Hamlin, 'The American Spirit in Architecture' in the *Pageant of America* contains valuable illustrative material. There are a number of good biographies: M.G.Van Rensselaer, *Henry Hobson Richardson;* A.H.Granger, *Charles Follen McKim;* and C.H.Moore, *Daniel H.Burnham, Architect and Planner of Cities.* Louis Sullivan, *Autobiography of an Idea* is a brilliant and chaotic autobiography of one of the most influential American architects; see also his *Kindergarten Chats,* and the biography by Hugh Morrison. The *Autobiography of Frank Lloyd Wright* is similarly provocative and disorganized, and see Frederick Gutheim, *F.L.Wright on Architecture.* There is a good discussion of some aspects of architecture in Mumford's *Brown Decades.*

Charles H.Caffin has written popular histories of painting and sculpture: *The Story of American Painting* and *American Masters of Sculpture.* Alan Burroughs, *Limners and Likenesses: Three Centuries of American Painting* is a good brief survey. Samuel Isham, *History of American Painting* is more elaborate but antiquated; J.C.Van Dyke, *American Painting and its Traditions,* interpretative. Homer St.Gaudens, *The American Artist and his Times* is admirably illustrated. Cecilia Beaux, *Background with Figures* is a charming autobiography by one of the best of contemporary painters. Other autobiographies are *Art Young, His Life and Times,* which presents one of the greatest of contemporary American cartoonists; George Biddle, *An American Artist's Story;* and Thomas Hart Benton, *An Artist in America.* E.H.Blashfield has told the story of *Mural Painting in America,* Frank Weitenkampf of *American Graphic Art,* and William Murrell of *American Graphic Humor* (2 vols.). Of the numerous biographies of painters, the best are: Kenyon Cox, *Winslow Homer;* Lloyd Goodrich, *Winslow Homer;* W.H.Downes, *Life and Works of Winslow Homer;* George Inness, Jr., *Life, Art and Letters of George Inness;* Elizabeth McCausland, *George Inness;* R.F.Mather, *Homer Martin;* Henry C.White, *Life and Art of Dwight Tryon;* R.Cortissoz, *John LaFarge;* W.H.Downes, *John Singer Sargent, His Life and Work;* E.R. and J.Pennell, *James McNeill Whistler,* and Elizabeth L.Cary, *The Works of James McNeill Whistler.* A good general study is Wolfgang Born, *American Landscape Painting.* Fairfax Downey, *Portrait of an Era as drawn by C.D.Gibson* is entertaining and well illustrated. For sculpture see the classic *History of American Sculpture* by Lorado Taft, and Adeline Adams, *The Spirit of American Sculpture*. Royal Cortissoz, *Augustus St.Gaudens* is excellent, but the student should consult the *Reminiscences of Augustus St.Gaudens* (2 vols.). Ferdinand Schevill has written a biography of *Karl Bitter*.

EDUCATION. Paul Monroe (ed.), *Cyclopaedia of American Education* (5 vols.) is invaluable. On primary and secondary education there are three satisfactory texts: E.P.Cubberley, *Public Education in the United States;* E.G.Dexter, *History of Education in the United States;* and R.G.Boone, *Education in the United States*. E.E.Brown, *Making of our Middle Schools* is useful. Thomas Woody, *A History of Woman's Education in the United States* (2 vols.) is indispensable. Merle Curti, *Social Ideas of American Educators* is a pioneer work in the field and immensely valuable; it should be supplemented by Howard Beale, *Are American Teachers Free?* E.W.Knight, *Public Education in the South* has been largely supplanted by Charles W.Dabney, *Universal Education in the South* (2 vols.). On the effect of the Civil War on Southern education, see Knight's *Influence of Reconstruction on Education in the South* and J.L.M.Curry, *History of the Peabody Fund*. C.F.Thwing's two volumes on higher education are almost alone in the field: *History of Higher Education in the United States* and *History of Higher Education in the United States Since the Civil War*. Practically every college and university has its 'history.' For Harvard University see S.E.Morison, *History of Harvard University* and Henry James, Jr., *Charles W.Eliot* (2 vols.). Fabian Franklin, *Life of Daniel Coit Gilman* tells the story of the founding of Johns Hopkins; A.D.White, *Autobiography*, of Cornell; and T.Stanley Hall, *Confessions of a Psychologist*, of Clark. Some good college histories are Jonas Vilas, *The University of Missouri*, Walter Dyson, *Howard University*, Thomas Le Duc, *Piety and Intellect at Amherst College, 1865–1912*, Robert Fletcher, *A History of Oberlin College Through the Civil War*, Edwin Mims, *History of Vanderbilt University*, Carl Becker, *Cornell University: Founders and the Founding*, Merle Curti and Vernin Carstensen, *The University of Wisconsin* (2 vols.); a staggering number of others are in preparation.

W.B.Parker's biography of *Justin Morrill* tells the story of the Morrill Act. E.D.Ross has written a study of the land-grant colleges: *Democracy's College*. For the McGuffey Readers see Harvey C.Minnich, *William Holmes McGuffey and his Readers*. On the public library, see A.E.Bostwick, *The American Public Library;* Robert D.Leigh, *The Public Library in the United States;* S.S.Green, *The Public Library Movement in the United States;* and W.I.Fletcher, *Public Libraries in America*.

XIII and XIV. *IMPERIALISM, WORLD POWER, AND EMPIRE*

GENERAL. S.F.Bemis and G.G.Griffin, *Guide to the Diplomatic History of the United States* is so thorough and well organized that it obviates the necessity for a detailed bibliography here. Mr.Bemis' *Diplomatic History of the United States* is the most satisfactory treatment of the whole period covered in these chapters, though T.A.Bailey, *A Diplomatic History of the American People* is somewhat easier reading. A.K.Weinberg, *Manifest Destiny: A Study of Nationalist Expansionism* is useful for all periods. B.M.Williams, *Economic Foreign Policy of the United States* is useful at every point. Dexter Perkins, *Hands Off! A History of the Monroe Doctrine* is a brilliant example of synthesis, thoroughly scholarly and unfailingly interesting. The same can be said for J.Bartlett Brebner, *The North Atlantic Triangle: The Interplay of Canada, the United States, and Great Britain*. A number of more specialized volumes trace American relations with particular states or regions: J.M.Callahan, *American Foreign Affairs in Mexican Relations, American Foreign Affairs in Canadian Relations, American Relations in the Pacific,* and *Cuba and International Relations;* J.H.Latané, *Diplomatic Relations of the United States and Latin America;* J.Fred Rippy, *The United States and Mexico;* G.H.Stuart, *Latin America and the United States;* C.L.Jones, *Caribbean Interests of the United States;* and P.J.Treat, *Japan and the United States, 1853–1921.* For relations with Britain see the pioneer work of Richard Heindel, *The American Impact on Britain, 1898–1914* and L.M.Gelder, *The Rise of Anglo-American Friendship*. Alfred L.P.Dennis, *Adventures in American Diplomacy, 1896–1906* covers many phases of our foreign affairs. For additional references see bibliography in §§ XVI and XIX.

DIPLOMATIC CONTROVERSIES. A.F.Tyler, *Foreign Policy of James G.Blaine* and D.S.Muzzey, *James G.Blaine* are satisfactory on *Pan-Americanism*. S.B.Stanton has written the history of the *Behring Sea Controversy*. For Samoa see G.F.Ryder, *Foreign Policy of the United States in Relation to Samoa*. For Hawaii, J.W.Pratt, *Expansionists of 1898* is definitive, but see also E.J.Carpenter, *America in Hawaii* and J.W.Foster, *American Diplomacy in the Orient*. P.E.Corbett is exhaustive on *The Settlement of Canadian-American Disputes*. The Venezuelan affair can best be studied in the biographies of Cleveland and Olney listed in § X. For the Monroe Doctrine see D.Y.Thomas, *A Hundred Years of the Monroe Doctrine;* A.Alvarez, *The Monroe Doctrine,* and Dexter Perkins, *Hands Off!*

THE RISE OF IMPERIALISM. J.W.Pratt, *Expansionists of 1898* is particularly good on the emotional and psychological background of imperialism and the philosophy which was developed to justify the new departure. Additional material may be found in the biographies of Admiral Mahan by C.C.Taylor and W.D.Puleston, and in Mahan's autobiography, *From Sail to Steam*. Richard West, *Admirals of American Empire* deals with Dewey, Schley, Sampson, and Mahan. Harold and Margaret Sprout, *The Rise of American Naval Power,* and George T. Davis, *A Navy Second to None* go down to the Second World War. Henry Pringle's *Theodore Roosevelt,* and C.H.Bowers' *Albert Beveridge and the Progressive Era* are on leading imperialists. See, too, Gordon O'Gara, *Theodore Roosevelt and the Rise of the Modern Navy.* For world-wide manifestations of imperialism, see J.A.Hobson, *Imperialism and the Philosophy of Jingoism* and Parker T.Moon, *Imperialism and World Politics.* Albert K.Weinberg, *Manifest Destiny* is a brilliant survey and criticism of the entire subject.

THE SPANISH WAR. Events leading up to the Spanish War are described in some detail in F.E.Chadwick, *Relations of the United States and Spain: Diplomacy* and in H.E.Flack, *Spanish-American Diplomatic Relations preceding the War of 1898.* Walter Millis, *The Martial Spirit* is lively and, on the whole, accurate. E.J.Benton has written on the *International Law and Diplomacy of the Spanish-American War,* and J.W.Pratt, *Expansionists of 1898* covers the whole story of the forces making for — and against — expansion, and is indispensable to any understanding of the war. Two volumes analyze in some detail the influence of the jingo press: Marcus Wilkerson, *Public Opinion and the Spanish-American War,* and Joseph Wisan, *The Cuban Crisis as Reflected in the New York Press.* On the *Maine* see Charles D.Sigsbee, *The Maine: a Personal Narrative.* Col.H.H.Sargent, *The Campaign of Santiago de Cuba* (3 vols.) is the definitive account of the principal military and naval campaigns. F.E.Chadwick, *Relations of the United States and Spain: the War* (2 vols.) is comprehensive and has a bibliography of the published records. Theodore Roosevelt's *Rough Riders,* which Mr.Dooley called '*Alone in Cubia,*' reproduces the flavor and enthusiasm of the time. John D.Long, *The New American Navy* (2 vols.) is by the Secretary of the Navy; A.T.Mahan, *Lessons of the War with Spain* is a bit of special pleading for a big navy; and R.A.Alger, *The Spanish-American War,* special pleading for Mr.Alger. There is abundant material in other personal accounts: W.S.Schley, *Forty-Five Years under the Flag;* N.A.Miles, *Serving the Republic;* Joseph Wheeler, *The Santiago Campaign;* John Bigelow, *Reminiscences of the Santiago Campaign;* Frederick Funston, *Memories of Two Wars;* Stephen Bonsal, *The Fight for Santiago;* and George Dewey, *Autobiography.*

THE TREATY OF PARIS AND ANTI-IMPERIALISM. The annual *Foreign Relations of the United States,* containing instructions to the American delegates, is supplemented by *Spanish Diplomatic Correspondence and Documents, 1896–1900,* and by *Papers on the Treaty of Paris,* 55th Cong.3d Sess.Sen.Doc.No.62. The volumes by Chadwick and Benton, listed above, may be supplemented by the account in Royal Cortissoz, *Life of Whitelaw Reid* (2 vols.). The literature on anti-imperialism is large; the most characteristic material can be found in the biographies and autobiographies of the anti-imperialists: The *Autobiography of Andrew Carnegie;* George F.Hoar, *Autobiography of Seventy Years* (2 vols.); and, for the other side of the picture, *Selections from the Correspondence of Theodore Roosevelt and Henry Cabot Lodge* (2 vols.). Bryan's position on the Treaty is well stated in M.Curti, *Bryan and World Peace.* Moorfield Storey and Marcial P.Lichauco, *The Conquest of the Philippines by the United States, 1898–1925* is a passionate protest; cf. M.A.DeW.Howe, *Portrait of an Independent, Moorfield Storey;* there is much, too, in Pratt's *Expansionists of 1898.* A summary of the anti-imperialist movement by Fred Harrington appeared in the *Miss. Val.Hist.Rev.*,xxii.

The constitutional aspects of imperialism may be studied in W.F. Willoughby, *Territories and Dependencies of the United States;* C.F.Randolph, *Law and Policy of Annexation;* and C.E.Magoon, *Legal Status of the Territory . . . Acquired by the United States during the War with Spain.* The Insular cases have been published separately by the government; they may be found conveniently in any case-book of constitutional law.

THE AMERICAN COLONIAL SYSTEM. W.H.Haas, *The American Empire* is a general survey of American colonial holdings and administration. Dean C.Worcester, *The Philippines, Past and Present* is a balanced account of the Islands and their administration to 1913; C.B. Elliott, *The Philippines to the end of Commission Government* (2 vols.) is more detailed. José S.Reyes, *Legislative History of America's Economic Policy toward the Philippines* develops that phase with great detail. For Hawaii, see especially H.W.Bradley, *American Frontier in Hawaii* and S.K.Stevens, *American Expansion in Hawaii, 1842–1898.* H.Hagedorn, *Leonard Wood* (2 vols.) makes out a case for that unpopular Governor. Nicholas Roosevelt, *The Philippines: a Treasure and a Problem* is a more recent survey. Grayson Kirk, *Philippine Independence* surveys the movement to its consummation. W.H.Calcott has written a useful survey of *The Caribbean Policy of the United States, 1890–1920.* Knowlton Mixer, *Porto Rico* is a history of American occupation of that Island; for Haiti see H.P.Davis, *Black Democracy,* and for the Dominican Republic, Sumner Welles, *Naboth's Vineyard* and M.M.Knight, *Americans in Santo Domingo.* On Cuba see L.H.Jenks, *Our Cuban Colony;* G.H. Stuart, *Cuba and its International Relations;* A.G.Robinson, *Cuba and the Intervention;* H.Hagedorn, *Leonard Wood;* and C.J.Chapman, *History of the Cuban Republic.* Scott Nearing and Joseph Freeman, *Dollar Diplomacy* is a vigorously biased criticism of American Caribbean policy.

THE OPEN DOOR. There is a large literature on American interests in the Far East. Foster Rhea Dulles has given a brief but critical survey of our relations with China: *China and America since 1784*. J.W.Foster, *American Diplomacy in the Orient* is an excellent general survey. A.W. Griswold, *The Far Eastern Policy of the United States* is brief and lucid. Paul S.Reinsch, *An American Diplomat in China* is by a diplomat who was also an historian. Tyler Dennett, *Americans in Eastern Asia* and his biography of *John Hay* are written with thoroughness and learning. W.W. Willoughby, *Foreign Rights and Interests in China* is concerned with the relations of China to the great Powers; additional material of a general character can be found in Paul H.Clyde, *Modern and Contemporary Far East* and G.H.Blakeslee, *Contemporary Politics in the Far East*. Foster R.Dulles, *Forty Years of American-Japanese Relations* covers the period from the beginning of the new century. Two volumes presenting the Oriental point of view are M.J.Bau, *The Open Door Doctrine* and H.Chung, *The Oriental Policy of the United States*. For a highly critical evaluation of American policy in the Far East see J.Barnes (ed.), *Empire in the East*. P.H.Clemens, *The Boxer Rebellion* is scholarly.

SOURCE SELECTIONS. R.J.Bartlett (ed.), *The Record of American Diplomacy, passim*. Commager, *Documents*, 5th ed., Nos.268, 281, 305, 329–331, 340, 345–352, 360, 362, 385, 386, 412, 446.

XV. *THE PROGRESSIVE MOVEMENT*

GENERAL. There is no adequate history of the Progressive movement, but the literature, personal and topical, is both extensive and excellent. A thought-provoking interpretation is John Chamberlain, *Farewell to Reform*, which should be read in connection with the *Autobiography of Lincoln Steffens*. A great deal of material can be found in the volumes of the American Life Series: A.M.Schlesinger, *Rise of the City;* Ida Tarbell, *Nationalization of Industry;* and especially, H.U.Faulkner, *Quest for Social Justice*. The bibliographies of all these volumes are comprehensive and critical. Mark Sullivan, *Our Times*, vols.ii and iii give the social background in a breezy, journalistic style. There are a number of volumes of a general interpretative nature: Herbert Croly, *Progressive Democracy* and *The Promise of American Life;* Walter Weyl, *The New Democracy;* and Thomas N.Carver, *Essays in Social Justice* are the most illuminating. Joseph Dorfman, *Thorstein Veblen and his America* covers the entire period and has a wealth of valuable material, as has his *American Economic Thought*, vol.iii. George P.Geiger, *Philosophy of Henry George* and Arthur E.Morgan, *The Philosophy of Edward Bellamy* and *Edward Bellamy* are satisfactory for two of the intellectual leaders of the progressive movement. C.C.Regier, *Era of the Muckrakers* is a pedestrian presentation of the subject with a useful bibliography. Louis Filler, *Crusaders for American Liberalism* contains a number of entertaining essays on some less known crusaders and muckrakers.. No one has yet improved on E.A.Ross, *Sin and Society* for an analysis of the social implications of modern corporate business. For the problem of wealth see the classic *History of Great American Fortunes* by Gustavus Myers; M.Josephson, *The Robber Barons;* and the more technical W.I.King, *National Income and its Purchasing Power,* The changing political philosophy of the period can be followed in C.E.Merriam, *American Political Ideas;* Edward R.Lewis, *History of American Political Thought;* and V.L.Parrington, *Beginnings of Critical Realism in America.* There are interesting essays in Chester McA.Destler, *American Radicalism, 1865–1901.* There is a wealth of material in the biographical and autobiographical literature listed below.

PERSONAL LITERATURE. The personal literature is so voluminous that we can scarcely do more than list part of it. LaFollette's *Autobiography* is indispensable but, like Theodore Roosevelt's *Autobiography* and the *Memoirs* of W.J.Bryan, must be used with caution. Lincoln Steffens' *Autobiography* is perhaps the most suggestive book of its kind for the subject, but almost equally good is William Allen White's charming *Autobiography;* see also Walter Johnson, *William Allen White's America* and *Selected Letters of William Allen White.* Ben Lindsey, *The Beast* tells the story of the fight on the corrupt political ring which ruled Colorado. Tom Johnson has written *My Story;* F.C.Howe, the *Confessions of a Reformer;* Brand Whitlock, *Forty Years of It,* which should be supplemented by his *Letters* (Allan Nevins, ed.); Ray Stannard Baker, an *Autobiography;* Oscar Ameringer, *If You Don't Weaken;* Mary Vorse, *A Footnote to Folly,* and C.E.Russell, *Bare Hands and Stone Walls.* In addition see the biographies of *Henry D.Lloyd* by Caro Lloyd; *Moorfield Storey* by M.A.DeW.Howe; *Beveridge* by Claude Bowers; and *Edward Atkinson* by H.F.Williamson.

HUMANITARIAN REFORM. For the battle with the slum, see the vivid personal account by Jacob Riis, *The Battle with the Slum* and the scholarly study by R.D.DeForest and L. Veiller, *The Tenement House Problem.* Every student should know Jane Addams, *Forty Years at Hull House* and Lillian Wald, *The House on Henry Street* and *Windows on Henry Street.* There are two biographies of Jane Addams: James W.Linn, *Jane Addams* and Winifred E.Wise, *Jane Addams of Hull House.* In addition, for the settlement house see the scholarly study by Edith Abbott, *The Tenements of Chicago, 1908–1935.* The rise of the city can best be studied in Mr. Schlesinger's admirable volume of that title; for a sociological approach see the notable work by R.S. and Helen Lynd, *Middletown* and *Middletown in Transition.* For the temperance movement see

Mary Earhart, *Frances Willard: From Prayers to Politics.* For charities see F.D.Watson, *The Charity Organization Movement in the United States* and the classic *American Charities* by Amos G.Warner. The new attitude toward crime is traced in Sheldon Glueck, *Crime and Justice;* C.R.Henderson edited the famous four-volume investigation of the Russell Sage Foundation, *Studies in Correction and Prevention of Crime.* The race question can be studied in R.S.Baker, *Following the Color Line,* Walter White, *Rope and Faggot,* and A.F.Raper, *The Tragedy of Lynching,* as well as in the books on the Negro listed in the bibliography in § I. On Indian reform see Howe's biography of *Moorfield Storey,* above, and Oliver LaFarge (ed.), *The Changing Indian.* J.A.Krout has traced the *Origins of Prohibition* in America, and E.H.Cherrington, *The Evolution of Prohibition in the United States.* On the peace movement see Merle Curti, *The Peace Crusade,* and on woman suffrage, Mary Gray Peck, *Carry Chapman Catt.* No attempt has been made to list here the volumes mentioned in the text.

POLITICAL REFORM. For political corruption see Lord Bryce, *The American Commonwealth,* R.C.Brooks, *Corruption in American Politics and Life,* and the *Autobiography of Lincoln Steffens.* B.P.DeWitt, *The Progressive Movement* is concerned chiefly with the political aspects of the movement; for politics see also F.E.Haynes, *Social Politics in the United States* and *Third Party Movements in the United States;* Claude Bowers, *Beveridge and the Progressive Era;* and the biographies of Roosevelt, Bryan, and Wilson listed elsewhere. Corruption in municipal politics can be read in Lincoln Steffens' classic *Shame of the Cities,* Fremont Older, *My Story,* Carter Harrison, *Stormy Years,* Fred Howe, *The City, the Hope of Democracy,* and, best of all, Brand Whitlock, *Forty Years of It.* W.D.Foulke, *Fighting the Spoilsmen* is a general account of the struggle for honesty in politics. Clifford W.Patton, *The Battle for Municipal Reform* is less dramatic than these personal accounts but probably more reliable. LaFollette's reforms in Wisconsin are celebrated in Fred Howe, *Wisconsin, an Experiment in Democracy,* C.C.McCarthy's *The Wisconsin Idea,* Edward Fitzpatrick, *McCarthy of Wisconsin* (not to be confused with the later Senator), and Edward N.Doan, *The LaFollettes and the Wisconsin Idea.* We still want a good biography of LaFollette. For U'Ren in Oregon see Allen H.Eaton, *The Oregon System.*

Here, as elsewhere, the story can be followed in imaginative literature. See, for example, Henry Adams, *Democracy;* F.Marion Crawford, *An American Politician;* Winston Churchill, *Coniston* and *Mr.Crewe's Career;* Brand Whitlock, *The Thirteenth District* and *The Turn of the Balance;* Theodore Dreiser, *The Titan* and *The Financier;* Booth Tarkington, *The Turmoil* and *The Midlanders;* William Allen White, *In the Heart of a Fool* and *A Certain Rich Man;* David G.Phillips, *The*

Plum Tree, and John W.De Forest, *Honest John Vane* and *Playing the Mischief.*

SOURCE SELECTION. Commager, *Documents,* 5th ed., Nos.301, 313, 371, 376, 384, 406, 407, 432, 433.

XVI. *THE REIGN OF ROOSEVELT*

GENERAL. James Ford Rhodes, *The McKinley and Roosevelt Administrations* falls far below the level of his larger *History.* F.A.Ogg, *National Progress* and H.Howland, *Theodore Roosevelt and his Time* are thin general histories of the Roosevelt and Taft administrations. M.Josephson, *The President Makers* is mostly straightforward political history, and a convenient summary. *Theodore Roosevelt, an Autobiography* is the best single volume on that President and his administration, but must be used with utmost caution. Roosevelt appears at his worst in *Selections from the Correspondence of Theodore Roosevelt and Henry Cabot Lodge* (2 vols.) and at his best in his delightful *Letters to his Children.* Various editions of Roosevelt's *Works* testify to his energy and versatility. The official biography by Joseph B.Bishop, *Roosevelt and his Time* (2 vols.) is most disappointing. W.R.Thayer, *Theodore Roosevelt: an Intimate Biography* reflects personal loyalty; the best biography of Roosevelt is that of Henry Pringle, and the best study of T.R.'s relation to progressivism is George E.Mowry, *Theodore Roosevelt and the Progressive Movement.* W.F.McCaleb, *Theodore Roosevelt* is valuable for the analysis of the Tennessee Coal and Iron Company episode. Lewis Einstein, *Roosevelt, his Mind in Action* is discriminating and thoughtful. Albert Shaw, *A Cartoon History of Roosevelt's Career* is both entertaining and informative. Roosevelt flits in and out of most of the biographies and autobiographies of the period, but see especially the *Autobiography of Lincoln Steffens,* N.W. Stephenson's *Aldrich,* Philip Jessup's *Elihu Root* (2 vols.), Tyler Dennett's *John Hay,* William Allen White's *Autobiography,* Gifford Pinchot's *Breaking New Ground,* Bower's *Beveridge,* and A.Nevins' *Henry White.*

THE EXTENSION OF GOVERNMENT REGULATION. For trust and railway regulation, see references in §§ V and VI. B.H.Meyer has written a *History of the Northern Securities Case;* additional material can be found in F.B.Clark, *Constitutional Doctrines of Justice Harlan.* A.H.Walker, *History of the Sherman Act* has succinct accounts of the important cases. The struggle for pure food and drug legislation can be followed in Mark Sullivan, *Our Times,* vols.i, ii; Bowers, *Beveridge and the Progressive Era;* and H.W.Wiley, *An Autobiography.* C.C.Regier, *The Era of the Muckrakers* gives an introduction to the literature of exposure.

The best older authority on conservation is C.R.Van Hise, *Conservation of Natural Resources in the United States.* Roosevelt, *Autobiography* and Gifford Pinchot, *The Fight for Conservation* reflect better the passions of the period. Pinchot's mature evaluation of this fight can be read in his autobiographical *Breaking New Ground.* For reclamation A.B.Darling (ed.), *The Public Papers of Francis G.Newlands* (2 vols.) is indispensable. On irrigation see F.H.Newell, *Irrigation in the United States;* W.E. Smythe, *Conquest of Arid America;* and B.H.Hibbard, *History of Public Land Policies.* Willard G.Van Name, *Our Vanishing Forest Reserves* is a severe arraignment of the U.S. Forest Service; Stuart Chase, *The Tragedy of Waste, Rich Land, Poor Land,* Russell Lord, *Behold Our Land,* Fairfield Osborn, *Our Plundered Planet,* and William Vogt, *Road to Survival* all emphasize the enduring nature of the problem of conservation. No student interested in the subject should fail to consult a file of *The Land,* a quarterly devoted to conservation.

FOREIGN AFFAIRS. The general works listed in §§ XIII and XIV cover the Roosevelt period. For Panama see J.B.Bishop, *The Panama Gateway,* W.J.Abbott, *Panama and the Canal,* and three more recent works: Dwight Miner, *The Fight for the Panama Route;* Miles P.Du Val, *Cadiz to Cathay;* and W.D.McCain, *The United States and the Republic of Panama;* H.C.Hill, *Roosevelt and the Caribbean;* the biographies of T.R. by Pringle and McCaleb are valuable. H.G.Miller, *The Isthmian Highway* is a general historical treatise. There is a wealth of material in the Congressional investigations: 'The Story of Panama,' *Hearings on the Rainey Resolution,* House Comm. on Foreign Affairs, 1912; *Diplomatic History of Panama,* 63d Cong.2dSess.Sen.Doc.474; and *Senate Committee on Interoceanic Canals,* 59th Cong.2dSess.Sen.Doc.401. J.B. and F.Bishop collaborated on an excellent biography of *Goethals, Genius of the Panama Canal;* M.C.Gorgas and B.J.Hendrick on a biography of *W.C.Gorgas, His Life and Work.* H.C.Hill, *Roosevelt and the Caribbean* punctures the legend of Roosevelt's defiance of the Kaiser and has illuminating chapters on Cuba and Central America. For Roosevelt's Cuban policy see David H.Lockmiller, *Magoon in Cuba: A History of the Second Intervention.*

For world politics see A.Nevins, *Henry White,* which traces the background of the Algeciras conference; Tyler Dennett, *John Hay,* and A.Weinberg, *Manifest Destiny.* A special subject is adequately covered in Gordon C.O'Gara, *Theodore Roosevelt and the Rise of the Modern Navy.* Tyler Dennett, *Roosevelt and the Russo-Japanese War* is exhaustive and fascinating. For the problem of Japanese immigration see S.L. Gulick, *The American Japanese Problem;* K.K.Kawakami, *The Real Japanese Question;* R.D.McKenzie, *Oriental Exclusion;* and J.E.Johnsen (ed.), *Japanese Exclusion.*

SOURCE SELECTIONS. Commager, *Documents,* 5th ed., Nos.355, 356, 360–63, 367, 369–72, 375.

XVII. *THE TAFT ADMINISTRATION*

GENERAL. Henry F.Pringle, *The Life and Times of William Howard Taft* (2 vols.) is detailed, impartial, and critical. The best approach to the Taft administration is through the biographies of other political figures: Bowers, *Beveridge,* Stephenson, *Aldrich,* Pringle, *Roosevelt,* Jessup's *Root,* etc. *Roosevelt and Taft, the Letters of Archie Butt* (2 vols.) is an intimate account of great value. M.A.DeW.Howe, *George von L.Meyer, His Life and Public Service* is a biography of Taft's Secretary of the Navy; O.S.Straus, *Under Four Administrations: from Cleveland to Taft* is by Roosevelt's Secretary of Commerce. For the Payne-Aldrich tariff see the standard histories of the tariff by Taussig, Tarbell, and Stanwood. The rise of insurgency can be traced in Bowers, *Beveridge.* Kenneth W. Hechler, *Insurgency* is far superior to the average doctoral dissertation. For the Ballinger-Pinchot controversy, see Rose M.Stahl, *The Ballinger-Pinchot Controversy,* and A.T.Mason, *Bureaucracy Convicts Itself: The Ballinger-Pinchot Controversy.*

FOREIGN AFFAIRS. Canadian relations may be studied in Keenleyside, *Canada and the United States,* and the U.S.Tariff Commission, *Reciprocity with Canada.* L.E.Ellis, *Reciprocity, 1911* is definitive on that unhappy venture. For dollar diplomacy see S.Nearing and J.Freeman, *Dollar Diplomacy;* Herbert Croly, *Willard Straight;* F.V.Field, *American Participation in the Chinese Consortiums;* and D.G.Munro, *The Five Republics of Central America.* A.T.Bailey has analyzed the 'Lodge Corollary' in *Pol.Sci.Qt.,* xlviii.

THE ELECTION OF 1912. All the works on Roosevelt, listed above, and Wilson, listed below, deal with the election of 1912. The most careful analyses are in Pringle's *Roosevelt* and *Taft,* in K.W.Hechler, *Insurgency: Personalities and Policies of the Taft Era,* and in George Mowry, *Theodore Roosevelt and the Progressive Movement.* More ephemeral in character are V.Rosewater, *Backstage in 1912,* and O.K.Davis, *Released for Publication.* Mark Sullivan, *Our Times,* vol.iii reflects much of the color of the campaign. W.J.Bryan reported the *Story of Two Conventions,* but failed to do justice to his own role in the second. For the Baltimore convention see especially, R.S.Baker, *Woodrow Wilson, Life and Letters,* vol.iii and Wayne Williams, *William Jennings Bryan.* Champ Clark, *My Quarter-Century of American Politics* (2 vols.) and William F. Combs, *Making Woodrow Wilson President* are biased.

SOURCE SELECTIONS. Commager, *Documents,* 5th ed., Nos. 373–87. Ruhl Bartlett (ed.), *Record of American Diplomacy, passim.*

XVIII. *THE NEW FREEDOM*

WOODROW WILSON. R.S.Baker and W.E.Dodd (eds.), *The Public Papers of Woodrow Wilson* (6 vols.) are, of course, indispensable. R.S. Baker has published eight volumes of the authorized biography, *Woodrow Wilson, Life and Letters;* all the volumes are pleasantly written, but only the fifth and sixth can be called scholarly. Of the many brief biographies of Wilson, that by Herbert Bell is probably the most satisfactory, especially for background. The biographies by W.E.Dodd, Tumulty, Daniels, and W.A.White are of a more personal nature. James Kerney, *The Political Education of Woodrow Wilson* is a shrewd study of one neglected phase of Wilson's development by a New Jersey journalist. Easily the best account of Wilson's intellectual and political development before 1912 is Arthur Link, *Wilson: The Road to the White House,* the first volume of what promises to be the definitive life of the President. Eleanor Wilson McAdoo, *The Woodrow Wilsons* reveals aspects of Wilson's character not presented to the public. *The Intimate Papers of Colonel House,* arranged as a narrative by Charles Seymour (4 vols.), leave the President little part in his administration, but are a rich storehouse of material. On the relations between House and Wilson see further, G.S. Viereck, *The Strangest Friendship in History.* Many of the members of Wilson's official family wrote memoirs; Bryan, *Memoirs;* David F.Houston, *Eight Years with Wilson's Cabinet* (2 vols.); W.C.Redfield, *With Congress and Cabinet;* W.G.McAdoo, *Crowded Years; The Letters of Franklin K.Lane;* the *Recollections* of Thomas R.Marshall; and the material collected in Burton J.Hendrick, *Life and Letters of Walter Hines Page* (3 vols.).

DOMESTIC POLICIES. The best accounts are in Seymour, *Pre-War Years* and Baker, *Woodrow Wilson,* vols.iii, iv. William Diamond's *Economic Thought of Woodrow Wilson* is valuable chiefly for its negative evidence. On the Underwood tariff see the standard histories by Taussig, Tarbell, and Stanwood, and H.P.Willis, 'The Tariff of 1913,' *Journal Pol.Econ.,*xxii. For the Federal Reserve system see E.W.Kemmerer, *The A.B.C. of the Federal Reserve System;* Carter Glass, *An Adventure in Constructive Finance;* P.M.Warburg, *The Federal Reserve System* (2 vols.); and W.P.G.Harding, *Formative Period of the Federal Reserve System.* A.D.Noyes, *War Period of American Finance, 1908–1925* gives the background. The *Report* of the Pujo Committee is in 62d Cong.3d Sess. House Report No.1593, and the *Report* of the Industrial Commission of 1915 in 64th Cong.1stSess.Sen.Doc.No.415. Louis Brandeis, *Other People's Money* summarized the report of the Pujo Committee in terms that all could understand; the significance of conditions revealed in the second report is set forth in A.A.Berle and G.C.Means, *Modern Corporation and Private Property.* Other aspects of financial concentration can be read in

L.Corey, *The House of Morgan;* Thomas Lamont, *Henry P.Davison;* and Cyrus Adler, *Jacob H.Schiff, His Life and Letters* (2 vols.). For the Clayton Act see bibliography of trusts, § VI; for the Federal Trade Commission, Thomas C.Blaisdell, *The Federal Trade Commission* and G.C. Henderson, *The Federal Trade Commission.* A criticism of trust legislation can be read in F.A.Fetter, *The Masquerade of Monopoly.* R.Fuller has written on *Child Labor and the Constitution* and W.S.Holt on *The Federal Farm Loan Bureau.* An amiable picture of the Wilson administration is given by its chief politician, Josephus Daniels, in *The Wilson Era: Years of Peace, 1910–1917.*

FOREIGN AFFAIRS. E.F.Robinson and V.J.West, *The Foreign Policy of Woodrow Wilson* consists largely of extracts from documents. Harley Notter, *Origins of the Foreign Policy of Woodrow Wilson* is easily the most perspicacious and scholarly survey of that subject. J.Fred Rippy, *The United States and Mexico,* J.M.Callahan, *American Foreign Policy in Mexican Relations,* and C.W.Hackett, *The Mexican Revolution and the United States* describe our relations with that Republic. There is a wealth of material in George Stephenson, *Lind of Minnesota.* No one has yet explained Wilson's curious Caribbean policy. For Bryan's peace treaties see his own *Memoirs* and M. Curti, *Bryan and World Peace.* For the Japanese problem see K.Sato, *Japan and the California Problem* and E.G.Mears, *Resident Orientals on the Pacific Coast.*

SOURCE SELECTIONS. Commager, *Documents,* 5th ed., Nos.389–398, 402, 404, 410–412.

XIX. *THE ROAD TO WAR*

GENERAL. The literature on the causes of America's entry into the World War is, for the most part, controversial. Since many of the basic documents and personal papers have not yet been made available to scholars, we cannot for some time expect any definitive treatment of the subject. Important documentary collections are: the annual *Foreign Relations of the United States; The Public Papers of Woodrow Wilson;* J.B.Scott (ed.), *Survey of International Relations between the United States and Germany, 1914–1917; German Official Documents relating to the World War* (2 vols.); and Carleton Savage (ed.), *Policy of the United States toward Maritime Commerce in War, 1914–1918.* Personal accounts which illuminate various aspects of the coming of the war are: The *Memoirs* of W.J.Bryan; *War Memoirs* of Robert Lansing; *The Intimate Papers of Colonel House* (4 vols.); *The Letters and Journals of Brand Whitlock* (2 vols.); D.F.Houston, *Eight Years with Wilson's Cabinet* (2 vols.); B.J.Hendrick, *The Life and Letters of Walter Hines Page* (3 vols.); J.Graf von Bernstorff, *My Three Years in America* and *Memoirs;* and Stephen

Gwynn (ed.), *Letters and Friendships of Sir Cecil Spring-Rice*. There is valuable material in the *War Memoirs of David Lloyd George* (6 vols.) and *Memories and Reflections* by Herbert Henry Asquith.

The best general accounts are in F.L.Paxson, *American Democracy and the World War,* vol.i, 1913–1917, well balanced and judicious, and C.C. Tansill, *America Goes to War,* learned and detailed but marred by hostility to Wilson.

PROPAGANDA. The literature on propaganda is large and growing, and almost all of it exaggerates the role of propaganda in the determination of policy. For this general subject, see Thomas A.Bailey, *The Man in the Street, Impact of American Public Opinion on American Foreign Policy;* H.C.Peterson, *Propaganda for War;* H.Lavine and J.Wechsler, *War Propaganda in the United States;* and H.D.Lasswell, *Propaganda Technique in the World War*. For German propaganda see John P.Jones and P.M.Hollister, *German Secret Service in America* and G.S.Viereck, *Spreading Seeds of Hate*. For the more important question of the attitude of Americans toward the belligerents the following are illuminating: R.H.Heindel, *The American Impact on Britain, 1898–1914;* L.M.Gelber, *The Rise of Anglo-American Friendship;* C.E.Schieber, *The Transformation of American Sentiment toward Germany, 1870–1914;* and C.J.Child, *The German-American in Politics, 1914–1917*.

THE FIGHT FOR NEUTRAL RIGHTS. S.B.Fay, *Origins of the World War* (2 vols.) and B.E.Schmidt, *The Coming of the War* (2 vols.) give conflicting interpretations. C.H.Grattan, *Why We Fought* and Walter Millis, *The Road to War* present vigorous but tendentious criticisms of American policy. The more conservative interpretation is presented with a masterly command of the source material by Charles Seymour in *American Diplomacy during the World War* and, in more generalized form, in *American Neutrality*. On American policy toward neutrals, see the monograph with that title by Thomas Bailey. Newton D.Baker, *Why We Went to War* overemphasizes the submarines. Alice Morrissey, *The American Defense of Neutral Rights, 1914–1917,* Edgar Turlington, *Neutrality: The World War Period,* and J.W.Garner, *International Law and the World War* (2 vols.) are strictly legalistic. Alex M.Arnett, *Claude Kitchen and the Wilson War Policies* is highly critical of Wilson; Josephus Daniels, *The Wilson Era: Years of War and After* highly favorable.

SOURCE SELECTIONS. Commager, *Documents,* 5th ed., Nos.400, 405, 408, 409, 416–418.

XX. *WAR AND PEACE*

MOBILIZATION. Waldo G.Leland and Newton D.Mereness have prepared an *Introduction to the Official Sources for the Economic and Social*

History of the World War. The most valuable history of all aspects of mobilization is Benedict Crowell and Robert F.Wilson, *How America Went to War* (6 vols.). Frederick Palmer, *Newton D.Baker: America at War* (2 vols.) is admirable for military organization and may be supplemented by Arthur Bullard, *Mobilizing America*. More specialized studies of phases of mobilization are: W.F.Willoughby, *Government Organization in War Times and After;* E.N.Hurley, *The New Merchant Marine;* W.D.Hines, *War History of American Railroads;* W.G.McAdoo, *Crowded Years;* Samuel Gompers, *American Labor and the War;* E.L. Bogart, *Direct and Indirect Costs of the World War;* J.M.Clark, *Costs of the World War to the American People;* J.R.Mock and C.Larson, *Words that Won the War: The Story of the Committee on Public Information 1917–1919;* Norman Thomas, *Conscientious Objectors in America;* and Z.Chafee, *Free Speech in the United States*.

MILITARY AND NAVAL HISTORY. Leonard P.Ayres, *The War with Germany* is a statistical summary sponsored by the War Department. J.M.McMaster, *The United States in the World War* (2 vols.) and J.S.Bassett, *Our War with Germany* are detailed and dull. C.R.M.F. Crutwell, *A History of the Great War, 1914–1918* and Liddell Hart, *A History of the World War* are by English military experts; the former neglects the American contribution and is otherwise one-sided. For the naval history of the War see Admiral Albert Gleaves, *A History of the Transport Service;* Edward Hurley, *The Bridge to France;* Thomas G.Frothingham, *Naval History of the World War;* Admiral Sims and B.J.Hendrick, *The Victory at Sea;* and Elting Morison, *Admiral Sims and the Modern American Navy*. On the submarine warfare see R.H. Gibson and M.Prendergast, *German Submarine War, 1914–1918*. The literature on military participation is large. John J.Pershing, *My Experiences in the World War* (2 vols.) is characterized by honesty and modesty; it should be supplemented by the *Report* of General Pershing, in *Annual Report* of the U.S.War Department, 1918. Thomas G.Frothingham, *American Re-enforcement in the World War* is clear and well organized. Books by commanding officers are: R.L.Bullard, *Personalities and Reminiscences of the War;* J.G.Harbord, *The American Army in France;* and H.Liggett, *Commanding an American Army*. Other useful accounts are Frederick Palmer, *America in France* and *Our Greatest Battle* (the Meuse-Argonne); Shipley Thomas, *History of the A.E.F.;* Dale Van Every, *The A.E.F. in Battle;* and J.C.Wise, *The Turn of the Tide*. David Lloyd George, *War Memoirs* (6 vols.) contain the liveliest appreciation and criticism of the American contribution by any Englishman, and Edouard Requin, *America's Race to Victory* by a Frenchman. G.S.Viereck (ed.), *As They Saw Us* has articles by Foch, Ludendorff, and others on the American contribution. The *Journal* of Brand Whitlock continues where his famous *Belgium* left off, and reflects better than almost any other source the emotions of war time. The Historical Branch of the U.S.Army has inaugurated a 17-volume documentary history of World War I: *The United States Army in the World War, 1917–1919*.

THE TREATY AND PEACE. Robert C.Binkley, 'Ten Years of Peace Conference History,' *Journal of Modern History,* i. and 'New Light on the Paris Peace Conference,' *Pol.Sci.Qt.,* xlvi are invaluable for an introduction to the literature. The standard history of the Conference is Harold W.V.Temperley, *et al., History of the Peace Conference* (6 vols.). For Wilson's contribution see the documents and narrative in R.S.Baker, *Woodrow Wilson and World Settlement* (3 vols.); Baker, *What Wilson Did at Paris;* E.M.House and C.Seymour (eds.), *What Really Happened at Paris;* and the valuable David Hunter Miller, *The Drafting of the Covenant* (2 vols.). Robert Lansing, *The Big Four* and *The Peace Negotiations, a Personal Narrative;* A.Nevins, *Henry White;* and Frederick Palmer, *Bliss, Peacemaker* give the history from the point of view of the other delegates. James T.Shotwell, *At the Paris Peace Conference* is by a trained historical observer. B.M.Baruch has written of *The Making of the Reparations and Economic Sections of the Treaty.* Some light on the contributions of the Inquiry gleams from C.H.Haskins and R.H.Lord, *Some Problems of the Peace Conference.* K.F.Nowak, *Versailles* presents a German interpretation and is highly critical of Wilson. The much-touted interpretation of Wilson in J.M.Keynes, *Economic Consequences of the Peace* is really superficial and misleading; Harold Nicolson, *Peace Making, 1919* is more perspicacious. Two highly critical volumes, indispensable but to be used with caution, are Thomas A. Bailey, *Woodrow Wilson and the Lost Peace* and *Woodrow Wilson and the Great Betrayal.*

For the League of Nations and the struggle over ratification see: J.S.Bassett, *The League of Nations;* J.H.Latané, *Development of the League of Nations Idea: documents and correspondence of Theodore Marburg* (2 vols.); D.F.Fleming, *The United States and the League of Nations, 1918–1920;* H.C.Lodge, *The Senate and the League of Nations;* A.Nevins, *Henry White;* and W.S.Holt, *Treaties Defeated by the Senate.* A critical — but not too critical — biography of Lodge is Karl Schriftgiesser, *The Gentleman from Massachusetts.* Allan Cranston, *The Killing of the Peace* is a capital study of how this idealistic plan for peace was wrecked by partisanship and bad management.

SOURCE SELECTIONS. James B.Scott (ed.), *Official Statements of War Aims and Peace Proposals; German Official Documents* (2 vols.); D.F.Fleming, *The United States and the League of Nations;* R.S.Baker, *Woodrow Wilson and World Settlement* (3 vols.); Commager, *Documents,* 5th ed., Nos.418, 423–429, 435, 436, 442. David H.Miller, *Diary of the Peace Conference* (21 vols.) is privately printed.

XXI. *WORLD POLITICS*

THE LEAGUE AND EUROPE. S.F.Bemis, *Diplomatic History of the United States* is the best guide for all aspects of American foreign relations since 1920; Bailey's *Diplomatic History of the American People* is better written but less comprehensive. Frank Simonds has written three thoughtful volumes: *American Foreign Policy in the Post-War Years; How Europe Made Peace without America;* and *Can America Stay at Home?* There is suggestive material in Dexter Perkins, *America and Two Wars,* and in Crane Brinton, *The United States and Great Britain.*

D.F.Fleming, *The United States and World Organization, 1920–1933* is easily the most judicious survey. John Spencer Bassett, *The League of Nations* carries the story to 1929; thereafter see the annual volumes of C.P.Howland, *Survey of American Foreign Relations* and Walter Lippmann and W.O.Scroggs, *The United States in World Affairs.* C.A.Berdahl, *The Policy of the United States with respect to the League of Nations* is a good analysis, and Kenneth Colgrove, *The American Senate and World Peace* valuable for that particular aspect of a troublesome problem. J.T.Shotwell has published two volumes on *The Origins of the International Labor Organization.* On the Kellogg Pact, see David Hunter Miller, *The Peace Pact of Paris.* Manley O.Hudson, *The Permanent Court of International Justice* is by an American member of the Court. The best book on the World Court is Denna F.Fleming, *The United States and the World Court;* H.G.Moulton and Leo Pasvolsky, *War Debts and World Prosperity* is the only good study of that complicated subject. On American foreign investments see R.W.Dunn, *American Foreign Investments;* Max Winkler, *Foreign Bonds, An Autopsy;* and U.S.Dept. of Commerce, Trade Information Bull.No.676, 'An Estimate of American Investments Abroad.'

LATIN AMERICA AND THE FAR EAST. On the Washington Conference see: R.L.Buell, *The Washington Conference;* C.Leonard Hoag, *Preface to Preparedness;* Y.Ichihashi, *The Washington Conference;* and G.H.Blakeslee, *The Pacific Area.* H. and M.Sprout, *Toward a New Order of Sea Power: American Naval Policy and the World Scene, 1918–1922* gives something of the background of the Conference. The *Report* of the Conference is in 67th Cong.2dSess.Sen.Doc.No.126. For the curious history of our Siberian expedition, see W.S.Graves, *America's Siberian Venture, 1918–1920* and F.S.Schuman, *American Policy toward Russia since 1917.* Additional references to Far Eastern Policy may be found in §§ XIII and XIV.

On Mexico see C.W.Hackett, *The Mexican Revolution and the United States, 1910–1926;* C.L.Jones, *Mexico and its Reconstruction;* J.Fred Rippy, *The United States and Mexico;* the masterly study by Frank Tannenbaum, *Mexico;* Samuel F.Bemis, *The Latin-American Policy of the*

United States; and Dexter Perkins, *The United States and the Caribbean.* Edgar Turlington, *Mexico and her Foreign Creditors* and Max Winkler, *Investments of United States Capital in Latin-America* are basic to an understanding of American policy. Harold Nicolson, *Dwight Morrow* is an admirable appreciation of the work of that diplomat. See also, on Latin-American policy, J.Fred Rippy, *The Bankers in Bolivia;* M.M. Knight, *Americans in Santo Domingo;* A.C.Millspaugh, *Haiti under American Control;* R.L.Buell, *American Occupation of Haiti;* Carleton Beals, *The Crime of Cuba;* and Harry Guggenheim, *The United States and Cuba.* For Canada, see Edgar McInnis, *The Unguarded Frontier: A History of American-Canadian Relations.*

SOURCE SELECTIONS. Commager, *Documents,* 5th ed., Nos.447–49, 457, 460, 466, 467, 477, 484–486.

XXII. '*NORMALCY*' *AND REACTION*

GENERAL. Dwight Dumond, *Roosevelt to Roosevelt* is a useful general account of the period, particularly good for the history of the reaction and the analysis of the relations of business and politics. There is good material in other texts dealing chiefly with the twentieth century: O.T. Barck and N.M.Blake, *Since 1900;* Harvey Wish, *Contemporary America;* and Henry B.Parkes, *Twentieth Century America.* See also the numerous economic-history texts listed above. George Soule, *Prosperity Decade: 1917–1929* is the best study of the era of normalcy. Preston Slosson, *The Great Crusade and After* is a general social history; F.L.Allen, *Only Yesterday,* an informal and journalistic study of the decade of the twenties; J.T.Adams, *Our Business Civilization,* a thoughtful interpretation. There is a wealth of material in *Recent Economic Changes in the United States* (2 vols.) and in *Recent Social Trends in the United States.*

Much of the personal material is journalistic in character. The best general study of the transition from Wilson to Harding is F.L.Paxson, *Post War Years: Normalcy, 1918–1923.* Karl Schriftgiesser, *This Was Normalcy, 1920–32* is journalistic but penetrating. John D.Hicks has a volume on the twenties in preparation. The best analysis of Harding is the article in the *Dictionary of American Biography* by Allan Nevins; there is a good picture of Harding in Mark Sullivan, *Our Times,* vol.vi, and a biography by Willis Fletcher Johnson, who has also written a life of *George Harvey.* The scandals of the Harding administration are set forth, somewhat sensationally, in Morris Werner, *Privileged Characters* and in M.E.Ravage, *Teapot Dome.* There are studies of both Harding and Coolidge in W.A.White, *Masks in a Pageant;* Mr.White has also written a biography of Calvin Coolidge, *A Puritan in Babylon.* Claude Fuess, *Calvin Coolidge* is less penetrating. The political history of this decade has been neglected; the only adequate study of the election of 1924 is Kenneth McKay, *The Progressive Movement.* For ' Al ' Smith see Henry Pringle's *A.E.Smith: a Critical Study,* and Governor Smith's own *Up from the City Streets.* R.V.Peel and R.C.Donnelly have prepared useful handbooks on *The 1928 Campaign* and *The 1932 Campaign.* Hoover's campaign speeches are collected in *The New Day,* and Hoover's philosophy set forth in his *American Individualism* and *The Challenge to Liberty.* Hoover's administration has been well covered in *The Hoover Administration,* ed.by W.S.Myers and W.H.Newton; *The Hoover Policies,* ed.by R.L.Wilbur and A.M.Hyde; and *The Foreign Policies of Herbert Hoover,* by W.S.Myers, all of them highly partisan. There is no satisfactory biography.

ECONOMIC POLICIES. Two reports of Presidents' Committees, *Recent Economic Changes in the United States* and *Recent Social Trends in the United States,* are valuable for the material assembled and perhaps for the conclusions. There is valuable material in two general works, Louis Hacker, *The Rise of American Capitalism* and Thomas C.Cochran and William Miller, *The Age of Enterprise.* A.A.Berle and G.C.Means, *The Modern Corporation and Private Property* is a masterly analysis of the separation of ownership and control. L.Corey's *Decline of American Capitalism* and *Crisis of the Middle Class* are Marxist criticisms. For the growth of trusts during these years see H.W.Laidler, *Concentration of Control in American Industry* and The Twentieth Century Fund, *Big Business, Its Growth and Its Place,* ed. by A.L.Bernheim. On the distribution of wealth see W.I.King, *Wealth and Income of the People of the United States*; Harold G.Moulton, *Income and Economic Progress;* and Federal Trade Commission, *Report on National Wealth and Income, 1928,* in 69th Cong.1st Sess.Sen.Doc.No.126.

The story of demobilization is told in vol.vi of Crowell and Wilson, *How America Went to War.* More general material can be found in Dixon Wecter, *When Johnny Comes Marching Home.* The Transportation Act of 1920 has received elaborate study: R.MacVeagh, *The Transportation Act of 1920;* D.B.Locklin, *Railroad Regulation since 1920;* W.M.Splawn, *Government Ownership and Operation of Railroads.* On the Railroad Labor Board see the volume of that title by Harry D.Wolf. A.R.Ellingwood and W.Coombs, *The Government and Railroad Transportation* contains the necessary documents. For the water-power struggle see J.G. Kerwin, *Federal Water Power Legislation,* H.S.Rauschenbusch and H.W. Laidler, *Power Control,* and Rauschenbusch, *The Power Fight.* One aspect of recent legislative development is analyzed in A.F.Macdonald, *Federal Aid, a Study in the American Subsidy System.* W.Thompson's *Federal Centralization* has not been brought up to date, but is useful for background. For the tariff see the illuminating analysis of the Act of 1930 by E.E.Schattschneider, *Politics, Pressures, and the Tariff,* and J.M.Jones,

Tariff Retaliation. For the Trusts and the Federal Trade Commission see bibliography under § XVIII. The struggle for foreign trade and markets may be followed in: B.H.Williams, *Economic Foreign Policies of the United States;* R.W.Dunn, *American Foreign Investments;* Max Winkler, *Investments of United States Capital in Latin America;* and Hiram Motherwell, *The Imperial Dollar.*

For prohibition, Charles Merz, *The Dry Decade* is satisfactory up to 1929. Peter Odegard, *Pressure Politics* is concerned with the enactment of the Eighteenth Amendment. See also: H.Feldman, *Prohibition, its Economic and Industrial Aspects;* The Federal Council of Churches of Christ in America, *The Prohibition Situation;* and the *Annals* of the American Academy of Pol. and Social Science, cix. The *Wickersham Report* is in 71st Cong.3rd Sess.House Doc.No.722.

Marquis James, *History of the American Legion* and M.Duffield, *King Legion* cover only the early history and are far from satisfactory. On the bonus see W.W.Waters, *B.E.F. The Whole Story of the Bonus Army;* Roger Burlingame, *Peace Veterans;* and the National Industrial Conference Board, *The World War Veterans and the Federal Treasury.*

AGRICULTURAL DISTRESS. Many of the books noted in the bibliography in § IX are useful for this period as well. Nathan Fine, *Labor and Farmer Parties in the United States* has some material on the farm bloc; P.R.Fossum, *Agricultural Movement in North Dakota,* on the Farmer-Labor party. James E.Boyle, *Farm Relief, a Brief on the McNary-Haugen Plan* is effective. See also: E.R.A.Seligman, *The Economics of Farm Relief;* J.D.Black, *Agricultural Reform in the United States;* W.S. Holt, *The Federal Farm Loan Bureau;* Arthur Capper, *The Agricultural Bloc;* and E.G.Nourse, *American Agriculture and the European Market.* Carey McWilliams, *Ill Fares the Land* is a general story of farm distress; it should be read in connection with Steinbeck's wonderful *Grapes of Wrath* — the best history of the impact of the depression on the farmer that has yet been written. Many of the volumes listed in the following section deal with the background of agrarian distress.

THE DEPRESSION. The best general account is Dixon Wecter, *The Great Depression;* almost equally good is Broadus Mitchell, *Depression Decade:* these two books should take care of the needs of most students. Gilbert V.Seldes, *The Years of the Locust: America, 1929–1932* is a general popular account of the depression. L.Corey, *Decline of American Capitalism* and *Crisis of the Middle Class* are tendential. There is some material in Myers and Newton, *Hoover Administration,* and a severe criticism of the Hoover policies in Rexford G.Tugwell, *Mr.Hoover's Economic Policies.* The article by Edwin F.Gay in *Foreign Affairs,* vol.x.529 is by a learned and thoughtful economist. W.Z.Ripley, *Main Street and Wall Street* and W.B. Donham, *Business Adrift* are by professional economists. Paul Douglas and Aaron Director have written on the *Problem of*

Unemployment and Abraham Epstein on *Insecurity*. For a critical interpretation of the prosperity of the twenties see Stuart Chase, *Prosperity, Fact or Myth?*

IMAGINATIVE LITERATURE. In the absence of substantial studies of the depression era, the best material is probably to be found in imaginative literature. A useful guide through this is Halford E.Luccock, *American Mirror: Social, Ethical, and Religious Aspects of American Literature, 1930–1940*. There is relevant material, too, in H.S.Commager, *The American Mind*, and in Maxwell Geismar, *Writers in Crisis* and *The Last of the Provincials*. Only a sampling of the imaginative literature can be suggested here, but all students should be familiar with such novels as Thomas Wolfe, *Look Homeward Angel* and *The Web and the Rock;* Scott Fitzgerald, *The Beautiful and Damned, Tender is the Night, The Great Gatsby,* and *The Last Tycoon;* Ring Lardner, *Collected Short Stories;* Sinclair Lewis, *Babbitt;* John Steinbeck, *Grapes of Wrath;* John Dos Passos, *U.S.A.;* Erskine Caldwell, *Tobacco Road* and *God's Little Acre;* William Faulkner, *Light in August* and *The Hamlet;* Fielding Burke, *Call Home the Heart;* Josephine Herbst, *If I Had Four Apples;* Richard Wright, *Native Son;* Dorothy Canfield, *Seasoned Timber;* John P.Marquand, *Wickford Point;* Carl Sandburg, *The People, Yes;* and the plays of Clifford Odets.

SOURCE SELECTIONS. Commager, *Documents*, 5th ed., Nos. 424, 430–433, 437–441, 450–456, 458, 459, 461, 462, 468, 470, 472.

XXIII. *AMERICAN SOCIETY BETWEEN TWO WARS*

AMERICAN SOCIETY. A number of recent books have attempted to paint a picture of American society in the second quarter of the century, or to interpret the American character. Harold Laski, *The American Democracy* is a severely critical indictment of American materialism and intolerance, but has invaluable chapters on the professions. H.S.Commager, *The American Mind* interprets the American character and deals specifically with such things as politics, law, history, literature, and architecture. Denis Brogan, *The American Character* is the best foreign analysis of America since Bryce's *American Commonwealth*. Margaret Mead, *Male and Female* and *Keep Your Powder Dry* both attempt to discover what is fundamentally American; the point of view is that of the social anthropologist. Lloyd Morris, *Postscript to Yesterday* is particularly good on cultural aspects of twentieth-century America; his *Not So Long Ago* describes social changes. On social characteristics and change see, too, Mark Sullivan, *Our Times,* vol.vi; Charles and Mary Beard, *America in Midpassage;* David Cohn, *The Good Old Days* — an attempt to interpret social history through the Sears, Roebuck catalogues; and a series of essays on 'Recent Social Trends' in the *American Journal of Sociology* for May 1942. John Gunther's encyclopedic *Inside U.S.A.* describes chiefly the war years, but is valuable for the earlier period as well.

Much of value is to be found in such general books as Preston Slosson, *The Great Crusade and After,* Dixon Wecter, *The Age of the Great Depression,* Broadus Mitchell, *The Depression Years,* Gilbert Seldes, *The Years of the Locust,* and J.T.Adams, *Our Business Civilization.* Robert and Helen Lynd, *Middletown* and *Middletown in Transition* are masterly case studies of life in a typical midwestern town and illuminate the social history of the whole country. Some aspects of prosperity are touched on in Paul Mazur, *American Prosperity.* For urbanization see, in addition to the books by the Lynds, J.V.Thompson, *Urbanization, its effects on Government and Society,* and N.P.Gist and L.A.Halbert, *Urban Society.*

For Leisure, see M.M.Davis, *The Exploitation of Pleasure* and J.P. Sizer, *The Commercialization of Leisure.* On sport and play, S.F.Dulles, *America Learns to Play* is invaluable and covers broad ground. See also R.B.Weaver, *Amusements and Sports in American Life.* There is no satisfactory study of the social effect of the automobile, but for the moving pictures see L.C.Rosten's amusing *Hollywood,* Lewis Jacobs, *The Rise of the American Film,* Margaret Thorp, *America at the Movies,* and W.M.Seabury, *The Public and the Motion Picture Industry.* There are some suggestive chapters in Gilbert Seldes, *The Seven Lively Arts.* On the radio, see Paul Schubert, *The Electric World: the Rise of Radio.* Lloyd Morris, *Not So Long Ago* has chapters on the automobile, the radio, the movies, and so forth. Llewellyn White, *The American Radio* is primarily concerned with the problem of control and of freedom of the air.

INTOLERANCE. There is a considerable literature on the intolerance of the period. General accounts are: E.S.Bates, *This Land of Liberty;* Walter Lippmann, *American Inquisitors;* Winifred E.Garrison, *Intolerance;* Gustavus Myers, *History of Bigotry in the United States;* Osmond K.Fraenkel, *Our Civil Liberties;* and Morris L.Ernst, *The First Freedom.* Particular phases of intolerance are examined in Maynard Shipley, *The War on Modern Science;* Zechariah Chafee, *Free Speech in the United States;* E.M.Borchard, *Convicting the Innocent;* Arthur G.Hays, *Let Freedom Ring* and *Trial by Prejudice;* George Seldes, *Freedom of the Press;* Howard Beale, *Are American Teachers Free?;* John M.Mechlin, *The Ku Klux Klan.* For intolerance and the race problem see the classic study by Gunnar Myrdal, *The American Dilemma,* Rupert Vance, *All These People,* and Bernard H.Nelson, *The Fourteenth Amendment and the Negro since 1920.* The literature on the Mooney-Billings and Sacco-Vanzetti cases is large. The Wickersham Committee report on the Mooney-Billings case is in 71st Cong.2d Sess.House Doc.No.252, and see H.H.Hunt, *The Case of Mooney and Billings.* The Records of the Sacco-Vanzetti case were published in six volumes; a shorter documentary study is O.K.Fraenkel, *The Sacco-Vanzetti Case.* F.Frankfurter, *The Case of Sacco and Vanzetti* is a masterly examination of the evidence. Louis Joughin and Edmund Morgan have compiled *The Legacy of Sacco and Vanzetti.* For the deportation delirium, see the chapters in Frederic Howe's *Confessions of a Reformer,* and Jane Clark, *The Deportation of Aliens from the United States.* Much is to be found, too, in the autobiography of the editor of *The Nation,* Oswald G.Villard, *Fighting Years.*

LITERATURE. See the general works listed in bibliography of § XII. Oscar Cargill, *Intellectual America* is an ambitious and vivacious effort to trace the sources of contemporary American literature. Joseph Wood Krutch, *The Modern Temper* is a penetrating study of the American mind during the post-war years. Harry Hartwick, *The Foreground of American Literature* is a series of studies of the major novelists, with a useful bibliography. A.H.Quinn, *American Fiction* and Fred L.Pattee, *The New American Literature, 1890–1930* are superficial. The urbanity of Percy H.Boynton's *Some Contemporary Americans, More Contemporary Americans,* and *America in Contemporary Fiction* sometimes conceals the soundness and maturity of judgment.

For poetry, see Alfred Kreymborg, *A History of American Poetry;* Amy Lowell, *Tendencies in Modern American Poetry;* Conrad Aiken, *Scepticisms;* J.L.Lowes, *Convention and Revolt in Poetry;* Louis Untermeyer, *New Era in American Poetry;* Harriet Monroe, *Poets and Their Arts;* and Babette Deutsch, *This Modern Poetry.*

Arthur H.Quinn, *History of the American Drama from the Civil War to the Present* is adequate for that subject; Joseph W.Krutch, *The American Drama since 1918* is less exhaustive but more penetrating.

Few of the biographical or critical studies of recent writers are of much value, but the following may be consulted with profit: Dorothy Dudley, *Forgotten Frontiers: Dreiser and the Land of the Free;* E.L.Masters, *Vachel Lindsay;* Herman Hagedorn, *Edwin Arlington Robinson;* Emery Neff, *E.A.Robinson,* in the new *American Men of Letters* series; and F.O. Matthiessen, *The Achievement of T.S.Eliot.* L.C.Powell, L.Adamic, and George Sterling have all written appreciations of Robinson Jeffers. The critical and comprehensive bibliographies in Spiller, *et al., Literary History of the United States* make it superfluous to list large numbers of books here. For some of the writers omitted from the Spiller bibliography, see the bibliography in Commager, *The American Mind.*

THE ARTS AND MUSIC. See the bibliography in the Introduction. In addition consult, on painting and painters, Martha Cheney, *Modern Art in America;* Augustus St.Gaudens, *The American Artist and his Times;* Frederick Wight, *Milestones of American Painting in our Century;* Samuel Kootz, *Modern American Painters;* Robert Henri, *The Art Spirit;* Helen A.Read, *Robert Henri;* Elizabeth Cary, *George Luks;* Guy P.duBois, *William Glackens;* Royal Cortissoz, *Guy Pène duBois;* Constance Rourke, *Charles Sheeler;* and the many books and articles listed in the bibliography of Oliver W.Larkin, *Art and Life in America.* On music see John T.Howard, *Our Contemporary Composers;* Aaron Copland, *Our New Music;* Isaac Goldberg, *Tin Pan Alley;* Herbert Graf, *The Opera and its Future in America;* Lazare Saminsky, *Living Music of the Americas;* and the elaborate bibliography in the third edition of John T.Howard, *Our American Music.* For the role of the Federal Arts Project see W.Whitman, *Bread and Circuses,* Grace Overmyer, *Government and the Arts,* and the forthcoming study of the *Index of American Design* by Holger Cahill.

SCIENCE AND SOCIAL SCIENCE. Notwithstanding the efforts to popularize the findings of science, the literature is far from adequate. Perhaps naturally, more has been written on medicine and doctors than on other sciences or scientists. S.M.Rosen and L.F.Rosen have written a general study of *Technology and Society,* which should be read along with Lewis Mumford's *Technics and Civilization.* Bernard Jaffe has given us a useful general study, *Men of Science in America: the Role of Science in the Growth of Our Country,* and a study of recent developments in *Outposts of Science.* Bernhard J.Stern's *Society and Medical Progress* is concerned with the social implications of medicine, as is his *American Medical Practice in the Perspectives of a Century.* Other useful studies of medicine are Harold Ward, *New Worlds of Medicine,* M.M.Davis, *America Organizes Medicine,* H.E.Sigerist, *Medicine and Human Welfare,* and George Gray, *The Advancing Front of Medicine.* Admirable biographies of eminent doctors are Helen Clapsattle, *The Doctors Mayo* and S.R. and F.T.Flexner, *William Henry Welch and the Heroic Age of American Medicine.* Two other useful biographical studies are Rackham Holt, *George Washington Carver* and L.Barnett, *The Universe and Dr. Einstein.*

There is no general study of the social sciences, and there are few satisfactory monographs on particular social sciences. Useful material can be found in the books listed above for American Society. There is a fairly comprehensive bibliography in Commager, *The American Mind,* Part II. Morton G. White, *Social Thought in America* deals with the interrelations of pragmatism and socio-economic ideas. For economics see Joseph Dorfman, *Economic Mind in American Civilization,* vol.iii and his *Thorstein Veblen and His America;* and Paul Homan, *Contemporary Economic Thought,* which has chapters on Veblen and Mitchell. Howard Odum (ed.), *American Masters of Social Sciences* has a few good essays, as has W.T.Hutchinson (ed.), *Essays in American Historiography.* For sociology see G.A.Lundberg, *et al., Trends in American Sociology;* H.E. Barnes and Howard Becker, *Social Thought from Lore to Science;* Charles H.Page, *Class and American Sociology;* and F.N.House, *The Development of Sociology.* E.A.Ross, *Seventy Years of It,* Richard T.Ely,

Ground under Our Feet, and John R.Commons, *Myself* are autobiographies by members of the Wisconsin school. Harold Fields, *The Refugee Problem in the United States* suggests something of refugee contributions as well as problems.

SOURCE SELECTIONS. Chiefly on intolerance, Commager, *Documents,* 5th ed., Nos.455–56, 463–65, 471, 487, 499, 511, 513, 528, 532, 533, 544, 559, 570, most of them with bibliographical references.

XXIV and XXV. *THE NEW DEAL*

GENERAL. There is already an immense literature on the New Deal and on Franklin D.Roosevelt; the stream of books on Roosevelt, indeed, promises to rise to flood proportions. Indispensable for any understanding of the period are *The Public Papers and Addresses of Franklin D.Roosevelt* (13 vols.), magnificently edited by Roosevelt himself and Judge Samuel Rosenman. The annotations themselves constitute a running history of the New Deal and its many special agencies. Of the general accounts of the New Deal see C.A. and Mary Beard, *America in Midpassage* and Basil Rauch, *The History of the New Deal, 1933–1938;* others are in preparation. The members of the Roosevelt administration have been highly articulate. The best of the personal accounts are Robert Sherwood, *Roosevelt and Hopkins* — invaluable for the war as for the peace years; Raymond Moley, *After Seven Years;* James Farley, *Behind the Ballots;* Frances Perkins, *People at Work;* Harold Ickes, *The Autobiography of a Curmudgeon;* Henry Stimson, *On Active Service in Peace and War; The Memoirs of Cordell Hull* (2 vols.); and James Byrnes, *Speaking Frankly.*

There is as yet no satisfactory biography of Roosevelt. Perhaps the best of the current works is that by Frances Perkins, *The Roosevelt I Knew.* The material in Sherwood's *Roosevelt and Hopkins* is invaluable. Karl Schriftgiesser has written a general book on *The Amazing Roosevelt Family, 1613–1942.* Two volumes of Roosevelt's personal letters have been published, edited by his son Elliott, but these carry the story only up to the Presidency. Eleanor Roosevelt, *This Is My Story* and *This I Remember* are lively personal accounts, remarkable for what they omit as well as for what they include. John Gunther, *Roosevelt in Retrospect* is a remarkable character analysis.

For the election of 1932 and subsequent elections, consult R.V.Pell and T.C.Donnelly, *The 1932 Election;* E.E.Robinson, *They Voted for Roosevelt: The Presidential Vote, 1932–1944;* and Charles W.Stein, *The Third Term Tradition.* There is interesting material on some of the New Dealers in J.T.Salter (ed.), *The American Politician,* and in such personal accounts as James Farley, *Jim Farley's Story* and E.J.Flynn, *You're the Boss.*

Accounts of the early phases of the New Deal, now mostly outdated, are C.A.Beard, *The Future Comes;* C.A.Beard and G.H.Smith, *The Old Deal and the New;* Ernest K.Lindley, *Half Way with Roosevelt;* Schuyler Wallace, *The New Deal in Action;* Stuart Chase, *The New Deal;* and George Soule, *The Coming American Revolution*. Criticism and protest can be read in Herbert Hoover's *The Challenge to Liberty* and, from another direction, in Norman Thomas, *After the New Deal, What?* and Benjamin Stolberg, *Economic Consequences of the New Deal.*

SPECIAL NEW DEAL REFORMS. For the background of the farm problem, see R.G.Tugwell, *Stricken Land,* and chapters in Dixon Wecter, *Depression Decade* and Broadus Mitchell, *Era of the Great Depression.* The history of the AAA is fully set forth in E.G.Nourse, J.S.Davis, and J.D.Black, *Three Years of the AAA* and Henry A.Wallace, *New Frontiers* and *America Must Choose.* Cary McWilliams, *Factories in the Field* and *Shadows on the Land* examine some continuing farm problems. No student should fail to read John Steinbeck's *Grapes of Wrath.* On the Hull program see J.C.Pearson, *Reciprocal Trade Agreements;* J.M.Letiche, *Reciprocal Trade Agreements in World Economy;* Alvin Hansen, *America's Role in World Economy;* and the *Memoirs of Cordell Hull.*

For the NRA see M.F.Gallagher, *Government Rules Industry;* A.A. Berle, *et al., America's Recovery Program;* L.S.Lyon, *et al., The National Recovery Administration;* and Hugh Johnson, *Blue Eagle, from Egg to Earth.* The findings of the famous TNEC are faithfully summarized in David Lynch, *The Concentration of Economic Power.*

For labor under the New Deal the following are useful: Carroll Dougherty, *Labor under the NRA;* R.R.Brooks, *Unions of their Own Choosing;* Herbert Harris, *American Labor and Labor's Civil War;* Edward Levinson, *Labor on the March;* Mary Vorse, *Labor's New Millions;* Horace R.Cayton, *Black Workers and the New Unions;* S.T.Williams and Herbert Harris, *Trends in Collective Bargaining;* H.R.Northrup, *Organized Labor and the Negro;* and J.Rosenfarb, *The National Labor Policy and How it Works.*

For unemployment and social security see: Abraham Epstein, *Insecurity;* I.M.Rubinow, *The Quest for Security;* Paul Douglas, *Social Security in the United States;* P.Douglas and A.Director, *The Problem of Unemployment;* Donald S.Howard, *The WPA and Federal Relief Policy;* Arthur MacMahon, *et al., The Administration of Federal Work Relief;* Lewis Meriam, *Relief and Social Security;* A.Epstein, *The Challenge of the Aged*; Marietta Stevenson and Ralph Spear, *The Social Security Program;* and the *Report* of the President's Committee on Economic Security, 15 January 1935. Relief is somewhat inadequately covered in the following: M.D.Lane and F.Steegmuller, *America on Relief;* A.D.Gayer, *Public Works in Prosperity and Depression;* Josephine C.Brown, *Public Relief, 1929–1939;* Grace Adams, *Workers on Relief;* and J.F.Isakoff, *The Public*

Works Administration. Bette and E.K.Lindley, *A New Deal for Youth* deals with the NYA; and Grace Overmyer, *Government and the Arts* and W.Whitman, *Bread and Circuses,* with the arts and theatre projects.

For housing reform see Carol Aronovici, *Housing the Masses;* M.W. Straus and T.Wegg, *Housing Comes of Age;* Louis Post, *The Challenge of Housing;* and L.H.Pink, *The New Day in Housing.*

For the background of the TVA see H.S.Rauschenbusch, *The Power Fight* and H.S.Rauschenbusch and H.W.Laidler, *Power Control.* C.L. Hodge, *The Tennessee Valley Authority* is quasi-official. There are enthusiastic appreciations of the TVA and its conservation program in Stuart Chase, *Rich Land, Poor Land,* Willson Whitman, *God's Valley,* R.Lord, *Behold Our Land,* and J.F.Carter, *The Future is Ours.* R.L.Neuberger and S.B.Kahn present an inadequate biography of the leader in the fight for the TVA, *George W.Norris.* Philip Selznick, *TVA and the Grass Roots* is a sociological study. The administrative aspect of TVA is adequately handled in C.L.Hodge, *The Tennessee Valley Authority,* and in C.Herman Pritchett, *The Tennessee Valley Authority: A Study in Public Administration.* Best of all is David E.Lilienthal, *TVA: Democracy on the March,* by the indomitable chairman of the Authority. There are interesting reflections on the TVA in his *This I Believe.* For an English view see Julian Huxley, *TVA: Adventure in Planning.* Various government publications contain material of great value: *General Report of the National Resources Board,* 1 December 1934; *Report of the Mississippi Valley Committee,* 1934 (2 vols.); *The Future of the Great Plains;* U.S.Dept. of Agriculture, *The Western Range;* and the *Annual Reports of the Tennessee Valley Authority.*

Securities regulation is covered by R.L.Weissman, *The New Wall Street;* the findings of the Senate Committee, 1933–34, are summarized somewhat dramatically in Ferdinand Pecora, *Wall Street under Oath.* Roy G.Blakey and Gladys C.Blakey, *The Federal Income Tax* and Sidney Ratner, *The Social History of Taxation* are good introductions to that complex subject. Henry J.Bittermann covers *State and Federal Grants-in-Aid.* There are three useful studies of money and the money policy of the government: A.Nussbaum, *Money in the Law;* G.G.Johnson, *The Treasury and Monetary Policy, 1933–1938;* and J.D.Paris, *Monetary Policies of the United States, 1932–1938.* For cartels, see the study by that name by Wendell Berge.

JUDICIAL REFORM. The literature on the court and court reform is voluminous, but there is no substitute for reading the leading decisions, most of which are noted in the text and presented in Commager, *Documents.* There is a wealth of material, as yet not fully exploited, in the six volumes of the *Hearings* of the Senate Judiciary Committee, U.S. 75th Cong.1st Sess. The best summary of the Supreme Court fight is Robert Jackson's *Struggle for Judicial Supremacy.* E.S.Corwin's *The Twilight of the Supreme Court, Court Over Constitution, The Supreme Court and the Commerce Power, Constitutional Revolution, Ltd.*, and *Total War and the Constitution* contain reflections by the most learned of our constitutional scholars. There is an admirable statement of the whole problem of judicial review in R.K.Carr, *The Supreme Court and Judicial Review,* and another in Benjamin Wright, *The Course of American Constitutional Law.* Other studies inspired by the reform bill are Morris Ernst, *The Ultimate Power;* Irving Brant, *Storm Over the Constitution;* Charles P. Curtis, *Lions under the Throne;* B.H.Levy, *Constitution, Tool or Testament;* and Wesley McCune, *The Nine Young Men* — which deals with the new Roosevelt court. H.S.Commager, *Majority Rule and Minority Rights* is highly critical of judicial review. C.Herman Pritchett, *The Roosevelt Court* is the most recent analysis of actual cases and decisions, but relies overmuch on statistics. There are a number of judicial biographies that command the attention of students: A.T.Mason, *Brandeis,* S.J.Konefsky, *Chief Justice Stone and the Supreme Court,* and John P. Frank, *Mr. Justice Black* are particularly helpful. Mark DeW.Howe is writing a definitive biography of Justice Holmes, and Paul Freund is preparing a study of the judicial career of Brandeis. Some of the problems raised by the Jehovah's Witnesses and other minority groups can be studied in H.H.Stroup, *The Jehovah's Witnesses;* Carl Zollman, *American Church Law;* Alvin Johnson and Frank Yost, *Separation of Church and State in the United States;* A.W.Johnson, *Legal Status of Church-State Relationships in the United States;* and Joseph Blau (ed.), *Cornerstones of Religious Freedom in America.*

SOURCE SELECTIONS. Commager, *Documents,* 5th ed., Nos.475–87, 493–505, 507–12, 515–20, 525, 529, 531.

XXVI. *THE COMING OF THE SECOND WORLD WAR*

We are still too close to the events leading up to the War to have a satisfactory historical perspective on them. Much of the literature on the coming of the war is highly colored; much of it, however, has a quasi-official character and is invaluable to the future historian. As time has not yet sifted the good from the bad, the useful from the misleading, the permanent from the ephemeral, we fall back here on a mere listing of the more helpful books.

THE BREAKDOWN OF COLLECTIVE SECURITY. General works: C.Grove Haines and Ross Hoffman, *Origins and Background of the Second World War,* with full bibliographies; Kenneth Ingram, *Years of Crisis, 1919–1945;* D.E.Lee, *Ten Years;* F.L.Schuman, *International Politics;* J.W.Wheeler-Bennett, *The Pipe-Dream of Peace. The Story of the*

Collapse of Disarmament; Merze Tate, *The Disarmament Illusion;* James T.Shotwell, *On the Rim of the Abyss;* Vera M.Dean, *Europe in Retreat;* and Sir Nevile Henderson, *Failure of a Mission.* On Italian Fascism, see G.A.Borgese, *Goliath, The March of Fascism;* G.Salvemini, *Under the Axe of Fascism* and *The Fascist Dictatorship in Italy;* C.T.Schmidt, *The Corporate State in Action;* and the Ciano *Diaries.* On Germany and Hitler, see Konrad Heiden, *Der Fuehrer;* R.A.Brady, *Spirit and Structure of German Fascism;* Franz L.Neuman, *Behemoth, The Structure and Practice of National Socialism;* Gustav Stolper, *German Economy, 1870–1940;* Herman Rauschning, *The Revolution of Nihilism* and *The Voice of Destruction;* S.H.Roberts, *The House that Hitler Built;* F.L.Schuman. *Germany Since 1918;* and C.E.R.Gedye, *Betrayal in Central Europe.* For Russia, see Frederick Schuman, *Soviet Politics at Home and Abroad;* Isaac Deutscher, *Stalin: A Political Biography;* Rudolf Schlesinger, *The Spirit of Post-War Russia: Soviet Ideology, 1917–1946;* and Julian Towster, *Political Power in the U.S.S.R., 1917–1947.* Winston Churchill's speeches constitute a running commentary on the European crisis; see especially *While England Slept* and the first volume of his great war history, *The Gathering Storm.*

AMERICAN FOREIGN POLICY IN THE THIRTIES. Nicholas J. Spykman, *America's Strategy in World Politics;* Charles G.Fenwick, *American Neutrality, Trial and Failure;* F.H.Simonds, *American Foreign Policy in the Post-War Years;* C.A.Beard, *The Open Door at Home;* Philip C.Jessup, *International Security: The American Role in Collective Action for Peace;* F.B.Sayre, *The Way Forward;* J.Fred Rippy, *America and the Strife of Europe;* R.L.Buell, *Isolated America;* Dexter Perkins, *America and Two World Wars;* W.H.Dulles and H.F.Armstrong, *Can America Stay Neutral?;* H.F.Armstrong, *When There is No Peace;* E.M. Earle, *Against This Torrent;* Lewis Mumford, *Men Must Act;* Hubert Herring, *And So to War;* Basil Rauch, *Roosevelt: From Munich to Pearl Harbor;* Walter Johnson, *The Battle against Isolation;* Thomas Bailey, *The Man in the Street;* Walter Lippmann, *U.S.War Aims* and *U.S.Foreign Policy.* The material in biographies and autobiographies listed above is invaluable; note especially the *Memoirs of Cordell Hull,* Henry Stimson, *On Active Service,* and Sherwood's *Roosevelt and Hopkins.*

THE WESTERN HEMISPHERE. See books listed in § XXI. In addition, Carnegie Endowment, *The International Conferences of the American States* (2 vols.); C.L.Jones, *The Caribbean Since 1900;* G.H.Stuart, *Latin America and the United States;* S.F.Bemis, *Latin America and the United States;* M.W.Williams, *The Peoples and Policies of Latin America;* J.Fred Rippy, *The Caribbean Danger Zone;* A.P.Whitaker, *Americas to the South;* Duncan Aikman, *The All-American Front;* Charles Wertenbaker, *A New Doctrine for the Americas;* Frank Tannenbaum, *Mexico;* Charles G.Fenwick, *The Inter-American Regional System;* Ray Josephs,

Latin America: Continent in Crisis; Arthur P.Whitaker, *The United States and South America: The Northern Republics.*

THE PACIFIC AND THE FAR EAST. Hugh Byas, *Government by Assassination;* Otto Tolischus, *Tokyo Record;* T.A.Bisson, *American Policy in the Far East, 1931–1940;* Stanley K.Hornbeck, *The United States and the Far East;* Harold S.Quigley, *The Far Eastern War;* John K.Fairbank, *The United States and China;* Foster R.Dulles, *China and America since 1784* and *Forty Years of American-Japanese Relations;* A.W.Griswold, *The Far Eastern Policy of the United States;* Joseph C.Grew, *Ten Years in Japan;* Edwin H.Falk, *From Perry to Pearl Harbor.* The United States Department of State has published two volumes on Foreign Relations: *Japan, 1931–41,* and one volume covering relations with China. The fullest account of prewar American diplomacy so far is in *Investigation of the Pearl Harbor Attack,* Report of the Joint Committee (79th Cong.2d Sess.Doc.No.244).

THE COMING OF THE WAR. Forrest Davis and E.K.Lindley, *How War Came;* Basil Rauch, *Roosevelt, From Munich to Pearl Harbor;* Winston Churchill, *The Second World War: Their Finest Hour,* and H.S. Commager, *The Story of the Second World War.*

SOURCE SELECTIONS. *The Public Papers and Addresses of Franklin D.Roosevelt, 1937 to 1941* are essential. Wilfred Funk (ed.), *Roosevelt's Foreign Policy, 1933–1941; Peace and War: United States Foreign Policy, 1931–1941,* Dept. of State Publication, No.1983; Ruhl Bartlett (ed.), *Record of American Diplomacy;* Commager, *Documents,* 5th ed., Nos. 488–92, 506, 514, 521–24, 526–27, 530–31, 534, 540.

XXVII. *WORLD WAR II: THE FRAMEWORK*

The literature on the home front during World War II is as yet scanty and ephemeral. For the political story see references in § XXVI and especially the invaluable *Roosevelt Papers,* 1941 to 1945 volumes. Something of the story of organizing the armed forces can be read in the official reports and histories: G.C.Marshall, H.H.Arnold, and E.J.King, *War Reports;* Kent Greenfield (ed.), *United States Army in World War II,* vols.i and ii; W.F. Craven and J.L.Cate (eds.), *Army Air Forces in World War II,* vol.i. There is valuable material, too, in the personal accounts, such as D.D. Eisenhower, *Crusade in Europe;* William D.Leahy, *I Was There;* R. Sherwood, *Roosevelt and Hopkins;* the *Memoirs of Cordell Hull;* Stimson's *On Active Service,* and others. Oliver LaFarge, *The Eagle in the Egg* tells the story of the Air Transport Command; Stewart Alsop and Thomas Braden, *Sub Rosa* is a history of the O.S.S.

Of the many journalistic books describing life in America during the war, John Gunther, *Inside U.S.A.* and John Dos Passos, *State of the Na-*

tion are probably the most rewarding. Jack Goodman (ed.), *While You Were Gone* is a report by various hands, some more expert than others, of conditions on the home front. Bruce Catton, *The War Lords of Washington* is a popular account of wartime politics in the national capital. On economic preparedness, Donald M.Nelson, *Arsenal of Democracy* is certainly the most interesting of various books that have appeared. There is valuable material, too, in Seymour E.Harris, *Economics of America at War* and in Sumner S.Schlichter, *The American Economy.* A particular but important aspect of wartime economy is explored in the Smaller War Plants Corporation: *Economic Concentration and World War II.* The War Production Board Historian and Staff has prepared the first volume of a history of *Industrial Mobilization for War,* and D.Norick, *et al., Wartime Production Controls* describes the experience of the War Production Board. For Lend-Lease see the account by its administrator, Edward R.Stettinius. For administration, see Leonard D.White (ed.), *Civil Service in Wartime;* Luther Gulick, *Administrative Reflections from World War II;* and Pendleton Herring, *The Impact of War.* E.S.Corwin, *Total War and the Constitution* is the best thing so far on that subject. James P.Baxter III, *Scientists at War* is a wholly admirable survey of that difficult subject.

SOURCE SELECTIONS. Commager, *Documents,* 5th ed., Nos.525, 529, 532–33, 538, 551, 558.

XXVIII and XXIX. *FIGHTING AND WINNING THE WAR*

The literature on the war is immense and growing, and promises to rival in volume that for the Civil War. It is, of course, a world-wide literature. We shall confine ourselves here largely to American war literature and to those books that reveal some qualities insuring permanence or that, in the absence of anything else, are useful guides until better books appear.

GENERAL. The student will do well to start with the official reports of the commanders-in-chief; those of Generals Marshall and Arnold and Admiral King have been conveniently collected in a single volume, *War Reports,* edited by Walter Millis. The U.S.Army Historical Branch has embarked upon an ambitious official history of the army operations, which may run to about 100 volumes; six of these have already been published under the general editorship of Kent R.Greenfield: *The United States Army in World War II.* The Air Force has limited its program more modestly to some six or seven volumes; three of these, *Army Air Forces in World War II,* have appeared under the editorship of W.F. Craven and J.L.Cate. No student of air power can neglect the official *United States Strategic Bombing Survey* for both the European and the Japanese theaters. S.E.Morison has published six volumes of his semi-official *History of United States Naval Operations in World War II.* On the work of the engineers see the inadequate study by Randolph Leigh, *American Enterprise in Europe.* Some of the best military history is to be found in the *American Forces in Action* series, prepared by the War Department Historical Division; they are particularly valuable for their maps.

The best personal account is that by the greatest of living military and political historians, Winston Churchill; three volumes of his *Second World War* have so far appeared, and more are on the way. Churchill's six volumes of wartime speeches are indispensable: *While England Slept; Blood, Sweat, and Tears; The Unrelenting Struggle; The End of the Beginning; On to Victory;* and *The Dawn of Liberation.* The material in such books as Sherwood's *Roosevelt and Hopkins* and the other personal accounts listed in § XXVII is invaluable.

There are already a number of shorter histories of the war, none based wholly on source material, but some of value. Perhaps the most satisfactory general account so far is Edgar McInnis, *The War,* an annual survey in six volumes. H.S.Commager has put together a compilation of accounts in *The Story of the Second World War.* Walter Phelps Hall, *Iron out of Calvary* covers the whole global contest briefly and interpretatively. Cyril Falls, *The Second World War* is clear and objective; J.F.C.Fuller, *The Second World War* technical and highly opinionated. R.W.Shugg and H.A.DeWeers, *World War Two: A Concise History* is just what its title indicates. The only chronology of the war to appear so far is that put out by His Majesty's Stationery Office. Two competent historians, Henry Pringle and Hanson Baldwin, have in preparation comprehensive histories of the war. Francis Brown (ed.), *The War in Maps* is based on the admirable but highly general maps that appeared in the *New York Times.* There are several comprehensive English histories of the war, the best of which is probably Sir Ronald Storrs and Philip Graves (eds.), *The War,* a record by quarters, running to over twenty volumes. Russian histories are notoriously unsatisfactory, but the student can profitably consult W.E.D.Allen and Paul Misatoff, *The Russian Campaigns of 1941–43* and *The Russian Campaigns* of 1944–45. For American wartime relations with Russia see John R.Deane, *The Strange Alliance,* Joseph E.Davies, *Mission to Moscow,* and, for a slightly later period, Walter B.Smith, *My Three Years in Moscow.* Harrison Salisbury, *Russia on the Way* is a sympathetic account by an able journalist.

SEA POWER AND THE BATTLE OF THE ATLANTIC. There are several interpretative volumes on the role of sea power in the war: Bernard Brodie, *Sea Power in the Machine Age* and W.D.Puleston, *The Influence of Sea Power in World War II* are the best. Gilbert Cant has written a general book on *America's Navy in World War II* and one on *The War at Sea,* which covers the battle for the Atlantic. For this chapter of sea war, however, see S.E.Morison, *Battle for the Atlantic*. D.S.Ballantine, *U.S.Naval Logistics in World War II* and Theodore Roscoe, *United States Submarine Operations in World War II* are satisfactory for those specialized subjects. For the naval convoys to the Arctic see Robert Carse, *There Go the Ships*.

THE PACIFIC WAR. There are a number of general accounts of the war with Japan; most of these will be superseded when S.E.Morison completes his 13-volume history of *U.S.Naval Operations in World War II*. Meantime see Gilbert Cant, *The Great Pacific Victory;* Frazier Hunt, *MacArthur and the War Against Japan;* Foster Hailey, *Pacific Battle Line* (to the end of 1943); Walter Karig and Wellbourne Kelley, *Battle Report* (3 vols.); and, for the views of a crack intelligence officer, Ellis Zacharias, *Secret Mission*. On the fall of the Philippines see Lewis H.Brereton, *The Brereton Diaries,* John Hersey, *Men on Bataan,* and C.P.Romulo, *I Saw the Fall of the Philippines*. S.E.Morison has a volume on Midway. Guadalcanal promises to be the most-written-of Pacific battle. S.E.Morison covers it in one of his volumes; the War Dept. *History* gives a volume to the Army story, and the U.S.Marines Historical Branch has a volume on the Marines at Guadalcanal. A superior journalistic account is John Hersey, *Into the Valley*. For New Guinea see Pat Robinson, *The Fight for New Guinea* and George H.Johnston, *The Toughest Fighting in the World*. There are two monographs on the battle of Leyte Gulf: James A.Field, *The Japanese at Leyte Gulf* and Vann Woodward, *The Battle for Leyte Gulf*. On China and relations with Chiang Kai-Shek see Robert Hotz, *With General Chennault,* Theodore White (ed.), *The Stilwell Papers,* and Jack Belden, *Retreat With Stilwell*. For Burma, one of the best accounts is *Victory in Burma,* put out by the British Information Services, but see also Charles J.Rolo, *Wingate's Raiders*. An interesting Japanese explanation of the course of the war is Masuo Kato, *The Lost War*. The literature on Hiroshima and the atom bomb is large and growing larger. The classic account is John Hersey, *Hiroshima;* the best technical explanation Henry D.Smyth, *Atomic Energy for Military Purposes;* the best interpretation Bernard Brodie (ed.), *The Absolute Weapon: Atomic Power and World Order*.

THE MEDITERRANEAN THEATER. Relations with Vichy are carefully discussed in William Langer, *Our Vichy Gamble;* the even more delicate relations with Spain in Ambassador Carlton J.H.Hayes, *Wartime Mission in Spain* and — from a different point of view — in T.J.Hamilton, *Appeasement's Child*. A lively picture of the situation in the eastern Mediterranean is painted by Philip Guedalla, *Middle East 1940–1942*. There are several first-rate English books on the North African campaigns: the official account is Sir B.L.Montgomery, *El Alamein to the River Sangro*. Alan Morehead, *African Trilogy* tells the whole story, but should be supplemented by his *Three against Rommel* and his biography of Montgomery. A.C.Clifford, *Conquest of North Africa* is critical and unfailingly interesting. Strategicus, *From Dunkirk to Benghazi* is by an anonymous but erudite British military critic. One of the best of all the accounts of this and subsequent campaigns is Sir Francis de Guingand, *Operation Victory*. The story of the landings can be read in S.E.Morison, *Operations in North African Waters,* in D.D.Eisenhower, *Crusade in Europe,* and in Harry C.Butcher, *Three Years with Eisenhower*. For the Italian campaign see Christopher Buckley, *The Road to Rome* and Alan Morehead, *Eclipse,* both British accounts. The *American Forces in Action* series on the Italian campaign are particularly good: *Anzio Beachhead, Salerno, From Volturno to the Winter Line,* and *The Winter Line*. The best account of the fighting from the soldiers' point of view is in Ernie Pyle, *Brave Men*.

THE EUROPEAN THEATER. On the air war see the invaluable summary volume of the *U.S.Strategic Bombing Survey, Overall Report*. H.H. Arnold, *Global Mission* is disappointing. Much of interest can be found in Asher Lee, *The German Air Force* and in Sir Arthur (Bomber) Harris, *Bomber Offensive*. The best general accounts of the invasion and the assault on Germany are Dwight D.Eisenhower, *Crusade in Europe,* Sir Bernard L.Montgomery, *Normandy to the Baltic,* and Sir Francis de Guingand, *Operation Victory*. See also Sir Giffard Martel, *Our Armored Forces* and Alan Melville, *First Tide*. The planning of the invasion is told in masterly fashion in Sir Frederick Morgan, *Overture to Overlord*. American accounts of the invasion and the Normandy campaign are John Gunther, *D Day,* Charles Wertenbaker, *Invasion,* W.W.Chaplin, *The Fifty-two Days,* Ernie Pyle, *Brave Men,* and Everett Hollis, *Unconditional Surrender*. There is an admiring account of Patton in B.G.Wallace, *Patton and his Third Army*. The battle of the Bulge can be followed in Robert E.Merriam, *Dark December* and in S.L.A.Marshall, *Bastogne*. Two fascinating studies of German defeat are B.H.Liddell Hart, *The Other Side of the Hill: The German Generals Talk* and Milton Shulman, *Defeat in the West*. No one should neglect the fascinating historical detective work in H.R.Trevor-Roper, *The Last Days of Hitler*.

SOURCE SELECTIONS: Louisa W.Holborn, *War and Peace Aims of the United Nations, 1939–1945* (2 vols.). Commager, *Documents,* 5th ed., Nos.536, 541, 542, 550, 552–54, 556, 560, 565, 566.

XXX. *THE TRUMAN ADMINISTRATION*

The literature on the domestic scene during the postwar years is, as we might expect, ephemeral and fragmentary. The most valuable material is to be found in the files of the *New York Times, Fortune Magazine,* the *New Yorker,* the *Nation,* the *Atlantic,* and *Harpers,* and in such scholarly journals as the *Political Science Quarterly, The American Political Science Review,* the *American Economic Review,* and so forth. For general accounts John Gunther, *Inside U.S.A.* is useful. On politics see the masterly survey by V.O.Key, *Southern Politics in State and Nation.* C.A.M.Ewing, *Presidential Elections from Lincoln to F.D.Roosevelt* and *Congressional Elections, 1896–1944* are statistical, as is Edgar E.Robinson, *They Voted for Roosevelt.* On the third and fourth terms, see C.W.Stein, *The Third Term Tradition.* For minor parties see William B.Hesseltine, *The Rise and Fall of Third Parties from anti-Masonry to Wallace,* and Murray and Susan Stedman, *Discontent at the Polls: Farmer and Labor Parties, 1827–1948.* James McG.Burns, *Congress on Trial* is a critical analysis of the war and postwar Congresses. Stephen K.Bailey, *Congress Makes a Law* is directed specifically to the Employment Act of 1946. There is a one-volume summary of the Hoover Report, and a study by Frank Gervasi, *Big Government: Meaning and Purpose of the Hoover Commission Report.* For economics in general see Seymour Harris (ed.), *Economic Reconstruction.* There are two useful studies of the problem of the national debt: Seymour Harris, *The National Debt and the New Economics* and Henry C.Murphy, *The National Debt in War and Transition.* For labor see Henry Miller and Emily C.Brown, *From the Wagner Act to Taft-Hartley;* Charles O.Gregory, *Labor and the Law;* C.E.Warne and K.W. Lumpkin, *et al., Labor in Post War America;* and Harold Metz, *Labor Policy of the Federal Government.* There is a substantial and growing literature on the ever-recurring problem of civil rights. The best general introduction is *To Secure These Rights: Report of the President's Committee on Civil Rights.* There are illuminating reflections on the Negro situation in the South in Ellis Arnall, *The Shore Dimly Seen* and in Hodding Carter, *Southern Legacy.* The Constitutional situation can be traced in Milton Konvitz, *The Constitution and Civil Rights.* On Japanese relocation see Carey McWilliams, *Prejudice: the Japanese-Americans, Symbol of Racial Intolerance* and Morton Grodzins, *Americans Betrayed.* A.Frank Reel has written on *The Case of General Yamashita.* Howard Mumford Jones has brought together some notable pleas for intellectual freedom in his *Primer of Intellectual Freedom.* Some of the essays in John Chase (ed.), *Years of the Modern* survey the problems of the forties and fifties, and H.S.Commager, *The American Mind* attempts to interpret the American character at mid-century.

XXXI. *THE RESPONSIBILITIES OF WORLD POWER*

GENERAL POSTWAR INTERNATIONAL RELATIONS. The annual volumes of *The United States in World Affairs, 1945–47, 1947–48, 1948–49,* edited by John C.Campbell, are quite invaluable, and contain elaborate bibliographies. Along with these surveys the student should read *Foreign Affairs*, a quarterly that contains not only important articles, but documents and bibliographies. For interpretation no student should neglect the almost daily column by Walter Lippmann or his two brief volumes: *U.S.Foreign Policy* and *U.S.War Aims*. A different point of view emerges from Sumner Welles, *Time for Decision*. Edgar A.Mowrer, *The Nightmare of American Foreign Policy* is, as the title indicates, highly critical of postwar policy. Two studies of global strategy are Hanson Baldwin, *The Price of Power* and Sherman Kent, *Strategic Intelligence for American World Policy*. Thomas A.Bailey, *The Man in the Street* analyzes the impact of public opinion on the conduct of foreign policy. There are a number of volumes dealing with U.S. relations with particular countries in the postwar era; some of the best are Ephraim Speiser, *The United States and the Near East;* John K.Fairbanks, *The United States and China;* Crane Brinton, *The United States and Britain;* and Arthur P. Whitaker, *The United States and Latin America: The Northern Republics.*

RELIEF AND RECOVERY. Seymour Harris, *European Recovery Program* and ed. *Foreign Economic Policy for the United States;* Herman Finer, *The United Nations Economic and Social Council;* Clair Wilcox, *A Charter for World Trade;* J.W.Begen, *Money in a Maelstrom* (for Bretton Woods); Julian Huxley, *UNESCO: Its Purpose and Philosophy;* Eugene Kulischer, *Europe on the Move* (for the Displaced Persons).

LIQUIDATING THE WAR. Two important books by top officials are James F.Byrnes, *Speaking Frankly* and Lucius D.Clay, *Decision in Germany*. There are a number of books on the problems of military government. W.Friedmann, *The Allied Military Government of Germany* is by an Englishman and covers the whole ground; for the American problem see Julian Bach, *America's Germany,* Saul K.Padover, *Experiment in Germany,* Harold Zink, *American Military Government in Germany,* and Carl J.Friedrich, *et al., American Experiences in Military Government in World War II*. For the war-crimes trials see Robert H.Jackson, *The Case against the Nazi War Criminals* and *The Nurnberg Case;* Sheldon Glueck, *The Nurnberg Trials and Aggressive War;* Albert Deutsch, *Doctors of Infamy, the Story of the Nazi Medical Crimes;* and the article by Secretary Henry L. Stimson, 'The Nuremberg Trials: Landmark in Law' in *Foreign Affairs,* January 1947. For the Japanese situation see A.Frank Reel, *The Case of General Yamashita;* W.C.Johnstone, *The Future of Japan;* W.Fleisher, *What To Do with Japan;* Ruth Benedict, *The Chrysanthemum and the Sword;* U.S.Dept. of State Publication 2671, *Occupation of Japan: Policy and Progress.*

THE UNITED NATIONS. Floyd A.Cave, *et al., The Origins and Consequences of World War II* deals chiefly with the U.N. Leland M. Goodrich and Edvard Hambro, *Charter of the United Nations* contains essential documents with commentary. See further, Vera M.Dean, *The Four Cornerstones of Peace;* P.Bidwell, *The United States and the United Nations;* Kenneth Colgrove, *The American Senate and World Peace;* E.S.Corwin, *The Constitution and World Organization;* Emery Reeves, *Anatomy of Peace;* and J.B.Whitton (ed.), *The Second Chance: America and the Peace.*

ATOMIC ENERGY. David Bradley, *No Place to Hide* describes the Bikini experiments. P.M.S.Blackett, *Fear, War and the Bomb* is by an English scientist critical of the American policy; Sir Gerald Dickens, *Bombing and Strategy* confines itself to analysis rather than interpretation. See also Bernard Brodie, *The Absolute Weapon;* Julie E.Johnson, *The Atomic Bomb;* Dexter Masters (ed.), *One World or None;* E.L. Woodward, *Some Political Consequences of the Atomic Bomb;* and Norman Cousins, *Modern Man is Obsolete.*

RUSSIA AND THE COLD WAR. The best accounts of wartime relations with Russia are in Sherwood, *Roosevelt and Hopkins;* William D. Leahy, *I Was There;* Edward R. Stettinius, *Roosevelt and the Russians;* J.R.Deane, *The Strange Alliance;* Joseph E.Davies, *Mission to Moscow;* Barbara Ward, *The West at Bay;* and Vera M.Dean, *The United States and Russia.* For Yalta the books by Sherwood, Leahy, and Stettinius, above, are friendly to Roosevelt, and Elliott Roosevelt, *As He Saw It* is critical of Churchill. See also R.A.Winnacker, *'Yalta, Another Munich?'* in the *Virginia Quarterly Review,* vol. 24. For post-Yalta developments see Walter B.Smith, *My Three Years in Moscow,* James Byrnes, *Speaking Frankly,* and Lucius Clay, *Decision in Germany.* On the Pötsdam agreement see Sumner Welles, *Where Are We Heading?* and B.G.Ivanyi and A.Bell, *Route to Potsdam.* The containment policy was first clearly formulated by George Kennan in 'Sources of Soviet Conduct' *Foreign Affairs,* vol. 25 (1947); its argument is severely handled in Walter Lippmann, *The Cold War.* On the North Atlantic Pact see Marina Salvin, *The North Atlantic Pact* (International Conciliation pamphlets).

STATISTICAL TABLES

Admission of States to the Union 898

Areas of Perfected Homestead Entries, Years Ending June 30 898

Table of Population of the United States, 1870–1940 899

Presidents and Their Cabinets, 1865–1949 900

Presidential Vote, 1789–1948 902

Justices of the United States Supreme Court 906

Political Control in the Presidency and in Congress 1865–1951 907

Foreign-Born Population, by Country of Birth 908

Immigration Quotas, 1930 909

Immigration, by Country of Last Permanent Residence, 1831–1947 910

Urban and Rural Population 911

Urban and Rural Income, 1929 911

Public Debt of the United States 912

Public Lands of the United States 912

United States Government Receipts and Expenditures, 1789–1949 .. 913

Speakers of the House of Representatives, 1863–1949 913

Summary of Manufactures, 1859–1947 914

Labor Union Membership, 1897–1945 914

Labor Force 915

Railroad Mileage, by Decade, 1830–1940 915

Foreign Trade — Value of Exports and Imports, 1821–1945 916

Production of Chief Metals in the United States, 1850–1934 917

Production of Selected Agricultural Commodities, 1800–1946 918

Statistics of Public Elementary and Secondary Schools, 1870–1946 919

Statistics of American Participation in the First World War 920

United States Participation in World War II 921

Reverse Lend-Lease Aid Received by United States, by Category. 921

Lend-Lease Aid, by Category 922

Lend-Lease Aid, by Country 923

ADMISSION OF STATES TO THE UNION

State	Ent'd Union	State	Ent'd Union
Alabama	1819	Nebraska	1867
Arizona	1912	Nevada	1864
Arkansas	1836	New Hampshire	1788
California	1850	New Jersey	1787
Colorado	1876	New Mexico	1912
Connecticut	1788	New York	1788
Delaware	1787	North Carolina	1789
Florida	1845	North Dakota	1889
Georgia	1788	Ohio	1803
Idaho	1890	Oklahoma	1907
Illinois	1818	Oregon	1859
Indiana	1816	Pennsylvania	1787
Iowa	1846	Rhode Island	1790
Kansas	1861	South Carolina	1788
Kentucky	1792	South Dakota	1889
Louisiana	1812	Tennessee	1796
Maine	1820	Texas	1845
Maryland	1788	Utah	1896
Massachusetts	1788	Vermont	1791
Michigan	1837	Virginia	1788
Minnesota	1858	Washington	1889
Mississippi	1817	West Virginia	1863
Missouri	1821	Wisconsin	1848
Montana	1889	Wyoming	1890

AREAS OF PERFECTED HOMESTEAD ENTRIES, YEARS ENDING JUNE 30

	Acres		Acres		Acres		Acres		Acres
1868	355,086	1885	3,032,679	1902	4,342,748	1919	6,524,760	1936	1,764,958
1869	504,302	1886	2,663,532	1903	3,576,964	1920	8,372,696	1937	1,914,806
1870	519,728	1887	2,749,037	1904	3,232,717	1921	7,726,740	1938	1,361,943
1871	629,162	1888	3,175,401	1905	3,419,387	1922	7,307,034	1939	1,088,938
1872	707,410	1889	3,681,709	1906	3,526,749	1923	5,594,259	1940	652,484
1873	1,224,891	1890	4,060,593	1907	3,740,568	1924	4,791,436	1941	389,970
1874	1,585,782	1891	3,954,588	1908	4,242,711	1925	4,048,910	1942	187,507
1875	2,068,538	1892	3,259,897	1909	3,699,467	1926	3,451,105	1943	101,529
1876	2,590,553	1893	3,447,232	1910	3,795,863	1927	2,583,627	1944	50,506
1877	2,407,828	1894	2,929,947	1911	4,620,197	1928	1,815,549	1945	34,692
1878	2,662,981	1895	2,980,809	1912	4,306,068	1929	1,700,950	1946	29,368
1879	2,070,842	1896	2,790,242	1913	10,009,285	1930	1,371,073	1947	25,987
1880	1,938,235	1897	2,778,404	1914	9,291,121	1931	1,352,861		
1881	1,928,205	1898	3,095,018	1915	7,180,982	1932	1,209,894	Total	247,466,340
1882	2,219,454	1899	3,134,140	1916	7,278,281	1933	906,578		
1883	2,504,414	1900	3,477,843	1917	8,497,390	1934	1,123,673		
1884	2,945,575	1901	5,241,121	1918	8,236,438	1935	1,640,393		

Source: Commissioner of the General Land Office

TABLE OF POPULATION OF THE UNITED STATES, 1870–1940

Estimates taken from the United States censuses

State	1870	1880	1890	1900	1910	1920	1930	1940
New England								
Maine	626,915	648,936	661,086	694,466	742,371	768,014	797,423	847,226
New Hampshire	318,300	346,991	376,530	411,588	430,572	443,083	465,293	491,524
Vermont	330,551	332,286	332,422	343,641	355,956	352,428	359,611	359,231
Massachusetts	1,457,351	1,783,085	2,238,947	2,805,346	3,336,416	3,852,356	4,249,614	4,316,721
Rhode Island	217,353	276,531	345,506	428,556	542,610	604,397	687,497	713,346
Connecticut	537,454	622,700	746,258	908,420	1,114,756	1,380,631	1,606,903	1,709,242
Middle Atlantic								
New York	4,382,759	5,082,871	6,003,174	7,268,894	9,113,614	10,385,227	12,588,066	13,479,142
New Jersey	906,096	1,131,116	1,444,933	1,883,669	2,537,167	3,155,900	4,041,334	4,160,165
Pennsylvania	3,521,951	4,282,891	5,258,113	6,302,115	7,665,111	8,720,017	9,631,350	9,900,180
South Atlantic								
Delaware	125,015	146,608	168,493	184,735	202,322	223,003	238,380	266,505
Maryland	780,894	934,943	1,042,390	1,188,044	1,295,346	1,449,661	1,631,526	1,821,244
Dist. of Columbia	131,700	177,624	230,392	278,718	331,069	437,571	486,869	663,091
Virginia	1,225,163	1,512,565	1,655,980	1,854,184	2,061,612	2,309,187	2,421,851	2,677,773
West Virginia	442,014	618,457	762,794	958,800	1,221,119	1,463,701	1,729,205	1,901,974
North Carolina	1,071,361	1,399,750	1,617,949	1,893,810	2,206,287	2,559,123	3,170,276	3,571,623
South Carolina	705,606	995,577	1,151,149	1,340,316	1,515,400	1,683,724	1,738,765	1,899,804
Georgia	1,184,109	1,542,180	1,837,353	2,216,331	2,609,121	2,895,832	2,908,506	3,123,723
Florida	187,748	269,493	391,422	528,542	752,619	968,470	1,468,211	1,897,414
South Central								
Kentucky	1,321,011	1,648,690	1,858,635	2,147,174	2,289,905	2,416,630	2,614,589	2,845,627
Tennessee	1,258,520	1,542,359	1,767,518	2,020,616	2,184,789	2,337,885	2,616,556	2,915,841
Alabama	996,992	1,262,505	1,513,401	1,828,697	2,138,093	2,348,174	2,646,248	2,832,961
Mississippi	827,922	1,131,597	1,289,600	1,551,270	1,797,114	1,790,618	2,009,821	2,183,796
Arkansas	484,471	802,525	1,128,211	1,311,564	1,574,449	1,752,204	1,854,482	1,949,387
Louisiana	726,915	939,946	1,118,588	1,381,625	1,656,388	1,798,509	2,101,593	2,363,880
Oklahoma	....	....	258,657	790,391	1,657,155	2,028,283	2,396,040	2,226,434
Texas	818,579	1,591,749	2,235,527	3,048,710	3,896,542	4,663,228	5,824,715	6,414,824
North Central								
Ohio	2,665,260	3,198,062	3,672,329	4,157,545	4,767,121	5,759,394	6,646,697	6,907,612
Indiana	1,680,637	1,978,301	2,192,404	2,516,462	2,700,876	2,930,390	3,238,503	3,427,796
Illinois	2,539,891	3,077,871	3,826,352	4,821,550	5,638,591	6,485,280	7,630,654	7,897,241
Michigan	1,184,059	1,636,937	2,093,890	2,420,982	2,810,173	3,668,412	4,842,325	5,256,106
Wisconsin	1,054,670	1,315,497	1,693,330	2,069,042	2,333,860	2,632,067	2,939,006	3,137,587
Minnesota	439,706	780,773	1,310,283	1,751,394	2,075,708	2,387,125	2,563,953	2,792,300
Iowa	1,194,020	1,624,615	1,912,297	2,231,853	2,224,771	2,404,021	2,470,939	2,538,268
Missouri	1,721,295	2,168,380	2,679,185	3,106,665	3,293,335	3,404,055	3,629,367	3,784,664
North Dakota } South Dakota }	14,181	135,177						
North Dakota			190,983	319,146	577,056	646,872	680,845	641,935
South Dakota			348,600	401,570	583,888	636,547	692,849	642,961
Nebraska	122,993	452,402	1,062,656	1,066,300	1,192,214	1,296,372	1,377,963	1,315,834
Kansas	364,399	996,096	1,428,108	1,470,495	1,690,949	1,769,257	1,880,999	1,801,028
Mountain								
Montana	20,595	39,159	142,924	243,329	376,053	548,889	537,606	559,456
Idaho	14,999	32,610	88,548	161,772	325,594	431,866	445,032	524,873
Wyoming	9,118	20,789	62,555	92,531	145,965	194,402	225,565	250,742
Colorado	39,864	194,327	413,249	539,700	799,024	939,629	1,035,791	1,123,296
New Mexico	91,874	119,565	160,282	195,310	327,301	360,350	423,317	531,818
Arizona	9,658	40,440	88,243	122,931	204,354	334,162	435,573	499,261
Utah	86,786	143,963	210,779	276,749	373,351	449,396	507,847	550,310
Nevada	42,491	62,266	47,355	42,335	81,875	77,407	91,058	110,247
Pacific								
Washington	23,955	75,116	357,232	518,103	1,141,990	1,356,621	1,563,396	1,901,874
Oregon	90,923	174,768	317,704	413,536	672,765	783,389	953,786	1,089,694
California	560,247	864,694	1,213,398	1,485,053	2,377,549	3,426,861	5,677,251	6,907,387
	38,558,371	50,155,783	62,947,714	75,994,575	91,972,266	105,710,620	122,775,046	131,669,275

PRESIDENTS AND

President and Vice-President	Secretary of State	Secretary of Treasury	Secretary of War
Andrew Johnson..................1865	W. H. Seward....1865	Hugh McCulloch..1865	E. M. Stanton.1865 U. S. Grant....1867 L. Thomas....1868 J. M. Schofield.1868
Uslysses S. Grant-Schuyler Colfax...1869 Henry Wilson 1873	E. B. Washburne 1869 Hamilton Fish...1869	Geo. S. Boutwell..1869 W. A. Richardson.1873 Benj. H. Bristow..1874 Lot M. Morrill....1876	J. A. Rawlins..1869 W. T. Sherman 1869 W. W. Belknap 1869 Alphonso Taft.1876 J. D. Cameron.1876
Rutherf'd B. Hayes-Wm. A. Wheeler 1877	W. M. Evarts....1877	John Sherman....1877	G. W. McCrary 1877 Alex. Ramsey..1879
Jas. A. Garfield-Chester A. Arthur..1881	James G. Blaine..1881	Wm. Windom.....1881	R. T. Lincoln..1881
Chester A. Arthur.................1881	F. T. Frelinghuy- sen...........1881	Chas. J. Folger....1881 W. Q. Gresham...1884 Hugh McCulloch..1884	R. T. Lincoln..1881
Grover Cleveland-T. A. Hendricks..1885	Thos. F. Bayard..1885	Daniel Manning...1885 Chas. S. Fairchild..1887	W. C. Endicott.1885
Benjamin Harrison-Levi P. Morton..1889	James G. Blaine..1889 John W. Foster..1892	Wm. Windom ....1889 Charles Foster....1891	R. Proctor.....1889 S. B. Elkins...1891
Grover Cleveland-Adlai E. Stevenson 1893	W. Q. Gresham...1893 Richard Olney...1895	John G. Carlisle...1893	D. S. Lamont..1893
Wm. McKinley-Garret A. Hobart...1897 Theodore Roosevelt 1901	John Sherman...1897 Wm. R. Day.....1897 John Hay.......1898	Lyman J. Gage...1897	R. A. Alger....1897 Elihu Root....1899
Theodore Roosevelt...............1901 Chas. W. Fairbanks 1905	John Hay.......1901 Elihu Root......1905 Robert Bacon....1909	Lyman J. Gage...1901 Leslie M. Shaw...1902 G. B. Cortelyou...1907	Elihu Root....1901 Wm. H. Taft..1904 Luke E. Wright 1908
William H. Taft-James S. Sherman..1909	P. C. Knox......1909	F. MacVeagh.....1909	J. M. Dickinson 1909 H. L. Stimson..1911
Woodrow Wilson-Thos. R. Marshall 1913	Wm. J. Bryan...1913 Robert Lansing..1915 Bainbridge Colby 1920	W. G. McAdoo....1913 Carter Glass......1918 D. F. Houston....1920	L. M. Garrison.1913 N. D. Baker...1916
Warren G. Harding-Calvin Coolidge 1921	Chas. E. Hughes.1921	Andrew W. Mellon 1921	John W. Weeks 1921
Calvin Coolidge....................1923 Charles G. Dawes 1925	Chas. E. Hughes.1923 Frank B. Kellogg 1925	Andrew W. Mellon 1923	John W. Weeks 1923 Dwight F. Davis 1925
Herbert C. Hoover-Charles Curtis..1929	Henry L. Stimson 1929	Andrew W. Mellon 1929 Ogden L. Mills....1932	James W. Good 1929 Pat. J. Hurley. 1929
Franklin Delano Roosevelt- John Nance Garner.............1933 Henry A. Wallace..1941 Harry S. Truman..1945	Cordell Hull.....1933 E. R. Stettinius, Jr. 1944	Wm. H. Woodin..1933 Henry Morgenthau, Jr. 1934	Geo. H. Dern..1933 H. A. Woodring 1936 H. L. Stimson..1940
Harry S. Truman.................1945 Alben W. Barkley 1949	James F. Byrnes..1945 Geo. C. Marshall.1947 Dean G. Acheson.1949	Fred M. Vinson...1945 John W. Snyder...1946	Robt. H. Patter- son.........1945 K. C. Royall...1947 Gordon Gray..1949

President	*Secretary of Agriculture*	
Grover Cleveland	Norman J. Colman	1889
Benjamin Harrison	Jeremiah M. Rusk	1889
Grover Cleveland	J. Sterling Morton	1893
William McKinley	James Wilson	1897
Theodore Roosevelt	James Wilson	1901
William H. Taft	James Wilson	1909
Woodrow Wilson	David F. Houston	1913
	Edward T. Meredith	1920

THEIR CABINETS

SECRETARY OF NAVY	SECRETARY OF INTERIOR	POSTMASTER-GENERAL	ATTORNEY-GENERAL	OTHER MEMBERS
Gideon Welles.....1865	John P. Usher..1865 James Harlan...1865 O. H. Browning.1866	Wm. Dennison..1865 A. W. Randall..1866	James Speed.....1865 Henry Stanbery..1866 Wm. M. Evarts..1868	*Secretary of commerce and labor* Established Feb. 14, 1903.
Adolph E. Borie...1869 Geo. M. Robeson..1869	Jacob D. Cox...1869 C. Delano......1870 Zach. Chandler..1875	J. A. J. Creswell.1869 Jas. W. Marshall 1874 Marshall Jewell.1874 James N. Tyner 1876	E. R. Hoar......1869 A. T. Ackerman..1870 Geo. H. Williams 1871 Edw. Pierrepont .1875 Alphonso Taft...1876	George B. Cortelyou.....1903 Victor H. Metcalf......1904–6
R. W. Thompson..1877 Nathan Goff, Jr. ..1881	Carl Schurz.....1877	David M. Key..1877 Horace Maynard 1880	Chas. Devens....1877	O. S. Straus 1907–9 Chas. Nagel..1909
W. H. Hunt......1881	S. J. Kirkwood..1881	T. L. James....1881	W. MacVeagh...1881	(Department
W. E. Chandler...1881	Henry M. Teller 1881	T. O. Howe.....1881 W. Q. Gresham..1883 Frank Hatton...1884	B. H. Brewster...1881	divided, 1913.) *Secretary of commerce*
W. C. Whitney....1885	L. Q. C. Lamar..1885 Wm. F. Vilas...1888	Wm. F. Vilas...1885 D. M. Dickinson 1888	A. H. Garland...1885	W. C. Redfield 1913
Benj. F. Tracy....1889	John W. Noble..1889	J. Wanamaker..1889	W. H. H. Miller..1889	Joshua W. Alexander..1919
Hilary A. Herbert.1893	Hoke Smith....1893 D. R. Francis...1896	W. S. Bissell....1893 W. L. Wilson...1895	R. Olney........1893 J. Harmon.......1895	H. C. Hoover.1921 H. C. Hoover.1925 W.F.Whiting.1928
John D. Long.....1897	C. N. Bliss.....1897 E. A. Hitchcock.1899	James A. Gary..1897 Chas. E. Smith..1898	J. McKenna.....1897 J. W. Griggs.....1897 P. C. Knox......1901	R. P. Lamont.1929 R. D. Chapin.1932 D. C. Roper..1933
John D. Long.....1901 Wm. H. Moody...1902 Paul Morton......1904 C. J. Bonaparte...1905 Victor H. Metcalf.1907 T. H. Newberry...1908	E. A. Hitchcock.1901 J. R. Garfield...1907	Chas. E. Smith..1901 Henry C. Payne.1902 Robt. J. Wynne.1904 G. B. Cortelyou.1905 G. von L. Meyer 1907	P. C. Knox 1901 W. H. Moody....1904 C. J. Bonaparte..1907	Harry L. Hopkins...1939 Jesse Jones...1940 Henry A. Wallace.......1945 W. Averell Harriman......1946
G. von L. Meyer..1909	R. A. Ballinger..1909 W. L. Fisher....1911	F. H. Hitchcock.1909	G. W. Wickersh'm 1909	Charles W. Sawyer....1948
Josephus Daniels..1913	F. K. Lane.....1913 J. B. Payne.....1920	A. S. Burleson...1913	J. C. McReynolds 1913 Thos. W. Gregory 1914 A. M. Palmer....1919	*Secretary of labor*
Edwin Denby.....1921	Albert B. Fall...1921 Hubert Work...1923	Will H. Hays...1921 Hubert Work...1922 Harry S. New...1923	H. M. Daugherty.1921	Established March 4, 1913.
Edwin Denby.....1923 Curtis D. Wilbur..1924	Hubert Work...1923 Roy O. West....1928	Harry S. New...1923	H. M. Daugherty.1923 Harlan F. Stone..1924 John G. Sargent..1925	W. B. Wilson.1913 J. J. Davis.1921–29 Wm. N. Doak 1930
Chas. F. Adams...1929	Ray L. Wilbur..1929	Walter F. Brown 1929	Wm. D. Mitchell.1929	Frances Perkins '33 L. B. Schwellenbach....1945
Claude A. Swanson 1933 Chas. Edison.....1940 Frank Knox......1940 James V. Forrestal.1944	Harold L. Ickes.1933	James A. Farley 1933 Frank C. Walker.......1940	H. S. Cummings .1933 Frank Murphy...1939 Robt. H. Jackson.1940 Francis Biddle...1941	M. J. Tobin 1948 *Secretary of defense*
James V. Forrestal.1945 John L. Sullivan...1947 Francis P. Matthews 1949	Harold L. Ickes.1945 Julius A. Krug..1946	Robt. E. Hannegan....1945 Jesse L. Donaldson....1947	Tom C. Clark....1945 J. H. McGrath...1949	James V. Forrestal......1947 Louis A. Johnson........1949

President	*Secretary of Agriculture*	
Warren G. Harding	Henry C. Wallace	1921
Calvin Coolidge	Howard M. Gore	1924
	W. M. Jardine	1925
Herbert C. Hoover	Arthur M. Hyde	1929
Franklin D. Roosevelt	Henry A. Wallace	1933
	Claude R. Wickard	1940
Harry S. Truman	Clinton P. Anderson	1945
	Charles F. Brannan	1948

PRESIDENTIAL VOTE, 1789–1948

Yr.	Candidate	Party	Popular Vote	Per Cent	Electoral Vote
1789	**Washington**...	....	....	....	69
1789	Adams........	....	....	....	34
1789	Jay..........	....	....	....	9
1789	Harrison......	....	....	....	6
1789	Rutledge......	....	....	....	6
1792	**Washington**...	Federalist........	....	....	132
1792	Adams........	Federalist........	....	....	77
1792	Clinton.......	Dem.-Rep........	....	....	50
1792	Jefferson......	Dem.-Rep........	....	....	4
1792	Burr..........	....	....	....	1
1796	**Adams**.......	Federalist........	....	....	71
1796	Jefferson......	Dem.-Rep........	....	....	68
1796	Pinckney.....	Federalist........	....	....	59
1796	Burr.........	Dem.-Rep........	....	....	30
1796	S. Adams.....	Dem.-Rep........	....	....	15
1796	Ellsworth.....	Federalist........	....	....	11
1800	**Jefferson**.....	Dem.-Rep........	....	....	73
1800	Burr.........	Dem.-Rep........	....	....	73
1800	Adams	Federalist	....	....	65
1800	C. C. Pinckney	Federalist........	....	....	64
1800	Jay..........	Federalist........	....	....	1
1804	**Jefferson**.....	Dem.-Rep........	....	....	162
1804	C. C. Pinckney	Federalist........	....	....	14
1808	**Madison**......	Dem.-Rep........	....	....	122
1808	C. C. Pinckney	Federalist........	....	....	47
1808	G. Clinton ...	Independent......	....	....	6
1812	**Madison**......	Dem.-Rep........	....	....	128
1812	De W. Clinton	Fusion...........	....	....	89
1816	**Monroe**.......	Dem.-Rep........	....	....	183
1816	King.........	Federalist........	....	....	34
1820	**Monroe**.......	Republican.......	....	....	231
1820	Adams.......	Ind. Republican..	....	....	1
1824	**Adams**.......	....	108,740	32.	84
1824	Jackson.......	....	153,544	43.	99
1824	Clay.........	....	47,136	13.	37
1824	Crawford.....	....	46,618	12.	41
1828	**Jackson**......	Democrat........	647,231	55.97	178
1828	Adams.......	Federal..........	509,097	44.03	83
1832	**Jackson**......	Democrat........	687,502	54.96	219
1832	Clay.........	Whig............	530,189	42.39	49
1832	Floyd........	Whig............	33,108	2.65	11
1832	Wirt.........	Anti-M...........			7
1836	**Van Buren**....	Democrat........	761,549	50.83	170
1836	Harrison......	Whig............	736,656	49.17	73
1836	White........	Whig............			26
1836	Webster......	Whig............			14
1836	Mangum......	Whig............			11
1840	Van Buren....	Democrat........	1,128,702	46.82	60
1840	**Harrison**......	Whig............	1,275,017	52.89	234
1840	Birney........	Liberty..........	7,059	.39	...

PRESIDENTIAL VOTE, 1789–1948—*Continued*

Yr.	Candidate	Party	Popular Vote	Per Cent	Electoral Vote
1844	**Polk**	Democrat	1,337,243	49.55	170
1844	Clay	Whig	1,299,068	48.14	105
1844	Birney	Liberty	62,300	2.31	...
1848	**Taylor**	Whig	1,360,101	47.36	163
1848	Cass	Democrat	1,220,544	42.50	107
1848	Van Buren	Free Soil	291,263	10.14	...
1852	**Pierce**	Democrat	1,601,474	51.03	254
1852	Scott	Whig	1,380,678	43.99	42
1852	Hale	Free Soil	156,149	4.98	...
1856	**Buchanan**	Democrat	1,838,169	45.34	174
1856	Frémont	Republican	1,341,264	33.09	114
1856	Fillmore	American	874,534	21.57	8
1860	Douglas	Democrat	1,375,157	29.40	12
1860	Breckinridge	Democrat	845,763	18.08	72
1860	**Lincoln**	Republican	1,866,352	39.91	180
1860	Bell	Union	589,581	12.61	39
1864	McClellan	Democrat	1,808,725	44.94	21
1864	**Lincoln**	Republican	2,216,067	55.06	216
1868	Seymour	Democrat	2,709,613	47.23	80
1868	**Grant**	Republican	3,015,071	52.67	214
1872	Greeley	Democrat	2,834,079	43.83	66
1872	O'Conor	Ind. Democrat	29,408	.45	...
1872	**Grant**	Republican	3,597,070	55.63	292
1872	Black	Temperance	5,608	.09	...
1876	Tilden	Democrat	4,284,885	50.94	184
1876	**Hayes**	Republican	4,033,950	47.95	185
1876	Cooper	Greenback	81,740	.97	...
1876	Smith	Prohibition	9,522	.11	...
1876	Walker	American	2,636	.03	...
1880	Hancock	Democrat	4,442,035	48.23	155
1880	**Garfield**	Republican	4,449,053	48.31	214
1880	Weaver	Greenback	307,306	3.34	...
1880	Dow	Prohibition	10,487	.11	...
1880	Phelps	American	707	.01	...
1884	**Cleveland**	Democrat	4,911,017	48.89	219
1884	Blaine	Republican	4,848,334	48.27	182
1884	Butler	Greenback	133,825	1.33	...
1884	St. John	Prohibition	151,809	1.51	...
1888	Cleveland	Democrat	5,540,050	48.66	168
1888	**Harrison**	Republican	5,444,337	47.82	233
1888	Streeter	Union Labor	146,897	1.29	...
1888	Fisk	Prohibition	250,125	2.20	...
1888	Cowdrey	United Labor	2,808	.03	...
1892	**Cleveland**	Democrat	5,554,414	46.04	277
1892	Harrison	Republican	5,190,802	43.02	145
1892	Bidwell	Prohibition	271,058	2.24	...
1892	Weaver	People's	1,027,329	8.51	22
1892	Wing	Socialist	21,164	.19	...
1896	**McKinley**	Republican	7,035,638	50.88	271
1896	Bryan	Democrat	6,467,946	46.77	176

PRESIDENTIAL VOTE, 1789–1948—*Continued*

Yr.	Candidate	Party	Popular Vote	Per Cent	Electoral Vote
1896	Levering	Prohibition	141,676	1.03	...
1896	Bentley	National	13,969	.10	...
1896	Matchett	Socialist Labor	36,454	.27	...
1896	Palmer	Nat. Democrat	131,529	.95	...
1900	**McKinley**	Republican	7,219,530	51.69	292
1900	Bryan	Democrat	6,358,071	45.51	155
1900	Woolley	Prohibition	209,166	1.49	...
1900	Barker	People's	50,232	.37	...
1900	Debs	Socialist Democrat	94,768	.67	...
1900	Malloney	Socialist Labor	32,751	.23	...
1900	Leonard	United Christian	518	.00	...
1900	Ellis	Union Reform	5,098	.04	...
1904	**Roosevelt**	Republican	7,628,834	56.41	336
1904	Parker	Democrat	5,084,401	37.60	140
1904	Swallow	Prohibition	259,257	1.91	...
1904	Debs	Socialist	402,460	2.98	...
1904	Watson	People's	114,753	.85	...
1904	Corregan	Socialist Labor	33,724	.25	...
1904	Holcomb	Continental	830	.00	...
1908	**Taft**	Republican	7,679,006	51.58	321
1908	Bryan	Democrat	6,409,106	43.05	162
1908	Chafin	Prohibition	252,683	1.69	...
1908	Debs	Socialist	420,820	2.83	...
1908	Watson	People's	28,131	.19	...
1908	Hisgen	Independence	83,562	.56	...
1908	Gillhaus	Socialist Labor	13,825	.10	...
1908	Turney	United Christian	461	.00	...
1912	**Wilson**	Democrat	6,286,214	41.82	435
1912	Roosevelt	Progressive	4,126,020	27.45	88
1912	Taft	Republican	3,483,922	23.17	8
1912	Debs	Socialist	897,011	5.97	...
1912	Chafin	Prohibition	208,923	1.39	...
1912	Reimer	Socialist Labor	29,079	.20	...
1916	**Wilson**	Democrat	9,129,606	49.28	277
1916	Hughes	Republican	8,538,221	46.07	254
1916	Hanly	Prohibition	220,506	1.19	...
1916	Benson	Socialist	585,113	3.16	...
1916	Reimer	Socialist Labor	13,403	.07	...
1916	Misc.	....	41,894	.23	...
1920	**Harding**	Republican	16,152,200	61.02	404
1920	Cox	Democrat	9,147,353	34.55	127
1920	Debs	Socialist	919,799	3.47	...
1920	Christensen	Farmer Labor	26,541	.10	...
1920	Watkins	Prohibition	189,408	.72	...
1920	Cox	Socialist Labor	31,175	.12	...
1920	Macauley	Single Tax	5,837	.02	...
1924	**Coolidge**	Republican	15,725,016	54.1	382
1924	Davis	Democrat	8,385,586	28.8	136
1924	La Follette	Independent, Progressive, and Socialist	4,822,856	16.6	13

PRESIDENTIAL VOTE, 1789–1948—*Continued*

Yr.	Candidate	Party	Popular Vote	Per Cent	Electoral Vote
1924	Faris	Prohibition	57,551		...
1924	Nations	American	23,867		...
1924	Wallace	Com. Land	2,778	.5	...
1924	Johns	Socialist Labor	38,958		...
1924	Foster	Workers'	33,361		...
1928	**Hoover**	Republican	21,392,190	58.2	444
1928	Smith	Democrat	15,016,443	40.8	87
1928	Thomas	Socialist	267,420		...
1928	Foster	Workers'	48,770		...
1928	Reynolds	Socialist Labor	21,603	1.0	...
1928	Varney	Prohibitionist	20,106		...
1928	Webb	Farm-Labor	6,390		...
1932	**Roosevelt**	Democrat	22,821,857	57.3	472
1932	Hoover	Republican	15,761,841	39.6	59
1932	Thomas	Socialist	884,781		...
1932	Reynolds	Socialist Labor	33,276		...
1932	Foster	Communist	102,991		...
1932	Upshaw	Prohibition	81,869	3.1	...
1932	Harvey	Liberty	53,425		...
1932	Coxey	Farm-Labor	7,309		...
1936	**Roosevelt**	Democrat	27,751,612	60.7	523
1936	Landon	Republican	16,681,913	36.4	8
1936	Lemke	Union	891,858		...
1936	Thomas	Socialist	187,342		...
1936	Browder	Communist	80,181	2.9	...
1936	Colvin	Prohibition	37,609		...
1936	Aiken	Socialist Labor	12,729		...
1940	**Roosevelt**	Democrat	27,243,466	54.7	449
1940	Willkie	Republican	22,304,755	44.8	82
1940	Thomas	Socialist	99,557		...
1940	Babson	Prohibition	57,812		...
1940	Browder	Communist	46,251	.5	...
1940	Aiken	Socialist Labor	14,861		...
1944	**Roosevelt**	Democrat	25,602,505	52.8	432
1944	Dewey	Republican	22,006,278	44.5	99
1944	Thomas	Socialist	80,518		...
1944	Watson	Prohibition	74,758		...
1944	Teichert	Socialist Labor	45,336	2.7	...
1944	Misc. Independent	....	216,289		...
1948	**Truman**	Democrat	24,045,052	50.5	304
1948	Dewey	Republican	21,896,927	43.75	189
1948	Wallace	Progressive	1,137,957		...
1948	Thurmond	States' Rights	1,168,687		38
1948	Thomas	Socialist	95,908		...
1948	Watson	Prohibition	95,075	5.75	...
1948	Misc. Independent	....	49,611		...

JUSTICES OF THE UNITED STATES SUPREME COURT

Name *Chief Justices in Italics*	Service		Name *Chief Justices in Italics*	Service	
	Term	Yrs.		Term	Yrs.
John Jay, N.Y.	1789–1795	6	William B. Woods, Ga.	1880–1887	7
John Rutledge, S.C.	1789–1791	2	Stanley Matthews, Ohio	1881–1889	8
William Cushing, Mass.	1789–1810	21	Horace Gray, Mass.	1881–1902	21
James Wilson, Pa.	1789–1798	9	Samuel Blatchford, N.Y.	1882–1893	11
John Blair, Va.	1789–1796	7	Lucius Q. C. Lamar, Miss.	1888–1893	5
Robert H. Harrison, Md.	1789–1790	1	*Melville W. Fuller*, Ill.	1888–1910	22
James Iredell, N.C.	1790–1799	9	David J. Brewer, Kan.	1889–1910	21
Thomas Johnson, Md.	1791–1793	2	Henry B. Brown, Mich.	1890–1906	16
William Paterson, N.J.	1793–1806	13	George Shiras, Jr., Pa.	1892–1903	11
John Rutledge, S.C.	1795–1795	..	Howell E. Jackson, Tenn.	1893–1895	2
Samuel Chase, Md.	1796–1811	15	Edward D. White, La.	1894–1910	16
Oliver Ellsworth, Conn.	1796–1799	4	Rufus W. Peckham, N.Y.	1895–1910	14
Bushrod Washington, Va.	1798–1829	31	Joseph McKenna, Cal.	1898–1925	27
Alfred Moore, N.C.	1799–1804	5	Oliver W. Holmes, Mass.	1902–1932	29
John Marshall, Va.	1801–1835	34	William R. Day, Ohio	1903–1922	19
William Johnson, S.C.	1804–1834	30	William H. Moody, Mass.	1906–1910	4
Brock. Livingston, N.Y.	1806–1823	17	Horace H. Lurton, Tenn.	1910–1914	5
Thomas Todd, Ky.	1807–1826	19	Charles E. Hughes, N.Y.	1910–1916	6
Joseph Story, Mass.	1811–1845	34	Willis Van Devanter, Wyo.	1911–1937	26
Gabriel Duval, Md.	1811–1836	25	Joseph R. Lamar, Ga.	1911–1916	6
Smith Thompson, N.Y.	1823–1843	20	*Edward D. White*, La.	1910–1921	11
Robert Trimble, Ky.	1826–1828	2	Mahlon Pitney, N.J.	1912–1922	12
John McLean, Ohio	1829–1861	32	Jas. C. McReynolds, Tenn.	1914–1941	27
Henry Baldwin, Pa.	1830–1844	14	Louis D. Brandeis, Mass.	1916–1939	23
James M. Wayne, Ga.	1835–1867	32	John H. Clark, Ohio	1916–1922	6
Roger B. Taney, Md.	1836–1864	28	*William H. Taft*, Conn.	1921–1930	9
Philip P. Barbour, Va.	1836–1841	5	George Sutherland, Utah	1922–1938	16
John Catron, Tenn.	1837–1865	28	Pierce Butler, Minn.	1922–1939	17
John McKinley, Ala.	1837–1852	15	Edward T. Sanford, Tenn.	1923–1930	7
Peter V. Daniel, Va.	1841–1860	19	Harlan F. Stone, N.Y.	1925–1941	16
Samuel Nelson, N.Y.	1845–1872	27	*Charles E. Hughes*, N.Y.	1930–1941	11
Levi Woodbury, N.H.	1845–1851	6	Owen J. Roberts, Pa.	1930–1945	15
Robert C. Grier, Pa.	1846–1870	24	Benjamin N. Cardozo, N.Y.	1932–1938	6
Benj. R. Curtis, Mass.	1851–1857	6	Hugo Black, Ala.	1937–....	..
John A. Campbell, Ala.	1853–1861	8	Stanley Reed, Ky.	1938–....	..
Nathan Clifford, Me.	1858–1881	23	Felix Frankfurter, Mass.	1939–....	..
Noah H. Swayne, Ohio	1862–1881	20	William O. Douglas, Conn.	1939–....	..
Samuel F. Miller, Iowa	1862–1890	28	Frank Murphy, Mich.	1940–1949	9
David Davis, Ill.	1862–1877	15	*Harlan F. Stone*, N.Y.	1941–1946	5
Stephen J. Field, Cal.	1863–1897	34	James F. Byrnes, S.C.	1941–1942	2
Salmon P. Chase, Ohio	1864–1873	9	Robert H. Jackson, N.Y.	1941–....	..
William Strong, Pa.	1870–1880	10	Wiley B. Rutledge, Iowa	1943–1949	6
Joseph P. Bradley, N.J.	1870–1892	22	Harold H. Burton, Ohio	1945–....	..
Ward Hunt, N.Y.	1872–1882	10	*Fred M. Vinson*, Ky.	1946–....	..
Morrison R. Waite, Ohio	1874–1888	14	Thomas C. Clark, Texas	1949–....	..
John M. Harlan, Ky.	1877–1911	34	Sherman Minton, Ind.	1949–....	..

POLITICAL CONTROL IN THE PRESIDENCY AND IN CONGRESS
1865–1951

Congress	*Year*	*President*		*Senate*	*House*
39	1865–1867	Johnson	R	R	R
40	1867–1869			R	R
41	1869–1871	Grant	R	R	R
42	1871–1873			R	R
43	1873–1875			R	R
44	1875–1877			R	D
45	1877–1879	Hayes	R	R	D
46	1879–1881			D	D
47	1881–1883	Garfield	R	37D–37R, 1 Independent, 1 Readjuster	R
48	1883–1885	Arthur		R	D
49	1885–1887	Cleveland	D	R	D
50	1887–1889			R	D
51	1889–1891	Harrison	R	R	R
52	1891–1893			R	D
53	1893–1895	Cleveland	D	D	D
54	1895–1897			R	R
55	1897–1899	McKinley	R	R	R
56	1899–1901			R	R
57	1901–1903	McKinley	R	R	R
58	1903–1905	Roosevelt		R	R
59	1905–1907	Roosevelt	R	R	R
60	1907–1909			R	R
61	1909–1911	Taft	R	R	R
62	1911–1913			R	D
63	1913–1915	Wilson	D	D	D
64	1915–1917			D	D
65	1917–1919			D	D
66	1919–1921			R	R
67	1921–1923	Harding	R	R	R
68	1923–1925	Coolidge		R	R
69	1925–1927	Coolidge	R	R	R
70	1927–1929			48R 47D 1 In.	R
71	1929–1931	Hoover	R	R	R
72	1931–1933			48R 47D 1 In.	D
73	1933–1935	Roosevelt	D	D	D
74	1935–1937			D	D
75	1937–1939			D	D
76	1939–1941			D	D
77	1941–1943			D	D
78	1943–1945	Roosevelt	D	D	D
79	1945–1947	Truman		D	D
80	1947–1949	Truman	D	R	R
81	1949–1951			D	D

FOREIGN-BORN POPULATION, BY COUNTRY OF BIRTH

Country of Birth	Number							
	1870	1880	1890	1900	1910	1920	1930	1940
Total foreign born	5,567,229	6,679,943	9,249,560	10,341,276	13,515,886	13,920,692	14,204,149	11,419,138
Europe	4,936,618	5,744,311	8,020,608	8,781,780	11,791,841	11,882,053	11,748,399	9,700,744
Northwestern Europe	3,124,638	3,494,484	4,380,752	4,202,683	4,239,067	3,830,094	3,728,050	2,825,671
England	555,046	664,160	909,092	840,513	877,719	813,853	809,563	621,975
Scotland	140,835	170,136	242,231	233,524	261,076	254,570	354,323	279,321
Wales	74,533	83,302	100,079	93,586	82,488	67,066	60,205	35,360
Ireland	1,855,827	1,854,571	1,871,509	1,615,459	1,352,251	1,037,234	178,832a 744,810b	106,416a 572,031b
Norway	114,246	181,729	322,665	336,388	403,877	363,863	347,852	262,088
Sweden	97,332	194,337	478,041	582,014	665,207	625,585	595,250	445,070
Denmark	30,107	64,196	132,543	153,690	181,649	189,154	182,238	138,175
Iceland	....	....	....	....	....	....	....	2,104
Netherlands	46,802	58,090	81,828	94,931	120,063	131,766	133,133	111,064
Belgium	12,553	15,535	22,639	29,757	49,400	62,687	64,194	53,958
Luxemburg	5,802	12,836	2,882	3,031	3,071	12,585	9,048	6,886
Switzerland	75,153	88,621	104,069	115,593	124,848	118,659	113,010	88,293
France	116,402	106,971	113,174	104,197	117,418	153,072	135,592	102,930
Central and Eastern Europe	1,784,449	2,187,776	3,420,629	4,136,646	6,024,041	6,134,845	5,897,799	4,958,368
Germany	1,690,533	1,966,742	2,784,894	2,663,418	2,311,237	1,686,108	1,608,814	1,237,772
Poland	14,436	48,557	147,440	383,407	937,884	1,139,979	1,268,583	993,479
Czechoslovakia	....	....	....	....	....	362,438	491,638	319,971
Austria	70,797	124,024	241,377	432,798	845,555	575,627	370,914	479,906
Hungary	3,737	11,526	62,435	145,714	495,609	397,283	274,450	290,228
Yugoslavia	....	....	....	....	....	169,439	211,416	161,093
Serbia	....	....	....	....	4,639	....	....	....
Montenegro	....	....	....	....	5,374	....	....	....
Russia and	4,644 (Russia and Lithuania, Latvia and Estonia, Finland)	35,722 (Russia and Lithuania, Latvia and Estonia, Finland)	182,644 (Russia and Lithuania, Latvia and Estonia, Finland)	423,726 (Russia and Lithuania)	1,184,412	1,535,563	1,347,234	1,040,884
Lithuania							24,223	165,771
Latvia and								18,636
Estonia								4,178
Finland				62,641	129,680	149,824	142,478	117,210
Rumania	....	....	....	15,032	65,923	102,823	146,393	115,940
Bulgaria	....	....	....	....	11,498	10,477	9,399	8,888
Turkey in Europe	302	1,205	1,839	9,910	32,230	5,284	2,257	4,412
Southern Europe	25,853	58,265	206,648	530,200	1,525,875	1,911,213	2,106,295	1,896,886
Greece	390	776	1,887	8,515	101,282	175,976	174,526	163,252
Albania	....	....	....	....	....	5,608	8,814	....
Italy	17,157	44,230	182,580	484,027	1,343,125	1,610,113	1,790,429	1,623,580
Spain	3,764	5,121	6,185	7,050	22,108	49,535	59,362	47,707
Portugal	4,542	8,138	15,996	30,608	59,360	69,981	73,164	62,347
Other Europe	1,678	3,786	12,579	2,251	2,858	5,901	16,255	19,819
America	....	807,230	1,088,245	1,317,380	1,489,231	1,727,017	2,102,209	1,509,855
Canada and Newfoundland	....	717,157	980,938	1,179,922	1,209,717	1,138,174	1,310,369	1,065,480
Canada French	....	....	302,496	395,126	385,083	307,786	370,852	273,366
Other	....	....	678,422	784,796	819,554	817,139	915,537	770,753
Newfoundland	....	....	....	....	5,080	13,249	23,980	21,361
West Indies	....	16,401	23,256	25,435	47,635	78,962	106,241	30,534
Mexico	....	68,399	77,853	103,393	221,915	486,418	641,462	377,433
Central and South America	....	5,273	6,198	8,630	9,964	23,463	44,137	36,408

a Northern Ireland. b Irish Free State.

IMMIGRATION QUOTAS, 1930

Country or Area	*Quota*	*Country or Area*	*Quota*
Afghanistan	100	Muscat (Oman)	100
Albania	100	Nauru (British mandate)	100
Andorra	100	Nepal	100
Arabian Peninsula	100	Netherlands	3,153
Australia (including Tasmania, Papua, and all islands appertaining to Australia)	100	New Guinea, Territory of (including appertaining islands) (Australian mandate)	100
Austria	1,413	New Zealand	100
Belgium	1,304	Norway	2,377
Bhutan	100	Palestine (with Trans-Jordan) (British mandate)	100
Bulgaria	100	Persia	100
Cameroon (British mandate)	100	Philippine Islands	50
Cameroon (French mandate)	100	Poland	6,524
China	100	Portugal	440
Czechoslovakia	2,874	Ruanda and Urundi (Belgium mandate)	100
Danzig, Free City of	100	Rumania	377
Denmark	1,181	Russia, European and Asiatic	2,712
Egypt	100	Samoa, Western (mandate of New Zealand)	100
Estonia	116	San Marino	100
Ethiopia (Abyssinia)	100	Saudi Arabia (Hejaz and Nejd and its Dependencies)	100
Finland	569	Siam	100
France	3,086	South Africa, Union of	100
Germany	25,957	South West Africa (mandate of the Union of South Africa)	100
Great Britain and Northern Ireland	65,721	Spain	252
Greece	307	Sweden	3,314
Hungary	869	Switzerland	1,707
Iceland	100	Syria and the Lebanon (French mandate)	123
India	100	Tanganyika (British mandate)	100
Iraq (Mesopotamia)	100	Togoland (British mandate)	100
Irish Free State	17,853	Togoland (French mandate)	100
Italy	5,802	Turkey	226
Japan	100	Yap and other Pacific Islands under Japanese mandate	100
Latvia	236	Yugoslavia	845
Liberia	100		
Liechtenstein	100		
Lithuania	386		
Luxemburg	100		
Monaco	100		
Morocco (French and Spanish zones and Tangier)	100		

IMMIGRATION, BY COUNTRY OF ORIGIN: 1901 TO 1949

[Data are totals, not annual averages, and are for periods ending June 30. Data prior to 1906 refer to country whence aliens came; thereafter, country of last permanent residence. Because of boundary changes and changes in list of countries separately reported, data for certain countries not comparable throughout.]

Country	1901–1910	1911–1920	1921–1930	1931–1940	1941–1945	1946	1947	1948	1949
All countries, total	8,795,386	5,735,811	4,107,209	528,431	170,952	108,721	147,292	170,570	188,317
Europe, total	8,136,016	4,376,564	2,477,853	348,289	53,066	52,852	83,535	103,544	129,592
Belgium	41,635	33,746	15,846	4,817	2,479	1,718	2,465	2,041	2,057
Bulgaria [1]	39,280	22,533	2,945	938	162	8	51	119	22
Czechoslovakia	....	3,426	102,194	14,393	753	267	2,053	2,310	2,018
Denmark	65,285	41,983	32,430	2,559	532	194	999	1,335	1,239
Finland	....	756	16,691	2,146	395	29	514	492	567
France	73,379	61,897	49,610	12,623	11,020	5,708	7,285	5,550	4,816
Germany	341,498	143,945	412,202	117,621 (Germany and Austria)	6,836 (Germany and Austria)	2,598	13,900	19,368	55,284
Austria [2]	2,145,266 (Austria and Hungary)	453,649	32,868			130	1,545	2,271	4,447
Hungary		442,693	30,680	7,861	732	49	803	947	748
Great Britain:									
England	388,017	249,944	157,420	21,756	13,101	30,922	20,147	21,257	16,634
Scotland	120,469	78,357	159,781	6,887	705	1,586	2,962	4,504	4,075
Wales	17,464	13,107	13,012	735	139	1,044	679	642	440
Greece	167,519	184,201	51,084	9,119	1,073	367	2,370	2,250	1,734
Ireland	339,065	146,181	220,591	13,167	1,059	1,816	2,574	7,534	8,678
Italy	2,045,877	1,109,524	455,315	68,028	935	2,636	13,866	16,075	11,695
Netherlands	48,262	43,718	26,948	7,150	1,160	355	2,936	3,999	3,330
Norway	190,505	66,395	68,531	4,740	700	248	1,967	2,447	2,476
Poland [3]	....	4,813	227,734	17,026	1,675	335	745	2,447	1,673
Portugal	69,149	89,732	29,994	3,329	2,934	578	633	890	1,282
Rumania	53,008	13,311	67,646	3,871	381	19	93	273	155
Spain	27,935	68,611	28,958	3,258	1,215	227	260	404	409
Sweden	249,534	95,074	97,249	3,960	884	643	1,848	2,260	2,847
Switzerland	34,922	23,091	29,676	5,512	2,155	766	1,779	2,026	1,967
Turkey in Europe	79,976	54,677	14,659	737	133	71	105	93	69
U.S.S.R. (Russia)	1,597,306	921,201	61,742	1,356	192	72	170	84	24
Yugoslavia	....	1,888	49,064	5,835	425	65	221	478	198
Other Europe	665	8,111	22,983	8,865	1,291	401	565	1,448	708
Asia, total	243,567	192,559	97,400	15,344	3,368	1,633	5,823	10,739	6,438
China	20,605	21,278	29,907	4,928	1,368	252	3,191	7,203	3,415
Japan	129,797	83,837	33,462	1,948	358	14	131	423	529
Turkey in Asia	77,393	79,389	19,165	328	111	16	22	16	40
Other Asia	15,772	8,055	14,866	8,140	1,531	1,351	2,479	3,097	2,454
America, total	361,888	1,143,671	1,516,716	160,037	109,714	46,066	52,753	52,746	49,334
Canada and Newfoundland	179,226	742,185	924,515	108,527	53,506	21,324	24,342	25,485	25,156
Mexico	49,642	219,004	459,287	22,319	22,674	7,146	7,558	8,384	8,083
Central America	8,192	17,159	15,769	5,861	8,606	2,338	3,386	2,671	2,431
South America	17,280	41,899	42,215	7,803	6,667	2,633	3,094	3,046	3,107
West Indies	107,548	123,424	74,899	15,502	17,248	5,898	6,728	6,932	6,733
Other America	....	....	31	25	1,013	6,727	7,645	6,228	3,824
Africa	7,368	8,443	6,286	1,750	1,696	1,516	1,284	1,027	995
Australia and New Zealand	11,975	12,348	8,299	2,231	2,636	6,009	2,821	1,218	661
Pacific Islands (not specified)	1,049	1,079	427	780	472	572	1,049	1,286	1,272
All other countries	[4] 33,523	1,147	228	....	....	73	27	10	25

[1] Includes Serbia and Montenegro prior to 1920.
[2] Austria included with Germany 1938–45.
[3] From 1899 to 1919 Poland is included with Austria-Hungary, Germany, and Russia.
[4] Includes 32,897 persons returning to their homes in the United States. After 1906 such aliens have been included in immigration statistics as nonimmigrants; prior to that year, aliens were recorded by countries whence they came (see headnote).

Source: Department of Justice, Immigration and Naturalization Service; releases.

URBAN AND RURAL POPULATION

Urban population: Places over 2500

Census Year	Urban Population		Rural Population		Census Year	Urban Population		Rural Population	
	Number	Per Cent of Total	Number	Per Cent of Total		Number	Per Cent of Total	Number	Per Cent of Total
1940	74,423,702	56.5	57,245,573	43.5	1860	6,216,518	19.8	25,226,803	80.2
1930	68,954,823	56.2	53,820,233	43.8	1850	3,543,716	15.3	19,648,160	84.7
1920	54,157,973	51.2	51,552,647	48.8	1840	1,845,055	10.8	15,224,398	89.2
1910	41,998,932	45.7	49,973,334	54.3	1830	1,127,247	8.8	11,738,773	91.2
1900	30,159,921	39.7	45,834,654	60.3	1820	693,255	7.2	8,945,198	92.8
1890	22,106,265	35.1	40,841,449	64.9	1810	525,459	7.3	6,714,422	92.7
1880	14,129,735	28.2	36,026,048	71.8	1800	322,371	6.1	4,986,112	93.9
1870	9,902,361	25.7	28,656,010	74.3	1790	201,655	5.1	3,727,559	94.9

URBAN AND RURAL INCOME

PER CAPITA PERSONAL INCOME, BY GEOGRAPHIC DIVISIONS AND STATES, 1929

Adapted from Leven, Moulton, Warburton, *America's Capacity to Consume*, Table 17, p. 173.

State and Region	Entire Population	Non-Farm Population	Farm Population	State and Region	Entire Population	Non-Farm Population	Farm Population
Southeast	*$ 365*	*$ 535*	*$ 183*	Maryland.....	$ 799	$ 881	$ 323
Virginia.......	431	594	182	West Virginia.	485	602	157
North Carolina.	317	472	167				
South Carolina.	261	412	129	*Middle States*	*715*	*854*	*262*
Georgia.......	343	532	147	Ohio.........	795	893	255
Florida........	548	577	419	Indiana......	614	748	221
Kentucky......	398	605	148	Illinois........	987	1,091	299
Tennessee.....	346	529	137	Michigan.....	869	983	283
Alabama.......	331	527	141	Wisconsin....	682	807	389
Mississippi.....	287	530	173	Minnesota....	610	802	248
Arkansas......	311	503	185	Iowa.........	485	659	214
Louisiana......	438	603	186	Missouri......	675	851	189
Southwest	*564*	*683*	*366*	*Northwest*	*590*	*703*	*426*
Oklahoma.....	503	699	243	North Dakota.	422	588	302
Texas.........	531	690	298	South Dakota.	420	614	268
New Mexico...	476	549	354	Nebraska.....	521	698	281
Arizona.......	744	795	567	Kansas.......	569	686	376
				Montana.....	698	856	435
Northeast	*881*	*946*	*366*	Idaho........	609	647	559
Maine.........	645	689	474	Wyoming.....	777	841	648
New Hampshire	652	689	379	Colorado.....	690	772	470
Vermont.......	633	761	351	Utah.........	600	629	496
Massachusetts..	975	976	898				
Rhode Island..	881	881	859	*Far West*	*921*	*953*	*818*
Connecticut....	1,008	1,028	630	Nevada......	1,000	1,041	811
New York.....	1,365	1,417	493	Washington...	841	887	651
New Jersey....	1,002	1,011	704	Oregon.......	757	817	563
Delaware......	1,315	1,550	368	California.....	1,085	1,066	1,246
Pennsylvania...	815	865	305				

PUBLIC DEBT OF THE UNITED STATES

(On basis of Treasury Statements)

June 30	Gross Debt	Per Cap.	June 30	Gross Debt	Per Cap.	June 30	Gross Debt	Per Cap.
	Dollars	Dollars		Dollars	Dollars		Dollars	Dollars
1870	2,436,453,269	63.19	1921	23,976,250,608	221.09	1936	33,778,543,494	263.01
1880	2,090,908,872	41.69	1922	22,964,079,190	208.97	1937	36,424,613,732	281.63
1885	1,578,551,169	28.11	1923	22,349,687,755	200.10	1938	37,164,740,315	285.41
1890	1,122,396,584	17.92	1924	21,251,120,427	186.86	1939	40,439,532,411	308.29
1895	1,096,913,120	15.91	1925	20,516,272,174	177.82	1940	42,967,531,037	325.19
1900	1,263,416,913	16.56	1926	19,643,183,079	167.50	1941	48,961,443,536	368.74
1905	1,132,357,095	13.60	1927	18,510,174,266	156.04	1942	72,422,445,116	537.80
1906	1,142,522,970	13.50	1928	17,604,290,563	146.69	1943	136,696,090,330	1,001.46
1910	1,146,939,969	12.69	1929	16,931,197,748	139.40	1944	201,003,387,221	1,445.67
1915	1,191,264,068	11.83	1930	16,185,308,299	131.38	1945	258,682,187,410	1,853.21
1916	1,225,145,568	11.96	1931	16,801,485,143	135.42	1946	269,422,099,173	1,907.62
1917	2,975,618,585	28.57	1932	19,487,009,766	156.12	1947	258,286,383,109	1,793.23
1918	12,243,628,719	115.65	1933	22,538,672,164	179.32	1948	252,292,246,513	1,721.29
1919	25,482,034,419	246.09	1934	27,053,141,414	213.75	1949	252,770,359,860	1,695.46*
1920	24,297,918,412	228.32	1935	28,700,892,624	225.71			

* Subject to revision.

PUBLIC LANDS OF THE UNITED STATES

Source: General Land Office, Department of the Interior

Acquired:	Acres
State cessions following Revolution	266,427,520
Louisiana purchase (1803)	529,911,680
Oregon territory (by discovery)	183,386,240
Purchased from Spain (1819):	
Florida	37,546,240
West of Mississippi River	8,598,400
Mexican cession (1848)	338,680,960
Purchased from Texas (1850)	78,892,800
Gadsden purchase (1853)	18,988,800
Total	1,462,432,640
Less water area	20,232,320
Land area of public domain	1,442,200,320
Alaska purchase (1867)	378,165,760

The disposition to June 30, 1940, of the public domain in the United States proper has been approximately as follows:

Title passed from the United States:	
Homesteads (approx.)	285,000,000
Cash sales and miscellaneous disposals (approx.)	419,117,998
State grants for educational or other purpose	181,975,263
Canal and river improvement grants to States	6,842,921
Wagon-road grants to States	3,359,188
Grants to States in aid of railroads	38,208,638
Railroad grants to corporations	94,239,448
Total area disposed of	1,028,743,456
Pending and unperfected entries	2,373,542
Title remaining in the United States:	
National forests, estimated net area of public lands	134,515,000
National Parks and Monuments	13,864,245
Indian reservations (estimated net)	55,192,183
Military, naval, miscellaneous reservations (approx.)	3,336,000
Unappropriated, but withdrawn (part estimated)	199,842,600
Miscellaneous disposals	4,333,294
Grand total (exact public land area)	1,442,200,320

UNITED STATES RECEIPTS AND EXPENDITURES, 1789–1950

Source: Treasury Department; annual statements for year ending June 30

Yearly Average	Receipts	Expend-itures	Yearly Average	Receipts	Expend-itures	Yearly Average	Receipts	Expend-itures
	$1,000	$1,000		$1,000	$1,000		$1,000	$1,000
1789–1800[1]	5,717	5,776	1871–1875	336,830	287,460	1908	601,862	659,196
1801–1810[2]	13,056	9,086	1876–1880	288,124	255,598	1909	604,320	693,744
1811–1820[2]	21,032	23,943	1881–1885	366,961	257,691	1910	675,512	693,617
1821–1830[2]	21,923	16,162	1886–1890	375,448	279,134	1911	701,833	691,202
1831–1840[2]	30,461	24,495	1891–1895	352,891	363,599	1912	692,609	689,881
1841–1850[2]	28,545	34,097	1896–1900	434,877	457,451	1913	724,111	724,512
1851–1860	60,237	60,163	1901–1905	559,481	535,559	1914	734,673	735,081
1861–1865	160,907	683,785	1906	594,984	570,202			
1866–1870	447,301	377,642	1907	665,860	579,129			

1915	$697,910,827	$760,586,802	1933	$2,021,212,943	$4,622,865,028
1916	782,534,548	734,056,202	1934	3,064,267,912	6,693,899,854
1917	1,124,324,795	1,977,681,751	1935	3,729,913,845	6,520,965,945
1918	3,664,582,865	[6]12,696,702,471	1936	4,068,936,689	8,493,485,919
1919	5,152,257,136	18,514,879,955	1937	[3]4,978,600,695	7,756,021,409
1920	6,694,565,389	6,403,343,841	1938	5,761,623,749	6,938,240,347
1921	5,624,932,961	5,115,927,690	1939	5,103,396,943	8,965,554,983
1922	4,109,104,151	3,372,607,900	1940	5,264,663,044	9,182,682,204
1923	4,007,135,481	3,294,627,529	1941	7,227,281,383	13,386,553,742
1924	4,012,044,702	3,048,677,965	1942	12,696,286,084	34,186,528,816
1925	3,780,148,685	3,063,105,332	1943	22,201,501,787	79,621,932,152
1926	3,962,755,690	3,097,611,823	1944	43,891,672,699	95,315,065,241
1927	4,129,394,441	2,974,029,674	1945	44,761,609,047	98,702,525,172
1928	4,042,348,156	3,103,264,855	1946	40,026,888,964	60,703,059,573
1929	4,033,250,225	3,298,859,486	1947	40,042,606,290	39,288,818,629
1930	4,177,941,702	3,440,268,884	1948	42,210,770,493	[7]33,791,300,649
1931	[5]3,115,556,923	[5]3,577,434,003	1949	38,245,667,810	[8]40,057,107,858
1932	1,923,913,117	[4]4,659,202,825	1950	37,044,733,557	40,166,835,915

(1) Average for period March 4, 1789, to Dec. 1, 1800.
(2) Years ended Dec. 31, 1801, to 1842; average for 1841–1850 is for the period Jan. 1, 1841, to June 30, 1850.
(3) Receipts from 1937 on have deducted, appropriations to Federal old-age and survivors insurance trust fund.
(4) Expenditures for years 1932 through 1946 have been revised to include Government Corporations (wholly owned), etc. (net).
(5) Effective January 3, 1949, amounts refunded by the Government, principally for the overpayment of taxes, are being reported as deductions from total receipts rather than as expenditures. Also, effective July 1, 1948, payments to the Treasury, principally by wholly owned Government corporations for retirement of capital stock and for disposition of earnings, are excluded in reporting both budget receipts and expenditures. Neither of these changes affects the size of the budget surplus or deficit. Beginning 1931 figures in each case have been adjusted accordingly for comparative purposes.
(6) Figures for 1918 through 1946 are revised to exclude statutory debt retirements (sinking fund, etc.).
(7) Excludes $3 billions transferred to Foreign Economics Cooperation Trust Fund.
(8) Includes $3 billions representing expenditures made from the Foreign Economics Cooperation Trust Fund.

SPEAKERS OF THE HOUSE OF REPRESENTATIVES

(Continued from Volume I)

Name	State	Time	Name	State	Time
Schuyler Colfax......	Ind.	1863–1869	Champ Clark........	Mo.	1911–1919
James G. Blaine......	Me.	1869–1875	Fred'k H. Gillett.....	Mass.	1919–1925
Michael C. Kerr.....	Ind.	1875–1876	Nich. Longworth.....	Ohio	1925–1931
Samuel J. Randall....	Pa.	1876–1881	John N. Garner......	Tex.	1931–1933
Joseph W. Keifer.....	Ohio	1881–1883	Henry T. Rainey.....	Ill.	1933–1934
John G. Carlisle......	Ky.	1883–1889	Joseph W. Byrns.....	Tenn.	1935–1936
Thomas B. Reed.....	Me.	1889–1891	Wm. B. Bankhead....	Ala.	1936–1940
Charles F. Crisp.....	Ga.	1891–1895	Sam Rayburn........	Tex.	1941–1947
Thomas B. Reed.....	Me.	1895–1899	Joseph W. Martin, Jr.	Mass.	1947–1949
D. B. Henderson.....	Ia.	1899–1903	Sam Rayburn........	Tex.	1949–....
Joseph G. Cannon....	Ill.	1903–1910			

SUMMARY OF MANUFACTURES, 1859–1947

Year	Establishments	Wage-Earners	Capital (In thousands)	Wages (In thousands)	Value of Products (In thousands)
1859	140,433	1,311,246	$ 1,009,856	$ 378,879	$ 1,885,862
1869	252,148	2,053,996	1,694,576	620,467	3,385,860
1879	253,852	2,732,595	2,790,273	947,954	5,369,579
1889	355,405	4,251,535	6,525,051	1,891,220	9,372,379
1899	512,191	5,306,143	9,813,834	2,320,938	13,000,149
1909 [1]	246,491	6,615,046	18,428,270	3,427,038	20,672,052
1919 [1]	290,105	9,096,372	44,466,594	10,533,400	62,418,079
1929 [2]	210,959	8,838,743	....	11,620,973	70,434,863
1939 [2]	184,230	7,886,567	....	9,089,941	56,843,024
1947 [3]	240,881	14,294,304	....	37,689,527	74,425,875

[1] Figures for 1909 and 1919 do not include hand and neighborhood industries or establishments with products valued at less than $500.

[2] For all establishments having products valued at $5000 or more.

[3] For all establishments employing one or more persons.

LABOR UNION MEMBERSHIP: 1897 TO 1945

Year	All Unions, Total Membership	American Federation of Labor		Congress of Industrial Organizations		Independent or Unaffiliated Unions, Total Membership
		Number of affiliated unions	Total membership	Number of affiliated unions	Total membership	
	1,000 members	Number	*1,000 members*	Number	*1,000 members*	*1,000 members*
1897	440	58	265			175
1900	791	82	548			243
1910	2,116	120	1,562			554
1919	4,046	111	3,260			786
1920	5,034	110	4,079			955
1921	4,722	110	3,907			815
1922	3,950	112	3,196			754
1923	3,629	108	2,926			703
1924	3,549	107	2,866			683
1925	3,566	107	2,877			689
1926	3,592	107	2,804			788
1927	3,600	106	2,813			787
1928	3,567	107	2,896			671
1929	3,625	105	2,934			671
1930	3,632	104	2,961			671
1931	3,526	105	2,890			636
1932	3,226	106	2,532			694
1933	2,857	108	2,127			730
1934	3,249	109	2,608			641
1935	3,728	109	3,045			683
1936	4,164	111	3,422			742
1937	7,218	100	2,861	32	3,718	639
1938	8,265	102	3,623	42	4,038	604
1939	8,980	104	4,006	45	4,000	974
1940	8,944	105	4,247	42	3,625	1,072
1941	10,489	106	4,569	41	5,000	920
1942	10,762	102	5,483	39	4,195	1,084
1943	13,642	99	6,564	40	5,285	1,793
1944	14,621	100	6,807	41	5,935	1,879
1945	14,796	102	6,931	40	6,000	1,865

LABOR FORCE

Year	All Persons 10 Years Old and Over					Women in Labor Force or Gainfully Occupied, 15 Years Old and Over		
	Population 10 years old and over	Number of persons engaged in —				Total number	Married	
		All occupations: Number	All occupations: Per cent of population 10 and over	Non-agricultural pursuits	Agricultural pursuits		Number	Per cent
	1	2	3	4	5	6	7	8
1820	6,487,815	2,881,000	44.4	812,042	2,068,958	....	....	....
1830	8,639,412	3,931,537	45.5	1,159,084	2,772,453	....	....	....
1840	11,629,006	5,420,000	46.6	1,700,049	3,719,951	....	....	....
1850	16,452,835	7,697,196	46.8	2,795,314	4,901,882	....	....	....
1860	22,429,625	10,532,750	47.0	4,325,116	6,207,634	....	....	....
1870	29,123,683	12,924,951	44.4	6,075,179	6,849,772	....	....	....
1880	36,761,607	17,392,099	47.3	8,807,289	8,584,810	....	....	....
1890	47,413,559	23,318,183	49.2	13,379,810	9,938,373	3,712,144	515,260	13.9
1900	57,949,824	29,073,233	50.2	18,161,235	10,911,998	4,997,415	769,477	15.4
1910	71,580,270	37,370,794	52.2	25,779,027	11,591,767	7,639,828	1,890,661	24.7
1920	82,739,315	42,433,535	51.3	30,984,765	11,448,770	8,346,796	1,920,281	23.0
1930	98,723,047	48,829,920	49.5	38,357,922	10,471,998	10,632,227	3,071,302	28.9
1940	110,443,129	52,148,251	47.2	42,985,704	9,162,547	13,840,000	5,040,000	36.4

RAILROAD MILEAGE

By Decade, 1830–1940

1830	23	1890	163,597
1840	2,818	1900	193,346
1850	9,021	1910	240,293
1860	30,626	1920	252,845
1870	52,922	1930	249,052
1880	93,262	1940	233,670

FOREIGN TRADE — VALUE OF EXPORTS AND IMPORTS: 1821–1945

Year	Exports	Imports	Excess of exports (+) or imports (−)
1821	65,074	62,586	+2,489
1830	73,850	70,877	+2,973
1840	132,086	107,142	+24,944
1850	151,899	178,138	−26,240
1860	400,122	362,166	+37,956
1870	450,927	462,378	−11,450
1880	852,782	760,989	+91,793
1890	909,977	823,287	+86,690
1900	1,499,462	929,771	+569,691
1910	1,918,835	1,645,505	+273,330
1920	8,663,724	5,783,610	+2,880,114
1930	4,013,305	3,499,723	+513,582
1931	2,917,568	2,731,418	+186,150
1932	2,434,394	1,705,739	+728,655
1933	2,060,687	1,702,981	+357,706
1934	2,202,110	2,944,451	−742,341
1935	2,303,635	4,142,995	−1,839,360
1936	2,495,477	3,749,525	−1,254,049
1937	3,407,229	4,807,068	−1,399,839
1938	3,107,411	4,170,416	−1,063,006
1939	3,192,314	5,978,047	−2,785,733
1940	4,029,815	7,433,280	−3,403,465
1941	5,152,891	4,374,500	+778,391
1942	8,081,618	3,101,745	+4,979,873
1943	12,905,086	3,511,045	+9,394,041
1944	15,247,687	4,056,479	+11,191,208
1945	9,879,419	4,256,938	+5,622,481

PRODUCTION OF CHIEF METALS IN THE UNITED STATES, 1850–1934

(Data by Bureau of Mines, U.S. Department of Commerce)

YEAR (CAL.)	GOLD	SILVER	COPPER	LEAD	IRON ORE	PIG IRON	STEEL
	Dollars	*Dollars*	*Long tons*	*Short tons*	*Long tons*	*Long tons*	*Long tons*
1850	50,000,000	50,900	650	22,000	....	563,755	....
1860	46,000,000	156,800	7,200	15,600	....	821,223	....
1870	50,000,000	16,434,000	12,600	17,830	3,031,891	1,665,179	68,750
1871	43,500,000	23,588,300	13,000	20,000	....	1,706,793	73,214
1872	36,000,000	29,396,400	12,500	25,880	....	2,548,713	142,954
1873	36,000,000	35,881,600	15,500	42,540	....	2,560,963	198,796
1874	33,490,900	36,917,500	17,500	52,080	....	2,401,262	215,727
1875	33,467,900	30,485,900	18,000	59,640	....	2,023,733	389,799
1876	39,929,200	34,919,800	19,000	64,070	....	1,868,961	533,191
1877	46,897,400	36,991,500	21,000	81,900	....	2,066,594	569,618
1878	51,206,400	40,401,000	21,500	91,060	....	2,301,215	731,977
1879	38,900,000	35,477,100	23,000	92,780	....	2,741,853	935,273
1880	36,000,000	34,717,000	27,000	97,825	7,120,362	3,835,191	1,247,335
1881	34,700,000	37,657,500	32,000	117,085	....	4,144,254	1,588,314
1882	32,500,000	41,105,900	40,467	132,890	....	4,623,323	1,736,692
1883	30,000,000	39,618,400	51,574	143,957	....	4,595,510	1,673,535
1884	30,800,000	41,921,300	64,708	139,897	....	4,097,868	1,550,879
1885	31,801,000	42,503,500	74,052	129,412	....	4,044,526	1,711,920
1886	35,869,000	39,482,400	70,430	130,629	....	5,683,329	2,562,503
1887	33,136,000	40,887,200	81,017	145,700	....	6,417,148	3,339,071
1888	33,167,500	43,045,100	101,054	151,919	....	6,489,738	2,899,440
1889	32,967,000	46,838,400	101,239	156,397	14,518,041	7,603,642	3,385,732
1890	32,845,000	57,242,100	115,966	143,630	16,036,043	9,202,703	4,277,071
1891	33,175,000	57,630,000	126,839	178,554	14,591,178	8,279,870	3,904,240
1892	33,015,000	55,662,500	154,018	173,305	16,296,666	9,157,000	4,927,581
1893	35,955,000	46,800,000	147,033	163,982	11,587,629	7,124,502	4,019,995
1894	39,500,000	31,422,100	158,120	162,686	11,879,679	6,657,888	4,412,032
1895	46,610,000	36,445,500	169,917	170,000	15,957,614	9,446,308	6,114,834
1896	53,088,000	39,654,600	205,384	188,000	16,005,449	8,623,127	5,281,689
1897	57,363,000	32,316,000	220,571	212,000	17,518,046	9,652,680	7,156,957
1898	64,463,000	32,118,400	235,050	222,000	19,433,716	11,773,934	8,932,857
1899	71,053,400	32,858,700	253,870	210,500	24,683,173	13,620,703	10,639,857
1900	79,171,000	35,741,100	270,588	270,824	27,553,161	13,789,242	10,188,329
1901	78,666,700	33,128,400	268,782	270,700	28,887,479	15,878,354	13,473,595
1902	80,000,000	29,415,000	294,423	270,000	35,554,135	17,821,307	14,947,250
1903	73,597,700	29,322,000	311,627	282,000	35,019,308	18,009,252	14,534,978
1904	80,464,700	33,456,024	362,739	307,000	27,644,330	16,497,033	13,859,887
1905	88,180,700	34,222,000	402,637	307,514	42,526,133	22,992,380	20,023,947
1906	94,373,800	38,256,400	409,735	336,200	47,749,728	25,307,191	23,398,136
1907	90,435,700	37,299,700	387,945	352,381	51,720,619	25,781,361	23,362,594
1908	94,560,000	28,050,600	420,791	311,666	35,983,336	15,936,018	14,023,247
1909	99,673,400	28,455,200	487,925	352,839	51,155,437	25,795,471	23,955,021
1910	96,269,100	30,854,500	482,214	375,402	56,889,734	27,303,567	26,094,919
1911	96,890,000	32,615,700	489,836	391,995	41,092,447	23,649,547	23,676,106
1912	93,451,500	39,197,400	555,031	392,517	57,017,614	29,726,937	31,251,303
1913	88,301,023	40,864,871	546,645	411,878	61,980,437	30,966,152	31,300,874
1914	94,531,800	40,067,700	513,454	512,794	41,439,761	23,332,244	23,513,030
1915	101,035,700	37,397,300	619,647	507,026	55,526,490	29,916,213	32,151,036
1916	92,590,300	48,953,000	860,648	552,228	75,167,672	39,434,797	42,773,680
1917	83,750,700	59,078,100	842,018	548,450	75,288,851	38,621,216	45,060,607
1918	68,646,700	66,485,129	852,024	539,905	69,658,278	39,054,644	44,462,432
1919	60,333,400	63,533,652	574,294	424,433	60,965,418	31,015,364	34,671,232
1920	51,186,900	60,801,955	539,759	476,849	67,604,465	36,925,987	42,132,934
1921	50,067,300	53,052,000	225,708	398,222	29,490,978	16,688,126	19,783,797
1922	48,849,100	56,240,048	424,235	468,746	47,128,527	26,825,060	35,602,926
1923	51,734,000	60,134,839	640,625	543,841	69,351,442	39,721,415	44,943,696
1924	52,277,000	43,822,814	729,576	566,407	54,267,419	30,874,765	37,931,939
1925	49,860,200	45,911,864	747,710	654,921	61,907,997	36,116,311	45,393,524
1926	48,269,600	39,136,497	776,617	680,685	67,623,000	38,698,417	48,293,763
1927	45,418,600	34,266,328	751,849	668,320	61,741,100	35,858,232	44,935,185
1928	46,165,400	34,200,567	815,134	626,202	62,197,088	37,401,648	51,544,180
1929	45,651,400	32,687,754	894,135	672,498	73,027,720	41,757,215	56,433,473
1930	47,247,600	19,538,029	622,495	573,740	58,408,664	29,905,366	40,699,483
1931	49,527,200	8,970,294	465,496	390,260	31,131,502	17,952,613	25,945,501
1932	50,626,000	6,762,578	287,504	255,337	9,846,916	8,549,649	13,681,162
1933	65,721,379	8,158,554	200,892	259,616	17,553,188	13,027,343	23,232,347
1934	108,641,311	21,165,667	218,506	299,841	24,587,616	15,676,889	26,055,289

AGRICULTURAL COMMODITIES — PRODUCTION, BY CHIEF KINDS: 1800 TO 1946

NOTE. — Data are for the crop or growth year. Blank lines indicate that data are not available.

YEAR	CORN	WHEAT	RICE (in terms of cleaned)	SUGAR		COTTON		TOBACCO
				Beet (chiefly refined)	Cane (chiefly raw)	Running bales	500-pound bales	
	1,000 bushels	*1,000 bushels*	*1,000 pounds*	*1,000 pounds*	*1,000 pounds*	*Thousands*	*Thousands*	*1,000 pounds*
1800	....	....	67,234	....	....	154	73	....
1810	....	....	78,805	....	....	286	178	....
1820	....	....	53,292	....	....	576	335	....
1830	....	....	81,352	....	....	1,026	732	....
1840	377,532	84,823	84,253	....	120,851	1,635	1,348	219,163
1850	592,071	100,486	102,776	....	247,577	2,454	2,136	199,753
1860	838,793	173,105	106,279	....	274,725	3,849	3,841	434,209
1870	1,124,775	254,429	54,889	896	178,304	4,352	4,025	345,045
1875	1,450,276	313,728	83,861	224	172,480	4,631	4,302	609,455
1880	1,706,673	502,257	111,869	1,120	285,302	6,606	6,357	469,395
1885	2,057,807	399,931	150,195	1,344	302,754	6,576	6,369	610,500
1890	1,650,446	449,042	136,800	7,748	497,170	8,653	8,562	647,535
1894	1,615,016	541,873	109,821	45,006	729,394	9,901	10,026	766,870
1895	2,534,762	542,119	168,665	65,452	543,636	7,162	7,147	745,000
1896	2,671,048	522,963	96,886	84,080	644,176	8,533	8,516	760,035
1897	2,287,628	606,202	116,302	90,492	708,252	10,899	10,986	703,275
1898	2,351,323	768,148	136,991	72,736	568,788	11,278	11,526	909,090
1899	2,645,796	655,143	219,278	163,458	322,548	9,393	9,346	870,250
1900	2,661,978	599,315	253,139	172,164	623,772	10,102	10,124	851,980
1901	1,715,752	762,546	388,035	369,212	728,650	9,583	9,508	885,550
1902	2,773,954	686,959	319,293	436,812	745,806	10,588	10,630	959,505
1903	2,515,093	663,115	560,750	481,208	556,140	9,820	9,851	976,375
1904	2,686,624	555,571	586,000	484,226	829,990	13,451	13,438	856,595
1905	2,954,148	706,026	377,972	625,842	781,204	10,495	10,576	938,865
1906	3,032,910	740,509	495,972	967,224	544,320	12,983	13,274	972,510
1907	2,613,797	628,764	520,500	927,256	788,480	11,058	11,106	885,620
1908	2,566,742	642,818	608,056	851,768	828,800	13,086	13,241	835,645
1909	2,611,157	683,927	572,417	1,024,938	663,452	10,073	10,005	1,053,818
1910	2,852,794	625,476	680,833	1,020,344	710,080	11,568	11,609	1,142,320
1911	2,474,635	618,166	637,056	1,199,000	721,748	15,553	15,694	940,935
1912	2,947,842	730,011	695,944	1,385,112	325,147	13,489	13,703	1,117,415
1913	2,272,540	751,101	715,111	1,466,802	601,075	13,983	14,153	991,605
1914	2,523,750	897,487	656,917	1,444,108	493,240	15,906	16,112	1,036,745
1915	2,829,044	1,008,637	804,083	1,748,440	277,240	11,068	11,172	1,157,425
1916	2,425,206	634,572	1,135,028	1,641,314	621,799	11,364	11,448	1,206,785
1917	2,908,242	619,790	964,972	1,530,414	491,680	11,248	11,284	1,325,530
1918	2,441,249	904,130	1,072,389	1,521,900	568,800	11,906	12,018	1,444,505
1919	2,678,541	952,097	1,185,806	1,452,902	250,000	11,326	11,411	1,444,206
1920	3,070,604	843,277	1,434,667	2,178,000	360,000	13,271	13,429	1,509,212
1921	2,928,442	818,964	1,090,944	2,041,000	668,000	7,978	7,945	1,004,928
1922	2,707,306	846,649	1,157,306	1,350,000	604,000	9,729	9,755	1,254,304
1923	2,875,292	759,482	923,278	1,762,000	336,000	10,171	10,140	1,517,583
1924	2,223,123	841,617	906,750	2,180,000	180,000	13,639	13,630	1,244,928
1925	2,798,367	668,700	917,667	1,826,000	284,000	16,123	16,105	1,376,008
1926	2,546,972	832,213	1,167,361	1,794,000	96,000	17,755	17,978	1,289,272
1927	2,616,120	875,059	1,236,028	2,186,000	144,000	12,783	12,956	1,211,311
1928	2,665,516	914,373	1,217,611	2,122,000	272,000	14,297	14,477	1,373,214
1929	2,521,032	823,217	1,098,167	2,036,000	436,000	14,548	14,825	1,532,625
1930	2,080,421	886,470	1,248,028	2,416,000	430,000	13,756	13,932	1,648,229
1931	2,575,611	941,674	1,239,250	2,312,000	368,000	16,629	17,097	1,564,487
1932	2,931,281	756,927	1,156,083	2,714,000	530,000	12,710	13,003	1,017,317
1933	2,399,632	551,683	1,045,861	3,284,000	500,000	12,664	13,047	1,371,131
1934	1,461,123	526,393	1,084,639	2,320,000	534,000	9,472	9,636	1,081,629
1935	2,303,747	626,344	1,095,889	2,370,000	766,000	10,367	10,638	1,297,155
1936	1,507,089	626,766	1,383,889	2,608,000	874,000	12,141	12,399	1,155,328
1937	2,651,284	875,676	1,482,556	2,576,000	924,000	18,252	18,946	1,562,886
1938	2,542,238	930,801	1,452,861	3,370,000	1,160,000	11,620	11,943	1,378,534
1939	2,580,985	741,210	1,416,800	3,288,000	1,008,000	11,420	11,817	1,880,629
1940	2,547,146	814,646	1,455,200	3,512,000	6,640,000	12,318	12,566	1,460,441
1941	2,651,889	941,970	1,383,500	2,982,000	8,380,000	10,552	10,744	1,261,839
1942	3,068,562	969,381	1,655,200	3,238,000	9,200,000	12,496	12,817	1,408,394
1943	2,965,980	843,813	1,677,800	1,870,000	9,960,000	11,083	11,247	1,406,190
1944	3,088,110	1,060,111	1,761,500	1,958,000	8,740,000	11,924	12,230	1,954,699
1945	2,880,933	1,108,224	1,837,900	2,366,000	9,500,000	8,852	9,015	1,994,262
1946	3,287,927	1,155,715	....	2,846,000	8,500,000	8,574	8,640	2,312,080

Source: Dept. of Agriculture, Agricultural Marketing Service, except as noted; annual report, Agricultural Statistics.

STATISTICS OF PUBLIC ELEMENTARY AND SECONDARY SCHOOLS

1870–1910

	1870	1880	1890	1900	1910
Total population	38,558,371	50,155,783	62,622,250	75,602,515	91,972,266
Population 5–17 years, inclusive	12,055,443	15,065,767	18,543,201	21,404,322	24,239,948
Pupils enrolled in public schools	6,871,522	9,867,505	12,722,581	15,503,110	17,813,852
Per cent of population 5–17, inclusive	57.00	65.50	68.61	72.43	73.49
Number of teachers	200,515	286,593	363,922	423,062	523,210
Total expenditure for education (thousands of dollars)	63,397	78,095	140,507	214,965	426,250
Per capita of total population	$1.64	$1.56	$2.24	$2.84	$4.64
Per capita of enrollment	$9.23	$7.91	$11.04	$13.87	$23.93

1920–1946

	1920	1930	1936	1940	1946
Total population	105,710,620	122,775,046	128,429,000	131,669,275	141,235,000
Population 5–17 years, inclusive	27,728,788	31,571,322	31,547,000	29,745,246	28,235,000
Pupils enrolled in public schools	21,578,316	25,678,015	26,367,098	25,433,542	23,299,941
Per cent of population 5–17, inclusive	77.8	81.3	83.6	85.5	80.5
Number of teachers	679,533	854,263	870,963	875,477	831,026
Total expenditure for education (thousands of dollars)	1,036,151	2,316,790	1,968,898	2,344,049	2,906,886
Per capita of total population	$9.80	$18.87	$15.33	$17.77	$20.58
Per capita of enrollment	$48.02	$90.22	$74.38	$91.64	$123.20

(Data by U.S. Office of Education)

STATISTICS OF AMERICAN PARTICIPATION IN THE FIRST WORLD WAR

Total armed forces, including Army, Navy, Marine Corps, etc.	4,800,000
Total men in the Army	4,000,000
Men who went overseas	2,086,000
Men who fought in France	1,390,000
Greatest number sent in one month	306,000
Greatest number returning in one month	333,000
Tons of supplies shipped from America to France	7,500,000
Total registered in draft	24,234,021
Total draft inductions	2,810,296
Greatest number inducted in one month	400,000
Graduates of Line Officers' Training Schools	80,568
Cost of war to April 30, 1919	$21,850,000,000
Cost of Army to April 30, 1919	$13,930,000,000
Battles fought by American troops	13
Months of American participation in the war	19
Days of battle	200
Days of duration of Meuse-Argonne battle	47
Americans in Meuse-Argonne battle	1,200,000
American casualties in Meuse-Argonne battle	120,000
American battle deaths in war	50,000
American wounded in war	206,000
American deaths from disease	57,500
Total deaths in the Army	115,000

From Leonard P. Ayres, *The War with Germany. A Statistical Summary* p. 11. Washington. Government Printing Office, 1919.

UNITED STATES PARTICIPATION IN WORLD WAR II

(All data are as of 31 August 1945)

Item	Total	Army (Inc. AAF)	Navy	Marine Corps	Coast Guard
Registered in Draft [a]	50,680,137	....	....	....	......
Draft Inductions, Total [b]	10,189,773	8,397,356	1,549,285	227,001	16,131
1 Nov. '40 to 31 Aug. '45 only	9,867,707	8,096,248	1,534,241	221,087	16,131
Number Who Served, Total	15,145,115	10,420,000	3,883,520	599,693	241,902
Overseas only [c]	11,411,581	7,300,000	3,378,662	512,788	220,131
Battle Casualties, Total [d]	1,122,879	948,574	83,550	89,194	1,561
Battle Deaths, Total	304,014	237,049	46,469	19,910	586
Killed in Action	} 267,899	175,407	36,488	} 19,641	572
Died of Wounds		26,706	9,072		13
Died while Prisoner or Missing	36,115	34,936	909	269	1
Wounded in Action	673,665	571,822	33,726	67,142	975
Captured or Missing	145,200	139,703	3,355	2,142	....
Died of Disease	21,856	[e] 14,730	[e] 5,862	900	364
Prisoners Captured, Total	3,710,000				
German	3,500,000				
Italian	175,000				
Japanese	35,000				
Enemy Submarines Destroyed, Total	[f] 290	....	....	....	3
German	174	....	....	....	3
Italian	5	....	....	....	0
Japanese	111	....	....	....	0

[a] Represents total registrations of age groups 18–64 years during the period October 1940 through March 1947.

[b] Total figures are for the entire draft period, 1 November 1940–30 November 1946.

[c] Estimated.

[d] Tentative.

[e] Tentative.

[f] Does not include number sunk by mines. A total of 996 enemy submarines were sunk by the Allies during the years 1939–45, of which 893 were sunk by known causes.

Source: U.S. Army Historical Branch.

REVERSE LEND-LEASE AID RECEIVED BY THE UNITED STATES, BY CATEGORY

(Cumulative to September 30, 1946)

Category	Amount
Capital installations	$1,664,915,000
Foodstuffs	512,875,000
Clothing	91,089,000
Petroleum and coal products	1,684,629,000
Air Force supplies and equipment	474,622,000
Other military supplies and equipment	1,189,739,000
Shipping and other transportation	1,349,421,000
Other services	504,744,000
Raw materials and food shipped to United States	347,288,000
Total	$7,819,322,000

LEND-LEASE AID, BY CATEGORY

March 11, 1941–September 30, 1946

Category	Amount
Ordnance	$ 1,433,601,000
Ammunition	2,957,410,000
Aircraft:	
Bombers	$ 2,692,592,000
Pursuit and fighter planes	1,783,824,000
Other planes	844,417,000
Total	$ 5,320,833,000
Aeronautical material	$ 3,247,718,000
Ordnance vehicles and parts:	
Tanks	$ 2,595,067,000
Other ordnance vehicles	848,786,000
Spare engines and parts	338,100,000
Total	$ 3,781,953,000
Motor vehicles and parts:	
Trucks	$ 1,829,758,000
Automobiles	2,275,000
Other vehicles and parts	714,902,000
Total	$ 2,546,935,000
Watercraft:	
Combatant vessels	$ 1,663,846,000
Naval auxiliary and small craft	994,989,000
Merchant vessels	899,302,000
Other equipage, services, supplies, and materials	499,305,000
Total	$ 4,057,442,000
Petroleum products	$ 2,731,199,000
Military clothing	639,036,000
Signal equipment and supplies	1,236,888,000
Engineer equipment and supplies	808,648,000
Chemical warfare equipment	236,551,000
Other military equipment and supplies	966,763,000
Industrial equipment and commodities	$ 8,360,623,000
Food	5,828,716,000
Other agricultural products	852,913,000
Total transfers	$45,007,229,000
Services rendered	3,594,136,000
Lend-lease costs not charged to foreign Governments	2,090,744,000
Total lend-lease aid	$50,692,109,000

LEND-LEASE AID, BY COUNTRY
(Thousands of Dollars)

Country	Mar. 11, 1941, to V-J Day (Sept. 2, 1945)	Sept. 2, 1945, to Sept. 30, 1946	Total, Mar. 11, 1941, to Sept. 30, 1946
British Empire	$30,949,870	$442,491	$31,392,361
U.S.S.R.	11,058,833	239,050	11,297,883
France and Possessions	2,842,082	391,777	3,233,859
China	870,435	694,263	1,564,698
Netherlands and Possessions	182,000	66,896	248,896
Belgium	90,278	68,320	158,598
Greece	71,697	3,907	75,604
Norway	45,820	6,683	52,503
Yugoslavia	32,000	36	32,036
Turkey	27,397	60	27,457
Saudi Arabia	14,988	2,543	17,531
Poland	16,874	80	16,954
Liberia	7,237	0	7,237
Ethiopia	5,152	100	5,252
Iran	4,798	0	4,798
Iceland	4,797	12	4,809
Egypt	1,016	44	1,060
Czechoslovakia	349	154	503
Iraq	4	0	4
American Republics:			
Argentina	0	0	0
Bolivia	5,155	456	5,611
Brazil	326,913	4,738	331,651
Chile	21,499	381	21,880
Colombia	8,120	7	8,127
Costa Rica	155	0	155
Cuba	6,083	10	6,093
Dominican Republic	1,594	20	1,614
Ecuador	6,979	562	7,541
Guatemala	1,779	0	1,779
Haiti	1,437	6	1,443
Honduras	374	0	374
Mexico	38,468	149	38,617
Nicaragua	902	0	902
Panama	84	0	84
Paraguay	1,963	2	1,965
Peru	18,553	480	19,033
Salvador	894	0	894
Uruguay	7,132	9	7,141
Venezuela	4,407	11	4,418
Not charged by country	1,900,805	189,939	2,090,744
Total lend-lease aid	$48,578,923	$2,113,186	$50,692,109

THE CONSTITUTION OF THE UNITED STATES OF AMERICA

☆

WE,
THE PEOPLE OF THE UNITED STATES,
IN ORDER TO
FORM A MORE PERFECT UNION,
ESTABLISH JUSTICE,
INSURE DOMESTIC TRANQUILLITY,
PROVIDE FOR
THE COMMON DEFENCE,
PROMOTE THE GENERAL WELFARE,
AND SECURE
THE BLESSINGS OF LIBERTY
TO OURSELVES
AND OUR POSTERITY,
DO ORDAIN AND ESTABLISH THIS
CONSTITUTION
FOR THE UNITED STATES OF
AMERICA.

ARTICLE I

Section 1

All legislative Powers herein granted shall be vested in a Congress of the United States, which shall consist of a Senate and a House of Representatives.

Section 2

The House of Representatives shall be composed of Members chosen every second Year by the People of the several States, and the Electors in each State shall have the Qualifications requisite for Electors of the most numerous Branch of the State Legislature.

No Person shall be a Representative who shall not have attained to the Age of twenty-five Years, and been seven Years a Citizen of the United States, and who shall not, when elected, be an Inhabitant of that State in which he shall be chosen.

Representatives and direct Taxes shall be apportioned among the several States which may be included within this Union, according to their respective Numbers, which shall be determined by adding to the whole Number of free Persons, including those bound to Service for a Term of Years, and excluding Indians not taxed, three fifths of all other Persons. The actual Enumeration shall be made within three Years after the first Meeting of the Congress of the United States, and within every subsequent Term of ten Years, in such Manner as they shall by Law direct. The Number of Representatives shall not exceed one for every thirty Thousand, but each State shall have at Least one Representative; and until such enumeration shall be made, the State of New Hampshire shall be entitled to chuse three, Massachusetts eight, Rhode-Island and Providence Plantations one, Connecticut five, New-York six, New Jersey four, Pennsylvania eight, Delaware one, Maryland six, Virginia ten, North Carolina five, South Carolina five, and Georgia three.

When vacancies happen in the Representation from any State, the Executive Authority thereof shall issue Writs of Election to fill such Vacancies.

The House of Representatives shall chuse their Speaker and other Officers; and shall have the sole Power of Impeachment.

Section 3

The Senate of the United States shall be composed of two Senators from each State, chosen by the Legislature thereof, for six Years; and each Senator shall have one Vote.

Immediately after they shall be assembled in Consequence of the first Election, they shall be divided as equally as may be into three Classes. The Seats of the Senators of the first Class shall be vacated at the Expiration of the second Year, of the second Class at the Expiration of the fourth Year, and of the third Class at the Expiration of the sixth Year, so that one-third may be chosen every second Year; and if Vacancies happen by Resignation, or otherwise, during the Recess of the Legislature of any State, the Executive thereof may make temporary Appointments until the next Meeting of the Legislature, which shall then fill such Vacancies.

No Person shall be a Senator who shall not have attained to the Age of thirty Years, and been nine Years a Citizen of the United States, and who shall not, when elected, be an Inhabitant of that State for which he shall be chosen.

The Vice President of the United States shall be President of the Senate, but shall have no Vote, unless they be equally divided.

The Senate shall chuse their other Officers, and also a President pro tempore, in the Absence of the Vice President, or when he shall exercise the Office of President of the United States.

The Senate shall have the sole Power to try all Impeachments. When sitting for that Purpose, they shall be on Oath or Affirmation. When the President of the United States is tried, the Chief Justice shall preside: And no Person shall be convicted without the Concurrence of two thirds of the Members present.

Judgment in Cases of Impeachment shall not extend further than to removal from Office, and disqualification to hold and enjoy any Office of honor, Trust or Profit under the United States: but the Party convicted shall nevertheless be liable and subject to Indictment, Trial, Judgment and Punishment, according to Law.

SECTION 4

The Times, Places and Manner of holding Elections for Senators and Representatives, shall be prescribed in each State by the Legislature thereof; but the Congress may at any time by Law make or alter such Regulations, except as to the Places of chusing Senators.

The Congress shall assemble at least once in every Year, and such Meeting shall be on the first Monday in December, unless they shall by Law appoint a different Day.

SECTION 5

Each House shall be the Judge of the Elections, Returns and Qualifications of its own Members, and a Majority of each shall constitute a Quorum to do Business; but a smaller Number may adjourn from day to day, and may be authorized to compel the Attendance of absent Members, in such Manner, and under such Penalties as each House may provide.

Each House may determine the Rules of its Proceedings, punish its Members for disorderly Behavior, and, with the Concurrence of two thirds, expel a Member.

Each House shall keep a Journal of its Proceedings, and from time to time publish the same, excepting such Parts as may in their Judgment require Secrecy; and the Yeas and Nays of the Members of either House on any question shall, at the Desire of one fifth of those present, be entered on the Journal.

Neither House, during the Session of Congress, shall, without the Consent of the other, adjourn for more than three days, nor to any other Place than that in which the two Houses shall be sitting.

Section 6

The Senators and Representatives shall receive a Compensation for their Services, to be ascertained by Law, and paid out of the Treasury of the United States. They shall in all Cases, except Treason, Felony and Breach of the Peace, be privileged from Arrest during their Attendance at the Session of their respective Houses, and in going to and returning from the same; and for any Speech or Debate in either House, they shall not be questioned in any other Place.

No Senator or Representative shall, during the Time for which he was elected, be appointed to any civil Office under the Authority of the United States, which shall have been created, or the Emoluments whereof shall have been encreased during such time; and no Person holding any Office under the United States, shall be a Member of either House during his Continuance in Office.

Section 7

All Bills for raising Revenue shall originate in the House of Representatives; but the Senate may propose or concur with Amendments as on other Bills.

Every Bill which shall have passed the House of Representatives and the Senate, shall, before it become a Law, be presented to the President of the United States; If he approve he shall sign it, but if not he shall return it, with his Objections to that House in which it shall have originated, who shall enter the Objections at large on their Journal, and proceed to reconsider it. If after such Reconsideration two thirds of that House shall agree to pass the Bill, it shall be sent, together with the Objections, to the other House, by which it shall likewise be reconsidered, and if approved by two thirds of that House, it shall become a Law. But in all such Cases the Votes of both Houses shall be determined by Yeas and Nays, and the Names of the Persons voting for and against the Bill shall be entered on the Journal of each House respectively. If any Bill shall not be returned by the President within ten Days (Sundays excepted) after it shall have been presented to him, the Same shall be a Law, in like Manner as if he had signed it, unless the Congress by their Adjournment prevent its Return, in which Case it shall not be a Law.

Every Order, Resolution, or Vote to which the Concurrence of the Senate and House of Representatives may be necessary (except on a question of Adjournment) shall be presented to the President of the United States; and before the Same shall take Effect, shall be approved by him, or being disapproved by him, shall be repassed by two thirds of the Senate and House of Representatives, according to the Rules and Limitations prescribed in the Case of a Bill.

SECTION 8

The Congress shall have Power To lay and collect Taxes, Duties, Imposts and Excises, to pay the Debts and provide for the common Defence and general Welfare of the United States; but all Duties, Imposts and Excises shall be uniform throughout the United States;

To borrow Money on the credit of the United States:

To regulate Commerce with foreign Nations, and among the several States, and with the Indian Tribes;

To establish an uniform Rule of Naturalization, and uniform Laws on the subject of Bankruptcies throughout the United States;

To coin Money, regulate the Value thereof, and of foreign Coin, and fix the Standard of Weights and Measures;

To provide for the Punishment of counterfeiting the Securities and current Coin of the United States;

To establish Post Offices and post Roads;

To promote the Progress of Science and useful Arts, by securing for limited Times to Authors and Inventors the exclusive Right to their respective Writings and Discoveries;

To constitute Tribunals inferior to the supreme Court;

To define and punish Piracies and Felonies committed on the high Seas, and Offences against the Law of Nations;

To declare War, grant Letters of Marque and Reprisal, and make Rules concerning Captures on Land and Water;

To raise and support Armies, but no Appropriation of Money to that Use shall be for a longer Term than two Years;

To provide and maintain a Navy;

To make Rules for the Government and Regulation of the land and naval Forces;

To provide for calling forth the Militia to execute the Laws of the Union, suppress Insurrections and repel Invasions;

To provide for organizing, arming, and disciplining the Militia, and for governing such Part of them as may be employed in the Service of the United States, reserving to the States respectively, the Appointment of the Officers, and the Authority of training the Militia according to the discipline prescribed by Congress;

To exercise exclusive Legislation in all Cases whatsoever, over such District (not exceeding ten Miles square) as may, by Cession of particular States, and the Acceptance of Congress, become the Seat of the Government of the United States, and to exercise like Authority over all Places purchased by the Consent of the Legislature of the State in which the Same shall be, for the Erection of Forts, Magazines, Arsenals, dock-Yards, and other needful Buildings; — And

To make all Laws which shall be necessary and proper for carrying into Execution the foregoing Powers, and all other Powers vested by this Constitution in the Government of the United States, or in any Department or Officer thereof.

Section 9

The Migration or Importation of such Persons as any of the States now existing shall think proper to admit, shall not be prohibited by the Congress prior to the Year one thousand eight hundred and eight, but a Tax or duty may be imposed on such Importation, not exceeding ten dollars for each Person.

The Privilege of the Writ of Habeas Corpus shall not be suspended, unless when in Cases of Rebellion or Invasion the public Safety may require it.

No Bill of Attainder or ex post facto Law shall be passed.

No Capitation, or other direct, tax shall be laid, unless in Proportion to the Census or Enumeration herein before directed to be taken.

No Tax or Duty shall be laid on Articles exported from any State.

No Preference shall be given by any Regulation of Commerce or Revenue to the Ports of one State over those of another: nor shall Vessels bound to, or from, one State, be obliged to enter, clear, or pay Duties in another.

No Money shall be drawn from the Treasury, but in Consequence of Appropriations made by Law; and a regular Statement and Account of the Receipts and Expenditures of all public Money shall be published from time to time.

No Title of Nobility shall be granted by the United States: And no Person holding any Office of Profit or Trust under them, shall, without the Consent of the Congress, accept of any present, Emolument, Office, or Title, of any kind whatever, from any King, Prince, or foreign State.

Section 10

No State shall enter into any Treaty, Alliance, or Confederation; grant Letters of Marque and Reprisal; coin Money; emit Bills of Credit; make any Thing but gold and silver Coin a Tender in Payment of Debts; pass any Bill of Attainder, ex post facto Law, or Law impairing the Obligation of Contracts, or grant any Title of Nobility.

No State shall, without the Consent of the Congress, lay any Imposts or Duties on Imports or Exports, except what may be absolutely necessary for executing it's inspection Laws: and the net Produce of all Duties and Imposts, laid by any State on Imports or Exports, shall be for the Use of the Treasury of the United States; and all such Laws shall be subject to the Revision and Controul of the Congress.

No State shall, without the Consent of Congress, lay any Duty of Tonnage, keep Troops, or Ships of War in time of Peace, enter into any Agreement or Compact with another State, or with a foreign Power, or engage in War, unless actually invaded, or in such imminent Danger as will not admit of delay.

ARTICLE II

Section 1

The executive Power shall be vested in a President of the United States of America. He shall hold his Office during the Term of four Years, and, together with the Vice President, chosen for the same Term, be elected, as follows

Each State shall appoint, in such Manner as the Legislature thereof may direct, a Number of Electors, equal to the whole Number of Senators and Representatives to which the State may be entitled in the Congress: but no Senator or Representative, or Person holding an Office of Trust or Profit under the United States, shall be appointed an Elector.

The electors shall meet in their respective States, and vote by ballot for two Persons, of whom one at least shall not be an Inhabitant of the same State with themselves. And they shall make a List of all the Persons voted for, and of the Number of Votes for each; which List they shall sign and certify, and transmit sealed to the Seat of the Government of the United States, directed to the President of the Senate. The President of the Senate shall, in the Presence of the Senate and House of Representatives, open all the Certificates, and the Votes shall then be counted. The Person having the greatest Number of Votes shall be the President, if such Number be a Majority of the whole Number of Electors appointed; and if there be more than one who have such Majority, and have an equal Number of Votes, then the House of Representatives shall immediately chuse by Ballot one of them for President; and if no Person have a Majority, then from the five highest on the List the said House shall in like Manner chuse the President. But in chusing the President, the Votes shall be taken by States, the Representation from each State having one Vote; A quorum for this Purpose shall consist of a Member or Members from two thirds of the States, and a Majority of all the States shall be necessary to a Choice. In every Case, after the Choice of the President, the Person having the greatest Number of Votes of the Electors shall be the Vice President. But if there should remain two or more who have equal Votes, the Senate shall chuse from them by Ballot the Vice President.

The Congress may determine the Time of chusing the Electors, and the Day on which they shall give their Votes; which Day shall be the same throughout the United States.

No Person except a natural born Citizen, or a Citizen of the United States, at the time of the Adoption of this Constitution, shall be eligible to the Office of President; neither shall any Person be eligible to that Office who shall not have attained to the Age of thirty five Years, and been fourteen Years a Resident within the United States.

In Case of the Removal of the President from Office, or of his Death, Resignation or Inability to discharge the Powers and Duties of the said Office, the same shall devolve on the Vice President, and the Congress may by Law provide for the Case of Removal, Death, Resignation or Inability, both of the President and Vice President, declaring what Officer shall then act as President. and such Officer shall act accordingly, until the Disability be removed, or a President shall be elected.

The President shall, at stated Times, receive for his Services, a Compensation, which shall neither be encreased nor diminished during the Period for which he shall have been elected, and he shall not receive within that Period any other Emolument from the United States, or any of them.

Before he enter on the Execution of his Office, he shall take the following Oath or Affirmation:—"I do solemnly swear (or affirm) that I will faithfully execute the Office of President of the United States, and will to the best of my Ability, preserve, protect and defend the Constitution of the United States."

SECTION 2

The President shall be Commander in Chief of the Army and Navy of the United States, and of the Militia of the several States, when called into the actual Service of the United States; he may require the Opinion, in writing, of the principal Officer in each of the executive Departments, upon any Subject relating to the Duties of their respective Offices, and he shall have Power to grant Reprieves and Pardons for Offences against the United States, except in Cases of Impeachment.

He shall have Power, by and with the Advice and Consent of the Senate, to make Treaties, provided two thirds of the Senators present concur; and he shall nominate, and by and with the Advice and Consent of the Senate, shall appoint Ambassadors, other public Ministers and Consuls, Judges of the supreme Court, and all other Officers of the United States, whose Appointments are not herein otherwise provided for, and which shall be established by Law: but the Congress may by Law vest the Appointment of such inferior Officers, as they think proper, in the President alone, in the Courts of Law, or in the Heads of Departments.

The President shall have Power to fill up all Vacancies that may happen during the Recess of the Senate, by granting Commissions which shall expire at the End of their next Session.

SECTION 3

He shall from time to time give to the Congress Information of the State of the Union, and recommend to their Consideration such Measures as he shall judge necessary and expedient; he may, on extraordinary Occasions, convene both Houses, or either of them, and, in Case of Disagreement between them, with Respect to the Time of Adjournment, he may adjourn them to such Time as he shall think proper; he shall receive Ambassadors and other public Ministers; he shall take Care that the Laws be faithfully executed, and shall Commission all the Officers of the United States.

Section 4

The President, Vice President and all civil Officers of the United States, shall be removed from Office on Impeachment for, and Conviction of, Treason, Bribery, or other high Crimes and Misdemeanors.

ARTICLE III

Section 1

The judicial Power of the United States, shall be vested in one supreme Court, and in such inferior Courts as the Congress may from time to time ordain and establish. The Judges, both of the supreme and inferior Courts, shall hold their Offices during good Behaviour, and shall, at stated Times, receive for their Services, a Compensation, which shall not be diminished during their Continuance in Office.

Section 2

The judicial Power shall extend to all Cases, in Law and Equity, arising under this Constitution, the Laws of the United States, and Treaties made, or which shall be made, under their Authority; — to all Cases affecting Ambassadors, other public Ministers and Consuls; — to all Cases of admiralty and maritime Jurisdiction; — to Controversies to which the United States shall be a Party; — to Controversies between two or more States; — between a State and Citizens of another State; — between Citizens of different States, — between Citizens of the same State claiming Lands under Grants of different States, and between a State, or the Citizens thereof, and foreign States, Citizens or Subjects.

In all Cases affecting Ambassadors, other public Ministers and Consuls, and those in which a State shall be Party, the supreme Court shall have original Jurisdiction. In all the other Cases before mentioned, the supreme Court shall have appellate Jurisdiction, both as to Law and Fact, with such Exceptions, and under such Regulations as the Congress shall make.

The Trial of all Crimes, except in Cases of Impeachment, shall be by Jury; and such Trial shall be held in the State where the said Crimes shall have been committed; but when not committed within any State, the Trial shall be at such Place or Places as the Congress may by Law have directed.

SECTION 3

Treason against the United States, shall consist only in levying War against them, or in adhering to their Enemies, giving them Aid and Comfort. No Person shall be convicted of Treason unless on the Testimony of two Witnesses to the same overt Act, or on Confession in open Court.

The Congress shall have Power to declare the Punishment of Treason, but no Attainder of Treason shall work Corruption of Blood, or Forfeiture except during the Life of the Person attainted.

ARTICLE IV

SECTION 1

Full Faith and Credit shall be given in each State to the public Acts, Records, and judicial Proceedings of every other State. And the Congress may by general Laws prescribe the Manner in which such Acts, Records and Proceedings shall be proved, and the Effect thereof.

SECTION 2

The Citizens of each State shall be entitled to all Privileges and Immunities of Citizens in the several States.

A person charged in any State with Treason, Felony, or other Crime, who shall flee from Justice, and be found in another State, shall on Demand of the executive Authority of the State from which he fled, be delivered up, to be removed to the State having Jurisdiction of the Crime.

No Person held to Service or Labour in one State, under the Laws thereof, escaping into another, shall, in Consequence of any Law or Regulation therein, be discharged from such Service or Labour, but shall be delivered up on Claim of the Party to whom such Service or Labour may be due.

SECTION 3

New States may be admitted by the Congress into this Union; but no new State shall be formed or erected within the Jurisdiction of any other State; nor any State be formed by the Junction of two or more States, or Parts of States, without the Consent of the Legislatures of the States concerned as well as of the Congress.

The Congress shall have Power to dispose of and make all needful Rules and Regulations respecting the Territory or other Property belonging to the United States; and nothing in this Constitution shall be so construed as to Prejudice any Claims of the United States, or of any particular State.

SECTION 4

The United States shall guarantee to every State in this Union a Republican Form of Government, and shall protect each of them against Invasion; and on Application of the Legislature, or of the Executive (when the Legislature cannot be convened) against domestic Violence.

ARTICLE V

The Congress, whenever two thirds of both Houses shall deem it necessary, shall propose Amendments to this Constitution, or, on the Application of the Legislatures of two thirds of the several States, shall call a Convention for proposing Amendments, which, in either Case, shall be valid to all Intents and Purposes, as Part of this Constitution, when ratified by the Legislatures of three fourths of the several States, or by Conventions in three fourths thereof, as the one or the other Mode of Ratification may be proposed by the Congress; Provided that no Amendment which may be made prior to the Year One thousand eight hundred and eight shall in any Manner affect the first and fourth Clauses in the Ninth Section of the first Article; and that no State, without its Consent, shall be deprived of its equal Suffrage in the Senate.

ARTICLE VI

All Debts contracted and Engagements entered into, before the Adoption of this Constitution, shall be as valid against the United States under this Constitution, as under the Confederation.

This Constitution, and the Laws of the United States which shall be made in Pursuance thereof; and all Treaties made, or which shall be made, under the Authority of the United States, shall be the supreme Law of the Land; and the Judges in every State shall be bound thereby, any Thing in the Constitution or Laws of any State to the Contrary notwithstanding.

The Senators and Representatives before mentioned, and the Members of the several State Legislatures, and all executive and judicial Officers, both of the United States and of the several States, shall be bound by Oath or Affirmation, to support this Constitution; but no religious Test shall ever be required as a Qualification to any Office or public Trust under the United States.

ARTICLE VII

The Ratification of the Conventions of nine States, shall be sufficient for the Establishment of this Constitution between the States so ratifying the Same.

DONE in Convention by the Unanimous Consent of the States present the Seventeenth Day of September in the Year of our Lord one thousand seven hundred and Eighty seven and of the Independence of the United States of America the Twelfth. IN WITNESS whereof We have hereunto subscribed our Names.

G° Washington
Presid^{t} and deputy from Virginia

NEW HAMPSHIRE	John Langdon Nicholas Gilman
MASSACHUSETTS	Nathaniel Gorham Rufus King
CONNECTICUT	Wm. Saml. Johnson Roger Sherman
NEW YORK	Alexander Hamilton
NEW JERSEY	Wil: Livingston David Brearley Wm. Paterson Jona: Dayton
PENNSYLVANIA	B Franklin Thomas Mifflin Robt. Morris Geo. Clymer Thos. FitzSimons Jared Ingersoll James Wilson Gouv Morris
DELAWARE	Geo: Read Gunning Bedford jun John Dickinson Richard Bassett Jaco: Broom
MARYLAND	James McHenry Dan of St. Thos. Jenifer Danl. Carroll
VIRGINIA	John Blair — James Madison Jr.

NORTH CAROLINA	WM. BLOUNT RICHD. DOBBS SPAIGHT HU WILLIAMSON
SOUTH CAROLINA	J. RUTLEDGE CHARLES COTESWORTH PINCKNEY CHARLES PINCKNEY PIERCE BUTLER
GEORGIA	WILLIAM FEW ABR BALDWIN

Attest WILLIAM JACKSON *Secretary*

AMENDMENTS

ARTICLE I

[THE FIRST TEN ARTICLES PROPOSED 25 SEPTEMBER 1789; DECLARED IN FORCE 15 DECEMBER 1791]

Congress shall make no law respecting an establishment of religion, or prohibiting the free exercise thereof; or abridging the freedom of speech, or of the press; or the right of the people peaceably to assemble, and to petition the Government for a redress of grievances.

ARTICLE II

A well regulated Militia, being necessary to the security of a free State, the right of the people to keep and bear Arms, shall not be infringed.

ARTICLE III

No Soldier shall, in time of peace, be quartered in any house, without the consent of the Owner, nor in time of war, but in a manner to be prescribed by law.

ARTICLE IV

The right of the people to be secure in their persons, houses, papers, and effects, against unreasonable searches and seizures, shall not be violated, and no Warrants shall issue, but upon probable cause, supported by Oath or affirmation, and particularly describing the place to be searched, and the persons or things to be seized.

ARTICLE V

No person shall be held to answer for a capital, or otherwise infamous crime, unless on a presentment or indictment of a Grand Jury, except in cases arising in the land or naval forces, or in the Militia, when in actual service in time of War or public danger; nor shall any person be subject for the same offence to be twice put in jeopardy of life or limb; nor shall be compelled in any Criminal Case to be a witness against himself, nor be deprived of life, liberty, or property, without due process of law; nor shall private property be taken for public use, without just compensation.

ARTICLE VI

In all criminal prosecutions, the accused shall enjoy the right to a speedy and public trial, by an impartial jury of the State and district wherein the crime shall have been committed, which district shall have been previously ascertained by law, and to be informed of the nature and cause of the accusation; to be confronted with the witnesses against him; to have compulsory process for obtaining Witnesses in his favor, and to have the Assistance of Counsel for his defence.

ARTICLE VII

In suits at common law, where the value in controversy shall exceed twenty dollars, the right of trial by jury shall be preserved, and no fact tried by a jury shall be otherwise re-examined in any Court of the United States, than according to the rules of the common law.

ARTICLE VIII

Excessive bail shall not be required, nor excessive fines imposed, nor cruel and unusual punishments inflicted.

ARTICLE IX

The enumeration in the Constitution, of certain rights, shall not be construed to deny or disparage others retained by the people.

ARTICLE X

The powers not delegated to the United States by the Constitution, nor prohibited by it to the States, are reserved to the States respectively, or to the people.

ARTICLE XI

[PROPOSED 5 MARCH 1794; DECLARED RATIFIED 8 JANUARY 1798]

The Judicial power of the United States shall not be construed to extend to any suit in law or equity, commenced or prosecuted against one of the United States by Citizens of another State, or by Citizens or Subjects of any Foreign State.

ARTICLE XII

[PROPOSED 12 DECEMBER 1803; DECLARED RATIFIED 25 SEPTEMBER 1804]

The Electors shall meet in their respective states, and vote by ballot for President and Vice-President, one of whom, at least, shall not be an inhabitant of the same state with themselves; they shall name in their ballots the person voted for as President, and in distinct ballots the person voted for as Vice-President, and they shall make distinct lists of all persons voted for as President, and of all persons voted for as Vice-President, and of the number of votes for each, which lists they shall sign and certify, and transmit sealed to the seat of the Government of the United States, directed to the President of the Senate; — The President of the Senate shall, in the presence of the Senate and House of Representatives, open all the certificates and the votes shall then be counted; — The person having the greatest number of votes for President, shall be the President, if such number be a majority of the whole number of Electors appointed; and if no person have such majority, then from the persons having the highest numbers not exceeding three on the list of those voted for as President, the House of Representatives shall choose immediately, by ballot, the President. But in choosing the President, the votes shall be taken by states, the representation from each state having one vote; a quorum for this purpose shall consist of a member or members from two-thirds of the states, and a majority of all the states shall be necessary to a choice. And if the House of Representatives shall not choose a President whenever the right of choice shall devolve upon them, before the fourth day of March next following, then the Vice-President shall act as President, as in the case of the death or other constitutional disability of the President. The person having the greatest number of votes as Vice-President, shall be the Vice-President, if such number be a majority of the whole number of Electors appointed, and if no person have a majority, then from the two highest numbers on the list, the Senate shall choose the Vice-President; a quorum for the purpose shall consist of two-thirds of the whole number of Senators, and a majority of the whole number shall be necessary to a choice. But no person constitutionally ineligible to the office of President shall be eligible to that of Vice-President of the United States.

ARTICLE XIII

[PROPOSED 1 FEBRUARY 1865; DECLARED RATIFIED 18 DECEMBER 1865]

SECTION 1

Neither slavery nor involuntary servitude, except as a punishment for crime whereof the party shall have been duly convicted, shall exist within the United States, or any place subject to their jurisdiction.

SECTION 2

Congress shall have power to enforce this article by appropriate legislation.

ARTICLE XIV

[PROPOSED 16 JUNE 1866; DECLARED RATIFIED 28 JULY 1868]

SECTION 1

All persons born or naturalized in the United States, and subject to the jurisdiction thereof, are citizens of the United States and of the State wherein they reside. No State shall make or enforce any law which shall abridge the privileges or immunities of citizens of the United States; nor shall any State deprive any person of life, liberty, or property, without due process of law; nor deny to any person within its jurisdiction the equal protection of the laws.

SECTION 2

Representatives shall be apportioned among the several States according to their respective numbers, counting the whole number of persons in each State, excluding Indians not taxed. But when the right to vote at any election for the choice of electors for President and Vice President of the United States, Representatives in Congress, the Executive and Judicial officers of a State, or the members of the Legislature thereof, is denied to any of the male inhabitants of such State, being twenty-one years of age, and citizens of the United States, or in any way abridged, except for participation in rebellion, or other crime, the basis of representation therein shall be reduced in the proportion which the number of such male citizens shall bear to the whole number of male citizens twenty-one years of age in such State.

SECTION 3

No person shall be a Senator or Representative in Congress, or elector of President and Vice President, or hold any office, civil, or military, under the United States, or under any State, who, having previously taken an oath, as a member of Congress, or as an officer of the United States, or as a member of any State legislature, or as an executive or judicial officer of any State, to support the Constitution of the United States, shall have engaged in insurrection or rebellion against the same, or given aid or comfort to the enemies thereof. But Congress may by a vote of two-thirds of each House, remove such disability.

SECTION 4

The validity of the public debt of the United States, authorized by law, including debts incurred for payment of pensions and bounties for services in suppressing insurrection or rebellion, shall not be questioned. But neither the United States nor any State shall assume or pay any debt or obligation incurred in aid of insurrection or rebellion against the United States, or any claim for the loss or emancipation of any slave; but all such debts, obligations and claims shall be held illegal and void.

SECTION 5

The Congress shall have power to enforce, by appropriate legislation, the provisions of this article.

ARTICLE XV

[PROPOSED 27 FEBRUARY 1869; DECLARED RATIFIED 30 MARCH 1870]

SECTION 1

The right of citizens of the United States to vote shall not be denied or abridged by the United States or by any State on account of race, color, or previous condition of servitude.

SECTION 2

The Congress shall have power to enforce this article by appropriate legislation.

ARTICLE XVI

[PROPOSED 12 JULY 1909; DECLARED RATIFIED 25 FEBRUARY 1913]

The Congress shall have power to lay and collect taxes on incomes, from whatever source derived, without apportionment among the several States, and without regard to any census or enumeration.

ARTICLE XVII

[PROPOSED 16 MAY 1912; DECLARED RATIFIED 31 MAY 1913]

The Senate of the United States shall be composed of two senators from each State, elected by the people thereof, for six years; and each Senator shall have one vote. The electors in each State shall have the qualifications requisite for electors of the most numerous branch of the State legislature.

When vacancies happen in the representation of any State in the Senate, the executive authority of such State shall issue writs of election to fill such vacancies: PROVIDED, That the legislature of any State may empower the executive thereof to make temporary appointments until the people fill the vacancies by election as the legislature may direct.

This amendment shall not be so construed as to affect the election or term of any senator chosen before it becomes valid as part of the Constitution.

ARTICLE XVIII

[PROPOSED 18 DECEMBER 1917; DECLARED RATIFIED 29 JANUARY 1919]

After one year from the ratification of this article, the manufacture, sale, or transportation of intoxicating liquors within, the importation thereof into, or the exportation thereof from the United States and all territory subject to the jurisdiction thereof for beverage purposes is hereby prohibited.

The Congress and the several States shall have concurrent power to enforce this article by appropriate legislation.

This article shall be inoperative unless it shall have been ratified as an amendment to the Constitution by the legislatures of the several States, as provided in the Constitution, within seven years from the date of the submission hereof to the States by the Congress.

ARTICLE XIX

[PROPOSED 4 JUNE 1919; DECLARED RATIFIED 26 AUGUST 1920]

The right of citizens of the United States to vote shall not be denied or abridged by the United States or by any States on account of sex.

The Congress shall have power, by appropriate legislation, to enforce the provisions of this article.

ARTICLE XX

[PROPOSED 2 MARCH 1932; DECLARED RATIFIED 6 FEBRUARY 1933]

Section 1

The terms of the President and Vice-President shall end at noon on the twentieth day of January, and the terms of Senators and Representatives at noon on the third day of January, of the years in which such terms would have ended if this article had not been ratified; and the terms of their successors shall then begin.

Section 2

The Congress shall assemble at least once in every year, and such meeting shall begin at noon on the third day of January, unless they shall by law appoint a different day.

Section 3

If, at the time fixed for the beginning of the term of the President, the President-elect shall have died, the Vice-President-elect shall become President. If a President shall not have been chosen before the time fixed for the beginning of his term, or if the President-elect shall have failed to qualify, then the Vice-President-elect shall act as President until a President shall have qualified; and the Congress may by law provide for the case wherein neither a President-elect nor a Vice-President-elect shall have qualified, declaring who shall then act as President, or the manner in which one who is to act shall be selected, and such person shall act accordingly until a President or Vice-President shall have qualified.

Section 4

The Congress may by law provide for the case of the death of any of the persons from whom the House of Representatives may choose a President whenever the right of choice shall have devolved upon them, and for the case of the death of any of the persons from whom the Senate may choose a Vice-President whenever the right of choice shall have devolved upon them.

SECTION 5

Sections 1 and 2 shall take effect on the 15th day of October following the ratification of this article.

SECTION 6

This article shall be inoperative unless it shall have been ratified as an amendment to the Constitution by the legislatures of three-fourths of the several States within seven years from the date of its submission.

ARTICLE XXI

[PROPOSED 20 FEBRUARY 1933; ADOPTED 5 DECEMBER 1933]

SECTION 1

The eighteenth article of amendment to the Constitution of the United States is hereby repealed.

SECTION 2

The transportation or importation into any State, Territory or possession of the United States for delivery or use therein of intoxicating liquors, in violation of the laws thereof, is hereby prohibited.

SECTION 3

This article shall be inoperative unless it shall have been ratified as an amendment to the Constitution by convention in the several States, as provided in the Constitution, within seven years from the date of the submission hereof to the States by the Congress.

ARTICLE XXII

[PROPOSED 2 JUNE 1924; RATIFICATION PENDING]

SECTION 1

The Congress shall have power to limit, regulate, and prohibit the labor of persons under eighteen years of age.

SECTION 2

The power of the several States is unimpaired by this article except that the operation of State laws shall be suspended to the extent necessary to give effect to legislation enacted by the Congress.

INDEX

A.B.C. Conference, 508
A.B.C. powers, 442
ABC–1 Staff agreement, 661
Abbey, Edwin, 301
Abda command, 709
Abrams, Jacob, 558
Acheson, Dean, 786, 819
Act for Preventing the Transportation of Malefactors (1788), 184–5
Act of Havana, 653
Adair *v.* United States, 170, 620
Adams, Andy, 92–3
Adams, Charles F., 63, 69, 70, 228
Adams, Charles F., Jr., 116
Adams, Henry, 58, 66–7, 191–2, 250, 264–5, 283, 296, 297, 303, 579, 796
Adams, John Quincy, 325
Adams, Samuel Hopkins, 397
Adamson Law (1916), 168, 438
Addams, Jane, 163, 180, 369
Adjusted Compensation Act, 524–5
Adkins case, 620
Agassiz, Louis, 183, 269
Agricultural Adjustment Act (1938), 621–2
Agricultural Adjustment Administration (A.A.A.), 591–3, 616
Agricultural Marketing Act (1929), 535
Agriculture, 7, 14, 94, 98, 99, 111, 123, 124, 126, 146, 151, 314; agrarian revolt, 207–13; agricultural revolution, 189–91; collapse in twenties, 534–6; crop systems, 23–5; farm-land values, 23–5; farm problem, 198–207; mechanization, 191–4; New Deal legislation, 590–95, 621–2; scientific, 194–8; World War II, 688–9
Agriculture, Dept. of, 97, 195–6, 200
Aguinaldo, Emilio, 334, 336, 338
Air Forces, U.S., 482–3, 671, 674–5, 685, 701–2, 731–4
Akerman, Amos T., 59
Alabama, U.S.S., 63
Alabama Midlands case (1897), 119
Alaska, 60, 342, 413
Albemarle, N.C., 28
Alcock, John, 128
Aldrich, Nelson W., 231, 234, 411, 413
Aldrich, Thomas Bailey, 187 n.
Aldrich-Vreeland Bill, 432
Aleutian Islands, 752
Alexander, Gen. Sir Harold, 718–20, 721–2
Algeciras Conference, 401
Alien Registration Act, 789
Allied Control Council, 806
Altgeld, John P., 156, 163, 183, 382
Aluminum, 683
Aluminum Company of America, 533
Amalgamated Copper Co., 138
Amalgamated Garment Workers, 159
America First Committee, 654
American Association for the Advancement of Science, 398
American Bankers Association, 530
American Farm Bureau Federation, 212
American Farmer, 195
American Federation of Labor (A.F. of L.), 147, 157–9, 600, 601–2, 687, 780, 782
American Railway Union, 162–3
American Sugar Refining Co., 138
American Telephone and Telegraph Co., 140
American Tobacco Co., 138, 393
Ames, Oakes, 72
Amnesty Act (1872), 54
Anderson, Gen. Richard H., 15
Anderson, Sherwood, 140–41, 564
Andrews, Sidney, 13
Antin, Mary, 183

Anti-Saloon League, 377
Anti-submarine warfare, 482–3, 693, 699–706, 735–6
Anti-trust laws, 143, 215, 388–9, 391–2, 394, 596
Anzio beachhead, 728
Appleby, George, 192
Appleby, John, 129
Arabic, S.S., 458
Architecture, 295–300
Aristophanes, 6
Army, U.S., 671–7
Arnold, Gen. H. H., 671
Arthur, Chester A., 83, 84, 214, 216, 219, 220, 221–5
Arts, 269, 300–304, 571–3
Ascham, Roger, 785
Asquith, Lord, 455
Astronomy, 576–7
Atlanta, Ga., 13, 15, 23
Atlantic, Battle of, 698–706
Atlantic and Pacific Railroad, 108
Atlantic Charter, 660, 814
Atlantic Pact, 827
Atomic bomb, 694–7, 775–6, 796–7, 823
Atomic energy, 577, 818–21
Atomic Energy Commission, 791, 820
Atomic Research Committee, 695
Attlee, Clement, 806
Auschwitz, 766
Australian ballot, 104, 381
Austria, 445, 502, 609
Automobiles, 150, 551–2, 681, 685
Aviation, 523–4, 685; *see also* Air Forces, U.S.
Aycock, Charles B., 305, 382

Babcock, Orville, 61, 73
Babcock, Stephen M., 197
Bacon Resolution, 347
Baer, George F., 164
Bailey, L. H., 310
Bailey *v.* Drexel Furniture Co. (1922), 169 n.
Baker, Newton D., 383, 429, 478
Bakunin, M. I., 154
Bancroft, H. H., 87
Bank holiday, 587
Bankhead Cotton Control Act (1934), 591
Bankhead-Jones Farm Tenant Act, 621
Banking, 7, 9–10, 14, 33, 40, 47, 57, 71, 206–7, 209, 211, 241, 250, 252, 431–5
Banks, Gen. N. P., 32
Barbey, Adm. Daniel E., 754, 771, 774
Barkley, Alben, 792
Barnard, Henry, 305, 308
Barron *v.* Baltimore, 561
Baruch, Bernard, 471, 820
Bastogne, 750
Bataan, 708
Baxter, James P., 691–2
Bayard, Thomas F., 321
Bayly, Sir Lewis, 482
Beach, Moses Yale, 361
Beard, Charles and Mary, 124–5
Beecher, Henry Ward, 276
Belgium, 446, 449
Belknap, William W., 59, 73–4
Bell, Alexander Graham, 128, 183
Bellamy, Edward, 143, 255, 369
Belsen, 766
Beneš, Eduard, 639
Benét, S. V., 205, 571
Bennett, James Gordon, 183, 290, 291
Benson, William S., 481
Berger, Victor, 476
Bering Sea controversy, 320
Berkeley, George, Bishop, 783
Berliner, Elilie, 183
Bernstorff, Count von, 448, 463
Bessemer, Henry, 127, 132
Bethmann-Hollweg, Moritz von, 463
Beveridge, Albert J., 395, 412, 413
Biddle, Francis, 788
Biddle, George, 573
Bigelow, John, 58
Bikini Lagoon, 819
Bill of Rights, 560–62
Bimetallists, 248

Bingham, John, 44
Bishop, J. B., 392n.
Bismarck, Otto von, 332
Bitter, Karl, 183, 304
Bituminous Coal Act, 616, 621
Black, Hugo, 619, 623
Black codes, 17–18
Black-Connery Bill, 599
Black Friday (24 Sept. 1869), 66
Blaine, James G., 76, 214, 216–17, 219, 225–6, 231, 232, 316, 318–19, 320
Blanchard, Jonathan, 96
Bland, Dick, 251, 256, 258, 261
Bland-Allison Silver Act (1878), 221, 246
Boer War, 321
Bohr, Niels, 694, 696
Bolshevism, 491
Bonneville Dam, 605
Bonus, veterans', 524–5
Booth, John Wilkes, 34
Borah, William E., 646–7
Borie, Adolph E., 59
Bougainville, 753–4
Boutwell, George S., 59, 64, 67
Bowles, Samuel, 291–2
Bradford, Roark, 122
Bradley, Joseph P., 67, 77–8
Bradley, Gen. Omar N., 672, 747
Bragg, E. S., 225
Brandeis, Louis D., 172, 429, 557, 617
Brazil, 702–3
Brest-Litovsk negotiations, 483
Bretton Woods Conference, 801
Briand, Aristide, 499
Bricker, John, 761
Bridgman, Percy W., 577
Bristow, Benjamin H., 59, 73
Broadcasting stations, 552
Bromfield, Louis, 140
Brookings Institution, 598
Brooks, James, 72
Brown, Arthur, 128
Brown, Joseph E., 29
Brush, Charles, 126
Bryan, Charles W., 516
Bryan, William J., 159, 186, 207, 240, 242, 248–9, 251, 255, 338, 340–41, 360, 380, 393, 401, 409, 422–3, 426, 433–4, 438–9, 449, 452, 457, 499, 555, 588; campaign of 1896, 256–65
Bryant, William Cullen, 278, 289, 291
Bryce, James, 362, 365, 382, 401, 414, 450
Buchanan, James, 33, 214
Buchenwald, 766
Buckner, Gen. Simon B., 775
Budd, Ralph, 688
Buffalo, 90, 91
Bulgaria, 744–5
Bulge, Battle of, 750–51
Bunau-Varilla, Philippe, 403, 404
Burbank, Luther, 197
Burchard, Rev. S. D., 226
Burgess, John W., 42, 323
Burke-Wadsworth Bill, 653
Burleson, A. S., 429
Burma, 709, 768–9, 775
Burnham, Daniel, 297, 299
Burroughs, William S., 128
Bush, Vannevar, 672, 692–3, 695, 696
Business, 10–11, 106, 153, 166, 189, 190, 209, 218, 242, 243, 251, 257, 259, 261, 263, 264, 324, 330, 357, 371, 435–8, 440, 459
Bussey, Benjamin, 195
Butler, Benjamin, 44, 61, 64
Butler, Nicholas Murray, 309
Butler, Pierce, 617
Byrd, Harry F., 761
Byrnes, James F., 619, 682, 761, 807

Cabet, Étienne, 154
Cable, 7, 9
Calamity Jane, 90
Caldwell, Erskine, 568
Calhoun, John C., 30
California alien land laws, 186
California Workingmen's party, 185
Calles, Plutarco E., 443, 509
Cameron, Don, 69, 74
Canada, 62, 63, 182, 415, 448, 595, 645, 698–9

Canadian Pacific Railway, 109, 110
Canal Zone, 404–5
Cannon, Joseph G., 411, 413
Cardozo, Benjamin N., 611
Carey Act (1894), 97, 197, 400
Carleton, Mark Alfred, 196–7
Carlisle, John G., 245–6, 251–2
Carnegie, Andrew, 28, 132–4, 183, 312–13, 363
Carnegie Steel Co., 158, 162
Carpet-baggers, 42, 43, 46 ff., 52, 54, 55
Carranza, August V., 442, 443
Carver, George Washington, 197
Casablanca Conference, 721–2
Case bill, 781
Cassino, 729
Castle, William R., Jr., 511
Castro, Gen. Cipriano, 405
Cather, Willa, 205, 284
Catholicism, 274, 440, 443
Cattle industry, 90–95, 97
Censorship, 554, 555
Centennial Exposition (1876), 75, 128, 297–8
Central Pacific Railroad, 106, 107, 108, 112, 113, 114, 115, 185
Cervera y Topete, Adm. Pascual, 332, 333
Chadwick, Sir James, 696
Chamberlain, Joseph, 321
Chamberlain, Neville, 639–40, 648
Chandler, Zachary, 68, 77
Channing, W. E., 277, 587
Charleston, S. C., 13, 23
Chase, Salmon P., 45, 49–50, 69, 70
Chase, Samuel, 617
Chase, Stuart, 200
Chennault, Gen. Claire L., 768
Cherbourg, 740–41
Chiang Kai-shek, 660, 663, 768–9, 824
Chicago, Burlington & Quincy R. R. *v.* Iowa, 117
Chicago, Milwaukee & St. Paul R. R. *v.* Minnesota, 118
Child labor, 599, 623
China, 414–15, 439, 503–8, 637–8, 660–61, 663, 682; immigration from, 185–6, 231; Open Door policy, 350–53, 504–6
China Incident, 508
Chinese Exclusion Act (1882), 155, 185
Chisholm Trail, 91
Chivington, Colonel, 82
Church, A. D., 192
Churchill, Winston, 115
Churchill, Winston S., 640, 650–51, 653, 659, 660, 668–9, 718, 724, 730, 743, 765, 768, 804, 821, 822, 827
Cincinnati Prison Conference, 376
Cities, growth of, 11
Civil Rights Act, 51
Civil Rights Cases (1883), 51
Civil Service Commission, 223, 233
Civil Service reform, 64, 68–9, 227
Civil Service Reform League, 233
Civil War, cost, 3–5; Northern prosperity, 8–12; objectives, 1–3; revolutionary developments, 5–8; Southern devastation, 12–15; *see also* Reconstruction
Civil Works Administration, 607
Civilian Conservation Corps (C.C.C.), 603, 606
Clarendon Convention, 63
Clark, Bennett, 763
Clark, Champ, 416, 422
Clark, Adm. Joseph J., 758
Clark, Gen. Mark W., 726–7
Clay, Gen. Lucius, 808, 810–11
Clayton Anti-trust Act (1914), 167, 436–7
Clayton-Bulwer Treaty, 401
Clemenceau, Georges, 490, 491
Cleveland, Grover, 84, 94, 143, 145, 162–3, 169, 187, 214, 215, 218, 240 ff., 250–53, 255, 256–7, 316 ff., 319 ff., 324, 326, 327, 398; administration, 225–35
Clews, Henry, 71, 152–3
Coal strike (1902), 150, 164–5
Cobb, Frank I., 292, 466–7
Cockburn, Sir Alexander, 64

Cockran, Bourke, 251
Coeur d'Alene strike, 250
Coinage Act (1873), 245
Coker, David A., 197
Colby, Bainbridge, 613
Cold war, 821–7
Colfax, Schuyler, 56, 72
Collective bargaining, 154, 599, 601
Collective security, 632, 640
Collector *v*. Day, 620
Colombia, 402–5, 438
Colonial system, 343–50
Colorado Fuel and Iron Company, 150
Columbia, S. C., 13, 15, 23, 28, 54, 55
Combinations, 531–4
Combined Chiefs of Staff, 667, 672, 710, 719, 737
Command of the Army Act, 44
Commerce, Department of, 388, 391
Commission of Economy and Efficiency, 413
Commission plan, 384
Committee for Industrial Organization, *see* Congress of Industrial Organizations
Committee on Industrial Relations, 436
Committee on Public Information, 473–4
Committee to Defend America by Aiding the Allies, 654
Commodity Credit Corporation, 536, 594
Commons, John R., 178
Communism, 637, 790, 796, 804, 824–5
Communist Labor party, 556
Compton, A. H., 696
Comstock Lode, 86–7
Conant, James B., 672, 693
Confederacy, 4, 5
Conference for Progressive Political Action, 517
Congress of Industrial Organizations (C.I.O.), 149, 160, 601–2, 622, 687, 762, 780, 782
Conkling, Roscoe, 64, 219, 220–21, 222, 223, 225
Conscription, *see* Draft
Conservation, 191, 397–400, 412–13, 603–5
Constitution, U.S., 142, 150, 341–2; amendments, 6, 7, 37 ff., 43, 45, 49 ff., 116, 141, 142, 170, 171, 375, 378, 414, 525–7; and Reconstruction, 49–52
Contract Labor law (1864), 155
Cooke, Jay, and Co., 71, 75
Coolidge, Calvin, 213, 214, 496, 503, 512, 514, 516–18, 524, 529, 533, 535, 641
Cooper, Peter, 128, 131, 143, 362
Coppage *v*. Kansas, 620
Coral Sea, Battle of, 712–13
Corn Products Refining Company, 436
Cornell, Alonzo B., 220
Cornell University, 309
Corporations, 135–6
Corporations, Bureau of, 391
Corregidor, 708, 709
Corwin, E. S., 788
Cotton, 25–6, 29, 193, 194, 451, 591–2
Cotton tax, 19, 21
Council of Foreign Ministers, 806, 808–9
Council of National Defense, 460, 469
Council-manager plan, 384
Couzens, James, 533
Cox, Jacob D., 59, 69, 70
Cox, James, 513–14
Coxey, Jacob, 253–4
Cram, Ralph Adams, 299
Crane, Stephen, 283
Credit, 537–8
Crédit Mobilier, 48, 72, 106
Creel, George, 473–4, 488
Creswell, J. A. J., 59
Crete, 659
Cripple Creek coal strike (1904), 160
Cripps, Sir Stafford, 802
Croly, Herbert, 294, 361

Cromwell, William N., 402, 403
Crop-lien system, 23–5
Crowder, Enoch H., 344
Cuba, 60–61, 325, 328, 329, 330–34, 343–5, 346, 406, 595
Culberson, Charles A., 382
Culin, Sergeant, 741
Cullom Committee (1886), 119
Cummings *v.* Missouri, 51
Cummins, Albert, 382
Cunningham, Adm. Sir Andrew, 719
Currency, *see* Money
Curtis, Benjamin R., 45
Curtis, George W., 225, 294
Curtis, Gen. William, 68
Curtiss, Glenn, 128
Cushing, Caleb, 315
Custer, Gen. George, 83
Czechoslovakia, 639–40, 808

Dachau, 766
Dakota Territory, 90, 92, 98, 101
Daladier, Édouard, 640
Damrosch, Walter, 183
Dan, Adam, 183n.
Dana, Charles A., 290
Daniels, Josephus, 429, 480
Darlan, Adm. Jean, 721
Darrow Committee, 598
Darwin, Charles, 269, 270
Darwinism, 274–5, 276, 277
Daugherty, Harry, 514, 515–16
Davidson College, 305
Davis, David, 70, 77
Davis, Jefferson, 5, 30, 33–4, 41
Davis, John W., 516, 526, 613
Davis, Norman, 497
Dawes, Charles G., 501
Dawes Act (1887), 82, 84, 229–30, 378
Dayton trial, 555
Death rates, 578
De Bow, J. D. B., 195
Debs, Eugene V., 162–4, 390, 423, 476, 514
Deere, John, 192
Defense, Department of, 792
Deflation, 113, 238
De Gaulle, Gen. Charles, 721
De Jonge *v.* Oregon, 560
Delano, Columbus, 59
De Leon, Daniel, 183
De Mille, Cecil B., 553
Democracy, 2, 631
Democratic party, 7 n., 8, 33, 34, 40, 45, 48, 52, 53, 55–7, 65, 67, 71, 76–8, 206–7, 211, 218–21, 225–7, 231–3, 235, 236–7, 240–42, 247, 251–2, 256–8, 259, 261, 263–5, 323–4, 331, 339, 340–41, 349, 393, 409, 414, 421–4, 425–6, 429, 435, 438, 444, 456, 459–60, 488, 513, 516–19, 526–7, 530, 542, 580–82, 612–15, 626, 655–7, 759–62, 791–4
Dempster, A. J., 694
Denby, Edwin, 515
Denmark, 346, 649
Dennett, Tyler, 408
Dependent Pension Bill, 229
Deportation, 557
Depressions, 75, 525, 536–46, 606–8
Destroyer transfer, 653, 672
Devers, Gen. Jacob L., 748, 765
Dewey, George, 331–2, 334
Dewey, John, 270 ff., 308, 311
Dewey, Thomas E., 654, 760–62, 792–3
Diaz, Porfirio, 439–40
Dickinson, Emily, 279
Dingley tariff (1897), 319, 341
Direct primary, 381
Disability Pension Act (1890), 233
Disney, Walt, 553
Displaced Persons, 799–800
Dixiecrat party, 793
Dodge, Gen. G. M., 106, 107
Doenitz, Adm. Karl, 684, 693, 699, 703–5, 706
Doheny, Edward L., 515
Doherty, Henry L., 533
Dole, Sanford B., 317
Dollar diplomacy, 415, 439
Domagk, Gerhard, 578
Dominican Republic, 439

Donne, John, 640
Donnelly, Ignatius, 69, 239, 240–41
Donovan, Maj. Gen. W. J., 679
Doolittle, Gen. James H., 710
Dorset, Marion, 197
Dos Passos, John, 565, 571
Douglas, Stephen A., 106
Douglas, William O., 619, 761, 792
Douglass, Frederick, 16
Draft, 653, 659–60, 673–4
Drago doctrine, 406
Draper, John William, 275
Dreiser, Theodore, 283, 565
Drew, Daniel, 74
Droughts, 603–4
Drugs, government supervision of, 397
Dry farming, 98
Dumbarton Oaks Conference, 814
Dunkirk, 649–50, 651
Dunne, Finley P., 339, 391 n.
Durham, N. C., 23, 28
Duryea, Charles, 127
Dwight, John Sullivan, 266

Eakins, Thomas, 295, 302, 572, 573
East, 9, 10, 80, 86, 94, 95, 100, 114, 118, 125, 150, 151, 189, 204, 207, 212, 237, 239, 249, 264
Eastman, George, 129
Eastman, Joseph B., 522
Eastport, Me., 62
Eden, Anthony, 815
Edison, Thomas A., 126 ff., 553
Edman Act (1898), 168
Edmunds, George F., 143
Education, 15, 19, 20–21, 48, 304–13, 348, 784–5
Eggleston, George Cary, 13
Eichelberger, Gen. R. L., 718
Eighteenth Amendment, 378, 525–7
Einstein, Albert, 576, 695, 821
Eisenhower, Gen. Dwight D., 669, 672, 719, 721, 736–8, 743, 745, 746, 748, 749, 763–5, 792
Eliot, Charles W., 152, 309, 399
Eliot, T. S., 567
Elkins Act, 395
Emancipation, 2, 6, 16, 21
Embargoes, 452, 462, 637, 638, 643–4, 661–2
Emergency Banking Law (1933), 587
Emergency Fleet Corporation, 470
Emerson, Ralph Waldo, 267, 278
Emma Mine swindle, 73
Employers' Liability Act (1908), 168
Engemann, Colonel, 764
Engineers, U.S.A., 676–7
Engle, Paul, 571
Ericson, John, 183
Erosion, 604
Esch-Cummins Transportation Act, 524
Espionage Act (1917), 476
Espionage and Sedition Acts, 557–8
Ethiopia, 636
European Advisory Commission, 805–6
Evans, Oliver, 126
Evans, Adm. Robley D., 331
Evarts, William M., 45, 220
Evening Post, Chicago, 171
Evening Post, N. Y., 289
Evolution, 269, 272, 274, 555
Ezekiel, Mordecai, 590

Fagan, Mark, 383
Fair Employment Practices Committee, 786–7
Fair Labor Standards Act, 623
Fairbank, John, 353
Fall, Albert B., 515
Faraday, Michael, 126
Farley, James A., 613, 615, 761
Farm Relief and Inflation Act (1933), 588
Farm Security Administration, 621
Farmers' Alliances, 210–12
Farmers' Non-Partisan League, 212
Farming, *see* Agriculture
Farrell, James, 565
Farrell, Gen. T. F., 696
Faulkner, William, 568

Federal Aid Road Act, 438
Federal Arts Project, 573
Federal Children's Bureau, 413
Federal Council of Churches, 165–6
Federal Deposit Insurance Corporation, 589
Federal Emergency Relief Administration, 606
Federal Farm Board, 535–6, 541
Federal Farm Credit Administration, 589
Federal Farm Loan Acts, 435, 594
Federal Housing Administration, 608
Federal Land Banks, 536
Federal Reserve Act (1913), 434–5
Federal Reserve system, 434–5, 537, 587, 589, 590
Federal Trade Commission, 533, 590, 598, 606
Federal Trade Commission Act, 436
Federal Water Power Commission, 606
Fenians, 60, 62
Fenton, Reuben, 69
Ferber, Edna, 102–3
Fessenden, William P., 37, 45
Fetterman, W. J., 82
Field, Cyrus, 128
Field, Stephen D., 127
Field, Stephen J., 253
Fifteenth Amendment, 6, 7, 18, 45, 50 ff.
Filipino Insurrection, 347
Fillmore, Millard, 214
Finance, 7, 8, 202, 251, 453, 472–3
Finland, 648–9
Finlay, Dr. Carlos, 343
Fish, Hamilton (1808–93), 59–63
Fish, Hamilton (1888–), 657, 763
Fisk, Jim, 66
Fiske, John, 276
Fitzhugh, George, 15
Fleming, W. L., 53
Fletcher, Rear Adm. F. J., 713–15
Florida, C.S.S., 63
Foch, Ferdinand, 484, 486, 487
Food Administration, 471–2
Foods, government supervision of, 396–7
Foraker Act, 345
Forbes, Col. Charles R., 515
Force Acts of 1870, 53, 65, 219
Ford, Henry, 127, 147
Ford Motor Company, 622
Fordney-McCumber tariff, 529
Forest Reserve Act (1891), 398
Fosdick, Raymond, 576
Four Brotherhoods, 159
Four freedoms, 657
Four Power Treaty, 506–7
Fourier, F. M. C., 154
Fourteen Points, 475–6, 487, 490
Fourteenth Amendment, 6, 7, 18, 37, 39–40, 41 ff., 49 ff., 116, 117, 141, 142, 170, 171
France, 60, 75, 407–8, 529, 637, 639–40, 646–50, 652, 665; *see also* World War I; World War II
Franco-Prussian War, 75
Frankfurter, Felix, 172, 590, 619
Franklin, Benjamin, 126, 361, 363
Franks, Sir Oliver, 803
Franz, Ferdinand, Archduke, 445
Free silver, 241, 245, 246, 257–61
Freedmen, 16–23
Freedmen's Bank, 73
Freedmen's Bureau, 15, 18–19, 20, 305
Freedmen's Bureau Bill (1866), 39, 51
Freight rates, 113–15, 119
Frémont, John C., 56
French, Daniel Chester, 303
French Indo-China, 661, 662
Frick, Henry, 134, 162
Friedeburg, Adm. H. G. von, 767
Froebel, Friedrich, 308
Froude, James A., 405
Fuller, George, 302
Fuller, Melville W., 342

Gage, Lyman, 432
Gallup polls, 638, 654, 662

Galvani, Luigi, 126
Garfield, Harry A., 472
Garfield, James A., 216, 221–2, 319
Garland, Hamlin, 100, 198, 204, 205, 208–9, 284, 306
Garland, Richard, 198
Garland case, 51
Garrison, L. M., 429
Gary, Elbert, 134
Gary, Joseph E., 156
Gas Ring, 48, 74
Gastonia, N. C., 28
Gay, Edwin F., 537–8
General Electric Company, 533
General Managers' Association of Railroads, 162
General Motors Corporation, 602
Geneva, 63–4
Geneva Disarmament Conference, 635
George, Henry, 143, 240, 368
George, Milton, 210
George, Walter F., 143, 626
Germany, 75, 133, 405–8, 634, 635–6, 637, 639–40; postwar, 805–12; *see also* World War I; World War II
Geronimo, 83
GI Bill of Rights, 690, 779, 785
Gilbert, Cass, 299
Gilbert Islands, 754–5
Gilman, Daniel Coit, 309, 311
Giraud, Gen. Henri, 721
Gitlow *v.* New York, 562
Gladstone, W. E., 63, 274
Glasgow, Ellen, 205, 286
Glass, Carter, 433–4
Glass-Steagall Banking Act (1933), 589
Glidden, J. F., 97
Godkin, E. L., 69, 183, 268, 293–4, 365
Goebbels, Joseph Paul, 650, 749
Goering, Hermann, 685
Goethals, George W., 405
Gold Act (1900), 431
Gold standard, 7, 243, 247, 249, 258, 259, 260, 587–8
Gompers, Samuel, 157–8, 159, 169, 183, 423, 437
Good Roads Bill, 254
Goodhue, Bertram, 300
Good-neighbor policy, 510–11, 644–5
Goodyear, Charles, 126
Gordon, Gen. J. B., 29
Gore-McLemore Resolutions, 458
Gorgas, William C., 343, 405
Gould, Jay, 66, 138, 155
Grady, Henry, 23, 26–7
Grain and Cotton Stabilization Corporations, 536
Grand Army of the Republic, 228–9, 231, 233
Grand Coulee Dam, 400, 605
Granger cases, 116–18
Granger movement, 207, 208–10, 211, 212
Grant, Ulysses S., 33, 36, 45, 50–51, 219, 222–3, 722; administrative scandals, 71–6; character, 58–60; domestic politics, 64–8; election, 56–7; foreign policy, 60–64; and Liberal Republican movement, 69–71
Great Britain, 61, 62–4, 75, 133, 249, 401–2, 405–6, 529, 531, 637, 639–40, 646–53, 659, 682–3, 692, 802–3; *see also* World War I; World War II
Great Northern Railway, 101, 109, 110
Greater East Asia Co-prosperity Sphere, 660
Greece, 658–9, 825–6
Greeley, Horace, 69, 70–71, 289–90, 291
Green, William, 159
Greenbacks, 7, 56, 57, 65–7, 221, 239, 243, 244
Greenhalge, Governor, 254
Greenland, 658
Greer, U.S.S., 660, 698
Gresham, Walter Q., 318
Grew, Joseph, 638, 776
Grey, Sir Edward, 441, 459
Grey, Zane, 106

Griffith, D. W., 553
Grimes, James W., 45, 71–2
Gromyko, Andrei, 820
Groves, Gen. L. R., 696
Grundy, Joseph R., 513, 515
Guadalcanal, 716–17
Guam, 346
Guffey Coal Act, 599

Hadley, A. N., 129
Hague, The, 401, 405–6, 498
Hague *v.* C.I.O., 561
Haig, Gen. Douglas, 484
Haile Selassie, 636, 659
Haiti, 439, 510
Hale, Edward Everett, 277
Hall, G. Stanley, 310
Halliday, Ben, 82
Halliday's Overland Stage, 106
Halsey, Adm. William F., 710, 717, 718, 752, 754, 770–73
Hammer *v.* Dagenhart, 619, 623
Hampton, Wade, 19, 54, 55, 239
Hancock, W. S., 221
Hanford, Wash., 696
Hanna, Mark, 257–8, 263, 330, 383, 386 n., 392, 393, 402
Hansen, Niels Ebbesen, 197
Hard money, 56, 57
Harding, W. G., 214, 496, 497, 506, 512, 513–16, 520, 529
Harlan, John M., 3, 120, 142–5, 170 n., 394
Harlan County, Kentucky, 150, 165
Harmon, Judson, 422
Harper, W. R., 310
Harper's Weekly, 294
Harriman, E. H., 390
Harriman group, 138–9
Harris, Sir Arthur, 731
Harris, William T., 270
Harrison, Benjamin, 102, 143, 145, 214, 216, 231–3, 240, 241, 317, 319, 398
Harrison, Francis B., 349
Hart, Adm. Thomas C., 708
Harvard Law School, 273–4
Harvard University, 309
Harvey, George, 421–2
Hatch Act (1887), 196; (1939), 625–6
Havana, Act of, 653
Hawaii, 316, 346–7; Republic of, 317, 342
Hawes-Cutting Act (1932), 349
Hawley-Smoot tariff, 530, 535, 541
Hay, John, 283, 335, 350–52, 401–4, 407
Hay-Pauncefote Treaty, 441
Hayes, Rutherford B., 54, 55, 76–8, 82, 84, 101, 214, 216, 218, 219–21
Haymarket riot, 156, 162–3
Hearst, William Randolph, 291, 292–3, 324, 422
Heilprin, Michael, 183
Heineman, Capt. P. R., 704
Hemingway, Ernest, 571
Henderson, John B., 45
Henderson, Leon, 689
Hendricks, B. J., 370
Henri, Robert, 302
Henry, Joseph, 126
Henry Street Settlement, 180, 372
Hepburn Act (1906), 396
Hepburn Committee of N. Y., 137–8
Herald, N. Y., 290
Herbart, J. F., 308
Herbert, George, 367
Herndon *v.* Lowry, 560–61
Herrick, Robert, 283–4
Herrin massacre, 165
Hertling, Chancellor, 485
Hewitt, Abram S., 77–8, 132–4
Hewitt, Rear Adm. H. K., 720–21, 726–7
Hickok, Wild Bill, 90
Hildreth, Richard, 129
Hill, Adm. Harry W., 755
Hill, James J., 108, 109–10, 138, 183, 259, 392 n.
Hill group, 138–40
Hindenburg, F. M. Paul von, 463, 483, 635
Hines Embargo, 660

Hippisley, Alfred E., 351
Hirohito, Emperor, 722 n., 776
Hiroshima, 776, 819
Historical romance, 568–9
Hitler, Adolf, 633, 635, 639, 641, 646–8, 650, 652, 658–9, 661, 665, 667, 668, 691, 693, 703, 705, 722–3, 735, 737–8, 742, 749, 767
Hoar, George F., 59, 143, 338
Hobson, Richard P., 331
Hoe, Robert, 128
Hoffer, George, 197
Holden *v.* Hardy (1898), 171
Holley, Alexander, 127, 134
Holmes, O. W., 170, 171, 273, 278, 357, 558, 559, 617, 619
Holt, Benjamin, 129
Home Building Association, 212
Home Owners' Loan Corporation, 589, 608
Homer, Winslow, 302, 572, 573
Homestead Act, 95, 96, 196
Homestead Co., 90
Homestead Law (1862), 7
Homestead strike (1892), 162, 237, 250
Homma, Gen. Masaharu, 708
Hong Kong, 665
Hood, Raymond, 299
Hoover, Herbert, 127, 213, 214, 471–2, 502, 512, 515, 516, 518–20, 525, 526–7, 530, 531–7, 541–2, 580, 582, 595, 603, 660, 798
Hopkins, Harry, 692, 823
House, Edward M., 422, 428, 459, 508
Houston, David F., 429
Howard, L. O., 201
Howard, Gen. O. O., 18
Howe, Edward, 284
Howe, Elias, 126
Howe, Frederic, 383
Howells, W. D., 255–6, 285, 369
Huerta, Victoriana, 440–42
Huertas, General, 404
Hughes, Charles Evans, 382, 417, 461, 495–6, 501, 514, 558–9, 560, 601
Hughes, John J., Bishop, 178
Hull, Cordell, 430, 511, 595, 644, 662
Hull House, 180, 372
Humanitarianism, 371–9
Hunt, Richard M., 295, 296, 298–9
Huntington, Collis P., 106, 107, 115
Hurly, Edward, 470
Hurst, Sir Cecil, 492
Hussey, Obed, 192
Hutchins, Robert M., 562
Huxley, Thomas, 276
Hydroelectric power, 533–4
Hydrogen bomb, 821

Iceland, 659
Idaho Territory, 87, 101
Illinois Central Railway, 112
Imagist poets, 568
Immigration, 11, 29, 95–6, 98, 124–5, 146, 151–2, 174–6, 206, 231; governmental regulation, 184–8
Immigration Acts, 186, 187, 507
Impeachment, 44
Incendiary bomb, 694
Independent, 294
Indian Bureau, 223, 234
Indian Rights Association, 378
Indians, 73–4, 79, 81–5, 90, 91, 94, 97, 103, 229, 378
Industrial Commission, 160
Industry, 7, 8, 9–11, 26–9, 123, 126, 127, 135, 140, 146, 150, 158, 165, 206, 264, 314; labor conflicts, 160–66; New Deal regulation, 595–9; production in World War II, 679–85
Inflation, 588–9
Ingalls, John J., 102
Ingersoll, Col. Robert, 8, 276
Inland Waterways Commission, 399
Inness, George, 300
Inouye, Vice Admiral, 712
Insular Cases, 341–2
Insull, Samuel, 533
Insurance, old-age and unemployment, 609–11

International American Conference (1889), 319
International Bank for Reconstruction, 801
International Harvester Co., 138, 394, 436
International Industrial Assembly, 154
International Labor Organization, 497
International Mercantile Marine, 390
International Military Tribunal, 809–10
International Monetary Conferences, 248
International Monetary Fund, 801
International Nickel Company of Canada, 533
International Trade Organization, 801
International Workers of the World, 160, 165, 423
Interstate Commerce Act (1887), 118, 119, 137, 215, 227, 395
Interstate Commerce Commission, 119–20, 396, 413, 436, 521–2
Intolerance, 555–62
Inventions, 105, 126–31
Investment business, reform of, 589–90
Iron Industry, 131–2
Irrigation, 98, 400
Isham, Samuel, 572
Ishii, Viscount, 506
Isolationism, World War I, 446–7; World War II, 632–3, 641–2, 660
Italy, 634, 636–7; *see also* World War II
Iwo Jima, 774

Jackson, Helen Hunt, 84, 378
Jackson, Robert H., 619, 790, 809
James, Henry, 285–6
James, William, 270, 271, 273, 293, 294
Japan, 401, 407–8, 414–15, 438, 498, 634, 635, 637–8; Chinese policy after World War I, 503–8; postwar, 812–13; *see also* World War II
Japanese-Americans, 788
Java, 709
Jeffers, Robinson, 567–8
Jefferson, Thomas, 30, 123, 124, 191, 198, 354, 427, 615, 662
Jewell, Marshall, 59
Jewett, Sarah Orne, 281
Joffre, Gen. Joseph, 478
Johns Hopkins University, 309–10, 311
Johnson, Andrew, 32, 33, 34–42, 44, 45, 51, 52, 56, 57, 62, 63, 65, 101, 208
Johnson, Hiram, 382
Johnson, Gen. Hugh S., 596
Johnson, Tom, 383
Johnson Act, 642
Joint Board Estimate, 671
Joint Chiefs of Staff, 710, 716, 751
Joint Committee of Fifteen, 37, 38, 39
Joint Resolution (1898), 331, 346
Joint Stock Land Banks, 536
Jones, Eliot, 137
Jones, 'Golden Rule,' 383
Jones Act (1916), 349
Jones Merchant Marine Act, 522–3
Jones-White Bill, 523
Journal, N. Y., 292, 324, 326, 329
Journalism, 288–94, 326, 561
Julliard *v.* Greenman, 67

Kakuta, Admiral, 714
Kamikaze planes, 774–5
Kansas and Pacific Railroad, 91
Kearney, Dennis, 185
Keller, A. G., 579
Kellogg, Frank B., 509
Kellogg Pact, 499, 508
Kelly, Oliver H., 205, 208, 209
Kelly, William, 127, 132
Kennan, George, 826
Kenney, Gen. George C., 752, 771
Kesselring, F. M. Albert, 727–8
Key, David M., 219

Keynes, John M., 690
King, Maj. Gen. E. P., 708
King, Adm. Ernest J., 700, 705, 710, 716
Kipling, Rudyard, 322
Kluge, F. M. Gunther von, 742, 746
Knapp, Seaman, 197
Knight, E. C., 392
Knights of Labor, 147, 154, 155–6, 157, 158, 601–2
Knights of St. Crispin, 147, 154–5
Knights of the White Camelia, 53
Know-Nothing movement, 184
Knox, Philander C., 392, 401, 414–15
Knox *v.* Lee, 67
Kohlsaat, H. H., 386 n.
Konoye, Prince, 660, 662
Korea, 813
Kreisler, Fritz, 477
Krutch, Joseph W., 563
Ku Klux Act, 65
Ku Klux Klan, 52–3, 555–6
Kurita, Admiral, 772–3

Labor, 5, 7, 14, 25–8, 99, 142–3, 145, 178, 202, 218, 241, 437; background of movement, 146–53; discrimination, 786–7; industrial conflicts, 160–66; legislation, 166–73; and New Deal, 599–602, 622–4; organized, 153–60; Truman administration, 780–82; World War II, 686–8
Labor, Bureau of, 168
Labor, Dept. of, 188
Ladd, Dr. E. E., 397
La Farge, John, 300–301
Lafayette Escadrille, 450
LaFollette, Robert M., 357, 360, 380–82, 396, 399, 412, 413, 417–18, 419, 420, 464, 533
LaFollette, Robert M., Jr., 602
LaFollette Seamen's Act (1915), 168, 437–8
LaGuardia, Fiorello, 799
Laissez-faire, 115, 116, 118, 123, 124, 143, 152, 167, 169, 191, 380
Lamar, L. Q. C., 94, 227
Land, Rear Adm. E. S., 678
Land, redistribution of, 23–4
Landis, Kenesaw M., 395
Landon, Alfred M., 613–15
Lane, Franklin K., 429
Lane, John, 192
Langdell, C. C., 273
Langford, M. P., 88–9
Langley, Samuel P., 128
Lanier, Sidney, 15, 75–6, 279, 282
Lansing, Robert, 452–3
Lansing-Ishii agreement, 506
Lasker, Albert D., 523
Lassalle, Ferdinand, 154
Lathrop, Julia, 413
Laughlin, J. Laurence, 249
Laurier, Sir Wilfrid, 416
Laval, Pierre, 636
Law, 272–4
Lawrence, E. O., 694
Lawson, Thomas, 370
Lazear, Dr. Jesse W., 343
Lea, Homer, 796
League of Nations, 492–7, 508, 633, 635, 636
Lease, Mary, 240, 255
Lee, Robert E., 5, 33, 37
Lee, Rear Adm. Willis A., 717
Lehman, Herbert, 799
Lend-Lease, 657–8, 669, 672, 679, 799, 801–2, 822, 921–3
Leopold, King, 649
Lesseps, Vicomte Ferdinand de, 402
Lewis, John L., 160, 602, 660, 687, 762, 780–81
Lewis, Sinclair, 564, 571
Leyte, P. I., 769–74
Liberal Republican party, 69–71, 76, 230
Liberty ships, 678, 685
Libraries, 312–13
Lie, Jonas, 302
Lieber, Francis, 183
Liebig, Baron von, 195
Lilienthal, David E., 791, 819, 821
Liliuokalani, Queen, 317

Lincoln, Abraham, 1–4, 31–4, 35, 37, 40, 44, 49, 56, 101, 106, 222, 786
Lindbergh, Charles A., 128, 657
Lindsey, Ben, 370, 375
Lippmann, Walter, 292
Literature, 278–88, 562–71
Little Rock and Fort Smith Railroad, 76
Little Steel formula, 687
Lloyd, Henry D., 143, 215, 255, 361, 363, 370, 371
Lloyd George, David, 454, 462, 490, 491
Local No. 144, 157
Locarno Treaty, 636
Lochner *v.* New York, 171
Lodge, Henry Cabot, 225, 314, 323–4, 326, 338, 401–2, 418, 451, 494
Lodge, Mrs. Henry Cabot, 264
Lodge corollary, 415
Lôme, Enrique de, 329
London, Declaration of, 453
London Economic Conference, 588
London Naval Treaty (1930), 497–8
Long, Huey P., 561
Long, John D., 332
Longfellow, Henry Wadsworth, 278
Los Alamos, N. M., 696
Louisiana, University of, 305
Lowden, Frank, 513
Lowell, James Russell, 1, 278
Lowell, Josephine Shaw, 379
Ludendorff, Gen. E. F. W., 463, 476, 484, 487
Lundeen plan, 609–10
Lusitania, S.S., 449, 451, 456–8
Lynd, Robert and Helen, 579
Lyon, Mary, 312

McAdoo, William G., 428–9, 452, 470, 526
MacArthur, Gen. Douglas, 662, 672, 707–8, 709, 712, 716, 717–18, 752–4, 756, 769 ff., 812
McCardle case, 50
McClellan, Gen. George B., 56
McCormick, Cyrus, 192
McCormick Harvester Co., 156, 203
McCosh, James, 270
McCoy, J. G., 91
McCrary Bill, 118
McCulloch, Hugh, 13–14
McEnery Resolution, 347
McGuffey Readers, 306
Mackay, Angus, 197
McKay, Gordon, 126
McKim, C. F., 297, 298–9
McKim, Mead, and White, 297
McKinley, William, 145, 234–5, 242, 257–8, 261, 263, 264, 319, 328–30, 334, 336–9, 341, 346, 385, 386 n., 388, 398, 514
McKinley tariff bill (1890), 233–5, 237, 252, 319, 327, 330
McLaughlin, A. C., 274
MacLeish, Archibald, 570
MacMonnies, Frederick, 295, 303–4
McNutt, Paul V., 686
McReynolds, James C., 429, 617
Macune, C. W., 210
McVeagh, Wayne, 364
Madero, Francisco I., 440
Madison, James, 455
Maginot Line, 649
Magnesium, 683
Mahan, A. T., 322–3, 332
Mahone, William, 29
Maine, U.S.S., 329
Makin, 755
Malay Barrier, 709
Malaya, 660, 661, 663, 665
Manchukuo, 507–8, 635, 644
Manhattan District, 696
Manila, P. I., 334, 336, 707–8, 774
Mann, Horace, 305, 307
Mann-Elkins Act (1910), 413
Manufacturing, 10–11, 14, 26–7, 189, 190, 202
Marconi, Guglielmo, 128
Marcy, William L., 316
Marginal farming, 593
Marianas Islands, 756–7
Markham, Edwin, 282–3
Marquand, J. P., 565

Marriage, 550
Marshall, Gen. George C., 668, 669, 670, 672, 674, 700, 726, 727, 766, 803, 824
Marshall, John, 610, 616
Marshall Islands, 755–6
Marshall Plan, 804, 826–7
Martin, F. T., 218, 363
Martin, Homer, 300
Marx, Karl, 154
Mason, Lowell, 575
Massachusetts Ten-Hour Act (1874), 169
Masters, Edgar Lee, 564
Materialism, 549–54
Mathews, Walter, 277
Max, Prince, 487
Maximilian, Emperor, 60
Maximum Freight Rate case (1897), 119
Mayo, Henry T., 441–2
Medical Corps, U.S.A., 675–6
Medicine, 578–9
Mellon, Andrew W., 515, 533
Melville, H., 278
Mencken, Henry L., 563
Mennonites, 109
Merchant marine, 522–3, 678
Merchant Marine Act (1916), 438
Mergenthaler, Ottmar, 128
Merrill, Adm. Aaron S., 753
Merritt family, 132
Mesabi range, 132
Methodist Church, 377
Mexico, 60, 438, 439–43, 464, 509–10
Middle West, 1, 29, 91, 116, 190, 194, 204, 239, 264
Middleton, Gen. Troy, 750
Midway, Battle of, 713–15
Midway Islands, 60
Migration, 105
Miles, Gen. N. A., 333
Mill villages, 28, 149–50
Millay, Edna St. Vincent, 560, 571, 646
Miller, David Hunt, 492
Miller, Col. Thomas W., 515
Milligan case, 50
Mills, Roger Q., 231
Minerals, 10
Mining, 85–90, 95, 131, 150, 181
Missouri, U.S.S., 776
Mitchell, Charles E., 538
Mitchell, John, 164–5
Mitscher, Adm. Marc A., 755, 770 ff.
Mobile Address, 508
Mohler, George, 197
Molotov, Vyacheslav M., 718, 803, 815
Money, 7, 56–7, 65–7, 218–19, 241, 242–56, 257, 431–5, 801
Monopoly, 135–44, 153, 436, 596–8
Monroe Doctrine, 60, 315, 318, 320, 322, 326, 350, 405–6, 645; Lodge corollary, 415; modification, 508–11; Roosevelt corollary, 406–7, 510–11
Monte Cassino, 729
Montgomery, Gen. Sir B. L., 718, 723, 740, 745–6, 767
Montgomery, Ward and Company, 210
Moody, John, 389
Moody, William H., 395
Moody, William Vaughan, 282, 339–40, 353
Morehead, Alan, 723–4
Morey, Charles R., 303
Morgan, Gen. Sir Frederick, 736
Morgan, J. P., 134, 138, 252, 389, 390, 392, 403, 532, 533
Morgan, John T., 326
Morgan-Belmont group, 138–9
Morgenthau, Henry, Jr., 805
Mormons, 79, 97, 103
Morocco, 408
Morrill, Justin, 196
Morrill Act (1862), 7, 195, 196, 309, 310
Morrill tariff (1861), 6
Morrow, Dwight W., 443, 509–10
Morse, Samuel, 128
Moscow Conference (1943), 805, 814
Most, Johann, 156
Mount Holyoke College, 312
Moving pictures, 553–4

Muckrakers, 366–70
Muller *v.* Oregon (1908), 172
Munich Conference, 640, 646
Municipal Bankruptcy Act, 616
Munn *v.* Illinois (1876), 116
Murphy, Frank, 602, 619
Murphy, Thomas, 73
Murray, 'Alfalfa Bill,' 382
Muscle Shoals, 533, 603, 604
Music, 573–5
Mussolini, Benito, 634, 636, 639, 641, 647, 668, 722, 725, 767
Myers, Gustavus, 370

Nagasaki, 776, 819
Nagumo, Adm. Chuichi, 707, 713–15
Napoleon III, 60
Nast, Thomas, 226, 294
Nation, N. Y., 233, 293–4
National Association for the Advancement of Colored People, 378
National Banking Acts (1863 and 1864), 7, 10
National Conference of Charities and Correction, 374
National Conservation Association, 399
National Cordage Company, 250
National debt, 4, 9, 528, 690
National Defense Act (1916), 460
National Defense Research Committee, 692
National Labor Board (N.L.B.), 599–600
National Labor Relations Board (N.L.R.B.), 600–601, 618, 623–4
National Labor Union, 147, 154–5
National Monetary Commission, 432
National Origins Act (1929), 188
National Protective Agency, 377
National Recovery Administration (N.R.A.), 513, 595–600, 607
National Typographical Union, 154
National Union Convention, 40
Nationalism, 555
Nationalist Clubs, 255, 369
Natural resources, 9, 10, 26, 532–3; conservation, *see* Conservation
Navy, U.S., 332–3, 480–83, 498, 671–2, 673, 677–8, 710–18; *see also* Anti-submarine warfare
Navy Department frauds, 48, 72
Negroes, 2, 6, 7, 15, 23, 25, 33, 38, 39–43, 52–5, 57, 71, 73, 150, 191, 193, 199, 239, 785–7; freedmen, 16–23; reconstruction, 45–9
Nelson, Donald, 670, 679, 680, 683
Netherlands, 456, 659
Netherlands East Indies, 665, 666
Neutrality, World War I, 447, 453–9; World War II, 642–4, 651–2
Neutrality Acts, 638
Nevins, Allan, 59–60, 289
New Deal, 168, 357, 760; conservation and utilities regulation, 603–6; evaluation, 626–31; farm legislation, 590–95, 621–2; financial legislation, 587–90; industrial regulation, 595–9; labor legislation, 599–602, 622–4; philosophy, 582–7; political and administrative reform, 624–6; relief and security legislation, 606–11; and Supreme Court, 615–21
New England, 1, 26, 27, 28, 29, 150, 189
'New Freedom,' 423, 435
New Haven Railroad, 437
'New Nationalism,' 416–18, 423
New Orleans, La., 23, 55
New Republic, 294
New York City, 48, 56, 74, 179–80, 372–4
Newell, Frederick H., 398, 400
Nicaragua, 61, 402, 438–9, 510
Nimitz, Adm. Chester W., 710, 711, 713–14, 770
Nineteenth Amendment (1920), 375
Nisei, 788
Nishimura, Admiral, 772
Nobel Prize, 576
Normandy, Battle of, 740–42
Norris, Frank, 283

Norris, George W., 412, 413, 533
Norris-LaGuardia Act, 167, 600
North, 2, 3, 4, 5, 6–12, 18, 19, 20, 26, 29, 31, 33, 36, 37, 48, 53, 55, 71, 105, 150, 194, 207, 219, 237; prosperity, 8–12
North Africa, 665, 718–24
North American Conservation Commission, 399–400
North Carolina, University of, 305
Northcliffe, Lord, 472–3
Northern Pacific Railroad, 91, 101, 107, 108, 112, 250, 398
Northern Securities Company, 392, 522
Northwest Ordinance (1787), 103
Norton, Andrews, 275
Norton, Charles Eliot, 293
Norway, 649
Noyes, Alexander, 252
Nye committee, 453, 642, 670, 763

O. Henry, 266, 362
Oak Ridge, Tenn., 696
Oberlin College, 312
Obregon, Alvaro, 443, 509
Oersted, Hans C., 126
O'Fallon decision (1929), 522
Office of Foreign Relief, 799
Office of Petroleum Administration, 683
Office of Price Administration, 689
Office of Scientific Research and Development, 693, 695
Office of Strategic Services, 679
Office of War Mobilization, 681–2
'Ohio idea,' 56, 57, 65
Oil Creek, Pa., 10
Oil industry, 10, 515, 530–31, 683–4
Okinawa, 774–5
Old-age insurance, 609–10
Oldendorf, Adm. Jesse B., 772
Older, Fremont, 383
Oliver, James, 129
Olney, Richard, 145, 162–3, 320–21
Omnibus Bill of 1889, 102
Omnibus Flood Control Bill, 603
O'Neil, John, 62
O'Neill, Eugene, 566, 571
Open Door policy, 350–53, 504–6
Oppenheimer, J. R., 696
Orders of Council, 454–5
Oregon, U.S.S., 401
Organic Act (1902), 348
Orlando, Vittorio, 490, 491
Osmeña, Sergio, 771
Otto, N. A., 127
Overland Stage Line, 108
Overlord, operation, 736–42
Owen, Robert, 154
Ozawa, Admiral, 772

Pacific Railway Bill, 106, 112, 196
Pacific theater, 706–18, 751–9, 767–76
Paine, Thomas, 624
Palma, Tomás Estrada, 406
Palmer, A. Mitchell, 557
Pan-American Conferences, 319, 320, 645
Pan-Americanism, 318–19
Panama Canal, 401–5
Panama Canal Company, 402–3, 405
Panay, U.S.S., 638
Panics (1857), 154; (1873), 67, 75, 113, 114, 116, 374; (1893), 114, 250
Pantelleria, 724
Papini, Giovanni, 271
Papua, 717–18
Paris, Pact of, 499
Paris, Treaty of (1898), 337, 341, 344
Paris Peace Conference, 489, 492
Parker, Alton B., 393, 422
Parker, Theodore, 275
Pas de Calais, 740
Patch, Gen. Alexander M., 743
Patent Office, U.S., 126
Patman Bill, 525
Patrick Henry, S.S., 678
Patrons of Husbandry, 205, 207, 208–10, 211, 212
Patterson, Robert P., 691
Patton, Gen. George S., 672, 694, 720, 725, 731–2, 742, 743, 745, 748, 764, 765

Pauncefote, Sir Julian, 401–2
Payne, Sereno, 411–12
Payne-Aldrich tariff, 412, 423, 430
Pearl Harbor, 663–4, 665, 681, 706–7
Pecora, Ferdinand, 589
Pedro, Emperor Dom, 128
Peek, George, 590
Peffer, W. A., 240
Peik *v.* Chicago & Northwestern R. R., 117
Peirce, Charles, 270
Pendleton, George, 57
Pendleton, Gen. William N., 15
Pendleton Civil Service Reform Bill, 222, 223
Pennell, Joseph, 302
Penrose, Boies, 516
Pensions, 4, 228, 234, 609–10
Perkins, Frances, 150
Perry, Matthew C., 315
Pershing, Gen. John, 443, 484, 485–6, 487
Pestalozzi, J. H., 308
Pétain, Henri, 650
Phelps-Dodge case, 620
Philip, Capt. John W., 331
Philippine Commission, 347
Philippine Independence Act (1934), 350
Philippine Islands, 338–9, 340, 342, 347–50, 662, 663, 665, 707–8, 769–74
Philippine Sea, Battle of, 757–8
Phillips, David Graham, 217, 370
Phillips, Wendell, 46, 143
Philosophy, 269–78
Phipps, Henry, 134
Physics, 577
Pierce, Franklin, 214
Pierce, John D., 305
Pinchot, Gifford, 398, 399, 412–13, 417, 533
Pingree, Hazen, 382
Pinkerton detectives, 149, 162, 153
Pious Fund dispute, 401, 498
Planter aristocracy, 5–6
Platt, Charles, 300
Platt, Thomas C., 386
Platt Amendment, 343–4, 406
Playfair, Lord, 195
Ploesti, Rum., 734
Plummer, Henry, 87
Plutonium, 696
Poetry, 278–9, 282–3, 287, 567–71
Poland, 647–8
Politics, *see individual presidents and political parties*
Poll taxes, 787
Pools, 137
Populist party, 143, 156, 211, 212, 235, 239–41, 255, 256, 258, 261, 323–4, 381
Port Moresby, N. Guinea, 712, 716
Porter, Katherine Ann, 566
Portsmouth, Treaty of, 407–8
Portugal, 705
Postal Telegraph Co., 140
Potsdam Conference, 775, 806, 810, 812
Potter law, 116
Pound, Roscoe, 273
Powderly, Terence V., 155, 156
Powell, Maj. J. W., 80, 94
Powell *v.* Alabama, 561
Pragmatism, 269, 270–72, 277
Prairie Farmer, 202–3
Presidential Succession Act, 791
Press, *see* Journalism
Progressive movement, and American life, 354–7; and democracy, 357–66; humanitarianism, 371–9; muckrakers, 366–71; in politics, 379–84
Progressive party, 419–20, 423–4, 461
Progressive Republican League, 417
Prohibition, 377–8, 525–7
Propaganda, 449–51
Property tax, 46
Property values, 14
Prosperity, 549–54
Protestantism, 274, 277
Proximity fuse, 694
Public Works Administration (P.W.A.), 604, 607
Puerto Rico, 342, 345–6

Pujo Committee, 411, 432–3, 436
Pulaski, Tenn., 52
Pulitzer, Joseph, 183, 291, 292, 324
Pullman, George, 164
Pullman Palace Car Co., 138, 162
Pullman strike (1894), 150, 158, 162–3, 167, 218, 254
Pupin, Michael, 183
Pure Food and Drugs Act, 397
Pyle, Ernie, 728, 741

Quebec conferences, 736, 770, 805

Rabaul, 665, 709, 716, 753–4
Rabi, Isidor I., 696
Radar, 693, 694, 712, 735
Radical Republicans, 20, 30, 31, 33, 35, 37–41, 43 ff., 50 ff., 55 ff., 61, 64, 69, 71
Radicals, 556–60
Radio, 552–3
Railroad Brotherhoods, 780
Railroad Retirement Act, 599
Railroad strike (1877), 150
Railroads, 3, 7, 9, 10, 14–15, 26, 29, 33, 40, 46, 47, 57, 72 ff., 90, 95, 96, 101, 105–7, 125, 137, 138–40, 142, 162, 178, 190, 203, 206–7, 209, 211, 214, 218, 221, 229, 237, 238, 240, 521–2, 688; abuses, 113–16; community of interests, 139; Federal and local aid, 111–13; growth, 105–8; regulation, 395–6, 116–20; and West, 108–11
Railway Labor Board, 521–2
Raskob, John J., 538
Rauschenbusch, Walter, 277
Rawlins, John A., 61
Rayburn Securities Act, 436
Raymond, Henry J., 290–91
Reading Railroad, 250
Reciprocal Trade Agreements, 800–801
Reclamation Act (1902), 97, 197, 400
Reconstruction, and Congress, 37–45; and Constitution, 49–52; during Civil War, 31–4; Johnson's policy, 34–7; Negroes, 45–9; restoration of white rule, 52–5
Reconstruction Acts (1867), 42, 44, 51
Reconstruction Finance Corporation (R.F.C.), 536, 542–6, 582, 587, 589, 594
Reconversion, World War II, 777–9
Reed, Stanley F., 619
Reed, Thomas B., 232, 234
Reed, Walter, 405
Regionalism, 569–70
Reid, Whitelaw, 68, 128
Reinhardt, Gen. Walther, 485
Relief, unemployment, 606–8
Religion, 274–8
Rent Control Law, 791
Renwick, James, 295
Reparations, 500–503
Republic Steel Corporation, 602
Republican, Springfield (Mass.), 291
Republican party, 7–8, 19, 20, 30 ff., 61, 64, 69 ff., 77, 78, 102, 106, 125, 195, 206, 207, 211, 217, 218, 225, 230–33, 235, 236, 240, 251–3, 256–8, 261, 263, 265, 319, 323–4, 330, 331, 339, 342, 349, 385, 386, 393, 409, 411, 414, 419, 422, 438, 456, 459, 513–14, 516–20, 526–30, 533, 535, 580, 613–15, 654–7, 759–62, 791; and League of Nations, 495–7
Resettlement Administration, 593–4, 604
Reuben James, U.S.S., 698
Reynaud, Paul, 650
Richardson, Henry H., 268, 296, 298
Richardson, William A., 67
Richmond, Va., 13, 15, 23
Riis, Jacob, 179–80, 183, 255, 369, 373, 374
Rio de Janeiro Treaty, 827
Ripley, W. Z., 522
Ritty, James, 128
Roberts, Owen J., 592–3, 619
Robeson, George M., 72
Robin Moor, S.S., 658
Robinson, Edwin A., 567

Rockefeller, John D., 137, 363, 389–90
Rodman, Rear Adm. Hugh L., 483
Rölvaag, O. E., 100, 183, 201, 204–5, 284–5
Rommel, F. M. Erwin, 722, 723, 737–8
Roosevelt, F. D., 172, 202, 224, 344, 349, 400, 436, 437, 480, 510–11, 513, 523, 525, 632, 668–9, 767, 769, 786, 798, 804, 813–14; election of 1932, 580–82; election of 1936, 612–15; election of 1940, 654–7; election of 1944, 759–63; New Deal, *see* New Deal; *see also* World War II
Roosevelt, James, 792
Roosevelt, Theodore, 145, 148–9, 158, 164–5, 169–70, 180, 182, 186, 224, 225, 233, 240, 263, 330 ff., 333, 334, 346, 350, 357, 360, 363–4, 366–7, 373, 380, 381, 385–8, 410–11, 416–20, 421, 423, 461, 488–9; big-stick policy, 401–7; conservation program, 397–400, 603; and government regulation, 394–7; and trusts, 388–94; and world politics, 407–9
Root, Elihu, 343, 386, 401, 419
Root-Takahira agreement (1908), 504
Rose, Sir John, 63
Ross, E. A., 358
Ross, Ronald, 405
Rough Riders, 385
Rowan, Lieutenant, 331
Royal Air Force, 701, 705, 730–33
Royal-Dutch Shell Oil Company, 531
Royce, Josiah, 311
Rubber industry, 684
Ruffin, Edmund, 195
Rumania, 744
Rundstedt, F. M. Karl von, 738, 746–7, 749, 751
Russell, Charles Edward, 370
Russell, Lord, 60
Russell, William E., 259
Russell Sage Foundation, 374
Russia, 60, 506, 637, 647, 648–9, 658, 659, 665–9, 682, 702, 730, 744–5, 776, 796–7, 803, 806–9, 820–26
Russo-Japanese War, 407–8

Sacco-Vanzetti case, 559–60
Sackville-West, Sir Lionel, 232
Saint-Gaudens, Augustus, 183, 297, 303
St. Paul and Pacific Railway, 109
Salisbury, Lord, 320–22, 401
Samar, Battle of, 772–3
Samoa, 317–18
Sampson, Adm. William T., 333
Sanborn, J. D., 73
Santa Fé Railroad, 108, 250
Santayana, George, 266–7
Santo Domingo, 60–61, 406–7, 439, 510
Sargent, John Singer, 295, 301–2
Saunders, William, 197
Savo Island, Battle of, 716
Scalawags, 46, 47, 54
Schechter case, 598, 601
Schenck, Robert, 73
Schenck *v.* United States, 558
Schley, Adm. W. S., 333
Schurz, Carl, 19, 61, 68, 69, 84, 183, 220, 223, 225
Schuschnigg, Kurt von, 639
Schwab, Charles, 28, 134
Science, 576–80; in World War II, 691–7
Scott, Dred, 51, 392
Scott, Gen. Hugh L., 478
Scott, Rear Adm. Norman, 717
Scottsboro case, 561
Sculpture, 303–4
Secession, 8
Sectionalism, 2
Securities and Exchange Commission, 590
Security business, reform of, 589–90
Sedition Act (1918), 476
Seidel, Emil, 383
Selden, George, 127
Selective Service, *see* Draft

Selective Service Act (1917), 478–9
Serbia, 445
Service forces, U.S.A., 675
Seventeenth Amendment (1913), 381, 414
Sewanee College, 305
Seward, William H., 35, 40, 60, 61, 63, 315–16, 318
Seymour, Horatio, 57
Shaler, Nathaniel, 267 n.
Share-crop system, 23–5
Sheldon, Edward A., 308
Shenandoah, C.S.S., 63–4
Shepard, Dr., 397
Shepherd, 'Boss,' 73
Sheridan, Gen. Philip H., 12, 98–9
Sherman, Adm. F. C., 753
Sherman, John, 9, 40, 143, 217, 223
Sherman, Gen. William T., 12, 36, 106
Sherman Anti-Trust Act (1890), 137, 143–5, 153, 164, 168, 233, 389, 390, 391–2, 393, 394, 414, 531
Sherman Silver Purchase Bill (1890), 233, 237, 247, 251, 256
Sherwood, Robert E., 814
Sholes, Christopher, 128
Shreve, Henry, 120
Siberia, 506, 507
Sicily, 724–5
Sickles, Gen. Daniel E., 43
Sigsbee, Capt. C. D., 329
Silver, 10, 245, 246, 257, 259, 263; *see also* Free silver
Simard, Captain, 714
Simpson, Jerry, 240
Sims, Rear Adm. William S., 481–2
Sinclair, Harry F., 515
Sinclair, Upton, 397
Singapore, 665
Singer, Isaac, 126
Single Tax, 368
Sino-Japanese War (1894–5), 350–51
Sixteenth Amendment, 414
Slavery, 2–3, 6
Sloan, John, 302
Smith, Adam, 130
Smith, Alfred E., 518–19, 526, 580, 581, 613
Smith, Donald, 109
Smith, Gen. Holland M., 755
Smith, Gen. Walter Bedell, 736
Smith-Connolly Act, 687
Smith-Hughes Act (1914), 438
Smith-Lever Act (1914), 438
Smoot, Reed, 513
Smythe *v.* Ames, 620
Social Security Act (1935), 173, 610–11, 618
Social Security Board, 609, 610
Socialism, 154, 159, 164, 558–9
Sociology, 579
Soil Conservation Act (1936), 621
Somers, Robert, 12
South, 2, 4, 5–6, 11–15, 19–21, 23–9, 33, 36, 37, 42, 46, 48, 50, 52–7, 65, 69, 71, 77, 100, 114, 150, 151, 189, 194, 199, 202, 204, 219, 226, 237, 239, 249, 304; devastation, 12–15; freedmen, 16–23; recovery, 23–30; *see also* Reconstruction
South Carolina, University of, 305
South End House, 372
Southern Pacific Railroad, 398
Spahr, Charles B., 362
Spain, 60, 61, 665
Spanish-American War, 293, 324, 329, 330–35, 385
Spanish Civil War, 636–7
Spargo, John, 374
Sparks, W. A., 229
Specie payments, 7
Specie Resumption Act (1875), 244
Speculation, 10
Spencer, Herbert, 171, 270
Spooner Act, 402
Sports, 554
Sprague, Adm. C. A. F., 773
Spring-Rice, Cecil, 451
Spruance, Adm. Raymond A., 714–15, 754, 755, 758, 775
Square deal, 387

Stalin, Joseph, 740, 744, 806
Standard Oil Company, 137–8, 142–3, 393, 394
Stanford, Leland, 106, 115
Stanley, William, 126
Stanton, Edwin M., 33, 35, 44, 51
Star Route frauds, 222
Stark, Adm. Harold R., 482, 668, 670
Steamboating, 120–22, 178
Stedman, Edmund, 279
Steel industry, 132–5, 681
Steffens, Lincoln, 370, 382
Steinbeck, John, 565–6
Steinmetz, Charles, 183
Stephens, A. H., 33
Stephens, Uriah S., 155
Stettinius, Edward, 815
Stettler *v.* O'Hara (1916), 172 n.
Steven, John L., 317
Stevens, John F., 110, 126
Stevens, Thaddeus, 21, 33, 37–8, 39, 41, 44, 46, 55
Stevenson, Robert Louis, 107
Stewart, William M., 89
Stilwell, Gen. Joseph, 768–9
Stimson, Henry, 349, 508, 644, 696–7, 818
Stock, Frederick, 477
Stock Exchange, New York, 75, 537
Stocks, 536–8
Stone, Harlan F., 593, 619
Stone, William, 458
Stone *v.* Farmers' Loan & Trust Co., 118
Storey, Moorfield, 378
Strasser, Adolph, 158
Strategic Bombing Survey, 732–3, 734
Straus, Nathan, 183
Strikes, 150, 162, 218, 221, 237, 292, 466–7, 600, 602, 622, 687, 780–81
Stromberg *v.* California, 561
Strong, William, 67
Submarines, World War I, 455–8, 463, 464, 482–3; World War II, 693, 699–706, 708, 735–6
Subsidies, 7
Suckow, Ruth, 205
Sudetenland, 639
Sugar, 327
Sugar Trust, 255
Sullivan, Louis, 268, 295, 298, 299
Sullivan, Mark, 474
Sumner, Charles, 21, 38, 39, 41, 46, 55, 60, 61, 63, 68, 69, 222
Sun, N. Y., 290
Supreme Court, 43, 45, 49–50, 51, 52, 67, 77, 118, 119, 144–5, 163–4, 168–9, 171–2, 173, 185, 186, 237, 253, 340, 341–2, 392, 416–17, 521–2, 560–62, 592–3, 598, 601, 610–11; and New Deal, 615–21
Sussex, 458
Sutherland, George, 617
Sutro, Adolph, 86
Swift *v.* Tyson, 620–21
Szilard, Leo, 695

Taft, Lorado, 304
Taft, Robert A., 654, 785, 804
Taft, William Howard, 145, 187, 344, 347–8, 406, 408–10, 423, 498, 510, 521; diplomacy, 414–16; ineptitude of administration, 410–14; and Progressive party, 416–20
Taft-Hartley Act, 781–2, 790
Tallmadge, T. E., 296
Tammany Hall, 225, 231, 237, 383
Tanner, James, 233
Tarawa, 755
Tarbell, Ida, 370
Tariff Commission (1882), 230
Tariffs, 6, 9, 33, 40, 56, 57, 64, 67–8, 69, 70, 123, 133, 143, 203, 218, 227, 230–31, 234, 241, 242, 252–3, 257, 319, 411–12, 415–16, 429–31, 528–30, 535, 633
Tarkington, Booth, 286–7
Taxation, 19, 21, 46 ff., 54, 115, 211, 254, 255, 364, 473, 528, 620, 690
Teapot Dome scandal, 515
Tedder, Gen. Sir Arthur, 736
Teheran Conference, 814
Telegraph, 7, 9
Teller, Henry M., 258

Teller Amendment, 331, 343
Temperance Movement, 376–7
Ten Years' War of 1868–78, 325
Tenant farming, 594
Tennessee Valley Authority (T.V.A.), 534, 603, 604–6, 683
Tenure of Office Act, 44, 227
Tesla, Nikola, 183
Texas *v.* White, 49–50
Textile industry, 27, 149–50, 160, 165, 181
Thailand, 707
Thayer, John M., 203
Thirteenth Amendment, 6, 16, 18, 38
Thomas, Lorenzo, 44
Thomas, Theodore, 183
Thompson, Holland, 27–8
Thomson, J. Edgar, 132
Thornhill *v.* Alabama, 561
Thurmond, J. Strom, 793
Tilden, Samuel J., 76–8
Tillman, Ben, 239, 255, 259
Times, N. Y., 290–91, 450
Tizard Mission, 692
Tobacco, 592
Tobruk, 718
Tojo, Gen. Hideki, 662–3, 668, 722
Torch, Operation, 719–21
Totalitarianism, 634–5
Townbridge, J. T., 17
Townsend plan, 609
Toyoda, Admiral, 756, 771–2
Trade Agreements Act (1934), 595
Transcendentalism, 269
Trans-Missouri Freight Association case (1897), 137
Transportation, 14, 26, 98, 105–22, 125, 135, 138, 146, 150, 189, 202, 390; government liquidation, 521–4; railroads, *see* Railroads; steamboating, 120–22
Traux *v.* Corrigan (1921), 168 n.
Treasury Dept., 251–2
Trenton Iron Works, 131
Tribune, Chicago, 18, 450
Tribune, N. Y., 128, 289–90, 362
Trident conference, 736
Trieste, 809
Triple Entente, 414–15
Troy Female Academy, 312
Truk, 756
Truman, Benjamin, 36
Truman, Harry S., 761–2, 806; civil rights program, 785–90; and education, 784–5; election of 1948, 790–94; labor problems, 780–82; reconversion problem, 777–9; social changes, 782–4
Truman Doctrine, 825–6
Trumbull, Lyman, 40, 45, 68 ff.
Trusts, 135–40, 141–5, 215, 218, 221, 231, 255, 388–94, 435–8
Truth in Securities Act (1933), 590
Tugwell, Rexford G., 593
Turkey, 825–6
Turkish Petroleum Company, 531
Turner, Frederick Jackson, 99
Turner, Jonathan B., 196
Turner, Rear Adm. R. K., 668, 754, 755, 775
Tutuila, 346
Twain, Mark, 120, 121, 280–81, 339
Tweed Ring, 48, 74
Twenty-First Amendment, 527
Twenty-One Demands, 504
Tydings, Millard R., 626
Tydings-McDuffie Bill, 349
Tyler, John, 34
Tyndall, John, 276

Un-American Activities Committee, 789–90
Unconditional-surrender doctrine, 722–3, 805
Underwood, Oscar W., 422, 430
Underwood Tariff, 428–31, 528
Unemployment legislation, 606–11
Union League, 18, 20
Union Pacific Railway, 72, 91, 106, 107, 110, 112, 113, 250, 390
Unions, *see* Labor
United Mine Workers, 160, 164, 687, 780

United Nations, 667, 810, 814; Atomic Energy Commission, 819–21; Charter, 815–17; Monetary and Financial Conference, 801; UNRRA, 799–800
United States Employment Service, 607
United States Housing Authority, 608
United States Leather Co., 138
United States Rubber Co., 138
United States Shipping Board Act (1916), 460, 470
United States Steel Corp., 134–5, 138, 148, 181, 389–90, 394, 532–3, 602
United States *v.* Cruikshank (1875), 51
United States *v.* E. C. Knight and Co. (1895), 144–5
United States *v.* Greenhut, 144
United States *v.* Harris (1883), 51
United States *v.* Reese (1875), 51
Universal Declaration of Human Rights, 810
Upjohn, Richard, 295
Uranium, 577, 695–6
Urbanization, 364–6, 551, 783
Urey, H. C., 694
Utah, 104
Utilities, regulation of, 605–6

V-1 and V-2 buzz bombs, 693–4, 735, 742
Vance, Rupert, 26
Vandenberg, Arthur, 654, 804, 815
Vandenberg Resolution, 827
Vanderbilt, Cornelius, 74
Van Devanter, Willis, 617, 619
Van Doren, Carl, 285
Vanzetti, Bartolomeo, 559–60
Vatican Council (1870), 274
Veblen, Thorstein, 363, 368, 562, 690
Venezuela, 405–6; boundary dispute, 320–22, 326
Versailles Treaty, 491, 494, 633, 635–6
Veterans' benefits, 524
Vicksburg, Arkansas, 32
Victor Emmanuel II, King, 722 n.
Villa, Pancho, 443
Villard, Henry, 108, 183
Villard, O. G., 294
Virgin Islands, 61
Virginius, 62
Volstead Act, 525–6

Wabash case (1886), 118, 119
Wade, Benjamin, 35, 44, 46
Wade-Davis Manifesto, 32–3
Wage and hour standards, 599, 622–3
Wagner-Connery Act (1935), 600–601
Wagner-Steagall Act, 621
Wainwright, Gen. J. M., 709
Waite, David H., 239
Waite, Morrison R., 116–17
Wald, Lillian D., 180
Walker, Edwin, 162–3
Walker, Horatio, 302
Wallace, H. C., 515
Wallace, Henry A., 590, 656, 761, 792, 793 n.
Walsh, Thomas J., 515, 533
Wanamaker, John, 232–3
War-crimes trials, 809–11
War debts, 500–503, 505
War Department, 35, 44, 106
War Industries Board, 471
War Labor Board, 687
War Maritime Commission, 684
War Production Board, 679–81, 684
Ward, J. Q. A., 303
Warehouse Act (1916), 211, 435
Warner, Olin L., 303
Warren, Charles, 642–3
Washington, Booker T., 20, 310, 378, 420
Washington and Lee University, 305
Washington College, 37
Washington Conference, 506–7
Washington Territory, 87, 101
Washington Treaty (1871), 63; (1922), 497–8
Watkins, J. H., 197
Watson, Elkanah, 194–5

Watson, Tom, 16, 239, 255, 261
Watt, James, 126
Watterson, Harvey, 36
Watterson, Henry, 70, 263
Wealth, concentration of, 11–12
Weaver, Baird, 239
Weaver, James B., 221, 241, 588
Webb, J. W., 73
Webb, Walter P., 80
Webb-Kenyon Act (1913), 378
Webster, Daniel, 316
Webster Spellers, 306
Weeks, J. W., 515
Weirton Steel Company, 600
Welles, Gideon, 35, 40, 69
Welles, Sumner, 805
Wells, David A., 68, 69
Wesleyan University, 196
West, 2, 3, 5, 7, 9–11, 29, 33, 75, 79, 114, 175, 190, 194, 202, 226, 249, 264; cattle industry, 90–95; disappearance of frontier, 95–100; Indian problem, 81–5; mining frontier, 85–90; political organization, 100–104
West, Andrew F., 421
Western Rural, 210
Western Union Company, 128, 140
Westinghouse, George, 192
Weyerhaeuser Timber Company, 398
Weyler, General, 328, 329
Wharton, Edith, 286
Wheat, 592
Wheeler, Burton K., 657, 659
Wheeler, Joe, 331
Wheeler-Rayburn Act (1935), 606
Whipple, Henry B., Bishop, 84
Whiskey Ring, 71, 73
Whiskey trust, 144
Whistler, James McNeill, 295, 301
White, Andrew D., 276, 309
White, Edward D., 392
White, Henry, 408
White, Sanford, 303
White, William Allen, 238, 262–3, 287, 515, 654
Whitlock, Brand, 142, 383, 480
Whitman, Walt, 3, 9, 268, 278, 279, 281
Whitney, Anita, 556–7
Whitney, Asa, 106
Whitney, Eli, 126
Wickersham Commission, 527
Wigner, Eugene, 695
Wiley, Harvey W., 397
Wilhelm, Kaiser, 321, 449, 463, 487
Wilkinson, Adm. T. S., 753, 754, 771
Willard, Emma, 312
Willard, Frances, 377
Williams, George H., 59
Willkie, Wendell, 655–7, 760
Wilson, Gen. Maitland, 727
Wilson, William B., 429
Wilson, William L., 251
Wilson, Woodrow, 145, 159, 187, 212, 224, 311, 344, 349, 354–5, 360, 364, 380–82, 414–15, 508, 511, 520, 528–9, 557, 580, 584, 814; banking and currency reform, 431–4; election of 1912, 420–24; election of 1916, 461; foreign affairs, 438–44; inaugural, 425–8; regulation of business, 435–8; Underwood tariff, 428–31; war message, 467–8; *see also* World War I
Wilson-Gorman tariff, 253, 319, 429, 430
Windom, William, 234
Windom Committee (1874), 118
Wines, Frederick, 376
Wingate, Brig. Orde, 768
Winona & St. Peter R. R. *v.* Blake, 117
Wolfe, Thomas, 565
Woman's Christian Temperance Union, 377
Wood, Gen. Leonard, 343, 349, 513
Workmen's Compensation Act (1916), 438
Works Progress Administration, 607–8
World, N. Y., 291, 292, 324
World Bank, 801
World power, 795–8; atomic energy

control, 818–21; cold war, 821–7; liquidation of war, 804–13; peace organization, 813–18; relief and reconstruction, 798–804
World War I, 123, 158, 166, 187, 207, 212, 533, 642, 670; air forces, 482–3; American entry, 461–8; American public opinion, 445–53, 473–7; debts and reparations, 500–503, 505; industrial and financial mobilization, 469–73; liquidation of government activities, 520–27; naval and military operations, 477–94; neutral rights, 453–9; preparedness, 458–60; submarine warfare, 455–8, 463, 464, 482–3; trade, 451–3
World War II, 175; agriculture, 688–9; air war, 730–35; approach, 632–46; basic considerations, 665–9; Battle of the Atlantic, 698–706; and consumer, 689–91; German defeat, 744–51, 763–7; invasion of France, 735–44; Japanese aggression, 660–64; labor, 686–8; military preparedness, 669–79; North Africa, 718–24; outbreak, 646–51; Pacific theater, 706–18, 751–9, 767–76; production, 679–85; science, 691–7; Sicily and Italy, 724–9, 745; U. S. preparations, 651–60
World's Fair, Chicago (1893), 297
Wright, Carroll, 147
Wright, Elizur, 276
Wright, Frank Lloyd, 298, 300
Wright, Orville and Wilbur, 128
Wyant, Alexander, 300
Wyoming Stock Growers' Association, 92, 94
Wyoming Territory, 101

Yalta Conference, 806, 814–15, 822–3
Yamamoto, Adm. Isoroku, 711–15, 752
Yamato, 713, 773, 775
Yeats, William B., 566 n.
Yellow fever, 343
Young, Owen D., 501
Yugoslavia, 658, 745

Zimmerman note, 464